Nineteenth-Century Literature Criticism

Guide to Gale Literary Criticism Series

For criticism on	Consult these Gale series
Authors now living or who died after December 31, 1999	*CONTEMPORARY LITERARY CRITICISM (CLC)*
Authors who died between 1900 and 1999	*TWENTIETH-CENTURY LITERARY CRITICISM (TCLC)*
Authors who died between 1800 and 1899	*NINETEENTH-CENTURY LITERATURE CRITICISM (NCLC)*
Authors who died between 1400 and 1799	*LITERATURE CRITICISM FROM 1400 TO 1800 (LC)* *SHAKESPEAREAN CRITICISM (SC)*
Authors who died before 1400	*CLASSICAL AND MEDIEVAL LITERATURE CRITICISM (CMLC)*
Authors of books for children and young adults	*CHILDREN'S LITERATURE REVIEW (CLR)*
Dramatists	*DRAMA CRITICISM (DC)*
Poets	*POETRY CRITICISM (PC)*
Short story writers	*SHORT STORY CRITICISM (SSC)*
Literary topics and movements	*HARLEM RENAISSANCE: A GALE CRITICAL COMPANION (HR)* *THE BEAT GENERATION: A GALE CRITICAL COMPANION (BG)*
Asian American writers of the last two hundred years	*ASIAN AMERICAN LITERATURE (AAL)*
Black writers of the past two hundred years	*BLACK LITERATURE CRITICISM (BLC)* *BLACK LITERATURE CRITICISM SUPPLEMENT (BLCS)*
Hispanic writers of the late nineteenth and twentieth centuries	*HISPANIC LITERATURE CRITICISM (HLC)* *HISPANIC LITERATURE CRITICISM SUPPLEMENT (HLCS)*
Native North American writers and orators of the eighteenth, nineteenth, and twentieth centuries	*NATIVE NORTH AMERICAN LITERATURE (NNAL)*
Major authors from the Renaissance to the present	*WORLD LITERATURE CRITICISM, 1500 TO THE PRESENT (WLC)* *WORLD LITERATURE CRITICISM SUPPLEMENT (WLCS)*

ISSN 0732-1864

Volume 165

Nineteenth-Century Literature Criticism

Criticism of the
Works of Novelists, Philosophers, and Other
Creative Writers Who Died between 1800
and 1899, from the First Published Critical
Appraisals to Current Evaluations

Jessica Bomarito
Russel Whitaker
Project Editors

THOMSON
GALE

Detroit • New York • San Francisco • San Diego • New Haven, Conn. • Waterville, Maine • London • Munich

Nineteenth-Century Literature Criticism, Vol. 165

Project Editors
Jessica Bomarito and Russel Whitaker

Editorial
Kathy D. Darrow, Jeffrey W. Hunter, Jelena O. Krstović, Michelle Lee, Rachelle Mucha, Thomas J. Schoenberg, Noah Schusterbauer, Lawrence J. Trudeau

Data Capture
Frances Monroe, Gwen Tucker

Indexing Services
Laurie Andriot

Rights and Acquisitions
Lori Hines, Lisa Kincade, Kim Smilay

Imaging and Multimedia
Dean Dauphinais, Robert Duncan, Leitha Etheridge-Sims, Lezlie Light, Michael Logusz, Dan Newell, Kelly A. Quin, Denay Wilding

Composition and Electronic Capture
Amy Darga

Manufacturing
Rhonda Dover

Associate Product Manager
Marc Cormier

LIBRARY OF CONGRESS CATALOG CARD NUMBER 84-643008

ISBN 0-7876-8649-2
ISSN 0732-1864

Contents

Preface vii

Acknowledgments xi

Literary Criticism Series Advisory Board xiii

Preface

Since its inception in 1981, *Nineteeth-Century Literature Criticism* (*NCLC*) has been a valuable resource for students and librarians seeking critical commentary on writers of this transitional period in world history. Designated an "Outstanding Reference Source" by the American Library Association with the publication of is first volume, *NCLC* has since been purchased by over 6,000 school, public, and university libraries. The series has covered more than 450 authors representing 33 nationalities and over 17,000 titles. No other reference source has surveyed the critical reaction to nineteenth-century authors and literature as thoroughly as *NCLC*.

Scope of the Series

NCLC is designed to introduce students and advanced readers to the authors of the nineteenth century and to the most significant interpretations of these authors' works. The great poets, novelists, short story writers, playwrights, and philosophers of this period are frequently studied in high school and college literature courses. By organizing and reprinting commentary written on these authors, *NCLC* helps students develop valuable insight into literary history, promotes a better understanding of the texts, and sparks ideas for papers and assignments. Each entry in *NCLC* presents a comprehensive survey of an author's career or an individual work of literature and provides the user with a multiplicity of interpretations and assessments. Such variety allows students to pursue their own interests; furthermore, it fosters an awareness that literature is dynamic and responsive to many different opinions.

Every fourth volume of *NCLC* is devoted to literary topics that cannot be covered under the author approach used in the rest of the series. Such topics include literary movements, prominent themes in nineteenth-century literature, literary reaction to political and historical events, significant eras in literary history, prominent literary anniversaries, and the literatures of cultures that are often overlooked by English-speaking readers.

NCLC continues the survey of criticism of world literature begun by Thomson Gale's *Contemporary Literary Criticism* (*CLC*) and *Twentieth-Century Literary Criticism* (*TCLC*).

Organization of the Book

An *NCLC* entry consists of the following elements:

- The **Author Heading** cites the name under which the author most commonly wrote, followed by birth and death dates. Also located here are any name variations under which an author wrote, including transliterated forms for authors whose native languages use nonroman alphabets. If the author wrote consistently under a pseudonym, the pseudonym will be listed in the author heading and the author's actual name given in parenthesis on the first line of the biographical and critical information. Uncertain birth or death dates are indicated by question marks. Single-work entries are preceded by a heading that consists of the most common form of the title in English translation (if applicable) and the original date of composition.

- The **Introduction** contains background information that introduces the reader to the author, work, or topic that is the subject of the entry.

- A **Portrait of the Author** is included when available.

- The list of **Principal Works** is ordered chronologically by date of first publication and lists the most important works by the author. The genre and publication date of each work is given. In the case of foreign authors whose works have been translated into English, the list will focus primarily on twentieth-century translations, selecting those works most commonly considered the best by critics. Unless otherwise indicated, dramas are dated by first performance, not first publication. Lists of **Representative Works** by different authors appear with topic entries.

- Reprinted **Criticism** is arranged chronologically in each entry to provide a useful perspective on changes in critical evaluation over time. The critic's name and the date of composition or publication of the critical work are given at the beginning of each piece of criticism. Unsigned criticism is preceded by the title of the source in which it appeared. All titles by the author featured in the text are printed in boldface type. Footnotes are reprinted at the end of each essay or excerpt. In the case of excerpted criticism, only those footnotes that pertain to the excerpted texts are included. Criticism in topic entries is arranged chronologically under a variety of subheadings to facilitate the study of different aspects of the topic.

- A complete **Bibliographical Citation** of the original essay or book precedes each piece of criticism.

- Critical essays are prefaced by brief **Annotations** explicating each piece.

- An annotated bibliography of **Further Reading** appears at the end of each entry and suggests resources for additional study. In some cases, significant essays for which the editors could not obtain reprint rights are included here. Boxed material following the further reading list provides references to other biographical and critical sources on the author in series published by Thomson Gale.

Indexes

Each volume of *NCLC* contains a **Cumulative Author Index** listing all authors who have appeared in a wide variety of reference sources published by Thomson Gale, including *NCLC*. A complete list of these sources is found facing the first page of the Author Index. The index also includes birth and death dates and cross references between pseudonyms and actual names.

A **Cumulative Nationality Index** lists all authors featured in *NCLC* by nationality, followed by the number of the *NCLC* volume in which their entry appears.

A **Cumulative Topic Index** lists the literary themes and topics treated in the series as well as in *Classical and Medieval Literature Criticism, Literature Criticism from 1400 to 1800, Twentieth-Century Literary Criticism,* and the *Contemporary Literary Criticism* Yearbook, which was discontinued in 1998.

An alphabetical **Title Index** accompanies each volume of *NCLC*, with the exception of the Topics volumes. Listings of titles by authors covered in the given volume are followed by the author's name and the corresponding page numbers where the titles are discussed. English translations of foreign titles and variations of titles are cross-referenced to the title under which a work was originally published. Titles of novels, dramas, nonfiction books, and poetry, short story, or essay collections are printed in italics, while individual poems, short stories, and essays are printed in roman type within quotation marks.

In response to numerous suggestions from librarians, Thomson Gale also produces an annual paperbound edition of the *NCLC* cumulative title index. This annual cumulation, which alphabetically lists all titles reviewed in the series, is available to all customers. Additional copies of this index are available upon request. Librarians and patrons will welcome this separate index; it saves shelf space, is easy to use, and is recyclable upon receipt of the next edition.

Citing *Nineteenth-Century Literature Criticism*

When citing criticism reprinted in the Literary Criticism Series, students should provide complete bibliographic information so that the cited essay can be located in the original print or electronic source. Students who quote directly from reprinted criticism may use any accepted bibliographic format, such as University of Chicago Press style or Modern Language Association style.

The examples below follow recommendations for preparing a bibliography set forth in *The Chicago Manual of Style,* 14th ed. (Chicago: The University of Chicago Press, 1993); the first example pertains to material drawn from periodicals, the second to material reprinted from books:

Guerard, Albert J. "On the Composition of Dostoevsky's *The Idiot." Mosaic: A Journal for the Interdisciplinary Study of Literature* 8, no. 1 (fall 1974): 201-15. Reprinted in *Nineteenth-Century Literature Criticism.* Vol. 119, edited by Lynn M. Zott, 81-104. Detroit: Gale, 2003.

Berstein, Carol L. "Subjectivity as Critique and the Critique of Subjectivity in Keats's *Hyperion."* In *After the Future: Postmodern Times and Places,* edited by Gary Shapiro, 41-52. Albany, N. Y.: State University of New York Press, 1990. Reprinted in *Nineteeth-Century Literature Criticism.* Vol. 121, edited by Lynn M. Zott, 155-60. Detroit: Gale, 2003.

The examples below follow recommendations for preparing a works cited list set forth in the *MLA Handbook for Writers of Research Papers,* 5th ed. (New York: The Modern Language Association of America, 1999); the first example pertains to material drawn from periodicals, the second to material reprinted from books:

Guerard, Albert J. "On the Composition of Dostoevsky's *The Idiot." Mosaic: A Journal for the Interdisciplinary Study of Literature* 8. 1 (fall 1974): 201-15. Reprinted in *Nineteenth-Century Literature Criticism.* Ed. Lynn M. Zott. Vol. 119. Detroit: Gale, 2003. 81-104.

Berstein, Carol L. "Subjectivity as Critique and the Critique of Subjectivity in Keats's *Hyperion." After the Future: Postmodern Times and Places.* Ed. Gary Shapiro. Albany, N. Y.: State University of New York Press, 1990. 41-52. Reprinted in *Nineteeth-Century Literature Criticism.* Ed. Lynn M. Zott. Vol. 121. Detroit: Gale, 2003. 155-60.

Suggestions are Welcome

Readers who wish to suggest new features, topics, or authors to appear in future volumes, or who have other suggestions or comments are cordially invited to call, write, or fax the Associate Product Manager:

Associate Product Manager, Literary Criticism Series
Thomson Gale
27500 Drake Road
Farmington Hills, MI 48331-3535
1-800-347-4253 (GALE)
Fax: 248-699-8054

Acknowledgments

The editors wish to thank the copyright holders of the criticism included in this volume and the permissions managers of many book and magazine publishing companies for assisting us in securing reproduction rights. We are also grateful to the staffs of the Detroit Public Library, the Library of Congress, the University of Detroit Mercy Library, Wayne State University Purdy/Kresge Library Complex, and the University of Michigan Libraries for making their resources available to us. Following is a list of the copyright holders who have granted us permission to reproduce material in this volume of *NCLC*. Every effort has been made to trace copyright, but if omissions have been made, please let us know.

COPYRIGHTED MATERIAL IN *NCLC*, VOLUME 165, WAS REPRODUCED FROM THE FOLLOWING PERIODICALS:

Canadian Journal of Netherlandic Studies, v. 5, fall, 1984; v. 13, fall, 1992. Both reproduced by permission of the author.—*ELH,* v. 62, spring, 1995; v. 70, winter, 2003. Copyright © 1995, 2003 The Johns Hopkins University Press. Both reproduced by permission.—*English Journal,* v. 74, March, 1985 for "Catherine Earnshaw: Mother and Daughter" by Linda Gold. Copyright © 1985 by the National Council of Teachers of English. Reproduced by permission of the publisher and the author.—*The Lovingood Papers,* v. 4, 1965. Copyright © 1967 by The University of Tennessee Press. Reproduced by permission of The University of Tennessee Press.—*Modern Language Notes,* v. 112, December, 1997. Copyright © 1997 The Johns Hopkins University Press. Reproduced by permission.—*Prospects: An Annual of American Cultural Studies,* v. 25, 2000. Copyright © 2000 Cambridge University Press. Edited by Jack Salzman. Reprinted with the permission of Cambridge University Press.—*Southern Folklore Quarterly,* v. 34, June, 1970. Copyright © 1970 by The University Press of Kentucky. Reproduced by permission of The University Press of Kentucky.—*The Southern Quarterly,* v. 25, winter, 1987. Copyright © 1987 by the University of Southern Mississippi. Reproduced by permission.—*Southern Studies: An Interdisciplinary Journal of the South,* v. 22, summer, 1983 for "Sut Lovingood: Backwoods Existentialist" by Elaine Gardiner. Copyright © 1983 by Southern Studies Institute. Reproduced by permission of the publisher and author.—*Studies in American Fiction,* v. 15, autumn, 1987. Copyright © 1987 Northeastern University. Reproduced by permission.—*Studies in American Humor,* new series, v. 3, 1995. Copyright © 1995 American Humor Studies Association. Reproduced by permission.—*Studies in the Novel,* v. 28, summer, 1996; v. 32, winter, 2000. Copyright © 1996, 2000 by North Texas State University. All reproduced by permission.—*Studies in Short Fiction,* v. 9, spring, 1972. Copyright © 1972 by Studies in Short Fiction. Reproduced by permission.—*Thalia: Studies in Literary Humor,* v. 1, winter, 1978-79. Copyright © 1978-79 by Jacqueline Tavernier-Courbin. Reproduced by permission.—*The University of Mississippi Studies in English,* new series, v. 2, 1981. Copyright © 1981 The University of Mississippi. Reproduced by permission.—*University of Toronto Quarterly,* v. 47, winter, 1977-78. Copyright © University of Toronto Press 1977-78. Reproduced by permission of University of Toronto Press Incorporated.—*The Victorian Newsletter,* fall, 1988 for "The Gothic Form of *Wuthering Heights*" by George E. Haggerty. Reproduced by permission of the publisher and author.—*Victorian Studies,* v. 27, summer, 1984. Copyright © Indiana University Press. Reproduced by permission.

COPYRIGHTED MATERIAL IN *NCLC*, VOLUME 165, WAS REPRODUCED FROM THE FOLLOWING BOOKS:

Baker, Gary L. From "Max Havelaar: A Romantic Novel for Social Fluidity," in *The Low Countries: Multidisciplinary Studies.* Edited by Margriet Bruijn Lacy. University Press of America, Inc., 1990. Copyright © 1990 by University Press of America, Inc. All rights reserved. Reproduced by permission.—Baker, Gary Lee. From "Object of Desire and Undesired Knowledge in Multatuli's *Woutertje Pieterse,*" in *The Low Countries and Beyond.* Edited by Robert S. Kirsner. University Press of America, Inc., 1993. Copyright © 1993 by University Press of America, Inc. All rights reserved. Reproduced by permission.—Caron, James E. From "Playin' Hell: Sut Lovingood as Durn'd Fool Preacher," in *Sut Lovingood's Nat'ral Born Yarnspinner: Essays on George Washington Harris.* Edited by James E. Caron and M. Thomas Inge. The University of Alabama Press, 1996. Copyright © 1996 The University of Alabama Press. All rights reserved. Reproduced by permission.—Eagleton, Terry. From *Myths of Power: A Marxist Study of the Brontës.* The Macmillan Press Ltd, 1975. Copyright © Terry Eagleton 1975. All rights reserved. Reproduced with permission of Palgrave Macmillan.—Fisher, IV, Benjamin Franklin. From "George Washington Harris and Supernaturalism," in *Sut Lovingood's Nat'ral Born Yarnspinner: Essays on George Washington Harris.* Edited by James E. Caron and M. Thomas Inge. The University of Alabama Press, 1996.

PHOTOGRAPHS AND ILLUSTRATIONS APPEARING IN *NCLC*, VOLUME 165, WERE RECEIVED FROM THE FOLLOWING SOURCES:

Thomson Gale Literature Product Advisory Board

Wuthering Heights

Emily Brontë

(Also wrote under the pseudonym Ellis Bell) English novelist and poet.

The following entry presents criticism of Brontë's novel *Wuthering Heights* (1847). For information on Brontë's complete career, see *NCLC,* Volume 16. For further information on *Wuthering Heights,* see *NCLC,* Volume 35.

INTRODUCTION

First published under the pseudonym Ellis Bell, Brontë's *Wuthering Heights* remains one of the most popular and widely discussed novels of nineteenth-century literature. Over the years the work has invited a range of interpretations by prominent scholars, who have generally regarded it as an eloquent and haunting representation of the human condition. In certain respects *Wuthering Heights* is a quintessential Gothic novel: it incorporates many of the traditional devices and motifs of the genre, including the doomed love affair, the gloomy, foreboding setting, and the recurrent suggestions of supernatural phenomena. At the same time, however, the novel's weighty philosophical themes, combined with its poetic prose style and inventive narrative structure, lend it a distinctly modern sensibility, and the work ultimately transcends the limitations of any particular category. Its protagonist, the enigmatic and destructive Heathcliff, has secured a permanent position as one of the most original and complex characters in literature. A larger-than-life figure—the embodiment of pure human emotion—Heathcliff has posed a unique challenge to generations of scholars, consistently defying straightforward critical analysis. Indeed, Heathcliff's ambiguity and intensity, coupled with Brontë's broader examination of humanity's struggle to survive in an insensate and irrational universe, lie at the heart of the novel's profound psychological power.

PLOT AND MAJOR CHARACTERS

Set in the inhospitable landscape of the Yorkshire moors, *Wuthering Heights* tells the story of the powerful, and ultimately fatal, emotional bond that develops between Catherine Earnshaw and her adopted brother, Heathcliff. Although the work is characterized by a convoluted chronology and an unorthodox structure, it is also meticulously logical and adheres to an ingenious symmetry. The novel opens with the figure of Lockwood, a stranger traveling through the moors, as he seeks accommodations in the region. In the course of his search he meets Heathcliff, who is the landlord of two estates—Thrushcross Grange and Wuthering Heights—and the central figure of the novel. Despite Heathcliff's somber, gruff manner, Lockwood initially perceives him as a sympathetic and good-hearted man and decides to rent Thrushcross Grange from him. During the course of two visits to Wuthering Heights, however, Lockwood begins to recognize Heathcliff's sinister nature, particularly in his spiteful attitude toward his daughter-in-law, Catherine, and in his generally inhospitable conduct. When a snowstorm forces a reluctant Lockwood to spend the night at Wuthering Heights, he finds his sleep disturbed by a harrowing dream of a young girl who shatters the window of his room and begins scraping her wrists along the jagged glass. When Lockwood recounts the dream, Heathcliff descends into a state of rage and despair, and as Lockwood leaves the room he overhears his host imploring the girl, whose name is also Catherine, to open the window. Upon returning to Thrushcross Grange, Lockwood asks the servant, Nelly Dean, the reason behind his host's peculiar outburst. Here the narrative shifts to the perspective of Nelly, who has been on intimate terms with Heathcliff and the other main characters of the novel for most of her life, and the novel's central plot begins to emerge.

Nelly recounts the complex story of two households, beginning with the day when the original owner of Wuthering Heights, a prosperous merchant named Earnshaw, returns from a trip to Liverpool with an orphan boy, whom he names Heathcliff. An exotic, dark-skinned figure, Heathcliff develops an immediate emotional affinity with Earnshaw's daughter, Catherine, and the two quickly become close, acting as brother and sister. Nelly describes the history of this intimate companionship, while also relating the bitter rivalry that emerges between Heathcliff and Earnshaw's elder son, Hindley, who resents the foundling's presence. For most of his childhood, Heathcliff is treated by Earnshaw as a son, and he devotes his youth to exploring the rugged beauty of the surrounding landscape and inventing elaborate games with Catherine. After Earnshaw's death, however, Heathcliff's fortunes change radically. Hindley assumes control over the management of the household, and he abruptly revokes Heathcliff's status as a member of the family, forcing him to become the house servant. At once distressed and confused by Heathcliff's degraded status, the now adolescent Catherine persists with her normal attitude toward her adopted brother, although Heathcliff's shame and indignation place a strain on their relationship. One evening while Catherine and Heathcliff are roaming the moors, they come upon Thrushcross Grange, home of the Lintons. As Catherine peers through a window into the Lintons' living room, she beholds a picture of sophistication and elegance, and she imagines for the first time a very different life than the one she knows at Wuthering Heights. Shortly after this experience, Heathcliff decides that life under Hindley's control is unbearable, and he runs away. During his absence, Catherine becomes engaged to Edgar Linton, the heir to Thrushcross Grange. As she explains her feelings to Nelly, Catherine describes the torment she feels over her decision, particularly because it undermines her closeness to Heathcliff. When she utters her famous declaration, "I *am* Heathcliff," she suggests not only the overpowering empathy she feels for her adopted brother, but also the impossibility of loving him as a person separate from herself. In the end she perseveres in her plan and marries Linton.

A few years later, Heathcliff, now a wealthy and urbane young man, returns to Wuthering Heights. He recounts little about his travels or his elevation in fortune, seeking only to resume his intimacy with Catherine. His attention to his adopted sister stirs jealousy in Linton, however, provoking a violent confrontation between the two men. As Heathcliff recognizes that his former relationship with Catherine is now impossible, he becomes resentful and withdrawn. At this point in the novel, Heathcliff's elaborate plot to revenge himself begins to unfold. He conspires to marry Linton's sister, Isabella, although he despises her, while simultaneously bullying Hindley into a state of alcoholism and incapacitation. When Catherine dies suddenly during the birth of her daughter, Catherine, Heathcliff sinks into a state of despair, and any remaining shred of compassion dies inside of him. Upon Hindley's death Heathcliff assumes control over Wuthering Heights, forcing Hindley's son, Hareton, to become a household servant, while denying him even a rudimentary education; and Heathcliff manages to marry his feeble and sickly son, Linton, to young Catherine, in the process gaining ownership of Thrushcross Grange. As Nelly relates the final details of this sordid chain of events, which includes the death of Linton, the narrative returns to the present and to Lockwood's point of view. Lockwood is present to witness Heathcliff's final unraveling: still inconsolable over the death of Catherine, he withdraws even further, declining any kind of social interaction and eventually refus-

ing food. Meanwhile, Lockwood observes a growing intimacy between Hareton and young Catherine, who teaches the abused young man to read. Heathcliff dies a short time later and is buried in a grave next to Catherine's; meanwhile, Hareton and young Catherine marry and take over the management of the two estates.

MAJOR THEMES

Wuthering Heights examines the struggles between morality, intellect, and passion that rage inside the human psyche. Throughout the novel, Brontë opposes images of refinement and security with visions of brute, violent force, creating a vigorous tension that underlies the relationships between the novel's central characters and lends the work its unique power. Indeed, each character seems caught in a state of perpetual conflict, driven by both external and internal impulses. When Catherine decides to marry Linton, she falls sway not only to society's notion of a sensible union between a man and a woman, but also to her own belief that happiness, to some extent, arises from a state of security and harmony. At the same time, however, her inexplicably powerful feelings toward Heathcliff, which she experiences as an essential aspect of her personality, make such rational notions of happiness seem hollow and unattainable. Even Heathcliff, who in many respects is the embodiment of irrationality and cruelty, elicits some sympathy from the reader, particularly in his abiding loyalty to the memory of Catherine, as well as in his ability to rise above his degraded condition to become an educated, prosperous, and attractive man. Although Heathcliff's rage is so extreme at times that he repels everyone around him—including most readers—in the end his anguish resonates with anyone who has ever suffered loss, lending him his unique humanity. Dualities, then—between civilization and nature, security and danger, affection and brutality, kindness and malice—dominate the novel.

Brontë's use of symbolism also plays a crucial role in *Wuthering Heights*. The novel abounds with vivid images of landscape, weather, home, and animals, all charged with profound meaning. Several scholars, notably Thomas Moser and Carol Jacobs, have focused on Brontë's use of windows and doorways as central images in the work, describing them both as openings into different realms of feeling and experience and at the same time as barriers that imprison the individual characters. Dogs play a key part in amplifying the novel's potent sense of foreboding. In some of the novel's most unforgettable scenes, dogs are victims of blind cruelty, as when Heathcliff hangs Isabella's dog and when Hareton tortures and kills a litter of puppies. In other instances, the presence of dogs contributes to an air of menace, or dogs become agents of savage and implacable violence, as when Lockwood finds himself at-tacked by the dogs at Thrushcross Grange. Through these powerful images, Brontë's readers become aware, on a visceral level, of the forces of irrationality and am-biguity that pervade the novel.

CRITICAL RECEPTION

Wuthering Heights met with general perplexity upon its original publication. Although some critics admired the work's powers of expressiveness and emotion, they also voiced disappointment in the rawness of the novel's prose style, as well as in its seemingly disjointed struc-ture. Some critics, upon discovering that the author was a woman, even described their uneasiness about the work's subject matter, declaring that the novel's unre-mitting sadism constituted inappropriate material for a female author. By the turn of the century, however, most scholars of Victorian literature acknowledged the work's singular genius and hailed Brontë as one of the most important woman novelists of the nineteenth cen-tury. Most later-twentieth-century criticism has focused on the psychological aspects of the novel, particularly as they relate to the character of Heathcliff. Both Dor-othy van Ghent and Harold Bloom have paid particular attention to the demonic qualities in Heathcliff, regard-ing him as an allegorical representation not only of hu-man existence, but of the creative act itself. Recent crit-ics have begun to explore more elaborate frameworks for interpreting the novel. Among these scholars are Terry Eagleton, who has examined the work's self-mythologizing qualities within a Marxist context, and Barbara Munson Goff, who has pointed out parallels between Brontë's explorations of human character and the evolutionary theories of Charles Darwin.

PRINCIPAL WORKS

Poems by Currer, Ellis, and Acton Bell [as Ellis Bell; with Charlotte and Anne Brontë] (poetry) 1846

*Wuthering Heights [as Ellis Bell] (novel) 1847

Life and Works of the Sisters Brontë. 7 vols. [with Char-lotte and Anne Brontë] (novels and poetry) 1899-1903

The Shakespeare Head Brontë. 19 vols. [with Charlotte and Anne Brontë] (novels, poetry, and letters) 1931-38

Gondal Poems (poetry) 1938

The Complete Poems of Emily Jane Brontë (poetry) 1941

**This edition of *Wuthering Heights* was published with Ann Brontë's *Agnes Grey*.

CRITICISM

G. W. Peck (review date June 1848)

SOURCE: Peck, G. W. "*Wuthering Heights.*" *American Review*, n.s., 1, no. 6 (June 1848): 572-85.

[*In the following excerpt, Peck finds that the "coarse" style and vulgar subject matter of* Wuthering Heights *might exert a negative influence on female readers, but concedes that the novel is a work of great intelligence and imaginative power.*]

Respecting a book so original as [*Wuthering Heights*],[1] and written with so much power of imagination, it is natural that there should be many opinions. Indeed, its power is so predominant that it is not easy after a hasty reading to analyze one's impressions so as to speak of its merits and demerits with confidence. We have been taken and carried through a new region, a melancholy waste, with here and there patches of beauty; have been brought in contact with fierce passions, with extremes of love and hate, and with sorrow that none but those who have suffered can understand. This has not been accomplished with ease, but with an ill-mannered con-tempt for the decencies of language, and in a style which might resemble that of a Yorkshire farmer who should have endeavored to eradicate his provincialism by taking lessons of a London footman. We have had many sad bruises and tumbles in our journey, yet it was interesting, and at length we are safely arrived at a happy conclusion.

The first feeling with which we turn back to recall the incidents passed through, is one of uneasiness and gloom; even the air of summer, so reviving to city dwellers, does not dispel it. To write or think about the tale, without being conscious of a phase of sadness, is impossible; which mood of the mind, if it appear to the reader, let him not attribute to an over susceptibility, unless he has read the book with no such impression himself.

We shall take for granted that a novel which has excited so unusual an attention, has been or will soon be in the hands of most of our readers of light literature, and shall therefore write rather *from* than *upon* it. We will not attempt an outline of the story; it is so void of events that an outline would be of small assistance to any who have not read it, and would only be tedious to those who have. It is a history of two families during two generations, and all transpires under their two roofs. The genealogy is a little perplexing, and as an assis-tance to the reader's recollection we give it in a note.[2]

If we did not know that this book has been read by thousands of young ladies in the country, we should es-teem it our first duty to caution them against it simply on account of the coarseness of the style. We are so far pedantic as to agree with John Kemble in thinking that "oblige" is more becoming to royal mouths than "obleege." With ladies who should be habituated to the use of forms of speech like those which occur in every page of this book, we can see how a gentleman should altogether fail in any attempt at love-making, though he might be able to hold discourse with a western boatman in his own dialect, and be so well accustomed to the language of bar-rooms and steamboat saloons, that he could hear the eyes and souls of those around him "condemned," to use the words of Mrs. Isabella Heathcliff, "to a perpetual dwelling in the infernal regions," without experiencing the slightest inconvenience. . . .

Suppose this book were not written with so much power and subtlety, and with so large an infusion of genuine truth and beauty, the judgment of the public would at once condemn it on account of its coarseness of style. It would then be seen how much of the coarseness was affected and how much natural. But ought the other qualities of the book, which render us almost insensible, while we are reading it, to a language which, to say the least, was never that of well-bred ladies and gentlemen, to excuse this language—even considering the coarseness wholly unaffected and unavoidable—a part of the substance of the writer's very self?

We think not. The book is original; it is powerful; full of suggestiveness. But still it is *coarse*. The narrative talks on in a way that if an attempt to imitate it be ever made in a parlor, the experimenter should be speedily ejected. It ought to be banished from refined society, because it does not converse in a proper manner. Setting aside the profanity, which if a writer introduces into a book, he offends against both politeness and good morals, there is such a general roughness and savageness in the soliloquies and dialogues here given as never should be found in a work of art. The whole tone of the style of the book smacks of lowness. It would indicate that the writer was not accustomed to the society of gentlemen, and was not afraid, indeed, rather gloried, in showing it. . . .

But the taint of vulgarity with our author extends deeper than mere snobbishness; he is rude, because he prefers to be so. In the outset he represents himself as a misanthropist, and confesses to a degree of reserve which it would puzzle a psychologist to explain:—

> The "walk in" was uttered with closed teeth, and expressed the sentiment, "Go to the Deuce!" Even the gate over which he leaned manifested no sympathizing movement to the words; and I think that circumstance determined me to accept the invitation: I felt interested in a man who seemed more *exaggeratedly reserved* than myself.

"Exaggeratedly reserved"—another Jeamesism.

While enjoying a month of fine weather at the sea-coast, I was thrown into the company of a most fascinating creature, a real goddess, in my eyes, as long as she took no notice of me. I "never told my love" vocally; still, if looks have language, the merest idiot might have guessed I was over head and ears; she understood me, at last, and looked a return—the sweetest of all imaginable looks—and what did I do? I confess it with shame—shrunk icily into myself, like a snail, at every glance retired colder and farther; till, finally, the poor innocent was led to doubt her own senses, and, overwhelmed with confusion at her supposed mistake, persuaded her mamma to decamp.

This is a phase of human nature which we had rather not understand. If it ever was real with any living man, he was a very bad-hearted one, and a conceited. More likely the real truth with one who would write himself so affected a personage, was just the reverse—that some gay girl, seeing in him a person on agreeable terms with himself, experimented on him for her diversion, till she made him "deucedly miserable." It is evident that the author has suffered, not disappointment in love, but some great mortification of pride. Possibly his position in society has given him manners that have prevented him from associating with those among whom he feels he has intellect enough to be classed, and he is thus in reality the misanthropist he claims to be. Very likely he may be a young person who has spent his life, until within a few years, in some isolated town in the North of England. It is only by some such supposition that his peculiarities of style and thought can be accounted for. He is one who is evidently unfamiliar with, and careless of acquiring, the habits of refined society.

We regret the necessity of proving his intentional and affected coarseness by examples. In the first place, several of the characters swear worse than ever the troops did in Flanders. Now, setting out of the question the morality or immorality of this practice, it is, as we have already observed, an offence against politeness; not such a great one, however, but it is esteemed venial when used effectively by military or naval gentlemen, who have seen some service. It is not permitted to civilians in general society, though a little Mantalini "demmit," escaping between the teeth in the heat of an argument, is readily overlooked. But common, rough swearing is a worse breach of decorum than disregarding the conveniences for tobacco saliva. And how much more in writing than in conversation! For a writer is presumed to be deliberate; he corrects his proofs at leisure. If a writer, therefore, permits his characters to swear, and that grossly, (not like gentlemen,) he does it *knowingly*; he is aware that it is not customary or mannerly, and every time he does it, he is, therefore, intentionally rude.

But the writer's disposition to be coarse is, perhaps, still more clearly shown by examples like the following:—

I was surprised to see Heathcliff there also. He stood by the fire, his back toward me, just finishing a stormy scene to poor Zillah, who ever and anon interrupted her labor to pluck up the corner of her apron, and heave an indignant groan.

"And you, you worthless——" he broke out as I entered, turning to his daughter-in-law, and employing an epithet as harmless as duck, or sheep, but generally represented by a dash.

Had the writer been simply, unconsciously coarse, he would, in this instance, have said "slut" or "bitch," without adverting to the harmlessness of the word. But by alluding to its harmlessness, he at once uses it, and offers a defence of it. This as plainly evinces a conscious determination to write coarsely, as if he had quoted and defended a passage from Rabelais. He knew the word to be a low word, though not an immodest one, and he determined to show his bold independence by using and defending it. He was anxious to extend the resources of the English language. This and hundreds of other sentences show that he has got the maggot in his brain, that low words are the strongest, and low manners the most natural. He desired to write a book with "no nonsense about it," and he has, therefore, been led into the affecting boorishness. . . .

The influence which this book cannot but have upon manners, must be bad. For the coarseness extends farther than the mere style; it extends *all through*; and the crude style and rude expressions are too much in keeping with the necessary situations. It deals constantly in exaggerated extremes of passion. From the beginning to the end, there is hardly a scene which does not place the actors in the most agonizing or antagonizing predicament possible. Let the reader run over the principal events of the story in his mind, and consider what a series of scenes it would make, if dramatized and placed upon the stage.

Mr. Lockwood visits Mr. Heathcliff, and is attacked by sheep dogs in his parlor. He visits him again and is caught in the snow; the dogs fly at him, his nose bleeds, Zillah pours a pint of ice water down his back and puts him to bed in a haunted chamber, where he has a terrible dream.

Mrs. Dean then begins her tale, and in the first chapter we have a fight between Heathcliff and Hindley. Then Mr. Earnshaw dies in his chair. Heathcliff and Cathy run away to the grange, and he is degraded for it. They lead a dreadful life with Hindley, who becomes a drunkard. Edgar Linton visits Catherine and falls in love; she, after nearly knocking him over with a blow on the face, accepts him.

But we will not continue the catalogue of scenes of the most disgusting violence, of which the remainder of the book is almost wholly made up. Catherine's election of Linton and her reasons for it, as it is the main incident of the story, may be most properly taken to examine the *naturalness* of the passion. She at last makes a confidant of Nelly:—

"Nelly, I see now, you think me a selfish wretch, but did it never strike you that if Heathcliff and I married we should be beggars? whereas, if I married Linton, I can aid Heathcliff to rise, and place him out of my brother's power."

"With your husband's money, Miss Catherine?" I asked. "You'll find him not so pliable as you calculate upon; and, though I'm hardly a judge, I think that's the worst motive you've given yet for being the wife of young Linton."

"It is not," retorted she, "it is the best! The others were the satisfaction of my whims; and for Edgar's sake, too, to satisfy him. This is for the sake of one who comprehends in his person my feelings to Edgar and myself. I cannot express it; but surely you and everybody have a notion that there is, or should be, an existence of yours beyond you. What were the use of my creation, if I were entirely contained here? My great miseries in this world have been Heathcliff's miseries, and I watched and felt each from the beginning; my great thought in living is himself. If all else perished, and *he* remained, I should still continue to be; and, if all else remained, and he were annihilated, the universe would turn to a mighty stranger. I should not seem a part of it. My love for Linton is like the foliage in the woods: time will change it, I'm well aware, as winter changes the trees. My love for Heathcliff resembles the eternal rocks beneath: a source of little visible delight, but necessary. Nelly, I *am* Heathcliff—he's always in my mind—not as a pleasure, any more than I am always a pleasure to myself—but as my own being; so don't talk of our separation again—it is impracticable; and——"

She paused, and hid her face in the folds of my gown; but I jerked it forcibly away. I was out of patience with her folly.

"If I can make any sense of your nonsense, miss," I said, "it only goes to convince me that you are ignorant of the duties you undertake in marrying, or else that you are a wicked, unprincipled girl."

Now, if Catherine could have found Heathcliff the same night; if he had not run away just at that juncture, and left her to a long brain fever, and finally to a marriage with Linton; if they could have met but an instant, the reader is made to feel that all would be well. What she here utters was but the passing fancy of an extremely capricious, ungoverned girl; her better reason, could it have availed in time, might have brought her to her senses. And so we are wrought upon to love her to the last. . . .

Yet with all this faultiness, **Wuthering Heights** is, undoubtedly, a work of many singular merits. In the first place it is not a novel which deals with the shows of society, the surfaces and conventionalities of life. It does not depict men and women guided merely by motives intelligible to simplest observers. It lifts the veil and shows boldly the dark side of our depraved nature. It teaches how little the ends of life in the young are rough hewn by experience and benevolence in the old. It goes into the under-current of passion, and the rapid hold it has taken of the public shows how much truth there is hidden under its coarse extravagance. . . .

Next to the merit of this novel as a work of thought and subtle insight, is its great power as a work of the imagination. In this respect it must take rank very high, if not among the highest. It is not flowingly written; the author can hardly be an easy writer. Yet he has the power, with all his faults of style, of sometimes flashing a picture upon the eye, and the feeling with it, in a few sentences. The snow-storm which occurs in the second and third chapters of the first volume, is an example. But the effect of the description is often marred by consciously chosen fine words; as for instance, the word "shimmering" in one of the extracts first quoted.

The dialogue is also singularly effective and dramatic. The principal characters all talk alike; yet they stand before us as definite as so many individuals. In this respect the book reminds us of the *Five Nights of St. Albans*. It is like that also somewhat, in the tone of the fancy; the dream in the opening might have been conceived by the author of the *Five Nights*; the effect is so like some of his own. Yet this novel has none of the loftiness of that splendid romance; and whatever it may be as a work of genius and ability, is not worthy to be named with it as a work of art.

That it is original all who have read it need not be told. It is *very* original. And this is the reason of its popularity. It comes upon a sated public a new sensation. Nothing like it has ever been written before; it is to be hoped that in respect of its faults, for the sake of good manners, nothing will be hereafter. Let it stand by itself, a coarse, original, powerful book,—one that does not give us true characters, but horridly striking and effective ones. It will live a short and brilliant life, and then die and be forgotten. For when the originality becomes familiarized, there will not be truth enough left to sustain it. The public will not acknowledge its men and women to have the true immortal vitality. Poor Cathy's ghost will not walk the earth forever; and the insane Heathcliff will soon rest quietly in his coveted repose.

We are not aware that anything has been written upon the rank that ought to be assigned to such works as **Wuthering Heights** in fictitious literature. In conversation we have heard it spoken of by some as next in merit to Shakspeare for depth of insight and dramatic power; while others have confessed themselves unable to get through it. But all agree that it affects them somewhat unpleasantly. It is written in a morbid phase of the mind, and is sustained so admirably that it communicates this sickliness to the reader. It does in truth lay bare some of the secret springs of human action with wonderful clearness; but still it dissects character as with a broad-axe—chops out some of the great passions, sets them together and makes us almost believe the combinations to be real men and women. It abounds in effective description, is very individual, and preserves the unity of its peculiar gloomy phase of mind from first to last. Yet the reader rises from its conclusion with the feeling of one passing from a sick chamber to a comfortable parlor, or going forth after a melancholy rain, into a dry, clear day.

Notes

1. *Wuthering Heights. A Novel.* By the Author of *Jane Eyre.* New York: Harper & Brothers. 1846.

2. Old Mr. Earnshaw of Wuthering Heights has two children, Hindley and Catherine. He finds Heathcliff, a gipsy boy, in Liverpool streets, and brings him home. When he dies, Hindley brings home a foreign wife, Frances. Old Mr. and Mrs. Linton, of Thrushcross Grange, have two children, Edgar and Isabella. In 1778 Hindley's wife gives birth to a son, Hareton, and dies. Old Mr. and Mrs. Linton die, and Edgar Linton marries Catherine Earnshaw. Heathcliff marries Isabella. Mrs. Linton (Catherine) gives birth to a daughter, and dies; the daughter takes her name. Heathcliff's wife dies, leaving a son, Linton. Hindley Earnshaw dies. Heathcliff's son, Linton, marries Edgar Linton's daughter Catherine. Edgar Linton dies. Heathcliff's son dies. Heathcliff himself dies; and finally Hareton Earnshaw and the widow of Heathcliff's son are left with a fair prospect of a happy marriage.

Galaxy (review date February 1873)

SOURCE: "The Life and Writings of Emily Brontë (Ellis Bell)." *Galaxy* 15, no. 2 (February 1873): 226-38.

[*In the following excerpt, the anonymous reviewer praises Brontë's evocation of life on the English moors in* Wuthering Heights, *while criticizing the novel as too improbable and grim to be read as realistic. The reviewer pays particular attention to the character of Heathcliff, concluding that the extreme intensity of his passion and brutality ultimately renders him implausible.*]

No amount of sophistry would persuade any one that Heathcliff was a noble nature, warped by adverse circumstances; or that the elder Catherine was anything but fierce, faithless, and foolish; or that such a swift succession of acts of coarse cruelty was probable or even possible in any Yorkshire manor-house, however isolated; or, finally, that an upper servant could ever have adorned a narrative with passages so eloquent and so elegant as those with which Nelly Dean not unfrequently adorns hers. But if *Wuthering Heights* admits in some respects neither of defence nor eneomium, still less does it deserve the wholesale condemnation and unqualified abuse which have been heaped upon it. Though a brutal, it is not a sensual book; though coarse, it is not vulgar; though bad, it is not indecent. The passion of Heathcliff for Catherine, though it is "a passion such as might boil and glow in the essence of some evil genius," is still a passion of soul for soul; and full of savage ferocity as the whole story is, it contains some exquisite pictures of childlike simplicity and innocence, which open upon us like glimpses of blue in a stormy sky; and there are bits of moorland, and dimly lighted and quaint interiors, and here and there a grand outline of distant hills, and grander stretch of sky, which are drawn by a master hand, and are like lilies among thorns, as compared with the coarseness, fierceness, and brutality of the rest of the narrative. In regard to the creation of Heathcliff—that strange being, neither man nor demon, nor apparently bearing any relation to anything in the heavens above or in the earth beneath—Charlotte Brontë has thus written in her eloquent preface to *Wuthering Heights*: "Whether it is right or advisable to create beings like Heathcliffs, I do not know: I scarcely think it is. But this I know; the writer who possesses the creative gift owns something of which he is not always master—something that at times strangely wills and works for itself. . . ."

The scene of *Wuthering Heights* is laid in an old north country manor-house, in the West Riding of Yorkshire, and the time is early in the present century. The hero of the book is a foundling, or waif, or stray. picked up by the master of the house in a journey to Liverpool, and educated by him together with his children. The elder of these children, the son and heir, treats him with extreme cruelty and injustice, and his revenge for this treatment, and his passionate attachment for the younger child, a little girl, form the keynote of the story, in which, however, plot is so entirely subordinate to delineation of character and description of scenery, that the extracts we shall make are selected for their intrinsic beauty or power, and not in order to illustrate the development of the plot.

Emily shared Charlotte's rare power of making the unreal vividly real to the reader. Throughout the whole of this narrative, the atmosphere of reality is so well kept up, that we recall it afterward as an experience, and seem to have lived through the lives and to have seen the places which it describes.

The grim old manor-house, with its belt of stunted firs, "all blown aslant" by the fierce winds; the wide, gray moor stretching away into the distance on every side; the sombre interior and sombre inmates of the "Heights"—how vividly real they are made to us! How strangely familiar is the aspect of the desolate chamber where Lockwood lies down to sleep, with the moaning wind for a lullaby and the frozen fir bough drawing its icy fingers ceaselessly along the lattice. How marvellously is the picture of his nightmare given, blending as it does so naturally with the black, stormy night, the wild wind, and the dreary old house; and how admirably is the deathless passion of Heathcliff for Catherine introduced, in all its weird power, as, "believing himself to be alone," he wrenches open the lattice and stretches out hands of wild yearning to the pitiless night, with that cry of anguish: "Cathy! oh my heart's darling! Hear me this once, Catherine, at last!" The keynote of his life's tragedy is struck in that vain appeal; and the deep night, the driving snow, the moaning wind form a fitting accompaniment to its passion and its pain. . . .

Heathcliff's conduct proceeds in a great measure from the entire absorption of all his faculties in one idea; but even admitting that view of the case, he is not human, and not being human he is not real. We do not feel this at first; the pure but powerful narrative style in which his history is written, the perfect and direct simplicity with which all his acts and feelings are described, the exquisite fidelity to nature, and to nature in some of her simplest and most every-day aspects, manifested in the description of his surroundings, the absence of melodrama, and finally, the great "though unconscious art with which the whole is managed," all combine to make us forget while we read, and shudder at the wickedness and woe of that lost soul, that such a living man could have existed. Not that many worse men than Heathcliff have not existed, but just such a character could not exist; and the longer we analyze it the more fully we are convinced that he is no man, but the freak of a fine though fevered fancy, in that fancy's infancy. We have already quoted what Charlotte Brontë alleges as an excuse for the creation of such a being, namely, that those who are possessed of the creative faculty own something which they cannot control. Perhaps another excuse may be found in the fact that when a woman's imagination possesses virile fire and power, it is apt in its first essays to project itself as far as possible from the beaten track of feminine grace and refinement, to delight in the sombre and the lurid, and to indulge in displays of strength which are too often uncouth and savage, because unmeasured and uncontrolled. There is a "sowing of wild oats" in art and literature as well as in life; that is, if we take the "sowing of wild oats" to mean what it originally did mean, the first outbreaks of the tumult of youth—tumult inevitable in strong and varied natures, and not to be regretted, because tumult means life, and out of such outbreaks gradually grows the power which, when properly directed, will do a great work in the world. Such is the only explanation, such the only excuses which can now be given for the faults of **Wuthering Heights.** Its beauties will speak for themselves to all who can appreciate genius and power and originality, and a careful study of those beauties will convince all such that the author of this book might have achieved almost anything had time, a wider and more genial experience, and a larger culture been vouchsafed to her.

Hugh Walker (essay date 1910)

SOURCE: Walker, Hugh. "The Women Novelists." In *The Literature of the Victorian Era.* 1910. Reprint, pp. 707-52. Cambridge: Cambridge University Press, 1913.

[*In the following excerpt, Walker praises the "extraordinary power" of* Wuthering Heights *but finds Brontë's portrayal of human nature overly dark.*]

All that has been said in adverse criticism of Charlotte Brontë might be said with much greater force of her sister Emily (1818-1848); and all that can be said in extenuation and excuse applies to her likewise with greater force. She died at thirty; she had seen less of the world than even Charlotte; her excessive reserve confined her still more narrowly within the narrow circle that was open to her; and finally, her own nature was more unyielding and had closer kinship with the harsh natures around her than her sister's. Her character was rather repellent than attractive; but yet it won the unstinted love and devotion of her sister. And however little Emily might be loved, hers was a nature that commanded respect. Her pride was morbid: it is painful to read how in her last illness even her sisters dared not notice her failing step and laboured breathing and her frequent pauses as she climbed the staircase. But this pride, when it took the form of courage, was magnificent. An incident recorded in *Shirley* actually occurred to her. Being bitten by a dog she believed to be mad, she applied cautery with her own hand, telling no one till the danger was over; and she thrashed her own bulldog, Keeper, with the bare hands till she conquered him, though she had been warned that he would spring at the throat of anyone who struck him. "I have never seen her parallel in anything," writes her sister in the *Biographical Notice.* "Stronger than a man, simpler than a child, her nature stood alone."

The book she wrote stands alone too. **Wuthering Heights** is a novel of extraordinary power, going far, with her poems, to justify the opinion of Arnold, that the author's soul

> Knew no fellow for might,
> Passion, vehemence, grief,
> Daring, since Byron died.

But it is a book not to be read with pleasure. The first picture of the Heights is revolting from its brutal inhumanity. To those who know only the softer southern life, the wild stories and the rugged characters of Yorkshire seem to be here exaggerated almost beyond the bounds of belief; and however those stories may explain, they do not justify in art such a picture. The book is spoilt because its author has not known how to humanise it. If Charlotte Brontë's work is impaired because she makes too deep the shadows and shows too little the lights of life, Emily sins in that way tenfold more grievously. And yet there is an irresistible attraction in all that remains of this austere and sombre genius. What might not such "passion, vehemence, grief, daring," have accomplished if years had brought a mellower wisdom to guide them? Emily Brontë was clearly the inferior of her sister in artistic sense; and what she has accomplished, with the exception of her noble poems, is far less valuable. Even in the hands of Time she might have proved an intractable pupil, and have marred other novels as she marred **Wuthering Heights** by the very excess of the qualities which made her great. But she had immense reserves of power clamorously demanding an outlet; and it is hard to resist the belief that she would, sooner or later, in verse if not in prose, have found one worthy of herself.

John Cowper Powys (essay date 1916)

SOURCE: Powys, John Cowper. "Emily Brontë." In *Suspended Judgments: Essays on Books and Sensations.* 1916. Reprint, pp. 313-36. New York: American Library Service, 1923.

[*In the following excerpt, Powys offers an impressionistic and meditative reading of* Wuthering Heights. *Powys examines the novel's romantic elements, while suggesting that Brontë's rich evocation of the Yorkshire moors lends the work emotional intensity.*]

I cannot think of Emily Brontë's work without thinking of a certain tree I once saw against a pallid sky. A long way from Yorkshire it was where I saw this tree, and there were no limestone boulders scattered at its feet; but something in the impression it produced upon me—an impression I shall not lightly forget—weaves itself strangely in with all I feel about her, so that the peculiar look of wintry boughs, sad and silent against a fading west, accompanied by that natural human longing of people who are tired to be safely buried under the friendly earth and "free among the dead," has come to be most indelibly and deeply associated with her tragic figure.

Those who know those Yorkshire moors know the mysterious way in which the quiet country lanes suddenly emerge upon wide and desolate expanses; know how they lead us on, past ruined factories and deserted quarries, up the barren slopes of forlorn hills; know how, as one sees in front of one the long white road vanishing over the hill-top and losing itself in the grey sky, there comes across one's mind a strange, sad, exquisite feeling unlike any other feeling in the world; and we who love Emily Brontë know that this is the feeling, the mood, the atmosphere of the soul, into which her writings throw us.

The power of her great single story, *Wuthering Heights,* is in a primary sense the power of romance, and none can care for this book for whom romance means nothing.

What is romance? I think it is the instinctive recognition of a certain poetic glamour which an especial kind of grouping of persons and things—of persons and things seen under a particular light—is able to produce. It does not always accompany the expression of passionate emotion or the narration of thrilling incidents. These may arrest and entertain us when there is no romance, in my sense at any rate of that great word, over-shadowing the picture.

I think this quality of romance can only be evoked when the background of the story is heavily laden with old, rich, dim, pathetic, human associations. I think it can only emerge when there is an implication of thickly mingled traditions, full of sombre and terrible and beautiful suggestiveness, stimulating to the imagination like a draught of heavy red wine. I think there must be, in a story of which the flavour has the true romantic magic, something darkly and inexplicably fatal. I think it is necessary that one should hear the rush of the flight of the Valkyries and the wailing upon the wind of the voices of the Eumenides.

Fate—in such a story—must assume a half-human, half-personal shape, and must brood, obscurely and sombrely, over the incidents and the characters.

The characters themselves must be swayed and dominated by Fate; and not only by Fate. They must be penetrated through and through by the scenery which surrounds them and by the traditions, old and dark and superstitious and malign, of some particular spot upon the earth's surface.

The scenery which is the background of a tale which has the true romantic quality must gather itself together and concentrate itself in some kind of symbolic unity; and this symbolic unity—wherein the various elements of grandeur and mystery are merged—must present itself as something almost personal and as a dynamic "motif" in the development of the plot.

There can be no romance without some sort of appeal to that long-inherited and atavistic feeling in ordinary human hearts which is responsive to the spell and influ-

Emily Brontë, 1818-1848.

ence of old, unhappy, lovely, ancient things; things faded and falling, but with the mellowness of the centuries upon their faces.

In other words, nothing can be romantic which is *new.* Romance implies, above everything else, a long association with the human feelings of many generations. It implies an appeal to that background of our minds which is stirred to reciprocity by suggestions dealing with those old, dark, mysterious memories which belong, not so much to us as individuals, as to us as links in a great chain.

There are certain emotions in all of us which go much further and deeper than our mere personal feelings. Such are the emotions roused in us by contact with the mysterious forces of life and death and birth and the movements of the seasons; with the rising and setting of the sun, and the primordial labour of tilling the earth and gathering in the harvest. These things have been so long associated with our human hopes and fears, with the nerves and fibres of our inmost being, that any powerful presentment of them brings to the surface the accumulated feelings of hundreds of centuries.

New problems, new adventures, new social groupings, new philosophical catchwords, may all have their vivid and exciting interest. They cannot carry with them that sad, sweet breath of planetary romance which touches what might be called the "imagination of the race" in individual men and women.

Wuthering Heights is a great book, not only because of the intensity of the passions in it, but because these passions are penetrated so profoundly with the long, bitter, tragic, human associations of persons who have lived for generations upon the same spot and have behind them the weight of the burden of the sorrows of the dead.

It is a great book because the romance of it emerges into undisturbed amplitude of space, and asserts itself in large, grand, primitive forms unfretted by teasing irrelevancies.

The genius of a romantic novelist—indeed, the genius of all writers primarily concerned with the mystery of human character—consists in letting the basic differences between man and man, between man and woman, rise up, unimpeded by frivolous detail, from the fathomless depths of life itself.

The solitude in which Emily Brontë lived, and the austere simplicity of her granite-moulded character, made it possible for her to envisage life in larger, simpler, less blurred outlines than most of us are able to do. Thus her art has something of that mysterious and awe-inspiring simplicity that characterises the work of Michelangelo or William Blake.

No one who has ever read *Wuthering Heights* can forget the place and the time when he read it. As I write its name now, every reader of this page will recall, with a sudden heavy sigh at the passing of youth, the moment when the sweet tragic power of its deadly genius first took him by the throat.

For me the shadow of an old bowed acacia-tree, held together by iron bands, was over the history of Heathcliff; but the forms and shapes of that mad drama gathered to themselves the lineaments of all my wildest dreams.

I can well remember, too, how on a certain long straight road between Heathfield and Burwash, the eastern district of Sussex, my companion—the last of our English theologians—turned suddenly from his exposition of St. Thomas, and began quoting, as the white dust rose round us at the passing of a flock of sheep, the "vain are the thousand creeds—unutterably vain!" of that grand and absolute defiance, that last challenge of the unconquerable soul, which ends with the sublime cry to the eternal spark of godhead in us all—

> Thou, thou art being and breath;
> And what thou art can never be destroyed!

The art of Emily Brontë—if it can be called art, this spontaneous projection, in a shape rugged and savage, torn with the storms of fate, of her inmost identity—can be appreciated best if we realise with what skill we are plunged into the dark stream of the destiny of these people through the mediatory intervention of a comparative stranger. By this method, and also by the crafty manner in which she makes the old devoted servant of the house of Earnshaw utter a sort of Sophoclean commentary upon the events which take place, we are permitted to feel the magnitude of the thing in true relief and perspective.

By these devices we have borne in upon us, as in no other way could be done, the convincing sense which we require, to give weight and mass to the story, of the real continuity of life in those savage places.

By this method of narration we have the illusion of being suddenly initiated into a stream of events which are not merely imaginary. We have the illusion that these Earnshaws and Lintons are really, actually, palpably, undeniably, living—living somewhere, in their terrible isolation, as they have always lived—and that it is only by some lucky chance of casual discovery that we have been plunged into the mystery of their days.

One cannot help feeling aware, as we follow the story of Heathcliff, how Emily Brontë has torn and rent at her own soul in the creation of this appalling figure. Heathcliff, without father or mother, without even a Christian name, becomes for us a sort of personal embodiment of the suppressed fury of Emily Brontë's own soul. The cautious prudence and hypocritical reserves of the discreet world of timid, kindly, compromising human beings has got upon the nerves of this formidable girl, and, as she goes tearing and rending at all the masks which cover our loves and our hates, she seems to utter wild discordant cries, cries like those of some she-wolf rushing through the herd of normal human sheep.

Heathcliff and Cathy, what a pair they are! What terrifying lovers! They seem to have arisen from some remote unfathomed past of the world's earlier and less civilised passions. And yet, one occasionally catches, as one goes through the world, the Heathcliff look upon the face of a man and the Cathy look upon the face of a woman.

In a writer of less genius than Emily Brontë Heathcliff would never have found his match; would never have found his mate, his equal, his twin-soul.

It needed the imagination of one who had both Heathcliff and Cathy in her to dig them both out of the same granite rock, covered with yellow gorse and purple ling, and to hurl them into one another's arms.

From the moment when they inscribed their initials upon the walls of that melancholy room, to the moment when, with a howl like a madman, Heathcliff drags her from her grave, their affiliation is desperate and absolute.

This is a love which passes far beyond all sensuality, far beyond all voluptuous pleasure. They get little good of their love, these two—little solace and small comfort.

But one cannot conceive their wishing to change their lot with any happier lovers. They are what they are, and they are prepared to endure what fate shall send them.

When Cathy admits to the old servant that she intends to marry Linton because Heathcliff was unworthy of her and would drag her down, "I love Linton," she says—"but *I am* Heathcliff!" And this "*I am* Heathcliff" rings in our ears as the final challenge to a chaotic pluralistic world full of cynical disillusionment, of the desperate spirit of which Emily Brontë was made.

The wild madness of such love—passing the love of men and women—may seem to many readers the mere folly of an insane dream.

Emily Brontë—as she was bound to do—tosses them forth, that inhuman pair, upon the voyaging homeless wind; tosses them forth, free of their desperation, to wander at large, ghosts of their own undying passions, over the face of the rainswept moors. But to most quiet and sceptical souls such an issue of the drama contradicts the laws of nature. To most patient slaves of destiny the end of the ashes of these fierce flames is to mingle placidly with the dark earth of those misty hills and find their release in nothing more tragic than the giving to the roots of the heather and the bracken a richer soil wherein to grow.

None of us know! None of us can ever know! It is enough that in this extraordinary story the wild strange link which once and again in the history of a generation binds so strangely two persons together, almost as though their association were the result of some æon-old everlasting Recurrence, is once more thrown into tragic relief and given the tender beauty of an austere imagination.

Not every one can feel the spell of Emily Brontë or care for her work. To some she must always remain too ungracious, too savage, too uncompromising. But for those who have come to care for her, she is a wonderful and a lovely figure; a figure whose full significance has not even yet been sounded, a figure with whom we must come more and more to associate that liberation of what we call love from the mere animalism of sexual passion, which we feel sometimes, and in our rarer moments, to be one of the richest triumphs of the spirit over the flesh.

It may be that Emily Brontë is right. It may be that a point can be reached—perhaps is already being reached in the lives of certain individuals—where sexual passion is thus surpassed and transcended by the burning of a flame more intense than any which lust can produce.

It may be that the human race, as time goes on, will follow closer and closer this ferocious and spiritual girl in tearing aside the compromises of our hesitating timidity and plunging into the ice-cold waters of passions so keen and translunar as to have become chaste. It may be so—and, on the other hand, it may be that the old sly earth-gods will hold their indelible sway over us until the "baseless fabric" of this vision leaves "not a rack behind"! In any case, for our present purpose, the reading of Emily Brontë strengthens us in our recognition that the only wisdom of life consists in leaving all the doors of the universe open.

Cursed be they who close any doors! Let that be our literary as it is our philosophical motto.

Alice Meynell (essay date 1918)

SOURCE: Meynell, Alice. "Charlotte and Emily Brontë." In *Hearts of Controversy*, pp. 77-99. London: Burns & Oates, 1918.

[*In the following excerpt, Meynell discusses the enigmatic qualities of Brontë's prose.*]

Whereas Charlotte Brontë walked, with exultation and enterprise, upon the road of symbols, under the guidance of her own visiting genius, Emily seldom or never went out upon those avenues. She was one who practised little or no imagery. Her style had the key of an inner prose which seems to leave imagery behind in the way of approaches—the apparelled and arrayed approaches and ritual of literature—and so to go further and to be admitted among simple realities and antitypes. . . .

Emily Brontë seems to have a quite unparalleled unconsciousness of the delays, the charms, the pauses and preparations of imagery. Her strength does not dally with the parenthesis, and her simplicity is ignorant of those rites. Her lesser work, therefore, is plain narrative, and her greater work is no more. On the hither side—the daily side—of imagery she is still a strong and solitary writer; on the yonder side she has written some of the most mysterious passages in all plain prose.

And with what direct and incommunicable art! "'Let me alone, let me alone,' said Catherine. 'If I've done wrong, I'm dying for it. You left me too . . . I forgive you. Forgive me!' 'It is hard to forgive, and to look at those eyes and feel those wasted hands,' he answered. 'Kiss me again, and don't let me see your eyes! I forgive what you have done to me. I love my murderer—but *yours!* How can I?' They were silent, their faces hid against each other, and washed by each other's tears." "So much the worse for me that I am strong," cries Heathcliff in the same scene. "Do I want to live? What kind of living will it be when you——Oh God, would you like to live with your soul in the grave?"

Charlotte Brontë's noblest passages are her own speech or the speech of one like herself acting the central part in the dreams and dramas of emotion that she had kept from her girlhood—the unavowed custom of the ordinary girl by her so splendidly avowed in a confidence that comprised the world. Emily had no such confessions to publish. She contrived—but the word does not befit her singular spirit of liberty, that knew nothing of stealth—to remove herself from the world; as her person left no image, so her "I" is not heard in her book. She lends her voice in disguise to her men and women; the first narrator of her great romance [*Wuthering Heights*] is a young man, the second a servant woman; this one or that among the actors takes up the story, and her great words sound at times in paltry mouths. It is then that for a moment her reader seems about to come into her immediate presence, but by a fiction she denies herself to him. To a somewhat trivial girl (or a girl who would be trivial in any other book, but Emily Brontë seems unable to create anything consistently meagre or common)—to Isabella Linton she commits one of the most memorable passages of her work, and one which has the rare image—I had almost written the only image, so rare is it: "His attention was roused, I saw, for his eyes rained down tears among the ashes. . . . The clouded windows of hell flashed for a moment towards me; the fiend which usually looked out was so dimmed and drowned." But in Heathcliff's own speech there is no veil or circumstance. "I'm too happy; and yet I'm not happy enough. My soul's bliss kills my body, but does not satisfy itself." "I have to remind myself to breathe, and almost to remind my heart to beat." "Being alone, and conscious two yards of loose earth was the sole barrier between us, I said to myself: 'I'll have her in my arms again.' If she be cold, I'll think it is this north wind that chills me; and if she be motionless, it is sleep." What art, moreover, what knowledge, what a fresh ear for the clash of repetition; what a chime in that phrase: "I dreamt I was sleeping the last sleep by that sleeper, with my heart stopped, and my cheek frozen against hers."

Emily Brontë was no student of books. It was not from among the fruits of any other author's labour that she gathered these eminent words. But I think I have found the suggestion of this action of Heathcliff's—the disinterment. Not in any inspiring ancient Irish legend, as has been suggested, did Emily Brontë take her incident; she found it (but she made, and did not find, its beauty) in a mere costume romance of Bulwer Lytton, whom Charlotte Brontë, as we know, did not admire. And Emily showed no sign at all of admiration when she did him so much honour as to borrow the action of his studio-bravo.

Heathcliff's love for Catherine's past childhood is one of the profound surprises of this unparalleled book; it is to call her childish ghost—the ghost of the little girl—when she has been a dead adult woman twenty years that the inhuman lover opens the window of the house on the Heights. Something is this that the reader knew not how to look for. Another thing known to genius and beyond a reader's hope is the tempestuous purity of those passions. This wild quality of purity has a counterpart in the brief passages of nature that make the summers, the waters, the woods, and the windy heights of that murderous story seem so sweet. The "beck" that was audible beyond the hills after rain, the "heath on the top of Wuthering Heights" whereon, in her dream of Heaven, Catherine, flung out by angry angels, awoke sobbing for joy; the bird whose feathers she—delirious creature—plucks from the pillow of her deathbed ("This—I should know it among a thousand—it's a lapwing's. Bonny bird; wheeling over our heads in the middle of the moor. It wanted to get to its nest, for the clouds had touched the swells and it felt rain coming"); the two only white spots of snow left on all the moors, and the brooks brim-full; the old apple-trees, the smell of stocks and wallflowers in the brief summer, the few fir-trees by Catherine's window-bars, the early moon—I know not where are landscapes more exquisite and natural. And among the signs of death where is any fresher than the window seen from the garden to be swinging open in the morning, when Heathcliff lay within, dead and drenched with rain?

None of these things are presented by images. Nor is that signal passage wherewith the book comes to a close. Be it permitted to cite it here again. It has taken its place, it is among the paragons of our literature. Our language will not lapse or derogate while this prose stands for appeal: "I lingered . . . under that benign sky; watched the moths fluttering among the heath and harebells, listened to the soft wind breathing through the grass, and wondered how anyone could ever imagine unquiet slumbers for the sleepers in that quiet earth."

Finally, of Emily Brontë's face the world holds only an obviously unskilled reflection, and of her aspect no record worth having. Wild fugitive, she vanished, she escaped, she broke away, exiled by the neglect of her contemporaries, banished by their disrespect, outlawed by their contempt, dismissed by their indifference. And such an one was she as might rather have taken for her own the sentence pronounced by Coriolanus under sentence of expulsion; she might have driven the world from before her face and cast it out from her presence as he condemned his Romans: "*I banish you.*"

John K. Mathison (essay date September 1956)

SOURCE: Mathison, John K. "Nelly Dean and the Power of *Wuthering Heights*." *Nineteenth-Century Fiction* 11, no. 2 (September 1956): 106-29.

[*In the following essay, Mathison examines the character of Nelly Dean, evaluating her role as both the principal narrator and moral authority in* Wuthering Heights. *Mathison argues that Nelly's inadequacies as a storyteller, in particular her failure to offer genuine insight into the motives and failures of the other characters, ultimately make the reader more sympathetic to the violent, self-destructive passions of Heathcliff and Catherine.*]

The memorable quality of **Wuthering Heights,** its power, has often been mentioned; numerous elements of the work have been considered the source of this power. No one element can be expected to account completely for it, and no combination of causes is likely to produce an answer that is fully satisfying. But examinations of the various elements in the structure of the novel have suggested clear connections between method and results, between technique and meaning.[1]

In this essay I am attempting a partial explanation of the power of the book through a detailed examination not of the general question of the use of a narrator but specifically of the fully developed character of Nelly Dean. Nelly Dean is not a mere technical device: we cannot forget as the story progresses that we are hearing it from her rather than from the author. She is a minute interpreter. She tells us what events mean, what is right or wrong, what is praiseworthy or despicable or unforgivable behavior. Her morality is a result of her training, experiences, and reading, combined with her native temperament. The reader's degree of acceptance of her explanations and moral judgments determines his understanding of the meaning of the story and its power over him.

Nelly is an admirable woman whose point of view, I believe, the reader must reject. She is good-natured, warmhearted, wholesome, practical, and physically healthy. Her interpretation of her reading and her experiences, her feelings on various occasions, are, to a large extent, the consequence of her physical health. When the reader refuses to accept her view of things,

which he continually does and must do, he is forced to feel the inadequacy of the normal, healthy, hearty, good-natured person's understanding of life and human nature. He is consequently forced into an active participation in the book. He cannot sit back and accept what is given him as the explanation of the actions of the characters. He must continually provide his own version.

For the reader to disagree with Nelly would be easy, if Nelly were not admirable. But to prevent the reader's turning Nelly into a cliché of simple and narrow piety, Emily Brontë has provided Joseph. He makes clear through his actions and his explicit statements to Nelly that she is not conventionally or rigidly pious. Her condemnations and approvals do not result from an unintelligent or fanatical acceptance of rigid rules of conduct. Joseph is sure she is destined for hell because of her warmth and human kindness, and because of her enjoyment of such pleasures as folk song and dancing. Joseph's strictures intensify the reader's favorable impressions of Nelly, the favorable impressions that make his rejection of her views more intense and significant.

And enough other servants are introduced to increase still further our realization of Nelly's superiority, intellectual and moral. Her pipe-smoking successor at the Grange[2] is apparently what might be expected of a servant. One need not more than mention Zillah, who has some mental alertness, to be made strongly aware of Nelly's superiority.

But more strongly than her superiority is shown by contrast with Joseph, with Zillah, or with the servant Lockwood finds at the Grange on his return, it is shown by the affection of the major characters, including Heathcliff, for her, as seen not in their words but in their behavior to her. And of course there is her narrative, full as it is of her ideas. In spite of all her fine qualities, nevertheless, she fails to understand the other characters and, more important, fails in her behavior in important crises of the action. From the emphasis on her admirable qualities, and from her final inadequacy, the reader is led to see that the insight of the normal, wholesome person cannot penetrate into all feelings justly: the reader becomes the active advocate of the extremes of passion of Cathy and Heathcliff, troublesome as they are to a peaceful, domestic routine.

Emily Brontë could not have succeeded in a direct attempt to demand our sympathy for or understanding of two such characters as Heathcliff and Cathy. Approached directly, the reader would not have to exercise his own perceptions; he would remain passive. Some readers might say that such violent behavior is exciting enough to read about in romantic novels, but that in real life it would not do to encourage such people as Cathy and Heathcliff. To other readers, the novel might have appeared merely as a tremendous protest against conventional standards, but the interest in it would be merely biographical, sociological, or psychological.

By indirection, Emily Brontë has produced not a personal protest but a work of art. The reader's reaction is not, of course, the precise opposite of any of those mentioned above, not a simple stamp of approval bestowed on Heathcliff and Cathy, but a realization that the "normal" person is often incapable of feeling for the tortured, emotionally distraught person, and that the latter's tortured failure to understand himself and the sources of his misery partly results from the failure of imagination of the majority. The question is not whether Heathcliff and Cathy are good or bad. They are the result of psychological isolation and misunderstanding working on a particular native temperament, and the "good" are as much the doers of the damage as the "bad," either Hindley or Joseph.

The better we come to know Nelly, the more we recognize her lack of understanding of the principals. To know her we need to watch her character as it is revealed through her opinions, and, even more, through her reports of her own actions. It is this person, whom we come to know well, whose judgments we finally interpret. Not abstract judgments of a merely nominal narrator, they are the particular limited judgments of a person of a distinct emotional and intellectual viewpoint. Knowing the judge, or interpreter, knowing the giver of advice as well as the advice given, we realize the inadequacy of the interpretation, the advice, and the judgments; we become as we read active interpreters, protesters, explicators, and possibly judges.

II

Nelly's physical vigor is emphatically part of her character. Impressing us generally from her account of her actions throughout the novel, her abundant good health is specifically alluded to as well. Her one illness, a bad cold after she had been obliged to sit for a long while in "soaked shoes and stockings," was a great surprise to her; up to the time of the narrative it is the only indisposition in her life that she can recall. By this accident, which most would accept as in the course of things, her spirits were depressed: "It is wearisome, to a stirring active body—but few have slighter reasons for complaint than I had" (p. 257). Elsewhere, responding to the terrors of Cathy, who fears that everyone she knows may die and leave her alone, Nelly confidently boasts: ". . . I am strong, and hardly forty-five. My mother lived till eighty, a canty dame to the last" (p. 244). Numerous examples of illness, decline, wasting away, and death in her experience make little impression on her, who feels herself so strong. Although she once remarks "I am stout, and soon put out of breath" (p. 286), this reference confirms rather than contradicts her feeling of "ruddy" health; the picture is that of the Shepherd's wife in *The Winter's Tale*:

> when my old wife liv'd, upon
> This day she was both pantler, butler, cook;
> Both dame and servant; welcom'd all, serv'd all,
> Would sing her song and dance her turn; now here,
> At upper end o' the table, now i' the middle;
> On his shoulder, and his; her face o' fire
> With labour and the thing she took to quench it . . .

(IV, iii, 55-61)

Her own health makes her a poor sympathizer with the illnesses of others; she tends to view even those illnesses in the novel which end in death as partly willful, partly acting. The physique and the temperament which goes with it of the weak or sick she cannot really believe in. An early example is her view of Hindley's consumptive wife; throughout the book further examples abound, to the last case of the frail son of Isabella whom she finds revolting largely because he will not exert himself and be vigorous. But to resume, of Hindley's wife, who had expressed fear of dying, she says:

> I imagined her as little likely to die as myself. She was rather thin, but young, and fresh complexioned, and her eyes sparkled as bright as diamonds. I did remark, to be sure, that mounting the stairs made her breathe very quick, that the least sudden noise set her all in a quiver, and that she coughed troublesomely sometimes: but, I knew nothing of what these symptoms portended, and had no impulse to sympathize with her. We don't in general take to foreigners here, Mr. Lockwood, unless they take to us first.

(pp. 46-47)

Since Nelly regards the idea of her own death as absurd, she sees no reason that Hindley's wife should be entitled to a fear of death. Such nonsense is just what one expects of foreigners (from a different county of England). This passage, very early in the novel, makes the reader aware of Nelly's fallibility of judgment combined with her satisfaction with her own attitudes. It conditions our expectations regarding her probable actions in later episodes, and helps us know her and hence discount her judgments and substitute our own. These early suspicions are confirmed when Cathy becomes ill:

> . . . Mr. Kenneth, as soon as he saw her, pronounced her dangerously ill; she had a fever.
>
> He bled her, and he told me to let her live on whey, and water gruel; and take care she did not throw herself down stairs, or out of the window; and then he left. . . .
>
> Though I cannot say I made a gentle nurse, and Joseph and the master were no better; and though our patient was as wearisome and headstrong as a patient could be, she weathered it through.

(p. 92)

Why should Cathy have chosen to come down with a fever, become dangerously delirious, and consequently be "wearisome" to healthy, reasonable people?

If we knew less of Nelly we might be able to sympathize with her jogging of Lockwood during his illness: "'You shouldn't lie till ten. There's the very prime of the morning gone long before that time. A person who has not done one half his day's work by ten o'clock, runs a chance of leaving the other half undone'" (p. 64). As it is, however, we know her advice is little more than justification of her own natural urges to be "busy and stirring" always; it is her failure to grasp the possibility of people's being less vigorous than herself.

Most serious is her deficiency in Cathy's later illness and delirium, foreshadowed by the illness already mentioned. Inevitably, she views it as an act:

> "Catherine ill?" he [Edgar Linton] said, hastening to us. "Shut the window, Ellen! Catherine! why . . ."
>
> He was silent; the haggardness of Mrs. Linton's appearance smote him speechless, and he could only glance from her to me in horrified astonishment.
>
> "She's been fretting here," I continued, "and eating scarcely anything, and never complaining, she would admit none of us till this evening, and so we couldn't inform you of her state, as we were not aware of it ourselves, *but it is nothing.*" [italics mine]
>
> (pp. 134-135)

One might suppose Ellen's "it is nothing" were a well-meant if unsuccessful effort to cheer Edgar, if the scene ended at this point, and if we had not begun to know Nelly rather well, but as it continues, it becomes clear that she really considers the illness both willful and minor:

> "Her mind wanders, sir," I interposed. "She has been talking nonsense the whole evening; but let her have quiet and proper attendance, and she'll rally. Hereafter, we must be cautious how we vex her."
>
> "I desire no further advice from you," answered Mr. Linton. "You knew your mistress's nature, and you encouraged me to harass her. And not to give me one hint of how she has been these three days! It was heartless! Months of sickness could not cause such a change!"
>
> I began to defend myself, thinking it too bad to be blamed for another's wicked waywardness!
>
> (pp. 135-136)

As Edgar Linton says, Nelly had had a lifetime of experience with Cathy, but the last quoted sentence alone makes clear the triumph of constitution and temperament over experience. Nelly never will grasp the less wholesome, physically or emotionally.

It may need to be said that objectively it would be possible for the reader to find Cathy a difficult person. But the healthy Nelly's complacent self-justification and lack of surmise of stronger passions and more highly strung temperaments, make the reader Cathy's advocate

in the context, and while he reads they lower his enthusiasm for the vigorously normal and, it appears, consequently obtuse.

Nelly's health is only one, though a significant, feature of the total character. Her "philosophy" on all sorts of matters is presented in detail. It is primarily a matter of avoiding any really strong passions, but continually encouraging a good deal of "natural affection." Children must "take to her." On a visit to the Heights she encounters the five-year-old Hareton near the building, and he begins to throw stones at her, and curses, distorting "his baby features into a shocking expression of malignity" (p. 115). Her reaction is unperceptively conventional.

> You may be certain this grieved, more than angered me. Fit to cry, I took an orange from my pocket, and offered it to propitiate him.
>
> He hesitated, and then snatched it from my hold, as if he fancied I only intended to tempt and disappoint him.
>
> (p. 115)

Here, too, she is clearly more concerned with her picture of herself as affectionately motherly, than with understanding.

She believes in forgiving one's enemies, but she herself, not having to struggle hard in this respect, does not realize that for others placid domestic normality may not be the strongest drive. After a serious crisis in which Hindley had confined Heathcliff (during childhood) fasting in the garret for more than twenty-four hours, she broke Hindley's commands by letting him into the kitchen to feed him: "he was sick and could eat little . . ."; he remained "wrapt in dumb meditation."

> On my inquiring the subject of his thoughts, he answered gravely—
>
> "I'm trying to settle how I shall pay Hindley back. I don't care how long I wait, if I can only do it, at last. I hope he will not die before I do!"
>
> "For shame, Heathcliff!" said I. "It is for God to punish wicked people; we should learn to forgive."
>
> "No, God won't have the satisfaction that I shall," he returned. "I only wish I knew the best way! Let me alone, and I'll plan it out: while I'm thinking of that, I don't feel pain."
>
> But, Mr. Lockwood, I forget these tales cannot divert you. I'm annoyed how I should dream of chattering on at such a rate . . . I could have told Heathcliff's history, all that you need hear, in half a dozen words.
>
> (p. 63)

Nelly is sorry for Heathcliff and sneaks him some supper. As usual she compromises, helping Heathcliff a little and disobeying Hindley a little. Perhaps that is what was possible. But in her role as narrator she looks back upon the event, having seen the whole history of the subsequent years, and takes it in stride, still blaming Heathcliff conventionally for his lapses, still blaming others moderately, and still keeping her picture of herself as normally affectionate and good. Heathcliff should have listened to her and forgiven his enemies.

She allows, of course, for normal selfishness. Since the marriage of Cathy to Edgar Linton does take place, she hopefully finds signs that there is a "deep and growing happiness" in their union. At least she is able to be a bustling housekeeper; there are no domestic storms. But this happy period ended. "Well, we *must* be for ourselves in the long run; the mild and generous are only more justly selfish than the domineering—and it ended when circumstances caused each to feel that the one's interest was not the chief consideration in the other's thoughts" (p. 97). To her this situation is normal. No allowance is made for the enduring passion of Cathy and Heathcliff. No doubt Cathy's marriage would have appeared more successful had she forgotten Heathcliff, but it is too easy for Nelly to take this stand for the reader to go along with her. He begins to sympathize with the course that Cathy and Heathcliff did take.

Later when the reader might have been exasperated with a tantrum of Cathy's, Nelly's stolidity makes him take Cathy's part against the printed interpretation:

> The stolidity with which I received these instructions was, no doubt, rather exasperating; for they were delivered in perfect sincerity; but I believed a person who could plan the turning of her fits of passion to account, beforehand, might, by exerting her will, manage to control herself tolerably even while under their influence; and I did not wish to "frighten" her husband, as she said, and multiply his annoyances for the purpose of serving her selfishness.
>
> (p. 124)

For Nelly to control "fits of passion" and "manage to control herself while under their influence" have never required a struggle. She is too ruddy, healthy, physically busy and emotionally placid to know what such a struggle would be. When a few pages later she confidently announces that "the Grange had but one sensible soul in its walls, and that lodged in my body" (p. 127), we agree, but the value we place on being "sensible" is far lower than hers.

Nelly is as much opposed to cold lack of visible affection as to violent passion. Normally approving of Edgar Linton, she fails to understand the feeling behind his apparent coldness and is quite ready to condemn him in his treatment of Isabella:

> "And you won't write her a little note, sir?" I asked imploringly.

> "No," he answered. "It is needless. My communication with Heathcliff's family shall be as sparing as his with mine. It shall not exist!"

> Mr. Edgar's coldness depressed me exceedingly; and all the way from the Grange, I puzzled my brains how to put more heart into what he said, when I repeated it; and how to soften his refusal of even a few lines to console Isabella.
>
> (p. 155)

She is "depressed" by "coldness," although all she wants from Edgar is a few futilely affectionate, meaningless, brotherly words not calculated to achieve any helpful result. That there is more "heart" in his coldness than in her superficiality does not occur to her. To make things well, and it really seems so to those like her, she will soften his refusal, in some compromising way, and thus receive the congratulations of her own conscience. On arriving at the Heights a few minutes later, she is actually able to say, "There never was such a dreary, dismal scene as the *formerly cheerful* house presented" [italics mine] (pp. 155-156).

The reader's first view of the house had been Lockwood's on his first visit, the history Nelly has told started with the discord resulting from the introduction into the house of the orphan Heathcliff (and the reactions to this say little enough in favor of the Earnshaws), and he has subsequently been concerned with Heathcliff, Cathy, and their agonized growing up in the house, not to mention Hindley, Joseph, and Hindley's consumptive wife. The reader, consequently, cannot help placing a low value on the judgment of the wholesome Nelly, and he reassesses her narrative with quite a different emphasis.

Edgar, except for his coldness to Isabella, is admired by Nelly. No unleashed and distressing passions are usually his, but a sensible and quiet affection, comforting to the housekeeper. Referring to Edgar's mourning for his deceased wife, Nelly approvingly says: "But he was too good to be thoroughly unhappy long. *He* didn't pray for Catherine's soul to haunt him: Time brought resignation, and a melancholy sweeter than common joy. He recalled her memory with ardent, tender love, and hopeful aspiring to the better world, where, he doubted not, she was gone" (p. 194). How much of this is Nelly's attribution, and how much was Edgar's real state remain doubtful; surely the part about "melancholy sweeter than common joy" is something she picked up from her boasted reading in the Linton library, but much is her natural wholesomely sentimental feeling about the decorous way for a bereaved husband to act. Possibly, too, Emily Brontë is indicating a tendency in Nelly to show off her elegance to impress Lockwood, a gentleman.

Of those aspects of experience which threaten to upset her outlook she forbids discussion, admitting her uneasiness, but willing to push aside the difficulty. Cathy, wishing to reveal a seriously troubling dream to Nelly is abruptly halted: "'Oh! don't, Miss Catherine!' I cried. 'We're dismal enough without conjuring up ghosts and visions to perplex us. Come, come, be merry, and like yourself! Look at little Hareton—*he's* dreaming nothing dreary. How sweetly he smiles in his sleep!'" (p. 84). Apart from the unwillingness to hear the dream, for Nelly to characterize Cathy as "merry and like yourself" is a stretch in making the desired the actual at any time during Cathy's adolescence, and her preference for babies is again apparent. Cathy replies: "'Yes; and how sweetly his father curses in his solitude! You remember him, I dare say, when he was just such another as that chubby thing—nearly as young and innocent'" (p. 84). Nelly interrupted her story to explain the situation to Lockwood:

> I was superstitious about dreams then, and am still; and Catherine had an unusual gloom in her aspect, that made me dread something from which I might shape a prophecy, and foresee a dreadful catastrophe.
>
> She was vexed, but she did not proceed. Apparently taking up another subject, she recommenced in a short time.
>
> "If I were in heaven, Nelly, I should be extremely miserable."
>
> "Because you are not fit to go there," I answered. "All sinners would be miserable in heaven."
>
> "But it is not for that. I dreamt, once, that I was there."
>
> "I tell you I won't hearken to your dreams, Miss Catherine! I'll go to bed," I interrupted again.
>
> (p. 84)

Little help can the distracted girl get from the only one from whom she can even try to get it. Nothing must interfere with Nelly's determination to impose her own meaning on events, and that meaning must be ordinary and cheerful. But Cathy and Heathcliff persist in a fatal tendency to try to confide in Nelly. Even at the end of his life Heathcliff confesses to her, although, dreading to hear anything unsettlingly appalling, she half refuses to listen.

The customary always triumphs with Nelly. Admirable feelings in Heathcliff, if strange or uncustomary, are shut out of her mind. Far from admirable attitudes in Edgar are approved without question, if they would be shared by most normal people in his station. When Isabella is attracted to Heathcliff, Nelly observes it merely as a new trouble to Edgar: "Leaving aside the degradation of an alliance with a nameless man, and the possible fact that his property, in default of heirs male, might pass into such a one's power, he had sense to comprehend Heathcliff's disposition . . ." (p. 106). No reader can approve such merely conventional objections, introduced without a qualm. Such attitudes had

been responsible for much of the maiming of Heathcliff already. And Heathcliff is here blamed, as often, merely for not knowing his place.

Nelly is similarly imperceptive when Isabella, who has really suffered from Heathcliff, reviles him. Nelly's attempt is simply to "hush" her railings. To Isabella's "would that he could be blotted out of creation, and out of my memory!" Nelly replies, "Hush, hush! He's a human being . . . Be more charitable; there are worse men than he is yet!" (p. 183). What appears is her hatred of extremes; she does not want even Heathcliff to be unique, but merely a normally bad man, one of the well-known class of sinners. What she advocates is some conventional verbal charity and to forget, to proceed as if nothing had happened.

Nelly is a woman whom everyone in her circle, employers, the children of employers, the other servants in the neighborhood, the people of Gimmerton, and Lockwood have recognized as superior, and admirable. How superior to Joseph, Zillah, and to various other characters the reader readily perceives. To insist that she should have shown a fuller understanding of Cathy and Heathcliff would be to show a lack of understanding of what is possible or probable. From day to day she did her best, with regard to her own welfare and peace of comfort; few would have done better.

Nonetheless, her character, a representation of the normal at its best, is inadequate to the situation. As will be shown, failing to understand them, she advises them poorly, and her actions in relation to them are also harmful. Emily Brontë does not plead for them. She lets us see them as they were seen and dealt with by a good woman. The reader must progressively lower his estimate of the value of the normal and healthy, develop a comprehension of and sympathy for genuine emotions however extreme and destructive, and in so doing become an active interpreter of the meaning of the novel. The reader's active involvement and sympathy with the conventionally despicable makes the power of the book.

III

Resulting from qualities in themselves admirable, Nelly's judgments based on her understanding of events and other people result in advice and action which are parts of the total harm done to Cathy and Heathcliff. Describing the first days of Heathcliff in the Earnshaw household, she makes it apparent to the reader that her presence there will do nothing to better the little Heathcliff's situation. Speaking of the child's silent endurance of Hindley's torments, she says:

> This endurance made old Earnshaw furious when he discovered his son persecuting the poor, fatherless child, as he called him. He took to Heathcliff strangely, believing all he said (for that matter, he said precious

little, and generally the truth), and petting him up far above Cathy, who was too mischievous and wayward for a favourite.

So, from the very beginning, he bred bad feeling in the house . . .

(p. 38)

Heathcliff is, at this early point in the story, obviously blameless, yet Nelly sides with the persecutors, concerned with the trouble caused by an unusual, and hence somehow wrong situation. Looking back through the years, she can only suppose that all would have been well had Mr. Earnshaw never had so freakish a notion as to introduce a waif into the neighborhood, not that the waif become warped through continued mistreatment and helpless suffering. The parenthetical words, whose significance she disregards, reveal the almost inevitable obtuseness of interpretation by a person of her type.

One page further on, another anecdote makes a point opposite from what Nelly intends it to. Heathcliff's colt (a gift from old Earnshaw) becoming lame, the boy tries to exchange it for Hindley's sound one. "'You must exchange horses with me; I don't like mine, and if you won't I shall tell your father of the three thrashings you've given me this week, and show him my arm, which is black to the shoulder'" (p. 39). The result is that Hindley "cuffs his ears," then threatens him with an iron weight, which he finally hurls at him, hitting him in the chest. Nelly prevents Heathcliff from revealing this blow to old Earnshaw, and Hindley suddenly says: "'Take my colt, gipsy, then! . . . And I pray that he may break your neck; take him, and be damned, you beggarly interloper! and wheedle my father out of all he has, only afterwards show him what you are, imp of Satan—and take that, I hope he'll kick out your brains!'" (p. 40). Of the words or blows, which were more damaging to young Heathcliff may be debated, but Nelly's actively taking the part of Hindley certainly contributes to the harm. And beyond that, she teaches Heathcliff to lie about the episode: "I persuaded him easily to let me lay the blame of his bruises on the horse; he minded little what tale was told since he had what he wanted. He complained so seldom, indeed of such stirs as these, that I really thought him not vindictive—I was deceived, completely, as you will hear" (p. 40). From the beginning, Nelly deals with Heathcliff through a policy of expediency, preserving outward tranquillity, preventing "stirs" in the family. Later when events demand even more of her, we recollect her habitual patterns of behavior, and know she will continue to fail, with increasingly serious results.

After old Earnshaw's death when Hindley becomes "Master," Nelly is not much troubled by the resulting deliberate degradation of Heathcliff. "He bore his deg-radation pretty well at first, because Cathy taught him what she learnt, and worked or played with him in the fields. They both promised fair to grow up as rude as savages . . ." (p. 47). More surprising is her assumption that the fanatical Joseph's discipline would have been successful unless there was something basically wrong with Heathcliff and Cathy: "The curate might set as many chapters as he pleased for Catherine to get by heart, and Joseph might thrash Heathcliff till his arm ached; they forgot everything the minute they were together again, at least the minute they had contrived some naughty plan of revenge . . ." (pp. 47-48). Another of her methods of helping Heathcliff is seen slightly later in a reproof: "'You are incurable, Heathcliff, and Mr. Hindley will have to proceed to extremities, see if he won't'" (p. 53).

Dramatically, with no recourse to the essay technique of Fielding as he restores the wayward Tom Jones to the favor of the reader, the reader's sympathies are being directed powerfully toward Heathcliff, and Cathy. More powerfully, perhaps, because unless he is making a deliberate analysis of the book he does not feel his sympathies being directed by a device of the author. Fielding's reader, directly exhorted, may argue back; Emily Brontë's reader reacts spontaneously in favor of Heathcliff.

The most Nelly can admit is that Hindley was a bad "example" for Heathcliff. This way of going to ruin—evil companions showing the way to vice—is familiar, and she makes allowance for Heathcliff in this way. It is a qualified allowance, for Heathcliff, she says, seemed "possessed of something diabolical at that period" (p. 68). Her evidence is that Heathcliff rejoiced to see Hindley degrade himself. But the portrait of Heathcliff is far from the depravity suggested in miscellaneous remarks:

In the first place, he had, by that time, lost the benefit of his early education: continual hard work, begun soon and concluded late, had extinguished any curiosity he once possessed in pursuit of knowledge, and any love for books or learning. His childhood's sense of superiority, instilled into him by the favours of old Mr. Earnshaw, was faded away. He struggled long to keep up an equality with Catherine in her studies, and yielded with poignant though silent regret: but he yielded completely; and there was no prevailing on him to take a step in the way of moving upward, when he found he must, necessarily, sink beneath his former level.

(pp. 70-71)

It is hard to see how Nelly could account for Heathcliff's behavior at the same time both by diabolical possession and as she does here, but her ability to describe accurately, and yet disregard the facts in favor of explanation by a conventional formula, is a major feature of her character and her inadequacy as a counselor.

Usually, of course, Cathy and Heathcliff are being simultaneously influenced. When Cathy returns from her stay at Thrushcross Grange, Nelly is deceived by the surface improvement in her manners (p. 54). But Heath-cliff's consequent desire for reform and self-improvement gets discouragingly brisk treatment:

> "Nelly, make me decent, I'm going to be good."
>
> "High time, Heathcliff," I said; "you have grieved Catherine; she's sorry she ever came home, I dare say! It looks as if you envied her, because she is more thought of than you."
>
> (p. 58)

Nelly, complacently quoting herself in such passages, still realizes no shortcomings in herself (her questions to Lockwood on moral problems from time to time never touch such failings). Had Heathcliff told his story, excusing all his actions through harsh portraits of these adults, the effect would be reversed: the reader would excuse the adults and blame Heathcliff, saying that they were no worse than most normal conventional people, and that others have survived better in worse circumstances.

Nelly's major failure (though few could have done better) is in the decisive episode during which Cathy reveals her intention of marrying Linton, despite her lack of love for him, and her intense love for, her identity with, Heathcliff. Nelly dissembles her knowledge of Heathcliff's presence, but worse, her knowledge of his departure at the worst possible moment: "Having noticed a slight movement, I turned my head, and saw him rise from the bench, and steal out, noiselessly. He had listened till he heard Catherine say it would degrade her to marry him, and then he stayed to hear no farther" (p. 85). And when Catherine wants to be assured that Heathcliff, unlike herself, does not know what deep love is, Nelly answers equivocally, "'I see no reason that he should not know, as well as you . . . and if *you* are his choice, he'll be the most unfortunate creature that ever was born!'" (*ibid.*), automatically putting Cathy in the wrong, getting herself over a difficult moment. What this moment has done is let Heathcliff overhear and leave, and the plans for marriage to Edgar go forward; Nelly has not let Cathy know that Heathcliff has heard her say that it would degrade her to marry him, but has not heard her say the words describing her real feelings, leading up to "I am Heathcliff." Nelly's view of the scene, in which her own inconvenience is more important than either Heathcliff's or Cathy's sufferings, is summarized by herself at the conclusion of Cathy's tremendous confession: "She paused, and hid her face in the folds of my gown; but I jerked it forcibly away. I was out of patience with her folly!'" (p. 86).

The reader, prepared by earlier passages in which Nelly has shown, on lesser occasions, her inevitable adherence to expediency or her own comfort, is not surprised by the major failure here: moral habits are not likely to be overcome in a crisis where there is little time for struggle and deliberation. Heathcliff enters and leaves while Cathy is talking and Nelly cannot but act from habit, on the spur of the moment, but the defects revealed in this scene are her customary ones. Here, perhaps more than anywhere, the reader is sharply aware not only of her failure as an interpreter of the past, but more important, of her failure as a counselor at the time of the action. Both failures co-operate to affect the reader and produce the power of the scene.

The following page, on which Nelly admits that Heathcliff had heard much, confirms the disaster: Cathy searches for Heathcliff during the storm, and stays up all night in wet clothes while Nelly, at one here with Joseph, is chiefly concerned about the interruption in the household routine, even after Heathcliff is clearly gone and Cathy has come down with a serious illness. This whole passage, too well remembered to need detailed citation, is the turning point. We see it as Nelly tells it. Our necessity of disagreeing completely with the narrator's version, made very easy owing to the great detail, gives our total sympathy to Cathy and Heathcliff. We give, perhaps, more than they deserve; we become unduly severe towards Nelly, but to make us feel powerfully the inadequacy of the "steady reasonable kind of body," Emily Brontë's technique could not be improved. Neither a direct plea nor a narrator who was a moralizing, narrow-minded, hypocritically pious guardian could have placed us so completely with Heathcliff and Cathy. It needs above all Nelly's admirable qualities including particularly the affection she arouses in both Cathy and Heathcliff, and the awareness that her failure is the result of them. Heathcliff and Cathy would have fared better with worse parental guidance. The failure of the ordinarily good being made apparent, the reader, attempting to supply the fuller comprehension, becomes fully involved in the novel.[3]

To emphasize the significance of the whole scene, Emily Brontë has Nelly sum up her attitude:

> One day, I had the misfortune, when she provoked me exceedingly, to lay the blame of his disappearance on her (where indeed it belonged, as she well knew). From that period for several months, she ceased to hold any communication with me, save in the relation of a mere servant. Joseph fell under a ban also; he *would* speak his mind, and lecture her all the same as if she were a little girl . . .
>
> (p. 93)

Later on, a dialogue between Heathcliff and Nelly emphasizes this superficiality of hers by contrasting her explanation with his. To his inquiry, after Cathy's marriage and illness, concerning her condition, Nelly first replies, "I blamed her, as she deserved, for bringing it all on herself," and continues, "the person [Edgar] who is compelled, of necessity, to be her companion, will only sustain his affection hereafter, by the remembrance of what she once was, by common humanity, and a sense of duty!" She is speaking not out of any true knowledge of Edgar, but out of her determination to edify Heathcliff. His refusal to be edified produces his reply and reveals once more Nelly's inadequacy: "'That is quite possible,' remarked Heathcliff, forcing himself to seem calm, 'quite possible that your master should have nothing but common humanity and a sense of duty to fall back upon. But do you imagine that I shall leave Catherine to his *duty* and *humanity?* and can you compare my feelings respecting Catherine, to his?'" (p. 157).

Heathcliff finally forces her to agree to arrange an interview between him and Cathy; her motives are not a genuine feeling for the two, but the desire to avoid an "explosion":

> Was it right or wrong? I fear it was wrong, though expedient. I thought I prevented another explosion by my compliance; and I thought, too, it might create a favourable crisis in Catherine's mental illness: and then I remembered Mr. Edgar's stern rebuke of my carrying tales; and I tried to smooth away all disquietude on the subject, by affirming, with frequent iteration, that that betrayal of trust, if it merited so harsh an appellation, should be the last.
>
> (p. 163)

Worse is the smugness in reporting the actual meeting when she sarcastically remarks "it seemed Heathcliff *could* weep on a great occasion like this" (p. 171). And conventionally, she weeps herself for Heathcliff after Cathy's death:

> "She's dead!" he said; "I've not waited for you to learn that. Put your handkerchief away—don't snivel before me. Damn you all! she wants none of *your* tears!"
>
> I was weeping as much for him as her: we do sometimes pity creatures that have none of the feeling either for themselves or others; and when I first looked into his face, I perceived that he had got intelligence of the catastrophe; and a foolish notion struck me that his heart was quelled, and he prayed, because his lips moved, and his gaze was bent on the ground.
>
> "Yes, she's dead!" I answered, checking my sobs, and drying my cheeks. "Gone to heaven, I hope, where we may, every one, join her, if we take due warning, and leave our evil ways to follow good!"
>
> "Did *she* take due warning, then?" asked Heathcliff, attempting a sneer. "Did she die like a saint? Come, give me a true history of the event. How did . . ."
>
> (p. 176)

The death of Cathy and its repercussions, however, do not end Nelly's failures that result from the great good fortune, for her own survival, of her native endowments. There remain young Cathy and the sickly son of

Isabella for her to fail to comprehend. Dealing with them, she reveals her unimpaired self-confidence. Suspecting that young Cathy is corresponding with Linton, rather than question Cathy as might seem her duty as a guardian, she automatically uses the method of trying all her household keys on Cathy's locked drawer:

> . . . I emptied the whole contents into my apron, and took them with me to examine at leisure in my own chamber. . . .
>
> Some of them struck me as singularly odd compounds of ardour and flatness; commencing in strong feeling, and concluding in the affected, wordy way that a schoolboy might use to a fancied, incorporeal sweetheart.
>
> Whether they satisfied Cathy, I don't know, but they appeared very worthless trash to me.
>
> After turning over as many as I thought proper, I tied them in a handkerchief and set them aside, re-locking the vacant drawer.
>
> (p. 238)

Catherine's agony on realizing that the letters have been discovered is great, but Nelly sympathizes with her not at all, since to her both the letters and their author are contemptible.

Still harsher is her treatment of Cathy after the revelation of the visits to Wuthering Heights:

> "Now, Ellen, you have heard all; and I can't be prevented from going to Wuthering Heights, except by inflicting misery on two people—whereas, if you'll only not tell papa, my going need disturb the tranquillity of none. You'll not tell, will you? It will be very heartless if you do."
>
> "I'll make up my mind on that point by to-morrow, Miss Catherine," I replied. "It requires some study; and so I'll leave you to your rest, and go think it over."
>
> I thought it over aloud, in my master's presence; walking straight from her room to his, and relating the whole story, with the exception of her conversations with her cousin, and any mention of Hareton.
>
> (p. 268)

Though Edgar, no doubt, should know of the activities of his daughter, Nelly's methods are shown first in her promise to Cathy to consider the problem (the easy and immediate way of "smoothing over" that difficulty), second, in her immediate and unreflective revelation to Edgar, and third, in her holding back from Edgar those items that might cause her some trouble with him. Most revelatory of all, of course, is the more than satisfied manner in which she narrates the whole episode to Lockwood.

One can also contrast the superficiality of Nelly's understanding even with that of young Cathy in two passages very close together (pp. 304 and 307). Cathy, now his daughter-in-law, says in the former,

"Mr. Heathcliff, *you* have *nobody* to love you; and, however miserable you make us, we shall still have the revenge of thinking that your cruelty arises from your greater misery! You *are* miserable, are you not? Lonely, like the devil, and envious like him? *Nobody* loves you—*nobody* will cry for you, when you die! I wouldn't be you!"

The realization of cruelty as the consequence of misery is beyond Nelly who had once explained his character as due to the evil example of Hindley. To emphasize Nelly's inability to understand, immediately after the passage just quoted, Emily Brontë has Heathcliff tell Nelly of his opening of Cathy's grave, and the reader is more than ever aware of the torments he has suffered, especially when he ends, "It was a strange way of killing, not by inches, but by fractions of hairbreadths, to beguile me with the spectre of a hope, through eighteen years." To this she comments to Lockwood:

> Mr. Heathcliff paused and wiped his forehead—his hair clung to it, wet with perspiration; his eyes were fixed on the red embers of the fire; the brows not contracted, but raised next the temples, diminishing the grim aspect of his countenance, but imparting a peculiar look of trouble, and a painful appearance of mental tension towards one absorbing subject. He only half addressed me, and I maintained silence—*I didn't like to hear him talk* [italics mine].

And while he had been talking, she had interrupted him with, "'You were very wicked, Mr. Heathcliff!' I exclaimed; 'were you not ashamed to disturb the dead?'" (p. 305), quick to register conventional horror at a breach of custom, but apparently oblivious of the overwhelming torment that had caused the breach. Here, with particular intensity, the reader revolts from accepting the wholesome, normal person as a criterion of thought and behavior, and tends to accept any passion so long as it is real, and in so doing becomes his own active interpreter of the true state of affairs and is powerfully affected by the genuine insight into human emotion.

Yet he may not be allowed to forget that Nelly is a fine woman nevertheless; she is once more contrasted with Joseph when Lockwood finds both of them together on his unexpected visit in September 1802, just after, furthermore, he had encountered her cloddish successor at the Grange (see p. 324):

> . . . at the door, sat my old friend, Nelly Dean, sewing and singing a song, which was often interrupted from within, by harsh words of scorn and intolerance, uttered in far from musical accents.
>
> "Aw'd rayther, by th' haulf, hev 'em swearing i' my lugs frough morn tuh neeght, nur hearken yah, hah-siver!" said the tenant of the kitchen, in answer to an unheard speech of Nelly's. "It's a blazing shaime, ut Aw cannut oppen t' Blessed Book, bud yah set up them

glories tuh sattan, un' all t' flaysome wickednesses ut iver wer born intuh t' warld. . . . O Lord, judge 'em, fur they's norther law nur justice amang wer rullers!"

> "No! Or we should be sitting in flaming fagots, I suppose," retorted the singer. "But wisht, old man, and read your Bible like a christian, and never mind me. This is 'Fairy Annie's Wedding'—a bonny tune—it goes to a dance."
>
> (pp. 326-327)

With this picture of Nelly's natural attractiveness and gaiety in mind we reach her narration of Heathcliff's end, his "queer" end, as she calls it (p. 328).

As any reader of the novel will have guessed, Nelly was taken by surprise at Heathcliff's death: as with all the other now dead characters, she had supposed him sound in all ways:

> "But what do you mean by a *change,* Mr. Heathcliff?" I said, alarmed at his manner, though he was neither in danger of losing his senses, nor dying; according to my judgment he was quite strong and healthy; and, as to his reason, from childhood, he had a delight in dwelling on dark things, and entertaining odd fancies. He might have had a monomania on the subject of his departed idol; but on every other point his wits were as sound as mine.
>
> (p. 344)

Such phrases as "delight in dwelling on dark things," "monomania on the subject of his idol" are perhaps a climax in Nelly's brushing aside of all powerful emotion, and above all, it should be noted that the only thing that here alarms her is Heathcliff's unwholesome manner.

As his death approaches, Nelly finally begins to worry about him; she fears for a short time, as the only way of explaining him, that he must be some "ghoul, or a vampire" (p. 350) but rejects that explanation and tries to conjure up some type of parentage that would account for his nature, but concludes by turning her attention aside to a serious abnormality, that he will not be able to have a proper tombstone, since his age and true name are unknown: "We were obliged to content ourselves with the single word, 'Heathcliff.' . . . If you enter the kirkyard, you'll read on his headstone, only that, and the date of his death" (p. 350). Her final words show how well for her own tranquillity she has settled the whole violent tale, when in response to Lockwood's half jest that the ghosts of Cathy and Heathcliff will be the future inhabitants of Wuthering Heights, "'No, Mr. Lockwood,' said Nelly, shaking her head. 'I believe the dead are at peace, but it is not right to speak of them with levity'" (p. 358).

We have received the story almost entirely from Nelly, a representative of an admirable type of person, a character developed in great detail and with great skill, no obvious technical device, but a genuinely memorable character. In the circumstances in which she has been forced to live, she has revealed the futility of a tolerant, common-sense attitude which is the result of a desire merely to avoid trouble, to deny serious problems, and of a failure to grasp genuinely the emotions of others; the futility of compromise which is a mere improvisation from day to day in the interest of averting "explosions," of the futility of a constant attempt to preserve surface decorum and tranquillity on the grounds that what does not appear will not do any harm, and she has made the reader feel that her action has been throughout the best that can be expected of the type she represents. The reader continually decreases in sympathy with a type that he would usually admire, as she goes healthily and happily singing about her household duties and amusing the babies, since her so consistently emphasized good qualities turn out to be of so little use.

Thus, constantly rejecting her explanations, the reader substitutes his own, based always on the available evidence which she supplies but does not take into account or understand, and he becomes through his own perceptions increasingly sympathetic with the thoughts, feelings, and deeds of Heathcliff and Cathy.

The engaging of the reader actively as one who does a large part of the work of comprehending is an important cause of the power of the novel. As Nelly contentedly provides her superficial interpretations of motive, and contentedly recounts her inadequate parental behavior, we are constantly directed toward feeling the inadequacy of the wholesome, and toward sympathy with genuine passions, no matter how destructive or violent.

Notes

1. I shall make no attempt to refer to previous studies of *Wuthering Heights* in the course of my essay. The essays listed below, as well as others, have all given readers valuable help in elucidating various causes of the power of the novel. My own essay does not intend to challenge or refute any of them, but to make one further suggestion toward this elucidation, through the consideration of one other aspect in detail. For criticism of *Wuthering Heights* from the time of its publication until 1948, one may consult Melvin R. Watson, "*Wuthering Heights* and the Critics," *The Trollopian,* III (1948), 243-263. Another article by Mr. Watson, "Tempest in the Soul: The Theme and Structure of *Wuthering Heights,*" *Nineteenth-Century Fiction,* IV (1949), 87-100, in comparing the structure of the novel to that of an Elizabethan play, and in considering Nelly Dean technically valuable as a means of dividing the action into convenient acts, has a closer bearing on my essay. Other essays which give some consideration to Nelly Dean are:

William E. Buckler, "Chapter VII of *Wuthering Heights*: A Key to Interpretation," *NCF,* VII (1952), 51-55; Boris Ford, "*Wuthering Heights,*" *Scrutiny,* VII (1939), 375-389; and Dorothy Van Ghent, "On *Wuthering Heights,*" *The English Novel, Form and Function* (New York: Rinehart, 1953), pp. 153-170. Two other essays particularly valuable in the elucidation of *Wuthering Heights* are G. D. Klingopulos, "The Novel as Dramatic Poem (II): 'Wuthering Heights,'" *Scrutiny,* XIV (1947), 269-286, and Mark Schorer, "Fiction and the Matrix of Analogy," *Kenyon Review,* XI (1949), 539-560. Mr. Klingopulos asserts that "the author's preferences are not shown, do not reveal themselves unambiguously even to analysis" (p. 271). Mr. Schorer, in a very convincing demonstration of the consequences of the metaphorical language in a work of fiction, believes that Emily Brontë reached a conclusion she did not quite intend. "At the end the voice that drones on is the perdurable voice of the country, Nelly Dean's. No more than Heathcliff did Emily Brontë quite intend that homespun finality" (p. 549). It is not necessary to explain the ways in which my analysis differs from these in this note. Finally, three other essays should be mentioned: Richard Chase, "The Brontës, or Myth Domesticated," *Forms of Modern Fiction,* ed. William Van O'Connor (Minneapolis: University of Minnesota Press, 1948), pp. 102-119; C. P. Sanger, "The Structure of *Wuthering Heights,*" *The Hogarth Essays,* XIX (London: Hogarth Press, 1926), 24 pp.; and Dorothy Van Ghent, "The Window Figure and the Two-Children Figure in *Wuthering Heights,*" *NCF,* VII (1952), 189-197.

2. *Wuthering Heights,* p. 324. This page reference and all subsequent ones are to the Rinehart Edition [(New York, 1950)] with an Introduction by Mark Schorer.

3. A very different case of the same fundamental problem is shown with Lady Russell in *Persuasion.* Lady Russell is admirable but has certain qualities (dislike of wit and cleverness, and veneration of position) which cause her to fail as an adviser to Anne. Unless an admirable character in Anne's original social group had been shown wanting, it would not be clear that Anne was correct in emotionally and intellectually abandoning her family and their values. (Her one regret on marriage is that she has no friends or relations to introduce to Wentworth who will add to his social pleasures.) If she were only abandoning the stand of her absurd father and sister, she could still have accepted the group as Emma did in marrying Knightley. But with the inclusion of Lady Russell, the best type that the group can offer, Anne's revolt from the group itself is complete.

Thomas Moser (essay date June 1962)

SOURCE: Moser, Thomas. "What Is the Matter with Emily Jane? Conflicting Impulses in *Wuthering Heights.*" *Nineteenth-Century Fiction* 17, no. 1 (June 1962): 1-19.

[*In the following essay, Moser asserts that structural flaws of* Wuthering Heights *contribute to, rather than obscure, the novel's intense emotional power.*]

I

Ever since C. P. Sanger,[1] over thirty years ago, charted the elaborate time scheme of *Wuthering Heights*[2] and showed the symmetrical arrangement of characters, commentators have been writing in awestruck terms of the novel's design. Even Dorothy Van Ghent, the most perceptive of its critics, calls *Wuthering Heights* "finely wrought."[3] Others have drawn analogies to music and have—inevitably—invoked the sacred name of Beethoven. Moreover, critics have insisted generally that the structure is truly artful; it supports the meaning. The form fits the subject—in Lord David Cecil's homely phrase—"like a glove."[4]

I would suggest that the nineteenth-century view of *Wuthering Heights* as a powerful and imperfect book comes closer to the truth than recent assertions of its exquisite shape. I would suggest, too, that Charlotte Brontë's frequently maligned description of her sister as a most unconscious artist bears rereading:

> Her imagination, which was a spirit more sombre than sunny, more powerful than sportive, found in such traits material whence it wrought creations like Heathcliff, like Earnshaw, like Catherine. Having formed these beings, she did not know what she had done. If the auditor of her work, when read in manuscript, shuddered under the grinding influence of natures so relentless and implacable, of spirits so lost and fallen; if it was complained that the mere hearing of certain vivid and fearful scenes banished sleep by night, and distrubed mental peace by day, Ellis Bell would wonder what was meant, and suspect the complainant of affectation. . . .
>
> Whether it is right or advisable to create things like Heathcliff, I do not know: I scarcely think it is. But this I know; the writer who possesses the creative gift owns something of which he is not always master—something that at times strangely wills and works for itself.
>
> (pp. xxxiii, xxxv)

The two most distinctive features of the design of *Wuthering Heights* are its multiple narrators (who cause the chronological involutions) and its two generations of love triangles. The narrative method is indeed a brilliant invention. Mrs. Van Ghent reveals two of its uses: the narratives of Nelly Dean and Lockwood place the drama "in the context of the psychologically familiar"; the dis-

placement "into past time and into the memory of an old woman functions in the same way as dream displacements: it both censors and indulges, protects and liberates."[5] Even more important, it seems to me, these narrators, the epicene Lockwood and the prudent Nelly, are obtuse; they misinterpret the action and in their characters act as ironic contrasts to Heathcliff and Cathy. But in the second half of the novel the method essentially breaks down: the narrators cease to serve as ironic screens and the novel suffers seriously. Mark Schorer's stimulating and complex interpretation of *Wuthering Heights* relies not only upon the narrative perspective but also upon the continuance of the story through another generation. "One of the most carefully constructed novels in the language," it is carried on long enough to show that convention and the "cloddish world" survive and that Heathcliff's passion is "meaningless at last" (p. xiii). But is this what the novel shows? Does not the creation of the second generation serve chiefly to mar the structure by contradicting the novel's true subject? Probably Emily Brontë at no time consciously accepted her true subject; in the closing pages of *Wuthering Heights* she certainly rejects it—to the obvious detriment of her art.

How does one determine a novel's "true subject"? To try to discuss this in a few sentences is absurd; yet an oversimplified answer may help to clarify the problems posed by *Wuthering Heights.* A novel's true subject is the one that, regardless of the novelist's conscious intention, actually informs the work, the one that elicits the most highly energized writing. To put it another way, a novelist has found the true subject of his book when he dramatizes the truth he cannot escape rather than the illusion he longs to make "true."[6]

Lord David Cecil's account of the true subject of *Wuthering Heights* ("philosophy," he terms it) has been conspicuously influential. He calls Emily Brontë a "mystic" who views the cosmos as the "expression of certain living spiritual principles . . . the principle of storm . . . and the principle of calm." These principles do not conflict. "They are the component parts of a harmony." The final impression that *Wuthering Heights* leaves is one of "cosmic order," "harmonious, complete."[7] Despite the ingenuity of this reading, it hardly describes the common reader's response to *Wuthering Heights,* or his recollection of it. One admires and rereads the novel for the grand passion of Heathcliff and Cathy. Lord David's discussion must be seen then as rationalization rather than interpretation. Most commentators, in fact, evince a longing to tame the novel, to make their pleasure in it somehow respectable. This would explain the reiterated references to Emily Brontë as a mystic, and the evident comfort that enthusiasts take in the notion that Cathy and Heathcliff's love is "sexless," meaning, presumably, that intercourse is not even implied.

II

Lord David's essay commands assent at least in its stress on the characters as representative of universal forces. It is rather the vagueness of his definitions and their generality of application which seem dubious. Mrs. Van Ghent and Richard Chase give, I think, much more persuasive symbolic readings. The former describes Heathcliff as "essentially, anthropomorphized primitive energy,"[8] and the latter calls him "sheer dazzling sexual"[9] force. I would be even more specific. Over a century ago Emily Brontë dramatized what Freud subsequently called the id. She discovered and symbolized in Heathcliff and, to a lesser extent, in Cathy that part of us we know so little about, the secret wellspring of vitality, the child that lurks within everyone, even within so ordinary a person as Nelly Dean or one so weak as Lockwood. Somehow, Emily Brontë penetrated to that most obscure part of the psyche and "characterized" it. The primary traits which Freud ascribed to the id apply perfectly to Heathcliff: the source of psychic energy; the seat of the instincts (particularly sex and death); the essence of dreams; the archaic foundation of personality—selfish, asocial, impulsive.

I do not mean to say that **Wuthering Heights** is a sport, a modern novel born by chance in the nineteenth century. It clearly belongs to the tradition of tales of overwhelming, self-consuming love described in Denis de Rougemont's *Love in the Western World*. More particularly, it has close affinities in terms of character, situation, and recurrent imagery with *Clarissa*; both novels come from the same kind of imagination—English, Puritan, essentially feminine. Nor do I wish by a Freudian reading of symbols to exclude mythic interpretations. By stressing a perhaps restrictive reading, I hope to throw into sharper relief the novel's weaknesses—and strengths.

The basic childishness of Cathy and Heathcliff and their impulse to lose themselves in the world of external nature need no analysis. Mrs. Van Ghent's brilliant essay makes these quite clear. But Heathcliff as the embodiment of sexual energy requires detailed explanation not only because critics have largely ignored this role but also because Emily Brontë apparently tried to disguise the truth from herself. The large body of evidence suggesting that Emily Brontë felt Heathcliff to be pure sexual force lies just beneath the surface, in a series of scenes involving Heathcliff, Cathy, and, in most cases, an ineffectual male. Each scene dramatizes a dispute of some sort over entrance through a door or window. Heathcliff always wins, and the images suggest that the victory is a sexual conquest.[10]

The *locus classicus* for this pattern is the eleventh chapter. Edgar has just learned that Heathcliff intends to marry his sister, and he determines to throw Heathcliff

out of the house. To this end he orders three servants to wait in the passage while he enters the kitchen where Heathcliff and Cathy converse. When he demands Heathcliff's "instant departure," the latter responds in a way calculated to cast doubt on Edgar's masculinity: "Cathy, this lamb of yours threatens like a bull!" (p. 121). Edgar tries to signal the servants for help, but Cathy slams the door to the passage and locks it, saying that she will swallow the key before Edgar shall get it and that she wishes that Heathcliff may flog Edgar sick:

> It did not need the medium of a flogging to produce that effect on the master. He tried to wrest the key from Catherine's grasp; and for safety she flung it into the hottest part of the fire; whereupon Mr. Edgar was taken with a nervous trembling, and his countenance grew deadly pale. For his life he could not avert that access of emotion—mingled anguish and humiliation overcame him completely. He leant on the back of a chair, and covered his face.

> (p. 121)

Notice here that Cathy throws the key into the fire, which throughout the novel is associated with Heathcliff and Cathy, and opposed to Edgar. (Cathy says earlier of Heathcliff, "Whatever our souls are made of, his and mine are the same, and Linton's is as different as a moonbeam from lightning, or frost from fire" [p. 85].) Notice too that Edgar's response to the defeat at Cathy's hands far exceeds the apparent danger of a beating by Heathcliff. It is almost as if Edgar senses in this defeat his sexual inferiority to Heathcliff and Cathy. Certainly Cathy views the situation in these terms: "Oh! Heavens! In old days this would win you knighthood! . . . We are vanquished! we are vanquished! Heathcliff would as soon lift a finger at you as the king would march his army against a colony of mice" (pp. 121-122).

In the ensuing action, Edgar appears to put Heathcliff to rout; he strikes him across the throat, taking his breath momentarily, and walks out the back door, through the yard, to summon the servants from the front of the house. Heathcliff vows immediate vengeance: "I'll crush his ribs in like a rotten hazel-nut" (p. 122). But Nelly, to prevent violence, tells one of her white lies. Edgar, she says, has sent only his servants to the back door and is himself in hiding. Heathcliff thus finds himself trapped by Cathy's earlier stratagem against Edgar. The front door of the kitchen remains locked, the key in the fire. But Heathcliff does not tremble; he quickly remedies the loss of the key by seizing from the fireplace a poker, smashing the lock, and making his escape through the "inner door" (p. 123).

Cathy's response to the drama has sexual overtones. "Very much excited," she hastens upstairs to the parlor, throwing herself on the sofa: "A thousand smiths' hammers are beating in my head!" (p. 123). She directs

Nelly not to permit Isabella to approach and lies in wait for Edgar. She tells Nelly to remind Edgar of her "passionate temper, verging, when kindled, on frenzy," and to "dismiss that apathy" out of her face (pp. 123-124). Edgar appears, not in anger but in sorrow. His lack of fire enrages Cathy. She stamps her foot: "Your cold blood cannot be worked into a fever—your veins are full of ice-water—but mine are boiling, and the sight of such chilliness makes them dance" (p. 124). When Edgar asks her to choose between him and Heathcliff, she tells him to leave her and rings the bell until it breaks with a twang. Then she lies on the sofa dashing her head against the arm and gnashing her teeth. Edgar and Nelly cannot understand her feelings, and she rushes into her bedroom, locks the door, and remains for three days, Edgar staying in the library. When she finally lets Nelly in, she is clearly dying. Her description of her first night alone in the bedroom dramatizes her complete absorption with Heathcliff. She had fallen unconscious and had not begun to awaken until dawn.

> "I thought as I lay there, with my head against that table leg, and my eyes dimly discerning the grey square of the window, that I was enclosed in the oak-panelled bed at home. . . . I was a child; my father was just buried, and my misery arose from the separation that Hindley had ordered between me and Heathcliff—I was laid alone, for the first time, and, rousing from a dismal doze after a night of weeping—I lifted my hand to push the panels aside, it struck the tabletop!"
>
> (p. 132)

Cathy asks Nelly to open the window for her, Nelly refuses, and Cathy throws it open herself and leans out, "careless of the frosty air that cut about her shoulders as keen as a knife" (p. 133). Finally Edgar appears. Shocked by her haggard countenance, he takes her in his arms. "Ah! you are come, are you, Edgar Linton? . . . You are one of those things that are ever found when least wanted, and when you are wanted, never!" (p. 135). She goes on to make what seems a most curious remark, in view of the fact that Edgar is embracing her: "What you touch at present, you may have; but my soul will be on that hill-top, before you lay hands on me again. I don't want you, Edgar, I'm past wanting you" (p. 135).

These three scenes—the kitchen, the upstairs parlor, and Cathy's bedroom three days later—need little comment. In the kitchen battle over the key, Cathy reveals her contempt for Edgar's masculinity by seizing the key and locking the door, and Heathcliff shows himself master by breaking the lock with the poker. When Cathy hurries up to the parlor to lie on the sofa, her longing for love gives Edgar another chance. All may be well between them if he will come, not blaming Cathy but loving and wanting her. Instead, he shows no feeling at all while Cathy, raging at his utter inadequacy, breaks the bellpull. Sexual frustration clearly contributes to her

collapse after Edgar's failure. Cathy's dream of the time Hindley first removed Heathcliff from her bed (he was thirteen and she was twelve) reaffirms that only her foster-brother and childhood lover can alleviate her suffering. Edgar is useless, she tells him, and his masculine attentions are no longer wanted. Heathcliff must come through that window to satisfy Cathy. (Since Emily Brontë cannot let this happen, on the literal level—because Heathcliff and Cathy are "one"? because Emily Brontë wrote under some kind of incest taboo? because she would have curtailed her story?—she has Heathcliff snatch Isabella away from Thrushcross Grange at the very time that Cathy is calling for him through the window and telling Edgar that she'll be dead "before you lay hands on me again.")

III

The kitchen scene offers the most vivid example of Heathcliff as sexual force, but it is far from unique. In fact, it is only one of many following the same pattern. Emily Brontë repeatedly portrays Heathcliff as breaking through a barrier, identified with Cathy, which an ineffectual male either attempts to break and cannot or attempts futilely to defend. Sometimes a fourth party is present, chiefly as a witness to narrate the scene later to the reader. (Mrs. Van Ghent interprets windows in *Wuthering Heights* as symbolic of the barrier between the "human" and the "other" world;[11] windows and doors seem also to admit of another more specific reading.)

The early scenes of this type all show, as might be expected, Edgar as the ineffectual male. In the first, Heathcliff appears only as a potential invader of Thrushcross Grange the night he and Cathy, still children, are caught peeking through the windows at Edgar and Isabella. The Lintons take in Cathy and send away Heathcliff. But he lurks outside and later tells Nelly: "If Catherine had wished to return, I intended shattering their great glass panes to a million fragments" (p. 52). The next such scene occurs three years after Heathcliff's departure (a departure that was signalized by a huge bough falling across the roof of Wuthering Heights and knocking stones into the kitchen fire). Heathcliff returns in September, 1783. Here is Nelly's and the reader's first view of him, on the porch of Thrushcross Grange: "He leant against the side, and held his fingers on the latch, as if intending to open for himself" (p. 98). Instead he opens it for Nelly to take his message upstairs; Cathy joins him immediately and later flies up the stairs "breathless and wild" (p. 99) with the wonderful news of his return. For the next three months Heathcliff visits more and more frequently until the violent scene in the kitchen, after which he steals Isabella away. The last of the invasion scenes during Cathy's life occurs two months later, when Heathcliff has returned to learn that she lies on the point of death. He tells Nelly he will fight his way into Thrushcross Grange if she will not let him in. As usual she gives in so as to prevent violence. Actually, Heathcliff manages alone, walking past the watchdog and into the house. "He did not hit the right room directly; she motioned me to admit him; but he found it out, ere I could reach the door, and in a stride or two was at her side, and had her grasped in his arms" (pp. 167-168). He and Cathy embrace tumultuously; Cathy collapses, not from the power of Heathcliff's love but from despair at the sound of Edgar's approaching step. Heathcliff at last withdraws to the garden and Cathy never regains consciousness.

Cathy dies early Monday morning, March 20, 1784, and is buried the following Friday. That night Heathcliff enacts his most violent invasion, this time into Wuthering Heights with Hindley acting as the ineffectual male striving to bar the door. The latter may seem a strange choice for this role; nevertheless, not only is he no match for Heathcliff, but he is also less than the master of women. Some years earlier, Nelly, virtually his foster sister, renders him, literally and symbolically, harmless by taking "the shot out of the master's fowling piece" (p. 76). Hindley, drunk, seizes a carving knife and orders Nelly to open her mouth:

He held the knife in his hand, and pushed its point between my teeth: but, for my part, I was never afraid of his vagaries. I spat out, and affirmed it tasted detestably—I would not take it on any account.

> "Oh!" said he, releasing me . . .

>   (pp. 77-78)

The night after Cathy's funeral finds Hindley similarly armed, holding a "curiously constructed pistol, having a double-edged spring knife attached to the barrel" which he normally carries concealed in his waistcoat. Isabella admires the pistol:

> I surveyed the weapon inquisitively; a hideous notion struck me. How powerful I should be possessing such an instrument! I took it from his hand, and touched the blade. He looked astonished at the expression my face assumed during a brief second. It was not horror, it was covetousness. He snatched the pistol back, jealously . . .

>   (p. 149)

Heathcliff returns from the cemetery and finds the kitchen door locked. As he walks around the house through the snow, Hindley and Isabella agree to keep him out. "Do!" says Isabella. "Put the key in the lock, and draw the bolts" (p. 185). Hindley determined to murder Heathcliff and asks silence of Isabella. But although she wants Heathcliff dead, Isabella, like all the other characters in the novel, cannot finally see harm done him. Impulsively, she shouts a warning through the lattice. Heathcliff knocks the casement to the floor

and, when Hindley rushes forward to shoot, reaches through and wrenches the weapon away. It goes off harmlessly and the spring knife closes, not on Heathcliff, but on Hindley's wrist. Heathcliff "then took a stone, struck down the division between two windows, and sprung in" (p. 188).

The scene seems incomplete. Why should Heathcliff bother to break through simply to get at Isabella, whom he detests? One hundred and twenty pages and eighteen years later the reader finally discovers Heathcliff's mission that night. He had been digging up Cathy's newly filled grave when he felt her warm breath upon him:

> "Her presence was with me; it remained while I re-filled the grave, and led me home. . . . Having reached the Heights, I rushed eagerly to the door. It was fastened; and, I remember, that accursed Earnshaw and my wife opposed my entrance. I remember stopping to kick the breath out of him, and then hurrying upstairs, to my room, and hers—I looked round impatiently—I felt her by me—I could *almost* see her . . ."

>   (p. 306)

Clearly, Heathcliff's victory over Hindley, like those over Edgar, is part of his quest for Cathy.

Even Lockwood, with his minimal role in the lives of the lovers, is permitted to play the ineffectual male once. His lack of masculinity needs no documentation. The only time a woman ever responded to him, Lockwood, as he himself admits, "shrunk icily into myself, like a snail; at every glance retired colder and farther" (p. 4). While calling on his landlord, Heathcliff, Lockwood is snowbound and spends the night. The housekeeper puts him, unbeknownst to Heathcliff, in the old panelled bed where Cathy and Heathcliff had slept as children. Here Lockwood dreams his memorable dream: that the waif Cathy knocks on the window to be let in and that he tries to silence the cry by unhasping the casement but cannot because the "hook was soldered into the staple, a circumstance observed by me when awake" (p. 24). In his dream he breaks the glass and finds his hand clasped by a tiny hand; terrified; he scrapes the wrist on the broken pane and finally screams so loudly as to waken himself and arouse Heathcliff. When he tells Heathcliff the dream, he is sent out of the room. But Lockwood surreptitiously observes Heathcliff: "He got on to the bed, and wrenched open the lattice, bursting, as he pulled at it, into an uncontrollable passion of tears. 'Come in! come in!' he sobbed. 'Cathy, do come. Oh do—*once* more!'" (p. 28).

This is the last time Heathcliff violently removes a barrier between himself and Cathy. And Lockwood's role is obviously more that of witness than opponent. There are, however, two other occasions at the end of Heathcliff's life when no other male is present and opposition is only implied. When the sexton is digging another grave, Heathcliff has Cathy's coffin uncovered. He strikes that side of the coffin loose which will be next to his: "and I bribed the sexton to pull it away, when I'm laid there, and slide mine out too" (p. 305). Eight months later Nelly finds Heathcliff lying dead in his and Cathy's panelled bed, with the window swinging to and fro and with eyes that "would not shut" (p. 356). Nelly reports that Heathcliff was buried as he had wished. Presumably, then, Heathcliff's intention was fulfilled, that "by the time Linton gets to us, he'll not know which is which!" (p. 305).

Not only is Heathcliff a consistently successful invader. He also bars the way to others and establishes himself as sole keeper of the keys. The first page of the novel shows Heathcliff leaning over the gate, hands in his waistcoat, while Lockwood burbles a request to enter. This image of Heathcliff standing menacingly at the entrance to Wuthering Heights recurs frequently throughout the novel. Even more striking is Heathcliff's tenacity when Isabella and later the younger Cathy try to deprive him of house keys. Isabella, coming to Wuthering Heights for the first time after her marriage, wanders through the house looking for the bedroom she will share with her husband. Joseph warns her that Heathcliff's is just the one she cannot see, so she sleeps in a chair in Hareton's room until Heathcliff finds her. Isabella reports to Nelly his reaction: "I told him the cause of my staying up so late—that he had the key to our room in his pocket. The adjective *our* gave mortal offense. He swore it was not, nor ever should be mine . . ." (p. 153).

Although Emily Brontë refers frequently to Heathcliff's violent treatment of the children in the second half of the novel, she dramatizes it only once. This is the time when Heathcliff captures the younger Cathy in order to force her to marry his son Linton. The subsequent action makes an interesting contrast to Edgar's battle for the kitchen key with the other Cathy many years before. Her daughter, black eyes flashing, says, "Give me that key—I will have it!" (p. 285). She snatches at the "instrument" and almost gets it out of Heathcliff's loosened fingers. He warns her to stand off, but she ignores the warning and applies her teeth to his hand. (Her mother, in the earlier battle, had threatened to swallow the key to keep it from Edgar.) Heathcliff suddenly and deliberately releases the key. But he shows none of Edgar's humiliation. For when Cathy goes to secure the key, he seizes her, pulls her on his knee, and administers a "shower of terrific slaps on both sides of the head" (p. 286). A touch on the chest stops Nelly when she tries to interfere; Heathcliff picks the key off the floor and, "perceiving us all confounded, rose, and expeditiously made the tea himself" (p. 287).

The actions and the language of the scenes examined above—surely the most memorable scenes in the novel—indicate that, whether she "knew" it or not,

Emily Brontë was writing a passionate paean to Eros. The novel moves relentlessly toward its necessary end—the complete physical union of Cathy and Heathcliff. Moreover, although Emily Brontë frustrates this union on the literal level until both are buried, and thus makes a "story," symbolically she accomplishes it in almost every scene Cathy and Heathcliff play together. At the same time she soundly defeats all the other characters (particularly the Thrushcross Grange inmates) whenever they attempt to curb Heathcliff in his quest for Cathy.

IV

E. M. Forster says that **Wuthering Heights** is one of those novels that asks of the reader the "suspension of the sense of humour."[12] This comment applies with much more force to the second half (with the exception of a few scenes) than it does to the first. The violence of the scenes just discussed does not seem laughably melodramatic. It is perfectly in keeping with the characters. As Mrs. Van Ghent says, "Heathcliff might *really* be a demon."[13] Again, Cathy's wild speeches to Nelly and Edgar in her bedroom after three days of isolation are completely appropriate to her. And these are perhaps the loveliest pages of the novel.

That Emily Brontë loses control of the second half of her novel and writes insincerely is suggested by her attempts to endow the thin-blooded Thrushcross Grange people with the emotional language of Heathcliff and Cathy. This occurs in Isabella's account of Heathcliff to Nelly immediately after Cathy's death and almost precisely in the middle of the novel:

> "I gave him my heart, and he took and pinched it to death; and flung it back to me—people feel with their hearts, Ellen, and since he has destroyed mine, I have not power to feel for him, and I would not, though he groaned from this, to his dying day; and wept tears of blood for Catherine!"
>
> (p. 183)

From Cathy's lips a speech like this would be convincing. But there is no evidence that Isabella's love for Heathcliff is anything but self-infatuation or that she ever had a heart to feel with, let alone to give. The younger Cathy employs the same kind of inappropriately emotional language to express sympathy for Linton Heathcliff, whom even Nelly Dean scorns. The scene, like many of the later ones, parodies an earlier. Hareton locks out Linton and Cathy, and Linton shrieks in helpless rage until he falls in a fit. Cathy expostulates: "Ellen, I was ready to tear my hair off my head! I sobbed and wept so that my eyes were almost blind" (p. 265). Had her mother said this about her lover, we would be convinced. But not here.

Emily Brontë at first persuades the reader when she consistently and movingly implies that a future of ecstasy will reward Heathcliff's and Cathy's quest for each other. The second half of the book promises a resolution on the realistic level through a younger generation, with Cathy playing her mother's role, Hareton playing Heathcliff's, and Linton playing Edgar's. The reader, however, will hardly accept the new terms of the perfect relationship between the sexes. Emily Brontë asks us to admire the younger Cathy's quest, first for a patient, in Linton, and then for a pupil, in Hareton. And both boys desire, not union with an equal, but unsexed bliss with a mother.

Cathy from the beginning is related to Linton like a sentimental nurse to a sickly child, "stroking his curls, and kissing his cheek, and offering him tea in her saucer, like a baby" (p. 213). Later she arranges his pillows, offers her shoulder or her knee as support for his head. She views marriage with him as perpetuating this relationship.

> "I'm a woman—and I'm certain Linton would recover quickly if he had me to look after him—I'm older than he is, you know, and wiser, and less childish, am I not? And he'll soon do as I direct him, with some slight coaxing—He's a pretty little darling when he's good. I'd make such a pet of him, if he were mine."
>
> (p. 256)

Linton's saccharine speeches (quite out of character) suggest that Emily Brontë actually feels Cathy praiseworthy in her attitude toward him: "believe that if I might be as sweet, and as kind, and as good as you are, I would be, as willingly and more so, than as happy and healthy. And, believe that your kindness has made me love you deeper than if I deserved your love. . . ." On this Cathy modestly comments: "I felt he spoke the truth" (p. 267). Love, which in the older generation is the expression of vital energy, dwindles, in the younger, to the pleasure of nursing and to gratitude at being mothered.

Also characteristic of the younger Cathy are her heroic debates with Heathcliff in which she plays either the little heroine of Victorian stage melodrama spurning the cruel villain or the embattled champion of woman's rights castigating the dissolute male:

> "Mr. Heathcliff, *you* have *nobody* to love you; and, however miserable you make us, we shall still have the revenge of thinking that your cruelty arises from your greater misery! You *are* miserable, are you not? Lonely, like the devil, and envious like him? *Nobody* loves you—*nobody* will cry for you, when you die! I wouldn't be you!"
>
> (p. 304)

Such speeches recur with alarming frequency in the last fifty pages of the book and suggest, painfully, Emily Brontë's identification with her moralizing heroine.

While Linton is made for his part, Hareton apparently needs the rough edges rubbed off before he can be Cathy's next suitable minion. The roughness is only ap-

parent, however, since Hareton early tries to ingratiate himself with Cathy. Heathcliff, it is true, had marked him for his own: "Now, my bonny lad, you are mine! And we'll see if one tree won't grow as crooked as another, with the same wind to twist it!"[14] (p. 198). Hareton, however, proves himself no oak of the Heathcliff-Cathy variety. After Linton's death, Emily Brontë and the second Cathy speedily deprive him of his male sexual force. First he is incapacitated for the masculine sport of hunting. Not only does his gun burst but his arm is injured and he is "condemned to the fireside and tranquillity" which, Nelly tells us, "suited Catharine" (p. 330). Hareton has recourse to his other masculine sport, smoking, but Cathy, like her mother with Edgar's key, takes Hareton's pipe from his mouth, breaks it, and throws it behind the fire. Although Hareton swears and takes another pipe, his smoking is never mentioned again, and a few minutes later we see him accept from Cathy a handsome book wrapped in white paper and tied with a bit of ribbon. Hareton trembles, his face glows, and soon his lessons have begun, Cathy's hand upon his shoulder. Presently all Wuthering Heights suffers feminization. Under Cathy's tutelage Hareton clears out Joseph's black currant trees for a flower bed while she puts primroses in her beloved's porridge.

How Lord David and most other Brontë critics can take seriously the affair between Cathy and Hareton remains a mystery. Their love story belongs with countless pieces of sub-literary fiction in women's magazines; it is simply a superficial stereotyped tale of feminine longings. Emily Brontë gives her heroine first a spoiled and then a tractable child to play with—a "love affair" without any of the concomitant inconveniences of sex. As the novel loses its force, the reader's mind inevitably wanders away from the work of art to its creator, the intense, inhibited spinster of Haworth. Her careful arrangement of symmetrical sets of characters, rather than signifying her continuing involvement with her subject, denotes simply that she has abandoned it.

V

For the structure that is organic form comes neither from intricate time schemes nor the neat repetition of character types. It rises from deep within the artist and relates directly to his felt awareness of life. Yet there is one aspect of the **Wuthering Heights** chronology which does express Emily Brontë's sense of Heathcliff's magical sexual power. Let us look with the eye of a month-counting neighborhood gossip at three important marriages and subsequent blessed events. A little calendar work reveals that Heathcliff's presence was vital to the conception of all three children of the second generation.

No one knew where Hindley met Frances or when they married. Certain it is that Hindley brought her with him when he returned from college for his father's funeral in October 1777; the next June, the ninth month after their arrival at Wuthering Heights, saw the birth of Hareton, last of the Earnshaws. Heathcliff has, of course, little personal impact upon Hindley's relations with Frances, and one could attribute Hareton's conception after their arrival to the potent atmosphere of Wuthering Heights. But Emily Brontë shows in detail the immense effect Heathcliff has on relations between Cathy and Edgar. They marry in April, 1783, and "for the space of half a year, the gunpowder lay as harmless as sand, because no fire came near to explode it." However, "on a mellow evening in September" (p. 97), Heathcliff finally returns. Cathy glows with delight at his appearance, and he flashes glances at her, his "eyes full of black fire," while Edgar grows "pale with pure annoyance" (p. 101). That night Edgar cries in bed. At first Cathy is irritated, but Heathcliff's return has wiped out the "misery" of her marriage and has reconciled her "to God, and humanity" (pp. 104-105). She makes peace with Edgar; the morrow finds her exuberantly vivacious and Edgar no longer peevish. He permits her to visit Wuthering Heights that afternoon with Isabella; "she rewarded him with such a summer of sweetness and affection, in return, as made the house a paradise for several days, both master and servants profiting from the perpetual sunshine" (p. 105). This one blissful period in their marriage ends soon with the quarrel over Heathcliff and Isabella. But clearly within those few days when Heathcliff's fire first nears Cathy's gunpowder, Cathy and Edgar conceive their child. The second Cathy arrives March 20, 1784, in the seventh month after Heathcliff's appearance, "a puny, seven months' child" (p. 174).

Heathcliff proves himself as potent a literal as symbolic father. He carries Isabella away in January 1784, and within twenty-four hours she wants to be back in Thrushcross Grange. Apparently Emily Brontë imagines them sleeping together only the first night. Certainly she stresses the fact that Heathcliff never permits the detested Isabella to enter his Wuthering Heights bedroom. Nevertheless, the following September, in the ninth month after their elopement, Isabella gives birth to Linton Heathcliff.

When E. M. Forster said that Emily Brontë tried to hide the clock in her book, he did not mean, one trusts, all this! Of course it is impossible to know whether Emily Brontë consciously arranged the births of Hareton and Cathy so that Heathcliff could influence their conceptions and whether she meant that Linton was conceived at Heathcliff's and Isabella's first and only sexual encounter. My own guess is that Emily Brontë did not consciously manipulate the time scheme here, but that her vision of Heathcliff as the energy that invests the universe, together with her woman's sense of the biological rhythms of life, produced these strangely appropriate results.

Her sense of Heathcliff's potency does not wholly desert her during the second half of the novel. Only this can explain all the improbable circumstances which "cause" the second Cathy to be drawn time after time, against the wills of her father, Nelly, and herself, to Wuthering Heights. Only his power can account for Isabella's half-conscious longing, after he has driven her away, for him to follow her, give her a new wedding ring, and take her back. Why else should Nelly fail to shout when help is near, and why should she irrationally blame herself rather than Heathcliff when she and Cathy are captured? In the later pages, he looms over Wuthering Heights like the source of a gigantic magnetic field; fitfully, reluctantly, unconsciously, its victims acknowledge that its power is good.

From Heathcliff as energy, however, to the words of Lockwood which close the book is a long step indeed; so, too, is the shift from the Lockwood and Nelly of the opening pages to their roles at the end. At the beginning both exist as ironic and, at times, ludicrous contrasts to the principals. Lockwood's sexual timidity effectively enhances Heathcliff's vigor, and Nelly's prudent complacency puts into strong relief Cathy's passion, but Emily Brontë's handling of her two narrators in the second half partakes of the general decline in quality. Nelly Dean becomes more and more an official voice of the author. No irony intervenes as she sings the younger Cathy's praises to Linton. Even worse are Lockwood's coyly banal observations on the love play of Cathy and Hareton. He hears her voice, "sweet as a silver bell," threatening Hareton with a hairpulling if he mispronounces, and Hareton in "softened tones," demanding a kiss if he speaks correctly. Cathy leans over him, her "light shining ringlets blending, at intervals, with his brown locks," as she superintends his studies. "The task was done," says Lockwood, "not free from further blunders, but the pupil claimed a reward and received at least five kisses, which, however, he generously returned" (pp. 325-326).

The first Cathy and Heathcliff are pretty well distilled out of the novel by its last page. Country people insist that Heathcliff "walks," but Nelly shows little sign of uneasiness. The novel ends with these words, much quoted and highly praised, spoken by Lockwood at the graves of the lovers:

> I lingered round them, under that benign sky; watched the moths fluttering among the heath and hare-bells; listened to the soft wind breathing through the grass; and wondered how anyone could ever imagine unquiet slumbers, for the sleepers in that quiet earth.
>
> (p. 358)

In view of what we know of Heathcliff, perpetually vibrant with passion, and of Cathy ceaselessly haunting him, we must find this passage profoundly ironic. There is, however, no evidence that Emily Brontë perceived that irony.

Mark Schorer's reading of the novel describes what may well have been Emily Brontë's ultimate conscious attitude toward her creation. He suggests that she "begins by wishing to instruct her narrator, the sentimental dandy Lockwood, in the nature of a grand passion, and that somehow she ends by instructing herself in the vanity of human wishes" (p. xiv). She tries to take Cathy and Heathcliff at their own valuation, to exalt the moral magnificence of unmoral passion. "Her novelistic art had to evaluate her world" (p. x), and through her arrangement of the generations, "as neat and tidy as the cupboard of a spinster" (p. xi), and by screening the narrative through the perspectives of two conventional people, she sees "what her unmoral passions come to. Moral magnificence? Not at all; rather, a devastating spectacle of human waste: ashes" (p. xiii). Probably Mr. Schorer is right, that this was Emily Brontë's conscious response to her work. Yet, as her sister said, she did not really understand what she was writing. Otherwise, she could not have tried to pass off as real and important those illusory figures, Hareton and the younger Cathy. Surely the authentic Emily Brontë does not believe that real love can be exemplified by this couple, so oblivious to the primitive forces that underlie life. The authentic Emily Brontë who wrote the masterpiece we return to is the creator of Heathcliff, vibrating with energy, and Cathy, scorning the pusillanimous Edgar to cry across the moors to her demon lover.

Notes

1. "The Structure of *Wuthering Heights*," *The Hogarth Essays,* No. XIX (London, 1926).

2. New York, 1950. All citations made in the text will be from this edition, the Rinehart. It includes the preface Charlotte Brontë wrote to the second edition (1850) as well as an interpretive introduction by Mark Schorer.

3. Van Ghent, *The English Novel: Form and Function* (New York, 1953), p. 153. I should here like to acknowledge a considerable debt both to Mrs. Van Ghent and to Albert J. Guerard for suggestions concerning this paper.

4. Cecil, *Early Victorian Novelists* (London, 1934), p. 185.

5. Van Ghent, pp. 155, 160.

6. *As I Lay Dying* provides an example of a novel in which the author's intention conflicts with the true subject. Addie Bundren's long, explicitly philosophical monologue gives the intended subject: the cleavage between thought and action. Faulkner apparently wishes in this novel to rank his characters according to the ability of each to unite thought and action, and in these terms, Addie comes first, Anse last. But whatever the intended subject, *As I Lay Dying* succeeds primarily as a comic novel, the dramatization of man enduring amid a welter of absurd disasters. This is what energizes the novel, and the central figure is Anse—almost the type of the comic hero—selfish, amoral, buffeted on all sides, but, somehow, always landing on his feet.

7. Cecil, pp. 151, 152, 167, 164.

8. Van Ghent, p. 154.

9. Chase, "The Brontës, or Myth Domesticated," *Forms of Modern Fiction,* ed. William Van O'Connor (Minneapolis, 1948), p. 109.

10. I first noticed this pattern while studying a similar and recurrent scene in the novels of Joseph Conrad: an older man attempts to kill the hero at the door of the heroine's boudoir, but the heroine intervenes, disarms the older man, and drops the weapon at the hero's feet. Conrad seems unconsciously to imagine the older man as an impotent voyeur; the disarming figures as a symbolic statement of his impotence. But since the hero frequently identifies himself with the older man, the heroine's contemptuous gesture of dropping the weapon at the hero's feet tends to cast doubt on his masculinity too. Emily Brontë's scene differs from Conrad's in the important respect that although females may assist Heathcliff and may help to disarm his opponents, they never disarm him nor is there ever any implication that he really needs help.

Other affinities between Conrad and Emily Brontë have been noticed, particularly their common use of multiple narrators and involuted chronology. I suspect that the resemblance in the present instance reflects chiefly the uneasiness of both about sexual matters. In Conrad's early, major novels, the scene plays an unimportant part, but in the later, inferior works, it is crucial, betraying Conrad's doubts about his intended theme of "affirmation." In *Wuthering Heights,* this scene lies at the very heart of the novel's meaning. I need not say, I trust, that only a few novels will respond to this kind of examination—those in which unconscious creation plays a large part and in which sex is a central subject. Although characters in *Middlemarch* stand in doorways, hold objects, and even drop them, the novel will yield no extra meaning by undergoing this kind of analysis. In *Middlemarch,* everything is held up to the light; George Eliot requires no second guessing.

11. Van Ghent, pp. 160-163.

12. Forster, *Aspects of the Novel* (New York, 1927), p. 211.

13. Forster, p. 154.

14. Heathcliff's tree metaphor is appropriate since both he and the first Cathy are consistently associated with trees. The pine bough scratching the window, in Lockwood's dream, becomes Cathy's fingers, and her marriage to Edgar resembles putting "an oak in a flower-pot" (p. 163). When Heathcliff leaves Wuthering Heights a branch strikes the roof, and he beats his head bloody against a tree trunk at Cathy's death. The lovers become a single tree in Cathy's image: whoever tries to separate them will "meet the fate of Milo" (p. 85), the Greek athlete caught by the tree he was trying to split and torn to death by wolves.

F. R. Leavis and Q. D. Leavis (essay date 1969)

SOURCE: Leavis, F. R., and Q. D. Leavis. "A Fresh Approach to *Wuthering Heights*." In *Lectures in America,* pp. 85-138. London: Chatto & Windus, 1969.

[*In the following excerpt, Leavis and Leavis discuss the dominant themes in Brontë's* Wuthering Heights, *comparing the novel to the works of Shakespeare, Dickens, and Dostoevsky.*]

I would first like to clear out of the way the *confusions* of the plot [of *Wuthering Heights*] and note the different levels on which the novel operates at different times. It seems clear to me that Emily Brontë had some trouble in getting free of a false start—a start which suggests that we are going to have a regional version of the sub-plot of *Lear* (Shakespeare being generally the inspiration for those early nineteenth-century novelists who rejected the eighteenth-century idea of the novel). In fact, the Lear-world of violence, cruelty, unnatural crimes, family disruption and physical horrors remains the world of the household at Wuthering Heights, a characteristic due not to sadism or perversion in the novelist (some of the physical violence is quite unrealized)[1] but to the Shakespearian intention. The troubles of the Earnshaws started when the father brought home the boy Heathcliff (of which he gives an unconvincing explanation and for whom he shows an unaccountable weakness) and forced him on the protesting family; Heathcliff 'the cuckoo' by intrigue soon ousts the legitimate son Hindley and, like Edmund, Gloucester's natural son in *Lear,* his malice brings about the ruin of two families (the Earnshaws and the Lintons, his rival getting the name Edgar by attraction from *Lear*). Clearly, Heathcliff was originally the illegitimate son and Catherine's half-brother, which would explain why though so attached to him by early associations and natural sympathies, Catherine never really thinks of him as a possible lover either before or after marriage;[2] it also explains why all the children slept in one bed at the Heights till adolescence, we gather (we learn later from

Catherine (Chapter XII) that being removed at puberty from this bed became a turning-point in her inner life, and this is only one of the remarkable insights which *Wuthering Heights* adds to the Romantic poets' exploration of childhood experience). The favourite Romantic theme of incest therefore must have been the impulsion behind the earliest conception of *Wuthering Heights.* Rejecting this story for a more mature intention, Emily Brontë was left with hopeless inconsistencies on her hands, for while Catherine's feelings about Heathcliff are never sexual (though she feels the bond of sympathy with a brother to be more important to her than her feelings for her young husband), Heathcliff's feelings for her are always those of a lover. As Heathcliff has been written out as a half-brother, Catherine's innocent refusal to see that there is anything in her relation to him incompatible with her position as a wife, becomes preposterous and the impropriety which she refuses to recognize is translated into social terms—Edgar thinks the kitchen the suitable place for Heathcliff's reception by Mrs Linton while she insists on the parlour. Another trace of the immature draft of the novel is the fairy-tale opening of the Earnshaw story, where the father, like the merchant in *Beauty and the Beast,* goes off to the city promising to bring his children back the presents each has commanded: but the fiddle was smashed and the whip lost so the only present he brings for them is the Beast himself, really a 'prince in disguise' (as Nelly tells the boy he should consider himself rightly); Catherine's tragedy then was that she forgot her prince and he was forced to remain the monster, destroying her; invoking this pattern brought in much more from the fairy-tale world of magic, folklore and ballads, the oral tradition of the folk, that the Brontë children learnt principally from their nurses and their servant Tabby.[3] This element surges up in Chapter XII, the important scene of Catherine's illness, where the dark superstitions about premonitions of death, about ghosts and primitive beliefs about the soul, come into play so significantly;[4] and again in the excessive attention given to Heathcliff's goblin-characteristics and especially to the prolonged account of his uncanny obsession and death. That this last should have an air of being infected by Hoffmann too is not surprising in a contemporary of Poe's; Emily is likely to have read Hoffmann when studying German at the Brussels boarding-school and certainly read the ghastly supernatural stories by James Hogg and others in the magazines at home. It is a proof of her immaturity at the time of the original conception of *Wuthering Heights* that she should express real psychological insights in such inappropriate forms.

In the novel as we read it Heathcliff's part either as Edmund in *Lear* or as the Prince doomed to Beast's form, is now suspended in boyhood while another influence, very much of the period, is developed, the Romantic image of childhood,[5] with a corresponding change of tone. Heathcliff and Catherine are idyllically and innocently happy together (and see also the end of Chapter V) roaming the countryside as hardy, primitive Wordsworthian children, 'half savage and hardy and free'. Catherine recalls it longingly when she feels she is dying trapped in Thrushcross Grange. (This boy Heathcliff is of course not assimilable with the vicious, scheming and morally heartless—'simply insensible'—boy of Chapter IV who plays Edmund to old Earnshaw's Gloucester.) Catherine's dramatic introduction to the genteel world of Thrushcross Grange—narrated with contempt by Heathcliff who is rejected by it as a ploughboy unfit to associate with Catherine—is the turning-point in her life in *this* form of the novel; her return, got up as a young lady in absurdly unsuitable clothes for a farmhouse life, and 'displaying fingers wonderfully whitened with doing nothing and staying indoors'⁶ etc. visibly separates her from the 'natural' life, as her inward succumbing to the temptations of social superiority and riches parts her from Heathcliff. Heathcliff's animus against his social degradation by his new master Hindley is barbed by his being made to suffer (like Pip at the hands of Estella in *Great Expectations*)⁷ taunts and insults—mainly from Edgar Linton—based on class and externals alone. They are suffered again (thus making Emily Brontë's points inescapable) in the second half of the novel by Hindley's son Hareton at the hands of Catherine's and Edgar's daughter Cathy as well as from his other cousin Linton Heathcliff, Isabella's son. And this makes us sympathetic to Heathcliff as later to Hareton; we identify here with Nelly who with her wholesome classlessness and her spontaneous maternal impulses supports Heathcliff morally while he is ill-used (and even tries to persuade Catherine not to let Edgar supplant him in her life)—she retains this generous sympathy for him until she transfers it to her foster-child Hareton when in turn he becomes a victim (of Heathcliff's schemes). Her sympathy for Heathcliff's hard luck, even when she sees that his return is a threat to the Lintons' happiness, is at odds with her loyalty to her new master Edgar, and leads her to consent to some ill-advised interviews between Catherine and the desperate Heathcliff—though she also feels that to consent to help him there is the lesser of two evils (as it probably was), and she has no doubts about her duty to protect Isabella from becoming Heathcliff's victim.

Nelly Dean is most carefully, consistently and convincingly created for us as the normal woman, whose truly feminine nature satisfies itself in nurturing all the children in the book in turn.⁸ To give this salience we have the beginning of Chapter VIII when the farm-girl runs out to the hayfield where Nelly is busy to announce the birth of 'a grand bairn' and to give her artless (normal feminine) congratulations to Nelly for being chosen to nurse it since it will soon be motherless: 'I wish I were you, because it will be all yours when there is no

missus'. Nelly's greater sensibility in realizing that from the bairn's point of view this is not altogether a matter for rejoicing is shown in the next chapter when she says 'I went into the kitchen, and sat down to lull my little lamb to sleep . . . I was rocking Hareton on my knee, and humming a song that began

> *It was far in the night, and the bairnies grat,*
> *The mither beneath the mools heard that . . .'*

The ballad is evidently one expressing the widespread belief, in folk-song and folk tale, that a prematurely dead mother cannot rest in the grave but returns to suckle the babe or help her child in the hour of need,⁹ an indication of what is going on in Nelly's compassionate mind. But the whole episode of Hareton's birth and childhood exposes Catherine's insensibility, that her self-centred nature is essentially loveless. (Her only reference to her own pregnancy later is the hope that a son's birth will 'erase Isabella's title' to be Edgar's heir.) Yet Nelly's limitations are made clear and the novelist's distinct position of true insight, where necessary. Like Dolly in *Anna Karénina* who is also the normal maternal woman, Nelly is inevitably too *terre-à-terre* (Vronsky's complaint about Dolly), therefore unable to sympathize with difficulties that seem to her the result only of will, and a perverse will at that ('"I should not have spoken so, if I had known her true condition, but I could not get rid of the notion that she acted a part of her disorder"'). These limitations and not ill-will are of course the reason why Nelly makes some mistakes in trying to act for the best in situations where no easy or right solution offered itself. But in doing Catherine full justice ('"she was not artful, never played the coquette"') and giving her sound advice in her 'perplexities and untold troubles', Nelly convinces us of her right to take a thoroughly disenchanted view of Catherine's disposition. In fact, both Heathcliff and Edgar know the truth about Catherine and Hindley is under no illusions—'"You lie, Cathy, no doubt"' he remarks (correctly) of her explanation of Edgar Linton's visit in his absence. One of the most successful indications of the passage of time is Nelly Dean's change, from the quick-moving and quick-witted girl who for little Hareton's sake copes with the drunken murderous Hindley, to the stout, breathless, middle-aged woman who, though still spirited, cannot save Cathy from a forced marriage.

To hark back to Heathcliff: it follows from this 'social' development of the theme that Heathcliff should go out into the world to make his fortune and come back to avenge himself, 'a cruel hard landlord', 'near, close-handed' and given over to 'avarice, meanness and greed', plotting to secure the property of both Earnshaws and Lintons and also to claim equality with them socially—we are now in the Victorian world of *Great Expectations* where money, as Magwitch the convict learnt, makes a gentleman. Emily Brontë took no trouble to explain the hiatus in Heathcliff's life—irrelevant to her purposes—and in fact it is enough for us to gather that he comes back a professional gambler at cards; a real flaw however is wholly inadequate illustration of the shared life and interests of himself and Catherine that makes it plausible that on his return she should be so absorbed in conversing with him as to cut out immediately and altogether her young husband. After all, we reflect, they couldn't always have been talking about their childhood escapades—that is to say, we recognize a failure in creative interest here in the novelist; nor do we ever hear what they talk about till Catherine attacks him over Isabella and they quarrel, when it becomes clear even to Catherine that he can be only the monster he has been made by his history. This aspect of him is kept before us from now till the end and accounts for his brutalities and violent outbreaks. For various reasons, therefore, after envisaging several alternative conceptions of Heathcliff, Emily Brontë ended by keeping and making use of them all, so that like Dostoievski's Stavrogin he is an enigmatic figure only by reason of his creator's indecision, like Stavrogin in being an unsatisfactory composite with empty places in his history and no continuity of character. [And like Iago and Stavrogin, Heathcliff has been made the object of much misdirected critical industry on the assumption that he is not merely a convenience.] There is nothing enigmatic about either Catherine, we note, and this points to the novelist's distribution of her interest.

There are various signs that the novelist intended to stress the aspect of her theme represented by the corruption of the child's native goodness by Society and to make this part of the explanation of Catherine's failure in life. She evidently had in mind the difficulties and dangers inevitable in civilizing children to enter the artificial world of class, organized religion, social intercourse and authoritarian family life. This is the point of Catherine's childhood journal that Lockwood reads, which gives a caricature of the torments suffered by children in the enforcement of the Puritan Sabbath, and another caricature is the account given by the boy Heathcliff of the parlour life of the broken-in Linton children as seen from the other side of the window by a Noble Savage whose natural good instincts have not been destroyed like theirs. More impressive is the beautifully rendered exemplary relation between the child Catherine and the adults as reported by Nelly in Chapter V. Her father's attempts to improve her, or tame her to an approved pattern,[10] resulted only in 'a naughty delight to provoke him: she was never so happy as when we were all scolding her at once, and she defying us with her bold, saucy look, and her ready words; turning Joseph's religious curses into ridicule, baiting me, and doing just what her father hated most'—'Mr. Earnshaw did not understand jokes from his children', Nelly notes, 'he had always been strict and grave with them'.

After behaving as badly as possible all day, she sometimes came fondling to make it up at night. 'Nay, Cathy' the old man would say, 'I cannot love thee; go, say thy prayers, child, and ask God's pardon. I doubt thy mother and I must rue that we ever reared thee!' That made her cry, at first; and then, being repulsed continually hardened her, and she laughed if I told her to say she was sorry for her faults, and beg to be forgiven. . . . It pleased the master rarely to see her gentle—saying 'Why canst thou not always be a good lass, Cathy?' And she turned up her face to his, and laughed, and answered, 'Why cannot you always be a good man, father?'

We note that the child is allowed the last word—and a very telling rejoinder it is. Emily Brontë, the girl in the family most sympathetic to the black-sheep brother, was the most recalcitrant to the domestic training of her rigid aunt, to schooling, and to orthodox religion; she had plainly thought about the psychological effects of conventional disciplines and taken this opportunity to report adversely in the strongest terms a novelist can use—by showing their part in destroying the possibilities of a happy childhood and maturity.

But this originally naïve and commonplace subject—the Romantics' image of childhood in conflict with society—becomes something that in this novel is neither superficial nor theoretic because the interests of the responsible novelist gave it, as we have seen above, a new insight, and also a specific and informed sociological content. The theme is here very firmly rooted in time and place and richly documented: we cannot forget that Gimmerton and the neighbourhood are so bleak that the oats are always green there three weeks later than anywhere else, and that old Joseph's Puritan preachings accompany his 'overlaying his large Bible with dirty bank-notes, the produce of the day's transactions' at market; and we have a thoroughly realistic account of the life indoors and outdoors at Wuthering Heights as well as at the gentleman's residence at the Grange. In fact, there would be some excuse for taking this, the pervasive and carefully maintained sociological theme which fleshes the skeleton, for the real novel. This novel, which could be extracted by cutting away the rest, was deliberately built, to advance a thesis, on the opposition between Wuthering Heights and Thrushcross Grange, two different cultures of which the latter inevitably supersedes the former. The point about dating this novel as ending in 1801 (instead of its being contemporary with the Brontës' own lives)—and much trouble was taken to keep the dates, time-scheme and externals such as legal data, accurate[11]—is to fix its happenings at a time when the old rough farming culture based on a naturally patriarchal family life, was to be challenged, tamed and routed by social and cultural changes that were to produce the Victorian class consciousness and 'unnatural' ideal of gentility.[12]

Notes

1. *v.* Appendix B [in *Lectures in America*].

2. The speech (Chap. IX) in which Catherine explains to Nelly why she couldn't marry Heathcliff—on social grounds—belongs to the sociological *Wuthering Heights*. But even then she intends, she declares, to keep up her old (sisterly) relations with him, to help him get on in the world—'to *rise*' as she significantly puts it in purely social terms.

3. Tabby had, Mrs Gaskell reports, 'known the "bottom" or valley in those primitive days when the faeries frequented the margin of the "beck" on moonlight nights, and had known folk who had seen them. But that was when there were no mills in the valleys, and when all the woolspinning was done by hand in the farm-houses round. "It wur the factories as had driven 'em away", she said.'

4. *v.* Appendix C [in *Lectures in America*].

5. I am referring to the invaluable book, *The Image of Childhood*, [(1967)], by P. Coveney, though this does not in fact deal with *Wuthering Heights*.

6. This very evident judgment of Nelly's on the gentility with which Catherine has been infected by her stay at Thrushcross Grange (lavishly annotated in the whole scene of her return home in Chap. VII) is clearly endorsed by the author, since it is based on values that are fundamental to the novel and in consonance with Emily's Wordsworthian sympathies. It is supplemented by another similar but even more radical judgment, put into old Joseph's mouth, the indispensable Joseph who survives the whole action to go on farming the Heights and who is made the vehicle of several central judgments, as well as of many disagreeable Calvinistic attitudes. Resenting the boy Linton Heathcliff's contempt for the staple food, porridge, made, like the oat-cake, from the home-grown oats, Joseph remembers the boy's fine-lady mother: 'His mother were just soa—we wer a'most too mucky tuh sow t'corn fur makking her breead.' There are many related judgments in the novel. We may note here the near-caricature of Lockwood in the first three chapters as the town visitor continually exposing his ignorance of country life and farming.

7. A regular Victorian theme, springing from the consciousness and resentment by creative artists of a new class snobbery and expressed in such widely different novels as *Alton Locke, North and South, Felix Holt, Dombey and Son, Great Expectations,* as well as *Wuthering Heights* which is earlier than all these.

8. David Copperfield's Peggotty is the same type, registered through the nursling's eyes (she is supplemented, as he grows out of her, by his great-aunt Betsy Trotwood) and Dickens's testimony to such truths is important. It will be noticed that Peggotty has to mother not only David but also his permanently immature mother. Our nineteenth-century fiction and memoirs are full of such nurses (sometimes they are spinster aunts), bearing witness to the living reality (*v.,* e.g., Lord Shaftesbury's nurse, the Strachey nurse, and the Darwin nurse in Gwen Raverat's autobiography *Period Piece*). Nelly Dean seems to have incurred a good deal of unjustified ill-will, and perverse misrepresentation in consequence, from Catherine's defenders. That Peggotty and Miss Trotwood haven't (so far—or so far as I know) must be due less to Dickens's fairly unambiguous presentation of David's Dora and (but to a less degree) of David's mother, than to the fact that Doras are not now in esteem.

9. Hence Nelly's indignant rebuke to Hareton's father in Chap. IX takes the form of telling him: '"Oh! I wonder his mother does not rise from her grave to see how you use him".'

10. Significantly, because old Joseph 'was relentless in worrying him about ruling his children rigidly', as religion required.

11. *v.* C. P. Sanger's *The Structure of 'Wuthering Heights'* ([1926;] a Hogarth Press pamphlet).

12. Other pre-Victorian novelists noted and resented the effects on children too. In the original preface to her children's classic *Holiday House* (1839), Catherine Sinclair wrote: 'In these pages the author has endeavoured to paint that species of noisy, frolicsome, mischievous children, now almost extinct, wishing to preserve a sort of fabulous remembrance of days long past, when young people were like wild horses on the prairies, rather than like well-broken hacks on the road.'

U. C. Knoepflmacher (essay date 1971)

SOURCE: Knoepflmacher, U. C. "*Wuthering Heights*: A Tragicomic Romance." In *Laughter and Despair: Readings in Ten Novels of the Victorian Era*, pp. 84-108. Berkeley: University of California Press, 1971.

[*In the following essay, Knoepflmacher discusses the tension between conflicting elements of tragedy and comedy in* Wuthering Heights. *Knoepflmacher asserts that the unpredictable, often irrational behavior of the novel's characters make it a radical work compared to other mid-nineteenth-century British novels.*]

The modern reader who has come to regard *Wuthering Heights* as one of the finest Victorian novels cannot but wonder why the public which responded to Dickens,

Thackeray, and George Eliot failed to recognize the excellence of Emily Brontë's work. *Wuthering Heights* was published in 1847, the same year which marked the publication of Thackeray's successful *Vanity Fair* and Trollope's unsuccessful *The Macdermots of Ballycloran,* as well as of Charlotte Brontë's *Jane Eyre* and Anne Brontë's *Agnes Grey.* Like Trollope's, Emily Brontë's first novel was published by Thomas Newby; despite Newby's attempt to capitalize on the success of *Jane Eyre* (by pretending that "Currer Bell," its author, and "Ellis Bell," the pseudonymous author of *Wuthering Heights,* were one and the same), Emily Brontë's masterpiece was as ill received as Trollope's clumsy *Macdermots.* Yet while Trollope tried again and again until he succeeded later with *The Warden,* Emily Brontë was granted no second chance to conquer the Victorian reading public. She died of tuberculosis on December 19, 1848.

The notion that *Wuthering Heights* was too much removed from the ordinary "reality" that Victorian readers could find in the novels of Trollope and Thackeray is belied by the contemporary success of Charlotte's own work, *Jane Eyre,* which—with its supernatural omens and eerie voices, the madwoman in the attic, the split chestnut tree, the burning manor, and the maimed Rochester—depends far more unequivocally on mystery and melodrama than does *Wuthering Heights.* In her preface to a posthumous edition of *Wuthering Heights* (1850) in which she capitalized on her own prestige to draw attention to Emily's work, Charlotte deplored her sister's unfamiliarity with "what is called 'the world'" and guardedly defended the novel as a "rude and strange production."[1] According to Charlotte, Emily was possessed by a daemon she could not master, working "passively under dictates you neither delivered nor could question."[2] Her attempts to excuse the supposed excesses of Emily's imagination miss the mark as much as her efforts to moralize *Wuthering Heights.*[3] Charlotte had once shared the childhood dreamworld of Emily, yet either she never quite penetrated the qualities of her sister's imagination, or, if she did, she shrank from them in her eagerness to make Emily's novel palatable to the Victorian reader.

Charlotte's reprinting of her sister's novel did not help to persuade Victorian readers of its merits. *Wuthering Heights* continued to be neglected. In 1860, one of Emily's cousins wrote: "I wish my cousin had never written *Wuthering Heights,* although it is considered clever by some." Why did the novel fail to attract a contemporary audience? The reasons for its failure in the nineteenth century are probably the reasons for its success in the twentieth century.[4] The Victorians did not reject Emily's work because, as Charlotte assumed, they found it to be too fantastic and subjective a work. (Charlotte also made the mistake of declaring Thackeray to be a Jane-Eyre-like reformer, "the first social re-

generator of the day.") They rejected it because under the guise of the comic amusement of the novel, which they had come to expect, they found a disturbing, unexplained vision of anarchy and decay.

Both *Jane Eyre* and *Wuthering Heights* can be traced back to the mythical domain of "Angria" invented by the Brontë children after their readings in Shakespeare and Byron. When Angria was dissolved in 1831 with Charlotte's departure for school, Emily and Anne proceeded to form a second fantasy world, the island of Gondal.[5] The poems that Emily wrote about the inhabitants of this imaginary realm were discovered by the surprised Charlotte, who found them to be "condensed, vigorous and genuine" (the same adjectives apply to *Wuthering Heights*).[6] The Gondal cycle, recently reconstructed by Mrs. Fannie Ratchford,[7] demonstrates that Emily's imagination, far from being lyrical and subjective, was essentially dramatic, relying on complementary points of view.

In writing *Wuthering Heights* Emily relied on this same dramatic talent to objectify her vision. Unlike the earnest Charlotte, who projected her fantasies and aspirations through the single-minded figure of Jane Eyre, Emily relied on irony and self-division to complicate her own responses to reality. The indignant feminist who acts as Charlotte's narrator is treated without the protective irony enforced by Lockwood and Nelly Dean, the two narrators of Emily's novel. In *Wuthering Heights,* as in *Barchester Towers* and in *Vanity Fair,* the mode is dramatic; there is no direct spokesman for the implied author. Whereas the self-righteous Jane Eyre imposes, through the forcefulness of her personality, her own order on the world around her, and her own view on us, the pair of comic observers who act as our guides in *Wuthering Heights* are even more fallible than Thackeray's equivocal Showman or Trollope's evasive narrator. The civilized Lockwood and the commonsensible Mrs. Dean qualify, and are qualified by, the turbulent, irrational world of Cathy and Heathcliff.

Emily Brontë knew that her bent, like Charlotte's, was romance; yet she was also astute enough to recognize that the dominant mode of the English novel was comic. Byron, who had written "Childe Harold" and *Manfred,* had also composed the comic *Don Juan*; Shakespeare, whose *King Lear* Lockwood remembers so incongruously when he is beset by Heathcliff's dogs, had blended humor and melodrama, laughter and terror. Emily's dramatic powers allowed her to control the fantasy world she had once shared with her brother and sisters. Her inventiveness allowed her to devise a framework in which the outer veneer of social comedy encases the truths of fantasy and myth.

In *Vanity Fair,* as we have seen, Thackeray was able to express his pessimistic outlook within the traditional framework of the comic novel by throwing out the dictionary definitions of good and evil and thereby forcing the reader to reassess reality itself. Though sharing this aim, Emily Brontë is far more radical in her departures. Thackeray's Showman refuses to act as our moral guide; yet his equivocations help to establish definable attitudes in the reader. The guide provided to the reader in the opening pages of **Wuthering Heights** proves to be totally unreliable. We cross the threshold of Heathcliff's mansion together with Lockwood only to find that the assumptions we have shared with this city man become totally untenable. Lockwood is a refugee from civilized society. His witty tone and extreme self-consciousness make him a distinct cousin of the jesting misanthropist who acts as Thackeray's narrator. Yet this Thackerayan figure, whose manners are urbane and whose outlook is comic, cannot cope with the asocial world he finds beyond the "threshold" of Wuthering Heights. His education becomes the reader's own, although, eventually, our understanding will surpass his.

Once inside the mansion Lockwood commits one blunder after another. Each overture, each phrase that he utters, results in a new misconception. In desperation, Lockwood cries out to the girl he has twice misidentified: "I want you to *tell* me my way, not to *show* it" (ch. 2). He demands to be led back to the sanity of Thrushcross Grange. After Lockwood is imprisoned by the snowstorm, the guide he demands will appear to him in a nightmare. Although the disturbing dream which he defends himself against was intended for Heathcliff—whose sensibilities are totally unlike his own, despite Lockwood's earlier, jocular identification of his host—the dream, though not telling Lockwood the way out of the labyrinth he has entered, begins to show us a new way of creating order. Lockwood, however, bound by his ordinary perceptions, fails to see that the creature outside the window is, potentially, a guide whose call for pity can rescue him from the "sin no Christian need pardon." Next day he relies on Heathcliff to conduct him back to the Grange. The snow-covered landscape has become treacherous: a "billowy, white ocean" has erased all landmarks, covering "rises and depressions in the ground: many pits, at least, were filled to a level" (ch. 3). Heathcliff follows stones erected to "serve as guides in the dark"; he warns the stumbling Lockwood to "steer to the right or left, when I imagined I was following, correctly, the winding of the road." Just as the external topography has altered from what "yesterday's walk left pictured" in Lockwood's mind, so has his neatly ordered inner world been disrupted by contradictions he has yet to sort out. Heathcliff stops at the gate of the Grange. Within its confines the exhausted Lockwood yields to a new "guide," Nelly Dean. Yet even her more sedate attempts to impose order and sanity on the reality he has experienced prove to be insufficient.

The reader is lured with Lockwood into the irrational world of **Wuthering Heights.** Like Lockwood, we have had barely time to take note of the lavish engravings on the front door, the date "1500," and the name "Hareton Earnshaw" before we are faced with incongruities we must decipher. The Heights lacks any "introductory lobby or passage," just as Emily Brontë's novel lacks the introductory passages furnished by a Trollope or Thackeray. Lockwood's initial experience is our own. As we stand on the threshold with him we too ponder between "speedy entrance" or "complete departure." On crossing the threshold we are mystified. Unsure of the causes for our mystification, we, like Lockwood, make the mistake of being overconfident. Soon, however, we are on the defensive. Our instinctive reaction is to flee, to be told the way out. Emily Brontë's Victorian readers took this way out. Confused by the discrepancy between Lockwood's polite diction and the atmosphere into which he is thrust, they must have been as confused as he is to find that a lady's furry "favourites" turn out to be a heap of dead rabbits. Yet the modern reader, more attuned to incongruity, gradually accepts the challenge. Whereas Lockwood represses the meaning of the two dreams he has experienced, we are willing to analyze their content. While Lockwood is content to lie on his back for most of the novel, willing to be entertained by Nelly's account, we continue to wander through a maze of conflicting attitudes, shifts in point of view, and abrupt changes in tone.

For a long while the reader is thwarted. Expectations misfire. Doors that seem open are shut; gates that seem closed turn out to provide us with an unexpected means of passage. Hovering between comic realism and the exaggerations of melodrama, this novel constantly avoids either extreme. In Thackeray's scheme, too, satire and sentiment qualify each other. But in **Wuthering Heights** these two modes merge and interpenetrate. Unlike *Vanity Fair,* Emily Brontë's novel moves toward a resolution. The social-comical realism of Lockwood and Nelly clashes with the asocial tragic myth enacted by Cathy and Heathcliff, but a new comic mode—represented by the idyll of the second Cathy and Hareton—bridges the chasm and ultimately provides the passage that seemed so impossible to find. In the novel's closing scene, Lockwood flees through the back door of the Heights. The reader, however, is rewarded for his endurance. He welcomes the restoration of order, and he wonders, with the departing Lockwood, how anarchy could ever have disrupted the benign face of "that quiet earth" (ch. 34).

1

Like *Vanity Fair,* **Wuthering Heights** traces the fortunes of three generations. Whereas time moves in a straightforward progression in Thackeray's novel, Emily Brontë's use of two narrators permits her to devise a more subtle time scheme. The novel begins in the winter of 1801; but after chapter three, when Lockwood yields to Nelly's narrative, the plot moves simultaneously in two directions. Nelly's long flashback accounts for the "some quarter of a century" (ch. 3) that separates Lockwood's present from the events recorded in the notebook he has read; at the same time, as the prostrate Lockwood listens to the housekeeper's story, the weeks keep gliding by. By the end of chapter thirty, after Nelly has finished her tale, Lockwood decides to spend the "next six months in London." He returns in September of 1802, and, in a new flashback, Nelly now fills him in on the events that have occurred in his absence. The novel finishes on a forward thrust. Heathcliff's agony has ended, and the union of a new set of lovers promises a future far more wholesome than the one projected in *Vanity Fair.*

Thus it is that although the novel carries the reader through almost three decades it gives us the impression that only a year has elapsed. In *Vanity Fair* (where the nineteen monthly parts contributed to the sense of wasted decades which Thackeray wants to produce) the reader is asked to share the weariness felt by Dobbin and the Showman. The reader of **Wuthering Heights,** however, can shake off Lockwood as soon as he recognizes that the destructive past fits into a cycle of regeneration. Refreshed by the abrupt turn of events which have taken place during Lockwood's absence and without Nelly's usual interference, we thus are finally freed from our dependence on the two narrators who have until then controlled our responses.

For the first thirty chapters, however, we depend on Lockwood's and Nelly's points of view. Both characters fail us precisely at those points where they could have taken an active part in the story. Although their own actions are significant, both are essentially passive figures. Lockwood comes to the country because he has resisted involvement. Having toyed with the affections of a "most fascinating creature, a real goddess," he fled her company as soon as this imaginary attachment threatened to be confounded by actuality. His evasion has gained him "the reputation of deliberate heartlessness" (ch. 1). He makes two trips to Wuthering Heights in the opening chapters and but two more in the final portions of the book. The rest of the time, between these visits, he is either laid up in bed or away in London. Only his "fancy" (the term he uses in contradistinction to Heathcliff's term, "imagination") remains active. After his unsettling experience at the Heights, Lockwood is diverted by Nelly's story of the Earnshaw and Linton families. Although his tone is patronizing ("Excepting a few provincialisms of slight consequence, you have no marks of the manners which I am habituated to consider as peculiar to your class" [ch. 7]), Lockwood actually wants Nelly to simplify experience for him. To him she is an uncomplicated rustic who

lives "more in earnest . . . and less in surface change, and frivolous external things" than the Londoners of his acquaintance (ch. 7). Lockwood the city man needs Nelly the provincial. Her story permits him to order his excited mind; it allows him to fan his fancy in safe and unviolent ways.

Lockwood's reactions remain as stereotyped as before; his involvements continue to be imaginary. After Nelly's account of the two Catherines, he finds it possible to consider the young woman he has met at the Heights in a completely new light. He tells himself to "beware of the fascination that lurks in Catherine Heathcliff's brilliant eyes" (ch. 14). From his earlier pose of "a fixed unbeliever in any love of a year's standing," he lapses into fancying "a love for life here almost possible" (ch. 7). But as his bodily health returns, Lockwood's fancy abates. He goes to the Heights and looks at the real Cathy, and he is relieved to find that actuality does not match his romantic preconceptions: "She's a beauty, it is true, but not an angel." The union of Cathy and Hareton defeats his constructing more mental castles. In the opening part of the book, on finding himself locked out by Joseph, this wooden Lockean angrily protests: "I would not keep my doors barred in the day time" (ch. 2). Yet at the end of the novel, it is Lockwood himself who deliberately bars the door and hastily escapes romance in plain daylight.

Nelly, on the surface, seems a far more active character than Lockwood. She bustles around as a go-between and acts as an officious duenna; she is a witness to all the crucial scenes. Yet, for all her meddling, Nelly remains curiously inactive whenever she might have exerted a crucial influence on events through compassion and feeling. Her first reaction to the alien child brought by Mr. Earnshaw is as defensive as Lockwood's reaction to the child in his dream. She ignores the little intruder, hoping that it might leave the Heights. As the adult Heathcliff says sarcastically to her, later in the novel: "you'll force me to pinch the baby, and make it scream, before it moves your charity" (ch. 27). When the elder Catherine dies, Nelly reports the event casually, without any display of emotion.

The dire effect of Nelly's inaction is best illustrated in the crucial scene in which Catherine confides to her that she will marry Edgar Linton although she loves Heathcliff. The housekeeper knows that Heathcliff has overheard the first part of Catherine's speech, yet instead of recalling Heathcliff or telling Catherine to run after him, she remains silent, thus contributing to the misfortunes that will be visited on two generations of Earnshaws and Lintons. Not only does she refuse to acknowledge that her passivity has contributed to Heathcliff's misunderstanding and escape but she also self-righteously lays "the blame of his disappearance on [Catherine] (where indeed it belonged . . .)" (ch. 9).

After Heathcliff's return she refuses her sympathy to the morbid trio at the Grange: Isabella, in love with love, secludes herself, "always silent"; Edgar, in love with Catherine, locks himself in his study "among books that he never opened"; Catherine, in love with Heathcliff, shuts herself in her chambers and fasts for three full days. Yet Nelly, the talkative meddler, holds off all communication and merely congratulates herself for her own sanity amidst this disorder: "I went about my household duties, convinced that the Grange had but one sensible soul in its walls, and that lodged in my body" (ch. 12).

Although Nelly, like Lockwood, distrusts passion and emotion, she is by no means the villainess that at least one critic has made her out to be.[8] Of all characters, she best loves the second Cathy, "my own sweet little mistress," and is willing to serve the girl's interests. But, significantly enough, Nelly can do nothing to avoid this Cathy's subjection to Heathcliff. Whereas she could easily have prevented the first Catherine's union to Edgar Linton and thereby have helped to avert her mistress' irresolvable conflict of allegiances, Nelly cannot, despite her efforts to the contrary, prevent the second Catherine's unfortunate marriage to Heathcliff's son. Nelly falls sick precisely during the time that her ward steals away for her visits with Linton Heathcliff ("I was laid up, and during three weeks I remained incapacitated . . . a calamity never experienced prior to that period, and never, I am thankful to say, since" [ch. 23]). She is locked in by Heathcliff during Cathy's nuptials and kept a prisoner for five days (ch. 27). When she returns to the Grange, she is incapable of altering the dying Edgar Linton's testament. Her self-induced inaction contributed to the first Catherine's alienation from Heathcliff; her enforced inaction now contributes to the second Catherine's suffering—even though this suffering proves to be a necessary prelude for the younger Cathy's growth to a stage beyond the arrested development of her mother.

Lockwood's own paralysis is, as we have already seen, amply suggested in the opening chapters. Like the gregarious Nelly, he is, for all his antisocial pose, an eminently social creature with little understanding for the isolatoes dwelling at the Heights. Although he professes to be a misanthrope eager to be "removed from the stir or society," he cannot really identify himself with that "capital fellow," Heathcliff: "It is astonishing how sociable I feel myself compared with him" (ch. 1). Lockwood's second visit to the Heights incapacitates him even further. His new impressions confirm his inability to penetrate the drama of its inhabitants. His frame of reference proves to be wholly inadequate. His diction is full of the formulas of polite conversation: "amiable lady," "proper person," "ministering angel." He is as shocked by the incivilities of Joseph, Hareton, Heathcliff, and Cathy as he is rattled by his discovery that by

no stretch of his "fancy" can a heap of dead rabbits be construed to be a lady's pets.

Like Nelly, Lockwood finds that only "by assuming the cheerful" (ch. 2) can he manage to settle his mind. Threatened by the nightmare in Cathy's chamber, he tries on awaking to bring his imagination under control. Heathcliff, on hearing about the dream, strikes his "forehead with rage"; Lockwood, on the other hand, steadfastly refuses to yield to his host's "access of violent emotion" (ch. 3). He looks at his watch, that symbol of regularity, and self-consciously begins to soliloquize on the length of the night: "Not three o'clock yet! I could have taken oath it had been six. Time stagnates here—we must surely have retired to rest at eight!" (ch. 3). Lockwood's obdurate cheerfulness sets off Heathcliff's melodramatic outburst somewhat in the way that Becky Sharp's calculated good humor qualifies and yet is qualified by Amelia's tear-floods. Taken by itself, Heathcliff's action of beating his forehead may seem excessively histrionic; yet the turbulence of his emotions seems preferable to the complacency of Lockwood, who looks at his watch so methodically and refuses to betray the violence which had led him to rub the bloody wrists of the apparition in his nightmare. He merely "fancies" a tear in Heathcliff's eyes. By way of contrast, the unbridled, irrational behavior of his host seems preferable by far.

Lockwood's external calmness, however, is deceptive. He has been shaken by his encounter with visions more unusual than those his rational fancy is able to concoct. When he returns to the Grange he gratefully yields to Nelly Dean's ministrations, almost too feeble to enjoy "the cheerful fire" prepared for him (ch. 3). His ailments are not purely physical: "I was excited, almost to a pitch of foolishness, through my nerves and brain" (ch. 4). He relies on Nelly to purge this unwanted "foolishness"; her logic must counter the illogic he has experienced. The housekeeper who is so proud of her "sensible soul" is glad to oblige. Her reaction to dreams is, after all, not unlike Lockwood's own (to Catherine's query about "queer dreams," she rejoins, "Come, come, be merry, and like yourself!" [ch. 9]); when, "half dreaming," she yields to fantasies of her own, she welcomes the dawn that restores her to "common sense" (ch. 34). Bodily health and the mental sanity that come with such health are what she prizes most. Nelly delights in nursing the strong; she rejects the weak and abnormal. Heathcliff appeals to her only after the "dangerously sick" boy responds to her care (ch. 4); she likes the second Catherine because—like Hareton whom she has bottle-fed—this child is healthy, a far better investment for her sympathies than the shrieking Catherine or the stupid Frances, Hareton's tubercular mother, who is insensible of her approaching death. Like Dr. Kenneth the physician, Nelly can be cruelly blunt. She dismisses Linton Heathcliff as a "bit of a sickly slip" (ch. 23) and tries to intimidate the morose youngster: "do you imagine that beautiful young lady, that *healthy,* hearty girl, will tie herself to a little *perishing* monkey like you?" (ch. 27; italics added).

Although the woman who reserves her heart for those who are healthy, sensible, and sane shares Lockwood's shortcomings, her point of view cannot be dismissed as easily as that of her "heartless" listener. Lockwood flees; Nelly remains firmly anchored in the world of Cathy and Hareton. Her view of life ultimately blends with that of her favorites. She is most reliable, because most intimately involved, when she tells the younger Cathy's story; she is a far less able interpreter of the romance of Catherine and Heathcliff. Still, even if her indifference to the first set of lovers reveals her limitations, Nelly Dean also becomes the vehicle for Emily Brontë's own definite reservations about the romantic exaggerations of Heathcliff and Catherine. Her comic stance, unlike Lockwood's, helps to preserve the novel's balance. When the enraged Hindley tries to force his carving knife down Nelly's throat, she tells him that she would much prefer to be shot, "if you please," since she dislikes the taste of his blade (ch. 9). Her answer has the effect of reducing bombast into slapstick. We are disarmed by Nelly's cheerfulness because, by converting this "blasphemer" against God and the universe into a harmless fool, she has helped us to disarm Hindley's nihilism. The reader who listens with Lockwood to Nelly's story gradually is led to acknowledge that her instinct of self-preservation saves us from the vortex of self-destruction that engulfs her romantic counterparts.

Wordsworth, a Romantic, claimed that in his sonnets, Shakespeare had "unlocked his heart"; Browning, a Victorian, ridiculed that claim. In *Wuthering Heights,* a work that is both Romantic and Victorian, Nelly Dean and Lockwood provide the ironic frame which encases the novel's heart. This outer frame is not detachable. If the passion of Heathcliff and Catherine lies at the emotional core of the novel, Nelly's comic vision is vindicated by her two nurslings, Cathy and Hareton. We are allowed to unlock the novel's inner core only through Nelly's guarded account. Paradoxically enough, it is this balanced housekeeper who provides us with the keys to a story about the imbalances of the heart.

2

Wuthering Heights ultimately relies on the comic convention of a happy ending through the harmony of marriage. Just as the marriage of Mr. Arabin and Eleanor Bold in *Barchester Towers* erases the conflicts that agitated poor Mr. Harding, so does the union of Hareton and the second Cathy help to restore the happiness denied to the previous inhabitants of Wuthering Heights and Thrushcross Grange. But the losses incurred in this novel are far more severe than those that disrupt Trollope's world of provincial clergymen. At the center of *Wuthering Heights* lies a tragic vision of waste and disjunction which even goes beyond the grim picture of irreconcilables that Thackeray had presented in *Vanity Fair.* This tragedy relies on severance—the severance between old Earnshaw and his children, between the worlds of the Heights and the Grange, and, most cruelly, between Catherine and the two men in her life: Heathcliff and Edgar Linton.

Catherine Earnshaw tries to explain to Nelly the nature of her oneness with Heathcliff by resorting to an account of one of her "queer dreams." Nelly, "superstitious about dreams," quickly rejects this irrational means of explanation. In desperation, Catherine is thus forced to express herself in metaphoric terms:

> I was only going to say that heaven did not seem to be my home; and I broke my heart with weeping to come back to earth; and the angels were so angry that they flung me out, into the middle of the heath on the top of Wuthering Heights; where I woke sobbing for joy. That will do to explain my secret, as well as the other. I've no more business to marry Edgar Linton than I have to be in heaven; and if the wicked man in there had not brought Heathcliff so low, I shouldn't have thought of it. It would degrade me to marry Heathcliff now; so he shall never know how I love him; and that, not because he's handsome, Nelly, but because he's more myself than I am.
>
> (ch. 9)

Catherine assumes that her marriage to Edgar Linton will not destroy her essential oneness with Heathcliff: "Nelly, I *am* Heathcliff—he's always, always in my mind—not as a pleasure, any more than I am always a pleasure to myself—but as my own being—so, don't talk of our separation again." Catherine's very diction is expressive of her own internal division, her split between the two antithetical realities that William Blake had labeled "innocence" and "experience." The girl who tries to rely on irrational dreams to explain her feelings, whose semiconscious being responds to the asocial energies represented by Heathcliff, nonetheless finds her conscious, social self yielding to the ordered existence represented by Edgar Linton, Nelly's favorite. She hovers between stasis and change, between the intuitive affinities of a world of essences ("My love for Heathcliff resembles the eternal rocks") and the self-conscious acceptance of a temporal world of growth ("My love for Linton is like the foliage in the woods. Time will change it"). Unable to exist in both of these orders, she falls from innocence into experience and thus precipitates Heathcliff's own self-division and incompleteness. She argues that if he were annihilated, "the Universe would turn to a mighty stranger" for her. Her words apply to Heathcliff's own estrangement after her death: until his own demise, Heathcliff will live in that estranged universe. He searches for Cathy in the dreamworld she failed to maintain. Only in that realm, re-created by Heathcliff's superior imagination, can the two lovers eventually be reunited and attain the oneness of mythical beings, freed from time and change. Unlike the second generation of lovers, they cannot find fulfillment in a temporal world of change and disruption.

This disruption begins with Heathcliff's introduction to the Heights. The founding enters a world no longer bound by the reasonable social and ethical values still operating in Trollope's Barsetshire. The Christian ethic, so often invoked by Nelly to counter Catherine's and Heathcliff's presumed heresies, has lost its hold; by the end of the novel, Nelly informs us laconically that Gimmerton Kirk no longer has a "minister now." Instead of Trollope's benevolent bishop, the figure who opens Nelly's narrative is that of the "severe" and forbidding Old-Testament "master," Mr. Earnshaw. The door latch is raised, the master appears, and his expectant family confront the alien creature hidden in his greatcoat.

A century earlier, old Earnshaw would have been represented by Fielding's Squire Allworthy as an emblem of natural benevolence. In Emily Brontë's darkened world, however, Earnshaw's kindness is suspect: "I was never so beaten with anything in my life; but you must e'en take it as a gift of God, though it's dark almost as if it came from the devil" (ch. 4). The provider who had earlier promised gifts to the children eating porridge at his table and promised a "pocketful of apples and pears" to Nelly herself soon starves the affection of his dependents. Oblivious of the crushed fiddle expected by Hindley, impervious to having lost the whip Cathy had demanded, he becomes strangely obsessed by the sullen boy who shows no signs of gratitude. His irrational attraction to Heathcliff puzzles Nelly as much as Heathcliff's attraction for Catherine. Earnshaw indulges his adopted son, but he is unduly harsh to the daughter who later claims that she is Heathcliff. Through Nelly's eyes, we witness the incongruity of the master's behavior. Yielding to the influences of the curate and of the canting Joseph, the old man frowns on Cathy's laughter, is jealous of her vigor, and wishes that she be tamed by sickness: "I cannot love thee; thou'rt worse than thy brother" (ch. 5). When he reproaches her for not always being a good lass, Cathy pertly asks, "Why cannot you always be a good man, father?" Conventional goodness—still desired by Heathcliff when he asks Nelly to make him "decent" so that he can be "good"—can no longer order existence at the Heights.

After old Earnshaw's death, the energies he had stifled burst out. Hindley and Catherine cannot take their place in the adult institutional world now represented by the Grange. Both revert to the freedom and unrestraint of childhood. Hindley chooses the vapid Frances, a figure of perennial mirth, as a partner in his attempts to re-

gress into a world of childhood games, but this world proves too frail to resist the realities of death and change. Incapable of assuming the role of a mother, Frances dies on giving birth to a son; bereft of a playmate, Hindley eschews the responsibilities of master and father. Losing the "benefit of his early education," he sinks into the chaos of total irrationality: Hareton, his son, runs a chance of either "being squeezed and kissed to death" or of "being flung into the fire, or dashed against the wall" (ch. 9).

Unlike her older brother, Catherine retains the companionship and affection of her own mate, Heathcliff. Whereas Hindley's attachment to Frances is an infantile regression, Cathy and Heathcliff are children who live a life of healthy unconstraint; "rude as savages," they are stronger by far than the new master of the Heights. Yet Cathy's division is not totally unlike her brother's. Hindley shakes off his education and reverts to savagery; Catherine, though secure in the "absolute heathenism" she shares with Heathcliff, becomes attracted to the civilizing influences of the Grange. Whereas Hindley capriciously hovers between alternate moods, his sister's conflicting allegiances make her far more deeply and irreconcilably divided. Hindley's childhood games merely signified an evasion of his adult role; Cathy, on the other hand, refuses to be arrested in her development. In her speech to Nelly she implies that she feels she can somehow retain her identity with all that which is represented by Heathcliff while moving into the different order of reality to which she now aspires. Her wishes prove to be impossible. By expecting that she can possess both Edgar Linton and Heathcliff she becomes untrue to each man and to the antithetical modes of existence each stands for.

Heathcliff's return only confirms the discord Catherine has created. He, too, has tried to submerge his earlier self by adopting the ways of civilization. But his genteel exterior only disguises the energies he shared with Cathy. These energies are now bent on destruction. He exploits Isabella's affections and deprives Hindley's son of his patrimony. Even at his most satanic and brutal, however, Heathcliff still remains true to that self which is Catherine. Like Hindley, he lashes out against a universe that has become meaningless. His recriminations to the dying Catherine are made, ironically enough, against the background provided by the chiming bells of the Gimmerton church, where Edgar and Nelly have gone for their devotions. Heathcliff bitterly accuses Catherine for having betrayed her own instincts: "You have killed yourself" (ch. 15). Upon her death, he accuses Edgar of being her murderer. Yet it is he who, by returning, has induced the woman who is pregnant with Edgar's child to long for her old freedom. This freedom is, for her, now only possible through the release of death.

When Nelly informs Heathcliff that Catherine has died on giving birth to the second Cathy, he rejects the housekeeper's pious hope that she may wake "in another world." He asks that she may wake "in torment" and demands that her ghost haunt him "as long as I am living" (ch. 16). His fullest expression of his love thus comes in a curse. In life, their union was denied by all kinds of barriers and obstacles. Catherine's death creates a new barrier, but Heathcliff denies the physical barrier of the grave as well as the spiritual barrier implied in Nelly's allusion to "another world." Catherine's notion of retaining Heathcliff while married to Edgar Linton proved to be an impossible longing; Heathcliff's desire to have her ghost with him at all times seems even more fantastic. Throughout the novel, however, he incessantly seeks out her ghost: he pushes Lockwood aside after he finds that the apparition in Lockwood's dream had claimed to be walking the earth "these twenty years" (ch. 3); he almost kills Hindley when his former tormentor tries to lock him out of the Heights.

Heathcliff's devotion to a Cathy who has been liberated from the confinement of time and space is finally rewarded. Wishing to die, Catherine had fasted for three days upon Heathcliff's return; after her death, we discover from Isabella that Heathcliff failed to eat a meal for nearly a week (ch. 17). At the end of the novel, the Heathcliff who refuses Nelly's food ("seemingly, I must not eat") dies in his paneled bed with the window swung open besides his corpse (ch. 34). Has he been recalled by Cathy? Before expiring, he stated that he was near sight of his haven—"hardly three feet to sever me!" His reunion with Catherine's ghost may be imaginary, but his imagination belongs to a different order than Isabella's fancied love for him or Lockwood's fancied love for the second Cathy. It is capable of breaking barriers. He and Cathy may well have fused in a world of myth that defies ordinary understanding.

The story of Heathcliff and Catherine thus ends as mysteriously as it had begun. Nelly dismisses the account of the little shepherd boy who claims to have seen "Heathcliff and a woman, yonder." The rational housekeeper who is so afraid of dreams remarks that the child "probably raised the phantoms from thinking, as he traversed on the moors alone, on the nonsense he had heard his parents and companions repeat" (ch. 34). Relying on her own eyes, she sees "nothing." Nelly's skepticism seems too defensive, too assertive in her need to vindicate common sense at the expense of inexplicable powers of intuition. Although her report is confirmed by Lockwood, who wonders how any one could ever imagine "unquiet slumbers" for the sleepers buried next to the moor, we remember that, on closing his eyes, Lockwood had stared at the ghostly "child's face" in his dream. Phantoms, it would seem, are raised, not "from thinking," but from the suspension of thought. It is significant that the pair who, in life, found that their union was possible only as thoughtless children, "half savage, hardy, and free," should be seen, after death, by another small child.

3

Heathcliff's and Catherine's love has proved mutually destructive; it is resolved only through their survival as mythical creatures roaming the moors. As phantoms whose essence is denied by both Nelly Dean and Lockwood, they exist in a reality removed from ordinary experience. Their afterlife is not that affirmed by orthodox Christian belief—be it Nelly's unquestioning belief in a beneficent Providence or Joseph's fanatical belief in a God of damnation. Organized religion deteriorates in the course of the novel: old Earnshaw's loveless righteousness degenerates into Heathcliff's frank cult of hate. Gimmerton Kirk, whose curate had originally set Earnshaw against his children and later failed to soothe Edgar's bereavement over the loss of his wife, crumbles into ruins by the end of the novel. Only through the love of Hareton, a Heathcliff who does not degenerate, and of the second Cathy, a Catherine who survives an error in judgment, can Emily Brontë lend meaning to the temporal world the first pair of lovers have vacated.

The union of Hareton and Cathy provides a fulfillment that does not require a suspension of disbelief, but, quite to the contrary, can be achieved in the ordinary, probable world presided over by Nelly Dean. The restoration effected by Hareton and his bride completes a cycle. Hindley's son and Catherine's daughter correct the imbalance of the previous two Earnshaw generations and manage to counter the changes introduced by Heathcliff and his offspring. Heathcliff recognizes his own Catherine in both Hareton and the second Cathy. In both, the infusion of outside blood, that of Frances and of Edgar Linton, has humanized the Earnshaw strain. The second Cathy is blond like her father; like Edgar, she is capable of extending love to others. In marked contradiction to her mother, who married Edgar Linton in order to receive from him the solicitude she had been denied by her father and her elder brother, Cathy first marries the younger Linton Heathcliff out of an almost maternal need to give the sickly youth the same affection and care she has received from her own father: "I'm certain Linton would recover quickly if he had me to look after him" (ch. 23). Secure about her father's love for her, Cathy cannot be persuaded by Heathcliff that Edgar must have hated her for being the cause of her mother's death. Moreover, her intuition allows her to divine that Heathcliff's own professions of hate are but expressions of his own thwarted love. She says to him: "I don't hate you. Have you ever loved *anybody*, in all your life, uncle? *never*?" (ch. 27). Her words cause Heathcliff to flee. She triumphs over Heathcliff again when she reminds him that her strength comes from the reciprocation of love: "I know he loves me and for that reason I love him. Mr. Heathcliff, *you* have *nobody* to love you . . . *nobody* will cry for you, when you die! I wouldn't be you!" (ch. 29).

Cathy—the daughter of the woman who wanted to "be" Heathcliff—is wrong in assuming that he will die uncried for. She has not yet taken notice of Hareton's own capacity for love. On seeing Heathcliff's corpse, Nelly's reaction is one of fear—she is afraid of the face that has been contorted into a sneer and afraid that Dr. Kenneth may blame her for not having fed her master. Hareton, on the other hand, sits by Heathcliff's corpse "weeping in bitter earnest" (ch. 34). Heathcliff's attempt to revenge himself on the third generation of Earnshaws by converting them into haters thus proves to be unsuccessful. Though brutalized as a Caliban, Hareton loves the master who tried to supplant his father.

The laughter of Cathy and Hareton comes to signify the restoration of sanity in the disrupted world of *Wuthering Heights.* This laughter is that of comedy, closer in tone to that of Nelly Dean than to that so seldom indulged in by the previous tenants at the Heights. The first Catherine's merriment grates on her father, who preferred the serious Heathcliff to the little girl who was always "singing, laughing, and plaguing everybody who would not do the same" (ch. 5). Heathcliff's first alienation from his former playmate occurred when she returned from the Grange and declared him to be "funny and grim." Like Dickens' Pip, mocked by Estella, Heathcliff cannot bear her ridicule: "I shall not stand to be laughed at" (ch. 7). When he returns, it is he who wants to laugh at others, although his laughter is bitter and hollow. Heathcliff banishes the cheerful Nelly. He taunts Isabella and Hindley, mocks Lockwood, deprecates Edgar, and sneers at Linton, his own son. Significantly enough, his revenge misfires when the more healthy laughter of others again penetrates Wuthering Heights.

In chapter thirty-three the second Cathy is sticking primroses in Hareton's plate of porridge. A "smothered laugh" is heard. When Heathcliff turns fiercely on Cathy and says, "I thought I had cured you of laughing," Hareton sheepishly admits that it was he who had laughed. Despite the sternness of old Earnshaw and the sullenness of Joseph, who distrusts any form of amusement, laughter—imported from the social world of the Grange—intrudes in the asocial world of the Heights. Ironically enough, it is Hareton, whom Heathcliff has tried to degrade into a replica of the crude being that the first Catherine had laughed at after her contact with the Grange, who now defies his master's attempt to smother joy.

The fact that Hareton's laugh occurs over a plate of food is equally significant. We have seen how the death wishes of the first Catherine and of Heathcliff and ex-

pression through their deliberate starvation. Hareton and the second Catherine, on the other hand, feed each other. Sure that "she was starved," Hareton clumsily presses some food on the second Catherine when she comes to the Heights as Heathcliff's captive (ch. 30). Cathy admits that she has been "starved a month and more," but she fails to recognize Hareton's own starvation for love and his hunger for knowledge. When Hareton asks her to read to him, she mistakes his overture as a "pretence at kindness" (ch. 30). Soon, however, she discovers that his kindness is unfeigned. Like Heathcliff, Hareton is compacted of good and evil; but unlike Catherine, Cathy does not reject his coarseness, but proceeds to civilize him and to bring out the good. Together, they uproot the twisted bushes at the Heights and import "plants from the Grange." Presumably, in moving to the Grange, they will in turn implant Earnshaw vitality into the too-ordered gardens of the Lintons.

Although it is false to ignore the positive ending made possible by Cathy's ability to reclaim Hareton, it is equally easy to exaggerate the happiness of this happy ending. Emily Brontë's return to a comic mode allows her to illustrate the redemptive powers of a quasi-Christian love. Still, the story of Hareton and Cathy is clearly subordinated to that of the first set of lovers. Heathcliff's tragedy cannot be dispelled. As a denier, a Faustian figure who questions the meaning of existence in this world and in the next, Heathcliff, though checked and countered by Emily Brontë's art, remains a self-projection who acts out some of her own anguish and doubt. It is the withering of love, more than its eventual restoration, that remains at the emotional core of *Wuthering Heights.*

In his first dream in the third chapter, Lockwood, "with Joseph for a guide," had entered the Chapel of Gimmerton Sough to hear the preacher Jabes Branderham. The sermon is on "Seventy Times Seven," the unpardonable sin. The text is taken from Matthew, 18:21-22: "Then came Peter to him, and said, Lord, how often shall my brother sin against me, and I forgive him? till seven times? / Jesus saith unto him, I say not unto thee, Until seven times: but, Until seventy times seven." Lockwood is bored by the preacher's interminable sermon; the man who later uses Nelly to divert him from boredom accuses the preacher of the "sin no Christian need pardon." The preacher in turn accuses Lockwood of challenging his authority. But the unpardonable sin is committed by Lockwood in his next dream, when he rejects the child that pleads to be let in from the cold. Lockwood's failure to respond to the "child's face looking through the window" makes him guilty of the same lovelessness which was so ruinous to the descendants of the man who admitted the alien child into his house. In the same chapter of Matthew, Jesus tells His disciples that "whoso shall receive one such little child in my name receiveth me." To those who deny love to the innocent, damnation will occur: "But whoso shall offend one of these little ones which believe in me, it were better for him that a millstone were hanged about his neck, and that he were drowned in the depth of the sea" (18:5-6).

Cruelty toward the innocent is the chief sin in **Wuthering Heights.** This cruelty is shared by almost all the adult characters; moreover, it is often self-inflicted. There is no original sin, no absolute evil; no character is purely and wantonly malicious. In a novel in which the characters themselves are constantly blaming someone else for their misfortunes, the reader, prevented from pointing an accusing finger at any one of them, cannot declare, "Thou art the man!" Heathcliff blames Catherine for her willingness to marry Edgar; Catherine, in turn, blames Hindley for forcing her into a union with a man she cannot really love. Hindley has his own scapegoats. He blames God, his Heavenly Father, for killing the one object of his love, Frances, just as he blames old Earnshaw, his earthly father, for loving Heathcliff the Ishmaelite instead of his rightful son. Earnshaw, however, has merely rationalized his perverse attraction to the foundling by telling himself that he is following the dictates of a just God. It is in that Justicer's spirit that he reproaches Nelly for her cruelty to the boy. But the deity he believes in is devoid of feeling. Out of justice comes injustice. Although this process proves reversible, Emily Brontë's novel nonetheless relies on this cruel arch-paradox.

Despite the novelist's efforts to vindicate her belief in goodness and love, **Wuthering Heights** achieves its harmony not because of its final synthesis but rather because of its recognition of paradox and contradiction. Although the plot represents a triumph for the benign social forces of the Grange, it is in the garden at that Grange, and not at the Heights, that the cleavage which will separate Catherine from Heathcliff first becomes manifest. By having Edgar and Isabella fight over their dog so fiercely that they almost tear the animal apart, the author shows that the Lintons' civilized ways are only skin deep. Emily Brontë seems to share Heathcliff's disgust with the "petted things" who quarrel over a "heap of warm hair" (ch. 6). His mockery, to Nelly, of these "good children" only helps to expose the incongruity of the housekeeper's notions of what constitutes conventional "good."

The vitality of Heathcliff and the first Catherine is used as a foil to expose the precariousness of the Lintons' ordered way of life. As the second Cathy's "uncle," Heathcliff merely parodies the family structure on which life at the Grange is based. It is no coincidence that the elder Mrs. Linton, who nurses Catherine after the girl's unsuccessful search for Heathcliff in the rainstorm, should have "reason to repent of her kindness" (ch. 9).

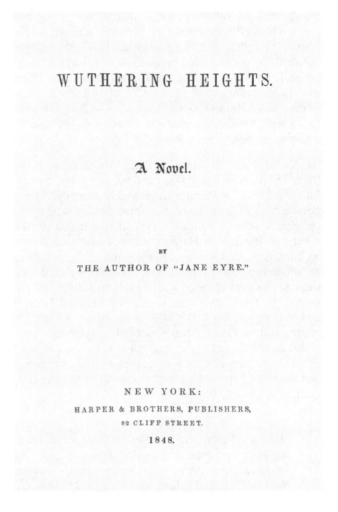

WUTHERING HEIGHTS.

A Novel.

BY

THE AUTHOR OF "JANE EYRE."

NEW YORK:
HARPER & BROTHERS, PUBLISHERS,
82 CLIFF STREET.
1848.

Title page of Wuthering Heights, *1848.*

Both she and her husband die from the fever Catherine had contracted. Good can come out of evil, but the test of anarchy and disease seems necessary. Edgar Linton must confront such a test and suffer in its process before the author is willing to endorse his humaneness.

By her willingness to interpenetrate opposites, Emily Brontë achieves artistically what Catherine Earnshaw was unable to do. Catherine wanted to retain Edgar and Heathcliff, to live suspended between responsibility and freedom, civilization and eros, Victorian acquiescence and Romantic rebellion. Finding herself unable to span Edgar's social order and the life of instinct that she shared with Heathcliff, Cathy chooses to die, hoping to transcend a finite world of irreconcilables. The suspension she despairs of, however, is made possible by the novelist's construction of a form which encompasses these same alternatives. **Wuthering Heights** relies on the resemblances between opposites and the disjunction of alikes. Opposites blend: the Heathcliff who oppresses Hindley's son eventually matches the Hindley who oppressed Heathcliff; victim and tyrant become alike.

Similarities are sundered: the Catherine who vows that she *is* Heathcliff survives, yet becomes altered, in the Linton daughter hated by Heathcliff. Only Joseph, oblivious to paradox and contradiction, always remains himself, unswerving in his self-righteousness, as eager to depreciate Heathcliff in the eyes of Hindley as he is to depreciate Hindley's son in the eyes of his new master. Joseph the fanatic, sure of his point of view, is an anomaly in Brontë's world.

By blending the illogic of Heathcliff's story with the logical realism of Nelly Dean and her nurslings, by fusing pessimism and hope, tragedy and comedy, Emily Brontë was able to resist the formulas by which her characters want to reduce reality. It is a tribute to the reality of **Wuthering Heights,** as well as to the novelist's integrity, that she was able to control the polarities on which her vision is built. The novelists we shall consider in the next chapter were unable to follow her example. In Meredith's *The Ordeal of Richard Feverel* and in George Eliot's *The Mill on the Floss,* the tension maintained in Emily Brontë's novel is no longer possible; in both works, the equipoise between romance and realism breaks down as comedy yields to pathos and the sins of the fathers irrevocably destroy their children.

Notes

1. "Editor's Preface to the New Edition of Wuthering Heights," reprinted in *Wuthering Heights: An Authoritative Text With Essays in Criticism,* Norton Critical Edition, ed. William M. Sale, Jr. (New York, 1963), pp. 10, 9. All future references in the text are to this edition.

2. *Ibid.,* p. 12.

3. "For a specimen of true benevolence and homely fidelity, look at the character of Nelly Dean; for an example of constancy and tenderness, remark that of Edgar Linton" (*Ibid.,* p. 11).

4. *Wuthering Heights* has stimulated a greater variety of distinguished critical essays than most other Victorian novels. The reader is referred to the essays reproduced in the Norton Critical Edition, as well as to the more comprehensive selection by Richard Lettis and William E. Morris in *A Wuthering Heights Handbook* (New York, 1961).

5. For the full story of "Angria" and "Gondal," see Fannie E. Ratchford, *The Brontës' Web of Childhood* (New York, 1941).

6. "Biographical Notice of Ellis and Acton Bell," *Ibid.,* p. 4.

7. In *Gondal's Queen: A Novel in Verse by Emily Jane Brontë* (Austin, 1955).

8. James Hafley, "The Villain in *Wuthering Heights,*" *Nineteenth-Century Fiction,* XIII (December 1958), 199-215; reprinted in Lettis and Morris, *A Wuthering Heights Handbook,* pp. 182-197.

Elliott B. Gose, Jr. (essay date 1972)

SOURCE: Gose, Elliott B., Jr. "*Wuthering Heights.*" In *Imagination Indulged: The Irrational in the Nineteenth-Century Novel,* pp. 59-71. Montreal: McGill-Queen's University Press, 1972.

[*In the following essay, Gose examines storytelling motifs in* Wuthering Heights *and argues that the work's principal strength lies in its tension between opposing qualities of symbolism, or fairy tale, and realism. By weaving together these conflicting styles, Gose suggests, Brontë expanded the traditional boundaries of the novel form.*]

It would be an error to claim that the fairy-tale patterns are the only figurative patterns in **Wuthering Heights.** But they are very important because of the levels of meaning they open up, and they do provide an obvious area for further investigation of the relation between romance and the novel. The brevity of most fairy tales and the lack of complexity in their structure, description, and characterization make the task of recognizing and interpreting their symbols if not easy at least simpler and more straightforward than it is with a novel like **Wuthering Heights** where the symbols appear as part of the realistic fabric. I shall therefore enter into a more detailed consideration of the novel with a passage that has two immediate virtues: it reads like the beginning of a fairy tale; it names several things that clearly carry some symbolic weight.

Nelly Dean starts her story for Lockwood not only in the style of a fairy tale but with the incident that begins the Beauty-and-Beast type of tale—the father about to go on a trip. Like that father, Mr Earnshaw promises each of the three children a present on his return. He addresses first Hindley, his oldest:

> "Now, my bonny man, I'm going to Liverpool today . . . What shall I bring you? You may choose what you like; only let it be little, for I shall walk there and back; sixty miles each way, that is a long spell!"

> Hindley named a fiddle, and then he asked Miss Cathy; she was hardly six years old, but she could ride any horse in the stable, and she chose a whip.

> He did not forget me [says Nelly]; for he had a kind heart, though he was rather severe, sometimes. He promised to bring me a pocketful of apples and pears, and then he kissed his children good-bye, and set off.

> It seemed a long while to us all—the three days of his absence—and often did little Cathy ask when he would be home. . . . Just about eleven o'clock, the door-latch was raised quietly and in stept the master. He

threw himself into a chair, laughing and groaning, and bid them all stand off, for he was nearly killed—he would not have such another walk for the three king-doms.

"And at the end of it, to be flighted to death!" he said, opening his great coat, which he held bundled up in his arms. "See here, wife! I was never so beaten with any-thing in my life; but you must e'en take it as a gift of God, though it's as dark almost as if it came from the devil."

(pp. 36-37, second ellipsis mine)

Again like the father in "Beauty and the Beast," Mr Earnshaw brings home trouble instead of presents for his children. Unlike that father, however, the trouble he brings is the beast itself; all three children are con-fronted with the creature responsible for their not re-ceiving presents. Although Mr Earnshaw offered to bring whatever they wanted that he could carry, what he actually carries home is a gift that none of them would have chosen, not even the father. Heathcliff's ini-tial appearance is symbolic: the pronoun *it* applied to him indicates an alien, subhuman nature, an object of fate. Since he is "as dark almost" as if he comes "from the devil" we can adopt Dorothy Van Ghent's view of him as a "daemonic archetype." But we must qualify this view with that of Kettle, who connects Heathcliff's energy with "moral emotion" (p. 147).[1] We shall delve further into his symbolic name and nature presently, but for now we must at least see this gift from the father as a means for a testing by fortune of Hindley and Cathe-rine.

This brings us to the three simpler symbols in the pas-sage above, the objects the children originally asked for. Hindley had wanted a fiddle, Catherine a whip. Similarly, he cries upon seeing the fiddle, smashed, she threatens upon hearing the whip was lost while her fa-ther tended "the stranger." Although we might expect the desires and reactions of the two to be reversed, we should remember that, when children speak from their heart's desire, they often ask for what they really want, which may very well be the opposite of what they are conventionally supposed to want. Taking the gifts sym-bolically, we may say that Hindley wants to develop the finer, more cultural, less active side of his nature. His gift is crushed. Catherine wants to develop the rougher, more physical and active side of hers, and indeed has already begun to do so. She is consequently soon able to accept Heathcliff. Hindley, on the other hand, sees his hopes for refinement being thwarted by his father's subsequent favouring treatment of this alien. Ironically, in rejecting what Heathcliff stands for, he rejects self-knowledge. His dark side emerges negatively, in de-structiveness, including self-destruction.

Nelly Dean, who is Hindley's age (p. 196) and calls herself "his foster sister" (p. 68), had not asked for any-thing but was promised "a pocketful of apples and

pears." She is presumably also disappointed, but, whereas we never after see Hindley with a fiddle or Catherine with a whip, we do see Nelly with fruit and can judge from later scenes its symbolic overtones. Her use of it in a scene where she is trying to entice Hare-ton shows the meaning clearly. He swears at her, not recognizing his old nurse after a separation of ten months. "This grieved, more than angered me," reports Nelly. "Fit to cry, I took an orange from my pocket, and offered it to propitiate him" (p. 115). This act shows the same kind of encouragement of deprived humanity which she had earlier demonstrated with Heathcliff. The first time the Linton children come to visit the Heights, Nelly tries to make Heathcliff presentable enough to take part in the Christmas dinner. Unfortunately Hind-ley intervenes, ordering Heathcliff "into the garret till dinner is over. He'll be cramming his fingers in the tarts, and stealing the fruit, if left alone with them a minute" (p. 60). Like other self-fulfilling prophecies, this one comes true when Heathcliff dashes "a tureen full of hot apple sauce" against Edgar Linton. But this aggressive use of fruit should not obscure the nourish-ing use intended by Nelly.

Her life-giving warmth is quite apparent in the descrip-tion she gives of the kitchen the night before these events.

Putting my cakes in the oven, and making the house and kitchen cheerful with great fires befitting Christmas eve, I prepared to sit down and amuse myself by sing-ing carols. . . . I smelt the rich scent of the heating spices; and admired the shining kitchen utensils, the polished clock, decked in holly, the silver mugs ranged on a tray ready to be filled with mulled ale for supper; and, above all, the speckless purity of my particular care—the scoured and well-swept floor.

I gave due inward applause to every object, and, then, I remembered how old Earnshaw used to come in . . . from that I went on to think of his fondness for Heath-cliff, and his dread lest he should suffer neglect after death had removed him; . . . It struck me soon, how-ever, there would be more sense in endeavouring to re-pair some of his wrongs than shedding tears over them—I got up and walked into the court to seek [Heathcliff].

(pp. 56-57)

The emotional gamut here is from applause for the physical, to memory of affection, to sadness, to deter-mination.

This thought sequence would not be worth remarking if it did not lead to the interesting advice that Nelly gives Heathcliff when she finds him.

You're fit for a prince in disguise. Who knows, but your father was Emperor of China, and your mother an Indian queen, each of them able to buy up, with one week's income, Wuthering Heights and Thrushcross

Grange together? And you were kidnapped by wicked sailors, and brought to England. Were I in your place, I would frame high notions of my birth.

(p. 59)

Because of his dark skin, Heathcliff is connected with the devil by his foster father, is called a gipsy by the Lintons, and is here offered a third possibility, a royal eastern parentage by Nelly Dean. As Dorothy Van Ghent phrases this possibility: "If Heathcliff is really of daemonic origin, he is, in a sense, indeed of 'high birth,' a 'prince in disguise,' and might be expected, like the princes of fairy tale, to drop his 'disguise' at the crisis of the tale and be revealed in original splendor" (p. 168). Unlike Hareton, however, who later does shine forth, Heathcliff remains untransformed because rejected by Catherine. He does disappear at one point, to return after Catherine's marriage to a different person, but he is changed by loneliness and hate rather than transformed by love. On the other hand, we have Nelly's reaction to his return: "I was amazed more than ever, to behold the *transformation* of Heathcliff." His face "looked intelligent, and retained no marks of former degradation. A half-civilized ferocity lurked yet in the depressed brows, and eyes full of black fire, but it was subdued" (pp. 100-101, my italics). Although subdued, this "black fire" is characteristic of the violent Heathcliff we come to know. In our fairy-tale sense he is untransformed and never turns into a bright prince of light or gold.[2]

An extension of the symbolism of darkness associated with Heathcliff is indicated by Catherine's earlier characterization of him as "bleak, hilly, coal country" (p. 73). This image suggests not only his exterior appearance but his interior being, compressed to rich dark fuel. Similar associations attach to his name. The *heath* is bleak, while *cliff* connects with Catherine's description of her love for Heathcliff, which "resembles the eternal rocks beneath—a source of little visible delight, but necessary" (p. 86). Cliff and rocks together connect with Peniston Crag, the landmark whose cave is associated with fairy power (p. 210).

Like the magician in "The Glass Coffin," Heathcliff because he is rebuffed has chosen to strive for revenge, to bring down pride. Just as the magician transformed the brother of the woman he loved into a stag, Heathcliff played a key role in the dehumanization of both Hindley and Hareton. Just as the magician became a vicious black bull after casting his spells, Heathcliff becomes a vicious person until he is finally opposed. One important difference between the novel and any of the fairy-tale analogues we have noted is, of course, the complexity of *Wuthering Heights.* Heathcliff perverts Hareton's nature, yet wins Hareton's love. Heathcliff stops his revenge because he sees the spirit of Catherine in the face of Cathy (pp. 340, 342) and of Hareton (p.

343). He wins not mere death but presumably union with the spirit of Catherine.

In his single-minded effort to create revenge, Heathcliff works with the negative force of destruction. In doing so he acts counter to Nelly Dean. Through most of the novel she is a frustrated mother, as we have seen in her unsuccessful attempts to help Heathcliff and Hareton. But by the end she is fulfilled in the coming marriage of Hareton and Cathy, whom she calls "in a measure, my children" (p. 341), having nursed them when their mothers died soon after each was born.

In the fairy-tale pattern, Nelly takes the role of helpful provider, the good fairy who offers the young man a token and advice for achieving his destiny, or for finding his true identity. If she is motherly in addition this only confirms the findings of psychoanalysis that the good fairy represents one side of the mother, just as the bad fairy represents another. Sometimes, indeed, the fairy who appears good at first (offering sweets to eat, as in "Hänsel and Gretel") may turn out to be a witch who really means harm. It has, in fact, been argued that Nelly is the villain of the novel.[3] Certainly it is true that Catherine at one point views Nelly as a potential witch. "'I see in you, Nelly,' she continued, dreamily, 'an aged woman—you have grey hair, and bent shoulders. This bed is the fairy cave under Peniston Crag, and you are gathering elf-bolts to hurt our heifers; pretending, while I am near, that they are only locks of wool. That's what you'll come to fifty years hence: I know you are not so now'" (p. 130).[4] Then finding that Nelly has not told her husband what she wished, Catherine bursts out, "Nelly is my hidden enemy—you witch! So you do seek elf-bolts to hurt us!" (p. 136). As Heathcliff points out to Catherine in their last interview, however, she is her own "hidden enemy." Nelly does meddle, has human failings, but she always acts from good motives, by her standard. That standard is based on a natural sympathy with the comfortable, orderly world of Thrushcross Grange. She is at home in its cultivated comfort and its orchard of fruit trees. But she has known Catherine and Heathcliff as children at the Heights, and she is willing to compromise and allow room for their values. In their generation, however, the world of the Heights cannot be reconciled with that of the Grange. Nelly is successful only with the next generation, Hareton and Cathy.

Having cleared Nelly of being a witch, we seem to be well on our way to demonstrating that the characteristic atmosphere of *Wuthering Heights* is sweetness and light. Any reader's experience is quite different, of course: we all know that *wuthering* really is descriptive of "atmospheric tumult" (in Lockwood's decorous phrase). We also know that the first half of the novel is the best place to look for the violence which we have already admitted to be in the novel. In turning our attention there, I propose, however, to begin with another fairy-tale scene, also apparently filled with sweetness and light. Here is Heathcliff's description of the living room at Thrushcross Grange as seen by him and Catherine. "It was beautiful—a splendid place carpeted with crimson, and crimson-covered chairs and tables, and a pure white ceiling bordered by gold, a shower of glass-drops hanging in silver chains from the centre, and shimmering with little soft tapers" (p. 49). This is the palace where lives the prince whom Catherine will marry. Taken inside, she finds there a fulfilment of her wish to be queen. "Then the woman servant brought a basin of warm water, and washed her feet; and Mr. Linton mixed a tumbler of negus, and Isabella emptied a plateful of cakes into her lap, and Edgar stood gaping at a distance. Afterwards, they dried and combed her beautiful hair, and gave her a pair of enormous slippers, and wheeled her to the fire" (p. 52). All we need is the marriage itself and we shall know that Catherine and Edgar will live happily ever after. The marriage takes place, and a certain kind of happiness does follow; but it is not the kind forecast by the two scenes above, nor does it last very long. Why not?

The problem is that Catherine cannot decide which kind of fairy tale she is participating in. Or, to put it from her point of view, she cannot decide which kind of identity to choose, the easy one of material comfort, or the difficult one of sympathy with an outcast. The second corresponds to "Beauty and the Beast" or perhaps to "The Frog Prince." There the father makes the princess go through with her bargain, after which the frog, like the Beast, is transformed into a handsome prince. But Catherine has lost her father by the time marriage becomes a possibility. Her brother, as the new authority, separates her from Heathcliff and pushes her toward Edgar Linton. But, if she cannot function as the princess who helps the beast to become human, why should she not choose another role, and become the poor little girl who is taken into the king's palace and herself transformed into a queen? She could make this shift, on one condition: that she had never committed herself to the first role, never made a promise to the beast (or frog). But she has committed herself, has already so bound up her identity with Heathcliff's that she can choose a destiny demanding another identity only at the cost of splitting her nature.

That split is evident in her delirium following Heathcliff's return after her marriage to Edgar Linton. Nelly tries to restrain her from looking in the mirror, where Catherine sees a face which she does not recognize as her own. When Nelly finally convinces her, Catherine makes a strange comment.

> "There's nobody here!" I insisted. "It was *yourself,* Mrs. Linton; you knew it a while since."

"Myself!" she gasped, "and the clock is striking twelve! It's true, then, that's dreadful!"

(p. 131)

As Nelly confirms further on (p. 132), the clock really has struck twelve midnight. In her delirium, however, Catherine puts a different kind of weight on the fact than Nelly. We discover that she dreamed she was back at Wuthering Heights, "the whole last seven years of my life [grown] a blank" (132). The face in the mirror appears alien because she expected to see her earlier self. What is true and dreadful is that she is actually at the Grange. Heathcliff's reappearance has made her aware of the split, of her mistake in marrying Edgar. The clock striking twelve brings it home because midnight, the traditional time of change, indicates the end of the spell, the enchantment which made the girl who belonged in the cinders appear as a princess. She cannot fool herself any longer.

We have made Catherine sound perhaps too culpable in our analysis (though we have not been as hard on her as Heathcliff is just before her death). One detail from her dream may give us a clue to balancing our judgement. "I was a child; my father was just buried, and my misery arose from the separation that Hindley had ordered between me and Heathcliff—I was laid alone, for the first time" (p. 132). This makes clear that the original split occurred, not when Catherine deserted Heathcliff for the Lintons, but when she was separated from him by authority. Her fairy-tale task is to work and suffer to heal the split, as she is well aware. Her rationalization to Nelly for marrying Edgar is that it will help Heathcliff. But this move is a mistake, as Nelly tries to tell her; she is actually choosing physical comfort when only suffering will resolve the problem.

But once again we are being too hard on Catherine. Circumstances separated her from Heathcliff before she ever agreed to marry Edgar, and they held her at the Grange before she ever agreed to enter and allow herself to be charmed. I am thinking of a scene the very opposite of Catherine on a sofa being waited on, of the incident which in fact causes that scene to take place. Earlier outside, Heathcliff and Catherine had started to run, and she had fallen. "'Run, Heathcliff, run!' she whispered. 'They have let the bull-dog loose, and he holds me!'" (p. 50). Heathcliff continues,

> The devil had seized her ankle, Nelly; I heard his abominable snorting. . . . I got a stone and thrust it between his jaws, and tried with all my might to cram it down his throat. A beast of a servant came up with a lantern, at last, shouting—
>
> "Keep fast, Skulker, keep fast!" . . .
>
> The man took Cathy up; she was sick—not from fear, I'm certain, but from pain. . . .

"How her foot bleeds!" . . .

"She may be lamed for life!"

(pp. 50-52)

She is not lamed for life physically, but she does not recover her psychic freedom until death liberates her spirit.

The connection between physical and psychical impressions and reactions was covertly present in an earlier scene between Lockwood and the Heights' dogs. When they attacked him, he defended himself with a poker and afterward answered Heathcliff's query whether he was bitten, "If I had been, I would have set my signet on the biter" (p. 6). But in fact they were about to set their sign on him. Wanting to leave, he picked up a lantern outside, at which Joseph sicked Gnasher and Wolf on him. Again he was not bitten, just knocked down, "but they would suffer no resurrection, and I was forced to lie till their malignant masters pleased to deliver me." Once on his feet, he trembled and threatened, and "the vehemence of my agitation brought on a copious bleeding at the nose" (p. 16). He finally stayed at the Heights to dream first of being attacked by men with staves in a chapel near a graveyard, and then of his own aggression, sawing a girl's wrist on a broken window while "the blood ran down and soaked the bedclothes" (p. 25). Lockwood had been initiated by the forces of power and violence, into the inner world of darkness.

Like Catherine after her indoctrination, he had to stay in bed at Thrushcross Grange for a few weeks, but, whereas he recuperated in a house that suited his social nature, she became acclimated to an unfamiliar environment. Also like hers his blood flowed after contact with ferocious dogs. In her case, however, there was a physical wound, and a psychic scar. Her contact with the beast led to the more genteel initiation inside the house, and the two together form the upper and lower half of the force that tests the strength of her spirit. That is, we can contrast the "lower" dog bite in the dark on Catherine's leg with the "upper" combing of her beautiful hair in the light.

Similarly, we have noted a fairy-tale pattern of reconciliation between the low beast and the high beauty. But Skulker is no transformable beast; he is a watchdog, the brute force by which those who own protect what they have from those who own not. But he is also the necessary prelude to a test. Fairy tales are full of palaces and castles guarded by beasts and monsters. To fail in dealing with them is to come under an alien power. The nature of the new identity "forced" on Catherine is revealed when she returns to the Heights. Nelly reports, "I removed the habit, and there shone forth, beneath a grand plaid silk frock, white trousers and burnished

shoes; and, while her eyes sparkled joyfully when the dogs came bounding up to welcome her, she dare hardly touch them lest they should fawn upon her splendid garments" (p. 54). Catherine is now too clean and bright to be touched by dirty dogs, too high to live intimately with such beasts as Heathcliff. "If the wicked man [her brother, Hindley] in there had not brought Heathcliff so low," she would not have considered marrying Edgar. But "it would degrade me to marry Heathcliff, now" (pp. 84-85). In fairy tales the pride of the person who is unwilling to stoop is invariably punished severely.

The polarized thinking responsible for Catherine's predicament is made a paramount psychological and moral theme in the novel. Even at the very beginning, it is tellingly embodied in Lockwood's responses, again in fairy-tale terms. Leaving aside such obvious blunders as his mistaking dead rabbits for live cats, we may look at the mistake he makes about the younger Catherine's position in the household. Finding his error in assuming her to be Heathcliff's wife, he again puts his foot in it by suggesting to Hareton that "you are the favoured possessor of the beneficent fairy" (p. 12). Not only is this superficial compliment, "favoured possessor," denied by "a brutal curse" from Hareton; its twin, "the beneficent fairy," is shown to be equally wrong as a characterization of Cathy. She quickly gets into an argument with Joseph in which she threatens to ask his "abduction as a special favour" (p. 13). She then takes "a long, dark book" from the shelf, mentions "the Black Art" and again threatens Joseph, "I'll have you modelled in wax and clay" (p. 14). Lockwood for once is able to interpret correctly: "The little witch put a mock malignity into her beautiful eyes, and Joseph, trembling with sincere horror, hurried out" (p. 14). She is only playing the witch, then, but she is playing it for real, as a means of holding her own with Joseph. It is this vitality that Lockwood instinctively shrinks from.

Lockwood's incapacity with a marriageable woman is, however, indicated even before his blunders with Cathy. He tells the reader a revealing anecdote about himself. "While enjoying a month of fine weather at the seacoast, I was thrown into the company of a most fascinating creature, a real goddess in my eyes, as long as she took no notice of me. I 'never told my love' vocally; still, if looks have language, the merest idiot might have guessed I was over head and ears; she understood me, at last, and looked a return—the sweetest of all imaginable looks—and what did I do? I confess it with shame—shrunk icily into myself, like a snail" (p. 4).[5] Lockwood understands that "looks have language," and yet he immediately turns around and acts as though they do not. Left alone with the dogs, as mentioned before, and "imagining they would scarcely understand tacit insults, I unfortunately indulged in winking and making faces at the trio" until he "so irritated madam, that she suddenly broke into a fury, and leapt on my knees" (p. 5). In case any reader is in doubt as to the parallel between these two contiguous scenes, the name of "madam" is presently revealed as "Juno"—a real goddess who, we might say, pays Lockwood back for his earlier refusal of engagement with her sex. More to our purpose is the point that his insistence on consciously idealizing women seems to be balanced by an unconscious hostility to them. His calling a woman a goddess or a good fairy seems to call up the bitch and the witch to remind him that human nature has connections with the physicality of animals and the twisted spirituality of aggression. Essentially these themes are also present in his two dreams.[6]

Although Lockwood is too defensively bound up in himself to learn from his experiences, Cathy can modify her nature, as a brief comparison with her mother will indicate. Catherine, learning intransigence in the face of Hindley's unfair authority, was indoctrinated into a life of civility and ease during her enforced stay at the Grange. Her daughter, being spoiled by comfort and indulgence at the Grange, is indoctrinated into a life of hardship and neglect at the Heights. The mother could only retreat to the Heights in fantasy or to the grave in reality as an escape from the split embodied in husband and first love. The daughter is able to learn through suffering the patience and humility needed to love another and transform him. More than this, though, as we have seen, she transforms her dependent egoism into a rebellious self-reliance which is equally necessary to survival. The girl who was used to being called "angel" learns to depend on her potential as witch; the lady who has been treated as a queen is finally condemned by Joseph as a "quean" (that is a "jade, wench, slut") for encouraging Hareton to pull up Joseph's thorny bushes and plant flowers at the Heights. As this act shows, she is trying to reconcile the creative with the destructive.

Hardly an unsophisticated fairy tale, *Wuthering Heights* incorporates its oppositions in the same subtle way a fairy tale does. We do not consciously register the fairy-witch, goddess-bitch, queen-quean pairs or their final reconciliation except in the sense of a generalized tempering of Cathy's nature by the end. But, as often in a fairy tale, a structure that feels powerful on reading turns out on examination to have such oppositions and resolutions within it.

Despite the presence of fairy-tale motifs in *Wuthering Heights,* it is not simply a fairy tale. Emily Brontë wrote a novel; the fairy tale is by our definition a form of romance. The transformation of the brother into a stag in "The Glass Coffin" is, for instance, an impossibility which the reader allows without thinking to employ realistic standards. Like other works of the romance type, the fairy tale demands an indulgence which frees it from the bonds of particularized verisimilitude. It may then give full rein to the tendency to make be-lieve, though it may at the same time redeem its licence by treating seriously some problem of human nature. It may even call in question the reality of the everyday world it has left behind, usually by means of the make believe which inspired the original departure from the everyday (see *Through the Looking Glass*). Such questioning will consequently strike most readers as the game it often is.

Wuthering Heights works differently. It tries to keep in contact with the everyday, but insists at the same time in pushing beyond simple realism. Thus, for contemporaries of Emily Brontë, the oddity of the novel, as of Blake's poetry earlier, lay in its inability to be superficial or sentimental. She did not indulge in crude realism or spiritual perversity to shock the philistines as the late Victorians often did; rather she carried on the search started by the Romantic movement to discover the place of the individual in the universe.

Such a search obviously included due respect for the ravages of the flesh, just as it also accepted the possibility of the separate existence of the spirit.[7] Lockwood has an intimation of this possibility in his dream of the waif Catherine outside his window; Catherine and Heathcliff, before their respective deaths, also affirm it. And I think the reader of the novel is intended to register it as a latent permissible reality. Just before the end of *Wuthering Heights,* Nelly tells of meeting "a little boy with a sheep and two lambs." He is frightened and tells of having encountered the ghosts of Catherine and Heathcliff on the moor. Nelly's conclusion is interesting: "I saw nothing; but neither the sheep nor he would go on" (p. 357). Lockwood can see nothing either. Visiting the graves under a "benign sky," he wonders "how anyone could ever imagine unquiet slumbers, for the sleepers in that quiet earth" (p. 358). Since these words end the novel, they are often taken as expressing their author's final position. It seems to me evident that they are a last ironic revelation of Lockwood's character. First of all, he has forgotten his dream, with its accurate cry from Catherine, "I've been a waif for twenty years" (p. 25). Second, his logic has a flaw. Suppose the sky were not benign? Suppose it were "wuthering," what would one be able to imagine for those two passionate sleepers then? Like Nelly, Lockwood by choice belongs to the calm and regulated life of the Grange. But I believe the reader who has experienced the tumult of the novel is invited to imagine that spirits do roam, not visible to the rational eye, but as a sufficient testimony to the durability of psychic energy.

This notion may be romantic, but is it novelistic? Balanced as it is against the brute force of temporal circumstance, I believe it is, for this spiritual state is given a physical correlative in the elemental world of the moors, the place where young Catherine and Heathcliff were free from the tyranny of Hindley. The elements of wind and rain as nonhuman thus become a lyric part of the circumstances of the novel.[8] The final freedom of Heathcliff and Catherine there may stretch the form of the novel, but without breaking it.

Notes

1. Dorothy Van Ghent, *The English Novel: Form and Function* (New York: Rinehart & Co., 1953), p. 164. She argues that, unlike the other examples of this archetype with which she deals, Heathcliff cannot be connected with "ethical thought." Kettle's best analysis is of the Blakean morality of Heathcliff's statement, "The more the worms writhe, the more I yearn to crush out their entrails! It is a moral teething" (pp. 161-62).

2. Edgar says of Heathcliff just before this description, "He never struck me as such a marvellous treasure."

3. James Hafley, "The Villain in *Wuthering Heights*," *Nineteenth-Century Fiction*, 13, (December 1958).

4. "Elf-bolts, the ancient British flint arrow-points." Mrs. Gutch, *North Riding of Yorkshire . . . County Folklore* (London: D. Nutt, 1901), p. 181.

5. Cathy later gives a smile "as sweet as honey" (p. 333) to Hareton; obviously, Lockwood could never have responded to such a stimulus.

6. For consideration of the dreams, see Dorothy Van Ghent. See also Edgar F. Shannon, Jr., "Lockwood's Dreams and the Exegesis of *Wuthering Heights*," *Nineteenth-Century Fiction*, 14 (September 1959).

7. For a comprehensive analysis of the relation of physical destructiveness to spiritual union in *Wuthering Heights*, see J. Hillis Miller, *The Disappearance of God* (Cambridge: Harvard University Press, 1963), Chapter 4. Miller also analyses the relation between the Catherine-Heathcliff and the Cathy-Hareton love stories.

8. On the elements, see again Dorothy Van Ghent. See also Elliott B. Gose, Jr., "*Wuthering Heights*: the Heath and the Hearth," *Nineteenth-Century Fiction*, 21 (June 1966).

Ronald B. Hatch (essay date 1974)

SOURCE: Hatch, Ronald B. "Heathcliff's 'Queer End' and Schopenhauer's Denial of the Will." In *Heathcliff*, edited by Harold Bloom, pp. 92-105. New York: Chelsea House Publishers, 1993.

[*In the following essay, originally published in* Canadian Review of Comparative Literature *in 1974, Hatch offers a detailed analysis of the character of Heathcliff,* *examining his actions within the context of Schopenhauer's concept of the will. Hatch asserts that Heathcliff's violent nature is the product of his unrealized sense of self.*]

'I wish to be as God made me,' Emily Brontë was wont to reply, leaving her questioners mystified. And her readers to this day have been similarly discomfited by the enigmatic self-sufficiency of *Wuthering Heights.* In her 1964 survey of Brontë scholarship, Mildred G. Christian rightly noted that 'the contradictory judgments on *Wuthering Heights* are the most striking fact in its critical history.'[1] The major reason for the contradictory judgments is that readers have reacted in different ways to Heathcliff and Cathy. While some readers have maintained that Cathy and Heathcliff are invested with positive values, others have seen them representing negative qualities which are exorcized in the end. The two poles can be illustrated by Ruth M. Adams, who maintains that 'Catherine and Heathcliff themselves illustrate the perverse values that prevail in *Wuthering Heights*,'[2] and Edgar F. Shannon, Jr, who advances the antithetical reading when he concludes that the novel 'results in a paradigm of love,'[3] in which Emily Brontë shows that Heathcliff 'is not innately demonic and that hate is subservient to love.'[4] A survey of recent criticism reveals that no consensus has been reached about the novel's ultimate direction. This diversity of opinion of course bears witness to the complexity and greatness of *Wuthering Heights* in its ability to engender different responses. What is needed, however, is an examination of those incidents in the novel which permit opposing interpretations. Since most of the disagreements arise over Heathcliff, I intend to offer a close reading of Heathcliff's actions, especially those near the end of the novel, in order to point out where and why readers diverge in their opinions, and hopefully thereby to clarify some of Emily Brontë's assumptions in the portrayal of her principal characters.

Surprisingly enough, little detailed attention has so far been devoted to a close examination of Heathcliff's death, a curious omission when, as Melvin R. Watson has commented, 'Heathcliff *is* the story.'[5] In part this failure to attend closely to Heathcliff is a result of the emphasis given to the structure of the novel. In his important article 'Nelly Dean and the Power of *Wuthering Heights*,' John K. Mathison showed that the structure of the novel serves the purpose of maintaining the reader's sympathy with Heathcliff until the end of the book.[6] The reader's desire to overcome the narrative limitations of Nelly and Lockwood permits him to bear with more of Heathcliff's violence than would have been the case had Heathcliff told the story. Yet emphasis on the structure of the novel has at times obscured an important question—what is the reader's final opinion of

Heathcliff? While the rhetorical devices may allow the reader to maintain sympathy with Heathcliff, surely they alone cannot turn Heathcliff into a sympathetic hero.

Readers of **Wuthering Heights** have often been self-conscious and apologetic about their sympathy towards Heathcliff. F. H. Langham, for instance, argues that 'Hindley's brutality, tyranny, and murderous violence far outdo anything of which Heathcliff can be accused on the evidence.'[7] And Langham asserts that the reader continues to sympathize with Heathcliff because of the justice of Heathcliff's desire 'to hold a place in the scheme of things.'[8] Yet Heathcliff's violence obviously troubles Langham, for he remains unwilling to credit Heathcliff with positive values, and his rather lame conclusion is that, 'for all this, in Heathcliff's behaviour there is an excess from which moral sympathy does turn away.'[9] Yet this reading, like so many, ignores the ending of the book, and therefore never entertains the possibility that the narrative method functions to gain enough of the reader's sympathy to keep his attention until the end of the novel when Heathcliff can undergo a redeeming process.

The phrase 'redeeming process,' it should be noted, has been applied to the character of Heathcliff, and not to the novel as a whole. Elliott Gose, in his interesting article, '**Wuthering Heights**: The Heath and the Hearth,'[10] has already shown that the novel embodies 'figurative image and narrative patterns,' whereby the perversion of Heathcliff and Cathy is resolved in the second generation—in Cathy II and Hareton. Gose places the change in the novel's direction near the end when Cathy resists Heathcliff's will in the incident concerning the uprooting of Joseph's mulberry bushes:

> The moral teething is complete; someone has finally resisted tyranny, and Heathcliff, seeing the pattern of his youth repeated, gives up.[11]

But the use of such a phrase as 'Heathcliff . . . gives up' indicates that Gose does not believe a positive change occurs in Heathcliff. What I wish to argue is that not only does a positive change occur at this point, but that Heathcliff learns something about himself and embodies this positive change.[12]

The first clear indication of Heathcliff's change in personality occurs near the end of the novel when Heathcliff meets Hareton rushing from the house after the younger Catherine has tormented him into throwing his books in the fire. Surprised, Heathcliff lays hold of Hareton's shoulder and asks: 'What's to do now, my lad?'[13] But Hareton refuses to answer, and Heathcliff sighs:

> 'It will be odd, if I thwart myself! . . . But, when I look for his father in his face, I find *her* every day more! How the devil is he so like? I can hardly bear to see him.'
>
> (ch xxxi p 240)

Such a statement serves both to tease and to appease the reader's expectations. Certainly Heathcliff's sudden change of mind seems to demand an explanation; and in part an explanation is offered when Heathcliff 'explains' that he sees Cathy Earnshaw in Hareton. But why this should deprive him of the will to act remains unclear. The passage seems designed to persuade the reader to accept the change while awaiting further developments. Yet most unexpectedly, at this point when the reader's curiosity about Heathcliff has been fully aroused, the novel's focus shifts abruptly. It will be recalled that Lockwood himself overheard Heathcliff's above-quoted comment while waiting at the Heights to tell him of his intended departure from Thrushcross Grange. Although Lockwood's diary brings the reader to the very point when Heathcliff's change commences, to the point where Lockwood could, if he wished, begin to observe new events for himself, Lockwood himself never witnesses the change. At this point Lockwood returns to London, and breaks off his diary with no evident curiosity about Heathcliff's future. Only when he returns briefly on a chance visit eight months later, in September 1802, does Lockwood hear from Nelly the story of Heathcliff's 'queer end.'

As a result, the nature of Heathcliff's 'queer end' appears as something of an epilogue, and no doubt this is one reason why Heathcliff's death has not received the attention which is its due. Yet to fail to take account of this section is to run the danger of becoming a Lockwood, and to remain unaware of and uninterested in the crucial change towards which the story has been moving.

Although the implications of Heathcliff's death are not spelled out, many clues are given that indicate its seriousness and importance. In her account, Nelly repeatedly emphasizes the changes in Heathcliff's character preceding his death. For instance, Heathcliff brought her to the Heights from Thrushcross Grange because he was becoming 'more and more disinclined to society' (ch xxxii p 246). What this means at the sparsely populated Heights is that Heathcliff does not want to be alone with the younger Catherine. Nelly reports that Heathcliff told her he was 'tired of seeing Catherine' (ch xxxii p 245), that he disliked the way Catherine stared at him with her 'infernal eyes' (ch xxxiii p 251). Heathcliff of course also dislikes Catherine's open defiance. And undoubtedly Gose is correct when he places the change of direction in the novel at the point where Catherine and Hareton uproot Joseph's mulberry bushes for a garden of plants and flowers imported from the

Grange. Yet Heathcliff's change is not directly contingent on Catherine's defiance. Actually, the defiance itself arouses his anger, and for a moment, as Heathcliff holds Catherine by the hair, it seems that he may murder her. But as his anger reaches its peak, he suddenly stops:

> his fingers relaxed, he shifted his grasp from her head to her arm, and gazed intently in her face. Then, he drew his hand over his eyes, stood a moment to collect himself apparently, and turning anew to Catherine, said with assumed calmness—
>
> 'You must learn to avoid putting me in a passion, or I shall really murder you, some time!'
>
> (ch xxxiii p 253)

Quite clearly Heathcliff is prevented from hitting Catherine this time because of something he sees in her eyes—the same thing he saw earlier in Hareton's eyes—a resemblance to his own Cathy. Nelly, it will be remembered, comments that Hareton and Catherine Linton have eyes that 'are precisely similar, and they are those of Catherine Earnshaw' (ch xxxiii p 254).

To the reader interested in understanding Heathcliff's change, the crucial confrontation appears a short time later when Heathcliff finds Hareton and Catherine reading by the fire after he has forbade any further relationship. Nelly first relates how 'they lifted their eyes together, to encounter Mr Heathcliff,' and then makes the above-quoted comment of how similar their eyes are to those of Catherine Earnshaw. Yet the loquacious Nelly has almost nothing to say about Heathcliff's reaction at this important juncture. She merely comments:

> I suppose this resemblance disarmed Mr Heathcliff: he walked to the hearth in evident agitation, but it quickly subsided, as he looked at the young man; or, I should say, altered its character, for it was there yet.
>
> (ch xxxiii p 254)

Unusually vague at this point, Nelly can only 'suppose' that the resemblance disturbed Heathcliff. Thus, curiously enough, Emily Brontë deliberately eschews all overt explanation of Heathcliff's behaviour, leaving it open to the reader's interpretation. This no doubt explains why the novel has generated so many widely varying explanations.

Although the positive reasons for Heathcliff's discomposure may remain mysterious, Emily Brontë takes pains to tell us the reasons that *do not* affect Heathcliff. Heathcliff himself states that he forsakes the chances of revenge neither from pity nor because he has lost the power:

> 'I could do it [take revenge]; and none could hinder me. But where is the use? I don't care for striking, I can't take the trouble to raise my hand! That sounds as

> if I had been labouring the whole time, only to exhibit a fine trait of magnanimity. It is far from being the case—I have lost the faculty of enjoying their destruction, and I am too idle to destroy for nothing.'
>
> (ch xxxiii p 255)

Heathcliff's inaction could be construed as altogether unmotivated. But such an 'explanation' requires careful qualification, since Heathcliff himself understands the apparent absurdity of his change of heart, and thus anticipates the reader's possible objection:

> 'It is a poor conclusion, is it not,' he observed, having brooded a while on the scene he had just witnessed. 'An absurd termination to my violent exertions? I get levers and mattocks to demolish the two houses, and train myself to be capable of working like Hercules, and when everything is ready, and in my power, I find the will to lift a slate off either roof has vanished!'
>
> (ch xxxiii pp 254-5)

Although Heathcliff's seeming lack of motivation has led a number of critics to ask whether the novel does not fail artistically in the last section, surely such a reaction misses the point: Emily Brontë recognized that Heathcliff's end was 'queer'; she wanted the reader to puzzle over its meaning.

For the reader to understand Heathcliff's death, the novel demands an intuitive leap from the designedly ambiguous evidence to the ultimate meaning of Heathcliff's change. The very structure of the novel indicates that such a leap is imperative. Since neither Nelly nor Lockwood understands Heathcliff, the reader must overcome the narrators' lack of perception by means of his own insight. Thus the reader finds himself in a position remarkably akin to that described by eighteenth- and early nineteenth-century philosophers where it seemed problematic that man could ever know the 'ultimate reality' (the Kantian Ding-an-sich) when he was limited to his perception of sense data or surface phenomena.[14] Interestingly, Heathcliff at the end of the novel seems to transcend his previous limitations to attain a new mode of perception. The unusual nature of this change is difficult to explain without the context of Romantic metaphysical thought, but is clarified when compared with some strikingly similar examples cited by Schopenhauer in his major work *Die Welt als Wille und Vorstellung* (usually translated as *The World as Will and Idea*).[15] Schopenhauer describes an experience and an attitude to the phenomenal world of which Emily Brontë provides a concrete character example. The one account, while it does not necessarily give rise to the other, helps us to understand it.

Schopenhauer, following Kant, believed that all objects in the material world were but the objectification of another dimension. In Kantian terms this other dimension was called the noumenal world; Schopenhauer preferred to call it 'the Will.' Schopenhauer claimed:

every individual is transitory only as phenomenon, but as thing-in-itself is timeless, and therefore endless. But it is also only as phenomenon that an individual is distinguished from the other things of the world; as thing-in-itself he is the will which appears in all, and death destroys the illusion which separates his consciousness from that of the rest: this is immortality. His exemption from death, which belongs to him only as thing-in-itself, is for the phenomenon one with the immortality of the rest of the external world.[16]

Steeped in the writings of Plato and Kant, Schopenhauer believed that man could never be happy in this world until he had grasped the basic fact that the phenomenal world which he saw around him, and of which he was a part, was only a shadow of the real world; until he did so, he would continue to pursue unreal ends that would prove transitory. To gain such an understanding, the individual must see through the transitory nature of the world conditioned by the Kantian categories of time and space to the eternal noumenal world where space and time cease to exist.[17] As soon as the individual understood that all phenomena were mere objectifications of the one Will, he would then see the absurdity of striving for transitory and unreal goals, and attempt to realize himself as part of the underlying world Will.

Schopenhauer said that the first step in recognizing that the phenomenal world was only a shadow of the Will would be taken when a man recognized, 'in all beings his own inmost and true self.'[18] What Schopenhauer describes is precisely what happens to Heathcliff. His change commences when he sees the resemblance of the younger Catherine and Hareton to his Cathy, and when he perceives that they are living out the patterns of his own youth. Seeing through exterior appearances, he begins at this point to understand that his life force (Will) is identical with that working in Catherine and Hareton. No longer does he see people merely as phenomena; he is able to see through to their noumenal existence. Of Hareton, he says:

> 'Five minutes ago, Hareton seemed a personification of my youth, not a human being. I felt to him in such a variety of ways, that it would have been impossible to have accosted him rationally. . . . His startling likeness to Catherine connected him fearfully with her.'
>
> (ch xxxiii p 255)

Heathcliff realizes that Nelly (and possibly the reader as well) will misunderstand him when he says that Hareton resembles Catherine Earnshaw. As Hindley's son, Hareton is Cathy's nephew, and would have the Earnshaw features. But Heathcliff is not referring simply to a family resemblance. He says, 'That, however, which you may suppose the most potent to arrest my imagination, is actually the least, for what is not connected with her to me?' (ch xxxiii p 255). Moreover Heathcliff is

beginning to perceive that *all* individuals are mere objectifications of the single world force. Everywhere he looks he finds that 'the most ordinary faces of men and women,' even his own features 'mock [him] with a resemblance' to his Cathy (ch xxxiii p 255). Even objects begin to resemble Cathy: 'I cannot look down to this floor, but her features are shaped on the flags! In every cloud, in every tree—filling the air at night, and caught by glimpses in every object by day, I am surrounded with her image!' (ch xxxiii p 255).

So far what has been described of Heathcliff's change is consonant with Romantic neo-platonism in general. But Schopenhauer's innovation in Kantian thought was his claim that as soon as an individual understood completely that phenomenally different objects were all products of the same world Will, then the individual's volition would cease, since he would see that all differences in the world were only seeming differences. This applies to Heathcliff, since his volition ceases as soon as he sees the spirit of his Cathy in the world around him. His new knowledge of the nature of the world quiets his will.[19]

Interestingly enough, as soon as Heathcliff begins his change, he once again becomes the principal figure of interest. In the middle section of the novel, Heathcliff occupies less of our attention as the stories of the second generation 'people of calm'—Hareton, Catherine, and Linton—are developed at length. That Heathcliff should become a relatively minor figure in the middle section is only natural, since his sole interest at this time is his desire for revenge. Miriam Allott notes: 'At the very point where his need for vengeance dies, Heathcliff does in fact fully revive *as* Heathcliff, that is to say, as the powerfully compelling and complex figure of the first part of the story.'[20] However, this description is only partly correct. When Heathcliff resumes his place at centre stage, he is not the old Heathcliff, but a changing Heathcliff. Our interest revives because of his change and his 'queer end.'

Heathcliff's death, sometimes described as suicide, has long been a source of confusion, but it becomes less so when seen in relation to Schopenhauer's description. In terms remarkably similar to those of Emily Brontë, Schopenhauer gives a full explanation of the type of 'suicide' which Heathcliff represents:

> There is a species of suicide which seems to be quite distinct from the common kind, though its occurrence has perhaps not yet been fully established. It is starvation, voluntarily chosen on the ground of extreme asceticism. All instances of it, however, have been accompanied and obscured by much religious fanaticism, and even superstition. Yet it seems that the absolute denial of will may reach the point at which the will shall be wanting to take the necessary nourishment for the support of the natural life. This kind of suicide is so far

from being the result of the will to live, that such a completely resigned ascetic only ceases to live because he has already altogether ceased to will. No other death than that by starvation is in this case conceivable (unless it were the result of some special superstition); for the intention to cut short the torment would itself be a stage in the assertion of will.[21]

When Schopenhauer says that the reason for this type of death is 'extreme asceticism,' he means that the person becomes so completely absorbed in the attainment of the spiritual life that he neglects the material world. In Heathcliff's case, his 'spiritual reunion' with Cathy so completely overpowers him that he cannot be reached by normal motives. So powerfully does his vision of reunion with Cathy affect him, that he unwittingly starves himself. When Schopenhauer described such starvation cases, he was not speaking entirely theoretically, but attempting to explain a number of historic incidents. He cites several examples, including one which occurred in England in the 1830s, with which Emily Brontë might easily have been acquainted.[22] Certainly Heathcliff's death follows closely Schopenhauer's pattern.

As Schopenhauer explains, a death such as Heathcliff's is actually the opposite of suicide: the person dies, not because he hates the world, but because he has discovered he need not take the world seriously. In fact, such a person cannot be said to 'will' at all. He dies because he has completely lost all will—even the will to eat. The frequently made claim that Heathcliff 'deliberately wills his own death'[23] is a distortion of the text. When Nelly asks Heathcliff whether he has a 'feeling of illness' or whether he is 'afraid of death,' Heathcliff is surprised:

> 'Afraid? No! . . . I have neither a fear, nor a presentiment, nor a hope of death. Why should I? With my hard constitution, and temperate mode of living, and unperilous occupations, I ought to, and probably *shall* remain above ground, till there is scarcely a black hair on my head.'
>
> (ch xxxiii p 256)

To suggest that he deliberately *does* anything is patently absurd; something happens to him over which he has no control.[24]

Indeed, Heathcliff's comments suggest that he is losing all control over his body. He says, 'And yet I cannot continue in this condition! I have to remind myself to breathe—almost to remind my heart to beat!' (ch xxxiii p 256). The passage could be treated as hyperbole, designed to show that Heathcliff is losing all interest in life. However, Schopenhauer discussed this very question of the possibility of a person's losing all interest in willing and so forgetting to breathe. Noting that the question whether breathing belongs to the set of voluntary or involuntary movements is disputed, Schopen-hauer concludes that although various people have attempted to explain breathing as a mixed function, it can actually be included in the set of voluntary actions:

> However, we are finally obliged to number it [breathing] with expressions of will which result from motives. For other motives, i.e., mere ideas, can determine the will to check it or accelerate it, and, as is the case with every other voluntary action, it seems to us that we could give up breathing altogether and voluntarily suffocate. And in fact we could do so if any other motive influenced the will sufficiently strongly to overcome the pressing desire for air.[25]

In Heathcliff's case, a motive exists almost strong enough to overcome his desire for air. He exclaims:

> 'I have a single wish, and my whole being and faculties are yearning to attain it. They have yearned towards it so long, and so unwaveringly, that I'm convinced it *will* be reached—and *soon*—because it has devoured my existence. I am swallowed in the anticipation of its fulfilment.'
>
> (ch xxxiii p 256)

The 'single wish' is, of course, his desire for reunification with Cathy.

In his discussions of the possibility of an enlightened individual's dying as a result of starvation or suffocation, Schopenhauer generally conceived of the case in terms of the individual's denial of his will. Heathcliff's death, however, may not appear immediately to follow this pattern, since Heathcliff claimed that his will was swallowed up by the single desire of rejoining Cathy. Moreover, the question still remains as to why Heathcliff should become assured of his reunification with Cathy at the moment when he sees in the growing relationship between Catherine and Hareton a reminder of his love for Cathy. Both points are clarified when one recalls what Cathy meant to Heathcliff. Their relationship is not presented as an ordinary love affair, but as the meeting and mingling of two people such that each completes the other. When Cathy explained to Nelly—'I *am* Heathcliff'—she was expressing the feeling that Heathcliff and she were the same substance. It will be recalled that in her dream at the Grange, Cathy found that her 'misery arose from the separation that Hindley had ordered' between Heathcliff and herself (ch xii p 107). She does not mean that they are united sexually, but that they are made of the same 'stuff.' Heathcliff's recognition of his own life patterns in the lives of Hareton and Catherine teaches him that Cathy and he, although phenomenally different, are in essence part of the one Universal Will. This knowledge enables him to understand that he has not lost Cathy, that they are still one. Their bodies are only transitory phenomena; their real nature has never been divided or separated because it partakes of the Universal Will. As a result of this new knowledge, Heathcliff loses all interest in existing as a part of nature, surrenders all volition, and thus delivers himself from any individual existence.[26] He has become conscious that his own nature is identical with the kernel of the world, and thus identical with Catherine's nature.

In the mind of the layman, Schopenhauer's philosophy of the denial of the will has been misconstrued; the belief has arisen that he advocated suicide as a remedy to existence in a world of sorrow. But Schopenhauer always maintained strongly that one could not escape this world merely through death; suicide, he contended, was not a denial of the will, but an assertion of the will. To escape the phenomenal world forever, and so overcome death, one had to attain consciousness of the essential oneness of all objects. Consequently if Heathcliff is to be reunified with Cathy in a noumenal existence, it is not enough that Cathy should have died, but that she should have died eternally to this world.

But is this the case? Although Cathy's death resembles Heathcliff's in a number of important respects, Emily Brontë has chosen to de-emphasize those positive results which arise from Heathcliff's achievement in denying his will. Hints are given that suggest Cathy gives up the world freely for a better world, but the full implications of her death are left to be worked out later in Heathcliff's death. In her comment following Cathy's death, Nelly sums up the reader's puzzled reaction to Cathy:

> To be sure, one might have doubted, after the wayward and impatient existence she had led, whether she merited a haven of peace at last.
>
> (ch xvi pp 137-8)

Yet the sight of Cathy's corpse convinces Nelly that Cathy has achieved peace:

> One might doubt in seasons of cold reflection, but not then, in the presence of her corpse. It asserted its own tranquillity, which seemed a pledge of equal quiet to its former inhabitant.
>
> (ch xvi p 138)

As was the case with Heathcliff, critical opinion has divided over the quality of Cathy's death. The reason for this is that Emily Brontë has again deliberately created an ambiguity. For instance, after the quarrel between Heathcliff and Edgar that causes her fatal illness, Cathy locks herself in her room and asks Nelly to tell Edgar that she is 'in danger of being seriously ill.' Then she adds: 'I wish it may prove true. He has startled and distressed me shockingly! I want to frighten him' (ch xi p 100). These comments seem those of a confused girl, not those of a Schopenhauerian saint. And at this point in the novel, surely Cathy is confused. Although she realizes early that she and Heathcliff are one, she is untrue to this perception when she attempts to compro-

mise with the social world by marrying Edgar. Later, however, when confronted with Heathcliff and her husband, she is forced to choose between them. For a time she tries to blame her plight on Nelly, but soon realizes the failure of her attempted compromise and chooses death as the only solution. When Edgar finally discovers Cathy in her distracted mood, after she has locked herself in her room for three days, she has already made her decision. She tells Edgar:

> 'What you touch at present, you may have; but my soul will be on that hilltop before you lay hands on me again. I don't want you, Edgar; I'm past wanting you.'
>
> (ch xii p 109)

This speech might be regarded as another act of petulance on Cathy's part, originating from her irritation at Edgar's failing to come to her immediately, but the following events show this interpretation to be false. As soon as Cathy recognizes that she has no further use for the conventional social world, but requires the freedom represented by the moors, she loses her will. She does not commit suicide. In fact she no longer talks about refusing to eat; she simply acquiesces to all around her.

An important reason for the reader's uncertainty about Cathy's death is that the structure of the novel does not permit him to observe Cathy's crisis. The narrative takes the reader to the beginning of Cathy's change, but then, when the reader is most interested in understanding Cathy's anger and remorse, Emily Brontë interposes the story of Heathcliff's marriage to Isabella. As was noted in the case of Heathcliff's change, the reader remains uninformed of the meaning of the crisis; moreover, with Cathy, the reader is not even permitted to observe the change. Again the novel *forces* him to infer a great deal. After her narration of the events of Heathcliff's marriage, Nelly describes the new Cathy:

> The flash of her eyes had been succeeded by a dreamy and melancholy softness; they no longer gave the impression of looking at the objects around her; they appeared always to gaze beyond, and far beyond—you would have said out of this world.
>
> (ch xv p 131)

Thus Emily Brontë again presents us with a *fait accompli*. Although she permits us to observe the beginning of Cathy's change, we are not allowed to witness the process. This type of narrative structure is designed to invite reader-participation and interpretation.

That Cathy near her death understands more about the nature and implications of her relationship with Heathcliff than does Heathcliff is revealed during Heathcliff's last visit to her at the Grange.[27] After the first wild embrace, Heathcliff looks at Cathy, and sees that she is dying. He cries out: 'Oh, Cathy! Oh, my life! how can I bear it?' (ch xv p 132). Cathy, however, perceives at once that Heathcliff is concerned primarily, not with *her* death, but with *his* own coming separation from her. Unafraid of death, Cathy is angered at Heathcliff's own selfish fears; she attempts to help him overcome his egoistic desires, and begs him to help her recapture their original feeling of oneness. When Heathcliff continues resentful, Cathy affirms that the ordinary, perceived world (including the phenomenal aspect of Heathcliff) does not interest her any longer:

> 'That is not *my* Heathcliff. I shall love mine yet; and take him with me—he's in my soul. And,' added she, musingly, 'the thing that irks me most is this shattered prison, after all. I'm tired, tired of being enclosed here. I'm wearying to escape into that glorious world, and to be always there; not seeing it dimly through tears, and yearning for it through the walls of an aching heart; but really with it, and in it. Nelly, you think you are better and more fortunate than I; in full health and strength. You are sorry for me—very soon that will be altered. I shall be sorry for *you*. I shall be incomparably beyond and above you all.'
>
> (ch xv p 134)

Whereas Cathy understands that the earthly Heathcliff is not the real Heathcliff, and that later she will take the real Heathcliff to her 'glorious world,' Heathcliff at this point still believes that death will separate them forever and does not understand that he can follow her. This lesson he learns only at the end of the novel. Cathy's highly mystical statement that the selfish Heathcliff, concerned only with his own suffering, is not the real Heathcliff, that the real Heathcliff lives in her soul, is clarified for the reader when Heathcliff, near the time of his death, finally realizes that he is united to Cathy in essence.

At the time of Cathy's death, however, Heathcliff does not understand how he can be reunified with Cathy; therefore he believes that in her death he has lost all chance to satisfy his desires to be one with another person. Again Schopenhauer is astute in describing what will happen to a man of immense will who finds that all his longings for the infinite must remain unsatisfied:

> If, now, a man is filled with an exceptionally intense pressure of will,—if with burning eagerness he seeks to accumulate everything to slake the thirst of his egoism, and thus experiences, as he inevitably must, that all satisfaction is merely apparent, that the attained end never fulfils the promise of the desired object, the final appeasing of the fierce pressure of will, but that when fulfilled the wish only changes its form, and now torments him in a new one; and indeed that if at last all wishes are exhausted, the pressure of will itself remains without any conscious motive, and makes itself known to him with fearful pain as a feeling of terrible desolation and emptiness; if from all this, which in the case of the ordinary degrees of volition is only felt in a small measure, and only produces the ordinary degree of melancholy, in the case of him who is a manifesta-

tion of will reaching the point of extraordinary wickedness, there necessarily springs an excessive inward misery, an eternal unrest, an incurable pain; he seeks indirectly the alleviation which directly is denied him,—seeks to mitigate his own suffering by the sight of the suffering of others, which at the same time he recognises as an expression of his power. The suffering of others now becomes for him an end in itself, and is a spectacle in which he delights . . .[28]

Schopenhauer's description helps us to understand Heathcliff's violence; it is the result of his immense will that cannot find an object.

The extent of Heathcliff's absorption in his own ego causes his violence against other people, especially Linton and Catherine. His violence offers proof that he has not understood the basic identity of his own nature with that of others. Yet he is dimly aware that some sort of reunion with Cathy would be possible if only he could find the means. It will be recalled that at Cathy's death he had cried: 'Not *there*—not in heaven—not perished—where?' (ch xvi p 139). In a vague, intuitive way, Heathcliff understands that Cathy has not been annihilated;[29] yet he cannot understand in what way she still exists. Ironically, all the time Heathcliff implores Cathy to come *in* to him, and he attempts to go *out* to her, he denies such a union by continually asserting his will over other people.

Heathcliff's awareness of his unreadiness to join Catherine is implicit in his much misunderstood explanation for his cruelty to Isabella. He says: 'It is a moral teething, and I grind with greater energy, in proportion to the increase of pain' (ch xiv p 128). Morality is usually associated with actions done for the benefit of others. But Heathcliff does not want to go to the orthodox heaven, and therefore does not attempt to lay up good works. For Heathcliff, to be moral means to realize fully his innermost being, that is, to achieve a state of mind in which he can be unified with Cathy—a state of grace that has no connection with good works. As Schopenhauer comments:

> In the might with which the bad man asserts life, and which exhibits itself to him in the sufferings which he inflicts on others, he measures how far he is from the surrender and denial of that will, the only possible deliverance from the world and its miseries.[30]

His cruelty to others does not, of course, make Heathcliff worthy of Cathy; it simply shows him the distance he has to travel to attain the ideal of willessness.[31] In a similar way, Baudelaire was to develop his perversities to feel their human significance, to discover in a negative fashion the humanity he was abusing. For a person such as Heathcliff, the greatest danger is to abandon the search for his own higher self in the pursuit of social relations and personal happiness.

This Schopenhauerian account also makes sense of the puzzling dual ending of ***Wuthering Heights.*** It will be recalled that although Lockwood feels that Cathy, Heathcliff, and Edgar are at peace in the grave under the benign sky, the local people do not agree. The shepherd boy claims to have seen Heathcliff and a woman wandering the moors at night. G. D. Klingopulos has suggested that the ending of the novel is ambiguous, leaving the reader uncertain which interpretation to accept.[32] Indeed, Allan Brick has asserted that Lockwood's statement is merely another instance of his naiveté.[33] Yet there is no reason why these two endings should be contradictory. Both accounts are true. Lockwood is correct if one assumes that as object, Heathcliff and Cathy are dead; their phenomenal existence is completed. But their noumenal existence can never be finished. As people, they were simply the objectification of the universal will which is the eternal force of the universe. Their intrinsic 'other' selves—manifestations of the eternal will—are still alive vitalizing the world.

Notes

1. Mildred G. Christian, 'The Brontës.' *Victorian Fiction: A Guide to Research,* ed. Lionel Stevenson (Cambridge, Mass. 1964) 244. See also J. H. Miller's statement: '*Wuthering Heights* is . . . a work with which no reader has felt altogether at ease.' *The Disappearance of God* (Cambridge, Mass. 1963) 162.

2. Ruth M. Adams, '*Wuthering Heights*: The Land East of Eden.' *Nineteenth-Century Fiction* XIII (June 1958) 6. This belief in the 'perversity' of the novel's values is often presented in a qualified form; Miriam Allott, for example, has suggested that Emily Brontë's piety forced her to reject the qualities Heathcliff represents. Professor Allott, however, concedes that the 'rejection' of Heathcliff is by no means final. See '*Wuthering Heights*: The Rejection of Heathcliff?' *Essays in Criticism* VIII (January 1958) 46.

3. 'Lockwood's Dreams and the Exegesis of *Wuthering Heights.*' *Nineteenth-Century Fiction* XIV (September 1959) 109.

4. Shannon, *Nineteenth-Century Fiction* XIV 105.

5. Melvin R. Watson, 'Tempest in the Soul: The Theme and Structure of *Wuthering Heights.*' *Nineteenth-Century Fiction* IV (September 1949) 89. The best account to date of Heathcliff's actions in relation to the novel's themes is Frederick T. Flahiff's recent introduction to the Macmillan edition of *Wuthering Heights* (Toronto 1968).

6. *Nineteenth-Century Fiction* XI (September 1956) 106-29.

7. F. H. Langham, '*Wuthering Heights.*' *Essays in Criticism* XV (July 1965) 310. See also Arnold Kettle, *An Introduction to the English Novel* (London 1951) I 107-22.

8. F. H. Langham, 310.

9. Ibid., 311.

10. Elliott Gose, '*Wuthering Heights*: The Heath and the Hearth.' *Nineteenth-Century Fiction* XXI (June 1966). Gose is attempting to refute (quite successfully, I believe) the arguments of Richard Chase and Wade Thompson that the central characters are portrayed as perverse. See Richard Chase, 'The Brontës: A Centennial Observance.' *Kenyon Review* IX (Autumn 1947) 487-506; Wade Thompson, 'Infanticide and Sadism in *Wuthering Heights.*' *PMLA* LXXVIII (March 1963) 69-74.

11. Elliott Gose, 18.

12. Richard Chase, in the article cited in n 10. alleges that no such learning process takes place, but he has offered no evidence for this belief.

13. *Wuthering Heights,* ed. William M. Sale Jr, Norton Critical Edition (New York 1963) 239 (ch xxxi). All future page references are to this edition and are indicated parenthetically.

14. See Allan R. Brick, '*Wuthering Heights*: Narrators, Audience, and Message.' *College English* XXI (November 1959) 83-4.

15. It is impossible to argue that Emily Brontë had actually read any of the works of Schopenhauer, since the extent of her reading is unknown. However, Charlotte Brontë's characterization of Emily as an immature genius, secluded from the world, and relying entirely on her own imagination is no longer acceptable (Charlotte's preface to the 1850 edition of *Wuthering Heights*). Even if it were not that Charlotte herself, in another passage, describes the extreme dependence of the entire family on books and study, Emily's period as a schoolteacher at Law Hill, Halifax, and her period abroad studying at the Hégers' in Brussels indicate that she had more opportunity to read and study than Charlotte revealed. By the time they left Brussels, Emily and Charlotte both read French fairly fluently, and Charlotte mentions her sister's rapid progress in learning German (letter to Ellen Nussey, July 1842), but the extent of Emily's knowledge of German literature remains uncertain. However in the 1830s and 1840s it was unnecessary to read German in the original to learn something of German philosophy. The Brontës' favourite journal, *Blackwood's,* reviewed and commented on a great deal of German literature and philosophy. Moreover, Emily Brontë's period in Brussels was 'at a time when romanticism was in flood in the French-speaking countries,' and she would surely

receive some account of the major figures in the home of Madame Héger (see John Hewish, *Emily Brontë: A Critical and Biographical Study* [New York 1969] 34).

16. Arthur Schopenhauer, *The World as Will and Idea,* trans. R. B. Haldane and J. Kemp, 11th impr. (London 1964) I 364 (bk IV sec 54). The first edition appeared late in 1818 (with the date 1819). The second edition appeared in 1844 in two volumes. The first volume was a slightly altered reprint of the first edition; the second volume consisted of a commentary on the first edition. The first English translation appeared in 1883.

17. Although it is unwise to place undue emphasis on Emily Brontë's short French *devoirs* which she wrote in Brussels for M. Héger, one cannot help noting their similarity to some of Schopenhauer's ideas. In 'The Butterfly,' Emily Brontë writes: 'Nature is an inexplicable puzzle, life exists on a principle of destruction; every creature must be the relentless instrument of death to the others, or himself cease to live.' This vision of a universe without meaning is transformed, however, when she recognizes that man's soul can escape into a 'new heaven' at death. Compare also her essay on King Harold where she describes him transformed on the field of battle, ready to yield to Death, whose touch will strike 'off his chains.' See *Five Essays Written in French,* trans. L. W. Nagel (Austin, Texas 1948).

18. *The World as Will and Idea* I 489 (bk IV sec 68).

19. In a curious, but extremely insightful essay on 'affinities' between Lord Byron and Emily Brontë, Margiad Evans pointed out that the clue to Emily Brontë's writing was her 'pacifism towards death.' 'Byron and Emily Brontë: An Essay.' *Life and Letters* LVII (June 1948) 203.

20. *Essays in Criticism* VIII 45.

21. *The World as Will and Idea* I 518 (bk IV sec 69).

22. Schopenhauer notes: 'Old examples of this may be found in the "Breslauer Sammlung von Natur- und Medicin-Geschichten," September 1799, p 363; in Bayle's "Nouvelles de la république des lettres," February 1685, p 189; in Zimmermann, "Ueber die Einsamkeit," vol. I p 182; in the "Histoire de l'Académie des Sciences" for 1764, an account by Houttuyn, which is quoted in the "Sammlung für praktische Aerzte," vol. I p 69. More recent accounts may be found in Hufeland's "Journal für praktische Heilkunde," vol. X p 181, and vol. XLVIII p 95; also in Nasse's "Zeitschrift für psychische Aerzte," 1819, part III p 460; and in the "Edinburgh Medical and Surgical Journal," 1809, vol. V p 319. In the year 1833 all the papers announced that the English historian, Dr Lingard, had died in January at Dover of voluntary starvation; according to later accounts, it was not he himself, but a relation of his who died.' *The World as Will and Idea* I 518-19 (bk IV sec 69).

23. Wade Thompson, *PMLA* LXXVIII 73.

24. That Heathcliff knows something is happening to him is evinced by his statement to Nelly: 'There is a strange change approaching' (ch xxxiii p 255), but clearly he has no idea what shape this change will take.

25. *The World as Will and Idea* I 151 (bk II sec 23).

26. D. H. Lawrence in his insistence that what man sees as the universe and as himself is 'not much more than a mannerism' and that the 'one glorious activity of man' is 'the getting himself into a new relationship with a new heaven and a new earth,' is the British novelist whose position most closely resembles that of Emily Brontë. See 'The Crown.' *Phoenix II,* ed. W. Roberts and H. T. Moore (New York 1968) 415.

27. Frederick Flahiff has recently suggested the possibility that Cathy has been aware of the 'substantial identification' existing between herself and Heathcliff from the time she was a little girl. See introduction to the Macmillan edition of *Wuthering Heights* (1968) xxxiii. While I agree with Flahiff that Heathcliff becomes aware of his unity with Cathy only at the end of the novel, I find that Emily Brontë's depiction of Cathy is much more complex that Flahiff concedes. Cathy, it seems to me, is quite capable of making mistakes in her assessment of what is important to her; clearly one such mistake is her marriage to Edgar in order to obtain conventional happiness.

28. *The World as Will and Idea* I 470 (bk IV sec 65).

29. Compare Heathcliff's threat to Nelly: 'You shall prove, practically, that the dead are not annihilated!' (ch xxxiv p 263).

30. *The World as Will and Idea* I 474 (bk IV sec 65).

31. The crucial point is that Heathcliff comes to *understand* his own life force in relation to the world order. The novel does not show, as J. H. Miller contends, 'that the suffering sin brings will be sufficient expiation for that sin' and will allow the sinner 'to escape to heaven' (*The Disappearance of God,* 200). For Emily Brontë, suffering does not create expiation; it may, however, be the precursor to an individual's awareness of his proper relation to the noumenal world, which would then show the individual the way to achieve his intrinsic immortality.

32. 'The Novel as Dramatic Poem (II): *Wuthering Heights.*' *Scrutiny* XIV (1946-7) 85.

33. *College English* XXI 226.

Frank Kermode (essay date 1975)

SOURCE: Kermode, Frank. "Chapter 4." In *The Classic: Literary Images of Permanence and Change*, pp. 117-41. New York: Viking Press, 1975.

[*In the following excerpt, Kermode offers a close reading of* Wuthering Heights. *In the process of evaluating other critical interpretations of the novel, Kermode identifies the various qualities that in his view make the work a modern "classic."*]

Horace provided a rule of thumb, sensible so far as it goes, when he said: *est vetus atque probus, centum qui perfecit annos,* he did not know the word 'classic' in the literary sense, but Pope was right to put it into his imitation of Horace's line:

> Who lasts a century can have no flaw,
> I hold that Wit a Classic, good in law.[1]

What they leave out is any account of the temporal agencies of survival, the most important of which is a more or less continuous chorus of voices asserting the value of the classic; and of course they say nothing about the difficulties that arise in consequence of periodic changes in language, generic expectation, ideology, and so forth. The imperialist view of the classic accommodates all these, as we have seen. It does so by modifications of the basic model (renovations, translations, and the like) and by other means we can broadly call allegorical. But ultimately it rests on the notion of a moment privileged, timeless yet capable of contemporaneity with all others, a classic in which all lesser classics participate. If we were to think of theirs as a scientific theory we should reject it either as we reject Ptolemaic astronomy (because discrepancies between the model and observational data require too many new rules—epicycles, *translationes*—for the model itself to remain credible; a new model is required) or more simply because it is not, as Popper would say, testable. It is easy to see that such criteria have no relevance. And yet such models change, by other and perhaps obscurer laws. We are less able to rest easy with the imperial model in its purity.

A new model would require us in the first place to abandon the notion of the absolute classic and consider, more simply, the Horatian case, the text which continues to be read several generations after it was written. A classic, then, is a book that is read a long time after it was written; one might want to qualify this by adding 'without institutional constraint', 'by the competent' and perhaps other rules. Once we made this new start we can see some of the problems in quite a different light. *Translationes* become transitions from a past to a present system of beliefs, language, generic expectations; renovations become very specific attempts to establish the relevance of a document which has had a good chance of losing it. The *querelle* persists, but with major changes in the historiographical assumptions of the two sides.

These are some of the topics I have to consider in this last chapter. There are others, all related to the ones I have mentioned; the most important is the extreme variety of response characteristic of the modern reading of the classic. But I daresay it is best to approach these questions by way of a single familiar text; and I have chosen **Wuthering Heights** for what I take to be good reasons. It meets the requirement that it is read in a generation far separated from the one it was presented to; and it has other less obvious advantages. It happens that I had not read the novel for many years; furthermore, although I could not be unaware that it had suffered a good deal of interpretation, and had been the centre of quarrels, I had also omitted to read any of this secondary material. These chances put me in a position unfamiliar to the teacher of literature; I could consider my own response to a classic more or less untrammelled by too frequent reading, and by knowledge of what it had proved possible, or become customary, to say about it. This strikes me as a happy situation, though some may call it shameful. Anyway, it is the best way I can think of to arrive at some general conclusions about the classic, though I daresay those conclusions will sound more like a programme for research than a true ending to this briefer exercise.

I begin, then, with a partial reading of **Wuthering Heights** which represents a straightforward encounter between a competent modern reader (the notion of competence is, I think, essential, however much you may think this demonstration falls short of it) and a classic text. However, in assuming this role, I could not avoid noticing some remarks that are not in the novel at all, but in Charlotte Brontë's Biographical Notice of her sisters, in which she singles out a contemporary critic as the only one who got her sister's book right. 'Too often,' she says, 'do reviewers remind us of the mob of Astrologers, Chaldeans and Soothsayers gathered before the "writing on the wall", and unable to read the characters or make known the interpretation.' One, however, has accurately read 'the Mene, Mene, Tekel, Upharsin of an original mind' and 'can say with confidence, "This is the interpretation thereof"'. This latterday Daniel was Sidney Dobell, but a modern reader who looks him up in the hope of coming upon what would after all be a very valuable piece of information is likely to be disappointed. Very few would dream of doing so; most would mistrust the critic for whom such claims were made, or the book which lent itself to them. Few would believe that such an interpretation exists, however frequently the critics produce new 'keys'. For we don't think of the novel as a code, or a nut, that can be broken; which contains or refers to a meaning all will agree upon if it can once be presented *en clair*. We need little persuasion to believe that a good novel is not a message at all. We assume in principle the rightness of the plurality of interpretations to which I now, in ignorance of all the others, but reasonably confident that I won't repeat them, now contribute.

When Lockwood first visits Wuthering Heights he notices, among otherwise irrelevant decorations carved above the door, the date *1500* and the name *Hareton Earnshaw*. It is quite clear that everybody read and reads this (on p. 2) as a sort of promise of something else to come. It is part of what is nowadays called a 'hermeneutic code'; something that promises, and perhaps after some delay provides, explanation. There is, of course, likely to be some measure of peripeteia or trick; you would be surprised if the explanation were not, in some way, surprising, or at any rate, at this stage unpredictable. And so it proves. The expectations aroused by these inscriptions are strictly *generic*; you must know things of this kind before you can entertain expectations of the sort I mention. Genre in this sense is what Leonard Meyer (writing of music) calls 'an internalized probability system'.[2] Such a system could, but perhaps shouldn't, be thought of as constituting some sort of contract between reader and writer. Either way, the inscriptions can be seen as something other than simple elements in a series of one damned thing after another, or even of events relative to a story as such. They reduce the range of probabilities, reduce randomness, and are expected to recur. There will be 'feedback'. This may not extinguish all the informational possibilities in the original stimulus, which may be, and in this case is, obscurer than we thought, 'higher', as the information theorists say, 'in entropy'. The narrative is more than merely a lengthy delay, after which a true descendant of Hareton Earnshaw reoccupies the ancestral house; though there is little delay before we hear about him, and can make a guess if we want.

When Hareton is first discussed, Nelly Dean rather oddly describes him as 'the late Mrs. Linton's nephew'. Why not 'the late Mr. Earnshaw's son'? It is only in the previous sentence that we have first heard the name Linton, when the family of that name is mentioned as having previously occupied Thrushcross Grange. Perhaps we are to wonder how Mrs. Linton came to have a nephew named Earnshaw. At any rate, Nelly's obliquity thus serves to associate Hareton, in a hazy way, with the house on which his name is *not* carved, and with a family no longer in evidence. Only later do we discover that he is in the direct Earnshaw line, in fact, as Nelly says, 'the last of them'. So begins the provision of information which both fulfils and qualifies the early 'hermeneutic' promise; because, of course, Hareton, his inheritance restored, goes to live at the Grange. The two principal characters remaining at the end are Mr. and Mrs. Hareton Earnshaw. The other names, which have intruded on Earnshaw—Linton and Heathcliff—are extinct. In between there have been significant recursions to the original inscription—in Chapter XX Hareton cannot read it; in XXIV he can read the name but not the date.

We could say, I suppose, that this so far tells us nothing about **Wuthering Heights** that couldn't, with appropriate changes, be said of most novels. All of them contain the equivalent of such inscriptions; indeed all writing is a sort of inscription, cut memorably into the uncaused flux of event; and inscriptions of the kind I am talking about are interesting secondary clues about the nature of the writing in which they occur. They draw attention to the literariness of what we are reading, indicate that the story is a story, perhaps with beneficial effects on our normal powers of perception; above all they distinguish a *literary* system which has no constant relation to readers with interests and expectations altered by long passages of time. Or, to put it another way, Emily Brontë's contemporaries operated different probability systems from ours, and might well ignore whatever in a text did not comply with their generic expectations, dismissing the rest somehow—by skipping, by accusations of bad craftsmanship, inexperience, or the like. In short, their internalized probability systems survive them in altered and less stringent forms; we can read more of the text than they could, and of course read it differently. In fact, the only works we value enough to call classic are those which, and they demonstrate by surviving, are complex and indeterminate enough to allow us our necessary pluralities. That 'Mene, Mene, Tekel, Upharsin' has now many interpretations. It is in the nature of works of art to be open, in so far as they are 'good'; though it is in the nature of authors, and of readers, to close them.

The openness of **Wuthering Heights** might be somewhat more extensively illustrated by an inquiry into the passage describing Lockwood's bad night at the house, when, on his second visit, he was cut off from Thrushcross Grange by a storm. He is given an odd sort of bed in a bedroom-within-a-bedroom; Catherine Earnshaw slept in it and later Heathcliff would die in it. Both the bed and the lattice are subjects of very elaborate 'play'; but I want rather to consider the inscriptions Lockwood examines before retiring. There is writing on the wall, or on the ledge by his bed: it 'was nothing but a name repeated in all kinds of characters, large and small— *Catherine Earnshaw*, here and there varied to *Catherine Heathcliff*, and then again to *Catherine Linton*'. When he closes his eyes Lockwood is assailed by white letters 'which started from the dark, as vivid as spectres— the air swarmed with Catherines'. He has no idea whatever to whom these names belong, yet the expression 'nothing but a name' seems to suggest that they all belong to one person. Waking from a doze he finds the name *Catherine Earnshaw* inscribed in a book his candle has scorched.

It is true that Lockwood has earlier met a Mrs. Heathcliff, and got into a tangle about who she was, taking first Heathcliff and then Hareton Earnshaw for her husband, as indeed, we discover she, in a different sense, had also done or was to do. For she had a merely apparent kinship relation with Heathcliff—bearing his name as the wife of his impotent son and having to tolerate his ironic claim to fatherhood—as a prelude to the restoration of her true name, Earnshaw; it is her mother's story reversed. But Lockwood was not told her first name. Soon he is to encounter a ghost called Catherine Linton; but if the scribbled names signify one person he and we are obviously going to have to wait to find out who it is. Soon we learn that Mrs. Heathcliff is Heathcliff's daughter-in-law, *née* Catherine Linton, and obviously not the ghost. Later it becomes evident that the scratcher must have been Catherine Earnshaw, later Linton, a girl long dead who might well have been Catherine Heathcliff, but wasn't.

When you have processed all the information you have been waiting for you see the point of the order of the scribbled names, as Lockwood gives them: *Catherine Earnshaw, Catherine Heathcliff, Catherine Linton.* Read from left to right they recapitulate Catherine Earnshaw's story; read from right to left, the story of her daughter, Catherine Linton. The names Catherine and Earnshaw begin and end the narrative. Of course some of the events needed to complete this pattern had not occurred when Lockwood slept in the little bedroom; indeed the marriage of Hareton and Catherine is still in the future when the novel ends. Still, this is an account of the movement of the book: away from Earnshaw and back, like the movement of the house itself. And all the movement must be *through* Heathcliff.

Charlotte Brontë remarks, from her own experience, that the writer says more than he knows, and was emphatic that this was so with Emily. 'Having formed these beings, she did not know what she had done.' Of course this strikes us as no more than common sense; though Charlotte chooses to attribute it to Emily's ignorance of the world. A narrative is not a transcription of something pre-existent. And this is precisely the situation represented by Lockwood's play with the names he does not understand, his constituting, out of many scribbles, a rebus for the plot of the novel he's in. The situation indicates the kind of work we must do when a narrative opens itself to us, and contains information in excess of what generic probability requires.

Consider the names again; of course they reflect the isolation of the society under consideration, but still it is remarkable that in a story whose principal characters all marry there are effectively only three surnames, all of which each Catherine assumes. Furthermore, the Earnshaw family makes do with only three Christian names, Catherine, Hindley, Hareton. Heathcliff is a family name also, but parsimoniously, serving as both Christian name and surname; always lacking one or the other, he wears his name as an indication of his difference, and this persists after death since his tombstone is inscribed with the one word *Heathcliff*. Like Frances, briefly the wife of Hindley, he is simply a sort of interruption in the Earnshaw system.

Heathcliff is then as it were between names, as between families (he is the door through which Earnshaw passes into Linton, and out again to Earnshaw). He is often introduced, as if characteristically, standing outside, or entering, or leaving, a door. He is in and out of the Earnshaw family simultaneously; servant and child of the family (like Hareton, whom he puts in the same position, he helps to indicate the archaic nature of the house's society, the lack of sharp social division, which is not characteristic of the Grange). His origins are equally betwixt and between: the gutter or the royal origin imagined for him by Nelly; prince or pauper, American or Lascar, child of God or devil. This betweenness persists, I think: Heathcliff, for instance, fluctuates between poverty and riches; also between virility and impotence. To Catherine he is between brother and lover; he slept with her as a child, and again in death, but not between latency and extinction. He has much force, yet fathers an exceptionally puny child. Domestic yet savage like the dogs, bleak yet full of fire like the house, he bestrides the great opposites: love and death (the necrophiliac confession), culture and nature ('half-civilized ferocity') in a posture that certainly cannot be explained by any generic formula ('Byronic' or 'Gothic').

He stands also between a past and a future; when his force expires the old Earnshaw family moves into the future associated with the civilized Grange, where the insane authoritarianism of the Heights is a thing of the past, where there are cultivated distinctions between gentle and simple—a new world in the more civil south. It was the Grange that first separated Heathcliff from Catherine, so that Earnshaws might eventually live there. Of the children—Hareton, Cathy, and Linton—none physically resembles Heathcliff; the first two have Catherine's eyes (XXXIII) and the other is, as his first name implies, a Linton. Cathy's two cousin-marriages, constituting an endogamous route to the civilized exogamy of the south—are the consequence of Heathcliff's standing between Earnshaw and Linton, north and south; earlier he had involuntarily saved the life of the baby Hareton. His ghost and Catherine's, at the end, are of interest only to the superstitious, the indigenous now to be dispossessed by a more rational culture. . . .

Earnshaws persist, but they must eventually do so within the Linton culture. Catherine burns up in her transit from left to right. The quasi-Earnshaw union of Heathcliff and Isabella leaves the younger Cathy an easier passage; she has only to get through Linton Heathcliff, who is replaced by Hareton Earnshaw, Hareton has suffered part of Heathcliff's fate, moved, as it were, from Earnshaw to Heathcliff, and replaced him as son-servant, as gratuitously cruel; but he is the last of the Earnshaws, and Cathy can both restore to him the house on which his name is carved, and take him on the now smooth path to Thrushcross Grange.

Novels, even this one, were read in houses more like the Grange than the Heights, as the emphasis on the ferocious piety of the Earnshaw library suggests. The order of the novel is a civilized order; it presupposes a reader in the midst of an educated family and habituated to novel reading; a reader, moreover, who believes in the possibility of effective ethical choices. And because this is the case, the author can allow herself to meet his proper expectations without imposing on the text or on him absolute generic control. She need not, that is, know all that she is saying. She can, in all manner of ways, invite the reader to collaborate, leave to him the supply of meaning where the text is indeterminate or discontinuous, where explanations are required to fill narrative lacunae. . . .

Instances of this are provided by some of the dreams in the book.[3] Lockwood's brief dream of the spectral letters is followed by another about an interminable sermon, which develops from hints about Joseph in Catherine's Bible. The purport of this dream is obscure. The preacher Jabes Branderham takes a hint from his text and expands the seven deadly sins into seventy times seven plus one. It is when he reaches the last section that Lockwood's patience runs out, and he protests, with his own allusion to the Bible: 'He shall return no more to his house, neither shall his place know him any more.' Dreams in stories are usually given a measure of oneiric ambiguity, but stay fairly close to the narrative line, or if not, convey information otherwise useful; but this one does not appear to do so, except in so far as that text may bear obscurely and incorrectly on the question of where Hareton will end up. It is, however, given a naturalistic explanation: the rapping of the preacher on the pulpit is a dream version of the rapping of the fir tree on the window.

Lockwood once more falls asleep, but dreams again, and 'if possible, still more disagreeably than before'. Once more he hears the fir-bough, and rises to silence it; he breaks the window and finds himself clutching the cold hand of a child who calls herself Catherine Linton.

He speaks of this as a dream, indeed he ascribes to it 'the intense horror of nightmare', and the blood that runs down into the bedclothes may be explained by his having cut his hand as he broke the glass; but he does not say so, attributing it to his own cruelty in rubbing the child's wrist on the pane; and Heathcliff immediately makes it obvious that of the two choices the text has so far allowed us the more acceptable is that Lockwood was not dreaming at all.

So we cannot dismiss this dream as 'Gothic' ornament or commentary, or even as the kind of dream Lockwood has just had, in which the same fir-bough produced a comically extended dream-explanation of its presence. There remain all manner of puzzles: why is the visitant a child and, if a child, why Catherine *Linton*? The explanation, that this name got into Lockwood's dream from a scribble in the Bible is one even he finds hard to accept. He hovers between an explanation involving 'ghosts and goblins', and the simpler one of nightmare; though he has no more doubt than Heathcliff that 'it'—the child—was trying to enter. For good measure he is greeted, on going downstairs, by a cat, a brindled cat, with its echo of Shakespearian witchcraft.

It seems plain, then, that the dream is not simply a transformation of the narrative, a commentary on another level, but an integral part of it. The Branderham dream is, in a sense, a trick, suggesting a measure of rationality in the earlier dream which we might want to transfer to the later experience, as Lockwood partly does. When we see that there is a considerable conflict in the clues as to how we should read the second tapping and relate it to the first we grow aware of further contrasts between the two, for the first is a comic treatment of 491 specific and resistible sins for which Lockwood is about to be punished by exile from his home, and the second is a more horrible spectral invasion of the womb-like or tomb-like room in which he is housed. There are doubtless many other observations to be made; it is not a question of deciding which is the single right reading, but of dealing, as reader, with a series of indeterminacies which the text will not resolve.

Nelly Dean refuses to listen to Catherine's dream, one of those which went through and through her 'like wine through water'; and of those dreams we hear nothing save this account of their power. 'We're dismal enough without conjuring up ghosts and visions to perplex us,' says Nelly—another speaking silence in the text, for it is implied that we are here denied relevant information. But she herself suffers a dream or vision. After Heathcliff's return she finds herself at the signpost: engraved in its sandstone—with all the permanence that Hareton's name has on the house—are 'Wuthering Heights' to the north, 'Gimmerton' to the east, and 'Thrushcross Grange' to the south. Soft south, harsh north, and the rough civility of the market town (something like that of Nelly herself) in between. As before, these inscriptions provoke a dream apparition, a vision of Hindley as a child. Fearing that he has come to harm, she rushes to the Heights and again sees the spectral child, but it turns out to be Hareton, Hindley's son. His appearance betwixt and between the Heights and the Grange was proleptic; now he is back at the Heights, a stone in his hand, threatening his old nurse, rejecting the Grange.

And as Hindley turned into Hareton, so Hareton turns into Heathcliff, for the figure that appears in the doorway is Heathcliff.

This is very like a real dream in its transformations and displacements. It has no simple narrative function whatever, and an abridgement might leave it out. But the confusion of generations, and the double usurpation of Hindley by his son and Heathcliff, all three of them variants of the incivility of the Heights, gives a new relation to the agents, and qualifies our sense of all narrative explanations offered in the text. For it is worth remarking that no naturalistic explanation of Nelly's experience is offered; in this it is unlike the treatment of the later vision, when the little boy sees the ghost of Heathcliff and 'a woman', a passage which is a preparation for further ambiguities in the ending. Dreams, visions, ghosts—the whole pneumatology of the book is only indeterminately related to the 'natural' narrative. And this serves to muddle routine 'single' readings, to confound explanation and expectation, and to make necessary a full recognition of the intrinsic plurality of the text.

Would it be reasonable to say this: that the mingling of generic opposites—daylight and dream narratives—creates a need, which we must supply, for something that will mediate between them? If so, we can go on to argue that the text in our response to it is a provision of such mediators, between life and death, the barbaric and the civilized, family and sexual relations. The principal instrument of mediation may well be Heathcliff: neither inside nor out, neither wholly master nor wholly servant, the husband who is no husband, the brother who is no brother, the father who abuses his changeling child, the cousin without kin. And that the chain of narrators serve to mediate between the barbarism of the story and the civility of the reader—making the text itself an intermediate term between archaic and modern—must surely have been pointed out.

What we must not forget, however, is that it is in the completion of the text by the reader that these adjustments are made; and each reader will make them differently. Plurality is here not a prescription but a fact. There is so much that is blurred and tentative, incapable of decisive explanation; however we set about our reading, with a sociological or a pneumatological, a cultural or a narrative code uppermost in our minds, we must fall into division and discrepancy; the doors of communication are sometimes locked, sometimes open, and Heathcliff may be astride the threshold, opening, closing, breaking. And it is surely evident that the possibilities of interpretation increase as time goes on. The constraints of a period culture dissolve, generic presumptions which concealed gaps disappear, and we now see that the book, as James thought novels should, truly 'glories in a gap', a hermeneutic gap in which the

reader's imagination must operate, so that he speaks continuously in the text. For these reasons the rebus—*Catherine Earnshaw, Catherine Heathcliff, Catherine Linton*—has exemplary significance. It is a riddle that the text answers only silently; for example it will neither urge nor forbid you to remember that it resembles the riddle of the Sphinx—what manner of person exists in these three forms?—to which the single acceptable and probable answer involves incest and ruin.

* * *

I have not found it possible to speak of *Wuthering Heights* in this light without, from time to time, hinting—in a word here, or a trick of procedure there—at the new French criticism. I am glad to acknowledge this affinity, but it also seems important to dissent from the opinion that such 'classic' texts as this—and the French will call them so, but with pejorative intent—are essentially naïve, and become in a measure plural only by accident. The number of choices is simply too large; it is impossible that even two competent readers should agree on an authorized naïve version. It is because texts are so naïve that they can become classics. It is true, as I have said, that time opens them up; if readers were immortal the classic would be much closer to changelessness; their deaths do, in an important sense, liberate the texts. But to attribute the entire *potential* of plurality to that cause (or to the wisdom and cunning of later readers) is to fall into a mistake. The 'Catherines' of Lockwood's inscriptions may not have been attended to, but there they were in the text, just as ambiguous and plural as they are now. What happens is that methods of repairing such indeterminacy change; and, as Wolfgang Iser's neat formula has it, 'the repair of indeterminacy' is what gives rise 'to the generation of meaning'.[4]

Having meditated thus on *Wuthering Heights* I passed to the second part of my enterprise and began to read what people have been saying about the book. I discovered without surprise that no two readers saw it exactly alike; some seemed foolish and some clever, but whether they were of the party that claims to elucidate Emily Brontë's intention, or libertarians whose purpose is to astonish us, all were different. This secondary material is voluminous, but any hesitation I might have had about selecting from it was ended when I came upon an essay which in its mature authority dwarfs all the others: Q. D. Leavis's 'A Fresh Approach to *Wuthering Heights*'.[5]

Long-meditated, rich in insights, this work has a sober force that nothing I say could, or is intended to, diminish. Mrs. Leavis remarks at the outset that merely to *assert* the classic status of such a book as *Wuthering Heights* is useless; that the task is not to be accomplished by ignoring 'recalcitrant elements' or providing sophistical explanations of them. One has to show 'the nature of its success'; and this, she at once proposes, means giving up some parts of the text. 'Of course, in general one attempts to achieve a reading of a text which includes all its elements, but here I believe we must be satisfied with being able to account for some of them and concentrate on what remains.' And she decides that Emily Brontë through inexperience, and trying to do too much, leaves in the final version vestiges of earlier creations, 'unregenerate writing', which is discordant with the true 'realistic novel' we should attend to.

She speaks of an earlier version deriving from *King Lear,* with Heathcliff as an Edmund figure, and attributes to this layer some contrived and unconvincing scenes of cruelty. Another layer is the fairy-story, Heathcliff as the prince transformed into a beast; another is the Romantic incest-story: Heathcliff as brother-lover; and nearer the surface, a sociological novel, of which she has no difficulty in providing, with material from the text, a skilful account. These vestiges explain some of the incongruities and inconsistencies of the novel—for example, the ambiguity of the Catherine-Heathcliff relationship—and have the effect of obscuring its 'human centrality'. To summarize a long and substantial argument, this real novel, which we come upon clearly when the rest is cut away, is founded on the contrast between the two Catherines, the one willing her own destruction, the other educated by experience and avoiding the same fate. Not only does this cast a new light on such characters as Joseph and Nelly Dean as representatives of a culture that, as well as severity, inculcates a kind of natural piety, but enables us to see Emily Brontë as 'a true novelist . . . whose material was real life and whose concern was to promote a fine awareness of human relations and the problem of maturity'. And we can't see this unless we reject a good deal of the text as belonging more to 'self-indulgent story' than to the 'responsible piece of work' Emily was eventually able to perform. Heathcliff we are to regard as 'merely a convenience'; in a striking comparison with Dostoevsky's Stavrogin, Mrs. Leavis argues that he is 'enigmatic . . . only by reason of his creator's indecision', and that to find reasons for thinking otherwise is 'misguided critical industry'. By the same token the famous passages about Catherine's love for Heathcliff are dismissed as rhetorical excesses, obstacles to the 'real novel enacted so richly for us to grasp in all its complexity'.[6]

Now it seems very clear to me that the 'real novel' Mrs. Leavis describes *is* there, in the text. It is also clear that she is aware of the danger in her own procedures, for she explains how easy it would be to account for *Wuthering Heights* as a sociological novel by discarding certain elements and concentrating on others, which, she says, would be 'misconceiving the novel and slighting

it'. What she will not admit is that there is a sense in which all these versions are not only present but have a claim on our attention. She creates a hierarchy of elements, and does so by a peculiar archaeology of her own, for there is no *evidence* that the novel existed in the earlier forms which are supposed to have left vestiges in the only text we have, and there is no reason why the kind of speculation and conjecture on which her historical argument depends could not be practised with equal right by proponents of quite other theories. Nor can I explain why it seemed to her that the only way to establish hers as the central reading of the book was to explain the rest away; for there, after all, the others *are*. Digging and carbon-dating simply have no equivalents here; there is no way of distinguishing old signs from new; among readings which attend to the text it cannot be argued that one attends to a truer text than all the others.

It is true that 'a fine awareness of human relations', and a certain maturity, may be postulated as classic characteristics; Eliot found them in Virgil. But it is also true that the coexistence in a single text of a plurality of significances from which, in the nature of human attentiveness, every reader misses some—and, in the nature of human individuality, prefers one—is, empirically, a requirement and a distinguishing feature of the survivor, *centum qui perfecit annos*. All those little critics, each with his piece to say about *King Lear* or *Wuthering Heights,* may be touched by a venal professional despair, but at least their numbers and their variety serve to testify to the plurality of the documents on which they swarm; and though they may lack authority, sometimes perhaps even sense, many of them do point to what is *there* and ought not to be wished away.

A recognition of this plurality relieves us of the necessity of a *Wuthering Heights* without a Heathcliff, just as it does of a *Wuthering Heights* that 'really' ends with the death of Catherine, or for that matter an *Aeneid* which breaks off, as some of the moral allegorists would perhaps have liked it to, at the end of Book VI. A reading such as that with which I began Chapter 1 is of course extremely selective, but it has the negative virtue that it does not excommunicate from the text the material it does not employ; indeed, it assumes that it is one of the very large number of readings that may be generated from the text of the novel. They will of course overlap, as mine in some small measure does with that of Mrs. Leavis.

And this brings me to the point: Mrs. Leavis's reading is privileged; what conforms with it is complex, what does not is confused; and presumably all others would be more or less wrong, in so far as they treated the rejected portions as proper objects of attention. On the other hand, the view I propose does not in any way require me to reject Mrs. Leavis's insights. It supposes that the reader's share in the novel is not so much a matter of knowing, by heroic efforts of intelligence and divination, what Emily Brontë really meant—knowing it, quite in the manner of Schleiermacher, better than she did—as of responding creatively to indeterminacies of meaning inherent in the text and possibly enlarged by the action of time.

We are entering, as you see, a familiar zone of dispute. Mrs. Leavis is rightly concerned with what is 'timeless' in the classic, but for her this involves the detection and rejection of what exists, it seems to her irrelevantly or even damagingly, in the aspect of time. She is left, in the end, with something that, in her view, has not changed between the first writing and her reading. I, on the other hand, claimed to be reading a text that might well signify differently to different generations, and different persons within those generations. It is a less attractive view, I see; an encouragement to foolishness, a stick that might be used, quite illicitly as it happens, to beat history, and sever our communications with the dead. But it happens that I set a high value on these, and wish to preserve them. I think there is a substance that prevails, however powerful the agents of change; that *King Lear,* underlying a thousand dispositions, subsists in change, prevails, by being patient of interpretation; that my ***Wuthering Heights,*** sketchy and provocative as it is, relates as disposition to essence quite as surely as if I had tried to argue that it was Emily Brontë's authorized version, or rather what she intended and could not perfectly execute.

This 'tolerance to a wide variety of readings' is attacked, with considerable determination, by E. D. Hirsch, committed as he is to the doctrine that the object of interpretation is the verbal meaning of the author; I think he would be against me in all details of the present argument. For example, he says quite firmly that interpretations must be judged entire, that they stand or fall as wholes; so that he could not choose, as I do, both to accept Mrs. Leavis's 'realist' reading and to reject her treatment of Heathcliff.[7] But as I said in Chapter 2, Hirsch makes a mistake when he allows that the 'determinations' (*bestimmungen*) of literary texts are more constrained than those of legal texts; and a further difficulty arises over his too sharp distinction between criticism and interpretation. In any case he does not convince me that tolerance in these matters represents 'abject intellectual surrender'; and I was cheered to find him in a more eirenic mood in his later paper. He is surely right to allow, in the matter of meaning, some element of personal preference; the 'best meaning' is not uniform for all.

This being so one sees why it is thought possible, in theory at any rate, to practise what is called 'literary science' as distinct from criticism or interpretation: to consider the structure of a text as a system of signifiers,

as in some sense 'empty', as what, by the intervention of the reader, takes on many possible significances.[8] To put this in a different way, one may speak of the text as a system of signifiers which always shows a surplus after meeting any particular restricted reading. It was Lévi-Strauss who first spoke of a 'surplus of signifier' in relation to shamanism, meaning that the patient is cured because the symbols and rituals of the doctor offer him not a specific cure but rather a language 'by means of which unexpressed, and otherwise inexpressible, psychic states can be immediately expressed'.[9] Lévi-Strauss goes on to make an elaborate comparison with modern psychoanalysis. But as Fredric Jameson remarks, the importance of the concept lies rather in its claim for the priority of the signifier over the signified: a change which itself seems to have offered a shamanistic opportunity for the expression of thoughts formerly repressed.[10]

The consequences for literary texts are much too large for me to enter on here; among them, of course, is the by-passing of all the old arguments about 'intention'. And even if we may hesitate to accept the semiological method in its entirety we can allow, I think, for the intuitive rightness of its rules about plurality. The gap between text and meaning, in which the reader operates, is always present and always different in extent.[11] It is true that authors try, or used to try, to close it; curiously enough, Barthes reserves the term 'classic' for texts in which they more or less succeed, thus limiting plurality and offering the reader, save as accident prevents him, merely a product, a consumable. In fact what Barthes calls 'modern' is very close to what I am calling 'classic', and what he calls 'classic' is very close to what I call 'dead'.

There is, in much of the debate on these matters, a quality of outrageousness, of the *outré,* and there is no reason why this should not be taken into account. We should, however, recall that in any *querelle* it is the modern that is going to display it most palpably. The prime modern instance is the row between Raymond Picard and Roland Barthes, which followed the publication of Barthes's *Racine* in 1963. The title of Picard's brisk pamphlet puts the point of the quarrel with a familiar emphasis: "Nouvelle Critique ou nouvelle imposture" (1965), and it contrives to make Barthes sound like the critic, deplored by all though read by few, who said that Nelly Dean stood for Evil. Barthes makes of the violent but modest drama of Racine something unrestrainedly sexual; if the text doesn't fit his theory he effects a 'transformation'; he uses neologisms to give scientific dignity to absurdities, and makes of the work under consideration 'an involuntary rebus, interesting only for what it doesn't say'.[12]

Barthes's reply is splendidly polemic; the old criticism takes for granted its ideology to the degree that it is unconscious of it; its vocabulary is that of a schoolgirl (specifically, Proust's Gisèle, Albertine's friend) seventy-five years ago. But the world has changed; if the history of philosophy and the history of history have been transformed, how can that of literature remain constant? Specifically the old criticism is the victim of a disease he calls *asymbolie*; any use of language that exceeds a narrow rationalism is beyond its understanding. But the moment one begins to consider a work as it is in itself, symbolic reading becomes unavoidable. You may be able to show that the reader has made his rules wrong or applied them wrongly, but errors of this kind do not invalidate the principle. And in the second more theoretical part of this very notable document Barthes explains that in his usage a symbol is not an image but a plurality of senses; the text will have many, not through the infirmity of readers who know less history than Professor Picard, but in its very nature as a structure of signifiers. 'L'oeuvre propose, l'homme dispose.' Multiplicity of readings must result from the work's 'constitutive ambiguity', an expression Barthes borrows from Jakobson. And if that ambiguity itself does not exclude from the work the authority of its writer, then death will do so: 'By erasing the author's signature, death establishes the truth of the work, which is an enigma.'[13]

I have suggested that the death of readers is equally important, as a solvent of generic constraints. However much we know about history we cannot restore a situation in which a particular set of arbitrary rules of a probability system is taken for granted, internalized. To this extent I am firmly on Barthes's side in the dispute; and I have found much interest in his later attempts—which don't, however, command anything like total agreement—to describe the transcoding operations by which, in contemplating the classic, we filter out what can now be perceived as mere ideological deposits and contemplate the limited plurality that remains.[14]

Barthes denies the charge that on his view of the reading process one can say absolutely anything one likes about the work in question; but he is actually much less interested in defining constraints than in asserting liberties. There are some suggestive figures in his recent book *Le Plaisir du texte* (1973), from which we gather that authorial presence is somehow a ghostly necessity, like a dummy at bridge, or the shadow without which *Die Frau ohne Schatten* must remain sterile; and these are hints that diachrony, a knowledge of transient dispositions, may be necessary even to the *nouvelle critique* competently practised. Such restrictions on criticism *à outrance* can perhaps only be formulated in terms of a theory of competence and performance analogous to that of linguistics.

Though I am more than half-persuaded (largely by Dr. Jonathan Culler) that such a theory could be constructed, I am certainly not to speak of it now. It will

suffice to say that in so far as it is thought possible to teach people to read the classics it is assumed that knowledge of them is progressive. The nature of that knowledge is, however, as Barthes suggests, subject to change. Secularization multiplies the world's structures of probability, as the sociologists of religion tell us, and 'this plurality of religious legitimations is internalized in consciousness as a plurality of possibilities between which one may choose'.[15] It is this pluralism that, on the long view, denies the authoritative or authoritarian reading that insists on its identity with the intention of the author, or on its agreement with the readings of his contemporaries; or rather, it has opened up the possibilities, exploited most aggressively by the structuralists and semiologists, of regarding the text as the permanent locus of change; as something of which the permanence no longer legitimately suggests the presence and permanence of what it appears to designate.

I notice in a very recent book on *The Early Virgil*— though it is by no means a Formalist or Structuralist study—what seems a characteristic modern swerve in the interpretation of the Fourth Eclogue; the author believes that the *puer* is the poem itself, that the prophecy relates to a new golden age of poetry, an age which the Eclogue itself inaugurates; and this, like the author's remarks on the self-reflexiveness of the whole series of eclogues, seems modern, for it insists in some measure on the literarity of the work, its declared independence of the support of external reference. Even the arithmological elements in its construction serve to confirm it in this peculiar status.[16] And we see how sharply this form of poetic isolation differs from the privileged status accorded the Eclogue by the 'imperialist' critics of my first chapter: there would be, for Mr. Berg, no question of Christian prophecy in the Eclogue—there is not even any question of a reference to some recent or impending political event involving Antony or Octavius or Pollio himself. By the same token no interpretation of Virgil which depends on the assumption, in however sophisticated a form it may be presented, that his *imperium* was to be transformed into the Christian Empire, his key words—*amor, fatum, pietas, labor*—given their full significance in an eternal pattern of which he could speak without actual knowledge, would be acceptable to this kind of criticism. When we say now that the writer speaks more than he knows we are merely using an archaism; what we mean is that the text is under the absolute control of no thinking subject, or that it is not a message from one mind to another.

The classic, we may say, has been secularized by a process which recognizes its status as a literary text; and that process inevitably pluralized it, or rather forced us to recognize its inherent plurality. We have changed our views on change. We may accept, in some form, the view proposed by Michel Foucault, that our period-discourse is controlled by certain unconscious constraints, which make it possible for us to think in some ways to the exclusion of others. However subtle we may be at reconstructing the constraints of past *epistèmes,* we cannot ordinarily move outside the tacit system of our own; it follows that except by extraordinary acts of divination we must remain out of close touch with the probability systems that operated for the first readers of the *Aeneid* or of **Wuthering Heights.** And even if one argues, as I do, that there is clearly less epistemic discontinuity than Foucault's crisis-philosophy proposes, it seems plausible enough that earlier assumptions about continuity were too naïve. The survival of the classic must therefore depend upon its possession of a surplus of signifier; as in *King Lear* or **Wuthering Heights** this may expose them to the charge of confusion, for they must always signify more than is needed by any one interpreter or any one generation of interpreters. We may recall that, rather in the manner of Mrs. Leavis discarding Heathcliff, George Orwell would have liked *King Lear* better without the Gloucester plot, and with Lear having only one wicked daughter—'quite enough', he said.

If, finally, we compare this sketch of a modern version of the classic with the imperial classic that occupied me earlier, we see on the one hand that the modern view is necessarily tolerant of change and plurality whereas the older, regarding most forms of pluralism as heretical, holds fast to the time-transcending idea of Empire. Yet the new approach, though it could be said to secularize the old in an almost Feuerbachian way, may do so in a sense which preserves it in a form acceptable to changed probability systems. For what was thought of as beyond time, as the angels, or the *majestas populi Romani,* or the *imperium* were beyond time, inhabiting a fictive perpetuity, is now beyond time in a more human sense; it is here, frankly vernacular, and inhabiting the world where alone, we might say with Wordsworth, we find our happiness—our felicitous readings—or not at all. The language of the new Mercury may strike us as harsh after the songs of Apollo; but the work he contemplates stands there, in all its native plurality, liberated not extinguished by death, the death of writer and reader, unaffected by time yet offering itself to be read under our particular temporal disposition. 'The work proposes; man disposes.' Barthes's point depends upon our recalling that the proverb originally made God the disposer. The implication remains that the classic is an essence available to us under our dispositions, in the aspect of time. So the image of the imperial classic, beyond time, beyond vernacular corruption and change, had perhaps, after all, a measure of authenticity; all we need do is bring it down to earth.

Notes

1. *Ep.* [*Epistles*], II, i, 39; *Imitations of Horace,* 1st Ep. of 2nd Book, 55-6.

2. Leonard B. Meyer, *Music, the Arts and Ideas,* 1967, 8 (speaking of musical styles).

3. My subsequent reading in *Wuthering Heights* criticism (which has certainly substantiated my vague sense that there was a lot of it about) has taught me that the carved names, and Lockwood's dreams, have attracted earlier comment. Dorothy Van Ghent's distinguished essay asks why Lockwood, of all people, should experience such a dream as that of the ghost-child, and decides that the nature of the dreamer—'a man who has shut out the powers of darkness'—is what gives force to our sense of powers 'existing autonomously' both without and within. (*The English Novel: Form and Function,* 1953.) Ronald E. Fine suggests that the dreams are 'spasms of realism' and that Emily Brontë arranged the story to fit them, or as he says, lets the dreams generate the story. He emphasizes their sexual significance, and the structural relations between them, explained by the generative force of a basic dream of two lovers seeking to be reunited ('Lockwood's Dream and the Key to *Wuthering Heights*', *Nineteenth Century Fiction,* xxiv, 1969-70, 16-30). Ingeborg Nixon suggests that 'the names must have been written by Catherine after her first visit to Thrushcross Grange as a child . . . but they form a silent summary of the whole tragic dilemma'; they indicate three possibilities for Catherine, who of course chooses *Linton.* This is to give the inscriptions the most limited possible 'hermeneutic' sense, reading them back into a possible chronology and ignoring their larger function as literary or defamiliarizing signs ('A note on the Pattern of *Wuthering Heights*', *English Studies,* xlv, 1964). Cecil W. Davies notices that 'Heathcliff' is an Earnshaw name, and argues that this makes him 'in a real, though non-legal sense, a true inheritor of Wuthering Heights' ('A Reading of *Wuthering Heights*', *Essays in Criticism,* xix, 1969). Doubtless C. P. Sanger's justly celebrated essay ('The Structure of *Wuthering Heights*' (1926)) is partly responsible for the general desire to fit everything that can be fitted into legal and chronological schemes; but the effect is often to miss half the point. All these essays are reprinted, in whole or in part, in the Penguin Critical Anthology, *Emily Brontë,* ed. J.-P. Petit, 1973. Other collections include one by Miriam Allott in the Macmillan Casebook series (1970), Thomas A. Vogler's *Twentieth-Century Interpretations of 'Wuthering Heights'* (1965) and William A. Sale's Norton edition (1963).

4. 'Indeterminacy and the Reader's Response', in *Aspects of Narrative,* ed. J. Hillis Miller, 1971, 42.

5. F. R. Leavis and Q. D. Leavis, *Lectures in America,* 1969, 83-152.

6. For a different approach to Mrs. Leavis's reading see D. Donoghue, 'Emily Brontë: On the Latitude of Interpretation', *Harvard English Studies,* i, ed. M. W. Bloomfield, 1970; reprinted in *Emily Brontë,* ed. J.-P. Petit, 1973, 296-314, 316.

7. *Validity in Interpretation* [1967], 168.

8. F. Jameson, *The Prison-House of Language,* 1972, 195, compares the Frege-Carnap distinction between *Sinn* (unchanging formal organization) and *Bedeutung* (the changing significance given to the text by successive generations of readers).

9. *Structural Anthropology,* 1968, 198.

10. Jameson, 1972, 196.

11. '. . . commentaries or interpretations are generated out of an ontological lack in the text itself . . . a text can have no ultimate meaning . . . the process of interpretation . . . is properly an infinite one' (Jameson, 176, paraphrasing Jacques Derrida).

12. Picard, 135.

13. Barthes, *Critique et Vérité,* 1966, 52-3.

14. The 'cultural code' of *S/Z* (1970) serves some of the purposes of Mrs. Leavis's archaeological categories, though she is inclined to retain the period elements that he drops.

15. P. L. Berger, 'Secularization and the Problem of Plausibility,' extracted from *The Sacred Canopy* (1967) in *Sociological Perspectives,* ed. K. Thompson and J. Tunstall, 1971, 446-59; developing the thesis of Berger and T. Luckmann, *The Social Construction of Reality,* 1967.

16. William Berg, *The Early Virgil,* 1973.

John Beversluis (essay date 1975)

SOURCE: Beversluis, John. "Love and Self-Knowledge: A Study of *Wuthering Heights*." In *Heathcliff,* edited by Harold Bloom, pp. 106-13. New York: Chelsea House Publishers, 1993.

[*In the following essay, originally published in* English *in 1975, Beversluis examines the powerful emotional bond that develops between Heathcliff and Catherine in* Wuthering Heights. *While traditional critical interpretations argue that Catherine's famous assertion, "I am Heathcliff," exemplifies a unique affinity between the two characters, Beversluis finds that her assertion is inconsistent with her behavior toward Heathcliff and is a mark of her self-deception.*]

The Catherine-Heathcliff relationship has traditionally been defined in terms of reciprocal love, a love not merely sexual or romantic, but metaphysical, in character: an 'affinity' arising from a shared moral response to the world. Clifford Collins, for example, asserts that the love of Catherine for Heathcliff '. . . is the opposite of love conceived as social and conventional acceptance, the love Catherine has for Edgar which has only her conscious approval. What she feels for Heathcliff is a powerful undercurrent, an acceptance of identity below the level of consciousness. . . . It is an extension of the deepest layers of the self into another. . . .'[1] Similarly, Lord David Cecil holds that the deeper feelings of Emily Brontë's characters are '. . . only roused for someone for whom they feel a sense of affinity, that comes from the fact that they are both expressions of the same spiritual principle. Catherine does not "like" Heathcliff, but she loves him with all the strength of her being. For he, like she, is a child of the storm; and this make a bond between them, which interweaves itself with the very nature of their existence.'[2]

In this paper I wish to question the traditional interpretation of *Wuthering Heights.* More particularly, I wish to re-examine the relationship of Catherine to Heathcliff in order to determine whether the claim regarding an alleged 'affinity' between them is a plausible claim.

All such readings of *Wuthering Heights* rely heavily upon the following well-known passage:

> 'It would degrade me to marry Heathcliff now; so he shall never know how I love him; and that, not because he's handsome, Nelly, but because he's more myself than I am. Whatever our souls are made of, his and mine are the same, and Linton's is as different as a moonbeam from lightning, or frost from fire. . . . I cannot express it; but surely you and everybody have a notion that there is, or ought to be, an existence of yours beyond you. What were the use of my creation if I were entirely contained here? My great miseries in this world have been Heathcliff's miseries, and I watched and felt each from the beginning; my great thought in living is himself. If all else perished, and *he* remained, I should still continue to be; and, if all else remained, and he were annihilated, the Universe would turn to a mighty stranger. I should not seem a part of it. My love for Linton is like the foliage in the woods. Time will change it, I'm well aware, as winter changes the trees. My love for Heathcliff resembles the eternal rocks beneath—a source of little visible delight, but necessary. Nelly, I *am* Heathcliff—he's always, always in my mind—not as a pleasure, any more than I am always a pleasure to myself—but as my own being. . . .'[3]

It is, of course, true that this passage, the so-called 'I *am* Heathcliff' speech, must be central to any plausible interpretation of Catherine's relationship to Heathcliff. It is not the fact, but the kind, of centrality ascribed to this passage by the traditional interpretation that I question. Mary Visick provides a clear and representative statement of the traditional thesis. 'In the great scene with Nelly,' she writes, 'in which [Catherine] weighs up her love for the two young men and talks, for the first and only time, of her real feelings for Heathcliff as "more myself than I am," the usually hidden self looks out, and we know what she really is. . . .'[4]

It seems to me, on the contrary, that an examination of Catherine's behaviour toward Heathcliff yields results which are quite incompatible with such talk about her 'hidden', but none the less 'real', self. As I read **Wuthering Heights,** this passage can serve neither as the criterion for revealing to us the real Catherine nor for determining the character of her actual relationship to Heathcliff. I shall argue that it serves, rather, as a clear instance of her self-deception, of the false way she has of picturing herself to herself.

In this paper, then, I put fourth an interpretation of **Wuthering Heights** which constitutes a reversal of the traditional one. I will try to show that the passage I have quoted cannot bear the weight that the traditional interpretation demands that it carry. Catherine's impassioned avowals regarding Heathcliff must not be examined and assessed in isolation; rather, they must be examined in conjunction with her *total* behaviour toward him. If they are examined in this way, her behaviour is seen as contrasting significantly with her avowals, not as consistent with them. And it is her total behaviour, not simply her avowals, which defines her psychologically decisive response to Heathcliff.

* * *

In making the 'I *am* Heathcliff' speech, Catherine believes herself to be torn merely between which of two men she ought to marry. Her existential conflict is, of course, more fundamental than this. Indeed, her momentary indecision is only a symptom of this more radical conflict, a conflict involving the necessity of choosing between two very different ways of life. For, clearly, Edgar and Heathcliff do not share a common world.

The surface of this obvious fact does not, to be sure, escape Catherine's attention. But she fails utterly to grasp its full significance. We can go further. She fails even to perceive the full content of this fact. One of the chief reasons for these failures in her pre-occupation (one might almost say her obsession) with a certain picture of herself; she sees herself as powerfully, even irresistibly, attracted to Heathcliff. The traditional interpretation accepts this picture as authentically descriptive of her actual relationship to Heathcliff; I do not. In what follows I will attempt to show why.

I begin with a disclaimer. Surely such an attraction is in evidence during their early years at Wuthering Heights. As children, both reject and mock authority and the attempts on the part of authority to control them. They are wild, intractable children, who flourish in their role as 'rude savages'. They are always together. Their favourite form of amusement is to run off and spend the entire day on the moors. Their forthcoming punishment 'became a thing to laugh at'; they forgot it the minute they were reunited. As a child, Catherine's worst punishment is to be kept from Heathcliff. When her father dies, it is to Heathcliff that she turns for consolation. There is, then, throughout their childhood, a powerful bond between them.

What is not sufficiently recognized, however, is that it is a bond of a fundamentally negative character: they identify with one another in the face of a common enemy, they rebel against a particular way of life which both find intolerable. It is not enough, however, simply to reject a particular way of life; one cannot define oneself wholly in terms of what he despises. One must carve out for oneself an alternative which is more than a systematic repudiation of what he hates. A positive commitment is also necessary. The chief contrast between Catherine and Heathcliff consists in the fact that he is able to make such a commitment (together with everything it entails) while she is not. And, when the full measure of their characters has been taken, this marks them as radically dissimilar from one another, whatever their temporary 'affinities' appear to be. It requires only time for this radical dissimilarity to become explicit.

Their visit to Thrushcross Grange provides a dramatic anticipation of the change which is soon to come about in their relationship. The Lintons examine Heathcliff and ridicule him. To our surprise, Catherine participates in the ridicule. This quite unexpected behaviour on her part proves to be an ominous forecast of the quality of their subsequent relationship. After five weeks have elapsed, Catherine returns to Wuthering Heights, 'her ankle thoroughly cured, and her manners much improved'. But a more important change is immediately apparent. Heathcliff discovers that the girl who returns is no longer the 'dirty, wild counterpart of himself', but a 'lady' who has 'taken readily to fine clothes and flattery'. She finds him 'black and cross', 'funny and grim' in comparison to Edgar and Isabella. She avoids touching him, fearing that her clothing had 'gained no embellishment from its contact with his'. When he finally dashes from the room in humiliation, her response is that of the perfected conventional specimen: she cannot comprehend how her remarks could have produced such an exhibition of 'bad temper'. Bad temper! Such a description—an infallible index of the fully respectable, but unperceiving, sensibility—is concerned only with the socially unacceptable behaviour. What a 'scene' he's making! She fails totally to grasp his inner anxiety, his humiliation, the fact that she has violated him. She has become in her own person a paradigm of the very respectability, empty and loveless, against which they both had formerly rebelled, and she fails to perceive it. One might be inclined to say that after this incident Heathcliff loses her little by little. It would be more accurate to say that he gradually comes to the realization that she was never his at all.

But this incident is significant in a second way. Not only does it mark a turning-point in Catherine's relationship to Heathcliff; it signals a change in her behaviour *in general*. From now on her rebellion becomes remarkably moderate. Whereas earlier she was 'never so happy as when everyone was scolding her at once', defying them with her 'bold, saucy look, and her ready words', she now adopts a different strategy. She discovers silence to be an excellent tactic in that its employment enables one to make one's compromises almost without detection. Almost. Nelly Dean tells us (an unusually perceptive comment from her) that Catherine began to develop 'a double character without exactly intending to deceive anyone'. When Edgar calls Heathcliff 'a vulgar, young ruffian', or describes him as being 'worse than a brute', Catherine does not rise to his defence. Indeed, she makes no protest whatever; instead, she takes care not to act like him in the presence of his cultured detractors. Long before they marry, she dares not treat Edgar's sentiments with indifference, 'as if depreciation of her playmate were of scarcely any consequence to her'. She and Heathcliff spend increasingly less time together. When he touchingly produces a calendar showing how much more time she has spent with the Lintons than with him, she rebuffs him most insensitively. She calls him 'foolish' for noticing such things. And she adds that she gets 'no good' from seeing him, that he might as well be 'dumb or a baby' for all he says to amuse her, and that it is 'no company at all when people know nothing and say nothing.'

Where, one wants to ask, is the 'affinity' of which she speaks? The real Heathcliff is now intolerable to her. More and more she seeks out the society of the Lintons. Yet, when Edgar proposes marriage, she is in some sense torn, indecisive. She vacillates. It is while in this state of mind that her famous 'I *am* Heathcliff' speech occurs. In the light of her total behaviour toward him, how is this passage to be interpreted? Does it, as so many readers have supposed, exhibit the 'real' Catherine, the Catherine who still belongs, and who will always belong, to Heathcliff? I believe the answer to be, No. The passage is psychologically revealing, but not in *that* way. Her avowals regarding Heathcliff, I observed earlier, must be examined in conjunction with, and in the light of, her total behaviour toward him.

We discover who the real Catherine is in much the same manner in which we discover who anyone really is. We observe. We do not, that is to say, wish to be present only when a person is on the brink of making a resolu-

tion, or intending to turn over a new leaf. Nor are we unduly impressed with mere talk. We have hope at such times; but we neither exaggerate their importance nor (after a while) take them at face value, dissociating them from past performances and disconnecting them from future ones. So with Catherine Earnshaw. Her 'I *am* Heathcliff' speech would, perhaps, be tolerable as an acknowledgement of her past indifference toward him; as an expression of her past and present 'affinity' for him, it is not tolerable. In fact, it is outrageous. Nelly Dean is unimpressed by it; and no one, not even Nelly Dean, is an infallibly wrong judge of character. While the fact that she did not tell Catherine of Heathcliff's presence can never be condoned, her response to Catherine's speech is singularly appropriate. 'I was,' she says, 'out of patience with her folly.' Folly! It is exactly the right word. Catherine has persuaded herself that there is still some affinity on her part toward Heathcliff. But she has deceived herself. This is merely the picture of herself of which she is enamoured: Catherine and Heathcliff together on the moors as in the past. They are, however, no longer children tormenting the adults and running away for the afternoon. Catherine's participation in Heathcliff's life has by this time become imaginative rather than real. His reality pulls her up short; he is intolerable in his concreteness. In her moments of lucidity she realizes that Heathcliff's way of life exacts a price, and that she is neither willing nor able to pay it. Yet, the idealization of that way of life continues to exercise an intermittent hold upon her imagination. It is part of her double character: the wanting of two fully romanticized worlds—Edgar's and Heathcliff's—coupled with the inability of making a genuine commitment to either of them as they are.

But it is also only a picture of Heathcliff of which she is enamoured. For all her alleged 'affinity' for him, Catherine does not comprehend that his way of life is no longer to be assessed as a prolonged tantrum directed at life and its obstacles. Heathcliff has self-consciously chosen his way of life, decided what he shall become. Catherine, on the other hand, never outgrows her own tantrums, never chooses what she is to be. Although both she and Heathcliff are capable of violent action, their violence springs from different sources. Hers is emotional, arbitrary, prompted by and directed to what is immediate; his is willed, principled, teleological. Hers is grounded in irritation and self-pity; his is motivated by the desire to destroy one world and create a new one. And Catherine, by virtue of her marriage to Edgar, identifies herself with the world Heathcliff wants destroyed. She is seduced by the surface of that world, thereby showing her lack of commitment to Heathcliff and the values his way of life embodies. But she marries Edgar still hoping in some bizarre sense not to lose Heathcliff, thereby showing her lack of commitment to Edgar.

Critics ponder her chief motive for marrying Edgar. Was it his good looks? His money? The status such a marriage would enable her to achieve? Her desire to help Heathcliff? It seems to me that she has no clear motive. She simply drifts into the marriage unreflectively. And she acts in bad faith to everyone concerned.

In marrying Edgar, however, she does not betray her deepest self, for she has no self recognizable enough to betray. Nor, strictly speaking, does she betray Heathcliff, for her adult relationship to him is never defined unambiguously enough so as to constitute the condition under which an act of betrayal could *significantly* occur. Indeed, Catherine's defining characteristic appears to be her incapacity for significant action. She has preferences, does this rather than that, is found here and not there; but, because of her inability to choose, she does not act in the full, agonizing sense of the word. Her 'I *am* Heathcliff' speech, then, taken in conjunction with her total behaviour, does not reveal her love and lasting 'affinity' for him; on the contrary, it reveals her inability to love or to commit herself to anyone.

In short, Heathcliff is desirable to her only as an imaginative possibility, not as a person. Instead of abandoning the conception for the reality, she marries Edgar (another imaginative possibility) only to reject him because he is not Heathcliff. And so, in a curious sense, her imagination wins out over both. It is little wonder, therefore, that she becomes wholly incapable of living in the present, and that the specific form which her illness takes is that of a regression to the symbols and experiences of her childhood. Since the present has become unbearable, she opts for a new ideal. This time it is not Heathcliff as such, but the past, a time when her self was still undivided. What she fails to understand is that it was undivided then only because there were no choices to be made, no consequences to be endured. Nothing was unalterable. All that was needed in order for the world to come back into focus was a noisy tantrum and a day on the moors. But it was a world that can never be again. And there was room for Heathcliff in it only because it was not a world at all.

A retreat into the past conjoined with a projection of her own flaws upon others characterizes Catherine's last days on earth. She is not, however, a tragic figure; she is merely a pathetic one. She suffers, but her suffering is self-inflicted. She is not even capable of meaningful remorse; the form of her suffering is almost wholly that of self-pity, whining. It is not that her 'wrong' is a violation of her nature, and that she cannot right it. It is, rather, that she can bear the weight of no reality whatever, neither Edgar's nor Heathcliff's.

And so, never content with what is, she becomes an incurable dreamer, a dreamer obsessed with what might have been and with what (she believes) once was. She becomes given to contrasting the actual with the ideal, and to employing the latter as the basis (and the justification) for her rejection of the former. The world of her daily experience is now intolerable to her when compared to the past and what she has persuaded herself to believe was her 'real' life, her 'real' identity. She cannot see that the past was not as she now envisions it. Again she is the victim of a picture. She fails to comprehend that the past was as intolerable then as the present now appears to be. Indeed, it was so intolerable that she rejected it for the sake of her (now intolerable) present. Hence, grasping at everything, she attains nothing. And the responsibility for this she confidently assigns to others. She has been 'abominably treated'. Self-deception is no longer a mere tendency; it has become a vocation.

That this is so may be seen by noticing her settled responses to both Edgar and Heathcliff. During one of Edgar's visits prior to their marriage she, supposing that he is not observing her, pinches Nelly for alleged insubordination, then denies that she did so, and, when trapped in her lie, proceeds to slap them both. Edgar, somewhat disquieted by this spectacle, prepares to leave. Catherine, however, prevents him from doing so; she prevails upon him by employing her usual strategy: 'Well, go, if you please—get away. And now I'll cry— I'll cry myself sick.' Edgar is manipulated. He stays. He is 'a soft thing'. 'He's doomed', says Nelly Dean, 'and flies to his fate'. Again, she is right.

Catherine's treatment of Edgar after their marriage, however, is equally outrageous. She continues to see Heathcliff despite Edgar's protests; then, later, she belittles him for not having had the courage to put a stop to these visits, assuring him that Heathcliff would 'as soon lift a finger against him as the king would march his army against a colony of mice'. Edgar, however, remains with her, toward the end caring for her as devotedly as any mother would have nursed an only child, 'enduring all the annoyances that irritable nerves and a shaken reason could inflict', sacrificing his own health and knowing no limits of joy when she is once again out of danger. Yet, for Catherine, Edgar is 'one of those things that are ever found when they are least wanted. . . .' 'Return to your books,' she tells him. 'I'm glad you have a consolation, for all you had in me is gone.' Edgar has pity for her; better, he has compassion and commitment. And she loathes him for it.

Where Edgar is gentle and forbearing, Heathcliff is hard. 'I have no pity! I have no pity! The more the worms writhe, the more I yearn to crush out their entrails. It is a moral teething, and I grind with greater energy, in proportion to the increase of pain.' Earlier he had told her: 'I want you to be aware that I *know* you have treated me infernally—infernally! Do you hear? And if you think that I don't perceive it, you are a fool;

and if you think that I can be consoled by sweet words you are an idiot.' Shortly before her death he reaffirms this. She has told him that he and Edgar have broken her heart, that they have killed her. For the last time he reveals her to herself. It is she who is cruel and false. '*Why,*' he asks her, 'did you despise me? *Why* did you betray your own heart . . . ? I have not one word of comfort. You deserve this. You have killed yourself. Yes, you may kiss me and cry; and wring out my kisses and tears. They'll blight you—they'll damn you. . . . Because misery, and degradation, and death, and nothing that God or Satan could inflict would have parted us, *you,* of your own will, did it. . . . I have not broken *your* heart—*you* have broken it. . . . It is hard to forgive, and to look at those eyes, and feel those wasted hands. . . . I love my murderer—but *yours!* How can I?'

Indeed, how can he? It is impossible. And yet, of course, he does. He loves her despite the fact that her great miseries have not lately been his. But he remembers or thinks he does. Was there not a time? Surely she could not have forgotten? Hence, his rage, his violent protest, his accusations. He is reminding her.

This, too, is part of his 'moral teething'. But how, we ask, can such apparently brutal tactics count as moral? The answer to this question can only be formulated in terms of Heathcliff's earlier choices and his commitment to their consequences. The moral quality of which he speaks attaches not to his actions, but to his person. Whatever we may say of his hardness, his cruelty, his revenge, it is not mere hardness, mere cruelty, mere revenge. It is, rather, the behavioural manifestation of his own values, of a self undivided by fantasy and unmoved by tears and tantrums. Heathcliff sees that Catherine, because of her inability to choose, has negated the possibility of achieving an identity, and with it, negated her capacity to act, to hope, to love. He sees and despairs. But not simply because Catherine does not know the truth about herself. For part of what Heathcliff knows is that knowledge is not the issue. Not even self-knowledge, unless self-knowledge means the capacity to *acknowledge,* to acknowledge, who (and what) one is—in terms of one's actions—and to forgo the evasive, and essentially uncostly, policy of appealing to one's inner states, one's 'hidden' self. The real person is not, in this sense, hidden from us. On the contrary, it lies open for all who have eyes to see. The difficulty is not one of insufficient or ambiguous evidence; it is, rather, one of a capacity for discernment. And so Heathcliff's outburst, while perhaps deplorable as an isolated incident, is none the less intelligible as a teleological assault upon Catherine's carefully nurtured myth of having been abominably treated. His hardness is kinder than the softness of Edgar: it is therapeutic in intention. For Edgar desires only Catherine's physical recovery, whereas Heathcliff desires her inner purification, her

moral cleansing. When the sickness is 'unto death', the kindness of silence is not kindness at all; it is an acquiescence in the destruction of the self.

Immanuel Kant began the *Critique of Pure Reason* with the words: 'Human reason has this peculiar fate that in one species of its knowledge it is burdened by questions which, as prescribed by the very nature of reason itself, it is not able to ignore, but which, as transcending all its powers, it is also not able to answer.' This phenomenon occurs not only in man's cognitive life, but in his affectional life as well. That is, not only are there questions which cannot be answered; there are also desires that cannot be satisfied. And, like the questions, those desires are the deepest, the most recurring, the most definitive of human needs. Yet they remain desires for illusory objects. Nothing objectively real or achievable answers to them. And if it is perilous to ignore them, it is much more perilous to act for the sake of them, to allow their pursuit to become constitutive of one's way of life. They must be exposed, unmasked. Catherine's inability to risk such self-exposure is precisely what renders her permanently inaccessible to Heathcliff. Heathcliff sees this. Catherine does not. This is why Heathcliff despairs.

Notes

1. 'Theme and Conventions in *Wuthering Heights*', *The Critic* (Autumn, 1947), 43-5.

2. *Early Victorian Novelists* (New York, 1935), p. 56.

3. *Wuthering Heights* (New York, 1963), pp. 72-4.

4. *The Genesis of* Wuthering Heights (Hong Kong, 1958), p. 45.

Terry Eagleton (essay date 1975)

SOURCE: Eagleton, Terry. "*Wuthering Heights.*" In *Myths of Power: A Marxist Study of the Brontës,* pp. 98-121. London: Macmillan Press Ltd, 1975.

[*In the following essay, Eagleton examines the mythic qualities of* Wuthering Heights, *interpreting the novel as a dialectic in which the individual and society—or, passion and order—contend for dominance. Eagleton asserts that unlike Charlotte Brontë, who strives to smooth out the rough surfaces of such tensions in her novel* Jane Eyre, *Emily Brontë merely represents these realities as they are, without trying to shape them according to a larger ideal. By refusing to manipulate her art to reconcile these conflicting forces, Eagleton argues, Brontë creates a vision of life that is at once tragic, honest, and aesthetically harmonious.*]

If it is a function of ideology to achieve an illusory resolution of real contradictions, then Charlotte Brontë's novels are ideological in a precise sense—myths. In the fabulous, fairy-tale ambience of a work like *Jane Eyre,* with its dramatic archetypes and magical devices, certain facets of the complex mythology which constitutes Victorian bourgeois consciousness find their aesthetically appropriate form. Yet 'myth' is, of course, a term more commonly used of *Wuthering Heights*; and we need therefore to discriminate between different meanings of the word.

For Lucien Goldmann, 'ideology' in literature is to be sharply distinguished from what he terms 'world-view'. Ideology signifies a false, distortive, partial consciousness; 'world-view' designates a true, total and coherent understanding of social relations. This seems to me a highly suspect formulation: nothing, surely, could be more ideological than the 'tragic vision' of Pascal and Racine which Goldmann examines in *The Hidden God* [(1964)]. Even so, Goldmann's questionable distinction can be used to illuminate a crucial difference between the work of Charlotte and Emily Brontë. Charlotte's fiction is 'mythical' in the exact ideological sense I have suggested: it welds together antagonistic forces, forging from them a pragmatic, precarious coherence of interests. *Wuthering Heights* is mythical in a more traditional sense of the term: an apparently timeless, highly integrated, mysteriously autonomous symbolic universe. Such a notion of myth is itself, of course, ideologically based, and much of this chapter will be an attempt to de-mystify it. The world of *Wuthering Heights* is neither eternal nor self-enclosed; nor is it in the least unriven by internal contradictions. But in the case of this work it does seem necessary to speak of a 'world-view', a unified vision of brilliant clarity and consistency, in contrast to the dominant consciousness of Charlotte's novels. Goldmann's distinction is valuable to that limited extent: it enforces an appropriate contrast between the elaborated impersonality of Emily's novel, the 'intensive totality' of its world,[1] and Charlotte's tendentious, occasionally opportunist manipulation of materials for ideological ends, her readiness to allow a set of practical interests to predominate over the demands of disinterested exploration. If *Wuthering Heights* generally transcends those limits, it is not in the least because its universe is any less ideological, or that conflictive pressures are absent from it. The difference lies in the paradoxical truth that *Wuthering Heights* achieves its coherence of vision from an exhausting confrontation of contending forces, whereas Charlotte's kind of totality depends upon a pragmatic integration of them. Both forms of consciousness are ideological; but in so far as Emily's represents a more penetrative, radical and honest enterprise, it provides the basis for a finer artistic achievement. *Wuthering Heights* remains formally unfissured by the conflicts it dramatises; it forges its unity of vision from the very imaginative heat those conflicts generate. The book's genealogical structure is relevant here: familial relations at once provide the substance of antagonism and mould that substance into intricate shape, precipitating a tightly integrated form from the very stuff of struggle and disintegration. The genealogical structure, moreover, allows for a sharply dialectical relation between the 'personal' and 'impersonal' of a sort rare in Charlotte: the family, at once social institution and domain of intensely interpersonal relationships, highlights the complex interplay between an evolving system of given unalterable relations and the creation of individual value.

One is tempted, then, to credit Goldmann's dubious dichotomy between ideology and world-view to this extent: that if 'ideology' is a coherence of antagonisms, 'world-view' is a coherent perception of them.[2] An instance of such coherent perception may be found in Emily Brontë's early essay, **'The Butterfly'**:

> All creation is equally insane. There are those flies playing above the stream, swallows and fish diminishing their number each minute: these will become in their turn, the prey of some tyrant of air or water; and man for his amusement or his needs will kill their murderers. Nature is an inexplicable puzzle, life exists on a principle of destruction; every creature must be the relentless instrument of death to the others, or himself cease to live.[3]

This, clearly enough, is ideological to the point of prefiguring Social Darwinism; but it is difficult to imagine Charlotte having written with this degree of generalising impersonal poise, this fluent projection of fearful private vision into total, lucid statement. Charlotte, indeed, seems to have recognised something of this difference with her sister. 'In some points', she once wrote, 'I consider Emily somewhat of a theorist; now and then she broaches ideas which strike my sense as much more daring and original than practical.'[4] Defining the issue as a contrast between theory and practice seems significant: the cautious empiricist greets the totalising visionary with a mixture of respect and reservation. It certainly seems true of Charlotte that her *imaginative* daring is not coupled with any equivalent moral or intellectual boldness. Hunsden, Rochester, Shirley, Paul Emmanuel: all combine a civilised moderation with their Romantic radicalism, which could hardly be said of Heathcliff. Heathcliff, as Lockwood finds to his cost, is precisely *not* a rough diamond; he conceals no coy Hunsden-like affection beneath his barbarous behaviour.

The difference between Charlotte and Emily can be expressed another way. The spite, violence and bigotry which in *Wuthering Heights* are aspects of the narrative are in parts of Charlotte's fiction qualities of the narration. *Wuthering Heights* trades in spite and stiff-neckedness, but always 'objectively', as the power of its tenaciously detailed realism to survive unruffled even the gustiest of emotional crises would suggest. Malice and narrowness in Charlotte's work, by contrast, are occasionally authorial as well as thematic, so that characters and events are flushed with the novelist's ideological intentions, bear the imprint of her longings and anxieties. This, as I have argued, is less true of *Jane Eyre,* where a subtler epistemology grants the objective world its own relative solidity: we feel the menacingly autonomous existence of Brocklehurst, Mrs Reed, even Bertha, as we do not with Père Silas, Madame Walravens or Job Barraclough. Because these figures are so directly the spontaneous precipitates of authorial fantasy, they have both the vividness and the vacuity of Lucy Snowe's dazed perceptions. We are almost never at a loss what to think about a Charlotte character, which could hardly be said of *Wuthering Heights.* No mere critical hair-splitting can account for the protracted debate over whether Heathcliff is hero or demon, Catherine tragic heroine or spoilt brat, Nelly Dean shrewd or stupid. The narrative techniques of the novel are deliberately framed to preserve these ambivalences; those of Charlotte Brontë allow us fairly direct access to a single, transparent, controlling consciousness which maintains its dominance even when its bearer is in practice subdued and subordinated.

I have said that *Wuthering Heights* remains unriven by the conflicts it releases, and it contrasts as such with those Charlotte works which are formally flawed by the strains and frictions of their 'content'. Charlotte's fiction sets out to reconcile thematically what I have crudely termed 'Romance' and 'realism' but sometimes displays severe structural disjunctions between the two; *Wuthering Heights* fastens thematically on a near-absolute antagonism between these modes but achieves, structurally and stylistically, an astonishing unity between them. Single incidents are inseparably high drama and domestic farce, figures like Catherine Earnshaw contradictory amalgams of the passionate and the pettish. There seems to me an ideological basis to this paradoxical contrast between the two sisters' works. Charlotte's novels, as I have suggested, are ideological in that they exploit fiction and fable to smooth the jagged edges of real conflict, and the evasions which that entails emerge as aesthetic unevennesses—as slanting, overemphasis, idealisation, structural dissonance. *Wuthering Heights,* on the other hand, confronts the tragic truth that the passion and society it presents are not fundamentally reconcilable—that there remains at the deepest level an ineradicable contradiction between them which refuses to be unlocked, which obtrudes itself as the very stuff and secret of experience. It is, then, precisely the imagination capable of confronting this tragic duality which has the power to produce the aesthetically superior work—which can synchronise in its internal structures the most shattering passion with the most rigorous realist control. The more authentic social and moral recognitions of the book, in other words, generate a finer artistic control; the unflinching-

ness with which the novel penetrates into fundamental contradictions is realised in a range of richer imaginative perceptions.

The primary contradiction I have in mind is the choice posed for Catherine between Heathcliff and Edgar Linton. That choice seems to me the pivotal event of the novel, the decisive catalyst of the tragedy; and if this is so, then the crux of *Wuthering Heights* must be conceded by even the most remorselessly mythological and mystical of critics to be a social one. In a crucial act of self-betrayal and bad faith, Catherine rejects Heathcliff as a suitor because he is socially inferior to Linton; and it is from this that the train of destruction follows. Heathcliff's own view of the option is not, of course, to be wholly credited: he is clearly wrong to think that Edgar 'is scarcely a degree dearer [to Catherine] than her dog, or her horse'.[5] Linton lacks spirit, but he is, as Nelly says, kind, honourable and trustful, a loving husband to Catherine and utterly distraught at her loss. Even so, the perverse act of *mauvaise foi* by which Catherine trades her authentic selfhood for social privilege is rightly denounced by Heathcliff as spiritual suicide and murder:

> '*Why* did you betray your own heart, Cathy? I have not one word of comfort. You deserve this. You have killed yourself. Yes, you may kiss me, and cry; and ring out my kisses and tears: they'll blight you—they'll damn you. You loved me—then what *right* had you to leave me? What right—answer me—for the poor fancy you felt for Linton? Because misery and degradation, and death, and nothing that God or Satan could inflict would have parted us, *you,* of your own will, did it. I have not broken your heart—*you* have broken it; and in breaking it, you have broken mine.'[6]

Like Lucy Snowe, Catherine tries to lead two lives: she hopes to square authenticity with social convention, running in harness an ontological commitment to Heathcliff with a phenomenal relationship to Linton. 'I *am* Heathcliff!' is dramatically arresting, but it is also a way of keeping the outcast at arm's length, evading the challenge he offers. If Catherine is Heathcliff—if identity rather than relationship is in question—then their estrangement is inconceivable, and Catherine can therefore turn to others without violating the timeless metaphysical idea Heathcliff embodies. She finds in him an integrity of being denied or diluted in routine social relations; but to preserve that ideal means reifying him to a Hegelian essence, sublimely untainted by empirical fact. Heathcliff, understandably, refuses to settle for this: he would rather enact his essence in existence by becoming Catherine's lover. He can, it seems, be endowed with impressive ontological status only at the price of being nullified as a person.

The uneasy alliance of social conformity and personal fulfilment for which Charlotte's novels works is not, then, feasible in the world of *Wuthering Heights*;

Catherine's attempt to compromise unleashes the contradictions which will drive both her and Heathcliff to their deaths. One such contradiction lies in the relation between Heathcliff and the Earnshaw family. As a waif and orphan, Heathcliff is inserted into the close-knit family structure as an alien; he emerges from that ambivalent domain of darkness which is the 'outside' of the tightly defined domestic system. That darkness is ambivalent because it is at once fearful and fertilising, as Heathcliff himself is both gift and threat. Earnshaw's first words about him make this clear: "'See here, wife! I was never so beaten with anything in my life: but you must e'en take it as a gift of God; though it's as dark almost as if it came from the devil.'"[7] Stripped as he is of determinate social relations, of a given function within the family, Heathcliff's presence is radically gratuitous; the arbitrary, unmotivated event of his arrival at the Heights offers its inhabitants a chance to transcend the constrictions of their self-enclosed social structure and gather him in. Because Heathcliff's circumstances are so obscure he is available to be accepted or rejected simply for himself, laying claim to no status other than a human one. He is, of course, proletarian in appearance, but the obscurity of his origins also frees him of any exact social role; as Nelly Dean muses later, he might equally be a prince. He is ushered into the Heights for no good reason other than to be arbitrarily loved; and in this sense he is a touchstone of others' responses, a liberating force for Cathy and a stumbling-block for others. Nelly hates him at first, unable to transcend her bigotry against the new and non-related; she puts him on the landing like a dog, hoping he will be gone by morning. Earnshaw pets and favours him, and in doing so creates fresh inequalities in the family hierarchy which become the source of Hindley's hatred. As heir to the Heights, Hindley understandably feels his social role subverted by this irrational, unpredictable intrusion.

Catherine, who does not expect to inherit, responds spontaneously to Heathcliff's presence; and because this antagonises Hindley she becomes after Earnshaw's death a spiritual orphan as Heathcliff is a literal one. Both are allowed to run wild; both become the 'outside' of the domestic structure. Because his birth is unknown, Heathcliff is a purely atomised individual, free of generational ties in a novel where genealogical relations are of crucial thematic and structural importance; and it is because he is an internal *émigré* within the Heights that he can lay claim to a relationship of direct personal equality with Catherine who, as the daughter of the family, is the least economically integral member. Heathcliff offers Catherine a friendship which opens fresh possibilities of freedom within the internal system of the Heights; in a situation where social determinants are insistent, freedom can mean only a relative independence of given blood-ties, of the settled, evolving, predictable structures of kinship. Whereas in Charlotte's

fiction the severing or lapsing of such relations frees you for progress up the class-system, the freedom which Cathy achieves with Heathcliff takes her down that system, into consorting with a 'gypsy'. Yet 'down' is also 'outside', just as gypsy signifies 'lower class' but also asocial vagrant, classless natural life-form. As the eternal rocks beneath the woods, Heathcliff is both lowly and natural, enjoying the partial freedom from social pressures appropriate to those at the bottom of the class-structure. In loving Heathcliff, Catherine is taken outside the family and society into an opposing realm which can be adequately imaged only as 'Nature'.

The loving equality between Catherine and Heathcliff stands, then, as a paradigm of human possibilities which reach beyond, and might ideally unlock, the tightly dominative system of the Heights. Yet at the same time Heathcliff's mere presence fiercely intensifies that system's harshness, twisting all the Earnshaw relationships into bitter antagonism. He unwittingly sharpens a violence endemic to the Heights—a violence which springs both from the hard exigencies imposed by its struggle with the land, and from its social exclusiveness as a self-consciously ancient, respectable family. The violence which Heathcliff unwittingly triggers is turned against him: he is cast out by Hindley, culturally deprived, reduced to the status of farm-labourer. What Hindley does, in fact, is to invert the potential freedom symbolised by Heathcliff into a parody of itself, into the non-freedom of neglect. Heathcliff is robbed of liberty in two antithetical ways: exploited as a servant on the one hand, allowed to run wild on the other; and this contradiction is appropriate to childhood, which is a time of relative freedom from convention and yet, paradoxically, a phase of authoritarian repression. In this sense there is freedom for Heathcliff neither within society nor outside it; his two conditions are inverted mirror-images of one another. It is a contradiction which encapsulates a crucial truth about bourgeois society. If there is no genuine liberty on its 'inside'—Heathcliff is oppressed by work and the familial structure—neither is there more than a caricature of liberty on the 'outside', since the release of running wild is merely a function of cultural impoverishment. The friendship of Heathcliff and Cathy crystallises under the pressures of economic and cultural violence, so that the freedom it seems to signify ('half-savage and hardy, and free'[8]) is always the other face of oppression, always exists in its shadow. With Heathcliff and Catherine, as in Charlotte's fiction, bitter social reality breeds Romantic escapism; but whereas Charlotte's novels try to trim the balance between them, *Wuthering Heights* shows a more dialectical interrelation at work. Romantic intensity is locked in combat with society, but cannot wholly transcend it; your freedom is bred and deformed in the shadow of your oppression, just as, in the adult Heathcliff, oppression is the logical consequence of the exploiter's 'freedom'.

Just as Hindley withdraws culture from Heathcliff as a mode of domination, so Heathcliff acquires culture as a weapon. He amasses a certain amount of cultural capital in his two years' absence in order to shackle others more effectively, buying up the expensive commodity of gentility in order punitively to reenter the society from which he was punitively expelled. This is liberty of a kind, in contrast with his previous condition; but the novel is insistent on its ultimately illusory nature. In oppressing others the exploiter imprisons himself; the adult Heathcliff's systematic tormenting is fed by his victims' pain but also drains him of blood, impels and possesses him as an external force. His alienation from Catherine estranges him from himself to the point where his brutalities become tediously perfunctory gestures, the mechanical motions of a man who is already withdrawing himself from his own body. Heathcliff moves from being Hindley's victim to becoming, like Catherine, his own executioner.

Throughout *Wuthering Heights,* labour and culture, bondage and freedom, Nature and artifice appear at once as each other's dialectical negations and as subtly matched, mutually reflective. Culture—gentility—is the opposite of labour for young Heathcliff and Hareton; but it is also a crucial economic weapon, as well as a product of work itself. The delicate spiritless Lintons in their crimson-carpeted drawing-room are radically severed from the labour which sustains them; gentility grows from the production of others, detaches itself from that work (as the Grange is separate from the Heights), and then comes to dominate the labour on which it is parasitic. In doing so, it becomes a form of self-bondage; if work is servitude, so in a subtler sense is civilisation. To some extent, these polarities are held together in the yeoman-farming structure of the Heights. Here labour and culture, freedom and necessity, Nature and society are roughly complementary. The Earnshaws are gentlemen yet they work the land; they enjoy the freedom of being their own masters, but that freedom moves within the tough discipline of labour; and because the social unit of the Heights—the family—is both 'natural' (biological) and an economic system, it acts to some degree as a mediation between Nature and artifice, naturalising property relations and socialising blood-ties. Relationships in this isolated world are turbulently face-to-face, but they are also impersonally mediated through a working relation with Nature. This is not to share Mrs Q. D. Leavis's view of the Heights as 'a wholesome primitive and natural unit of a healthy society';[9] there does not, for instance, seem much that is wholesome about Joseph. Joseph incarnates a grimness inherent in conditions of economic exigency, where relationships must be tightly ordered and are easily warped into violence. One of *Wuthering Heights'* more notable achievements is ruthlessly to de-mystify the Victorian notion of the family as a pious, pacific space within social conflict. Even so, the Heights does pin to-

gether contradictions which the entry of Heathcliff will break open. Heathcliff disturbs the Heights because he is simply superfluous: he has no defined place within its biological and economic system. (He may well be Catherine's illegitimate half-brother, just as he may well have passed his two-year absence in Tunbridge Wells.) The superfluity he embodies is that of a sheerly human demand for recognition; but since there is no space for such surplus within the terse economy of the Heights, it proves destructive rather than creative in effect, straining and overloading already taut relationships. Heathcliff catalyses an aggression intrinsic to Heights society; that sound blow Hindley hands out to Catherine on the evening of Heathcliff's first appearance is slight but significant evidence against the case that conflict starts only with Heathcliff's arrival.

The effect of Heathcliff is to explode those conflicts into antagonisms which finally rip the place apart. In particular, he marks the beginnings of that process whereby passion and personal intensity separate out from the social domain and offer an alternative commitment to it. For farming families like the Earnshaws, work and human relations are roughly coterminous: work is socialised, personal relations mediated through a context of labour. Heathcliff, however, is set to work meaninglessly, as a servant rather than a member of the family; and his fervent emotional life with Catherine is thus forced outside the working environment into the wild Nature of the heath, rather than Nature reclaimed and worked up into significant value in the social activity of labour. Heathcliff is stripped of culture in the sense of gentility, but the result is a paradoxical intensifying of his fertile imaginative liaison with Catherine. It is fitting, then, that their free, neglected wanderings lead them to their adventure at Thrushcross Grange. For if the Romantic childhood culture of Catherine and Heathcliff exists in a social limbo divorced from the minatory world of working relations, the same can be said in a different sense of the genteel culture of the Lintons, surviving as it does on the basis of material conditions it simultaneously conceals. As the children spy on the Linton family, that concealed brutality is unleashed in the shape of bulldogs brought to the defence of civility. The natural energy in which the Linton's culture is rooted bursts literally through to savage the 'savages' who appear to threaten property. The underlying truth of violence, continuously visible at the Heights, is momentarily exposed; old Linton thinks the intruders are after his rents. Culture draws a veil over such brute force but also sharpens it: the more property you have, the more ruthlessly you need to defend it. Indeed, Heathcliff himself seems dimly aware of how cultivation exacerbates 'natural' conflict, as we see in his scornful account of the Linton children's petulant squabbling; cultivation, by pampering and swaddling 'natural' drives, at once represses serious physical violence and breeds a neurasthenic sensitivity which allows selfish impulse free rein. 'Natural' aggression is nurtured both by an excess and an absence of culture—a paradox demonstrated by Catherine Earnshaw, who is at once wild and pettish, savage and spoilt. Nature and culture, then, are locked in a complex relation of antagonism and affinity: the Romantic fantasies of Heathcliff and Catherine, and the Romantic Linton drawing-room with its gold-bordered ceiling and shimmering chandelier, both bear the scars of the material conditions which produced them—scars visibly inscribed on Cathy's ankle. Yet to leave the matter there would be to draw a purely formal parallel. For what distinguishes the two forms of Romance is Heathcliff: his intense communion with Catherine is an uncompromising rejection of the Linton world.

The opposition, however, is not merely one between the values of personal relationship and those of conventional society. What prevents this is the curious impersonality of the relationship between Catherine and Heathcliff. Edgar Linton shows at his best a genuine capacity for tender, loving fidelity; but this thrives on obvious limits. The limits are those of the closed room into which the children peer—the glowing, sheltered space within which those close, immediate encounters which make for both tenderness and pettishness may be conducted. Linton is released from material pressures into such a civilised enclave; and in that sense his situation differs from that of the Heights, where personal relations are more intimately entwined with a working context. The relationship of Heathcliff and Catherine, however, provides a third term. It really is a personal relationship, yet seems also to transcend the personal into some region beyond it. Indeed, there is a sense in which the unity the couple briefly achieve is narrowed and degutted by being described as 'personal'. In so far as 'personal' suggests the liberal humanism of Edgar, with his concern (crudely despised by Heathcliff) for pity, charity and humanity, the word is clearly inapplicable to the fierce mutual tearings of Catherine and Heathcliff. Yet it is inadequate to the positive as well as the destructive aspects of their love. Their relationship is, we say, 'ontological' or 'metaphysical' because it opens out into the more-than-personal, enacts a style of being which is more than just the property of two individuals, which suggests in its impersonality something beyond a merely Romantic-individualist response to social oppression. Their relationship articulates a depth inexpressible in routine social practice, transcendent of available social languages. Its impersonality suggests both a savage depersonalising and a paradigmatic significance; and in neither sense is the relationship wholly within their conscious control. What Heathcliff offers Cathy is a non- or pre-social relationship, as the only authentic form of living in a world of exploitation and inequality, a world where one must refuse to measure oneself by the criteria of the class-structure and so must appear inevitably subversive. Whereas in Charlotte's novels the love-relationship takes you into society, in **Wuthering Heights** it drives you out of it. The love between Heathcliff and Catherine is an intuitive intimacy raised to cosmic status, by-passing the mediation of the 'social'; and this, indeed, is both its strength and its limit. Its non-sociality is on the one hand a revolutionary refusal of the given language of social roles and values; and if the relationship is to remain unabsorbed by society it must therefore appear as natural rather than social, since Nature is the 'outside' of society. On the other hand, the novel cannot realise the meaning of that revolutionary refusal in social terms; the most it can do is to *universalise* that meaning by intimating the mysteriously impersonal energies from which the relationship springs.

Catherine, of course, *is* absorbed: she enters the civilised world of the Lintons and leaves Heathcliff behind, to become a 'wolfish, pitiless' man. To avoid incorporation means remaining as unreclaimed as the wild furze: there is no way in this novel of temporising between conformity and rebellion. But there is equally no way for the revolutionary depth of relationship between Heathcliff and Catherine to realise itself as a historical force; instead, it becomes an elusive dream of absolute value, an incomparably more powerful version of Charlotte's myth of lost origins. Catherine and Heathcliff seek to preserve the primordial moment of pre-social harmony, before the fall into history and oppression. But it won't do to see them merely as children eternally fixated in some Edenic infancy: we do not see them merely as children, and in any case to be 'merely' a child is to endure the punitive pressures of an adult world. Moreover, it is none of Heathcliff's fault that the relationship remains 'metaphysical': it is Catherine who consigns it to unfulfilment. Their love remains an unhistorical essence which fails to enter into concrete existence and can do so, ironically, only in death. Death, indeed, as the ultimate outer limit of consciousness and society, is the locus of Catherine and Heathcliff's love, the horizon on which it moves. The absolutism of death is prefigured, echoed back, in the remorseless intensity with which their relationship is actually lived; yet their union can be achieved only in the act of abandoning the actual world.

Catherine and Heathcliff's love, then, is pushed to the periphery by society itself, projected into myth; yet the fact that it seems *inherently* convertible to myth spotlights the threshold of the novel's 'possible consciousness'. I take that phrase from Lukács and Goldmann to suggest those restrictions set on the consciousness of a historical period which only a transformation of real social relations could abolish—the point at which the most enterprising imagination presses against boundaries which signify not mere failures of personal perception but the limits of what can be historically said. The force Heathcliff symbolises can be truly realised only in some more than merely individu- alist form; *Wuthering Heights* has its roots not in that narrowed, simplified Romanticism which pits the lonely rebel against an anonymous order, but in that earlier, more authentic Romantic impulse which posits its own kind of 'transindividual' order of value, its own totality, against the order which forces it into exile. Heathcliff may be Byronic, but not in the way Rochester is: the novel counterposes social convention not merely with contrasting personal life-styles but with an alternative world of meaning. Yet it is here that the limits of 'pos- sible consciousness' assert themselves: the offered to- talities of Nature, myth and cosmic energy are forced to figure as asocial worlds unable to engage in more than idealist ways with the society they subject to judge- ment. The price of universality is to be fixed eternally at a point extrinsic to social life—fixed, indeed, at the moment of death, which both manifests a depth chal- lengingly alien to the Lintons and withdraws the char- acter from that conventional landscape into an isolated realm of his own.

Nature, in any case, is no true 'outside' to society, since its conflicts are transposed into the social arena. In one sense the novel sharply contrasts Nature and society; in another sense it grasps civilised life as a higher distilla- tion of ferocious natural appetite. Nature, then, is a thoroughly ambiguous category, inside and outside so- ciety simultaneously. At one level it represents the un- salvaged region beyond the pale of culture; at another level it signifies the all-pervasive reality of which cul- ture itself is a particular outcropping. It is, indeed, this ambiguity which supplies the vital link between the childhood and adult phases of Heathcliff's career. Heathcliff the child is 'natural' both because he is al- lowed to run wild and because he is reduced as Hind- ley's labourer to a mere physical instrument; Heathcliff the adult is 'natural' man in a Hobbesian sense: an ap- petitive exploiter to whom no tie or tradition is sacred, a callous predator violently sundering the bonds of cus- tom and piety. If the first kind of 'naturalness' is anti- social in its estrangement from the norms of 'civilised' life, the second involves the unsociality of one set at the centre of a world whose social relations are inhu- man. Heathcliff moves from being natural in the sense of an anarchic outsider to adopting the behaviour natu- ral to an insider in a viciously competitive society. Of course, to be natural in both senses is at a different level to be unnatural. From the viewpoint of culture, it is unnatural that a child should be degraded to a savage, and unnatural too that a man should behave in the ob- scene way Heathcliff does. But culture in this novel is as problematical at Nature. There are no cool Arnoldian touchstones by which to take the measure of natural de- generacy, since the dialectical vision of *Wuthering Heights* puts culture into question in the very act of ex- ploring the 'naturalness' which is its negation. Just as being natural involves being either completely outside

or inside society, as roaming waif or manipulative land- lord, so culture signifies either free-wheeling Romantic fantasy or that well-appointed Linton drawing-room. The adult Heathcliff is the focus of these contradictions: as he worms his way into the social structure he be- comes progressively detached in spirit from all it holds dear. But *contradiction* is the essential emphasis. Heath- cliff's schizophrenia is symptomatic of a world in which there can be no true dialectic between culture and Na- ture—a world in which culture is merely refuge from or reflex of material conditions, and so either too estranged from or entwined with those conditions to offer a viable alternative.

I take it that Heathcliff, up to the point at which Cathy rejects him, is in general an admirable character. His account of the Grange adventure, candid, satirical and self-aware as it is, might itself be enough to enforce this point; and we have in any case on the other side only the self-confessedly biased testimony of Nelly Dean. Even according to Nelly's grudging commentary, Heathcliff as a child is impressively patient and uncom- plaining (although Nelly adds 'sullen' out of spite), and the heart-rending cry he raises when old Earnshaw dies is difficult to square with her implication that he felt no gratitude to his benefactor. He bears Hindley's vindic- tive treatment well, and tries pathetically to keep cultur- ally abreast of Catherine despite it. The novel says quite explicitly that Hindley's systematic degradation of Heathcliff 'was enough to make a fiend of a saint';[10] and we should not therefore be surprised that what it does, more precisely, is to produce a pitiless capitalist landlord out of an oppressed child. Heathcliff the adult is in one sense an inversion, in another sense an organic outgrowth, of Heathcliff the child. Heathcliff the child was an isolated figure whose freedom from given ge- nealogical ties offered, as I have argued, fresh possibili- ties of relationship; Heathcliff the adult is the atomic capitalist to whom relational bonds are nothing, whose individualism is now enslaving rather than liberating. The child knew the purely negative freedom of running wild; the adult, as a man vehemently pursuing ends progressively alien to him, knows only the delusory freedom of exploiting others. The point is that such freedom seems the only kind available in this society, once the relationship with Catherine has collapsed; the only mode of self-affirmation left to Heathcliff is that of oppression which, since it involves self-oppression, is no affirmation at all. Heathcliff is a self-tormentor, a man who is in hell because he can avenge himself on the system which has robbed him of his soul only by battling with it on its own hated terms. If as a child he was outside and inside that system simultaneously, wan- dering on the moors and working on the farm, he lives out a similar self-division as an adult, trapped in the grinding contradiction between a false social self and the true identity which lies with Catherine. The social self is false, not because Heathcliff is only apparently brutal—that he certainly is—but because it is contradic-torily related to the authentic selfhood which is his pas-sion for Catherine. He installs himself at the centre of conventional society, but with wholly negative and in-imical intent; his social role is a calculated self-contradiction, created first to further, and then fiercely displace, his asocial passion for Catherine.

Heathcliff's social relation to both Heights and Grange is one of the most complex issues in the novel. Lock-wood remarks that he looks too genteel for the Heights; and indeed, in so far as he represents the victory of capitalist property-dealing over the traditional yeoman economy of the Earnshaws, he is inevitably aligned with the world of the Grange. Heathcliff is a dynamic force which seeks to destroy the old yeoman settlement by dispossessing Hareton; yet he does this partly to re-venge himself on the very Linton world whose weapons (property deals, arranged marriages) he deploys so effi-ciently. He does this, moreover, with a crude intensity which is a quality of the Heights world; his roughness and resilience link him culturally to *Wuthering Heights,* and he exploits those qualities to destroy both it and the Grange. He is, then, a force which springs out of the Heights yet subverts it, breaking beyond its constric-tions into a new, voracious acquisitiveness. His capital-ist brutality is an extension as well as a negation of the Heights world he knew as a child; and to that extent there is continuity between his childhood and adult pro-tests against Grange values, if not against Grange weap-ons. Heathcliff is subjectively a Heights figure opposing the Grange, and objectively a Grange figure undermin-ing the Heights; he focuses acutely the contradictions between the two worlds. His rise to power symbolises at once the triumph of the oppressed over capitalism and the triumph of capitalism over the oppressed.

He is, indeed, contradiction incarnate—both progressive and outdated, at once caricature of and traditionalist protest against the agrarian capitalist forces of Thrush-cross Grange. He harnesses those forces to worst the Grange, to beat it at its own game; but in doing so he parodies that property-system, operates against the Lin-tons with an unLinton-like explicitness and extremism. He behaves in this way because his 'soul' belongs not to that world but to Catherine; and in that sense his true commitment is an 'outdated' one, to a past, increasingly mythical realm of absolute personal value which capi-talist social relations cancel. He embodies a passionate human protest against the marriage-market values of both Grange and Heights at the same time as he cal-lously images those values in caricatured form. Heathc-liff exacts vengeance from that society precisely by ex-travagantly enacting its twisted priorities, becoming a darkly satirical commentary on conventional mores. If he is in one sense a progressive historical force, he be-longs in another sense to the superseded world of the Heights, so that his death and the closing-up of the

house seem logically related. In the end Heathcliff is defeated and the Heights restored to its rightful owner; yet at the same time the trends he epitomises triumph in the form of the Grange, to which Hareton and young Catherine move away. Hareton wins and loses the Heights simultaneously; dispossessed by Heathcliff, he repossesses the place only to be in that act assimilated by Thrushcross Grange. And if Hareton both wins and loses, then Heathcliff himself is both ousted and victori-ous.

Quite who has in fact won in the end is a matter of critical contention. Mrs Leavis and Tom Winnifrith both see the old world as having yielded to the new, in con-trast to T. K. Meier, who reads the conclusion as 'the victory of tradition over innovation'.[11] The critical con-tention reflects a real ambiguity in the novel. In one sense, the old values have triumphed over the disrup-tive usurper: Hareton has wrested back his birthright, and the qualities he symbolises, while preserving their authentic vigour, will be fertilised by the civilising grace which the Grange, in the form of young Catherine, can bring. Heathcliff's career appears from his perspective as a shattering but short-lived interlude, after which true balance may be slowly recovered. In a more obvi-ous sense, however, the Grange has won: the Heights is shut up and Hareton will become the new squire. Heath-cliff, then, has been the blunt instrument by which the remnants of the Earnshaw world have been transformed into a fully-fledged capitalist class—the historical me-dium whereby that world is at once annihilated and el-evated to the Grange. Thrushcross values have entered into productive dialogue with rough material reality and, by virtue of this spiritual transfusion, ensured their continuing survival; the Grange comes to the Heights and gathers back to itself what the Heights can yield it. This is why it will not do to read the novel's conclusion as some neatly reciprocal symbolic alliance between the two universes, a symmetrical symbiosis of bourgeois realism and upper-class cultivation. Whatever unity the book finally establishes, it is certainly not symmetrical: in a victory for the progressive forces of agrarian capi-talism, Hareton, last survivor of the traditional order, is smoothly incorporated into the Grange.

There is another significant reason why the 'defeat' of Heathcliff cannot be read as the resilient recovery of a traditional world from the injuries it has suffered at his hands. As an extreme parody of capitalist activity, Heathcliff is also an untypical deviation from its norms; as a remorseless, crudely transparent revelation of the real historical character of the Grange, he stands askew to that reality in the very act of becoming its paradigm. It *is* true that Heathcliff, far from signifying some merely ephemeral intervention, is a type of the histori-cally ascendant world of capital; but because he typifies it so 'unnaturally' the novel can move beyond him, into the gracefully gradualistic settlement symbolised by the union of Hareton and young Catherine. Heathcliff is finally fought off, while the social values he incarnates can be prised loose from the self-parodic mould in which he cast them and slowly accommodated. His undisguised violence, like the absolutism of his love, come to seem features of a past more brutal but also more heroic than the present; if the decorous, muted milieu of the Grange will not easily accommodate such passionate intensities, neither will it so readily reveal the more unpleasant face of its social and economic power. The 'defeat' of Heathcliff, then, is at once the transcending of such naked power and the collapse of that passionate protest against it which was the inner secret of Heathcliff's outrageous dealings.

We can now ask what these contradictions in the figure of Heathcliff actually amount to. It seems to me possible to decipher in the struggle between Heathcliff and the Grange an imaginatively transposed version of that contemporary conflict between bourgeoisie and landed gentry which I have argued is central to Charlotte's work. The relationship holds in no precise detail, since Heathcliff is not literally an industrial entrepreneur; but the double-edgedness of his relation with the Lintons, with its blend of antagonism and emulation, reproduces the complex structure of class-forces we found in Charlotte's fiction. Having mysteriously amassed capital outside agrarian society, Heathcliff forces his way into that society to expropriate the expropriators; and in this sense his machinations reflect the behaviour of a contemporary bourgeois class increasingly successful in its penetration of landed property. He belongs fully to neither Heights nor Grange, opposing them both; he embodies a force which at once destroys the traditional Earnshaw settlement and effectively confronts the power of the squirearchy. In his contradictory amalgam of 'Heights' and 'Grange', then, Heathcliff's career fleshes out a contemporary ideological dilemma which Charlotte also explores: the contradiction that the fortunes of the industrial bourgeoisie belong *economically* to an increasing extent with the landed gentry but that there can still exist between them, socially, culturally and personally, a profound hostility. If they are increasingly bound up objectively in a single power-bloc, there is still sharp subjective conflict between them. I take it that **Wuthering Heights,** like Charlotte's fiction, needs mythically to resolve this historical contradiction. If the exploitative adult Heathcliff belongs economically with the capitalist power of the Grange, he is culturally closer to the traditional world of the Heights; his contemptuous response to the Grange as a child, and later to Edgar, is of a piece with Joseph's scorn for the finicky Linton Heathcliff and the haughty young Catherine. If Heathcliff exploits Hareton culturally and economically, he nevertheless feels a certain rough-and-ready *rapport* with him. The contradiction Heathcliff embodies, then, is brought home in the fact that he combines Heights violence with Grange methods to gain power over both

properties; and this means that while he is economically progressive he is culturally outdated. He represents a turbulent form of capitalist aggression which must historically be civilised—blended with spiritual values, as it will be in the case of his surrogate Hareton. The terms into which the novel casts this imperative are those of the need to refine, in the person of Hareton, the old yeoman class; but since Hareton's achievement of the Grange is an ironic consequence of Heathcliff's own activity, there is a sense in which it is the capitalist drive symbolised by Heathcliff which must submit to spiritual cultivation. It is worth recalling at this point the cultural affinities between the old yeoman and the new industrial classes touched on by David Wilson;[12] and F. M. L. Thompson comments that by the early 1830s a depleted yeomanry were often forced to sell their land either to a large landowner, or to a local tradesman who would put a tenant in.[13] On the other hand, as Mrs Gaskell notes, some landed yeomen turned to manufacture. Heathcliff the heartless capitalist and Hareton the lumpish yeoman thus have a real as well as an alliterative relation. In so far as Heathcliff symbolises the dispossessing bourgeoisie, he links hands with the large capitalist landowner Linton in common historical opposition to yeoman society; in so far as he himself has sprung from that society and turned to amassing capital outside it, still sharing its dour lifestyle, he joins spiritual forces with the uncouth Hareton against the pampered squirearchy.

In pitting himself against both yeomanry and large-scale agrarian capitalism, then, Heathcliff is an indirect symbol of the aggressive industrial bourgeoisie of Emily Brontë's own time, a social trend extrinsic to both classes but implicated in their fortunes. The contradiction of the *novel,* however, is that Heathcliff cannot represent at once an absolute metaphysical refusal of an inhuman society and a class which is intrinsically part of it. Heathcliff is both metaphysical hero, spiritually marooned from all material concern in his obsessional love for Catherine, and a skilful exploiter who cannily expropriates the wealth of others. It is a limit of the novel's 'possible consciousness' that its absolute metaphysical protest can be socially articulated only in such terms—that its 'outside' is in this sense an 'inside'. The industrial bourgeoisie is outside the farming world of both Earnshaws and Lintons; but it is no longer a *revolutionary* class, and so provides no sufficient social correlative for what Heathcliff 'metaphysically' represents. He can thus be presented only as a conflictive unity of spiritual rejection and social integration; and this, indeed, is his personal tragedy. With this in mind, we can understand why what he did in that two years' absence has to remain mysterious. The actual facts of his return, as an ambitious *parvenu* armed with presumably non-agrarian wealth and bent on penetrating agrarian society, speak eloquently enough of the real situation of the contemporary bourgeoisie; but it is clear that such social realities offer no adequate symbolism for Heathcliff's unswerving drive, which transcends all social determinants and has its end in Catherine alone. The novel, then, can dramatise its 'metaphysical' challenge to society only by refracting it through the distorting terms of existing social relations, while simultaneously, at a 'deeper' level, isolating that challenge in a realm eternally divorced from the actual.

It seems clear that the novel's sympathies lie on balance with the Heights rather than the Grange. As Tom Winnifrith points out, the Heights is the more homely, egalitarian place; Lockwood's inability at the beginning of the book to work out its social relationships (is Hareton a servant or not?) marks a significant contrast with the Grange. (Lockwood is here a kind of surrogate reader: we too are forestalled from 'reading off' the relationships at first glance, since they are historically moulded and so only historically intelligible.) The passing of the Heights, then, is regretted: it lingers on in the ghostly myth of Heathcliff and Catherine as an unbanishable intimation of a world of hungering absolution askew to the civilised present. Winnifrith declares himself puzzled by Mrs Leavis's point that the action of Hareton and Catherine in replacing the Heights' currant-bushes with flowers symbolises the victory of capitalist over yeoman, but Mrs Leavis is surely right: flowers are a form of 'surplus value', redundant luxuries in the spare Heights world which can accommodate the superfluous neither in its horticulture nor in its social network. But though the novel mourns the death of Wuthering Heights, it invests deeply in the new life which struggles out of it. In so far as Heathcliff signifies a demonic capitalist drive, his defeat is obviously approved; in so far as his passing marks the demise of a life-form rougher but also richer than the Grange, his death symbolises the fleeing of absolute value over the horizon of history into the sealed realm of myth. That death, however tragic, is essential: the future lies with a fusion rather than a confrontation of interests between gentry and bourgeoisie.

The novel's final settlement might seem to qualify what I have said earlier about its confronting of irreconcilable contradictions. *Wuthering Heights* does, after all, end on a note of tentative convergence between labour and culture, sinew and gentility. The culture which Catherine imparts to Hareton in teaching him to read promises equality rather than oppression, an unemasculating refinement of physical energy. But this is a consequence rather than a resolution of the novel's tragic action; it does nothing to dissolve the deadlock of Heathcliff's relationship with Catherine, as the language used to describe that cultural transfusion unconsciously suggests:

> 'Con-*trary*!' said a voice as sweet as a silver bell—
> 'That for the third time, you dunce! I'm not going to tell you again. Recollect or I'll pull your hair!'

> 'Contrary, then', answered another, in deep but softened tones. 'And now, kiss me, for minding so well.'

> 'No, read it over first correctly, without a single mistake.' The male speaker began to read; he was a young man, respectably dressed and seated at a table, having a book before him. His handsome features glowed with pleasure, and his eyes kept impatiently wandering from the page to a small white hand over his shoulder, which recalled him by a smart slap on the cheek, whenever its owner detected such signs of inattention. Its owner stood behind; her light, shining ringlets blending, at intervals, with his brown locks, as she bent to superintend his studies; and her face—it was lucky he could not see her face, or he would never have been so steady. I could; and I bit my lip in spite, at having thrown away the chance I might have had of doing something besides staring at its smiting beauty.[14]

The aesthetic false moves of this are transparently dictated by ideological compromise. 'Sweet as a silver bell', 'glowed with pleasure', 'shining ringlets', 'smiting beauty': there is a coy, beaming, sentimental self-indulgence about the whole passage which belongs more to Lockwood than to Emily Brontë, although her voice has clearly been confiscated by his. It is Jane and Rochester in a different key; yet the difference is as marked as the parallel. The conclusion, while in a sense symbolically resolving the tragic disjunctions which precede it, moves at a level sufficiently distanced from those disjunctions to preserve their significance intact. It is true that *Wuthering Heights* finally reveals the limits of its 'possible consciousness' by having recourse to a gradualist model of social change: the antinomies of passion and civility will be harmonised by the genetic fusion of both strains in the offspring of Catherine and Hareton, effecting an equable interchange of Nature and culture, biology and education. But those possibilities of growth are exploratory and undeveloped, darkened by the shadow of the tragic action. If it is not exactly true to say that Hareton and Catherine play Fortinbras to Heathcliff's Hamlet, since what they symbolise emerges from, rather than merely imposes itself upon, the narrative, there is none the less a kernel of truth in that proposition. Hareton and Catherine are the products of their history, but they cannot negate it; the quarrel between their sedate future at Thrushcross Grange and the spectre of Heathcliff and Catherine on the hills lives on, in a way alien to Charlotte's reconciliatory imagination.

There is another reason why the ending of *Wuthering Heights* differs from the ideological integration which concludes Charlotte's novels. I have argued that those novels aim for a balance or fusion of 'genteel' and bourgeois traits, enacting a growing convergence of interests between two powerful segments of a ruling social bloc. The union of Hareton and Catherine parallels this complex unity in obvious ways: the brash vigour of the petty-bourgeois yeoman is smoothed and sensitised by the cultivating grace of the squirearchy. But the crucial difference lies in the fact that the yeomanry of *Wuthering Heights* is no longer a significant class but a historically superannuated force. The transfusion of class-qualities in Charlotte's case rests on a real historical symbiosis; in *Wuthering Heights* that symbolic interchange has no such solid historical foundation. The world of the Heights is over, lingering on only in the figure of Hareton Earnshaw; and in that sense Hareton's marriage to Catherine signifies more at the level of symbolism than historical fact, as a salutary grafting of the values of a dying class on to a thriving, progressive one. If Hareton is thought of as a surrogate, symbolic Heathcliff, then the novel's ending suggests a rapprochement between gentry and capitalist akin to Charlotte's mythical resolutions; if he is taken literally, as a survivor of yeoman stock, then there can be no such historical balance of power. Literally, indeed, this is what finally happens: Hareton's social class is effectively swallowed up into the hegemony of the Grange. Symbolically, however, Hareton represents a Heathcliff-like robustness with which the Grange must come to terms. It is this tension between literal and symbolic meanings which makes the ending of *Wuthering Heights* considerably more complex than the conclusion of any Charlotte Brontë novel. Read symbolically, the ending of *Wuthering Heights* seems to echo the fusion of qualities found in Charlotte; but since the basis of that fusion is the absorption and effective disappearance of a class on which the novel places considerable value, Emily's conclusion is a good deal more subtly shaded than anything apparent in her sister's work.

Wuthering Heights has been alternately read as a social and a metaphysical novel—as a work rooted in a particular time and place, or as a novel preoccupied with the eternal grounds rather than the shifting conditions of human relationship. That critical conflict mirrors a crucial thematic dislocation in the novel itself. The social and metaphysical are indeed ripped rudely apart in the book: existences only feebly incarnate essences, the discourse of ethics makes little creative contact with that of ontology. So much is apparent in Heathcliff's scathing dismissal of Edgar Linton's compassion and moral concern: 'and that insipid, paltry creature attending her from *duty* and *humanity*! From *pity* and *charity*! He might as well plant an oak in a flower-pot, and expect it to thrive, as imagine he can restore her to vigour in the soil of his shallow cares!' The novel's dialectical vision proves Heathcliff both right and wrong. There *is* something insipid about Linton, but his concern for Catherine is not in the least shallow; if his pity and charity are less fertile than Heathcliff's passion, they are also less destructive. But if ethical and ontological idioms fail to mesh, if social existence negates rather than realises spiritual essence, this is itself a profoundly social fact. The novel projects a condition in which the available social languages are too warped and constric-

tive to be the bearers of love, freedom and equality; and it follows that in such a condition those values can be sustained only in the realms of myth and metaphysics. It is a function of the metaphysical to preserve those possibilities which a society cancels, to act as its reservoir of unrealised value. This is the history of Heathcliff and Catherine—the history of a wedge driven between the actual and the possible which, by estranging the ideal from concrete existence, twists that existence into violence and despair. The actual is denatured to a mere husk of the ideal, the empty shell of some tormentingly inaccessible truth. It is an index of the dialectical vision of *Wuthering Heights* that it shows at once the terror and the necessity of that denaturing, as it shows both the splendour and the impotence of the ideal.

Notes

1. See Lukács, *The Historical Novel* [(London, 1962)], esp. chs. 1-2.

2. A coherence which is partial, limited, defined as much by its absences and exclusions as by its affirmations, and so (*pace* Goldmann) ideological.

3. Quoted by J. Hillis Miller, *The Disappearance of God* (Cambridge, Mass.[: Harvard University Press], 1963) p. 163.

4. Quoted by Leavis, *Lectures in America* [(London: Chatto and Windus, 1969)], p. 127.

5. *Wuthering Heights* [from *The Life and Works of Charlotte Brontë and Her Sisters,* 6 vols. (London: John Murray, 1920)], ed. Ward and Shorter, ch. 14, p. 155.

6. Ch. 15, p. 168.

7. Ch. 4, p. 36.

8. Ch. 12, p. 130.

9. Leavis, p. 99.

10. Ch. 8, p. 66.

11. *Brontë Society Transactions,* no. 78 (1968).

12. *Modern Quarterly Miscellany,* no. 1 (1947).

13. [F. M. L. Thompson,] *English Landed Society in the Nineteenth Century* [(Oxford: Taylor and Francis Books, Ltd., 1971)], p. 233.

14. Ch. 32, pp. 319-20.

Walter E. Anderson (essay date winter 1977-78)

SOURCE: Anderson, Walter E. "The Lyrical Form of *Wuthering Heights.*" *University of Toronto Quarterly* 47, no. 2 (winter 1977-78): 112-34.

[*In the following essay, Anderson examines the way in which Brontë's concept of death serves as the unifying theme of* Wuthering Heights.]

. . . heaven did not seem to be my home; and I broke my heart with weeping to come back to earth; and the angels were so angry that they flung me out, into the middle of the heath on the top of Wuthering Heights; where I woke sobbing for joy.

In *Wuthering Heights* death—or rather, life in death—is the supreme value. By understanding this we can understand that Brontë's central aim is to express the reality of Heathcliff's and Catherine's life and love continuing on the moors, as they attain immortal union with the living earth itself. Properly considered, this fact allows us to explain such unresolved critical questions about the book as the function of the second-generation characters and of Heathcliff's hatred of both them and life in this world. Brontë achieves in *Wuthering Heights* a singular power which most of her critics have felt. The crucial issue remains one of integrating all the novel's parts and meanings by a hypothesis adequate to its form and effect as a whole. The fundamental paradox of death against life cannot be resolved by synthesizing such concepts as storm and calm, or the house of the valley and the house of the moors, or the civilized family and the wild family inhabiting them. Nor finally are we to suppose, I shall argue, that the tempest of passion emerging in the course of the story is quelled or the issues resolved by the Hareton-Cathy relationship in a harmonious combination of Earnshaw energy and Linton calm. Brontë works within the conventional constraints of ordinary themes and a quasi-realistic plot structure, but her accomplishment lies in transcending them. She creates a radically new form, through which she endues Catherine's and Heathcliff's existences after death with living force. She shifts the planes of reality to such a degree that ordinary life gradually comes to seem less vital than death. The book induces in us not simply a belief, but the vivid sense that Catherine and Heathcliff's union is fulfilled after death upon the literally living earth. Heathcliff's conviction, when he reopens Catherine's grave, that she is not there, 'not under me, but on the earth,' parallels the reader's final impression that these lovers do not rest quietly in the grave but walk together as spirits on the Heights.

I

Catherine and Heathcliff's love is from the beginning a *donnée*. The formal sufficiency of the story is determined, therefore, not by a representation of the gradual emergence of their love, but by the need to define its transcendent nature and express its peculiar power. In *Wuthering Heights* we have, in place of a logical structure and a realistic plot, a symbolic action progressing towards 'lyric' revelation[1] and shaped according to a probability and necessity with other-worldly implications. Change and fluctuation in this action are subsumed finally under the realization of a timeless, static world, as constant as Catherine and Heathcliff's love and as enduring as the moors.

Brontë invites us to release her principal subject from ordinary limits and values and to focus on a transcendental vision. The book belongs to Catherine and Heathcliff, but they do not belong to this world. They draw away from all earthly hopes, yielding completely to another expectation. By concentrating on their love for each other, by causing them to deny a lasting affection with any other person, Brontë sufficiently expresses a love and a life which even death cannot sunder or alter. As she lies dying, Catherine says to Heathcliff: 'Will you forget me—will you be happy, when I am in the earth? Will you say twenty years hence, "That's the grave of Catherine Earnshaw. I loved her long ago, and was wretched to lose her; but it is past. I've loved many others since—my children are dearer to me than she was, and, at death, I shall not rejoice that I am going to her, I shall be sorry that I must leave them!" Will you say so, Heathcliff?'[2] Of course, he does not. By raising the issue Brontë points to the meaning and formal nature of her novel. Catherine defines the arc Heathcliff's career will eventually complete. Once she is dead he refers to life not as living but as remaining above ground, suspended in an abyss. He endures those twenty years of separation, and hates their children, to rejoice all the more in attaining his real life out of this world. When these lovers approach their ends, their eyes glitter with keen perception, but not of the objects around them: 'they appeared always to gaze beyond, and far beyond—you would have said out of this world' (p 131; cf pp 260-4). We are meant to focus on the peculiar reality of their life in death, not on the relatively common existences of those they leave behind.

Through Catherine and Heathcliff's uncompromising love, which admits no resolution short of total union with the earth, Brontë overcomes the isolation from each other and from nature we inevitably feel in life. She denies her lovers a marriage in this world to sustain their yearning for an eternal consummation. Catherine and Heathcliff defeat death by expecting to live completely only in death—not in any heavenly spiritual realm, but by means of the total commingling of their dust and therewith their souls. When Catherine reveals her dream of having gone to heaven and how unhappy she was there, Nelly says: 'All sinners would be miserable in heaven.' Catherine takes this chance to explain: 'it was not that.' Rather, it 'did not seem to be my home . . . and the angels were so angry that they flung me out, into the middle of the heath on the top of Wuthering Heights; where I woke sobbing for joy' (p 72). Catherine's and Heathcliff's wildness, even their wickedness, stresses their repudiation of a union in this world or in heaven for one with tumultuous nature.

In the well-known passage in which Catherine declares 'I *am* Heathcliff!' she says: 'I cannot express it, but surely you and everybody have a notion that there is, or should be an existence of yours beyond you. What were the use of my creation if I were entirely contained here? . . . my great thought in living is himself . . . he's always, always in my mind . . . as my own being—so, don't talk of our separation' (pp 73-4). We have here no ordinary intimation of immortality. Catherine refuses to accept an existence confined within her personal self, separate not from God or heaven, but from the beloved *in* whom she would live (cf pp 107, 133). Catherine reaches beyond the limitation of self towards 'Heathcliff' who *is* herself in the other—an existence of *yours* beyond *you*. Heathcliff also speaks of her as his soul, his life (p 139), in a literal, not figurative, sense. To be perfect soul mates, they must become death mates. From the windows of their prisons they see the graveyard near the moors, which promises them triumph, not defeat. To speak of their love as tragic or destructive—even self-destructive—is nothing to the purpose.

The love story will appear perplexing if we try to interpret its moral, psychological, and emotional involutions in terms appropriate either to the normal social world or to any orthodox Christian belief about the next. Whereas the Christian God and heaven are wholly distinct and other, these two lovers, possessing the same soul or being, become each other's 'all in all' (p 107) by uniting in the middle of the heath, on top of Wuthering Heights. Upon Catherine's death, Nelly believes her spirit is 'at home with God' (p 137), but Heathcliff demands to know where she is: 'Not *there*—not in heaven—not perished—where?' (p 139). In this novel, to go to heaven is really to perish. Heathcliff may pray 'like a Methodist,' but the 'deity' he implores is Catherine (p 144). And Heathcliff is Catherine's source of life: 'my great thought in living is himself. If all else perished, and *he* remained, I should still continue to be, and, if all else remained, and he were annihilated, the Universe would turn to a mighty stranger. I should not seem a part of it' (p 74). As a demiurgic, primordial force of raw energy, Heathcliff is like the moor itself; and his fiendishness better comprehends the violent aspect of the living world than does any pantheistic conception. Heathcliff is, in Catherine's words, 'a fierce, pitiless, wolfish man,' 'an arid wilderness of furze and whinstone,' which conceals no subterranean 'depths of benevolence' (pp 89-90). Their furious passion is like a tempest on the moors (p 76). When Catherine expresses her feeling for Heathcliff with the ideas that she *is* Heathcliff and that *he* is as 'necessary as the rocks,' we understand, finally, the novel's expression of a life at one with the *heath* and the *cliffs*.

Critics have questioned whether Heathcliff and Catherine's relationship is sexual, non-sexual, perversely sexual, asexual, or pure. The riddle is not to be solved by any one of these terms, for in some senses their love is both sexually dynamic and chaste. Their violent confrontations convey their passionate desire, but its force

must not be spent in this world. Catherine's death determines that these lovers reach each other only through the grave. Heathcliff's desire throughout the entire action is shown in his straining towards the dead Catherine 'as a tight-stretched cord vibrates—a strong thrilling, rather than trembling' (p 258). After Catherine and Heathcliff become adults only one can be left physically alive to prevent their coming together in the flesh. After a single passionate embrace with Heathcliff, Catherine must die, keeping them apart until they meet in dust. Brontë paradoxically reverses the traditional metaphoric comparison of the sexual act with death by switching vehicle and tenor. The lovers embrace really to die, and, in dying, they live forever with the intensity of a sexual embrace in a chaste fusion with the animated earth.

Catherine says she will marry Edgar Linton because 'it would degrade me to marry Heathcliff now' (p 72), that is, now that she has tasted life at Thrushcross Grange. But Catherine never really changes. Her language, like her character, must be taken not primarily in its conventional, literal sense but for its general, symbolic function. Despite her apparently divided character, she actually exhibits an underlying singlemindedness equal to Heathcliff's. We might say, with Nelly, that Catherine adopts 'a double character without exactly intending to deceive anyone' (p 62). The question is, why does Brontë move her in two directions at once? In the first place, Catherine's marriage to Linton obviates a union between her and Heathcliff. Second, her and Edgar's marriage demonstrates the meaninglessness of their socially conventional union: existing only for the present, it discloses how much she and Heathcliff can dispense with. Catherine and Linton's temporal association is the inverse measure of what Catherine and Heathcliff come to possess in their eternal union. After she accepts Edgar's proposal, Catherine avows she loves Heathcliff and cannot love Edgar, except superficially, and only for 'the present' (p 71): 'My love for Linton is like the foliage in the woods. Time will change it, I'm well aware, as winter changes the trees. My love for Heathcliff resembles the eternal rocks beneath—a source of little visible delight, but necessary' (p 74). Catherine knows that she has 'no more business to marry Edgar Linton,' than 'to be in heaven' (p 72). Yet Brontë has her marry the decent, humane man and move to Thrushcross Grange, the home of beauty and social grace, to demonstrate ultimately her profound dedication to another kind of life altogether. Catherine repeatedly expresses her rejection of both Edgar and the Grange, just as she rejected a conventionally pleasant vision of heaven. Married to 'a stranger' and exiled from what had been 'her world,' Catherine feels at Thrushcross Grange like an outcast in an abyss (p 107). The story leaps over three years of Catherine's married life to resume with Heathcliff's sudden return (p 81). Catherine then renews her struggle towards Heathcliff, affirming, prior to her death, how much she loves him. From an overview of the novel's goal, we see that a union in this world between her and Heathcliff would be a degradation. Brontë focuses not on what they forfeit on the earth, but on what they realize in it.

To think that these lovers destroy their love and themselves through mismatches is to neglect the formal reasoning which overrides the apparent bearing of events. Both Edgar and Catherine's this-worldly marriage and Heathcliff and Isabella's terminate at the same time (in successive chapters, 16 and 17), leaving Heathcliff and Catherine's to come. 'What you touch at present, you may have,' Catherine tells Edgar a short time before she dies, 'but my soul will be on that hilltop before you lay hands on me again. I don't want you Edgar; I'm past wanting you. Return to your books, I'm glad you possess a consolation, for all you had in me is gone' (p 109). Edgar will find further consolation in their daughter Cathy, who takes possession of his heart after Catherine's death. And as the two men who have loved Catherine in such different ways approach their own deaths, Heathcliff rejoices whereas Edgar begins 'to shrink and fear it' (p 205).

The word *affinity* has often been used to describe Heathcliff and Catherine's attraction for each other, but *identity* is more accurate.[3] 'Whatever our souls are made of,' Catherine says, 'his and mine are the same' (p 72). Neither character is an incomplete half—merely masculine or feminine—seeking ordinary wholeness through love. As persons, both Heathcliff and Catherine are complete in themselves, being incomplete only in their separation. When her death is near, Heathcliff rages at her: 'Do I want to live? What kind of living will it be when you—oh, God! would *you* like to live with your soul in the grave?' (p 135). Heathcliff arranges for the sexton to remove the facing sides of his and Catherine's coffins when they are both dead so that 'by the time Linton gets to us, he'll not know which is which' (pp 228-9). Both lovers are opposed to the meek and patient Edgar, who is excluded from the eternal marriage bed where Catherine's and Heathcliff's two selves merge into a single identity through fusion with the living earth. Their graves are located 'on a green slope, in a corner of the kirkyard, where the wall is so low that heath and bilberry plants have climbed over it from the moor' (p 140; cf p 266).

Heathcliff and Catherine's love appropriately takes on a paradoxical model of expression whenever they compare the life they look forward to with the life they are living. The central idea is clearly communicated to the reader when Catherine eagerly contemplates her death:

> 'Oh, you see, Nelly! he would not relent a moment to keep me out of the grave! *That* is how I'm loved! Well, never mind! That is not *my* Heathcliff. I shall love mine

yet; and take him with me—he's in my soul. And,' she added, musingly, 'the thing that irks me most is this shattered prison, after all. I'm tired, tired of being enclosed here. I'm wearying to escape into that glorious world, and to be always there; not seeing it dimly through tears, and yearning for it through the walls of an aching heart, but really with it, and in it. Nelly, you think you are better and more fortunate than I; in full health and strength. You are sorry for me—very soon that will be altered. I shall be sorry for *you*. I shall be incomparably beyond and above you all. I *wonder* he won't be near me!'

(p 134)

The opening sentences of this passage are more ironic than first appears, for *that,* in a sense, is how Heathcliff loves Catherine. She wonders whether he will be near her, but we do not. We have already seen (in the third chapter) his tearful yearning for her. They need only wait twenty years, one generation—a short time within the perspective of eternity—before meeting in and on the moors whose wind is 'so full of life, that it seemed whoever respired it, though dying, might revive' (p 211). Catherine's exultation here over a complacent Nelly is not bravado; it anticipates her triumph in death.

In an earlier passage, when Heathcliff is present only in her imagination, Catherine foresees and accepts the conditions of their love:

> 'It's a rough journey, and a sad heart to travel it; and we must pass by Gimmerton Kirk, to go that journey! We've braved its ghosts often together, and dared each other to stand among the graves and ask them to come. But Heathcliff, if I dare you now, will you venture [that is, into the grave to seek her]? If you do, I'll keep you. I'll not lie there by myself; they may bury me twelve feet deep, and throw the church down over me, but I won't rest till you are with me. I never will!'

> She paused, and resumed with a strange smile, 'He's considering—he'd rather I'd come to him! Find a way, then! not through the Kirkyard. You are slow! Be content, you always followed me!'

(p 108)

Prior to this moment, Nelly would not open the window to Catherine's room lest she catch her death of cold. For Catherine, however, death provides 'a chance of life,' and she opens it herself. She seeks a way through the kirkyard, knowing that Heathcliff will eventually follow. He will find no better way to life.

Before dying Catherine wishes to hold Heathcliff 'till [they] were both dead,' and he embraces her so intensely it seems doubtful she will emerge alive (pp 133-4). In a sense she does not, for she dies that night in childbirth. Seeing them together, Nelly tells Lockwood, she felt that she was not 'in the company of a creature of [her] own species' (p 134), and she is right. Catherine and Heathcliff become strangers to everyone alive because they exist only in their dedication to each other and to death. Before Heathcliff retreats to his room to die, his last exchange is with Cathy (Linton) Heathcliff: 'Will *you* come, chuck? I'll not hurt you. No! to you, I've made myself worse than the devil. Well, there is *one* who won't shrink from my company! By God! she's relentless' (p 263). And as he contemplates his imminent union with Catherine, Heathcliff ecstatically proclaims: 'I'm too happy, and yet I'm not happy enough. My soul's bliss kills my body, but does not satisfy it' (p 262). His body will be satiated only with its dissolution along with hers. 'Strange happiness!' Nelly says; to be sure, but this is the essential strangeness at the heart of the book.

The idea of this novel's form and meaning which I have been forwarding will explain the highly restricted function of both Heathcliff's hate and the symmetrical replication of the first-generation characters in the second. Because critics of *Wuthering Heights* generally have taken the ostensible plot of revenge involving Hareton Earnshaw, Cathy Linton, and Linton Heathcliff as an independent development in its own right rather than as a screen for fully projecting the central love story, many problems of interpretation have arisen. Perhaps the most important of these involves the supposed incongruities in the novel, given the apparent shift from a story of grand passion to one of sordid revenge after Catherine's death midway in the action (chap 16). But instead of losing control of her subject in the second half of her novel, Brontë ingeniously manages to augment its power by substituting the second generation for the first, once Catherine is present only as a memory or a ghost. As I shall attempt to show in the next two sections, the logical extension of the plot with a revenge motive constitutes only an apparent complication; the story continues to express its single concern, though in a different mode. The structure is peculiar because the subject is fundamentally paradoxical. Although the later action grows out of the earlier, it does not introduce new consequences and goals of its own, but points back to the affairs of the first half. Because her action has much to do with hate and love, but nothing to do with the accomplishment of revenge, Brontë abruptly terminated Heathcliff's seeming struggle to destroy his enemies before the novel closes. Her purpose in the literal action is not to complete Heathcliff's revenge but through his desire for revenge, to express his hatred of the world and, correlatively, his love of Catherine. The idea of revenge permits full dramatization of Heathcliff's rejection of all those ordinary human values the other characters represent. Renunciation would not be emotionally powerful enough, and hate is more nearly the mirror image of love than mere rejection or indifference. After serving as echoes of the first-generation characters, the members of the second either die or fade into the dim background of the normal world as Catherine and Heathcliff come forward to assume their immortal life.

The story, like Heathcliff himself, is monomaniacal, having at its centre only 'one absorbing subject' (p 230; cf p 256). One common focus connects the apparently different parts as Brontë converts the hate/revenge motif to an expression of the principal subject, centring in Heathcliff's love of Catherine. The strange happiness Heathcliff enjoys at the close is the happiness of a soul outstripping the body, just as the book's strange power evolves from a form outstripping its literal action. Brontë did not shrink from her 'mad' vision, but held it in her mind's eye until she had found the complex form to give it nearly perfect expression.

II

Given her conception of Catherine and Heathcliff's love, why did Brontë choose to make her hero a fiend? The question touches the book's morality, a subject which has aroused its critics as much as any other. *Wuthering Heights* has been judged moral, immoral, amoral, and even pre-moral, but, as with the question of sexuality, this one admits no simple either/or solution. Although we acknowledge Heathcliff's diabolism, we cannot deny him our primary sympathy. The problem disappears once we grasp the connection between his savagery and his love, and between our feelings towards him and the way Brontë renders her material.

Despite Heathcliff's viciousness, he retains our sympathy to the end, for our feelings are never as convinced of his cruelty as is our reason. We believe in his ferocious power, but we do not fear him. Brontë never represents Heathcliff's malevolence without extenuation, and the harm he perpetrates does not live after him. That the reader is meant to acquit him of wrongdoing is reflected, though in a curiously indirect manner, by those critics who have attempted to fix the blame for all the mayhem on one of the other characters. Even the inoffensive Nelly Dean and the innocuous Lockwood have been charged and convicted. There is good reason, at least, for our feeling ambivalent towards Heathcliff. Just when destruction of those he hates is within his grasp, he arbitrarily restrains his hand. And although he takes the trouble to prevent Edgar Linton from protecting Cathy by modifying his will, he never bothers to make one of his own: 'How to leave my property, I cannot determine,' he says (p 262)—a curious indifference for a man bent on destruction. Also, Heathcliff despises his son Linton enough to wish him dead, yet he carefully preserves the sickly youth far longer than he might otherwise have lived. The 'father's selfishness' is made to contribute to Linton's comfort (p 171). Heathcliff's motive is revenge, since he gains Cathy's property after she marries Linton Heathcliff and he dies. Yet

Cathy ultimately comes into possession of her estate and forms a happy alliance with Hareton, who is restored to his rights. I would suggest that Brontë has arranged matters in this way to limit the consequences of Heathcliff's diabolical machinations. In this section, then, I shall argue that Heathcliff's hate, not his hatefulness, is the subject expressed, and in the next, that his power to achieve revenge, not its accomplishment, is the matter represented.

In the first and second chapters we witness Heathcliff's savagery, and in the third we learn that its cause is love. These are the two major poles of the book. Consequently we see all his fiendishness in light of his misery over being separated from Catherine. Brontë communicates the nature of Heathcliff's love in association with his rejection of the world and all earthly affections. Had he not loved Catherine so well, he could not hate all others as he does; did Brontë not have him renounce the world so completely, she could not fully represent his longing for death. She did not allow Heathcliff and Catherine to die at the same time, but continued the story with a second set of characters to express the intensity of Heathcliff's torment and longing.

Very soon after the book opens, Lockwood's nightmare occasions the scene which reveals Heathcliff's ferocity to be but a corollary of his love:

> He got on to the bed and wrenched open the lattice, bursting, as he pulled at it, into an uncontrollable passion of tears.
>
> 'Come in! come in!' he sobbed, 'Cathy, do come. Oh, do—*once* more! Oh! my heart's darling, hear me *this* time—Catherine, at last!'
>
> There was such anguish in the gush of grief that accompanied this raving, that my compassion made me overlook its folly.
>
> (p 33)[4]

What is folly to Lockwood makes sense to us. To deny Heathcliff's assurance of Catherine's presence is to deny the novel. His love, as fresh and vital as it was when she died eighteen years before, continually intimates that its consummation is still to come. Aware from the book's start that Catherine is dead and yet somehow still alive, we can accept the termination of the worldly portion of their affair. From the beginning Brontë endows their love with eternality by presenting the past within the present as well as by Heathcliff's confident expectation of future fulfilment.

At strategic moments during the novel's second half, Brontë reminds us of the lovers' closeness by Heathcliff's continual wandering on the moors and at the Heights in search of Catherine. Only when he feels her spirit nearby, is he 'unspeakably consoled' (p 230). Twice he uncovers her coffin, the better to contemplate

the ultimate transformation, 'of dissolving with her, and being more happy still!' (pp 228-9). For these reasons, Heathcliff's words near the end of the novel provide an apt commentary on its form: 'it is by compulsion that I notice anything alive, or dead, which is not associated with one universal idea' (p 256). His violent outbursts towards others give the impression of temporary distraction, having no permanent effect. All the objects of his hate function as 'an aggravation of the constant torment' he suffers (p 255). Of his son Linton, he says, I 'hate him for the memories he revives' (p 170). Likewise we are often reminded of Heathcliff's sense of Catherine through Cathy: 'He looked up, seized with a sort of surprise at her boldness, or, possibly, reminded by her voice and glance of the person from whom she inherited it' (p 215). But, unlike Edgar, he must not feel too much of Catherine in Cathy for he is not to compromise his love of the mother by loving the daughter. Instead, he insists, 'I don't love you!' (p 218). 'Keep your eft's fingers off; and move, or I'll kick you! . . . How the devil can you dream of fawning on me? I *detest* you!' (p 219). Recognizing the underlying cause of Heathcliff's hate, we adjust the surface action to the reality of his undeviating love for Catherine, the subject represented on nearly every page of the work. His 'entire world is a dreadful collection of memoranda that she did exist, and that [he has] lost her!' (p 255). Thus, his 'monomania on the subject of his departed idol' (p 256) provokes his rage but at the same time continually interrupts his intention to destroy and allays our concern for his would-be victims.

It remains to demonstrate how Brontë shapes her material to evoke the desired response in the reader. I think it is safe to say that we feel more indignant towards Alec D'Urberville during his first carriage ride with Tess in *Tess of the d'Urbervilles* than we ever feel towards Heathcliff. Compared with Thomas Hardy, Brontë is a great spendthrift of malice and violent passions, but always to avoid isolating Heathcliff's malignity for moral reprobation. She makes us so familiar with fiendishness that she diffuses the disgust while she sustains the terrific. The effect Hardy achieves with Alec depends on his comparative parsimony in the distribution of evil. Brontë's purpose is quite different.[5] For contrast we need only imagine the effect had Heathcliff possessed the only violent temper or appalling hatred in the world of this novel. Or suppose that Isabella Linton had been as amiable as Tess, with Heathcliff seducing her against her will. Instead Brontë has Isabella rush headlong into her miserable marriage against all that advice and observation can do to dissuade her.

Brontë enlists our sympathy for Heathcliff by telling the story of his childhood conflicts with Hindley Earnshaw and Edgar Linton, thereby raising our antipathy against those who inspire his lust for revenge. When Heathcliff throws hot applesauce into young Edgar's face, Nelly

Dean's reaction directs our own. She 'rather spitefully' scrubs Edgar, 'affirming it served him right for meddling' (p 55). Nelly is there later to condemn the wretched Linton Heathcliff for the same want of spirit she observed in his uncle. She discovers him to be 'the worst-tempered bit of a sickly slip that ever struggled into its teens! Happily, as Mr. Heathcliff conjectured, he'll not win twenty!' (p 195). And earlier, Nelly 'began to dislike, more than to compassionate, Linton, and to excuse his father, in some measure, for holding him cheap' (p 179). Strong resemblances are drawn between the ineffectual Edgar and the abject, ill-natured Linton—who emphatically 'does not resemble his father' (p 205; cf pp 206, 211). 'Where is *my* share in thee, puling chicken?' Heathcliff asks (p 169). Our favour turns to Heathcliff and Catherine, to whom all vital qualities rebound, qualities which define the norms of the novel, as Edgar's conventional values and vapid gentility do not. By stressing the opposition between Heathcliff's and Catherine's potency and Linton's and Edgar's weakness, Brontë forcefully imparts the idea that these lovers have not exhausted their vitality in living. In our imaginations, they bear more strength into the grave than the others possess in life.

Although we never lose a sense of Heathcliff's potential for evil, he elicits our sympathy when exercising his passion against Edgar, Isabella, Hindley, or Linton. Even though we appreciate the mutuality of Hindley and Heathcliff's hatred, Brontë consistently turns our feelings against the former. Heathcliff delights in Hindley's destruction, but his role in it is, on consideration, negligible. He instigates nothing. Hindley's self-ruination is well underway before Heathcliff returns to the Heights, and he ends by drinking himself to death. Like Heathcliff, Hindley idolizes his beloved, and after she dies he also curses and defies both God and man (pp 60-1). But unlike Heathcliff, Hindley 'gave himself up to reckless dissipation.' His self-destruction distinctly contrasts with Heathcliff's course. Although both men are notable for savage sullenness and ferocity, Hindley degrades himself 'past redemption' (p 61). With Frances dead, he is lost. Before terminating Hindley's perverse career, Brontë devotes more of the action to his destructive intentions towards Heathcliff than the reverse, as one of the major confrontations between them shows.

For many days following Catherine's death, Heathcliff is away from the Heights mourning at her grave. When he returns home one night during a snowstorm—anticipating, we learn later, the presence of Catherine's ghost in her room—he discovers that Hindley and Isabella have conspired to bar his entrance. Hindley holds a gun and a knife, intending to assassinate Heathcliff, who breaks in and disarms him. The gun discharges, causing the knife to recoil and slash the would-be murderer's arm. Heathcliff proceeds to thrash the villain, but only

with one free hand, be it noted, since he holds Isabella with the other. Sometime later, Heathcliff tells Nelly that he then rushed directly to Catherine's bedroom, but that is not what Isabella recounts in her detailed narration of events. Instead, Heathcliff carries Hindley to the settle, binds up his wound, and advises him to sleep off his drunkenness. Of course Joseph supposes Heathcliff to be the devil in the mischief, and Isabella has to labour 'to satisfy the old man that Heathcliff was not the aggressor' (p 148). Here, as usual, Brontë realizes as much violence as possible consistent with exonerating Heathcliff. She seeks a maximum of blood and malice with a minimum of harm and blame, as is epitomized in one phrase in particular: Heathcliff 'bound up [Hindley's] wound with brutal roughness' (p 147). Rough though he is, he binds the wound.

In this episode Heathcliff's hate and revenge motives are, as always, subordinated to the love which is their cause. The next morning Heathcliff stands at the fireplace oblivious of Hindley, despite the latter's murderous assault the night before. 'His basilisk eyes were nearly quenched by sleeplessness, and weeping,' Isabella tells Nelly, 'his lips devoid of their ferocious sneer and sealed in an expression of unspeakable sadness' (p 148). Our attention is then diverted to Isabella's vindictiveness: 'I couldn't miss this chance of sticking in a dart,' she says. 'Fie, fie, Miss,' Nelly interrupted, 'one might suppose you had never opened a Bible in your life.'

The entire pattern of this seventeenth chapter establishes a frame for many episodes to follow. Brontë consistently embeds Heathcliff's savagery within a larger scheme of others' malice or disagreeableness and of his overriding love for Catherine. Only thus qualified does she permit a savage eruption, which is quelled when Heathcliff's thoughts turn to 'the subject of his departed idol.' Isabella experiences 'pleasure in being able to exasperate' Heathcliff, whom she taunts for mourning over what she supposes to be 'senseless dust and ashes': 'Heathcliff, if I were you, I'd go stretch myself over her grave and die like a faithful dog. The world is surely not worth living in now, is it?' (p 146). Indeed it is not; and there is nothing Heathcliff would prefer to doing as she says. No plot requirement delays him, for he is in a similar posture in the thirty-third chapter, the third, the seventeenth, and many others. The formal requirement is expressionistic—a full and powerful revelation of the novel's spiritual core. Isabella complains about that 'monster' Heathcliff, wondering how Catherine could have loved him, for she better than anyone knew his true nature. The reader understands these lovers' mutual obsession: their alienation from others only emphasizes the harmony prevailing between them.

Cathy Linton later taunts Heathcliff as Isabella did. When Linton Heathcliff spitefully tells Cathy that her mother hated her father and loved his, she calls him a liar (p 192). Yet her confrontations with Heathcliff deflect the reader's attention from his harshness towards her to his love for Catherine: 'I don't hate you, I'm not angry that you struck me. Have you never loved *anybody*, in all your life, uncle? *never?*' (p 219). Unwittingly, she evokes the true state of affairs by connecting Heathcliff's cruelty with its cause: 'Mr. Heathcliff, *you* have *nobody* to love you; and, however miserable you make us, we shall still have the revenge of thinking that your cruelty rises from your greater misery! You *are* miserable, are you not? Lonely, like the devil, and envious like him? *Nobody* loves you—' (p 228). By such means Brontë continually directs the reader to an ever fresh apprehension of the central subject.

Cathy is not crushed by Heathcliff's contempt. She pities him more than she hates him, and retains her boldness in the face of his savage outbursts. Brontë employs similar devices in delineating Heathcliff's and Hareton's dispositions towards each other. When Heathcliff dies, only Hareton mourns him. If we consider Hareton rationally as he kisses the dead savage face and bitterly weeps, we may be perplexed, as Nelly is, that 'the most wronged' should feel such grief upon the death of his persecutor (p 264). But we are never completely convinced that Heathcliff has wronged him. Brontë's treatment of Heathcliff's and Hareton's relationship further discloses her double-dealing technique both in portraying the fiend/no-fiend Heathcliff and in representing a revenge/no-revenge plot. In Heathcliff's supposed revenge on Hindley through Hareton, Brontë reveals his violent will, but simultaneously acquits him of wrongdoing. 'If he were the devil, it didn't signify,' Hareton tells Cathy, and Brontë tells the reader.

When we meet Hareton as a little boy during one of Nelly's rare visits to the Heights (chap 11), we find that his brutalization is well underway as a consequence of Hindley's sottish neglect. Hareton's chief lesson, he tells Nelly, has been to avoid 'Devil daddy,' who he knows cannot abide him. Heathcliff encourages the alienation, to be sure, but at the same time he becomes the boy's protector: 'he pays Dad back what he gies to me—he curses Daddy for cursing me' (p 95). Through dissipation Hindley not only wastes his son's heritage, but nearly kills him. Once, attempting to escape from his father's drunken clutches, Hareton falls from an upper story and would at least have been maimed had Heathcliff not caught him (pp 68-9). Heathcliff diabolically regrets having saved the lad, yet those who witness 'his salvation' rejoice nonetheless. We might say that he preserves Hareton's life with 'brutal roughness.' In accord with the patterns already traced, Nelly immediately turns her wrath upon Hindley for abusing his son: 'He hates you—they all hate you,' she exclaims. 'Have mercy on this unfortunate boy' (p 68). Hindley responds by drinking a tumbler of brandy and discharging a sequel of curses too blasphemous to record. By

comparison with Hindley, Heathcliff commits mostly sins of omission against Hareton.

While Heathcliff rants, after Hindley's death, about making one tree grow as crooked as another, Hareton lovingly strokes his cheek, a gesture which resembles Cathy's snuggling up to him after he viciously slaps her face (pp 154, 219). Ironically, we recognize the 'gold' in Hareton because Heathcliff virtually loves the lad in spite of himself (p 178). Charlotte Brontë felt that the single link connecting Heathcliff with humanity is 'his rudely confessed regard' for Hareton.[6] She was wrong to conclude, however, that he had ruined the young man. When the time is ripe for aborting the putative revenge plot, Cathy promptly falls in love with Hareton, who renews himself by virtue of his noble spirit (p 254). The boy happily never had more than 'a dim notion of his inferiority' (p 177), a fact which mitigates the effect of Heathcliff's malevolence. Perhaps the most remarkable instance of Brontë's calculated ambiguity is Heathcliff's triumphant boast of surpassing the cruelty of Hindley's persecution of him by making his victim love him (p 178). All victims should have so rare an oppressor.

III

Cathy Linton, Hareton Earnshaw, and Linton Heathcliff are not very memorable characters, and I am not surprised to learn that, like myself, other readers remember distinctly only Catherine and Heathcliff shortly after reading ***Wuthering Heights***. 'Great as the novel is,' E. M. Forster writes, 'one cannot afterwards remember anything in it but Heathcliff and the elder Catherine.'[7] Even if this reaction is typical, it ought not to reflect disparagingly on Emily Brontë's conduct of the story, as Forster's reservation does. Much of her art goes to securing just that effect. Her masterful control becomes apparent once we realize that she creates chains of associated ideas which cut loose from the present occurrence and reach to something deeper and, for her, more real. What is momentarily present is nothing but an occasion for releasing again the framing situation which precedes and overrides those events involving the second generation.[8] The latter half of the novel appears more accidental, less probable, poorer in effect than the first only if we take the revenge plot too literally. Critics who do so become dissatisfied when later developments fail to produce the effects their premises logically dictate. Actually, the improbabilities and forced plotting in the novel serve Brontë's positive intention. Even the demise of several characters immediately after they outlive their usefulness assists in denying the literal action more than a slight natural probability. It is just possible, as it were, and no more than half-real. In the words of an early reviewer, Brontë achieves a 'nice provision of the possible even in the highest effects of the supernatural.'[9] We reserve our fullest belief for the realm in which Catherine and Heathcliff ultimately abide.

The second-generation characters' importance formally depends not on their existences in their own right but on their reprojection of the original principals—Catherine, Edgar, and the young Heathcliff. The children amplify, by repetition, the original sets of events. Consequently their traits detach from them as individuals to reflect their generic source. At the same time, the paleness of the reflection shows us how little of what matters in Brontë's world *could* be mirrored in these relatively ordinary creatures. Several critics have noticed the symmetrical pedigree of the generations, but we must go further. Brontë purposely denies the children distinctive traits of their own because she wishes them to fade away, leaving only Catherine and Heathcliff. The second generation dimly personifies the first, recreating the structure of the original relationships. The plot does not progress for the sake of logical complications, but for symbolic revelation. The revenge plot is a red herring. Intentionally so. Brontë sustains it only superficially to abort it after exhausting its restricted functions. Before the novel closes, the idea of Heathcliff's hatred and revenge also fades from our memory, leaving only the image of his living love for Catherine. Everyone eventually gives way to these two lovers, as life in this world gives place to life in death.

By the end of the book only four of the chief actors remain: Catherine and Heathcliff, perfectly united as ghostly lovers in the grave and on the moors; and Cathy and Hareton, happily restored to everything they almost lost. But the living pair resolve nothing. They recede into relative insignificance, whereas the dead pair come forward into greater life. The shift in the planes of reality is given sharp focus in Nelly and Lockwood's final exchange. Nelly duly believes that 'the dead are at peace,' but, she says, reports persist that Catherine's and Heathcliff's ghosts wander on the moors and near the Heights. Just then Nelly and Lockwood see Cathy and Hareton returning from a ramble. Lockwood says, '*they* are afraid of nothing . . . Together they would brave Satan and all his legions' (pp 265-6). The words have some applicability to Cathy and Hareton but much more to Catherine and Heathcliff. We automatically shift from the lesser to the greater: we know who feared nothing, not even death itself, and who outbraved both heaven and hell. Cathy and Hareton lend an aura of corporeality to the spiritual pair. Towards the domesticated lovers at Thrushcross Grange, we, like Heathcliff, become comparatively 'regardless' how they go on together and 'can give them no attention any more' (p 255).

As substitutes, Cathy, Hareton, and Linton image the young Catherine, Heathcliff, and Edgar. Brontë introduces the idea of substitution early in the novel when Isabella tells Nelly that Heathcliff looked upon her as 'Edgar's proxy in suffering, till he could get a hold of him' (p 123). Heathcliff's getting a hold of Edgar does not signify; only his declaration of the desire counts. But to sustain the original situation, Edgar must be present in principle once communication between him and Heathcliff almost ceases after Catherine's death. Isabella's son Linton now provides the perfect proxy. When Heathcliff looks at Linton, he affirms the boy's resemblance to Edgar; and Edgar was convinced 'that as his nephew resembled him in person he would resemble him in mind' (pp. 205-6, 211).

The fullest and most explicit statement of the idea that the second generation is absorbed into the first comes near the close, when Heathcliff tells Nelly his feelings towards Cathy and Hareton. The passage evinces Brontë's own reasoning about her formal intentions:

> 'Five minutes ago, Hareton seemed a personification of my youth, not a human being. I felt to him in such a variety of ways, that it would have been impossible to have accosted him rationally.
>
> 'In the first place, his startling likeness to Catherine connected him fearfully with her. That, however, which you may suppose the most potent to arrest my imagination, is actually the least, for what is not connected with her to me? and what does not recall her? . . . I am surrounded with her image! The most ordinary faces of men and women—my own features—mock me with a resemblance. The entire world is a dreadful collection of memoranda that she did exist, and that I have lost her!
>
> 'Well, Hareton's aspect was the ghost of my immortal love, of my wild endeavours to hold my right, my degradation, my pride, my happiness, and my anguish—'
>
> (p 255)

This passage clearly indicates that Brontë deprived the second generation of a fully independent existence because she meant it to mirror the past, not to introduce an extended action posing new consequences and goals. Hareton is, by substitution, the 'ghost' of Heathcliff's earlier self. His struggling towards Cathy revives the idea of Heathcliff's original struggle towards her mother. Cathy and Hareton serve as a sympathetic reminder of Heathcliff's love and loss, even his unappeasable pride. Remembering his own life, Heathcliff admires Hareton and would set him against Linton, as he himself opposed Edgar: 'twenty times a day, I covet Hareton, with all his degradation[.] I'd love the lad had he been some one else. But I think he's safe from *her* [Cathy's] love. I'll pit him against that paltry creature [Linton] unless it bestir itself briskly' (p 176; cf pp 99-100). Of Hareton, he says; 'When I look for his father in his face, I find *her* every day more! How the devil is he so like? I can hardly bear to see him' (p 240). Thus does Brontë sustain, in an immediate way, Heathcliff's aspiring love for Catherine.

The Cathy-Linton relationship also excites Heathcliff's remembering consciousness, indelibly fixed on the fact that Catherine belongs to him, not to Edgar. Cathy and

Linton's marriage repeats Catherine and Edgar's, proving again how thoroughly null and void it was and is. Cathy's feelings for Linton are as contradictory as Catherine's were for Edgar: 'You're not much, are you, Linton?' she says to him after one of his peevish fits (p 193). Her courage before Heathcliff starkly contrasts with Linton's timidity, as when she abjures the weeping wretch: 'Rise, and don't degrade yourself into an abject reptile' (p 212). We recall Edgar Linton's 'nervous trembling' before the threatening Heathcliff, which prompted Catherine in revulsion to call him 'a suckling leveret' (p 100). Cathy's discovery that she is not like Linton (p 168) echoes Catherine's acknowledgment that her soul and Edgar were 'as different as a moonbeam from lightning, or frost from fire' (p 72). Still, Cathy insisting she loves Linton, marries him. But like her mother's marriage, Cathy's has been invalidated before it occurs. After she and Linton marry, we see him in his usual enfeebled state, sucking a piece of candy. Brontë exhibits him at his spiteful worst before mercifully allowing him to die; and his timely death prevents our feeling the marriage had been consummated. Everything we know about Linton betrays his impotence. 'No—don't kiss me,' he says to Cathy during their courtship. 'It takes my breath—dear me!' (p 190). He can 'contribute to her entertainment' even less than Edgar could to Catherine's (cf pp 208, 86). Upon Linton's death, Cathy turns to Hareton in life as Catherine turned to Heathcliff in death.

Soon after Hareton ventures towards 'higher pursuits,' Heathcliff gazes after him admiringly and sighs: 'It will be odd, if I thwart myself!' (p 240). The real trend of events in the second part of *Wuthering Heights* leads to Heathcliff's baffling, not accomplishing, his great revenge. He does not bother to do his worst because he has but one objective, and in that he is not thwarted. By extending Heathcliff's life twenty years beyond Catherine's, Brontë validates his unalterable commitment. She makes this intention almost explicit when Heathcliff unseals his thoughts to Nelly by telling her what occurred on the night that he thrashed Hindley: 'I looked round impatiently—I felt her by me—I could *almost* see her, and yet I *could not*! . . . And, since then, sometimes more, and sometimes less, I've been the sport of that intolerable torture! Infernal—keeping my nerves at such a stretch, that, if they had not resembled catgut, they would, long ago, have relaxed to the feebleness of Linton's' (p 230). After producing her full effect Brontë brings Heathcliff to a 'strange change' (p 255). He rather arbitrarily decides to hold his hand and strike at nothing, even though 'now would be the precise time,' he realizes, to revenge himself completely on 'the representatives' of his old enemies (p 255). This final attenuation of the revenge plot has been well prepared for and does not jar with the peculiar system of probability informing the world of this novel.

Heathcliff's decision not to revenge himself appears, he says, to be 'an absurd termination to my violent exertions' (p 254); it 'sounds as if I had been labouring the whole time, only to exhibit a fine trait of magnanimity' (p 255). Brontë seems here to reflect upon the form she has created, upon the point of her own labour. Those critics who sense a certain clumsiness in this episode try to explain it either by penetrating what they suppose to be its moral and psychological implications or by concluding that the novel splits into incongruous halves, with the second marred by improbabilities and irresolution. Heathcliff's change seems too sudden and inadequately motivated by the rationalization he provides: 'I don't care for striking, I can't take the trouble to raise my hands! . . . I have lost the faculty of enjoying their destruction, and I am too idle to destroy for nothing' (p 255). Quibbling over his motives is, I would suggest, beside the point. The revenge plot has been stretched on a cord which snaps, hurtling Heathcliff towards Catherine.

Although the revenge plot abruptly snaps, in doing so it loses none of its qualitative significance, for its impact is transferred from a worldly to an other-worldly terminus. The symbolic action firmly establishes Heathcliff's control over fate. He makes his will felt in a series of successes which ultimately imply that he brings to his real goal the same success and control. Heathcliff, who begins as an unwanted, sometimes persecuted waif, in time becomes sole master over Wuthering Heights, Thrushcross Grange, and their inhabitants. As a young man he went away for three years, to return rich and independent, the image of a man who has dominated circumstances. Heathcliff proceeds to win control of the Heights from Hindley, who had hoped to master him and whose rage and hatred come to nothing, as if to underscore his comparative ineffectuality. Heathcliff's power and control are reaffirmed continually throughout the action, but at the very moment he might exercise his accumulated strength in destruction, he holds his hand, for there is to be no mere worldly stop to his energetic forward movement. Qualitatively his power seems augmented by its suspension, confirming his ability to guide fortune where he chooses, to achieve the single goal for which he cares. That he will fulfil the strange fate Brontë has imagined for him is, in short, given full credibility by the pattern of power which he displays throughout. Brontë must at this point hasten towards her conclusion so that the reader does not lose the impression of this symbolic pattern, but transmutes it to a conviction that Heathcliff reaches Catherine in spirit.

By the thirty-third chapter, all mediation through resemblances, memoranda, personifications, and associations may be discarded as Brontë drives Heathcliff, far from spent or altered, *directly* towards his source. All his thoughts turn exclusively towards Catherine, whom he sees before him as if she were in the same room. Heathcliff now thinks solely of his single wish, convinced that 'it *will* be reached—and *soon*—because it has devoured my existence' (p 256). The book is devoured by the same goal. The line disappears in the circle.

Heathcliff dies, not exhausted and will-less, but at the height of his strength and passion, a fact Brontë emphasizes by keeping him in perfect health until his self-willed end. He takes his life into the grave. Not surprisingly, Dr Kennedy was 'perplexed to pronounce of what disorder the master died.' His fast, Nelly is persuaded, 'was the consequence of his strange illness, not the cause' (p 264). During his last days Heathcliff's grimly smiling countenance communicated 'both pleasure and pain, in exquisite extremes' (p 261), an image fitting perfectly the book's formal polarity. The 'joyful glitter in his eyes' remains in the 'life-like gaze of exultation' on the face of the corpse (p 264). Yet it is also 'sarcastic, savage,' expressing both his fearless anticipation of death ('he looks girning at death,' says Joseph) and his contempt for this world (his eyes 'would not shut; they seemed to sneer at my attempts,' says Nelly). Heathcliff's anguish is quieted as he attains his 'soul's bliss.'

IV

Most of the events in **Wuthering Heights** are *faits accomplis*. What has happened cannot be changed and therefore induces acceptance and belief. The complicated narrative view frequently shifts from the present to the past and the future perfect; the world of Wuthering Heights alternately seems close and remote, as we are assaulted with savage action or lulled with quiet summary. The most concrete, natural, immediate events support the most visionary, giving the whole a quality of reality. Throughout the novel, life lends reality to death. The shifting temporal perspective evokes a sense of omnitemporality, which contributes to our belief in the eternity of Heathcliff's love for Catherine. These two are released from the time boundary which consumes the lives of all the other characters.[10] We view the action through a narrative casement ranging from single to quadruple thickness: events touch Lockwood more or less closely as he experiences them first-hand or through Nelly, at one, two, or three removes. The function and effect of the peculiar narrative technique of this novel, as it specifically involves Nelly Dean as narrator to Lockwood, remain to be considered.

I have already touched on Nelly's function in diverting, at crucial points, the moral onus from Heathcliff onto one of the other characters. She frequently sides with Heathcliff against Edgar, Isabella, and Linton, yet she feels more at home with the platitudinous Lintons. Although her commonsense humanity often promotes our charitable view of Heathcliff as he interacts with the other characters, on one point she consistently opposes

him: his love for Catherine after she marries Edgar. Nelly's commitment to the normal social world naturally makes her a stranger to Catherine's and Heathcliff's passion. She listens, but does not learn; knows the whole story, but fails to apprehend its implications. Her view is not only inadequate, but ultimately irrelevant to the significance of their love.[11] Her good-natured, commonplace sense of things does, however, make an inestimable contribution to Brontë's mode of expressing the central love story and its goal.

Nelly's view of human nature is almost always reliable whenever she judges normal relationships. Her attitude towards Edgar and Catherine's marriage, for example, is as reasonable as Edgar's own; and when Catherine confesses her feelings towards Edgar, Nelly finds no sense in her 'nonsense' except that she is ignorant of the duties she undertakes in marrying (p 74). She is equally uncomprehending when she opposes Heathcliff after he returns from his three-year exile. Because illness had altered Catherine, Nelly imagines that anyone compelled to be her companion 'will only sustain his affection hereafter by the remembrance of what she once was, by common humanity, and a sense of duty!' (p 125). Heathcliff scorns the idea of leaving Catherine to Edgar's '*duty* and *humanity*,' as he tries to impress upon her the distinction between their feelings. She makes no pretence of understanding him. To her his talk is insane, as Catherine's is delirious. When Heathcliff tells her that he exhumed Catherine's body, Nelly quite naturally exclaims: 'you were very wicked, Mr. Heathcliff! were you not ashamed to disturb the Dead?' (p 229). In contrast, Edgar's response to Catherine's death strikes her as proper: 'he was too good to be thoroughly unhappy long. *He* didn't pray for Catherine's soul to haunt him. Time brought resignation, and a melancholy sweeter than common joy. He recalled her memory with ardent, tender love, and hopeful aspiring to the better world, where, he doubted not, she was gone' (p 151). Edgar had, in addition, 'earthly consolation and affections' to divert him, Nelly approvingly notes, in his daughter Cathy, who soon 'wielded a despot's sceptre in his heart' (p 152). In another book these might have been the norms for judgment, but in **Wuthering Heights** they are not. Paradoxically the values rest, instead, in Heathcliff's hating the children and denying Catherine any rest until he joins her. Nelly neither comprehends nor sympathizes with such passions.

By continually raising, through Nelly, the social, moral perspective, Brontë precludes the reader's judging events according to any conventional sense of the world. Because we see that Nelly's judgments of Heathcliff and Catherine, as well as any advice or remedy she offers them, are irrelevant, we give ourselves wholly up to an appreciation of that love for the extraordinary thing it is. What we perceive as impertinent in Nelly's position, we understand to be inappropriate in ourselves.

Thus near the end of the book, when Heathcliff rapturously declares his anticipation of shortly joining Catherine and Nelly feels called on to 'offer some advice' which would make him 'happier' (p 262), we can only smile at their irreconcilable notions of happiness. Her advice has no more to do with these lovers than they have to do with shame or fear.

Brontë does not, I would suggest, construct her indirect narration, then, because the reader would become passive and not exercise his own perception and judgment if the story were approached directly.[12] The direct method of, say, Jane Austen or Thomas Hardy exacts the most active kind of moral awareness and discrimination from the reader. Brontë's indirect narration functions, instead, to make us morally passive but imaginatively flexible. A shift of view is called for because Catherine and Heathcliff fulfil their love outside this world, a transcendence which becomes the ground for evaluation and appreciation. The nature of their love places it beyond all conventional standards. The reader, therefore, adopts a view not morally superior to Nelly's, but completely different in sensibility—as different as Heathcliff's love is from Edgar's.

The effete Lockwood, who foolishly imagines himself another Heathcliff (see chaps 1 and 2), is even less capable than Nelly of judging or appreciating these lovers' experience. He is a *poseur,* both as misanthrope and as lover, leading us to appreciate Heathcliff's authenticity, however savage its expression. Lockwood learns the story of these lovers while idly passing time in the sick room or casually moving in and out of the world of the Heights. Brontë never intended that either he or Nelly should be instructed in her lover's grand passion, but she did not wish to obscure it for her readers.

Just as Nelly embodies the ordinary moral perspective, the old servant Joseph voices the full rigour of divine law, which we also feel to be irrelevant—if not irreverent. Nelly articulates our response to him adequately: 'He was, and is yet, most likely,' she informs Lockwood, 'the wearisomest, self-righteous pharisee that ever ransacked a Bible to rake the promises to himself, and fling the curses on his neighbours' (p 42). Yet Nelly, like Joseph, reviles Heathcliff for his unchristian life, warning him, as he approaches his end, how unfit he is for heaven. But we share Heathcliff's attitude, not hers: 'No minister need come; nor need anything be said over me. I tell you. I have nearly attained *my* heaven; and that of others is altogether unvalued and uncoveted by me!' Heathcliff requires only that the sexton heed his special instructions 'concerning the two coffins' so that his and Catherine's meeting will not be spoiled (p 263; cf pp 228-9). Nelly may be shocked by his 'godless indifference,' but we find it harmonious with both the strange happiness Brontë has prepared for him and the strange power she has devised for us.

Everyone else in **Wuthering Heights** is given a place in the world as we know it; only Catherine and Heathcliff belong to another. It is their experience which we carry away from the book, leaving all the rest behind, as they themselves do. Nelly's idea of happiness is realized in Cathy and Hareton's union; but their love is only the afterglow of the conflagration we have witnessed. At the close of the story, Lockwood visits Catherine's and Heathcliff's graves and notices that 'decay had made progress' upon the church walls. How much more quickly does flesh decay. We are reminded of the dissolution Heathcliff long desired as the perfect consummation of his 'immortal love.' Lockwood wonders 'how any one could ever imagine unquiet slumbers for the sleepers in that quiet earth' (p 266), but we do not. Within the story we accede to the conviction that ghosts 'can, and do exist, among us' (p 229), that 'the dead are not annihilated' (p 263). The wind blowing on the boldly swelling heath is the respiration of a living world.[13]

Notes

1. I adopt the word *lyrical* as a general descriptive term to point up the radical formal difference between *Wuthering Heights* and those novels—Fielding's, Austen's, and Hardy's, for example—shaped by a principle of logically progressive plots. In discussing similar forms in 'Novelists as Storytellers,' Sheldon Sacks formulates the concept of 'a *plot* of "lyric" revelation' (*Modern Philology,* 73 [May 1976], 109). Sacks borrows the phrase 'fluctuating stasis' from Leonard M. Meyer's general description of such forms: in the imaginative world of such a work, progress as normally conceived is absent, since 'the distinction among past, present, and future becomes obscured, is static' (see *Music, the Arts, and Ideas* [Chicago: University of Chicago Press 1967], p 169).

   In the course of formulating my conclusions about Brontë's technique, I was influenced by Erich Auerbach's analysis of Virginia Woolf and Marcel Proust, 'The Brown Stocking,' in *Mimesis: The Representation of Reality in Western Literature,* trans Willard R. Trask (Princeton: Princeton University Press 1953), pp 525-53. Brontë should be placed in the tradition of the novel which leads to Woolf and Proust rather than to Conrad and Lawrence through Hardy. Brontë in some ways anticipates the technical goals of stream-of-consciousness narrative, but whereas a writer like Woolf may oppose exterior events directly to the representation of the processes of consciousness itself, Brontë discloses the remembering consciousness of Heathcliff by playing events off against each other in parallel fashion—the Edgar/Heathcliff, Linton/Hareton conflicts and the

Catherine/Edgar, Cathy/Linton marriages—as well as through parallel characters—Catherine/Cathy, Edgar/Linton, and Heathcliff/Hareton. She adapted the methods of realistic, logical plot-action novels to her own peculiar ends, as I hope to show.

2. *Wuthering Heights: An Authoritative Text with Essays in Criticism,* ed William M. Sale, Jr (New York: Norton 1963), p 133. Page references to the novel are given in the text.

3. See Cecil W. Davies's fruitful pursuit of this idea in 'A Reading of *Wuthering Heights,' Essays in Criticism,* 19 (July 1969), 254-72.

4. Compare Heathcliff's anguish here with his rage immediately after Catherine dies. Nelly observes that he 'dashed his head against the knotted trunk; and, lifting up his eyes, howled, not like a man, but like a savage beast getting goaded to death with knives and spears' (p 139). The exaggeration of Heathcliff's passions symbolically expresses an extra-ordinary existence. As Virginia Woolf has observed, 'it is as if she [Brontë] could tear up all we know human beings by, and fill these unrecognizable transparencies with such a gust of life that they transcend reality': '*Jane Eyre* and *Wuthering Heights,'* in *The Common Reader* (New York: Harcourt, Brace 1925), p 165.

5. An early reviewer of *Wuthering Heights* intuited an effect Brontë intended, but he thought it disclosed an intrinsic flaw: 'like all spendthrifts of malice and profanity, however, he ['Ellis Bell'] overdoes the business. Though he scatters oaths as plentifully as sentimental writers do interjections, the comparative parsimony of the great novelists in this respect is productive of infinitely more effect': *The North American Review,* October 1848, rpt in *The English Novel: Background Readings,* ed Lynn C. Bartlett and William R. Sherwood (Philadelphia: Lippincott 1967), pp 197-8.

6. 'Editor's Preface To the New Edition of *Wuthering Heights* [1850],' in Sale, ed, pp 11-12.

7. *Aspects of the Novel* (New York: Harcourt, Brace 1927), pp 209-10.

8. In the preceding two sentences I adopt some of Auerbach's phrasing from his analysis of *To the Lighthouse* to suggest the relationship between Brontë's and Woolf's techniques. These authors radically differ, of course, in their general thematic intentions. *Wuthering Heights* does not, for example, breathe 'an air of vague and hopeless sadness'; and if it is 'hostile to reality,' it is so in a very different sense from Woolf's novel (see Auerbach, p 551). Brontë is as certain of her transcendent reality as Austen is of her social reality.

9. Sidney Dobell in the *Palladium,* September 1850, in Sale, ed, p 280.

10. Compare Thomas A. Vogler's provocative treatment of time and point of view in *Wuthering Heights,* 'Story and History in *Wuthering Heights,'* in *Twentieth-Century Interpretations of Wuthering Heights,* ed T. A. Vogler (Englewood Cliffs, NJ: Prentice-Hall 1968), pp 85ff.

11. John K. Mathison provides a valuable analysis of Nelly Dean's role and the reader's response to it in 'Nelly Dean and the Power of *Wuthering Heights,' Nineteenth-Century Fiction,* 11 (September 1956), 106-29. Mathison argues that we are released from Nelly's point of view, because of its inadequacy, to become sympathetically involved with 'conventionally despicable' characters (p 118). But for him our gain is exclusively a more 'genuine insight into human emotion' (p 127), specifically of 'the tortured, emotionally distraught person' (p 109).

12. Cf Mathison, p 109.

13. I wish to thank Professor Ralph Wilson Rader, who read the original version of this essay and generously suggested ways to draw out more fully the implications of its argument.

Barbara Munson Goff (essay date summer 1984)

SOURCE: Goff, Barbara Munson. "Between Natural Theology and Natural Selection: Breeding the Human Animal in *Wuthering Heights*." *Victorian Studies* 27, no. 4 (summer 1984): 477-508.

[*In the following essay, Goff presents an unorthodox reading of* Wuthering Heights, *analyzing the novel's central themes within the framework of the radical new theories of evolution that began emerging in the mid-nineteenth century.*]

> [*Wuthering Heights*] is the unformed writing of a giant's hand; the "large utterance" of a baby god.
>
> [Sidney Dobell], *Palladium* (September 1850).
>
> . . . . .

> There can be no interest attached to the writer of *Wuthering Heights*—a novel succeeding *Jane Eyre* and purporting to be written by Ellis Bell—unless it were for the sake of a more individual reprobation. For though there is a decided family likeness between the two, yet the aspect of the Jane and Rochester animals in their native state, as Catherine and Heathfield [*sic*], is too odiously and abominably pagan to be palatable even to the most vitiated class of English readers.
>
> [Elizabeth Rigby, Lady Eastlake], *Quarterly Review* (December 1848).[1]

Contemporary reviewers respond both more and less consciously than modern critics to what lies between the lines of a novel. The two reviews excerpted above represent extremes, to be sure, of reaction to *Wuthering Heights,* reactions unmediated by subsequent general opinion or even accurate information about its authorship. The novel remains, to this day, one which students either love or hate and one which critics and scholars find endlessly fascinating. The fact that virtually every *ism* of the eighteenth, nineteenth, and twentieth centuries has been proposed as a candidate for the novel's hidden agenda bears witness to its apparent theoretical vigor. The above reviews indicate not only extremes of reaction to the novel but also a context more appropriate to its period as well as its author: namely the theological implications of contemporary thinking in the natural sciences. Both Sidney Dobell and Lady Eastlake recognize that there is something fundamentally theological going on, the obvious difference being that the "baby god" is speaking pagan to Eastlake. She has understood all too well, perhaps even better than many modern critics, that something biological is also going on between the lines. Her vehemence is instructive, for it will be matched, a dozen years later, by the outrage effected by Charles Darwin's *Origin of Species* (1859).

Darwin's notebooks of the late 1830s and 1840s, the period of the Brontës' intellectual maturity, demonstrate that the pieces of the evolutionary puzzle had fallen in place decades before the publication of the *Origin*[2]. These notebooks and the later autobiography indicate his reticence to proselytize for the "materialism" in which he so firmly believed, despite the fact that he was able to provide "material," biological bases for the moral and even religious instincts in man. As a scientist, he lacked the protection of Emily Brontë's fiercely maintained cover of pseudonymity, not to mention the possibility of narrative indirectness. But he was able to devise, in the years before notoriety, a persona of sorts: that of a harmless, though scrupulously careful investigator of topsoils and fossils, gentians and flatworms. This somewhat eccentric country gentleman also circulated a number of ingenuous questions to several well-known breeders of domestic animals.[3]

While always alert to the dangerous unorthodoxy of the theory they are elaborating, Darwin's notebooks often suggest a decided giddiness in the triumph of his materialism over the patently ridiculous explanations provided by natural theology. Having weathered the initial vengeance, Darwin became increasingly bold to go the distance of his early conclusions, publishing *The Descent of Man* in 1871 and *The Expression of the Emotions in Man and Animals* the following year. It is impossible to know where Emily Brontë might have gone with her own theories after *Wuthering Heights* or even to define the motives behind her determination to publish the novel, as provocative in its own way as Darwin's theory. It can nevertheless be said that, for both of them, truth had been revealed in a nature relatively untampered with by mankind, and that error proceeded from a human refusal to recognize the fundamental connection between humans and animals. These premises brought both Darwin and Brontë to very similar conclusions about human vis-a-vis animal "nature," at much the same time and "in the [same] air." Both were, more or less deliberately, building a case against the prevailing state of British biology and theology, dominated as both were by William Paley's "Argument from Design," and, more or less concomitantly, against the social and psychological complacency that this natural theology had seemed to justify. This paper places Emily Brontë in what seems then her most appropriate context: the transition from the "design" of Paley's natural theology to Darwin's description of the "mechanism" of natural selection. I argue that Brontë, like Darwin, utterly rejected the anthropocentrism and notions of progress that had served natural theologians as both first and final cause; that Brontë, like Darwin, based her conclusions on observation and knowledge of the manipulations of "selection" on the part of animal breeders, as well as on close and relatively objective observation of animal behavior; that Brontë, more aggressively than Darwin, had come to conclusions about the literal descent of Victorian man from his essential animal nature; that Brontë's conclusions, like Darwin's, grew out of a reverence for the pitiless economy of nature; that Brontë, unlike both Darwin and the natural theologians, was perfectly comfortable with a personal God who operated as ruthlessly as Darwin's "mechanism"; and that—to return this argument to the novel that plays out its propositions—*Wuthering Heights* represents this "God" of hers, this "mechanism," in the character of Heathcliff.

I

Virtually all critics of *Wuthering Heights* have addressed themselves to the rhetoric of animality in the novel, finding in the trope a structural device, a feature of characterization, a clue to Brontë's Renaissance sources, an element of her philosophy of nature, and so on. Few have been as willing as Eastlake to grant animality more than metaphorical status. Those who have seem as unable as Eastlake to extricate themselves from that Great Chain of Being Darwin had aimed to subvert: "brutish," "inhuman," "ferocious" are terms we are all assumed to understand as pejoratives. J. Hillis Miller's definition of life at Wuthering Heights as "a return [to an animal state] reached only through the transgression of all human law" exemplifies this position among modern critics, the difference between his reading and Eastlake's lying mainly in his attribution of the moral outrage to the author herself.[4] Darwin had been at great pains to reserve terms like "brutish," "savage," and "cruel" for human behavior, and goes to some lengths in his later works to catalogue the social, psychological, and even moral virtues of animals.[5] Our interpretations of the rhetoric of animality, even before

Darwin and certainly after, depend entirely on where the reader ranks human behavior and human law in the hierarchy of nature. Brontë and Darwin both seem to have preferred the moral instincts—and even the company—of dogs.[6]

Evolution had been, as we say, "in the air" since the 1830s, but that atmosphere was created largely by geologists and paleontologists. Little suggests that Emily Brontë had been influenced by that literature: Catherine's love for Heathcliff is, after all, "like the *eternal* rocks beneath" (italics mine).[7] Nor is evolution per se (the development of new species over eons) the question or issue for Brontë, whose own sense of natural selection operates over both a shorter (since "1500") and a longer ("eternal") temporal framework. She is concerned only with the moral, social, psychological, and theological implications of natural science. Darwin himself had attempted, in the same years, to distinguish the issues by sorting his speculations and observations into notebooks on "transmutation" and "metaphysics." We do know that both Charlotte and Emily Brontë were avid students of natural history, delighting in such animal lore as the "Dogiana" columns of *Chambers's Edinburgh Journal*.[8] Similarly anecdotal accounts of animal behavior also fed Darwin's notebooks and speculations. My own evidence suggests that Brontë knew, also, a great deal about the history and practice of sheep-breeding in Yorkshire and that these facts became as crucial to her understanding of human nature as they had to Darwin's theory of natural selection. Studying Brontë's work in the context of contemporary natural science confirms what had formerly been only an intuitive response to *Wuthering Heights*: that the novel is a hypothetical experiment in the breeding of human beings, conducted to suggest how the breed has been corrupted from its "native state" by the very civilization that the Lady Eastlakes arbitrate.

In a truly "Fresh Approach to *Wuthering Heights*," Q. D. Leavis first elucidated the line of sociological argument in the novel, a line more vigorously pursued by Terry Eagleton's Marxist study. These analyses of the novel's commentary on the social and economic deterioration of a nineteenth-century rural community leave little more to be said. The importance of such commentary has been clear ever since C. P. Sanger revealed Brontë's knowledge of English property law.[9] But all three of these critics readily admit that the social commentary is not what arouses contemplation on the first or even tenth reading of *Wuthering Heights*. The novel is about far more fundamental, eternal human problems and overwhelms us with its remorseless—if not easily definable—sense of the workings of things.

Anyone at all familiar with Emily Brontë's poetry and personality knows that she had no interest whatsoever in "society"—in any sense of the word. She did not go particularly out of her way for people, aside from her own family and servants, and was distant and diffident even with her sisters' friends. "All that I, a stranger, have been able to learn about her," Elizabeth Gaskell remarks, "has not tended to give either me, or my readers, a pleasant impression."[10] Though Brontë's poetry reveals a private struggle to reconcile herself to her disappointment in human folly and weakness,[11] she seems never to have altered her social behavior toward those she considered unjustifiably privileged, pampered, weak. An indefatigable worker herself, she clearly respected the industriousness of the working classes. Later biographers, therefore, came away with far better impressions by consulting family servants and local tradesmen, or their descendants. *Wuthering Heights* itself testifies to the close attention Brontë had paid the working people among whom she grew up, to her fondness for their "plain-speaking" and matter-of-fact vision of the ways of the world and of their supposed "betters." Brontë was schooled by them, and her sense of debt and admiration is, as Leavis suggests, a source for the sociological warp of the novel's fabric.

But is it necessary to postulate, as Leavis does, *two* novels—a "sociological" and a "real" *Wuthering Heights*—going on in tandem? We clearly get two stories for the price of one, the first ending with the simultaneous death of the first heroine and birth of the second, but the distinctions between these two novels are those of decorum and genre rather than subject. The sociology of *Wuthering Heights* is, furthermore, consistent with its theories of biology, psychology, and theology—a common thread that runs through both novels: Brontë is constructing an "argument from design" that accounts for her vision of both nature and human history, and she is of one mind about both. Dobell's "'large utterance' of a baby god" far more aptly accounts for our sense of sureness and coherence in the novel's metaphysics, despite surface confusions of character and time.[12] Dictating the words of its numerous inadequate or partial narrators is a consciousness at least as sure of itself and presumptuous as that of Milton "justify[ing] the ways of God to man." Our awareness of this consciousness is literally "metaphysical," speaking over and above the words that create the characters and events. We know what we know of the novel's truth in much the same way that the "truth" is revealed to a religious visionary, who sees through the apparent surfaces of things.

One of the few things that we know about Emily Brontë, from her designatedly personal poems, is that she felt God speaking to her on the moors. That God speaks in the "Book of Nature" as well as in the Bible is the premise upon which natural theology had been based for centuries. It was most definitely the moral of Reverend Brontë's numerous sermons and publications on the Crow Hill Bog Burst of 1824, an event that Emily

Brontë had witnessed when she was six.[13] Such sermons were in the brimstone for Romantics, fundamentalists, and Haworth Sunday Schoolers alike. Personal revelation was, however, another matter entirely, one at odds with Anglican orthodoxy. Behind the anonymity of "Ellis Bell," Emily Brontë became as determined as Darwin to present the whole picture of human nature and as driven as an Old Testament prophet to speak the truth, regardless of its effect on an audience for whose moral weaknesses she, like the prophets and her own Joseph, felt little pity.

Emily Brontë was not merely shy and reclusive but downright ascetic and misanthropic. *Wuthering Heights* is animated by her contempt for humanity and its fallen ways. But it also offers salvation for those readers willing to accept the harshness of its vision, for it describes, in terms and forms familiar to its audience from gothic romance, the possibility of a union with the awesome and destructive powers of nature/God that transcends normal experience. Rather than trying to describe such experience directly, as Brontë does in her poetry, *Wuthering Heights* allows us only to glimpse it through the eyes and mouths of speakers who are themselves, as we gather by degrees, at a loss for coming to terms with it or with its incarnation, Heathcliff. Nelly Dean, sharing the superstitions of the Yorkshire peasantry, is at least open to "supernatural" experience, though she reduces it to familiar ghosts, demons, and fairies. Brontë presents her own caveat to the reader by having Nelly, the best of her narrators, explain to Lockwood—the most short-sighted and also, I think, Brontë's personal archetype of the reader of novels and "artificial man of cities"—"You'll judge as well as I can, all these things, at least you'll think you will, and that's the same" (chap. 17). The reader's judgment of *Wuthering Heights* is ultimately a matter of coming to terms with Heathcliff. The more intellectually provocative modern analyses of the novel have, I think, made a poorer showing in this respect than the more romantic, symbolic, or mystical readings that characterized appreciations of the novel in its first hundred years. The worst offender in this regard may be Q. D. Leavis herself, who rebukes those critics for not understanding that "[Heathcliff] is merely a convenience," a plotting device (Leavis, p. 96).

The novel's chief interest, for narrators and readers alike, is psychological, as is Leavis's otherwise superb analysis of the characters; she may thus be excused for her technical reduction of Heathcliff. He is not very complicated psychologically and does not "develop" at all. He exits from the novel, leaving its readers and characters in the same state as Mr. Earnshaw was upon introducing him into the family circle thirty-two years before: "I was never so beaten with anything in my life; but you must e'en take it as a gift of God, though it's as dark almost as if it came from the devil" (chap. 4). I will not elaborate the subsequent identification of Heath-

cliff with the devil on the part of all the characters—or Charlotte Brontë's more grisly specification, a "Ghoul." More to my point is Nelly's alternative version of ways in which Heathcliff confounds categorization and human intercourse: "I did not feel as if I were in the company of a creature of my own species; it appeared that he would not understand, though I spoke to him; so I stood off, and held my tongue, in great perplexity" (chap. 15). Heathcliff is, if possible, identified as an animal even more frequently than as a demon. Heathcliff's power transcends that of mere humans and, I believe, is the power that Brontë equates with nature, if not God Himself. Again, Eastlake's reading is accurate: Brontë was a pagan in the most wholesome and primal sense of the word, and, as the parson's daughter, was especially vulnerable to suggestions of "devilment." Like William Blake, Brontë used the strategy of simply reversing charges on such words as reason and energy, good and evil, heaven and hell (and also, like Darwin, animal and human). Her authoritative absence from the novel allows us, even forces us, to "think we will [have judged]" Heathcliff when, in fact, we have merely confirmed our own presumptions. Salvation has always been a risky theological proposition, but we have never been denied the freedom to go to hell in our own handbaskets.

The most distressing reading of Heathcliff as evil, "indeed . . . unredeemed"—distressing because it would seem to validate decades of misunderstanding—is Charlotte Brontë's. In her "Preface" to the 1850 edition of *Wuthering Heights,* she doubts "whether it is right or advisable to create beings like Heathcliff" and attempts to excuse her sister on grounds that she "did not know what she had done," not being "a lady or a gentleman accustomed to what is called 'the world.'" It is difficult to believe that such an intelligence as Charlotte's failed so completely to comprehend her sister's, or that she really believes that Nelly Dean, good hearted though she may be, is the spiritual center of *Wuthering Heights.* Reviews such as Eastlake's, however, forced an awareness of the power of her sister's unorthodoxy on her. Having opened the can of worms in the first place, Charlotte must have felt especially obliged to defend her late sisters from snobbish reviewers and their charges of crudeness and blasphemy. It is possible to find, between the lines of Charlotte's introductory essays, yet another assault on a "vitiated class of English readers" (the one to which Lockwood, Eastlake, and most of us belong) to place beside the one mounted by *Wuthering Heights* itself, Charlotte being relatively adept at the art of sarcasm.

Emily Brontë seems to have defied categorization, for even Charlotte is unable—or unwilling—to define her sister's creed for so sympathetic an audience as Charlotte's own editor, W. S. Williams, who had offered the three sisters the opportunity to come to London to see more of "what is called 'the world'":

> Ellis [Emily Brontë], I imagine, would soon turn aside from the spectacle [of London] in disgust. I do not think he admits it as his creed that 'the proper study of mankind is man'—at least not the artificial man of cities. In some points I consider Ellis somewhat of a theorist: now and then he broaches ideas which strike my sense as more daring and original than practical; his reason may be in advance of mine, but certainly it often travels a different road. I should say Ellis will not be seen in his full strength till he is seen as an essayist.[14]

The prospect of discourse of more "full strength" than *Wuthering Heights* begs credulity. I, nonetheless, find this passage Charlotte's truest assessment of her sister's achievement, accurate as well as insightful. Her estimate of her sister's true strength is echoed in the probably independent judgment of M. Héger, their schoolmaster in Brussels, who told Gaskell that "Emily had a head for logic, and a capability of argument, unusual in a man, and rare indeed in a woman. . . . Impairing the force of this gift, was her stubborn tenacity of will, which rendered her obtuse to all reasoning where her own wishes, or her sense of right, was concerned" (Gaskell, p. 230). The rectitude of Emily Brontë's "creed"—whatever it was—is emphasized again in the praise of another of the few people who know her personally, Charlotte's friend, Ellen Nussey: "Emily's extreme reserve seemed impenetrable, yet she was intensely lovable; she invited confidence in her moral power."[15]

None of these testimonials to Brontë's character is able to divorce the toughness of her mind from her passionate intensity. The same may also be said of *Wuthering Heights,* an emotional experience matched in rawness only by the *Lear* it so clearly resembles. As with *Lear,* we are presented with "unaccommodated man," "the thing itself," the "poor, bare, forked animal[s]" mankind becomes when bereft of artificial dominion over animal nature. As with *Lear,* it is equally difficult to locate an authoritative voice in the work, internal evidence continuously refuting all suggested formulations. Yet we do not come to the conclusion, as we can with *Lear,* that *Wuthering Heights* is simply nihilistic. Even Samuel Johnson would have approved of the novel's ending, for the virtuous seem finally to prosper. But what then is its creed, its argument, its moral?

I nominate an intuitive, religious version of the theory of natural selection, derived, as Darwin's was, from close observation of nature and a profound respect for its driving forces, the simultaneity of creation and destruction, the laws of conservation of matter and energy. *Wuthering Heights* shows these driving forces,

embodied in Heathcliff, at work over three generations. Adaptation is, indeed, in evidence, but it is adaptation to an environment whose deterioration gathers momentum with the accommodations of civilization. Brontë differs from Darwin, however, in a significant respect: try as he might to avoid and deny it, Darwin could not help but suggest that evolution was progressive. Brontë's view is more traditionally orthodox, suggesting, literally, the *descent* of man, sin originating in our fall from animal nature. "Methodical selection," in man as in animals, has not improved the breed.

II

> Emily, half-reclining on a slab or stone, played like a young child with the tadpoles in the water, making them swim about, and then fell to moralising on the strong and the weak, the brave and the cowardly, as she chased them with her hand.[16]

Ellen Nussey is recalling one of Brontë's rare moments of volubility. *Wuthering Heights* similarly moralizes on the strong and the weak, and virtually everyone is weak except for Catherine and Heathcliff, Joseph and Zillah, the survivors at the Heights. Nelly, Hareton, and Cathy Linton are also survivors, but, as I shall argue, they pave the way for vitiation of the breed by their voluntary domestication at Thrushcross Grange. The third generation is, therefore, absolutely necessary to Emily Brontë's moral because it is in them that specific strengths and weaknesses of the human animal can be expressed and assessed.

Were *Wuthering Heights* merely a romantic novel, it would have concluded where romantic novels, William Wyler's film version, and many readers' memories of it leave off: with Catherine and Heathcliff dying happily ever after. The sequel might have begun with the posthumous birth of the lonely, lovely, soon-to-be-landless daughter. But that was not Brontë's strategy. *Wuthering Heights* is, instead, a kind of botanical experiment, the grafting of a bourgeois romance of marriage and property onto a gothic romance of love and death. It is the grafting that attracts those of us who read the novel theoretically, trying to discover what it is really about. Leavis asserts that "*Wuthering Heights* became a responsible piece of work, once Brontë began to see it as a way to alert her own (Early Victorian) generation [to the dangers of rapid social and ecological change]" (Leavis, p. 101). J. Hillis Miller defines the strategy of *Wuthering Heights* as that of "a detective story. First the reader encounters the corpse of a dead community. Then the novel explains, by a process of retrospective reconstruction, how things came to be as they are."[17]

Miller's "retrospective reconstruction" is more aptly characteristic of Brontë's temperament than Leavis's "way to alert," for Leavis's position assumes that Brontë thinks it possible for humans to reverse the direction of change. For Brontë, as for the Old Testament prophets, it was already too late. Miller, arguing for Brontë's overwhelming sense of doom, thus comes closer to the sociological truth of the novel from an analysis of her religious background. The "soul" of the community had long since been sold; clerical weakness was simply the most obvious symptom, for the Brontës as for William Cowper and George Crabbe before them. I am, however, equally unsatisfied by Miller's version of Brontë's creed, despite agreeing that Brontë herself, in a certain mood, can be heard in Joseph's unsolicited commentary on the action at the Heights. Miller depicts Brontë as wandering between the doom of her aunt's Methodism and the optimistic salvation of her father's evangelical Anglicanism, both of which conspired to make her distrust her mystical experiences of God's immanence and lament their "insufficiency" (Miller, "Emily Brontë," pp. 181-186). For Winifred Gérin, however, Brontë's experiences were themselves sufficient to overwhelm both doctrine and doubt. She locates Brontë's frustration in an obsession with her inability to summon the visions at will (Gérin, chaps. 10-13, 18).

Both of these versions of Brontë's theology are compelling and well supported. Brontë's view of the world was dim, even grim. But "moralising" on the tadpoles comes closer than traditional theologies to the epistemology that informs both **Wuthering Heights** and Darwin's theory of natural selection. All of the characters, except Heathcliff, are varying mixtures of strength and weakness, cowardice and bravery. The traits they exhibit as children become exacerbated with age. Most of the characters, save Heathcliff, confess to a sense of being unable to help themselves when they behave badly, Catherine Earnshaw being the most extreme example.[18] Her daughter, Cathy Linton, is a significant exception, for she always acts, even misbehaves, deliberately: the child con-artist develops into the only character sufficiently willful to stand up to Heathcliff.[19] In short, Emily Brontë's "retrospective reconstruction of how things came to be as they are" speaks for a biological/psychological destiny, the irreversibility of human nature, regardless of whether her position rests on notions of humankind's fall or an individual's psychological endowment. **Wuthering Heights** is an hypothetical experiment in the expression of such parental sins or temperamental traits over several generations.

Modern readers of Emily Brontë are, in fact, fortunate to have at least a glimpse of Ellis Bell as a "theorist," albeit inchoate, in the surviving French *devoirs* performed for M. Héger on more or less assigned topics. Though it would be even worse than having our own freshman English papers produced as evidence of our mature thought—worse because of Brontë's linguistic handicap—the essays suggest the "full strength" of the voice to which Charlotte Brontë alludes and are, moreover, consistent with the theoretical nature of **Wuther-**

ing Heights, composed three to five years later. Of particular psychological interest are **"Portrait: King Harold before the Battle of Hastings"** and two entirely imaginary letters, one to a mother and the other from a brother to a brother. A bit of relevant sociology can be found in **"The Palace of Death,"** in which Death appoints, as its viceroy, Intemperance, identified as the only true vice because it thrives on the surfeit made possible by Civilization.

More pertinent to Brontë's own natural theology are **"The Cat," "The Butterfly,"** and **"Filial Love."** Each of these essays argues that humanity's fall was not shared by the more pristine animals, with the single exception of cats, whose "hypocrisy, cruelty, and ingratitude" are matched only by humans'. **"The Cat"** opens with the assertion that the speaker loves them, in spite of their human nature, and concludes that cats "owe all their greed and bad qualities to the forefather of humankind, for assuredly, the cat was not wicked in Paradise."[20] The essay on **"The Butterfly"** opens with a description of nature as "an enigma, it exists on a principle of destruction," yet closes with the assertion that God is, in fact, "the god of justice and mercy; then, assuredly, each pain that he inflicts on his creatures, be they human or animal, rational or irrational, . . . is but a seed for that divine harvest which will be reaped when sin [has dispensed] its last drop of venom" (Gérin, p. 272). Brontë presents the same data as her contemporary, Alfred Lord Tennyson, showing numerous aspects of "Nature, red in tooth and claw," but without resorting to Tennyson's divorce of either "man" or God from animals or "Nature." Humanity's fall, for Brontë, is the result of a continuously reenacted failure to accept the larger simultaneity of creation and destruction, the larger rationality of apparent irrationality and individual suffering. The essays are, in short, her own renditions of "the argument from design," pushing, however, beyond natural theology to Darwin's rebuttal of anthropocentrism.

No discussion of biology or religion in England during the first half of the nineteenth century can avoid the literature of natural theology. It is, therefore, surprising that, for all the discussions of the Brontës' love of "nature" and animals and for all the analyses of animal imagery in **Wuthering Heights,** there has been no serious examination of the novel in relation to natural theology.[21] It is inconceivable that the Brontës could have escaped exposure: natural history was a subject of great interest to them. Charlotte Brontë lists "Bewick and Audubon and Goldsmith [the *History of Animated Nature*] and White's *Natural History [of Selbourne]*" in her recommended reading for Ellen Nussey.[22] Emily copied drawings from Thomas Bewick's *British Birds* (1797), and all three sisters did naturalistic portraits of the family pets. Given their obvious interest in natural history, it is probably a persistent sentimentalism (and possibly sexism) regarding the Brontës' intellectual isolation that has prevented us from seeing them relatively aggressively pursuing scientific interests. Charlotte Brontë remarks on this very point in a letter to Ellen Nussey concerning the lectures given by her father and the curate William Weightman at the Keighley Mechanics Institute, at least one of which the girls were allowed to attend: "[B]oth are spoken of very highly in the newspaper, and it is mentioned as a matter of wonder that such displays of intellect should emanate from the village of Haworth, situated amongst the bogs and mountains, and, until very lately, supposed to be in a state of semi-barbarism. Such are the words of the newspaper."[23]

Such interest in the natural sciences would have certainly been encouraged by Patrick Brontë. As a schoolmaster in Ireland he had instituted field trips and nature studies. He attended Cambridge in the very years of Archdeacon Paley's initial impact and vouchsafed to the local surgeon that he had kept up his scientific studies in the interim.[24] His library included textbooks in anatomy, pharmacology, chemistry, and a sadly annotated copy of T. J. Graham's *Domestic Medicine* (Lock and Dixon, pp. 486, 373). He furthermore participated in the activities of Keighley Mechanics Institute and subscribed to its library. A weekly trek to exchange armloads of books was a task rotated through the family, and the children, much to the horror of some, were allowed to read anything. Two copies of Paley's *Moral Philosophy* and another "Paley" (in the "Beauties of Literature" series) are listed in the 1841 catalogue of the Keighley Mechanics Institute Library.[25] Patrick Brontë's sermon on the Crow Hill Bog Burst, furthermore, one of the few of his that survive, opens with the scientific explanation of the phenomenon, as well as Biblical analogues, but proceeds specifically to contrast responses of scientists "who only looked at second causes and grovelled here below" with that of "one who saw by faith through nature to Nature's God" (Lock and Dixon, pp. 250-251). The exempla and language of Emily's early essays similarly resonate with the language and method of natural theology.

Paley's *Natural Theology: or, Evidences of the Existence and Attributes of the Deity, Collected from the Appearances of Nature* was a virtual encyclopedia of natural history, anatomy, meteorology, and astronomy, describing phenomena and then explaining them in terms of final causes. The following passage is typical—and almost makes one lament the loss of teleology for the prose of science:

> Neither ought it, under this head, to be forgotten how much the instinct *costs* the animal which feels it; how much a bird, for example, gives up, by sitting upon her nest; how repugnant it is to her organization, her habits, and her pleasures. An animal, formed for liberty, submits to confinement, in the very season when every thing invites her abroad: what is more; an animal delighting in motion, made for motion, all whose motions are so easy and so free, hardly a moment, at other times, at rest, is, for many hours of many days together, fixed to her nest, as close as if her limbs were tied down by pins and wires. For my part, I never see a bird in that situation, but I recognize an invisible hand, detaining the contented prisoner from her fields and groves, for a purpose, as the event proves, the most worthy of the sacrifice, the most important, the most beneficial.

> But the loss of liberty is not the whole of what the procreant bird suffers. Harvey tells us, that he has often found the female wasted to skin and bone by sitting upon the eggs.[26]

This passage from Paley, like so many others, bespeaks a sentiment, tone, and attitude often encountered in the poetry and prose of Emily Brontë, and is only slightly more vivid and anthropomorphic than Darwin's own descriptions of animal behavior.[27] Take, for example, the following passage from Brontë's essay, **"Filial Love"**: "Parents love their children, it is a principle of nature; the doe fears not the dogs when her little one is in danger, the bird would die on her nest: this instinct is a portion of the divine soul which we share with all animals that exist, and has not God placed in the heart of the infant a comparable feeling?" (Gérin, p. 269). Naturally. But Brontë goes on to find little evidence for this instinct in the contemporary world.

Certainly one would not have to have studied Paley to make these observations. But Paley has used, in the cited chapter, the sagacity of the butterfly in knowing where best to deposit the caterpillar larvae as his trump argument for instinct as meta-utilitarian, therefore divinely inspired. **"Filial Love"** itself goes on to locate, in the fact of God's having to articulate the Fifth Commandment, her evidence of humanity's fall from instinct/nature/God, and her next surviving essay, **"The Butterfly,"** written less than a week later, discusses the caterpillar-butterfly metamorphosis as exemplary of God's creation of life from death and destruction, of beauty from ugliness, of the soul's release from the misery of this world, and—most originally—of our presumption in defining these qualities anthropocentrically. These essays read, in short, very much like critical commentaries on passages in Paley, providing alternative readings of his own "evidences." Darwin adopted the same technique in his notebooks: copying out or referring to passages from the natural theologians, questioning the conclusions to which the authors had come and substituting his own "materialist" interpretation of the observation in question.

Even if Emily Brontë had never studied Paley, the literature of natural theology informed the prose she grew up on—Anglican sermons and the periodicals the Brontë children pored over. Another coincidence lurks in the fact that Paley's chief apologist and editor in the

Brontës' own time was a professor at the Royal College of Surgeons by the name of Sir Charles Bell. Bell, a forerunner in the field of comparative anatomy, had come to popular attention as the author of the fourth Bridgewater Treatise: *The Hand: Its Mechanism and Vital Endowments as Evincing Design.*[28] The Bridgewater Treaties, which were also to be found in the Keighley library, pushed natural theology to its absurd extreme: where Paley found assurance and comfort in his conviction that all the apparent evil and irrationality in nature could be explained from a God's-eye view, the authors of the Bridgewater Treatises were bound to assert that man himself is God's final cause, that, in the title of the second volume, "External Nature" had been "Adapt[ed] to Man." Bell strongly qualifies the idea that the world was made *for* man by stressing the hand and the attendant technology which "convert the being who is weakest in natural defence to the ruler of animate and inanimate nature" (C. Bell, p. 18). Bell thus reiterates the often overlooked point that environments themselves are not stable, but continuously altered by humans, albeit with God's imprimatur, in order to achieve their own adaptation and survival.

If one examines the work of the Brontë sisters from the perspective of contemporary thought on the plasticity of human nature, a classic debate along the typical lines of the "nature-nurture" controversy emerges. Bell himself so deftly aims for equilibrium between the forces of nature and nurture that I want to suggest him as a possible source for their choice of the pseudonym. The Brontës had access not only to the series of Bridgewater Treatises, but also to a "Phenomena of Nature (Bell's) 2 copies," and, in all likelihood, his edition of Paley, which by their time had become the standard—and required reading in the British universities.[29] As an allusion it certainly signifies their work better than the middle name of the newly arrived curate, Arthur Bell Nicholls, despite the fact he would eventually become Charlotte's husband.[30]

Charlotte's novels can themselves be seen as hypothetical experiments in altering the environments of characters familiar to her, in order to bring them to more personally satisfying (for good or ill) ends than actual circumstances had permitted. *Shirley* is the most immediately relevant: what if a woman of Emily's fortitude and will had been graced with money and power? The novel became, for Charlotte, a tribute to Emily, who sickened and died in the course of its composition: Shirley Keeldar's ferocity increases in direct proportion with Emily's own stoicism and recalcitrance. The novel captures virtually every memorable incident in Emily's life that has come down to us, including the obsession with animals and an almost pagan worship of nature. But to make these experiments work out as novels, Charlotte frequently resorted to "fudging" coincidences that beg belief and weaken her plots. Anne Brontë's

novels are neither hypothetical nor experiments. Her avowed intention is "to tell the truth, for truth always conveys its own moral to those who are able to receive it."[31] Indeed, she did little more than change the names in recounting episodes from her own and her brother's experiences and clearly implied the morals to be drawn from them. In the nature-nurture debate, Anne thus takes a middle position, believing both that humanity is fallen (though salvageable) and that, at least in her brother's case, unhappy circumstances and human cruelty provide occasion for further deterioration.[32]

Anne and Emily's Gondal saga had more than satisfied, perhaps even exhausted, their need for private fantasies with romantic paper dolls (or wooden soldiers). Emily Brontë's hypothetical experiment in **Wuthering Heights** is neither a game of supposition nor a "moralising" from direct observation. Emily was more philosophical and far more despairing of the possibility of the perfectibility of human life than her sisters. In the hypothetical debate she takes the extreme side of "nature": people are what they are, no matter what they are, no matter what the circumstances, and what they are is fallen from nature itself.

Wuthering Heights shows civilization, the process by which people "adapt external nature," as a reversal of the order of nature, making "the being weakest in natural defence" unnaturally strong and unnaturally brave. Edgar Linton, for example, can only bring himself to confront Heathcliff with the accommodation of "a brace of pistols" and a goon squad of peasants. Only the vicious taunting of his mate is sufficient stimulus to bring out the "animal" in him, and a power beyond his control forces him to go for Heathcliff's jugular (chap. 11). It is the moment when we most admire him; usually we are invited only to feel painfully sorry for him. Thrushcross Grange (a place where wealth, in this case the fruits of the labor of peasants, is collected, counted, and stored away) typifies this reversal of God's natural order. If Thrushcross Grange—it is difficult even to pronounce—is the heaven that so many of the characters tell us it is, then "heaven [does] not seem to be [Catherine's] home" (chap. 9)—nor Emily Brontë's.

All sociological issues are, by this definition of Brontë's "creed," post-lapsarian, and her commentaries, however telling, merely symptomatic of a more profound vitiation of the species, human beings having become the "artificial [men] of cities." Artificial wealth has made it possible for the inhabitants of Thrushcross Grange, including the tenant Lockwood, to cut themselves off from the land, do no work for a living, and act out a town scenario in the midst of rugged moors, which they keep out of sight and mind by the gardens, fences, and hedges of Thrushcross Park. The Grange allows for the proliferation of moral runts, whose very survival is made possible by peasants and servants. They sicken, even die, at the slightest provocation. Had they been born at Wuthering Heights, Hareton Earnshaw would have hung them by the chairback. Emily Brontë's contempt for them is exceeded only by Heathcliff's. **Wuthering Heights** is indeed a "retrospective reconstruction" of how humankind got into this sorry state, suggesting that the species has been weakened by poor breeding methods, hyperdomestication, and the hyper-"adaptation of external nature" to humanity's fallen nature.

III

[The Westmorland sheep were] sik as God set upon the land, so they never change any.

J. Lawrence, *General Treatise on Cattle* (1809).[33]

Though we tend, in retrospect, to blame natural theology and its "argument from design" for crippling the progress of science—certainly constraining, for example, the acceptance of Darwinism in England—it nonetheless made possible the pursuit of scientific investigation within institutions that maintained subscription to the Thirty-Nine Articles and royal charters. Natural theology had, since the Renaissance, underpinned natural history, making it possible for priests of such diverse temperaments as Robert Herrick and Gilbert White to pursue their inclinations without compromising their Holy Orders. Anglican natural theology screened the "paganism" of an Emily Brontë and the "presumption" of the natural sciences from the obscurantist hell-fires of Calvinism. Gavin de Beer points out, furthermore, that Paley "had, in fact, [provided] a catalogue of adaptations that was shortly to come in very useful [for Darwin]."[34] Darwin was very well aware of his own debt to Paley, pointing out in his *Autobiography* that the necessity to "get up Paley" for exams at Cambridge was "the only part of the academic course which, as I then felt, and as I still believe, was of the least use to me in the education of my mind."[35]

Brontë's vision of the natural order of things, as I have suggested, was very close to Darwin's, based, as it may have been, on the same sources—both written and observed—and the same sense of wonder in the beauty, economy, justice, and apparent wisdom of "Nature," in Brontë's case, or "natural selection" in Darwin's. All of Brontë's works bespeak her belief in the "argument from design" and the identity of "Nature" with "God," but differ in her insistence on confronting the thorniest issues: cats with rats' tails hanging from their mouths, schoolgirls crushing caterpillars, the "nest of little skeletons" (chap. 12) that drives Catherine to despair. The design of Brontë's universe is far more brutal than Paley's: these cases are not the exceptions, but the rule. And for both Darwin and Brontë, unnecessary cruelty was the distinct feature of human behavior. In nature, death and destruction on a massive scale are necessary for the proliferation of life and variety.

Darwin and Brontë shared interest in another line of inquiry, namely the vast body of practical knowledge and lore concerning the breeding of domestic animals, which had been rapidly developing since the middle of the eighteenth century. Indeed, Darwin opens his *Origin* with an appeal to the *prima facie* evidence of species variation in the "methodical selection" conducted by breeders of animals.[36] The success of Robert Bakewell's New Leicester sheep, a hybrid that produced high quality meat and wool, towards the end of the eighteenth century, and the general interest in "rural improvement" and "scientific agriculture" gave rise to a number of experiments in what Darwin terms "unconscious, or methodical selection," most notably the attempt on the part of farmers in the West Riding to create an animal with long fine wool that was also hardy enough to survive the terrain. The local variety most admired for its fitness was the "heath sheep," or Linton, named after the market from which they were exported to the Highlands in the middle of the eighteenth century. George Culley's description of the Linton sheep reveals much about the mood of the times:

The Heath Breed have large spiral horns, black faces [their distinctive feature], and black legs, a fierce wild-looking eye and a short, firm carcass . . . covered with long, open, coarse, shagged wool; the fleeces . . . sold in 1792 for 6d. per lb. They are an exceedingly active and hardy race, run with amazing agility, and seem the best adapted of all others to high, exposed heathy, mountainous districts . . . what a pity they are not covered with a finer and more valuable fleece! There is no doubt but it might be improved. Indeed it is scarce possible to make it coarser.[37]

Another agriculturalist displaces the value of "improvement" even further from the animals themselves: "If it were possible to give these animals a less restless nature, and ample fleece of finer wool, without impairing the hardiness and other qualities which fit them so peculiarly for their bleak and barren situations, it would prove the greatest benefit that could be conferred on moorland property."[38] The actual "improvement" of the Linton's coarse wool was eventually accomplished by diet and "the vigorous culling of weak ewes and small lambs, and only keeping such as are of the best size and shape" (Trow-Smith, p. 140). Such also was the fate of the Lintons of Thrushcross Grange.

Another variety of sheep is of more than passing interest to the reader of **Wuthering Heights,** the Penistone:

In the West Riding, and on the borders of Lancashire, a breed of short-woolled sheep has existed from time immemorial. They are horned, with mottled or spotted faces and legs; some of them, however, are white-faced. They are called the Penistone sheep, from the town situated between Sheffield and Huddersfield, to which they are usually driven for sale. . . . Towards the north it has been oftener crossed with the heath sheep, and then the legs and faces are black or grey, or spotted: but the fleece is not improved, becoming more coarse and open . . . The short-woolled sheep are diminishing in the West Riding, and the long wools are found wherever the pasture is good enough to support them.[39]

William Youatt thus describes, in 1837, what was well known to be one of the casualties of these breeding experiments, the loss of the "pure" Penistone variety by crosses with the Lintons, the "heath sheep" to which he refers. Only the Westmorland sheep, referred to at the head of this section, seem to have escaped the permanent deterioration of the Linton cross.

Emily Brontë was probably not familiar with the literature of animal husbandry. None of these treatises, not even Arthur Young's classic (and popular) compendium, the *Annals of Agriculture* (1784-1809), is recorded as being in the Keighley library, despite the fact that such Mechanics Institutes were models for the American agricultural colleges. The Brontës' great-great grandfather, however, had been a cattle trader in Ireland, his foster-son Welsh Brunty ferrying the cattle to market in Liverpool.[40] To Patrick Brontë's credit, he was never ashamed of his humble origins, and some of that family lore and knowledge must have been passed on to his children. Charlotte Brontë has Shirley Keeldar taking great and active interest in the management and husbandry of her cattle. Local newspapers, furthermore, were full of agricultural information, and such "country matters" would certainly have been known by the peasants and servants whose conversation Emily Brontë attended to. No competing explanation for her nomenclature in *Wuthering Heights* is quite so compelling as this, even taking into account that the attributes of the two varieties of sheep reverse those of the characters: the ruggedness, fierce eyes, coarse wool, and black faces of Linton sheep being more like Heathcliff, and the fine fleece of the Penistone closer to the features of the Linton characters. Penistone Crags, furthermore, indicates the "Nature" that Heathcliff represents, apart from the house with which he is associated. The Lintons are, however, hyperdomesticated, with the exception of Cathy, who loves the moors and is taken to Penistone Crags by Hareton. With reference to the sheep, furthermore, Emily would have been able to observe only the *ex post facto* evidence, the worse aspects of the crossbred sheep that were grazing in the 1830s; she, or her sources, may have been confused about the pedigree of the traits.

Emily did have available to her, however, the second Bridgewater Treatise, John Kidd's *On the Adaptation of External Nature to the Physical Condition of Man.*[41] Kidd, the Regius Professor of Medicine at Oxford, opens with a lengthy philosophical speculation on the "animal" nature of human beings, emphasizing their emotional and moral similarities. Later chapters deal with the differences between wild and domesticated varieties and with the anatomical effects of domestication. Though I think Emily Brontë would have stubbornly denied the Bridgewater premise, that humans have a God-given right and ability to subjugate nature, Kidd's treatise would have provided much information as well as grist for her particular theoretical mill.

The evidence that Emily Brontë had animal breeding in mind is not only remarkable in itself but reverses, also, most interpretations of the status of "civilization" in the novel. That the novel is literally about domestication—the dialectics of the two houses—is obvious on a first reading. Our difficulty in deciding which of the two houses harbors more perversity is itself a reflection of the reader's own social priorities. Sociological critics like Leavis, Eagleton, and myself have little trouble deciding against Thrushcross Grange, but find ourselves in difficulty when it comes to arguing for Heathcliff and/or Wuthering Heights: there seems so much blatant cruelty and destructiveness on the premises. Considering that action, however, within the context of the realities of rural life—a context not available to most urbane reviewers and critics and, consequently, not brought to bear on the action—goes far toward explaining it as one of the hard facts of a harder way of life, the wisdom of which Brontë accepts.[42] Comparing Brontë's vision of nature with Darwin's, finally, goes far toward elucidating the theories of both.

Take, for example, the constant routine of culling. People for whom animals are an economic system—and Lockwood has to be told that the nursing pointer is "not kept for a pet" (chap. 1)—do not sentimentalize or anthropomorphize them. Hareton's hanging the litter of puppies is not necessarily the act of gratuitous cruelty Isabella implies, especially if we recall the cruelty of our first glimpse of Edgar and herself, who "had nearly pulled [a little dog] in two between them" (chap. 6). Heathcliff clearly does recall the incident, for he pointedly attempts to finish off the job of murder when he elopes with Isabella (chap. 12). Heathcliff's callousness is exhibited by all those whose own bodies are commodities: thus Nelly's contempt for the urchin Heathcliff and Zillah's for the puny Linton Heathcliff. They, like Catherine and Heathcliff, have no use for pampered, "petted things" of any species (chap. 6).

Then there is the trapping and shooting—another apparent business venture of Hareton's, to judge by the "heap of dead rabbits" in the corner on Lockwood's first visit. This is a skill Hareton has learned from Heathcliff, as we know from the incident of the lapwings (chap. 12). One of the dubious benefits of civilization is that most of us avoid direct confrontation with the slaughter on which our comfort depends. Those who do it for us, again, do not anthropomorphize the animals upon whose death their own survival more directly depends—erring perhaps too far in the opposite direction. In her essay, **"The Butterfly,"** Emily Brontë, like Paley before her but unlike her contemporary Tennyson, comes to terms with the necessity of death and the obvious indifference of nature, and even God, to human sentiments. The "nest of little [lapwing] skeletons" is God's, winter's, or the mother's work, not Heathcliff's; Catherine's plea that he spare the mother (who wouldn't return anyway) is an act of supererogation, however indicative of her own, more tender feelings.

If those who work with animals are less "humane" than those of us who indulge ourselves in them, they also feel a stronger sense of obligation to them, if only on grounds of enlightened self-interest. Emily Brontë took sole responsibility for the care and feeding of the household menagerie and fulfilled her obligations up through the last night of her life. An interchange on this point is instructive. Hareton, Heathcliff, and Cathy Linton argue about how to deal with Lockwood in the snowstorm. Hareton volunteers to go halfway with him, to the park, to which Heathcliff responds, "You'll go with him to hell! . . . And who is to look after the horses, eh?" Cathy surprises Lockwood by "murmur[ing], 'A man's life is of more consequence than one evening's neglect of the horses'" (chap. 2). Emily Brontë did not feel her own life to be worthy of an evening's neglect of the dogs: though Hareton's attempt to answer the needs of the stranger, the sheep, and the horses is the most admirable response of all, I have no doubt that a Lockwood does not sit as high as a horse in Emily Brontë's own hierarchy of animals.

"Breeding" in the common parlance of the nineteenth century refers, of course, to the proper nurturance of "civilized" behavior. I have already suggested the ways in which Brontë implies that such "civilized," "artificial" behavior has weakened the breed of animals at Thrushcross Grange. A far more venal definition of breeding characterizes the notions of "bad breeding" that so frequently prevented marriage-for-love in the eighteenth and nineteenth centuries, thus indicating another way in which "methodical selection" had vitiated the upper-middle classes: superficial, invented standards, such as those applied to the sheep of Yorkshire, had not produced survivors. It is interesting to note, in this context, Nelly's use of the term: "[For Cathy to] sneer at [Hareton's] imperfect attempt [at reading] was very bad breeding" (chap. 24). While Nelly seems to refer to "manners," she is in fact rebuking Cathy for a failure in human decency and a snobbishness about the Heights that Nelly has deplored through two generations of Lintons already. Such behavior is, indeed, part of Cathy's psychological endowment—"bad breeding."

Wuthering Heights selects for a different sort of animal, infinitely more rugged and surviving with little apparent variation for at least 300 years. Outsiders—except Heathcliff—do not hold up well there: the mistresses predecease its own offspring, the men and the peasants, who are virtually immortal. It takes years of willful dissipation for Hindley to kill himself off, and his father, like an animal or an American Indian, seems simply to know when life is draining out of him. Catherine has inherited both traits, her brother's self-destructiveness and her father's ability to die at will. Catherine and Hindley, furthermore, share a fatal attraction to "what is called 'the world.'" Hindley comes down from university, having "grown sparer, and lost his colour, and spoke and dressed quite differently"; he brings with him a "half-silly . . . rather thin but young, and fresh complexioned" wife, in the words of Nelly Dean (chap. 6). The ultimate cause of Hindley's self-destruction, and the proximate cause of Edgar Linton's, is uxoriousness, an overdependence and overfondness that Catherine, in her better nature, calls being "like two babies, kissing and talking nonsense by the hour—fool's palaver that [Heathcliff and I] should be ashamed of" (chap. 3).

Heathcliff is even more rugged than the native stock at the Heights, and Catherine has always recognized him as the neighborhood's prize stud. When he returns from "the world," though his "cheeks were sallow . . . his manner was even dignified." When Heathcliff is thus groomed with wealth and power, Isabella Linton herself plumps (or more romantically, wastes) for him.

Heathcliff's pedigree is dubious and perhaps irrelevant, for the cities, as Emily Brontë well knows, are an environment in which more than one variety of "artificial man" survives. Thus the suggestion that Brontë is a proto-Social Darwinist misrepresents both. While Social Darwinism seemed to accommodate natural selection to natural theology and/or the idea of progress, it did so in order to justify the status quo of the ruling class: "fitness" most definitely included the ability to attain and maintain wealth. **Wuthering Heights,** however, suggests again and again that money instead selects for weakness, that it is the poor who are more "fit" for survival—or, at least, that those who do survive the harshness of their "artificially" brutal lives are virtually indestructible if feral. When Heathcliff disappears into "the world," he returns a success, by its standards, a rich man. Heathcliff thus possesses the ability to appropriate any and all forms of power: human kindness, animal ferocity, human abusiveness, the natural elements, money, land, and finally even death and the grave itself, as seen in his "Ghoul"-ish burial arrangements. Rather than Leavis's "plotting device," Heathcliff is a sort of first cause, a Prime Mover, a principle of creation and destruction in whose aura life is both conceived and terminated for the other characters in the novel. Heathcliff attains the status of a "mechanism" in Darwin's terminology, that which drives nature and thus human destiny, the natural selector. Only the equal ferocity of human willfulness—embodied here in Catherine—eludes him. Had Darwin himself been at less pains to eliminate irrelevant speculation on the attributes of Paley's watchmaker from the wonders of the watchworks, he might have identified this mechanism, as easily as Brontë herself seems to, with God.

Darwin's notion of "natural selection" falls, with appropriate scientific detachment, squarely between the implicit optimism of Alexander Pope's "Whatever is, is right" and the resignation of Martin Heidegger's "The Dreadful has already happened." Natural selection can, however, be directed by the operations of chance and will, for the mechanism, in Darwin's scheme, is itself conducted by "sexual selection," or the natural selection of traits that make one potential mate more attractive than another. The mechanism is tampered with in the "methodical selection" of breeders, and usually to the ruin of the breed. Hareton is the only offspring of sexual selection in the third generation, the product of the true love match between Hindley and Frances. Hindley and Frances are themselves temperamentally well matched, delighting equally in each other and in cruelty to their unwanted charges, Catherine and Heathcliff. They are both tough—Nelly admires the stoicism with which Frances confronts her terminal illness—but Frances is, unfortunately, "a rush of a lass" (chap. 8), unable to adapt to the harshness of the Heights environment, and dies when childbirth wracks her already-consumptive frame.

Cathy Linton and Linton Heathcliff are hybrids, breedings arranged "methodically," according to artificially established norms rather than by mutual, natural attraction. Linton Heathcliff is the worst throwback of them all, "blending" (in the pre-Mendelian parlance) both the ferocity of the poor (from his father) and the willfulness and selfishness of his mother, Isabella, the only character in the novel who has no commendable qualities in the eyes of anyone. Even Linton Heathcliff has one or two moments of strength and bravery, for all his physical and emotional weakness: he rebukes Cathy's self-centeredness and defends his foster-brother Hareton from her abuse. Linton also knows himself: "I cannot help showing my nature to you, I regret and repent it, and shall regret and repent it till I die!" (chap. 14). In this, he is even more admirable than Lockwood, who also knows his weaknesses, but neither regrets, repents, nor changes. Lockwood's one moment of strength and decency, also in defense of Hareton, comes off poorly, more like a correction of Cathy's vocabulary: "'Mr. Hareton is desirous of increasing his amount of knowledge,' I said, coming to his rescue. 'He is not *envious* but *emulous* of your attainments'" (chap. 31).

Catherine Linton is in a class by herself, the most adaptable of all characters: she is able to survive the ruggedness of the Heights but thrives in the civility of the Grange. Her mother's willful temperament, a quality

not admired in either of them by anyone in the novel, is sufficient, at least, to hold Heathcliff at bay. Her father's overfondness expresses itself as, rather, a fierce loyalty to those she loves, but she can be equally fierce in her contempt. Methodical selection has produced one case of hybrid vigor. Cathy is, furthermore, the character most worth saving, and most in need of it. And she is saved—by her forced confrontation with death.

The ultimate mating would, of course, have been that of Catherine and Heathcliff. The attraction between them is asexual, though intensely physical. Indeed, Brontë invokes elementary physical forces—heat, magnetism, electricity—to describe their contact. Could "the world" or even nature withstand the union of their energies? The conclusion of **Wuthering Heights** suggests that it could not, that they exist, together, only as ghosts at Penistone Crags. But there is the ghost-child—a product, perhaps, of supernatural selection—who identifies herself to Lockwood as "Catherine Linton," "a waif for twenty years."[43] The ghost-child's desperation parallels that of her "half-brother" Linton, when he is locked out of the house by Joseph (chap. 24). Linton curses; the child pleads for Lockwood's mercy. Lockwood, who had himself been locked out in the storm only hours previous, not only denies the child entrance but performs the most gratuitous violence in the novel. So much, Brontë makes clear from the very beginning, for the humanizing gentility of the upper classes.

The relationship between Catherine and Heathcliff invokes, as I have suggested, physics more than biology. It exists on a higher energy level than "society" and is thus identified always with Penistone Crags, moorland unadaptable by man and uninhabitable, almost, by the animals whose nature man has altered in an attempt to transform supposed "waste lands" into profitable "property." Wuthering Heights itself can barely withstand the energy level of Heathcliff, for all its native ruggedness. Lockwood's encounter with the ghost-child introduces a point about the relative strengths of the two different breeds, reiterated throughout the novel, which is suggestive of not only the Law of Conservation of Energy but Sigmund Freud's description of the mechanism of repression. Though the inhabitants of Thrushcross Grange are physically weak, they are not endowed with less energy than the hard-working, rough-talking Heights breed. They merely affect lassitude for the sake of gentility. When roused, their virulence exceeds that of the natives of the Heights. Isabella, in fact, thrives in the ambience of emotional and physical violence and pain there, "covet[ing]" Hindley's deadly weapons and "delight[ing]" in plotting her revenge on Heathcliff: "'ignoble as it seems to insult a fallen enemy, I couldn't miss the chance of sticking in a dart; his weakness was the only time when I could taste the delight of paying wrong for wrong'" (chap. 17). Compare this with Heathcliff himself: "'I have no pity! I have no pity! The more the worms writhe, the more I yearn to crush out their entrails! It is a moral teething, and I grind with greater energy, in proportion to the increase of pain'" (chap. 14). There is a world of difference in Isabella's "tast-[ing] delight" in revenge and the pain of Heathcliff's "moral teething." It is the fact that "worms" continue to writhe that arouses Heathcliff's urge to destroy them, just as the speaker of Brontë's **"The Butterfly"** "crush[es] out [the] entrails" of the flower-destroying caterpillar. Human injustice and cruelty evoke both pain and energy in him. It is here, in Heathcliff's determination to select for humane traits, that we find the sociological, moral, and theological center of the novel.

IV

Teeth are contrived to eat, not to ache; their aching now and then, is incidental to the contrivance, perhaps inseparable from it: or even, if you will, let it be called a defect in the contrivance; but it is not the *object* of it.

William Paley, *Moral Philosophy.*[44]

Perhaps Paley's own *exemplum* of teeth provided Brontë with a source for what is, for me, the most provocative moment in the novel: Heathcliff's declaration of the state of "moral teething." Regardless of whether Brontë refers consciously to Paley, her variation on his theme measures precisely the distance between natural theology and Darwin. Paley, for his part, seems to go out of his way not to cite the function of teeth most typically associated with "Nature, red in tooth and claw." Brontë herself, like Darwin, confronts the necessity of "murder" in nature head-on, as the precondition for finding the terms in which to accept its ultimate, natural "rightness," morality. The moral distinction of humans from animals, for both Brontë and Darwin, is one (to reverse Darwin's phrase) of kind and not degree: the development of a thriving agriculture precluded the necessity for ruthless overkill to guarantee survival. Human brutality, "savageness" in the midst of plenty, is an index, for Brontë, of how far we have fallen from the instincts of natural humaneness. God rebukes the speaker of Brontë's **"The Butterfly"** because she squashes the "ugly" caterpillar by presenting the simultaneous vision of the exquisite butterfly: death and destruction in nature are thus tempered by life and variety. Heathcliff is far more justified in his "yearn[ing] to crush out . . . entrails," for he has, indeed, been personally abused and deprived by the human worms. Nor would Cathy or Hareton transform into anything more beautiful than caterpillars without Heathcliff's intervention.

The notion of "moral teething" seems in need of a gloss, for the passage is cited repeatedly, especially by readers who do not reverence Heathcliff, as paradigmatic of his "sadism."[45] This interpretation seems grossly to overlook the details of the text—Heathcliff only "yearn[s]" and one "grind[s]" one's own teeth—but an obvious

fact about grinding and teething: the processes hurt only the teether. Post-Darwinian, sadder-but-wiser enlightenment, moreover—as distinct from Paley's insistent Panglossianism—demonstrates how and why aching teeth are indeed "inseparable from [the contrivance]." Mammals cannot grow to an adaptive adulthood without the process of teething, nor, to return to Brontë's analogy, can humans develop morally without an aching awareness of the weakness of oneself and others.

Heathcliff's return to the scene of his pain is, if anything, more masochistic than sadistic. He came to Wuthering Heights already having learned how to survive Liverpool. He next had to learn how to survive Hindley's brand of meanness. But with Catherine, he learned also how to love and to trust—only to be betrayed by her. Bereft of his "human" soul in Catherine, he is left to contend only with the "worms." That these worms thrive—to endow the world with nothing but worms—generates Heathcliff's "greater energy" and spiritual pain. His state of "moral teething" thus corresponds with that of the Old and New Testament, or at least Miltonic God: Heathcliff is both ruthless in his wrath and broken-hearted by the fall of his "angel," the fall of Man from Himself, the human fall from nature—initiated, literally, by Catherine's fall at Thrushcross Grange. Once Heathcliff has determined, like the successful Yorkshire sheep-breeder, to cull "the weak ewes and small lambs" from the Linton stock, he becomes both natural and methodical selector. The "greater energy" with which he "grind[s]" is not simply a principle of life and death, but also one of absolute and inexorable justice: Brontë herself seems to "taste the delight" of Heathcliff's "paying wrong for wrong"—though she defines the injuries quite differently from Isabella.

Brontë gives us a third generation and "second" novel to show us this principle in action, to "justify the ways of [her] God to man." The Creator is often apparently cruel. Heathcliff's treatment of these children evokes the always problematic fact of "the sins of the fathers," a point upon which modern genetics is even more emphatic than old-time religion. But exactly how cruel is Heathcliff? Hareton and Linton both love him. How terrible is it to have raised Hareton as a hard-working, proud, self-sufficient farmer? Once Heathcliff has acquired the Grange, who would inherit both it and Wuthering Heights? What good did violin lessons do Hindley and a "plaid silk frock" Catherine? Heathcliff is, rather, determined to keep Hareton pristine, to suppress any expression of that fatal attraction for gentility that has destroyed Hareton's father and aunt.

It is Cathy Linton who poses the moral quandary for the reader. She never comes around to "loving" Heathcliff—and I suppose we can understand that, for she is the one who is most seriously abused by him, financially, verbally, physically, and emotionally. Cathy alone is defiant and unafraid of him, her birthright from her mother, and is never chastened or swayed from her own willfulness. But Heathcliff seems to have a long-range plan for her also, beyond the enforced marriage to his moribund son. He teaches her the true value of life by rubbing her nose in death, forcing her to witness the prolonged agony of Linton's spiritual and physical weakness. It is, of course, Cathy's own innate sympathy with suffering (her mother's legacy) and her loyalty to the family (her father's) that give her the strength for her ordeal. That it is all part of Heathcliff's "design" is revealed by his first word to her when it is over:

> [Heathcliff] went up, held the light to Linton's face, looked at him, and touched him; afterwards he turned to her.
>
> "Now—Catherine," he said, "how do you feel?"
>
> She was dumb.
>
> "How do you feel, Catherine?" he repeated.
>
> "He's safe, and I'm free," she answered, "I should feel well—but," she continued with a bitterness she couldn't conceal, "you have left me so long to struggle against death, alone, that I feel and see only death! I feel like death!"
>
> And she looked like it, too! I gave her a little wine.
>
> (chap. 30)

Nelly, in her inimitable style, undercuts the high seriousness of the whole scene. Cathy Linton has survived Heathcliff's ordeal and now knows death. She is also saved, as well as "free." Nelly, whom Charlotte Brontë has characterized in the "Preface" as "a specimen of true benevolence," in one gesture both belies her mixed feelings for Cathy and administers a communion. Cathy Linton is about to begin to become humane, able now to begin to love Hareton and to be worthy of his love for her. She is now also "free" to marry him—and equally free to corrupt his strength with her own relative frailty.

One of the reasons for ***Wuthering Heights***' narrative and dramatic success is, as I have been suggesting, Emily Brontë's identification with the strengths and weaknesses of all of the characters she creates, with the exception of Heathcliff, who is an ideal, a projection of her understanding of God. Brontë herself struggled, more successfully than Catherine, to "[be] Heathcliff," that Designer/Nature/God who is "always, always in my mind," whose soul is identical with her own. Her sister Charlotte seems to have understood this, for the description of Emily's terminal illness in the "Biographical Notice" of the 1850 edition alludes unmistakably to Heathcliff's "greater energy":

> Yet, while physically she perished, mentally, she grew stronger than we had yet known her . . . indeed, I have not seen her parallel in anything. Stronger than a

man, simpler than a child, her nature stood alone. The awful point was, that, while full of ruth for others, on herself she had no pity; the spirit was inexorable to the flesh; from the trembling hand, the unnerved limbs, the faded eyes, the same service was enacted as they had rendered in health.

Wuthering Heights is about the colossal stupidity, arrogance, even impiety of anthropocentrism. So, also, is Darwin's *Origin of Species*: Darwin describes the denial of species variation in the face of the obvious evidence of our own "methodical selection" as our "ignor[ance of] all general arguments, and refus[al] to sum up in [our] minds slight differences accumulated during many successive generations" (chap. 1, p. 29). Darwin's suggestion that "methodical selection" itself indicates not only arrogance, what we call today "playing God," but also ignorance is even more evident in his original term for the breeding of animals, "unconscious selection." The following passage (also from *Origin*) illustrates Darwin's own vision of humankind's reduction of nature to an "abnormal" state of artifice, unfit for survival—a view that closely matches Brontë's in its contempt for the civilized admiration of "external[s]" and for the human arrogance, ignorance, "unconscious[ness]" of the subtler design of nature:

> On the views here given of the all-important part which selection by man has played, it becomes at once obvious, how it is that our domestic races show adaptation in their structure or in their habits to man's wants or fancies. We can, I think, further understand the frequently abnormal character of our domestic races, and likewise their differences being so great in external characters and relatively so slight in internal parts or organs. Man can hardly select, or only with much difficulty, any deviation of structure excepting such as is externally visible; and indeed he rarely cares for what is internal. He can never act by selection, excepting on variations which are first given to him in some slight degree by nature.
>
> (chap. 1, pp. 38-39)

Darwin is only more hopeful than Brontë that Nature/Justice/Heathcliff—"selection"—will always have the last word.

A final point from Charles Bell may also go far toward explaining the method of Brontë's madness, or at least, in the words of her sister's "Preface," the "advisab[ility of creating] characters like Heathcliff." Bell, in the fourth Bridgewater Treatise, is deploring the fact that we seem more aware of God in the apparent evil of the Design than in its obvious perfection: "Debased in some measure by a habit of inattention, and lost to all sense of the benevolence of the Creator, [one] is roused to reflection only by overwhelming calamities, which appear to him magnified and disproportional; and hence arises a conception of the Author of his being more in terror than in love" (C. Bell, pp. 13-14). Brontë creates a character whose "terror" may arouse the debased and "vitiated" reader of novels to a conception of his love, given, as she tells us in **"The Butterfly"** and as Bell asserts here, that mankind seems actually to prefer to fix on destruction and ugliness rather than on creation and beauty.

In one final attempt to read between the lines of Charlotte Brontë's misleading "Preface," I suggest that even she realizes that "Heathcliff, indeed, stands unredeemed," because Heathcliff alone needs no redemption. "Moral teething," growing up, understanding how weak, how cowardly how cruel the human "worms" can be, is redemption in itself, and it hurts. Brontë's "Love"—for God, for humans, and for animals—is humanity's only redeeming social value, the sense of "an existence of yours beyond you," in the words of Catherine Earnshaw (chap. 9). Love hurts too. The blessing and the curse of love, in Emily Brontë's scheme, is that it is beyond one's own control, one's powers of manipulation, one's own will. Love is fatal to solipsism, and it is no wonder Lockwood is "a fixed unbeliever" in it (chap. 7).

The novel ends with Hareton about to bite the apple, about to leave the self-sufficiency of the Heights for the debilitating dependency of the Grange, out of love for Cathy. The ending seems to be a happy one. Even Heathcliff had described the Grange as a paradise at first sight: "'We saw—ah! it was beautiful—a splendid place carpeted with crimson, and crimson-covered chairs and tables, and a pure white ceiling bordered by gold, a shower of glass drops hanging in silver chains from the centre, and shimmering with little soft tapers . . . [Catherine and I] should have thought ourselves in heaven!'" (chap. 6). By the end of the novel, all of us know better, except Hareton, who is as ignorant of it as he is of the ways of "the world." Nelly knows better too, but, as Hindley's "foster-sister," she has perhaps acquired the fatal attraction for gentility and is only slightly less culpable because she is a servant. Thrushcross Grange is, for her, a step up the social Chain of Being. Nelly welcomes the move as an escape from the hard, unlettered ruggedness of the Heights, as wetnursing Hareton had formerly provided "relief from [her] rake" (chap. 8).

Lockwood is, as I have suggested, not only stupidly anthropocentric, but egocentric, solipsistic, and spiritually, if not physically, the most recessive character in the novel, lacking even Linton Heathcliff's ability to love—or insatiable need for it. In Miller's words, the man who "has been a fixed unbeliever in any love of a year's standing witness[es] a love that has lasted beyond the grave" (Miller, p. 169). Like the narrator of Paley's *Natural Theology*, Lockwood "cross[es] a heath" and stumbles upon phenomena in need of explanation.[46] Undaunted by the wrongheadedness of all his

hypotheses, Lockwood proceeds to the end, unredeemed by his experience of Heathcliff and unable to rise above a worldliness that leaves Catherine and Heathcliff in their graves, "sleepers in that quiet earth," reports to the contrary notwithstanding. There is a consolation, however: his refusal to love eliminates his traits for the future.

The true ending of **Wuthering Heights** pushes beyond Lockwood's vision, beyond the "second" novel, into the future. It is as poignant and unresolved as that of *Paradise Lost.* Hareton, like Milton's Adam, has just fallen as a result of love. Despite the fact that Hareton and Cathy walk the moors by night, the genes for gentility have won the day. We are left to wonder how many generations it will take for a little Edgar and Isabella Earnshaw to be discovered "nearly pull[ing] a little dog in two between them." Nelly, to be sure, and Hareton, as it seems, are perfectly delighted to have "the world" on Cathy Linton's terms, to move with her back to Thrushcross Grange, which is where, I suppose, a farmer with an acquired taste for primroses in his porridge belongs.

We are left only with the satisfaction that Wuthering Heights remains relatively untouched by Cathy's corruption. She had attempted a plantation scheme, replacing Joseph's currant bushes with flowers. Heathcliff, as one of his final acts in this world, puts an end to her efforts and declares that the fruit-bearing bushes be restored, Joseph thus "regain[ing]" for his beloved currants, their "blissful seat." That Emily Brontë is, again, of one mind with Heathcliff may be inferred from this final observation from Ellen Nussey, who laments the transformation of the Haworth Parsonage into a tourist attraction: where it had formerly, she tells us, "possessed only a few stunted thorns and shrubs, and a few currant bushes which Emily and Anne treasured as their own bit of fruit garden [it] is now a perfect Arcadia of floral culture" (Nussey, p. 83). Joseph and Zillah, the last of the true-bred peasants, repossess Wuthering Heights in the original terms of Nature's lease. When they die, however, the species will have become extinct, unable to adapt to the hyperadapted local environment. Such had, in fact, become the reality for this endangered species by Emily Brontë's own time, forty years later. The Heights stands as its fossil, and **Wuthering Heights,** her requiem for a lost natural and humane life and her assault on that "vitiated class of English readers" who drove the sheep away and refuse to believe that ghosts and God still walk the "waste" land.

Notes

1. Excerpted in *Wuthering Heights: A Casebook,* ed. Miriam Allott (London: Macmillan, 1970), pp. 61, 48.

2. Paul H. Barrett, comp. and ed., *Metaphysics, Materialism, and the Evolution of Mind: Early Writ-*

ings of Charles Darwin (Chicago: University of Chicago Press, 1980).

3. The "Questions for Mr. Wynne" have been included in *Metaphysics, Materialism, and the Evolution of Mind,* pp. 163-165. See also Gavin de Beer's collection, *Questions about the Breeding of Animals* (1840; rpt. ed., London: Society for the Bibliography of Natural History, 1968).

4. J. Hillis Miller, "Emily Brontë" in *The Disappearance of God: Five Nineteenth-Century Writers* (Cambridge, Massachusetts: Belknap Press, 1963), p. 168.

5. Charles Darwin, *The Descent of Man and Selection in Relation to Sex* (1871; rev. ed., New York: D. Appleton and Co., 1897), chaps. 3 and 4.

6. The *Origin of Species* does not press the human question. In its famous concluding paragraphs, however, Darwin confesses a personal preference for "descen[t] from that heroic little monkey . . . or from that old baboon . . . as from a savage who delights to torture his enemies."

7. Emily Brontë, *Wuthering Heights: An Authoritative Text,* ed. William M. Sale, Jr. (1847; rev. ed., New York: Norton, 1972), chap. 9. Subsequent quotations from the novel will be indicated in the text by parenthetical chapter references.

8. I mention the publications of the Chambers family here because one of their editorial hands—that of Robert Chambers—also produced, anonymously in 1844, *Vestiges of Creation,* the book that fed Tennyson's despair.

9. Q. D. Leavis, "A Fresh Approach to *Wuthering Heights*" in *Lectures in America,* by F. R. Leavis and Q. D. Leavis (New York: Pantheon, 1969); Terry Eagleton, *Myths of Power: A Marxist Study of the Brontës* (New York: Harper and Row, 1975); C. P. Sanger, *The Structure of Wuthering Heights* (1926; rpt. ed., Folcroft, Pennsylvania: Folcroft Library Editions, 1972).

10. Elizabeth Gaskell, *The Life of Charlotte Brontë* (1844; rpt. ed., Harmondsworth: Penguin, 1975), p. 379.

11. See, for example, "I am the only being whose doom," "'Well, some may hate, and some may scorn,'" and "It is too late to call thee now," nos. 11, 123, 135 in *The Complete Poems of Emily Jane Brontë,* ed. C. W. Hatfield (New York: Columbia University Press, 1941).

12. Dobell's review is, in fact, the one specifically cited by Charlotte Brontë in her "Biographical Notice of Ellis and Acton Bell" as having "discerned the real nature of *Wuthering Heights*." The

"Biographical Notice" and "Editor's Preface to the New Edition of *Wuthering Heights*" of 1850 are reprinted in every modern edition of the novel. All subsequent references to Charlotte Brontë's remarks, unless otherwise noted, are taken from these prefaces and will be indicated in the text.

13. John Lock and W. T. Dixon, *A Man of Sorrow: The Life, Letters and Times of the Rev. Patrick Brontë, 1777-1861,* 2d ed. (Westport, Connecticut: Meckler Books, 1979), pp. 249-252. Winifred Gérin, *Emily Brontë: A Biography* (Oxford: Clarendon Press, 1971), p. 6.

14. Charlotte Brontë to W. S. Williams, 15 February 1848, in Clement Shorter, *The Brontës: Life and Letters,* 2 vols. (1908; rpt. ed., New York: Haskell House, 1969), I, 396-397.

15. Quoted by Gérin in *Emily Brontë,* p. 94, but not in Ellen Nussey's own "Reminiscences" as reprinted by The Brontë Society (see note 16).

16. Ellen Nussey, "Reminiscences of Charlotte Brontë," *Brontë Society Transactions,* II, Pt. 10 (1899), 76.

17. Miller, "Emily Brontë," p. 178. Miller's more recent discussion, "*Wuthering Heights*: Repetition and the Uncanny," in *Fiction and Repetition* (Cambridge: Harvard University Press, 1982), pp. 42-72, develops his points about the narrative strategy of the novel, without indicating a significantly revised interpretation.

18. For an important discussion of Catherine Earnshaw's inability to control her behavior, see Leavis, pp. 116 and following. But the phenomenon extends beyond Catherine and Edgar to Isabella, Linton, Nelly, and even Lockwood himself.

19. For the sake of convenience and clarity, I use "Catherine" to designate the mother and "Cathy" to designate the daughter.

20. The complete *oeuvre* is reproduced as an appendix in Gérin, including the marginal comments of the Hégers. Translations may be found in the 1947 and 1950 editions of the *Brontë Society Transactions* and in Fannie Ratchford, *Five Essays by Emily Brontë* (Austin: University of Texas Press, 1948). Emily Brontë's French never rises too far above my own, seeming to be translations from English; I have therefore translated them quite literally for this paper.

21. W. H. Marshall's promising titular reference in "Hareton Earnshaw: Natural Theology on the Moors," *Victorian Newsletter,* 21 (Spring 1962), 14-15, referred to Robert Browning's "Caliban upon Setebos" rather than Paley. In a recent study, Richard Benvenuto discusses ways in which

Brontë's "The Butterfly" anticipates Darwin, but finds it "doubtful that Brontë knew of the scientific research that would culminate in the theory of natural selection." Richard Benvenuto, *Emily Brontë* (Boston: Twayne, 1982), p. 78. Revolutionary theories such as Darwin's, however, do not have their sources in "research" so much as in an overwhelming sense of the inadequacy or wrongheadedness of current explanations. Brontë, I believe, shared this with Darwin—and had available to her the same materials as Darwin did, before he stepped on board the *Beagle* and gathered evidence.

22. Charlotte Brontë to Ellen Nussey, 4 July 1834, in Shorter, I, 111.

23. Charlotte Brontë to Ellen Nussey, 9 April 1840, in Shorter, I, 178.

24. Annette B. Hopkins, *The Father of the Brontës* (Baltimore: Johns Hopkins University Press, 1958), p. 17.

25. Clifford Whone, "Where the Brontës Borrowed Books," *Brontë Society Transactions,* XI, Pt. 60 (1950), 344-358.

26. William Paley, *Natural Theology* (1802; rpt. ed., Houston, Texas: St. Thomas Press, 1972), pp. 225-226.

27. For an interesting analogue to this passage from Paley in Darwin, see *The Descent of Man*: "At the proper season these birds seem all day long to be impressed with the desire to migrate; their habits change; they become restless, are noisy, and congregate in flocks. Whilst the mother bird is feeding, or brooding over her nestlings, the maternal instinct is stronger than the migratory; but the instinct which is more persistent gains the victory, and at last, at a moment when her young ones are not in sight, she takes flight and deserts them. When arrived at the end of her long journey, and the migratory instinct has ceased to act, what an agony of remorse the bird would feel, if, from being endowed with great mental activity, she could not prevent the image constantly passing through her mind, of her young ones perishing in the bleak north from cold and hunger." Darwin, *The Descent of Man,* chap. 4, p. 113.

28. The Bridgewater Treatises were a series of books whose publication was supported by the estate of the Earl of Bridgewater. Bridgewater had directed that these books should be written by persons nominated by the President of the Royal Society, to demonstrate "the Power, Wisdom, and Goodness of God, as manifested in the Creation, illustrating such work by all reasonable arguments." Charles Bell, *The Hand* (London: William Pickering, 1834), p. v.

29. Whone, p. 353. If the numbering system indicates the order of acquisition, Bell's "Phenomena of Nature" was one of their first. It may also be the librarian's designation for *The Hand*. Other volumes in the series appear as "Bridgewater's [*sic*] Treatises on Animal and Vegetable Physiology" (p. 346) or under the author's name, with equally adventitious titles.

30. Though Gérin suggests Nicholls as the source of the name, she does not suggest that he may have been drawn into the secret: it would have been a good strategy for Charlotte Brontë to have done so, for mail addressed to a "Mr. Bell" might thus have fallen into the proper hands. Nicholls was, however, not much admired by the sisters at this point. At risk, furthermore, of attacking my own suggestion twice, I must admit that my sense of Charlotte Brontë's wit persuades me that "Bell" was merely a French pun, the Belles, and (worse yet) "Ellis" was "Hell's Belle."

31. Acton Bell, "Preface," *The Tenant of Wildfell Hall* (1848; rpt. ed., New York: Penguin, 1979).

32. Valentine Cunningham locates a similar distinction in the three sisters' views of human nature by examining the degree to which each seems to have been influenced by Methodism, in *Everywhere Spoken Against: Dissent in the Victorian Novel* (Oxford: Clarendon Press, 1975), pp. 113-126. His conclusions support the larger point: that it is virtually impossible to distinguish psychology, sociology, or biology from theology in this period. The issues and reactions raised by Edward O. Wilson's "sociobiology" demonstrate the degree to which these distinctions remain unclear, even among scientists, in our own time.

33. J. Lawrence, cited in Robert Trow-Smith, *A History of British Livestock Husbandry, 1700-1900* (London: Routledge and Kegan Paul, 1959), p. 141.

34. Gavin de Beer, "Biology Before the *Beagle,*" in Philip Appleman, *Darwin: A Norton Critical Edition* (2d ed., New York: Norton, 1979), p. 10.

35. Charles Darwin, *The Autobiography of Charles Darwin and Selected Letters,* ed. Francis Darwin (1892; rpt. ed., New York: Dover, 1958), p. 19.

36. Charles Darwin, *On the Origin of Species by means of Natural Selection* (1859; rpt. ed., New York: Atheneum, 1967), chaps. 1, 4.

37. George Culley, *Observations on Live Stock, containing Hints for Crossing and Improving The Best Breeds of the Most Useful Kinds of Domestic Animals* (3d ed., London: G. G. and J. Robinson, 1801), pp. 143, 145.

38. William Fullarton, *General View of the Agriculture the County of Ayr* (1793) in Trow-Smith, p. 140.

39. William Youatt, *Sheep: Their Breeds, Management, and Diseases* (London: Simplan, Marshall and Co., 1837), p. 303.

40. The saga of Welsh Brunty, a foundling from Liverpool who brought the Brunty family to financial ruin because they opposed his marriage to his "foster-sister," beggars credulity and is probably a piece of *ex post facto* embroidery or blarney on someone's part, though not necessarily John Cannon's. John Cannon, *The Road to Haworth* (New York: Viking Press, 1981).

41. John Kidd, *On the Adaptation of External Nature to the Physical Condition of Man, Principally with Reference to the supply of his wants and the exercise of his intellectual faculties* (Philadelphia: Carey, Lea and Blanchard, 1835). It is worth noting, for example, that Kidd cites the cat as the animal least affected by domestication, "less subjugated to man than horses or dogs" (chap. 9). In her essay, "The Cat," Brontë argues that the cat is the animal most like man himself and thus less submissive to mastery.

42. Q. D. Leavis is one of the few modern critics to emphasize the fact that Wuthering Heights is a working (however marginally) farm. Charlotte Brontë herself reiterates the point in her "Preface" to justify not only the "ruggedness" of the language but also the frank discussion of such matters as wet-nursing and alcoholism, not usually encountered in the genteel fiction of the times.

43. A child of Catherine Linton would be, legally, named Linton, regardless of paternity. If, as Sanger demonstrates, Brontë knew property and estate law, she certainly knew this point re: legitimacy. Heathcliff's "Cathy" was never both a child *and* a Linton.

44. William Paley, *The Principles of Moral and Political Philosophy* (1785, 11th American ed.; rpt. ed., Houston: St. Thomas Press, 1977), pp. 60-61. The section from which this passage is taken was quoted by Paley himself in *Natural Theology* (p. 347). Not one, but "2 copies" of the "*Moral Philosophy*" are listed in the Keighley catalogue. (See above, note 25.) Readers may share my horror that both of Paley's works have been reprinted by an Episcopal press in Houston as its contribution to the Creation Science movement: know-nothingism thus makes strange bedfellows of American nostalgia for High Church Anglicanism and fundamentalism.

45. Miller, for example, introduces his discussion of this passage with the statement, "No other figure in English literature takes so much pleasure in causing pain *to others*" (italics mine), "Emily Brontë," p. 196.

46. The famous opening proposition of Paley's *Natural Theology*, p. 1.

Linda Gold (essay date March 1985)

SOURCE: Gold, Linda. "Catherine Earnshaw: Mother and Daughter." *English Journal* 74, no. 3 (March 1985): 68-73.

[*In the following essay, Gold compares the divergent portraits of female psychology that emerge in Brontë's two Catherines.*]

When I was in college, I heard a story about a fifteen-year-old girl who attended the 1939 film version of ***Wuthering Heights*** with her mother. "Oh, mother," the girl gushed upon leaving the theater, "do you think there could be love like that?" "I don't know," her mother replied tartly, "but if there is, I don't approve of it." I laughed then, a laugh of recognition, for what adolescent girl has not fantasized about a man so passionately in love with her that he cries, "How can I live without my life?" "How can I live without my soul?" And of course, I laughed also at the mother's tongue-clucking disapprobation. She seemed so much like— well, a mother.

As a novice teacher, I told the story to my classes, who responded much as I had done. At what point, then, did I begin to feel the same ring of recognition at the mother's comment? Was I beginning, as she had, to outgrow Heathcliff? What is Heathcliff that he should or could be outgrown? As I continued to teach the novel, other questions surfaced, the same questions, it seemed year after year. And slowly the dialectic posed by the anecdote seemed the dialectic posed by the two halves of the novel. It is the dialectic between the girl's infatuation with mythologized romantic love in all its seductive, destructive potential and the woman's rejection of this myth. It is the dialectic between Catherine Earnshaw and Catherine Linton Heathcliff Earnshaw; it is a woman's struggle with herself; it traces her maturation from girl to woman. The landscape depicted in ***Wuthering Heights*** is not only an external one; it is internal as well.

The maturation of Catherine Earnshaw resembles the development of the personality described by Freud. The first generation and its intense struggles evoke the early conflicts in the emergent personality. The intense symbiosis of Catherine, Heathcliff, and Linton suggests an interaction within the personality of the id, the ego, and the superego.[1] Not only are the lives of the three characters inextricably bound, but ultimately they are buried in what Heathcliff envisions as a single coffin. After convincing the sexton digging Linton's grave to remove the earth from Catherine's coffin lid, Heathcliff

> struck one side of the coffin loose—and covered it up—not Linton's side, damn him. I wish he'd been soldered in lead—and I bribed the sexton to pull it away, when I'm laid there, and slide mine out too. I'll have it made so, and then, by the time Linton gets to us, he'll not know which is which.

The three here literally merge into one.

As the story suggests, no one's mother approves of Heathcliff; he is the id personified. Although everything about his character bespeaks his wildness and distance from civilization, he enters the Earnshaw home not from without but from within: Earnshaw draws the boy Heathcliff from under his own greatcoat. Nelly Dean describes the first encounter of the "wild gipsy brat" with the Earnshaws: "When it was on its feet, it only stared round, and repeated over and over some gibberish that nobody could understand." The origins and parentage of this bestial child are a mystery. When Lockwood encounters the adult Heathcliff at Wuthering Heights, Heathcliff has become one with a setting as primitive and remote from civilization as he is. All of its inhabitants, canine and human, are snarling, unrestrained, and exemplary of the word "wuthering"—"descriptive of the atmospheric tumult to which its station is exposed in stormy weather." Like the id, Heathcliff remains primitive and unmodified by the passage of time. As a child, he runs barefoot and dirty through the moors; later, at Catherine's death, he "groaned in a sudden paroxysm of ungovernable passion . . . he dashed his head against the knotted trunk; and, lifting up his eyes, howled, not like a man, but like a savage beast." When he hears from Lockwood of Catherine's spectral appearance at the window of Wuthering Heights, he wrenches open the window and bursts into an "uncontrollable passion of tears."

Linton, on the other hand, is consummately civilized. His home is Thrushcross Grange, whose name and appearance suggest gentility and cultivation. Edgar is fair-haired, polite, correct, wealthy, and gentlemanly. It is he who, as the conscience, forces Catherine to choose between her husband and Heathcliff, and who, coolly, from the cerebral retreat of the library, severs ties with his sister Isabella when she disobeys his dictates. Edgar never shirks his duty or tolerates dereliction in others.

Then, there is Catherine, who is the ego. Yet Catherine is female, and the reality she faces offers her few genuine choices. There is little outlet for her primal desires; there is a single culturally-endorsed position—that of wife. When this female ego confronts and tests reality, she must confront also her lack of power and freedom in this male world. Freud would suggest she must confront her lack of a penis; it has been suggested, more reasonably, that she must confront the lack of power and freedom experienced by those who "lack" a penis. According to Freud, the woman might experience some relief from penis envy by giving birth to a male child and, through identification with this male child, experience the gratification of "phallic activity." The woman is forced to vicarious satisfaction because direct action is denied her. And, indeed, in Emily Brontë's novel and in her life, a pattern of woman speaking or acting through masculine personae emerges: the Brontë family expects that it is Bramwell who will achieve artistic success; Emily Brontë publishes her novel under the pseudonym Ellis Bell. Nelly Dean tells her story to Lockwood who tells it to the reader. The ego, that part of the personality which faces the world, must be male. And so Catherine, Brontë's female child, first attempts to emerge through her male children, Edgar Linton and Heathcliff. She must attempt to live through men if she is to live at all. Catherine resolves this dilemma through narcissistic identification with two men.

That Catherine identifies with Heathcliff is clear. As children, they are nearly inseparable, running together on the moors and mocking together Joseph's superstitious and tedious pieties. As Catherine says to Nelly Dean, "Nelly, I *am* Heathcliff—he's always, always in my mind, not as a pleasure, any more than I am always a pleasure to myself, but as my own being."

But she also identifies with Edgar Linton. It is the visit to Thrushcross Grange and Catherine's resulting injury which ends her earlier exclusive identification with Heathcliff. For this visit, marked by a debilitating wound and the resulting ministrations of the Lintons, coincides with Catherine's emergence as a woman, an emergence which requires that she attempt to take her place in a world which so rigidly defines her. After a five-week sojourn at the Grange, she returns to the Heights, having transformed herself into a lady.

> Instead of a wild, hatless little savage . . . there lighted from the handsome black pony a very dignified person, with brown ringlets falling from the cover of a feathered beaver and a long cloth habit which she was obliged to hold up with both hands that she might sail in.

Hindley remarks when he sees Catherine, "I should scarcely have known you—you look like a lady now." To complete her identification with Linton, she marries him, assuming his name, his life, and his social position.

After her decision to marry Linton, Catherine describes her feelings for the two men to Nelly:

> My love for Linton is like the foliage in the woods. Time will change it, I'm aware, as winter changes the

trees. My love for Heathcliff resembles the eternal rocks beneath—a source of little visible delight, but necessary.

Here Catherine's description captures the primal and timeless quality of the id as well as its relationship to the rest of the personality. The id is not "visible" or conscious. Linton, like civilization, is more apparent, as trees can be seen more readily than underlying rock. Yet it is the id which is the constant necessary basis for the personality.

It is not Catherine's intention to fragment her personality: she aims at synthesis. Although she feels that it would "degrade" her to marry Heathcliff or to surrender totally to her instinctual self, she continues to see Heathcliff as "more myself than I am." Her intention, therefore, is to maintain her union with both men, and to use Linton's position to help Heathcliff "rise." However, this attempt is frustrated by Heathcliff's flight. Catherine is successful as Linton's wife as long as Heathcliff, with whom she has identified her primal urges, is absent. Nelly describes Catherine during this period as "infinitely better than I dared expect." Yet this calm is seen as temporary and a denial of Catherine's true nature. "The gunpowder lay as harmless as sand, because no fire came near to explode it." But, as Nelly says, "It ended. Well, we must be for ourselves in the long run."

When Heathcliff returns, so does the conflict within Catherine. But, because the conflict is not external to her, the reconciliation she attempts is impossible. Freud describes such a dilemma in *The Ego and the Id*.

> If they (the ego's object identifications) obtain the upper hand and become too numerous, unduly powerful, and incompatible with each other, a pathological outcome will not be far off.[2]

If the conflict between diverse identifications becomes too acute, the ego loses control. Because Catherine has split apart her personality through her identification with these two men, no synthesis is possible. The only possible resolution is Catherine's death.

Catherine's decline begins soon after Heathcliff's return, with the ensuing battle between Heathcliff and Linton. Catherine is at first overjoyed at Heathcliff's return and naively expects cooperation between the two men. As Heathcliff enters the Linton parlor, Catherine "sprang forward, took both his hands, and led him to Linton; and then she seized Linton's reluctant fingers and crushed them into his."

Catherine vainly hopes that she can achieve the integration of her divided self, but this hope is as futile as her effort to crush the two hands into one. As she despairs of wholeness, she cries to Nelly, "I'll try to break their hearts by breaking my own," suggesting that to her the

three hearts are one. When Edgar, ever the moralizer, forces what is in effect a dissolution of her own personality by offering his ultimatum: "It is impossible for you to be my friend and his at the same time; and I absolutely require to know which you choose," Catherine is driven into a frenzy.

> There she lay dashing her head against the arm of the sofa and grinding her teeth, so that you might fancy she would crash them to splinters.

So begins Catherine's slow and deliberate death. Catherine curses Edgar's rectitude and isolation in his library by saying "What in the name of all that feels has he to do with books when I am dying?" The agitated Catherine begins to rend apart a pillow, as she is being rent apart, and to identify the feathers of the wild birds which fill it, as if she recognizes the wildness that lies beneath every thin covering of civilization.

Catherine seeks death as a release from the unendurable tension created by her inability to synthesize the fragmented segments of her personality, a fragmentation necessitated by the constricting environment which provides no outlet for her psychic energy. Shortly before she dies, she confides to Nelly:

> Oh, I wish I were out of doors—I wish I were a girl again, half savage, and hardy and free . . . and laughing at injuries, not madding under them. Why am I so changed? . . . I'm sure I should be myself were I once among the heather on those hills . . . Open the window again wide, fasten it open!

When Nelly refuses, claiming she won't "give Catherine her death," of cold, Catherine replies, "I'm not helpless yet, I'll open it myself."

And Catherine does release herself, through death. And with her death comes the beginning of reconciliation. The locket she wears, filled with a blond lock of Edgar Linton's hair, is removed by Heathcliff, who replaces Linton's pale lock with a dark one of his own. But Nelly twines the pale and dark together within Catherine's locket heart, for she recognizes both as parts of Catherine. And in death, Catherine achieves the peace she has sought. Nelly describes Catherine's dead face: "her brow smooth, her lids closed, her lips wearing the expression of a smile. No angel in heaven could be more beautiful than she appeared and partook of the infinite calm in which she lay."

But the novel, as students persist in pointing out, does not end with Catherine's death. The youthful and passionate Catherine Earnshaw both dies and lives transformed in the person of her daughter and namesake, Catherine Linton. Therefore, it can be argued that the entire saga of two generations of Earnshaws, Lintons, and Heathcliffs is the odyssey of a single personality, parts of which are "male" and parts of which are "female." This personality begins with Catherine Earnshaw and ends with Catherine Linton Heathcliff Earnshaw, or a Catherine Earnshaw who has incorporated and reconciled those elements represented by Linton (superego) and Heathcliff (id). According to Freud, when the id is frustrated in the attainment of its desires by contact with reality, the ego provides a series of substitutions; this energy may be sublimated or directed toward a more socially acceptable object. Energy within the personality, like physical energy, is not destroyed, but transformed. What Catherine cannot achieve—freedom from tension, reconciliation of the opposing forces in her nature—is finally achieved by the daughter. For, in one sense, Catherine does not die at all, for shortly before her death, she gives birth to another Catherine, Catherine Linton, a partial synthesis of the opposing forces within her personality.

Catherine achieves her "spring through the window," her return to girlhood, both through her death and through young Catherine, who is born as Catherine dies "having never recovered sufficient consciousness to miss Heathcliff or to know Edgar." As Catherine lies in newfound repose, the infant "wails out of life." Catherine's conflict is both reborn and transformed in the infant who possesses Catherine's vitality and spirit tempered by the Lintons' gentleness. Young Catherine is

> a real beauty in face, with the Earnshaws' handsome dark eyes but the Lintons' fair skin and small features and yellow curling hair. Her spirit was high, but not rough, and qualified by a heart, sensitive and lively to excess in its affections. The capacity for intense attachments reminded me of her mother; still she did not resemble her; for she could be soft and mild as a dove, and she has a gentle voice, and pensive expression. Her anger was never furious, her love never fierce; it was deep and tender.

Through her two marriages, young Catherine achieves the serenity her mother was denied, for marriage is a melding of male and female into one, a reconciliation of male and female within the personality. Her first marriage is to the repellent Linton Heathcliff, whom Nelly describes as "the worst tempered bit of a sickly slip that ever struggled into his teens." Linton like the unfortunate proposed child of George Bernard Shaw and a famous actress, who inherited his looks and her brains, is the worse of eros and civilization, a joke of genetics. He combines the Lintons' constitutional weakness, described by Nelly as "listless apathy," with Heathcliff's infantile self-absorption and hysterical emotional dependency. Despite his questionable appeal, Catherine is drawn to him and he to her, and like her mother, defies Edgar Linton to maintain their relationship. When Nelly warns young Catherine that Edgar Linton has ordered that the friendship between Catherine and Heathcliff must not be revived, the girl replies

defiantly, "It has been revived." This love contains further echoes of the struggles of the previous generation. Each describes his or her dream of heaven, evoking Catherine's famous dream. "He wanted to lie in an ecstasy of peace; I wanted to sparkle and dance in a glorious jubilee . . . I said his heaven would be only half alive and he said mine would be drunk. . . ." The frustrated effort to achieve a shared male-female nature is represented by the pair's unsuccessful attempt to share two balls found in a heap of old toys belonging to their parents. "One was marked C. and the other H. I wished to have the C. because that stood for Catherine and the H. might be for Heathcliff, his name; but the bran came out of H. and Linton didn't like it."

Young Catherine, by doing what her mother did not do, by marrying Heathcliff, in a sense, validates her mother's fear of degradation. Marriage at the Heights becomes a thralldom surpassing that of thralldom at the Grange. Catherine, desperate at the news of Edgar's dying but imprisoned by Heathcliff and his son, leaps from a window at the Heights to reunite herself with that part of herself dying with her father, as her mother once leapt through a window at the Grange.

> She dare not try the doors, lest the dogs should raise an alarm; she visited the empty chamber and examined their windows, and, luckily, lighting on her mother's she got easily out of its lattice.

After Edgar's death, Catherine returns to Wuthering Heights, to be "buried alive." The Catherine Lockwood discovers and addresses as "Mrs. Heathcliff" is sullen, cruel and a bit depraved. On her face is an expression which hovers between "scorn and a kind of desperation." Accused by the sanctimonious Joseph of heading "raight to t' divil, like (her) mother before (her)," the "little witch" practices the black art on the red cow. But Wuthering Heights and a life as "Mrs. Heathcliff" is not Catherine's final destination. For the H., which "might be" for Heathcliff, might also be for Hareton.

After the deaths of Linton Heathcliff and Heathcliff, Hareton's cultivation and consequent ascendence begin. With Catherine's marriage to Hareton Earnshaw the reconciliation of conflicting elements is furthered. For Hareton is to Catherine and Heathcliff what young Catherine is to the elder Catherine and Edgar Linton: a harmonious synthesis of opposing forces. Hareton undoubtedly resembles and is allied with Heathcliff throughout the novel. Heathcliff unwittingly rescues the toddler Hareton after Hareton is tossed from the stairwell by Hindley. During Nelly's first encounter with Hareton after Catherine's marriage, the child sits at the crossroads between the two houses and extols Heathcliff's maniacal torment of Hindley. As a young man, Hareton admires and imitates the actions of Heathcliff: both prefer activities like demonstrations of poor table manners and the hanging of dogs. And the sullen "brute" Lockwood encounters is strongly reminiscent of the boy Heathcliff. But not only does Heathcliff see himself in Hareton, he sees Catherine, who is Hareton's aunt, as well. "But when I look for his father in his face, I see *her* more everyday." Through the marriage of these two, Catherine becomes Catherine Earnshaw again; Hareton and Catherine (H. and C.) begin a placid domestic life at Thrushcross Grange, having tamed those primal elements which caused such depths of torment and such heights of ecstasy.

But not entirely. For one part of Catherine's untamed nature, that part which leapt through the window at her death, remains. This part is represented by the plaintive wailing of the unsatisfied Catherine Linton at the window of Wuthering Heights; Catherine Linton (and Lockwood is puzzled by the spectre's identification of herself as "Catherine Linton" and not "Catherine Earnshaw") attempts to gain access to that fragment of herself imprisoned within the house, that fragment of herself represented by her daughter, then Catherine Heathcliff. This part is also represented by Heathcliff, whose spirit leaps also from the window to roam the moors again. This fragment is a part of the id, that part concerned with intimations of eternity, the "oceanic feeling" Freud describes. Part of the primitive, infantile id, this part of the personality cannot separate itself from its environment and thus shares the life of all around it. And so, what is seen at the novel's end is not the complete domestication or integration of this androgynous personality, but a redistribution of psychic energy which allows this personality to come to terms with its environment. As Freud writes in *Civilization and its Discontents*:

> But have we a right to assume the survival of something that was originally there, alongside of what was later derived from it? Undoubtedly . . . In the animal kingdom we hold to the view that the most highly developed species have proceeded from the lowest; and yet we find all the simple forms still in existence today. In the realm of the mind . . . what is primitive is so commonly preserved alongside of the transformed version which has arisen from it that it is unnecessary to give instances as evidence. When this happens, it is usually in consequence of a divergence in development: one portion . . . of an attitude or instinctual impulse has remained unaltered, while another portion has undergone further development.[3]

This "further development" is socialization and acceptance of "reality"; "further development" is seen in the happy marriage of Catherine Linton and Hareton Earnshaw. However, part of this personality's primal energy, irrepressible and indestructible, remains uncompromised in the ghostly presence on the moors of "Heathcliff and a woman."

The dialogue between mother and daughter in the introductory anecdote and in the novel emerges as a wom-

an's dialogue with herself. The girl so smitten with the film is eager and responsive but naive; the mother, pragmatic but constricting. Paired with Hareton, Catherine the daughter is contentedly acculturated but pallid; indeed, few readers remember that she occupies the novel at all. Paired with Heathcliff, Catherine the mother, unfettered, passionate, utterly memorable, discovers that although heaven does not seem to be her home, neither can she fully occupy the earth. The novel's ending both offers and withholds a resolution: Catherine the woman remains fragmented, spirit and body, wanton and wife, male and female. Catherine's anguished desire to be herself expresses a uniquely female suffering: nowhere does she exist as herself, whole and entire.

Notes

1. The id, according to Freud, is that basic, primal, unrestrained part of the personality in which resides the human being's most basic drives. The id is motivated by the pleasure principle, since the id aims at almost all times to seek pleasure and to avoid pain. Residing in the id are eros, the sexual impulse, and the death instinct. Both drives—eros and the death instinct—seek a similar end—a freedom from tension which Freud saw as the end of all organ matter. It is impossible, however, for the id to achieve its ends without interaction with the external environment. Hence—the ego, that part of the personality which engages in reality testing. The id announces its primitive needs and the ego intercedes with the external environment, modifying the pleasure principle with the reality principle, forcing the id to postpone release of its energy until gratification can reasonably be achieved. The third part of the personality, the superego, is concerned with the innumerable "shoulds" of civilization. It is the voice of parents, of the church, of social convention. It consists of the "ego-ideal", which offers the ideals to which the ego should aspire, and the conscience, which scolds the ego when it has erred.

2. Freud, Sigmund. *The Ego and the Id*, (New York: Norton, 1960), pp. 20-21.

3. Freud, Sigmund. *Civilization and Its Discontents* (New York: Norton, 1960), p. 16.

George E. Haggerty (essay date fall 1988)

SOURCE: Haggerty, George E. "The Gothic Form of *Wuthering Heights*." *Victorian Newsletter*, no. 74 (fall 1988): 1-6.

[*In the following essay, Haggerty examines the Gothic elements of* Wuthering Heights, *arguing that Brontë's radical manipulation of the novel form helps the book overcome the limitations of the genre.*]

Emily Brontë's remarkable novel has often been placed within the Gothic tradition in fiction, and it is indeed from within that tradition that this harrowing tale of a solitary gypsy youth who first liberates and then nearly destroys a pair of Yorkshire families finds its conventional vocabulary and its range of images.[1] But Brontë was no mere scribbler attempting to resuscitate the greying features of a dying form. For like no other writer before or since, Emily Brontë in *Wuthering Heights* looks into the heart of Gothic fiction, as it were, uncovers the most deeply rooted formal problems which Gothic novelists themselves were never able to resolve, and forges a solution to those problems out of the literary smithy of her own soul.

The problem in the Gothic novel, as I have argued elsewhere, is fundamentally a problem of language. Indeed the novel itself, as a form, posed difficulties for writers primarily concerned with the expression of subjective fantasy.[2] The key to understanding the distinction between intention and form in the Gothic novel lies in the very nature of the language which the Gothicists employed. Roman Jakobson's now famous article "Two Aspects of Language and Two Types of Aphasic Disturbances" argues that "The development of a discourse may also take place along two different semantic lines: one topic may lead to another either through their similarity or through their contiguity. The METAPHORIC way would be the most appropriate term for the first case and the METONYMIC way for the second, since they find their most condensed expression in metaphor and metonym respectively. In aphasia one or the other of these two processes is restricted or totally blocked . . ." (90).[3] Within the Gothic novel itself, there is a constant tension between these two uses of language. The result is a kind of literary aphasia, if you will, rendering literary expression both unsatisfying and self-defeating. In a sense, the very metonymic nature of the novel, inherently concerned with the contextualization of experience and the socialization of the private, formally contradicts the metaphorical demands of the Gothic, which began with a dream and developed by means of a series of fantasy situations and characters, at times carefully developed and at times blandly automatic, but rarely fully integrated into the demands of the novel's content and scope.

We might, for instance, consider the techniques in *The Monk* (1795) whereby Lewis attempts to involve his villain Ambrosio in actions that express the extremes of psychological horror at the same time that they advance the plot and expand our sense of his character. For this purpose, Lewis devises such scenes as the murder of a lady to whom he is confessor and for whose daughter he has developed unexampled lust, as well as the scene in which he later rapes and murders the supplicating girl herself. These scenes are vivid and distressing, and the revelations concerning his relation to his victims (they are his mother and sister) are meant as the final measure of damnation.

The difficulty Lewis encounters in this dramatic rendition of Ambrosio's Gothic role is that brand of sensationalism which results from Lewis's own kind of aphasia. Metaphorical ramifications of Ambrosio's predicament are powerful enough, but the metonymical aspect of his presentation feels gratuitous and strangely unconvincing. In outright ghost stories within the novel, however—the superficially ridiculous tale of the Bleeding Nun, for instance—Lewis devises an internal narrator whose record of private experience begins to contain the metaphorical dimensions of subjectivity within the bounds of the metonymical. "I listened . . . I felt . . . I shuddered . . . I heard . . . I started": Raymond de Cisternas tells us of his encounter with the gory religious (159). Raymond contains his tale within the personal at the same time that he insists on vivid contextual detail. The internal tale, that is, suspended from the novel form, momentarily sustains and intensifies Lewis's Gothic intention, and it seems that he has managed to construct a linguistic system which can temporarily resolve the tension between metaphor and metonym in his work. Lewis was incapable, however, of sustaining these effects or discovering an idiom which could render the personal effectiveness of the tale, so capable of incorporating the metaphorical within the metonymical, formally compatible with novelistic expression.

Brontë was not only aware of such formal inconsistency in the Gothic novel, she seems to have structured her own work both to mirror these tensions and to demonstrate the linguistic as well as thematic means of their resolution.[4] *Wuthering Heights,* in other words, directly confronts the formal dilemma facing every Gothic novelist and works out with literary exactitude the means of identifying Gothic intention and the novel form.

Brontë does this in the first place by writing instead of a conventional novel an extended tale, what Northrop Frye calls a romance.[5] The distinction between novel and tale is of course not merely one of semantics: Brontë employs internal narrators who tell their own accounts of the action which transpires. These private accounts already have a tale-like force because they attempt to explore the subjective and personal. Unlike the internal narrators in novels such as *The Monk* or *Melmoth the Wanderer* (1820), however, Brontë's narrators are impervious to the threats of other-worldly presences. They are created out of the formal stuff of novels, Lockwood and Nelly Dean, and they thereby indirectly place the novelistic version of experience against something deeper and more powerful. In so creating them, Brontë challenges novelistic form with Gothic meaning as it had never before been challenged. Lockwood, it could be said, attempts to novelize the events he witnesses and indeed to force a novelistic resolution to the action; but his very failure to be convincing is the measure of the inadequacy of his response.[6] His inadequacy, however, is not merely temperamental: it is the inadequacy of a certain kind of novelistic language that his failure both exposes and censures. Nelly, too, attempts to mould her material into novelistic form, and again her failure becomes itself a metaphor for the limits of interpretation.[7] Their metonymical presence, in other words, becomes a sign for the metaphorical absence of the experience they relate. Brontë thereby uses the novel to display the limits of its own expressive power.

Lockwood's inadequacy when he first confronts the largely "second generation" Wuthering Heights has been richly remarked.[8] His structures of response, like those of other Gothic heroes before him, are incapable of interpreting the terms of his experience correctly. In addition to mistaking a heap of dead rabbits for cats and assuming a marital relation between Heathcliff and the second Cathy, Lockwood demonstrates a general anxiety in the face of what he does not understand and an urge for meaning which results in endless misconstruction. This anxiety is of course vividly represented in his attempts to "read" the various inscriptions which he discovers around his bed, and in his brutal reaction to the pleading Catherine Linton of his dream, whose wrist he rubs to and fro on the broken window pane "till the blood ran down and soaked the bedclothes" (30). The repressed fear and aggression suggested by this dream begin to represent the kind of disfiguration of the tale that socializing, civilizing, contextualizing, novelizing versions of it perpetrate (see Musselwhite). In other words, Lockwood is the first critic of **Wuthering Heights,** and he literally attempts to tear it to shreds.

Challenged by Heathcliff to explain his midnight raving, Lockwood finds himself unwittingly incapable of using language in a way which Heathcliff can understand:

> "The truth is, sir, I passed the first part of the night—" here, I stopped afresh—I was about to say "perusing those old volumes;" then it would have revealed my knowledge of their written, as well as their printed contents; so, correcting myself, I went on—"in spelling over the name scratched on the window-ledge. A monotonous occupation, calculated to set me asleep, like counting, or—"
>
> "What can you mean by talking in this way to me!" thundered Heathcliff with savage vehemence. "How— how *dare* you, under my roof?—God! he's mad to speak so!" And he struck his forehead with rage.
>
> (32)

Lockwood begins this explanation of the immediate cause of his dream by calling upon "truth." But of course truth is just what his polite conversation is struc-

tured to evade. Lockwood's repression of the truth and his mode of self-editing suggest at once the effeteness of literary language as well as its intentional duplicity. This language reveals more than it hides, however, because its blithe urbanity is a measure of its inability to contain the essential reality it has not even begun to understand. Heathcliff's reaction emphasizes both what Lockwood of madness because he seems oblivious to the power behind his words. Lockwood feels indeed that he can control language as he chooses and here use it to lead him through a difficult moment. To him Heathcliff's reaction clearly seems as akin to madness as his own prattling does to Heathcliff.

We feel that communication between these two characters is impossible, and critics have been quick to attribute this to Lockwood's citified urbanity (see, for instance, Knoepflmacher 88-89). If we look closer, however, we can describe this disruption in more specific terms. Lockwood clearly suffers a "similarity disorder" in the terms I outlined from Jakobson above, while Heathcliff seems the victim of the converse contiguity disorder. Lockwood sees little beyond the immediate contextualizing syntax of his words, and Heathcliff sees nothing but their profound significance. Lockwood is all form and Heathcliff is all meaning. It would take more than a midnight chat to bring such characters into communication. Their anger indeed is nothing more than the frustration they experience at seeming to speak the same language while being constitutionally unable to understand each other. To describe Lockwood, then, as an "unreliable narrator" is to distort his central function here. His ruthless distortions of the truth are a part of his breeding. They emerge from what it means to be a member of society. His interpretations therefore may be unreliable, but they are intrinsic to the nature of Brontë's enterprise. His metonymic superficiality is necessary to the measure of what it cannot understand. Without Lockwood, that is, Heathcliff would be beyond our power of comprehension as well. Lockwood and Heathcliff cannot communicate with each other, but together they begin to convey the nature of the novel.

Nelly Dean has also been accused of misinterpretation and manipulation.[9] She is without question unsympathetic to her "friends" Heathcliff and Catherine and does indeed act counter to their mutual understanding and even physical survival. Yet Nelly is not therefore to be censured as "unreliable" but understood as central to Brontë's technique. For Nelly too represents the novelizing force of interpretation and contextualization, and her pernicious inadequacy is but a measure of the limitations of her form for understanding and those of upright and well-meaning people.

Nelly gives Lockwood, for instance, this description of events at the Grange after Catherine's hysterical scene upon Linton's dismissal of Heathcliff:

While Miss Linton moped about the park and garden, always silent, and almost always in tears; and her brother shut himself up among books that he never opened—wearying, I guessed, with a continual vague expectation that Catherine, repenting her conduct, would come of her own accord to ask pardon, and seek a reconciliation—and while *she* fasted pertinaciously, under the idea, probably, that at every meal, Edgar was ready to choke for her absence, and pride alone kept him from running to cast himself at her feet, I went about my household duties, convinced that the Grange had but one sensible soul in its walls, and that lodged in my body.

I wasted no condolences on Miss, nor any expostulations on my mistress, nor did I pay any attention to the sighs of my master. . . .

I determined they should come about as they pleased for me; and though it was a tiresomely slow process, I began to rejoice at length in a faint dawn of its progress, as I thought at first.

Mrs. Linton, on the third day, unbarred her door; and having finished the water in her pitcher and decanter, desired a renewed supply, and a basin of gruel, for she believed she was dying. That I set down to a speech meant for Edgar's ears; I believed no such thing, so I kept it to myself, and brought her some tea and dry toast.

(103)

To catalogue Nelly's behavior here is less important than to analyze her attitude by means of the language with which she expresses it. The first paragraph is but a single sentence, the subject of which, in the final clause, is "I." This is not merely to say that Nelly is an egoist and that she interprets experience primarily in relation to herself, but even more importantly to demonstrate that her language itself is incapable of finding any other center but that "I." This is not a story about Nelly Dean, but she tells it nevertheless from the only perspective she knows—her own. Nelly's impatience and even seeming cruelty in scenes such as these is more than a comment on the recalcitrance of servants. Nelly can express no more than she understands: a world of contiguity, cause and effect, action and reaction. "[W]earying, I guessed," "under the idea, probably," 'I went about . . . convinced," "I wasted no condolences," "I determined," "she believed she was dying . . . I believed no such thing. . . ." Nelly continually asserts her assumptions and beliefs because without them the experience of this household would seem arbitrary and meaningless. She treats everything representationally because, like Lockwood, she has no other linguistic terms with which to treat them: Nelly is all presence; the absence of metaphor has no meaning for her.

The central characters in the novel, on the other hand, if Catherine and Heathcliff can be called such, understand only metaphor. Like their Gothic predecessors, they inhabit a world which for them is so charged with meaning that it is almost unbearable. They speak a language which moves among these meanings with only the barest concern for contiguous syntactical structure. In Catherine's final "madness," for instance, her mind wanders among what Nelly calls "associations," in a realm of fantasy.[10] As she pulls feathers from a torn pillow, she murmurs:

"That's a turkey's . . . and this is a wild duck's; and this is a pigeon's. Ah, they put the pigeons' feathers in the pillow—no wonder I couldn't die! Let me take care to throw it on the floor when I lie down. And here's a moor-cock's; and this—I should know it among a thousand—it's a lapwing's. Bonny bird; wheeling over our heads in the middle of the moor. It wanted to get to its nest, for the cloud touched the swells, and it felt rain coming. This feather was picked up from the heath, the bird was not shot; we saw its nest in the winter, full of little skeletons. Heathcliff set a trap over it, and the old ones dare not come. I made him promise he'd never shoot a lapwing, after that, and he didn't. Yes, here are more! Did he shoot my lapwings, Nelly? Are they red, any of them? Let me look."

(105)

Catherine gives way completely to the metaphorical mode—goes mad, that is—when it is clear that social acceptance of her feelings for Heathcliff—their contextualization, if you will—is impossible. Syntactic coherence therefore gives way to noncontiguous assertions of meaning and associations of significance. The specific terms of this speech, although interesting, are in turn less important than its own "significance" in the novel's structure. For placed against Nelly's prim and even destructive morality or Lockwood's civilization, this madness suggests a world of wind, and light, and energy—and love.[11] That is not to say that Catherine's speech is not heart-rendingly pathetic, but rather that this very pathos is but the measure of our own inability to share in Catherine's vision. "You're wandering," Nelly imaginatively suggests. "I'm not wandering, you're mistaken," Catherine answers. Nelly is mistaken, and we are as well, insofar as we attempt to force Catherine into our own restrictive linguistic structures. Meanings, for Catherine, reside in a heap of feathers, in a lapwing, in a cloud. She sees Heathcliff in them all because he is the only character in the work who understands her, who speaks her language.

Heathcliff's own program of revenge after Catherine's death is an attempt to overturn the established order of things and to assert the primacy of his private vision. Like a Gothic hero, he tries to disrupt the contiguity of experience and make present the absent meanings of metaphor. This behavior too is a kind of madness; but while Catherine's madness was self-destructive, Heathcliff's is self-assertive. As such, it brings the realms of metaphor and metonym into vivid confrontation. The world of private meanings is pitted against the world of public ones. And if there is to be resolution in the novel, our concern must be with more than which side wins:

"Catherine Earnshaw, may you not rest, as long as I am living! You said I killed you—haunt me, then! The murdered *do* haunt their murderers, I believe. I know that ghosts *have* wandered on the earth. Be with me always—take any form—drive me mad! only *do* not leave me in this abyss, where I cannot find you! Oh God! it is unutterable! I *cannot* live without my life! I *cannot* live without my soul!"

(139)

Heathcliff is in his own way both as pathetic and as inaccessible as Catherine. If throughout the second half of the novel, as this quotation suggests, he inhabits a world of ghosts, he in that sense makes his private motivation his only meaning, becoming, to the public eye, mad; his frustrated attempts to gain control of the Earnshaw and Linton families bespeak the impossibility of translating that madness directly into social action. More than a Gothic villain, he becomes like the Gothic novelist him-or herself in attempting to introduce private subjective meanings into an objective public world without first finding the formal means to accomplish such a union.

In the action of the second half of **Wuthering Heights,** Brontë attends directly to these concerns and not only demonstrates the nature of the resolution to her own story here but also works out the terms of effective Gothicism in the novel. From one point of view, the story of the second generation is the outline of Heathcliff's frustrated revenge and ultimate death. From another, it is the story of young Catherine's discovery of Heathcliff's world, her forced marriage to his son Linton, her confrontation with the reality of death, and her ultimate toleration and then love of Hareton Earnshaw. Only by understanding these in relation to one another can we get a sense of Brontë's achievement.[12]

Both Linton and Hareton are sons of Heathcliff, the former physically and the latter spiritually (see Eigner 96-99). As his sons they come to represent both the two sides of Heathcliff's own personality and their relation to the worlds the novel depicts. Linton is the pathetic outward sign of Heathcliff's attempt to control the world of contiguity in the novel. He is the implement of Heathcliff's revenge, and in that role his simpering weakness provides outward manifestation of the impotence of Heathcliff's plan. As Linton becomes more clearly a tool of his father's revenge, he becomes less a person with whom we can sympathize, an almost allegorical figure of peevishness and perverted self-vindication. Indeed, this is what Heathcliff himself must seem to those who only know him from without. Ironically Linton's death complements his weakness as representative of the ultimate failure which Heathcliff must experience in his attempt at this kind of resolution. It leaves Heathcliff with everything, but nothing.

If Linton comes to represent this impotent program of revenge, this attempt to assert private meaning in the public world, Hareton clearly represents the other private Heathcliff that the novel seems so to celebrate: "Well, Hareton's aspect was the ghost of immortal love," Heathcliff says, "of my wild endeavours to hold my right, my degradation, my pride, my happiness, and my anguish—" (255). Hareton, for Heathcliff, belongs to that metaphorical world of madness and private meaning. At the same time, it is important that Hareton is not really Heathcliff's son, because that would include Heathcliff in the kind of worldly success that had failed with Linton's death. As a spiritual son, however, Hareton offers the terms whereby Heathcliff's private vision can be made public reality, limited and awkward at first, but ultimately approaching something like resolution.

Hareton's love is perhaps the most capacious of anyone's in the novel. It does not insist on complete possession nor is it absolutely exclusive. We can see this most clearly in the scene where Cathy forces a confrontation between herself and Heathcliff as objects of Hareton's love. Because he loves them both, he does everything within his power to avoid the confrontation while attempting to offend neither of them. When the confrontation does occur, "Hareton attempted to release [Cathy's] locks, entreating [Heathcliff] not to hurt her that once" (253). Hareton's actions suggest that violence between the generations is not necessary. When Heathcliff drops his hand from her head—whether as a result of Hareton's entreaties or of Catherine's looks—he has begun to realize how unrealistic his stance has become in relation to his own desires. In seeing their love he is reminded of his own, and, in his own words, "it partly contributes to render me regardless how he and his cousin go on together. I can give them no attention, any more" (255). Our ability to see Hareton partly as a manifestation of what was best about Heathcliff makes the union between Cathy and Hareton much more than the mere domestic resolution which Nelly and Joseph would make it. Instead it dramatizes the psychological regeneration which reaches fruition for both generations in Heathcliff's death.

By focusing our attention on the second generation as a reflection and reinterpretation of the first, Brontë accomplishes both thematic and formal resolution. Much has been said about resolution and reintegration in **Wuthering Heights.**[13] It is nevertheless important to note that this resolution is not, finally, a triumph of public values over private ones. Nelly and Lockwood are not the winners in **Wuthering Heights,** as much as their homely domesticity and urbane gentility may lead us to think so. Brontë insists instead that we look beyond the world of metonymic language if not into a world of pure metaphor, at least into a realm where private vision can be given public meaning after all.

The process of reunion with Catherine, of course, begins for Heathcliff almost immediately after her death, but Brontë has constructed the action so that we do not experience his torment except in the excessive revenge to which it drives him. The result is to force us to experience the most discomfort at the very moments at which Heathcliff feels the greatest distance from Catherine. That we only recognize this in retrospect is Brontë's method of preventing us from scrutinizing too carefully the terms of her other-worldly resolution. If we were to see Heathcliff roaming the moors night after night, the meaning Brontë places on these excursions would become banal. There is also, I think, the possibility that we would not remain at all sympathetic to his suffering in the midst of his savagery. For this reason, Brontë has Nelly narrate most of the denouement of the story after Heathcliff has died. Finally, lest an overexplicitness dispel the impact she seeks, Brontë allows Nelly to describe, but rarely to interpret, Heathcliff's actions just before his demise. This momentary refusal to contextualize places Heathcliff beyond the metonymical scope of language into a realm we can only approach by means of analogy:

> . . . I peeped in. Mr. Heathcliff was there—laid on his back. His eyes met mine so keen and fierce, I started; and then he seemed to smile.
>
> I could not think him dead, but his face and throat were washed with rain; the bed clothes dripped, and he was perfectly still. The lattice, flapping to and fro, had grazed one hand that rested on the sill; no blood trickled from the broken skin, and when I put my fingers to it, I could doubt no more—he was dead and stark!
>
> I hasped the window; I combed his black long hair from his forehead; I tried to close his eyes—to extinguish, if possible, that frightful life-like gaze of exultation, before anyone else beheld it. They would not shut; they seemed to sneer at my attempts, and his parted lips and sharp, white teeth sneered too!
>
> (264)

In this final look, just as in all his inexplicable looks over Nelly's shoulder throughout the last section of the novel, we see more than Brontë allows Nelly to articulate. The setting and the pose strongly suggest that he is reaching out to his beloved Catherine at last. The rain is a cleansing, soothing image when compared to the blood Lockwood produced in similar circumstances. Heathcliff's sneer forbids us to share his final vision, but it is this final refusal to articulate his private reality which places him at last beyond the contextualizing force of the novel itself.

Those critics who resist Brontë's attempt to resolve the relationship between Catherine and Heathcliff in a transcendent realm ignore the peculiar nature of the action she has constructed.[14] As a resolution of the public world of the novel, the mere death of Heathcliff and the succession of the second generation is sufficient. Yet the work insists on a reading that accomplishes more than

this metonymical completion. Brontë pays careful attention to a kind of growing supernatural awareness on Heathcliff's part, our interest in which can but supersede our concern with a happy ending for the young lovers. "I have a single wish," Heathcliff says, "and my whole being and faculties are yearning to attain it. They have yearned towards it so long, and so unwaveringly, that I'm convinced it *will* be reached—and *soon*—because it has devoured my existence. I am swallowed in the anticipation of its fulfillment" (256). The power of metaphor here is to liberate Heathcliff from the confines of his separation at the same time that it makes him less likely to continue in this world. Heathcliff is consumed within his own anticipation just as his language, and metaphorical language in general in the novel, becomes self-absorbed and ultimately self-reflexive. There is no public role for Heathcliff and Catherine, except within our own imaginations; and that is the realm within which Brontë finally tries to place them. As a physical union, if united at all, they are united in the grave. As a spiritual union, on the other hand, they reach beyond the grave and animate the novel with a spirit of other-worldliness both palpable and convincing.[15]

Cathy and Hareton have been called substitutes for Heathcliff and Catherine, and surely Brontë means us to understand their final happiness in those terms. It is not simply perverse, on the other hand, to note that Heathcliff is responsible for that union and that it is his own spirit that gives it life. Cathy takes it upon herself to tame this spirit, as it were, a project most readily accomplished by teaching Hareton to read and write. As he struggles to form words to her specification, she offers him kisses as a reward. She finds as well that his immense private world of love can be shared and realized publicly. When she first attempts this, of course, she risks the force of Heathcliff's wrath and his insistence that her love will make Hareton a beggar, but after his death Lockwood grumbles that "*they* are afraid of nothing" (265). At the close of the novel, they are set to marry and move into the Grange: they seem poised to realize their private happiness in a public form.

Cathy and Hareton do offer a resolution, then, which combines metaphor and metonymy in a reintegration of linguistic modes. They are neither haunted by private meanings nor trapped within public ones. The image of their indoor/outdoor existence at the Heights, with windows open to the sun and the fire blazing within, suggests this union of public and private, in contrast both to the darkness of the churchyard graves of Heathcliff and Catherine and the coldness of Lockwood's response to them.

It is not a weak compromise, then, that Brontë offers to the Gothic dilemma. She has depicted instead a world in which literary forms can collide without destroying a work but instead giving it life. Cathy and Hareton survive all attempts to make them anything but themselves. The tale, at its close, remains open to all the possibilities of language; the public has been contained within the private, and the private within the public. In *Wuthering Heights,* Brontë has liberated language from the rigid dichotomies of the Gothic novel and found instead an idiom capable of animating the social form with the private fantasy. At the end of *Wuthering Heights* we do not question whether Cathy and Hareton will be happy or whether Catherine and Heathcliff will realize their union. Instead, we set down the novel with satisfaction: this is the first truly successful Gothic novel. Walpole's "ancient and modern romance" have at last been blended so as to produce one of the most profound personal statements in English.

> I lingered round [the graves], under that benign sky; watched the moths fluttering among the heath and hare-bells; listened to the soft wind breathing through the grass; and wondered how anyone could ever imagine unquiet slumbers for the sleepers in that quiet earth.
>
> (266)

Lockwood's closing speech reminds us of how much there is to comprehend at the close of *Wuthering Heights* and how much lies beyond comprehension. For like Lockwood, we can only look and wonder. That is the measure of Brontë's achievement here.

Notes

1. The most useful study in this regard remains Kiely 233-51. See also Moers 35-39, Trickett 338-47, Windsor. For the most illuminating study of the Gothic in the mid-nineteenth century, see Sedgwick.

2. See also Kiely 17, Sedgwick 12-14, and Weiskel 14, 112.

3. See also Weiskel 30 and Gillis 80.

4. The most useful formal study of *Wuthering Heights* is that of Anderson 112-34. See also Garrett 1-17 and Miller 85-100.

5. (304-305). Frye's use of the term romance is confusing in this context, for he distinguishes the romance in other places as "myth" and "mode." Here he considers substituting "tale" for "romance," but decides that "tale" "appears to fit a somewhat shorter form."

6. Lockwood's narrative presence has been widely discussed. See especially Knoepflmacher 84-108 and McCarthy 48-64.

7. The classic indictment of Nelly Dean is presented by Hafly. See also Mathison, 333-53, Knoepflmacher 92-93, and McCarthy 56-58.

8. See, for instance, Kiely 238-39, Knoepflmacher 88-89, and McCarthy 51.

9. In addition to those critics listed above, n. 7, see also Musselwhite 157.

10. The process whereby such thinking came to be labelled madness is provocatively discussed in Foucault. See esp. 87-93 and the discussion of the relation of madness to passion to be found in chapter IV. For a post-Freudian reading of this passage, see Homans 16-18.

11. The imagery of *Wuthering Heights* is emphasized in such classic studies as that of Van Ghent 187-208.

12. Interesting discussions of the second generation in *Wuthering Heights* are included in Knoepflmacher 105-08, Garrett 8; Eigner 96-99, Burgan 395-413, and Armstrong 243-64.

13. See Burgan 404-11 and Armstrong 253-54 for recent considerations of the "resolution" of *Wuthering Heights.* For Burgan, the ending is "designed . . . to answer the problems posed by the beginning," both dramatically and psychologically (404-405); while Armstrong suggests the suppression of Romantic concerns in a Victorian resolution (253-54).

14. See Leavis 85-138 and Kettle 140-55. A useful answer to such studies is to be found in Grudin, 389-407.

15. This discussion is much indebted to Ralph W. Rader, "The Coherent Incoherence of *Wuthering Heights*," a paper delivered at the annual meeting of the Modern Language Association, Los Angeles, December, 1982.

Works Cited

Anderson, Walter E. "The Lyrical Form of *Wuthering Heights.*" *The University of Toronto Quarterly* 47 (1977-78): 112-34.

Armstrong, Nancy. "Emily Brontë In and Out of Her Time." *Genre* 15 (1982): 243-64.

Brontë, Emily. *Wuthering Heights.* Ed. William Sale. Norton Critical Edition. New York: W. W. Norton, 1972.

Burgan, Mary. "Some Fit Parentage": Identity and the Cycle of Generations in *Wuthering Heights.*" *Philological Quarterly* 61 (1982): 395-413.

Eigner, Edward. *The Metaphysical Novel in England and America.* Berkeley and Los Angeles: U of California P, 1978.

Foucault, Michel. *Madness and Civilization: A History of Insanity in the Age of Reason.* Trans. Richard Howard. New York: Random House, 1965.

Frye, Northrop. *The Anatomy of Criticism: Four Essays.* Princeton: Princeton UP, 1957.

Garrett, Peter, K. "Double Plots and Dialogical Form in Victorian Fiction." *Nineteenth-Century Fiction* 32 (1977): 1-17.

Gillis, Pamela Marsden. *The Paradox of Privacy: Epistolary Form in "Clarissa."* Gainesville: UP of Florida, 1984.

Grudin, Peter D. "*Wuthering Heights*: The Question of Unquiet Slumbers." *Studies in the Novel* 6 (1974): 389-407.

Hafly, James. "The Villain in *Wuthering Heights*." *Nineteenth-Century Fiction.* 13 (1958): 109-25.

Haggerty, George E. "Fact and Fancy in the Gothic Novel." *Nineteenth-Century Fiction* 39 (1985): 379-91.

Homans, Margaret. "Repression and Sublimation of Nature in *Wuthering Heights*." *PMLA* 93 (1978): 9-19.

Jakobson, Roman. "Two Aspects of Language and Two Types of Aphasic Disturbances." Jakobson, Roman and Morris Halle. *The Fundamentals of Language.* The Hague: Mouton, 1956.

Kettle, Arnold. *An Introduction to the English Novel.* London: Hilary House, 1951.

Kiely, Robert. *The Romantic Novel in England.* Cambridge: Harvard UP, 1972.

Knoepflmacher, U. C. *Laughter and Despair: Readings in Ten Novels of the Victorian Era.* Berkeley and Los Angeles: U of California P, 1971.

Leavis, Q. D. "A Fresh Approach to *Wuthering Heights*." Leavis, F. R. and Q. D. *Lectures in America.* London: Chatto & Windus, 1969.

Lewis, M. G. *The Monk: A Romance.* Ed. Howard Anderson. London: Oxford UP, 1973.

Mathison, John K. "Nelly Dean and the Power of *Wuthering Heights*." *Wuthering Heights.* Ed. William Sale. Norton Critical Edition. New York: W. W. Norton, 1972.

McCarthy, Terence. "The Incompetent Narrator of *Wuthering Heights*." *Modern Language Quarterly* 42 (1981): 48-64.

Miller, J. Hillis. "*Wuthering Heights* and the Ellipses of Interpretation." *Notre Dame English Journal* 12 (1980): 85-100. This essay is reprinted in a slightly altered form in Miller, J. Hillis. *Fiction and Repetition: Seven English Novels.* Cambridge: Harvard UP, 1982.

Moers, Ellen. "Female Gothic: Monsters, Goblins, and Freaks." *The New York Review of Books* 21 (April 4, 1974): 35-39.

Musselwhite, David. "*Wuthering Heights*: The Unacceptable Text." *Literature, Sociology, and the Sociology of Literature.* Ed. Francis Barker, et al. Proc. of the Conference Held at the Univ. of Essex. July, 1976. Colchester: U of Essex P, 1977. 154-60.

Sedgwick, Eve Kosofsky. *The Coherence of Gothic Convention.* 1980. New York: Methuen, 1986.

Trickett, Rachell. "*Wuthering Heights*: The Story of a Haunting." *Brontë Society Transactions* 16 (1975): 338-47.

Van Ghent, Dorothy. *The English Novel: Form and Function.* New York: Harper & Row, 1967.

Weiskel, Thomas. *The Romantic Sublime: A Study in the Nature of Transcendence.* Baltimore and London: The Johns Hopkins UP, 1976.

Windsor, Dorothy. "The Continuity of the Gothic: The Gothic Novels of Charlotte Brontë, Emily Brontë, and Iris Murdoch." Diss. Wayne State U, 1979.

Eric P. Levy (essay date summer 1996)

SOURCE: Levy, Eric P. "The Psychology of Loneliness in *Wuthering Heights*." *Studies in the Novel* 28, no. 2 (summer 1996): 158-77.

[*In the following essay, Levy explores the central psychological themes of* Wuthering Heights, *analyzing qualities of loneliness, cruelty, and pity in the novel's characters.*]

As Walter Allen has observed, **Wuthering Heights** "is utterly unlike any other novel."[1] Historically, the most celebrated aspect of its uniqueness concerns the portrayal of character. According to E. M. Forster, "the emotions of Heathcliff and Catherine Earnshaw function differently to other emotions in fiction."[2] But the psychological strangeness of these two figures has undermined their intelligibility. Bernard Paris points out several critics who do not regard Heathcliff as "a mimetic character"—that is, one whose function is to represent a person.[3] Similarly, Joyce Carol Oates finds Catherine's unusual fixation on her own childhood inaccessible to analysis: "why, as a married woman of nineteen, she should know herself irrevocably 'changed'—the novel does not presume to explain."[4] Mr. Lockwood, the primary narrator of the novel, has also aroused perplexity. David Sonstream judges Lockwood's character to be incoherent because he "is alternately happy warrior and repressive milksop."[5] Dorothy Van Ghent sees Lockwood's famous nightmare of Catherine's ghost as somehow extraneous to its dreamer and the result of autonomous "powers of darkness."[6] Ruth Adams argues that the nightmare "contaminates" Lockwood with the violence proper to Wuthering Heights.[7]

The difficulty of explaining these three characters has led many critics to approach Emily Brontë's fiction with the aid of psychological theory. Freud is the theorist most frequently invoked[8] but there are several others, as evident for example in Paris's attempt to define Heathcliff in the nomenclature of Karen Horney as an "arrogant-vindictive personality" and in Pratt's Jungian linking of both Heathcliff and Catherine with the "[d]ying-god archetype."[9] Other critics found the explication of character on fundamental oppositions detected in the text and corresponding (in most cases) to the two households depicted in the novel, Wuthering Heights and Thrushcross Grange. Even a short list of these polarities is impressively varied: "the land of storm" and "the home of calm" (Cecil), Hell and Heaven (Gilbert and Gubar), "the Sexual" and "the Spiritual" (Prentis), classless society and hierarchal society (Winnifreth), disappearing farm culture and emerging Victorian gentility (Q. D. Leavis), savagery and civilization (Reed), patriarchal society and negated feminine authority (Lavabre).[10]

Though each interpretation enhances our understanding of the novel, none has approached consensual acceptance. Indeed, in 1964 Mildred Christian could already observe that "[t]he contradictory judgments on *Wuthering Heights* are the most striking fact in its critical history."[11] More recently, both Miller and Baldridge have insisted that the novel lacks any central or formative principle by which its meaning can be comprehensively explicated.[12] Mid such boisterous disagreement, there remains the opportunity to combine the psychological and polarizing approaches in order to explain Heathcliff, Catherine, and Lockwood in terms of a distinctly Brontëan psychology embedded in the text and founded on the fundamental polarities of their own experience.

The prominent role played by Catherine's ghost in the lives of both Heathcliff and Lockwood can serve as an introduction. As we shall see, the most important afterlife in the world of Emily Brontë is the life after childhood—the persistence in adulthood of the attitude toward love acquired in childhood. *Wuthering Heights* explores two types of defective love in childhood, each barring the path to fulfilling love in adulthood. For reference purposes, they can be named descriptively as Unlove and Overlove. The Earnshaw family of Wuthering Heights is the representative household of Unlove where childhood is an experience of neglect, abuse, and rejection. In contrast, the Linton family of Thrushcross Grange is the representative household of Overlove with its tendency to overprotect and coddle children, treating them as "petted things."[13] In one family, the implied message transmitted to the child might be rendered as "You don't belong here"; in the other, "You're too weak ever to leave." The most devastating consequence of either type of defective love is that the adults emerging from it have difficulty separating the need for love from the fear of abandonment. Their need for love is exceeded only by their distrust of it. The distrust of the Unloved results from the expectation of rejection;

that of the Overloved stems from an overwhelming dependence which, feeling itself too weak to survive rejection, can trust only a love unable to leave.

As we shall find later, certain characters in the novel, such as Hindley, Edgar, and Isabella, provisionally solve the conflict between the need for love and the fear of abandonment through finding relationships offering love without the countervailing threat of rejection or separation. Yet, other characters, namely Heathcliff, Catherine, and Lockwood, remain more actively at war with love in their adult lives. Some force, as inexorable as the wind sweeping over the moors, seems to have bent their lives into a pattern of frustration that their own struggle for relief only aggravates. Their need for love is expressed, not through loving, but through the anguish of loneliness. Paradoxically, though they do not know it, this loneliness is the one condition necessary for the fulfillment of their most profound fantasy concerning perfect love: a love, that is, perfectly protected against the threat of abandonment that in childhood these sufferers learned that love entails.

To uncover this fantasy is to probe the Brontëan notion of the unconscious, for it exploits the conscious misery inflicted by loneliness in order to prove that satisfactory love with another in real life is impossible: satisfaction must be sought exclusively in the fantasies that frustration in real life arouses. As a result of the distrust of love so painfully acquired in childhood, the only love these figures can accept in adulthood is one sustained by fantasy, because that is the only love that guarantees secure possession. But those in whom this need for fantasy resides are ignorant of its presence. They regard their loneliness as a tormenting affliction whereas, by encouraging fantasy, it actually fulfills their own deepest wish: the wish that love remain no more than wishing, for only in that way can inviolable intimacy be assured.

This preliminary paradox entails another that we shall also clarify in the course of our study. The obverse of the unconscious need to confine intimacy to fantasy is the need for conscious preoccupation with loneliness. The need for fantasy requires that the waking awareness of the subject it controls focus regularly on the pain of loneliness and the memory of loss. Otherwise, the need for the fantasy of intimacy might be displaced by genuine intimacy—in which case, the subject would be left defenseless in his relation with real love, just as in childhood when the need for the protection of fantasy was first unconsciously conceived. In different ways, both the Unloved and Overloved unwittingly exploit their own suffering of loneliness not only to perpetuate the need for the fantasy of intimacy, as we have just noted, but also—and most ironically—to approximate the type of love which that fantasy concerns: an intimacy secure from loss, for it is based on the sharing, not of love, but rejection.

As a result of the Unlove that they were made to suffer, both Heathcliff and Catherine, by opposite means and in distinct circumstances, turn loneliness into a community of rejection over which they wield absolute control. Heathcliff does this by persecuting those he hates; Catherine, by persecuting those she loves. Yet, by thus avenging the pain of rejection, they simultaneously increase it; the more each mistreats others, the more estranged from them each becomes. Hence, cruelty to others ultimately becomes cruelty to themselves. But the meaning of their loneliness is transformed by this antagonism. Instead of suffering as the helpless victim of rejection, each now suffers as its unassailable source. Whereas loneliness formerly derived from humiliating rejection, it now expresses a complacent aloofness: neither needs those he or she hurts; instead, loneliness expresses contempt for company. But at the same that loneliness implies rejection of others, it also reinforces the sense of worthiness to be loved by another—a confidence which, as rejection in childhood taught them, love inevitably undermines. Only loneliness can make them feel worthy of love, because only through loneliness can each simultaneously avenge rejection and reverse the personal debasement resulting from it.

The Overloved (or, more precisely, as we shall see, the type thereof represented by Lockwood) shows the same tendency to manipulate loneliness, but the loneliness manipulated is founded on a principle of exclusion contrary to that underpinning the isolation of the Unloved. Whereas the Unloved tries through cruelty to *universalize* rejection in order to exalt himself above it, the Overloved tries through the need for pity to *monopolize* rejection so that in his mind he becomes its most helpless victim. Both the Unloved and Overloved strive toward the same goal: a love secure from the threat of rejection. But each side employs a different, though unconscious, strategy for achieving this objective. The Unloved separates love from the threat of rejection by making loneliness confirm eligibility for intimacy. The Overloved (in the example to be examined) separates love from the threat of rejection by pursuing an intimacy that is no more than self-pity for his own loneliness. This reliance on pity is not displayed by the Unloved who learned in childhood that to expose one's vulnerability is to risk increasing it. Hence, the only pity the Unloved wants is cruelty. Aggravating the pain of loneliness is the only way to relieve it because through that suffering, as earlier suggested, the very meaning of isolation is changed.

* * *

Our inquiry into these matters can best begin with Heathcliff. The most bizarre example of his resistance to pity occurs during his agony in the garden of Thrushcross Grange, immediately after Catherine's death. Despite the intensity of his suffering, Heathcliff repulses Nelly's compassion: "he held a silent combat with his inward agony, defying, meanwhile, my sympathy with an unflinching, ferocious stare" (p. 203). Here Heathcliff struggles to control not so much his pain as the pity it would evoke. Indeed, a few moments later he yields unrestrainedly to his agony in a manner certain to increase it: "He dashed his head against the knotted trunk; and lifting up his eyes, howled, not like a man, but like a savage beast getting goaded to death with knives and spears" (pp. 204-05). But, as Nelly observes, the very excessiveness of Heathcliff's suffering makes it repellent to pity: "It hardly moved my compassion—it appalled me" (p. 205).

Her remark exposes the central paradox of Heathcliff's character: his own suffering puts him as far beyond the reach of pity as does the cruelty that he makes others suffer. He is as cruel to himself as he is to others. On the superficial level, banging his head against the tree expresses Heathcliff's grief at his loss and frustration at his helplessness to overcome it. But underneath these emotions is something far more significant: the will to intensify his own suffering. Heathcliff needs his suffering even more than he needs Catherine. This paradox becomes especially vivid in the period following Catherine's death. For even after accepting the *fact* of her demise, Heathcliff still suffers like a "beast getting goaded to death"—but one goaded now by nothing more than anguished yearning to see her ghost: "It was a strange way of killing, not by inches, but by fractions of hair-breadths, to beguile me with the spectre of a hope, through eighteen years!" (p. 351).

To understand Heathcliff's pain-obsessed relationship with Catherine is to understand his psychological core and the role played by Unlove in forming it. His preoccupation with her ghost gives literal expression to the meaning her love came to have for him when she was still living. Indeed, Heathcliff himself draws the connection: "She showed herself, as she often was in life, a devil to me!" (p. 351). For Heathcliff, love has always been associated with the pain of absence, rejection, and disappointment. This pattern, of course, was initiated by the abusive regime of Hindley. But it was repeated by Catherine, when she wounded Heathcliff by deciding to marry Edgar.

But in the course of the novel, Heathcliff's relationship with the dead Catherine can be seen as an attempt to *overcome* all the defects in the relationship with the live one, even as it mirrors them. At the deepest level, his obsession with the ghost is motivated by the unconscious fantasy of finally turning the tables on love. This is the fundamental wish of the Unloved: to transform disappointment, rejection, and absence into their contraries by the sheer intensity of the pain they cause. The first evidence of this transformation appears in Heathcliff's account of his desperate effort to disinter Catherine's corpse on the night after her burial. The episode is remarkable for its attribution to Catherine of two opposite traits: pity and cruelty. Just as he is about to force open the coffin, Heathcliff suddenly senses her presence above him: "I relinquished my labour of agony, and turned consoled at once, unspeakably consoled" (p. 350). But a few minutes later—and, as we have just seen, for years afterward—the ghost's pitying presence becomes the instrument of cruelty: "I ought to have sweat blood then, from the anguish of my yearning, from the fervour of my supplications to have but one glimpse! I had not one" (p. 351).

This paradoxical fusing of pity and cruelty makes sense when we recall the attitude toward pity created in Heathcliff by Unlove. Despite his emotional agony, pity is vehemently refused; for, as a result of his experience in childhood, Heathcliff has learned that to depend on another for emotional support is to risk increasing his own sense of helplessness. Hence, his unconscious wish as victim in his relationship with Catherine is to suffer so acutely that he becomes independent of pain. In this way, her cruelty ultimately approximates pity—but only if Heathcliff dies of it. At bottom, as we shall see, Heathcliff's yearning for Catherine becomes no more than the *eroticization* of his own wish for death, and death itself becomes the *idealization* of his relationship with Catherine.

These unconscious fantasies appear very clearly near the end of the novel. Though Heathcliff is now able to see the ghost, his suffering intensifies: "It's unutterably too much for flesh and blood to bear, even mine" (p. 410). But here, very obviously, cruelty is the purveyor of pity; for the more Heathcliff suffers, the more imminent seems the consolation of relief: "it has devoured my existence—I am swallowed in anticipation of its fulfillment" (p. 395). The ravenous intensity of Heathcliff's obsession with Catherine's ghost consumes his attention. He becomes oblivious to virtually everything—except his preoccupation with the ghost. He forgets to eat, and even has "to remind [himself] to breathe—almost to remind [his] heart to beat!" (p. 395). The inevitable consequence of this condition is his own death, as Nelly one morning discovers: "I tried to close his eyes—to extinguish, if possible, that frightful, life-like gaze of exultation. They would not shut—they seemed to sneer at my attempts, and his parted lips, and sharp, white teeth sneered too!" (p. 411).

The meaning of Heathcliff's exultation in death can be clarified by the one occasion when he displays that same emotion in life: Hindley's funeral. At that time, Nelly observes "something like exultation in [Heathcliff's] aspect" (p. 230), and the reason for it is obvious: triumphant revenge against the pain and humiliation that Hindley made him suffer in childhood. This link between exultation and revenge implies that Heathc-

liff's own death also concerns revenge against pain and humiliation that he has been made to suffer. But this time, the victim of revenge is none other than himself—or, more precisely, as we shall see, his own life. By allowing obsession with the Ghost to usurp the awareness necessary to sustain his own life, Heathcliff avenges himself on the humiliating sense of neglect that life made him suffer. He makes death signify *his* rejection of life as unworthy of attention. His "life-like gaze" (p. 411) in death views the living with the same "sneer" of contempt with which Unlove once regarded him.

Yet, the undying antagonism between Heathcliff and life can be fully explained only in the context of the afterlife that his death implies. At the end of novel, we read that Heathcliff's ghost is spotted with Catherine's "on *every rainy night* since his death" (my emphasis, p. 412). As we shall see, the posthumous relation between Heathcliff and Catherine signifies not so much a supernatural reality as the deepest fantasy rooted in their hearts as a result of their experience with Unlove: to have a love that sneers at the need for love, to have a love based on the sharing of rejection.

The condition of "rainy night" associated with Heathcliff and Catherine's afterlife will clarify this fantasy. Near the beginning of the novel, Mr. Lockwood reads a crucial passage in Catherine's childhood diary: "we cannot be damper, or colder, in the rain than we are here" (p. 27). She is referring to one of many occasions (in this case, at nighttime) when Hindley expelled Heathcliff and Catherine from the warm hearth. In this diary entry, the nocturnal rain becomes a more attractive environment than the house in which she lives; for she writes that Heathcliff "proposes that we . . . have a scamper on the moors. A pleasant suggestion" (p. 26). We see here the essence of the childhood love between Heathcliff and Catherine: it is a sharing of the state of exclusion from love—a state symbolized by the nocturnal rain. The love that bonds them under that desolate rain is their only escape from the abuse and rejection they suffer in their home, Wuthering Heights. Their love, in other words, is founded on rejection. That is the first principle on which their love depends. The connection between nocturnal rain and the sharing of separation from love is dramatically reinforced elsewhere in the novel. The death of Mr Earnshaw, an event that exposes both Heathcliff and Catherine to the brutal regime of Hindley, their elder sibling, is marked by a violent nocturnal storm (p. 84), as is the sudden departure of Heathcliff after hearing of Catherine's plan to marry Edgar (p. 124)—a man whose love will eventually make Catherine rue the absence of Heathcliff.

The relationship between Heathcliff and Catherine thrives as long as vulnerability to the same domestic source of Unlove (i.e., Hindley) unites them. Entry into adulthood frees them from that environment, yet even greater discord follows. Each meets the other in mere oppugnancy. Heathcliff reproaches Catherine for abandoning him: "Catherine . . . I *know* you have treated me infernally—infernally!" (p. 138). Catherine is just as convinced that Heathcliff has abandoned her: "You have killed me and thriven on it" (p. 195). Yet in the midst of this embittered opposition, each protests passionately that he or she loves the other—and only the other. It could not be otherwise. Even as a married couple, the result would have been the same. Without a third party on whom to blame the pain of rejection, Heathcliff and Catherine are doomed both to love and resent each other with equal intensity. For, as we have seen, their love is founded on a paradox: no love unless they share the pain of rejection. In childhood, Hindley inflicted that pain on them. In adulthood, they must inflict it on each other. That is what love formed by Unlove means for them.[14]

The "rainy night" image connected with their afterlife suggests that only death can restore the condition defining their love in childhood: joint escape from the pain of rejection. Whereas in childhood the source of rejection was located *inside* the home, in adulthood that source is eventually identified with life itself which, after Catherine's death, denies Heathcliff all hope of love: "The entire world is a dreadful memoranda that she did exist, and that I have lost her!" (p. 394). The open window "flapping to and fro" (p. 410) near Heathcliff's corpse suggests that in death he escapes at last from the unpleasant confines of life and shares love once again with Catherine *outside* in the rain.[15] Indeed, the night of his death is marked by another tremendous downpour (p. 364).

The same syndrome finds different expression in Catherine. At bottom, her sickness in adulthood is the need to feel abused by love in order thus to replicate the environment of Unlove indispensable to the intimacy she and Heathcliff once enjoyed. Unable to understand the motive for her own actions, Catherine fulfills this need through fostering rivalry between Heathcliff and Edgar. First, she jilts Heathcliff by marrying Edgar, and then rejects Edgar for forbidding her to receive Heathcliff in the marital home. Finally, she accuses both men of hurting her: "You and Edgar have broken my heart, Heathcliff! And you both come to bewail the deed to me, as if you were the people to be pitied!" (p. 195).

From Catherine's distorted perspective, the Heathcliff whose love she seeks to restore is not the Heathcliff whom her actions wound: "That is not *my* Heathcliff. I shall love mine yet; and take him with me—he's in my soul" (p. 197). The suffering that she causes the living Heathcliff does not concern her; for the love she wants to revive exists only in the past: the close bond between herself and Heathcliff in the lonely childhood they endured. Death becomes the fantasy of the past resur-

rected, while the present with its self-imposed misery becomes both a goad to end her life *and* the means of simulating the circumambience of Unlove in which her love for Heathcliff flourished long ago.[16]

The great irony of Heathcliff's love for Catherine's ghost is that, during her adulthood, there is a kind of ghost inside Catherine—a part perpetuating the perspective of childhood, long after childhood is over. We see this clearly when a delirium precipitated by Edgar's ultimatum that she choose between himself and Heathcliff causes Catherine to forget temporarily her adult identity and to reenter the most traumatic moment of her childhood: "the whole last seven years of my life grew a blank! I did not recall that they had been at all. I was a child; my father was just buried, and my misery arose from the separation that Hindley had ordered between me, and Heathcliff" (p. 153). Yet when Catherine suddenly remembers that she is no longer that forlorn child but an adult married to Edgar, her "despair" (p. 153) instead of abating actually intensifies: "But, supposing at twelve years old, I had been wrenched from the Heights, and every early association, and my all in all, as Heathcliff was at that time, and been converted, at a stroke, into Mrs. Linton . . . the wife of a stranger; an exile, and outcast thenceforth, from what had been my world—You may fancy a glimpse of the abyss where I grovelled!" (p. 153).

In contrast to Lockwood's nightmare (to be examined later) where the adult injures the ghostly child, here the part persisting from childhood causes the adult pain: Catherine allows regret for the loss of childhood to bleed her to death, as it were. The more she regrets, the more intolerable adulthood becomes: "I wish I were a girl again, half savage and hardy, and free . . . and laughing at injuries, not maddening under them!" (p. 153). This scene dramatizes what might be called the *suicide of adulthood,* and it can be understood on two levels. The first is literal—or almost so. In her delirium, Catherine does indeed hasten her own death by opening her window for too long on a windy winter night while urging an imaginary Heathcliff to join her in the grave: "But Heathcliff, if I dare you now, will you venture? . . . they may bury me twelve feet deep . . . but I won't rest till you are with me" (p. 154). But more profoundly, Catherine's suicide of adulthood signifies not an action so much as a persistent attitude: her refusal to identify with her adulthood.

The depth of this refusal becomes intelligible when we consider an earlier crisis in the delirium scene. Here, Catherine fails to recognize her own reflection: "'Don't *you* see that face?' she enquired, gazing earnestly at the mirror" (p. 150). In fact, she recoils from her reflection with a terror as intense as that which grips Lockwood when he sees the child-ghost outside the window. Moreover, the part of Catherine here fearing her own reflection is associated, not with an adult at all, but with the same child-ghost that Lockwood sees on the other side of the window in his dream. Once Catherine recovers from the shock of terror, she sounds exactly like the ghost in Lockwood's dream who "wailed, 'Let me in!'" (p. 31). In Nelly's words, "our fiery Catherine was no better than a wailing child!" (p. 152). And like the ghost, she wails for reentry into the house of childhood: "Oh, if I were but in my own bed in the old house!" (p. 151).

* * *

Catherine knows herself only through regret for loss of childhood—the same emotion underneath Heathcliff's lust for revenge. But in Lockwood's famous dream we find the direct opposite: an overwhelming fear of *returning* to childhood, even as he regresses helplessly toward it. But before analyzing his dream, we must consider the context of its occurrence.

Near the beginning of the novel, Lockwood recounts a recent disappointment at a seaside resort where a young woman seemed to reciprocate his bashful attentions. Immediately, Lockwood shrank "icily into [himself] like a snail, at every glance retired colder and further; till, finally, the poor innocent was led to doubt her own senses, and . . . persuaded her mamma to decamp" (p. 7). However much Lockwood wants to respond to love, some reflex makes him withdraw every time the chance for love approaches: "By this curious turn of disposition I have gained the reputation of deliberate heartlessness, how undeserved, I alone can appreciate" (p. 7). As a result, Lockwood feels doomed to fulfill his mother's prediction that he "should never have a comfortable home" (p. 7). This reference to his mother hints strongly that the cause of Lockwood's adult loneliness is his experience with love in childhood. Indeed, right after the resort digression three incidents occur in which he visibly regresses to childhood.

Lockwood feels strangely drawn to his new landlord, Heathcliff and, despite the reluctant hospitality, persists in visiting him. During the first visit, while waiting in the parlor of Wuthering Heights for Heathcliff and Joseph to return from the cellar, Lockwood acts in a most unadult way, "winking and making faces" (p. 8) at the three large dogs near him. His regressive behaviour provokes the animals to attack, and Lockwood must cry out for rescue. A second attack occurs during Lockwood's next visit when, fed up with rude treatment, he suddenly snatches a lantern to illumine his path back to Thrushcross Grange, and is pinned by two ferocious dogs unleashed by Joseph. For a few moments, Lockwood loses his manhood entirely and thrashes on the ground in a helpless tantrum, while Heathcliff and Hareton scoff at his "rage and humiliation" (p. 21). Later, Lockwood is given Catherine's old bedroom to sleep in, and there has his dream of the child-ghost who wails piteously: "Let me in!" (p. 31).

Thus, his desperate struggle against that child-ghost culminates a series of regressions to childhood. Each involves a vivid polarity between heartless cruelty and piteous helplessness. In the resort incident (which Lockwood cites as an example of his uncontrollable reflex to withdraw from love), his apparently "deliberate heartlessness" (p. 7) is opposed to the girl's pitiful "confusion" (p. 7). In the two dog incidents, canine savagery is opposed to Lockwood's childish vulnerability; in the dream, the child-ghost's supplications are contrasted with Lockwood's fierce refusal.

Moreover, in the last three incidents of this series, the cruelty is explicitly directed against an *intruder figure*. The nightmare, of course, is a spectacular intruder dream with Catherine as the figure who must be repelled. In the two dog scenes, Lockwood himself is the intruder—one whose presence in the house is, at best, only warily tolerated. Indeed, he twice refers to his "intrusion" (p. 10, p. 35). By implication, the first incident in the series (Lockwood's reflex to withdraw from love) also concerns the attempt to repel an intruder, though to understand its nature we must remember the regression to childhood associated with all four incidents.

In both types of childhood presented in this novel, the intruder figure signifies, not the thief of property, but the *thief of love*. When Heathcliff, for example, is first brought into the home by Mr. Earnshaw, everyone there initially resents the intrusion of the tiny urchin, and Hindley never gets over his hostility at Heathcliff for being "a usurper of his parent's affections" (p. 47). Moreover, dogs often symbolize hostility toward this special kind of intruder. The *locus classicus* for such usage is Isabella's remark to Catherine: "You are a dog in the manger, Cathy, and desire no one to be loved but yourself!" (p. 126).

Once adulthood is reached, the mentalities formed in childhood by Unlove and Overlove have different ways of combatting the threat of the intruder and fulfilling the desperate need for secure possession of love. The Unloved protects himself from further loss of love by becoming the thief who steals it from others through making *them* suffer rejection. His or her resulting sense of isolation, as we saw in detail with Heathcliff and Catherine, sustains the unconscious fantasy of eventually receiving love without threat to the vulnerability needing it. In contrast, Lockwood seeks protection from the thief of love through increasing his own fear of intrusion.

Lockwood takes elaborate precautions to avoid heartbreak, whereas Heathcliff—through a lifetime of yearning for Catherine—ensures that his will never mend. When Lockwood meets Catherine's daughter, Cathy, he warns himself against yielding to his attraction for her: "let me beware of the fascination that lurks in Catherine

Heathcliff's brilliant eyes. I should be in a curious taking if I surrendered my heart to that young person, and the daughter turned out a second edition of the mother!" (p. 188). But Lockwood's reference to Cathy's mother is only an excuse; for, according to his own testimony, he always withdraws when his need for love is aroused. That is the intruder against which he must protect himself.

Lockwood's nightmare represents in symbolic form the emotional forces controlling a crucial aspect of his waking life: the insecurity caused by his own need for love. Part of Lockwood craves love; we can see this from his frustration after withdrawing from the resort girl. We see it expressed also in the ghost's petition to be let in: "I've been a waif for twenty years" (p. 31). But another part fears that to fall in love as an adult would be to revive the greatest fear of his childhood: the fear of one day being left like a waif without the protective love on which his weakness has come to depend. If he yields to love, he might become as helplessly dependent upon it as he was when a child. Even worse, if then he lost love, how would he ever get over the renewed need for it? Hence, Lockwood can feel secure in adulthood only by cruelly repressing the need for love that has haunted him ever since childhood. But by so doing, Lockwood attempts what might be called the *suicide of childhood,* as symbolized by his action of rubbing the child-ghost's wrists over the broken glass, "till the blood ran down and soaked the bedclothes" (p. 31). This suicide of childhood is the counterpart of the suicide of adulthood noted in Catherine. Paradoxically, in order to quell the fear of living like a waif that dominated his childhood, Lockwood lives like a kind of waif in adulthood, with no close emotional relationships and with not even (at least during his tenancy at Thrushcross Grange) a permanent home of his own.[17]

Thus, at the deepest level, the child-ghost in Lockwood's nightmare is an image of his own loneliness. But what he fears most about loneliness is not the pain of being alone but the desperate need for love that loneliness intensifies. For, as we discovered, Lockwood unconsciously connects his need for love with the helpless dependence that would overwhelm his adult identity, if ever given the chance.[18]

Yet, in addition to warding off dependence on love, Lockwood's loneliness actually serves as substitute for it by allowing him to remain the primary object of his own solicitude. Nothing gets more attention than his own self-pity for what he won't let himself have. We have already heard him complain of the frustration caused by his withdrawal reflex, but he also deplores the boredom that his solitude must endure: "I'm frequently very dull at the Grange—take my books away, and I should be desperate!" (p. 364). But that boredom is the inevitable consequence of the loneliness Lockwood must maintain in his adult life in order to avoid the risk of love. In fact, the books connected with his boredom are invoked in his dream as the very means by which to repel the ghost symbolizing his need for love: "I . . . hurriedly piled the books up in a pyramid against it, and stopped my ears to exclude the lamentable prayer" (p. 31).

Lockwood's nightmare can be clarified further if we turn now to the dream immediately preceding it. Here Lockwood sits in church, enduring an interminable sermon delivered by Jabes Branderham. Finally, enraged by tedium, Lockwood rises to denounce the preacher, only to find himself assailed by "the whole assembly, exalting their pilgrim's staves" (p. 29). Unfortunately, Lockwood is the only member of the congregation without a staff, and so he tries to snatch Joseph's. A general fracas ensues: "Every man's hand was against his neighbour" (p. 29). The cacophony of "rappings and counter-rappings" (p. 29) awakens Lockwood who then hears a real noise, caused by a branch of a windblown fir-tree rapping against the window panes. The confusion in the dream where each man fights his fellow vividly symbolizes Lockwood's psychomachy or internal conflict. One part, as we have seen, protests against the regime of boredom, while another part enforces it.

The phallic implications of Lockwood's status as the only man without a staff have been stressed by many critics.[19] But the novel itself suggests that a condition other than the Oedipal castration complex is implied, though we shall need a few moments to explain it. The motif of rebellion against the tedium of enforced religious observance first appears immediately prior to this dream when, before falling asleep, Lockwood reads in Catherine's childhood "diary" (p. 24) a description of the boring Sunday observance imposed at home on herself and Heathcliff by Joseph at the instigation of Hindley: "The service lasted precisely three hours" (p. 25). Moreover, Lockwood also reads that, when Catherine and Heathcliff later attempted to break the monotonous solemnity of Sunday evening by engaging in a little play, Hindley instantly repressed them: "I insist on perfect sobriety and silence" (p. 25). But there is yet another antecedent to Lockwood's dream of Branderham. Earlier that day, near the beginning of his impromptu visit to Wuthering Heights, Lockwood hears Cathy threaten Joseph who has just criticized her "idleness": "I warn you to refrain from provoking me, or I'll ask your abduction as a special favour" (p. 18). This emphasis on removal is echoed in Lockwood's declamation after enduring all he can take of Branderham's sermon: "Drag him down, and crush him to atoms, *that the place which knows him may know him no more!*" (p. 29, my emphasis).

In the context of this juxtapositioning with both Catherine's diary entry and Cathy's rebuking of Joseph, Lockwood's Branderham dream can be further explicated. In the dream, the staff is the universal attribute that all men in the congregation except Lockwood possess. Without a staff, he is unable to defend himself or successfully assert his rights. This helplessness corresponds to the childhood situation of Catherine and Heathcliff who, in the diary entry, were powerless to escape the regime of Hindley and his servant, Joseph.[20] But in contrast to this childhood impotence, Cathy, who as a young woman is abducted by Heathcliff and temporarily imprisoned in Wuthering Heights, manages to cow the offending Joseph and force him to retreat from the room. Her greater effectiveness is a function of her emergent adulthood. In contrast, Lockwood's staffless status in the dream indicates a lack, not of maleness, but of *man*hood (the large, "heavy-headed" [p. 27] appearance of Joseph's staff is significantly emphasized). On a crucial level, Lockwood is still a child, rebelling vainly against the tedious regime of adulthood.[21] But as we learned from our analysis of his second nightmare, the intolerable boredom of his adulthood derives precisely from the refusal to satisfy the need for love rendered problematic by his childhood.[22]

This interpretation of Lockwood's first dream is corroborated by the text. The image of the brandished staff occurs on two other occasions. The first concerns the aged Mr. Earnshaw's reaction to Hindley's abuse of Heathcliff: "[Mr. Earnshaw] seized his stick to strike him, and shook with rage that he could not do it" (p. 50). Here, the staff signifies the father's fury, not so much at his son, as at his own inability to punish him. The second image of the brandished staff concerns Joseph's visit to Thrushcross Grange in order to announce Heathcliff's demand for custody of his son, Linton. To reinforce his authority, Joseph gives "a thud with his prop on the floor" (p. 249). The tumult of rapping clubs in Lockwood's dream conflates these associations. On the one hand, through connection with the failure of the adult, Mr. Earnshaw, to discipline his child, Hindley, the rapping suggests Lockwood's own difficulty as an adult in quelling the need for love which he links with the dependence of the child. On the other hand, through connection with the imperious demand of the adult, Joseph, for possession of the child, Linton, the rapping suggests Lockwood's determination to master the childish impulse that threatens to overwhelm his adult identity—even if it means treating his own need for love as cruelly as Heathcliff treats Linton, or as Lockwood himself treats the ghost. Thus, the brandished staff attains in the fiction of Emily Brontë the force of an archetype whose recurrence in the text signifies the pervasive influence of the mentalities of Overlove and Unlove connected with it.

We can understand now the strange affinity that Lockwood feels for Heathcliff: they share the same need for loneliness. The only love in adulthood that they can completely trust is the one that loneliness makes them imagine; for such love is the only one over which they have complete control. But each has his own way of exploiting isolation or, to adapt Lockwood's image, each approaches loneliness from the opposite direction: "Mr Heathcliff and I are such a suitable pair to divide the desolation between us" (p. 3). One displays the attitude toward loneliness associated with the Unlove at Wuthering Heights; the other displays the attitude toward loneliness associated with the Overlove at Thrushcross Grange.

As Unloved, Heathcliff imposes loneliness on others in revenge against the lack of love he himself was forced to endure. Yet, the deepest motive of his cruelty is the need to increase his *own* isolation, since exclusion from others was the very condition on which his love for Catherine originally depended. Through his obsession with her ghost, Heathcliff makes his loneliness in adulthood simulate the only intimacy he knew in childhood: sharing with Catherine the state of banishment or expulsion from company. For their love, as we have seen, was first formulated as the joint enduring of rejection. In contrast, Lockwood makes loneliness prove that, instead of actually enjoying love, he will always remain separated from it, as if by a clear pane of glass. He can want, but never have; for what he lets himself have he might eventually lose, and then be left alone with his renewed dependence. But while loneliness protects Lockwood from the childish dependence that love would revive, it also gives him an Overlove more secure than any that real love in adulthood could provide. For as long as he remains alone, he can pity his own suffering of isolation.[23] Loneliness thus provides him with an Overlove more intimate than any other, for in it no one—not even the caregiver—gets between Lockwood and his need for indulgent attention.

Thus, both Heathcliff and Lockwood derive from loneliness a simulacrum of the type of love each requires. For Heathcliff, preoccupied with the ghost, loneliness enables the sharing of Unlove; for Lockwood, frustrated by self-imposed boredom and isolation, loneliness permits the perpetuation of Overlove. The opposition between Heathcliff and Lockwood—and, more especially, between the mentalities of Unlove and Overlove connected with them—can be further clarified by juxtaposing the two scenes in the novel involving a window-breaking and bloodletting struggle with a dreaded intruder: Lockwood's second nightmare and Heathcliff's nocturnal return from Catherine's grave.

In the latter scene, Hindley (intently observed by Isabella), frantically attempts to deny Heathcliff reentry into Wuthering Heights. When grappling with Heathcliff, who has just smashed his way through a window, Hindley falls "senseless with excessive pain" (p. 218), and does not regain consciousness for some time. Astonishingly, his insensate condition elicits one of the few gestures of pity ever displayed by Heathcliff, who terminates his retaliation in order to bind up Hindley's wound. Yet the brutal strength Heathcliff shows in this scene by breaking through the window and rendering Hindley helpless itself derives from Heathcliff's own pitiful helplessness in relation to the ghost. For, as we learn later, Heathcliff is focussing his attention here, not on Hindley at all, but on the ghost whom he at this moment is desperately striving to see: "I remember, that accursed Earnshaw and my wife opposed my entrance. I remember stopping to kick the breath out of him, and then hurrying upstairs, to my room, and hers—I looked round impatiently—I felt her by me—I could *almost* see her, and yet I *could not*!" (p. 350-51). Ironically, the thrashing Heathcliff gives Hindley becomes an analogue of the "intolerable torture" (p. 351) that Catherine's invisibility inflicts on Heathcliff.

The most obvious difference between these related scenes concerns the power of the intruder each portrays. In Lockwood's nightmare, the intruder is pathetically weak and can do little more than bleed; in the forced entry scene, Heathcliff the intruder is ruthlessly strong and inflicts a bleeding wound on the occupant, Hindley. But, as noted, Heathcliff's strength here derives paradoxically from "the anguish of his yearning" (p. 351) to see the ghost. In this regard, he resembles the pitiful ghost in Lockwood's dream. In fact, a little later he utters fervid "supplications" (p. 351) to Catherine's ghost, much as the child-ghost in the nightmare wails its own supplications to Lockwood. These connections between Lockwood's dream and Heathcliff's forced entry into Wuthering Heights underscore a fundamental distinction between these two characters. Heathcliff's strength stems from his need for *pity* from the ghost; Lockwood's strength derives from his *fear* of the ghost: "Terror made me cruel" (p. 31).

To understand this distinction, we must first of all understand the difference between pity and fear. Aristotle, the first thinker to connect these emotions with the spectacle of human suffering, can help us here. According to his analysis of tragedy, the crucial difference between pity and fear concerns the degree to which the witness or audience *identifies* with the pain of the sufferer: "pity is aroused by undeserved misfortune, and fear by that of one like ourselves."[24] Hence, in Aristotle's view, pity requires more emotional distance than fear. If the pain pitied gets too close to its witness, it changes into fear.

In Emily Brontë's universe, the pain or misfortune corresponding to that found by Aristotle in Greek tragedy is the loss of love. The mentalities formed by Unlove and Overlove have different ways of responding to this threat. Overlove characters try to maintain a distance between themselves and the pain of separation, either through fostering extreme dependence on love (as in the overly protective upbringing provided by Isabella to

Linton) or by resisting the need for love (as in the case of Lockwood) because of the risk of eventual loss. Appropriately, both these characters prominently display fear when threatened by the pain of separation. Lockwood does so in his nightmare when he repels the ghost representing the pain of separation threatened by his own need for love. Isabella, in the forced entry scene, is similarly "unnerved by terror" (p. 218) at the spectacle of Heathcliff's intrusion. Her overwhelming fear finds its deepest explanation in the fact that Heathcliff here is identified with the pain of separation, just as the ghost was in Lockwood's dream. He struggles successfully through the window, even though it is mullioned and defended, because he wants to re-enter the room that he and Catherine once shared in order to suffer the agony of loss more keenly—one might almost say more intimately.

Unlike those formed by Overlove, characters connected with Unlove do not need to maintain a distance between themselves and the pain of separation. In fact, as we have seen with Heathcliff and Catherine, they unite themselves with this pain, and seek their only fulfillment in love from it. Increasing the agony of loss guarantees relief from suffering it; for the victim hopes eventually to enter a state beyond the reach of pain. This is the only solution for one whom Unlove has made afraid of exposing his need for pity. For how is the Unloved to ask for pity, when his pain has always made him feel that he *deserves* his suffering? To borrow a simile from Nelly, the pain he suffers makes the Unloved feel like "a vicious cur that appears to know the kicks it gets are its desert, and yet hates all the world, as well as the kicker, for what it suffers" (pp. 71-72). The painful sense of rejection for which the Unloved needs pity makes him feel unworthy of receiving any kindness. To seek pity under these conditions would be to intensify the feeling of unfitness for it. Moreover, as noted earlier, to seek pity in such a hostile environment would only increase his vulnerability to further attack. Thus, the only pity the Unloved can accept is the cruelty of his own pain.

A brief consideration of Hindley's role in the forced entry scene will clarify this paradox. His ostensible motive for barring Heathcliff's return is murder. Devastated by the death in childbirth of his wife, Frances, Hindley seeks to avenge his pain by killing Heathcliff—the figure whom he has always identified with the pain of love. In childhood, Hindley persecuted Heathcliff for becoming the favorite of his father, Mr. Earnshaw: "the young master [Hindley] had learnt to regard his father as an oppressor rather than a friend, and Heathcliff as a usurper of his parent's affections" (p. 47). When Heathcliff returns in adulthood to Wuthering Heights, Hindley soon loses all his property to his enemy through gambling. Without realizing it, Hindley succumbs to this financial folly in order to *intensify* the pain of loss. In the masochistic tradition of Unlove, Hindley's unconscious aim is to suffer until he reaches the breaking point where he can suffer no more. This is especially evident in Hindley's declaration to Isabella just before assaulting Heathcliff: "Nobody alive would regret me, or be ashamed, though I cut my throat this minute—and it's time to make an end!" (p. 215). Here, it is impossible to determine exactly what Hindley intends to do: kill Heathcliff or kill himself. This ambiguity is reinforced by the strange duality of the weapon that Hindley employs to gain his objective: "a curiously constructed pistol, having a double-edged spring knife attached to the barrel" (p. 170).

Yet, Hindley's failure to kill Heathcliff must be understood as a success. Even more than revenge against Heathcliff, Hindley wants pity for his own suffering— and this is exactly what he achieves. After succumbing to the onslaught of his opponent whom he himself has enraged, Hindley, now unconscious and wounded by his own weapon, is tended by Heathcliff, whose solicitous action, though rough and hasty, underscores the relief implicit in the extremity of pain. Thus, in their desperate struggle on either side of the window, Heathcliff and Hindley are mirror images of the same mentality of Unlove. The violent cruelty of each derives from preoccupation with the loss of love he himself has been made to suffer. On the surface in both cases, revenge for that loss of love seems to be the dominant motive, but actually the most profound one is the wish to end the pain by increasing its intensity.

In contrast, the characters formed by Overlove show greater diversity in satisfying the needs that love in childhood created. There are three ways for them to do so. The first, implied by the chronic dependence of Linton, is to insist on remaining the recipient of indulgent attention. The second is to become the donor who provides Overlove to someone else. This is path followed by both Edgar and Isabella. As a husband, Edgar satisfies his need for Overlove vicariously, first indulging his temperamental spouse, Catherine, and then by overprotecting his daughter, Cathy. Isabella, Edgar's sister, eventually satisfies her need for Overlove through her self-destructive infatuation with Heathcliff—a man who makes no secret of despising her: "she persisted in forming a fabulous notion of my character, and acting on false impressions she cherished" (p. 183). But there is an unconscious method to her madness. After the separation that inevitably follows their elopement and her own impregnation, Isabella establishes a home in London where she creates a world of extreme Overlove at whose center is her sickly son, Linton. The third way of perpetuating Overlove after childhood is to provide it to oneself through self-pity for the misery of loneliness. As we have found, this is the course unwittingly pursued by Lockwood.

Notes

1. Walter Allen, *The English Novel: A Short Critical History* (New York: Dutton, 1954), p. 223. A similar judgment is offered by F. R. Leavis, *The Great Tradition: George Eliot, Henry James, Joseph Conrad* (1948; New York: Harcourt, 1963), p. 27.

2. E. M. Forster, *Aspects of the Novel* (New York: Harcourt, 1927), p. 145.

3. Bernard Paris, "'Hush, Hush! He's A Human Being': A Psychological Approach to Heathcliff," *Women and Literature* 2 (1982): 101-02. For a treatment of Heathcliff as an incarnation of sexual potency, see Thomas Moser, "'What is the Matter with Emily Jane?' Conflicting Impulses in *Wuthering Heights*," *Nineteenth-Century Fiction* 17 (1962): 1-19.

4. Joyce Carol Oates, "The Magnanimity of *Wuthering Heights*," *Critical Inquiry* 9.2 (1982): 441.

5. David Sonstream, "*Wuthering Heights* and the Limits of Vision," *PMLA* 86 (1971): 58.

6. Dorothy Van Ghent, *The English Novel: Form and Function* (New York: Harper & Row, 1961), pp. 160-61.

7. Ruth Adams, "*Wuthering Heights*: The Land East of Eden," *Nineteenth-Century Fiction* 13 (1958-59): 60.

8. For Freudian analyzes, see Beth Newman, "'The Situation of the Looker-On': Gender, Narration, and Gaze in *Wuthering Heights*," *PMLA* 105.5 (1990): 1029-1041; Michael D. Reed, "The Power of *Wuthering Heights*: A Psychoanalytic Examination," *Psychocultural Review: Interpretations in the Psychology of Art, Literature, and Society* 1 (1977): 21-42; and Leo Bersani, *A Future for Astyanax: Character and Desire in Literature* (Boston: Little, Brown, 1976), pp. 206-08.

9. Paris, p. 113; and Annis V. Pratt, "Archetypal Patterns in Women's Fiction," in *Jungian Literary Criticism,* ed. Richard P. Sugg (Evanston: Northwestern Univ. Press, 1992), p. 371.

10. Lord David Cecil, *Early Victorian Novelists* (Indianapolis: Bobbs-Merrill, 1935), p. 173; Sandra Gilbert and Susan Gubar, *The Madwoman in the Attic: The Woman Writer and the Nineteenth-Century Literary Imagination* (New Haven: Yale Univ. Press, 1979), pp. 249-308; Barbara Prentis, *The Brontë Sisters and George Eliot: A Unity of Difference* (London: Macmillan, 1988), p. 204; Tom Winnifreth, *The Brontës and Their Background: Romance and Reality,* 2nd ed. (London: Macmillan, 1988), p. 192; Q. D. Leavis, "A Fresh Approach to *Wuthering Heights*," *Lectures in*

America (New York: Pantheon, 1969), pp. 85-138; Donna K. Reed, "The Discontents of Civilization in *Wuthering Heights* and *Buddenbrooks*," *Comparative Literature* 41.3 (1989): 209-29; S. Lavabre, "Feminisme et Liberté Dans *Wuthering Heights*," *Cahiers Victoriens & Edouardiens* 34.2 (1991): 63-70. In contrast, Bersani denies that the novel "opposes the Grange to the Heights" (p. 204). Another group analyzes character in terms of family dynamics, without stressing an opposition between the two households depicted. For example, Paula Marantz Cohen, *The Daughter's Dilemma: Family Process and the Nineteenth-Century Domestic Novel* (Ann Arbor: Univ. of Michigan Press, 1991), advances the notion of "chronic triangulation" to elucidate the efforts of the nuclear family to "maintain its stability as a relatively closed relational system" (p. 90). Mary Burgan, "'Some Fit Parentage': Identity and the Cycle of Generations in *Wuthering Heights*," *Philological Quarterly* 61.4 (1982): 395-413, examines techniques of "manoeuvering for power" (p. 398).

11. Mildred G. Christian, "The Brontës," *Victorian Fiction: A Guide to Research,* ed. Lionel Stevenson (Cambridge, MA: Harvard Univ. Press, 1964), p. 244.

12. J. Hillis Miller, *Fiction and Repetition: Seven English Novels* (Cambridge: Harvard Univ. Press, 1982), p. 51; Cates Baldridge, "Voyeuristic Rebellion: Lockwood's Dream and the Reader of *Wuthering Heights*," *Studies in the Novel* 20.3 (1988): 285.

13. Emily Brontë, *The Clarendon Edition of the Novels of the Brontës: Wuthering Heights,* eds. Hilda Marsden and Ian Jack (Oxford: Clarendon Press, 1976), p. 59. Further references to this edition will be cited parenthetically in the text.

14. This interpretation of the love between Heathcliff and Catherine contrasts with prevailing opinions which can be arranged categorically:

(a) idealizing: George Levine, *The Realistic Imagination: English Fiction From Frankenstein to Lady Chatterley* (Chicago: Univ. of Chicago Press, 1981) views Heathcliff as "almost a Trollopean idealist—seeking purity in love . . . he turns, like a monster, into a blind destructive force" (p. 215); John T. Matthews, "Framing in *Wuthering Heights*," *Texas Studies in Literature and Language* 27.1 (1985): 25-61; Patrick Kelly, "The Sublimity of Catherine and Heathcliff," *The Victorian Newsletter* 86 (1994): 24-30. However, John Beversluis, *English* 120 (1975): 77-82, critiques the tendency to idealize the love between Heathcliff and Catherine (p. 106).

(b) infantilizing or regarding as pre-Oedipal: Anne Williams, "The Child is Mother of the Man: The Female Aesthetic of *Wuthering Heights*," *Cahiers Victoriens & Ed-*

ouardiens 34.2 (1991): 81-94; J. Hillis Miller, *The Disappearance of God: Five Nineteenth-Century Writers* (Cambridge: Harvard Univ. Press, 1963, p. 170), asserts that "The violence of Emily Brontë's characters is a reaction to the loss of an earlier state of happiness."

(c) emphasizing incest: Eric Solomon, "The Incest Theme in *Wuthering Heights*," *Nineteenth-Century Fiction* 14 (1969): 80-83; James Kavanagh, *Emily Brontë* (London: Methuen, 1985), p. 64; Jane Gallop, *The Daughter's Seduction: Feminism and Psychoanalysis* (Ithaca: Cornell Univ. Press, 1982), p. 145.

(d) universalizing: Prentis, p. 102, views the relation between Heathcliff and Catherine as "an exploration of the universal significance of love and hate."

(e) aestheticizing: Irene Taylor, *Holy Ghosts: The Male Muses of Emily and Charlotte Brontë* (New York: Columbia Univ. Press, 1990), p. 74: "They are not so much friends or lovers as they are male and female elements of a single being, fictional embodiments of the female artist and her male muse."

(f) problematizing: John Allen Stevenson, "'Heathcliff is Me!': *Wuthering Heights* and the Question of Likeness," *Nineteenth-Century Literature* 43.1 (1988): 60-81, writes that "we do not really know much about why Heathcliff and Catherine come together" (p. 65).

15. More conventionally, Margaret Homans, "Repression and Sublimation of Nature in *Wuthering Heights*," *PMLA* 93 (1978): 11, sees the window as a symbol of body trapping soul. Similarly, Stevie Davies, *Emily Brontë: The Artist as Free Woman* (Manchester: Carcanet, 1983), p. 116, interprets the window as a symbol of "the imagined border between the seen and unseen worlds."

16. Nevertheless, Kathleen Blake, *Love and the Woman Question in Victorian Literature* (Brighton: Harvester, 1983), pp. 150-51, interprets the yearning for childhood displayed by both Catherine in *Wuthering Heights* and Sue Brideshead in Hardy's *Jude the Obscure* as nostalgia for "a time before they grew up into sexual and thereby limited beings."

17. Many critics have been baffled by Lockwood's nightmare. Like Van Ghent and Adams, Williams, "The Child is Mother of the Man," regards this dream as "implicitly someone else's [i.e., Catherine's]" (p. 84). Related to this group, George E. Haggerty, "The Gothic Form of *Wuthering Heights*," *The Victorian Newsletter* 74 (1988): 1-6, explains Lockwood's fear of the ghost as a symptom of his "general anxiety in the face of what he does not understand" (p. 2). For critics who attempt more earnestly to interpret the nightmare, the most common response is to view it as an expression of sexual repression. See, for example, Ronald Fine, "Lockwood's Dreams and the Key

to *Wuthering Heights*," *Nineteenth-Century Fiction* 24 (1969-70): 16-30. Perhaps the most unusual interpretation is that of Patricia Yaeger, "Violence in the Sitting Room: *Wuthering Heights* and the Woman's Novel," *Genre* 21.2 (1988): 203-29. She treats the ghost's hand as an emblem of Brontë's status as a *woman* writer, and argues that the dream expresses "'Brontë's anxieties about female authorship' [intruding upon the novel form, traditionally a masculine domain]" (p. 222).

18. This analysis of Lockwood's dream is faintly anticipated by Robert M. Polhemus, *Erotic Faith: Being in Love From Jane Austen to D. H. Lawrence* (Chicago: Univ. of Chicago Press, 1990): "Cathy is not only the passionate lover; she is also the erotic history of childhood—the needs and urges formed back then and inefficiently suppressed later" (p. 86).

19. See, for example, "The Power of *Wuthering Heights*," p. 30.

20. Two other critics also link this dream with Joseph's repression of Heathcliff and Catherine. See U. C. Knoepflmacher, *Emily Brontë, Wuthering Heights* (Cambridge: Cambridge Univ. Press, 1989), p. 88; and Baldridge, p. 281.

21. Knoepflmacher, p. 88, also discusses Lockwood's childishness in the first dream: "The staff of male power is not yet required, for it belongs to the realm of Experience, not Innocence."

22. In approaching this dream, some critics have emphasized its Biblical allusions. See Edgar F. Shannon, "Lockwood's Dreams and the Exegesis of *Wuthering Heights*," *Nineteenth-Century Fiction* 14 (1959-60): 107 and Knoepflmacher, pp. 87-88. Others argue that it expresses a rebellion against bourgeois values. See Allan R. Brick, "*Wuthering Heights*: Narrators, Audience, and Message," *College English* 21 (1959-60): 80-86; and Baldridge, p. 282.

23. Nevertheless, there is a tendency for critics to see Lockwood as fundamentally different from the major characters in the novel. See Terence McCarthy, "The Incompetent Narrators of *Wuthering Heights*," *Modern Language Quarterly* 42 (1981): 48-64, 59; and Gideon Shunami, "The Unreliable Narrator in *Wuthering Heights*," *Nineteenth-Century Fiction* 27 (1973): 449-68, 465. To Nancy Armstrong, *Desire and Domestic Fiction: A Political History of the Novel* (New York: Oxford Univ. Press, 1987), pp. 195-96, Lockwood incarnates polite social conventions that fail to comprehend female sexuality.

24. Aristotle, *Poetics* 1453a 5-6 in *The Basic Works of Aristotle,* trans. Ingram Bywaters, ed. Richard McKeon (New York: Random House, 1941), pp. 1455-87.

Rebecca Steinitz (essay date winter 2000)

SOURCE: Steinitz, Rebecca. "Diaries and Displacement in *Wuthering Heights*." *Studies in the Novel* 32, no. 4 (winter 2000): 407-19.

[*In the following essay, Steinitz examines Brontë's use of the diary form to frame the central action of* Wuthering Heights.]

It is self-evident, if soon forgettable, that **Wuthering Heights** opens as a diary: "1801—I have just returned from a visit to my landlord."[1] Yet, though Lockwood's voice begins the novel, the dated entry, immediacy, and first person account of events and thoughts which characterize the diary soon give way to the recounting, through multiple narrators, of the complex story of the Earnshaws, the Lintons, and Heathcliff, a saga which takes place in the past, albeit a past which grows closer as the novel progresses. This diary, it would seem, functions primarily as a frame, an excuse for telling this story. In the novel's third chapter, however, we encounter something more insistently and explicitly a "regular diary" (p. 16), as Lockwood terms it: Catherine's passionate description of the day of injustices she and Heathcliff have just suffered, "scrawled in an unformed, childish hand" in the margins of an old religious book and stowed away in the confines of the cabinet bed.[2] These two diaries could not seem more different: Lockwood's appears to function primarily to transmit narrative; Catherine's as revelation of experience and subjectivity. Lockwood's has no physical specificity, no book or pages; Catherine's is emphatically material. Lockwood's moves through time, both the year of his tenantship at Thrushcross Grange and the decades of his story; of Catherine's we receive only the fragments of a single day (or perhaps two). Yet we do not need J. Hillis Miller's image of the novel as a set of "Chinese boxes of texts within texts" to see Catherine's diary as diametrically engaged with Lockwood's, the inner text to his outer.[3] Indeed, the formal prominence and stylistic differences of these two diaries insist upon critical attention.

Not surprisingly, such attention has been given, sometimes at great length. Yet, almost inevitably, critical narratives have subsumed the novel's diaries under some larger rubric. Often, that rubric has been textuality itself, as one or both diaries take their place among the novel's diverse books, letters and inscriptions. Robert McKibben instances Catherine's marginal scribbles as an example of the misuse of books which the novel's characters must overcome to live in peace with each other and their texts.[4] In contrast, like J. Hillis Miller, Carol Jacobs finds in the insufficiencies of the diary a marker for the unconquerable instabilities of fiction, textuality, and interpretation.[5] Feminist critics Margaret Homans, Patricia Yaeger, and Regina Barreca, reading gendered discourse in the novel, seize upon Lockwood's and Catherine's diaries as emblematic texts.[6] Even Jan Gordon, who offers one of the most sustained treatments of the ontological status of the diaries, particularly Lockwood's ultimately foregrounds the genre as an instance of textuality in tension with what he argues is the novel's dominant orality.[7] Yet, to see the diaries in **Wuthering Heights** as simply texts among other texts, or as mere thematic vehicles (say, a protest against religion or patriarchy in the case of Catherine's, or a paradigmatic instance of misreading in the case of Lockwood's), is to overlook their particularity as diaries.

In his magisterial *Telling Time: Clocks, Diaries, and English Diurnal Form, 1660-1785,* Stuart Sherman theorizes temporality as the primary locus for understanding both the diary and its appearances in fiction.[8] Diurnal form, he argues, offered diarists, journalists, and novelists a means of enacting the repetitive fullness of time and experience, a means to which, in the eighteenth century, all three kinds of writers reacted ambivalently, drawn to its copious potential, but repelled by its refusal to select and highlight significant details or events, its insistence on equality of representation. In this account, diaries in novels figure as a mode of representing and ordering time, a mode at once embraced and resisted in the eighteenth-century texts he discusses. I want to argue here, however, that in **Wuthering Heights,** materiality becomes the significant locus for the diaristic, a locus foregrounded in particular by Emily Brontë's idiosyncratic reorganization of diaristic temporality. That is, useful for its temporal schema, the diary ultimately works, both thematically and literally, as an object which itself promises a space for the realization of its writer's and readers' desires. Indeed, despite their many differences of status, both Catherine and Lockwood—the marginalized young farmer's daughter, and the gentleman, a socially central figure who insists upon marginalizing himself—use their diaries to deal precisely with their senses of displacement. In the novel, then, the diary itself becomes the proverbial place of one's own, but its very status as such reveals how, psychologically, textually, and materially, one's own place can never be secured.

Brontë's own quasi-diary serves as an effective starting-point for a consideration of her use of diaries in fiction, despite the fact that she is not known as a diarist and her diary is unconventional, especially in its temporality. Using Frank Kermode's distinction between *kairos*

and *chronos,* Sherman argues that the temporality of the diary is like that of the watch: the "*Tick, Tick, Tick*—of the *quotidian* as series and structure."[9] He opposes this aural repetition to two alternatives: theoretically, the clock's "*tick-tock*," which for Kermode symbolizes the progression of narrative; and, historically, the sound of the church bell which marks "occasional" time, itself generally subsumed into "narratives of signal occasions."[10] Sherman claims that in the seventeenth century, the diary as a genre, once a collection of notations of occasions, became characterized by a regular and endless succession of formally identical entries, entries which, in his description, depend upon their dailiness. In nineteenth-century diaries, however, what we might call the "*Tick, Tick, Tick*" of dailiness in fact coexists with the "*tock*" or peal of occasional time; almost invariably, diarists use the occasion of significant dates—New Year's Day, birthdays, wedding anniversaries, anniversaries of deaths—to take stock, to pray, to predict, in short, to mark the developments of their own personal narratives. Brontë's diary, consisting of four entries written years apart in 1834, 1837, 1841, and 1845, one on her brother Branwell's birthday and two on her own, registers only the "*tock*," the significant occasion.[11] Yet in registering that "*tock*" almost regularly over a dozen years, the diary has its own repetitive sequence, a sequence that insists on the ongoing openendedness of such personal narrative.

The entries themselves display an interest in time, both in the moment at hand, and in its progression. In 1834, for instance, Brontë notes, "Anne and I have been peeling apples for Charlotte to make us an apple pudding . . . Tabby said just now Come Anne pilloputate (i.e., pill a potato) Aunt has come into the kitchen just now and said where are your feet Anne Anne answered On the floor Aunt." In 1837, she speculates, "I guess that this day 4 years we shall all be in this drawing-room comfortable I hope it may be so. Anne guesses we shall all be gone somewhere comfortable We hope it may be so indeed." In 1841, she foresees "that at the time appointed for the opening of this paper we i.e. Charlotte, Anne, and I, shall be all merrily seated in our own sitting-room in some pleasant and flourishing seminary"; four years later, she marks the fact that the "school scheme has been abandoned." Even in their temporal preoccupation, however, these few quotations reveal how time, for Brontë, is in many ways a screen for space. The main question about the passage of time is *where* it will lead the diary's denizens. Will their feet still be on the floor? Will they be in the drawing room at Haworth? In an imaginary seminary's sitting-room? Though the 1841 entry begins with time, it immediately turns to a wide-ranging consideration of precise location:

> It is Friday evening, near 9 o'clock—wild rainy weather. I am seated in the dining-room alone, having just concluded tidying our desk boxes, writing this

Photograph of the moors and house believed to be the locale of Wuthering Heights.

document. Papa is in the parlour—aunt upstairs in her room. She has been reading *Blackwood's Magazine* to papa. Victoria and Adelaide [the geese] are ensconced in the peat-house. Keeper [the dog] is in the kitchen—Hero [a hawk] in his cage. We are all stout and hearty, as I hope is the case with Charlotte, Branwell, and Anne, of whom the first is at John White, Esq., Upperwood House, Rawdon; the second is at Luddended Foot; and the third is, I believe, at Scarborough, inditing perhaps a paper corresponding to this . . .

The Gondalians are at present in a threatening state, but there is no open rupture as yet. All the princes and princesses of the Royalty are at the Palace of Instruction.

What people do matters, but, except for the fictional Gondalians, always already dematerialized, it is consistently secondary to where they are.

Indeed, space is not just a thematic concern for the diary, but a material one as well. Nineteenth-century British diarists were quite deliberate about where and how they wrote their diaries, arranging and rearranging their sheets of paper, blank books, and printed diary volumes to suit their representational needs. The physical body of the diary thus developed its own iconic import.

Brontë composed her entries on single sheets of paper covered closely with text and sketches. In the 1837 entry, for example, she includes a sketch which illustrates the kitchen scene described in the main text, captions the sketch with a dialogue between its figures, and writes lengthwise along the edge of the page about the future (see illustration). Here the space of the page enables not just the physical reproduction of relationships between people, but a further reproduction of time, specifically in the relationship between the central present and its peripheral but essential future. Brontë herself foregrounds the diary's materiality by titling her 1841 entry "A PAPER to be opened / when Anne is / 25 years old, / or my next birthday after / if / all be well" (her capitalization). As an object, the diary has talismanic significance: here, the very opening of the "PAPER" will signal that all is well, that is, that the two sisters have survived and the material emblem of the past has arrived safely into the future.

It is easy to see the pervasive sense of emplacement in these entries as a response to anxiety, particularly when it is coupled with the graphically highlighted conditional, "if / all be well." As many biographers and critics have pointed out, the loss of the Brontës' mother in

1821, and of their older sisters, Elizabeth and Maria, in 1825, not to mention the location of the Haworth parsonage on the edge of the graveyard, made death a constant in their lives.[12] If people could be placed, and placed actively through what they were doing in the place where they were, their existence, and perhaps their continued existence, could be imaginatively guaranteed. Less mortally, collecting the locations of family members on a single page could psychologically alleviate the anxiety of separation, itself a negative portent: Elizabeth and Maria had gone away to board at Cowan Bridge School where they contracted the typhoid that killed them; economic exigencies had dispersed Brontë's siblings to "John White, Esq., Upperwood House, Rawdon; . . . Luddended Foot; and . . . Scarborough," metonyms for their teaching positions. In short, Brontë had tangible reasons to be anxious about where people were and where they belonged.

But if in her diary Brontë responds to anxiety by insistently locating, she threads her novel with dislocation, perhaps enacting more drastically that anxiety's existential depth. The cry of the ghostly Catherine at the window—"Let me in—let me in!" (p. 20)—articulates most trenchantly the anxiety of place in *Wuthering Heights.* "I'm coming home, I'd lost my way on the moor!" the ghost tells Lockwood, the stranger sleeping, perhaps dreaming, in her bed. Adrift in the vastness of the frightening world, here the moors, dark and cold, the ghost seeks only to secure a space for herself. The home she seeks, the old house with "the date '1500,' and the name 'Hareton Earnshaw'" (p. 4) carved on its lintel, and "*Catherine Earnshaw*," "*Catherine Heathcliff,*" and "*Catherine Linton*" (p. 15) scratched in its window ledge, itself memorializes claims for place so strong they are staked in writing on its very walls. Indeed, it seems as if almost everyone—from Catherine and the ancestral Hareton, to Hindley, Heathcliff, Joseph, and Nelly—demands Wuthering Heights for their own. Yet the house consistently refuses such demands. For strangers, like Lockwood, the young Heathcliff, and Isabella, who have inordinate trouble finding seats and beds within its walls, Wuthering Heights itself becomes the frightening and unfamiliar world in which one has no place. Even for those who might think it theirs, the house marks the difficulty, if not the impossibility, of permanently assuring one's own space: Lockwood violently thwarts the ghost's attempt to come in through the window, while at the novel's end, Hareton and Cathy reject the home claimed in their names by their forebears. In *Wuthering Heights,* then, the fundamental experience of place is displacement. The novel can be read as a series of attempts to address the sense of displacement, including, most notably for my purposes, the efforts of Catherine and Lockwood to do so through their diaries.

It should not be surprising that the young Catherine Earnshaw seeks a place of her own. Orphaned, harassed by her older brother, harangued by Joseph, attached primarily to the foundling Heathcliff, not to mention young and female, she finds little space readily available to her at Wuthering Heights, emotionally, physically, and structurally. Unlike Brontë, who uses her diary to articulate her preoccupation with space by locating all of her family members precisely, even to noting that Anne's foot is on the floor, Catherine instead uses hers to detail a series of struggles which replace emplacement with displacement. When rain prevents attendance at church, Joseph creates his own congregation: "Heathcliff, myself, and the unhappy plough-boy were commanded to take our Prayer-books, and mount. We were ranged in a row, on a sack of corn, groaning and shivering, and hoping that Joseph would shiver too, so that he might gives us a short homily for his own sake" (p. 16). Released downstairs, where Hindley makes clear his power to control the environment—"'You forget you have a master here,' says the tyrant. 'I'll demolish the first who puts me out of temper!'"—Catherine attempts to create a refuge, but fails again: "We made ourselves as snug as our means allowed in the arch of the dresser. I had just fastened our pinafores together, and hung them up for a curtain, when in comes Joseph . . . he compelled us to square our positions that we might receive, from the far-off fire, a dull ray to show us the text of the lumber he thrust upon us" (p. 17). When Catherine and Heathcliff rebel, Hindley steps in once more: "Hindley hurried up from his paradise on the hearth, and seizing one of us by the collar, and the other by the arm, hurled both into the back-kitchen, where, Joseph asseverated, 'owd Nick' would fetch us as sure as we were living; and, so comforted, we each sought a separate nook to await his advent."

I quote at length to demonstrate how repeatedly Catherine becomes the object of others, both grammatically and physically, even as she continually attempts to find a space for herself. Though Heathcliff may be aligned with her through much of her trouble, he too works to thwart her efforts: "I reached this book, and a pot of ink from a shelf, and pushed the house-door ajar to give me light, and I have got the time on with writing for twenty minutes; but my companion is impatient and proposes that we should appropriate the dairy woman's cloak, and have a scamper on the moors under its shelter" (p. 17). Finding "shelter" together means abandoning the only site which she successfully, at least so far, has carved out for herself. The provisional nature of that "shelter," a stolen piece of fabric, emblematizes the impossibility of finding a permanent place for oneself which the entire diary entry dramatizes. It seems not at all coincidental that the excerpts from the diary conclude with Catherine's fears about Hindley's treatment of Heathcliff: "'He . . . swears he will reduce him to his right *place*—'" (p. 18, emphasis added).

Hindley's oath, of course, references place as social status or class, not physical coordinate. He wants to return Heathcliff from his once-privileged position as favored adopted son to his apparent origins in the social depths. Yet Hindley articulates his strategy for doing so spatially: according to Catherine, "Hindley calls him a vagabond, and won't let him sit with us, nor eat with us any more, and, he says, he and I must not play together, and threatens to turn him out of the house if we break his orders" (p. 18). Hindley names Heathcliff as a "vagabond," one without a place, refuses him the familial spaces of Wuthering Heights, and asserts his power to render the younger boy homeless. It would seem as if the condition of displacement in the novel is at once material and social, the two inseparable.

Lockwood's sense of displacement, however, renders this preliminary conclusion moot, or at least inadequate. Lockwood is clearly a gentleman of considerable leisure and financial resources. He rambles from the seaside to the moors to London and then North for shooting. He rents capacious homes, complete with servants. Still, like Catherine, Lockwood suffers the anxiety of place and uses his diary to record his compensatory search for a space for himself, albeit fairly ludicrously. Lockwood begins the novel with the conviction that he has found a suitable location:

> 1801—I have just returned from a visit to my landlord—the solitary neighbour that I shall be troubled with. This is certainly a beautiful country! In all England, I do not believe that I could have fixed on a situation so completely removed from the stir of society. A perfect misanthropist's heaven—and Mr. Heathcliff and I are such a suitable pair to divide the desolation between us.
>
> (p. 3)

Clearly, his search for an appropriate locale corresponds to a search for self, and in his exultation at the idea that he has found both, he is just as clearly mistaken, as the ironies of his pleasure in the "beautiful . . . desolation" and his simultaneous claim to misanthropy and companionship in the final sentence suggest. His own "dear mother," Lockwood notes, "used to say I should never have a comfortable home" (p. 5), a statement whose truth is writ large and absurd in his flight from the seashore where he rejects the interest of the woman he desires, to Thrushcross Grange where he chafes at the constraints of his chosen solitude, and, eventually, back to London. At Thrushcross Grange, over the course of the diary and novel, Lockwood never seems comfortable with his chosen place and persona: despite his claim to misanthropy, he repeatedly visits the clearly inhospitable Wuthering Heights and solicits the company of his housekeeper, Nelly. Lockwood's displacement thus seems exaggeratedly self-selected, even as it is clearly and powerfully felt. At once, then, the novel universalizes the anxiety of place and points to its particularity for the socially dispossessed. Displacement, in all its varieties, becomes the human condition.

It may seem, so far, that my argument about diaries is as thematic as any cited above, that I am merely presenting diaries as vehicles not just for Brontë's concerns with textuality, gender, and class, but also for her interest in place. I want to suggest, however, that in her representation of the novel's diaries, Brontë works specifically with the genre's cultural connotations, in particular its material significance, valorizing these texts' ability to alleviate the anxiety of place, even as she ultimately problematizes that ability. Lockwood's description makes Catherine's diary most emphatically material: kept, in part, in an "injured tome . . . smelling dreadfully musty," its "faded hieroglyphics" "scrawled in an unformed, childish hand," it even includes "an excellent caricature of my friend Joseph, rudely yet powerfully sketched" (p. 16). Though her diary's actual marginality ("a pen and ink commentary—at least, the appearance of one—covering every morsel of blank that the printer had left") may physically replicate her social marginality, Catherine has made the diary into her place, claiming the margins as her own, as it were. Here she can tell her own story; here she can say how she feels; here she can express her opinion by caricature; and here we even find the indexical traces of her own "hand," which turn the diary into a rhetorical extension of her body. It seems that the most dispossessed young girl can still find a place for herself in a diary, even if that diary itself recounts a narrative of displacement. Again, then, the novel echoes the imperative found in Brontë's own diary: the urge to secure a space for the self through text written on paper: the diary as place.

Yet, in Catherine's diary, as in Brontë's, that urge surfaces only to be thwarted. Brontë's diary, with its hope that envisioning the future will ensure its arrival, certainly failed dramatically in its prescriptive purpose. Though the last entry ends "With best wishes for the whole house till 1848, July 30th, and as much longer as may be," no 1848 entry survives, if any was written. A short year after it would have been written, both Emily and Anne were dead. Obviously, a diary's textual representation of the future cannot ward off death, just as its textual representation of spatial desire cannot provide a social, physical or ontological place for a particular person. Less obviously, its failure to do so is not only literal, but also symbolic and material: creating an object which will persist, like the "PAPER to be opened / . . . / if / all be well," also creates an object which can be threatened. Catherine's diary emphasizes this contradiction. Burned by Lockwood's candle, piled up like bricks against the window, drenched by incoming snow, left behind when Cathy and Hareton vacate Wuthering Heights for Thrushcross Grange at the novel's end, it demonstrates, to an extreme, the potential dangers the material diary faces. Disfigured and abandoned, suffering almost as much as its writer, Catherine's diary finally articulates the frustration of location, making explicit the illusory nature of the diary's offer of a site for the self. Indeed, Lockwood's use of its volumes to keep Catherine's ghost out of her childhood home (p. 20), not four pages after we read her entries, symbolically underscores the immediate refusal of the genre's promise.

But what of Lockwood? Place is clearly a preoccupation of all three diaries, Brontë's, Catherine's, and Lockwood's, even if Brontë articulates her own preoccupation as emplacement, Catherine's as displacement, and Lockwood's as confusion. But, unlike the other two, Lockwood's diary seems distinctly immaterial. We receive no glimpse of the book or paper upon which he writes, not even a reference to the physical act of writing: the act which he performs is retelling, not transcribing, as he explains, "I have now heard all my neighbour's history, at different sittings, as the housekeeper could spare time from more important occupations. I'll continue it in her own words, only a little condensed. She is, on the whole, a very fair narrator and I don't think I could improve her style" (p. 120). Indeed, Lockwood's violent deployment of Catherine's diary could be seen to mark him as the diary's anti-materialist, that is, as one with no respect for the privileged textual materiality of the genre.

Unlike Catherine, however, Lockwood can procure physical spaces for himself. He can rent Thrushcross Grange; he can respond to the closed door at Wuthering Heights by announcing, correctly as it turns out, "I don't care—I will get in!" (pp. 7-8); he can order a servant to "prepare a corner of a sitting-room for me to sup in, and a bed-room to sleep in" (p. 232); he clearly could have settled into a home of his own with the "real goddess" he meets "While enjoying a month of fine weather at the sea-coast" (p. 5) before the events of the novel begin. His ability to procure such spaces, of course, derives directly from his more powerful social and economic position, made evident through indicators like the seaside vacation, the rented country house, and the hunting trips, as well as the essential privilege of gender. But what Lockwood lacks, at least in the body of the novel, are two things that Catherine has almost to excess: a family and a narrative. These, the familial and the narrative, are the spaces which he seems most to long for and least able to achieve, as epitomized by his subjunctively-expressed and partially-displaced desire to write Cathy into the heroine of his own romance: "'What a realization of something more romantic than a fairy tale it would have been for Mrs. Linton Heathcliff, had she and I struck up an attachment, as her good nurse desired, and migrated together into the stirring atmosphere of the town!'" (pp. 230-31).

In this context, the status of Lockwood's diary as frame becomes another key to understanding its apparent lack of materiality within the text. In one sense, the space emphasized by Lockwood's diary is, precisely, narrative space: the diary provides the space within which the story of the Earnshaws and Lintons can be told. Indeed, writing their story in his diary can be seen as a way for Lockwood to claim that story for his own, both to insinuate himself into it and to take material possession of it. But if this may seem yet another abstracted conception of materiality, it ultimately leads us to the most literal enactment thereof. It seems not incidental that frame, the term for narratives which enable the recounting of other narratives, also references the construction and structure of a building. For, in the end, Lockwood's diary can be seen as the most literally material aspect of *Wuthering Heights.* Housing the narrative, his diary becomes the book itself, the cover we hold, the pages we turn as we read. Ironically, while the novel may seem to emphasize the greater urgency of Catherine's need for space, by giving her a material diary within the text, it also points to the significantly greater possibilities Lockwood has for actually achieving a space of his own, by making his diary enclose the text itself. Yet the irony of Lockwood's material triumph is at least partly, if only partly, blunted by the persistence of Catherine's diary as an emotional focal point of the novel. As such, the two diaries once again reflect the gender and class differences between their writers, becoming almost a microcosm of the separate spheres: Catherine's stands for the enclosed world of emotional power, housed within Lockwood's material boundaries, an all-too-familiar structure of Victorian social and familial spaces.

It might be argued that the other texts of *Wuthering Heights* register displacement as significantly as do its diaries, and that they too do so materially as well as thematically. Certainly the carved names in the lintel and the windowsill, as well as Isabella's plaintive epistles, operate on these terms. But the formal and material prominence of Lockwood's and Catherine's diaries, as well as their ascription to the characters who stand at the novel's emotional periphery and center, establish their priority. That is, they reveal how Brontë's formal narrative strategy of enclosing the story of her main characters within the diary of a stranger, a diary which itself ultimately encloses the diary of one of those main characters, is in fact thematically essential to the full elucidation of the novel's concern with displacement.

Though the thrust of my argument has thus focused on the diary's thematic and material enactment of place, I want to conclude by returning to Sherman's frame of reference: time. Like Brontë's, Catherine's and Lockwood's diaries specifically abjure diurnality. While Catherine's text is clearly copious, the reader receives from Lockwood only two interrupted fragments of it. It is not even clear whether these fragments represent one day or two, for both are undated, and Lockwood writes of the second only that "the next sentence took up another subject" (p. 17). Lockwood's diary itself has only two dates: "1801" (p. 3) and "1802" (p. 231). Years, rather than days, these notations echo Brontë's own quadrennial entries. Within the text, he locates time more punctually and immediately, though still not diurnally. At the end of chapter 9, as the first installment of Nelly's tale ends with Catherine and Edgar's marriage, he references the present moment of diary-writing by the hour: "At this point of the housekeeper's story, she chanced to glance towards the time-piece over the chimney; and was in amazement on seeing the minute-hand measure half-past one . . . now that she is vanished to her rest, and I have meditated for another hour or two, I shall summon courage to go, also, in spite of aching laziness of head and limbs" (p. 70). When the next chapter begins, he marks the passing of "Four weeks' torture, tossing and sickness!" He even tries to account for the unrealistic idea that several chapters and many years of narrative could be written down in a single diary entry: "Another week over—and I am so many days nearer health, and spring! I have now heard all my neighbour's history, at different sittings, as the housekeeper could spare time from more important occupations. I'll continue it in her own words, only a little condensed" (p. 120). Yet all of these temporally-focused entries still evade dailiness, even as they do so self-consciously.

As in the diurnal diary, however, both Catherine's absolute fragmentariness, enforced for writer and reader alike by interruption, and Lockwood's ongoing sense of time passing, pose a resistance to temporal and textual closure. Ironically, as the novel itself reaches closure, in its very last paragraph, the diary is once again our direct means of narration: Lockwood, visiting the graves of Heathcliff, Edgar and Catherine at the edge of the churchyard, writes, "I lingered round them" (p. 256). This phrase, with its sense of abeyance, suggests at once a suspension of temporality and activity, and a future beyond the close of the book, when he will leave these buried bodies behind and move on with his life. At the same time, this last scene, captured so diaristically, works specifically to foreground the unattainability of place. As the diary, theoretically, continues forever, so does the quest for place which the novel embodies, a quest highlighted, in the transitory moments of this final entry, for all its major characters: Catherine, whose body rests in the churchyard, poised between the two men in her life, as her spirit presumably roams the moors with Heathcliff, the foundling whom she loved first and best; Lockwood, off to continue his restless travels; and Cathy and Hareton, who believe they can escape the legacy of Wuthering Heights simply by leaving the house behind.

Ultimately, I would argue, Brontë at once minimizes diaristic temporality and puts it to use in service of the materiality which is key to the genre's function in the novel. By using temporality to thematize placement and displacement at the novel's conclusion, Brontë returns us to the central concerns played out through materiality, and thus finally renders temporality subordinate. *Wuthering Heights* is not alone among nineteenth-century novels in this generic revaluation. While the temporality Sherman focuses on in the eighteenth century remains a crucial aspect of the diary's function in fiction, the placement and treatment of the material diary becomes a vital element of the genre's significance in a host of other nineteenth-century texts. Just a few such examples include the monster's discovery of Victor's diary in the pocket of his overcoat in *Frankenstein,* the torn pages of the diary Helen Huntingdon gives Gilbert Markham in *The Tenant of Wildfell Hall,* Fosco's inscribed invasion of Marian Halcombe's diary in *The Woman in White,* and Cecily's offer of her diary as a physical guarantor of her (lack of) veracity in *The Importance of Being Earnest.* Though these novels may not share the thematic preoccupations of Brontë's texts, they constitute their own diaries similarly, as physical repositories of character, plot, ideology, and meaning. As such, like Brontë's own idiosyncratic diary, they significantly reflect and reshape the artistic and ideological significance of the diary in nineteenth-century British fiction and culture.

Notes

1. Emily Brontë, *Wuthering Heights* (New York: Norton, 1990), p. 3. All subsequent references will be made parenthetically.

2. For the sake of clarity, I refer to Catherine Earnshaw Linton as Catherine, and to her daughter, Catherine Linton Heathcliff, as Cathy.

3. J. Hillis Miller, *Fiction and Repetition* (Cambridge: Harvard Univ. Press, 1982), p. 45.

4. Robert C. McKibben, "The Image of the Book in *Wuthering Heights,*" *Nineteenth-Century Fiction* 15 (1960): 159-69.

5. Carol Jacobs, "*Wuthering Heights*: At the Threshold of Interpretation," *Boundary 2: A Journal of Postmodern Literature* 7 (3): 49-71 (1979).

6. Margaret Homans, *Bearing the Word: Language and Female Experience in Nineteenth-Century Women's Writing* (Chicago: Univ. of Chicago Press, 1986), pp. 72-73; Patricia Yaeger, "Violence in the Sitting Room: *Wuthering Heights* and the Woman's Novel," *Genre* 11 (1988): 203-29; and Regina Barreca, "The Power of Excommunication: Sex and the Feminine Text in *Wuthering Heights,*" Regina Barreca, ed., *Sex and Death in Victorian Literature* (Bloomington: Indiana Univ. Press, 1990), pp. 227-40.

7. Jan Gordon, *Gossip and Subversion in Nineteenth-Century British Fiction: Echo's Economies* (New York: St. Martin's, 1996), pp. 97-154.

8. Stuart Sherman, *Telling Time: Clocks, Diaries, and English Diurnal Form, 1660-1785* (Chicago: Univ. of Chicago Press, 1996).

9. Ibid., p. 22.

10. Ibid., pp. 7, 42, 35. Sherman works through the distinction between the temporality of occasion and "diurnal form" in a comparison between Pepys and John Donne's *Devotions upon Emergent Occasions*. See pp. 36-48.

11. The diary papers, as they are known, can be seen in the museum at the parsonage at Haworth. All quotes here come from transcriptions included in the Norton edition of *Wuthering Heights* cited above, pp. 295-98.

12. For an analysis of the profound effect of those deaths on the surviving Brontës, see Kate Brown, "Plain and Lovely Bodies: Consolations of Form in the Fiction of Charlotte Brontë" (Diss. Univ. of California, Berkeley, 1996).

Daniel Cottom (essay date winter 2003)

SOURCE: Cottom, Daniel. "I Think; Therefore, I Am Heathcliff." *ELH* 70, no. 4 (winter 2003): 1067-88.

[*In the following essay, Cottom evaluates the Gothic elements in* Wuthering Heights, *examining the way in which Brontë's interpretation of this popular genre is rooted in the philosophy of René Descartes. According to Cottom, Descartes's notions of individuality and certainty play a key role in Brontë's development of her central characters.*]

Under Gothic conditions, thinking comes to be defined by way of the unhuman, especially in the form of art. Allowances must be made for the various aspects and kinds of Gothic literature, but key exemplars of the genre are consistent on this point.[1] In the activity of thought, one finds the unhuman coming alive and, in doing so, ruining not only the perspectives and sympathies but also the architecture of humanity. This ruination can then be made out to be the very proof of that humanity. Portraits stir and look back at their beholders, statues bleed, suits of armor walk, costumes disguise, invisible minstrels tantalize, picturesque scenes open themselves to nightmares: every mechanism of this genre adumbrates the proposal that, if thinking is to be, it will exist only through the aesthetic animation, sufferance, and internalization of that which is supposed to be foreign to thought.[2] By emphasizing its own romance

nature, which is designed to be enlivened through its readers' imaginative imprisonment in extravagantly hostile situations, the remote past, or exotic environments, the Gothic novel further embodied this proposal for its audience. As Ingmar Bergman recognized when he adapted this technique to the screen in his Gothic *Seventh Seal* (1957), in which Death appears to the Knight as the chess player he has seen him to be in a painting, all those restless works of art figure as synecdoches for the novel itself, which finds its fantasy of origins in the vivification of mouldering manuscripts into an appropriately modern genre.

An emphasis on this genre's artifice could figure as that which is exterior, anterior, or foreign to thought because of the immemorial traditions in which art was considered to be fundamentally irrational. In addition, the historical conditions of the late eighteenth and early nineteenth centuries made it possible to see art as specifically emblematic of all that was irrelevant, anachronistic, or distant in relation to the utilitarian tendencies of modern life. (It was with good reason that Immanuel Kant chose this historical moment to draw a *cordon sanitaire* around art that would sequester it from crafts, decorations, and commodities, and in his own fashion Georg Wilhelm Friedrich Hegel was addressing the same set of circumstances when he proclaimed art to be "a thing of the past.")[3] This is not to say, however, that the Gothic novel was opposed to the emerging demands of modern life—for instance, as a rebellion against Enlightenment reason—or in some other way strikingly at odds with contemporary historical developments.[4] On the contrary, the challenge this genre took up was that of justifying the ways of modernity to man.[5] In the Gothic novel art discovers its misanthropy, its unhuman motivation, as that which enables the modern sense of humanity to be instituted.

It follows that this genre may be read as a series of footnotes to the writings of René Descartes. Although Horace Walpole's *Castle of Otranto* (1764) is generally regarded as having inaugurated this genre, which crested in popularity at the end of the eighteenth and the beginning of the nineteenth century, Descartes's *Meditations* (1641) was actually the first Gothic novel. Understandably, its presentation and reception as a work of philosophy composed in the genre of the meditation has obscured its claim to this distinction, as has the century and a half delay between its publication and the great wave of imitations that popularized Gothicism as a cultural style. These might seem to be inconvenient facts for my argument. Nonetheless, Descartes's *Meditations* can be said to have laid the foundations not only for modern philosophy but also for influential works like Ann Radcliffe's *Mysteries of Udolpho* (1794) and their revisionary successors such as Emily Brontë's ***Wuthering Heights*** (1847). Comparison of the Gothic novel with this precursor text serves to illuminate both the one and the other. As the Gothic comes to seem a machine designed to manufacture the world of modern humanity, the comparison also serves to highlight the worldliness of Descartes's *cogito*: its implication in a specific history and will. We can see how the confrontation of the Cartesian ego and demon prefigures the Gothic encounter with the misanthrope and all that this entails in terms of the family and society at large. This comparison also clarifies the supremacy of aesthetic over logical premises in Descartes's thought and thus enables us to comprehend the vital role of art in Gothic metaphysics. We are then in a better position to appreciate the culmination of this relation between Cartesian and Gothic thought in the achievement of **Wuthering Heights,** which rewrites the Gothic in much the same way that this genre had rewritten Descartes: by drawing out the worldly implications of what seems to be its most clear and simple device, which in this case is the romantic love that is supposed to bring one human to identify with another.

Like certain Gothic novels, such as the Marquis de Sade's *History of Juliette* (1797), Charles Brockden Brown's *Wieland* (1798), and William Godwin's *St. Leon* (1799), the *Meditations* takes the form of a personal narrative interspersed with extended passages of philosophical reflection and argument. As in all Gothic literature, the protagonist of Descartes's treatise (Pierre Gassendi puckishly nicknamed him "Mind") experiences a melancholy seclusion from the world.[6] At first the seclusion is freely chosen, just as it is in many Gothic novels; but then it comes to bear all the trappings of the involuntary isolation that is one of the trademark motifs of Gothic plots. In this isolated state of being Descartes can no longer trust the evidence of his own senses. As he is forced to trade the presumption of a consentient perceptual reality for solipsistic and paranoid self-doubt, his thought-experiment sets the stage for every Gothic protagonist in centuries to come who would suffer the fate of losing confidence in his or her perceptions. ("Every thing now appeared to me an object of suspicion" is a sentence that could have been written by the seventeenth-century metaphysician but was in fact written, to register a characteristically Gothic moment, by the eighteenth-century celebrity Matthew "Monk" Lewis.)[7] Moreover, in many if not all Gothic novels, just as in the *Meditations,* the greatest crises associated with one's suspension in uncertainty are attributed to the machinations of an evil figure conceivably possessed of supernatural powers.

In the Gothic novel, as in the *Meditations,* Descartes's malignant demon is the figure of misanthropy through which the thought of modernity must pass if it is adequately to establish and estimate itself. For Descartes, as for those who followed him, the consequence is that the question of identity is driven into the foreground of consciousness by virtue of being put into extreme jeopardy. In both cases this jeopardy does not really arise from a preexisting crisis; it is itself the heuristic positing of a crisis that provides the imaginative rationale for the demand that identity be renovated. On this basis, identity is so terrorized that individuals may not be sure whether they are dreaming, may wonder whether they have fallen into madness, and may even become so hysterical as to lose all sense of connection with their own bodies. This experience of uncertainty may go so far as seemingly to cast into doubt the fundamentals of Christian belief, and the entertainment of such doubts would threaten authors of the Gothic works under consideration here with opprobrium and hostility, as well as fame, even as Descartes had been so threatened. Finally, we may note that, in most cases, divine providence is ritually reestablished by the end of Gothic novels; in this respect, too. Descartes set the pattern for their protagonists' journeys.

Of course, in making this comparison I do not mean to suggest that the *Meditations* was an influence, in the conventional sense of that term, on writers of Gothic fiction, many of whom were probably ignorant of Descartes's name, not to mention his metaphysics. Despite the similarities between his *Meditations* and Gothic novels, Descartes did not literally devise the form of these works, but he did anticipate their defining obsession with thinking of and through the unhuman, as exemplified most notably in the work of imaginative art. The *Meditations* deserves to be called the first Gothic novel because it asked its readers to prepare themselves for modernity by entertaining the thought that their very selves might be works of art, the unhuman product of a misanthropic demon. Like the Gothic novel, the *Meditations* argued that art must come to life so that doubt may die. Credulousness was to be assigned to a past thenceforth to be defined in terms of superstition, while modernity would be defined as the era that is able to confine the incredible within the realm of art, which essentially belongs to the past and so may be licensed to thrill the present.

Yet at the same time that it follows the model developed by Descartes, the Gothic novel significantly reformulates his project. In effect, it sets out to demonstrate why the meditative method ought to give way to that of the romance as the appropriate instrument for the formation of identity. Most notably, the modern romance makes seclusion a different state of affairs than the innocent reader of the philosophical work may take it to be. Crucial to the entire series of Descartes's meditations was the overt premise that they concerned only thought, not action, since he had taken care to isolate himself from all encumbrances and from all knowledge of and concerns about others—from all "worries," in a word—before he began this exercise. This seclusion was to provide the "free time" necessary to the rigorous tests of thought but was also required to safeguard that thought from accusations of irresponsibility or, worse, sinfulness or heresy (*M* [*Meditations*], 2:12). (Galileo Galilei's experience with the Inquisition, which had led Descartes to suppress the writings published posthumously as *The World* and the *Treatise on Man* [1664], was still a living memory for him—as well it had ought to have been, considering some of the initial responses to his work.)[8] "I know that no danger or error will result from my plan," he wrote, "and that I cannot possibly go too far in my distrustful attitude," since meditation "does not involve action" (*M*, 2:15). Saying so, however, did constitute an action, a very complex one, in fact, which the formal disavowal of any relation between one's literary self and other persons is designed to forestall the unequivocally real possibility that the author might be identified with and punished for his words. The overt premise of the *Meditations* thus undoes itself or, in Gothic terms, turns out to have a secret interior. The *cogito* is revealed (in Gassendi's formulation) as a creation of "artifice, sleight of hand and circumlocution" (*M*, 2:180). If it were not social through and through—even, and especially, in its disavowal of the existence of others—it would be unimaginable.

Catching a glimpse of this problem as it played itself out in Descartes's work, another of his commentators noted, "if you had not grown up among educated people, but had spent your entire life alone in some deserted spot, how do you know that the idea [of a perfect being] would have come to you? . . . [T]he fact that the natives of Canada, the Hurons and other primitive peoples, have no awareness of any idea of this sort seems to establish that" (*M*, 2:88).[9] Descartes simply dismissed this anthropological argument: "the objections you raise cannot occur to those who follow the road which I have indicated" (*M*, 2:109). As the Gothic novel would show, however, that which Descartes preferred to style as a road was, in fact, a labyrinth in which the *cogito* and evil demon were artfully implicated in one another, just as these critics had suggested.

In the world of the Gothic, no asylum is to be had. There is no such thing as free time, and seclusion is where the action is. What might otherwise appear as one's private study, that objective correlative to the philosophical promise of certainty in one's identity, is redesigned within the Gothic novel into something like a monastic cell or a chamber in a castle: sites emphatically impressed with a sense of communal relations, even for individuals locked in isolation within them. One is never less alone than when singled out in such circumstances, especially when one comes to recognize (as Gothic protagonists must) that seclusion is always doubtful. One can never be sure that rooms do not have a secret entrance invisible even to the closest inspection and yet accessible to unknown others on the outside. For this reason, even a seemingly willing seclusion is never secure as such; one can never be certain of being safe from others' eyes, ears, hands, or general influence.

Accordingly, the indubitable mark of history in Descartes's defensive *mise-en-scène,* which was designed to protect his hyperbolic doubt from reproach, was itself made hyperbolic in the role of the Inquisition in novels such as Lewis's *The Monk* (1796), Radcliffe's *The Italian* (1797), Percy Bysshe Shelley's *Zastrozzi* (1810), and Charles Robert Maturin's *Melmoth the Wanderer* (1820). Even as it follows the plot wrought by Descartes, the Gothic novel outdoes his meditations by faithfully calling into doubt their enabling premise and thus revealing his reasoning as always having been more dramatically than logically compelling.[10] Contingent as it is on its self-contradictory disavowal of home and all that pertains to it, from one's immediate family to the structures of wealth, rank, religion, and law in society at large, Descartes's *cogito* must be seen as having been tormented by a demonic other from the very beginning, before the evil genius was even introduced as such.

In the Gothic novel this disavowed society, or demon, finds its summary figure in the misanthrope. As if recognizing the unclear and indistinct social relations within the clear and distinct ideas apprehended through the light of reason in the *Meditations,* the Gothic registers the inescapability of misanthropy, the constitutive role of the unhuman, in the imagining of human existence within this work. In the Gothic misanthrope we can see the necessity of Descartes's contingencies, the tyrannical power of his identity, even his metaphysical desire for the experience of paranoia—and thus, in short, the art of his reason, uncannily alive. Thought simply cannot be isolated from action, much less from worries, the Gothic novel maintains—even as it honors Descartes by suggesting that to imagine otherwise is natural to the heroes and heroines of its drama, who could not play their roles if they were not susceptible to this delusion.

As logical premises turn out to be aesthetic, in Gothic literature's rewriting of Descartes, so, too, does the issue of identity turn out to be one of multiple, disjunctive, and contradictory identifications. This revision does not establish the Lacanian "fragmented subject" described by Robert Miles, however, but rather the misanthropic subject of unhuman motivations presupposed by the countervailing desire for humanity and registered in the Gothic preoccupation with the artwork that comes alive.[11] This unhuman subject is retrospectively created, called on to have existed, so that humanity may be given a distinctively modern place in metaphysics, history, and psychology. This subject's character, its unhuman lack of comprehensible agency and coherence, is an imaginative fiction necessary to the seeming proof of humanity's existence within a distinctively modern conception of thought. Like the spanking new ruins that typify Gothic aesthetics, this disaggregation is a sign not of an identity in distress or under assault but rather of one under construction. It is a modern humanity to be created through, as it is saved from, art. Taken to the Gothic extreme, then, as Oscar Wilde recognized in his reworking of this genre in *The Picture of Dorian Gray* (1890), modernity is created as an ageless contemporaneity that assigns living art to the sequestered past and multiple, disjunctive, and contradictory motivations to the realm of aesthetic reflection, as distinct from the logic of everyday life. Thus is Gothic horror—the Frankensteinian horror of viewing the unholy arts that go into the making of humanity—turned into modern entertainment.

Accompanying the definitively insecure seclusion in the realm of the Gothic is the inability to draw a clear distinction between others' existence and one's own. This existence in the other is the defining promise and distress of humanity. Therefore, if an inalienable certainty is to be found in this genre, it must be looked for in the fact that there exists a desire that humanity should be materialized through art, not in the recognition that a discrete I exists in reality. Because identity is thought by demonic historical agencies such as those of gender, class, religion, and nationality, epistemological questions are proven to be indissoluble from dramas in which characters must strive to identify themselves through their relations with others. In the Gothic novel, it is through the institution of the family that these unhuman agencies do their most creative thinking, and so the family is to this genre what the *cogito* is to the *Meditations,* the indubitable ground of primitive self-consciousness.

Along with social position, economic condition, religious denomination, and other kinds of historically specific identifications, Descartes's *Meditations* initially assigned the family to the categorically doubtful realm of imagination and brute materiality—which, after all, is precisely where it belongs, as far as the Gothic novel is concerned. When his respondents tried to bring family and community into their discussions of the mind, Descartes summarily dismissed their reasonings by declaring that any recourse to the supposed determinations of such contexts could lead only to an infinite regress in the search for certain knowledge. (Any authority attributed to one's immediate ancestors must in turn be accounted for in relation to their ancestors, and so on.)[12] Again, the Gothic novel is fully in agreement with him—one's familial relations *are* infinitely suspicious— but the significance of this point is construed rather differently. Instead of allowing protagonists to conceive of themselves as unique and disembodied intelligences, this recognition drives them into a congeries of shifting identifications in a world so saturated with mystery as

to provide no basis even for the axiomatic Cartesian definition of bodies as substances extended in space. In fact, the presumptive difference between immaterial identities and physical bodies is precisely what the imaginary and brute materiality of the family throws into confusion.[13] When he sees Catherine's features not only in the floor under his feet and in "every cloud, in every tree—filling the air at night, and caught by glimpses in every object by day," but also in his own features, Brontë's Heathcliff is doing little more than restating the literary tradition that arose out of this recognition.[14]

In *The Italian,* for instance, it is not sufficient to Radcliffe's purposes that her plot should be set in motion by a dispute over the nature of the family, with the hero's parents objecting to his fancied heroine because her background is insufficiently grand. Nor is it enough that the mother's agent in this family dispute, the misanthropic Father Schedoni, should be a mysterious figure who comes to be thought of as "a demon in the guise of a monk" and whose actions may be "more than human," with consequences that throw the hero's mind into "a tempest of conjecture and of horror."[15] It is still insufficient that the hero, Vicentio di Vivaldi, should confuse Schedoni with a second monk who had repeatedly emerged from shadowy ruins to utter enigmatic warnings to Vivaldi that he had best keep away from the heroine, Ellena Rosalba. It is not even enough that Schedoni should discover, at the very moment when he is about to murder Ellena, that she is his daughter— who then will be brought to love him not only as her father but as the man who has delivered her from the unknown assailant, whom readers know is none other than himself. Furthermore, we cannot rest easy in the revelation that Schedoni was born Count Ferando di Bruno and married Ellena's mother after murdering her first husband, who happened to be his own brother; and we are not yet at an end when we learn that Ellena was raised in obscurity by an aunt because Schedoni then went on, for good measure, to slay her mother. Readers are not allowed any respite until they learn why the proof "that removed every doubt of [Schedoni's] identity" as Ellena's father was, in fact, deceptive, and that he is actually Ellena's uncle and stepfather, not her progenitor.[16] (The confusion on this score is owing to the fact that her mother had a daughter by each di Bruno brother, the death of the second child having been mistaken for that of the first.) As a bonus, we learn that even though he had tried to do away with his wife and had thought himself successful, Schedoni failed. She has survived to greet her long-lost child and to usher her into the novel's pious conclusion, in which she serves neatly to counterbalance the Marchesa, whose fierce character had set this work into motion, much in the way that Hareton and Catherine Linton, at the end of **Wuthering Heights,** provide a formal counterbalance to the pair formed by Heathcliff and Catherine at the beginning of the events recounted in that novel.

In short, in *The Italian* the statement "I think" logically entails the conclusion, "Therefore, I am bedevilled with a family." Broadly sketched as being placed in conflict between stereotypically aristocratic and emergent middle-class conceptions, which are also associated with the differences between Italy, Catholicism, and the past, on the one hand, and the inference of an English and Protestant modernity, on the other, the family in this novel completely circumscribes self-consciousness without giving it a place to stand, much less safely seclude itself. In a world of families, we learn, multiple, disjunctive, and unstable identifications are normative. Far from offering comfort, the image of a self-assured *cogito* in this world must be positively terrifying, disrupting rather than securing the difference between mind and body. In other words, this image must turn out to be a Heathcliff-like Schedoni, whose "contempt and malignity" allow him to act as if he is not bound by family relationships, association, or name. Rather than comporting himself as a proper family man, Schedoni acts as a plotter, an artist who is able to manipulate Vivaldi for so long because this hero has yet to learn that superstition properly belongs to the past and to art. "The opinions you avowed were rational," says Schedoni to Vivaldi, "but the ardour of your imagination was apparent, and what ardent imagination ever was contented to trust to plain reasoning, or to the evidence of the senses?" Vivaldi fails to know artifice when he sees it because he has not learned to confine his desire for the incredible to art—and to accept that life as thus defined through its sequestration of art is an endlessly regressive, doubtful, and dissatisfying realm of conjoined imagination and brute materiality.[17]

This sketch of *The Italian* cannot begin to cover the representation of the family in all of Radcliffe's novels, much less in all of Gothic literature. Nevertheless, it should give some indication of why it is fair to say that this literature discovers the unclear and indistinct familial relations that await their reading within the clear and distinct identity apprehended through the natural light of reason in the *Meditations*. To be sure, other examples would bring other emphases. In *The Castle of Otranto,* for instance, Manfred insists that he will marry Isabella, who was to be his daughter-in-law before a giant helmet squashed her intended, despite the fact that he labors under the impediment of already being married. (Manfred goes on to slay his own daughter, Matilda, with the consequence that he frees Isabella to marry Frederic, who had been in love with Matilda but who now finds in Isabella "one with whom he could forever indulge the melancholy that had taken possession of his soul.")[18] In Godwin's *St. Leon,* having been rejected by his son and having recognized himself as the inadvertent cause of his wife's death, the titular protagonist feels duty-bound to protect his daughters by absenting himself from their lives, even by feigning his own death, only to find that it is his non-presence that then becomes a torture for them, because of the cloud it casts over their ancestral name and marital prospects. In Eleanor Sleath's *Nocturnal Minstrel* (1810), haunted by music from an unknown origin as well as by other apparitions, the widowed Baroness Fitzwalter must strive to negotiate for her independence, not only with her father and her king but also with suitors as importunate as Penelope's; the ghost who tells her that he will clarify "the mysterious fate of this family" turns out to be her undead husband, who has taken the opportunity afforded by the exaggerated report of his demise to test his wife's fidelity by spying upon her while also engaging her guests in spooky tricks.[19] Whatever the case may be in a particular work, however, the family in this genre cannot be bracketed off through a phenomenological reduction or through any other means, because it is impossible to isolate oneself from an institution constituted through identifications that can be neither delimited nor fully known. The advice one character in *The Monk* offers another typifies this Gothic condition: "But you must listen to me with patience. You will not be less surprised, when I relate some particulars of your family still unknown to you."[20] The family lives in the very walls that offered Descartes the illusion of quiet, peace, and free time in which to reflect upon himself while supposing "that no other human beings were yet known" to him (*M,* 2:102). When his thoughts were most focused on what he could know with certainty of himself, the Gothic novel suggests, Descartes was unthinkingly being thought by the institution of the family and all the other social powers represented in and through it—and his confusion on this score is exemplary of that which constitutes humanity as such. From the Gothic perspective, then, individuals are still likely to claim that identity is a discovery made through the natural light of reason. More fully represented, however, it is an effect created through imaginative art or, more specifically, through the unhuman motivations of art aptly represented by the overpowering, and hence terrifying, abstraction of the family, which is the most intimate version of the society his malignant genius represented in reality.

So the identity of modern humanity is portrayed as the product of a fundamental misanthropy. From this perspective, one might say that it was with good reason that Thomas Love Peacock satirically suggested, in *Nightmare Abbey* (1818), that the "delicious misanthropy and discontent" of modern books makes them "very consolatory and congenial."[21] For all its claim to the natural light of reason, the identity of modern humanity is drawn out of a drama of dissimulation, like that in which a monk takes a new name and leaves the world behind, as the saying goes, so that he may eventually be revealed as the very demon he was supposed to oppose. Despite the diversity of Gothic plots, *The Italian* is paradigmatic in this respect, and as viewed from the perspective thus afforded to us, we can see that Descartes's meditations prove too much. In defining the activity of thought by first willing away the influence of the family and all the social distinctions appertaining to it (rank, wealth, religion, nationality, and so on), he undoes himself in a distinctively modern way. He shows the necessity of a recourse to the very art that he will nonetheless disavow when he attributes all ruinous manipulations of bodies, images, and thoughts to the figure of the malignant demon. Just as his isolation anticipates the role of the dangerous confinement, romantic past, and exotic lands in Gothic literature, so does this demon play the role of the Gothic villain.

As if recognizing that the Cartesian I is dependent on this aesthetic creation, the malignant genius, and, even prior to that, on the aesthetics of a misanthropic seclusion prefiguring that demon, the Gothic novel portrays the ego and its challenging adversary as mutually constitutive characters in a literary drama, not as intellectual figures in a logical demonstration. In doing so it practically invites a Freudian reading, in which ego and demon are distinct agencies within the same psychic apparatus, as well as the Foucauldian revision of that reading, in which the repressive hypothesis that may lead to sympathy for the demon is shown to overlook how fully and openly this other's co-creation with the ego has been effected. At the same time, though, the Gothic novel thwarts such readings in advance through its insistence on identifying cultural with biological and social reproduction. In portraying thinking as historical action fashioned through unhuman motivations—the motivations of agencies that seem sadistically to lord it over the human figure, such as sexual impulses, kinship structures, economic systems, legal codes, and religious institutions—the Gothic genre takes for granted that consciousness holds no exalted privilege in its world. (From Jane Austen on, the lapses of consciousness featured in its drama have been the most obvious targets for mockery in this genre, but this satire appears more naïve than its intended target if one considers the assumptions it conveys about consciousness as a continuous and secure state of self-possession.) Moreover, this genre takes for granted that power is productive and jubilant in the creation of identities, not simply repressive, as nothing shows more clearly than its portrayal of the powerful nexus of relations that is the family, that thoroughly dubious thing compounded of imagination and brute materiality. In other words, far from being confronted and surpassed in these novels, misanthropy is made out to be the unsettling power that modernity must labor to confine to an art symbolically marked as dead, relegated to the past, even though it is this ghostly conception of artistic form that makes possible the in-

vention of modernity and all its privileged figures, including that favorite term of Radcliffe's, "humanity."

To think, in the Gothic novel, is to recognize one's existence in the other, the reality of one's present in the romance of the past. The implications of Descartes's proof of identity, through its testing at the hands of the malignant demon, thus become, for example, the identification of universal humanity through the creation of a Continental, Catholic, aristocratic demon. Of course, the design of Gothic misanthropy varies from work to work, just as Gothic plots do. For instance, in *The Recess* (1783-1785), embroiling her protagonists in religious factionalism, illegitimacy, secret marriages, and threats of incest, rape, and insanity, not to mention murder, Sophia Lee represented this existence in the other through the relation between Mary, Queen of Scots (the protagonists' mother) and Queen Elizabeth. (With characteristic Gothic logic, this relationship could then be reproduced within the aesthetic furnishings of the mind of one of the protagonists, Ellinor: "Taste, genius, and science, those rich columes with which enthusiastic fancy creates in peaceful minds a thousand light aerial structures, deep sunk, and broken in my heart, presented to the mental eye a ruin . . .—Misanthropy, black-visaged misanthropy, reigned there like a solitary savage, unconscious of the value of those treasures his rude hand every day more and more defaced.")[22] The beginning of *The Monk* finds the renowned Father Ambrosio overhearing a novice's tormented exclamation— "Oh God! What a blessing would Misanthropy be to me!"—counseling the novice that such a condition is wholly "imaginary," and then becoming a complete misanthrope himself—as well as the rapist of his sister and murderer of his mother—after he is seduced by the novice, who turns out to be a crossdressed and dreamily lubricious young woman.[23] *Melmoth the Wanderer* opens with John Melmoth leaving Dublin's Trinity College to visit the manse of his dying uncle, a confirmed misanthrope, where he first encounters the ancestral figure that is cursed forever to wander the earth, haunt his family, and corrupt his own existence—"that being, I will not call him a man," as another character refers to it. At one point, when "the demon of his superhuman misanthropy had now fully possessed" the ancestral wanderer, as he maliciously pours an account of the evils of modern civilization into the ear of an innocent island maiden, Maturin even felt it necessary to add a footnote complaining that the "worst sentiments" of his "worst characters" had been attributed, against all reason, to him. Bitterly and amusingly, with perfect Gothic logic, he thus reproduced the ego-demon as an author-reader relationship.[24]

The generically distinctive constant through all such variations is the recognition of oneself in the misanthropic other and thus the discovery of oneself in the unhuman and of the unhuman within oneself. Precisely because it mimes humanity, serving as its shadowy double, art is the exemplary figuration of the unhuman; and art's assumed distinction from nature, inanimation, secondary or representational mode of being, and suspect status in Platonic, Christian, and other metaphysics are accordingly brought to life in the Gothic. Melmoth, for instance, is introduced to the perturbations of his demonic ancestor through a portrait whose eyes seem to move, and uncannily affecting portraits appear as well in *The Monk* and *The Recess,* among other works. (As in Clara Reeve's 1778 "Preface to the Second Edition" of *The Old English Baron,* the animated picture and similar devices have long been criticized as excesses of the Gothic genre, but it is this criticism that appears excessive if one examines its governing assumptions about the existence of clear cut divisions between subjects and objects and between the probable and the marvelous.)[25] It is through such figurations of the undead nature of art that the Gothic defines modernity—defines modernity despite, and because of, the fact that the Gothic imperils its definition.

In *Wuthering Heights,* which is by no means the last but which is arguably the most brilliant work in this tradition, the undead nature of art is so powerfully realized that Charlotte Brontë, in her "Editor's Preface" to the second edition of her sister's novel, seemed terrified by it. Charlotte herself was no mean hand at the Gothic, of course, but she evidently could not accept how openly Emily had acknowledged the misanthropy at the heart of Gothic art and of the modern identity it was designed to entertain. Therefore, in writing of how her late sister had wrought "creations like Heathcliff, like Earnshaw, like Catherine" (*W* [*Wuthering Heights*], 368), she denigrated her ("I am bound to avow that she had scarcely more practical knowledge of the peasantry amongst whom she lived, than a nun has of the country people who sometimes pass her convent gates" [*W,* 368]), patronized her ("Having formed these beings, she did not know what she had done" [*W,* 368-69]), and lovingly condemned her ("Whether it is right or advisable to create beings like Heathcliff, I do not know: I scarcely think it is" [*W,* 370]). Even if it had not been provided, one might have wished to imagine such an editorial introduction to Emily Brontë's work, in which one sister plays ego to the other's demon; for the way Charlotte insists on placing her sister's identity in a family context that defines it in terms of ignorance, unreliability, and suspect morality—terms that cannot help but also suggest sibling rivalry—reproduce in the form of denial precisely what Emily Brontë's masterpiece affirms to be the nature of Gothic identity.[26]

The opening sentences of *Wuthering Heights* focus in on the subject of the Gothic as subject to misanthropy: "In all England, I do not believe that I could have fixed on a situation so completely removed from the stir of society. A perfect misanthropist's Heaven: and Mr.

Heathcliff and I are such a suitable pair to divide the desolation between us" (*W,* 1). Hindley and Catherine Earnshaw will also appear as exemplars of misanthropy, and even Edgar Linton fits the bill when, recoiling from Heathcliff, he betakes himself and his daughter to a melancholy seclusion like that of the protagonist in Friedrich Schiller's play *The Misanthropist Reconciled* (1790). Thus evoked from the outset, the general spirit of misanthropy is concentrated in the history of Heathcliff, who incarnates its unhuman agency in every aspect of his being, from the dubious circumstances of his birth and his disruptive insertion into a family on through to his animalic, devilish, and monstrous appearance as an object of superstition to Nelly Dean, among others, when he is an adult: "'But where did he come from, the little dark thing, harboured by a good man to his bane?' muttered Superstition" (*W,* 330). "It" is what Nelly calls him when Mr. Earnshaw first brings him home (*W,* 35), and as Charlotte Brontë recognized, an it is what he is and what he remains throughout the novel. "He's not a human being," his wife will flatly declare (*W,* 177): and as goes Heathcliff in this novel, so goes humanity. For instance, he is like the it that Lockwood experiences when his sleep at Wuthering Heights is interrupted by an apparition at the window by his bed: "As it spoke, I discerned, obscurely, a child's face looking through the window—Terror made me cruel; and, finding it useless to attempt shaking the creature off, I pulled its wrist on to the broken pane, and rubbed it to and fro till the blood ran down and soaked the bedclothes" (*W,* 23). Since this scene takes place three decades after that which introduces Heathcliff into the Earnshaw household but actually precedes it in the narrative, with only a few pages separating the two, readers are given the impression of an "itness" that is at once subjective and intersubjective—an impression that the rest of the novel is designed to elucidate as the condition of identity wrought through the unhuman agencies of identification. In Emily Brontë's portrayal, the unhuman is the foundation of modern identity; the misanthrope is the character demanded by its world; and the characteristic art of misanthropy is romantic love.

It is through this last intuition that her work in this genre outdoes her predecessors'. For the most part, love in Gothic novels is a perfunctory business, characterized formulaically as an index of virtue, sensibility, or morality. (Recall, for instance, how thin the incest-tinged love story is in Mary Shelley's *Frankenstein* [1818], as compared to the impassioned relation between Victor and his creation.) It was Emily Brontë's genius to see that, instead of being portrayed as a sign of the consciousness established through the aesthetic invention, sufferance, and internalization of otherness, romantic love could be portrayed more accurately as itself being the indubitably Gothic machinery that institutes humanity through the parlous process of identity formation. It would be through love that we would come to see the revelation of logical as aesthetic premises, the appearance of disturbing identifications in the place of certain identity, the emblematic embodiment of these identifications in the image of art that stirs itself into life, and—through all these aspects of the novel—the mutually constitutive relation of ego and demon.

Brought forward through Gothic terror and the allied Romantic feelings represented by works as disparate as Johann Wolfgang von Goethe's *Sorrows of Young Werther* (1774) and Charlotte Dacre's *Confessions of the Nun of St. Omer* (1805), the romantic love of Andreas Capellanus, which must be gratuitous and so can be manifested only in adulterous or extramarital passion, was thus legitimized as art. By showing Gothic art coming alive in love and so giving the experience of love the place traditionally occupied in the Gothic novel by that of dramatic uncertainty, Brontë reinterpreted her predecessors in this genre as effectively as they had reinterpreted Descartes. Like earlier Gothic novels, *Wuthering Heights* shows the familial dramas lurking in the dreamy architecture of the thinker's room, but Brontë also saw the sadomasochistic institution of romantic love in the structuring of the Gothic plot.[27] What is more, she saw the value of estimating such love as a matter that properly belongs to the past and that is supposed to appear in the present only in the form of art. It is this insight that accounts for what Terry Eagleton has described as "the curious impersonality of the relation between Catherine and Heathcliff," its famously "ontological" or "metaphysical" quality.[28] Catherine's and Heathcliff's love can be consummated only in imagination or in brute materiality—only in ghostly visitations or in the commingling of their remains—so that it may be formally assigned to the realm of art, as distinct from life. Like the mockery of romantic love that runs throughout the nineteenth-century novel, from the portrayals of Marianne Dashwood and Hetty Sorrell to those of David Copperfield and Emma Bovary and *Tuan Jim*, among so many others, this love story signifies modernity, which emerges from its dramatized failure. As distinct from many other novels that employ this device, however, *Wuthering Heights* keeps faith with the Gothic through its dramatized insistence that modernity recognize its existence in the other that is art. The unhuman motivations of art, Brontë suggests, are still those of the humanity that defines itself by framing the image of art's life as superstition.

In his response to Descartes's *Meditations,* Johannes Caterus had explained the argument about identity on which he agreed with the philosopher by making an allusion to Terence's *Andria*: "Davus is Davus and not Oedipus" (*M*, 2:67).[29] Like her predecessors in the Gothic genre, Brontë would have none of this. "I *am* Heathcliff!" Catherine Earnshaw exclaims, recognizing the foundation of her identity in the necessary existence of the other. Whereas her love for Edgar Linton "is like the foliage in the woods," subject to time and change, her love for Heathcliff "resembles the eternal rocks beneath—a source of little visible delight, but necessary" (*W*, 82). Brontë marks this identity through identifications with irony even as Catherine proclaims its perdurability, however, so as to make clear that love, like the Gothic family, is bound to be as unstable as it is fundamentally unhuman, no matter whether that unhuman nature is imaged as being animal, vegetable, or mineral—or demon or ghoul. At the very moment that Catherine is proclaiming her identification with Heathcliff and characterizing his existence as hers—"my own being" (*W*, 82)—he is stealing away, having heard only her earlier remarks that to marry him now would be a degradation for her. Like the events that followed upon his entrance into her family's household, his disappearance from it and subsequent fairytale transformation into a gentleman serve to emphasize that in being Heathcliff, Catherine is and yet is not Catherine, and in being Catherine, Heathcliff is and is not himself.[30] Accordingly, Heathcliff may reverse the subjects and objects in her statements—"I have not broken your heart—*you* have broken it—and in breaking it, you have broken mine" (*W*, 161)—and in her last meeting with him Catherine may say of Heathcliff, "That is not *my* Heathcliff. I shall love mine yet; and take him with me—he's in my soul" (*W*, 160).

Upon Heathcliff's return, Catherine had expressed her sense of things in a gleeful moment of self-dramatization: "The event of this evening has reconciled me to God and humanity! I had risen in angry rebellion against providence" (*W*, 99). Yet this quip is actually a serious riposte to the proof of divine security that Descartes considered himself to have found through his *cogito*. As much a blasphemy to God and insult to the family as it is a misanthropic rejection of humanity, the identification of Catherine and Heathcliff demands the Gothic ghost as its defining figure. No image could be adequate to their love that did not register its profoundly unhuman motivations, which can "take any form" because they derive their existence from the overwhelming and infinitely regressive number of cultural, biological, and social forms that reproduce themselves through the identifications out of which identity is composed. So Heathcliff, not really himself, calls out to the dead Catherine, "I know that ghosts *have* wandered on earth. Be with me always—take any form—drive me mad! only *do* not leave me in this abyss, where I cannot find you!" (*W*, 167).

This Gothicism that comes to life in the love of Catherine and Heathcliff is specifically literary in nature, in keeping with the nature of *Wuthering Heights* as a self-conscious reworking of literary tradition. Instead of paintings or statues or other *objets d'art*, the letters of the alphabet are the unhuman stuff that becomes animated, as when Lockwood has his nightmare vision of

Catherine Linton after reading her name scratched on a window ledge and scrawled in the books resting on that ledge.[31] The way letters become animated does not appear at all logical ("why did I think of *Linton*? I had read *Earnshaw* twenty times for Linton" [*W*, 23]), and Lockwood's response to this event is as lacking in humanity as was the reaction of Catherine, Hindley, and Nelly to the sudden delivery of Heathcliff from within Mr. Earnshaw's coat. By the end of the novel, of course, as the eighteenth has turned to the nineteenth century, the sadomasochistic tropes of the Gothic will have been toned down to the comic dimensions of the playful slaps and kisses exchanged in the reading lesson given to Hareton Earnshaw by the second Catherine. However, it is notable that Brontë did not reestablish a Providential security for the senses, in accordance with the Gothic pattern. Instead, as in the twentieth century's film noir versions of the Gothic, Brontë's narrative structure has the violent prehistory to this scene with Hareton and Catherine come out of the past to modify our impressions of that scene, and we are left with the image of a child's terrified blubbering at the sight of "Heathcliff and a woman, yonder, under t'Nab" (*W*, 336). To be sure, Lockwood's final words, as he describes the graves of Catherine, Edgar Linton, and Heathcliff, do make a gesture toward something like divine assurance: "I lingered round them, under that benign sky; watched the moths fluttering among the heath, and hare-bells; listened to the soft wind breathing through the grass; and wondered how any one could ever imagine unquiet slumbers for the sleepers in that quiet earth" (*W*, 338). The muted and willful nature of this assurance can hardly go unremarked, however, especially since readers will have noted from the first words of the narrative that Lockwood, the urbane modern gentleman who has decided to vacation among the moors, is not one whose perceptions can be trusted, to say the least.

Lockwood's impercipience is made clear when he makes embarrassing mistakes on his first visit to Heathcliff's household, as when he takes a pile of dead rabbits to be cherished cats; and he actually introduces himself with a story that illustrates the confounding cross-purposes in his actions of the immediate past. Nonetheless, although he has pronounced himself a misanthropist, in accordance with Gothic fashion, and secluded himself in this place far removed from "society," as the contemporary idiom would have it, he is no Descartes metaphysically trying to sort himself out. As a man of the present in this narrative's time scheme, Lockwood is comically self-assured even as he details his confusions and errors. It would appear that Cartesian doubt is a thing of the past, a matter that cannot touch a gentleman who knows how to dismiss a nightmare with the same absurd confidence with which he lets his readers know that, if he had been so inclined, he might have stolen a march on Hareton in the matter

of the second Catherine's affections. In short, Lockwood does not think, and he is not Heathcliff or anything like him.

Instead, Lockwood and Nelly figure as the dispiriting modern counterparts to the ego and demon of Descartes's *Meditations*. Lockwood is the silly ego that does not have the art to question itself, Nelly the tormentor as mere busybody (and so her "hidden enemy" [*W*, 129], says the first Catherine, not because Nelly Dean is of supernatural consequence but because she so decidedly is not). The fact that the structuring of **Wuthering Heights** has Nelly's oral narrative retold in Lockwood's writing reduces the demonic testing of identity to a gossip's test of one's patience. As told by Nelly to divert the ailing or bored Lockwood and as retold by Lockwood for what we can infer to be an intended audience of persons with pretensions to education and culture, this story is oriented to the need for entertainment, not to the need for such certainty as was sought by Heathcliff and Catherine Earnshaw.

It is significant, in this regard, that Lockwood appears as a failed or indecisive misanthrope—as so much of a dilettante in this respect, in fact, that he takes Heathcliff's vehement rejection of any desire for his company as a perverse incitement to pester him further. Like Nelly's tale, Heathcliff is entertainment to him. Lockwood's very existence as a tourist in this countryside, a consumer of the experiences it may provide, shows us that Wuthering Heights and everything around it have the nature of a resort for him, like the spa he had graced with his presence shortly before coming there. His recourse to such entertainment is necessarily ambivalent, however, for he must let it come alive enough to divert him with its power while still maintaining the critical distance from it that will assure him that he need not question his own identity—and so need not doubt that art is essentially a thing of the past. As a narrator, then, Lockwood is also a stand-in for **Wuthering Heights**'s readers, whom Brontë mocks through Lockwood's patronizing affection for Catherine Linton and Hareton and through the sentimental closure to the narrative that he takes them to have bestowed upon the graves of their forebears. At the same time, she offers readers who know better than to identify with Lockwood's modernity—the modernity she deliberately places almost half a century before her novel's publication, as if it ought to be regarded as being no less remote than any generic Gothic setting—a thoroughly self-mortifying conception of art. In this conception, it is a damned good thing that art should have the making and unmaking of us, for who could face the unimaginable alternative of simply belonging to humanity, like Nelly and Lockwood, without being scared to death?

Notes

1. For analyses of the qualifications important in the discussion of the Gothic as a genre, see Jacqueline

Howard, *Reading Gothic Fiction: A Bakhtinian Approach* (Oxford: Oxford Univ. Press, 1994); James Watt, *Contesting the Gothic: Fiction, Genre and Cultural Conflict, 1764-1832* (Cambridge: Cambridge Univ. Press, 1999); and Michael Gamer, *Romanticism and the Gothic: Genre, Reception, and Canon Formation* (Cambridge: Cambridge Univ. Press, 2000). Although to some extent the very term "Gothic novel" is doubly anachronistic, especially in relation to eighteenth-century works, the family resemblance among the writings on which I focus, as well as common scholarly usage, sufficiently justifies its use for my purposes here.

2. On this topic of art becoming life in the Gothic, see Maggie Kilgour, *The Rise of the Gothic Novel* (New York: Routledge, 1995), 85-87, 156-58.

3. G. W. F. Hegel, *Aesthetics: Lectures on Fine Art,* trans. T. M. Knox, 2 vols. (Oxford: Oxford Univ. Press, 1998), 1:11.

4. On this point, though not on all others, I am in agreement with the entertaining polemic against "a continuing consensus" that "subsumes the Gothic into an anti-Enlightenment rebellion." See Chris Baldick and Robert Mighall, "Gothic Criticism," in *A Companion to the Gothic,* ed. David Punter (Oxford: Basil Blackwell, 2000), 215.

5. See the valuable argument about the creation of "an autonomous realm of the aesthetic," in relation to "the historical coincidence of the expanding taste for commercial fictions of the supernatural and the project of a supernaturalised theory of capitalism." E. J. Clery, *The Rise of Supernatural Fiction, 1762-1800* (Cambridge: Cambridge Univ. Press, 1995), 9.

6. [Pierre Gassendi,] "Fifth Set of Objections," in the "Objections and Replies," in René Descartes, *Meditations on First Philosophy, The Philosophical Writings of Descartes,* trans. John Cottingham, Robert Stoothoff, and Dugald Murdoch, 2 vols. (Cambridge: Cambridge Univ. Press, 1984), 2:179-240. Hereafter abbreviated *M* and cited parenthetically by page number.

7. Matthew Lewis, *The Monk,* ed. Howard Anderson (Oxford: Oxford Univ. Press, 1980), 107.

8. See, for example, the danger of appearing impious suggested by the theologian Antoine Arnauld in the "Fourth Set of Objections," in Descartes, *Meditations,* 2:151-53.

9. The editors note that these replies were collected and largely composed by Marin Mersenne.

10. On the question of how the aesthetic conventions of the meditation figure in Descartes's work, see the volume edited by Amélie Oksenberg Rorty: *Essays on Descartes'* Meditations, ed. Rorty (Berkeley: University of California Press, 1986).

11. Robert Miles, *Gothic Writing 1750-1820: A Genealogy* (New York: Routledge, 1993), 3. For another characterization akin to Miles's, see Vijay Mishra, *The Gothic Sublime* (Albany: State Univ. of New York Press, 1994).

12. See the "Second Set of Objections," and Descartes's response, in Descartes, *Meditations,* esp. 2:98, 109.

13. See the discussion of a partial "collapse of Cartesian dualism" in the writings of Ann Radcliffe and Edmund Burke. Steven Bruhm, *Gothic Bodies: The Politics of Pain in Romantic Fiction* (Philadelphia: Univ. of Pennsylvania Press, 1994), 99-100.

14. Emily Brontë, *Wuthering Heights,* ed. Ian Jack (Oxford: Oxford Univ. Press, 1995), 324. Hereafter abbreviated W and cited parenthetically by page number. In relation to this point, see Terry Castle's "The Spectralization of the Other in *The Mysteries of Udolpho,*" in *The Female Thermometer: Eighteenth-Century Culture and the Invention of the Uncanny* (New York: Oxford Univ. Press, 1995), 120-40.

15. Radcliffe, *The Italian,* ed. Frederick Garber (Oxford: Oxford Univ. Press, 1981), 18 ("a demon"), 19 ("more than human"), 367 ("a tempest"). The first quotations here are initially made in reference to an unknown tormentor, but Schedoni soon comes to be suspected either of being this person or, as eventually turns out to be the case, of being the agent behind his actions.

16. Radcliffe, 239.

17. Radcliffe, 52, 397-98.

18. Horace Walpole, *The Castle of Otranto,* ed. W. S. Lewis (Oxford: Oxford Univ. Press, 1982), 110.

19. Eleanor Sleath, *The Nocturnal Minstrel,* 2 vols. (New York: Arno Press, 1972), 2:18.

20. M. Lewis, *The Monk,* 130.

21. Thomas Love Peacock, *Nightmare Abbey,* in *The Works of Thomas Love Peacock,* ed. H. F. B. Brett-Smith and C. E. Jones, 10 vols. (New York: AMS Press, 1967), 3:41.

22. Sophia Lee, *The Recess,* 3 vols. (New York: Arno Press, 1972), 3:11.

23. M. Lewis, *The Monk,* 51, 53.

24. Charles Robert Maturin, *Melmoth the Wanderer,* ed. Douglas Grant (London: Oxford Univ. Press,

1968), 39 ("that being"), 303 ("the demon"; "worst sentiments"; "worst characters"). As Grant notes, Samuel Taylor Coleridge had published a critique of one of Maturin's works ("Critique on Bertram"), in his *Biographia Literaria,* in which he accused the author of immorality and impiety (303).

25. The unease with such devices continues on into contemporary criticism; see, for example, George E. Haggerty's comment on "an incongruity of technique and subject that reaches almost to self-parody." *Gothic Fiction/Gothic Form* (University Park: The Pennsylvania State Univ. Press, 1989), 16.

26. See the commentary on Charlotte Brontë's "Editor's Preface," on her editing of her sister's work (U. C. Knoepflmacher, *Wuthering Heights: A Study* [Athens: Ohio Univ. Press, 1994], 111-13), and on her "Biographical Notice" of Emily (which is described as being "shaped by a dynamic similar to that of *Wuthering Heights* itself" [Knoepflmacher, 4]).

27. The sadomasochistic aspects of Gothic literature have been much remarked; see, for example, William Patrick Day, *In the Circles of Fear and Desire: A Study of Gothic Fantasy* (Chicago: Univ. of Chicago Press, 1985). For *Wuthering Heights,* in particular, see Laura Hinton, *The Perverse Gaze of Sympathy: Sadomasochistic Sentiments from Clarissa to Rescue 911* (Albany: State Univ. of New York Press, 1999), 147-70.

28. Terry Eagleton, *Myths of Power: A Marxist Study of the Brontës* (London: Macmillan, 1975), 107 ("curious"), 108 ("ontological"; "metaphysical"). See also Nancy Armstrong's argument that *Wuthering Heights* "locates desire elsewhere, in an extrasocial dimension of human experience"; in *Desire and Domestic Fiction: A Political History of the Novel* (New York: Oxford Univ. Press, 1987), 196.

29. I owe the identification of the allusion to Terence to the translators of this work.

30. This transformation is suggestive not only of fairytales, of course; see, for instance, Eagleton's argument about this transformation as that of a bourgeois *parvenu* (114-17), and Susan Meyer's argument about its relation to the American Revolutionary War, and to anti-imperialist threats generally, in *Imperialism at Home: Race and Victorian Women's Fiction* (Ithaca: Cornell Univ. Press, 1996), 115-16.

31. See the analysis of issues of textuality in *Wuthering Heights,* in Carol Jacobs, *Uncontainable Romanticism: Shelley, Brontë, Kleist* (Baltimore: The Johns Hopkins Univ. Press, 1989), 61-84. See also James H. Kavanagh's argument about how "the book" in this novel figures "as a complex image, the nexus of multiple associations linking cultural order and the control of language with sublimation and the self-control of desire" (*Emily Brontë* [Oxford: Basil Blackwell, 1985], 19), as well as Robert C. McKibben, "The Image of the Book in *Wuthering Heights,*" *Nineteenth-Century Fiction* 15 (September 1960): 159-69.

Bettina Tate Pedersen (essay date 2003)

SOURCE: Pedersen, Bettina Tate. "Suicidal Logic: Melancholy/Depression in Emily Brontë's *Wuthering Heights.*" In *Victorian Gothic,* edited by Karen Sayer and Rosemary Mitchell, pp. 110-23. Leeds: Leeds Centre for Victorian Studies, 2003.

[*In the following essay, Pedersen examines suicidal imagery in* Wuthering Heights. *Pedersen suggests that Brontë's graphic portrayals of her characters' self-destructive tendencies reflect the novel's larger themes of psychological disturbance, isolation, and loss.*]

> To the psychologist, mourning is a great riddle . . . But why is it that this detachment of the libido from its objects should be such a painful process is a mystery to us and we have not hitherto been able to frame any hypotheses to account for it.
>
> —Freud ([in Julia Kristeva,] *Black Sun* [(1989)] 98)

> Storytelling is always after the fact, and it is always constructed over a loss.
>
> —J. Hillis Miller (61)

> My depression points to my not knowing how to lose—I have perhaps been unable to find a valid compensation for the loss? It follows that any loss entails the loss of my being—and of Being itself. The depressed person is a radical, sullen atheist.
>
> —Kristeva (*Black Sun* 5)

As one would expect of a gothic novel, ***Wuthering Heights*** criticism is over-rich with readings of the novel's dualities. Stevie Davies sees it full of characters 'with childhood animosities, allegiances and obsessions',[1] never fully able to enter the symbolic realm of adulthood. Ellen Moers reads it as 'a novel about the erotic life of children'[2] thinking that 'the puzzles of ***Wuthering Heights*** may best be resolved if the novel is read as a statement of a very serious kind about a girl's childhood and the adult woman's tragic yearning to return to it'.[3] J. H. Miller avers critics wrongly see their readings as definitive keys that expunge all 'remainder' and unify the text as coherent and contained,[4] erasing the uncontained disturbance and puissance of *Wuthering Heights*' characters.[5] Indeed, Heathcliff and Catherine are characters 'experienced by the reader as continuing energies and presences [long] after their deaths'.[6] Concomitantly, three images of bleeding wrists[7] infuse their essences with suicidal ambiance. The persistent and disturbing logic of the 'suicide' is powerfully delineated in Julia Kristeva's 1989 study, *Black Sun: Depression and Melancholia,* which illuminates the melancholic's economy as one fundamentally predicated on irreconcilable loss and offers a way of reading these suicidal images and the characters' irreconcilable loss.

The first, and most graphic, occurs during Lockwood's dream: 'Terror made me cruel; and, finding it useless to attempt shaking the creature off, I pulled its wrist on to the broken pane, and rubbed it to and fro till the blood ran down and soaked the bed-clothes'.[8] The second appears when Heathcliff and Hindley fight in the kitchen of the Heights and Hindley's knife 'closed into its owner's wrist Heathcliff pull[ing] it away by main force, slitting up the flesh as it passed on'.[9] The third at Heathcliff's deathbed is his own abrased but bloodless hand.[10] These images carry potent connotations of suicide, the wrist being an idiosyncratic site of melancholic suicidal trauma. Dorothy Van Ghent concentrates here on the question the bleeding wrist image raises: 'why should the well-mannered urbanite [Lockwood], dream of giving *this* treatment to the ghost child?'.[11] In her view Lockwood lacks the 'emotional motivation' for dreaming up such unwarranted cruelty or despairing melancholia, raising yet another question about the connection between the emotional tenor of Catherine's marginal-diary notes and such latent violent images in Lockwood's dreams when he 'no longer [had his] imagination under control'.[12] Emily Brontë does not say, but this early image sets into motion the disturbance and profound sense of loss that precipitates and follows an act of suicide.

Kristeva acknowledges Freud's[13] identification of loss as 'everywhere the same *impossible mourning for the maternal object*'[14] and notes in her study of female depression/melancholia that without matricide suicide follows: 'The maternal object having been introjected, the depressive or melancholic putting to death of the self is what follows, instead of matricide. In order to protect the mother I kill myself while knowing—phantasmatic and protective knowledge—that it comes from her, the death-bearing she-Ghenna . . . Thus my hatred is safe and my matricidal guilt erased'.[15] Such an absence of matricide is evident in Heathcliff and Catherine, both unable to reconcile themselves to the loss of

the mother. From the moment Mr. Earnshaw brings Heathcliff home, it is clear Heathcliff is parentless. Earnshaw had seen 'it starving, and houseless, and as good as dumb in the streets of Liverpool, where he [had] picked it up and inquired for its owner. Not a soul knew to whom it belonged'.[16] Heathcliff is so far removed from the maternal relationship that Earnshaw inquires for the boy's owners not his parents or mother and refers to him as 'it'. Further, Mrs. Earnshaw possesses no desire to become his surrogate. She 'was ready to fling it out of doors'.[17] Even giving Heathcliff, 'the name of a son who [had] died in childhood'[18] awakens no feelings of tenderness or compassion but only lodges him deeper in nonexistence, absence, and loss.

Although Catherine initially spits 'at the stupid little thing',[19] she eventually aligns herself with him and fills the absence both of biological and would-be surrogate mother. In maternal function, Catherine nurtures, protects, admonishes, plays and even sleeps with Heathcliff.[20] Catherine soon identifies so completely with Heathcliff that distinction between her *self,* initially unified with Mrs. Earnshaw in rejecting Heathcliff, and the *other,* Heathcliff, collapse revealing their 'common experience of *object loss* and of a *modification of signifying bonds*'.[21] For both, the loss of the mother, who 'is almost wholly absent from the text, though its children rage and wail loudly enough to wake the dead',[22] is keenly felt. This loss of maternal object is simultaneously introjected into their respective psyches and projected onto each other and their relationship.

The totality of their identification is evident in their resistance to separation. Despite Hindley's attempt to separate them (relegating Heathcliff to the position of despised servant) and Catherine's extended stay with the Lintons at Thrushcross Grange (who become signifiers of loss and separation), Catherine continues to resist any real separation. She takes life-threatening measures to join Heathcliff in his imprisonment, creeping 'by the skylight of one garret, along the roof, into the skylight of the other, and [. . . only] with the utmost difficulty [. . . can Nelly] coax her out again. When she come[s], Heathcliff [comes] with her'.[23] Even Catherine's view of heaven changes to accommodate her soul's and psyche's union with Heathcliff: 'Heaven did not seem to be my home; and I broke my heart with weeping to come back to earth; and the angels were so angry that they flung me out, into the middle of the heath on the top of Wuthering Heights; where I woke sobbing for joy'.[24] To be in heaven is to be separated from Heathcliff, and this is precisely what her psyche cannot bear or acknowledge. Similarly the notion of separation seems inscrutable to Heathcliff,—for whom 'the notion of envying Catherine was incomprehensible . . . , but the notion of grieving her he understood clearly enough.'[25]

Their sense of an undivided self is disrupted, however, when Catherine decides to marry Edgar not long after returning from the Grange. Nelly identifies the incongruities in Catherine's plans but reads them as improperly motivated romance not as growing neurosis. Catherine looks for Nelly's support to assuage her own sense that 'in whichever place the soul lives—in my soul, and in my heart, I'm convinced I'm wrong!'.[26] Nelly simply does not understand what causes Catherine's dilemma. On one level, Catherine is genuinely trying to recognize and accept the reality that she and Heathcliff are two separate selves. Her plan to marry Edgar confirms this. Yet, she is unable to sever her psyche from Heathcliff's notwithstanding her impending marriage to another. She tells Nelly she loves Heathcliff "not because he's handsome, Nelly, but because he's more myself than I am. Whatever our souls are made of, his and mine are the same, and Linton's is as different as a moonbeam from lightning, or frost from fire".[27] In her mind they are one self, one psyche.

Judith Weissman suggests that Catherine's contradictory behaviour and thought derive from her inability to understand 'the strength of her true nature, which will draw her into self-starvation, madness, and finally, self-chosen death when Heathcliff returns, a few years later, to destroy her illusion of bourgeois respectability'.[28] Rather than the loss of 'bourgeois respectability' that converts Catherine's neurotic melancholia into psychosis, it is her resisting of matricide that maintains the 'unsplit' Catherine-Heathcliff self:

> My great miseries in this world have been Heathcliff's miseries, and I watched and felt each from the beginning; my great thought in living is himself. If all else perished and *he* remained, I should still continue to be; and, if all else remained, and he were annihilated, the Universe would turn to a mighty stranger. I should not seem a part of it. My love for Linton is like the foliage in the woods. Time will change it, I'm well aware, as winter changes the trees. My love for Heathcliff resembles the eternal rocks beneath . . . Nelly, I *am* Heathcliff—he's always, always in my mind—not as a pleasure, any more that I am always a pleasure to myself—but as my own being—so, don't talk of our separation again—it is impractical; and—[29]

Catherine simply cannot accept the loss of seeing Heathcliff as separated from her self. Her 'denial [is] the rejection of the signifier [Heathcliff—the sign which signifies the loss]'[30] as the man to whom she is not joined in any legally/symbolically-codified way.

Heathcliff's abrupt departure, having overheard her plans, drives her to hysteria and depression. Heathcliff's escape response is ultimately futile however. The loss of Catherine as maternal object become transitional is one that Heathcliff is compelled to deny and to project onto an 'other'. Such projection only masks the genuine pain, hatred, anger, and guilt (linked to/directed at Catherine) her loss evokes in him. When he confronts Catherine after his three-year absence, he simultaneously vents and masks his anger and guilt:

> 'I want you to be aware that I *know* you have treated me infernally—infernally! Do you hear? And if you think I can be consoled by sweet words you are an idiot; and if you fancy I'll suffer unrevenged, I'll convince you of the contrary, in a very little while! [. . .] I seek no revenge on you,' replied Heathcliff less vehemently [. . .] 'You are welcome to torture me to death for your amusement, only allow me to amuse myself a little in the same style, and refrain from insult, as much as you are able. Having levelled my palace, don't erect a hovel and complacently admire your own charity in giving me that for a home.'[31]

Heathcliff's loss engenders his melancholia. He and the depressed patients in Kristeva's study '*disavow the negation* [the necessary lack out of which language, signifiers, arise]: they cancel it out, suspend it, and nostalgically fall back on the real object (the Thing) of their loss, which is just what they do not manage to lose, to which they remain painfully riveted'.[32] Thus he can say at Catherine's deathbed, 'I forgive what you have done to me. I love *my* murderer—but *yours*! How can I?'.[33]

Edgar is, of course, Catherine's murderer in Heathcliff's view and receives the brunt of their anger. They project their concurrent hatred of and guilt over the other onto Edgar. He, like Nelly, stands outside their melancholia thus cannot read its signs as they do. The three-year separation and the division in their joint self that Edgar, as Catherine's husband, represents evaporates as if neither had occurred. Catherine and Heathcliff reconstitute their undifferentiated self in defiance of the actual constraints the Symbolic Order of marriage places on their undivided self: 'They were too much absorbed in their mutual joy to suffer embarrassment. Not so Mr. Edgar; he grew pale with pure annoyance'.[34]

Readers participate in both the melancholy perspective of Heathcliff and Catherine and the sane lucidity of Edgar and Nelly. It is this 'lucid' perspective that provokes the suicidal view of Catherine's murderer. Catherine is her own murderer, starving herself into a raving madness that kills her precisely because she refuses to acknowledge her position in the Symbolic Order as a self (a married woman in this instance) differentiated from Heathcliff, the 'other' whom she refuses to see as anything apart from her 'self.' We cannot help but recognize that 'violent sexuality seethes beneath the surface of [these] dark characters'.[35] Kristeva notes that 'the analysis of depression involves bringing to the fore the realization that the complaint against oneself is a hatred for the other, which is without doubt the substratum of an unsuspected sexual desire'.[36] This repressed sexual desire and rage is clearly evident in Heathcliff's revenge and in Catherine's scorn when Isabella vies for Heathcliff's affection:

> 'Heathcliff is—an unreclaimed creature, without refinement, without cultivation; an arid wilderness of furze and whinstone. I'd as soon put that little canary into the park on a winter's day as recommend you to bestow your heart on him! It is deplorable ignorance of his character, child, and nothing else, which makes that dream enter your head. Pray don't imagine that he conceals depths of benevolence and affection beneath a stern exterior! He's not a rough diamond—a pearl-containing oyster of a rustic; he's a fierce, pitiless, wolfish man [. . .] he'd crush you, like a sparrow's egg, Isabella, if he found you a troublesome charge [. . .]. There's my picture; and I'm his friend—so much so, that had he thought seriously to catch you, I should, perhaps, have held my tongue, and let you fall into his trap.'[37]

In Van Ghent's words, Catherine's behaviour belies 'a tension between two kinds of reality, a restrictive reality of civilized manners and codes, and the anonymous unregenerate reality of natural energies'.[38]

Catherine intuits that Edgar's stature as husband/signifier of separation can become the wedge that forces a rupture in their undifferentiated self and an acceptance of its negation when she warns: 'Quarrel with Edgar, if you please, Heathcliff, and deceive his sister; you'll hit on exactly the most efficient method of revenging yourself on me'.[39] Catherine's already acute sense of pride intensifies in an attempt to deny the impending negation of her union with Heathcliff. 'A depressive person's pride is immeasurable',[40] and Catherine's frees her from all culpability or responsibility projecting both onto Heathcliff and Edgar: 'I'm delightfully rewarded for my kindness to each! After constant indulgence of one's weak nature, and the other's bad one, I earn, for thanks, two samples of blind ingratitude, stupid to absurdity!'.[41] Her perspective denies her unfolding psychosis and the guilt of impending matricide. It also justifies her 'suicide' to punish her tormentors. Nelly's perspective that Catherine 'was so proud, it became really impossible to pity her distresses, till she should be chastened into more humility'[42] becomes important here.

Nelly's intransigent practicality functions such that 'the novel's language of desire is constantly being absorbed into a thick, muffling wall of incomprehension'.[43] She frequently describes Catherine's frenzies as 'scene[s]

she acted'[44] attributing them to physical illness or bad temper and becomes 'convinced that the Grange had but one sensible soul in its walls',[45] her. Though not comprehended, Catherine's melancholia manifests itself on three other levels in addition to her pride, and all are captured by Nelly's narrative. The first is the 'supreme, metaphysical lucidity'[46] and 'accelerated, creative cognitive process'[47] of Catherine's mind and language. The melancholic's 'considerable associative originality'[48] is manifest in Catherine's distraction with the bird feathers to which she attributes great importance though they are wholly unrelated to the seriousness of her life-threatening delirium. She

> seemed to find childish diversion in pulling the feathers from the rents she had just made, and ranging them on the sheet according to their different species: her mind had strayed to other associations. 'That's a turkey's,' she murmured to herself; 'and this is a wild-duck's; and this is a pigeon's. Ah, they put pigeons' feathers in the pillows—no wonder I couldn't die! Let me take care to throw it on the floor when I lie down. And here is a moor-cock's; and this—I should know it among a thousand—it's a lapwing's. Bonny bird; wheeling over our heads in the middle of the moor. It wanted to get to its nest, for the clouds touched the swell, and it felt rain coming. This feather was picked up from the heath, the bird was not shot; we saw its nest in the winter, full of little skeletons. Heathcliff set a trap over it, and the old ones dare not come. I made him promise he'd never shoot a lapwing after that, and he didn't. Yes, here are more! Did he shoot my lapwings, Nelly? Are they red, any of them? Let me look.[49]

Catherine's creative association here indicates her heightened and strained melancholic awareness: 'Such hyperactivity with signifiers reveals itself particularly by connecting distant semantic fields [. . . and] is co-extensive with the cognitive hyperlucidity of depressed persons, but also with the manic-depressive's inability to decide or choose'.[50] Catherine's own inability to chose between Edgar and Heathcliff, or perhaps more accurately between Heathcliff and herself, has led her into this melancholy/depressive state, and she remains unable to effect a separation of her *self* from Heathcliff's. '[T]he terms of Catherine's speech indicate a childlike terror of solitude ('being laid alone') conjured up by the hectic and nervous brilliance of her localising imagery',[51] Davies notes. Nelly accuses Catherine of 'wandering' to which Catherine responds defensively: 'I'm not wandering: you're mistaken, or else I should believe you really *were* that withered hag, and I should think I *was* under Penistone Crag, and I'm conscious it's night, and there are two candles on the table making the black press shine like jet'.[52]

Catherine's confusion of the Grange-room mirror with the Heights' black press illustrates her second melancholia symptom, an aversion to mirrors. Catherine cannot allow the mirror's reality nor the image of her *self* that it reflects; hence, she masks both by seeing the black press in the mirror's stead. Kristeva observes 'the depressed woman cannot put up with mirrors. Her image and that of others arouse within her wounded narcissism, violence, and the desire to kill—from which she protects herself by going through the looking glass and settling down in that other world where, by limitlessly spreading her constrained sorrow, she regains a hallucinated completedness'.[53] Although Catherine sees her image in the mirror, Nelly is 'incapable of making her comprehend it to be her own'.[54]

This aversion to mirrors explains why Catherine insists that the windows in her room be opened; 'I wish I were out of doors—I wish I were a girl again, half savage, and hardy, and free; and laughing at injuries, not maddening under them! Why am I so changed? why does my blood rush into a hell of tumult at a few words? I'm sure I should be myself were I once among the heather on those hills. Open the window again wide, fasten it open! Quick, why don't you move?'.[55] With the windows open, their reflective power is removed and the ability for her to 'pass through the looking glass,' becomes a possibility. Catherine's language remains impervious to Nelly whose only concern is the physical threat of cold winds.

The third symptom of Catherine's melancholia is her reconcatenating of Heathcliff lodged in her 'mourning for an archaic and indispensable object [. . . and] transposing, beyond loss and on an imaginary or symbolic level, the imprints of an interchange with the other articulated according to a certain order.'[56] While both have tried to effect a separation by marriage, neither has been successful; thus Catherine can say to Heathcliff: 'I wish I could hold you . . . till we were both dead! I shouldn't care what you suffered. I care nothing for your sufferings. Why shouldn't you suffer? I do!'[57] When her approbations do not elicit the expected signifier of Heathcliff, she reconstructs one that will preserve their joint self: 'That's not *my* Heathcliff. I shall love mine yet; and take him with me—he's in my soul.'[58]

Since Catherine cannot keep her undivided self by keeping both Edgar and Heathcliff, she intimates her suicidal intent to Nelly: 'Well, if I cannot keep Heathcliff for my friend, if Edgar will be mean and jealous, I'll try to break their hearts by breaking my own.'[59] Although Catherine labels Heathcliff as her 'friend,' because of his connection with repressed sexual desire his loss is not that of a friend but that of erotic object of desire. In Kristevan terms, this loss is experienced by woman

> as an assault on her genitality and, from that point of view, amounts to castration. At once, such a castration

starts resonating with the threat of destruction of the body's integrity, the body image, and the entire psychic system as well. [. . .] Even though a woman has no penis to lose, it is her entire being—body and especially soul—that she feels is threatened by castration. As if her phallus were her psyche, the loss of the erotic object breaks up and threatens to empty her whole psychic life. The outer loss is immediately and depressively experienced as an inner void.[60]

Catherine's only way of holding onto the integrity of the joint self she envisions with Heathcliff is to merge with the infinite, to 'pass through the looking glass.' For Catherine, life without being joined to Heathcliff is meaningless: 'In short, a devitalized existence that, although occasionally fired by the effort [she] make[s] to prolong it, is ready at any moment for a plunge into death. An avenging death or a liberating death, it is henceforth the inner threshold of my despondency, the impossible meaning of a life whose burden constantly seems unbearable'.[61]

Catherine's wilful suicide is both liberating and avenging. She exhibits the classic signs of mourning and despising the object of desire. Because she both loves Heathcliff as her *self* and hates him as signifier of her independent *self* she behaves in the typical fashion of a depressed person: "'I love that object . . . but even more so I hate it; because I love it, and in order not to lose it, I imbed it in myself; but because I hate it that other within myself is a bad self, I am bad, I am nonexistent, I shall kill myself." The complaint against oneself . . . [is thus] a complaint against another, and putting oneself to death but a tragic disguise for massacring an other.'[62]

Once Catherine dies, Heathcliff's own melancholia fills the horizon of the second half of the novel as Catherine's does the first. Virtually everything—the Heights, the Grange, Catherine's grave, Edgar, Cathy (born the night of Catherine's death), Hareton—becomes a signifier of Heathcliff's loss of Catherine, who has all along been his maternal object, his object of desire. Even her grave, which is perhaps the most fixed of all signifiers of absence, denies the reality of his loss. When he unearths the lid of Catherine's coffin, he finds that 'her flesh has not begun to decompose' which suggests 'there seems [to be] no final dissolution'.[63] Heathcliff, though 'knowingly disinherited of the Thing [object of desire . . .] wanders in pursuit of continuously disappointing adventures and loves; or else retreats, disconsolate and aphasic, alone with the unnamed Thing.'[64]

Indeed Heathcliff's pursuit of the 'Thing' becomes *the* fundamental signifier of Catherine's continued presence in his world: 'What he resists is her evacuation from reality. He does not resist, rather, welcomes, his own pain as a testament to the possibility of her immanence, invoking her to haunt him'.[65] At the moment when readers first encounter the suicidal bleeding wrist image, we are also confronted with Heathcliff's pleading for Catherine to haunt him: '"Come in! come in! . . . Cathy, do come in. Oh, do—*once* more! Oh! my heart's darling, hear me *this* time—Catherine, at last!"'.[66] Clearly Heathcliff has repeatedly begged Catherine to haunt him since Lockwood's dream occurs 17-18 years after Catherine's death.[67] Further, Nelly also relates Heathcliff's prayer to Catherine: '"Be with me always—take any form—drive me mad! Only *do* not leave me in this abyss, where I cannot find you! Oh God! it is unutterable! I *cannot* live without my life! I *cannot* live without my soul!"'.[68]

His sustained torment is not the only signifier of Catherine. Both Hareton and Cathy junior, or, perhaps more accurately, Heathcliff's hatred of the two are signifiers of Catherine. Heathcliff's unrecoverable loss manifests itself in the endless energy of destruction that he directs, first toward Edgar and Hindley, then toward Hareton and Cathy. It is during one of his violent struggles with Hindley that the second bleeding wrist image appears: 'The knife, in springing back, closed into its owner's [Hindley's] wrist. Heathcliff pulled it away by main force, slitting up the flesh as it passed on, and thrust it dripping into his pocket. . . . [Hindley] had fallen senseless with excessive pain and the flow of blood that gushed from an artery, or a large vein.'[69] This image reverberates with the suicidal depression that pervades the text. Heathcliff, like Catherine, becomes an omnipotent devourer, consuming the Earnshaw and Linton estates, fortunes, and heirs alike. This 'melancholy cannibalistic imagination[70] is a repudiation of the loss's reality and of death as well. It manifests the anguish of losing the other through the survival of self, surely a deserted self but not separated from what still and ever nourishes it and becomes transformed into the self—which also resuscitates—through such a devouring.'[71]

While Heathcliff's endless energy of destruction may appear as means of erasing Catherine and all her signifiers, it is the only means available to him of keeping Catherine alive. At precisely the moment when he can obliterate both Lintons and Earnshaws, he finds himself unwilling and impotent. It is 'an absurd termination to my violent exertions,' he tells Nelly:

> 'I get levers and mattocks to demolish the two houses, and train myself to be capable of working like Hercules, and when every thing is ready, and in my power, I find the will to lift a slate off either roof has vanished! My old enemies have not beaten me; now would be the precise time to revenge myself on their representatives: I could do it; and none could hinder me. But where is the use? I don't care for striking, I can't

take the trouble to raise my hand! That sounds as if I had been labouring the whole time, only to exhibit a fine trait of magnanimity. It is far from being the case—I have lost the faculty of enjoying their destruction, and I am too idle to destroy for nothing.'[72]

He intuits that to destroy them will be to destroy the signifiers of Catherine and simultaneously nullify his loss; 'To leave these signs in existence is to be tormented by the absence they all point to, but of which they also block the filling. To destroy them is to be left with nothing, not even with any signs of the fact that Cathy once existed and that he has lost her. There is no "use" in either destroying or not destroying'.[73] Like Catherine, he cannot face the inevitability of loss/separation, which his own neurosis has forced upon him:

> For such narcissistic depressed persons, sadness is really the sole object; more precisely it is a substitute object they become attached to [. . .]. In such a case, suicide is not a disguised act of war but a merging with sadness and, beyond it, with that impossible love, never reached, always elsewhere, such as the promises of nothingness, of death.[74]

Hence Heathcliff does not resist death as a signifier of separation; rather, he looks upon it as a merging with Catherine—the only means left to him of denying negation. 'I have a single wish,' he tells Nelly, 'and my whole being and faculties are yearning to attain it. They have yearned towards it so long, and so unwaveringly, that I'm convinced that it *will* be reached—and *soon*—because it has devoured my existence. I am swallowed in the anticipation of its fulfilment.'[75]

As with Catherine, Nelly confronts Heathcliff's psychotic melancholia with concern for physiological matters—his malnutrition—but does not believe his death either likely or imminent. It is indeed both, and at his deathbed the third suicidally resonant wrist appears. Nelly finds him and cannot 'think him dead, but his face and throat were washed with rain; the bedclothes dripped, and he was perfectly still. The lattice, flapping to and fro, had grazed one hand that rested on the sill; no blood trickled from the broken skin, and when I put my fingers to it, I could doubt no more—he was dead and stark!'[76] Heathcliff's torment, culminating in a wilful and ameliorating suicide produces a hand upon a windowsill with broken skin, but skin that does not bleed. Coming after the first two wrist images, both dripping with blood, this final image intimates that the melancholic suffering of negation has moved onto a metaphysical plane of symbiotic desire. Lockwood's obtuse observation confirms this: he 'lingered round [their graves], under that benign sky; watched the moths fluttering among the heath and hare-bells; listened to the soft wind breathing through the grass; and wondered how any one could ever imagine unquiet slumbers for the sleepers in that quiet earth.'[77] He may imagine such but no other character does.

Wuthering Heights not only embodies the 'unquiet slumbers' but also the suicidal reality of its melancholic, even psychotic, protagonists in handling their maternal loss. In analyzing its suicidally resonant images I aim not to repeat the error of erasing the novel's 'remainder' or to participate in Nelly's intransigent practicality, but rather to acknowledge the profound disturbance that perdures in this gothic novel. In foregrounding these images within the frame of Kristeva's work on melancholia, ***Wuthering Heights*'** realist mode, deeply grounded in human psychology, becomes apparent. Moreover, its unparalleled stature is confirmed in its 'remainder,' expressing love and desire that struggle to preclude the shining of black suns.

Notes

1. Stevie Davies, *Emily Brontë* (Bloomington: Indiana UP, 1988), 43.

2. Ellen Moers, *Literary Women: The Great Writers* (New York: Oxford UP, 1985), 102.

3. Moers, *Literary Women,* 102.

4. J. Hillis Miller, *Fiction and Repetition: Seven English Novels* (Cambridge, MA: Harvard UP, 1982), 50-51.

5. Similarly, Peter Garrett reads the novel as a case in point of the dialogical form—as a novel that 'resists any monological formulation'. P. K. Garrett, *The Victorian Multiplot Novel: Studies in Dialogical Form* (New Haven: Yale UP, 1980), 20. He, too, recognizes that 'to read [*Wuthering Heights*] in this way is not to claim mastery of [its] complexity or to unmask [its] latent contradictions but to continue the process of setting one perspective against another in which the [novel itself is] already engaged, a process which the conventions neither of narrative nor of critical argument can ever bring to more than a provisional conclusion' (20-21).

6. Stevie Davies, *Emily Brontë: The Artist as a Free Woman* (Manchester: Carcanet Press, 1983), 27.

7. My labeling all three of these images as 'wrists' is slightly inaccurate since it is Heathcliff's bloodless hand that is mentioned in the third instance. Nonetheless, following on the heels of the first two actually bleeding wrists, the similarity in all three images is inescapable.

8. Emily Brontë, *Wuthering Heights* (New York: Norton, 1972), 30.

9. Brontë, *Wuthering Heights,* 147.

10. Brontë, *Wuthering Heights,* 264.

11. Dorothy Van Ghent "The Window Figure and the Two-Children Figure in *Wuthering Heights*", *Nineteenth-Century Fiction,* 7 (Dec 1952): 189-190.

12. Brontë, *Wuthering Heights,* 32.

13. Kristeva problematizes the Oedipal foundation of Freud's theory by recognizing the work of D. W. Winnicot who discussed what he called 'transitional objects' and their role in the development of an independent *self*-image. These are objects (of desire) that chronologically and logically exist in the child's mind earlier than the concept of the mother as other. They comprise 'a series of *semi*-objects that stake out the transition from a state of indifferentiation to one of discretion (subject/object)'. Julia Kristeva, *Powers of Horror* (New York: Columbia UP, 1982), 32.

14. Julia Kristeva, *Black Sun: Depression and Melancholia* (New York: Columbia UP, 1989), 9.

15. Kristeva, *Black Sun,* 28.

16. Brontë, *Wuthering Heights,* 39.

17. Brontë, *Wuthering Heights,* 39.

18. Brontë, *Wuthering Heights,* 39.

19. Brontë, *Wuthering Heights,* 39.

20. In Winnicotian terms, Catherine becomes for Heathcliff a transitional object, taking the place of the maternal object.

21. Kristeva, *Black Sun,* 10.

22. Davies, *Emily Brontë,* 64.

23. Brontë, *Wuthering Heights,* 57.

24. Brontë, *Wuthering Heights,* 72.

25. Brontë, *Wuthering Heights,* 53.

26. Brontë, *Wuthering Heights,* 71.

27. Brontë, *Wuthering Heights,* 72.

28. Judith Weissman, *Half Savage and Hardy and Free: Women and Rural Radicalism in the Nineteenth-Century Novel* (Middletown, CT: Wesleyan University Press, 1987), 89.

29. Brontë, *Wuthering Heights,* 74.

30. Kristeva, *Black Sun,* 44.

31. Brontë, *Wuthering Heights,* 97.

32. Kristeva, *Black Sun*, 43-44.

33. Brontë, *Wuthering Heights*, 135.

34. Brontë, *Wuthering Heights*, 85.

35. Lori Hope Lefkovitz, *The Character of Beauty in the Victorian Novel* (Ann Arbor: UNI Research Press, 1987), 138.

36. Kristeva, *Black Sun*, 11.

37. Brontë, *Wuthering Heights*, 89-90.

38. Van Ghent, "The Window Figure."

39. Brontë, *Wuthering Heights*, 98.

40. Kristeva, *Black Sun*, 90.

41. Brontë, *Wuthering Heights*, 99.

42. Brontë, *Wuthering Heights*, 62.

43. Davies, *Emily Brontë*.

44. Brontë, *Wuthering Heights*, 78, 104.

45. Brontë, *Wuthering Heights*, 103.

46. Kristeva, *Black Sun*, 4.

47. Kristeva, *Black Sun*, 59.

48. Kristeva, *Black Sun*, 59.

49. Brontë, *Wuthering Heights*, 105.

50. Kristeva, *Black Sun*, 59.

51. Davies, *Emily Brontë*, 51.

52. Brontë, *Wuthering Heights*, 105.

53. Kristeva, *Black Sun*, 74.

54. Brontë, *Wuthering Heights*, 106.

55. Brontë, *Wuthering Heights*, 107.

56. Kristeva, *Black Sun*, 40.

57. Brontë, *Wuthering Heights*, 133.

58. Brontë, *Wuthering Heights*, 134.

59. Brontë, *Wuthering Heights*, 101.

60. Kristeva, *Black Sun*, 81-82.

61. Kristeva, *Black Sun*, 4.

62. Kristeva, *Black Sun*, 11.

63. Davies, *Artist*, 20.

64. Kristeva, *Black Sun*, 13.

65. Davies, *Emily Brontë*, 59.

66. Brontë, *Wuthering Heights*, 33.

67. Charles Percy Sanger "The Structure of *Wuthering Heights*," *Wuthering Heights* (New York: Norton, 1972): 229-230. Sanger's chronology situates Catherine's death in March 1784 and Lockwood's visit and dream in November 1801.

68. Brontë, *Wuthering Heights*, 139.

69. Brontë, *Wuthering Heights*, 147.

70. Kristeva is drawing on the work of Pierre Fédida's "Le Cannibalisme mélancolique," in *L'Absence* (Paris: Gillimard, 1978), 65; Kristeva, *Black Sun*, 262.

71. Kristeva, *Black Sun*, 12.

72. Brontë, *Wuthering Heights*, 255.

73. Miller, *Fiction & Representation*, 66.

74. Kristeva, *Black Sun*, 12-13.

75. Brontë, *Wuthering Heights*, 256.

76. Brontë, *Wuthering Heights*, 264.

77. Brontë, *Wuthering Heights*, 266.

FURTHER READING

Bibliography

Barclay, Janet M. *Emily Brontë Criticism, 1900-1968: An Annotated Check List.* New York: New York Public Library, 1974, 76 p.
    Lists critical writings published between 1900 and 1968 on *Wuthering Heights.*

Criticism

Barreca, Regina. "The Power of Excommunication: Sex and the Feminine Text in *Wuthering Heights.*" In *Sex and Death in Victorian Literature,* edited by Regina Barreca, pp. 227-40. London: Macmillan, 1990.
    Examines aspects of feminine discourse in *Wuthering Heights.*

Berg, Maggie. *Wuthering Heights: The Writing in the Margin.* New York: Twayne Publishers, 1996, 136 p.
    Offers a close reading of *Wuthering Heights,* along with an analysis of the work's social and historical context and a brief survey of its critical reception.

Bersani, Leo. "Desire and Metamorphosis." In *A Future for Astyanax,* pp. 189-229. Boston: Little, Brown and Company, 1976.

In-depth comparison of Brontë's narrative strategy in *Wuthering Heights* with the radical literary experimentation of the Comte de Lautréamont's *Chants de Maldoror,* paying particular attention to aspects of myth, metamorphosis, and authorial identity in the two works.

Bloom, Harold, ed. *Emily Brontë's Wuthering Heights.* New York: Chelsea House Publishers, 1987, 152 p.
Includes several critical interpretations of the novel by leading scholars.

———, ed. *Heathcliff.* New York: Chelsea House Publishers, 1993, 212 p.
Offers a number of full-length essays examining the character of Heathcliff, as well as several critical extracts of particular scholarly importance.

Harpham, Geoffrey Galt. "Walking on Silence: The Lamination of Narratives in *Wuthering Heights.*" In *On the Grotesque: Strategies of Contradiction in Art and Literature,* pp. 79-105. Princeton, N.J.: Princeton University Press, 1982.
Examines the relationship between Gothic imagery and manifestations of evil in *Wuthering Heights,* paying particular attention to the similarities between the character of Heathcliff and aspects of the grotesque in Christian art.

Homans, Margaret. "The Name of the Mother in *Wuthering Heights.*" In *Bearing the Word: Language and Female Experience in Nineteenth-Century Women's Writing,* pp. 68-83. Chicago: University of Chicago Press, 1986.
Discusses the relationship between language and female identity in *Wuthering Heights,* through a close analysis of the characters of Catherine Earnshaw and Cathy Linton.

Jacobs, Carol. "At the Threshold of Interpretation." In *Uncontainable Romanticism: Shelley, Brontë, Kleist,* pp. 61-81. Baltimore: Johns Hopkins University Press, 1989.
Examines the relationship between dreams and storytelling in the narrative technique of *Wuthering Heights.*

Klingopulos, G. D. "The Novel As Dramatic Poem (II): *Wuthering Heights.*" *Scrutiny* 14, no. 4 (September 1947): 269-86.
Argues that the prose style of *Wuthering Heights* is essentially dramatic in quality by comparing the major speeches in the novel to the writings of Elizabethan playwrights, both in tone and in ambition.

Knoepflmacher, U. C. *Wuthering Heights: A Study.* Athens: Ohio University Press, 1989, 138 p.

Comprehensive analysis of *Wuthering Heights,* discussing the work's narrative structure, major themes, and critical reception.

Maeterlinck, Maurice. *Wisdom and Destiny,* pp. 295-320. New York: Dodd, Mead and Co., 1898.
Offers a contemplative, personal meditation on *Wuthering Heights.*

McGuire, Kathryn B. "The Incest Taboo in *Wuthering Heights*: A Modern Appraisal." *American Imago* 45, no. 2 (summer 1988): 217-24.
Analyzes elements of incest and transgression in the relationship between Heathcliff and Catherine.

Miller, J. Hillis. "*Wuthering Heights*: Repetition and the 'Uncanny.'" In *Fiction and Repetition,* pp. 42-72. Cambridge: Harvard University Press, 1982.
Offers a deconstructionist interpretation of *Wuthering Heights.*

Newman, Beth. "'The Situation of the Looker-On': Gender, Narration, and Gaze in *Wuthering Heights.*" *PMLA* 105, no. 4 (October 1990): 1029-41.
Examines various aspects of the "gaze" in *Wuthering Heights,* while discussing the relevance of visual metaphors to a feminist critical interpretation of the novel.

Paglia, Camille. "Romantic Shadows: Emily Brontë." In *Sexual Personae: Art and Decadence from Nefertiti to Emily Dickinson,* pp. 439-59. New Haven, Conn.: Yale University Press, 1990.
Examines the tension between morality and paganism at the heart of *Wuthering Heights,* while arguing that Heathcliff's demonic power resides in his embodiment of both male and female sexual characteristics.

Parker, Patricia. "The (Self)-Identity of the Literary Text: Property, Propriety, Proper Place, and Proper Name in *Wuthering Heights.*" In *Identity of the Literary Text,* edited by Mario J. Valdés and Owen Miller, pp. 92-116. Toronto: University of Toronto Press, 1985.
Examines the ways that *Wuthering Heights* both conforms to and subverts Enlightenment concepts of order and linearity.

Reynolds, Thomas. "Division and Unity in *Wuthering Heights.*" *University Review* 32, no. 1 (October 1965): 31-7.
Examines the complex narrative framework of *Wuthering Heights.*

Seichepine, Marielle. "Childhood and Innocence in *Wuthering Heights.*" *Brontë Studies* 29, no. 3 (November 2004): 209-15.

Argues that *Wuthering Heights* introduces a darker, more perverse conception of childhood than any previously depicted in English literature.

Thomas, Ronald R. "Dreams and Disorders in *Wuthering Heights*." In *Dreams of Authority: Freud and the Fictions of the Unconscious,* pp. 112-35. Ithaca, N.Y.: Cornell University Press, 1990.

Examines aspects of madness, grief, and emotional disturbance in *Wuthering Heights.*

Traversi, Derek. "*Wuthering Heights*: After a Hundred Years." *Dublin Review,* no. 449 (spring 1949): 154-68.

Examines the novel's central themes, as well as its critical significance.

von Sneidern, Maja-Lisa. "*Wuthering Heights* and the Liverpool Slave Trade." *ELH* 62, no. 1 (spring 1995): 171-96.

Evaluates various aspects of *Wuthering Heights*—notably the novel's historical context and dominant imagery—against the backdrop of Liverpool's prosperous slave trade of the eighteenth century.

Watson, Melvin R. "Tempest in the Soul: The Theme and Structure of *Wuthering Heights*." *Nineteenth-Century Fiction* 4, no. 2 (September 1949): 87-100.

Examines the close relationship between Brontë's choice of narrative structure and the novel's central themes.

Yaeger, Patricia. "The Novel and Laughter: *Wuthering Heights*." In *Honey-Mad Women: Emancipatory Strategies in Women's Writing,* pp. 177-206. New York: Columbia University Press, 1988.

Discusses aspects of female emancipation and self-determination in *Wuthering Heights.*

Additional coverage of Brontë's life and career is contained in the following sources published by Thomson Gale: *Authors and Artists for Young Adults,* **Vol. 17;** *Beacham's Encyclopedia of Popular Fiction: Biography & Resources,* **Vol. 1;** *Beacham's Guide to Literature for Young Adults,* **Vol. 3;** *British Writers,* **Vol. 5;** *British Writers: The Classics,* **Vol. 1;** *British Writers Retrospective Supplement,* **Vol. 1;** *Concise Dictionary of British Literary Biography, 1832-1890; Dictionary of Literary Biography,* **Vols. 21, 32, 199;** *DISCovering Authors; DISCovering Authors: British Edition; DISCovering Authors: Canadian Edition; DISCovering Authors Modules: Most-studied Authors, Novelists,* **and** *Poets; DISCovering Authors 3.0; Exploring Novels; Feminism in Literature: A Gale Critical Companion,* **Vol. 2;** *Gothic Literature: A Gale Critical Companion,* **Vol. 2;** *Literature and Its Times,* **Vol. 1;** *Literature Resource Center; Nineteenth-Century Literature Criticism,* **Vols. 16, 35;** *Novels for Students,* **Vol. 2;** *Poetry Criticism,* **Vol. 8;** *Reference Guide to English Literature,* **Vol. 2;** *Twayne's English Authors; World Literature and Its Times,* **Vol. 3; and** *World Literature Criticism,* **Vol. 1.**

George Washington Harris
1814-1869

(Also wrote under the pseudonyms Mr. Free and Sugartail) American sketch writer.

The following entry provides an overview of Harris's life and works. For additional information on his career, see *NCLC,* Volume 23.

INTRODUCTION

Harris was one of the most eccentric and audacious of the nineteenth-century Southwestern humorists. Armed with a caustic wit and a keen ear for the popular vernacular of his day, Harris wrote numerous humorous and satirical sketches over the course of his career, and his writings appeared in the leading newspapers of his day, both in the North and the South. He remains most famous for creating the character of Sut Lovingood, a larger-than-life social outcast and practical joker whose observations about Christianity, politics, and sex contravened the literary and social conventions of the era. While Harris emerged from the same tradition as such "gentleman humorists" as A. B. Longstreet and Joseph Glover Baldwin, his storytelling represents a radical departure from the refined, decorous fiction of his predecessors. Irreligious, hard-drinking, and vengeful, Sut Lovingood inhabits a different world than his fictional antecedents, one where the boundaries between conventional morality, individual free will, and racial violence are obscured. Harris's raucous, often lewd depictions of frontier life have had a profound impact on generations of Southern writers, notably Mark Twain, William Faulkner, and Flannery O'Connor. Although Harris's use of obscure Southern dialect poses a unique challenge to modern readers, his sketches remain significant both as representative examples of the American tall tale and as vital documents of Southern political and social attitudes in the years leading up to the Civil War.

BIOGRAPHICAL INFORMATION

Harris was born in Allegheny City, Pennsylvania, on March 20, 1814. At the age of five he moved to Knoxville, Tennessee, with his half-brother, Samuel Bell, who taught him the metalworking trade. Harris received little formal education as a child, and throughout his late teens and early twenties he held a variety of jobs, among them steamboat captain, railroad worker, and

farmer. These years of wandering from job to job exposed the young Harris to a wide range of personalities, scenarios, and experiences that would later inform his fiction. During this period he met Mary Emeline Nance, whom he married in 1835. Critics generally believe that Harris launched his writing career around the year 1840 with the publication of several political articles in the *Argus and Commercial Herald,* a Democratic newspaper based in Knoxville. His first humor pieces began to appear in 1843 under the alias "Mr. Free." Published in the New York newspaper *Spirit of the Times,* these early sketches focused on sporting topics and employed the popular literary conventions of the day. Harris's distinctive colloquial style emerged two years later, with the publication of "The Knob Dance, a Tennessee Frolic." This sketch, published under the new pseudonym "Sugartail," introduced the character of Dick Harlan, a backwoodsman whose folksy, plainspoken diction embodies the narrative style that would reach its maturity in the Sut Lovingood sketches. Although Harris's sketches from these years had begun to attract a modest readership, he struggled to support his family, and throughout the early 1850s he moved frequently, piecing together a living as a silversmith, the supervisor of a glass factory, and a mine surveyor. In this last profession Harris met Sut Miller, who would become the inspiration for the character of Sut Lovingood.

Harris's breakthrough story, "Sut Lovingood's Daddy, Acting Horse," appeared in the November 4, 1854, issue of the *Spirit of the Times.* A year later Harris returned to Knoxville, where he devoted himself more seriously to his writing and became deeply involved in secessionist politics. The next few years marked the most productive period of Harris's literary career. He produced several of his most enduring humorous sketches, in addition to writing political propaganda in support of the Confederacy, often using Sut Lovingood as a fictional spokesman for his own anti-Union sentiments. Between 1854 and 1861 Harris published more than twenty-five new Sut Lovingood sketches in a variety of newspapers, among them the Nashville *Union & American,* the Savannah *Morning News,* and the New York *Picayune.* At the onset of the Civil War Harris left Knoxville, traveling with his wife and children to various towns throughout the South for the duration of the war. He resumed writing his Sut Lovingood sketches when the war ended, eventually compiling them into the 1867 collection, *Sut Lovingood, Yarns Spun by a "Nat'ral Born Durn'd Fool."* It would be the only book Harris would publish in his lifetime. After the death of his wife in 1867, Harris continued to publish sketches and satires with the aim of compiling them into a new collection. In October 1869 Harris married Jane E. Pride in Decatur, Alabama. He died of apoplexy two months later, during a trip to Lynchburg, Virginia.

MAJOR WORKS

Harris remains best known for *Sut Lovingood, Yarns Spun by a "Nat'ral Born Durn'd Fool."* A collection of twenty-four sketches, the book included only eight pieces previously published in newspapers, most of which were extensively revised. The sketches employ a wide range of literary styles and techniques, weaving together satire, parable, and exaggeration to evoke the vibrant, chaotic, and violent nature of frontier life. The early Sut Lovingood sketches generally take the form of a framed narrative, in which a gentleman, usually the author himself, introduces Sut's story. In the book's first sketch, "Sut Lovingood's Daddy, Acting Horse," Harris introduces many of the key elements of his literary style, including the sardonic character portrayals, the grotesque evocations of wilderness living, and Sut's distinctive mean streak. As Harris's style evolved, he began to rely exclusively on idiomatic speech to tell his stories, allowing Sut to emerge as a fully realized fic-

tional voice, as well as the embodiment of Southerners' rapidly growing antipathy toward the North. Sketches like "Sut Lovingood Escapes Assassination" and "Sut Lovingood's Adventures in New York" give free rein to Harris's prejudices, as Sut heaps scorn on a variety of Northeast character types. Sut's mean-spirited, antisocial behavior reaches new heights in "Sut Lovingood's Big Dinner Story," in which he exacts revenge on a society lady. In "Blown Up with Soda," Harris turns the tables on Sut—when Sut attempts to seduce small-town beauty Sicily Burns, he becomes the object of a cruel practical joke. "Blown Up with Soda" is especially noteworthy for its ribald treatment of the sexual tension between Sut and Sicily, as well as for its unusually frank descriptions of female anatomy.

Although *Sut Lovingood, Yarns Spun by a "Nat'ral Born Durn'd Fool"* offers a representative selection of Harris's sketches, it failed to include some of his classic stories, such as "Sut Lovingood's Chest Story," a bawdy tale of adultery involving Sicily Burns. The book also omits all of Harris's political satire sketches, which offer a sobering glimpse into Harris's vitriolic, anti-Union attitudes. Indeed, the majority of Harris's writings remained uncollected at the time of his death. In the early 1960s, however, the Sut Society, a group of scholars dedicated to generating interest in Harris's work, published the series *Lovingood Papers,* which included much of the author's previously uncollected material along with critical assessments of his works. In 1966 M. Thomas Inge edited *Sut Lovingood's Yarns,* an expanded edition of Harris's collection. *High Times and Hard Times,* a volume of Harris's unpublished sketches, followed in 1967.

CRITICAL RECEPTION

Although enormously popular with the reading public in Harris's lifetime, *Sut Lovingood, Yarns Spun by a "Nat'ral Born Durn'd Fool"* failed to elicit a substantial reaction from critics at the time of its publication, with the notable exception of Mark Twain, who was an early champion of the book. While Harris's sketches appeared in a number of prominent anthologies in the late 1800s, most editors and reviewers took pains to distance themselves from his work, which was regarded as obscene by the literary establishment of the period. Harris first gained significant critical recognition in the 1930s, when scholars like Constance Rourke and Walter Blair began to recognize the importance of Harris's writings in the development of American fiction, regarding him as the most significant humorist before Mark Twain. In the 1940s Donald Day wrote seminal articles on Harris's life and political satire sketches. Brom Weber, editor of a 1954 edition of Harris's stories titled *Sut Lovingood,* was among the first to assert that

Harris's stories contained a distinct social message. *Lovingood Papers,* a series containing Harris's unpublished sketches with commentary from such scholars as McClary, Weber, and Blair, was published from 1962 to 1965. In 1965 Milton Rickels published *George Washington Harris,* the first major full-length critical study of the author. One noteworthy dissenter to this chorus of praise was Edmund Wilson, who dubbed the Sut Lovingood stories "repellent," while describing Harris as a "peasant squatting in his own filth." In recent years scholars have examined the latent racism of the Lovingood tales, arguing that the anger and hostility depicted in Harris's writing played a distinct role in the development of segregationist rhetoric during the Reconstruction era.

PRINCIPAL WORKS

Sut Lovingood, Yarns Spun by a "Nat'ral Born Durn'd Fool," Warped and Wove for Public Wear (sketches) 1867; revised as *Sut Lovingood's Yarns: Edited for the Modern Reader,* 1966

Sut Lovingood Travels with Old Abe Lincoln (sketches) 1937

Sut Lovingood (sketches) 1954

High Times and Hard Times: Sketches and Tales by George Washington Harris (sketches and letters) 1967

CRITICISM

Henry Watterson (essay date 1882)

SOURCE: Watterson, Henry. "Sut Lovingood." In *Oddities in Southern Life and Character.* 1882. Reprint, pp. 415-38. Boston: Houghton, Mifflin & Co., 1910.

[*In the following excerpt, Watterson praises the authenticity of Harris's protagonist, Sut Lovingood, as well as the lively humor of his stories.*]

"Sut Lovingood" belongs to a class which is but little known even in the South. The gulf between him and Simon Suggs is impassable. He is no relation to Major Jones, or even to Ransy Sniffle. His ilk is small, his base of operations limited, and his lingo his own. But he is genuine. In spite of his amazing oddities and his audacious flights of fancy, he was, on his first appearance, recognized and welcomed as native and to the manner born.

George W. Harris, to whom "Sut" owes the honor of paternity, was a quiet, rather sombre gentleman, who lived and died in East Tennessee, where he was born and reared. His contributions were originally made to the "Union and American," of Nashville, and thence collected in a volume, issued by Dick & Fitzgerald. His humor is very rough, and often of the coarsest; but it is full of comic situation, plot, and phrasing.

One at least of "Sut's" adventures has crossed the Atlantic to do duty in one of the acts of a comedy by Sardou, and not a few of the conceits and oddities, with which his exploits abound, have reappeared in our domestic dramas. The hero himself, however, has never been attempted on the stage. He is a little too lively and a little too uncouth, perhaps, for presentation *in propriâ personâ.* Nevertheless, he is vastly funny, and in the hands of an American actor—such, for example, as Mr. Toole is to the comic life of London—would certainly prove effective.

There is, as will be observed, as little attempt at technical literary finish, either in description or proportion, in **"Sut Lovingood"** as in the rest of the sketches of which it is an example; the author seeming to aim merely at his point, and, this reached, to be satisfied to leave it to work out its own moral and effect.

George F. Mellen (essay date 11 February 1909)

SOURCE: Mellen, George F. "Sut Lovingood's Yarns." *Knoxville Sentinel* (11 February 1909): 4.

[*In the following essay, Mellen defends Harris's sketches against charges that they are indecent or offensive, insisting that beneath the surface of the author's grotesque caricatures of Southern life lies a subtle wit, a powerful command of the English language, and genuine pathos.*]

"Have you a copy of George W. Harris' **Sut Lovingood's Yarns**?"

The inquiry was put to the librarian of one of the two large libraries in the city which Harris made his home for the greater part of his life. It emanated from a professor of English in the institution which possessed the other large library.

The answer of the librarian was a negative. The seeker after Tennessee's most widely known book of humor doubtless thought it strange that his search should be so rewarded. Its author spent almost fifty years in Knoxville. The local color of his stories belonged to East Tennessee. The characters in the main were presented as types of the region.

It is true, the characters are grotesque in their exaggerations. In some of the passages, there are suggestions that offend. There is an indelicacy repulsive to those of squeamish tastes. One of Puritanic mould would exclude the work as inimical to decency. The ultra orthodox would denounce it as hurtful to religious worship and sentiment. In the preface, "Sut" gives fair warning to such critics. Speaking to his interlocutor, "George," he says: "I wants to put sum whar atween the eyebrows ove our book, in big winnin-lookin letters, the sarchin, meanin words, what sum pusson writ ontu a 'oman's garter onst, long ago—"

"Evil be to him that evil thinks," "George" interposes.

"Them's em, by jingo! I want em for a gineral skeer—speshully fur the wimin."

However, between the lids of *Sut Lovingood's Yarns* there is many a hearty laugh. There is much sound philosophy. Underneath the bald caricatures and the canny situations there is much of rollicking humor. Here and there are touches of pathos. In the sketch, **"Trapping a Sheriff,"** that is a fine passage which describes the sickly wife of the faithless husband, "Sheriff Doltin," calmly awaiting her end. After picturing her wan cheeks, shrunken form, and hacking cough, "Sut" says:

"Yit in spite ove all this, a sweet smile kiver'd her feeters, like a patch ove winter sunshine on the slope ove a mountin, an' hit staid thar as steddy an' bright as the culler dus tu the rose. I 'speck that smile will go back up wif her when she starts home, whar it mus' a-cum frum. She must onst been mons'us temtin tu men tu look at, an' now she's loved by the angils, fur the seal ove thar king is stamp'd in gold on her forrid. Her shoulder blades, as they show'd thru her dress, made me think they wer wings a sproutin' fur her flight tu that comfort and peace she desarves so well. She's a dealin' wif death now."

As a touch of unadulterated philosophy, this is excellent: "Ef ever you dus enything to enybody wifout cause, you hates em allers arterwards, an' sorter wants to hurt em agin. An' yere's anuther human nater: Ef enything happens to sum feller, I don't keer ef he's yure bes' friend, an' I don't keer how sorry yu is fur him, thar's a streak ove satisfackshun 'bout like a sowin thread a-runnin all through yer sorrer. Yu may be shamed ove hit, but durn me ef hit ain't thar."

While Harris spent most of his life in and about Knoxville, his last years were passed in Chattanooga, Trenton, Ga., and Decatur, Ala. When he died a sudden and mysterious death in Knoxville, December 11, 1869, his remains were taken to Chattanooga for interment. In this city he was intimate with William Crutchfield, who for one term, 1873-1875, represented the Chattanooga district in congress. Hesitating to whom he will dedicate his yarns, "George" makes the suggestion to "Sut" that this dedication would be appropriate: "To William Crutchfield. of Chattanooga, my friend in storm and sunshine, brave enough to be true, and true enough to be singular; one who says what he thinks, and very often thinks what he says." To this "Sut" philosophically objects: "Ef ever yu is grateful at all, show hit tu them what yu expeck will du yu a favor, never tu the 'tarnil fool what hes dun hit."

Harris was a versatile genius. Besides author, he was silversmith, engineer, steamboat captain, railroad constructor and postmaster. He was captain of the steamboat "Knoxville," which plied between Knoxville and Chattanooga. When the latter was used in conveying the Cherokee Indians westward, the name "Indian Chief" was substituted. There is little local coloring discernible in the sketches. Here and there are mentioned Black Oak Ridge, Hiwassee Copper Mine, Frog Mountain, indicating the region other than Knoxville wherein he found some of his characters and scenes. One reading the quotations from the *Yarns* should not regard the author lacking in ability to use choice English and to indulge in tender sentiment. A passage betraying these qualities and full of local color is in the sketch, **"Eaves-Dropping a Lodge of Free Masons."** To those still living, the names of places and men will recall fond memories. Inasmuch as "George" was a participant, "Sut" insists that he tell the story, who begins:

"But ever now, and here in the thickening twilight, I see gliding past in misty ranks, the forms of Jackson, Hu Lawson White, the Williamses, the Dunlaps, Haywood, Peck, Powell, McKinney, Pleasant Miller, the Andersons, Carrick White, and Mynatt Scott. In my boyish eyes they seemed giants, and manhood's more discriminating gaze sees them undiminished. The quiet grave has long ago claimed the last of the band, but memory preserves their fame and deeds of well-doing. There too is 'College Hill,' with its clear cool spring at the foot, the 'Bluff,' with its triple echo, the 'Flag Pond,' and its sunny-sided inhabitants, 'Old Aunt Edy's' cakes and beer, the White mill and its dripping dam, Scuffletown Crick, and its walnut trees, the 'Dardis lot with its forbidden grapes,' 'Witt's old field, and its forbidden blackberries,' the 'old church' and its graveyard. 'Tis strange how faithfully memory paints the paths and places belonging to our boyhood. The march of improvement first, then the march and crash of armies, have nearly swept away those, to me, almost sacred places. But they and those who 'were boys then,' still have a place in memory that time nor distance can take, nor the pressing, crowding, bloody events of now dim, nor sorrow obliterate with its tears."

Here, "Sut" interrupts "George's" sentiment and memories, with an outburst, "Oh, komplicated durnashun; that haint hit; yu's drunk," and proceeds to tell it in his own vernacular.

"College Hill" is now the University of Tennessee, with its varied life and numerous buildings. Where the "Flag Pond" stood is now the seat of a busy commerce. The wholesale houses on Jackson street, the railroad depot and yards of the Southern railway, and elevated thoroughfares tell little of the spreading bosom of the waters on which the village lads sailed their tiny crafts and into which they dashed and splashed. The "old church" was old Methodist Hill that stood with its graveyard across First creek. The forests on the neighboring hillside had been made resonant with the eloquence of Tennessee's most gifted and renowned orator, William T. Haskell, whose name Harris calls up in the sketch, **"Dad's Dog School."**

Despite his coarseness here and there, in healthy minds the *Yarns* of "Sut Lovingood" are provocative of merriment. They are in no sense intended to be faithful portrayals of the people among whom Harris dwelt and whom he loved. They are simply the outcome of a riotous imagination, which reveled in a keen sense of the ludicrous and grotesque. They are far removed from delicate, delicious humor, taking on its boisterous and outlandish phases.

Donald Day (essay date December 1945)

SOURCE: Day, Donald. "The Political Satires of George W. Harris." *Tennessee Historical Quarterly* 4, no. 4 (December 1945): 320-38.

[*In the following essay, Day examines Harris's sketches within the context of the political writing of the period. Day argues that Harris's contributions to the rich tradition of satirical journalism represent its high point in Civil War-era Tennessee, while offering the modern reader a vital glimpse into the prevailing political and social attitudes of the times.*]

Mark Twain had examples by the score when he wrote his rollicking sketch on "Journalism in Tennessee." The spirit of the early Tennessee press was bellicose, to put it mildly, and that bellicosity is best seen perhaps in political satires which occupy a sizable portion of all newspaper space in the South before and after the Civil War. These satires, saturated with the vigor and combativeness of a frontier people, furnish excellent illustrative material for the historian, the political scientist, and the student of American literature.

George W. Harris (1814-1869), long famous for the *Sut Lovingood Yarns,* perhaps raised the political satire to its peak of robustness. Harris, who was born in Allegheny City, Pennsylvania, spent most of his life in Knoxville, Tennessee. His schooling was meager, probably not exceeding eighteen months, but he learned to be a careful workman by serving an apprenticeship in a jewelry shop. When he came of age, he worked three years as captain of a steamboat; farmed for an equal period in the foothills of the Smokies; and then established a metal working shop in Knoxville, which he operated for seven years, making and repairing anything from the smallest screw to a steam engine. During the 1850's, when the economy and politics of Knoxville were changing rapidly, he established and managed a glass works, again captained a steamboat, established a sawmill, surveyed and managed the Ducktown copper mines, served as postmaster at Knoxville, became an important political figure in the state, and in the later years of the decade turned to railroading, which held him until his death.

Recent critics have noticed how this wide experience was tapped by Harris' imagination and Rabelaisian touch so that "scent, sound, form, color, and motion" become "not only vividly lifelike but also hilariously comic." His "keen eye and ear" which he used to "portray the frontier life with both realism and extravagance" help to give him on the comic level "something of what Melville" possesses on the tragic, "the rare kind of dramatic imagination that can get movement directly into words."[1] The purpose of this study is to examine some of Harris' political satires, not as humorous works, but against their background to determine their value as interpretative material.

Harris' first political writings are buried in the files of the Knoxville *Argus and Commercial Herald,* a newspaper established by the Democratic party in Tennessee when James K. Polk stepped down from the speakership of the House of Representatives in 1839 to wrest the governorship from the Whig incumbent, Newton Cannon.[2] As was the custom, political polemics appeared in the *Argus* over such pseudonyms as Cato, Cicero, Veritas, Franklin, Salmagundi, etc. Although it is known that Harris wrote a number of these sketches, a selection of the specific ones would rest on inconclusive evidence.[3]

Following this beginning, in so far as is known, Harris wrote no more political sketches until 1856. Perhaps he was too busy with his personal affairs; perhaps the political situation did not arouse his fighting spirit. Actually, during the decade from 1840 to 1850 there was almost a phenomenal evenness "with which the Whig and Democratic parties were balanced" in Tennessee. With a total vote between 100,000 and 125,000, no party received more than a 4,000 majority in the governor's election.[4] A plausible explanation for Harris' silence may be found in a statement which he later has Sut Lovingood make: "Ez a general thing, afore this, humuns hev hed but wun kind ove varmints to fite at a time."[5] It may have been, therefore, the new interest aroused by the realignment and reshuffling of groups into new party structures which in 1856 caused him to write on politics again.[6]

With a number of "varmints" to fight, Harris brings his comic character, Sut Lovingood, into the fray when on October 18, 1856, he published **"Playing Old Sledge for the Presidency—A Dream of Sut Lovingood's"** in the Nashville *Union and American*.[7] In this sketch Harris pictures the political campaigns of Buchanan, Fillmore, and Fremont for the Presidency as a game of old sledge (seven-up). In a dream Sut witnesses the game in a room at the Willard Tavern in Washington City. Another man [Seward] looks on "with one hand under his cotail, an tother a strokin ove his chin as he peeps into the hands of Fillmore and Freemount." He tries to peep at "Buck-cannon's" hand, but

> . . . the old feller hilt it under the shadder ov the table and sorter looked at it sideways his self, an was a watchin the peepin feller, too, all the while rite clost . . .

Clearly, Seward will go where he sees success but Buchanan—Harris' man—will have nothing to do with him. The two other players allow "peeps" and Sut sees that the game is "two pluck one and Buck-cannon" is bound to be skinned "ef his hide" doesn't "grow fast onto his bones" and Seward is the "darn'd snake in the grass" who will do it.

The points of the game—Harris' estimate of the chance for success of the players—stand at six for Buchanan, six for Fremont, and three for Fillmore. It is Buchanan's deal. He "licks his thumb" and deals the "kerds mity slow and keerful." Fremont has the right to stand or beg. Trump is turned and Sut first looks into Fillmore's hand and

> . . . thar was the *ace*, the king, the queen, the jack, the ten and the *juice* ove trumps . . . and thar the old feller sot, his belly kiverin the cheer all over, an nearly out tu his knees, as solemn, as big, and about as wise as an ole Dutch squire a tryin ove a bastardy case with good proof again the daddy . . . he looked jist like he had his fust big horn ove whisky fur the nite, and felt it in his boots.

Obviously, if Fremont stands (if the machinations of Seward move Fremont into the Native-American party and out of a separate candidacy), Fillmore will be elected President. But Fillmore's wisdom, well indicated by Sut's comparing him to the Dutch squire, is not equal to the occasion and Fremont begs (decides to run on his own). More cards are dealt to determine a new trump (issues before the people). Sut glances at Fremont's hand and says:

> I now swar, that when a man's six on a big game ove seven up, I never seed jist sich kerds. He hilt tother three aces, bound to be high let what cum—an out-an-out President at that. . . .

Sut looks to see "what suit" is "to make the President outen that darn mule eatin Fremont" when

> . . . thars nara no nothin in hell ef he [Buchanan] didn't turn jack jist as easy as ef thar'd been fifty-two of em in the deck [giving him seven points before Fremont has the chance to count his high], and then only leaned back and smiled loud fur a *President!*

Written several weeks before the election, this sketch gives an uncanny prediction of the result: that Buchanan might win by the shrewdest and luckiest manipulation of the political cards and would win only by the narrowest margin. Here is historian Schouler's summary of the election for comparison:

> "Black Republicanism" carried New England, swept the great state of new York . . . and . . . took vigorous and emphatic possession of the broad Northwest. . . . Pennsylvania had borne up her favorite son, Buchanan, by an electoral majority of scarcely more than 1,000, in a total over 460,000; Indiana's margin, too, was very close; and the transfer of these two States—or of Pennsylvania alone, with New Jersey or Illinois added to the Republican column—would have reversed the national result. . . .[8]

Sut goes beyond the election and dreams what will happen. Look at this:

> Fillmore . . . fainted as comfortable on the floor as an old maid at a quiltin when the kissin begins. Freemount's eyes turned green—the har on the back ove his hed ris up like the teeth ove a comb, his must-touch-us turned up towards his eyes, he brayed like a mule, an at one jump kivered old Fill as he lay, an then sot in tu bitin and chokin and a maulin ov him like the Devil beatin hominy.

Harris is predicting, of course, that the Native-American party, which Fillmore represents, will fold up after the election, which it does, and that the Republicans will fight for the fusion which Seward is unable to bring about before the election. Sut sees success in their endeavor for he says: "Now ef fusion means *mixin,* they war *fused,* about as well as two pints of bald face in a quart flask on a hard trottin hoss." Seward leaves them fighting, locks the door on the outside, and goes "strait to a prar' meetin in Ninth Street. . . ."

Harris' next political preachment is saturated with the growing hatred between the South and the North. He writes:

> Do not the belligerent demonstrations among our prominent men (?), in these latter days, strike you as savorin somewhat of the ridiculous—rather of the Bombastes Furioso school. The lie "passes" back and forth for some indefinite period of time (always before a full audience); then a call for friends; then a labored set of carefully worded and dated notes; then—*smoke.* . . . Meantime all the news mediums, viz: loafers, gossips, telegraphs, editors, and old women, exert their powers

lauding or decrying the animals whose trenchant horns are so soon to lock for life or death; when, lo! after all the supposed notoriety for "game" has been obtained, at vast expense of tongue and ink and shaky nerves, here stoops the mediating angel in a staid, Methodistic "cool" old man, "whose courage has never been doubted," because no sensible person ever thought it worthy of a test. . . . Presto, change!—a healing balm, written on gilt-edged paper, called an explanation, for which all parties looked as they did for their mint-juleps, comes dove-like amid the savage sanguinary crowd, and all's over; each principal struts, as well he may strut, under his cheaply earned honors![9]

The man referred to in this invective is "the redoubtable prize ox in the human cattle show," Henry Wilson of Massachusetts,[10] who

. . . reveling in animal strength, filling the eye with a redundancy of muscle, yet the veriest coward that ever truckled to an inferior foe—sows his insults broadcast, and then simply acts the poltroon.

Harris suggests "a four-year-old, well preserved hickory, in the hands of a brother blacksmith born south of Mason and Dixon's line" as a remedy and, for fear this is not enough, adds this significant anecdote:

Todkins was delivering himself of some rather pungent remarks, addressed point blank to Bynum . . . which were rounded off somewhat in this style: "And now you d—d villain, you sneaking dog-ear'd puppy, I mean to *grind up* my foot and make a scabbard for it in your loathsome carcass." Bynum, who had listened with an air of bewildered astonishment to the whole invective, without once looking at the inveigher, took my arm, and, after walking some distance in silence, remarked: "I am a *very* excitable man, and, when roused, very exceedingly dangerous. I do not wish to trust my judgment in this matter, and having full confidence in yours, I'd like to obtain your deliberate opinion. Do-you-not-think the general tenor of Todkins' remarks, as addressed to me, were tinged (perhaps slightly so) with—with—something savoring of personality?" I gravely replied, most decidedly not; that I viewed them as the most guardedly general remarks I had ever heard, and most particularly the climax. Bynum was magnanimously disposed to accept my interpretation, and proceeded towards dinner—*a continuation* of our walk. The next tableau was said B., "under steam," with Todkins in furious chase, armed with an old buggy shaft, which he was industriously "grinding up" to a sharp point with a dinner knife. Memo: *He didn't catch him.*

A good idea of Harris' attitude toward the North, which is probably a fairly accurate statement of the general prejudice in the South, emerges from this anecdote. Place in juxtaposition to this the prejudices of the Garrisons and the Phillips, based upon a South as pictured by Olmsted and Cairnes, and the stage is set for a refutation of Harris' memorandum: actually, Todkins [the South] does catch Bynum [the North] and a "right smart fracas" ensues.

As Harris' hatred for certain types of men in the North grew, particularly men from Massachusetts, he looked about and saw a transplanted man from that state leading good Tennesseans into the fold of the Republican party so Harris feared. This man was Horace Maynard, who had come to Knoxville in 1838 as a professor in the East Tennessee University; subsequently, had turned to law and politics; and, had been elected to Congress in 1857.[11] Sut tells it this way: "thar cum to this country, onst, a cussed sneaking lookin rep-tile, name Stilyards" who was

. . . hatched in a crack—in the frosty rocks, whar nutmaigs am made outen maple, an' whar wimmin paints clock-faces an' pints shoe-paigs, an' the men invents rat-traps, man traps, an' new fangled doctrins fur the aid ove the devil. In fac' hit am his gardin, whar he kin grow what won't sprout any whar else. . . . He cum among us a ole field school-marster—soon shed that shell, an' cum out as oily, slippery a lawyer as ever tuck a fee. Why, he'd a hilt his own in a pond full ove eels, an' a swallered the las durn one ove em, an' then sot the pond tu turnin a shoe-paig mill. Well he practiced on all the misfortinate devils roun that sarkit, till he got sassy, got niggers, got rich, got forty maulins fur his nastiness, an' tu put a cap sheaf ontu his stack ove raskality, got religion, an' got tu Congress.[12]

In 1858 Sut goes to New York and in commenting on the efforts of a "brass gun man" to stop him, says:

Shootin' ove strange varminty critters ain't his gift; he ain't sly enuff, an' he'll git kingdum cum some day soon ef he don't quit that trade. 'Spose he wer tu undertake tu shoot Ole Beacher, in open day, afore witnessis like he did me, why durn my melt ef the passon's sister didn't have his haslet outen him, an' a dryin' atop of thar church-steepil in a minit; ef thar's enything in looks, she'd be wus on him nor I wer.[13]

Later, after other hair-raising adventures, Sut rolls down a stair and among

. . . a winein' blades lookin' feller's laigs, what wer a blunderin along in a ole white hat, with a mud dauber's nest built in the crown, a throat latch made outen a piece ove ole sweaty saddil-girth, an a ole dirty white coat, with a small soap factory in full blast in one pocket and a patent nigger trap in t'uther; he uses his shut to clean stove pipes with, an' he gits his boots by stealin' a par ove leather fire buckets—hes em footed, an' then pulls 'em on by the bales, over a par ove britches what he hes had patented as a flea hatchin' mershean.

This curious creature is identified as Horace Greeley and Sut admits that

. . . he's the only man in New York what kin hold a candil for me tu act durn'd fool by, an' he works onder a disadvantige, fur I'm told he won't tetch a drap ove sperits. Oh! he's a mons'ous promisin' ole durn'd fool, ef he don't get sot back, ur thunderstruck!

In a series of four sketches published in 1859, Harris again blasts his "kith and kin" in Tennessee who are being metamorphosed into the same "varminty" species by joining the Opposition party. Since 1852, the Democrats had managed to retain control of the governorship of Tennessee. But the Opposition, with many "turncoats" from the Democrats and recruits from the Native-Americans, threatened to take over in 1859. Harris satirizes this danger by having Sut describe a convention of the Opposition as a meeting "ove permiscus varmints, ove the sneaking an stealin sort, whar good dogs, an steel traps, an guns aint allowed tu cum."[14] Sut warns his readers that

> Sum infurnal devilmint's agwine tu cum over hit sartin, I'se studied the nater ove beastes monsous well, particular the mean kind ove varmints, caze I spose they's sorter in tu me, and I tell you, sure es youre born, when they meets by waggin loads tu hold a pow-wow, hit dont mean eny good tu any critter but thar selfs.

The "keynoter" of the convention, an "Ole Boar," in expressing the primary aim of the "love-feast," justifies Sut's fears when he says: ". . . *we hasent et ontil we hes lost all ideas ove size, shape, smell ur taste, an thars but wun thing afore us and that this is 'VITTILS OR DEATH.'*" But even this most "praiseworthy" goal does not unite them at first. Sut has hopes:

> . . . I tell you, George, *that hellfired scent ove tharn is tu be thar ruin yet.* The pole-cat may look like a coon and talk like a coon, and the buzzard may sprinkle hisself with meal ontil he looks like *a Eagle*; but durn me, ef the smell dont tell on him in the aind; and when hit does, his time am cum sure.

The same diversity exists among the leadership of the convention. The "love-feast" is opened by an "ole coon, monsous grey"[15] who has a "bell tied roun his neck and hit tinckles when he racks roun the room." Soon, however, a younger "coon" begins to take charge. Sut says:

> He hes his den ni ontu Nashville. . . . I hearn him tell a passle ove possums, minks, and foxes, that ef ever they wanted tu taste vittils again, the less they follered and noticed that ar ole "anomaly" the better . . . and that his dried hide would fetch more money than the livin coon wer worth, an axed them tu think ove what he'd sed, and not tu onderstand him *as wantin murder done,* but only as speakin of relative value, in case Providence wer tu take hit intu his head that the coon with the faded tail's *time had come.*[16]

Sut shudders at what might happen if this strange assortment of "varmints" should become organized under effective leadership. He contemplates their success and its results:

> The coon would eat isecrem . . . ontil the har ontu his tail friz together hard enuff tu shell corn ontu. . . . The mink, he'd be wus on briled chicken nor surkit riders am . . . The wile boar, he'd—but never mind

. . . The buzzard, he'd hev young wimmin an fat boys killed and packed away aforehand tu spile . . . The skunk would eat cod-fish with otter ove rose sass ontil he perjuced a new smell . . . Nun on em hes any judgment, but you jist give em power an durn me fundamentally ef they doesn't interchange with wun anuther, thar taste, voice, shape, color, habit, an all but thar hungry, stealin, hidin nater. . . .

Summarized, this means to Sut (or Harris) "a battle fur life, ur vittils as they [the "varmints" or the Opposition] call hit, atween humans and humanity and the varmints and dam rascality" and with "every dam oncircumsized, onmitigated, stinkin, stealin varmint on yearth . . . in love-feas' agin the humans," Sut promises:

> I jist wish I may be methodically, numerically, an harmoniously dam ef thar'll be a perdatory varmint lef alive inter the corporate limits ove Tennessee by the middle ove August nex. I'm agwine intu that hunt. . . . I mean tu gin what time I ken spar frum necessary running whisky, frolics, gals, an kerds tu my country, an help save vittils fur the humans instead ove hevin groundhogs eat poundcake; buzzards, sassige; and pole cats fried chicken; while humans hev carron, 'simmons, minners and crawfish raw.[17]

The Democratic candidate for governor, Isham G. Harris, was elected in "the middle ove August nex," and the "vittils" were saved temporarily for the humans. But the very next year the "varmints" got together in a national "love-feast," nominated Abraham Lincoln as their "head coon," and then elected him as the chief "vittil provider" for the nation. Harris sends Sut Lovingood, a confessed "natral born durn'd fool," to conduct the new President safely to Washington, because he has "more confidence in MR. LINCOLN" than he has in the vice-president elect, Hannibal Hamlin. Sut tells of the danger to Lincoln:

> Es I wer a gittin thru Bald-timore I seed a feller a sittin ontu a barrel a filin at the lock ove a durned revolting pistil. Sez I, mister, are ye gwine tu war? Yes, sez he, I'm gwine tu bore ole ABE's years fur him es he cums along. I went a piece furder and seed another fat ole tub a cuttin a cheese with a nife a foot long. That's a monsous nife, mister, sez I. Y-a-w, sez he, I means tu feel ole ABE's haslet with hit, sez he. I rocked along an seed another feller a rubbin brite a orful cannon. . . . Gwine tu shute, sez I? Not just yet, sez he. . . . When are ye gwine tu shute, ef I mout be so bold? Day arter tomorrow, sez he. I'm jist gwine tu take ole ABE in the place what fust tetches a hoss . . .[18]

Sut rushes to meet "Old Abe" and warns him of the danger. Old Windin Blades' [Lincoln] eyes "sorter bulged and sorter spread, and his mouf swelled out" and he says, "I hain't prepared tu die, SUTTY, my sun. . . . I hes dun the things I hadn't orter. . . ."

Lincoln is made a coward, as he was according to the prevailing belief throughout the South, and to this fault Sut adds the following appropriate description:

. . . if he aint a long wun and a narrow wun I'm durned. His mouf, his paw, and his fotzes am the principil feeters, an his strikin pint is the war them ar laigs ove hizen gets under his body. They goes in at each aidge sorter like the prongs goes intu a pitch fork. Ove all the durned skeery lookin ole cusses fur a president ever I seed, he am decidedly the durndest. He looks like a yaller ladder with half the rungs knocked out.

While Sut is with "Mister Link-horn" on the journey to Washington, he tells him about an interesting institution in the South:

When we lects our Governers we lects a fool-killer fur every county, and furnishes him with a gun, sum asnic, strick-nine, an a big steel trap, an hit is his juty tu travel, say about wun day ahine the Suckit Rider. You see the Suckit Rider gethers the people tugether and hit makes hit more convenient, and he kills off the stock ove fools tu a considerabil extent every round he takes. Our fool-killers hev dun thar juty, and consekently the South hev seceded.[19]

"Old Abe" suggests that emasculation (perhaps equated with emancipation) is a more humane way to eliminate fools. Sut objects and states that "fools break out like measils" and adds:

Spose the fool-killer wer tu kill (as in juty bound he orter) every 'bolitionist now livin, woudent the same sile, an climit, and feedin what perjused the d—d ol cusses what burnt ole, palsied wimmen as witches, and perjused Jo Smith, an Ole Miller, an Miss Fox, an Wendil Phillips, an Misses Bloomer, with her breeches and shut, nex year perjuse just such another crop . . . ?

By the aid of a grotesque disguise, Sut finally gets Old Abe through Baltimore to Washington. On the way, however, Old Abe makes such a fool of himself that Sut says:

. . . jist tu think ove this cross barr'd great beastes bein ole Abe President ove the United States ove North Ameriky. I swar natral born durn'd fool is I no's I is, I felt shamed, sorter humbled, an I sorter felt like cuttin ove his throat an a sellin the hay [with which Lincoln is padded as a part of his disguise] tu pay fur my shame, an drink all the whisky on his carcuss tu make my self feel good agin. . . .[20]

Harris emerged from the Civil War an unreconstructed Democrat. His first known writing, significantly entitled **"Sut Lovengood Come to Life,"**[21] replies to a correspondent of the *Wisconsin State Journal,* who had come South for a few weeks, then had gone home and written his recommendations for reconstruction of that region over the pseudonym of Solomin Sunstroke. Sut, as the "Fool killer Gineril," under an appointment direct from the President decrees a sentence of death upon Solomin in an "Orfishul Dokymint" in which he decides:

Yure case am sich a mark'd one, that I felt like makin up sorter, fur yer maker's . . . stinginis, in jis givin yu no *sence* at all, by a few hours warning . . . sit down,

an' rite out a statemint, over what *yu hes been a duin,* jurin the las' war; that orful four yeres ove blood, an' bluster an' misin up ove things, an' totein off things, an' skeerin things. . . .

Sut further states that Solomin must do this "to 'nable the projuce ove" his "loins, tu stan' fair in avrige 'sciety." Particularly, Sut wants him to tell how much fighting he did, how "meney barrils ove" the "crimson tied" he "pussonly spilt" and to separate it into "mens, wimens, childrens, cattils, hogs, hens, pole cats, turnips. . . ." Then Solomin is to state how many "dullers and sents" he received for stolen plunder. Sut asks specifically

. . . ef yu hes misfortinately been the ruin for this worild, and the worild tu cum, ove eny feemails, (stait the number of laigs, ef over two) an' how many ove em, you can sartinly say, an' swar tu, gin it tu me, in roun' hundreds, flinging in the frackshun, an' class em intu three shades ove culler, jet black, ash black, an' saddil yaller. . . .

Solomin is to tell if he "remembers *ara case,*" where he "personely reconstructed a rebil, an' if so," how he "managed the cuss, an' . . . how many laigs an' arms had he, and what wer his heft." Finally, Sut concludes:

Hits rit on every hart in the world, what has a soul behine hit, tu set hit tu beatin, that ove all the cussed, low down varmints, what dishoner the name ove man, the suck-aig sneak, hu hides ahine the pettecoats at home a suckin the heart's blud ove his country, an' a *fattenen hisself on hit,* while she am strugglin for very life, a bleedin at every auger hole, gimlet hole, wurm hole an' crack, an' ater she has barly won the fight, weakly tryin tu stagger tu her feet again, creeps frum his safe place, an' jackal like, goes scentin roun' amung the dead, the dyin and the starvin, like a surchin fur sumthin like a dead fire coal, to tote home and lite wif a lucifer match, and then say, "See yere, they haint whipped yit!" . . . An' then keeps a bellerin fur sumbody else tu go down thar, an' grind em sum more, to feed his hell's hatred, ought to be spit on—by nuthin living but polekats, tail tu tail—stink tu stink.

Harris follows this blast with **"Sut Lovengood, On the Puritan Yankee,"** of whom he says: "Powerful ornary stock, . . . powerful ornary."[22] He begins like this:

The rale, pure puritan, yankee baby, has a naik like a gourd, a foot like a glut, an a belly like a mildew'd drum head. He gits his eyes open at five days, while uther purps have to wait nine, an' long afore that time he learns to listen ove a night, for his mam's snorin, when he sneaks in to suck on the sly, not that he's hongry . . . but bekaze stolen meat is sweet even this yearly, to the blue, bline, scrawny young trap maker . . . As the dorg vomits, as the mink sucks blood, as the snail slimes, as the possum sham's death so does the yankee cheat, *for every varmint has hits gif.*

In the cultivation of this "gif," the "puritan yankee" believes in "schools an' colleges, as a barber dus in strops, and hones, as bein good tools to sharpen razors on." Even in his "cussin thar's a cheat in the words, he'll try to smuggle in G-d d—n onder the whinin sham ove 'gaul darn.'"

Sut takes a vigorous swat at the "Mayflower" complex when he says:

> I kin sorter bar the idear ove my bein a nat'ral born'd durn'd fool, my dad a playin h—l actin hoss,[23] the sody bisness,[24] sister Sall's onlawful baby[25]—everything—everything, even the las' war an' THAD STEVENS—but fur the life ove me, I cant reconstruck myself on the idea ove the landin ove the *Mayflower*. What cud our Maker bin thinkin about, that he forgot to lay his finger on her rotten old snout, an' turn her down in the middil ove the soft sea, wif her pestiferus load of can-tin cheats an' moril diseases.

If either the Lord or the Indians had destroyed these early Puritans, he goes on to say, we would have "no wooden clocks, horn gun flints, nur higher law. No Mil-lerism, mormonism, nur free love. No abolishunism, spirit rappins, nur crowin hens. No Bloomer bit—briches I mean to say, no GREELEY, no SUMNER. Oh! my grashum hits too good to think about."

With conditions becoming steadily worse in the South, Harris consigns its tormentors in words to where many wished them in actuality. He has Sut dream that he is in hell for voting "the Radikil ticket" and while there wit-ness the coming ove the darndest sluice ov mean look-ing cusses."[26] Among these are "Stevens, Summer, Wade, Butler—surnamed the Beast—an' Wendell Phil-lips." The devil sorts out the "common cusses," and then takes

> . . . up a needil as long as a harpoon, and with a big quile ove trace chain . . . threaded it . . . and strung 'em on the chain . . . then hung the whole bunch over the aidge of the boat into the brimstone. Jehosophat, how they sizzled, an' sloshed, an' dove, an' sprinkled hot iron about wif thar tails. A string ove sun perch would have been jist no whar.

For punishment of the important "cusses," the devil ranges "a big bom mortar" and shoots them out of it, one at a time, point blank at the hatch hole. Thad Stevens begs that "a she nigger strung on the chain" be loaded with him. Satan refuses. Sumner begs "to be loaded head fust, as he sed he'd always traveled sturn fust throu life, and he wanted to finish his journey the same way." When Satan is ready for Wendell Phillips, he cannot be found. Sut concludes that "thar'll be peace in hell fur a while, if the devil kin only ketch Wendil an' reconstruct the durn'd raskil."

Harris crystalizes the hatred of the South for Grant in a curious series of sketches in which he parodies the New York *Ledger*'s publication of "The early life of Grant,

by his father."[27] The Knoxville *Press and Messenger* an-nounces in grandiose language **"The Forthcoming Early Life of Sut Lovengood, by His Dad,"**[28] and states that it is to be "the early and inner life of the greatest living man, *in his way*" (as a "na'tral born durn'd fool"). A rivalry is set up between Sut's father, Hoss Lovengood, and Grant's father, since their sons are so "palpably and unmistakably pitted against each other for the same prize." Hoss promises that Ulysses will not walk "over the track unmarked by whip or spur, to be proclaimed the durn'd fool of his day." A few comparisons will reveal the trend of the parody.

Grant's father begins his biography of his son, Ulysses, in this way:

> Robert Bonner, Esq.—Dear Sir: You inform me that you wish to publish some articles about General Grant; and, in order that they may be perfectly correct and re-liable, you request me to furnish them . . . Having ac-quired, when very young, some facility in the use of the pen, I was, for many years, made secretary of al-most every public meeting which I attended where clerical services were required. . . .[29]

Hoss Lovengood begins his biography of Sut like this:

> Mister Ramige, Dear Sir:—You sent me word, that you wanted to print sumthin about the yearly life ove my most notorious son "Sut," and as how I bein' his dad, (so far as eny body knows) you tho't I wer most knowin' ove his littil tricks, an' tharfoar the very feller to rite 'em down for you to print frum. Well, jist you count me I—doudle-en in. I ruther like hit, havin a strong honein arter a pen enyhow; hevin been often called on in my yearly days, to tally bushels at corn measurin's, to keep count at shootin matches, or games ove "ole Sledge," witnessin' notes ove han', an' ar-ticles for a hoss race, or a rastilin mach. In fac', almos' all short jobs ove writin done off han' . . .[30]

Grant's father gives a long genealogical account of the Grant family, tracing it "round the jails, onder the gal-luses, apast the soap works" and hitting "every durnd castil, an' throne, on the whole road." Hoss counters by saying that "my son Sut comes of as good, and pure durn'd fool stock, as most public characters now fig-urin' on top ove the pot." To prove this he catalogues the doings of his forebears from his "gran'dad," who "killed hisself a jumpin down a bluff . . . jist to save a half a mile gwine to the still house," to his father SUG-ARTAIL LOVENGOOD, who "jist sloshed along lazily . . . spiled" for everything except "multiplyin' childer."

Grant's father maintains that his wife is the best woman on earth and extols her virtues in glowing terms. Sut says:

> . . . every man thinks his own wife, the best woman in the world, But if all men thinks as I dus—a durnder lie never was told. When I fasten'd onto Betts Leather-laigs, for a mate, she wer a rale slide easey, smilin',

saft footed gal, but she soon spread an' hardened into the durndest, scaley heel'd, rule-a-roast 'oman, atwix h—l, an' breakfast. She stomp'd a heap ove her character onto her brats, in fac', I don't think eny ove 'em, takes arter me to a suspisious egstent. . . .

Ulysses is introduced in this way: "The leading passion of Ulysses, almost from the time he could go alone, was for horses. The first time he ever drove a horse alone, he was about seven and a half years old." Hoss says of Sut:

The leadin' passions uv "my son" SUT, from the time he could go alone, wer skeers—whiskey—obstinacy, an' hosses. The fust hoss, he ever druv, wer a muel, an' him he druv crazy, in two secon's an' a half, by comin' at him sturn formos' on his all fours, an' in his shut tail. That ar animule wer never worth a cuss arterwards. *His hart was broke.*

With Sut well introduced, Harris makes a clever shift whereby he metamorphoses Hoss Lovengood into Grant's father and Sut into Grant. The Civil War is portrayed as a circus

. . . with a little cuss ove a muil an' they call'd hit Lee. The ring marster; name Abe, call'd aloud for some able bodied boy, to ride this vishus cuss. Wel boy arter boy tried hit, an' got flung right, an' left. One lit head fust on the candy stand, then Abe mos' incontintly kick'd him out. Another, name John Pope, lit sturn fust amung the "nashun's wards," and Abe, in bootin' his rear, misfortinately stove out his brains. Another got flung clean into the Rapahancok. . . . In stepp'd "my son" SUT, an' offered to ride—got mountid, went— The people sot up a great shout, some few for the muel, an' a heap for "my son." So many hollered for him, that the ring-master wer feard to boot him out, although he wer a smashin' things bad . . . an' besides all that, go as hit would, the performince *wer payin'.*

By the use of this metamorphosis, Harris castigates and satirizes Grant most effectively. He terminates the "biography" by an announcement that Hoss is wrathy and will write no more because an imprudent friend and the prying public have questioned why "he had always treated Sut as the black sheep of his flock [as Jesse R. Grant actually had treated his son Ulysses] until he obtained for himself a national distinction." Harris says that he does not blame the old man for getting the "sulks," for in reality "he has been very cavilierly treated simply for thinking his very black crow was a very white one" and when, no one else volunteering, "he blew his own cracked horn . . . not dreaming that he would become the laughing stock of the continent."[31]

In September, 1868, Harris published **"Sut Lovengood's Allegory,"** a[32] sketch in which he and Sut look to the "good old days" which are hopelessly gone. Sut says:

Some ove you minds the boy that started to school one sleety mornin' an' slipp'd two steps backward for one forrid. He only got thar, you mine, by turnin' roun', an'

gwine tother way. Well! that's the world's fix to-day, an' if heaven is the hotel that they is aimin' to sleep in, if they don't turn an' go tother way, I'm dod-drabbited if they don't lie out.

In analyzing the situation, Sut tells how Brakebill serves his "billy goat." This "meterfistickal, free will, billy goat," in those "good old days," is "forty years ahead ove his day." He shows "many marks of progress, an' higher law" but since he is a "beast" nobody notices it. Finally, he goes too far. Sut says that he, "like mos' ove these yere human progress humbugs, jis' played hell with his-sef." Old Brakebill finds that

. . . the lambs had patches ove coarse har in their wool, an wer sproutin' beards . . . Venuses pups, too, seem'd to hev the very devil in 'em. While one ove 'em lived on the goose grass in the yard, another one butted the house cat blind . . . Then another sprouted periwinkle shells above his ears, an' smelt like a bottle ove hartshorn, with a mouse in hit. An old, one eyed goose laid aigs with har on hit . . .

This is a satire on "business" and "carpet-baggers" and "nigger-rule"—in short, "progress" coming to the South. At first old Brakebill does not know what to do about it, but

. . . one mornin' arter drams, he come acrost a bran new, curious, little cuss, lookin' like a cross twixt the devil an' a cookin stove, standin on hit's hine laigs, a suckin' the muley cow. Arter brainin' hit with a wagon standard, he jist sot down, an' whetted his knife, ontil it would shave the har off his arm. Now, boys, that's about all that any body now livin' know ove the matter. Only this much was noticed thararter: That Mister Benny, billy goat, instid ove chawing his cud, with a short quick, sassey nip, nip, nip, arter that mornin' . . . chaw'd hit arter the fashion ove an old, lazy cow, when she is standin' onder the shade ove the willers, belly full, an' bellydeep in the creek.

In spite of this militant threat, after Grant's election to the Presidency, Harris published a despairing sketch entitled **"Well! Dad's Dead."**[33] In it, he equates Sut's worthless old Dad with the decaying and dying remnant of the Old South, which, for the best interest of all concerned should take its last gasp and pass on. When Dad actually does die, Mam [equated with the new South] declares that "Gineril Washington never did a better thing in his whole life" and she grumbles that "he didn't ketch the idea twenty years sooner." [1848]. Sut disputes the contention of "good people, an' passuns" about the "onnatralness ove folks towards the sick" for, said he,

. . . the neighbors acted jist as natral to dad, as could be. Nara durn'd one ove 'em ever come nigh the old cuss, to fool 'im into believin' that he stood a chance to live, or even that they wanted him to stay a minit longer than he wer obleeged to, by givin him sups of warter, fannin' off the flies—axin him if he wer hongry, or any other meddlesome interfarances with nater—not them.

Even more than that, while he is "a kickin' his last kicks"

> . . . Old muddleg's wife come to the fence an' call'd mam out, to know if she coudent spar the frock she had on, in pay for sixty cents, that dad owed her husbun', for three drinks ove "hoss botts." That she thought mam mout afford to run in her petticoattail a while, as the weather wer good.

This passage may have been aimed at the North, with its horde of "carpet-baggers" streaming into the South taking what was left of an impoverished economy. Sut decides that such a course of action is proper, after all, because, as he says:

> Dad shave the hipocracy ove fixin' a dead man away nice, arter lettin' him starve. Many, many a time, has people spent enough in plantin' a corpse, that if they had even loan'd the half ove hit to the mortul a livin', hit would a put off a funeral. But then the cuss wudent a went, when his time had come. Thars the devil ove hit—flustratin' doctrines so bad, you know.

Dad is dead (as was the Old South) and Sut raises problems curiously appropriate to both of them. He says:

> . . . we cudent raise ara coffin, without diggn' one up, an' totein hit a long mile. We had an old accoutrement box, hit's true, but then mam wanted hit, to ketch rain water in. So, we just sot in, an' made a regular mummy out ove him, by sowin' him up, body, an' soul, in an old black bed spraid. . . .

Truly, the "Old South" is a "long mile" away and there is not enough left of physical goods to give it a proper burial. The "old accoutrement box," from which a hopeless war had been fought, serves now to catch nature's drippings for drink. Sut despondently expressed the only hope that remains in Harris' heart:

> Who knows, boys, but what he'll git dug up, some three thousan' years arter this, an' be sot up in a glass case, for a King Pharaoo, an' a devil ove a fuss rasied about the bed spraid bein' a royal mantle?

Well! Dad is dead and the thing to do is to bury him. Mam "com'b her har an' flour'd her face"; Sut borrows "Old Stump Snodgrasses' steers" and a loose sled; an, he loads Mam and the "childer" on. Mam says "hits the rule to go *slow*" but the steers run away when they smell the corpse. In the helter-skelter race the "childer" are thrown off and Mam is bumped back and forth as Dad's corpse rocks from side to side. Mam wonders "when the *devil* will go out ove *him*," and well she may for just as they reach the edge of the graveyard, Dad's corpse butts her off the sled with his head as he lunges from side to side. Sut looks back and

> . . . Mam wer left behine, about a hundred yards, tryin' her levil best to git out ove the jaws ove a tall, forked stump, [what was left of the old order] that had her fast by the waist.

Sut decides that he never did see "jist sich a glimmer ove arms and laigs a reachin' for the ground."

Sut forgets Mam's plight as he sees that the steers are "aimin' to run plum astradle ove the grave," so he places his foot "agin dad's head" and gives him a shove. "Hit shot him out, like an arrow, an' he chug'd in, as plum, and strait, as an 'oman lays a baby in the cradle."

With Dad (the Old South) properly buried, Harris pictures the aftermath:

> That night, when we wer all hunker'd round the hearth, sayin' nothin', an' waitin for the taters to roast, mam, she spoke up—"oughtent we to a scratch'd in a little dirt on him, say?" "No need, mam," sed Sall, "hits loose yearth, an' will soon cave in enuff."

Significantly, this sketch ended Harris' active writing career. He wrote two more forlorn little yarns, both devoid of his usual robustness, before joining Dad in his long sleep.

Notes

1. See particularly Franklin J. Meine, ed., *Tall Tales of the Southwest* (New York, 1930); Walter Blair, *Native American Humor* (New York, 1930); F. O. Matthiessen, *American Renaissance* (New York, 1941).

2. James Phelan, *History of Tennessee* (Boston, 1888), 354 ff.; Ulrich B. Phillips, "The Southern Whigs," *Essays in American History, Dedicated to Frederick Jackson Turner* (New York, 1910), 214; George F. Mellen, "The Tennessee Press," Chattanooga *News*, April 29, 1910.

3. "In Memory of George W. Harris," Knoxville *Daily Press and Herald*, December 14, 1869.

4. St. George L. Sioussat, "Tennessee and National Political Parties, 1850-1860," *Annual Report of the American Historical Association for 1914* (Washington, 1916), I, 246.

5. "Love-Feast ove Varmints," Nashville *Union and American*, April 30, 1859.

6. See James Schouler, *History of the United States of America Under the Constitution* (New York, 1880-1913), V, 349.

7. This sketch was reprinted as far away as Texas where it appeared in the *Southern Intelligencer* (Austin) for November 26, 1856.

8. Schouler, *History of the United States*, V, 356-357.

9. "Letter From Sut Lovingood of Tennessee," Nashville *Union and American*, June 24, 1858.

10. See *Dictionary of American Biography*, XX, 322-325, for a sketch of this ex-cobbler who was born Colbath and christened Jeremiah Jones. Schouler says: "Massachusetts, forsaking her proud traditions, gave the seat which Webster had once occupied to the Natick cobbler, Henry Wilson, Free Soil Whig, Free Soil Know-Nothing, and an indefatigable worker in such temporary coalitions as had brought Sumner to the Senate before him . . ." *History of the United States*, V, 336.

11. Oliver P. Temple, *Notable Men of Tennessee* (New York, 1909), 137-149.

12. "The Widow McCloud's Mare," George W. Harris, *Sut Lovingood, Yarns Spun by a "Nat'ral Born Durn'd Fool"* (New York, 1867), 37-38. Cited hereinafter as *Sut Lovingood, Yarns.*

13. "Sut Lovingood's Adventures in New York," Nashville *Union and American*, August 15, 1858.

14. "Sut Lovingood's Love-feast ove Varmints," Nashville *Union and American*, April 19, 1859.

15. Probably John Bell.

16. Nashville *Union and American*, April 30, 1859.

17. *Ibid.,* May 3, 1859.

18. "Sut Lovingood Travels With Old Abe as His Confidential Friend and Adviser," Nashville *Union and American*, February 28, 1861.

19. "Sut Lovingood With Old Abe on His Journey," Nashville *Union and American*, March 2, 1861. See article by Ernest E. Leisy, "Jesse Holmes, the 'Fool-Killer'," *Publications of the Texas Folk-Lore Society*, VIII (1930), 152-159; also O. Henry's story, "The Fool-Killer," in *The Voice of the City* (New York, 1913), 157-169.

20. "Sut Lovingood Lands Old Abe Safe at Last," Nashville *Union and American*, March 5, 1861.

21. Nashville *Union and American*, May 3, 1866.

22. *Ibid.,* October 16, 1866.

23. *Sut Lovingood, Yarns,* 19-28.

24. *Ibid.,* 75-85.

25. This yarn has not been found.

26. "Sut Lovingood's Dream," Lynchburg *Daily Virginian*, January 23, 1867.

27. New York *Ledger,* March 7, 14, 21, 1868.

28. April 30, 1868.

29. New York *Ledger,* March 7, 1868.

30. Knoxville *Press and Messenger,* April 30, 1868.

31. *Ibid.,* May 21, 1868.

32. *Ibid.,* September 17, 1868.

33. *Ibid.,* November 15, 1868.

Kenneth S. Lynn (essay date 1959)

SOURCE: Lynn, Kenneth S. "The Volcano—Part II." In *Mark Twain and Southwestern Humor*, pp. 112-39. Boston: Little, Brown and Company, 1959.

[*In the following excerpt, Lynn discusses the emergence of the "red-necked" protagonist in Southern fiction, asserting that Harris's Sut Lovingood remains the most representative example of this unique character type. Lynn examines the influence of Sut Lovingood on the later comic works of Mark Twain.*]

Isolated, outnumbered, haunted by its own guilt, the secessionist South was in no mood to hear moderation and temperance extolled. In place of the Gentleman, there emerged as the comic spokesman of the slavocracy a series of red-necked, dialect-drawling louts, like Bill Arp or Mozis Addums, whose opinion of the Union was that the "Gnashnul Dimmockracy of the North and South ar jined together like the rooms in a jale," and who boasted that he was an "outenout ole fashin, strait up and down, Staits rite, Jacksin, Kansis dimmokrat, bleevin in nuthun but what the party bleeved in, voting fur a dimmokrat aginst eny body, I don't keer hoo." Of all this raffish crew, by far the most colorful was an illiterate, whisky-drinking youth from the Tennessee mountains. A "queer looking long legged, short bodied, small headed, white haired, hog eyed, funny sort of genius," his name was Sut Lovingood. His literary début was made in the *Spirit of the Times* for November 4, 1854, although he was destined never to appear in Porter's pages again. For the *Spirit* pursued a policy of Whiggish conciliation to the bitter end, and Sut Lovingood's yarns were a stronger brand of Southwestern humor than the magazine cared to dispense. Thenceforward, Sut Lovingood appeared in Southern newspapers, principally in the Nashville *Union and American*, a fire-eating Democratic sheet.

Sut's creator, George Washington Harris, had been born in the North, in Allegheny City, Pennsylvania, but had moved to Knoxville, Tennessee, while still a boy. Leaving school after a year or so, he had a varied career in East Tennessee as a jeweler's apprentice, steamboat captain, metal worker, surveyor, politician, postmaster, copper mine manager, glass works manager, sawmill operator, and—at the last—railroad employee. During the 1840s he was a frequent contributor to the *Spirit of the Times* of "sporting epistles" and backwoods anecdotes. He learned to manage the Addisonian style with slick facility, while his command of the vernacular showed right from the start that "rare kind of dramatic imagination that can get movement directly into words" which F. O. Matthiessen admired in his later work. To Porter's readers, Harris became a well-known author. If he and the *Spirit* editor parted company after 1854, it was not for personal reasons; their split symbolized rather the larger secession of which Harris was now becoming the fanatical exponent.

The brainchild of that fanaticism was Sut Lovingood, born in the very year that Kansas-Nebraska inflamed the slavery controversy as never before. Students of Southern nationalism who are given to buttressing their books with quotations from the fantastic sociologizing of George Fitzhugh's *Cannibals All!,* or from the poems of Henry Timrod, or from the grandiloquent rhetoric of the "chivalry politicians," would do well to remember that birthday. For in ignoring Sut Lovingood, as they have, they not only overlook the most gifted humorist to come out of the Southwest before Mark Twain, but an author who has more to tell us than any other Southern writer of his time about the mind of a society at bay.

Many of the Sut Lovingood yarns are political satires. Consumed by hatred for the North, Harris went to extraordinary lengths to vilify Northern politicians. Following the Presidential election of 1860, he turned the full force of his invective on Abraham Lincoln, representing him as a coward and a fool, and savagely caricaturing his physical appearance. Harris's most violent humor, however, was reserved for fellow Tennesseans. For not only was Tennessee the last Southern state to leave the Union, but the eastern part of the state, particularly the region around Knoxville, was notorious for its anti-secessionist sentiments. In Knoxville itself, the eccentric Parson Brownlow, an itinerant Methodist preacher who had drifted into politics, conducted a brilliantly sarcastic campaign against disunion in the pages of the Knoxville *Whig*. The last Unionist paper in the Southeastern United States, the *Whig* was the moving spirit behind the East Tennessee "rebellion against the rebellion" in 1861. Harris, detesting Brownlow and despising Knoxville for its "treason" against the South, poured out his rage in a series of ferociously comic diatribes.

When the war came, Harris refused to live in such a contemptible city any longer and took his family away. For four years, he and his wife and their five children wandered through the South—from Chattanooga to Decatur, Alabama, to Trenton, Georgia, and beyond. No one knows exactly how they lived, or all that they did; one catches sight of Harris near Rome, Georgia, late in the war, passing through the Federal lines on muleback to procure some salt, but it is only a passing glimpse; the years of the South's agony were years of silence for

Harris. He came out of the war an unreconstructed Democrat, and soon Sut Lovingood was back at work spewing out his contempt for the South's newest crop of enemies: the carpetbaggers, the Radicals, "nigger rule," and Ulysses S. Grant. But Grant's election to the Presidency in 1868 was the last straw. Too bitter even to go on fighting, Harris managed to turn out three more comic sketches and then wrote no more. A year later, he was dead, under bizarre circumstances. In December of 1869, Harris traveled up to Lynchburg, Virginia, to transact some business for his railroad employers; on the way back, he became ill and had to be taken off the train when it reached Knoxville. He died without regaining consciousness on the night of December 11. A man who had spent his life believing that the horizons of his world were ringed with deadly enemies, he went to his grave amidst rumors that he had been the victim of foul play. "In behalf of a community, who deeply deplore the death of Captain Harris," wrote the Knoxville *Press and Herald* a few days later, "and who shudder to think of his horrible, lonely ride in a railway train, without one pitying glance or gentle hand to soothe his dying moments, we ask that whatever facts in the possession of anyone, tending to explain this most mysterious death, be published, that the world may know, whether Capt. George W. Harris died by the stroke of his God, or the poisoned chalice of a wicked man." The mystery as to whether or not Harris died by poison has never been cleared up. The only certainty is that he had lived by it.

IV

As always in Southwestern humor, the best of the Sut Lovingood stories are not Harris's overtly political satires, but rather those stories which issued from a deeper level of his imagination—which turn away from the "real world" of contemporary affairs and have their being in the realm of comic fantasy.

In these fantasies, Harris retained vestiges of the traditional forms of Whig comedy. We are, for example, made aware of a Gentleman, named George, who speaks a genteel language; and his occasional introductions of the action constitute a rudimentary "frame." But the striking thing about George is how shadowy a figure he is. Harris the secessionist had nothing but contempt for Whiggery's ideals, and as a consequence the voice of temperate gentlemanliness is as severely restricted in his comedy as the vernacular Clown's had once been. At best, Harris's Gentleman is heard for as long as a short paragraph; in some stories, he does not speak at all. His role is as peripheral as that of the end-man in a minstrel show: popping in occasionally from the wings, he feeds lines to the star performer, the once-despised Clown.

To a degree, Harris's choice of a teen-aged youth as his hero reveals once again the vestigial influence of the gentlemanly tradition upon his imagination. William

Byrd's *Dividing Line* had represented the North Carolina frontiersman as a childish figure, who should be seen and not heard; the Self-controlled Gentleman in "The Big Bear of Arkansas" had condescendingly referred to Jim Doggett as a child of the woods; James K. Paulding had conceived of Nimrod Wildfire as just an overgrown boy. In the Southwestern tradition, the Clown was funny precisely because he was unselfconsciously infantile, even when he was technically an adult. Whooping and hollering and jumping into the air, he behaved with childlike unrestraint in no matter what company; his vernacular speech—grotesque, drawling, ungrammatical—was a sort of baby-talk. Regarded as a child in spirit, the Clown tended more and more to become a child in fact, thus establishing an image of the vernacular character which has lasted down to the present. From the boy-Quixote of "Georgia Theatrics" to Sut Lovingood, from Huck Finn to Nick Adams to Holden Caulfield, the most memorable vernacular voices in American literature have been the voices of children. However, what differentiates Harris from Longstreet and the earlier humorists, and makes him the forerunner of Mark Twain and Hemingway and Salinger, is that he negotiates the crucial transition from regarding the child with the patronizing attitude of the fond adult, who "knows better" about everything in life, to looking at the adult world through the eyes of a child and judging it by the standard of values of a child. Richard Malcolm Johnston made the child his hero in the same decade as did Harris, but Johnston nevertheless continued to view the child as Longstreet had: in detachment, and at a distance. In the Sut Lovingood yarns, the child becomes the author's persona. Although Harris christened gentlemanly George with his own name, it is more significant that Harris was known all through East Tennessee by the nickname of "Sut." On those comparatively rare occasions in the yarns when George is on stage, we view the child-hero from an external and superior vantage point, but not until *Huckleberry Finn* would an American book sustain a child's point of view more faithfully than the Sut Lovingood stories.

Paradoxically, Harris the secessionist was driven to adopt a child's point of view for the same reason that had prompted Johnston the Unionist to make children the moral center of his stories—namely, that in all societies children are to a greater or lesser degree aliens, barred by their youthfulness and inexperience from full membership in the tribe, and kept in ignorance of its mysteries. If a vernacular view of the world has so often been a child's view as well, in modern American literature, it is because both represent unofficial—or even anti-official—ways of seeing things. Harris in the pro-Union atmosphere of Knoxville and Johnston in a university where one could not teach if one did not hate the North both felt themselves strangers in the community, and their imaginative sympathy with the children of their fiction is symptomatic of their alienation.

However, just as Harris and Johnston had nothing in common politically, so their child-heroes are different. Edmund Wilson's succinct summary of what sort of youth Sut Lovingood is makes it clear that Sut could hardly have symbolized Richard Malcolm Johnston's piously Whiggish hope that the future would bring forth a more self-controlled South: "The deadpan homicides and corpses of the early Mark Twain," Wilson has written, "are given a certain dignity by the stoicism of the pioneer, and the nihilistic butcheries of Ambrose Bierce a certain tragic force by his background of the Civil War. But Sut Lovingood is something special. He is not a pioneer contending against the wilderness; he is a peasant squatting in his own filth." An outsider in the community, Sut is further cut off from love and human connection by reason of his estrangement from his half-crazy family; like old Mr. Flood in E. A. Robinson's poem, the boy has a whisky jug for his closest friend; in all the heterogeneous company of orphans and castaways who make up the heroes of American literature, there is no one more lost or miserable than Sut Lovingood. Lonely, afraid, often half-drunk, he imagines himself surrounded by enemies, as in a bad dream. Everywhere he looks, he sees a fundamental disorder; in Sut's view, normal human arrangements have degenerated in a frenzy of superstition, lust, and hypocrisy. Nor is evil a thing of the past in Sut's world. When the youth tells, as he does in one of his yarns, about a doctor who is a grave-robber, a planter who is an adulterer, a sheriff who is a coward and a Negro parson who is a common thief, he is not reminiscing in the manner of the Self-controlled Gentleman about former unpleasantnesses, he is describing society *as it now is*. The triumph of the moral light over the moral dark, and all the other Whig reassurances as well, have quite faded away in Sut's yarns, along with the virtual disappearance of the gentlemanly style. The vernacular narration of this outcast is not intended to instruct the reader in the virtues of the temperate life—indeed, just the reverse. For Sut's humor blocks critical awareness in order to release a tremendous burst of emotion; he is concerned not to reprove society, but to revenge himself upon it. Although Sut never comes to explicit revolt, his sadistic practical jokes—on women, on his parents, on Yankees and Negroes, on Methodist preachers who resemble Parson Brownlow, on anyone who has had an education or who smacks of a genteel upbringing—constitute his war against the world. While his despised victims scream, knowing Sut laughs in enjoyment. His one hero is Wirt Staples, a mountain bully-boy who is everything that this weak, ugly youth wishes he could be:

> His britches wer buttoned tite roun his loins, an' stuffed 'bout half intu his boots, his shut bagg'd out abuv, an' wer es white es milk, his sleeves wer rolled up tu his armpits, an' his collar wer es wide open es a gate, the mussils on his arms moved about like rabbits onder the skin, an' ontu his hips an' thighs they play'd like the swell on the river, his skin wer clear red an' white, an'

his eyes a deep, sparklin', wickid blue, while a smile fluttered like a hummin bird roun his mouf all the while.

Whenever Wirt is kicking a sheriff, or booting a Negro through a window, or riding horseback through a court-room, Sut is there to cheer him on with laughter.

Yet no matter how hard Sut laughs, he can never get rid of his harrowing guilt-complex and his implacable self-contempt. No matter how well he succeeds in humiliating his enemies, he always comes back to the characterization of himself as a coward and a "durn'd fool," and to the terrible assertion that he was born without a human soul and would be glad to be dead, except that he is afraid of dying. No other detail about the boy's life is more important than this. For if there can be little doubt that Harris's depiction of Sut is a ghastly caricature of his own furious, inner life—that the youth's antisocial pranks were Harris's symbolic way of getting even with contemptible Knoxville—the fact of Sut's corrosive sense of guilt rounds out an even more significant correspondence. Sut Lovingood's haunted imagination reflects like a cracked mirror the frantic state of mind of the secessionist South. Perhaps the first juvenile delinquent in American literature, Sut Lovingood is a rebel without a cause; but his guilty contempt for himself, and his paranoid hatred of the enemies whom he sees all about him, tell us much about those rebels of the Lost Cause whom the Southern intellectual, George Tucker, described in 1861 as "crazed in the fancies of imaginary evils, and of their strange remedies." More intensely than any other figure in American literature, Harris's hero embodies the worst aspects of the slavocracy, even as the name "Sut" is an ugly contraction of "South."

The youth also represents, however—and it is this complexity which makes him such a fascinating character—a prototypical Huck Finn, whose youthful refusal to submit to orthodoxy compels our sympathy as well as our despair. Sut's ingratiating qualities were what Faulkner was thinking of in 1956 when he responded to a question about his favorite characters in literature:

> My favorite characters are Sarah Gamp. . . . Mrs. Harris, Falstaff, Prince Hal, Don Quixote and Sancho, of course. Lady Macbeth I always admire. And Bottom, Ophelia and Mercutio. . . . Huck Finn, of course, and Jim. Tom Sawyer I never liked much—an awful prig. And then I like Sut Lovingood from a book written by George Harris about 1840 or '50 in the Tennessee mountains. He had no illusions about himself, did the best he could; at certain times he was a coward and knew it and wasn't ashamed; he never blamed his misfortunes on anyone and never cursed God for them.

Sut is an appealing character, in other words, because unlike the adult society in which he lives he has no pretensions. His realism is oftentimes unpleasant, but it is always candid, and he infallibly sees himself for who he is. The romantic notions of what their life was like which beguiled so many Southerners of the period seem particularly preposterous by comparison with Sut's vernacular honesty. Thus in a post-Civil War story called—with grotesque humor—**"Well! Dad's Dead,"** Sut turns an account of the death of his father into an appeal to the South to give up its absurd illusions that the dead past could somehow be recaptured. The appeal is entirely typical of Sut's imagination. Huck and Sut are very different children in many respects (for example, Sut has a sex life, Huck does not), but they are very much alike in their mutual refusal to take any stock in dead people. As in *The Adventures of Huckleberry Finn*, the tension between myth-minded adults and literal-minded Sut is a source of comic delight.

In the Sut Lovingood stories, too, the style is the man—or rather, the youth—and there is a wonderful, lifesaving freshness to Sut's language which almost always redeems his adventures from sordidness. In the teeth of a frightful world, his spontaneous metaphors and original images generate laughter and renewed hope. Sut's admiration for Wirt Staples may be a deplorable sign of his nihilism, but the passage in which he describes his feelings toward Wirt's wife is an affirmation of life. As F. O. Matthiessen has said, the description is a hymn to fertility—a hymn, it must be added, with an ache in its music, for Sut affirms a life which is beyond his youthful grasp. At the very heart of his vernacular style is the wistfulness, and the awed attention to details, of a lost and lonely boy:

> Wirt's wife got yearly supper, a rale suckit-rider's supper, whar the 'oman ove the hous' wer a rich b'lever. Thar were chickens cut up, an' fried in butter, brown, white, flaky, light, hot biskit, made wif cream, scrambil'd aigs, yaller butter, fried ham, in slices es big as yure han, pickil'd beets, an' cowcumbers, roas'in ears, shaved down an' fried, sweet taters, baked, a stack ove buckwheat cakes, as full ove holes es a sifter, an' a bowl of strained honey, tu fill the holes. . . . Fur drinks, she hed coffee, hot, clar an' brown, an' sweet milk es cold es a rich man's heart. Ontu the dresser sot a sorter lookin potbellied bottil, half full ove peach brandy, watchin a tumbler, a spoon, an' a sugar bowl. Oh! massy, massy, George! . . . I gets dorg hongry every time I sees Wirt's wife, ur even her side-saddil, ur her frocks a-hangin on the closeline.
>
> Es we sot down, the las' glimmers ove the sun crep thru the histed winder, an' flutter'd on the white tabilcloth an' play'd a silver shine on her smoof black har, es she sot at the head ove the tabil, a-pourin out the coffee, wif her sleeves push'd tight back on her white roun' arm, her full throbbin neck wer bar to the swell of her shoulders, an' the steam ove the coffee made a movin vail afore her face, es she slowly brush'd hit away wif her lef han', a-smilin an' a-flashin hur talkin eyes lovinly at her hansum husbun. I thot ef I were a picter-maker, I cud jis' take that ar supper an' that ar 'oman down on clean white paper, an' make more men

hongry, an' hot tu marry, a-lookin at hit in one week, nor ever ole Whitfield converted in his hole life; backsliders, hippercrits, an' all, I don't keer a durn.

V

Two years before his death, Harris collected the best of the Sut Lovingood stories and brought them out as a book. Generally ignored by the reviewers, the collection received its most interesting notice in a West Coast publication called the *Alta California*. Written by a young author whose mind was crammed with impressions of life, but who still had not figured out exactly what to do with them, the review responded enthusiastically to the vernacular humor of the yarns. Whether Harris was gratified—or even aware—that the author of "The Celebrated Jumping Frog of Calaveras County" had liked his stories is unrecorded. As for the reviewer, he may be pardoned if he did not give much thought to Harris's book, for after all, he was about to sail for Europe for the first time. Nevertheless, the time would come when Mark Twain would have occasion to remember Sut Lovingood.

Brom Weber (essay date 1962)

SOURCE: Weber, Brom. "A Note on Edmund Wilson and George Washington Harris." *Lovingood Papers* 1 (1962): 47-53.

[*In the following essay, Weber evaluates Edmund Wilson's 1955 review of* Sut Lovingood. *Weber takes Wilson to task for failing to recognize the complexity of Harris's humor.*]

Mr. Edmund Wilson, one of our most distinguished American men-of-letters, has had an ambivalent relation with George Washington Harris since 1955. In that year Mr. Wilson reviewed the present writer's edition of *Sut Lovingood* (Grove, 1954) for the *New Yorker* (May 7, 1955). On the one hand Mr. Wilson granted Harris an acknowledgement of his "real literary merit"; on the other hand Harris' writing was mistakenly regarded as political literature. Recently, perhaps still wrestling with the nature of Harris' accomplishment, Mr. Wilson reprinted his review almost verbatim in *Patriotic Gore* (1962). The result has been to mar a book in many respects deeply felt and intellectually profound, for Mr. Wilson's essentially negative though still ambivalent attitude to Harris has not been made more persuasive or precise with age. In the context of *Patriotic Gore,* furthermore, it is easier to discover why Mr. Wilson was initially wrong about Harris and has remained so, for the book reveals a carelessness with focus and detail fatal for serious scholarship and criticism.

The *New Yorker* review lacked focus because it ranged haphazardly between Harris, the 1954 edition, and the book's editor, without making clear the identity of the review's subject. Additional confusion was created by Mr. Wilson's uncertainty about the purpose of the 1954 edition. On the one hand he granted that the book was a modern treatment designed for the "average reader"; on the other hand he persisted in discussing the book as though it were a scholarly edition published for the "serious student of literature."

The aura of confusion surrounding the review is now heightened by its inclusion in *Patriotic Gore,* ostensibly a study of American Civil War literature. The book's principle of selection is mystifying, for its pages discuss such non-Civil War writers as Adelaide Crapsey and Ezra Pound while overlooking the Civil War literature of the humorists whom Abraham Lincoln read and enjoyed to the day of his death: "Artemus Ward," "Orpheus C. Kerr," and "Petroleum V. Nasby." Additional mystification is created when *Patriotic Gore* devotes many of its pages to the character and editorial procedure of the 1954 edition—hardly a Civil War product— and goes so far afield as indiscriminately to include the 1954 dustjacket in its category of materials relating to Civil War literature.

Mr. Wilson's treatment of the dustjacket epitomizes the responsibility of his approach to Harris, for he has attempted to find both Harris and the contents of the 1954 edition guilty of association with the book's wrapper. Using a tactic familiar in some book-reviewing circles, Mr. Wilson asserts that Sut "is depicted on the jacket as a stalwart and bearded mountaineer, a portrayal that has nothing in common with the dreadful, half-bestial lout of the original illustrations." (p. 509) This is careless as well as petty. In one original illustration Sut stands barefooted, wearing overalls; in a second illustration Sut is as respectably dressed and featured as a minister portrayed in another of the original illustrations; Mr. Wilson's adjectival outburst is unjustified by either of the illustrations. Worse yet, the 1954 dustjacket artist— certainly not Harris nor the editor of the 1954 edition— obviously portrayed the spirit of the Southwestern school of humor to which Harris belongs. It would have been equally trivial and extravagant for Wilson to have applauded Harris and his editor because the dustjacket, with a hearty wrenching, can be said to have offered a brilliant allegorical key to Sut's bestiality. After all, the dustjacket figure was printed in black ink (EVIL) and overprinted with yellow ink (COWARDICE, DEGENERACY, FASCISM) and red ink (MURDER or, rather, GORE).

The expansive range of Mr. Wilson's attention to Harris is not always fortified by a scrupulous concern for accuracy of fact and interpretation. In truth, *Patriotic Gore* is not as finished as it should be. In the area of verifiable facts, for example, the book gives us "Professor H. Foster" (p. vi) instead of Professor Charles H. Foster; "John Sherman . . . the candidate from Illinois"

(p. 373) instead of John Sherman, the candidate from Ohio; "*Ode by James Russell Lowell Recited at the Harvard Commencement, July 21, 1865*" (p. 472) instead of "Ode Recited at the Harvard Commemoration, July 21, 1865"; "J. Franklin Meine" (p. 511) instead of Franklin J. Meine; and George Ade's "*Fables in Slavery*" (p. 587) instead of *Fables in Slang*. Matters of interpretation are also handled in a cavalier fashion. It is flippant, I suggest, to write of Melville's *Billy Budd* as though it were a pill designed to combat insomnia, decrying its structure on the ground that "its huge units . . . make it one of the most inappropriate works for reading in bed at night, since it is easy to lose consciousness in the middle of one." (p. 637)

But for our immediate concern the acid test of Mr. Wilson's literary acumen is his reading of Harris' text. How, with the best will in the world, can one defend this misreading of **"Mrs. Yardley's Quilting"**?

> In the case of an old lady who loves to make quilts, he [Sut] rides into her quilting party with a horse he has driven frantic, ripping up all the quilts and trampling the hostess to death. This is Sut's only recorded human murder. . . .
>
> (pp. 514-15)

The sentimental progression from "old lady" to "murder" makes for touching rhetoric, but it has no basis in Harris' story. Neither the 1867 edition nor the 1954 edition justify the belief that Sut rode a horse into a quilting party or the belief that Sut or a horse trampled the old lady to death. The text clearly indicates that the old lady died of a broken heart because a nine-diamond quilt she valued had been torn. The point missed by Mr. Wilson is that in **"Mrs. Yardley's Quilting"** Harris ridiculed the conventions of nineteenth-century sentimental fiction in a manner that is one of his major achievements. There is no real need, of course, to defend Harris against reading as typically unreliable as the one quoted above from *Patriotic Gore*. They are not worth much as scholarship and are not too valuable even for intuitive criticism.

The truth is that Mr. Wilson embodies the best attributes of the genteel tradition modernized by exposure to the twentieth century, but that those attributes do not include a sensitive appreciation of American humor in its full range. He cannot comprehend the complexity of a humor which, like that of Harris, is frolicsome and serious all in one. I have elsewhere (*an Anthology of American Humor*, 1962) tried to demonstrate that this is the dominant characteristic of American humor at its best, and of most of our major American writers too, from the seventeenth century down to our own time. Nor is American humor unique in its combination of "low" and "high" elements, for parallels are plentiful in European literatures.

The genteel tradition is dominated by the eighteenth-century view, developed in England and imported into American culture where it was nurtured by sentimentalists, that humor is wholly benevolent and compassionate. Credence was given to this misconception by adherents to Turner's frontier theory, who hypothesized that the violence and grimness of American humor—actually present since the seventeenth century—has been grafted onto humor by the American frontier experience. With the frontier officially buried in the 1890's, there was no longer any need to muddy American culture with frontier barbarities. Turned back on nineteenth-century "frontier" humorists such as Mark Twain, the modernized genteel tradition can only find aimless brutalities and vulgarities in writings which actually hold much more. Mr. Wilson writes that "all that was lowest in the lowest of the South found expression in Harris's book." True enough, but much that was also highest in the South was also given expression by Harris. My introduction to the 1954 edition, which made this point, is quoted in *Patriotic Gore*, so that it is more appropriate now to quote from another writer, one who has succinctly set forth the importance and quality of Harris' achievement which have eluded Mr. Wilson:

> It may well appear that Harris' imagery will bear close scrutiny, that it is art of no mean order. Sut appears to seek sheer fun, but the imagery associated with him enlarges his stature to a figure ambiguously comic and mythic, hopelessly desiring an impossible freedom, pursuing intensity of experience in the flesh, and an abandonment of the obsessive and irrational. Subtly communicated is the hint of large hopes of what man might be on the frontiers of the new world, and bitter disappointment in what he really was. Sut is hard and cruel because in the moral void of the American backcountry of his experience he can assert his individuality only through violence. The stories recount crude practical jokes; the imagery supplies the counterpoint, sounding a world only occasionally satisfying, but more often harsh, hypocritical, wicked, transitory, and meaningless.
>
> (Milton Rickels, "The Imagery of George Washington Harris," *American Literature*, May 1959, p. 187)

It is characteristic of Mr. Wilson's ambivalent approach to Harris that he does not find it inconsistent to balance his violation of Harris' substance with a deep concern for the purity of Harris' text in other respects. *Patriotic Gore* asserts, for example, that as editor of the 1954 edition I sought to "clean up" the text by my treatment of Harris' dialect. On this matter Carvel Collins has written: "Every critic and scholar I know of who has quoted brief illustrative passages from ***Sut Lovingood's Yarns*** has felt it not only proper but necessary to make Sut's speech more understandable: here Mr. Weber has changed the whole book, and has done it consistently and on sensible principles." (*New Mexico Quarterly Re-*

view, Summer 1955, p. 263) Mr. Wilson's handling of this matter is not as circumspect as Mr. Collins' nor can it do more than distract readers from Harris' significant achievements.

Mr. Wilson inaccurately guesses that my treatment of Harris' dialect was inspired by a "suggestion" put forth by Bernard DeVoto. Much more pertinent to the literary history antedating the 1954 edition is the fact that De-Voto himself (in *Mark Twain's America,* 1932) provided a precedent for my treatment of the dialect. Furthermore, Walter Blair (in *Native American Humor,* 1937) and F. O. Matthiessen (in *American Renaissance,* 1941) also treated Harris in a manner similar to my own. The implication created by Mr. Wilson that there was a gap between DeVoto's "suggestion" and my procedure in the 1954 edition is misleading. Indeed, the full facts were available to Mr. Wilson in the introduction to the 1954 edition.

Modern textual scholars are not agreed upon the treatment to be accorded a text selected for reprinting. Much depends upon whether the reprinting is designed for scholars or for the general reader, or both, as well as upon individual characteristics of the primary document. In Perry Miller's *Major Writers of America* (1962), for example, Edward Taylor's poetry is reprinted in as verbatim a transcription of the original manuscripts as possible. But in *The American Puritans* (Anchor, 1956), not designed like *Major Writers of America* for students but for general readers instead, Mr. Miller felt it proper to follow the precedent set by Samuel Eliot Morison's edition of William Bradford and to prepare a modern text. Individual characteristics of a primary document which will affect the handling of its text for reprinting include printer's errors and the author's errors of spelling, punctuation, and paragraphing.

In my judgment, a modern edition of Harris' 1867 text was desirable. With all due respect to Harris' art, his dialect is one of his least valuable achievements. Its faults include inconsistent misspellings for humorous effect as well as the careless rendition of dialect terms in a confusing and unsystematic variety of form. A prime requisite for first-person narration, which Sut employs, is that the narrator use only one language—his own—rather than several languages interchangeably. To credit Harris with the scientific consistency of a philologist or a writer sufficiently concerned with dialect to have made **Sut Lovingood** an inviolable dialectal document is to violate the text by failing to read it with a responsive eye and ear. Under the circumstances as I saw them, I had to decide whether or not the best interests of Harris, American literature, and the reader would be served by verbatim reprinting of the flawed dialect and other flaws. I decided against verbatim reprinting because, like DeVoto, Blair, and Matthiessen before me, I believed that Harris' importance rested upon literary

virtues other than his dialect and punctuation. Furthermore, I was preparing a text for the general reader. I was not interested in preserving Harris as an unreadable curio known to a handful of initiates, his condition prior to 1954 and one which, ironically, a fervent concern for his dialectual purity tends to foster.

Earlier in this note I commented upon Mr. Wilson's waving of a dustjacket before the eyes of his reader. That gratuitous gesture is matched in spirit by a reticence concerning scholars in the field of American humor whose names or contributions have been slighted by misprinting or omission in *Patriotic Gore.* Mr. Wilson cites the late Bernard DeVoto, Constance Rourke, and F. O. Matthiessen as those who "in the late thirties of the present century . . . began to take an interest in Sut Lovingood." True, but not the whole truth. Franklin J. Meine's *Tall Tales of the Southwest* (1930) discussed Harris earlier than DeVoto, Rourke, and Matthiessen; the book also reprinted six Harris stories. Walter Blair's *Native American Humor* (1937) provides us with the first extensive critical and scholarly commentary on Harris as well as with four Harris stories. Both Meine and Blair are still alive and deserve credit for their efforts. The omission of Walter Blair's name from the pages of *Patriotic Gore* is especially puzzling, for this admirer of Harris is the most distinguished scholar in the field of American literary humor. Mr. Wilson cites Kenneth Lynn's *Mark Twain and Southwestern Humor* (1960) as having shown that Southwestern humorists used the frame device to establish their "cultural superiority" and their general distance from lower-class characters such as Sut. It just happens that Walter Blair had earlier set forth this theory with persuasive detail in *Native American Humor* (1937). One wonders why Mr. Wilson neglected either to praise or negate Mr. Blair's scholarship.

All notes end best when they end happily, and this one is no exception. It is pleasant to observe that Edmund Wilson's interest in George Washington Harris testifies to the latter's growing importance.

Walter Blair (essay date 1965)

SOURCE: Blair, Walter. "Harris' Best: 'Bill Ainsworth's Quarter Race.'" *Lovingood Papers* 4 (1965): 16-20.

[In the following essay, Blair discusses the origins of Harris's story "Bill Ainsworth's Quarter Race."]

Beginning late in the eighteenth century and for about a hundred years thereafter, quarter races were popular throughout the old Southwest as sporting events and as subjects for sketches. Since these competitions ranked with cheaper sports such as cock-fighting, deer-driving, 'possum-hunting, partridge-netting and gander-pulling, they could be held even when hard times halted more expensive events. And they were run almost everywhere there were two horses (even plow-horses), two riders, and two or more sportsmen eager to make a wager.

At the start they were simple affairs: horses and riders were lined up at a post from which they raced a distance of about a quarter of a mile; hence the name, although in time a race for a longer distance was also likely to be called a quarter race. In the early days, because such a contest could not be run on a proper race track, superb horsemanship was necessary. When the race was held in a clearing, the rider not only had to jockey for the lead but also had to steer his steed around boulders, logs, and stump-holes. When it was held on unimproved village streets, deep dust or mud might make the going almost as rough; and pedestrians, wagons, and even entrants in simultaneous races hampered speedy movement. Godly citizens often took stern measures against such events. The trustees of Lexington, Kentucky, for instance, in 1798 levied fines "for firing guns and running horses within the bounds of the in-lots"; a few years later the folk of Greensboro, Alabama, literally threatened to shoot sportsmen who raced horses in the streets; and in 1821 the General Assembly of the sovereign state of Kentucky levied a ten-dollar fine for the running of horse races "on the public highways."

The contests were frowned upon by solid townsfolk for another reason—because a crowd that gathered for a quarter race, like any other frontier assemblage, was pretty sure to turn the affair into a social occasion. Stump speeches, games of chance, shooting matches, foot races, no-holds-barred fights, and dances that were nearly as rambunctious erupted all over the place. Drinking parties too, of course. The remark of the Arkansas pioneer who said that she hadn't a drop of whiskey when she actually had a barrel of it indicated an attitude: "Why, goodness gracious! What do you reckon one barrel of whiskey is to me and my children when we're out of milk?"

Such affairs naturally appealed to the writers interested in color and action, particularly to George Washington Harris, a peerless chronicler of lively Southwestern functions. If a reminiscent passage that Harris wrote in 1846 is to be believed, by the time Sut's creator was fifteen he himself had "ridden a few quarter races" and knew a thing or two about guiding a horse over a dangerous course. Thereafter Harris must have watched many races in the Knobs and on the Knoxville track owned by his brother-in-law, Pryor Nance.

Like several other Southwesterners who later became well known as humorous writers, Harris started his career as a contributor to *The Spirit of the Times* by writ-

ing "sporting epistles," four of which were published in 1843. The first epistle of that year, though apparently not the first that Harris wrote, appeared on February 11 and was signed with his current pseudonym, "Mr. Free." It mentioned quarter racing as a sport that was being enjoyed around Knoxville during a time of "scarcity and pressure." A second, in the issue for April 15, was called **"Quarter Racing in Tennessee,"** and recounted a recent race held at the Stock-Creek Paths "in that rare place for sport south of the Holston River, known as 'South America,'" between F. K.'s horse Little Breeches and W. R. B.'s Brown Mary. A third, in the June 17 issue, lamented the cancellation of spring races in Knoxville because of hard times and looked forward to the imminent running for the Peyton Stake in Nashville. The fourth, printed on September 2, mentioned the quarter race on July 4 in Tuck-a-Lucky Cove "between those notorious crowders, Terrapin and Snapping Turtle," "a fast thing, beyond all previous conception, and so extremely close, that the judges decided it a draw race."

Soon after, Harris began writing contributions that no longer pretended to be sporting reports, some in conventional—and rather stuffy—literary English and some in the vernacular. That he planned an even more ambitious venture was indicated by a Tennessee contributor to *The Spirit* for November 15, 1845, who announced that Harris and a contributor who signed himself "The Man in the Swamp" planned to collaborate on a book, *Smokey Mountain Panther*, "illustrative of the manners and customs of East Tennessee—containing an account of Bear and Panther fights, quarter racing, Card playing . . . etc."

The book, and hence the promised account of quarter racing, never appeared; but more than two decades later, in the Knoxville *Press and Messenger* for June 4, 1868, Harris published **"Bill Ainsworth's Quarter Race."** Here the humorist's creation Sut, who by now had become famous as a political satirist and spinner of yarns, recounts the great race of 1833 between Kate, Hunter's fast Alabama mare, and Ainsworth's even faster horse, Ariel.

This narrative, published late in Harris' career, in fact about a year before his death, in my belief and that of a number of other Sutologists, is the author's best. Edmund Wilson, Harris' most famous detractor, would, I assume, find our liking for this piece incredible. For if Wilson ever read this sketch, he would be hard put to it to find support in it for his description of a Sut who is "avowedly sadistic" and "a peasant squatting in his own filth." It is hard to believe that even Wilson's ineffable delicacy would be offended by the bits about "a mess ove boys stonein a sqirrel, up a tree"; some other boys "chasin out the hogs with dorgs"; Jo and Tom emerging from "jis a fis' fight, with sticks . . . with bloody heads an' no shirts"; or about Sut's difficulty, referred to but never specified, when he caught "a flea, or a bug, off a young lady." These, nevertheless, are the only touches that I can find that might distress even the nicest sensibility. Nor could Wilson cite this piece to justify his astonishing claim that "in the Lovingood stories . . . the fun entirely consists of Sut's spoiling everybody else's fun," since the only prank that the "peasant" mountaineer plays is that of avoiding the telling of a story that he has promised to tell. Can it be that in guessing wherein the humor of Sut's stories lies Wilson missed things rather important to Harris' admirers?

Not, I believe, entirely. Wilson does say in passing that "the language [of Sut] is often imaginative," then hastily darts away from this grudging concession. But the language is one of Harris' chief assets in this piece and elsewhere. One may see the quality of the language here with some clarity by comparing some of Harris' own words with those of Sut since, like Mark Twain, Harris became a far more original, zestful, and exciting stylist when he spoke with the voice of a vernacular character rather than with his own. Here is Harris' voice in a story published on September 17, 1868:

> Those of us who have not yet reached the ferry, so dreaded by many, yet anxiously looked forward to by the footsore and weary ones, who have passed but few cool fountains, or hospitable shelters, along their bleak road, must well remember the good old days of camp meetings, battalion musters, tax gatherings, and shooting matches. Well! there was the house raisings too, and the quiltings, and the corn shuckins, where the darkey's happy song was heard for the last time. And then the moonlight dance in the yard. . . .

Compare Sut's voice in **"Bill Ainsworth's Quarter Race,"** slightly more than three months earlier:

> Ox carts . . . full ove har trunks an' kaigs, an' them full ove cider an' ginger cakes. While fat ole wimmen sot on top, in brass speks, an' frilled cap borders, kep' busy a drappin' fourpence ha'pennys into a black, press'd paper snuff box, with a red face an' cock'd hat, called the juke of Wellington, painted on the lid. While a favorit dater sot on the tail board, keepin off the flies with a green bush, lookin' soft an' sweet. . . . Young men, in their shirt sleeves, with the collar unbutton'd, an' a fresh cut hickory club in their han's, slung'd roun', winkin' at the red daters ove the cake wimmen, or listen'd to Claib Nance, sittin' the porch, playin' "Billy in the low groun's," like no other man ever has, or ever will, play that tchune.

Both passages are expressions of nostalgia, an attitude that mellows Harris' writings far more often than casual readers might guess. But while the first passage is abstract and is spotted with clichés in the elegant mode, the second is concrete and easy-going. The details in the first are evocative only for those who have experienced "the good old days"; those in the second convey what was delightful even to the uninitiated. Exactly the

right fragments in the scene are recalled to make unforgettable and wistfully appealing the fat old women, their snuff boxes (even—poignantly—the picture of Wellington on the cover), the "soft and sweet" daughters, the young men. Only when he talks of Claib Nance does Sut explicitly voice an attitude which carefully handled brush strokes in the rest of the passage already have conveyed.

A great charm of the entire sketch derives largely from a like choice and rendition of details throughout—a caressing of memories that the author obviously delights to recall. Again after all these years the two horses seem to live and breathe again: Kate, walking "with a limber, sassy step, that look'd like she cud step as fur agin, if she wanted to," and Ariel, his muscles moving "onder his glossy grey hide like cats crawlin' onder a carpet." So do card players, women, girls, boys, young men, old men, athletes, the sheriff, the tax collector, the Negro woman by the old spring house, Hunter, Ainsworth, Wash Morgan, and the enraptured crowd which watches the contest. The lingering over details is so thorough and at the same time so delighted as to give a quality of gusto typical of the most ebullient member of a school of almost uniquely zestful authors. A community is re-created, some of its folk not in the least comic, some amusing, but all of them partaking of life and knowing and conveying the joy of simply being alert and alive.

Whether the somewhat complex effect should be called a humorous one may be debatable, but surely the sympathetic reader's enjoyment is closely allied to that of humor. In pictorial art, the nearest thing to Harris' achievement seems to me to be a sixteenth-or seventeenth-century Flemish painting of some lively village festival. In American writing, the nearest thing I know is one of Mark Twain's evocative picturings of life in an antebellum Mississippi river town.

Milton Rickels (essay date 1965)

SOURCE: Rickels, Milton. "The Fool as Point of View." In *George Washington Harris*, pp. 95-106. New York: Twayne Publishers, 1965.

[*In the following essay, Rickels evaluates Harris's place in the Southern literary tradition. Rickels examines the ways in which Harris differs from earlier frontier humorists, such as A. B. Longstreet and Johnson J. Hooper, particularly in his use of a more lively and expansive prose style.*]

I

When William Faulkner, in the *Paris Review* interviews, was asked for his favorite fictional characters, he offered Dickens' Mrs. Gamp, Falstaff and Prince Hal,

Don Quixote and Sancho, Huck and Jim, and a few others; he devoted his longest discussion to the least-known character in his list: "And then I like Sut Lovingood from a book written by George Harris about 1840 or '50 in the Tennessee mountains. He had no illusions about himself, did the best he could; at certain times he was a coward and knew it and wasn't ashamed; he never blamed his misfortunes on anyone and never cursed God for them."[1] The august company seems surprising, and Faulkner's point that Sut is an admirable literary creation invites examination.

The framework device of the earlier Southwestern humorists—A. B. Longstreet, T. B. Thorpe, and Johnson J. Hooper—always gave the gentleman observer superior comprehension and a moral system competent to understand and judge the native backwoodsmen whose oral stories he reproduced. Harris, by the time he prepared *Yarns* [*Sut Lovingood, Yarns Spun by a "Nat'ral Born Durn'd Fool"*] for publication, had abandoned this framework except as the briefest convention and had endowed Sut with a vividness of language, expansiveness of spirit, and even a perceptive intelligence superior in vitality to those of gentleman George. Sut is a highly sophisticated point of view in the technical literary sense, a personality rich enough to evoke interest for itself and to perceive and refract the world. With careful craftsmanship, Harris exploits Sut's point of view to destroy in his reader old habits of perception and to introduce a fresh and original vision of the world.[2]

In time and place Sut is to some degree a local type. He shares a language, a social condition, a set of traditions that define the outward form of his existence. From the first, however, he is detached both in life and in spirit from his community. Outwardly, he seems often to be one of the insulted and the injured—to have reason, as Faulkner felt, to curse God; but he is not one of Dostoievski's introspective underground men, or one of Dickens' victimized and terrified poor. Although mean-souled and often cruel, Sut is at the same time large-spirited, triumphant, and free. To achieve Sut's triumph over life, Harris has chosen one of man's ancient modes of existence within society; Harris defines his broadest intention for Sut in his subtitle by terming Sut a "nat'ral born durn'd fool."

The reader is early aware that Harris is not using the term in any loose, careless, or general way. Instead, Sut is created in the literary tradition of the fool, a type which has since Classical antiquity been constantly reinvigorated by a parallel folk tradition.

Sut is always conscious of his mode of existence. In this sense, despite his constant disclaimers, his life is a free choice he has made for himself; his existence is the product of his own will. His choice frees him from the necessity of deceiving himself and thus provides him an authentic mode of being. His existence is not, like that of the average man, dead in the world of tradition, habit, and illusion.

In his preface, Sut calls himself an eternal fool. Writing prefaces, he tells George, "Smells tu me sorter like a durned humbug, the hole ove hit—a littil like cuttin ove the Ten Cummandmints intu the rine ove a watermillion; hits jist slashed open an' the inside et outen hit, the rine an' the cummandmints broke all tu pieces an' flung tu the hogs, an' never tho't ove onst—them, nur the 'tarnil fool what cut em thar" (ix). Harris' conception of his fool, then, is not the antic simpleton but the wise fool; Sut is the ironic hero who perceives the human condition and knows he himself is a fool to communicate his perceptions, to cut his ten commandments in the rind of a watermelon.

In **"Sut Lovingood's Daddy, Acting Horse,"** Harris provides one of the rare objective descriptions of Sut: a "queer looking, long legged, short bodied, small headed" creature. He is five times the fool any other member of the family could claim to be, excepting his dad, of course. Sut's dad is called a damned fool and he calls his son a damned fool; and variously throughout the sketch the Lovingoods, father and son, are cursed as eternal fools. At the opening of the book, Harris defines Sut primarily in action. He is a demonically ebullient creature, commanding and free.

For the following sketch, Harris chose **"Sut's New-Fangled Shirt,"** which is something of a falling-off from the opening; but Sut as fool is further developed by his telling a tale of his own ignorance. In Sut's authentic existence as fool, he always knows his own weakness and stupidity; and his expressions of comic despair are both recognition and acceptance of his life.

During 1858 Harris had begun considering more carefully how he might utilize the mode of Sut's existence to present a version of life. References in his sketches show that at the time he was reading Pope, Burns, Byron, and particularly Dickens and Shakespeare; from these sources he drew techniques and concepts to help him shape Sut's being. At the end of **"Sicily Burns's Wedding"** one of Sut's definitions introduces the element of irony possible to the point of view:

> Hit am an orful thing, George, tu be a natral born durn'd fool. Yu'se never 'sperienced hit pussonally, hev yu? Hits made pow'fully agin our famerly, an all owin tu dad. I orter bust my head open agin a bluff ove rocks, an' jis' wud du hit, ef I warnt a cussed coward. All my yearthly 'pendence is in these yere laigs—d'ye see 'em? Ef they don't fail, I may turn human, sum day, that is sorter human, enuf tu be a Squire ur school cummisiner.

(97)

To become "sorter human" is not plaintive longing, but the ironic man's disdainful scorn for unrealized and, to Sut, unrealizable humanity. Sut has chosen not to try to become human.

After rejecting the human condition, Sut also rejects the religious life. In **"Old Burns's Bull Ride"** Sut repeats his comic fear, but what he fears is pain of the body. He has no fear of the hereafter, for he has no soul:

> I'se a goner I 'speck, an' I jis' don't keer a durn. I'm no count, no how. Jis' look at me! Did yu ever see sich a sampil ove a human afore? I feels like I'd be glad *tu be* dead, only I'se feard ove the dyin. I don't keer fur hererater, fur hits onpossibil fur me tu hev ara soul. Who ever seed a soul in jis' sich a rack heap ove bones an' rags es this? I's nuffin but sum new-fangil'd sort ove beas', a sorter cross atween a crazy ole monkey an' a durn'd wore-out hominy-mill. I is one ove dad's explites at makin cussed fool invenshuns an' cum afore my time. I blames him fur all ove hit, allers a-tryin tu be king fool.
>
> (107)

Within the *Yarns* the image of mam as a worn-out kitchen machine and of dad as a lascivious beast is appropriate; behind the tale the mechanical inventiveness of Harris himself and of his foster father Samuel Bell provides possible psychological applications. But most important for the point of view he is constructing, Harris has freed him from any transcendental significance in making Sut soulless.

As has been argued in the discussion of **"Rare Ripe Garden Seed"** and **"Dad's Dog School,"** Harris' work embodies expression of anti-authoritarian and anti-rational feelings. Sut as fool personifies this concept in another of his characteristics, his mindlessness. Sut says he talks, acts, and "thinks at randum" because he has no "steering oar" to his brain. He then develops a comic biology to explain the imperfection of his mind:

> Well, I thinks peopil's brains what hev souls, am like ontu a chain made outen gristil, forkid at one aind; wun fork goes tu the eyes, an' tuther tu the years, an' tuther aind am welded tu the marrer in the backbone. . . . Idears start along the chain, an' every link is smarter nur the wun ahine hit, an' dergests em sorter like a paunch dus co'n, ur mash'd feed. . . . Now, in my case, thar's a hook in the chain, an' hits mos' ove the time onhook'd an' then my idears stop thar half made. Rite thar's whar dad failed in his 'speriment; puttin in that durn'd fool hook's what made me a natral born fool.
>
> (210-11)

Planning and thinking, says Sut, are "ginerly no count" (67). One's fate is determined by how one conducts himself at the moment of action. Harris, like W. G. Simms, feared that thought and contemplation enfeebled

life; both expressed a yearning to solve the problem of the conduct of life in moments of dramatic action.[3] Sut's conduct is uninfected by reason.

The elements of Sut's nature and his experience of life issue in a formulated philosophy. One of the primary elements of Sut's character is his search for joy. Such passages as "kissin an' fitin am the pepper an' salt ove all soshul getherins" (139) image his world and express his reason for being. His philosophy insists on the joy of sex: "Yere's my sentimints ontu folks: Men wer made a-purpus jis' tu eat, drink, an' fur stayin awake in the yearly part ove the nites: an' wimen wer made tu cook the vittils, mix the sperits, an' help the men du the stayin awake" (88). Sometimes the conflict between pleasure and the demands of social morality and religion are openly acknowledged, as in Sut's evaluation of Sicily Burns's function in the world:

> George, this worl am all 'rong enyhow, more temtashun than perventitive; ef hit wer ekal, I'd stand hit. What kin the ole prechurs an' the ugly wimen 'spect ove us, 'sposed es we ar to sich invenshuns es she am? Oh, hits jis' no use in thar talkin, an' groanin, an' sweatin tharsefs about hit; they mus' jis' upset nater ontu her head, an' keep her thar, ur shet up.
>
> (77)

Expressions of the joys, frustrations, and occasional horrors of sexual activity are possible to Sut because of his comic freedom as fool. The formal public man, George Washington Harris, abhorred, on a rational level, what he took to be Brigham Young's sexual license; and in his political satires he ridiculed the free-love utopias of nineteenth-century America. Harris found only the comic mode satisfactory to contain what he both abhorred and, at a deeper level, desired.

While Sut seeks joy, he also sees the harsh, bitter competition for existence. Harris' emphasis on the poverty and cruelty of the American backwoods implies a profound disappointment with life in the New World that was envisioned in his early Mr. Free essays. In **"Rare Ripe Garden-Seed,"** which came late in Harris' career, Sut speculates on the social cannibalism of village America:

> Well, es I wer sayin, mam wer feedin us brats ontu mush an' milk, wifout the milk, an' es I wer the baby then, she hilt me so es tu see that I got my sheer. Whar thar ain't enuf feed, big childer roots littil childer outen the troff, an' gobbils up thar part. Jis' so the yearth over: bishops eats elders, elders eats common peopil; they eats sich cattil es me, I eats possums, possums eats chickins, chickins swallers wums, an' wums am content tu eat dus, an' the dus am the aind of hit all. Hit am all es regilur es the souns from the tribil down tu the bull base ove a fiddil in good tchune, an' I speck hit am right, ur hit wudn't be 'lowed.
>
> (228)

Harris' familiarity with Pope's *Essay on Man* assures his acquaintance with the "Vast chain of being! which from God began," vibrating in perfect, holy harmony. Sut's concluding ironic submission to a guiding divinity and his mock-faith that "whatever is, is right" reinforce the satiric tone of his version of the heavenly order of the universe.

It is a mistake to see in the vision of human wickedness the grasp of original sin. There can be no knowledge of original sin without knowledge of the will of God and without sacrifice to make that will be done on earth. For Christianity, the will of God is expressed centrally in the Sermon on the Mount. The *Yarns* are not concerned with the knowledge of God or with the will of God; on the contrary, they are a symbolic escape from the discipline of love, as well as the discipline of authority. Sut exists outside Christianity.

Some of Sut's vitality lies in his being conscious of the discipline of love but his choosing to be free of it, and thus he is free to express the reality of his primitive hatreds. His explanation of his hatred of an encyclopedia salesman who expressed boredom at one of his tales goes beyond revenge to embody the human impulse to inflict and to contemplate pain:

> I hates ole Onsightly Peter, jis' caze he didn't seem tu like tu hear me narrate las' night; that's human nater the yearth over, an' yere's more univarsal onregenerit human nater: ef ever yu dus enything tu enybody wifout cause, yu hates em allers arterwards, an' sorter wants tu hurt em agin. An' yere's anuther human nater: ef enything happens [to] sum feller, I don't keer . . . how sorry yu is fur him, thar's a streak ove satisfackshun 'bout like a sowin thread a-runnin all thru yer sorrer. . . . An' yere's a littil more; no odds how good yu is tu yung things, ur how kine yu is in treatin em, when yu sees a littil long laiged lamb a-shakin hits tail, an' a-dancin staggerinly onder hits mam a-huntin fur the tit, ontu hits knees, yer fingers *will* itch tu sieze that ar tail, an' fling the littil ankshus son ove a mutton over the fence amung the blackberry briars. . . . Ur a baby even, rubbin hits heels apas' each uther, a-rootin an' a-snifflin arter the breas', an' the mam duin her bes' tu git hit out, over the hem ove her clothes, don't yu feel hungry tu gin hits jis' one 'cussion cap slap, rite ontu the place what sum day'll fit a saddil, ur a sowin cheer, tu show hit what's atwixt hit an' the grave; that hit stans a pow'ful chance not tu be fed every time hits hungry, ur in a hurry?
>
> (245-46)

In spite of the rationalizations, the piece expresses primarily the impulse to give pain. Beneath is a strong sense that life is struggle and disappointment; man's natural response to the cruel urgency of the infant is not always kindness but often an equally selfish cruelty.

This passage not only expresses Sut's vision of life but also reveals his power to observe and to verbalize as a commanding storyteller. He is no simple poor white,

and he goes considerably beyond Davy Crockett and the Big Bear of Arkansas in his grasp of his world. The movement of Harris' imagination toward myth is revealed in these presentations of Sut's vision of existence and in his numerous passages of advice to George about how to live. The impulse to give Sut supernatural characteristics is shown in the bird imagery associated with him. The farthest movement toward mythic birth does not appear in the *Yarns,* but in **"Sut Lovengood Lands Ole Abe Safe at Last,"** where Sut tells a newspaper reporter: "We kep a sand-hill crane, and Mam and him had a difficulty, and he chased her under the bed" (Weber, 232).[4] Our source of delight in the "mythy" Sut is not far to seek.

At his farthest symbolic meaning Sut escapes the Christian conception of man fulfilling himself by abandoning himself to Divine truth and goodness. Instead, he finds the significance of his existence within himself. He is the creator of his own being. His project is to identify himself and define himself to himself. Once he discovers his authentic desires, he wants to realize them in some condition of purity and permanence. By making Sut a self-conscious symbol of the essential poverty and mortality of human life, by restricting the meaning of his existence to the flesh's reality, by making comedy of the idea of resurrection (in **"Well! Dad's Dead"**), but by keeping undiminished in him the will of life to survive and enjoy itself, the fool Sut becomes the irrational comic figure who realizes the ancient yearning to escape death and to become God himself.[5]

II

By having Sut present his version of the world and the nature of his own being through self-analysis, Harris defines Sut's point of view as that of the fool as seer. He is outside the law, outside social morality, outside religion, even outside rational life. As fool, he can express the logically incompatible elements of comedy: cruelty and joy, logic and license, the knowledge of mortality and the insistence on permanence.[6] The summary reveals the parallels and affinities Sut has with the Fool of tradition.

Enid Welsford's *The Fool* [(1935)], a study of the "historical origin and role of the Fool as comic entertainer," defines the fool's esthetic significance as he appears in the folk tradition, in society, and in the literary tradition. The fool, according to Welsford's definition, is the one who gets slapped, the ancient scapegoat of mankind; but also he is emotionally and spiritually tough, none the worse for his slapping:

> For the genius of the fool is manifested by his power of deluding us into the belief that he can draw the sting of pain; by his power of surrounding us with an atmosphere of make-believe, in which nothing is serious, nothing is solid, nothing has abiding consequences.

Under the dissolvent influence of his personality the iron network of physical, social, and moral law, which enmeshes us from the cradle to the grave, seems—for the moment—negligible as a web of gossamer.[7]

The fool, Miss Welsford argues, does not lead to revolt against the law; on the contrary, he acts as preserver of social life by exposing pretension, by providing a safety-valve for our own unruliness, and by nourishing the sense in us "of secret spiritual independence of that which would otherwise be the intolerable tyranny of circumstance."[8]

The illusion of freedom must be created by relief from pressures. In Sut's experience, his defiance of order and propriety, and his urge to revenge himself on Sicily are all outward symbols of inner pressures. His desires are real and at the same time impossible. It is less the pressure from without than the pressure from within that Sut symbolizes. As fool, he is creator not of order, not of beauty, but of freedom.[9] He is free to create his being and to be that self.

III

Harris' work and his literary associations contain many hints about possible sources for the fool Sut. The American folk tradition is rich in terms for fools and in anecdotes about simpletons, antic clowns, and clever rogues. Many of these tales found their way into the *Spirit of the Times* and *Yankee Notions* during the years Harris contributed to those periodicals. In 1845 and 1846—when **"The Knob Dance"** was printed in the *Spirit* and reprinted in Porter's anthology, *A Quarter Race in Kentucky*—Johnson J. Hooper's crafty rogue Simon Suggs was also appearing in the same journal and volume. The young Suggs cheats his father at cards and runs away from home, the grown Suggs swindles a camp meeting, the middle-aged Suggs deceives his neighbors into electing him to a military office. Harris never makes Sut a sharper, but he may have found in Suggs's freedom from morality and social ties hints for a type freer even than the rogue.

Harris was fond of Alexander Pope; he paraphrased for comedy a line from the *Essay on Criticism*[10] and quoted from the *Essay on Man,* which is full of references to fools. According to Pope, man cannot escape being a fool; he can only learn and then mourn his condition. From Robert Burns, whom Harris also read and quoted (**Yarns,** 158), he could have found, had he needed, precedent for Sut's caustic satire on social pretensions and religious hypocrisy. Somewhat more remotely, **"Sut Lovengood's Adventures in New York"** echoes lines from Byron's *Don Juan,* Stanzas 128, and 132:

> This is the patent age of new inventions
> For killing bodies and for saving souls,
> All propagated with the best intentions.

A greater amount of evidence exists for the influence of Charles Dickens. Sut's victim in **"Old Skissim's Middle Boy"** is modeled, Harris writes, on "Charley Dickins's son, the fat boy" (67), from *Pickwick Papers.* In a headnote to **"Hen Baily's Reformation"** Harris calls his mock temperance tract to the attention of Dickens' Reverend Mr. Stiggins, leader of the Grand Junction Ebenezer Temperance Association (198). Some of Dickens' most ebullient satire on religious cant and affectation is focused on the Reverend Mr. Stiggins. More significant for the creation of Sut's view of life may have been Harris' reading of *Hard Times* (1854). He intended to title his last manuscript **High Times and Hard Times,** which seems in the nature of a special tribute. Dickens' work may have been useful to Harris both in content and in the technique it manifested. Dr. F. R. Leavis has pointed out that the appropriateness of the vocabulary, rhythm, and imagery to the burden of meaning in *Hard Times* places Dickens among the greatest masters of the English language.[11] These three elements are strong qualities in Harris' work.

Hard Times is Dickens' most comprehensive version of the inhumanities of Victorian civilization, particularly in the way its harsh philosophy fostered and sanctioned "the aggressive formulation of an inhumane spirit."[12] These inhumanities reduce workers to "hands" in Bounderby's factory; children to numbers in Gradgrind's school, where only "facts" are allowed; and life itself to the measure of the "deadly statistical clock very hollow." Sut's objection to the excessive order of Squire Hanley's life, his complaint that "we know too much," his dissertation against planning might all have been reinforced by the reading of Dickens.

One of the ways in which Harris transmuted material from Dickens is indicated in what is at first glance one of Sut's more original flights of fancy. Discussing circuit riders in **"Sicily Burns's Wedding,"** first published in 1858, Sut tells George: "Suckit-riders am surgestif things tu me. They preaches agin me, an' I has no chance tu preach back at them. Ef I cud I'd make the institushun behave hitsef better nur it dus. They hes sum wunderful pints, George. Thar am two things nobody never seed: wun am a dead muel, an' tuther is a suckit-rider's grave" (89). In *Pickwick Papers* the ingenious comic servant Sam Weller theorizes that postboys are immortal. He asks the medical student, Bob Sawyer:

> "Never . . . see a dead postboy did you?" inquired Sam, pursuing his catechism.
>
> "No," rejoined Bob, "I never did."
>
> "No," rejoined Sam, triumphantly, "Nor never vill; and there's another thing that no man never see, and that's a dead donkey. . . ."[13]

In conceptualizing objections to the utilitarian society, in the techniques of rhythm, dialect, and imagery, even in items of comic fantasy, Harris is indebted to Dickens.

When Sut is considered in his generalized form, however, he seems to have most affinities with the Renaissance Fool of court and stage: he is a lean, ugly creature; he leaps and runs; he has a rapid, commanding flow of talk; he is cruel or witty in repartee; he is sometimes privileged truthteller; he is sometimes the antic, diverting jester; he is sometimes the scapegoat; he is often the bitter seer. Harris could have learned most of this tradition of the fool from Shakespeare. *The Merchant of Venice,* from which Harris borrows twice in one sketch (67, 69), has a good traditional fool in Launcelot Gobbo. Launcelot tricks his father, can be both kind and cruel, and is the witty jester and privileged truthteller. Falstaff, Touchstone of *As You Like It,* and Feste of *Twelfth Night*—all represent the fool's flight from civilization, the freedom from law and order that many an American frontiersman yearned for.

The influence of one artist on another is never a simple matter, but Harris' utilization of material from other writers forms a significant pattern. His quotation from Pope reveals his interest in poetic techniques to control sound and speed of language. His utilization of material from Shakespeare and Dickens concentrates on the comic figures of Gobbo and Sam Weller, revealing his fascination with the clever, witty, free ironic character, and the capacity of such a point of view to refract a vision of life and evaluate a society. Byron and particularly Burns provide satiric elements. As one result, Sut becomes the most technically sophisticated point of view in Southwestern humor—one capable of exploring a variety of qualities of American and Southern life that lie obscurely along the fringes of perception.

Notes

1. Republished in Malcolm Cowley, ed., *Writers at Work* (New York, 1958), p. 137.

2. For a useful definition of comic points of view see John Gerber, "Mark Twain's Use of the Comic Pose," *PMLA,* LVII (June, 1962).

3. [William R. Taylor, *Cavalier and Yankee* (New York, 1961)], pp. 294-96.

4. Quotations from Weber's edition [*Sut Lovingood* (New York: Grove Press, 1954)] will be included in the text, with the editor's name within the parentheses.

5. For a psychological study of this impulse, see [Jean-Paul Sartre, *Being and Nothingness,* trans. Hazel E. Barnes (New York, 1956)], p. 566.

6. Wylie Sypher, "The Meanings of Comedy," in Sypher, ed., *Comedy* (Garden City, New York, 1956), p. 218.

7. Welsford, p. 321.

8. *Ibid.*

9. *Ibid.,* p. 326.

10. In "Sut Lovengood Reports What Bob Dawson Said after Marrying a Substitute." See also letter to Eastman, Nashville *Union & American,* June 16, 1858.

11. *The Great Tradition* (Garden City, New York, 1954), p. 297.

12. *Ibid.,* p. 274.

13. Editions of Dickens' *Posthumous Papers of the Pickwick Club* exist in great variety. The quotation is from Chapter 51.

Ormonde Plater (essay date June 1970)

SOURCE: Plater, Ormonde. "Before Sut: Folklore in the Early Works of George Washington Harris." *Southern Folklore Quarterly* 34, no. 2 (June 1970): 104-15.

[*In the following essay, Plater discusses elements of Southern folklore in Harris's early sketches.*]

Although the trickster-fool antics of Sut Lovingood, who flourished from 1854 until shortly before his creator's death in 1869, provide luxuriant evidence that George Washington Harris was familiar with oral tradition, in order to appreciate Sut's folk milieu we have to examine Harris's early, sometimes feeble attempts at humor. In these early writings, in the 1840's, the folk motifs fall into two main groups: wisdom and foolishness (corresponding to the trickster and the tricked), and humor concerning sex. The sketches often use animal life, especially serpents, various categories of bumpkins (Hoosiers, Irishmen, yokels, dandies, and strangers in general—traditionally numskulls), and a physical discomfort which ranges from facial ugliness to excruciating pain. In these areas of narrative folklore Harris broke few trails. Corroborative evidence shows that the motifs were common among the story-tellers of the Old Southwest; some are international in scope, occurring over many centuries in many different lands.[1]

In 1843 Harris made his first contribution to the New York *Spirit of the Times* in the form of four sporting epistles signed "Mr. Free." In the first,[2] he tells of a coon hunt in which he and Tom D., champion shooter and owner of the fabulous rifle "Old Turkey Reacher," follow the hounds into "Haunted Hollow" (an Irving touch). In the moonlight they spy what looks like a coon up a tree. Tom fires twelve times without hitting. He climbs the tree and fires his pistol, still without success. Tom descends rapidly, and the hunters leave. On the way home he decides that he has "encountered the 'Prince of Darkness' in the shape of a 'coon.'" But when they return in daylight, they find that the "coon" is a swelling on the tree.

Aside from motifs of the great marksman and his gun (X1120, X1121), the charmed rifle that won't hit the object aimed at, and the Devil in the form of an animal,[3] the nub of the sketch lies in the deflating self-deception of a famous hunter who mistakes a tree knot for a coon. Tom D. follows in the footsteps of Davy Crockett, who, according to an 1833 tale by an unknown author, had a similar encounter. Out on a moonlit night with his dog "old Ratler," the Colonel spies a coon in a tree, tries to grin it down (a magico-Munchausen feat), and finally finds the "coon" to be a large knot, from which he has grinned all the bark.[4] The motif (X939b) is repeated in the 1842 *Davy Crockett's Almanac*. Some men take Davy out to meet the ghost of a bear he hugged to death:

> I run up an' did see something looked tarnal like a bar's skull in a shirt.
>
> "So," says I, "here's for another death hug"; an' I jist walked directly up to it, got on one knee, and grinned a little lightnin to see by, an' if the hull thing war anything more than a barked tree with two big knot holes in it, then take my eyes for green grog bottles.[5]

Thomas D. Clark has noted the popularity of varmint tales on a frontier where varmints were numerous and provided many an entertaining or even hair-raising adventure.[6] In the humor of the Old Southwest, the element of realism tends to rise into fantasy. But in the Crockett and "Mr. Free" sketches the fantastic element is related to a large number of numskull motifs and tale-types concerning mistaken identity (J1750-1809; Types 1311-1323). The motif of the tree knot mistaken for a coon should be classified under J1771 (object thought to be animal).

If foolishness receives gentle treatment in the first epistle, in the second Harris's tone roughens slightly as he introduces the stereotype of the greenhorn. "A right *verdant* Hoosier," having walked eleven miles to see his first quarter race, goes into "Old Keats' Jug-grocery" (or tavern) for a dram of whiskey and misses the race.[7] The anecdote is related to motifs concerning short-sightedness in which a numskull, in possession of a valuable object, loses it through drunkenness or some other foolish act.[8]

In his third sporting epistle "Mr. Free" combines foolishness with animal exaggeration.[9] After suggesting that the confluence of the French Broad and Holston Rivers in East Tennessee contains fish weighing "forty, fifty, sixty, and even a hundred pounds each" and "catfish as tall as your own dear self" (William T. Porter, editor of

the *Spirit*, bore the nickname "Tall Son of York"), Harris tells a tall tale he "witnessed," about a man who mistook a braying mule for a lion escaped from a traveling menagerie. He also alludes to "a brute of that kind the Irishman shot as the father of all rabbits!"[10] The epistle closes with an anecdote about Col. S. whipping a mule that balks at a fork in the road. When a preacher reprimands him for cursing one of God's creation, the Colonel replies: "He is not of God's creation, Sir, but of man's invention."

Told in the yarn-spinner's own brand of stream-of-consciousness, this string of anecdotes touches folklore at every turn. Lies about the remarkable weight and length of fish are common (X1301.1*, X1301.2*). So are jokes about numskulls who mistake the identity of animals and objects; misunderstanding of animal cries—mainly of owls, roosters, and frogs—is widespread in the United States (listed under J1811). The anecdote about the Irishman shooting the mule, related to many jokes about the Irish (X621*), also fits into the category of mistaken-animal motifs (J1750) and recalls a Texas story of the 1930's in which a servant, sent to bring in the cows, chases rabbits instead (J1757). The final anecdote may refer to the creation of animals by God (A1701) and through transformation (A1710; cf. A2561.1, why mule is sterile), but the twist involves a clever retort based on church or clergy (J1260).

The last of the tour epistles abandons narrative motifs for a brief romp among East Tennessee folkways—quarter race, log-rolling, quilting, dance, and corn-shucking.[11] The dance introduces an element heretofore lacking in Harris's humor—sex. After food and drink, the folk of Tuck-a-lucky Cove repair to the dance floor, where the women, restrained by no stays or bustles, shed their shoes for a frolic that leads to hugging and kissing.

This provides a warm-up for a romp two years later, **"The Knob Dance—A Tennessee Frolic,"**[12] which borders on primitive frenzy, and in which the sexual element receives an emphasis startling even in the humor of the Old Southwest. The structure is a framework in which "Sugartail" allows Dick Harlan to tell, in dialect, about a dance hosted by Jo Spraggins which ends in a free-for-all. This kind of event, with its inevitable hugging, kissing, and fighting, was undeniably typical of frontier life, and Norris W. Yates has recorded the popularity of the backwoods dance in *Spirit* yarns.[13]

The sexual suggestiveness of **"The Knob Dance"** bears cataloguing, if only to demonstrate what Milton Rickels calls the frankness of "illicit sexual intercourse" in this and other *Spirit* yarns.[14] Dick Harlan opens by referring to "a *kiss* that cracks like a wagin-whip," and we are given to understand that if any girl dares to come in silk, the other girls will tear it off her. Dick rides up on a horse with Jule Sawyers, hugging him tightly, who says that if she falls and breaks a leg "she'd be fit fur nuthin but to nuss brats ollers arterwards." Before the dancing starts, boys and girls exchange winks and sly looks, Dick kisses Jule, a boy asks a girl to let him pin up her dress since her bare back "looks adzactly like the blaze on a white oak," Het Goins shows her stocking while tumbling on the bed, and Jim Clark and Peggy Willet disappear in the woods for "a coon's age" looking for fat pine:

> "Oh, here comes the lost 'babes in the wood,' an *no lite!*" "Whar's that lite! whar's that torch! I say, Peggy, whar *is* that bundle of lite wood?" "Why, I fell over a log an lost it, and we hunted clar to the foot of the holler for it, and never found it. It's no account, no how—nuthin but a little pine—who cares?"

(***High Times***, p. 48)

There is a reference to a "fool" who "when a gall puts hir arm round his neck will break and run." Dick sums up: "We had danced, kissed and drank ourselves into a perfect thrashin-machine apetite." When honey for the whiskey runs out, the men are advised to "run an kiss the galls fur sweetnin." The eventual fight breaks out over a girl whom a boy has been hugging. During the fight Dick pulls Jule off another girl and "put hir in a good humor by given hir about as many kisses as would cover a barn door." Dick ends his account with a statement of admiration for Jule's legs:

> Oh, my stars and possum dogs! they make a man swaller tobacker jist to look at 'em, and feel sorter like a June bug was crawlin up his trowses and the waistband too tite for it to git out. I'm agoin to marry Jule, I swar I am, and *sich* a cross! Think of a locomotive and a cotton gin! Who! whoopee!

(***High Times***, p. 52)

Those who prefer to interpret this playfulness at the level of "Post-Office" or some other form of mild petting will miss the rich humor implied in folk symbols of lovemaking. Gershon Legman, in his treatise on dirty jokes, writes of the tradition of the mountain hillbilly who boasts of only three entertainments: *"fightin', fuckin', an fishin'."*[15] **"The Knob Dance"** concerns only the first two. Jule Sawyers' remark that a fall from a pony would result in her nursing brats contains veiled allusions, on several levels, to the sex act. More obvious is the activity immediately preceding the dance. On a realistic level we can appreciate Jim Clark and Peggy Willet's absence in the woods, but the symbolic level suggests more. Coitus is implied in Peggy's fall over a log and loss of the pine torch, leading to a hunt which, she tells us coyly, went "clar to the foot of the holler." And what of Jule's legs which make Dick "feel sorter like a June bug was crawlin up his trowses and the waistband too tite for it to get out"? The June bug, suggesting a penis, prefigures Harris's later use of lizards and snakes beneath clothing. The motif is common, in folklore as in the humor of the Old Southwest.

Folklore in **"The Knob Dance"** is not limited to sexual humor. At the start of his tale, Dick Harlan refers to "knottin tigers' tails thru the bung-holes of barrels." This hunting motif, with a trickster twist, is related to the tall story, collected in North Carolina, Missouri, and elsewhere, of the boy who holds fast to a wolf's tail through a hole in a barrel (X1133.3; Type 1875).[16] A different kind of motif, involving clever verbal retorts, especially concerning drunkenness (J1320), is present in Jo Spraggins' account of his talk with a preacher. Liquored up and mistaking "a camp meetin for a political speechifyin" (J1772), Jo asks "'who was the bigest fool the Bible told of?' and he said 'Noah for he'd get *tite!'*" Next: "I axed him if he'd *'ever seen the Elephant?'* He said no, but he had seed *a grocery walk,* and he expected to see one *rot down* from its *totterin looks,* purty soon!" Beaten in the verbal contest, Jo rides off. Finally, there is the feat in which a fellow "nocked a hole in the bottom of a fryin pan over Dan Turner's head, and left it a hangin round his neck, the handle flyin about like a long que, and thar it hung till Jabe Thurman cut it off with a cold chissel next day!" In a lumberman's tale published in 1924, Paul Bunyan's wife wields a similar skillet, which serves the victim as black collar and tie (X945e).

The 1846 version of **"A Snake-Bit Irishman,"**[17] which Harris later rewrote from memory as a Sut story for his 1867 collection, ***Sut Lovingood's Yarns***, relates a trick played on a numskull. The basis for the joke lies in the folkloristic traits attributed to the Irish, who are loquacious, superstitious, and afraid of snakes since those creatures do not exist in Ireland (X621*, M318). The Irishman as noodle or fool is one of the oldest continuing traditions in American folklore; he shares the tradition with other ethnic characters, and it is interesting that Harris starts his yarn with the mock dialect of another of these, the Frenchman. The general category into which the Irishman fits, the greenhorn or stranger who both menaces frontier society and makes a fool of himself, includes the Yankee, who constitutes the main target for the frontiersman's ridicule and aggression in jokes like these.[18]

But the joke itself plays upon the fictitious danger resting in mistaken identity—a seven-foot length of deer gut which one of the Tennesseans ties to the sleeping Irishman's shirt-tail, and which the hunters cause him to mistake for a rattlesnake (under J1771). The story contains several other instances of mistaken identity. I do not agree with M. Thomas Inge when he says that Harris is in "error" (***High Times***, p. 55 n. 5) in referring to a "moccasin" with rattles. This is tall talk. Later in the tale, one of the tricksters wakes the Irishman with: "HU WEE! HUW WEE! *A big copper-headed black rattle-snake, eleven feet long, has crawled up my breeches and is tying himself into a double-bow-knot round my body!"* Copperheads aren't rattlers either. The motif in this last quotation, of a snake (or other creature) beneath clothes, suggests a phallic invasion common in the Old Southwest. It may help to list several fake-snake antecedents or analogues in the *Spirit of the Times,* a mere handful from a vast storehouse of snake yarns. "N. of Arkansas" [C. F. M. Noland] tells in his "Bulletin from Arkansas," *Spirit,* VI (1836), 229, of a volunteer soldier who, squatting on his heels, feels a snake-bite. He discovers that his spurs have stuck him. In "One of the Snake Stories," *Spirit,* XXI (1851), 64, credited to the Nashville *Gazette,* a man has his slave take three or four feet of a pig's small intestine, blow it up, tie it at the ends, and put this "snake" in the bed of a sleeping friend. Slightly distant is the account by Governor Alexander McNutt of Mississippi in the *Spirit,* XVII (1847), 67, of poor-white Jim who, flicked on the leg by a hanky, thinks he is being attacked by an alligator and falls into the river in fright.[19] The emphasis varies in each of these yarns. In Harris's story it is placed on convincing a newcomer of the existence of a non-existent animal (cf. J2349.8*), a widespread trick related to the snipe hunt (J2349.6*). One interesting aspect of the motif is the counterplay between reality and fantasy. The story-teller—or, here, the trickster-hunter—lies about remarkable kinds of snakes (X1321.3), whereas the Irishman believes these fanciful exaggerations (B765). The awakened Irishman yells that "he's got a shark hook on 'is tale!" (B765.16), that the snake is forty or sixty feet long (X1321.1.1), and that "he carries a lite to see how to bite by!" The oral material from which Harris drew these fanciful motifs plays a large role in American folklore.

Frightening allusion to snakes up breeches may involve sexual folklore which implies castration. Sex of a more robust sort returns in **"A Sleep-Walking Incident,"**[20] which, as Inge notes, is related to Chaucer's Reeve's Tale and Boccaccio's Day 9, No. 10, and perhaps to modern traveling-salesman jokes.[21] This is the famous "Tale of the Cradle" (K1345; Type 1363), in which two young men spend the night with a family in one room; the shifting of a cradle causes the travelers to sleep with the wife and the daughter. Vance Randolph has collected the tale in the Ozarks, and Leonard Roberts in the mountains of southeastern Kentucky.[22] "Sugartail's" version involves only one visitor, allegedly himself, but a more complicated family visited—man and wife, three maiden daughters, one married daughter with year-old child, and an eighteen-year-old boy named Tewalt. "Sugartail" wakes in the night to find himself in bed with the four girls and baby. He pretends sleep, throws his arm "across the heaving warm breast of *somebody,*" and the girls toss him out with great clatter. In the morning, he escapes the father's wrath. One familiar with the older *fabliau* may regret that Harris replaced sexual achievement with rejection.

Other changes involve the beginning and the ending of the tale. At bedtime "Sugartail" becomes disturbed over the bedding arrangements (there being only three beds for nine persons) and eventually undresses behind a quilt "in spite of stray eye-shots fired at me from the region of the fire-place," although the old lady has cautioned "the girls in an undertone not to *look.*" In 1845 the *Spirit* published two stories, one by Stephen A. Douglas, the other by Joseph M. Field, about a traveler's embarrassed disrobing before frontier wenches.[23] Hints of bare flesh were not always so coy in Harris's stories.

The story ends with a wager, enforced on "Sugartail" by the enraged father, which the traveler wins by trickery (N81). In a handicapped contest, he is allowed to race as far as a fence "about 150 yards off" before the old man fires after him. But Tewalt has passed him a hickory switch, and with the encouragement of one of the daughters he jumps the fence to safety. (See also K11, K500.)

Harris turned next to a numskull theme, the two bumpkins who come to town in **"There's Danger in Old Chairs!"**[24] These Hoosiers go into a hotel dining-room where two of the chairs bear the defunct steamboat names "Bolivar" and "Plough Boy." By coincidence, the names fit the Hoosiers, who, when they try to displace a couple of effeminate dandies from the chairs, are ejected from the hotel. The story may, as Inge claims, be "an undistinguished variation on an old theme,"[25] but my main concern here is the old theme, the countryman whose absurd ignorance of the great world causes him to act the fool (J1742). The theme is related to that of the rustic visitor, commenting on town or city or politics, whose American genealogy Walter Blair traces from Royall Tyler's *The Contrast* (1787) to Crockett and Jack Downing.[26] A typical bumpkin story, afloat during the year before **"There's Danger in Old Chairs!"** is Hamilton C. Jones's "McAlpin's Trip to Charleston,"[27] in which Angus McAlpin returns to North Carolina with tales of fantastic sights, of being entertained in a house where he hitched his horse to the door knob, hesitated to step on the rug (J1742.5.1), mistook a portrait for a man looking in the window (J1792), and botched up carving the turkey. The *Spirit* carried a similar tale in the same issue as Harris's sketch, December 4, 1847—T. W. Lane's "The Thimble Game":[28] Peter Wilkins, Jr., a farmer's son reputedly bright in swapping, goes to Augusta, Georgia, to sell a load of cotton and loses $451 in a thimble game. When his father accuses him of being a "fool," he returns to Augusta and loses a load of cotton in the same game. Although it is usually the dandy (or Yankee) who is the numskull,[29] trickster and fool in frontier humor frequently switch roles, and the bungling backwoodsman is a common motif. Other humorous visits to hotels are recorded in Henry P. Leland's "How Old Zeb Went to a 'Crack'

Hotel," *Spirit*, XXVI (April 5, 1856), 87, in which Zeb gets drunk, falls asleep in a dumbwaiter, and wakes up thinking he has been lowered to hell (the kitchen),[30] and in Harden E. Taliaferro's "Johnson Snow at a 'Hottle,'" *Southern Literary Messenger*, XXXV (February 1863), 97-101, in which two yokels in Raleigh misread signs and, taken in by a prankster, make fools of themselves in the "hottle" dining-room.[31]

Harris's long description of his two Hoosier's should remind us that humor of ugliness (X137) is at least as old as Chaucer. The ox-wagon driver is tall and thin, has big feet, sings "Barbara Allen nasally," and has thin and flaxen hair. His mate is "a *very* fat, overgrown green boy" with a nose "made after the pattern of a goose-wing broad axe." Redistribute some of these features and we get the Miller, the Reeve, and the Pardoner. Harris also mentions that the fat boy "got into a fight once, during which a man hit him on his nose with a handspike, when thirty-eight bats and a kingfisher blew out of it." (X916d, remarkable nose; see also X921 and X1783*, tall persons, X924 and X1782*, thin persons, and X923, fat persons.)

The joke turns on the absurd misinterpretation given the names on the chair, which recalls the misunderstanding of an animal cry in one of Harris's 1843 epistles. This motif is prominent in the folklore of fools, who tend to be literal (J2490), mistake the identity of objects (J1770), and misunderstand learned words (J1803). In a tale common in the South, a fool in the form of a deaf man replies absurdly to a preacher's remarks in church (Type 1698G). Misunderstanding is also a trait of the Negro servant who, when he sees Bolivar knock a dandy under the table, remarks: "De great golly! if he haint druv 'im frew de floor!" The Hoosiers land in the street unregenerate in their ignorance, as Bolivar indicates in his final comment:

> When he *raised* me I thought he was turning me inside out, that my starn would be ahead of my nose afore I went five feet, and that the bee martins would build in my har afore I lit. I *be* durn'd if I was sure I ever would lite at all.—Oh! durn his eternal picter, I say. But them *war* our cheers, and if I warn't afeard of being kicked into kingdom cum, I'd hev em—I *be* gaul durn'd if I didn't.

> **(High Times, p. 71)**

Bolivar's fright suggests two Munchausen hunting motifs: turning an animal inside out (X1124.2; Type 1889B) and being carried through the air by geese (X1258.1; Type 1881). Both motifs are so prevalent in the South that Harris could easily have appropriated narrative elements.

These four sporting epistles in 1843 and four tales in 1845-1847 constitute Harris's apprenticeship as a popular humorist. In the four tales, especially, using material

from narrative folklore, he approaches his maturity as a comic writer. Two of the tales deal with erotic happenings—a wild frolic and the titillating consequences, bordering on dream-wish, of sleeping-walking[32]—and two feature numskulls—an Irish Paddy and a couple of Hoosier bumpkins. Sex and foolishness were to furnish Harris with the basic human surroundings in which Sut Lovingood capers.

Notes

1. Index numbers for folklore motifs appear throughout this study. They refer to Stith Thompson, *Motif-Index of Folk-Literature*, rev. ed., 6 vols. (Bloomington, Ind., 1955-58), supplemented by Ernest W. Baughman, *Type and Motif-Index of the Folktales of England and North America* (The Hague, 1966). Index numbers for tale-types refer to Baughman and to Antti Aarne, *The Types of the Folktale*, trans. and enlarged by Stith Thompson (FFC No. 184; Helsinki, 1961).

2. "Sporting Epistle from East Tennessee," *Spirit*, XII (Feb. 11, 1843), 596-597. Reprinted in George Washington Harris, *High Times and Hard Times*, ed. M. Thomas Inge (Nashville, 1967), pp. 16-18.

3. Milton Rickels notes: "The folklore of heroic hunters and fabulous weapons was already common in the *Spirit* and had reached wide circulation in the Crockett books during the 1830's. The devil as animal was common, also. The Big Bear of Arkansas that Jim Doggett hunted through the Western woods in T. B. Thorpe's tale was such a shape shifter that Doggett came to believe he was 'hunting the devil himself.' Harris' attempts at humor are traditional, too: the hunter backs down the tree like an old she bear and runs home in fear" (*George Washington Harris* [New York, 1965], pp. 37-38). Thorpe's famous tale, "The Big Bear of Arkansas," first appeared in the *Spirit* on March 27, 1841.

4. *Sketches and Eccentricities of Col. David Crockett of West Tennessee* (New York, 1833), pp. 125-127. The incident became celebrated. See, for example, mention of "Davy Crockett's feat of grinning the bark off a white oak" in the anonymous "Anecdotes of Western Travel," *Polly Peablossom's Wedding; and Other Tales*, ed. T. A. Burke (Philadelphia, 1851), p. 182.

5. *Davy Crocket, American Comic Legend*, ed. Richard M. Dorson (New York, 1939), p. 160. For bibliographical data on the almanacs excerpted in Dorson's collection, see his "The Sources of *Davy Crockett, American Comic Legend*," *Midwest Folklore*, VIII (1958), 143-149.

6. Thomas D. Clark, *The Rampaging Frontier* (New York, 1939), pp. 39-56.

7. "Quarter Racing in Tennessee," *Spirit,* XIII (April 15, 1843), 79. Reprinted in *High Times,* pp. 19-22.

8. J2181, for instance, concerns numskulls who buy a charter from their landlord, get drunk and use the seal as a candle, and thereby forfeit the charter. This is a Norfolk Gothamite story recorded in W. A. Clouston, *The Book of Noodles* (London, 1888), pp. 17-18.

9. "Sporting Epistle from East Tennessee," *Spirit,* XIII (June 17, 1843), 187. Reprinted in *High Times,* pp. 23-27.

10. A mule. "Probably an allusion to another tall tale going the rounds" (*High Times,* p. 26 n. 5).

11. "Sporting Epistle from East Tennessee," *Spirit,* XIII (Sept. 2, 1843), 313. Reprinted in *High Times,* pp. 28-31.

12. *Spirit,* XV (Aug. 2, 1845), 267. Reprinted in *High Times,* pp. 44-53. The sketch has been widely anthologized, sometimes under the title "Dick Harlan's Tennessee Frolic."

13. See Clark, pp. 262-263, 272, and Norris W. Yates, *William T. Porter and the Spirit of the Times* (Baton Rouge, 1957), pp. 122-123. Yates notes that "The Knob Dance" seems to have inspired as many as six frolic yarns in the *Spirit* (pp. 124-126).

14. *George Washington Harris,* p. 40.

15. *Rationale of the Dirty Joke: An Analysis of Sexual Humor,* First Series (New York, 1968), p. 105.

16. See Ralph Steele Boggs, "North Carolina White Folktales and Riddles," *Journal of American Folklore,* XLVII (October-December 1934), 273-274.

17. *Spirit,* XV (Jan. 17, 1846), 549-550. Reprinted in *High Times,* pp. 54-58.

18. See Clark, p. 116; Richard M. Dorson, *Negro Folktales in Michigan* (Cambridge, Mass., 1956), pp. 175-176, 182-185; Rickels, p. 42; Arthur Palmer Hudson, ed., *Humor of the Old Deep South* (New York, 1936), pp. 451-452; and Richard Boyd Hauck, "The Literary Content of the New York *Spirit of the Times,* 1831-1856" (Ph.D. diss., Univ. of Illinois, 1965), p. 107.

19. For these analogues, I am indebted to Yates, pp. 65, 144, 114. Cf. Inge, *High Times,* p. 55 n. 4. See also "Philip Paxton" [Samuel Adams Hammett], *Spirit,* XIX (1849), 51-52, and Hammett, *A Stray Yankee in Texas* (New York, 1853), pp. 229-231; and anon., "How Uncle Jimmy Was Bitten by a Snake," *Spirit,* XXII (1853), 614. Some of these later yarns may have drawn upon Harris's story as well as on oral tradition.

20. *Spirit,* XVI (Sept. 12, 1846), 343. Reprinted in *High Times,* pp. 59-66.

21. *High Times,* pp. 37, 59 n. 2.

22. Vance Randolph, *Who Blowed Up the Church House? and Other Ozark Folk Tales* (New York, 1952), pp. 29-30. Leonard W. Roberts, *South from Hell-fer Sartin: Kentucky Mountain Folk Tales* (Lexington, Ky., 1955), p. 256. For other variants (with comments), see Legman, pp. 122, 354, 410, 747-748.

23. *Spirit,* XIV (1845), 617, and XV (1845), 9; repr. in *A Quarter Race in Kentucky, and Other Sketches,* ed. William T. Porter (Philadelphia, 1846), pp. 52-59. See Yates, pp. 132-133.

24. *Weekly Nashville Union,* XIII (Oct. 6, 1847), 3; Knoxville *Standard,* III (Oct. 19, 1847), 1; *Spirit,* XVII (Dec. 4, 1847), 480. Reprinted in *High Times,* pp. 67-71.

25. *High Times,* p. 37.

26. *Native American Humor* (San Francisco, 1960), pp. 40-41.

27. *Spirit,* XVI (July 11, 1846), 234; repr. in *Quarter Race in Kentucky.* For texts of Jones's works, see Richard Walser, "Ham Jones: Southern Folk Humorist," *Journal of American Folklore,* LXXVIII (October-December 1965), 295-316.

28. Credited to the *Georgia Constitutionalist,* and later published in *Polly Peablossom's Wedding*; repr. in *Tall Tales of the Southwest,* ed. Franklin J. Meine (New York, 1930), pp. 373-382.

29. As in "Anecdotes of Western Travel," in *Polly Peablossom's Wedding,* pp. 181-190.

30. Repr. as "A 'Crack' Hotel" in *With the Bark On,* ed. John Q. Anderson (Nashville, 1967), pp. 322-325. Zeb thinks the "crack" means the opening through which he fell to hell.

31. Repr. in Harden E. Taliaferro, *Carolina Humor,* ed. David K. Jackson (Richmond, 1938), pp. 73-84.

32. On the interest in somnambulism in the Old South, see Eston Everett Ericson, "Folklore and Folkway in the Tarboro (N. C.) *Free Press* (1824-1850)," *Southern Folklore Quarterly,* V (June 1941), 119.

Lewis Leary (essay date 1971)

SOURCE: Leary, Lewis. "The Lovingoods: Notes Toward a Genealogy." In *Southern Excursions: Essays on Mark Twain and Others,* pp. 111-30. Baton Rouge: Louisiana State University Press, 1971.

[*In the following essay, Leary examines the complicated relationships between the character Sut Lovingood and his family members. Leary also evaluates the resur-*

*gence of critical interest in Harris's stories in the sec-
ond half of the twentieth century, noting the stories' impact on such writers as Mark Twain, Robert Penn
Warren, and Flannery O'Connor, among others.*]

Sut Lovingood and his escapades, as described by
George Washington Harris, have never been quite forgotten. But during the past several years they have been
splendidly and generously memorialized, and most often in a manner which would have pleased Sut completely. Four books about him, who reminds us of "the
depravity ove man, when he am a boy,"[1] have appeared
since 1954, only one before that date; more than thirty
articles have seen print since 1950, as opposed to five
recorded in the previous half-century; a Sut Society has
been formed, and four issues of *The Lovingood Papers*
presented in annual volumes; and at least nine candidates have received advanced graduate degrees by writing learnedly about him. His admirers have become le-
gion, for Sut is them and Huck Finn and an advocate of
measures which neither they nor Huck would have
dared.

But Sut has not been without enemies who have called
attention to his violence, his sadism, his lack of polite
taste. "A dreadful bestial lout," he has been called, in
whom "all that was lowest of the South found expression."[2] Even his ability to speak as he should has been
questioned; his vagaries in spelling have been thought
"disastrous to his fame,"[3] though they certainly can be
thought to exemplify that fine American assumption,
variously attributed to Benjamin Franklin and Mark
Twain, that no man can be considered educated who
cannot spell a word in at least two different ways. But,
even worse, he has been accused of speaking as a Yankee speaks, his use of "du," "intu," "fer," and other
such words said to have been learned from the New
Englander Hosea Biglow.[4]

Not even all of his friends have been consistently re-
spectful. More than one in quoting him have taken polite pains to correct Sut's orthography so that he might
seem to speak more plainly and be less confusing to
modern readers. But true lovers of Lovingoodeana recognize that of course Sut is confusing and sometimes
confused, just the same as anyone else, and as who in
situations such as he finds himself would not be. Confusion is part of his character, even of his intention, and
should not be tampered with. No more than his relative
Huck did Sut want to be drawn to book learning or
civilized: "ove all the fools the woorild hes tu contend
wif, the edicated wuns am the worst; they breeds ni
ontu all the devilment a-gwin on," and he further wisely
cautions, "Ef yu ain't fond ove the smell ove cracklins,
stay outen the kitchin" (25)—a statement which Sut,
being human, may have purloined from a verse of the
mountain fiddle tune, "If you don't like my peaches,
stay outa my tree."

Nor has he been without other admirers who threaten to
turn his head completely. To be told that his stories possess "on the comic level something of what Melville
does on the tragic" would have caused Sut to choke on
his chitterlings, though he might have preened on hearing that his language was closer than that of "any other
writer to the indigenous and undiluted resources of the
American language, to the common man himself."[5] To
place him beside Falstaff and the Wife of Bath[6] would
have appalled his not unplacid sense of his unsullied
monosexual personality. To hear himself described as a
neglected, lost, and lonely child[7] would have sent him
gagging behind the woodshed. He might not have understood all the implications when he was called "a
peasant squatting in his own filth,"[8] surely the most
genteelly scatological image contrived in our time by a
major critic, but he surely would have agreed that he
was indeed a "genuine roughneck mountaineer riotously
bent on raising hell."[9] And he just might be proud to be
reminded that in his often outrageous tales "the antebellum humor of the South reaches its highest level of
achievement before Mark Twain."[10]

But most admirers of Sut seem to me to take him too
seriously. He does descend to intolerable depths, particularly in his treatment of the Negro—see, for an example, **"Sut at a Negro Night Meeting"** (128-37), but
especially in **"Sut Lovingood Come to Life"** (280).
But he rises sometimes also to minor heights: certainly
"Mrs. Yardley's Quilting" (114-22) and probably **"Sicily Burns's Wedding"** (76-83) and **"Sut Lovingood's
Chest Story"** (90-96) belong in any anthology of
American short fiction, humorous or not. But so each of
us have our heights and depths, though often not so
candidly revealed, or so successfully set forth. Read
rightly, this "natral born durn'd fool" (83) reveals cous-
inship with us all. It may be somewhat fancy to name
him the victim-hero of "scape-goat ritual and the nightmare dream . . . that concentrates our fears and hates"
in, and of, a society where "injustices are an inseparable part of existence,"[11] though there is certainly something about him to which the tatterdemalion in almost
everyone responds. It seems proper then briefly to review his lineage and his family ties, and to review them
simply, without stopping to designate literary antecedents.

When Sut first appeared in 1854, and side by side that
year on few library tables with Thoreau and his better-
controlled adventures in wildness beside Walden Pond,
the family name was Lovengood, which was probably
the way Sut pronounced it; it was changed from an aural, or oral, to a visual signification by the time the
yarns were collected in 1867, and has remained so ever
since. Of all the family, however spelled, Dad was most
often in Sut's mind, in admiration or filial terror. As the
young man exercised his "tremenjus gif . . . fur breedin skeers amung durned fools" (26), he had trouble

enough with Barbelly Bullen, the "Passun," who was an "infunel, hiperkritikal, pot-bellied, scaley-hided, whisky-wastin, stinkin ole groun'-hog" (52-53); with Dr. Gut-Fatty Gus Fagin, who called on Sut's old sweetheart when her husband was away (93); with Sheriff Dalton, who seemed not always as honest as he might be; with old Clapshaw, the "suckit-rider," whom Squire Bullen cuckolded; and with other burly, usually overweight, scoundrels, and all the thin ones, who were peddlers, Irishmen, or Yankees whose moral values were subject to correction. But his dad was more trouble than most: "he allers wer a mos' complikated durned ole fool" (35). When Ticktail, his horse, died, "starv'd fust, and froze arterwards" (so stiff, said Sut, that "we hed tu wait ni ontu seventeen days fur 'im tu thaw afore we cud skin 'im"), Sut's dad decided, "I'll be hoss *mysef,* an' pull the plow, whilst yu drives me." And he did, after "a-studyin pow'rful . . . how tu play the kar-acter ove a hoss puffectly" (34-35); another time he disguised himself as a cow in order to train Sut's puppy to hold fast—and almost lost his nose in doing it. Only a true-blue but transported Southerner could have recognized that "man reduced to the level of beast" is "crucial to the meaning" of the Sut stories.[12] Sut might have expanded that observation simply by saying, Man am beast.

For that reason, I think that readers must resist the more recent suggestion that in some symbolic sense Hoss Lovingood—that's Dad—is meant to represent a heavenly father: such an attribution is unfair both to father and son, and would have shocked Sut immeasurably. Lest anyone be tempted to the further step, it certainly cannot be documented that Sut was his father's only begotten son, on either side of the blanket. To attribute to him "supernatural characteristics" or to find in his escapades a "mythic quality"[13] places upon him responsibilities greater than he would be comfortable in accepting. Even without being sure of the meaning of all of the words, he would have responded to the better, though Yankee-born, assurance that "no cosmic relations about mythology disturbed Sut Lovingood."[14] He seems to me all boy, primitive, vengeful, ingenious.

But back to Dad. His playing horse or playing cow, "hit cudn't a-been did by eny uther peopil on this yearth, but us," for Lovingoods were all, from the beginning of their line, "plum clarified darn fool, frum aind to aind" (206). "Hit am an orful thing," said Sut, "tu be a natral born durn'd fool . . . an' all owin tu dad" (83), for he was the "king ove all durn'd fools" (77) and his influence was large; his perpetual proximity to trouble was inherited.

Even Dad's wife thought him an old fool who played "hoss better nur . . . husband," though she only "sed so when he warn't about" or when as horse he kicked at her. For Hoss Lovingood was "dod-dratted mean, an'

lazy, an' ugly, an' savidge, an' durn fool tu kill" (35). Sut had reason to keep all the space he could between himself and his dad. When Sut was a boy and Dad "fotch home a durnd wuthless, mangy, flea bitten, grey old fox houn, good fur nothin but tu swaller up what orter lined the bowels ove us brats," Sut "natrally tuck a distaste" to the dog, "an hed a sorter hankerin arter hurtin his feelins an discumfortin ove him every time dad's back wer turnd."

What Sut did to that poor dog does not bear retelling—it was awful, even by Sut standards: he gave him no "more peace ove mind nur a suckit rider dus in a baptis neiborhood at sacramint time when the ruver am up in good dippin order" (235). As a result, Dad turned his meanest, and "durn his onsanctified soul! flung five or six hundred onder my shut with the dried skin ofen a bull's tail, an gin me the remainder nex day with a waggin whip what he borrered frum a feller while he wer a waterin his hosses" (236). Later, when Sut taunted his father for acting like a horse stung by hornets (which Dad had done, and certainly had been), "knowin dad's onmollified nater," Sut set out for the copper-mine country of Tennessee (38), astride a "nick tailed, bow necked, long, poor, pale sorrel horse" of his own (33).

There we first meet him, "a queer looking, long legged, short bodied, small headed, white haired, hog eyed, funny sort of genius . . . who reined up in front of Pat Nash's grocery, among a crowd of mountaineers full of fun, foolery, and mean whiskey" (33). From this time on, Sut ("half dandy, half devil") was on his own, prey to all, and all his prey. He was often duped, but usually outduped the dupester, and his long legs—"the Lovingoods, durn em! knows nuffin but tu run when they gits skeerd" (57)—allowed him to live to dupe another day. Bees were his allies, and rampaging bulls, not people generally, certainly not those who got in the way of his own simplified notions of right and wrong. Almost always he is the only witness to what happened to him or to what he made happen to other people, and it can be suspected that he sometimes allowed imagination to improve on fact.

Like most of us, he had trouble with words: "Now why the devil can't I 'splain myself like yu?" he asked his friend George. "I ladles out my words at random, like a calf kickin at yaller-jackids" (114). He recognized himself to be only "a rack heap ove bones an' rags. . . . I'se nuffin," he admitted, "but sum newfangil'd sort ove beas', a sorter cross atween a crazy ole monkey an' a durn'd wore-out hominy-mill" (89). With few illusions, he knew of himself,

> *Fustly,* that I haint got nara a soul, nuffin but a whisky proof gizzard, sorter like the wust half ove a ole par ove saddil bags. *Secondly,* that I'se too durn'd a fool tu cum even onder millertary lor. *Thudly,* that I hes the

longes' par ove laigs ever hung tu eny cackus, 'sceptin only ove a grandaddy spider, an' kin beat *him* a usen ove em jis' es bad es a skeer'd dorg kin beat a crippled mud turkil. *Foufty,* that I kin chamber more cork-screw, kill-devil whisky, an' stay on aind, than enything, 'sceptin only a broad bottum'd chun. *Fivety,* an' lastly, kin git intu more durn'd misfortnit skeery scrapes than enybody, an' then run outen them faster, by golly, nor enybody.

(138)

Through all of his adventures and all of his skeers, even when he went traveling with Abraham Lincoln and saw New York—"that cussed n'isey, skary, strange-lookin' country"[15]—Sut seldom forgot his family in the clearing above the creek. If Hoss Lovingood was remembered more than most, it was, as has been suggested, with good reason. He was the root of Sut's troubles, having handed down the "famerly dispersishun tu make a durn'd fool ove myse'f jis' es ofen es the sun sets, an' fifteen times ofener ef thar's a half a chance. Durn dad evermore, amen!" (72-73). When old Burns's fox-hunting sons came after Sut "with hosses, houns, ho'ns, muskits, shotguns, cur dogs an' all," Sut got away by running fast, but he thought now his time "mos' cum"—fifty dollars reward was on his head, and it was Dad's fault: "I is one ove dad's explites at makin cussed fool invenshuns. . . . I blames him fur all ove hit. . . . He hes a heap tu count fur" (89).

"I'se allers hearn that hit tuck a mons'us wise brat tu know hits daddy," said Sut, "an' I thinks hit takes a wiser daddy tu know his own brats" (64). And Hoss had a cabin bulging full—seventeen children, including "the baby that haint named yet," and not including the "Prospect" which Betts Lovingood then carried. Sut tallied them carefully on his fingers, naming himself five times: "me . . . an' Sall, an' Jake (fool Jake we calls 'im fur short), an' Jim, an' Phineass, an' Callimy Jane, an' Sharlottyan, an' me, an' Zodiack, an' Cashus Clay, an' Noah Dan Webster, an' the twin gals (Castur and Pollox), an' me, an' Catherin Second, an' Cleopatry Antony, an' Jane Barnum Lind, an' me, an' Benton Bullion, an' the baby . . . an' me" (34). He did not commit himself on the paternity of his younger brothers and sisters, but of his own he was sure, though not always unequivocally. Most readers recognize him as the eldest son of Hoss and Betts Lovingood, as indeed he does seem to be.

However, in **"Rare Ripe Garden Seed"** he remembers his mother as holding him in her arms in such a way that he would be sure to get his infant's share of mush, because, Sut explains, "Whar thar ain't enuf feed, big childer roots littil childer outen de troff, an' gobbils up thar part" (174), which seems to imply that there were children older than he. It could be supposed that there were older siblings who did not survive, except that Sut's tally of the family corresponds exactly with Dad's

later statement that, in addition to Sut, "Seventeen other brats we cotch in my net, an' strung on my string" (300). One may reasonably assume that, like Mark Twain, Sut told the truth mainly, but was capable of an honest "stretcher" when a good story required it. Whatever the provenance of his brothers and sisters, Sut had no doubt of his own legitimate Lovingoodness: "Dad never wud speak sartin about eny ove our famerly but *me,* an' he counted fur that by sayin I wer by a long shot tu cussed a fool tu belong tu enybody else, so I *am* a Lovingood" (64).

Betts suspected Hoss of having been too friendly with "old Missus Simmons, what lived a mile below" (287) on the same creek which the Lovingoods used, and once the two had a hair-pulling, dress-ripping altercation, though ostensibly not for that reason. It was not, as has been said, "a fight . . . over dad,"[16] for though Betts Lovingood did have suspicions about the origin of Sall Simmons' "cum by chance childer," the immediate cause of animosity was that Betts had muddied the creek which the two housewives used in common by washing Sut in it: Sut it was who warned his dad, "I think they'se fightin' 'bout *you*" (289); Dad preferred to think not.

Sut always remembered his capable mam with affectionate awe. She was good with fist and fingernail, and had a quicker "lick with a hickory, or a clapboard, ove eny 'oman" (299), but she was in other respects a comfort. He recalled as a youngster "a standin' atwixt her knees" while she fed him "mush an' milk, wifout the milk": "I kin feel the knobs ove her jints a-rattlin a-pas' my ribs yet" (174). When the sheriff came "levyin ontu the bed an' cheers," Sut darted for safety "on all fours onder mam's petticoatails," so frightened that he failed to gobble down the bowl of mush she had hidden there: "I'se mad at mysef yet, fur rite thar I showd'd the fust flash ove the nat'ral born durn fool what I now is. I orter et hit all up, in jestis tu my stumick an' my growin" (175).

Mam was a slender woman who had not many teeth and too many children and not enough to feed them with, but she was a good mother, ambitious for her brood and not unwilling, when circumstances were right, to encourage them in devilment. Once she set Sut up as a merchant, "(I were about thuteen year ole I recon) wif a willer basket ove red ginger cakes an' sour apples." When the enterprise proved to be "a splendid failur" because Sut "et up the las' durn'd one, apples an' all, an los' the baskit a playin' mumble-the-peg," then Mam "got hostile" and applied appropriate and vigorous correction (287). At another time, however, when Sut was sixteen, old enough for simple pranking, she encouraged him in placing a Jimson burr under the tail of the horse on which intruded Squire Haney, who was fond "ove squelchin sin in the neighborhood" (212) and who now would squelch a Lovingood "*privit soshul famerly 'musement"* which had poor Hoss in trouble. Betts had a strong arm and a quick, sharp tongue, and she could use either of them or both, in correcting a family or a husband, in pummeling a neighbor into admitting that, yes, Betts was "a nat'ral born'd lady, every inch" (289), or in telling off this meddlesome Squire who dared announce all Lovingoods as depraved and tormentors of varmints (213).

But Sut mostly remembered his mam as a quiet woman "standin wif her arms cross'd a-restin em on her stumick" (35). Her concern was with "kitchen insex, bakin hoecake, bilin greens, and runnin' bar laiged" (77)—sometimes Sut was ashamed "ove mam's bar laigs" (211). As a mother, she was efficient and painstaking. Sut remembered once sitting on the fence "a-shavin seed-ticks ofen my laigs wif a barlow knife," watching her "in the yard . . . wif three ur four ove the childers' heads in her lap, bizzy rite in the middil ove a big still hunt arter insex" which she cracked "vigrusly atwixt her thumbs, an' then wiped her nails ontu her gown along her things" (207). She was even graceful as she "peaner'd her fingers down thru the har . . . clost arter a knowin old insex, what hed been raced before" and was scooting toward "the wrinkil onder the year-flap, but he never got thar," for Mam thumped him with her finger and "he got hissef busted like ontu a 'cussion-cap" (208).

As wife also, she assumed proper responsibilities. After Dad and Sut had done the plowing, "she and the brats," her husband conceded, "kin plant, an' tend, ur jis let hit alone, es they darn pleze" (35). He called her "Old Quilt," presumably because she was a warm comfort in bed. Surely it was from observation of his parents that Sut learned that "Men wer made a-purpus jis' tu eat, drink, an' fur stayin awake in the yearly part ove the nites; an' wimen wer made tu cook the vittils, mix the sperits, an' help the men du the stayin awake." There were other male and female responsibilities however: "fur the wimen tu raise the devil atwix meals, an' knit socks atwix drams, an' the men tu play short kerds, swap hosses wif fools, an' fite fur exersise" (77), but these seem to have seemed to Sut less elemental.

He admired his mam: she was "the very bes' 'oman that I ever know'd, in my whole life" (327), he once said. He was grateful to her especially for the long legs she had bequeathed him, so useful for "a-runnin from under" (26) the consequences of his retributive escapades. They allowed him to remain faithful to the "rale pure Lovingood idear ove what orter be dun under strong hurten an' a big skeer. Jis run over ur thru everthing yure durndest, till yu gits comfort, that's hit" (135). His legs and his skill in using them came naturally, a prenatal gift from Mam, who when carrying him "tuck a pow'ful skeer at a san-hill crane a-sittin on a peel'd well-pole, an' she out-run her shadder thuty yards in cumin half a mile. I speck I owes my laigs an' speed," he confessed, "tu that sarcumstance an' not tu eny fraud on mam's part" (64).

He had less to say about his brothers and sisters. It is possible to assume that "fool Jake" was mentally retarded (though not necessary so to assume), and Callimy Jane was "allers sayin sum durn'd fool thing, hevin no barin on the case"; her brother Benton hushed her by calling her—the context in which his remark is placed does not make it clear whether he spoke in affection or exasperation—a "littil narrer-tail'd tucky hen" (217). Benton was lively, but not quick enough to escape a whack from Mam which sent him "flyin outen his tracks over the fence, wif his hands flat ontu his starn" (218). None of the others are spoken of, except to be named, but Sall, perhaps the oldest after Sut, and she seemed a favorite. She was a practical girl, who picked up an ax to free Dad from a puppy which held fast to his nose (219) and made false bosoms out of gourds into each of which an acorn was stuck butt first (280). She had an "onlawful baby" (273), but she was the most helpful of all the family, except Sut, when it became necessary to bury Hoss Lovingood.

As far as Sut was concerned, the legitimate line of Lovingoods would die out, though I think it did not: "you never cotch me," he said, "foolin with ile stock, patunt rights, lottery tickets, cheap jewelry, ur marriage licunses" (276). Not that he was not, and naturally, everlastingly attracted to girls, women, and widows. Compared to most of the rest, Sicily Burns seemed to him "like a sunflower amung dorg fennil, or a hollyhawk in a patch ove smartweed," and "sich a buzzim! Jis' think ove two snow balls wif a strawberry stuck but-ainded intu bof on em" (69). That "ar gal cud make me . . . kill mam, not tu speak ove dad, ef she jis' hinted she wanted sich a thing dun." She "cud du more devilmint nur a loose stud hoss et a muster ground" (70). But Sicily was neither faithful nor kind, and she chose another, and was not faithful to him either.

Thereafter Sut turned to other girls, to a Sall who was larruped with a stirrup leather after Parson Bullen discovered her with Sut in a huckleberry patch (50-55), to Sal Yardley who was "fat enuf to kill," but who loved "kissin" and "wrastlin" and "didn't b'leve in corsets" (115). Like Ben Franklin, he knew the advantage of old maids—"ef yu gits one . . . out tu hersef, then she subsides an' is the smoofes, sleekes, saft thing yu ever seed." And widows!—"what they don't know, haint worth larnin" (118). He knew the difference between young girls and old girls, which was partly that the former twisted and turned and spoiled Sut's aim in kissing: "I is as awkward as a left-handed foot adze, with an injun rubber helve, when I is amung wimmen folks." As for kissing: "Hits sorter like hot soup, not very fattenin—jist a forerunnin shadder ove vittils, that's all" (329).

Indeed, Sut's preferences and adventures among women would provide matter for another definitive study. There were those whom he admired, like Wirt Staples' honest and hearty wife. There were those whom he feared, and with reason, like Betts Carr. He was attracted to those who had an occasional good word for him, like Mrs. Burns, but he avoided, when he could, those like Mary McKidrin who trapped men or who were meanly suspicious like the proprietress of Catfish Tavern. Best, however, were those who, though rough, were approachable, like Peg Davis, or even better than best, those who were fun at revivals. A calendar and a counting would reveal, I think, that like most of us Sut preferred good women for almost every occasion.

One girl he truly adored, but she "hed tu die," and slept now "onder the pea-vine an' the long grass of Big Frog Mount'in . . . in Tennessee, whar the south birds chirp and the bar growls, whar the wild harycane dus es hit pleases, an' whar thar's plenty of a'r tu breathe an' plenty ove room tu run." Kate Willis had been gentle— "she never told me a lie, never helped to sker me, an' alers stud up that I wur a human, spite of my looks an' behavior." Sut softened when he thought of her. "I haint got no soul," he admitted; "hits onpossible; an' I wouldn't hev one ef I could, only in hopes ove seein' her ag'in, an' hevin' her p'int out tu me the sunshine an' the green ove that purty place she used to talk so much about, whar nobody's arter you—whar thar's no skeer, nur no runnin', fur I railey wants tu rest."[17]

But the Lovingood line was an old one, and inevitably would survive, one way or another. Dad traced the family "back tu Joseph in Yegipt, an' sed hit wer pufeckly useless tu hunt furder fur better fool blood" (108). Sut cared less about genealogy; he had little patience with people who were always "on a fiddil string strain, a-lookin' up for a higher limb to roost on, an' wringin' in every chance far or onfar, what a h—l ove a feller that granmamey was, never seed a louse—smelt a bed bug, or hearn tell ove the eatch, in thar lives." His experience told him that "thar is some folks powerful feard ove low things, low ways, an' low pepil, an' everlastinly a-tryin' their durndest, to show that they aint low." As he saw it, "They ginerily has a pedigree wif one aind tied to thar sturn, an' tother one a-soakin' in *Noah's* flood, an' they'l trace hit back for you, round the jails, onder the galluses, apast the soap works, an' over the kitchens, ove four thousin years, an' if you'l notice clost, hit makes some ove the shortest kind ove dodges, to miss 'em all; but by golly, hit does miss 'em, an' hits every durn castil, an' throne, on the whole road" (260).

His father was more interested. "Sut," he assures us, "comes of as good and as pure durn'd fool stock, as most public caracters now figurin' on top ove the pot." His "great gran'dad, arter a long life spent doin' the durndes fool things done in them durn'd fool days, killed hissef a jumpin down a bluff, two hundred feet into a rocky dry branch, jist to save a half mile gwine to the stillhouse" (298). Earliest named in the family was Sugartail Lovingood, Sut's grandfather, who "never got whipp'd," said Dad, "as I knows ove, becaze he never did eny fightin'. He jist sloshed along lazily, an' this sort ove life spiled him for finanshul business, all except multiplyin' childer, ove which I am one." Dad's mother "was an 'oman hard to beat, or forget," with a sure hand in discipline and "a sharp eye for insex. A sunshiney, Sunday mornin', was a day ove doom, to all creepin' things, an'," he remembered, "we all had sore heads on Monday, an' scratchin' scasely ever begun afore Wensday" (299).

Dad himself was born, probably in or near Bertie County, "in Old Noth Caliney, clost to Firginney line, an' tuck my fust drink ove warter," he said, "outen Tar River, whar herrins, gourd martin boxes, an' tupemtime did mos' abound." While he was still a lad, the family moved to Bunkum County, close to the mountains: "I led two houn dogs, mam toted twins, an' the chances, with a dinner pot on her back, while dad, Sugartail Lovingood, rid the bull, a toatin' a rifle gun; the rest ove the childer follered durn'd permiskusly, pickin' huckilberys, an' fightin' the hole way." Not long afterwards, they returned to Bertie, "whar," Dad explained, "I boun' myself out, to the trade ove varmint huntin', corn shuckin', an' sich" (299). Then he set out for himself, and straightway suffered "a sevear, an' perlonged attack ove onintermitunt durn'd fool, jurin' which I got married" to Betts Leatherlaigs, "an' we imejuntly sot in to house keepin' in a bark camp, wher, sooner nor you would expeck, I foun' mysef the daddy (so called) ove 'my son' Sut . . . a mos' remarkabil son in his way" (300).

I am becoming increasingly convinced that Sut was not, as I had supposed, a Tennessean at all, but a native Tar Heel from the Old North State, who skipped over the line to Ducktown in the Tennessee copper country in flight from his dad. It was not Sut who said it, but he listened to and reported verbatim what an itinerant stranger said: "I wish I wer back in old Noth Calina, whar onest people ken sleep ove nites. . . . I'll tell you, mister, this yere Tennessee don't suit me" (94). I shall appreciate correction on this point.

Then, more than thirty years later, Hoss Lovingood died. The time pattern is obscure. Sut speaks of Dad's having "acted hoss . . . fifteen years before" his death (323), and it can be assumed, I think, that Sut had then been in his late teens, though it can be argued that he was a little older. At any rate, "Well, Dad's dead," said Sut. He "put off doing his good thing for an awful long time, but at last he did hit, like a white man. He died, by golly! Perfeckly squar—strait out, an' for keep."

Betts Lovingood grumbled "that he dident ketch the idear twenty years sooner, for then, she mout 'a done sumthin'"—like marrying again, perhaps. "But no, he hilt on, jist to spite her, ontil she broke off her last tooth, crackin' a corn bread crust, an' then he immegintly went" (321). Only his daughter Sall wept for Dad; as they sewed him into a bedspread shroud, she recalled that day when she had stitched him into a cowskin so that he could train Sut's pup to hold fast.

They all did what they could to bury Dad decently, but they had kept him too long, so that his smell frightened the steers that were to pull the funeral sled to the grave. Hoss proved cantankerous to the end: the bouncing sled bounced him so hard against wife and children who rode with him that they were bounced to the ground; only Sut sat firm, guiding the runaway steers toward the grave hole into which he shot Dad, though wrong end to, as they dashed past. Sall was sorry it had ended that way—"An' us tryin' our best to be sorry, an' solemn." Mam wanted "to plant a 'simmon sprout at his head . . . on account ove the puckery taste he has left in my mouth" (325).

And then Sut died, or is said to have, though evidence of that event comes to us at second hand, and no authenticated report survives. Especially suspicious seems the tradition that Parson Bullen, whom Sut disliked almost more than almost anyone, is said to have had the last word as he spoke at Sut's funeral: "We air met, my brethering, to bury this ornery cuss. He had hosses, an' he run 'em; he had chickens, an' he fit 'em; he had kiards, an' he played 'em. Let us try an' ricollect his virtues—ef he had any—an' forgit his vices—ef we can. *For of sich air the kingdom of heaven!*"[18]

But the last word may not have been said. It is not necessary here to concern ourselves with Sut's descendants. Others have done that,[19] discovering them among characters and escapades in the writings of William Faulkner, Erskine Caldwell, Truman Capote, Carson McCullers, and Flannery O'Connor. Further evidences of kinship have been suggested, including that between Sut's **"Well! Dad's Dead"** and Faulkner's *As I Lay Dying*,[20] and between the bull on rampage in **"Sicily Burns's Wedding"** and the horses let loose in "Spotted Horses," and attention is called to Sut's opening sentence in **"Rare Ripe Garden Seed,"** where he speaks of a "spotted hoss sirkus" (174).[21] Sut has been claimed "unmistakably an ancestor of Faulkner's Snopses,"[22] and **"Sut Lovingood's Daddy, Acting Horse"** to have a kind of kissing-kin relationship to a similar situation concerning the Armstids in *The Hamlet*,[23] but some have been more skeptical: these people simply grew up in the same region and heard the same tales.[24]

Robert Penn Warren seems to have read Sut, and Flannery O'Connor certainly—she told Milton Rickels so.[25] Faulkner knew him long and well. Joseph Blotner, his biographer, tells me that according to an inventory of Faulkner's books, an original (1867) edition of the *Yarns* was shelved in the living room of his house in Charlottesville, and that Brom Weber's simplified edition was in his bedroom. Yet, however he may have admired Sut, Faulkner seems not to have read him carefully, for he was only partially correct when he said that Sut "never blamed his misfortunes on anyone."[26] Surely, as has been noted above, Sut placed blame aplenty on his dad!

Walt Whitman did not like Sut's kind, though Hamlin Garland did. They were too uncommon for Whitman, too grotesque, without the good manners, quiet heroism, and generosity, or even the "good real grammar" which Whitman found among simple men, North or South.[27] Of course Mark Twain liked Sut, but William Dean Howells seemed to have some reservations about him. And Mark Twain also wrote a story of a boy, a bull, and some bees, and of their "larruping into the midst of . . . [a] prayerful congregation," so that "the meeting adjourns in stings and confusion" (pure Sut, with embellishments, though it may have been derived from others beside Sut), and Mark Twain intended the tale as one which the young prince's whipping boy would tell in *The Prince and the Pauper*. Advised by Howells, whose surer taste must have informed him that the tale of bulls and bees would be a distraction, boisterously out of place in a historical romance, Mark Twain withdrew it; but, always unwilling to let a good thing go, he published it in the Hartford *Bazar Budget*, and, years later, "he sneaked it into *Personal Recollections of Joan of Arc*."[28]

But closest kin of all is Huck. Almost everyone says so, but someone has yet to undertake the detailed, close study which will set forth the relationship complete. When that is done, I suspect that there may be found a genuine generation gap, so that the two will seem more different than alike, though I shall not anticipate the findings by saying why or in what respects they can be found to differ. Enough now to suggest that Sut, driven from the mountains, probably with a bounty on his head, found it advisable to feign death, flee the country, and change his name to Finn, to become, as deceit-filled as ever, Huck's deplorable Pap, whose first name is never revealed. He had some of Pap Finn's superficial attributes, including a great thirst for mountain dew and an apparent distaste for bathing.

The chronology, at any rate, is correct, if it is recalled that Mark Twain probably first put Pap on paper in the 1870's, soon after Sut's flight westward, and then, likely as not, pushed the action of what he wrote about him back some twenty years in order to disguise the relationship—telling the truth mainly—he was capable of that. (I resist however the suggestion that as Sut Finn, down from the mountains and ready to make a new start, the North Carolinian turned Tennessean, and then Mississippian, found place, his name misspelled, in Faulkner's *Absalom, Absalom!*) It is true that Sut never mentions having a son, but no one of his admirers would be likely to expect him to. Huck never mentioned his mother either, no more than Sut ever admitted having, or wanting, a wife. That Sut is reported to have died is irrelevant, for Sut, like Huck, was perfectly capable of being a lively presence at his own funeral. In short, anyone who discounts the suppositions set forth above, simply does not know Sut and his incalculable capabilities for mixing things up: "thar's a heap of whisky spilt," he has told us, "twixt the counter an' the mouf" (36).

Notes

1. George Washington Harris, *Sut Lovingood's Yarns,* ed. M. Thomas Inge (New Haven, Conn.: College and University Press, 1966), 60. Hereinafter citations from this source are given parenthetically within the text immediately following the quoted material or reference.

2. Edmund Wilson, "Poisoned," *New Yorker,* XXXI (May 7, 1955), 138-42, 145-47, reprinted in *Patriotic Gore: Studies in the Literature of the American Civil War* (New York: Oxford University Press, 1962), from which I quote, pp. 509, 517. Brom Weber, in "A Note on Edmund Wilson and George Washington Harris," *Lovingood Papers,* I (1962), 47-53, has proved, I think, that Mr. Wilson did not read Sut carefully. Henry Watterson, however, in *Oddities in Southern Life and Character* (Boston: Houghton, Mifflin and Co., 1883), 415, though a qualified admirer of Sut, partially disowns him as belonging "to a class which is but little known . . . in the South."

3. E. Hudson Long, *Mark Twain Handbook* (New York: Hendricks House, 1957), 2. J. Thompson Brown, in *The Library of Southern Literature* (Atlanta: Martin & Holt Co., 1909), V, 2101, may imply something of the same, but is certainly more correct, when he says, "Sut Lovingood has his own dialect." For myself, I would plead with all tamperers to allow him to keep it. As Walter Blair has said, in *Native American Humor, 1800-1900* (New York: American Book Co., 1937), 96n, "Sut's dialect is mastered after a little effort"; my experience tells me that the effort is worthwhile.

4. Jay B. Hubbell, *The South in American Literature* (Durham, N.C.: Duke University Press, 1954), 679.

5. F. O. Matthiessen, *American Renaissance* (New York: Oxford University Press, 1941), 644, 637.

6. M. Thomas Inge (ed.), *High Times and Hard Times,* by George Washington Harris (Nashville: Vanderbilt University Press, 1967), 3.

7. Milton Rickels, *George Washington Harris* (New York: Twayne Publishers, 1965), 129-31, has taken Kenneth S. Lynn properly to task for this kind of sentimental designation of Sut in *Mark Twain and Southwestern Humor* (Boston: Little, Brown and Co., 1960), 129-35; Mr. Lynn seems to me more temperate and closer to fact in his briefer treatment of Sut in *The Comic Tradition in America* (New York: Doubleday Anchor Books, 1958), 192-93.

8. Wilson, *Patriotic Gore,* 510.

9. Franklin J. Meine, *Tall Tales of the Southwest* (New York: Alfred A. Knopf, 1930), xxiv.

10. Blair, *Native American Humor,* 101.

11. As Milton Rickels does in *George Washington Harris,* 65, drawing for definition of the *pharmakas* from Northrop Frye's *The Anatomy of Criticism* (New York: Oxford University Press, 1957), 41-45; the quotations from Frye are, however, mine.

12. See Hennig Cohen, "Mark Twain's Sut Lovingood," *Lovingood Papers,* I (1962), 22.

13. Rickels, *George Washington Harris,* 85.

14. Matthiessen, *American Renaissance,* 641.

15. Inge (ed.), *High Times and Hard Times,* 126.

16. Rickels, *George Washington Harris,* 91.

17. Inge (ed.), *High Times and Hard Times,* 131.

18. The sketch in which Sut's death and funeral are recorded has not to my knowledge been found. Parson Bullen's brief eulogy is quoted in Henry Watterson, *The Compromises of Life and Other Lectures and Addresses* (New York: Duffield and Co., 1906), 60-61. Ben Harris McClary has discovered an obituary notice for William S. ("Sut") Miller, in the Athens, Tennessee, *Post,* August 20, 1858, whom he identifies as "The Real Sut," *American Literature,* XXVII (March, 1955), 105-106. I should prefer to think that the real Sut did not die, if indeed he did then, until fourteen years later.

19. Notably Willard Thorp, "Suggs and Sut in Modern Dress," *Mississippi Quarterly,* XIII (Fall, 1960), 168-72.

20. M. Thomas Inge, "William Faulkner and George Washington Harris," *Tennessee Studies in Literature,* VI (1962), 47-59.

21. William Van O'Connor, *The Tangled Fire of William Faulkner* (Minneapolis: University of Minnesota Press, 1954), 123.

22. Wilson, *Patriotic Gore,* 517.

23. Rickels, *George Washington Harris,* 45.

24. See, for example, Carvel Collins, "Faulkner and Certain Earlier Southern Fiction," *College English,* XVI (November, 1954), 92-97.

25. Rickels, *George Washington Harris,* 128.

26. See Malcolm Cowley (ed.), *Writers at Work* (New York: Viking Press, 1958), 137.

27. See Matthiessen, *American Renaissance,* 603.

28. Walter Blair, *Mark Twain and Huck Finn* (Berkeley: University of California Press, 1960), 242-43. See also E. Hudson Long, "Sut Lovingood and Mark Twain's *Joan of Arc,*" *Modern Language Notes,* LXV (1949), 37-39, and, especially, D. M. McKeithan, "Mark Twain's Story of the Bull and the Bees," *Tennessee Historical Quarterly,* XI (1952), 246-53.

Eugene Current-Garcia (essay date spring 1972)

SOURCE: Current-Garcia, Eugene. "Sut Lovingood's Rare Ripe Southern Garden." *Studies in Short Fiction* 9, no. 2 (spring 1972): 117-29.

[*In the following essay, Current-Garcia examines representations of Southern frontier life in Harris's Sut Lovingood sketches. While Current-Garcia finds much in the stories that is grotesque and repellent, he argues that the stories still serve as honest, imaginative, and exuberant portrayals of Southern life in the years before the Civil War.*]

Although George Washington Harris published only one book containing twenty-four short sketches and about two dozen more uncollected ones, the imaginative world he created in them, chiefly through the voice of his central character, Sut Lovingood, remains unsurpassed in nineteenth-century American fiction. It is not a pretty world—indeed, there is some justice in Edmund Wilson's truculent disparagement of the *Yarns* [*Sut Lovingood, Yarns Spun by a "Nat'ral Born Durn'd Fool"*] as "by far the most repellent book of any real literary merit in American literature"[1]—yet a world that reflects certain aspects of antebellum Southern frontier life with more exuberance and intensity than any other prior to Faulkner's world of Yoknapatawpha. Firmly rooted in the gritty soil of the folk, Sut's earthy responses to the basic human urges of survival and self-expression are not merely ribald fantasies or comic escapades. Metaphorically, they hold the mirror up to nature in the South, reflecting in authentic speech rhythm and flashing images traditionally Southern attitudes, virtues, and follies. Supreme individualism, audacity, independence, resistance to authority, above all a self-indulgent gratifi-

cation of the senses—what Wilbur Cash called the Southerner's downright hedonism[2]—these are the qualities that come vibrantly to life in the antics of Harris's zany barbarians.

Like many of his contemporary Southern yarnspinners, Harris first gained national attention through William T. Porter's sporting journal, *The Spirit of the Times,* with his four short **"Sporting Epistles from East Tennessee,"** which appeared in the *Spirit* between January and September, 1843.[3] Done in a conventional epistolary manner, these described such local activities as coon hunting, quarter racing, log rolling, and quilting, but with less originality than J. J. Hooper's "Chicken Man" yarn, "Taking the Census in Alabama," published the same year. Two years later Harris's work again showed up in the *Spirit,* this time in a form that bore promise of his eventual mastery in handling the frontier humor yarn. For in **"The Knob Dance—a Tennessee Frolic"** he allowed a fictional character to tell the story from his own point of view and in his own racy vernacular and thus succeeded in translating the sights and happenings of his regional experience into vivid, colorful language. The rich texture of backwoods American folk speech, M. Thomas Inge writes, has seldom been so imaginatively handled in depicting "the pursuit of food, dancing, fun, women, and fighting for the sheer hell of it" as in the description of a certain Jo Spraggins, who "can belt six shillins worth of corn-juice at still-house rates and travel—can out shute and out lie any feller from the Smoky Mounting to Noxville, . . ." (**High Times & Hard Times,** pp. 35, 46). With its dancing, shouting, fighting, flirting, and liquoring thrown together in frenzied confusion, **"The Knob Dance"** contained in embryo the rich elements that Harris would later combine and develop with more controlled artistry.

Little more of Harris's writing appeared in print, however, until 1854, the year when Sut Lovingood sprang into view, although it is known that in 1848 Porter rejected one of his yarns which he found "too highly seasoned to be published as it is."[4] During the interim Harris may have been too preoccupied with other activities—farming, silversmithing, running a glass factory and even a steamboat on the Tennessee River—to do much writing. But sometime in 1854 while serving also as superintendent of a surveying crew at the Ducktown copper mines, situated in Polk County, he evidently encountered his legendary hero in this isolated mountain community. Perhaps there was an actual counterpart named Sut Miller living there; more likely the fictive character who first appeared in the *Spirit*'s sketch **"Sut Lovingood's Daddy Acting Horse"** was a lucky but potent blend which served "to uncork the stopper of [Harris's] imagination in a way that nothing else in his imaginative life had."[5]

In this sketch Harris wove a ludicrously exaggerated fantasy about a mountain family so poor that the father, after the death of their horse Tickytail, had himself strapped to the plow in a futile effort to work the family corn patch, but wound up in the creek, fighting off a mass of angry ball hornets whose nest he had destroyed. Told in Sut's own inimitable dialect, this yarn set the tone and pattern for the creation of an imaginary community of beings, both human and sub-human, the like of which surpassed in its microcosmic variety the Anacharsis Klootz delegation that Melville dreamed of. Thereafter, for the last fifteen years of his life, Harris rounded out his characterization of Sut and Sut's unique world in a melange of hilarious escapades, employing him sometimes as a thinly disguised mouthpiece for his bitterly satirical denunciation of specific persons, institutions, and developments he disapproved of, but more often (and more successfully) as a comic observer and recorder of mankind's general and universal follies.

Hard on the heels of Sut's debut in the *Spirit,* Harris featured him in several more yarns, published, sometimes as political propaganda, in Tennessee newspapers during the later 1850's. By the end of 1858 he had written more than a dozen new Sut sketches and was vainly seeking a publisher to bring them out in book form. Obliged to wait nearly another full decade while suffering the bitter reverses of the war years and aftermath, he kept on writing throughout these harrowing times and by the spring of 1867 had published several more sketches, among them the most virulent of his anti-Yankee diatribes lampooning Lincoln, Sherman, Grant, and other well-known Northerners. He had also revised some of his old ones for the publication at last of his collection—*Sut Lovingood. Yarns Spun by a "Nat'ral Born Durn'd Fool,"* published by Dick and Fitzgerald of New York, just two years before his death.[6] Harris had finally made a book which, in Sut's eloquent prefatory comments, he would thank God for "'ef any poor misfortinit devil hu's heart is onder a millstone . . . kin fine a laugh, jis' one, sich a laugh as is remembered wif his keerless boyhood, atwist these yere kivers.'"[7]

Of the forty-odd sketches devoted to Sut, all but a few of the best are concentrated in the two dozen that comprise the 1867 collection. Beginning with **"Sut Lovingood's Daddy Acting Horse,"** Harris creates here a fantastically comic world, dominated by the central figure of Sut, who fulfills the role of the traditional fool as both narrator and hero (often victim) of as wild a series of adventures as may be found anywhere in literature. The underlying purpose throughout is to evoke laughter, and Harris achieves it by relying, for the most part, on several standard plot devices, notably the practical joke, in which incongruous acts based on fiendish schemes for revenge erupt into a chaos of disaster, bringing humiliation and pain to the principals involved and a general breakdown of the social order. In more than half the *Yarns,* Sut's motive as prankster is to dis-

SUT LOVINGOOD.

YARNS SPUN

BY A

"NAT'RAL BORN DURN'D FOOL.

WARPED AND WOVE FOR PUBLIC WEAR.

BY

GEORGE W. HARRIS.

"A little nonsense, now and then,
Is relished by the wisest men."

"Suppose I am to hang the morrow, and
Can laugh to-night, shall I not?"—OLD PLAY.

NEW YORK:
DICK & FITZGERALD, PUBLISHERS.

Title page of Sut Lovingood, Yarns Spun by a "Nat'ral Born Durn'd Fool," Warped and Wove for Public Wear, *1867.*

comfort his victims and to disrupt the community: twice he throws a camp meeting into confusion; he upsets a wedding, a Negro funeral, a quilting party, and a dance; and elsewhere he plays violent jokes on a lawyer, a doctor, a Yankee lecturer, a farmer, an Irishman at a hunting camp, a town drunkard, as well as on a number of preachers, sheriffs, school commissioners, and others easily identifiable as "depressing symbols of propriety, power, and authority." (Rickels, p. 77).

The jokes themselves, some harking back to the ancient slapstick of Aristophanes, would seem tiresomely dull were it not for the rich characterization of their perpetrator and his manner of relating them. For it is the mercurial ebullience of Sut—his actions and speech—that makes the garden of his world unique and charms his audience, whatever the reader's intellectual level, into sharing its heady flavor. "You see, las' year I went tu the big meeting at Rattlesnake Springs," Sut begins by way of explaining how he avenged the punishment inflicted on him and an unnamed girl friend by the hypocritical Parson Bullen, who caught them "sittin in a nice shady place convarsin . . . intu the huckil berry thickit, jis' duin nuffin tu nobody an' makin no fuss" (*Yarns,* p. 52). Because the Parson had broken his promise not to inform the girl's parents of her dalliance, Sut vowed to repay, with interest, her suffering and his own. At the next camp meeting, while seated penitentially beneath the pulpit platform, Sut quietly awaited an appropriate climax in the Parson's impassioned sermon on a text "pow'fly mixed wif brimstone, an' trim'd wif . . . the idear of Hellsaprints"; then, just as the preacher had stirred his largely female audience into frenzied apprehension with his vision of hell serpents crawling up and down inside their clothing, Sut stealthily untied his little sack of lizards, inserted it beneath the Parson's "britches-laig, an' sot into pinchin thar tails. Quick as gunpowder they all tuck up the bar laig, makin a nise like squirrils a-climbin a shell-bark hickory." (p. 54).

From this point on, Sut's narrative, told with mounting relish and increasingly colorful specific detail, builds up to a wild climax of action as the distraught Parson, stripped to the buff, scurries headlong over a mob of fainting women and vanishes into the woods. Yet in his quiet dénouement, Sut's revenge becomes doubly meaningful: Bullen's influence has been permanently weakened because "hoss, I tell yu thar ain't meny ove em [parsons] kin run stark nakid over an' thru a crowd ove three hundred wimen an' not injure thar karacters sum. Enyhow, hits a kind ove show they'd ruther see one at a time, an' pick the passun at that" (p. 57). Sut's meditative conclusions regarding feminine preferences for clerical exposure in a frontier society ramify in various non-theological directions, since his yarn as a whole has suggested through innuendo and specific detail not merely his own latitudinarian sexuality but that of an entire congregation.

Besides sheer pranksterism, the pleasures and agonies of sexual incontinence provide much of the comedy in Sut's escapades, especially when filtered through the screen of his elaborate ribaldry. Harris's most concentrated treatment of this theme occurs in two connected groups of four sketches each, all but one of which he included in his 1867 edition. The first group concern Sut's relationship with the temptress, Sicily Burns, a woman who "cud du more devilment nur a loose stud hoss et a muster ground, ef she only know's what tools she totes" (p. 70).[8] Beginning with the yarn entitled **"Blown Up With Soda,"** Sut exorcizes his own sense of humiliation by narrating the embarrassing lesson Sicily taught him in the art of love when she induced him to swallow a generous portion of what he took to be an aphrodisiac, only to discover, too late, that he had ingested an overdose of soda powder. "'Hole hit down, Mister Lovingood! Hole hit down! Hits a cure fur puppy luv,'" Sicily laughingly screams after him as he flees

the scene on horseback, foam streaming from his mouth like a river of soap suds. (p. 74).

During his flight Sut encounters "ole Clapshaw," the circuit-riding preacher, whom he detests above all others of his ilk because Clapshaw rather than Sut is to be rewarded, through marriage, with the gratification of Sicily's abundant physical endowments. And in **"Sicily Burns's Wedding"** Sut avenges his defeat upon both of them by upending a bushel basket of corn over the horns of the Burns's bull, steering the blindfolded beast in the direction of a stand of bee hives, and then letting nature from there on take its course. As Old Sock, "leader ove the bigges' an' the madest army ove bees in the worild," backs his way into the house where the wedding dinner party is just getting under way, he quickly reduces the entire household to a shambles, destroying furniture and crockery right and left, scattering food and dinner guests alike, and, before escaping out the front door, depositing among them a sizeable number of his angry attackers. The inevitable outcome, Sut mournfully prophesies in retrospect, was a "misfortinit" wedding, since Sicily and Clapshaw, denied the pleasures of the marriage bed for nearly a week, "never will gee tugether; got tu bad a start, mine what I tell yu" (p. 82). Here again it is not merely the wild sequence of events that enriches the comedy, but rather Sut's magnificently suggestive depiction of community mores and postures—his off-hand observations regarding Parson Bullen's distillery, Sicily's maddening influence, his Dad's utter folly, and "Clapshaw's ole mam . . . deaf as a dog-iron," fighting off bees like a windmill—that keeps his stage boiling with human action.

For the story of **"Old Burns's Bull Ride,"** Harris simply picked up the ending of the preceding sketch, allowing Sut to finish his account of the aftermath of the wedding party and dropping the sexual theme momentarily to tell of Sicily's father's wild ride astride ole Sock. He returned to it, however, in **"Sut Lovingood's Chest Story,"** the fourth sketch in the Sicily Burns series (omitted from the *Yarns* possibly because he considered it too bawdy or too bitter) in which Sut pays off his debt of vengeance in one of his most elaborate flights of comic fantasy. Having discovered, as he knew he would, that after a year of marriage Sicily no longer cares for her husband but is "runnin an oppersishun line to the ole chicken eater, in cahoote with a man powfull with pills and squts—Doctor Gus Fabin—an they wer making fast time, all connections, an the male wer kerried purfectly fust rate" (p. 91), Sut plans to frighten them both one evening while Clapshaw is away collecting debts. Spying upon the lovers yet alerting them to impending danger, he ingeniously contrives Doc's entrapment and disposal within a large clothes chest which, attached to his horse, plunges down the mountainside, clear out of Polk County. Sut's score against Sicily is thus finished, as he concludes laconically that she is wearing thin and has no roses in her cheeks.

By the time Harris completed his Sicily Burns series in 1858, his characterization of Sut had achieved such a level of sophistication that, as Rickels observes, "plot summary gives no idea of content [because] the language is too compressed" (p. 52). Sut's allusive comparison of his father's folly to the action of Joseph in eluding Potiphar's wife, for example, suggestively underscores in almost the same breath not only the well-known Old Testament incident and the traditional role of the cuckolded husband, but also his own maturing awareness of man's aggressive animal instincts. At bottom Sut's philosophy implies a desire for freedom from the restraints imposed on his natural impulses by the authority of church and state, society's conventions and parental tyranny; but the frequency with which sexual references are woven into the texture of his attacks against these and other emblems of institutionalized control throws a lurid spotlight on his creator's ambivalent motives. Rickels shrewdly attributes these attacks, as well as the fantastic imagery supporting them, to "Harris's real interest [in] the inner world of the spirit where yearning, delight, suffering, hatred, and the struggle for power are the true facts of existence" (p. 55). But the yearning, frustration, and hatred that Rickels senses, lurking like a dark strain in Harris's subconscious, are much more evident in a number of bitterly satiric sketches that Harris prudently omitted from the 1867 collection. These add little to his reputation as a comic artist because in them Sut, as a mere mouthpiece for Harris's vitriolic invective, is obliged to step out of character and to speak of persons, things, and events with which he would have been much less concerned, if at all, than his creator was.[9]

In the *Yarns,* Sut's boisterous idiom is fittingly attuned to humiliating exposures of unworthy types—liars, hypocrites, cheats, abusers of authority—who, like Sut himself, are recognizably human yet indigenous to the special world in which he lives and breathes.[10] Sut's proper world is therefore one in which the "yearning for unrestrained existence" (Rickels, p. 78) is a shared experience, and its expression becomes a vortex of frenetic activity involving the entire community. Though Sut himself remains at the center—the "eye" of the action—his family, friends, enemies, and mere acquaintances are all sucked into its swirling centrifuge. In **"Mrs. Yardley's Quilting"** and **"Bart Davis's Dance,"** for example, the comedy is perfectly suited to the mores of the community; it emerges richly and evenly, like that of a Breughel drawing, from the shared aims and overt reactions of Sut's fellow citizens toward him and toward one another:

> Everybody, he an' she, what wer baptized b'levers in the righteousnes ove quiltins wer thar, an' hit jis' so

happen'd that everybody in them parts, frum fifteen summers tu fifty winters, were unannamus b'levers . . . Hit were the bigges' quiltin ever Missis Yardley hilt, an' she hed hilt hundreds; . . . Es I swung my eyes over the crowd, . . . I thought quiltins, managed in a morril an' sensibil way, truly am good things— good fur free drinkin, good fur free eatin, good fur free huggin, good fur free dancin, good fur free fitin, an' goodest ove all fur poperlatin a country fas'.

(pp. 116-117)

As Sut warms up to his analysis of the joys of quilting parties, explicitly documenting the charms of free dancing, fighting, and love-making—especially among old maids and widows—the reader is swept along into his ensuing tale of outrageous trickery with as much gusto and anticipation as Sut himself reveals in the telling of it. And neither the demise of poor Mrs. Yardley from heartbreak over the loss of her "preshus nine dimunt quilt" nor the monumental retribution conferred on Sut's rear by old man Yardley's boot sole lessens our enjoyment of the outcome. We are there, savoring along with Sut, the excitement of stolen kisses in dark corners, the aroma of over-heated bodies, the tangy taste of "mountain dew," and the soft, sibilant sounds of bare shuffling feet. Free dancing, drinking, fighting, and love-making on the sly also figure prominently in **"Bart Davis's Dance,"** together with some of the most painful justice ever meted out to a hypocritical wearer of the cloth, ole Hardshell, the whiskey-guzzling "suckit-rider" who repays his host's generosity by preaching a hell-fire sermon on the evils of dancing and flirting. In both of these yarns the sense of plenitude, fertility, and exuberance is repeatedly evoked through imagery suggesting unrestrained sexual potency and appetitive assuagement.[11]

But Harris achieved his most ambitious—and his funniest—treatment of these urges while developing his favorite anti-authoritarian theme in the last four of his *Yarns.* Entitled successively **"Rare Ripe Garden Seed," "Contempt of Court—Almost," "Trapping a Sheriff,"** and **"Dad's Dog School,"** the first three develop an elaborate account of cuckoldry and revenge; while the fourth provides a fitting climax to the destruction of Sut's father, surpassing in antic suggestiveness the opening tale of the book, **"Sut Lovingood's Daddy Acting Horse."**

"Rare Ripe Garden Seed" offers a hilarious variation on the time-honored folk tale of marital infidelity and its consequences. The naïve but deliberate young blacksmith, Wat Mastin, whose wily mother-in-law tries to persuade him that her daughter, Mary, during his absence from home, gave birth to his child in less than half the normal span of gestation, finds it hard to reconcile this phenomenon with her explanation that as a result of the rare ripe seed purchased in April from a Yankee peddler—"'Everything cums in adzackly half the time hit takes the ole sort, an' yu *knows,* my darlin son, yu planted hit waseful'" (p. 180). Although Wat reluctantly accepts this reasoning, since it is strongly seconded by Sheriff John Doltin—the real father of the child—who shows up presently with gifts for both Mary and the baby, it takes him only a short while to smell out the true state of affairs between his wife and the Sheriff; so that with Sut's enthusiastic help an elaborate revenge is planned and executed in the next two episodes. Doltin, lured into a rendezvous with another young wife posing as Wat's, is publicly exposed by her towering husband, Wirt Staples, then stripped to the waist and sent flying down the road with a pair of turpentine-maddened tom cats clawing his bare back.

Summing up the implications behind Sut's exposure of masculine hypocrisy and feminine deceit in this series of adventures involving cuckoldry, entrapment, and revenge, Rickels calls attention to an element in Harris's writing that raises it far above mere comic buffoonery. "In Sut's world," he says, "explanations are always false. Human reason exists only as an instrument of the self in the struggle with others" (p. 80). As a commentary on Harris's artistry, this judgment suggestively distinguishes both the triumphant individualization of Sut himself, and Sut's function as a symbolic outlet of his community's extraordinary urge to be and to express itself—let come what may. In such a community, rare ripeness is a way of life: whether expressed in the fertility and speedy growth of beans and tomato plants, or in the swiftness to anger and retributive justice undertaken by an outraged husband, it is a quality that hotheaded Southerners impatient of legal restraints can appreciate and live with. Let Yankees reason and chop logic; Sut's ardent fellows will bend nature's irresistible thrust to match their own fiercely emotional inclinations.

Abundant evidence to support this view may be found in the last of the *Yarns,* "Dad's Dog School," a marvelous saga of Lovingood family exploits brought into focus on a quiet Sunday morning and subsumed under the rubric of wild irrationality. As Sut tells it, Dad decides over Mam's protest to teach Sugar how to hold on securely by having himself sewn, naked, inside a bull's hide and ordering Sut to sic the dog on him. Somewhat doubtfully Sut carries out his instructions; then steps aside to savor the consequences.

From the outset Dad's strategy misfires. The dog's first sally at his rear discloses the thinness of the protective covering in that area—a mere prelusory indication of the torture in store for him when Sugar, attacking next in front, gets "hissef a steeltrap holt ontu the pint ove his snout, an' his upper lip. Nose to nose they wer, an' no yearlin skin atwixt, not a durn'd inch" (p. 211). The ensuing dance of man and dog, delighting the younger children who mistakenly suppose things are all "gwine

jus' es dad wanted," is interrupted at this point by the arrival of the deacon, Squire Hanley, a paragon of respectability, order, and propriety, whose appearance, hymn book in hand astride his "pius ole Sunday hoss," momentarily makes Sut feel ashamed of himself, his family, and even "a mossel shamed ove the pup." But only momentarily. For the deacon's horrified inquiry—"'What's am yu tormentin them ar two varmints fur, on the Lord's Holy Sabbath?'"—earns Mam's scornful dismissal from their "'*privit soshul famerly 'musement . . .*'" and a burr under his horse's tail that sends both flying on their way.

Poor Dad, meanwhile, yowling in pain within the bull's hide, his muffled obscenities so distorted by the pup's grip on his nose and mouth that they pretend not to understand what he says, must now endure Mam's vigorous blows across the back with a bean pole as he and the pup continue their frenzied gyrations to the tune of Sut's ironic encouragement: "'Stan hit dad, stan hit like a man; hit may be a littil hurtin tu yer, but dam ef hit ain't the makin' ove the pup. Stay wif that hide, Sugar, my boy yu'se mity ni a deplomer'd dorg'" (p. 218). Under this twofold punishment, Dad's staying power rapidly wanes, his legs beginning to buckle; but the providential reappearance of his daughter Sal, an avenging *dea ex machina,* brings order out of chaos. Sizing up the situation at once, she angrily cries out "'Yu durn'd yaller son ove a b—h, *I'll* break yer holt,'" snatches up an axe and, with one sweeping overhanded blow, cleaves the pair asunder, though not without slicing off the end of Dad's nose and a portion of his upper lip, as well as the dog's snout, lower jaw, and one front paw. At the end, Sut observes drily that although Dad fainted and Sugar was "ruinated furever, es a dorg, . . . That wer the liveliest Sunday I ever seed at home." (p. 219).

Closing the book on this funniest of all the *Yarns,* one readily shares Rickels' view that besides expressing scorn for the comic anti-father, the yarn "also releases laughter at order, regularity, and reason itself" (p. 83). But by altering one's perspective slightly, it requires no great stretch of imagination to discover in **"Dad's Dog School"** a still deeper significance: to see it, namely, as the capstone of a rich comic allegory embodying the South's basic impulses and predicament in the antebellum period. Here at the climax, as Rickels observes, "energy overwhelms order. In this energy, exuberance, revenge, joy, hatred, fear, sexuality swirl together as irreducible facts; and the knowledge that all the impulses of life cannot be enjoyed at once is a knowledge to be fled in comedy" (p. 84). To a degree, this may be said of all the *Yarns,* the depth and richness of which emerge chiefly through Harris's controlled manipulation of figurative language in his development of character and action.

To reflect upon the impact of the book is to become aware of the truly Shakespearean flavor of action and folk encountered in it—old and young, ugly and handsome, mean and lovable, repellent and attractive—and all teeming, vibrant with felt life. There are Sut's mean, lazy father; his virago mother, solicitous toward her fifteen children but contemptuous toward her mate; Stilyards, the lawyer, who "look't like a cross atween a black snake an' a fireman's ladder"; "potbellied, scaley-hided, whiskey-wastin'" Parson Bullen; Bake Boyd and his Yankee" rayzure grinder"; old Skissim, the clock tinkerer; and luscious Sicily Burns, who stands out "amung wimen like a sunflower amung dorg fennil"; as well as old Burns, her father; Clapshaw, her husband; and Doc Fabin, her lover. There are old Mrs. Yardley and her fat daughter Sal; Bart Davis and Peg, "his ole quilt"; Hardshell and Black Silk; Hen Baily and old Rogers; Wat Mastin, the Mckildrins, Sheriff Doltin, Wirt Staples, Squire Hanley—and still the list is far from complete.

Above all, there is Sut himself, the consummate, "nat'ral born durn'd fool," an original through whom all the others as well as himself come vividly to life. The evolution of his highly sophisticated point of view may be seen first in his cool detachment, an unabashed awareness of his own and others' deficiencies and a triumphant determination to turn them to his own account; next, in his ironic contemplation of a wolfish world he never made, in which pain, frustration, and bitter disappointment are the human lot, yet capable of being met and at least partially offset by a self-indulgent but persistent quest for pleasures of the flesh; and finally, in his transcendent self-realization as creator of his own being. Far from becoming either a mere simpleton or an out-and-out rogue, Sut attains through Harris's imagination the heroic quality and stature of myth; so that there is about him and the world he evokes an air of permanence and transcendent reality.

Sut's world is necessarily a restricted one; hence the range of subject matter found in it is not great. Yet his vision of that world is so richly furnished with concrete imagery and so convincingly articulated through his spirited recreation of it that both its variety and complexity are inescapable. Harris's images (chiefly animal, mechanical, and occupational ones)[12] are compounded of elaborate metaphors and similes that tumble over one another with such rapidity in almost every paragraph that the first impression they create is one of speed, vibrancy, intensity; while his skill in choosing and combining details that can be seen, felt, heard, tasted, and smelled gives depth and solidity to that strange, yet quite imaginable world. Together, these images and details arouse mingled sensations of horror and delight, as well as vigorous responses toward basic human mo-

tives, attitudes, and relationships. In Sut's world, as in the Big Bear's creation state of Arkansaw, the very air you breathe "will make you snort like a horse."

However repellent they may be, Sut and his world symbolize—in one sense—the old South's vigor and fertility. Rare ripeness is implicit in Brom Weber's assertion that nowhere else in nineteenth-century American literature can one find "a similar portrait of primitive insular man in all his bestiality, glory, and humor."[13]

Notes

1. *Patriotic Gore* (New York: Oxford University Press, 1962), p. 509. Wilson's strictures had appeared several years earlier in a long essay-review of Brom Weber's 1954 edition, *Sut Lovingood,* published by Grove Press. Wilson's essay, entitled "Poisoned!" was printed in *The New Yorker,* 31 (1955), 150-54+. Perceptive analyses of the weaknesses in Wilson's criticism may be found in Brom Weber, "A Note on Edmund Wilson and George Washington Harris," *The Lovingood Papers* (1962), pp. 47-53; and in Milton Rickels, *George Washington Harris* (Twayne United States Authors Series New York: Twayne Publishers 1965), pp. 128-29.

2. *The Mind of the South* (New York: Alfred A. Knopf), pp. 46-55.

3. M. Thomas Inge, *High Times and Hard Times: Sketches and Tales by George Washington Harris* (Nashville: Vanderbilt University Press, 1967), pp. 10-31. References to quotations from this work will appear in parentheses in the text under the short title.

4. Quoted in Milton Rickels, *George Washington Harris,* p. 26. Page references to material in this work will appear hereafter in the text as *Rickels.*

5. Inge, *High Times & Hard Times,* p. 43.

6. *Rickels,* p. 33.

7. M. Thomas Inge, *Sut Lovingood's Yarns* (New York, 1966), p. 26. Page references to quotations from this work will appear hereafter in the text as *Yarns.*

8. Following "Blown Up With Soda," the other three yarns in this series are entitled "Sicily Burns's Wedding," "Old Burns's Bull-Ride," and "Sut Lovingood's Chest Story," pp. 69-96.

9. For example, using Sut as a convenient mouthpiece for channeling his invective, Harris adopted the old beast fable form to attack a variety of Tennessee politicians in a long four-part satire entitled "Sut Lovingood's Love Feast of Varmints." Similarly, shortly after Lincoln's election he viciously

attacked the new President in three connected sketches ("Sut Lovingood Travels with Old Abe as his Confidential Friend and Advisor," "Sut Lovingood with Old Abe on his Journey," and "Sut Lovingood Lands Old Abe Safe at Last") by having Sut pose as Lincoln's guide and companion, reminiscing over Lincoln's mysterious night ride through Baltimore to avoid rumored threats of assassination on his way to the White House. Here Lincoln is repeatedly described in Sut's vivid animal imagery as being not merely ugly, dirty, and flea-bitten, but also drunken and cowardly to the point of befouling himself under severe tension and fear of personal injury. In these and other satiric sketches published after the Civil War, Harris's vitriolic contempt for Northerners (for example, "Sut Lovingood, On the Puritan Yankee" and "Sut Lovingood's Dream: Tartarus, and What He Saw There") tended to weaken his artistic grasp and thus to reduce the comic effectiveness of Sut's behavior and expression. See *High Times & Hard Times,* pp. 222-292.

10. For sheer comic fantasy, not even all the *Yarns* themselves are on a par with the Sicily Burns series. Several, such as "Sut Lovingood's Sermon" and "Tripetown: Twenty Minutes for Breakfast," simply employ Sut's point of view as a medium for expressing Harris's disapproval of innkeepers, though they do reflect other colorful facets of the local scene; while "Sut at a Negro Night-Meeting" and "Frustrating a Funeral" somewhat tediously over-expose his contemptuous attitude toward Negroes. See *Yarns,* pp. 39, 59, 97, 101, 107, 128, 138, 152, 163.

11. The rich suggestiveness of Sut's imagery cannot be conveyed without extensive quotation. Consider, for example, the following passages: "One holesum quiltin am wuf three old pray'r meetins on the poperlashun pint, purtickerly ef hits hilt in the dark ove the moon, an' runs intu the night a few hours, an' April ur May am the time chosen. The moon don't suit quiltins whar everybody is well acquainted an' already fur along in courtin. . . . The mornin cum, still, saft, sunshiney; cocks crowin, hens singin, birds chirpin, tuckeys gobblin—jus' the day tu sun quilts, kick, kiss, squeal, an' make love" (p. 117). Or again, "Ef thar's a frolic enywhar in five mile, Bart is sure tu be thar, an' Peg, too, ef she's in travilin fix, which ain't more nur five months in the year. She goes fur two reasons: wun is, tu eat an' dance, an' tuther tu watch Bart. He hes two reasons also; wun is tu suck in all the whiskey floatin roun, an' tu du a heap ove things what needs watchin." (p. 144-45).

12. For a full discussion of Harris's imagery, see *Rickels,* Chapter 8, "The Texture of a Language," pp. 107-119.

13. Quoted in *Rickels,* p. 127.

St. George Tucker Arnold, Jr. (essay date winter 1978-79)

SOURCE: Arnold, St. George Tucker, Jr. "Sut Lovingood, the Animals, and the Great White Trash Chain of Being." *Thalia* 1, no. 3 (winter 1978-79): 33-41.

[*In the following essay, Arnold discusses parallels between animals and humans in* Sut Lovingood, Yarns Spun by a "Nat'ral Born Durn'd Fool."]

George Washington Harris' Sut Lovingood, as all critics considering the *Yarns* [*Sut Lovingood, Yarns Spun by a "Nat'ral Born Durn'd Fool"*] have noted, is a character intimately involved with creatures of all sorts. As they are to any other poor-white farm boy of rural East Tennessee, the bellows, yaps, whinnies, squeals, and snorts of the beasts are an expressive language to Sut. He senses the feelings of the non-human species as precisely as his own emotions. Harris is only being faithful to the hard-scrabble realities of mountain dirt-farm life when he assigns his character this minutely detailed knowledge of the natural world.

Yet the images of Sut's interactions with the critters go well beyond the demands of realistic depiction; animals are much more to Sut than they are to the average hick. As the creatures are redefined according to Sut's own peculiar sense of the hierarchy of man and beast, he truly demarks his own little cosmos, his own little world, made cunningly. It is a world complete with a consistent moral system, if a very novel one. This world is the work of an artist, however red his neck.

In this cosmos, the creatures often take on character traits more typically granted to humans; in rare cases, they even become tragic in a sense more appropriate to higher forms of life. Sut constantly proclaims his worthlessness, his inferiority to most living things. But his fine delineation of animal behavior, his imaginative projection of thoughts, personalities, individualized oddities of manner onto the creatures, creates a great deal of the humor that, for all his protestations to the contrary, proclaims Sut's humanity.

That Sut can tellingly penetrate the inner lives of the creatures—think like the animals—is only reasonable, since, as Milton Rickels has pointed out, one of Sut's interpretations of his own scruffily mythical genesis hints that he may be as much a part of the animal world as the human.[1] Among a variety of other explanations of his parentage, such as seeing himself a "cussed fool invention" of Hoss Lovingood's biological tinkering, Sut reports that he may have been conceived, not by his despicable father, but through a union of Mam and a pet sand-hill crane. ". . . mam and him had a difficulty, and he chased her under the bed."[2] The lingering memory of the run-in with the feathered rapist seems to have colored the hill woman's thinking on cranes, for at one point during Sut's gestation,

> Mam tuck a pow'ful skeer et a san-hill crane a-sittin on a peeled well-pole, an she out-run her shadder thuty yards in cumin half a mile. I spek I owes my laigs an' speed tu that sarcumstance an' not tu eny fraud on mam's part.[3]

Expanding another way on his odd nature, Sut flaunts his unconcern about the hereafter, since the life to come surely has no bearing on a being which is not human, but is some bizarre concatenation of a primate and a mechanism. ". . . hits onpossible fur me tu hev ara soul . . . I's nuffin but sum newfangil'd sort ove beas', a sorter cross atween a crazy ole monkey an' a durn'd wore-out hominy mill" (107).

In owning these strange alternative origins for his existence, Sut, in defensive reaction to his inability to claim for himself either the moral and intellectual attainments of humanity and the dignity they supply, or the instinctual imperatives of the beasts and the innocence they reflect, establishes himself somewhere outside of both. Still, he owns a self-deprecating connection to at least the lowest forms of animal life, and to those he sees as the most wrong-headed and perverse, in general terms. Rickels notes that Sut checks himself when about to say "durn my skin," substituting, "no, my haslets," suggesting that he has a hog's, not a man's internal organs.[4] Sut also claims kinship to the ungainly giraffe, citing length of appendages as the index of comparison. ". . . I'm kin tu *them* things; I knows by the neck an' laigs, an' I'm gwine to see if they has same famerly disposition."[5] Stories in the *Yarns* show Sut bearing out the worst of his self-accusations of bestiality. He is driven frantic by the feeling of entrapment that results when his pasted shirt dries, after he has sweated in it, in **"Sut's New-fangled Shirt."** Like a creature chewing off its own leg to escape a trap, Sut would rather skin himself alive to retain his freedom than remain encased in the shirt a moment longer.

The beast-man, or man-beast, or both, moves in a world of grotesques, where human and animal roles are frequently confused. But is it truly a world without pattern, as contended by some commentators on the *Yarns*? That Sut's universe is a chaos, with no design or meaning save that provided by his quest to satisfy his animal appetites, vent his self-loathing, and wreak vengeance on other humans who are less candid than he about the

baseness of their motives, has been suggested by Rickels. The self-image of himself as a soul-less being, the lascivious monkey/overused kitchen appliance combination, implies to Rickels that Sut appears ". . . as living or moving almost without mind or spirit—a suitable protagonist to celebrate the joys of action and the abandonment to the irrational, cruelty, hatred, and the euphoria of whiskey."[6]

This evaluation fails to give Sut adequate credit. Within his very singular view, he does demonstrate mind, spirit, and a moral perspective that suggests how both should be articulated. He possesses, as well, a personalized sense of the obligations bearing on all living things, animal and human. Sut, the self-proclaimed "nat'ral born'd durned fool," who has chosen to define himself as beyond the pale with regard to common sense, decency, or respectability, nonetheless places considerable emphasis on proper fulfillment of his role as community scourge of the hypocritical and the foolish, accompanying his status as town jester and laughingstock. He feels equally the pressure for other living things to measure up to their obligations, to perform their roles in what may be called Sut's personal version of the Great Chain of Being. While Rickels mentions the parallel he sees between Sut's sense of hierarchy and that which Sut's creator probably encountered in Pope's *Essay on Man,* he gives the similarity only passing mention.[7] However, the concept needs greater scrutiny.

The Fool's Great Chain reflects Sut's rigid, highly conservative folk consciousness of just what is incumbent upon those occupying each niche in the hierarchy. The order described, while greatly truncated from its ancient predecessor, has all the precise stratification of the medieval stair-stepping of creation, as delineated most thoroughly by Arthur O. Lovejoy in *The Great Chain of Being.*[8] The scheme envisions a cosmos encompassing all that is, in order of increasing spiritual complexity and dignity. It moves from the lowest forms of life—clams and such minimally sensate creatures—up through the more highly evolved beasts, thence into the orders of human society, slave up to monarch, progressing still higher to the ranks of celestial beings in God's presence—angels, archangels, cherubs, seraphs, thrones, dominations, powers. The whole of the Chain is topped by the Godhead Himself. The roles of all members of the order are demarked precisely; proper duty for each is defined by celestial imperative, and for humans, eternal life is the reward of reverent obedience to that duty.

The Fool's Chain, posited on an entirely existential outlook, excludes all celestial ranks of being—nothing higher than a bishop appears in the human link. Yet within Sut's reduced hierarchy—worms are the lowest reach of the order, at the farthest remove from bishops—it is a firm and consistent set of gradations, clearly demarked and firmly asserted in the *Yarns.*

The style of Sut's conservatism, if not the matter, echoes the reactionary outlook of the unreconstructed Confederate, George Washington Harris. Like his outspoken creator, Sut comments readily on what he sees as the proper duty of each living thing, pontificates fearlessly on what every member of every link in his limited Great Chain should be, and expects every man, fool, and frog to do his duty. The harshest criticisms he can level at any person or animal involve that human's or beast's violation of the role prescribed for him, her, or it in the Fool's order. The actions by others that bring down the most intense forms of Sut's scorn, and his vengeance, involve such disobedience.

One image of Sut's view of creation combines all living things in a primitive order of predation and competition, stronger creature eating weaker, and Sut accepts the harsh food-chain scheme stoically.

> Whar thar ain't enuf feed, the big childer roots little childer outen the troff, an' gobbils up thar part. Jis' so the yeath over: bishops eats elders, elders eats common peopil, they eats sich cattil es me, I eats possums, possums eats chickins, chickins swallers wums, an' wums am content to eat dus, an' the dus am the aind ove hit all. Hit am all es regilur es the souns frum the tribil down tu the bull base ove a fiddil in good tchune, an' I speck hit am right, ur hit wudn't be 'lowed.
>
> (228)

In this pattern of primitive Darwinian competition, the person, or human fool, or animal consuming the next creature down the chain—Sut conceives his vision as he recalls his infant memory of the sheriff seizing the family's furniture for nonpayment of debts—is but performing a natural duty, and is not to be criticized for the act. Not the sheriff, but fate itself is responsible. Faulkner's comments on Sut—"He had no illusions about himself, did the best he could; at certain times he was a coward and knew it and wasn't ashamed; he never blamed his misfortunes on anyone, and never cursed God for them"—may be extended to define Sut's outlook on duty or human and creature, if we omit the religious element to some degree where beasts are involved.[9]

When defining the sex roles appropriate to those on the human link of his Great Chain, Sut opines:

> Men were made a pupus jis' tu eat, drink, an' fer stayin' awake in the yearly part ove the nites; an' wimmen were made tu cook the vittils, mix the sperits, and help the men du the stayin awake. That's all, an' nuthin' more, onless hits fur the wimmen to raise the devil atwixt meals, an knit socks atwist drams, an' the men tu play short kerds, swap hosses wif fools, and fit fur exercise, at odd spells.
>
> (88)

He believes anyone can get along in the rough world, if he knows his gifts, his "pints," and honors those gifts by always pursuing the corporeal satisfactions available to him with energy and imagination, never compromising his liberty by signing on with a temperance society, never living too far from a still house, or too near to a church or a jail.

Sut provides examples of humans living up to these none-too-exalted, but consistent ideals of conduct throughout the *Yarns*. In Sut's order, as he applies it to the humanity immediately around him, the highest place goes to the verbally adroit, two-fisted male who reverences moonshine whiskey, and hates sheriffs and clergymen. Beneath him comes woman—sexually pliant, obedient woman, that is. Children are subordinate to woman; they are only barely distinct from small animals in Sut's hierarchy, and are often treated like gaggles or litters of tiny creatures. Beneath these ranks, and often slipping into unity with the most revolting animals in Sut's thoughts, are all human hypocrites. Among these are all clergymen, lawyers, judges, sheriffs, and men and women with inflated social pretensions, excessive vanity, or a poor sense of their proper sexual roles. (English professors are not specifically lambasted, but are surely not exempt from Sut's harsh scrutiny of the fallen Elect.)

A prime exemplum of manly behavior is Wirt Staples, as seen in **"Contempt of Court—Almost."** Wirt, "fitin fur exercise" after getting regally tanked up on three horns of a potent fresh run of "popskull," first trumpets his prowess in the great rip-roarer's traditional style of braggodoccio, and gains the town's complete attention by tossing a small Negro through a jeweller's window. He displays his opinion of Sheriff Doltin, cuckolder of Wirt's cousin, and flaunts his lack of awe for the county court, by knocking the adulterer senseless with a leg of venison, then galloping his horse straight through the courtroom, before Sut's approving eyes. "When the state-fair offers a premin fur *men,* like they now dus fur jackasses," Sut opines as he watches Wirt wreak his havoc, "I means to enter Wirt Staples, an' I'll git hit, ef thar's five thousand entrys" (253).

Among women, Sut is drawn by those whose strong point is in the "raisin the devil atwixt meals" direction, the potent, enticingly desirable creatures of Sicily Burns' stamp. After getting "blown up with soda" for submitting to Sicily's humiliating cure for puppy love, however, he recognizes that such strong-minded love-lies are in fact dangerous oddities without a proper place on the Great Chain. They are a form of the "rale he oman" whom Sut fears most of all the creatures for the savagery inspired in them by their abiding discontent with their subordinate place in the hierarchy. If such a "rale he oman" gets after him, Sut counsels George, straight man in the *Yarns,* "—jist you fight her like she wore whiskers or run like h—l." Such creatures will not abide the frustration grows from their unsatisfactory place, as they see it, and the effects of their discontent render them monstrous. ". . . theyse an ekal mixtry ove stud hoss, black snake, goose, peacock britches and d—d raskil. They wants tu be a man; an es they cant, they fixes up thar case by being devils."[10]

The female who truly does know her place, relishes it, and performs the duties that are her lot in the Great Chain, as Sut sees it, with flair, poise, and gratitude, is the young widow. Just as Wirt is the epitome of the fearless, violent, profane and witty male, the ideal twenty-five-year-old widow possesses all that is right, in Sut's vision, in the way of unaffected, acquiescent, sexually responsive female human nature, eager to serve man in kitchen and bedroom alike. The very thought of tasty young widows, of the sexual banquet they spread before a willing and vital lover, brings images of delicious indulgences to his hungry libido. "They hes all been to Jamakey an' larnt how sugar's made, an knows how tu sweeten wif hit. . . . All yu hes tu du is tu find the spoon, an' then drink cumfort till yer blind" (141). The widows' experience at the timeless rhythms of the sexual gallop recommend them above all others to Sut as the most rewarding steeds man can mount, "the rale sensibil, steady-goin, never-skeerin, never-kickin, willin, sperrited smoof pacers." When the lover-rider is positioned, and gives the reins a flick, ". . . away they moves like a cradil on cushioned rockers, ur a spring buggy runnin in damp san'." Their role, in Sut's estimate, is an honorable one, developing, editing, and pleasuring the men to the improvement of the race and its collective sexual gratification. "Widders am a speshul means, George, fur ripenin green men, killin off weak ones, an makin 'ternally happy the soun ones" (142).

When a human being fails in performing any of these Sut-defined duties, or adopts the role he sees belonging to the opposite sex, or misses both, strenuous measures must be applied to the violator to restore the balance of things, and the disciplinarian feels no qualms about altering his role to match the malcreant's aberrations. Hence "weaker sex" inhibitions must be discarded when a man locks horns with a Sicily Burns; no holds are barred. And God knows Sut shows her no quarter in the revenge he finally exacts for the soda sabotage. The judgment she receives also falls upon men who are in one way or another violating the code, who are not utilizing their own "pints" to emulate the Wirt Staples ideal. Thus Sut recognizes, with acute disgust, that the Fifth Avenue dandy he meets in New York has no place in any of the categories appropriate to the human segment of the Great Chain, let alone that of the virile young man. All the perversities of the baffling big city seem distilled and magnified, to the country critic, in the image of the prissy fop and his fellow.

> They haint neither man nur 'oman, 'caze they can't talk good nor fight like one, or kiss ur scratch feelin'ly like t'uther . . . as they can't fill or feel the instink ove

a man, nur do the juty ove an 'oman, they jest settles on a fence atween the two, an' turns inter the wust kind ove fool monkeys despised by wun, an' larft at by t'uther.[11]

This oddity perceived by Sut, the dandy is sentenced instantly to correction, and, fighting fire with fire, Sut goes after the creature he sees as extra-human, extra-animal in an appropriately atavistic fashion. Voluntarily regressing down the Chain of Being, he pursues the dandy in the style, and with the fighting techniques of various beasts: horse, mule, gander, dog. Sut drops to all fours behind the dandy, fetches a "rale fightin' hoss squeal," and boots him head-first through the back door of a crowded omnibus. When the angry driver shoots Mr. Dandy back out, Sut catches him, straddling his neck, brays, sinks his teeth into a "bill holt" on the fop's thigh, and streaks toward the river, "about es fast es a big dog kin go with a tin bucket a chasin' ove him." Sut spreads chaos about town, destroying an umbrella salesman, sending a man and his trotting surrey through a display window, gathering a retinue of pursuing policemen, who believe they are chasing a dog, and literally scaring the piss out of the dandy before flinging him into East River. Sut wonders "ef thar's eny law in this yere place agin drowndin such reptiles"; in the confused and unnatural city, there just might be, for city folks are odd beings: ". . . they're so durn'd curious, enyhow."[12]

In posing as an animal to humiliate the dandy, Sut certainly debases himself as well as his victim. He retains, however, his ironic remove from the pose. Ultimate degradation for a human in Sut's world results when a character not only poses as a lower being for effect, but actually loses his hold on his spot in the human link of the Great Chain as a result of his foolishness, when figurative regression seems to become literal. Sut's father, Hoss Lovingood, truly living up, or more accurately, down, to his name, performs such regression in **"Sut Lovingood's Daddy, Acting Horse,"** and **"Dad's Dog-School."** The essential "damn fool" qualities of Hoss convince him that, if he is to do a convincing job of replacing the family's recently deceased ploughhorse, he must reproduce not only the beast's function as tractor, but also evince the peculiarities of cantankerousness appropriate to a balky nag. He insists on Sut's fashioning him a harness of bark strips, and a coathanger bridle. For true unity with nature, he strips naked.

> When we got the birdil fix'd ontu Dad, don't yu bleve he sot intu chompin hit jes' like a rale hoss, an' tried to bite me on the arm. (he allers wer a mos' complikated durned ole fool.)
>
> (23)

In his consummately realistic impersonation of the beast, Hoss feels obliged, "tu keep up his karacter es a hoss," by tearing straight through a sassafras bush he encounters. A nest of hornets, their peace in the bush destroyed, set upon Dad, drive him through a bramble thicket, and chase him off a bluff into the river, stinging en route. Sut considers Dad's leap a weakness in the otherwise top-notch rendering of horsely character.

> Now rite thar, boys, he over-did the thing, ef actin hoss tu the scribe wer what he wer arter; fur thar's nara hoss ever foaldid durnd fool enuf to lope over eny such place; a cussed muel mout a dun hit, but dad warnt actin muel, tho' he orter tuck that karacter; hits adzactly sooted to his dispersition.
>
> (26)

The hilarious and disgusting spectacle of naked, thoroughly hornet-stung Dad enchants Sut, who richly detests the Lovingood *paterfamilias,* and the sense of Dad's repellent bestiality, the conviction that he is hardly human, grows for the reader with each of Sut's somewhat-less-than-helpful bits of counsel as enraged Dad pops his head above the water to curse Sut, then submerges to dodge another hornet. "'kick em—bite em—paw em—switch em wif uure tail, Dad,' sez I . . . I'll hev yure feed in the trot redy; yu won't need eny curyin tu-nite will yu?" (27)

The confusion of Dad with an animal goes to its most extreme in **"Dad's Dog-School,"** when the elder Lovingood, seeking to teach Sut's bull-pup tenacity, undertakes dog education. He strips—all regressions in the *Yarns* begin by the human discarding the symbols of civilization—and has Sut's sister sew him into a bull's hide. Sut is then to sick the dog on him, and try to pull the dog off, in hopes of showing Sugar, the dog, the need to hang on to his jawhold despite resistance. Dad's performance as bull is consummate.

> Torreckly I hearn Dad a-bellerin jis' the bes' sampil ove a yearlin's nise yu ever hearn, sceptin hit wer a scrimpshun too corase, an' a littil too fas': Dad wer excited. "Boor, woo woff—Bohua a huah"—fust rate, by the jinglin Jehosophat! thinks I, an' Sugar cock't his years an' barked.
>
> (281-82)

The image of the obscene old redneck, with the bull's horns and nose covering his face, carry the human clear out of the *homo sapiens* condition and into the bestial, even in his son's thoughts.

> (Sister Sall) had turn'd the head an' ho'ns back, raw side out, es high es dad's eye-brows, an' tied the nose to the naik, so he cud see the inimy. His face were smeer'd wif the blood an' fat . . . takin' the site altugether hit cudn't be beat, fur a big, ruff, skeery thing outen hell, ur a mad-hous.
>
> (282)

The canine instruction advances, with Mam flogging her helpless beast-mate with a beanpole—she is not pleased with the dog pedagogy, nor the insults she had

received—while the bulldog clings to Dad's nose with admirable staying power. The adult family members, and a meddling clergyman who happens by, alike react with amazed disgust to Dad's abandonment of his assigned place on the Great Chain for an animal role, his act played too well. Mam had earlier commented on his impersonation of the plough horse, "Yu plays hoss better nur yu dus husband," and now voices the family judgment, "Hu ever hearn ove the likes bein dun by the daddy ove a famerly, an' him a bal' headed man at that, a-shedin his hair fur the grave" (279). Even Sut voices his shame at Dad, one of the few places in the *Yarns* that he owns a capacity for the emotion.

The above examples, then, give some notion of how Sut expects men and women to behave in their places on the Great Chain, of how he honors those performing well, by his lights, and how he copes with those who are falling short of his standards. How does he treat the creatures when they are or are not coming up to snuff in terms of Sut's rules for evaluating the conduct of those below the human link in the Chain? It is soon apparent that, in his premeditated stunts, Sut selects any creature that is to serve a key comic function in any escapade by considering the beast's or bug's "pints"; he regards the creature in some of the ways he evaluates human reliability. That is, he looks to its consistency in behaving as it should according to his sense of its nature, its place on the Chain, when under the pressure of the particular bit of hell-raising in which it will play a role. He often sketches his idea of the animal's inner life during the stunt, honors it for doing well, downgrades it when inconsistent, and, perhaps most importantly for its characterization, bestows greatest credit when it displays ability to improvise. This quality, ability to think fast, to show flair, might even be called the animal equivalent of imagination. In saluting this quality, Sut shows that the highest level of animal accomplishment is that in which the animal reflects the same ability to "think on its feet" to compound the chaos while seeking its own escape, that is Sut's own greatest gift, the Fool's major "pint." In Sut's words, "all 'pends, et las' on what yu das . . . *at the moment ove ackshun.*" In this, Sut suggests that, just as Wirt Staples is the ideal against which all other human males are to be judged for manliness and quality of inspiration, the fool himself, the figurative half-human, half-creature, the quick-witted improvisor, is the standard against which comic animals serving Sut will be judged.

His scrutiny of the animal world runs upward from the insect world. In a tick, attempting to evade Mam's talented fingers while she is "on a still hunt arter insex," in the children's hair, Sut admires the evasive tactics of the "knowin ole insex, what hed been raced before" as it scurries over Sut's sibling's scalp, "aimin fur the wrinkle under the year-flap." The tick, like Sut on certain occasions, doesn't show enough imagination to effect his escape. ". . . but he never got thar; he got hissef busted like ontu a 'cussion-cap, 'bout a inch an a 'alf frum his den" (278-80).

In the hornets and bees Sut employs to disrupt a Negro night-meeting revival, and which add to the confusion at Dad's horse act and the fiascos at Sicily Burns' wedding, Sut sees admirable allies in his schemes, and kindred spirits when it comes to squaring accounts with enemies. The insects' fidelity to their calling, their place in creation as fanatically committed defenders of their hives and nests, pleases Sut greatly, for he too believes deeply in revenge. "Hit aint much wuf tu tell what the bees did, ur how soon they sot into duin hit," says Sut of the insects who have landed on the basket-blinded bull which has knocked down their hive outside Sicily's nuptials. "They am pow'ful quick-tempered little critters enyhow. The air wer dark wif 'em, and Sock (the bull) wer kivered all over . . . so clost yu cudent a-sot down a grain ove wheat fur bees" (91).

In the reptile kingdom, Sut finds the "pints" of quick-wittedness personified in the speedy lizard; the reptile's nervous scurrying and opportunism suggest to Sut the quality of keen observation and readiness to capitalize on a good chance that marks the alert human trickster. He salutes one of the bag of lizards he has released under Parson Bullen's pant-leg, in the midst of his "hell-sarpint" tirade to the camp meeting, when the reptile seeks escape by popping his head out of the frantic divine's collar. "[The lizard] wer a surveyin the crowd, when Ole Bullen struck at 'im, jis' too late, fur he'd dodged back again." The most imaginative of the lizards makes the most of a bad thing when he is flung into the crowd from Bullen's just-discarded pants.

> One ofe the smartest ove my lizards lit head-fust intu the buzzim ove a fat 'oman, es big es a skin'd hoss, an' ni ontu es ugly. . . . Smart to the las', by golly, he imejuntly commenced runnin down the center ove her breas'-bond, an' kep on, I speck.
>
> (55-56)

When the fat lady faints, Sut feels the reptile has achieved an ultimate triumph of determination and fidelity to lizardly mission, worthy of the Fool himself.

Frogs and snakes, in Sut's opinion, are also doing their best with their gifts when they expend all efforts possible to conceal themselves in niches and holes, if caught in the open, and frogs distinguish themselves by keeping clear of the snakes. In **"Sut Lovingood's Big Dinner Story,"** these impulses act on the peck container of striped garden frogs, one bullfrog, and a four-and-a-half-foot black-snake served up by Sut and Violet Watson to enliven social-climbing Misses Jarrold's fancy dinner party. The critters dominate the conversation and establish a certain unmistakable ambiance when

the frogs react to the appearance of their biological adversary from another dish. Just as Sut is ever alert for all comic openings in a figurative sense, the frogs and snake seek literal openings for refuge; Sut has to admire the creatures' ingenuity and explorative urgency. "One long-laiged, actif little cuss" pops into Mr. Jarrold's open mouth. Ejected by "a vomitin sort ove a jerk" from the old man, he does a flip on the table and shoots into the visiting parson's shirt. The parson "set tu dancin Killacrankey . . . powerful thankful fur what *he'd* received, I speck." The snake hides in Lawyer Gripes' hat, which the advocate dons, planning hasty exit, and the snake slithers down his back. Sut considers the reptile's thoughts in transit between Gripes' legs as the lawyer seizes his tail from behind his back.

> [The snake] wer obleged to strengthen his purchase, so he straightened out some ove his kinks . . . along that legul back-bone, ontil he come to the forks ove the road; then he wound around the turn, leavin' a laig on his right an' a laig on his left, an' started up hill agin . . . he seed a streak ove day light, an poked out ni ontu a foot ove hissef to 'zamine the open country a little.[13]

Gripes' gyrations, with a foot of the business end of a snake protruding from his fly, receive Sut's careful dramatization, as does the frantic lawyer's flight through the cornfield, with clothes, and finally snake, flying into the air above the corn tassels in the distance.

The frogs and snake in the dinner story are presented principally as keeping their spots on the Great Chain, but the huge frog which appears from under the railroad restaurant stove in **"Sut Lovingood at Bull's Gap"** makes shocking hops up the Great Chain, becoming a hostile Duncan Hines condemning the vile food and service at the trainstop. The frog mounts an overshoe floating in the slop and spilled whiskey on the restaurant floor.

> He hed a iron teaspoon crosswise intu his mouf . . . an sot intu paddlin hissef with his spoon, injun way, fust one side ove the heel and then tother across that ar pond.[14]

The frog steers to a hair trunk, mounts it, scratches his back with the spoon, and, after a few laps of the puddle, flings the spoon at Sut. He feels the time is then ripe for an oration, and commences.

> Then he squatted ontu the har trunk, spread his fore laigs wide . . . a facin the crowd, an in the mos' human-like way yu ever hearn in all yer born days, begun in an orful voice a croakin, "Bull's Gap—Bull's Gap—Bull's Gap."[15]

The wretched station, its awful food, so anger Sut that he feels the whole cosmos out of focus, the animal misplaced on the Great Chain, or monstrously sliding up it. He considers the frog an appropriate part of the perverse, nightmare station, where travellers have surely been poisoned for years. "The thought got thru my har that hit wer the ghostes ove some Frenchman what had got pizened with sumthin he'd et thar."

Further up the chain of being, Sut finds the hogs, dogs, horses, and cattle, the more highly evolved creatures which present the Fool greater challenges, and greater opportunities for making mayhem. While Sut largely has his way with the lower beasts, discounting the reincarnate Frenchman frog, the wiser and more powerful creatures are less tractable, and sometimes, the fool. Not for nothing does Sut opine that he must watch out lest he be sabotaged by certain creatures in their less inhibited moments. "Why, when I meets a 'nowin-lookin beast, I'se feared ove hit, an' watches tu see that hit don't git me inter sum cussed skeery scrape."[16] The comment is only half ironic, for in a few of the *Yarns*, such as **"Sut Lovingood's Hog Ride"** and **"Taurus in Lynchburg Market,"** Sut is truly the animal's victim, with the creature calling the tune as the Fool is done in by hog and bull. In the first Sut is literally caught with his pants down in a Nashville alley, and ridden about town on the hog's snout through the city's business district, spreading chaos and finally losing his britches. "I her'n the words 'dam fool' cum frum somewhar," he recalls. "Thinks I, mister, yuse hit hit to a dot, whether yu mean me ur this yer infernal sow."[17] Sut's attempt to halt the progress of a furious runaway bull in Lynchburg, which he essays by grabbing the bull's tail and taking several turns about a lamp post with the appendage, ends with Sut's leaping into the river, barely avoiding a goring in the seat of the pants.

Yet in most of his dealings with the larger quadrupeds, Sut triumphs. When demolishing Sicily Burns' wedding, he plays on his knowledge of bull nature; he knows that nature well from a near family connection in the Great Chain. "[Cow brutes] is the durnes' fools amung all the bestes ('scept the Lovingoods)," he observes when recounting his blinding Old Sock with a basket. ". . . when they gits intu tribulashun, they knows nuffin but to shot thar eyes, beller, an' back, an' keep a-backin" (90). Thus encumbered, Old Sock performs flawlessly, in best bull-headed fashion, by backing through the house, bashing through walls, destroying the crockery and furnishings, hurling guests about, and finally knocking over the bee-bench. The wedding destroyed, Sock exits, bellowing his misery from the assaults of the vengeful insects. Old Mr. Burns, victim of an ill-timed grab at the basket, is now Old Sock's rider.

As Sock tears down the road in the sequel story, **"Old Burns' Bull-Ride,"** Sut considers the beast's meditations. The trickster appreciates the animal's frenzy when influenced by a "skeer" such as Old Sock received. His rider's beating him savagely with brush snatched in

transit deters Sock not. "He didn't keer a durn fer enything, since his intercourse wif the bees, an his mistification in the baskit" (99). Enter another bull, that belonging to Burns' neighbor, Mills. Seeing something at which to direct his wrath, Old Sock attacks. The Mills' bull, assaulted by both Old Sock and his passenger, alters strategy after a few passes, to Sut's admiration.

> The Mills bull's a mity smart critter, to be only a cow beas', an' he preshiated adzactly Ole Burns power wif a hanful ove brush. So while Old Sock wer a gwine thru a gran' charge blind he tuck a circumbendibus roun. . . . He jis cum in atween his hine laigs.
>
> (100)

As the fight progresses, Old Burns progresses from Sock's back, to hanging upside down in a tree, to riding backwards on the Mills' bull's back. To secure his grip, Burns sinks his teeth into the bull's tail. Sut considers the bull's response to the unique sensation.

> [The bull] now dident begin tu onderstan' what wer atop ove 'im; hit wer somthin sartin what hed bof claws an' teef, an—*painter*—flash'd ontu his mine wif all the force the bill holt ontu his tail cud give hit . . . his pluck wilted, an' he jis turn'd tail . . . aimin fur North Caliney.
>
> (103)

The human durn'd fool enjoys the leather-headedness of the creatures he identifies with on the Great Chain, feeling that both bulls have done as well as he could have, in terms of stupidity displayed and carnage generated. The strain on both bulls is such that they lose their senses of place on the Chain; one becomes a pansy, the other goes berserk: "Mills' bull sought hissef anuther suckit, an' becum es morril es a draft-steer. Old Sock becum more depraved, an' run wile in the mountins, an' I is jis about es I wer, the durndes' fool in the mess" (104).

Horses, next link up in the four-footed portion of the chain, show more intricacy than bulls, which are, on the whole, true to their nature. Horses, by contrast, are more impressionable, more easily drawn into pretension. That Sut can admire a horse is seen in **"Bill Ainsworth's Quarter Race: A Story of Old Times (1833) in East Tennessee."** Sut—very un-Sut-like—dotes on the beauty of the mare Kate, and describes her splendid form by orienting her likeness up the Great Chain, treating her much as he does the beautiful Sicily Burns.

> She walked with a limber, sassy step. . . . She look'd right at every body an' thing roun' her es a human would . . . I hes seen wimmen in my time adzackly like Kate . . . an' every one ove 'em wer oncommon people, either for good or bad.[18]

But Kate is an atypical "hoss" in Sut's stories, just as the nostalgic *Yarn* in which she appears is not the normal Sut Story, for its sentimental tone. The horse's poise, boldness, self-confidence, and gifts as a racer, make her a "rale he oman" among her kind.

The more typical horse Sut pictures is seen in Squire Hanley's nag, presented in **"Dad's Dog-School."** The horse has lost its basic equine character—we recall Dad's dramatization of the essential qualities—and has adopted the sanctimonious style of its owner.

> His hoss wer ove a pius turn ove mine. . . . Nobody ever seed him kick, gallop, jump a fence, smell uther hosses, ur chaw a bridil. He wer never hearn squeal, belch, ur make eny onsightly soun . . . he hed scabs ontu his knees an' mud on his snout.
>
> (288)

The animal shares Hanley's condescending sorrow as they witness the spectacle of Dad-turned bull. "Even his pius ole hoss show'd a grieved spirit frum foretop tu lip" (286). This sort of selling out his spot on the Chain by the horse revolts Sut as much as Hanley's attempt to lecture the family on the impropriety of the Sunday dog academy; he and Mam collaborate to destroy the composure of horse and rider. Sut jams a burr under the horse's tail, then splits a clapboard "plum open, atwixt the root ove his tail, an the squire's." The horse goes quite mad, leaping in frenzy about the lot, despite Hanley's resistance, and finally bolts, leaving the squire in a nearby thicket. Sut is proud to have revealed simultaneously the animal's and his owner's common true nature. ". . . I show'd him that day tu be es durn's a ole hipperkirt es ever toted a saddil, ur a hyme book." In several stories in the *Yarns,* Sut treats horses unfaithful to their place in this way.[19]

In dogs, Sut sees creatures at a spot nearly parallel to horses in his Great Chain. But the dogs are more important, for, at their worst, they are even closer to true nat'ral born'd durn'd foolhood than bulls. Like horses, they have the capacity for devotion to their calling as dogs that can make them appear admirable at times. Resembling Kate the quarterhorse, in terms of dedication, Sut's bull-pup, Sugar, is a paragon of what his kind should be, "Ugly as a she ho'net, an' brave es a trap'd rat" (278) The dog's laudable qualities, his keeping his jaw-grip despite all the abuse he receives during the dog-school, fill Sut with affection and admiration. Sugar hangs onto Dad's bloody nose until an axe-blow delivered by Sister Sall finally chops off Sugar's, and part of Dad's respective snouts. The tragedy moves Sut with sorrow for Sugar and spite for Dad. Sut's crying as he drowns the maimed pup is the only evidence of such sentimental feeling for any creature Sut demonstrates; the scene is certainly one of the microscopically small number of tragic passages in the *Yarns.*

In Stuff-gut, the canine protagonist of **"Sut Lovingood's Dog,"** Sut demonstrates his ultimate identification with any animal; the feisty, tail-less mutt reflects Sut's idea of the Fool's role precisely. He expresses his approval of the dog, as Donald R. Knight has noted, by likening its movements to human gestures.[20] The similes project the dog up the Great Chain, as Sut recalls, "He hed a way ove walkin slow an' solemn like I've seed yung fellers do at a camp-meetin when approachin ove a gal . . . agwine sorter side ways an' mity keerful." Again, "he wagged his hole sturn, an' his hine feet slipped about on the groun, sorter like a fashunable gal walks when she thinks sum he feller is lookin at her" (150).

Like the Fool, his owner, Stuff-gut is hard to predict, tends to be a bit perverse, and works at cross purposes.

> . . . yu cud never set 'im ontu enything yu wanted tu, an' cudn't call 'im ofen enything he got arter on his own accord. He wer skeered all the time, an' stud redy tu run or steal . . . he wur jis' the rite sort ove a dog tu belong tu me—not wurth a durn, an' orter been killed afore his eyes got open.
>
> (150-51)

Thanks to a whim of Dad's, and a straw-cutting machine, the dog is missing his tail, just as Sut's genetic durn'd foolhood has left him missing his common sense. The animal is, literally, Sut on all fours. Following Sut to town, unwanted, Stuff-gut starts "'roun town on a stealing experdition ove his own, an' like his cussed fool owner, got hissef inter a fust rate scrape an' skeer, without half tryin." Emerging from the doggery with a goodly quantity of popskull internalized, Sut finds that town wags have tied a lantern full of smouldering powder to Stuff-gut with a string harness. The dog rockets by Sut, with all the hounds of the town in pursuit. Sut so feels his unity with the dog-fool, he senses Stuff's suffering personally, if stoically.

> When I seed him pass wit-out knowin me, I thot of Dad's ho' net tribulashun, an' felt that thar wur such a thing as a tribulashun at las'; an' then I got mad an' looked roun fur sum wun to vent rath on.
>
> (151-52)

Like many other bulls, horses and dogs Sut encounters, Stuff is changed in nature by the "skeer" he gets, going back to his primitive state. He ends up, again Sut-like, with the community up in arms against him.

> He tuck to the mountins, an' turn's wolf, an' tuck up the trade of sheep-killin fur a livin, an' the hole settlement is now out after his skalp. That trip tu town, like the cuttin-box, hes changed his dispersition agin, all showin the pow'ful changes that kin be made in ever a dog. I cum outen that scrape purty well . . .
>
> (155-56)

So only Sut, among the higher beasts, and a very select company of humans and critters, can truly maintain their spots on the Great Chain despite all catastrophes, but the struggle to do so is a major theme in the *Yarns.* Sut's Great Chain establishes an abiding pattern and a unifying principle amid the tumult and shouting, neighing and braying of the *Yarns.* While there are a number of breaks in the pattern, as has been indicated above, they are not enough to distract significantly from the overall impression of unity in Sut's worldview; his world is a consistent one and his feeling of hierarchy affecting all parts of the Chain is maintained with surprising steadiness. However quirky his values, they are values, and when Sut looks at the creation, he has a strong sense of what ought to be; the overall unity of this outlook is the major thread joining the *Yarns* into a firm artistic fabric.

Notes

1. Milton Rickels, *George Washington Harris* (New York: Twayne Pubs., 1965), p. 101. I should like to express my thanks to the National Endowment for the Humanities for the opportunity to pursue the research that made this study possible. It was composed during an N. E. H. Seminar-in-Residence directed by Hamlin Hill at the University of New Mexico. Professor Hill's counsel and encouragement were of great value during all phases of the writing.

2. George Washington Harris, "Sut Lovingood Lands Ole Abe Safe at Last," *Nashville Union and American,* XXV (March 5, 1861), 3. Reprinted in *High Times and Hard Times,* ed. M. Thomas Inge (Nashville: Vanderbilt Univ. Press, 1967), p. 272. Hereafter indicated as *HTHT.*

3. Harris, "Old Skissum's Middle Boy," *Sut Lovingood. Yarns Spun by a "Nat'ral Born Durn'd Fool"* (New York: Dick and Fitzgerald, 1867), p. 68. Cited hereafter as *Yarns.* Subsequent page references to this work will be given in parentheses in the text.

4. Rickels, "The Imagery of George W. Harris," *The Frontier Humorists,* ed. M. Thomas Inge (Hamden, Conn.: The Shoestring Press, 1975), p. 161.

5. Harris, "Sut Lovingood Escapes Assassination," *New York Atlas,* XXI (July 11, 1858), 6. Reprinted in *HTHT,* p. 129.

6. Rickels, "The Imagery of George W. Harris," p. 161.

7. Rickels, *George Washington Harris,* p. 100.

8. Arthur O. Lovejoy, *The Great Chain of Being* (Cambridge, Mass.: Harvard Univ. Press, 1936).

9. William Faulkner, interview; reprinted in *Writers at Work: The Paris Review Interviews,* ed. Malcolm Cowley (New York: Viking Press, 1958), p. 137.

10. Harris, "Sut Lovingood's Chest Story," *Nashville Union and American,* XXIX (June 30, 1858), I. Repr. in *HTHT,* p. 120.

11. Harris, "Sut Lovingood's Adventures in New York," *New York Atlas,* XXI (August 8, 1858), I. Repr. in *HTHT,* p. 135.

12. Harris, ed. Inge, 139.

13. Harris, "Sut Lovingood's Big Dinner Story," *Nashville Union and American* XXXIII (August 10, 1866), 4. Repr. in *HTHT,* p. 171.

14. Harris, "Sut Lovingood at Bull's Gap," *New York Atlas,* XXI (November 28, 1858), 6, Repr. in *HTHT,* p. 146.

15. Harris, *HTHT,* p. 147.

16. Harris, "Sut Lovingood's Adventures in New York," p. 138.

17. Harris, "Sut Lovingood's Hog Ride," *Nashville Daily Press and Times,* III (September 14, 1865), I. Repr. in *HTHT,* p. 161.

18. Harris, "Bill Ainsworth's Quarter Race, A Story of the Old Times (1833) in East Tennessee," *Knoxville Press and Messenger,* III (June 4, 1868), I. Repr. in *HTHT,* 199.

19. This is not to say that all Sut's vengeance schemes, without exception, consist of measured retribution shown equally to man and beast for their parallel violations of their Great Chain roles. In "Sut Lovingood's Chest Story," the finale of Sut's revenge on Sicily, Doc Fabin's big black horse is put through excruciating suffering for nothing more than the crime of being one of the pompous adulterer-doctor's affections.

Similar animal abuse, and Sut's calmly analytical reporting of the event, also mark accounts of animals' fates in "The Widow McCloud's Mare." Sut's expressing his dislike for lawyer Stilyards, a shyster who has just claimed a dog, mare, and clock in payment of legal fees, involves his destroying the advocate's new property as the dog is disembowelled, the mare's neck broken, and the clock smashed thanks to Sut. The animal victims are treated solely as chattel here, as Stilyards's ill-gotten gains.

But Edmund Wilson's charge that Sut "loves to kill dogs, cats, and frogs," is inaccurate. (*Patriotic Gore,* N.Y.: Oxford Univ. Press, 1962), p. 509). The only animal that might be seen as being wantonly destroyed for pure meanness is Sut's dad's fox hound, which pre-adolescent Sut blows up with a piece of meat spiked with a dose of fused powder; Sut justifies the killing in Great Chain survival terms, as the dog was, in his view, ". . . good fur nuthin but tu swaller up what orter lined the bowels of us brats." (*HTHT,* p. 149.)

20. Donald R. Knight, "Sut's Dog Imagery," *The Lovingood Papers,* ed. Ben Harris McClary (Knoxville: University of Tennessee Press, 1965), pp. 59-60.

Milton Rickels (essay date 1981)

SOURCE: Rickels, Milton. "George Washington Harris's Newspaper Grotesques." *University of Mississippi Studies in English,* n.s., 2 (1981): 15-24.

[*In the following essay, Rickels discusses key differences between Harris's sketches that were published only in newspapers and his sketches that were collected in* Sut Lovingood, Yarns Spun by a "Nat'ral Born Durn'd Fool." *Rickels suggests that publishing in newspapers allowed Harris greater artistic freedom in both his prose style and his subject matter.*]

The Southwestern humorist, George Washington Harris (1814-1869), published only one book, **Sut Lovingood** (1867).[1] Most of his writing was done for New York and Tennessee newspapers. By studying the revisions he made in his newspaper sketches when preparing them for book publication, and, more importantly, by comparing the work in the book with those sketches which appeared only in newspapers, it is possible to make some observations about what these two kinds of publication meant to his creative life.

Broadly speaking, newspapers afforded Harris more freedom of subject matter and technique than he was allowed or allowed himself in his book. And the more local the journal, the greater the freedom. William Trotter Porter and subsequent editors would not reprint in the nationally circulated New York *Spirit of the Times* material obviously political or partisan. Harris's satires on Abraham Lincoln, written for the Nashville *Union and American* in early 1858, did not appear in the *Spirit of the Times*[2] and naturally enough were excluded from his 1867 book. Harris's post-war anti-Republican Party satires were all printed in Southern newspapers.

Apart from such political functions, Harris exercised other freedoms of subject matter and technique in his newspaper work. Although an apparently avid newspaper reader, and a bookish man (borrowing creatively from Shakespeare, Burns, Dickens, and others), Harris drew much of his subject matter and his esthetic techniques from the culture of folk humor. The esthetics of folk humor is to a degree separable from the esthetics of the high culture in classical Greece, and clearly and elaborately separable in Medieval and Renaissance Europe. By Harris's mid-nineteenth-century time, the esthetic systems of humor in the high culture, the developing popular culture, and the folk cultures are embarrassingly tangled for critics who wish artists would stay neatly in their categories. Although perimeters of these esthetic systems overlap, their centers can be roughly defined. Newspapers were a central force in developing the techniques and value systems of popular American culture, and were often hospitable to literary experiments with the esthetics of folk culture.

One of Harris's sketches, written before his book was published but excluded from it, illustrates dramatically the distance between standard nineteenth-century humorous literary culture and the culture of folk humor. **"Sut Lovingood at Bull's Gap"** appeared first in the New York *Atlas,* and was quickly reprinted in the Nashville *Union and American.*[3] Thus, at least two editors thought their readers would enjoy it, but it seems equally likely to arouse loathing and disgust in both the nineteenth- and twentieth-century reader whose taste is formed on more standard literary fare.

The sketch itself is a plotless account which, improbably, has Sut spending the night in a tavern at Bull's Gap, Tennessee, where nineteenth-century passengers had to leave one train, ride twenty miles on a stage to board another line to go north through Virginia. After the opening description of Bull's Gap as a cold, wreckage-strewn mud hole, the sketch is divided into three sections: the first an impressionistic description of the cursing that erupted from the passengers as they entered the inn, the second an hallucinatory account of a bullfrog's appearance from under the stove at the inn, while the third, the longest section, presents a monstrous Dutchman, pictures his gluttonous eating, his nightmare in a room where Sut sleeps on the floor, his bursting his belly from his gross feeding, and Sut's sewing up his paunch. This plotless narration in Sut's voice does not develop character or conflict, but rather presents three broadly conceived creatures: the cheating, greedy landlord, the fool Sut, and the coarse Dutchman—the latter two engaged in eating, drinking, sleeping, and suffering grotesque discomforts in the disquietingly alien microcosm of the inn. Within the area of literate culture, perhaps only some newspapers of the age would present so estranged a comic world.

As is usual in Harris's better work, meaning lies less in plot or character than in the language, particularly in the system of images. The imagery is drawn not so much from the high literary culture nor from popular culture, as from the culture of folk humor. The main source of these images is the grotesque human body, the animal world, and the world of material objects, ugly, ineffectively serviceable, often broken. This system of images is unlike the images of classical esthetics, which emphasize the completeness of the human body, often seen as microcosm, so that by extension, the world's harmony, balance, and beauty appear.⁴ Instead, this characteristic set of images in the culture of folk humor works to bring down to the material level, to de-idealize, to degrade, to emphasize a world in process, constantly growing, changing and decaying.

The opening episode of cursing could not be presented directly in the nineteenth century, even in newspapers, but rather is described impressionistically. The shadowy crowd around the ineffective little stove at the inn was, according to the narrator Sut, both united and divided: "sum a cussin hit, sum a cussin tharsefs, sum a cussin Bull's Gap, sum a cussin wun another, sum a cussin the lake they stood in, sum a cussin that are shanty tavrin, sum a cussin fur supper, sum a cussin the strike nine snake whisky, an all a cussin their levil best. One monsous clever little fellow frum Nashville endorsed all the cussin, and then sot in an cussed the world."⁵

Mikhail Bakhtin, the Russian analyst of folk humor, points out that one of the formal categories of this verbal culture is made up of various genres of billingsgate such as curses, insults, and oaths.⁶ As Sut sees it, cursing is one of the communal human arts in his world,⁷ and he turns to the tavern keeper for praise of the performance: "I axed the tavrinkeeper how he liked that cussin es a specimint ove the gift in perfecshun. Oh, he sed, hit were ornary, not third rate in quality, an wantin powful in quantity; hardly listened tu hit; in fac, hit didn't even warm him up; wouldn't do as a sampil ove the art at all . . ." (145). The innkeeper then offers a comparative assessment of cursing which moves to a tall tale fantasy in praise of the previous night's performance to illustrate the shortcoming of the present achievement: "Sed he hed a crowd the nite afore what onderstood the business—sixty-seven ove em; an they wer so well trained that hit sounded like one man only sixty-seven times louder. Sed they cussed him pussonely, till his jackit buttons flew off an the ainds ove his har cotched fire; then they turned in ontu a stage agent an cussed him into a three week's spell ove fits an diarrear, but he hadn't much ove a constitushun no how; an then finished off by cussin wun ove the stage waggins ontil hit run off inter the woods without eny hosses tu hit" (146).

This strange fantasy of the power of curses first to injure, then to animate the inanimate is swiftly followed by the tavern-keeper's account of how he himself was regenerated by the preceding night's powerful cursing: "'Laigs,' sez he, 'I got the best nites sleep arter they got throu, what I've had in six months; never felt the fust durned bug, an would gin a duller if your crowd could jist cuss half es purfectly. Hits a monsous holesum quietin thing fur a man tu get a tip top cussin jist afore he goes tu bed, perticulerly if the wimmin ove the crowd jines in with that ar "nasty hog," and "aint you shamed ove herself, you stinkin brute you!" chorus ove theirn. I

tell you, mister, hits all I keeps tavrin fur'" (146). Sut sees the tavern-keeper as a con-man, willing to be cursed for bad food and lodging in order to make money out of his wretched victims. The reader enters a world of diarrhea, bed bugs, nasty hogs, and stinking brutes. The host's fantasy can also be seen, following the analysis of tall tale function in Constance Rourke, as a psychological defense mechanism, to exaggerate threats and danger in order to reduce and ridicule them.⁸ Finally, to move out of the rational and the psychological, one of the ancient religious functions of cursing was to destroy so that a new life could magically replace the old. In this comic inversion, the scapegoat himself is renewed and strengthened. This opening tribute to the power of curses and abusive language, this exalting of the forbidden language of oaths signals us that we have left the official, accepted world for one where men speak freely and with magic power.

The frog of the second episode, a battered iron spoon crosswise in his mouth, paddling Indian fashion across the lake covering the floor of the inn, rises as one of those disquieting, phantasmagoric images, like the animals in fairy tales that leave their categories as animals to undermine our faith in the stability of the world. Fear and flight are Sut's responses. The next day he is told he was drunk and only imagined the rowing, croaking frog, but later he sees its enormous skin and is confirmed in his vision.⁹

The third episode, an account of the Dutchman at dinner, centers on his gluttonous eating and the subsequent bursting of his belly. In Sut's words: "Well, he planted hissef at the tabil forninst a two year old chicken cock biled whole, an a big tin pan ove sourcrout what smelt sorter like a pile ove raw hides in August, an a bullit ladil wer socked inter hit. He jist fotch a snort an socked his fork up tu the hilt in the rump bone ove that misfortinate ole cock an started him down his throat head fust, and then begun tu hump hissef an grunt. Every yerk he gin the chicken went an inch, an he'd crook his neck sorter side-wise like a hen does with a lump ove dough stuck in her throat. When he swallered hit apast the rump, the laigs stuck out at each corner ove his mouf es wide apart as the prongs ove a pitchfork, an then he sot intu ladlin in the crout atween em. At last the toes ove the rooster went outen site, an he sent the ballance ove the crout arter him, now an then pitchin in, lef handed, a chunk ove bull-steak es sorter mile stones tu separate the ladles ove crout. He rubbed his belly an pernounced hit 'tam goot'" (148).

Eating, to the "sensitive" is often seen as bordering on the indelicate; the anorexy of extreme civilization regards eating and all its signs as repellent. In this episode, the "thundering" (i.e., farting) Dutchman, in his great size, in his reptilian swallowing, in his explosive digestive transformations presents play with the concept of the loathsome. Instead of shrinking away from eating and digesting, Harris details the process to image its bestial vigor.

Sut's own eating is equally grotesque. When he fears the disgusting beef he has swallowed whole may rise again, he calls for something to drink: "Then I drunk a bowl ove coffee made outen an ole chopped wool hat, an a stage driver's ole boot laig. The grease, sweat, glue, leather, blackin, an wool in ole hats an boots, makes a fust rate biled drink, when hit am sweetened with a mixtry of Orleans sugar, pissants an cock roaches . . ." (152). The items in the series reveal that what Sut takes into his body is even more astonishing than the Dutchman's food: insects, used clothing (hats and boots are traditionally comic food referents), and even human sweat. This, together with the prefixed pun in "pissants," are both forms of scatophagy and both traditionally comic in the ancient culture of folk humor.[10]

The set of images, and the ritual act of eating this kind of food, do not belong to standard literature, and even Harris's readers do not much comment on such passages as this. Ordinarily, we dismiss such fictional actions as coarse, grotesque (in the general sense), or, more perceptively, "Rabelaisian."[11] And perhaps one function of such passages is to allow the reader to express his dismay and thus to affirm his participation in the civilized world, to declare his cultural identity. But there is more here than an opportunity for self-gratulation. In Sut's world, eating is invested with rich meaning.

Harris's work abounds in images of hunger, threats of starvation. The present episode is interrupted by one of the narrator's characteristic digressions, in which Sut recalls an episode from his childhood. His father once brought home a dog, he says: "a durnd, wuthless, mangy flea-bitten grey old fox houn, good fur nuthin but tu swaller up what orter lined the bowels ove us brats" (149). In competition with the dog for food, Sut revenges (and thus protects) himself by stuffing a pig's bladder with gun powder, getting the dog to swallow it, and blowing the animal to bits.[12] Scarcity of food and precariousness of supply are central conditions of Sut's world. Sut's cruelty, his cowardice, his gluttony all have a rational dimension. In Sut's environment, life itself may depend on indifference to the concept of the loathsome.

But Sut's eating goes beyond the Dutchman's gluttony. Sut's symbolic consumption (we remember he is drinking coffee) of sweat and grease, pissant and cockroaches, is not only satire on innkeepers' food; it is a kind of triumphant dismissal of the significance, the reality, of loathing and disgust. In western culture, Stephen Greenblatt writes: "Since the onset of the early modern period, the archetypal rules, the earliest and

most systematic to which the child is exposed and in which he is trained, are those governing the definition and control of filth; it is these rules that determine the experience of disgust and, to a certain extent, the experience of personal identity."[13] In Sut's world, it may be maintained, the concept of the filthy is not only a traditional comic way of facing reality, but is intensified then dismissed as a response appropriate to those little creatures reduced by civilization to the experience of frequent shrinking away or rejection. Sut is not a mere belated scatophagus as implied by the image of sweat and the two prefixed puns, but a literary creation of mythy grandeur. This system of images is drawn, as Bakhtin says, from the grotesque body created in the culture of folk humor. This body is ever unfinished, always exceeding its limits, being born and dying, being dismembered, copulating, eating, drinking, and defecating. This body devours everything in its world. Again, we remind ourselves, the passage is not material filth, but words. Harris is creating a literature that moves toward unaccustomed symbolic transcendences.

In the concluding episode, Sut asleep (on the floor) in the Dutchman's room, dreams of the beef he has eaten as a living, sick, mutilated bull; but is awakened from this vision by the Dutchman, also asleep, crowing like a cock, then bellowing like a bull, both images of male assertiveness. Sut claps a chamber pot over his head, and the blinded man-animal runs across the room on his all-fours and butts his head into the wall with such violence that he splits his belly open. Sut repairs the wound: "I jist laid him ontu his back, tuck a nife fur a needil, an a ole bridil rein fur a thread, an sowed him up adzactly like ye sows up the mouf ove a par ove saddil bags with the strap, an then tied a knot on bof ainds ove the rein. While I wer makin the holes in the aidges ove the tare, he axed me to look inside fur the spurs of 'tat tam schicken cock an gut tem off,' but all I could see were his paunch, an hit looked adzackly like the flesh side ove a raw hide" (154). Although his rude surgery is, on the surface, a comically incongruous humanitarian act, Sut's report of it is detached and cold. There is no satiric move toward teaching, warning, or arousing compassion. Instead, Sut simply reports a glimpse into the secret interior of the human body. The scene, to the humanistically trained sensibility, is revolting, impossible, incomprehensible.[14]

After he finishes, Sut asks his patient how he feels, and the Dutchman replies, "Tam good"; his only fear is that he will leak lager beer. Later Sut learns that the Dutchman has recovered and, at Bristol, Virginia, has won a bet that he could drink beer faster than a muley cow could eat salted meal slop. He won, implying perhaps, that the Dutchman is leaking, but living with great gusto, unsubdued. Sut's last sentence exults that his bridle rein sewing has held the great indestructible belly together.

The cultural problem is to account for the sketch's relative popularity. It was reprinted half a dozen times in whole or in part, in different regions of the United States. Clearly, of all the print media, newspapers were most hospitable to this material. Here lay the greatest freedom to publish such traditional but sub-literary creations. Its popular appeal, its comic energy, must rest, to some degree, on its incongruous action, its defiance of manners, order, decency, even, as we have suggested, its indifference toward the very concept of the repellent, the loathsome, the filthy. In this it asserts freedom from deep esthetic and cultural concepts. In Sut's microcosm, all is debased, dismembered, rendered carnal, materialized, made familiar so that even the most awful catastrophes of nature and the human body are not endured so much as enjoyed. The tone is triumphant. Out of this filthy food, this muddy world of Bull's Gap, these accidents to the flesh, the curses of others and one's own excesses, the landlord, Sut, and the Dutchman rise enlarged and regenerated.

"Sut Lovingood Reports What Bob Dawson Said, After Marrying a Substitute" may serve as an example of the freedom newspapers offered Harris in creating the erotic grotesque. Published in the Chattanooga, Tennessee *Daily Union* in 1867, late in Harris's career, the attitude toward human sexuality is noticeably different from that expressed in the tales written a decade earlier. While Sut's response to women was always complex, combining fear and desire, the dominant tone of the imagery associated with Harris's earlier creation, Sicily Burns, expresses her vitality, her fleshly beauty, and her overwhelming desirability.

Bob Dawson's experience extends into the repellent. He does not transcend the disgusting in the erotic. On his wedding night Bob Dawson goes first to bed, where he eagerly awaits his bride. When she appears, he later reported: "She glode into the room like the embodiment of a Haleluigah, or a vision of unspeakable joy" (179). Saying that delicacy has no place between two who are one in marriage, she undresses by candlelight, divesting herself of layers of hoops and starched muslin, of padding for her legs, a false bosom, false teeth, a glass eye, and a wig. In horrified recapitulation, Bob says: "'False calves, false breasts, false teeth, false eye, false hair,' what next? The most horrible idear that ever burnt an' blazed in the brain of man, was now fast resolving itself into its dreadful shape in mine, an' her remark, 'Don't be impatient, Robert love; I is most through,' flashed it into its fiendish maturity. Without darin' even a glance at her, I was up *out-gone*; I went down them stair steps six at a bounce in my shirt tail through that festive throng in my shirt tail out of that house, out of that lot, out of that town, in my shirt tail" (181).

Now the "horrible idear," which must remain unprinted, is, of course, Dawson's fear that his bride's vagina, too, is false. This implication is not present in Hawthorne's "Mrs. Bullfrog," and surely only certain newspapers in 1867 would have allowed it to be hinted at so openly. It is, however, traditional. In the last decade my own students have collected two versions of it in the oral lore. Gershon Legman prints a version of the false vagina story in his *Rationale of the Dirty Joke* (1: 376), where he argues that the motif is older than his first printed version and probably reached the height of its popularity in the mid-nineteenth century.

The sketch concludes with Sut's returning to his own experience by way of an account of his sister Sal's homemade false breasts, constructed out of dry gourd halves with white oak acorns for nipples. The whole contraption Sut calls "palpititytators" and the wearers "palpititytator toters." This may not be a digression from the central motif. Legman argues that male interest in the female breasts is merely a psychological technique of displacement anyway.

It is possible to read the sketch simply as satire on women's wiles, as protest against cosmetic deceits and affectations in appearance and manners. Thus the story could be seen as a moral and social attack on falsity. But comic misogyny and satire on women is a very old tradition, and what is interesting in Harris is the particular set of images and actions he selects and what special meaning we can find in his esthetic.

However one responds to this type of traditional erotic grotesque, it expresses fear and hatred of the female. The anecdote has nothing to do with erotic pleasure. Instead, marriage, sexual activity, the female herself are sources of fear and anxiety. The comic function here is very narrow, very specific. Indeed, the whole anecdote is told in response to George's question of why Sut never married. Thus Bob Dawson's experience is exemplary. Sut concludes by connecting the false female with the experience of diminishing sexual desire. He tells George he will never again put his hand into the front of a woman's dress, concluding mournfully: "No, by giminy hoss, *that* appertite's dead, an' the ballance of 'em scept for sperrits ara sinkin fas'. . . ." The female (as in **"Sut Lovingood's Chest Story"**) is feared as the destroyer of male virility. As Vivian Mercier observes of Irish humor, the grotesque esthetic expresses, in this instance, "fear and hatred of sex."[15] The tone of the bedroom scene between Dawson and his bride is very much in the tradition of the Romantic grotesque as defined by Wolfgang Kayser in *The Grotesque in Art and Literature*. The microcosm seems alien, the tone gloomy, the woman inhuman, the world has become false. Dawson feels that his body floats between mattress and ceiling, like Mahomet's coffin. This grotesque contrasts significantly with the folk grotesque of **"Sut Lovingood at Bull's Gap."** The Dawson sketch instills, as Kayser says, "fear of life, rather than fear of death."[16]

From such a limited survey as this, it seems clear that some mid-nineteenth century newspapers gave Harris much more freedom than book publishers allowed. Harris used these freedoms to expand significantly his system of images and his themes. Within these broader latitudes he gave expression not to individual neuroses or to an eccentric vision but rather to some traditional cultural responses. Particularly with **"Sut Lovingood at Bull's Gap"** Harris preserved in print a full traditional esthetic system of grotesque bodily images from the culture of folk humor, presenting responses and celebrating values generally excluded from the values of the high culture.

Notes

1. For Harris's place in the history of American humor, see Walter Blair and Hamlin Hill, *America's Humor* (New York, 1978), pp. 213-221; for a recent foreign assessment, see Daniel Royot, *L'humour américain* (Lyon, 1980), pp. 244-245.

2. By 1858 William Trotter Porter was no longer making editorial selections for the *Spirit.* Indeed he died 15 August 1858. See Norris W. Yates, *William T. Porter and the SPIRIT OF THE TIMES* (Baton Rouge, 1959), pp. 190-195 and *passim.*

3. Available in book form in George Washington Harris, *High Times and Hard Times,* ed. M. Thomas Inge (Nashville, 1967), pp. 144-145. For Inge's comments see pp. 109-111. See also F. DeWolfe Miller, "Sut Lovingood at Bull's Gap." *The Lovingood Papers: 1962,* pp. 36-38; and Hans Bungert, "How Sut Lovegood [sic] Dosed His Dog," *The Lovingood Papers: 1963,* pp. 32-33. For an academic misreading, see Milton Rickels, *George Washington Harris* (New York, 1965), p. 58.

4. For a brief history of the idea of Vitruvian man, see Kenneth Clark, *The Nude: A Study in Ideal Form* (New York, 1956), pp. 15-27.

5. *High Times and Hard Times,* p. 145. Subsequent quotations will be from this source, with page references included in the text.

6. *Rabelais and His World,* trans. Helene Iswolsky (Cambridge, Mass., 1968), pp. 5, 15-18, 145-196.

7. For a well-known nineteenth-century example of the art of abusive language, see Vance Randolph, *Pissing in the Snow and Other Ozark Folktales* (Urbana, 1976), pp. 103-105.

8. *American Humor, A Study of the National Character* (New York, 1931), presents illuminating analyses of the large patterns of humor in our culture.

9. For analysis of the fantastic, see Bruno Bettelheim, *The Uses of Enchantment* (New York, 1976), pp. 5-7, 63, 66-67, 75, 143-135; and Tzvetan Todorov, *The Fantastic* (Cleveland, 1973), pp. 31-33, 35, 109-110, 120, 158-159.

10. Bakhtin, p. 330.

11. Franklin J. Meine, *Tall Tales of the Southwest* (New York, 1930), p. xxiv.

12. M. Thomas Inge locates five reprintings of this episode between 1859 and 1869. See his essay on Harris in *High Times and Hard Times,* pp. 110-111, and n. pp. 150-151. For an example of the humor of dismemberment, see Blair and Hill, p. 94. For dismemberment in the culture of folk humor, see Bakhtin, p. 318, and elsewhere.

13. "Filthy Rites," *University Publishing,* 9 (1979), 5.

14. Kayser, p. 35.

15. *The Irish Comic Spirit* (New York, 1962), p. 48.

16. Kayser, p. 185. See also Bakhtin, p. 50. It is illuminating to compare these two works with Feodor Dostoyevsky's comic evocations of the "darker" side of human experience in the Marmeladov and the Svidrigailov episodes in *Crime and Punishment.* For variants with other meanings see Randolph, *Pissing in the Snow,* pp. 60-61.

Larzer Ziff (essay date 1981)

SOURCE: Ziff, Larzer. "The Fool Killer: George Washington Harris and Sut Lovingood." In *Literary Democracy: The Declaration of Cultural Independence in America,* pp. 181-94. New York: Viking Press, 1981.

[*In the following excerpt, Ziff analyzes elements of sadism and depravity in* Sut Lovingood, Yarns Spun by a "Nat'ral Born Durn'd Fool." *According to Ziff, Harris's audacious celebration of such forbidden themes as sexuality, violence, and antiauthoritarianism represented a radical departure from traditional Southern writing and made him one of the most original American authors of the Civil War era.*]

The great popular success of *Uncle Tom's Cabin* increased desire in the South for a literature distinctive of that culture. It was not a desire of long standing. Before Garrison started his weekly, *The Liberator,* in 1831, southerners took pride in all American literature, regardless of regional origin, as their literature.[1] But the hostility of such publications as the abolitionist journal led to a concern that southern opinion have a literary outlet, and the more southern men of letters reflected on the matter, the more they were struck by what Poe had announced as a fact: the literary products of New England were a sectional literature masquerading as a national literature. The most prolific, and some would say the only, southern writer of note based in the South, William Gilmore Simms of Charleston, complained that not only were the Yankees regional in their writing, what was worse, they were not manly. The highest praise he could find for their work was conveyed in phrases such as "nice taste," "clever imitator," "delicate," "unobtrusive humor." But there was a native character the opposite of this, rough, original, and above all manly, and this he felt the North had evaded in its feeble writings.[2]

Simms himself attempted to capture such original native flavor in his novels, but nativism to him meant adherence to the code of manners practiced in the South, and the more urgent the political pressures from the North, the more refined became that code in his pages. By the 1850s he was, without quotation marks or qualification, calling his plantation owners "aristocrats" and entering into detailed illustration of the circumstances under which overseers might safely be honored with the friendship as well as the indulgence of their employers. James Fenimore Cooper, who also followed Scott in the framework of much of his fiction, had argued that there were real social distinctions in a democracy and undertook the task of demonstrating them in his novels. But Simms accepted the existence of a social hierarchy as fixed as the planets—elegant aristocracy, knightly retainers, sturdy yeomen, fiercely loyal slaves—and within that static frame was unable to start a resonant action because all human and social issues had been settled. He was left with the melodrama that could be stirred by sheer villainy, and his novels' better moments are generally those devoted to recording the talk of the low characters—deliberately staged in response to a formula by Shakespeare out of Scott—where his ear for speech, far finer than Cooper's, keeps such characters from becoming, like Cooper's, massive bores. Simms lacks, however, the dynamic sense of social issues that Cooper possessed so surely.

And Simms stood just about alone. His fiction was the sharpest kind of realism when compared with the confections of southern life as feudal idyll that were baked in answer to the threatening North. In these lesser novels characters named Iolia, Manolia, Roscius, and Cassanio moved languidly beneath the southern moon, exercising in speech and action an exquisite courtesy toward one another. The diction was Latinate and the syntax frequently periodic, although there were happy intervals in which the whole collapsed into a comic mélange that was unintended. A mountaineer, asked if he knows where Roscius is, stands at the door of his cabin and manfully attempts to maintain the standard of lofty speech set him by his acknowledged betters: "I have heard tell of no such youth. Them ravens you hear screaming over yon chasm can give you some account of him likely."[3]

The culture that was forced into such literary reaction had a high respect for learning, but was also separated from a good part of its own social reality. On one hand there is the illiteracy rate five times greater than that of New England; on the other, by 1860 there were twenty-three colleges in Virginia, enrolling 2,824 students, in contrast to eight colleges in Massachusetts, enrolling 1,733 students, some of them Virginians. Annually Virginia spent $50,000 more on her colleges than Massachusetts did.[4] The failure of southern literature to match northern in either quantity or quality did not stem from the absence of an educated class, but from the aspirations to which that class put its learning, as well as from the fact that status and therefore identity were withheld from a literate middle class of tradesmen and mechanics, who should have served as traffickers in ideas as well as goods. . . .

In the border states at some distance from the homes of the feudal ideal, however, a literature of the plain folk was beginning to find expression, a literature that surpassed that of the North in its expressive colloquialism, skillfully shifted points of view, and vital presentation of spontaneous feeling. The yarns and sketches from this region that began to find their way into local newspapers and thence into the sporting journals of the Northeast, not regarded as reading suitable for the home, were southern in their dialect, and southern in their undisguised hatred for the North (while genteeler southern writers disagreed or remonstrated, the writers in this tradition refreshingly hated). But as tied to the South as this region was by its acceptance of slavery, the energy of its literature came in some good part from a contempt for the ideal southern hierarchic social vision. Hill farmers, copper miners, and river men had their own version of southern culture, one that scorned authority and ridiculed sentiment. The fantasies that grew straight up from the roots of their anarchic culture were so passionate as frequently to be sickeningly sadistic, and the writing of their greatest creator, George Washington Harris, is so centered on cruel if comically intended scenes of revenge, detailed with such physiological precision, that the pleasure of his achievement is forever mixed with distaste for his climactic scenes of discomfort and dismemberment. But the ferocious antisentimentalism of Harris's sadistic scenes provides a valuable, one might almost say a relieving, contrast to the unexamined pieties of even so accomplished a moralist as Stowe. His celebration of the primal, his ability to slide persuasively into the epic and out again, his keen eye for animation, his subtle ear for the offbeat, anticlimactic, comic line, and his capacity to symbolize in incident the nexus of antiintellectualism, sexual vigor, antiauthoritarianism, and cruel physical force buried in the psyche of his folk make him one of the greatest American writers of his day, albeit one who has not written more than ten consecutive pages that can be read without wincing.

The paradox in his achievement is matched by the paradox in his life.[5] Born in Allegheny, Pennsylvania, in 1814, Harris migrated to the West, where by the age of nineteen he was captain of a steamboat on the Tennessee River. He went on to speculation in glassworks, supervision of a copper mine, and another spell as a steamboat captain, and in the course of his activities began writing sketches of local incidents and manners. In 1854 he seems to have encountered in extreme southeast Tennessee a man who served him as the basis for the character of Sut Lovingood, the "born fool" through whose eyes and voice the finest of his tales are realized.

Harris became a Presbyterian elder in Knoxville, was a sabbatarian and a hard-working machinist. Sut was irreligious and expressed strong doubts about his even possessing a soul; he was free with women and with the bottle, and shiftless. Harris was a Democrat, although his half brother Samuel Bell, who was mayor of Knoxville and stood to him as a father, was a pro-union Whig, as was his close friend William Crutchfield, to whom he dedicated *Sut Lovingood's Yarns* (1867). But Sut was an unthinking, anarchic Yankee-hater, more apt to set a mortal trap for a Whig than to talk to him. Sut is not developed ironically by Harris nor is he patronized by him. Rather he is a free spirit, the true alter ego of his creator; he expresses the passionate subrational forces repressed in the mechanically skilled Presbyterian elder, and he expresses them all the more forcefully for Harris's successful repression of them in his own life.

"It's an awful thing, George," Sut tells Harris, "to be a natural-born durned fool. You's never experienced it personally, have you? It's made pow'fully agin our family—and all owin to Dad."[6] But, of course, because he is a fool, Sut is free to act out what Harris must control, and throughout the accounts of his adventures Sut emphasizes his reliance in tight spots on the length and speed of his legs rather than on his wits: "I tell you . . . that running am the greatest invenshun on yearth when used keerfully."[7]

In Sut's world women are objects of sexual desire, and motherhood has no special aura, meaning, as it does, the end of the first flush of headlong youth. Jule Sawyers hugs Dick Harlan tightly as she rides behind him on the pony carrying them to the dance: "She says she didn't mind a fall but it mought break hir leg an then good bye frolics—she'd be fit fur nuthin but to nuss brats ollers afterwards."[8] Even Sut's own mother is presented without the pieties that glossed over the matron in northern literature; since she is a woman, her basic characteristic for the male who contemplates her is sexual force, even though that male is her son. When Sut considers that neither of his parents has the long legs that are his most distinctive feature, he explains the matter thus:

My long legs sometimes sorta bothers me. But then Mam took a pow'ful scare at a sand-hill crane a-sittin on a peeled well-pole, and she outrun her shadow thirty yards in comin half a mile. I expect I owes my legs and speed to that circumstance and not to any fraud on Mam's part.[9]

The explanation is vigorously unprudish, and the visualization—the sharpness of "peeled well-pole"—the unforced alliterative rhythms, and the ease with which hyperbole is accommodated through its presentation in precise detail—"thirty yards in runnin half a mile"—ground the outlook in a comprehensive and coherent perception of reality.

Sut's celebration of the sexual attraction of women is detailed in images drawn from his ragged environment, and the frankness of his physical observation is all the more welcome for this. Decades before Mark Twain attempted through the concrete, nature-bound diction of Huck Finn to elicit a feeling larger than the homely details in which it was expressed, Harris, whose work Twain knew well, was experimenting with shabby American circumstances:

She shows among women like a sunflower among dog fennel, or a hollyhock in a patch of smartweed. Such a bosom! Just think of two snowballs with a strawberry stuck butt-ended into both on 'em. She takes exactly fifteen inches of garter clear of the knot, stands sixteen an a half-hands high, and weighs one hundred and twenty-six in her petticoat tail afore breakfast. She couldn't crawl through a whiskey-barrel—with both heads stove out—nor sit in a common armchair, while you could lock the top hoop of a churn, or a big dog collar round the huggin place.[10]

The object of this rhapsody is Sicily Burns, a young woman who does not reciprocate Sut's desire for her and who plays a cruel practical joke on him to underline her preference for another man. Sut, in turn, will have his revenge upon Sicily with equal physical cruelty, and notable in such incidents is the perfect social and psychological equality of the sexes. Unlike the tender domestic creatures to the north and the pale, elegant, objects of chivalry to the south, women in Sut's country are as forthright as men and can be treated in the same way. His description of Sicily was a description of the only way women differ from men.

In the culture he so closely observes, Harris is able to construct similes of a scope to match those in the folk epics of other and older lands. They are genuine, unaffected for all their far-reaching nature, because they grow, as did the folk epics' similes, from an oral tradition in which emotion is likened to what is physically perceived, rather than being explained in a vocabulary created by the literate:

I'se heard in the mountains a first-rate, fourth-proof smash of thunder come unexpected and shake the earth, bringin along a string of lightnin as long as a quarter-track and as bright as a welding heat, a-racin down a big pine tree, tearin it into toothpickers, and raisin a cloud of dust and bark and a army of limbs with a smell sorta like the Devil were about, and the long, darning-needle leaves fallin round with a *tith-tith* quiet-sorta sound and even then a-quiverin on the earth as little snakes die. And I feel queer in my innards, sorta half-comfort, with a little glad and right smart of sorry mixed with it.

I'se seed the rattlesnake square hisself to come at me, a-sayin "Z-e-e-e-e" with that noisy tail of his'n, and I feel queer agin—monstrous queer. I've seed the Oconee River jumpin mad from rock to rock, with its clear, cool water . . . white foam . . . and music. . . . "Music." The rushin water does make music. So does the wind, and the fire in the mountain, and it gives me an uneasy queerness again. But every time I looked at that gal Sicily Burns, I had all the feelins mixed up—of the lightnin, the river, and the snake.[11]

At the other end of his spectrum of the sexual world is Sut's earthy recognition of male physiology. To look at Jule Sawyer's legs is to make a man "feel sorter like a June bug was crawlin up his trowses and the waistband was too tite for it to git out."[12] In the agonies of springtime love, Wat Mastin, the blacksmith, blunders about with "his hands socked down deep into his britches-pockets like he was feared of pickpockets"; but after his wedding night, "His coat . . . and his trousers looked just a scrimption too big, loose-like, and heavy to tote. I asked him if he felt sound. He said 'yas,' but he'd welded a steamboat shaft the day afore and were sorta tired-liked."[13]

And in his hymn to widows Sut exposes in fine detail the objects of his material culture, the manners of courtship in his society, and above all, in contrast with other regional cultures, the avidity with which greater experience is pursued:

Gals and ole maids ain't the things to fool time away on. It's widders, by golly, what am never-kickin, willin, spirited smooth pacers. They come close't up to the hoss-block, standin still with their purty, silky ears playin and the neck-veins a-throbbin, and waits for the word—which of course you give after you find your feet well in the stirrup—and away they moves like a cradle cushioned on rockers, or a spring buggy runnin in damp sand. A tech of the bridle and they knows you want 'em to turn, and they does it as willin as if the idea were their own. . . .

They has all been to Jamaicy and learnt how sugar's made, and knows how to sweeten with it. And, by golly, they is always ready to use it. All you has to do is to find a spoon, and then drink comfort till you're blind.

If you understands widder nature, they can save you a power of trouble, uncertainty, and time; and if you is enterprisin, you gits monstrous well-paid for it. The very sound of their little shoe-heels has a knowin click as they tap the floor.

When you has made up your mind to court one, just go at it like it were a job of rail-maulin. Wear yer workin clothes; and, above all, fling away your cinammon-oil vial and burn all your love songs. No use in tryin to fool 'em, for they sees plumb through their veils. No use in a pasted shirt; she's been there. No use in borrowin a cavortin fat hoss; she's been there. No use in hair-dye; she's been there. No use in cloves to kill whiskey breath; she's been there. No use in buyin closed curtains for your bed, for she has been there. Widders am a special means . . . for ripenin green men, killin off weak ones; and makin 'ternally happy the sound ones.[14]

Harris's diction is impressive, nouns and verbs effectively carrying the descriptive burden loaded by others onto the backs of adjectives and adverbs, and his syntax is equally effective, duplicating the drawn-out sentences of the storyteller but keeping their units in so simple and rhythmic a relation to one another that the reader visualizes what is said effortlessly and never has to trace back to fix the scene aright.

In addition to his sure gift for aural and visual effect, Harris developed a technique of shifted point of view that serves as an unforced reminder that the primal world of Sut is a world of magic. One tale centers on an all too typical practical joke played on Stilyards, an avaricious lawyer and congressman, Connecticut-born, as Sut is quick to explain, although he puts it more feelingly—"hatched in a crack in the frosty rocks, whar nutmaigs am made outen maple, an whar wimmin paints clock-faces." Sut comes upon him in the road just after he has taken as fees the dog and grandfather clock of a man for whom he lost a case and the big mare of a widow for whom he lost another. Stilyards wants to hire Sut to help him with the transport of his goods, but Sut persuades him to mount the mare, tie the dog's rope around her neck, and place the clock along his back and belt it to his waist. As Sut anticipated, the mare bolts, Stilyard jounces violently and helplessly, the clock begins an endless striking, further accelerating the horse, and the dog is jerked into so swift a run that, in a detail Harris typically refuses to withhold, his entrails stream behind. The scene is sharply set in motion before the reader, but it can no longer be expected to raise the hilarity it once provoked in barbershops.

Harris's literary tact, however, is superior to his sporadic tastelessness. The point of view shifts. Sut strolling homeward well satisfied with himself passes a cabin "whar a ole 'oman dress'd in a pipe an' a stripid apron wer a-standing on the ash-hopper lookin up the road like she wer 'spectin tu see somethin soon." Her words pour out. "Say yu mister, did yu meet anything onkommon up thar?" Sut shakes his head and she unwinds:

Mister, I'se plum outdun. Thar's sumthin pow'ful wickid gwine on. A crazy organ-grinder cum a-pas' yere jis' a small scrimpshun slower nur chain litenin, on a hoss wif no tail. His organ wer tied ontu his back, an' wer a-playin that good tchune, "Sugar in the Gourd," ur "Barbary Allin," I dunno which, an' his monkey wer a-dancin Hail Columby all over the road, an' *hits* tail wer es long as my clothes-line, an' purfeckly bar ove hare.[15]

Sut suggests that it was either the advance guard of a circus proclaiming its coming or the arrival of the millennium, "durn'd ef I know'd which." But the woman, with a shrewd eye for detail, disagrees and advances sounder theories:

> She 'lowed hit cudent be the merlennium, fur hit warnt playin hyme-tchunes; nur a sarkis either, fur the hoss warn't spotted. But hit mout be the Devil arter a tax collector, ur a missionary on his way tu China; hit look'd ugly enuf tu be one, an' fool enuf tu be tuther.[16]

The sudden sight of a spectacle that, however uncommon, has nevertheless been naturalistically explained to the reader as it erupts into the field of vision and assaults the understanding of a simple bystander endows it with a memorable and magic effect and provides Harris's yarn with a studied anticlimax that exceeds the actual scene in comedy, as was intended. It was a technique that William Faulkner, an enthusiastic Harris reader, was to use, for example, in *The Hamlet,* where naturalistically explained runaway Texas horses dash into Tull's carriage in apocalyptic furor. The comedy is fulfilled and its fulfillment partakes of a visitation of the supernatural into the lives of the folk, who believe in its imminent presence.

Harris's sure sense of the folk imagination, moreover, led him to techniques that were not again to be widely employed until the development of the twentieth-century comic strip and animated cartoon aimed at the imagination of the masses. No matter how his characters are maimed in one episode, they are soundly reassembled and ready for use in the next, like cartoon characters. And more impressive from a literary point of view, Harris animates in such a way as to be able to stop his frame and see what takes place in nature too swiftly for the eye to notice: "Bart loaned the parson a most tremendous contusion right in the bull curl. I seed the parson's shoe soles a-goin up each side of Bart's fist afore Bart had time to move it after he struck."[17]

The cruelty that Harris lovingly constructs time and again is the eruption of an omnipresent outrage at the sentimental view of life, which he equated with the hypocritical moralizing of the dominant culture. Like Harriet Beecher Stowe, he was a Calvinist, but unlike Stowe and with the ruthless thoroughness of one who has been exposed to the elemental facts of a world governed by sin, he presses home the inherent viciousness of all creatures. Acceptance of universal corruption enabled him to be comic, as temporizing with it led Stowe to be sentimental. Sut was the mouthpiece of his perception of the bottom of creation—deeper even than the teachings of the Presbyterian Church—and perhaps no

scene of cruelty is more discomfiting and yet more courageous than is Sut's outburst on the subject of innocence. Man is perverse, he broods; if something happens to your best friend you feel sorry for him, yet you sense a deep-down satisfaction:

> Or say a little calf, a-buttin first under the cow's forelegs and then the hind, with the point of its tongue stuck out, makin suckin motions, not yet old enough to know the bag-end of its mam from the hookin end . . . don't you want to kick it on the snout, hard enough to send it backwards—say fifteen foot—just to show it that buttin won't allers fetch the milk? Or a baby even, rubbin its heels a-past each other, a-rootin and a-snifflin after the breast, and the mam doin her best to git it out over the hem of her clothes: don't you feel hungry to give it one percussion-cap slap right onto the place what some day'll fit a saddle or a sewin-chair, to show it what's atwixt it and the grave; that it stands a pow'ful chance not to be fed every time it's hungry or in a hurry?[18]

Sut's perception of depravity goes beyond Calvinism to the soil that nurtures it. His world is one of poverty, illiteracy, and physical exertion, one in which sexual activity is a welcome outburst of the troubled self. It is a world of barely repressed passion, and reason is its enemy because reason comes from without to thwart or to manipulate it. The agents of reason are elected officials, clergymen, or lawyers, who exploit rather than improve, and Sut's anarchic hate of this condition leads him to attack authorities in all his practical jokes. His constant rage is, finally, the unconscious reaction of the proletarian in a society in which the rules operate to make him pay while others profit. His only weapons are force and flight; his principal expression is sexual love.

"Rare Ripe Garden-Seed," perhaps the greatest of Harris's stories, still finds its way into modern anthologies because of its relative freedom from sadism and because of the mythic quality of the folklore it develops. Sut approaches the tale through a monologue that explains why he hates sheriffs and was therefore willing, in the tale to follow, to assist friends in their revenge on one. Here with understated mastery he blends the elements of a class hate born of economic circumstances, elements that lie deeper than a mere desire for revenge against a particular personality.

> I tell you now, I minds my first big scare just as well as rich boys mind their first boots or seein the first spotted-horse circus. The red top of them boots am still a rich, red stripe in their minds, and the burnin red of my first scare has left as deep a scar onto my thinkin works.
>
> Mam had me a-standin atwixt her knees. I kin feel the knobs of her joints a-rattlin a-past my ribs yet. She didn't have much petticoats to speak of, and I had but one—and it were calico slit from the nape of my neck to the tail, held together at the top with a draw-string and at the bottom by the hem. . . .

Mam were feedin us brats onto mush and milk—without the milk—and as I were the baby then she held me so as to see that I got my share. When there ain't enough feed, big childer roots little childer outen the trough and gobble up their part.[19]

Onto the scene comes the sheriff to levy the bed and the chairs, and Sut's mother hisses like an animal in danger and the children scatter. No piece of writing from honestly concerned prewar socialists matches the proletarian eloquence of the scene created by the alter ego of the conservative Presbyterian elder of Knoxville.

As the war drew nearer, Sut turned more and more vicious on the subject of the North, and as Stowe on her level matched arguments with sentiments, so Harris on his matched them with violence. His outlook is summarized in Sut's haunting if terrible myth of why his region takes the stand it does:

> When we elects our Governors, we elects a fool-killer for every county and furnishes him with a gun, some arsenic, strychnine, and a big steel trap; and it is his duty to travel, say about one day, ahind the circuit rider. You see, the circuit rider gathers the people together, and it makes it more convenient, and the fool-killer kills off the stock of fools to a considerable extent every round he takes. Our fool-killers have done their duty, and consequently the South have seceded.[20]

Sut, the natural-born, damned fool, ends his career by celebrating the fool-killer. In a sense, Harris is now finished with his alter ego as the times move to put a finish to the conditions that spawned him. But from a broader point of view, Sut is no such fool as the fool-killer seeks out—these are sympathizers with abolition, idealistic philanthropists, and moral sentimentalists—and he survives to tell his tales because, of course, in them the fool and fool-killer are one. And though his culture went under during the war, it did not disappear; such folk were used to the shifts of survival constantly forced upon them from above.

The world of Sut Lovingood reappeared censored after the war as a region of charming local color, and survived into the twentieth century as the tobacco-road culture of sexual degeneracy and menacing violence that blended into blue-collar brutality as natives of the border states moved into the factories. But the art and outlook of George Washington Harris are not in such literature. Rather his comic vision born of a sense of universal depravity and his mythic celebration of the debased human condition can be seen in the writings of Faulkner, who valued his work and whose ultimate point of view was not that of the aristocracy of Simms but of the suspicious, pawky, lower-class observers of the spectacle. And Harris's voice, transmitted by another admirer, Mark Twain, and purified in the transmission, is present in the work of Hemingway, whose narrators distrust the words applied to actuality and seek the words actuality wears.

Like all writers, the American writer in the prewar period had to find his reader before he could find his voice and his genre. He did not need a large audience, but he had to be satisfied in his mind that there existed the kind of reader for whom he wrote. Harris was thwarted by this necessity, able only to imagine a readership that fell short of the full stretch of his genius, and consequently he warped his best work as he accepted the sporting journal as his medium. With far more modest literary powers but with a sure sense of a wide, middle-class audience, Stowe was encouraged to write better than she knew how to do, even as Harris wrote worse than he could.

The suspicion that American literature was really New England literature disguised is, finally, misfounded. The region of origin is secondary to the culture of the reader who is imagined, and American literature in that age attempted to speak to Americans.

Notes

1. Jay B. Hubbell, *The South in American Literature 1607-1900* (Durham, N.C., 1954), p. 261.

2. Ibid., p. 595.

3. John Donald Wade, *Augustus Baldwin Longstreet* (New York, 1924), p. 146.

4. Hubbell, *South,* pp. 346-47.

5. For details of his life see Milton Rickels, *George Washington Harris* (New York, 1965).

6. George Washington Harris, *Sut Lovingood,* ed. Brom Weber (New York, 1954), p. 54. The editor of this collection altered the original orthography in the reasonable belief that Harris's attempt to represent the sound of Sut's voice through misspellings was unnecessary for the effect he desired and presents an arbitrary obstacle to the modern reader. In my citations I rely on this edition as well as those that have the original orthography, and fear I may also have unconsciously let my own spellings intrude from time to time. At any rate, the words are Sut's.

7. George Washington Harris, *High Times and Hard Times,* ed. M. Thomas Inge (Nashville, 1967), p. 150.

8. Ibid., p. 47.

9. Harris, *Sut Lovingood,* p. 19.

10. Ibid., pp. 35-36.

11. Ibid., pp. 37-38.

12. Harris, *High Times,* p. 52.

13. Harris, *Sut Lovingood,* p. 124.

14. Ibid., pp. 178-79.

15. Ibid., p. 77.

16. Ibid., p. 78.

17. Ibid., p. 99.

18. Ibid., pp. 138-39.

19. Ibid., pp. 119-20.

20. Ibid., p. 277.

Elaine Gardiner (essay date summer 1983)

SOURCE: Gardiner, Elaine. "Sut Lovingood: Backwoods Existentialist." *Southern Studies* 22, no. 2 (summer 1983): 177-89.

[*In the following essay, Gardiner analyzes the worldview of Harris's protagonist, Sut Lovingood. Gardiner suggests that Sut can be seen as a forerunner of the absurd hero of twentieth-century literature.*]

In his 1965 study, *George Washington Harris*, Milton Rickels comments that Harris is "only now being discovered."[1] Rickels' book is, itself, the first full-length study of this nineteenth century humorist whom Mark Twain is known to have read and admired. It is with Harris' best known fictional creation, Sut Lovingood, that this study is concerned. In the one published volume about him, ***Sut Lovingood: Yarns Spun by a "Nat'ral Born Durn'd Fool"*** (1867),[2] and in the numerous individual sketches of Sut published in various newspapers and journals, a character emerges whom it is possible to examine in a modern light. Sut Lovingood—the self-professed "nat'ral born durn'd fool"; the practical, often sadistic joker; the rambunctious mountaineer of whom William Faulkner said, when naming his favorite fictional characters for a *Paris Review* interview, "I like Sut Lovingood. . . . He had no illusions about himself, did the best he could"[3]—can, surprisingly, be seen in the tradition of, or perhaps as a precursor to, what has come to be known as the absurd or existential anti-hero.

Professors Hennig Cohen and William Dillingham, co-editors of *Humor of the Old Southwest* (1964), seem to be the first critics to have looked at the *Yarns* explicitly in the light of existentialism and its literature. They say that "Sut's vision is frighteningly clear and his philosophy existential . . . he has decided to make out as best he can . . . ,"[4] remarks that echo Faulkner's. Likewise, many of Rickels' comments, in both his full-length study and his earlier article on imagery in the *Yarns*[5] [*Sut Lovingood's Yarns*], suggest an existential reading of Harris' work, though Rickels does not explicitly use the language of existentialism: "Sut is hard and cruel

because in the moral void of the American backcountry of his experience he can assert his individuality only through violence."[6]

Indeed, the available evidence indicates that Harris' intentions encompassed more than simply telling humorous tales. The skill and intelligence of his revisions reveal a concern with internal consistency and unity in the *Yarns* not necessary in a collection of purely comic or satiric tales. Consistency of locale, manners, customs, and types of tales would have guaranteed a well-integrated collection of tales of life in old Tennessee. Harris' work, however, has, in addition to the above, a unity of a different kind—an integrated and consistent vision of the world, a vision that is far from comic and that focuses on the plight of one individual in such a world—Sut Lovingood. It is interesting that Faulkner does not refer to Sut as a comic character, probably because the *Yarns* can hardly be skipped over as mere comic sketches if one notes the underlying consistency and horror of Sut's world vision. This is not to say that the *Yarns* are not funny; on the contrary, they are full of comedy, and sometimes, they are hilarious. Rickels says that "Sut's surfaces are those of realism, comic fantasy, and local color."[7] The key word here is "surfaces." Like the best of European existential comedy, Sut's surfaces are funny, but a look beneath the surface reveals something much different, an underlying despair. As Rickels points out, ". . . the laughter must come from the poor plots; the style, the imagery, communicates an infernal country in which no man could take joy."[8] It is this dark vision, then, which distinguishes Harris from most of the other Southwestern humorists. And it is this difference which makes us look ahead to the literature which followed Harris, in trying to understand Sut, as well as to the literature which preceded him; which makes us see Sut as absurd or anti-hero as well as rambunctious mountaineer, wise fool, and mythical creature.

Sut criticism has focused on the nature of Sut's character with little agreement; Sut is too complex for easy labels. Interpretations of his character tend to fall into three categories. To some, he is the "genuine naive roughneck mountaineer riotously bent on raising hell."[9] To others, Sut is something else; Edmund Wilson found him repellent, not funny; sadistic, not devilish; malevolent and sordid, not Rabelaisian.[10] A third critical view sees Sut as the "roughneck mountaineer" mentioned above, but with the concept of naivete removed. Sut's occupation, "raising hell," takes on a meaning and purpose beyond itself in this third vision of Sut and the American backwoods, a vision Rickels calls "a striking obverse to the Adamic myth, as R. W. B. Lewis called it: the idea of the 'authentic American as a figure of heroic innocence and vast potentialities'."[11] From this viewpoint, Sut is miserable. And knowing his misery to be essentially inescapable, he plunges himself into whatever animal pleasures are available—"eatin," "drinkin," and "huggin," as well as cruel practical joking. Rickels elaborates on this view: "Although at times Sut speculates that he might someday turn human, 'That is, sorter human,' he abandons himself to his animality in full consciousness of his misery and wretchedness. He expresses repeatedly in comic ambiguity his final despair: 'I'll drond mysef sumday'."[12] It is this third view which has affinities with the absurd man of existential literature. Appearing just three years after Dostoevsky's Underground Man, a prototype of later, serious existential figures, Sut is a prototype, perhaps, of the figures of existential comedy.

A basic tenet of existentialism is that a given individual (Sut, in this case) is "thrown" irrationally into the world and into a particular situation (for Sut, the Lovingood family in the Tennessee mountains). Sut's life begins in what Rickels calls, borrowing a term from William R. Taylor, an "anti-home" and with an "anti-father,"[13] usually known as Hoss Lovingood. It is a home with little love and less understanding. Sut has this to say about his father: "Thar never wer a man yet, so mean, but what some time, or other, done at least one good thing. Now, my Dad put off doin his good thing for an awful long time, but at last he did hit, like a white man. He died, by golly!"[14] Added to this lack of love and understanding and partially explaining it, perhaps, is the poverty and squalor in which the Lovingoods live: "Well, es I wer saying, mam wer feedin us brats ontu mush an' milk, wifout the milk, an' es I wer the baby then, she hilt me so es tu see that I got my sheer. Whar that ain't enuf feed, big childer roots littil childer outen the troff, an' gobbils up thar part" (174).

The Lovingood family does have a tradition, however; it can boast a long line of "durn'd fools." Sut's father writes proudly of this tradition in **"The Early Life of Sut Lovingood, Written By His Dad"** and reduces it to its absurd logical conclusion: "Well, 'My Son' Sut, comes of as good and as pure durn'd fool stock, as most public caracters now figurin' on top ove the pot. His great gran'dad, arter a long life spent doin' the durndes fool things done in them durn'd fool days, killed hissef a jumpin down a bluff, two hundred feet into a rocky dry branch, jist to save a half a mile gwine to the stillhouse" (298).

Sut's accidental birth into such a family is frequently referred to. His tendency toward durn'd fool seems to confirm, to most people and to himself, his paternity, but there are times when an even more irrational explanation for his birth is offered: "He run his eye twist along hit frum aind to aind, an sez he, 'Mister, you hes run powerfully to laigs; didn't a tellegraff pole fall across yer mom afore you wus bornd?' 'No,' sez I, 'but we kep a pet sand hill crane, an mom an him hed a differculty, an he chased her onder the bed'" (249). There

are other references to this crane in the **Yarns,** but this is the most explicit in its implications. It reinforces the grotesque aspects of Sut's creation and character; reinforces the mythic element, with its obvious analogy to Leda and the swan; and, finally, it reinforces the existential idea that to exist is to happen without reason. After man is in the world, he can ascribe his own reasons for existence, as Sut often does.

Sut's education, for the most part, seems to have been random; that is, by haphazard trial and error and bad example, although Dad does mention in his **"Life of Sut"** that the boy once "got smuggled into school" (305), a short-lived experiment. Examples of the more chaotic method abound, as in **"Sut Lovingood at Bull's Gap,"** an incident of which Sut says, "I think I got my fust noledge ove gittin away from imijut trubbil an cummin tribulashun frum him [an old fox] . . ." (235-36). In **"Sut Lovingood, His Autobiography,"** he explicitly uses the word "trial" in relation to his method of learning about himself and the world: "The nex' trial I made to fine my gif' wer trappin' fur varminty things . . ." (289).

Add to the above "givens" Sut's temporal and spatial environment—mid-nineteenth century backwoods Tennessee, and we have a good picture of his situation. Now we will look at Sut himself—his awareness, his suffering, and his defiant action as he responds to this situation.

David D. Galloway, in his book, *The Absurd Hero in American Fiction,* identifies the initial step in the development of the absurd hero as the "shocking recognition of the apparent meaninglessness of the universe."[15] Albert Camus calls this the recognition of the "absurd."[16] In either case, a prerequisite for recognition is consciousness. Sut is a conscious man. He sees himself, his situation, society and its institutions and types, and the world generally in a harsh, rarely mitigated light. As Faulkner said, he has few illusions. Perhaps the clearest utterance of his self-estimate occurs in **"Old Burns's Bull Ride"**:

> I'se a goner I 'speck, an' I jis don't keer a durn. I'm no count, no how. Jis' look at me! Did yu ever see sich a sampil ove a human afore? I feels like I'd be glad tu be dead, only I'se feard ove the dyin. I don't keer fur herearter, fur hits onpossibil fur me tu hev ara soul. Who ever seed a soul in jis' sich a rack heap ove bones an' rags es this? I's nuffin but sum newfangil'd sort ove beas', a sorter cross atween a crazy ole monkey an' a durn'd woreout hominy-mill. I is one ove dad's explites at makin cussed fool invenshuns, an' cum afore my time. I blames him fur all ove hit, allers a-tryin tu be king fool. He has a heap tu count fur, George—a heap.

(89)

In accord with his self-estimate, Sut does not expect to be treated with respect: "I hes allers notis'd nobody ever calls me Mister Lovingood, (ef they knows me,) onless they's mad at me" (160). He is not even surprised when he is dismissed as not human, a frequent occurrence.

Sut's most insistent view of himself is as a "durn'd fool," and he calls attention to it whenever he can, often several times in one yarn. He refers to this trait as his "nater," and others concur. His reputation for being a durn'd fool rests primarily on his continual practical joking. In **"Taurus in Lynchburg Market,"** after Sut escapes from an encounter with a bull, he tells us this: "They telegrafed tu Stantun fur a committee ove doctors, tu 'zamine me fur the honors ove the lunatic assalum. When they got thar, they foun' nuffin tu 'zamine but the karacter I hed lef fur bein a nat'ral born durn'd fool, an' a crack'd whisky flask" (112). It is what he *does*, then, which makes others dismiss him as a fool. It is interesting that George, the one person whom Sut confides in, never once calls him a fool.

Sut is as highly conscious of his family environment as of himself. His attitudes toward his family are fairly complex, ranging from downright shame to a sort of defiant pride when he speaks of the Lovingood fool tradition: "Our famerly am an' ole wun. Dad used tu trace hit back tu Joseph in Yegipt, an' he sed hit wer purfeckly useless tu hunt furder fur better fool blood" (108). Implicit in the pride and bragging is the need to redeem and vindicate, indicative of another and more deeply felt emotion regarding his home. Sut puts his family in a category all by themselves, often referring to them as not human, and when admitting they are human, differentiating them from other people. The difference is negative: ". . . hit cudn't a-been did by eny uther peopil on this yeath but us, fur hit am plum clarified dam fool" (206).

Sut's insights extend beyond himself and his own family. His consciousness of the world in general is no less acute and no less negative. His venom is particularly directed toward certain societal types, such as circuit riders, dandies, squires, traveling salesmen, tax collectors, and constables. Sut is capable of cutting down the hypocrisy and pretentiousness he sees in the most inimitable way: ". . . the most human view you gits ove 'em is when they is above you a climbin' up" (222). From his personal observations of the world, he devises his own chain of being in which he places himself somewhere between people and possums: ". . . Jis' so the yeath over: bishops eats elders, elders eats common peopil; they eats sich cattil es me, I eats possums, possums eats chickins, chickins swallers wums, an' wums am content tu eat dus, an' the dus am the aind ove hit all" (174-175). In a delightful description, he explains how the social climbers of the world go about their business: "They ginerily has a pedigree wif one aind tied to thar sturn, an' tother one a-soakin' in *Noah's*

flood, an' they'l trace hit back for you, round the jails, onder the galluses, apast the soap works, an' over the kitchens, ove four thousin years, an' if you'l notice close, hit makes some ove the shortest kind ove dodges, to miss 'em all; but by golly, hit does miss 'em, an' hits every durn castil, an' throne, on the whole road" (260). Sut sees the tremendous gap between himself and such people and knows that he is the better off for it. He, at least, has not deluded himself.

Sut discusses directly what he thinks about life in **"Sicily Burns's Wedding,"** and his statement is deceptively simple: "Men wer made a-purpose jis' tu eat, drink, an' fur stayin awake in the yearly part ove the nites: an wimmen wer made tu cook the vittils, mis the sperits, an' help the men du the stayin awake. That's all, an' nuthin more. . . . George, yu don't onderstan life yet scarcely at all, got a heap tu larn, a heap" (77). Life is so much and yet so little as Sut here expresses it. A less ambiguous statement is this one: "George, this worl am all 'rong enyhow, more temtashun than perventitive; ef hit wer ekal, I'd stand hit . . ." (70).

Sut's awareness, then, is complex. It is directed both inward, at himself and his family, and outward, at society and the world in general. His inner-directed awareness most often causes him anguish and shame while his outer-directed awareness arouses mostly anger and contempt. In many situations, the two kinds of feelings merge. Both kinds exemplify that Sut is an individual who feels things deeply.

In the existential tradition, both philosophical and literary, suffering plays an inevitable and important part. It is hard to read the *Yarns* and not believe that Sut suffers. He is of bad stock, unattractive, ungainly, uneducated, ill-mannered, and unloved—and knows it. It's the knowing that makes the difference, for Sut does have a vision of something better. In **"Blown Up With Soda,"** he compares what he feels in nature with what Sicily Burns makes him feel: "Music; the rushin warter dus make music; so dus the wind, an' the fire in the mountin, and hit gin me an oneasy queerness agin; but every time I look'd at that gal Sicily Burns, I hed all the feelins mix'd up . . ." (71). Sut knows that such a woman is not for the likes of him.

Sut's references to himself as a durn'd fool occur throughout the *Yarns.* Sometimes they are made boastfully, sometimes matter-of-factly, but all too often, they are said in a tone of sadness and inevitability. These laments are sometimes accompanied by threats of metamorphosis: "I'l turn buzzard, an' eat ded horses fur a livin; . . ." (137) or of destruction: "Hit am an orful thing, George, tu be a nat'ral born durn'd fool. Yu'se never 'sperienced hit pussonally, hev you? Hits made pow'fully agin our famerly, an all owin tu dad. I orter bust my head open agin a bluff ove rocks, an' jis' wud du hit, ef I warnt a cussed coward" (83).

Sut often expresses shame at himself and his family, as in this passage from **"Dad's Dog School"**: "A appertite tu run began tu gnaw my stumick, an' I felt my face a-swellin wif shame. I wer shamed ove dad, shamed ove mam's bar laigs an' open collar, shamed ove my-sef, an' dam, ef I minds right, ef I warn't a mossel shamed ove the pup" (211). References to his shame over the incident of dad's acting horse occur again and again: "I'se a durnder fool nor enybody outside a Assa-lum ur Kongriss, 'sceptin ove my own dad, fur he actid hoss, an' I haint tried that yet" (39). References also re-cur to incidents in which Sut has been disappointed or frustrated as when Sicily Burns plays a prank on him in **"Blown Up With Soda."** In **"Hen Baily's Reforma-tion,"** for instance, Sut remembers this earlier incident: "Durn'd ef his kerryins on didn't mine me ove my sody misery in a minnit" (157).

Anger is often a motivating force for Sut's actions, but usually it is mixed with some kind of hurt, as in **"Sut Lovingood, His Autobiography"**: "I cud hear frum 'em mos' every day, bemeanin' me the wust kine; at las' I hearn ove 'em callin me a *nusance!* This made me hos-tile as be durn'd; hit were the meanis soundin' name enybody had ever gin me, . . . 'nusance,' durn the nasty word; I hates hit tu this day" (291).

In **"Sut's New-Fangled Shirt,"** a yarn in which he threatens to drown himself several times, he expresses in one line most of the suffering that he feels, at one time or another, throughout the *Yarns*: "I'se sick—sham'd—sorry—sore—an'—mad tu kill I is" (39). Sut, then, feels as well as sees.

After consciousness and suffering, a third important theme of existentialism is engagement or action. "Man must choose to live his situation because it is beyond his power to separate himself from it."[17] To live one's situation is not to be passive. A passive Sut would be simply a victim. But a passive Sut is hard to imagine, for we see him playing joke after joke, often to the bor-der of sadism; damning hypocrisy and pretentiousness wherever he sees them; and proclaiming the life of "drinkin," "eatin," and "huggin" (117).

To live one's situation is to assert one's individual free-dom and to make decisions without reference to an out-side source for justification. "Escape from freedom . . . is a constant temptation. It takes the form of what might be termed a flight from self-consciousness into an illu-sory security."[18] Man, by acting rather than escaping, af-firms both his situation and himself.

Sut is aware of the possibilities of escape, the most fi-nal one being suicide. Another possibility he sometimes mentions is to someday turn "sorter human," to escape durn'd foolness. A third way out, and one which some existentialists take, is the way of faith, the Kierkegaard-

ian "leap." Sut never even gives the third possibility a serious thought. Religion is one of his primary objects of attack, or at least many of its representatives are, with circuit riders being his pet hate. He sees these people as cowards and hypocrites and prefers to rely on himself rather than take refuge in religion: "'Well, durn my rags ef gittin ove religun ain't the city ove rayfuge now-a-days; I hes a city ove rayfuge mysef, what I al-lers keeps along wif me,' and Sut looked down proudly at his legs" (204-205).

Thus Sut, like Camus, rejects two of the most obvious means of escape—suicide and religion. For Camus, to embrace either one is to destroy the absurd rather than to affirm and defy it, for the absurd is the product of the confrontation between man, with his expectations and ideals, and the irrational, ugly reality he encounters, what Camus calls "the unreasonable silence of the world."[19] Only if the disparity between the two is main-tained can the absurd be maintained. To destroy oneself is to destroy the self that dreams and thus that part of the dichotomy; to "leap into faith" is to destroy the irra-tional universe and give it meaning, thus breaking down the other half of the dichotomy. Sut actively maintains both sides. Like Sisyphus, he keeps pushing that rock up the hill *knowing* that it's going to roll back down. The two crucial points are that both Sut and Sisyphus are aware and that they affirm the absurd with joy.

An existential reading of the *Yarns,* then, proposes that because Sut has been "thrown" into a certain situation and given certain things, one of which is awareness, and because another of these givens is the fact that from the day he was born, others have expected him to be just another durn'd fool Lovingood, Sut, in extreme defiance, purposely determines to affirm and reinforce his situation to its utmost by being the durndest fool of all. He jumps into the *role* of fool; that is, he plays the part that is expected of him and that is very much an aspect of his character. But the fool role does require a mask, for its does not represent the entire human being. Underneath is Sut Lovingood—aware, feeling human being, who usually reveals himself only to George. Rickels also comments on this fool role: "Sut is always conscious of his mode of existence. In this sense, de-spite his constant disclaimers, his life is a free choice he has made for himself; his existence is the product of his own free will. His choice frees him from the neces-sity of deceiving himself and thus provides him an au-thentic mode of being."[20] The opening paragraph of **"Sut Lovingood's Sermon"** might serve as a sort of manifesto of what Sut has chosen to affirm as vigor-ously as he can:

> Hit takes a feller a long time, George, to fine out what his gif' am, his bes' pint, what game he's stronges' on. I knows hit tuck me a mortul while, but a las' I got hit narrer'd down to two things. Gittin intu trubbil wer

one, an' then runnin' out ove hit wer tuther. I wavered a good while which ove em' I'd bes' foller fur a livin', an' I studied, an' studied, an' sum how I cud see no way ove siperatin' 'em so at las' I made up my mine tu run the dubbil ingine, that is, take 'em together, an' I finds 'em to suit together jus ad-zackly, an' better nor all that, they bof suits me.

(287)

This explanation of Sut's studying to find his best point and then making up his mind to follow it suggests a very conscious and free choice on his part. His best point or his "gif" turns out to be two-fold—"gittin into trubbil" and "then runnin' out ove hit." He considers these fool things to do, and in doing them to their fullest, he affirms himself as durn'd fool.

It is Sut's legs, as much as anything else, which allow him to play the role of durn'd fool. Sut is constantly involved in what he refers to as "skeers." Anyone or anything can be the victim of a skeer, from the dog in **"Sut Lovingood's Hog Ride"** to Sut himself in many of the *Yarns.* The most recurrent pattern is for Sut to take aim at someone or something, often for no good reason, and to set a scare in motion. From there, the scare takes over, with Sut usually ending by taking a scare himself and running from the scene: ". . . in fac I *was* skeared by this time, fur I'd got more nor I'd paid fur" (224). This is when Sut's legs become important. Without his incredible "given" speed, he would not be able to constantly escape from his pursuers. Sut is sharply aware of the value of his legs to him: "George, never wer es proud ove these yere laigs afore (d'ye see em), only when I outrun ole Burns' houns. I'se tuck tu ilin ove em every day with frog ile; hit helps em powful, an' they'se my only pendance on this yeath; an I thinks I onderstands how to use em" (231).

Sut often refers to himself as a coward, and yet he continues to initiate actions which often end in a scare for him. As we have seen him able to feel anger, hurt, and shame, we also see him able to feel real fright: "I tuck a good holesum pull outen that bottil, an' tho't what a durn'd discumfortin thing a big skeer is" (172). But the scare is just part of the pattern of playing durn'd fool to the hilt, and there are special things to be done when one is scared. The whole process begins to take on an almost ritualistic aspect: "I likes that nigger; he's the only feller I ever seed what tuck in the rale pure Lovingood idear ove what orter be dun under strong hurtin an' a big skeer. Jis run over ur thru everything yure durndest, till yu gits cumfort" (135). To initiate the action, take a "skeer," and run; that is the pattern, and Sut, both comically and defiantly, goes through it again and again. He is totally aware of his own absurdity, but he has chosen to make it count for something. He has adopted an existential position of revolt in that he chooses to live in the face of his and the world's absurdity, and he has even chosen to play an absurd role.

Only the immediate is of importance to Sut: ". . . an' that minds me tu tell yu what I thinks ove plannin an' studdyin: hit am ginerly no count. All pends, et las' on what yu dus an' how yu kerries yursef at the moment ove ackshun" (63). In existentialism the moment of action is all that matters also, since man is "nothing else but the sum of his actions, nothing else but what his life is."[21] It is also important that, at the moment of action, man chooses what to do. Things don't simply happen to Sut, as he explains in **"Bart Davis' Dance."** He is talking to George about Obed Davis' skinned and slit face: "Yes, I see; how did it happen? Happen? Hit didn't happen at all, hit wer dun a-pupos, permeditated a-pupos" (144).

Part of defiantly playing the role of fool is for Sut to deny, whenever he can, his responsibility for things. Since a nat'ral born durn'd fool is ultimately innocent, and Sut is playing the role of fool, he can claim innocence. In a very real sense, however, he does feel unjustly blamed for many things: "I can't git jestis nowhar. . . ." (137), but he also feigns innocence in situations where he knows full well he has precipitated the catastrophe. This is not shirking responsibility or being hypocritical, but rather living more fully the absurd and undesirable situation in which he finds himself. Feeling soulless, Sut can also feel free of responsibility.

How do we reconcile, then, Sut's hedonistic philosophy with his vision of the world as "all 'rong"? Perhaps they don't seem so antithetical after all. The world *is* all wrong as far as Sut is concerned, and he is not any happier with himself than he is with the rest of the world. In fact, his contempt for himself is perhaps the greatest of all, and it is this which saves him from being despicable. It is part of the secret of his appeal. Sut knows that he cannot reform or save himself or the world, but he also knows that he can defiantly affirm them both by maintaining the whole absurd situation. Mean practical joking is one means of doing this. When Sut plays a practical joke on someone he despises, such as a hypocritical authority figure, he is perhaps letting his wrath take control; when he lashes out verbally at himself, he is reminding himself of his own unhappy condition. These might seem like lapses from the defiantly joyous state, but it is essential that Sut maintain the disparity between his dreams and expectations and the reality he encounters. Both his jokes and his verbal self-abuse remind him of the world he would rather have. It is really hard to imagine Sisyphus as happy going back down the hill, as going up. The state of joyous revolt or defiance is equally hard for Sut to maintain. And there *is* a world Sut indicates he would prefer—if it were possible. We see it in the description of Sicily Burns in the beginning of **"Blown Up With Soda,"** in the long passages on Mary Mastin in **"Trapping a Sheriff,"** and in his gentle puzzlement and good feeling about Missie

Burns in **"Old Burns's Bull-Ride."** These moments of longing are what Camus calls "the rock's victory,"[22] but they must remain only fleeting moments if the absurd hero is to transcend his situation.

So far, Sut follows the first two steps in Galloway's analysis of the development of the absurd hero. He recognizes the meaninglessness and absurdity, and he lives the conflict. The third step is the character's "assumption of heroic dimensions through living the conflict and making it his god."[23] Although Rickels argues that Harris denies Sut any "transcendence,"[24] Sut certainly makes the role of durn'd fool his god, and he does so with his eyes wide open, as Rickels himself observes: "Although at times Sut speculates that he might someday turn human, 'That is, sorter human,' he abandons himself to his animality in full consciousness of his misery and wretchedness."[25] Though he does not literally transcend his situation, Sut's combination of abandonment to the durn'd fool role and consciousness is what gives him a Sisyphean kind of transcendence, a heroic dimension.

Two final questions remain: does an existential revolt preclude comedy? Is Sut, finally, tragic or comic? The answer to the first question is no. One can as easily defy one's situation comically as seriously. The comic defiance demands something objective—in Sut's case, scapegoats on which to play jokes and lay blame and a good-humored audience ready to listen to his accounts of his antics. A more serious defiance, though it may erupt in an objective act like murder, as in William Styron's *Set This House on Fire,* more often takes the form of a turning inward and a gnawing upon the self, as in Dostoevsky's *Notes From Underground.* Whenever Sut gnaws on himself, it is never in solitude, but always with at least one listener—George. Usually, he directs his revolt outward.

Is Sut funny or tragic? An easy answer would be to call him tragicomic. But I think that I would have to call him comic. I qualify that by saying that I laugh *with* Sut but never *at* him, and this is a crucial distinction. Camus says, "One must imagine Sisyphus happy."[26] We must, likewise, imagine Sut comic and foolish, as well as happy, for to do otherwise would be to destroy the mighty, sustained affirmation he makes in the face of acute consciousness and despair. Sut himself expresses, in his preface, what it means to him to make us laugh:

> Ef eny poor misfortinit devil hu's heart is onder a millstone, hu's raggid children am hungry, an' no bread in the dresser, hu is down in the mud, an' the lucky ones a-trippin him every time he struggles tu his all fours, hu hes fed the famishin an' is now hungry hissef, hu misfortins foller fas' an' faster, hu is so foot-sore an' weak that he wishes he wer at the ferry—ef sich a one kin fine a laugh, jis' one, sich a laugh as is remembered wif his keerless boyhood, atwixt these yere kiv-

ers—then, I'll thank God that I *hes* made a book, an' feel that I got my pay in full.

(26)

We must remember Sut's total nature and what he has compromised with himself in making his affirmation of life under less-than-desirable conditions—the few pleasures he asks for rather than the larger ones he often desires. Sut Lovingood is a durn'd fool, but he is not a "nat'ral born" durn'd fool; he is a conscious fool.

Sut's brand of existentialism is, admittedly, primitive. He is not as consciously aware as Camus's Meursault, though certainly more passionate and engaged, nor is his vision yet enlarged to include the sense of compassion and responsibility for one's fellow man so important in Camus's later work, *The Plague,* and in the humanistic existentialism of Sartre. But he *is* an existentialist, though he would certainly disdain such a pompous-sounding title. He confronts his own alienation and creates meaning for himself through the confrontation.

The closing lines of **"Dad's Dog School,"** the story which ended the 1867 edition of the *Yarns,* strike me as one of the best summings-up of Sut and an appropriate end to this discussion. The scene is a typical one—Sut and a few friends around a campfire after the telling of a yarn:

> Boys, I'se sleepy now; yere's wishin (Sut raised on his elbow and held up his flask to the light) yu all good dreams, an' yu, George, may yu dream ove ownin three never-failin springs, so clost tugether yu kin lay on yure belly an' reach em all—the biggis' wun runnin ole whisky, the middil one strained honey, an' the leas' an' las'—cold warter, wif nara 'nat'ral born durn'd fool' in two miles tu bother yu, an' when yu wake up, may yu fine hit tu be a mortal fac'.

> Es tu me, ef I kin jis' miss dreamin ove hell ur ole Bullin's all I ax. Sum one ove yu move that ar saddil down yander by the corner ove the camp, further outen the way ove my laigs. Now le's snore sum; blow out the light.

(220)

Notes

1. Milton Rickels, *George Washington Harris* (New York, 1965), 7.

2. George Washington Harris, *Sut Lovingood, Yarns Spun By a "Nat'ral Born Durn'd Fool", Warped and Wove for Public Wear* (New York, 1867).

3. Malcolm Cowley, ed., *Writers at Work: 'The Paris Review' Interviews,* "William Faulkner," (New York, 1958), 137.

4. Hennig Cohen and William Dillingham, eds., *Humor of the Old Southwest* (Boston, 1964), 10.

5. Milton Rickels, "The Imagery of George Washington Harris," *American Literature,* 31 (1959), 173-87.

6. Rickels, "Imagery," p. 187.

7. Rickels, *GWH* [*George Washington Harris*], p. 29.

8. Rickels, "Imagery," p. 175.

9. Walter Blair, *Native American Humor* (Chicago, 1942), 97.

10. Edmund Wilson, "Poisoned," *The New Yorker,* 31 (May 1955), 24.

11. Rickels, "Imagery," p. 174.

12. Rickels, "Imagery," p. 181.

13. Rickels, *GWH,* p. 48.

14. George Washington Harris, *Sut Lovingood's Yarns,* M. Thomas Inge, ed. (New Haven, 1966), 321. All subsequent references are from this edition of the *Yarns.*

15. David D. Galloway, *The Absurd Hero in American Fiction* (Austin, 1966), 16.

16. Albert Camus, *The Myth of Sisyphus* (New York, 1955), 11.

17. Norman N. Greene, *Jean-Paul Sartre: The Existentialist Ethic* (Ann Arbor, 1961), 9-10.

18. Greene, p. 9.

19. Camus, p. 21.

20. Rickels, *GWH,* p. 96.

21. Jean-Paul Sartre, "Existentialism is a Humanism," in *Existentialism from Dostoevsky to Sartre,* Walter Kaufmann, ed. (New York, 1975), 358.

22. Camus, p. 90.

23. Galloway, p. 16.

24. Rickels, "Imagery," p. 181.

25. Rickels, "Imagery," p. 181.

26. Camus, p. 91.

William E. Lenz (essay date 1985)

SOURCE: Lenz, William E. "Four Variations of the Confidence Man." In *Fast Talk and Flush Times: The Confidence Man as a Literary Convention,* pp. 97-146. Columbia: University of Missouri Press, 1985.

[*In the following excerpt, Lenz analyzes the character of Sut Lovingood. Lenz asserts that Sut is in essence a "confidence man" of the Southern frontier, a man whose amorality, passion, and anarchic sense of humor embody the zeitgeist of antebellum Tennessee.*]

The American confidence man abuses the confidence of everyone he meets for personal advantage. Prowling the flush times, he exposes suspicion, dishonesty, naivete, and greed, marking by his success a pattern of faith betrayed that resembles the frontier cycle of boom and bust. Imitators of Captain Simon Suggs sprang up throughout the Old Southwest, some paying explicit homage to Hooper in collections like William T. Porter's *The Big Bear of Arkansas* (1845). The more talented of Hooper's successors varied the humorous convention, investing it with new meaning while retaining the confidence man's mastery of language, his manipulation of appearances, and his exploitation of ambiguities. Sometimes crossing the development of the confidence man with versions of older traditions of the confidence game, authors like Joseph G. Baldwin, George W. Harris, Herman Melville, and Kittrell J. Warren refocused the convention to express distrust of the flush times and to accommodate historical events ranging from the California Gold Rush to the Civil War. The fiction of these writers illustrates four distinct variations of the confidence man, the scope of the convention's historical development, and the proof of Melville's observation that "in new countries, where the wolves are killed off, the foxes increase."[1] . . .

SUT LOVINGOOD

In the gentlemen's magazines and Tennessee newspapers of the 1850s, George Washington Harris develops characteristics of the southwestern confidence man that differ markedly from Baldwin's. Harris's creation, whose misadventures are collected in the 1867 *Sut Lovingood. Yarns Spun by a "Nat'ral Born Durn'd Fool,"* shares neither the respectability of Ovid Bolus nor the success of Simon Suggs, Jr.[2] The flush times have become the hard times, but what Sut lacks in social graces he makes up for in "onregenerite pride" (229). And where Baldwin tightened the rhetorical reins of his cultured narrator over his immoral characters, Harris passes the reins over entirely to his vernacular character turned narrator, Sut.

In Sut's Tennessee, victimization is the way of all flesh, and brutality is a means of survival. The world of the *Yarns* is hostile, a nightmarish landscape in which people, animals, and even inanimate objects threaten to transform the self into inhuman things: merely by going to sleep a man can become a corpse in a coffin (**"Frustrating a Funeral"**), a simple trip to town can turn into a near-fatal dance with a crazed bull (**"Taurus in Lynchburg Market"**), and a new shirt can strip the skin off a man's back as painfully and professionally as a medieval instrument of torture (**"Sut's New-Fangled Shirt"**). Point of view is important in this unbalanced universe, as Sut explains in **"Sut Lovingood's Daddy, Acting Horse."** Sut's father is chased into a creek by an angry swarm of hornets.

He kep' up a rite peart dodgin onder, sumtimes afore they hit im, and sumtimes arterard, an' the warter wer kivered wif drownded ball ho'nets. Tu look at hit frum the top ove the bluff, hit wer pow'ful inturestin, an' sorter funny; I wer on the bluff myse'f, mine yu. Dad cudent see the funny part from whar he wer, but hit seem'd tu be inturestin tu him frum the 'tenshun he wer payin tu the bisness ove divin an' cussin.

(26)

Humor based on others' physical discomfort is a conventional southwestern technique for enduring frontier hardships by making light of them. In **"Old Burns's Bull Ride,"** as Walter Blair notes, Harris reworks a tale that had been told in print at least since 1834 by Henry Nott, William Thompson, and others,[3] and Sut retells traditional cruel stories of exploded Yankees, broken-up camp meetings, and snake-bit Irishmen (61, 157, 108). Like the snaps of Simon Suggs, these incidents are funny to the safely distanced observer and narrator, but in the *Yarns* Sut himself must cope with personal threats and injuries.

In **"Parson John Bullen's Lizards,"** first published in 1857,[4] Sut tangles with a preacher reminiscent of Jedidiah Suggs and the Reverend Bela Bugg. Like Hooper, Harris uses the popular narrative-frame technique, yet his reversal of Hooper's emphasis on what Kenneth Lynn has called the "Self-controlled Gentleman" shatters the reader's expectations of cruel devilry occurring only within the "cordon sanitaire."[5] The narrative begins with a reward poster for Sut's hide and is controlled throughout by vernacular points of view.

AIT ($8) DULLARS REW-ARD

'Tenshun Belevers And Konstables! Ketch 'Im! Ketch 'Im!

This kash wil be pade in korn, ur uther projuce, tu be kolected at ur about nex camp-meetin, *ur tharater,* by eny wun what ketches him, fur the karkus ove a sartin wun SUT LOVINGOOD, dead ur alive, ur ailin, an' safely giv over tu the purtectin care ove Parson John Bullin, ur lef' well tied, at Squire Mackjunkins, fur the raisin ove the devil pussonely, an' permiskusly discumfurtin the wimen very powerful, an' skeerin ove folks generly a heap, an' bustin up a promisin, big warm meetin, an' a makin the wickid larf, an' wuf, an' wus, insultin ove the passun orful.

Test,   JEHU WETHERO.
Sined by me,
JOHN BULLEN, the passun.

(48)

"George," who presents this advertisement to the reader, is all that remains of the cultured frame-narrator. He is merely an introductory device, a convenient bridge to help the reader cross over into the fantastic rhetorical world of the *Yarns.* George functions as a model of the reader, an amused listener who, having cut his teeth on Seba Smith's Jack Downing and James Russell Lowell's Hosea Bigelow, surrenders to Sut's comic misspellings, outrageous dialect, and grotesque actions.

At a Rattlesnake Springs camp meeting, Sut seeks not money, like Simon Suggs, but love. Sitting

in a nice shady place convarsin wif a frien' ove mine, intu the huckil berry thickit, jis' duin nuffin tu nobody an' makin no fuss, when, the fust I remembers, I woke up frum a trance what I hed been knocked inter by a four-year old hickory-stick, hilt in the paw ove ole Passun Bullin, durn his alligater hide; an' he wer standin a striddil ove me, a foamin at the mouf, a-chompin his teeth—gesterin wif the hickory club—an' a-preachin tu me so you cud a-hearn him a mile, about a sartin sins gineraly, an' my wickedness pussonely, an' mensunin the name ove my frien' loud enuf to be hearn tu the meetin 'ous.

(49-50)

Parson Bullen's artless attack symbolizes Sut's vulnerability to forces beyond his control; unlike Simon Suggs, Sut is not the shifty master of easily manipulated dupes. It is Parson Bullen, rather, who has the upper hand, and who makes Sut and his girlfriend the victims of his petty meanness. In exchange for Sall cooking supper for him, Bullen promises not to tell her mother of Sall's sitting with Sut, but once he has eaten he "went strait an' tole her mam" (51). Like Jedidiah Suggs, Parson Bullen embodies a hypocritical authority that delights in inflicting bodily pain—Sut is beaten and Sall is stropped.

Sut's spirit, however, remains unbruised. Pretending repentance, Sut joins the parson's next camp meeting at Rattlesnake Springs. As Parson Bullen's sermon on "hell-sarpints" reaches a crescendo,

when he wer a-ravin ontu his tip-toes, an' a-poundin the pulpit wif his fis'—onbenowenst tu enybody, I ontied my bag ove reptiles, put the mouf ove hit under the bottim ove his britches-laig, an' sot intu pinchin thar tails. Quick es gunpowder they all tuck up his bar laig, makin a nise like squirrils a-climbin a shell-bark hickory. He stop't preachin rite in the middil ove the word "damnation" . . . fetch a vigrus ruff rub whar a hosses tail sprouts: then he's stomp one foot, then tuther, then bof at onst. Then he run his han' atween his waisbun an' his shut an' reach'd way down, an' roun' wif hit; then he spread his big laigs, an' gin his back a good rattlin rub agin the pulpit, like a hog scratches hisself agin a stump, leanin tu hit pow'ful, an' twitchin, an' squirmin all over, es ef he'd slept in a dorg bed, ur ontu a pisant hill. About this time, one ove my lizzards scared an' hurt by all this poundin' an' feelin, an' scratchin, popp'd out his head from the passun's shut collar, an' his ole brown naik, an' wer a-surveyin the crowd, when ole Bullin struck at 'im, jis' too late, fur he'd dodged back agin. The hell desarvin ole raskil's speech now cum to 'im, an' sez he, "Pray fur me brethren an' sisteren, fur I is a-rastlin wif the great inimy rite now!"

(53-54)

In battling "the great inimy" Parson Bullen tears off his clothes, standing before his flock in only "a par ove heavy, low quarter'd shoes, short wollen socks, an' eel-skin garters tu keep off the cramp" (56). Stripped of the vestments of his profession, he vaults—"plum crazy"—over three hundred watchful "sisteren" screaming "take keer ove yerselves, the Hell-sarpints *hes got me!*" (56).

What has got Bullen, of course, is Sut's genius, which temporarily forces the parson out of the redemption business. Sut's trick resembles those of Thomas Singularity or Ned Brace more than those of Simon Suggs. In Harris's fiction, the development of the confidence man recrosses older traditions; having been made a comic butt, Sut assumes the role of prankster to make Bullen play the fool. Categories of normal experience break down as Sut switches roles with Bullen by making his metaphoric religious struggle into a physical, humorous one. Identity is revealed as a precarious substance when Sut transforms himself from victim to victimizer and the parson from a man of the spirit into a scratching animal of naked flesh. At this moment of triumph Sut surely seems "America's Till Eulenspiegel," as Walter Blair notes,[6] yet Sut's financial language echoes the rewards of the Suggsian confidence man, suggesting that in Tennessee profits are registered in different specie: "yere's the way I lifted [Bullen's] note ove han'"; "I paid him plum up fur hit, an' I means tu keep a payin him, ontil one ur tuther, ove our toes pints up tu the roots ove the grass" (51). The new country of the *Yarns* offers reduced opportunities for a confidence man; Polk County lacks the cash necessary for gambling, swapping, and confidence art. Here there are no crops taken to Augusta, and even the parson's eight-dollar reward for Sut's capture is offered "in korn, ur uther projuce, tu be kolected at ur about nex camp-meetin, *ur tharater*" (48). Drinking, dancing, fighting, playing pranks, making love—these are the activities available to Sut, for the unstable community could not afford to support a confidence man, who needs both social conventions to exploit and cash to survive. The country around Rattlesnake Springs is poor on both counts, but its poverty and instability promise other kinds of payment.

Sut sees women as one of Tennessee's most valuable resources. In **"Blown Up with Soda"** (1857)—a variation of Major Jones's courtship of Mary Stallins[7]—Sicily Burns proves as shiny and hard as a new double-eagle.

> "George, did yu ever see Sicily Burns? Her dad lives at the Rattilsnake Spring, clost ontu the Georgia line."
>
> "Yes, a very handsome girl."
>
> "Handsome! that ar word don't kiver the case; hit souns sorter like callin good whiskey strong water, when yu ar ten mile frum a still-hous, hit a rainin, an' yer flask only haf full. She shows among wimen like a sunflower amung dorg fennil, ur a hollyhawk in a patch ove smart-

weed. Sich a buzzim! Jis' think ove two snow balls wif a strawberry stuck but-ainded intu bof on em. She takes adzactly fifteen inches ove garter clar ove the knot, stans sixteen an' a 'alf hans hi, an' weighs one hundred an' twenty-six in her petticoatail afore brekfus'."

(75-76)

George's conventional description, "handsome," Sut perceives as inappropriate; his own language defines her as a precious substance to be admired, measured, and consumed. Sut desires her as Simon Suggs desires to beat "the Tiger," and Sut is similarly blinded by her attractions. She is not, of course, the fulfillment of Sut's fantasies, but a feminine prankster: "'Sutty, luv, I'se got sumthin fur yu, *a new sensashun*'" (80). As he tells George, "'I'd got the idear onder my har that hit wer *lov-powders,* an' I swaller'd the devil red hot from home, a-thinkin that. Luv-powders *frum her*! jis' think ove hit yerse'f solemnly a minit, an' sit still ef yu kin'" (81). The "new sensashun" Sicily gives him is ten doses of soda-powder garnished with nutmeg, a concoction that empties Sut's stomach as readily as the faro bank empties Simon's pockets. Although Simon occasionally plays the fool, an implicit acknowledgement of the confidence man's ancestry, Sut is subjected to repeated bad deals from various sharpers; the Fates themselves seem to have stacked the deck against him, indicative of a disorder in the comic world of the *Yarns* not present in *Simon Suggs*. Simon contends with his devilish father, but the alluring Sicily Burns makes Sut drink "the devil red hot." Unlike Simon's universe, Sut's is populated by other devils who do get the best of him, in large part because everyone is subject to imminent dislocation by impersonal forces, and in small because there are few social conventions adhered to; Sut can manipulate Parson Bullen by feigning repentance, a characteristic sham of the confidence man, but nothing can save him from the parson's hickory stick. And when Sut himself behaves in a conventional manner, as when he plays the obedient lover to Sicily, he sets himself up for victimization.

When Sicily Burns marries the "suckit rider" Clapshaw in **"Sicily Burns's Wedding"** (1858), she opens the door to Sut's revenge. Sut drives the Burns's bull into their beehives and then into Sicily's wedding reception; the result is sexual revenge and a reassertion of Sut's mastery over the chaotic universe.

> Sicily, she squatted in the cold spring, up tu her years, an' turn'd a milk crock over her head, while she wer a drownin a mess ove bees onder her coats. I went tu her, an' sez I, "Yu hes got anuther new sensashun haint yu?" Sez she—
>
> "Shet yer mouth, yu cussed fool!"
>
> Sez I, "Power'ful sarchin feelin bees gins a body, don't they?"

"Oh, lordy, lordy, Sut, these yere 'bominabil insex is jis' burnin me up!"

"Gin 'em a mess over SODY," sez I.

(95)

Momentarily satisfied that "her an' him cudent sleep tugether fur ni ontu a week" (96), Sut completes his triumph in **"Sut Lovingood's Chest Story."**[8] He discovers that although Sicily "never did feel warm tu old Clapshaw" (*HTHT* [*High Times and Hard Times*], 120), she has learned to keep off the chill with Doctor Gus Fabin, a grotesque man "four foot fourteen inches" tall. While spying on the adulterous pair, Sut disturbs their lovemaking and gains his chance: "Ole Gus Fatty" hides in a chest containing two hundred eggs and some lamp black, Sicily "flung on her dress terrectly," and Sut pretends to be too drunk to recognize the obvious. Sicily is glad to fix the "drunk" Sut some dinner, and while she is gone, Fabin asks if "he"—meaning Sut—is gone. Imitating Sicily's voice, Sut, like Hooper's Daddy Biggs at Cockerell's Bend, paints a picture of imminent apocalypse that sets Fabin to praying; his prayers do no good, however, for Sut has tied the chest to Fabin's huge horse, which Sut has carefully prepared to bring on the Day of Doom by smearing luminous fox fire on it and igniting firecrackers round its head. The horse races off, mixing Fabin, eggs, and lamp black into one unholy stew, and as Sut notes, he never laid eyes on

> the chest nor Gus Fatty arter that nite, an I *dont care a durn ef I never do.* Wonder ef Sicily misses much! Ole Clapshaw believes in "witches, an warlocks, an long nebbed things" more than he does in Sicily an his "growin" skeer ov ghostes keeps him at home o' nights. I railly think he's gettin to be a pious man. Poor Sicily, she's warin thin, her eyes am growin bigger, an she hes no roses on her cheeks. She *cant* laugh, an she *wont* cry. Haint hit orful to think ove?
>
> (*HTHT,* 125)

Of course to Sut and the reader it is not "orful to think ove," but humorous. As Milton Rickels concludes, when Sicily "binds herself with the institutions, she becomes respectable and has a social place to lose."[9] In as artful a manner, Sut manipulates the adulterous Sheriff Doltin and Mary Mastin in the **"Rare Ripe Garden-Seed"** trilogy (227-77). He is able to chasten the sheriff, stop Mary's roaming, and drive away the meddlesome Widder McKildrin because they value their social positions and are confident that the authority of the sheriff's title will mask infidelity.

This is not to suggest with critics like Brom Weber that Sut is an agent of morality or cosmic justice;[10] Sut functions more like the soul of anarchy, the traditional fool or the lord of misrule. Sut seeks not justice but freedom and revenge; like Simon Suggs, he is the agent of a comic deity, one who like Simon's satirizes Sut as well.

Sut is, as Walter Blair and Hamlin Hill demonstrate, a subversive character whose language, constructed of fantastic details and incongruous images, serves to "camouflage the underlying anarchy."[11] We are amused by Sut's victimization of Clapshaw largely because of Sut's victimization of language; coinages like *suckit rider, insex,* and even the innocent *buzzim* subvert traditionally held values and engage the reader in a rhetorical conspiracy against order. To decipher Sut's dialect is to share Sut's point of view.

That point of view is achieved by the conflation of the confidence man and the fool into a single vernacular narrator. By this stroke of genius, Harris creates a shifty character who, since he has no need of money, is freer than Simon Suggs,[12] and who, since he tells his own story, never suffers defeat. Although the undeniable butt of Sicily Burns's soda-powder trick, Sut triumphs over his humiliation by exaggerating his own ludicrousness. In retelling the story to George, Sut stresses his own foolishness, his own animal and mechanical characteristics, transforming the painful and embarrassing incident into a humorous narrative, his own comic illusion, his triumph.

> Jis' 'bout the time I wer ketchin my breff, I tho't I'd swaller's a thrashin-meersheen in full blast, wif a cuppil ove bull-dorgs, an' they hed sot intu fitin; an' I felt sumthin cumin up my swaller, monstrous like a hi pressur steamboat. I cud hear hit a-snortin, and scizzin. . . . Thar wer a road ove foam frum the hous' tu the hoss two foot wide, an' shoe mouf deep—looked like hit hed been snowin—a-poppin, an' a hissin, an' a-bilin like a tub ove soap-suds wif a red hot mole-board in hit. I gethered a cherry tree lim' es I run, an' I lit a-straddil ove ole Blackey, a-thrashin his hide like the devil beatin tan-bark, an' a-hissin wus nur four thousin mad gangers outen my mouf, eyes, nose, an' years.
>
> (81-82)

Even in defeat, Sut wrestles triumph from the incident by embellishing its fantastic details and casting himself as its outrageous star. He not only survives but overcomes his predicament, conquering threats to the self by transforming them into narrative art. His language acts as a distancing medium by which he separates himself and George from the painful event, turning what was humiliating into what is humorous. Like Simon Suggs and Ovid Bolus, Sut Lovingood uses language to master the new country; Sut creates fictions to control disorder and guarantee survival, substituting for one order of reality in which he is the victim another in which he is a comic hero.

M. Thomas Inge writes that from 1854 to 1869 Sut Lovingood is "a literary figure living partially in a world of reality and mostly in a world of his own making, and an ironical and literal mouthpiece for Harris' political opinions and satirical attacks."[13] Inge is certainly correct in distinguishing between Sut's two worlds; in reality, Sut victimizes preachers, sheriffs, doctors, and all visible representatives of order because they threaten his individual freedom. Sometimes he succeeds, and sometimes he is himself pranked or kicked. In either case, Sut's recreation of the event in bizarre and dislocating language diverts attention from the consequences of these actions: his own pain, seen at this remove, becomes comic, and his cruelty to others—which can culminate in death—becomes a cause for laughter. When George asks what killed Mrs. Yardley, Sut replies, "Nuffin, only her heart stop't beatin 'bout losin a nine dimunt quilt. True, she got a skeer'd hoss tu run over her, but she'd a-got over that ef a quilt hadn't been mix'd up in the catastrophy" (137). Sut separates commonsense cause from effect; Mrs. Yardley dies because she cares too much for quilts.

Sut's victimization of a normative language, though comic, is itself a threat to the social order, a challenge to conventional modes of expression, perception, and understanding. A favorite rhetorical device of Sut's—the catalogue—mixes categories of being in a fantastic new order. Sheriff Doltin's wife appears initially as a traditional symbol of Christian piety, but Sut's imagery swiftly propels her heavenward in a new incarnation.

> She were boney an' pale. A drunk Injun cud a-red a Dutch almanac thru her nose, and ther wer a new moon ove indigo onder her eyes, away back intu them, fifty foot or so. . . . Her wais wer flat, an' the finger cords on her han's wer mos' as high, an' look'd es tight, and show'd es clar thru the skin, es the strings ove a fiddil. The han' hitself wer white, not like snow, but like paint, and the forkid blue veins made hit look like a new map ove the lan' ove death. She wer a coughin wif her han' on her hart, like she hed no more spittil nur she hed tears, an' not much louder nor a crickit chirpin in a flute; yit in spite ove all this, a sweet smile kiver'd her feeters. . . . Her shoulder blades, as they show'd thru her dress, made me think they wer wings a sproutin fur her flight tu that cumfort and peace she desarves so well. She's a dealin wif death now. . . . *She* is ready, an' *I* raly wish she hed started.
>
> (256-57)

Sut's language asserts his mastery of reality, sounding a note of optimism in an almost claustrophobic, menacing universe. His tales prove that the individual can survive, but only if he is willing and able to reorder reality—usually by disordering others' perceptions.

In Henry Clay Lewis's "Curious Widow" (1850), three medical students elaborately wrap up an albino Negro cadaver's face to tempt their curious landlady. They anticipate her cries of horror as she opens the package, confident that the prank will teach her a hard lesson. Their expectations of terrible delight are defeated, however, for she "gazed upon its awfulness in silence as if her eyes were riveted to it forever."[14] After a moment she laughs, then composes herself and notes scornfully, "I was just *smiling aloud* to think what fools these students made of themselves when they tried to scare me with a dead nigger's face when I slept with a drunken husband for twenty years" (121). The knowledge she possesses is neither entirely comic nor reassuring; yet she stares into the disturbing face, confronts it, reads it, and finally laughs at it to survive, as she had survived twenty years with her drunken husband. It is this knowledge—of drunken husbands, battered flesh, and all the forces that threaten to annihilate and dehumanize the self—that Sut Lovingood shares with the reader and, in the act of sharing, masters. Sut is like the students who dissect life and discover the need to laugh at the grotesqueries they uncover, yet Sut resembles the landlady as well, who, improbably assaulted, laughs in the face of "awfulness" and thereby claims a desperate triumph. Harris collapses both visions of life into one point of view; as Sut explains, "hit am an orful thing, George, tu be a natral born durn'd fool. Yu'se never 'sperienced hit pussonally, hev yu?" (97).

Even the flexibility of the fool's point of view, however, could not withstand the chaos of the Civil War. Like many of his fellow Southern writers, Harris began to lose confidence in the security and superiority that had allowed him to record the fantastic doings of the Frog Mountain community in tales as temporally separate as **"A Snake-Bit Irishman"** (1846) and **"Blown Up with Soda"** (1857). Harris's own sense of order, not a fictitious Sheriff Doltin's, had come under attack. After 1860, as Inge concludes, Sut becomes more and more a vehicle for Harris's fears about the uncertain future of the South, a vindictive spokesman bitterly ridiculing Lincoln, Yankees, and humanity in general.[15] Sut's sense of humor evaporates in the **"Travels with Abe"** satires (1861), **"Sut Lovingood Come to Life"** (1866), and **"Sut Lovingood on the Puritan Yankee"** (1866). In Hoss Lovingood's four-part biography of Sut (1868), Harris parodies Jesse Root Grant's biography of his son, Ulysses S. Grant, and, though Harris's imitation is in spots amusing, the Civil War had dealt Harris's imagination a blow from which neither he nor Sut could hope to recover. In **"Sut Lovingood's Allegory"** (1868), Sut notes that "we aint as *good* as we wer forty years ago. We am too dam artifichul, interprizin an' *sharp*" (*HTHT,* 312). Anticipating the imaginative methods of Twain and Howells, Sut argues "for the sake ove this an' the nex generashun" (*HTHT,* 316) for a return to a simpler, more traditional way of life like that he portrayed in **"The Knob Dance—A Tennessee Frolic"** (1846). But in 1869 Harris died, embittered by the Yankee mechanisms of Reconstruction. The past was lost, Harris knew, with the Confederacy; and for Sut Lovingood—an enduring character combining confidence man, prankster, and fool—there would be no recovery.

Notes

1. Herman Melville, *The Confidence-Man: His Masquerade,* ed. Hershel Parker [(1971)], p. 2.

2. George Washington Harris. *Sut Lovingood. Yarns Spun by a "Nat'ral Born Durn'd Fool." Warped and Wove for Public Wear*, p. vii. Subsequent references unless otherwise noted will be to sketches revised by Harris and collected in this edition of the *Yarns* and will be cited parenthetically in the text.

3. Walter Blair, *Mark Twain and Huck Finn*, pp. 242-43.

4. Milton Rickels includes a fine bibliography listing the first known publication date of Harris's fictions in *George Washington Harris,* pp. 145-47, which I have followed throughout this chapter.

5. Kenneth S. Lynn, *Mark Twain and Southwestern Humor,* p. 64.

6. Walter Blair, *Native American Humor (1800-1900),* p. 101.

7. Rickels, in *George Washington Harris,* p. 30, notes Harris's debt to Thompson; the name *Stallins* may have been lifted from Longstreet's "The Fight."

8. "Sut Lovingood's Chest Story" can be found in M. Thomas Inge's excellent edition of Harris's previously uncollected works, *High Times and Hard Times: Sketches and Tales by George Washington Harris.* Subsequent references to this edition will be cited in the text using the abbreviation *HTHT.*

9. Rickels, *George Washington Harris,* p. 53.

10. See Brom Weber's introduction to *Sut Lovingood,* pp. ix-xxix.

11. Walter Blair and Hamlin Hill, *America's Humor: From Poor Richard to Doonesbury,* p. 216.

12. Rickels, *George Washington Harris,* p. 103.

13. Inge, *High Times,* p. 106.

14. The most available edition of Lewis's fiction is John Q. Anderson, *Louisiana Swamp Doctor: The Life and Writings of Henry Clay Lewis.* All references to "The Curious Widow" are from this collection and will be cited parenthetically in the text.

15. Inge, *High Times,* p. 106; see pp. 222-31 for an analysis of Harris's satires. See also Donald Day, "The Political Satires of George Washington Harris," *Tennessee Historical Quarterly* 4 (December 1945): 320-38 for a broader interpretation of Harris's political inclinations.

Bibliography

Anderson, John Q. *Louisiana Swamp Doctor: The Life and Writings of Henry Clay Lewis.* Baton Rouge: Louisiana State University Press, 1962.

Blair, Walter. *Mark Twain and Huck Finn.* Berkeley: University of California Press, 1960.

———. *Native American Humor (1800-1900).* New York: American Book Co., 1937.

Blair, Walter, and Hill, Hamlin. *America's Humor: From Poor Richard to Doonesbury.* New York: Oxford University Press, 1978.

Harris, George Washington. *Sut Lovingood, Yarns Spun by a "Nat'ral Born Durn'd Fool." Warped and Wove for Public Wear.* New York: Dick & Fitzgerald, 1867.

Inge, M. Thomas, ed. *High Times and Hard Times: Sketches and Tales by George Washington Harris.* Nashville, Tenn.: Vanderbilt University Press, 1967.

Lynn, Kenneth S. *Mark Twain and Southwestern Humor.* Boston: Little, Brown, 1959.

Rickels, Milton. *George Washington Harris.* New York: Twayne, 1965.

Weber, Brom. ed. *Sut Lovingood,* by George Washington Harris. New York: Grove, 1954.

David C. Estes (essay date winter 1987)

SOURCE: Estes, David C. "Sut Lovingood at the Camp Meeting: A Practical Joker Among the Backwoods Believers." *Southern Quarterly* 25, no. 2 (winter 1987): 53-65.

[*In the following essay, Estes examines Harris's attitude toward organized religion in his Sut Lovingood sketches. Estes argues that, while satirical depictions of revival meetings were common in other writings from the period, Harris's portrayals of religious hypocrisy represented a radical break from tradition, as they are imbued with a level of hostility and vindictiveness unprecedented in Southern fiction.*]

Backwoods preachers and circuit riders, and the revivals they lead, appear frequently in the humor of the Old Southwest. Yet George Washington Harris selected them as objects of satire more frequently than did other antebellum southern humorists. In depictions of the Protestant camp meeting, he turned his attention to one of the unique developments of the nineteenth-century American frontier experience. Its initial popularity coincided with the Second Great Awakening (1800-1805), at which time it became "almost instantly universalized along the southwestern frontier" (Johnson 40). The early meetings were characterized by lack of planning, disorderliness, emotionalism and immorality. But quickly the practice became systematized. By the end of the second decade of the century there were no longer camp meetings the size of that at Cane Ridge, Kentucky, which for six days in August 1801 had drawn between ten and twenty-five thousand worshipers to one of the most licentious of all such religious gatherings. Frequency and length of camp meetings, procedures for the service, and location all became set, and consequently more and more of them were held in permanent or semi-permanent facilities. By the 1830s and 1840s indoor revivals were frequent in the Old Northwest. Yet on the southwestern frontier, where winters were mild, the camp meeting remained popular up until the Civil War.

Easterners first became acquainted with this form of religious expression indigenous to the frontier through the accounts of travelers who were, for the most part, unsympathetic to the wild emotionalism they observed. For example, in *Diary in America,* Captain Frederick Marryat, whose judgments about frontier life were more complimentary than those of many others, expressed a disdainful distrust of camp meetings as shocking spectacles. He attended one such gathering near Cincinnati which

> . . . was a scene of horrible agony and despair. . . . Another of the ministers knelt down by some young men . . . who appeared to be almost in a state of phrenzy; and putting his hands upon them, poured forth an energetic prayer, well calculated to work upon their over excited feelings. Groans, ejaculations, broken sobs, frantic motions and convulsions succeeded. . . . I quitted the spot, and hastened away into the forest, for the sight was too painful, too melancholy. . . . It was a fever created by collision and contact, of the same nature as that which stimulates a mob to deeds of blood and horror.
>
> (278)

Furthermore, by calling attention to the drinking and sexual immorality easily found just outside the ring of worshipers, Marryat and other travelers created a popular image of the camp meeting as an orgy of self-indulgence and sensual excitement.

Writers of humorous ante-bellum frontier literature helped to popularize this image through depictions of licentious revivals and hypocritical parsons. The most well-known of such sketches is Johnson Jones Hooper's "Simon Suggs Attends a Camp Meeting." It is a literary ancestor of another famous revival described by Mark Twain in the chapter "The King Turns Parson" in *The Adventures of Huckleberry Finn.* The narrative pattern in both of these, as in numerous other sketches, is that a wandering trickster remains in a backwoods community only long enough to attend a revival where he profits from the hypocrisy of the believers by outwitting the preacher, who had expected to take advantage of them himself.

Harris's use of such scenes and characters, however, differs markedly from this dominant pattern. His racy accounts of Sut Lovingood's guerilla war against the conventional practices and values of his Tennessee community include five sketches which recount the main character's animosity toward the religious leaders of the community and his practical jokes on both them and their flock. All are included in the volume entitled *Sut Lovingood. Yarns spun by a "Nat'ral Born Durn'd Fool"* published in 1867, just two years before Harris's death. Of the five, two are devoted exclusively to the turmoil which Sut's tricks create at camp meetings—one for blacks and the other for whites. Quite naturally, Harris continues the satire of religious hypocrisy enjoyed by contemporary readers of the southwestern humorists. His pieces are unique, however, in their emphasis on Sut's substitution of physical pain for anticipated pleasure by means of his practical jokes. The purposes of his actions are also unique, for he intends to punish and reform hypocrites who have tormented him, without benefiting materially as Suggs and the Duke do. Sut compels the believers at the camp meeting to play games which shrewdly manipulate the possibilities inherent within the form of their worship service, and against their will the service comes to release the tormenting reality of human depravity they wish to ignore. Like Marryat, he emphasizes the dark psychological impulses from which the backwoods revival springs. Furthermore, Harris's use of the camp meeting is unique because the trickster Sut is not a vagabond. He remains part of the community dominated by the superficially religious who are the victims of his cruel jokes. By emphasizing Sut's continuing relationship with his neighbors, who refuse to reform themselves, Harris embodies a vision of the world as a place of continuous, unavoidable mutual torment.

According to his friend George, Sut is "queer looking, long legged, short bodied, small headed, white haired, hog eyed" (Harris, *Yarns* 33). Sut himself states the essential quality of his character that corresponds to this physical appearance: "Did yu ever see sich a sampil ove a human afore? . . . hits onpossibil fur me tu hev ara soul. . . . I's nuffin but sum new fangil'd sort ove beas', a sorter cross atween a crazy ole monkey an' a durn'd wore-out hominy-mill" (89). His soulless nature makes him a thoroughly sceptical enemy of the parson whose goal is to save everyone in the community. By claiming to be a beast with a monkey and a useless machine for parents, Sut thoroughly rejects all religious notions that human nature is redeemable. Frequently he refers to himself as a "nat'ral born durn'd fool." Milton Rickels argues that Sut is in the tradition of the wise fool. He is "the ironic hero who perceives the human condition and knows he himself is a fool to communicate his perceptions" (96). Unafraid to accept the universal validity of this self-knowledge, he therefore becomes a dangerous threat to the prestige and power of the religious leaders in particular when he begins to examine the essential character of his neighbors.

The various references Sut makes to preachers throughout his yarns reveal how thorough and complete his rejection of them is. The animosity visible in these comments and anecdotes prepares readers for the shocking practical jokes he plays on them and their flock at the two camp meetings he attends. In **"Sicily Burns's Wedding"** Sut sums up his feelings: "Suckit-riders am surjestif things tu me. They preaches agin me, an' I hes no chance tu preach back at them. Ef I cud I'd make the institushun behave hitsef better nur hit dus" (78). Time and time again he gives examples of their hypocrisy. For example, **"Bart Davis's Dance"** recounts how "a hard-shell preacher wif his mouf mortised intu his face in shape like a muel's shoe, heels down" disrupts a Saturday night frolic (145). Although he comes uninvited and objects to the dancing "an' p'raps the cussin an' kissin," he has no complaint about "the whisky part ove that inturtainment." After the moonshine begins to work on him, he stops the fiddler and begins to exhort the people about their sins. Led by the host who calls him a "cuss'd hiperkritikal, ongrateful ole mus-rat" (148), all the guests—including the women who are in their best black silk dresses—attack him, turning the dance into a chaotic brawl. Another hypocritical preacher who appears in several of Sut's yarns is Bullen, who has "a never-tirein appertite fur bal'-face" (77). He runs a still which produces poor quality whiskey that he doctors with red pepper and "the red water outen a pon' jis' below his barn" (76). Ironically, his customers are members of his congregation. Parson Clapshaw is also among Sut's tormentors, principally because he marries the enticing Sicily Burns. While speaking to George about them, Sut explains, "There am three varmits what kin charm wimmin an birds—the suckit rider, the cat, an the black snake. They kin du hit, an nun ove em ever misses a chance. Ef I hed a pet mockinbird an a darter, I'd make war on all cats an suckit riders—I'd fill the beryin groun with wun, and the big sink hole with tuther; an I'd hev a barrel ful ove hyme books an claws es medals ove my skill in clost shootin" (91). Domination by such hypocritically pious parsons is sufficient cause for the painful vindictiveness of the retaliatory tricks which are the hallmark of Sut's yarns.

The less well-known of Harris's two camp meeting sketches is entitled **"Sut at a Negro Night-Meeting."** Most probably, a major reason for its lack of popularity among critics is the racism implicit in its humor. Like his vicious satires against Abraham Lincoln published at the time of the 1861 inauguration, this sketch reveals some of the southern attitudes Harris emotionally defended that are offensive to modern sensibilities. Undeniably, the violence Sut's practical jokes create fits into the tradition of sadistic racist humor. One has only to recall that a stock figure in southern frontier humor is the slave who suffers physical discomfort because of some misfortune while unharmed, amused whites observe his situation. Despite the reliance on such humor, Sut's closing comments in the sketch suggest that he has had the higher purpose of chastising and reforming religious hypocrisy: "Thar haint been a nigger nite meetin hilt in the county since, an' they's mos' on em becum pius, an' morril" (136). He exposes the camp meeting as mere pretense which, in fact, condones and encourages the behavior that it preaches against. Yet Sut achieves his higher purpose here only because the slaves react stereotypically. In accordance with the conventions of the racist "scared darkey" type, the fright they suffer is sufficient to bring about their reform.

Sut accomplishes his educative goal by using practical jokes that substitute pain for anticipated pleasure. Harris achieves a total reversal by carefully integrating the tricks his hero plans with what the believers say and do in the normal course of the meeting. The huge meeting, worth "ni ontu five hundred thousin dullars in flush times" (128), is to be held at the Log Chapel camp grounds where the permanent facilities include both a church with pews and a large adjoining shed with benches. Before anyone else arrives, Sut hides several beef bladders under the preachers' seats in the church. They are filled with a gas which he describes as the "devil's own parfume" (129). In the shed, where the service will resume after the first interruption, he buries some plugged up hornets' nests under the straw placed around the benches "tu git happy in, an' du thar huggin an' wallerin on" (130). The trickster summarizes his plan of attack with menacing understatement: "hit [the straw] hid the inemy what I hed ambush'd thar fus'rate, an' arterwards wer put tu a diffrent use than gittin happy on."

Before the worshipers, if they can properly be called that, assemble in the church, Sut hides himself where he can watch the turmoil that will result when he pulls the string to release the stinking gas from the bladders. Before he can execute his plan, the two preachers "seed the bulge ove wun ove the bladders, stickin out frum onder the slab a littil." They wink knowingly at each other: "They wer bof on em showin thar instinks: the suckit rider tuck hit tu be the breast ove a fat roas hen, an' the Baptis' thot hit were the bulge ove a jug." The text on which the "potgutted, ball-heded Baptis' bull nigger" begins to preach is ironically appropriate for what follows: *Yu shall smell sweet-smellin yarbs, an' eat honey vittils dar, fur thars no stink, nur bitter, whar you's gwine, in Caneyan.* While speaking these words to the soul, the preacher is actually meditating on filling his own stomach. At this moment Sut pulls the string. The preacher stops short and sniffs around just like "ole steers du," and then "he shook his hed till his years slapt like a hog's when he's a-gittin mad" (131). Soon everyone abandons the church, overcome by the objectionable smell. One old man growls at the parson, "Preachin frum that fool tex what done hit" (132). Indeed, he is underscoring Harris's point that religious hypocrisy is responsible for the pain in the lives of all people—both those with souls and those, like Sut, without.

The second half of this sketch narrates events that ensue shortly thereafter when the slaves reassemble in the shed to continue with their plans for the evening. In fact, they seem pleased with the change in location. One of the leaders, anticipating "a warm activ meetin," says from the new pulpit that "hit wer all fur the bes' that they wer druv frum the hous'; grace allers spread hitsef better an' smoofer, outen doors then hit did in the hous'" (133). Another promises to pass the hat to collect for African missions, and Sut comments wryly that the only hats to be passed will be the loose ones the con man passes later "a runnin outen thar." One of the important reversals here is that the casting away of clothes in the straw for the purpose of sexual pleasure brings, instead, greater discomfort when the hornets attack. This second practical joke of the evening, like the first, is an ironic enactment of the sermon text: "*Thar shall be weepin an' railin an' chompin ove teef, bad, an' them wif no teef, shall smash thar gums tugether like ontu wolf traps*" (133). Just when the preacher has shed his coats and "wer a-tryin tu jump outen his trowsis wifout onbuttunin em" and the congregation "wer a-mixin, he an' she, hollerin an' beginin tu hug, an' rar, an' waller, rite peart, an' nat'ral like," Sut releases the furious hornets from the hidden nests. Enjoying the spectacle of discomfort he has fashioned in accordance with the preacher's text, Sut describes in full detail the depravity of the pious the hornet stings bring out into the open.

This yarn does not conclude at the camp meeting with the glee of the trickster over the painful education of the hypocrites—a glee which also reveals his racist attitudes. The final remarks are about the inescapable white community to which Sut belongs. Looking at the swollen hornet stings covering their slaves, the whites think that he has made them sick with smallpox. Although not actually a threat to personal health, they have become a threat to the community's established hierarchy. By reforming the slaves' piety and morality, Sut has attempted to make them purer than their hypocritical masters and mistresses, an intolerable situation necessitating retaliation by those unwilling to reform themselves. Their owners "sot in tu huntin fur *me,* wif shot guns an' dorgs," Sut complains. "But *du* yu see these yere laigs? They toted me outen thar safe an' soun. I can't git jestis nowhar, fur nuthin I du" (137). The whites chase him with dogs and guns—as if he were an escaped slave— because they realize that his practical jokes have the frightening capability of upsetting their comfortable, hypocritical customs. Their human desire for self-protection and Sut's equally powerful legs insure that the unavoidable battle between him and the community

will be a continuous torment to them all in which neither side will win total victory.

Sut's adventures recounted in **"Parson John Bullen's Lizards"** are firmly set within the context of his ongoing battle against the hypocritical community and, in particular, its pastor. Unlike the preachers in other sketches by Harris or by most humorists of his day, Bullen is not one who wishes to lead worshipers in a sexual orgy. Despite his notable faults of drinking and selling moonshine, he punishes promiscuity severely. At the previous year's camp meeting he discovered Sut and Sal in a huckleberry thicket. While she ran away, he beat Sut with a club, shouting their names for all to hear. In return for a promise not to tell her parents, the scared young woman cooked Bullen supper, but after eating it, he "went strait an' tole her mam" so that she was unable to avoid punishment and suffered from an "overhandid stroppin . . . wif a stirrup leather" (52). The believers who have gathered at the camp meeting the year following this incident share Bullen's disapproval of mixing promiscuity and worship. Although the availability of liquor indicates that most are probably not beyond reproach in their own behavior, they prefer a decorous orderliness and propriety at the camp meeting, unlike the slaves and quite unlike white worshipers in other ante-bellum humorous camp meeting sketches.

This piece explicitly reveals the primitive bestiality of human nature such conventional customs attempt to cover. The reality of its power will not be ignored, even in the midst of religious ceremonies when worshipers— and especially the clergy—might be expected to be the most holy. Harris makes his point by means of Sut's ability to force Bullen to play a different sort of game than he intends when he opens the service with a hymn, a reading and a sermon. Roger Caillois's sociological theory that game types distinguish civilized from primitive societies is particularly useful in interpreting the significance of Sut's practical joke at the camp meeting. By playing in a way particularly inappropriate to the community's agreed upon rules of conduct, the trickster unsettles deluded notions about life. He reveals that the very form of their communal religious expression— structured to provide emotional release, comfort and consolation—has inherent within it the very chaos and disorder of human life they desire to escape. Yet avoiding these realities is as impossible as is Sut's ending the attacks on Bullen, which he vows will continue "ontil one ur tuther, ove our toes pints up tu the roots ove the grass" (53).

Caillois's classification of games according to their sociological significance offers a perspective that reveals the essential differences between Sut and these people of his community. In the book *Man, Play, and Games* he contends that two opposing pairs of game categories emerge from a study of cultural history. The first pair includes two types of uninhibited games. Those under the label mimicry, or simulation, occur when the player "forgets, disguises, or temporarily sheds his personality in order to feign another" (18). Paired with these are games grouped under the heading vertigo or *ilinx* (Greek for *whirlpool*). These "consist of an attempt to momentarily destroy the stability of perception and inflict a kind of voluptuous panic upon an otherwise lucid mind" (23). Whereas mimicry presupposes an awareness of make-believe on the part of the player, vertigo seeks to erase such awareness through "disorder and panic, if not a total eclipse of consciousness" (75). Caillois emphasizes that "it is a question of surrendering to a kind of spasm, seizure, or shock which destroys reality with sovereign brusqueness" (23). These opposing categories can become associated through "the conjunction of mask and trance . . . which leads to an inexorable, total frenzy which in its most obvious forms appears to be the opposite of play. . . . The fit so provoked, being uninhibited, seems to remove the player . . . far from the authority, values, and influence of the real world" (75-76). The other paired categories include inhibited games, that is to say, games with "formal, . . . regulated, and protected activities" (76). The term *agôn* denotes competitive games that follow rules giving all players an equal chance so that merit determines the winner. Under the category *alea* (Latin for *a game of dice*) are games of chance in which the player passively follows the rules, awaiting an outcome independent of his will. The important difference between the two pairs is that the latter requires rules while the former "presume[s] a world without rules in which the player constantly improvises, trusting in a guiding fantasy or a supreme inspiration, neither of which is subjected to regulation" (75). Caillois argues that as a culture advances, inhibited games "lose their traditional dominance": "Whether it be cause or effect, each time that an advanced culture succeeds in emerging from the chaotic original, a palpable repression of the powers of vertigo and simulation is verified" (97). Of particular relevance to Sut Lovingood, his evidence suggests that uninhibited games are "reduced to roles that become more and more modern and intermittent, if not *clandestine and guilty*" (97; emphasis added). Even within each of the four groups, changes in games parallel the evolution of society; games originally "active, tumultuous, exuberant, and spontaneous" come to display "calculation, contrivance, and subordination to rules" (Trans. note viii).

One significant difference exists between the games about which Caillois writes and those which Sut plays in Harris's fiction. Caillois agrees completely with Johan Huizinga, author of the seminal *Homo Ludens,* on an essential characteristic of games or play: the player must remain free to choose whether or not to participate. This situation is not true, however, of the practical joke in which the trickster traps the unsuspecting and forces their unwilling participation. Caillois elaborates that as a voluntary activity play becomes "a source of joy and amusement" (6). Yet practical jokes intentionally bring some participants inescapable pain and discomfort. Although Caillois's study of games excludes practical jokes by definition, his insights remain applicable to this discussion. His cultural perspective suggests why, in a regulated society where inhibited games are preferred, uninhibited games must become practical jokes initiated by subversive tricksters who are "clandestine and guilty."

In Caillois's terms, at the camp meeting in **"Parson John Bullen's Lizards"** Sut introduces games of simulation and vertigo which the others condemn, preferring instead ones dominated by rules that are signs of a higher level of civilization and, in their eyes, of morality. Two world views clash in the backwoods community, and Harris indicates that the more primitive is the more potent because of its truthfulness. That the hypocritical believers must be tricked if they are to play what Sut has invented indicates their powerful resistance to the truths about human nature that are the theoretical basis of his gaming.

The frame of the sketch associates Bullen with games in the *agôn-alea* categories characterized by a sense of competition. Sut's friend George tells him about a "highly intelligible" notice posted "on every blacksmith shop, doggery, and store door, in the Frog Mountain Range" (51). It is a wanted poster "fur the karkus ove a sartin wun SUT LOVINGOOD, dead ur alive, ur ailin." The text calls on believers and constables to join the contest for a reward of eight dollars. The rules for these players are explicit: Sut must be "safely give over tu the purtectin care ove Parson John Bullin, ur lef' well tied, at Squire Mackjunkins." Most important is that the rules are known from the very outset, reflecting the regulation Caillois noted in games that predominate in civilized societies. Such a well-structured game allows "the satisfaction felt in overcoming an arbitrarily conceived and voluntarily accepted obstacle" (75), a type of pleasure not to be found in games of simulation and vertigo.

With a copy of the notice in hand, George asks Sut to explain what happened. After providing background about Bullen's injustice to him and Sal at the previous camp meeting, Sut revels in recounting his most recent practical joke. Unable to hide from the worshipers as in **"Sut at a Negro Night-Meeting,"** to accomplish his aim he must put on the unsuspicious disguise of a new convert in order to walk into the center of the camp meeting circle where he can be close enough to the parson to release seven or eight lizards up his pants leg. Sut's simulation is radically different from Bullen's approach to game playing, for his wanted notice is attested by Jehu Wethero and signed by himself. Bullen even adds his title, "the passun," to assure the players of his identity, thereby rejecting games of simulation. Sut, on the other hand, convincingly transforms his appearance: "I hed my face draw'd out intu the shape an' perporshun ove a tayler's sleeve-board, pint down . . . an' kivvered es much ove my straitch'd face es I could wif my han's, tu prove I wer in yearnis" (53). The reference to a tailor's equipment appropriately suggests clothing's ability to transform the human exterior without changing the inner nature, the very truth the practical joke on Bullen emphasizes.

As in **"Sut at a Negro Night-Meeting,"** Harris uses the conventional humorous technique of having statements made by the preacher during the service ironically foreshadow the spontaneous actions that are soon to occur as part of Sut's game. The words of the hymn are, "Thar will be mournin, mournin yere, an' mournin thar, / On that dredful day tu cum." And Bullen's sermon contains vivid details of how hell serpents will torture the bodies of sinners. He tells the women in particular that these evil creatures will "quile intu thar buzzims, an' . . . crawl down onder thar frock-strings, no odds how tite they tied 'em, an' . . . sum ove the oldes' an' wus ones wud crawl up thar laigs, an' travil *onder* thar garters, no odds how tight they tied *them*, an' when the two armys ove Hell-sarpents met, then—" (54). At this point the crowd begins to scream and holler, allowing Sut to put his practical joke into play by releasing the lizards. What he achieves, as his highly metaphoric description to George makes clear, is the immediate transformation of Bullen into an animal and the simultaneous frenzy that completely removes the preacher both mentally and physically from the reality of the camp meeting surrounding him.

Bullen's first reaction is to stop in mid-word and listen—"sorter like a ole sow dus, when she hears yu a whistlin fur the dorgs," the successful trickster comments. Then he begins slapping his body, but Sut's language indicates that his is no longer a human carcass, for his hands hit "about the place whar yu cut the bes' steak outen a beef" and also "whar a hosses tail sprouts." Still uncomfortable, he rubs his back "agin the pulpit, like a hog scratches hisself agin a stump." With all this ineffectual, frantic movement, "he wer a-cuttin up more shines nor a cockroach in a hot skillet." Coat, suspenders, shirt and pants are quickly flung away, sending lizards out into the congregation and leaving Bullen only "a par ove heavy, low quarter'd shoes, short woolen socks, an' eel-skin garters tu keep off the cramp" (56). Physically naked, showing his belly which is the size and color "ove a beef paunch," Bullen is now completely changed into a beast. This game of mimicry is not "a source of joy and amusement" for the hypocrite because the disguise reveals the truth of his inner nature. Furthermore, this game of mimicry is al-

lied with vertigo, for his "skeer hed druv him plum crazy." His actions in removing his trousers, in particular, suggest games of vertigo. To take them off, Bullen shakes and twists. Then he swings them around his head several times before throwing them away. Disoriented from the spinning motions, "he felt roun' in the air, abuv his head, like he wer huntin sumthin in the dark." Animal imagery continues in the references to this trance-like fear that impels him to run from the meeting ground "in a heavy lumberin gallop, like a ole fat waggon hoss, skared at a locomotive." The scene reminds Sut "ove a durnd crazy ole elephant, pussessed ove the devil, rared up on his hind aind, an jis' *gittin* frum sum imijut danger ur tribulashun."

Although the primary attention in this yarn is on Bullen, the worshipers are similarly affected. Transformed from humans into animals, some women yell like panthers at what they are seeing. One of the lizards lands on a woman who is "es big es a skin'd hoss, an' ni ontu es ugly." She shakes her dress, rolls down the hill and becomes tangled upside down in a huckleberry bush with her head in the creek. In contrast to the orderliness when Bullen opens the service, it becomes in the end a tumultuous scene of widely differing spontaneous reactions: some members of the congregation are screaming, some laughing, some crying, some trying to hide their embarrassment and others watching their pastor with curiosity. The chaos reaches its height when Bullen exits, running through the crowd: "When he jumpt a bainch he shook the yeath. The bonnets, an' fans clar'd the way an' jerked most ove the children wif em, an' the rest he scrunched."

Most interestingly, Sut's practical joke brings simulation and vertigo into association, a conjunction which Caillois believes "is so powerful and so inseparable that it is naturally part of the sphere of the sacred, perhaps providing one of the principal bases for the terror and fascination of the sacred" (76). What better setting, then, does Harris's region provide for such games than a camp meeting? Here, where civilized society is most vulnerable to Sut's guerilla warfare against its hypocrisy, it should also be the most ready to accept his revelation of eternal truths. Yet the believers refuse the instruction of the foolish trickster. They retaliate, instead, by mounting a hunt for Sut modeled on the games they prefer which reflect an illusory belief in a stable, regulated, orderly universe—untruthful games which Sut refuses to play.

Despite the shocking brutality of his practical jokes in the camp meeting sketches, Sut emerges as the sole admirable resident of this backwoods community because only he acknowledges the unavoidable chaos that destroys all hopes for a civilized life. Likewise, he is also the sole admirable trickster to attend a camp meeting in the humor of the Old Southwest. Unlike other selfish confidence men who look for ways to profit from the hypocrisy of the pious, he seeks to punish and reform. He claims scriptural authority for his practical jokes by basing them on the hymns and Biblical texts selected by the preachers. Thus when Sut attends a camp meeting, he becomes the true pastor because he alone teaches the flock that they are, indeed, beasts.

Works Cited

Caillois, Roger. *Man, Play, and Games.* Trans. Meyer Barash. 1958. New York: Free Press of Glencoe, 1961.

Harris, George Washington. *Sut Lovingood's Yarns.* Ed. M. Thomas Inge. New Haven, CT: College and UP, 1966.

Huizinga, Johan. *Homo Ludens: A Study of the Play-Element in Culture.* 1944. New York: Harper & Row, 1970.

Johnson, Charles A. *The Frontier Camp Meeting: Religion's Harvest Time.* Dallas: Southern Methodist UP, 1955.

Marryat, Frederick. *Diary in America.* Ed. Jules Zanger. 1839. Bloomington: Indiana UP, 1960.

Rickels, Milton. *George Washington Harris.* New York: Twayne, 1965.

John Wenke (essay date autumn 1987)

SOURCE: Wenke, John. "*Sut Lovingood's Yarns* and the Politics of Performance." *Studies in American Fiction* 15, no. 2 (autumn 1987): 199-210.

[*In the following essay, Wenke examines aspects of performance in the offbeat, often outrageous actions of Sut Lovingood, while also analyzing the political ramifications of his behavior.*]

In *Sut Lovingood's Yarns* George Washington Harris breathes the life and times of antebellum Tennessee, appropriating and transforming elements common to frontier humor, most notably the fool mask.[1] Mark Twain and William Faulkner found much to admire in Harris' vivid imagery, his zany comic situations, his precise, densely-textured renderings of the vernacular.[2] They relished especially the escapades of Harris' major comic creation, Sut Lovingood. In the fiction of the Old Southwest, Sut Lovingood looms as a wild man par excellence, an irreverent, earthy, illiterate, hard-drinking, yarn-spinning prankster.

However much he expresses the exuberant frontier spirit of iconoclastic frolic, Sut is not simply a hell-raiser out for a good time.[3] Instead, he repeatedly emerges as an "infunel mischief-maker," a self-conscious performer who doggedly and irrepressibly forces his anarchistic, self-reflexive designs into histrionic expression.[4] In the *Yarns* Sut engages in at least four kinds of performance: He variously appears as an actor and director, polemicist and story-teller. His activities respectively include role-playing and manipulation, declamation and narration. As actor and director Sut seeks to dominate the social script; he works to impose his will on others and thereby force his victims into enacting his designs. As polemicist and story-teller Sut offers recitations to an audience, usually made up of his friend and transcriber, George.

Characteristically, Sut attempts to reshape individual and social experience, to replace ostensibly civilized enterprises with anarchistic escapades. The conventional world of rule disintegrates as Sut enacts his play of misrule. His success as a performer hinges on his ability to shatter conventional formulations. "**Eaves-Dropping a Lodge of Free-Masons**" suggestively introduces Sut Lovingood's performative nature, especially his capacity for aggressive self-assertion. In this yarn Harris brings antithetical styles of narration into conflict. George sets out to recount a playful episode from his boyhood, the time when he and Lum Jones crashed a meeting of the Freemasons and got caught. George's rhetoric is dandified, effete, sentimental, nostalgic: "'Tis strange how faithfully memory paints the paths and places belonging to our boyhood—happy, ragged, thoughtless boyhood. The march of improvement first, then the march and crash of armies, have nearly swept away those, to me, almost sacred places." Sut Lovingood finds such language disgusting; in response he wrestles control of the narrative from George and resolves to tell it *"his* way":

> "Oh, komplikated durnashun! That haint hit," said Sut. "Yu's drunk, ur yure sham'd tu tell hit, an' so yu tries tu put us all asleep wif a mess ove durn'd nonsince. . . . Boys, jis' gin me a hoult ove that ar willer baskit, wif a cob in hits mouf, an' that ar tin cup, an' arter I'se spunged my froat, I'll talk hit all off in English."
>
> (p. 102)[5]

In "**Eaves-Dropping**" the stylistic antithesis points beyond commonplace distinctions between the literate George and the illiterate Sut, between region and education, east and west, "book-larnin" and "mother-wit."[6] Harris accentuates a stylistic *collision,* which issues in Sut's aggressive displacement of George as narrator. In taking over the verbal performance, Sut changes from auditor to teller, from witness to actor. Sut's unconventional, wild language of the hills replaces George's strained, hyper-civilized diction. In Harris' fiction, Sut's dynamic, chaotic, irreverent vernacular constitutes an authoritative reconstruction of a past world of action. George's style cannot remotely express the antic experience from boyhood, for sentimentality and cliché have come between speaker and event. The matter of George's past only comes to life in and through the manner of Sut's reconstruction. Wild events need wild words.

"Eaves-Dropping a Lodge of Free-Masons" highlights two elements basic to *Sut Lovingood's Yarns*: first, it presents the collision between narrative styles, which is but the verbal equivalent of a collision between competing systems of ordering self and society; second, it demonstrates Sut's preoccupation with using histrionic methods to dominate experience. What is not representative of the *Yarns* is the benign nature of Sut's usurpation. Here the transfer from George to Sut, from decorum to license, is smoothly realized, thanks to George's genial abdication. He simply lets Sut take over. More frequently, Sut's victims are unwitting dupes. In casting himself as actor and director, for instance, Sut works subversively to plunge representative structures of civilized rule into mayhem and confusion. Consequently Harris demonstrates not only the animalism latent beneath human exteriors, but also the more encompassing notion that civilization itself is but a shabby and fragile masquerade. Harris' backwoods fiction presses a sweeping indictment of civilization and its pretensions to order and respectability; the appearance of evolution covers up the actuality of bestialism. In the *Yarns* the performance of public roles constitutes a histrionic evasion of man's degenerate essence. If the establishment of acceptable public roles fosters the promulgation of acceptable codes of behavior, then the loss of these formulations necessarily undermines the social order. By working to disrupt convention, Sut Lovingood ushers in a saturnalia of confusion, violence, and suffering.

Sut's doings as actor and director, polemicist and storyteller must be understood as a quest for power. His will to power achieves expression in his various performative activities and has a distinctly political nature. Politics, in this sense, should not be taken to mean narrow partisan affiliations or what might be viewed as news of the day; rather its inclusive signification reflects Harris' preoccupation with the nature of human beings in society. His *Yarns* insistently examine the efficacy of essential structures of individual and communal existence: private identity and public role; law and authority; social convention and religious ritual; the nature of language as an expression of social standing. Politics constitutes the organization of public experience. In this enlarged sense of the *polis,* political reality provides the domain of the performing self.

The world of Sut's *"privit soshul famerly 'musement"* presents the misadventures—the failed performances—of Dad and Sut Lovingood (p. 213). Here Harris explores the relationship between role and essen-

tial identity as well as the possibilities and dangers inherent in trying to advance the cause of the self merely by changing costume. He examines whether it is possible, or even desirable, to make oneself the object of aesthetic transformation. In at least three of these tales that focus on more private Lovingood affairs, the role purports to extend one's normal possibilities of action. In adopting the roles of horse and cow, Dad tries to improve the family's condition. Sut adopts the costume of a lawyer in order to test out a new mode of self-expression. The process of changing from the essential self to the costumed self presupposes that the contingencies of experience will conform to the actor's intentions. In these yarns, however, the role fails to fulfill its intended function; what issues instead is the punishment of the actors.

In **"Sut Lovingood's Daddy, Acting Horse,"** Dad wishes to compensate for the death of Tickeytail, the family's only horse. He announces, "Sut, I'll tell yu what we'll du: I'll be hoss *mysef,* an' pull the plow whilst yu drives me . . ." (p. 35). Sut reports that Dad "sot on the fence a-lookin at us, an' a studyin pow'rful. I arterards foun' out, he wer a-studyin how tu play the kar-acter ove a hoss puffectly" (p. 35). Similarly in **"Dad's Dog School"** Dad dons the skin of a cow in order to teach the family dog to drive invading cows from their field. Dad describes his intentions to Sut: "I'll make yer sis Sall, thar, sow me up in Suggins's hide . . . an' I'll play ho'ned cattil rite squar intu Sugar's han" (p. 207).[7] Like his father, Sut changes costume. In **"Sut's New-Fangled Shirt"** the central joke is that a starched shirt will have "the vartu ove makin a lawyer outen me" (p. 41). He puts on the shirt "jis tu git tu sampil arter sumbody human" (p. 41). The starched shirt offers a synoptic image of the very world of law, order, civility, progress, and decorum that later becomes Sut's primary target.

Father and son run into trouble, becoming victims of their own histrionics. Rather than plowing a field or educating a dog or becoming lawyer-like, the Lovingood men fall prey to contingencies that generate from the very actions they have initiated. Like Mark Twain's Duke and King, like Tom Sawyer, who had a dream "and it shot him,"[8] like Hank Morgan, whose greatest effect encircles him victoriously with rotting, death-dealing corpses, Dad and Sut eventually lose control of their scenarios and suffer great pain. In taking on the "kar-acter" of a beast, Dad reverts to animalistic behavior: "When we got the bridil fix'd ontu dad, don't yu bleve he sot in tu chompin hit jis like a rale hoss, an' tried tu bite me on the arm. . . . I put on the geers, an' while mam wer a-tyin the belly ban' . . . he drapt ontu his hans, sed 'Whay-a-a' like a mad hoss wud, an' slung his hine laigs at mam's hed" (p. 35). What Dad and Sut find is that the conditions imposed by the enactment of each role preclude self-control. Repeatedly, what Sut calls "the show" (p. 209) gets out of hand. In **"Acting Horse"** Dad plows through a hornets' nest, strips naked, and runs madly but futilely to escape injury. In **"Dad's Dog School"** Sugar bites through the cowhide and mauls Dad's nose. In **"Sut's New-Fangled Shirt"** the pasted shirt sticks to Sut's skin, becomes, in effect, his second skin. Self and costume literally fuse. After putting on the shirt and doing a little work, Sut falls asleep. He dreams that "the judge ove the supreme cort had me sowed up in a raw hide" (p. 41), the inverse of his actual condition but a suggestive foreshadowing of Dad's own self-immurement in **"Dad's Dog School."** Sut awakens to find himself painfully imprisoned: "I now thort I wer ded . . . the cussed shut wer pasted fas' ontu me all over. . . . Hit sot tu me as clost es a poor cow dus tu her hide in March" (p. 41). In order to escape, Sut has to nail the shirt to a loft and jump off. Thus he skins himself. Not only is he bleeding and naked, but the shirt "looked adzactly like the skin ove sum wile beas' tore off alive . . ." (p. 42).

These yarns of private "'musement" provide touchstones that will explain Sut's more successful theatrical ventures. If the private domain demonstrates self-defeating role-playing, then the public domain manifests Sut's aggressive disruptions of convention. One purpose of the private world of Lovingood theatrics is to dramatize pitfalls, which Sut must avoid when taking on society. In order for his play of misrule to succeed, Sut must initiate the action and then make sure he does not get absorbed into the unfolding confusion; he must either stand to the side, out of harm's way, or work carefully to control the on-going action. In the public domain of performance, competing players vie for autonomy, for the power to determine the form of a particular social enterprise. These yarns find Sut matched directly against either some representative of authority or some form of ritual. When one of Sut's "skeers" works, he brings his victims to experience the same kind of humiliating defeat and physical pain that Sut and Dad experience in their private theatrics.

In the public arena, Sut emerges as an artist-in-life, a designer of scenes, a director of action, a manipulator, a trickster. He manufactures poses, controls perspectives, constructs scenarios. In waging war against such respectable types as preacher, doctor, lawyer, and sheriff, Sut Lovingood manages to disrupt a broad range of social rituals. In **"Sicily Burns's Wedding"** and **"Old Burns's Bull-Ride,"** Sut breaks up a wedding celebration; in **"Parson John Bullen's Lizards," "Sut at a Negro Night-Meeting,"** and **"Frustrating a Funeral,"** Sut upsets religious gatherings; in **"Mrs. Yardley's Quilting,"** Sut stampedes a horse and ruins the quilting party. In **"Rare Ripe Garden-Seed"** and **"Trapping a Sheriff,"** Sut varies the nature of his assault on authoritarians, exposing and punishing Sheriff Doltin for cuckolding Wat Mastin. Sut's art is often but not always im-

provisational. As he says, "plannin an' studdyin: hit am ginerly no count" (p. 63). Sut makes the most of a propitious instant. He describes the importance of timing as well as his sense of frenetic theatrical process: "All pends, et las' on what yu dus an' how yu kerries yursef *at the moment of ackshun*" (p. 63). Frequently one action sets off a chain reaction of chaotic events. In **"Mrs. Yardley's Quilting,"** for example, Sut impulsively tears down the line that spooks the horse that rampages through the yard and tramples Mrs. Yardley to death. Chaos is a motion, an action, away. In **"Sicily Burns's Wedding,"** Sut wishes to avenge a past slight; thus he "sot in a-watchin fur a chance tu du sumthin" (p. 78). Sut puts a basket over the head of Sock, the bull. As Sut expects, the bull runs amok and upsets a beehive. With the bees under the basket, Sock smashes through the house and destroys items representative of civilized life. The bull backs into a clock, a bed, and a cupboard: "Pickil crocks, perserves jars, vinegar jugs, seed bags, yarb bunches, paragorick bottils, aig baskits, an' delf war—all mix'd permiskusly, an' not worth the sortin." The bull then upsets the dinner table, scattering the crowd. Everything is "mix'd an' mashed, like hit had been thru a thrashin-meesheen" (p. 80), words that describe the effects of Sut Lovingood's antic artistry.

Sut's performances as actor and director are subversive in at least two ways. First, his antagonists never know what he is up to. If they did they could easily stop him. He rigs up his scenes, as it were, in the dark, Second, Sut works vigorously to undermine the social order, however skewed or parodic or hypocritical it might be to begin with. Significantly, Sut's subversion of convention generates from his recurrent success at trapping others into acting out the terms of his *own* self-definition. He, for one, baldly proclaims that he is a "natral born durn'd fool . . . [who] may turn human, sum day, that is sorter human . . ." (p. 83).[9] For the present, though, he admits that "hits onpossibil fur me tu hev ara soul. Who ever seed a soul in jis' sich a rack heap ove bones an' rags es this? I's nuffin but sum newfangil'd sort ove beas', a sorter cross atween a crazy ole monkey an' a durn'd wore-out hominy-mill" (p. 89). On first glance Sut's self-effacement accurately describes his debasement. But one must be careful: Harris's fiction is replete with instances of verbal ingenuity masquerading as illiterate rambling. Sut's assertions of worthlessness, cast here in metaphors of animalism and mechanism, do not simply describe his diminutive rank in the scale of being. Not only does Sut bring out the "damn fool" in others, but such key metaphors as "crazy ole monkey" and "wore-out hominy-mill" provide a synoptic account of Harris' indictment of human pretensions. As Harris repeatedly demonstrates, the human animal skulks somewhere between chaos and civilization. At one end of the behavioral range is the domain of animalism, primitivism, instinct, vent, and predation. At the other end is the context of man's moral, ethical, and technological endeavors. In Harris' fiction, barbarity is but the repressed underside of civility, the beast in the dark waiting to escape. The illusion of progress remains for only as long as man successfully controls social artifice. Take away the props and the appearance of civility comes undone. Sut's version of mere anarchy often plays itself out in terms of devolution, a sudden degeneration in one's ontological status. Metaphorically speaking, the machine breaks down; man becomes a monkey. Thus Sut's self-image as fool, monkey, and machine is not limited to himself but applicable across the board. Sut's peculiarity is not that he is a damn fool but that he admits it. In his theatrics he forces others to enact a scenario depicting their own essential confusion.

In his more complicated theatrics, Sut not only reduces his victim to a frenzied state of self-ridicule, but he does so by working to bring some notion of hell into histrionic presence. In becoming the "infunel mischief-maker" (p. 205) Sut combines planning and improvisation. He gathers his materials ahead of time but waits for the moment of action to declare itself. In **"Sut at a Negro Night-Meeting"** Sut procures a number of hornets' nests and stops up the entrances. He gathers beef bladders and turns them into stink bombs, filling them with a gas he describes as the "devil's own parfume" (p. 129). Sut hides in the thicket and waits to "open em . . . when I thort hit time tu take sich a sponsabil step." Just as the preacher rhapsodizes about heaven's "*sweet-smellin yarbs*" Sut releases the stink bombs (p. 130). Subsequently, he unleashes the hornets in response to the text: "*Thar shall be weepin an' railin an' chompin ove teef . . .*" (p. 133). Images of hell predominate. As one woman remarks, it is just like "de comin ob de debil . . ." (p. 131). Here the simulation of hell appropriately reflects the public domain of Sut's performances as actor and director. In **"Parson John Bullen's Lizards"** Sut himself enacts a role. He poses as a repentant sinner and goes to hear Bullen preach on hell-fire and hell-serpents. Sut brings his lizards along "a-purpus." Sut releases them up Bullen's leg and he stops "preachin rite in the middil ove the word 'damnation'" (p. 54). After the lizards overrun Bullen and cause him to flee naked to the woods, Sut muses, "didn't that ar Hell-sarpint sermon ove his'n, hev sumthin like a Hell-sarpint aplicashun?" (p. 58). In plying his infernal trade Sut works to eclipse his victims' sense of temporal (and eternal) well-being. One must smile, in fact, at Harris' subtlety of expression when Sheriff Doltin deftly, if unwittingly, describes Sut's most notable qualities as actor and director: "You've play'd hell." Sut replies, "folks generally sez that's my trade" (p. 194). Playing hell constitutes the central expression of Sut Lovingood's histrionic powers.

In **"Frustrating a Funeral"** Sut culminates his infernal masquerade when he takes on the role of Satan himself.

In this yarn Sut actualizes his most sweeping and successful disruption of authority and ritual. This yarn is also Sut's most disgusting (and perhaps most hilarious) play of misrule. **"Frustrating a Funeral"** depicts what might be called a gruesomely spirited improvisation. Sut transforms a somber, solemn occasion into an antic, tasteless escapade. He happens upon two black men, the dead Seize and the drunken Major. Sut very simply "swap't niggers" (p. 164). Sut takes Seize out of the coffin and replaces him with Major. What ensues is a gross desecration of a body spun into a wild, anarchistic comedy of entrapment. Sut first applies make-up to Major. He paints red and white stripes running outwardly from his eyes like spokes. After fastening horns to his head and festooning them with a dead black-snake, Major becomes "a purfeck dogratype ove the devil" (p. 164). Sut then goes to work on Seize:

> I'd got 'bout a tin cup full ove litnin bugs, an' cut off the lantern ove the las' durn'd one; I smear'd em all over his face, har an' years, an' ontu the prongs ove a pitch-fork; I sot him up in the corner on aind, an' gin him the fork, prong aind up in his crossed arms. I then pried open his mouf, an' let his teef shet ontu the back ove a live bull-frog, an' I smeard hits paws an' belly wif sum ove my bug-mixtry, an' pinned a littil live garter-snake by hits middil crosswise in his mouf, smeared like the frog plum tu the pint ove his tail. . . . Now, rite thar boys, in that corner, stood the dolefulest skeer makin mersheen, mortal man ever seed outen a ghost camp.
>
> (pp. 164-65)

An old preacher happens in, lifts the coffin lid, sees Major, and exclaims, "de debil hesef on top ob brudder Seize!" As he turns to run he spies the disguised Seize in the corner. At this point Sut takes on the voice of Satan: "*Hiperkrit, cum tu hell; I hes a claim ontu yu fur holdin the bag while Seize stole co'n*" (p. 165).

As Sut goes on to carry Seize from place to place, the night becomes the domain of Sut's diabolical theater. With his demonic prop and his satanic voice, Sut stalks the degenerate. His victims recognize their guilt and then run away. For example, Hunicutt, the white owner of the slaves, encounters Seize and hears the voice of Satan: "In the same doleful souns I used ontu Simon, I sed: 'Hunicutt, yu'se fell frum grace; I'll take yu down home *now*, leas' yu mout git good, *an' die afore yu fell again.*' Durn my picter ef I didn't cum mons'ous ni helpin the devil tu wun orful sinner, onexpected rite thar, in yearnist" (p. 166).

Sut enacts his *coup de grace* when he scares away the doctor, who moonlights as a body snatcher. After carting Seize and propping him on a bed, Sut hides to watch. He reports that there is "too much hell-sign on that bed even fur a bone-biler's narves." When the doctor freezes from fright, Sut speaks in the "same ole vise" and propounds his most chilling, most horrific threat: "Yu wants sum bones tu bile, dus yu? Didn't raise eny tu-night, did yu? I'se in that bisness mysef—follered hit ni ontu thuty thousand years. I'se a-bilin Ike Green's, an' Polly Weaver's, an' ole Seize's what yu pizen'd fur me, *an' they sent me arter yu*; les's go, my bilin hous' is warm—yu's cold—cum, sonny" (p. 167).

While Sut's performances as actor and director constitute his response to a perverted social order, his theatrics by no means correct the abuses perpetrated by the members of the social order. Sut only takes the *form* of a scourge or a moralistic force of retributive justice. Any salutary dispensation of justice must be seen as a mere offshoot of Sut's drive to undermine the particular political context before him. In fact Harris' fiction persistently reflects brutal, nihilistic, reactionary elements. Harris' preoccupation with bringing competing orders into collision has not even the remote intention of rectifying the ills of political reality. Rather than being anything as glorified as a social reformer or divine agent, Sut Lovingood merely satisfies his appetite for the outrageously disruptive. His motives are no more commendable than those of his adversaries. Like most of his victims, Sut is impelled by the innate desire to dominate experience.

The effects of Sut's theatrics, however, do not usually last very long. In fact his powers do not extend beyond the time when Sut is actively engaged in his performance. After a "skeer" has run its course, social authority tends to reconstitute itself. Whenever a representative authoritarian discovers that Sut is the source of the disturbance, that agent seeks to retaliate against him. For example, as Sut is about to have his way with Sal Yardley in **"Mrs. Yardley's Quilting,"** her father intervenes, kicks Sut in the tail, and drives him away. Repeatedly, Sut must take to the hills. Parson Bullen is reestablished and is trying to track him down. In an open confrontation Sut must use his long legs to effect his escape: "My pint am in takin aboard big skeers, an' then beatin enybody's hoss, ur skared dorg, a-running frum onder em agin" (p. 77). The comedy of Sut's long-legged flight displaces his brief period of ascendance. It is only after Sut finds a safe haven, in the company of George, that he can draw breath and tell his tales.

Sut's performances as verbal artist, as polemicist and story-teller, deserve brief mention for the ways in which they respectively provide both bitter complement and qualified counterpoint to Sut's disruptive, iconoclastic performances as actor and director. His polemics accentuate the *Yarns'* bleakness and anarchy, while the fusion of Sut's story-telling and George's transcription mildly mitigates the combative elements that characterize Sut's other performative modes.

Sut's polemical outbursts express the nihilistic nadir of Harris' portrait of man. The declamatory moments epitomize the viciousness, cruelty, and depravity of Sut Lovingood. His discourse on the "pints" of human life argues that the satisfaction of sensual appetite alone constitutes the informing purpose of human existence (p. 77). **"Sut Lovingood's Sermon"** offers a diatribe against innkeepers. At the end of **"Sicily Burns's Wedding"** and **"Old Burns's Bull-Ride,"** Sut's ribaldry gives way to self-loathing (pp. 83, 89). At the outset of **"Contempt of Court—Almost"** Sut makes a speech on "univarsal onregenerit human nater," describing in gruesome detail man's gleeful propensity for sadism (pp. 186-87). In another outburst he presents a Darwinistic view of predation: "Whar thar ain't enuf feed, big childer roots littil childer outen the troff, and gobbils up thar part. Jis' so the yeath over: bishops eats elders, elders eats common peopil, they eats sich cattil es me, I eats possums, possums eat chickins, chickins swallers wums, an' wums am content tu eat dus, an' the dus am the aind ove hit all" (pp. 174-75).

Readers might feel disgust at these misanthropic utterances; indeed, such passages anticipate the bleaker assumptions underlying American literary naturalism. But one must also recognize that such pronouncements frequently arise either before or after Sut gives an account of one of his escapades. His polemical outbursts function as set pieces, verbal counterparts to the madcap world of his role-playing and manipulation. These polemics offer Sut no more than frustrated substitutes for social control; these static pontifications describe the very conditions that render him impotent. At these moments the problems of experience loom as all-encompassing forces that dwarf the individual. Significantly, his polemics lack the exuberant catharsis of his disruptive play of misrule. In brief, his verbal assaults identify the conditions he seeks to displace; the very point of Sut's subversiveness is that the disenfranchised do have a chance to gain at least momentary power. If role-playing and manipulation give Sut a sense of control, then the absence of a clearly assailable or proximate opponent makes him all too self-conscious of his impotence.

Given the anarchy of his aesthetic, the debasement of his character, the nihilism of his polemics, one does well to wonder if Harris' penchant for so vigorously and sweepingly reviling the ceremonies of society makes him no more than a nay-saying Timon, a backwoods misanthrope, a confirmed man-hater. Despite the vehemence of Sut's encompassing negation, one can find a humane alternative in the creative partnership forged between Sut and his friend, George. The very making of the book becomes possible only through the fusion of Sut's illiterate yarn-spinning and George's assiduous transcription. Harris appears to be conscious of this division of labor: "Sumtimes, George, I wished I cud read an' write, jis' a littil; but then hits bes' es hit am, fur ove all the fools the world hes tu contend wif, the edicated wuns am the worst; they breeds ni ontu all the devilment a-gwine on. But I wer a-thinkin, ef I cud write mysef, hit wud then *raley* been my book" (p. 25). Sut's work will only come before the public if George, in Sut's words, "grease[s] hit good, an' let[s] hit slide down the hill hits own way" (p. 27). In Harris' fiction, having a literate Sut Lovingood would be too much like having a wild man tacitly committed to civilized discourse. Sut has to be able to make a book without being "tainted" by the necessity of authorial compromise. Sut has it both ways: He is source of the text, but the fact of his illiteracy dissociates him from true authorship. Sut has authority as teller; George assumes authority as reconstructor. Through George, Sut's aesthetic process becomes fixed as aesthetic product. With the congenial and educated George listening, Sut works his way into a yarn and claims to tell "what happened." Whatever "facts" may have existed are subsumed by Sut's conflation of retrospection and invention. As a fiction-maker, Sut performs in the present-tense time of telling; George's transcription completes this process insofar as he inscribes Sut's words on the page. Essentially, two artists are at work on the same material. For the reader, however, both activities inhabit the same space on the page. Sut's process is George's product; Sut's play of voice appears as George's artifact.[10]

In no other way does Harris fuse the forces that so destructively collide throughout the *Yarns.* While this verbal fusion of Sut's vent and George's transcription (possibly) celebrates the power of creative cooperation, such a fusion must also be seen as an unavoidable concomitant to Sut's illiteracy. It might even be that Harris was not aware of the humane implications of this synthesis; instead, he may simply have responded to the practical necessity of justifying the 1867 collection of an illiterate man's yarns.[11] For it is in the **"Preface,"** obviously composed after the yarns themselves, that Harris indicates that Sut is engaged in a book-making "perduckshun" and that he is not *"raley"* an author (p. 25). The fusion of story-telling and transcription should be recognized as literary expedient before it can mitigate Harris' reactionary politics. Interestingly, the **"Preface"** also finds Sut characterizing his audience and intention. The purpose of the *Yarns,* argues Sut, is to offer the disenfranchised the therapy of laughter. Sut wishes to tender relief to the downtrodden:

> Ef eny poor misfortinit devil hu's heart is onder a millstone, hu's raggid children am hungry, an' no bread in the dresser, hu is down in the mud, an' the lucky ones a-trippin him every time he struggils tu his all fours . . . hu is so foot-sore an' weak that he wishes he wer at the ferry—ef sich a one kin fine a laugh, jis' one, sich a laugh as is remembered wif his keerless boyhood, atwixt these yere kivers—then, I'll thank God that I *hes* made a book, an' feel that I hev got my pay in full.
>
> (p. 26)

In *Sut Lovingood's Yarns* one discovers a broad range of performative activities through which George Washington Harris considers the tortured, tenuous plight of political man. As actor and director, Sut dismantles antagonistic ways of life and savages innocent and guilty alike. As polemicist, he reductively portrays man as a vicious, soulless reprobate. As story-teller, Sut exuberantly reconstructs his antics for the benefit of friend George, who can take it all down and reconstruct multiple versions of Sut's play of misrule. It is this fusion of narration and transcription, finally, that contains the chaotic Lovingood world. Thus the wild process of Sut's verbal discharges consequently awaits deciphering in the unsightly product of George's careful labors.

Notes

1. For the classic study of frontier humor see Constance Rourke, *American Humor: A Study of the National Character* (New York: Harcourt, Brace, and Co., 1931); for further discussion of this subject see Walter Blair and Hamlin Hill, *America's Humor: From Poor Richard to Doonesbury* (Oxford: Oxford Univ. Press, 1978), pp. 92-221. The most important work on Harris is Milton Rickels, *George Washington Harris* (New York: Twayne, 1965). For Rickels' treatment of the fool mask see pp. 95-109. Other important studies of Harris' relation to the tradition of frontier humor are Ormonde Plater, "Before Sut: Folklore in the Early Works of George Washington Harris," *Southern Folklore Quarterly* 34 (1970), 104-15; Kenneth Lynn, *Mark Twain and Southwestern Humor* (Boston: Little, Brown, 1959), pp. 133-38; Eugene Current-Garcia, "Sut Lovingood's Rare Ripe Southern Garden," *Studies in Short Fiction* 9 (1972), 117-29.

2. For studies of Harris' influence on later writers see M. Thomas Inge, "William Faulkner and George Washington Harris: In the Tradition of Southwestern Humor," *Tennessee Studies in Literature* 7 (1962), 47-59; Current-Garcia, p. 117; Stephen M. Ross, "Jason Compson and Sut Lovingood: Southwestern Humor as Stream of Consciousness," *Studies in the Novel* 8 (1976), 278-90; R. J. Gray, "Southwestern Humor, Erskine Caldwell, and the Comedy of Frustration," *Southern Literary Journal* 8, No. 1 (1975), 3-26; Neil Schmitz, *Of Huck and Alive: Humorous Writing in American Literature* (Minneapolis: Univ. of Minnesota Press, 1983), pp. 30-39, 49-63.

3. Milton Rickels, in "The Imagery of George Washington Harris," *American Literature: A Journal of Literary History, Criticism, and Bibliography* 31 (1959), argues, "Sut appears to seek sheer fun, but the imagery associated with him enlarges his stature to a figure ambiguously comic and mythic . . ." (p. 187).

4. George Washington Harris, *Sut Lovingood's Yarns,* ed. M. Thomas Inge (New Haven: College and University Press, 1966), p. 205. All citations are from this text; page numbers will be noted parenthetically within the body of the essay.

5. For important studies of Harris' style see Rickels, *George Washington Harris,* pp. 107-19; Schmitz, pp. 49-59.

6. Schmitz, p. 36.

7. On Harris' treatment of the bestial see Blair and Hill, p. 221; Henning Cohen, "Mark Twain's Sut Lovingood," *The Lovingood Papers,* 1 (1962), 22; Ormonde Plater, "The Lovingood Patriarchy," *Appalachian Journal,* 1 (1973), 82-93; Noel Polk, "The Blind Bull, Human Nature: Sut Lovingood and the Damned Human Race," in *Gyascutus: Studies in Antebellum Southern Humorous and Sporting Writing,* ed. James L. W. West, III (Atlantic Highlands: Humanities Press, 1978), pp. 13-49.

8. Mark Twain, *Adventures of Huckleberry Finn* (Berkeley: Univ. of California Press, 1985), p. 343.

9. For discussions of Sut as "damned fool" see M. Thomas Inge, "Sut Lovingood: An Examination of the Nature of a 'Nat'ral Born Durn'd Fool,'" *Tennessee Historical Quarterly* 19 (1960), 231-51; Rickels, *George Washington Harris,* pp. 95-106; Ross, p. 238. See Rickels' discussion of Harris' imagery of beast and machine in "Imagery," p. 180.

10. For a complementary discussion of George as transcriber see Schmitz, pp. 49-51.

11. For an account of the conditions relating to the genesis, periodical publication, and eventual book publication of the yarns, see Rickels, *George Washington Harris,* pp. 44-48.

James E. Caron (essay date 1995)

SOURCE: Caron, James E. "An Allegory of North and South: Reading the Preface to *Sut Lovingood. Yarns Spun By a 'Nat'ral Born Durn'd Fool.'"* *Studies in American Humor,* n.s., 3, no. 2 (1995): 49-61.

[*In the following essay, Caron evaluates the various influences behind the Sut Lovingood sketches, including literary antecedents, regional anecdotes, historical personalities and events, and Harris's own life experiences.*]

It has been 126 years since the death of George Washington Harris in 1869, and in that time his sketches and tales have risen to the top rank in the crowded field of American comic writing before the Civil War. Few would dispute their artistry. Fewer still would dispute the three-dimensional comic vitality of Harris's most important creation, Sut Lovingood. Remarkably, Harris could draw upon very little formal education for the success he enjoyed in his avocation as a writer, as his biographer Donald Day makes clear. For the most part, that education consisted of buying many books by well-known authors and then reading and absorbing their themes and styles to help in the creation of his own distinctive brand of storytelling. Harris was less fortunate in his vocations and his efforts at financial success. By turns metalworker, steamboat captain, would-be planter, glassworks superintendent, sawmill owner, postmaster, surveyor, and railroad builder, Harris achieved respectability but not fortune. In this failure George Washington Harris was unremarkable, for the lives of many antebellum men fit the same pattern.

During one phase of his variegated working life, as surveyor for the copper mines at Ducktown, Tennessee, Harris probably met the inspiration for Sut Lovingood in a man named Sut Miller. Little is known about Sut or William S. Miller, but an obituary notice found in the August 20, 1858 issue of the Athens (Tennessee) *Post* by Ben Harris McClary suggests that Miller was indeed the genuine article: "Poor Sut! After having innumerable encounters and conflicts with man and beast—been shot several times, and consumed busthead enough to run an over-shot mill for forty days and nights, he died ignobly at last from a blow inflicted with the fist of a fellow-mortal."[1]

Yet, however much a wild man Sut Miller may have been, he was not a vagabond. McClary points out that Miller owned a farm near Ducktown valued at $400 in the 1850 census. Blanche Henry Clark's study on the number of small or non-slaveholding farmers in Tennessee puts that assessment into context. Also using 1850 census documents, Clarke's work makes clear that Sut Miller's land holdings placed him squarely in the yeoman class; his farm was possibly as large as one hundred acres with ten to fifteen improved. McClary notes that Sut's main crop in 1850 was corn, not unusual, but one is tempted to speculate how much of that corn became whiskey, especially once the mining boom at Ducktown took hold, as it had by 1854 when Harris ostensibly met Miller. Given the tenor of the boom times that Robert Barclay chronicles, an enterprising man with a steady supply of corn and his own still could probably make hard cash selling whiskey to the miners.

Speculation about Miller aside, any meeting he had with Harris no doubt played a role in the genesis of Sut Lovingood. Yet, we don't know how the two men George Washington Harris and Sut Miller felt about each other. We have a much better idea of how the characters "George" and Sut Lovingood feel about each other. Given Sut's propensity to talk and "George's" willingness to listen, given the welcome Sut seems to have in "George's" surveying camp, they seem to be good friends. Moreover, given that Sut seems to have known "George" as a little boy (if we believe Sut has first-hand knowledge of what happened to "George" and Lum Jones when they eavesdropped on a lodge of freemasons), one might claim that Sut and "George" have been friends for a long time.[2] But despite the sense of a friendly convocation of two projected by specific scenes within the tales, the preface for *Sut Lovingood. Yarns Spun by a "Nat'ral Born Durn'd Fool"* reveals a surprising antagonism between "George" and Sut when Sut comments on the making of the book:

> Sumtimes, George, I wishes I cud read an' write, jis' a littil; but then hits bes' es hit am, fur ove all the fools the worild hes tu contend wif, the edicated wuns am the worst; they breeds ni ontu all the devilment a-gwine on. But I wer a-thinkin, ef I cud write mysef, hit wud then raley been my book. I jis' tell you now, I don't like the idear ove yu writin a perduckshun, an' me a-findin the brains. 'Taint the fust case tho' on record by a durned site. Usin uther men's brains is es lawful es usin thar plunder, an jis' es common, so I don't keer much nohow.

(ix)

The startling aspect of this complaint is the barely concealed accusation that "George" is legally stealing the labor of Sut's mind. At the least, the implication runs, "George's" role as amanuensis allows him a claim of authorship that Sut resents but knows he can do nothing to change. This "George"-is-a-thief comment by Sut modifies any assumption of solid friendship and hints at the profoundly uneasy relation of "George" and Sut.

But Sut's comment does much more than expose the suppressed hostility of one character for another. I want to argue that this hostility between the textual figures "George" and Sut resonates within other narratives—e.g. biographical, historical, economic, and cultural. Analyses of fictional narrative rely on an interplay with other narratives like these. Moreover, as theorists like Hayden White have argued, this analytical interplay becomes structural entanglement when one considers that such "true" narratives are themselves shaped by the necessities of telling, just as fictional narratives are. I do not mean that a historical narrative, for example, is identical to a fictional one. But I do wish to examine their similarity and their difference as well as the critical habit of analyzing one type of narrative by foregrounding it with another.

This examination will illustrate how different kinds of narrative texts are tangled together as I discuss Sut's comment about "George's" role in making the book. For example, biographical knowledge of Sut Miller and George Washington Harris helps us to understand how a fiction comes from a life, how Sut Lovingood apparently is, in part, "generated" out of the events of Sut Miller's life. This move from a biographical narrative to a fictional one is the usual direction on a circuit between narratives that literary critics take. But might not the direction of the circuit be reversed so that the fictional hints at the biographical narrative? Thus, a textual figure might gloss its historical counterpart. I might infer something about the historical Sut from the character of the fictional Sut: Mr. Miller was probably as fond of telling yarns as he was of drinking and fighting. The relationship of Sut Lovingood and "George" in the preface, then, not only has a bearing on the fictional text, as one tries to reconstruct character psychology, but can also be read as a clue implying something about the relationship of Sut Miller and George Washington Harris. Furthermore, the relationship of Sut Lovingood and "George" can be read as an allegory about the cultural moment which "generated" *Sut Lovingood. Yarns Spun by a "Nat'ral Born Durn'd Fool."*

A good place to begin understanding how other narratives are implicated in *Yarns* is at the cultural and economic levels, for the key term in Sut's complaint, I would argue, is "perduckshun." The antagonism Sut expresses toward "George" in the preface allegorizes the historical clash between the cultures of the antebellum North and South and their different modes of economic production.

The South before the war was largely a self-sufficient, agrarian economy oriented toward markets existing outside its territory while the North, though also possessed of its share of self-sufficient farms, supported as well a manufacturing economy that not only was the locus of the South's markets but also the locus of the financial institutions that underpinned the entire market system. Simply stated, the South mostly had a rural, barter economy—the North an urban, money economy. In his capacity as a land surveyor who apparently hails from Knoxville, "George" is associated with a large influx of capital for developing copper mines, an investment that triggered an expansion of the historical Ducktown and necessitated the hiring of surveyors like George Washington Harris. In this aspect and in others, "George" represents the North within the allegory of the preface.

Sut of course represents the South.[3] More specifically, Sut as yarnspinner signifies the South's economy by virtue of his narrative production. The swapping of yarns symbolizes the homespun, decentralized, self-sufficient barter economy of the traditional South. Moreover, yarning, the oral production of narrative, is a practice redolent of a cultural ethic of leisure that the North frequently frowned upon, an ethic discussed in the work of David Bertelson, D. D. Bruce, Jr., and C. Vann Woodward, among others. To the antebellum traveler from the North, his southern countryman seemed to live a life of ease, or at least a life of idleness, whether rich planter or not. Indeed, the New Englander who travelled to the south, bringing his Puritan work ethic with him as part of his prejudices, often stereotyped the southerner as shiftless, willing to spend all day hunting, fishing, talking, and/or tending the still that consumed its share of the corn crop rather than improving his land or the cabin that sat upon it. In contrast, a southerner of the middling classes such as Sut Miller might feel that working beyond what was necessary to secure all of one's wants was an alien habit—especially if his background was a Celtic culture that valued hunting and lived as much on its livestock as on its farm produce, a possibility that was more likely than not according to Grady McWhiney in *Cracker Culture: Celtic Ways in the Old South*.[4] When we recall that much of Miller's tilled acreage in 1850 was planted in corn, which could entail whiskey production, it is possible to imagine how northerners, for their own cultural reasons, would have been disposed to view his lifestyle as primitive—even immoral—and to label him poor white trash, despite the fact that the worth of his farm put Miller into an economic middle class.

In the context of this sketch of two different cultures and economies, Sut Lovingood's lament about his inability to read and write and subsequent declaration that "hits bes' es hit am" affirm his place in the South's culture and economy. Sut is happiest when he is yarning in the presence of an audience. In a sense, he is most himself, feels his own presence most, when he tells a tale. The need to fashion a preface, on the other hand, reminds Sut that a book of yarns is not the same as yarning, and in that difference Sut not only feels inadequate because he cannot write, but he also feels alienated from his sense of self—a southern and rural sense that depends upon the production of oral narrative. Since "George" so obviously can participate in the production of books and written narrative, Sut projects the anger of his alienation onto his ostensibly friendly interlocutor. We might say that Sut unconsciously knows "George's" northernness and resents it.

The psychodynamic of Sut and "George," which underscores basic cultural and economic differences in antebellum America, is focused by a simple opposition. "Yarn" signifies the temporality of oral narrative, the presence of the audience, a sense of self in the teller. All of these features are associated with the South (Sut). "Book," on the other hand, conjures the image of readers whose activity isolates them from others; it also signifies the reification of commodity. "George," who fails miserably at yarning in **"Eaves-dropping a Lodge of Free-masons,"** nevertheless produces writing and thus adumbrates and advertises a marketable book of yarns rather than yarns. In this he complements his role as surveyor and affirms his place in the Northern mode of

capitalist production, a mode that unfairly profits from the labor of the South. That accusation, however, is not a legal one—such appropriation is as lawful as it is common, says Sut—but is based rather on a regional sense of values. Sut's comment to "George" is, at one level, the South noting that its labor enriches a group of people—financiers and middlemen—who apparently never work at all. Thus Sut's complaint against "George" in effect inverts the historical accusation by Yankees that the typical Southerner is shiftless and lazy. In the fictional text, Sut feels that his narrative production, based on and representing the technology of speech, is overridden, or at least overshadowed, by "George's" ability with the technology of writing. In the allegory I am weaving, that sense of second-best represents an historical event: the barter economy of the South, marked by leisure and decentralized production, was overridden during the war by the market economy of the North, itself marked by a work ethic that culminated its efficiency in the centralized factory production of commodities like books and Beecher Bibles.

My reading of Sut's antagonism toward "George," one that displaces their dynamic onto an historical setting, could be countered by insisting that the hostile feelings represented in the preface are usually submerged in the yarns themselves and that "George" and Sut remain friendly if not friends throughout.[5] After all, Sut does refrain from his usual means of expressing animus and maintaining his sense of community, namely, a full-scale episode of scapegoating. Perhaps we can attribute that restraint to how long he has known "George," possibly over thirty years. Moreover (this positive view could argue), as narrator and interlocutor they symbolize a process favored in the Old South for creating a sense of community. Richard Boyd Hauck elaborates the dynamics of oral storytelling—yarning—and its relation to community:

> When a story is told out loud, the voice of the teller reflects his awareness of his audience. [The teller] . . . must be able quickly to evoke and amplify common wisdom in order to establish a contract of belief so that the audience will accept his fantasy as a vital act of shared imagination which illuminates those hopes and fears [of the group] which would otherwise remain unspoken. . . . The final effect is a ritual of mutual understanding, and thus hundreds of southwestern yarns end with "Let's licker"—the universal signal for celebrating the achievement of fellowship through the act called story.
>
> (5, 6)

Yarning creates community in ritualistic fashion. The storyteller evokes communal beliefs and assumptions in his playful representations, and that sense of oneness is symbolized by the communal use of homemade liquor. Though Hauck's depiction of how yarning creates ritual community is idealized, much of *Yarns* fits his model.

As a representative instance, one might cite **"Blown Up with Soda,"** which ends with what Hauck claims is a traditional finish to yarning: "And the bottom of Sut's flask flashed in the sun light" (85). The dialect of *Yarns* is meant as a representation of oral narration. And, as Hauck shows, oral narration does create community in a palpable way, demanding the presence of its audience, even if it be only one person. Sut's tales often have a number of listeners, usually at the camp of "George's" surveying team, but sometimes they only have Sut's favored interlocutor as audience, a man who is apparently a boyhood acquaintance and thus disposed to listen with interest—"George" himself. According to Hauck's formulation, the special community of "George" the gentleman surveyor and Sut the wild mountaineer is emblematic of Southern community.

Indeed, one could supplement and strengthen the formulation: within that community is a sense of "communitas," Victor Turner's term for a ritual erasure of the usual hierarchy of society. The height of such potential equality in the Old South was of course the hunting camp. A man might gain entry to such a gathering simply on the strength of his prowess as storyteller, which partly accounts for the acceptance of Sut, wild man that he is, in the hunting camp of Judge Alexander. In *Yarns* the hunting camp is at times replaced by the camp of a surveying team lead by "George," but the rough equality, upheld by a general knowledge of who is leader, still remains. Indeed, one can imagine Sut playing the role of loyal retainer to the Judge or "George," as Boon Hogganbeck does for Major de Spain in Faulkner's "The Bear." In any case, clearly Sut is readily accepted in the camp. More importantly, his narratives, building on the masculine camaraderie that already exists, create a version of Turner's "communitas." As a yarnspinning fool, Sut ritually presents a temporary state of being wherein all men experience a truer sense of equality.[6]

It is this sense of community and "communitas" that forms the basis for any claim of friendship or, at the least, friendly acquaintance between "George" and Sut. Their antagonism in the preface, however, is not the only example of friction that could be cited. Consider, for example, their exchange in **"Rare Ripe Garden-Seed"** when "George" promises to shoot Sut if he were to show up in the former's church pew scandalously dressed. Even if we note the joking aspect of both incidents, the hostility is clear. Nevertheless, I do not wish to argue that these examples negate the ritualized equality that Hauck and Turner discuss. Rather, both the barely concealed hostility and the idealized image of friends telling stories should alert us to the complexity of Harris's representation of community. Sut's complaint against "George" in the preface, when the two seem the most cooperative, creates the effect of "communitas" plus the usual hierarchy of society; the force of hierarchy can be felt even within the apparently ideal

ritual moment. This representation is consistent with the complicated nature of Sut's central role in *Yarns*, the wise fool, an issue explored at length by Milton Rickles.[7]

It is also consistent with Sut's acceptance by men of higher social standing, like "George" and Judge Alexander, and with his friendship, mentioned in the dedication of the book, with two locally well-known, historical figures from Knoxville, Elbridge Eastman and William Crutchfield. Moreover, Harris's crossing of fictional and historical narratives (i.e. giving Sut friends who were historical figures) points to consistencies at levels other than the fictional text. Despite the apparent oddity, Sut's relationships with Eastman and Crutchfield would not have been unusual in the antebellum South, where even the best of men found it necessary to mix with others of less fortunate circumstances on a more or less equal basis. I do not mean that Sut Lovingood would be invited to tea at the plantation, but in public forums such as markets and law courts, the men clad in broadcloth were roughly on a par with those dressed in homespun jeans. We should imagine, for example, that Sut Miller, though apparently a ring-tailed roarer, maintained friendly and familiar relationships with prominent citizens of Ducktown, as befitted his yeoman status.

Yet, as the preface suggests, Sut does not—can not—forget a basic difference from "George" and others of his social status. Within my historical allegory, the South can not (will not?) forget its difference from the North. Since Sut does not scapegoat "George" despite their difference, reading the preface as an allegory of North and South might continue by noting that Sut's reluctant acquiescence to "George's" inclusion in his community, implied in his complaint about the making of the book, inverts the North's reluctance after the Civil War to let the South rejoin the United States.

If the dynamic between the textual figures of Sut and "George" suggests an allegory rooted in history, it also bears on the biographies of Sut Miller and George Washington Harris with which this essay began. Sut's complaint about "George," which is never answered, might also be Harris's way to underscore his own sense of separation from men like Sut Miller. It is probably no surprise that antebellum northerners writing about the South often stereotyped its people as lazy and even immoral. The more interesting point is how southerners treated each other and thus established their own sense of community. How is that sense of community affected when upper-class southerners, or aspirants to that upper class like Harris, easily see a comic character like Sut Lovingood in a man like Sut Miller—even while acknowledging his yeoman status and admiring his ability as a storyteller? One might argue that the separation Harris felt from Miller was a necessary distance for the wonderful comic vision of *Yarns.* One might even argue that the ambivalence Harris probably felt about Sut Miller was necessary to the creation of Sut Lovingood, who is both fool and fool killer. Such a formulation is close to Kenneth Lynn's thesis about the humor of the old southwest. Yet, ironically, separation and ambivalence undermine the idea of true community in the myth of the traditional South, a notion that not only Hauck argues for but one that Harris also seems to endorse through Sut as a comic embodiment of oral narratives.

Finally, my reading of the preface suggests what *Sut Lovingood. Yarns Spun by a "Nat'ral Born Durn'd Fool"* might have meant to Harris at a deep emotional level. Since it was published just after the Civil War, the book might signify his unconscious protest against the outcome of the war and the capitalist economy that provided the foundation for that outcome. Entailed in that protest, moreover, is a lament for the Old South and its cultural values, such as a fondness for all forms of oratory and the leisure time to indulge that fondness. Through Sut Lovingood's gift for yarning, Harris projects those cultural values, values signifying a way of life that—from the perspective of 1867—was apparently swept aside by the North's imposition of Reconstruction.[8]

Notes

1. See Inge for a discussion of whether Harris met Sut Miller before the first Sut sketch in 1854. Day only found evidence that Harris surveyed the copper mines in 1857 and says little about Harris's activities in 1854 (23, 26). Rickels says that "It seems probable that sometime in 1854 Harris visited the Ducktown copper mines of southeast Tennessee" (44).

2. See the beginning of the story called "Eavesdropping a Lodge of Free-Masons," wherein Sut seems to know first-hand what happened to "George" and Lum thirty-five years ago (114-16). And Sut does have white hair, suggesting either a vitamin deficiency or a commensurate age (19). Most commentators take literally a description of Sut by a Hard-shell Baptist preacher who refers to him as "youth" (184). One example is St. George Tucker Arnold Jr.'s article. However, Inge, in "Examination," argues that "Sut's very activities affirm his adulthood" (239). References to the preface and any specific stories are from *"Sut Lovingood. Yarns": A Facsimile of the 1867 Dick and Fitzgerald Edition.* ed. M. Thomas Inge. Page numbers will hereafter appear in the text.

3. In Kenneth Lynn's words, ". . . 'Sut' is an ugly contraction of 'South'" (p. 137).

4. Day, when discussing why Harris failed as a farmer, seems to suggest that even he at least par-

tially fit this Celtic culture model, noting the proximity of good hunting and good fishing streams near Harris's farm (10).

5. For a very different view of the relationship of "George" and Sut, one that emphasizes the positive, see John Wenke's article and Neil Schmitz's book, pp. 49-53.

6. Cf. Hauck's comments about Faulkner's depictions of a hunting community: ". . . it is almost the only successful form of community we can find, . . . [one] whose values transcend the traditional exclusions dictated by race and class" (8). Here and in his discussion of yarning, Hauck stresses a sense of harmony. Turner's formulation of "communitas" highlights the attribute of harmony as well but also stresses the temporary nature of the existence of "communitas": it is only part of the complete ritual process. Hauck, it should be noted, does go on to say that Faulkner's hunting community is a males-only preserve.

7. For a discussion of Sut's role as wise fool in relation to his community, see my "Playin' Hell: Sut Lovingood as Durn'd Fool Preacher," in *Sut Lovingood's Nat'ral Born Yarnspinner: Essays on George Washington Harris.* eds. James E. Caron and M. Thomas Inge.

8. "Sut Lovingood's Allegory," originally published in the Knoxville *Press and Messenger,* 17 September 1868, also reveals Harris' post-war nostalgia. Cf. Day, pp. 35-37.

Works Cited

Arnold, St. George Tucker, Jr. "Sut Lovingood, The Animals, and the Great White Trash Chain of Being." *Thalia* 1 (1979): 33-41.

Barclay, Robert E. *Ducktown Back in Raht's Time.* Chapel Hill: University of North Carolina Press, 1946.

Bertelson, David. *The Lazy South.* New York: Oxford University Press, 1967.

Bruce, D. D. Jr. "Play, Work and Ethics in the Old South." *Southern Folklore Quarterly* 40 (1977): 33-51.

Caron, James E. and M. Thomas Inge, eds. *Sut Lovingood's Nat'ral Born Yarnspinner: Essays on George Washington Harris.* Tuscaloosa, Alabama: University of Alabama Press, (forthcoming).

Clarke, Blanche Henry. *The Tennessee Yeoman, 1840-1860.* Nashville: Vanderbilt University Press, 1942.

Day, Donald. "The Life of George Washington Harris." *Tennessee Historical Quarterly* 6 (1947): 3-38.

Harris, George Washington. *"Sut Lovingood. Yarns": A Facsimile of the 1867 Dick and Fitzgerald Edition.* ed. M. Thomas Inge. Memphis: St. Lukes Press, 1987.

Hauck, Richard Boyd. "'Let's Licker'—Yarnspinning as Community Ritual." *American Humor: An Interdisciplinary Newsletter* 1 (1978): 5-10.

Inge, M. Thomas. "Sut Lovingood: An Examination of the Nature of a 'Nat'ral Born Durn'd Fool.'" *Tennessee Historical Quarterly* 19 (1960): 233-234.

Lynn, Kenneth. *Mark Twain and Southwestern Humor.* 1960. rpt. Westport, Connecticut: Greenwood Press, 1972.

McClary, Ben Harris. "The Real Sut." *American Literature* 27 (March, 1955): 105-106.

McWhiney, Grady. *Cracker Culture: Celtic Ways in the Old South.* Tuscaloosa, Alabama: University of Alabama Press, 1988.

Rickels, Milton Rickels. *George Washington Harris.* New York: Twayne Publishers Inc., 1965.

Schmitz, Neil. *Of Huck and Alice: Humorous Writing in American Literature.* Minneapolis: University of Minnesota Press, 1983.

Turner, Victor. *The Ritual Process: Structure and Anti-Structure.* 1969. rpt. Ithaca: Cornell University Press, 1977.

Wenke, John. "*Sut Lovingood's Yarns* [sic] and the Politics of Performance." *Studies in American Fiction* 15 (1987): 199-210.

White, Hayden. "The Question of Narrative in Contemporary Historical Theory." *History and Theory,* 23 (1984): 1-33.

———. *Metahistory.* Baltimore: Johns Hopkins University Press, 1973.

Woodward, C. Vann. "The Southern Ethic in a Puritan World." *American Counterpoint: Slavery and Racism in the North-South Dialogue.* New York: Oxford University Press, 1983.

Noel Polk (essay date 1996)

SOURCE: Polk, Noel. "The Blind Bull, Human Nature: Sut Lovingood and the Damned Human Race." In *Sut Lovingood's Nat'ral Born Yarnspinner: Essays on George Washington Harris,* edited by James E. Caron and M. Thomas Inge, pp. 148-75. Tuscaloosa: University of Alabama Press, 1996.

[*In the following essay, Polk offers a comprehensive analysis of Harris's* Sut Lovingood, Yarns Spun by a "Nat'ral Born Durn'd Fool," *examining the book's central themes, major characters, unique prose style, and critical history.*]

For Ben Harris McClary,
Milton Rickels, and Tom Inge:
They were here first.

so that they are without excuse:

21 Because that, when they knew God, they glorified *him* not as God, neither were thankful; but became vain in their imaginations, and their foolish heart was darkened.

22 Professing themselves to be wise, they became fools,

23 And changed the glory of the uncorruptible God into an image made like to corruptible man, and to birds, and fourfooted beasts, and creeping things.

24 Wherefore God also gave them up to uncleanness through the lusts of their own hearts, to dishonour their own bodies between themselves:

25 Who changed the truth of God into a lie, and worshipped and served the creature more than the Creator, who is blessed for ever. Amen.

* * *

28 And even as they did not like to retain God in *their* knowledge, God gave them over to a reprobate mind, to do those things which are not convenient;

29 Being filled with all unrighteousness, fornication, wickedness, covetousness, maliciousness; full of envy, murder, debate, deceit, malignity; whisperers,

30 Backbiters, haters of God, despiteful, proud, boasters, inventors of evil things, disobedient to parents,

31 Without understanding, covenant breakers, without natural affection, implacable, unmerciful;

32 Who knowing the judgment of God that they which commit such things are worthy of death, not only do the same, but have pleasure in them that do them.

—Romans I

I. GADFLY

In spite of the manifest difficulties of its language, the frequently savage and unpleasant nature of its humor, the intensity of its violence, and the vehemence of its author's hatred of so many of the agents of change in the mid-nineteenth century, George Washington Harris's **Sut Lovingood. Yarns Spun by a "Nat'ral Born Durn'd Fool"** has attracted a devoted readership for nearly 125 years.[1] The original edition of 1867 (Dick and Fitzgerald) stayed in print until well into the 1940s, and there have been as least six separate published editions of his works, including four of the **Yarns.** These editions, along with one published monograph-length study, at least three dissertations, and a spate of articles, form, quantitatively, a rather substantial body of scholarly materials on Sut Lovingood and his creator, most of which has emphasized the comedy of the *Yarns*[2]—and rightly so, for Harris's is possibly the most artistically complex sense of humor in American literature before Faulkner, saving perhaps only Melville—the brilliance of Harris's language, and the nature of Sut's numerous victims, as complete a catalog of stereotypical hypocrites and fools as can be found in any literary tradition. Here, however, I would like to focus on the book's supreme creation, Sut Lovingood himself. It is a mistake, I think, a serious underestimation of the *Yarns,* to see Sut as merely an irresponsible prankster who, like his literary forebears and peers in the southwestern humor "tradition," hates hypocrites, reformers, and Yankees and who plays his "pranks" just for revenge, and to assume that in his conflicts with authority Sut carries the moral force of Harris's approval because his victims are so manifestly deserving of Sut's vengeance.

In his book, Milton Rickels has stated that Harris "was always more interested in Sut as symbolic point of view than as a realistic construction,"[3] and, indeed, to the very large extent that Sut is a narrator, a storyteller, Rickels is absolutely correct. Sut is, of course, supremely, a storyteller. But he is not just a storyteller; Harris is careful to create a social context for him; he is in constant interaction with an assortment of cronies—including "George" and several intruders—and like any good raconteur, Sut is always mindful of his audience; much of the elaborated detail of his stories, including the tall-tale exaggeration, is his response to his auditors' laughter, calculated to create a desired effect—usually laughter, but frequently something else. In Sut's interaction with "George" and his other auditors Harris reveals a personality whose complexities are elaborated in Sut's wild tales.

In **"Sut Lovingood's Daddy, Acting Horse,"** for example, Sut names the members of his family, calling his own five times in a wonderfully comic display of bumptiousness; when a "tomato-nosed" man falls into the trap Sut has set, and points out the repetition, Sut responds immediately: "Yas, ole Still-tub, that's jis the perporshun I bears in the famerly fur dam fool, leavin out Dad in course."[4]

Sut's description of himself as a "nat'ral born durn'd fool" here and throughout the *Yarns* has generated much discussion of his character. Again, Rickels reasonably suggests that "Harris' conception of his fool . . . is not the antic simpleton but the wise fool; Sut is the ironic hero who perceives the human condition and knows he himself is a fool to communicate his perceptions" (96). But it is a great deal more complicated than this description allows. At the end of **"Sicily Burns's Wedding,"** for example, Sut opines that if his long legs do not fail him, he "may turn human sum day, that is sorter human, enuf tu be a Squire, ur school cummisiner" (97)—a remark that seems simple enough, one of many

cheap shots Sut takes throughout the *Yarns* at various pomposities. It is of course not without its implications, but Rickels may be taking Sut a bit too literally and miss his comic irony: "To become 'sorter human,'" Rickels suggests, "is not plaintive longing, but the ironic man's disdainful scorn for unrealized and, to Sut, unrealizable humanity. *Sut has chosen not to try to become human*" (97, emphasis added). Rickels builds from this premise an argument about Sut's character: "After rejecting the human condition," Rickels continues, "Sut also rejects the religious life. . . . He has no fear of the hereafter, for he has no soul" (97). By making Sut soulless, Harris has "freed him from any transcendental significance" (98). Finally, Rickels contends that Sut, "in another of his characteristics, his mindlessness" (98), personifies the antiauthoritarian and antirational feelings Harris expresses in his work. From being a wise fool to being mindless is a long and contradictory progression; but it is necessary for Sut to be mindless, apparently, in order for him to be a backwoods anarchist, opposed to both order and reason: "For Sut," Rickels has earlier argued, "every practical joke is a delight because it is a conspiracy against all order" (84).

This argument gives Harris little credit as a thinker and even less as an artist. Simply, I would rather argue, Sut is not mindless, and *he is no fool.* His repeated description of himself as a "nat'ral born durn'd fool" is the ironic self-deprecation that is part and parcel of any humorist's equipment and that neither he nor Harris expects the reader to take literally: the few characters in the *Yarns* who do are scorned and ridiculed for their lack of comprehension. But more than that, his self-deprecation is the main thematic device by which Harris stresses the differences between Sut and his victims and emphasizes the moral nature of the *Yarns.*

Certainly Harris was aware of the literary tradition of the Fool, and certainly he was capitalizing upon it; but he was also using another aspect of that tradition, the one personified by Socrates. Sut is a kind of backwoods Socrates who pricks holes in ballooned egos, brings hypocrites and fools to their knees before their peers: indeed, Socrates encounters the self-assured and smug sophists, Sut the self-assured and smug preachers, sheriffs, lawyers, and Yankees. Both Sut and Socrates continually expose fools and frauds for what they are, and both are therefore continually in trouble with civic and religious authorities. And both, I would suggest, have the same purpose in life. Sut's goal in **"Old Skissim's Middle Boy,"** for example—to awaken the fat, lethargic, and constantly sleeping boy—is, I propose, Harris's allegorical treatment of this famous passage in the *Apology:*

> the state is like a big thoroughbred horse, so big that he is a bit slow and heavy, and wants a gadfly to wake him up. I think the god put me on the state something

like that, to wake you up and persuade you and re-proach you every one, as I keep settling on you every-where all day long. Such another will not easily be found by you, gentlemen, and if you will be persuaded, you will spare me. You will be vexed, perhaps, like sleepers being awaked, and if you listen to Anytos and give me a tap, you can easily kill me; then you can go on sleeping for the rest of your lives.[5]

Under the circumstances, it seems clear that the hornets that appear and reappear throughout the *Yarns* are Har-ris's own symbolic "gadflies."

Thus when Sut calls himself a "nat'ral born durn'd fool," it is not merely self-deprecation: by doing so he can subtly suggest how eagerly his victims, his neigh-bors and friends, and his family delude themselves into thinking that they are something they are not. All the characters in the *Yarns* act horse or fool in one way or another and do so while asserting their righteousness, their respectability, and their general superiority to all other creatures; they do not, Sut and Socrates would ar-gue, "know themselves." Sut, however, like Socrates, does know himself, thoroughly, and is under no delu-sion about himself or society; he is, in short, wise pre-cisely because he does not pretend to know anything he does not know or be anything he is not.

Sut, then, is not a fool, and he is by no means, as Ed-mund Wilson, Sut's harshest critic, would have it, a "peasant squatting in his own filth."[6] It is his lazy and worthless Dad who so squats, and it is one indication of Sut's strength of mind and character that he has been able, with no more of this world's goods than his Dad, to escape and overcome the poverty and filth, both real and metaphorical, upon which his Dad tried to rear him. Sut's wisdom is heired from an incredible background of poverty and deprivation; perhaps because of that background, certainly not in spite of it, he is a singu-larly perceptive student of human nature: and though his vision of the world is understandably dark, it is per-sistently realistic and tough-minded.

Sut's vision is summed up in two philosophical set pieces that express in no uncertain terms his profound pessimism about "univarsal onregenerit human nater." The first, Rickels describes as a kind of Great Chain of Being (100).

> Whar thar ain't enuf feed, big childer roots littil childer outen the troff, an' gobbils up thar part. Jis' so the yeath over: bishops eats elders, elders eats common peopil; they eats sich cattil es me, I eats possums, pos-sums eats chickins, chickins swallers wums, an' wums am content tu eat dus, an' the dus am the aind ove hit all. Hit am all es regilur es the souns frum the tribil down tu the bull base ove a fiddil in good tchune, an' I speck hit am right, ur hit wudn't be 'lowed.

(228)

The second expresses among other things an attitude to-ward Innocence, in any form, that out-Claggarts Clag-gart:

> I hates ole Onsightly Peter, jis' caze he didn't seem tu like tu hear me narrate las' night; that's human nater the yeath over, an' yere's more universal onregenerit human nater: ef ever yu dus enything tu enybody wi-fout cause, yu hates em allers arterwards, an' sorter wants tu hurt em agin. An' yere's anuther human nater: ef enything happens [tu] sum feller, I don't keer ef he's yure bes' frien, an' I don't keer how sorry yu is fur him, thar's a streak ove satisfackshun 'bout like a sowin thread a-runnin all thru yer sorrer. Yu may be shamed ove hit, but durn me ef hit ain't thar. Hit will show like the white cottin chain in mean cassinett; brushin hit onder only hides hit. An' yere's a littil more; no odds how good yu is tu yung things, ur how kine yu is in treatin em, when yu sees a littil long laiged lamb a-shakin hits tail, an' a-dancin staggerinly onder hits mam a-huntin fur the tit, ontu hits knees, yer fingers will itch tu seize that ar tail, an' fling the littil ankshus son ove a mutton over the fence amung the blackberry briars, not tu hurt hit, but jis' tu disapint hit. Ur say, a littil calf, a-buttin fas' under the cow's fore-laigs, an' then the hine, wif the pint ove hits tung stuck out, makin suckin moshuns, not yet old enuf tu know the bag aind ove hits mam frum the hookin aind, don't yu want tu kick hit on the snout, hard enough tu send hit backwards, say fifteen foot, jis' tu show hit that buttin won't allers fetch milk? Ur a baby even, rubbin hits heels apas' each uther, a-rootin an' a-snifflin arter the breas', an' the mam duin her bes' tu git hit out, over the hem ove her clothes, don't yu feel hungry tu gin hit jis' one 'cussion cap slap, rite ontu the place what sum day'll fit a saddil, ur a sowin cheer, tu show hit what's atwixt hit an' the grave; that hit stans a pow'ful chance not tu be fed every time hits hungry, ur in a hurry? An' agin: ain't thar sum grown up babys what yu meets, that the moment yer eyes takes em in, yer toes itch tu tetch thar starns, jis' 'bout es saftly es a muel kicks in playin; a histin kine ove a tetch, fur the way they wares thar har, hat, ur watch-chain, the shape ove thar nose the cut ove thar eye, ur sumthin ove a like littil natur.

(245-47)

Nearly all commentators have noticed these superb pas-sages, but no one has yet discussed them as the most direct statements of themes that in fact darkly underlie all of the exuberant comedy of the *Yarns* and that give thematic and structural unity to the collection. Though my comments could and should be extended to the fu-gitive pieces collected by Inge in *High Times and Hard Times,*[7] I am limiting my discussion in this paper to the twenty-four sketches that Harris himself brought to-gether in the *Yarns,* for the reason that the *Yarns* is a deliberate book—not a random selection of things al-ready published, but a collection of mostly new mate-rial, apparently written specifically for this volume (only seven of the twenty-four had received prior publication). I do not, however, intend to make this a brief for the structural integrity of the *Yarns,* for that would take a much longer essay. What I would like to do is discuss a few of the numerous patterns of recurring images and themes that give philosophical weight and complexity to the comedy, to try to come to terms with Sut Lovingood as a character in his own right, and, finally, to suggest that the *Yarns* is not merely a minor masterpiece but a major work of American fiction.

II. BULLS

It is difficult to disagree with those who hold, like Rickels, that Sut is "outside the law, outside social morality, outside religion, even outside rational life" (102) and that each of his "practical jokes" is a "delight" because it is a "conspiracy against all order" (84). The actual sketches, however, suggest something considerably more complex: in the first place, no more than six of the twenty-four stories in the *Yarns* can even remotely be considered as having to do with "practical jokes" (**"A Razor Grinder in a Thunder-Storm," "Sut Assisting at a Negro Night-Meeting," "Frustrating a Funeral," "Parson John Bullen's Lizards," "The Snake-bit Irishman,"** and **"Mrs. Yardley's Quilting"**). In the second place, Sut causes the chaos in only ten out of the twenty-four sketches; and of those ten, four depict Sut's righteous (indeed, perhaps self-righteous) revenge against persons who have done him or others injustice (**"Parson John Bullen's Lizards," "Sicily Burns's Wedding," "The Snake-bit Irishman,"** and **"The Widow McCloud's Mare"**). Two are rather vicious jokes at the expense of Negroes (**"Sut Assisting at a Negro Night-Meeting"** and **"Frustrating a Funeral"**). Given the postwar social and political context in which these two were published, Sut's attitude toward the Negroes here is perhaps understandable: but even so, Harris is at pains to depict the Negroes as damn fools, with the same vices as their white owners. One story (**"Old Burns's Bull Ride"**) is simply a happy but unlooked-for extension of Sut's actions in **"Sicily Burns's Wedding."** One (**"Mrs. Yardley's Quilting"**) is a genuinely innocent practical joke. One (**"Old Skissim's Middle Boy"**), as I have suggested, is Sut's earnest, if metaphorical, attempt to do a good deed—to wake up the world. And only one, **"Sut Lovingood's Dog,"** represents Sut's angry and irrational and totally unjustified attack upon a fellow human being—and it is told with a definite pedagogical purpose.

Moreover, the actual violence depicted in the *Yarns* is largely the product of Sut's narrative imagination. We are not actually expected to believe—are we?—that the mole in **"Hen Baily's Reformation"** actually, literally, crawls up Hen's pantsleg and through his anus, chasing that lizard out of Hen's stomach, into his esophagus, and then out his mouth? or that bulls and Wirt Staples actually kick Negro children so that they fly through the air like footballs, creating havoc and destruction when they land? or, for that matter, that the soda powders Sicily Burns administers to Sut actually, literally, produce all the foam that Sut describes?:

> Thar wer a road ove foam frum the hous' tu the hoss two foot wide an' shoe mouf deep—looked like hit hed been snowin—a-poppin an' a-hissin, an' a-bilin like a tub ove soapsuds wif a red hot mole-board in hit.

(81-82)

This is not at all to say that violence is not a large part of Sut's world, or that he is unaware of it—indeed, he is all too aware of it, and the constant recurrence of astonishingly revolting images of violence is a conscious part of Sut's story-telling methods, a deliberate element of his attempt both to entertain and to teach. But to say that he *speaks* of violence is quite different from saying that he is an anarchist, a conspirator against all order.

Sut groups people into at least two classes, the wicked and the fools. There is plenty of overlapping, of course, but in general the wicked are those people who take advantage of other people, use them unfairly—economically, socially, legally, or sexually (e.g., Parson Bullen, Sheriff Doltin, Mary Mastin and her mother, Lawyer Stilyards, and Sicily Burns). The fools are characterized by a tendency to excess in whatever they do (Hen Baily's drunkenness, Mrs. Yardley's quilting, Skissim's boy's sleeping, and, of course, Dad's acting horse or bull or yearling): that is, the fools lose control of themselves. Sut is more often than not disgusted by the results of these excesses; he is certainly disgusted, even outraged, by Hen Baily's habitual drunkenness, as he is disgusted and shamed by Dad's excesses.

If it is possible to argue that Sut is opposed to excesses, and I think it is, it is then necessary to observe that he himself is not the Compleat Hedonist that he has been assumed to be. Critics generally describe him as a heavily excessive drinker, and he certainly is seldom without his flask. But we see him drunk only twice, in **"Sut Lovingood's Dog"** and **"Contempt of Court—Almost,"** and in both cases he uses his probable drunkenness as reasons, but not excuses, for his own violent behavior. He drinks regularly throughout the sketches but seldom enough to lose control of himself.[8] Nor does he exclude himself from the category of Fools—as we will see later in discussions of **"Sut Lovingood's Dog"** and **"Contempt of Court—Almost."** He knows only too well that he must maintain a constant and sober vigil over the irrational part of himself, lest he too cause the chaos he abhors.

Sut, then, is a civilizing force and not a destructive one in the Tennessee backwoods. He wants nothing more earnestly than to tame the chaos in which he lives. Sheriffs, lawyers, and preachers are so frequently his victims precisely because they are violators of the order they are specifically sworn to uphold, the order Sut knows is essential if civilization is to survive.

Harris announces this as a theme immediately, in the first two pages of the book. In **"Sut Lovingood's Daddy, Acting Horse,"** Sut is introduced in a vortex, astride the wildly bucking Tearpoke, who has apparently been "redpeppered" by some of Sut's friends as a practical joke:

> "Hole that ar hoss down tu the yeath." "He's a fixin fur the heavings." "He's a spreadin his tail feathers tu fly. Look out, Laigs, if you aint ready tu go up-'ards." "Wo, Shavetail." "Git a fiddil; he's tryin a jig." "Say, Long Laigs, rais'd a power ove co'n didn't yu?" "Taint co'n, hits redpepper."
>
> (19)

Before he can proceed with his tale about Tickeytail and Dad, however, Sut must, and does, bring Tearpoke under control, restore order:

> Sut's tongue or his spurs brought Tearpoke into something like passable quietude while he continued.
>
> (20)

The first paragraph, emphasizing the chaos, appears virtually unchanged in the story's first publication, in the *Spirit of the Times* (4 November 1854); the second was part of Harris's revision for the book version, an addition that argues that Sut is to be throughout the book an agent of order and not of chaos. The brief episode anticipates the situation in **"Taurus in Lynchburg Market,"** in which Sut actually risks his life in order to bring a raging bull under control. So the basic conflict in the *Yarns* is not at all that between Sut and the hypocrites of the world, or even that between right and wrong, but that between chaos and order, with Sut strongly on the side of order.

At the metaphorical center of that conflict is the image of the bull, which is traditionally, and in the *Yarns* specifically, a symbol of masculine power and virility: not just sexuality, though the connection between masculine sexuality and chaos is very significant in terms of the number of sexual sins committed in the *Yarns,* and especially in terms of the characterization of Sut's Dad in such grossly sexual, animalistic terms. In general, then, bulls symbolize an uncontrolled subservience to physical appetites. The bull also symbolizes political and social aggrandizement: the pursuit of sexual, legal, religious, economic power. In **"Sicily Burns's Wedding,"** for example, Sut gets his revenge on Sicily for her sexual humiliation of him. Thanks to Sut's "arrangements," the blinded bull Ole Sock backs through the house during Sicily's wedding dinner, his very phallic tail very erect, obviously displaying his genitals prominently, and frightening the entire wedding party with his brute sexuality: he passes through the bedroom first and destroys the bed (92), and moves on, wreaking havoc, through the house to the dining room, where Mrs. Clapshaw, the mother of the bridegroom, is hoisted by Ole Sock onto the dinner table. She so fears what she sees that she can only shout "rape, fire, an' murder" (93). Sut, then, uses the bull to desex, at least meta-

phorically, Sicily's marriage.[9] Sicily's feminine sexuality, which has so deceived, humiliated, and unmanned Sut, is simply overwhelmed by this unleashed masculine sexuality, which she cannot control as she can Sut's. In **"Old Burns's Bull Ride,"** the follow-up story, however, the conflict moves beyond sexuality when Ole Sock, with Burns riding quite accidentally and unwillingly, moves out into the world and encounters not women and effeminate men, but one of his own kind, Ole Mills, another bull. With tails hoisted very high they proceed to thrash each other, and the relatively innocent Burns, a victim of the capricious circumstance that put him on top of Ole Sock, dangles helplessly from a tree, upside down, while the bulls, violent, anarchic forces, rage all around him. So well the bull symbolizes the chaotic forces set loose in the Tennessee backwoods, not to mention in the whole nation, during the Civil War, to destroy civilization.

But it is more complex than that, for the bull is not just a destructive force; properly harnessed and controlled he is a tame and useful creature. Ole Sock is in fact generally a very domesticated beast who is regularly saddled and ridden (90). It is only when they are allowed to get away from the confines of their own pastures (the bull in **"Taurus"**) or are challenged on their own turf (Ole Mills), or are otherwise provoked that bulls lose control of themselves and go on destructive rampages. Thus in the *Yarns* bulls symbolize not just the abstract forces of chaos but the very concrete cause of much of it: onregenerit human nater. Harris is specific: "Now, George," Sut says, "ef yu knows the nater ove a cow brute, they is the durndes' fools amung all the beastes, ('scept the Lovingoods)" (90), and as epigraph to **"Taurus,"** Sut sings of the "blind bull, Human nater" (123): and so it is structurally and thematically no accident that Sut provokes Ole Sock by covering his head with a feeding basket, blinding him. Ole Sock totally disrupts Sicily's wedding celebration with a blind, malevolent, and backwards rush through the house.

III. DAD

Of course what Sut sings is that "Daddy *kill'd* the blind bull, Human nater" (emphasis added), and in doing so suggests a relationship between "Hoss" Lovingood and the image of the blind bull that is to be more fully and more meaningfully developed in the book's final story. The man Sut describes as "dod-dratted mean, an' lazy, an' ugly, an' savidge, an' durn fool tu kill" (22)—Dad— quickly becomes the touchstone in the *Yarns* for all the foolish and irrational behavior, the onregenerit human nater, that Sut continually animadverts against. Dad appears in only two of the sketches, **"Sut Lovingood's Daddy, Acting Horse,"** and **"Dad's Dog School,"** but their placement at the beginning and the end of the collection provides an important frame for the other twenty-two yarns. If the bull is the book's central metaphor, Dad is its figurative and literal frame of reference. He is the human exemplum of all the things the bull comes to symbolize, the *reductio ad absurdum* of all the irrational behavior in the book. By placing him at both the beginning and the end of the collection, Harris casts his shadow over everything that Sut says and does.

The two stories in which Dad appears are very much alike. In both he acts damn fool and gets himself severely punished for it. In both he reduces himself quite deliberately to an animal level, and in both he is stripped naked. In both Mam offers her unasked-for running commentary on the proceedings, caustic commentary that centers on Dad's ability to play "hoss better nur yu dus husban'" (23). In both Sut "assists," and in both an outsider intrudes.

As Sut tells the first story, their plow-horse Tickeytail dies, leaving the Lovingoods without a way to plant their crops: "Well we waited, an' wished, an' rested, an' plan'd, an' wished, an' waited agin, ontil ni ontu strawberry time, hopin sum stray hoss mout cum along" (22). The lazy Dad, instead of trying to buy or even borrow or steal another horse, uses the lack of one as his excuse to do nothing at all. When he does decide that no "stray hoss" is going to come along and save the day, he determines that he will himself pull the plow, and Sut will drive. But Dad is not content just to pull the plow, he must *become* a horse; Sut sees him "a-studyin how tu play the kar-acter ove a hoss puffectly" (22). Dad demands a bridle and bit and then whinnies and kicks when he drops to his all fours. Dad sounds the order/disorder theme clearly when he insists that he wants the bridle bit made "kurb, es he hedn't work'd fur a good while, an' said he mout sorter feel his keepin, an' go tu ravin an' cavortin" (23). Rave and cavort, of course, he does. Dad keeps up his "kar-acter" as a horse throughout, and we watch him gradually though deliberately slough his humanity, a sloughing that is total when he finally divests himself of reason: instead of going around a "sassafrack" bush, as a sensible person would, he "buljed squar intu an' thru hit" like a horse (24) and inflicts upon himself a severe hornet attack. Chaos and destruction ensue; Dad goes completely out of control, pulls out of Sut's hands the gears, which symbolize the restraints of rationality. As he runs through a fence, he leaves his one garment behind on a snag and is completely naked, stripped of all vestige of civilization and exposed, as it were, for the fool he is. Sut watches him run over the bluff and into the creek, then taunts him cruelly as he keeps ducking to get away from the pestiferous hornets, his just recompense for not acting like a rational human being.

"Sut Lovingood's Daddy, Acting Horse," then, is an essentially comic fable about man's propensity to divest himself of his humanity; but it is not difficult to see, especially from the point of view of **"Dad's Dog School,"**

the seriousness underlying the comic action, the tragic potential in the characters of Dad and of Sut. This potential is realized in **"Dad's Dog School,"** the book's masterful finale, in which all the important themes and images of the *Yarns* converge.

"Dad's Dog School" opens with Dad's determination to teach Sugar, the pup, to "hold fast"; school begins when Dad strips himself naked. In **"Acting Horse,"** his clothes were pulled from him accidentally when they snagged on a rail of the fence; here, in an unmistakably symbolic act, he deliberately and consciously strips himself of his clothes and, as we shall see, of his humanity. He forces Sall to sew him up into the hide of a yearling bull. Snorting and pawing the ground, he orders Sut to sick Sugar on and unwisely threatens punitive action if Sut should restrain the dog before he is "made." Of course the plan backfires: Sugar manages to get a death hold on Dad's nose through the mouth of the hide, to Dad's infinite displeasure. Sut perversely refuses to pull Sugar off, and Dad comes very close to being killed—he does lose part of his nose and a finger—when Sall separates him and Sugar with a swing of the axe.

But it is much more complicated than this simple plot would suggest. Sugar is a "bull pup," Sut tells us, as "Ugly es a she ho'net" (278), both of which images remind us of the other bulls and hornets in the book and which augur ill, very early in the story, for Dad. In the earlier story Dad "acted horse"; here he is just as intent on "acting bull." The hide, that of "a-tarin big black an' white yearlin bull beastes" (278) that they have killed some time before, suggests a specific association of Dad with the bull in **"Taurus in Lynchburg Market,"** which is also black and white; Dad Lovingood thus symbolically and literally becomes the bull that he has killed. Later in the story the "snout ove the hide what wer tied back on the naik, worked sorter loose, an' the fold hung down on dad's an' Sugar's snouts"; the fold covers Dad's eyes and, as Sut puts it, "my onregenerit dad wer blinefolded" (293). Dad's transmogrification is complete: he has literally, at this point, *become* the blind bull—"the blind bull, human nater."

It is a wonderfully complex image, for Dad has been "acting bull" all of his life; he is a bestial, destructive man whose rampant sexuality (he has apparently fathered eighteen children on Mam {21}) is almost a parody of the bull as symbol of masculine virility. But it is precisely to the extent that he has "acted bull" all of his life that he has "killed" his own human nature. Harris shows this in **"Dad's Dog School"** with a series of details that depict the diminishment of Dad's sexual virility and his humanity: it is, in the first place, a "yearling" bull that Dad becomes, an adolescent, as it were, in contrast to the fully grown Ole Sock and Ole Mills and the bull in **"Taurus."** Further, while the obviously phallic tails of the other rampant bulls remain very erect throughout the sketches in which they appear, the tail Dad assumes as part of his animal nature is very flaccid indeed: it "trail'd arter him *sorter dead like*" (282, emphasis added), Sut tells us; it "trail'd limber an' lazy, an' tangled sumtimes amung dad's hine laigs" (283), making it difficult for him to walk, much less, in his state, to function as a human being. After Sugar bites him on the nose, the tail becomes "stiff strait out, way high up, an' sweepin the air clar ove insex, all roun the yard" (284), but this is centrifugal force, Dad being twirled around the yard by the dog's unvitiated strength.

The story becomes even more explicit: whenever the tail points toward Mam, in what can only be a grotesque parody of Dad's sexual excesses with her, Mam hits him with a bean-pole (294-95), repulsing his advances and punishing him for his bestiality and for the lifetime of misery and poverty he has made for them all. Dad's debilitation, his dehumanization, is almost complete: he tries "tu rise tu the human way ove standin" (294) at one point but is not able to, with Sugar still clamped to his nose. Later he does manage to stand momentarily, but it is by this time an unbearable burden to "act human"; Sut notes that Dad "begun to totter on his hine laigs" (296) and that "his tail {wer} a-trimblin, a mons'ous bad sign in ho'ned cattil" (297).

The tail, however, is only one of two phallic symbols in the story; the other, obviously, is Dad's nose, which receives the brunt of the punishment. And when Sister Sall "tuck a chunk ofen dad's snout" (297), the implications are pretty clear: Dad is, finally, completely, if symbolically, emasculated by the excessive exercise of the very virility that makes, or made, a "man" of him. He becomes a beast because he refuses to act rationally; he kills his own human nature by refusing to control his bestial impulses. Whereas in **"Acting Horse"** he is merely punished for his foolishness, slapped on the wrist, so to speak, and then more or less restored to human status, here he is shown in his ultimate degradation. He loses all of what is left of his tenuous hold upon humanness; his descent to animality is total and, with his symbolic castration, so is his dehumanization; there is no suggestion of a chance that he will, this time, be restored.

Thus Dad receives his just deserts for his actions here as well as in **"Acting Horse."** But Dad is essentially unchanged from one story to the other, his behavior basically no different, and so his punishment here is merely the logical extension, a thematic intensification, of his punishment in the earlier story. The different element here is Sut himself, or perhaps it is more accurate to say that the different element is Sut's changed relationship to the action. His reactions here reveal a different aspect of his character and help explain his views of himself, of Dad, and of human nature in general.

In **"Dad's Dog School"** Sut has complete *control* of the situation. In **"Acting Horse"** he is primarily a bystander after Dad wrenches the reins loose from his hands. There is nothing he can do to help Dad out of his predicament; he cannot, as it were, save Dad from himself by holding onto the reins. Perhaps he would not have even if he could have—certainly he takes a dim view of "acting horse"—but he cannot, and so he contents himself with taunting Dad from the top of the bluff and entreating him a moral: "Better say yu wish yu may never see anuther ball ho'net, ef yu ever play hoss agin" (27). But in **"Dad's Dog School"** he is in complete control, he is in a position to save Dad from himself and refuses to, even though he clearly knows how much pain Dad is undergoing: "The childer all yell'd, an' sed 'Sick 'im'; they tho't hit wer all gwine jis' es dad wanted, the durn'd littil fools" (285). He not only allows but encourages the episode to proceed, painful page after painful page, and Mam joins him in humiliating Dad.

Part of the reason Sut refuses to stop it is, apparently, the years of stored-up resentment that he understandably feels, but the immediate cause is the intrusion into the "famerly devarshun" (286), as Sut calls this Sunday morning activity, of an outsider, Squire Haney.[10] This too is foreshadowed by a parallel incident in **"Acting Horse,"** when a stranger appears after all the excitement and sees only the aftermath of Dad's foolishness. He asks Sut to tell him "what ails" the man he has just seen back down the road, a "pow'ful curious, vishus, skeery lookin cuss. . . . His hed am es big es a wash pot, an' he hasent the fust durned sign ove an eye—jist two black slits" (28). Sut explains that the man is just "gittin over a vilent attack ove dam fool" (28), and the stranger asks, "Well, who is he eny how?" Sut bridles, expecting the man to say something derogatory about Dad or the rest of his family, "ris tu {his} feet, an' straiched out {his} arm" (28), preparatory to defending his family's honor, and says, defying him to criticize, "Strainger, that man is my dad" (28). But Sut has either misjudged or scared off the man; trouble is averted when the stranger looks at Sut's "laigs an' pussonel feeters" (28), recognizes the physical likenesses, especially the long legs, between Sut and Dad, and simply admits, "Yas, dam ef he aint" (28).

In **"Dad's Dog School,"** however, the intruder is not a stranger but a man well known to Sut and Mam for his hypocritical piousness. Sut sees him approach, "a regular two hundred an' twenty-five poun retribushun, arter us, an' our famerly devarshun sure enuf, armed wif a hyme book, an' loaded tu the muzzil wif brimstone, bilin pitch, forkid flames, an' sich uther nicitys es makes up the devil's brekfus'" (285-86). Up to this point, this story is a pretty typical one, not that much different from the others in the *Yarns*. But with the entry of Squire Haney the tone changes considerably; Sut begins to feel shame:

A appertite tu run began tu gnaw my stumick, an' I felt my face a-swellin wif shame. I wer shamed ove dad, shamed ove mam's bar laigs an' open collar, shamed ove myself, an' dam, ef I minds right, ef I warn't a mossel shamed ove the pup.

(286)

This is a convincing passage; Sut's shame at having an outsider witness the degradation of his family, even though the outsider be a hypocrite easily dealt with, is very real, and it is not, therefore, difficult to understand why Sut then sadistically allows Sugar to keep tormenting Dad, long after his point has been made. Harris's psychology is perfect. Sut turns from Squire Haney, the purveyor of his shame, to Dad, the cause of it; he lashes out, angrily and bitterly, with the only means he has at hand, by perversely following his orders not to pull Sugar off until he is "made." "Stan hit dad," he taunts, "stan hit like a man; hit may be a littil hurtin tu yu, but dam ef hit ain't the makin ove the pup" (296). Suddenly the story is not funny any more. Sut takes this opportunity, a gift, to flog Dad, to strike out at the one who is responsible for all of the misery and shame in his life; he works revenge against Dad and, by extension, against all the forces that make the world a difficult place in which to live. It is an opportunity not many have had, and Sut makes the most of it.

It is not a pretty picture: the worthless Dad, completely degenerated, his wife cursing and beating him with her every breath, and Sut, at this, the darkest point in an often dark book, unleashing all of his years of accumulated frustration and shame. And even though the story is told with the ironic rhetoric of the detached storyteller, it is clear that the episode, and his relations with Dad generally, have a profound effect upon Sut. Dad is for Sut a sort of foolish Everyman, in whose character are crystallized all of the faults of the human race, as Sut understands them, and his memory is a troubling one that hovers darkly over Sut's entire life: "I blames him fur all ove hit," he tells George earlier in the book, "allers a-tryin tu be king fool. He hes a heap tu count fur, George—a heap" (107).

IV. SUT

Profound as that effect is, though, Dad is not the only influence on Sut's vision. He is, of course, the dominant one, the one foremost in Sut's mind at all times, the standard of foolishness against which he measures all human behavior. He has seen nothing to make him alter the basic vision he has gleaned from his observations of his father; nearly everything has in fact tended to confirm it. In the world he knows, the Tennessee backwoods—and in the fugitive sketches collected in *High Times and Hard Times* the range is even further—people are vain and selfish and mean and do not understand that their disregard of the laws of decency and kindness is as debilitating to themselves personally as their flouting of the laws of society is to civilization as a whole. Sut knows it, though, and it is part of the burden of the *Yarns* to preach that particular gospel.

This is not a lesson Sut has learned easily, however, even with Dad's pristine example before him; and at least part of what the other stories in the *Yarns* do is to help us trace Sut's education in the ways of the world. **"Sut's New-Fangled Shirt,"** for example, the second story in the book, is among other things an allegorization of Sut's "birth" into the real world. In that story, Betts Carr, Sut's landlady, forces him to wear a heavily overstarched shirt, even though it is, to Sut, an "everlastin, infunel, new fangled sheet iron cuss ove a shut" (32) that makes him feel as though he's "crowded intu a ole bee-gum, an' hit all full ove pissants" (32). As he works and sweats, however, the shirt "quit hits hurtin, an' tuck tu feelin slippery" (33). Hot and tired, Sut climbs into his quarters in the loft and takes a nap. When he wakes, the shirt has dried again, this time cemented to his body, and is quite painful:

"I now thort I wer ded, an' hed died ove rhumaticks ove the hurtines' kind. All the jints I cud muve wer my ankils, knees, an' wrists; cudn't even move my hed, an' scarsely wink my eyes; the cussed shut wer pasted fas' ontu me all over, frum the ainds ove the tails tu the pints ove the broad-axe collar over my years."

(33)

He manages to get his pants off, so that he is naked save for the shirt. Removing a plank from the ceiling of the house, he nails the front and back tails of the shirt to the floor, and jumps through the opening; the shirt tears off, turning inside out as it does, and Sut hits the floor stark naked. It seems clearly a birth image, even to the shirt hanging there, to push the image as far as possible, as a grotesque parody of a placenta; it looks, Sut says, "adzactly like the skin ove sum wile beas' tore off alive, ur a bag what hed toted a laig ove fresh beef frum a shootin match" (35). It is, if birth it is, a violent, painful, and humiliating entrance into the world for Sut, who begins to learn about the world the moment he is born.

It is perhaps too much to say that Sut learns about life, in the course of the *Yarns,* in any systematic manner: it is neither possible or necessary to think that in each story he learns something different, or that from each person he encounters he learns a specific thing. But Sut is a keen observer of mankind, and over the years his initial observations, gleaned mostly from Dad, have been both confirmed and expanded. What Sut learns, and how he learns it, are very nicely summed up, condensed, into a superb story, **"Taurus in Lynchburg Market,"** which stands directly, and significantly, at the center of the book, the twelfth of twenty-four stories.[11]

At the beginning of **"Taurus"** Sut sings the important quatrain referred to earlier, which suggests the allegorical significance of the story Sut is to tell:

"Daddy kill'd the blind bull,
Human nater, human nater!
Mammy fried a pan full,
Sop an' tater, sop an' tater."

(123)

Sut sings this in reaction against George's reading, and obviously approving, Henry Wadsworth Longfellow's very sentimental poem, "Excelsior," which is about, as Sut describes it, a "feller . . . what starts up a mountin, kiver'd wif snow an' ise, arter sundown, wif nuffin but a flag, an' no whisky, arter a purty gal hed offer'd her bussum fur a pillar, in a rume wif a big hath, kiver'd wif hot coals, an' vittils" (124)—flouting, it seems to Sut, the laws of reason and common sense. He is not, however, merely teasing George; indeed, he is considerably upset that George could be so duped by a view of human nature as sentimental and naive as that of the Longfellow poem. To make his point, Sut rises "to his tiptoes, and elevate[s] his clenched fists high above his head" (124); such a fellow, he says, "am a dod durn'd, complikated, full-blooded, plum nat'ral born durn'd fool" (124). This is apparently one of a series of heroes whom George has admired and spoken of, for Sut then alludes to "Lum Jack . . . darin the litenin" (124). George responds, obviously irritated at Sut's attack, "Ajax, I suppose you mean" (124), and Sut speaks contemptuously of Ajax's heroic dare by pointing out a couple of facts that George has overlooked:

An' he wer a jack, ove the longes' year'd kine, fus', because eny fool mout know the litenin wudn't mine him no more nur a locomotum wud mine a tumble-bug. An' then, spose hit hed met his dar, why durn me ef thar'd been a scrimshun ove 'im lef big enuf tu bait a minner hook wif.

(124-25)

Sut knows what George doesn't know, that no individual has any control over the real world, and so his contempt is both for the hollowness and stupidity of Ajax's meaningless gesture and for George's willingness to be impressed by it. Sut relates his experience in Lynchburg, then, as a parable, to teach George a lesson about human nature and about the meaning of "heroism" and "sacrifice" in the real world.

"Taurus" is, again, a simple story. Visiting in the mountain city of Lynchburg, Virginia—and significantly it is a town, a center of civilization, and not just the usual backwoods settlement, where the episode takes place—Sut sees a "thuteen hunder' poun' black an' white bull" (126) rampaging violently through the town, causing destruction everywhere. His tail is "es strait up in the air es a telegraf pole" (126). At issue in **"Taurus,"** then, is the conflict between chaos and order, between civilization and anarchy. Sut takes sides in the conflict "agin the critter" (129), that is, against chaos. Seeing his chance, Sut grabs the bull's tail and wraps it around a light pole—which, like the "telegraf pole" to which Sut compares the bull's erect tail, is both a symbol of civilization and one of its products, one of the things that, bringing light into the darkness, helps make civilization possible. Sut's description of light poles as "mity good things . . . fur a feller tu straiten up on, fur a fresh start" (128-29), foreshadows Dad's inability, in **"Dad's Dog School,"** to stand up straight like a human being. Sut underscores the point that civilization is the instrument whereby brute natural chaotic forces can be tamed when he declares that the poles "can't be beat at stoppin bulls frum actin durn'd fool" (129). Sut steps in, puts himself at extreme risk, hoping to halt the destruction of Lynchburg, heroically taking sides "agin the critter."

What does he get for his trouble? The bull defecates on him, and he is abandoned by the very people whose civilization he is trying to save; one of the townspeople finds Sut's predicament funny and taunts him from behind the safety of a door. Sut tells George, "Ef hit hadn't been fur the cramp, skeer, an' that feller's bettin agin me, I'd been thar yet, a monument ove enjurance, parsavarance, an' dam fool, still holdin a dry bull's hide by the tail" (131). That is, he says, if he had had some help or even some moral support from anybody else, the fight would have been worth it, worth keeping up even indefinitely; but he gets none. All he gets, literally and metaphorically, is shat upon. All he can do alone is to put a couple of kinks in the tail of chaos (132).

This is not at all to suggest that Sut is right to undervalue heroism or that two kinks in that metaphorical tail is not a magnificent gesture in itself, perhaps the best that one can ultimately do. But it is no wonder that Sut is so bitter and disillusioned about mankind or that he is so exercised about George's sentimentality.

What, then, does Sut learn? He learns about wickedness and foolishness, of course, that it is human nature to be unregenerate, to court violence and self-destruction. But the implications of **"Taurus"** suggest that he learns even more: not just that people are capable of and delight in doing evil in all of its manifest forms; not just that they are capable of destroying themselves and their civilization through wickedness and folly; not just that they are capable of these things and more, but that like Dad they do them deliberately, consciously, and will not lift a hand either to save themselves or to help somebody else save them. It is a profoundly pessimistic vision.

It is, of course, a vision that he shares with many others, but Sut does not make the self-righteous mistake that many of his "victims" do, of separating himself from the rest of mankind in this regard; he does not believe he is different. Indeed, he knows himself too well to deny, and is too honest to avoid confessing, his own tendencies to lose control, to act irrationally. As early as **"Sut's New-Fangled Shirt,"** for example, he specifically associates himself with his Dad. The stiffened, starched shirt stands up against Betts Carr's cabin "like a dry hoss hide" (32), and Sut sweats "like a hoss" (32) when he wears it to work. Even more pointedly, Sut sleeping dreams that he has been "sowed up in a raw hide" and wakes to find the shirt pasted to him "es clost es a poor cow {is} tu her hide in March" (33).

Like all of his victims he is capable of meanness and violence, and two important episodes in the *Yarns* are in fact stories that Sut tells on himself. The lesser of the two is **"Sut Lovingood's Dog,"** a story in which Sut's dog is mistreated by someone (we are not told by whom) while Sut is inside a doggery, "gittin on a hed ove steam" (151). Incensed and, significantly, probably drunk, Sut "got mad an' looked roun fur sum wun tu vent rath on, an' seed a long-legged cuss, sorter ove the Lovingood stripe" (152) riding down the street on his horse. Without knowing whether the man is guilty or innocent, Sut decides "yu'll do, ef yu *didn't* start my dog on that hellward experdition" (152). Sut tries unsuccessfully to provoke a quarrel, and so in a cavemanlike rage hits the man with a rock: "I jist lent him a slatharin calamity, rite what his nose commenced a sproutin from atween his eyes, wif a ruff rock about the size ove a goose aig. Hit fotch 'im!" (152). During the ensuing fight, Sut puts a blazing box of matches into one of the man's coat pockets—but this is before he knows that in the other pocket the man is carrying two pounds of gunpowder. Telling it, Sut recognizes that he could easily have gotten himself killed or seriously injured. If he had known, he says, "durn me, ef I hedn't let him beat me inter a poultis, afore I'd a-sot him on fire" (153).

"Sut Lovingood's Dog" is primarily comic, and its moral is lightly stated. The other episode is deadly serious, however, and much more sobering in its effect. It appears in **"Contempt of Court—Almost"** in the wake of Sut's frank admission that he "hates ole Onsightly Peter," the snobbish and unwelcome encyclopedia salesman who has invited himself to join their camp, and of his long monologue on "universal onregenerit human nater" (245-47). The anecdote is intended, Sut says, "Jis' tu show the idear" of "universal onregenerit human nater," and he himself is the onregenerit human.

A foppish fellow enters a doggery where Sut is, again significantly, busy drinking; he looks at Sut "like {he} mout smell bad" (247), and Sut is perhaps understandably irritated by the man's arrogance and general manner. "Baw-keepaw, ole Champaigne Brandy," the fop orders, "vintage ove thuty-eight, ef yu please, aw"

(247). Sut's toes, he says, begin to tingle. He speaks to the stranger, again apparently trying to provoke a quarrel, but the man ignores him and turns to leave. Enraged and for no rational reason, Sut kicks the stranger as hard as he can. As the man flies out the door he turns, pulls a derringer, and fires twice. "I wer sorter fooled in the nater ove that feller," Sut confesses: "that's a fac'. The idear ove Derringers, an' the melt tu use em, bein mix't up wif es much durned finekey fool es he show'd, never struck me at all" (248-49). Sut of course "outruns" the bullets, but the point is lost on neither Sut nor the reader; like nearly everybody else in the book, Sut here loses control of his rational self and nearly destroys himself in the process. He knows, then, that he is no different from the rest of mankind, that he no less than anybody else will, upon the slightest provocation, act horse or bull or damned fool and so create the very chaos and destruction he abhors.

But the central episode of **"Contempt of Court—Almost,"** of which Sut's brush with the fop is introductory, entails a situation that seems to contradict the case for Sut as a proponent of order and that provides an essential insight into Sut's character. The one person in the *Yarns* whom Sut admires is Wirt Staples, who assists in righting the wrongs done by Sheriff Doltin to his rather slow-witted and cuckolded cousin Wat Mastin. Sut introduces Wirt in terms with which we have been describing his typical villains: Wirt is drunken and violent; coming out of a doggery he "histed his tail" (249), stepped out into the street "short an' high, like ontu a bline hoss" (250), and looked up and down the street "like a bull looks fur tuther one, when he thinks he hearn a beller" (250). "Wirt wer bilin hot; nobody tu gainsay him {that is, nobody to control him}, hed made him piedied all over; he wer plum pizen" (252). Bragging loudly and looking for a fight, he throws a little Negro boy up in the air and kicks him as he comes down so that he flies like a football through a watchtinker's window, wrecking the business and causing destruction generally. That is, even allowing for Sut's obvious exaggeration, clearly Wirt under the influence is very much like the bull of **"Taurus in Lynchburg Market."** And yet Sut sees him as the epitome of manhood:

> His britches wer buttoned tite roun his loins, an' stuffed 'bout half intu his boots, his shut bagg'd out abuv, an' wer es white es milk, his sleeves wer rolled up tu his armpits, an' his collar wer es wide open es a gate, the mussils on his arms moved about like rabbits onder the skin, an' ontu his hips an' thighs they play'd like the swell on the river, his skin wer clear red an' white, an' his eyes a deep, sparklin, wickid blue, while a smile fluttered like a hummin bird roun his mouf all the while. When the State-fair offers a premin fur *men* like they now dus fur jackasses, I means tu enter Wirt Staples, an' I'll git hit, ef thar's five thousand entrys.

(253)

Why this contradiction? It is only apparent, I think. In the first place, Sut insists that Wirt's drunkenness, and therefore his "acting bull," is a freak chance, unusual for Wirt: he "hed changed his grocery range, an' the sperrits at the new lick-log hed more scrimmage seed an' raise-devil intu hit than the old biled drink he wer used tu" (249). In the second place, Sut understands the world, of course, but understanding it is not quite the same thing as having to live in it. For the fact that he understands it as capricious and violent does not necessarily make living in it any easier—it can in fact make it more difficult. He is constantly on the run, Sut keeps saying, from one person or another, trying to escape whatever doom is about to overtake him. He is a man with many fears and anxieties, weary of constantly contending with this world and yet afraid of confronting the next: "I feels like I'd be glad *tu be* dead, only I'se feard ove the dyin" (106-07), he tells George. Sut has a great deal of courage and a lot of spiritual toughness, but in the end he realizes that the preachers and lawyers and sheriffs have the upper hand and that to get on in the world he must either avoid them entirely, outsmart them, or outrun them: he runs. What Sut admires about Wirt Staples is not at all his capacity for violence but his competence, his ability to deal with the world on its own terms, in a way that Sut is not able to. Wirt is big enough and strong enough not to have to be afraid of anything—not even the sheriff or the judge.

Finally, and this is perhaps more important, there is nothing mean or vicious or selfish about Wirt; he is not out to use or misuse anyone, and his marriage is the only healthy, harmonious relationship in the book. So he and his wife stand in vivid contrast to the other characters—even, to a certain extent, to Sut himself. They are fine examples of what human beings can be if they want to be and are willing to make the effort to be. Wirt, and not Dad, is obviously what Sut would like to be, what he would like human beings to be.

V. YARNS

A final perspective on the meaning of the *Yarns* can be gained by a brief look, here, at the book's magnificent preface. No book was ever so introduced, and no preface I know of functions so brilliantly as a structural component of the book it prefaces. The preface to the *Yarns* does much more than merely introduce the book: it establishes character, conflict, and theme; and it states, clearly but indirectly, the serious moral tone and purpose of the entire book.

Sut initially objects, though not very strenuously, to the inclusion of a preface in "his" book, arguing that because most prefaces preachily try to sum up the moral content of the book, readers usually ignore them:

> Smells tu me sorter like a durned humbug, the hole ove hit—a littil like curtin ove the Ten Cummandmints intu the rine ove a warter-million; hits jist slashed open an'

the inside et outen hit, the rine an' the cummandmints broke all tu pieces an' flung tu the hogs, an' never tho't ove onst—them, nur the 'tarnil fool what cut em thar.

> (ix)

Prefaces, no matter how serious, are as often disregarded as the Ten, and Sut agrees to have one very reluctantly, with a highly ironical and even slightly cynical disdain of the whole business: "But ef a orthur *mus'* take off his shoes afore he goes intu the publick's parlor," he continues, metaphorically describing the moral disorder in the world as dirt, "I reckon I kin du hit wifout durtyin my feet, fur I hes socks on" (ix).

His preface, however, makes its moral point not by discussing the book, as most prefaces do, but by discussing his readers, whom he divides into two large and perhaps all-encompassing classes, the lucky and the unlucky. The latter he describes in a highly moving passage that almost certainly wells up out of Harris's own experiences during his years of wandering:

> Ef eny poor misfortinit devil hu's heart is onder a millstone, hu's raggid children am hungry, an' no bread in the dresser, hu is down in the mud, an' the lucky ones a-trippin him every time he struggils tu his all fours, hu hes fed the famishin an' is now hungry hissef, hu misfortins foller fas' an' foller faster, hu is so foot-sore an' weak that he wishes he wer at the ferry—ef sich a one kin fine a laugh, jis' one, sich a laugh es is remembered wif his keerless boyhood, atwixt these yere kivers—then, I'll thank God that I *hes* made a book, an' feel that I hev got my pay in full.

> (xi)

This sentiment is directly related in many and obvious ways to **"Sut Lovingood's Sermon"** and **"Tripetown— Twenty Minutes for Breakfast"** and the diatribe in those sketches against the many unscrupulous "Perpryiters" who out of simple mean greed make rest, surcease from wandering, prohibitively expensive for those "poor misfortinit devils" who need it most. Sut's sympathies are clearly for these "unlucky" ones, and his compassion is all the more heartbreaking for the implicit recognition in the passage of the fact that any comfort he can offer, any laughter, any relief, can be only a momentary stay, and that they must eventually face the struggle again. This melancholy note is gently but firmly sounded even as early as the book's title page, in the legend, which states with Shakespearean simplicity that the laughter in the *Yarns* is inextricably commingled with the portent, the actual foreknowledge, of doom:

> "A little nonsense, now and then,
> Is relished by the wisest men."
> "Suppose I am to hang the morrow, and
> *Can* laugh tonight, shall I not?"

> —OLD PLAY

The only comfort that Sut can offer the unlucky is the catharsis of laughter—the satisfaction of seeing their oppressors brought humiliatingly low by one of the unlucky. The *Yarns* are full of the lucky ones, the "perpryiters" and sheriffs and preachers who take advantage of or mistreat other people out of greed or simply because they have the power to do so. It is generally the lucky ones who become Sut's victims, and it is these that he advises to stay away from his book:

> "I dusn't 'speck this yere perduckshun will sit purfeckly quiet ontu the stumicks ove sum pussons—them hu hes a holesum fear ove the devil, an' orter hev hit, by geminey. Now, fur thar speshul well-bein herearter, I hes jis' this tu say: Ef yu ain't fond ove the smell ove cracklins, stay outen the kitchin; ef yu is fear'd ove smut, yu needn't climb the chimbley; an' ef the moon hurts yer eyes, don't yu ever look at a Dutch cheese. That's jis' all ove hit.

> "Then thar's sum hu haint much faith in thar repertashun standin much ove a strain; they'll be powerful keerful how an' whar they reads my words. Now, tu them I haint wun word tu say: they hes been preached tu, an' prayed fur, now ni ontu two thousand years an' I won't dart weeds whar thuty-two poun shot bounces back."

> (ix-x)

Finally, Sut tells George that he wants "tu put sumwhar atween the eyebrows ove our book, in big winnin-lookin letters, the sarchin, meanin words, what sum pusson writ ontu a 'oman's garter onst, long ago," and George supplies the words: *"Evil be to him that evil thinks"* (xi). These words are indeed writ large throughout the book, for most of Sut's victims do in fact *think evil,* if we can understand "evil" to mean not just wickedness but foolishness too—any of the things that cause misery and chaos and destruction. And Sut's "tremenjus gif . . . fur breedin skeers amung durned fools" (xi) is his genius at producing for his victims the very retribution they most fear. Time and time again in the *Yarns* the evil that people do simply turns around, sometimes with and sometimes without Sut's help, and consumes the evil-doer in the very deed: think of Sut's Dad, of course, and Parson Bullen; the Irishman who most fears snakes is run out of camp by what he thinks is a snake; Hen Baily is nearly destroyed by his love of liquor; Sheriff Doltin is frightened by a man he believes to be Wat Mastin, a man he has deliberately wronged; and in **"Frustrating a Funeral"** Sut arranges for the sins of the past to come back and haunt all the main characters. That is, Sut's victims know they are doing evil at the time they are doing it, and so they walk in fear of the retribution they know they deserve. In producing that retribution, or a figment of it, Sut breeds his "skeers."

There is not, of course, in the *Yarns* or in life, a simple division of mankind into the lucky and the unlucky. It is rather Harris's metaphor for describing human relationships: all are capable of rapacity and meanness, and given the chance all are capable of using their fortuitously gained power over others for their own aggrandizement. At the whim of fate, common people become elders and elders become bishops, the worm becomes the chicken and the chicken becomes the possum (see 228); any may become, for the moment, a "lucky" one. And so it is with complete seriousness that Sut is able, finally, to dedicate his book *"tu the durndest fool* in the United States, an' Massachusets too, he or she"

DEDERCATED
WIF THE SYMPERTHYS OVE THE ORTHUR,
TU THE MAN UR 'OMAN, HUEVER THEY BE,
WHAT *DON'T* READ THIS YERE BOOK.

Obviously, the *durndest fool* is the man who persists in his own self-destruction, and Sut hopes that man will learn from his book not just how not, but *why* not, to destroy himself and his civilization.

But Sut is no optimist. He knows that nobody pays any attention to the Ten Commandments, or book prefaces, anyway, and Harris, in his warping and weaving of Sut's yarns, structures the book deliberately to confirm the bleak world view: the *Yarns* ends not with the bright ameliorating picture of Wirt Staples and his wife and their happy healthy relationship but with the much darker portrait of Dad and Mam and *their* relationship. And in that contrast lies much of the ultimate meaning of the *Yarns*: people must learn to control their animal nature if the institutions of civilization, and therefore civilization itself, are to survive, and they are capable of doing so. But they simply will not do it.

Perhaps it is too early in the study of Harris to start making claims for him as an important American author, but it is difficult to escape the conclusion that the *Yarns* is among the most ambitious and complex achievements in nineteenth-century American fiction, one that deserves and will repay a serious and sustained effort to come to grips with it. Its artistry is highly sophisticated and original, and its articulation of the human condition, especially that of the mid-nineteenth-century South, is among the most profound and moving that I know. It is a dark, pessimistic book, among the darkest in nineteenth-century American literature, precisely because it does not end on a hopeful note; no life-in-the-midst-of-death coffin buoys up from the dark depths to sustain life or give hope to those with the courage or the luck to survive. It is a darkness punctuated and illuminated all the way through by Harris's unmatched sense of humor; but it is ultimately unrelieved by any suggestion that humanity will ever be saved. In Harris's vision people are not being destroyed by forces beyond themselves, though of course those forces do exist in Harris's world. They are rather hell-bent on destroying themselves; and that is dark indeed.

Notes

1. I would like to thank Jim West for permission to reprint this essay[, originally published in *Gyascutus: Studies in Antebellum Southern Humor and Sporting Writing,* ed. James L. W. West (Atlantic Highlands, N. J.: Humanities Press, 1978), 13-49. The author has revised his article for this reprinting.] I am grateful to Jim Caron and Tom Inge for the chance to republish it, with some revisions, in this collection. Those who have read the essay in its earlier avatar will know how deep my gratitude runs, especially to Tom Inge.

2. See the bibliography at the end of the collection.

3. Milton Rickels, *George Washington Harris* (New York: Twayne, 1965), 48.

4. George Washington Harris, *"Sut Lovingood. Yarns": A Facsimile of the 1867 Dick and Fitzgerald Edition,* ed. M. Thomas Inge (Memphis: Saint Lukes Press, 1987), 21. Subsequent citations will be to this edition.

5. W. H. D. Rouse, trans., *Great Dialogues of Plato,* ed. Eric H. Warmington and Philip G. Rouse (New York: New American Library, 1956), 436-37.

6. Edmund Wilson, "'Poisoned!'" *New Yorker,* 7 May 1955, 138. The review is reprinted in this collection.

7. M. Thomas Inge, ed., *High Times and Hard Times: Sketches and Tales by George Washington Harris* (Nashville: Vanderbilt University Press, 1967).

8. Sut definitely likes his whiskey, but he is not an indiscriminate drinker, like Hen Baily, and in "Sut Lovingood's Love-Feast Ove Varmints," one of the fugitive sketches collected in *High Times and Hard Times,* Sut advises George not to take unnecessary risks when he drinks, giving sound advice: "Why, durn yer little fool pictur, are you gwine tu take yer warter afore you licker? Dont ye no that licker's the lightest an ef ye take hit fust, hit cums up thru the warter an makes a ekel mixtry an spiles all chance ove being pisened by hit? Allers take yer whisky fust, fur you don't allers know what mout be in hit. I'se monsus keerful about everything fur all natur's agin me" (243).

9. Sut's initial intention was to "shave ole Clapshaw's hoss's tail, go tu the stabil an' shave Sicily's mare's tail, an' ketch ole Burns out, an' shave his tail too" (90). Ormonde Plater, in "Narrative Folklore in the Works of George Washington Harris" (Ph.D. diss., Tulane University, 1969), 148, remarks that Sut intends to "de-sex" the marriage by symbolically defoliating Sicily's and Clapshaw's "pubes." But in light of what happens and in light of the tremendous metaphorical impor-

tance of tails throughout the *Yarns,* his comment seems a bit short of the mark.

10. Also called Squire Hanley the first two times his name is mentioned, *Yarns,* 285-86.

11. And, had "Sut Lovingood's Chest Story" been published in the *Yarns* following "Old Burns's Bull Ride," as the fourth story in the Sicily Burns tetralogy, as apparently the original plan had been, "Taurus" would have been squarely in the middle, the thirteenth story of twenty-five.

Benjamin Franklin Fisher, IV (essay date 1996)

SOURCE: Fisher, Benjamin Franklin, IV. "George Washington Harris and Supernaturalism." In *Sut Lovingood's Nat'ral Born Yarnspinner: Essays on George Washington Harris,* edited by James E. Caron and M. Thomas Inge, pp. 176-89. Tuscaloosa: University of Alabama Press, 1996.

[*In the following essay, Fisher discusses Gothic elements in Harris's Sut Lovingood stories. Although Fisher concedes that the sketches are predominantly realistic, he identifies distinct supernatural qualities in the writing, primarily in Harris's use of grotesque, often morbid imagery.*]

Sut Lovingood and the supernatural? An unlikely topic, many might suppose. In a class on southern literature, long ago, when Arlin Turner introduced the name of George Washington Harris, he mentioned no aspects of the mysterious in the Lovingood yarns. Instead, the renowned authority on southern studies emphasized traits of southwestern humor and the realism inherent in these writings. Another influential source in times past for introducing the Lovingood pieces, Wallace Stegner's *American Prose: 1840-1900, The Realistic Movement,* also placed them among texts of literary realism. We need not belabor here the prominence ascribed to Harris as humorist-realist in other anthologies. Like Dickens and Twain, he performed at his best for most readers as a comic author, and to such audiences any theory that might take away from that image has been suspect.

Nevertheless, Harris did venture into territories where natural and supernatural draw close. In "Realism and Fantasy in Southern Humor," published before his remarks mentioned above—which were delivered in 1963—Arlin Turner had managed to move Sut almost, but not quite, into the camp of the otherworldly. Milton Rickels has suggested that in the Lovingood yarns "the impulse to give Sut supernatural characteristics is shown in the bird imagery associated with him." Rickels's observation increased my own interest in the topic, and I offer forthwith my findings.[1]

I

Born in 1814, George Washington Harris wrote during the era of Dickens and Poe, themselves humorists and supernaturalists of no mean degree, as were surprising numbers of others among their contemporaries. Indeed, Kenneth S. Lynn once called attention to affinities between the comic impulses in the writings of Poe and Harris, but there has been little follow-up to his suggestions. We know how many tactics from terror tales in magazines and newspapers were adapted by Poe because of his familiarity with the journalistic world of the times; why not examine the methodology of supernaturalism in the fiction of Harris, who was also steeped in the newspaper and periodical world of the times?[2]

Internal evidence of Sut's supernatural bent is amply attested throughout the texts of the yarns proper. For example, in **"Old Skissim's Middle Boy"** the corpulent sluggard son of Skissim is overtly compared with the fat boy, Joe, from Dickens's *The Pickwick Papers*. The latter worthy terrifies his elderly mistress when he announces: "I wants to make your flesh creep." Instead of the anticipated account of blood-and-thunder or supernatural horrors, Joe agitates the old lady by informing her about the amorous intentions of her daughter and a man in the arbor.[3] Such reversals in a situation where supernaturalism might be expected are much a part of Harris's own procedures, although, like the fat boy, Sut Lovingood frequently conveys a "kind of dark and gloomy joy," creating through such tactics a genuine grotesquerie throughout the yarns. The ill-fated young man in **"Old Skissim's Middle Boy"** is actually made up by the vengeful Sut to resemble a being far more demon than human. Surely, through such methods, Harris grafted the twigs of sensational tales onto the hardy stock of native American humor and folklore. The resultant hybrids remain to this day a fresh subject for examination.

II

Sut's imaginative vision, and that of his friend "George" on at least one occasion, are positively morbid, running toward situations and, more restrictive and significant, dreams about the mysterious and ghostly. In the preface to ***Sut Lovingood. Yarns Spun by a "Nat'ral Born Durn'd Fool"*** appear solid examples of impulses toward death as well as attention to the figure of the devil in Sut's analogical imagination. He opens by comparing books without prefaces to coffin makers appearing in public without their customary black clothing. Sut continues in a manner adumbrating that of Huck Finn, whose fantasies consist largely of themes of illness, misfortunes, painful deaths, and wraiths. Educated fools, Sut adds, "breeds . . . devilment," and those who fear the devil—with good reason—will not enjoy the contents of this book. He emphasizes that it is rife with

"sicknin skeers," created by his innate and "tremenjus gif . . . fur breedin skeers amung durned fools." As if these examples might have but insufficiently demonstrated Sut's predilection toward scenes overspread by anxiety, torment of a physical nature, and supernatural creatures (epitomized by Satan himself), he concludes by dubbing a married man a "poor misfortinit devil" and by reaffirming the primary purpose of the *Yarns*: to offer a "gineral skeer."[4]

If in so brief a compass as this preface, Sut's rhetoric, the articulated expression of his imagination, runs to frights and demons, what evil may lurk in the ensuing pages? Although Sut's language is accorded high esteem by those intent upon finding in American colloquialisms the stuff of great literature, that expression may as readily yield illustrative substance for those who discern significance in his repeated drawing upon supernatural undercurrents. Multiple connotations, if not absolute wordplay, may constitute a greater portion of the art in these sketches than many others have remarked.

Centering upon nineteenth-century evangelical, or fundamentalist, religious ethics, Sut hints at suffering (in this world and in eternal environs) and ghostliness as well as appearances by the Prince of Darkness himself—to great literary advantage. Sut frequently comments that he himself has "nara a soul," so perhaps vampire lore also figures into his background. Readers used to hell-fire from the pulpit encounter it in different guises under Sut's tutelage. Indeed, hell-firedness provides staples of fear, or "skeers," in many of his yarns.

To illustrate: when in **"Eaves-dropping a Lodge of Free-masons"** the unfortunate Lum crashes through the ceiling and hangs suspended above the gathering of puzzled brothers, some of them hastily conclude that the devil has penetrated their midst. How appropriate that sentiment is: not long before this apocalyptic occurrence, Sut had described Lum and George as "little devils" and Lum, later, as a "skeer'd divil." Author Harris may have recollected the comic devil tales popular in *Blackwood's* and in that bible of contemporaneous American periodicals, William T. Porter's the *Spirit of the Times,* or, maybe, those of Irving, Poe, and Thackeray; here, instead of a genuine supernatural being experiencing defeat at the hands of a wily potential victim who ultimately bests him, young Lum suffers the ignominy of spanking at the hands of an unbefuddled lodge member.

As in numerous other burlesques of Gothic tradition, Lum's predicament is described in terms calculated to disperse horrors by means of intruding emphatic reality. Old Stack swings his piece of ceiling plank, "an' jis' busted hit intu seventeen an' a 'alf pieces at wun swollopin lick ontu the part ove Lum, what fits a saddil. Hit crack'd sorter like a muskit a-bustin, an' the tetchin sensashun shot Lum up thru the hole like a rocket" (*Yarns,* 119-20). Such reinstatement of reality firmly ends any notions of the horrific, at least that of other-worldly varieties, among the brotherhood and among readers.

Like many older hands at literary Gothicism—Mrs. Radcliffe, say, or nearer his own day, Poe—Harris undercuts exaggerated supernaturalism and the foolery of those who adulterate what should be rational perceptions with overdoses of nonsensical but sensational emotionalism. In this respect we must examine more closely the rhetoric, direct from the graveyard school of an earlier day, albeit still extant, vestigially at least, in the pages of sentimental magazines and other kindred literature, with which "George" begins his portion of this narration. He centers upon the old Knoxville courthouse, noting particularly its "steep gable front . . . its gloomy walls and ghostly echoes {as well as its} crime unveiled," all of which appropriately "belong to the past" (*Yarns,* 114). This sketching derives from much the same vein as Harrison Ainsworth's in *Rookwood* (1834), wherein the British novelist attempted a "romance in the bygone style of Mrs. Radcliffe." A like accoutrement appears in the "thickening twilight" accompanying and stimulating George's memories, for without doubt this tale is a "twilight story" akin to one offered by that old martinet of a lawyer, Mr. Tulkinghorn, in Dickens's *Bleak House,* as he outlines the unsavory past of Lady Dedlock, or to those eerie narratives entitled *Twilight Stories* (1873) by Rhoda Broughton. Gothic touches or not, George's memories quickly reveal the overly sentimental and lachrymose, especially when they take the form of reminiscences about the church and graveyard from childhood.

Sut can no longer tolerate his companion's sentimentality, so he takes over the thread of the story. He misses no opportunity to "skeer" or to create an atmosphere of anxiety and fearfulness during his outline of the boys' increasing foreboding while darkness descends upon their hiding place. They even suppose that it was "haunted": what a backdrop for their spying upon the secretive fraternity of Masons meeting below—because such groups were often suspected of diabolical pursuits. As if the youths had not sufficient "skeerin'," the Tyler of the lodge gives them sensational chase, threatening their lives, as they interpret his actions, when they attempt to escape. That bit of nightmare activity, verging very near the supernatural in its dreamlike aura, gives way as the boys flee the building, only to fall into what Harris euphemistically terms a "slush" hole, above which an outhouse had been removed, dash thence to the nearest creek for a wash, and, leaving all traces of that escapade behind, return naked to their homes. Persons they meet believe that they see "the cholery a-cumin" or frogs' ghosts, or spirits presaging an approaching famine (*Yarns,* 121). Sut leads into this con-

clusion by remarking sarcastically to George about the graveyard mentioned previously, as if Lovingood wishes to repeat his technique of taking over George's narrative materials but pruning them of sentimentality and irrational supernaturalism. The result is old-time Gothicism turned inside out with a vengeance.

In other ways Harris fashions his writing so that we find ourselves wondering what is and what is *not* of or in a world different from ours of the everyday stamp. **"Well! Dad's Dead"** gives us not merely the grotesque journey of the Lovingoods with old Hoss's corpse, which intermittently seems as lifelike and vital in death as ever he was in living days; the tale also affords a specimen of near supernaturalism in Mrs. Lovingood's harassed outburst: "I'd like to know when the devil *will* go out ove *him.*"[5] Such an ejaculation combines with the high jinks of shoving the seemingly recalcitrant corpse into the hole dug for it to effect "graveyard" humor substantially different from the concept of graveyard used above. This tale has been, rightly, called Poe-like in its macabre cast; in its bordering on the grotesque, furthermore, it suggests the work of Bierce and Faulkner.

A similar manipulation of circumstances to achieve a supernatural aura (that is dispelled in the conclusion) occurs in an early, non-Lovingood sketch, **"A Coon Hunt in Haunted Hollow."** The narrator, Mr. Free, and his friend Tom D.—patterned upon Thomas Bangs Thorpe's famous Tom Owen, the Bee Hunter—believe that they have sighted a raccoon high in a tree, located calculatedly enough, on Harris's part, in "Haunted Hollow." After many shots to bring down the coon prove vain, Tom worriedly concludes that he has been encountering Satan himself in animal form. Returning in daylight, the hunters discover that a growth on the tree trunk was their opponent. They vow never to mention the truth of this hunt to any save the "spirit" and in so doing they provide a neat bit of wordplay: this sketch was published in the *Spirit of the Times* (11 February 1843). Tom's personal inclination to believe in otherworldly visitants, as expressed succinctly in a snatch of Burns's "Tam O'Shanter": "Where ghaists and outlets nightly cry," prepares the way for this "spirit" in the close of the sketch.[6]

"The Snake-bit Irishman," a like creation, revolves around the ambiguities in the appearance-reality theme that recurs in so much American literature, and particularly American comic literature, in which the Lovingood yarns stand out as a high peak. Sut contrives to fashion a "snake" from deer guts, attaches it to his victim, and enjoys the ensuing melee. Dashing through the campfire, the Irishman in his terror does not realize that he has ignited the bogus "snake" but believes that it is a fiery or supernatural serpent intent on accomplishing his downfall (*Yarns,* 112). The components of darkness, isolation, and a threatening "spirit" draw together several strands of Gothic import. As in a Radcliffe novel, the being from what seems to be another world, so long as suspense is essential, turns out to be far less fearsome than the victim has supposed.

An additional, potentially fruitful document in this context is the obviously titled **"Saul Spradlin's Ghost,"** but because just the first of the two installments that appeared in a newspaper is available we can offer only surmises as to the outcome. From what is extant, we can conjecture that the "fat gourd" (**High Times,** 175) mentioned by Sut had in some way been mistaken for Saul's spirit. Sut's antagonism toward Parson Small, whose help is sought to lay the presumed spirit, seems certain to culminate in discomfiture for the sanctimonious clergyman, devolving from Sut's determination *"to help him lay Saul Spradlin's ghost"* (**High Times,** 176). In all probability, the parson's evident liking for widows would have been combined with Sut's ensuring that Small and perhaps one or (more likely) both widows, one old and one young, would have inflicted punishment or suffered it because the gourd might have been used to pound them. Or possibly the gourd's resemblance to Saul Spradlin in the flesh may have figured in some clandestine episode in bed if the ladies' attractions proved alluring to Mr. Small. This parson obviously delights in pleasures of the flesh, as we learn when Sut tempts him with visions of ample meals, and Sut is never behindhand at capitalizing on such impulses in others to victimize them. Because "George" knows about the ensuing "fright and stampede at Mrs. Hunter's" (perhaps one of the widows), we may lament the disappearance of part two of this tale, in which we would have discovered what Sut meant by remarking: "Instid ove layin {the ghost} as we aim'd tu do, we misfortinatly made a mistake in the cungerin an' raised the devil" (**High Times,** 175). We readers may rest assured, however, that raising the devil undoubtedly encompassed several implications of that colloquial phrase.

Another, more artistic production, wherein the seeming supernatural transcends the limitations of shoddy magazine-newspaper thrillers, is **"Sut Lovingood's Chest Story."** Here Sut finally gains revenge upon the philandering Sicily Burns, who had tricked him into ingesting too much soda and had taken wicked pleasure in his discomfiture when he tore away on horseback, looking like "a dreadful forewarning, ur a ghos', ur old Belzebub," according to the circuit rider Clapshaw, who encounters Sut in his misery (**Yarns,** 83).

The frequent recurrence of the word *devil* alerts one to Harris's careful modulations of elements that could originate in folk sources and in turn appeal to a folk, as well as a more sophisticated, mind. In other words, when Sut sets out to avenge his own emotional wounds,

he also accomplishes the end of Sicily's adulterous propensities. In such a situation, where the governance of the wages of sin is but too obvious, the intrusive implications about nonhuman agencies of punishment would strike terror across the unsophisticated religious beliefs of the adulterers. Sut's opening remarks about strong-minded women becoming devils foreshadow the violence and torments that follow. Indeed, because Sicily seems ever to direct the situations within those tales featuring her high jinks or seems, at least, to control them sufficiently for setting in motion a chain of catastrophic events, her demonic attributes are but natural. Intending initially to frighten only Gus Fabin's or "Gut Fatty's" great, black horse—itself an undeniable symbol of lustful human impulses—Sut decorates the "ole, black devil" with the phosphorescent fungus known as "fox fire," ties a charge of powder to the tail, and doses the animal with a sickening mixture of medicines (**Yarns,** d-e).[7] Seeing Sicily hurrying her illicit lover into a trunk (they supposing that a noise made by Sut might be that of her husband returning), Sut attaches the trunk to the horse. Next he torments the imprisoned Gus with visions of retribution consequent upon his adultery. The stroke of linking the sexually rampant man with the terrifying horse, which may symbolize a dominant animalism in the rutting relationship between Fabin and Sicily, is superb. The violent, erratic, and terrifying journey of the horse with its freight intensifies this theme. Once passion and violence gain sway, who can predict the outcome?

Following the horse and the battered Fabin, Sut encounters a North Carolinian, high in a tree whence he had scrambled, frightened by the spectacle of the apparently supernatural horse and rider. This man's thoughts are artistically fitting vehicles for the theme: "H——l's busted plumb open, an' this yere mountain's full ove the devils." He repeats, with variants: "we wus woke up by an arful yell, an' here cum the devil a-tarin es big es a corn crib, an' he had *hellfire harness on,* and a knot on the aind ove his tail es big es a turpintine still" (**Yarns,** g, h). To be sure, such visions as these, representative of chaos as they are, stem from reality, in this case the immoderate sexual passions of Sicily; and, "devil" that she is, no wonder ordinary mortals, in contrast to her own tempestuous but determined nature, grow literally and figuratively bewildered while confronting the results of her imposing presence and Sut's equally imposing handiwork in creating mixed displays of devilment.

Sut, of course, knows that there is no supernatural claptrap—of the sort so fascinating and delightful to unwitting readers. He sends off the woebegone Gus, remarking that folks in the region do not believe in "the devil what invented you," an observation wonderfully ambiguous in its ramifications. Sut's offhanded comments about Sicily's husband, who "believes in 'witches, an' warlocks, an' long nebbed {nosed} things' more than he does in Sicily," reveals additional psychological depths within this tale. Better, perhaps, to give credence to what we *know* are *false* ghosts than to the variety of deviltry Sicily manifests. Significantly, Sut adds that "she's warin thin, her eyes am growin bigger, an' she has no roses on her cheeks. She *cant* laugh, an' she *wont* cry" (*Yarns,* j). These characteristics typify those who in folklore are bewitched; here they devolve from Sicily's frustrated, negative sexuality. Of such substance is the making of literary art, prompting us to question just where naturalism turns into supernaturalism. Through Sut's vision, in this yarn and with frequency elsewhere, Harris implies that there is no easy solution to this dualism.

Another form of such diabolism occurs in **"Frustrating a Funeral,"** which in the table of contents for *Sut Lovingood. Yarns Spun by a "Nat'ral Born Durn'd Fool"* is subtitled "(never to be read by candle light)." This yarn is a veritable virtuoso's collection of horrifics, replete with a reworking of the popular nineteenth-century literary theme of live burials (shades of Poe!) and not just one but two devil figures to terrify beholders. An aura of drunkenness enlivens this story; early on "George" emphasizes Sut's easy access to whiskey, and, significantly, "kill-devil" whiskey is what brings about the death of one of the principals and the near burial of a living but intensely drunken man. Playing upon the heightened superstitions connected with funeral rites, Sut recounts his theft of the body of Caesar, or "Seize," presumably for a doctor's use in the laboratory. From his opening remark concerning premature burial, Sut goes on to apprise "George" of events surrounding the wake for the dead man, his own substitution of a drunken man for the corpse, and his making up both to resemble devils. First, Sut goes to work on Major, or "Maje," whom he has substituted for the corpse:

> I sot in an' painted red an' white stripes, time about, runnin out frum his eyes like ontu the spokes ove a wheel, an' cross-bar'd his upper lip wif white, ontil hit looked like boars' tushes, an' I fastened a cuppil ove yearlin's ho'ns ontu his hed, an' platted a ded black-snake roun the roots ove em, an' durn my laigs ef I didn't cum ni ontu takin a runnin skeer mysef, fur he wer a purfeck dogratype ove the devil, tuck while he wer smokin mad 'bout sum raskil what hed been sellin shanghis, an' a-pedlin matchless sanative all his life, then jinin meetin on his death-bed, an' 'scapin.

> (*Yarns,* 212-13)

As if to surpass this apparition, Sut turned to Seize:

> I'd got 'bout a tin cup full ove litning bugs, an' cut off the lantern ove the las' durn'd one; I smear'd em all over his face, har an' years, an' ontu the prongs ove a pitch-fork; I sot him up in the corner on aind, an' gin him the fork, prong aind up in his crossed arms. I then

pried open his mouf, an' let his teef shet ontu the back ove a live bull-frog, an' I smeared hits paws an' belly wif sum ove my bug-mixtry, an' pinned a littil live garter-snake by hits middil crosswise in his mouf, smeared like the frog plum tu the pint ove his tail. The pin kep him pow'ful bizzy makin suckils an' uther crooked shapes in the air. Now, rite thar boys, in that corner, stood the dolefulest skeer makin mersheen, mortal man ever seed outen a ghost camp.

> (*Yarns,* 213)

No wonder that episodes of terror and violence explode thereafter as various persons encounter this dreadful pair. Sut concludes this passage: "I tell yu now, I b'leves strong in ghosts, an' in forewarnins too." This comment is double edged; are we to interpret it as a straightforward admission, or, given Sut's fringe position in relation to the world about him, is this an ironic insinuation that means he disbelieves in otherworldly visitants? The devil-snake-horns motifs are redolent of rampant sexuality, of course, as they are in other Lovingood yarns.

Sut's ventriloquist's trickery materially assists in the emotional undoing of those who cross paths with these weird figures. Old Hunicutt comes into the death chamber first. Master of the dead slave Seize, he has evidently indulged an illicit passion for Mrs. Loftin. Aware of this affair, Sut, in the voice of the devil, threatens to take both of them to hell. In like manner he frightens the doctor, who had wanted Seize's body, out of his wits—and into a new line of work, that of a gristmill operator. This is a deft bit of comedy on Harris's part; doctors who experimented with cadavers were long thought to be in league with the devil. Later Sut goes to the funeral, informs the assembled group about several prominent persons' disappearances, and convinces them that he had seen Hunicutt and Mrs. Loftin on a burning ladder. The cook responds fittingly that she knew for three months previous that Mrs. Loftin would fetch the devil here before she was done—which persuasion led to an ironic kind of success.

En route to the burial ground, and with his wife sitting on top of his coffin, Maje begins to recover from his alcoholic stupor and, apropos of his hangover, mutters "Dis am the debil!" His words have the effect, naturally, of creating havoc among the mourners, as his speech puts his wife to flight and he pushes open the coffin lid, thus appearing in his full satanic glory before the others. Wright, who was the dispenser of "kill-devil" whiskey in his "doggery" (an unlicensed whiskey shop), supposed that his nefarious activities had marked him out as the devil's quarry, and Sut assists that mistake by speaking to him, again in an unearthly tone, about his time's being nearly up. Maje happens to see himself in a mirror and reacts as if he were facing off Satan. Again Sut's ventriloquism sends a sinner packing, although not before Maje meets the sheriff who, he thinks, can help him. We grow amused reading about yet another flight and pursuit that, to many who witnessed the spectacle, seemed unquestionably to be the devil intent on securing another victim.

This story ends with all of the customary pillars of the community gone and with Sut's notion, which preserves the context of his tale: "Why, the country's ruinated, an' hits haunted yet wif all sorts ove orful haunts; yu ken buy land thar fur a dime a acre, on tick at that" (**Yarns,** 226). The context is maintained equally well in his informing "George" that, after Wright's abandonment of the doggery, he had consumed all the remaining whiskey. Perhaps Sut's own "kill-devil" methods within his yarn were inspirited by that mammoth drinking feat, and if that is the case then **"Frustrating a Funeral"** is exceptionally close in its methods to one of Poe's "Tales of the Folio Club," in which drunken narrators related incidents of drunken characters. Perhaps the reason that Sut's story should never be read by candlelight is twofold: it may cause hair-raising effects in its readers or, given its liquorishness, it might ignite them if a flame were too near. Just so, the "frustrating" aspects within this tale extend far beyond the mere funeral qua funeral. Instead, frustration is handled as one of the primary motivators in life; all of the chief characters experience thwartings of their uppermost goals. And Sut himself sustains frustration—in getting Seize's body to the doctor. Elsewhere in his yarns, he had been subjected to frustrated actor symptoms, for example, when he attempted to court Sicily Burns. In this story, however, his actor's abilities come to us via some superb role playing, which places him among the foremost confidence men in American literary history.

III

C. Hugh Holman writes that if the southwestern humorists had not given a comic edge to their productions those works would be Gothic.[8] I hope, in such context, that my observations may afford a fresh perspective on the Lovingood canon. There realism and fantasy mingle, taking the American colloquial style and realistic mode into compelling territories. These aims and methods raise new questions about the nature of realism. More extensively than any of the other frontier humorists, Harris employs these blendings of terror and comedy.

In such contexts, though, the name of Henry Clay Lewis and his "Louisiana Swamp Doctor" yarns also come to mind. In "The Day of Judgment" a group of roisterers break up a camp meeting by turpentining a mule, setting fire to the hapless animal, and, themselves clad in long white robes made from sheets and with horns and loud yells to increase the pandemonium, running him amid the assembly. To that group, the eerie intruders and their awesome companion resemble nothing so much as fiends straight out of hell: "The thousand echoes of the swamp took up the sound, and the wildwood, if filled with screaming devils, could not have given back a more hideous outcry."[9] Ghost stories, including one in which a ghost-beset girl is found drowned in a churn of buttermilk, while away the time among the watchers over an ailing, elderly alcoholic in "My First Call in the Swamp." Elsewhere, "Dr. Tensas" tries in vain to conjure up the spirit of Major Subsequent in order that he might tell the story of his life himself ("The Man of Aristocratic Diseases"). In "A Struggle for Life," after combating a dwarfish slave who resembles an orangutan (and who seems to imbibe characteristics of both Poe's murderous ape in "The Murders in the Rue Morgue" and of the simian dwarf, Hop-Frog), the doctor passes through a period rather like those hypnagogic states recurrent within characters in Poe's writings. "Tensas's" sensations seem to be those of a dead person, although we ultimately learn that he has been stunned but not killed by his demonic assailant. This last is indeed an intensely Poesque piece, but in no way do Lewis's tales, taken collectively, offer the subtleties in handling conventions of the supernatural that we find in Harris's yarns. Lewis, in fact, excepting "A Struggle for Life" and, to a lesser extent, "The Day of Judgment," seems more inclined to smile away the otherworldly—about which he provides but few details—with an air of condescension, as if folklore and superstition were suitable for fleeting amusement and little else.

Conversely, the works of George Washington Harris demonstrate a more general functionalism in their supernatural substance, making Harris a transition figure between the grisly grotesque of Poe and the local-color vein of comic supernaturalism in Mary N. Murfree's stories or the diabolism in those of Virginia Frazer Boyle and Julia Peterkin (whose works bear no such stamp of hostile racism as is found in Harris's fiction).[10] Actually, we might profitably take note of similar techniques within the writings of a host of southern writers (in addition to those mentioned by Holman) well into this century, not the least of whom would be Ellen Glasgow—yet another whose name does not immediately come to mind when supernaturalism is the subject—in *The Shadowy Third*.

Notes

1. Turner's comments appear in the *Georgia Review* 12 (1958): 451-57; Rickels's are in *George Washington Harris* (New York: Twayne, 1965), 101.

2. Kenneth S. Lynn, *The Comic Tradition in America: An Anthology of American Humor* (Garden City: Doubleday, 1958), 193. See also Fred Madden, "A Descent into the Maelstrom: Suggestions of the

Tall Tale," *Studies in the Humanities* {Indiana, Pa.} 14 (1987): 127-38; Harry M. Bayne, "Poe's 'Never Bet the Devil Your Head' and Southwest Humor," *American Renaissance Literary Report: An Annual* 3 (1989): 278-79; and Benjamin Franklin Fisher IV, "Devils and Devilishness in Comic Yarns of the Old Southwest," *ESQ: A Journal of the American Renaissance* 36 (1990): 39-60.

3. Charles Dickens, *The Pickwick Papers,* ed. Andrew Lang (London: Chapman and Hall; New York: Charles Scribner's Sons, 1897), 1:459. The grotesque humor expands in the next chapter, 29, a tale in itself, "The Story of the Goblins Who Stole a Sexton."

4. George Washington Harris, *"Sut Lovingood. Yarns": A Facsimile of the 1867 Dick and Fitzgerald Edition,* ed. M. Thomas Inge (Memphis: Saint Luke's Press, 1987), x-xi. Further references will be cited in the text.

5. M. Thomas Inge, ed., *High Times and Hard Times: Sketches and Tales by George Washington Harris* (Nashville: Vanderbilt University Press, 1967), 210. Further references will be cited in the text.

6. The title of this sketch in *High Times* is "Sporting Epistle from East Tennessee," 15-18.

7. "Sut Lovingood's Chest Story" was added to Inge's facsimile edition of the yarns and is therefore paged with letters rather than numbers.

8. C. Hugh Holman, *Windows on the World: Essays on American Social Fiction* (Knoxville: University of Tennessee Press, 1979), 27-35. Holman demonstrates that the fine balance of humor with horror continues from southwestern humorists into recent writers like Faulkner, Caldwell, and O'Connor.

9. John Q. Anderson, ed., *Louisiana Swamp Doctor: The Writings of Henry Clay Lewis alias "Madison Tensas, M.D."* (Baton Rouge: Louisiana State University Press, 1962), 107. The pervasiveness of superstition in the Old Southwest is assessed by Everett Dick in *The Dixie Frontier: A Comprehensive Picture of Southern Frontier Life before the Civil War* (1948; reprint, New York: Capricorn Books, 1964), 30, 217-18, 220.

10. See Benjamin Franklin Fisher IV, "Mary Noailles Murfree's 'Special' Sense of Humor," *Studies in American Humor,* n.s., 4 (1985): 30-38; Fisher and Harry M. Bayne, "A Neglected Detective Novel: Henry Bellamann's *The Gray Man Walks,*" *Mystery FANcier* 12 (1990): 3-19; Melissa Yow, "Virginia Frazer Boyle: An Annotated Bibliography," *University of Mississippi Studies in English,* n.s.,

9 (1991): 205-34; and Irene Yates, "Conjures and Cures in the Novels of Julia Peterkin," *Southern Folklore Quarterly* 10 (1946): 137-49.

William E. Lenz (essay date 1996)

SOURCE: Lenz, William E. "Sensuality, Revenge, and Freedom: Women in *Sut Lovingood. Yarns Spun by a 'Nat'ral Born Durn'd Fool.'*" In *Sut Lovingood's Nat'ral Born Yarnspinner: Essays on George Washington Harris,* edited by James E. Caron and M. Thomas Inge, pp. 190-99. Tuscaloosa: University of Alabama Press, 1996.

[*In the following essay, Lenz discusses Harris's portrayal of women in his Sut Lovingood sketches, focusing in particular on his representations of female sensuality and its inherent power over men.*]

Henry Adams mourned and yet questioned the absence in nineteenth-century American literature of what he called an "American Venus," a woman who would insist on the classic potentialities of her sex as a natural and direct inheritance from Eve.

> The monthly-magazine-made American female had not a feature that would have been recognized by Adam. The trait was notorious, and often humorous, but any one brought up among Puritans knew that sex was sin. In any previous age, sex was strength. . . . Adams began to ponder, asking himself whether he knew of any American artist who had ever insisted on the power of sex, as every classic had always done; but he could think only of Walt Whitman; Bret Harte, as far as the magazine would let him venture; and one or two painters, for the flesh-tones. All the rest had used sex for sentiment, never for force; to them, Eve was a tender flower, and Herodias an unfeminine horror. American art, like American language and American education, was as far as possible sexless.[1]

Despite the deliberate playfulness and ambiguity of Adams's tone, his insistent rhetoric suggests an underlying seriousness to his search that is decidedly contemporary. "Why was she unknown in America?" Were there no surviving visions of Eve in the American Eden? Had a dynamic force—and one-half the race—been disconcertedly covered with fig leaves?

In the gentleman's magazines and Tennessee newspapers of the 1850s, however, George Washington Harris's Sut Lovingood vividly describes, in a stylized dialect both sexual and endemic, his numerous encounters with candidates for an American Eve.[2] Presenting Sut's pursuit in the tortured, self-consciously literary rhetoric of the conventional humorous frontier tale, Harris is able to insist, as the author of *Democracy* and *Esther* never could, on the cardinal power of sexuality. And although separated from Adams by much more than geography, Sut searches for an ideal woman possessing essential qualities—sensuality, vitality, and forcefulness—remarkably similar to those of Adams's elusive "American Venus." Seen in these terms, an examination of Harris's women, and of the themes governing their presentation, will result, it is hoped, in a greater appreciation of the *Yarns* [*Sut Lovingood, Yarns Spun by a "Nat'ral Born Durn'd Fool"*] and suggest avenues for further study.

In **"Sicily Burns's Wedding,"** Sut Lovingood informs simple George that "every livin thing hes hits pint, a pint ove sum sort."[3] The following lesson makes quite clear Sut's views concerning the points of men and women.

> Men wer made a-purpus jis' tu eat, drink, an' fur stayin awake in the yearly part ove the nites: an' wimen wer made tu cook the vittils, mix the sperits, an' help the men du the stayin awake. That's all, an' nuthin more, onless hits fur the wimen tu raise the devil atwix meals, an' knit socks atwix drams, an' the men tu play short kerds, swap hosses wif fools, an' fite fur exersise, at odd spells.
>
> (88)

Women exist for the pleasures of men, to feed, fuel, and satisfy their physical appetites, and Sut's emphasis on sensuality is central. In **"Parson John Bullen's Lizards,"** Sut divides women into eight categories according to their reactions to the parson's nude figure, and in **"Mrs. Yardley's Quilting"** he singles out widows as the most cooperative of women.

> Hits widders, by golly, what am the rale sensibil, steady-goin, never-skeerin, never-kickin, willin, sperrited, smoof pacers. They cum clost up tu the hoss-block, standin still wif thar purty silky years playin, an' the naik-veins a-throbbin, an' waits fur the word, which ove course yu gives, arter yu finds yer feet well in the stirrup, an' away they moves like a cradil on cushioned rockers, ur a spring buggy runnin in damp san'. A tetch ove the bridil, an' they knows yu wants em tu turn, an' they dus hit es willin es ef the idear wer thar own. I be dod rabbited ef a man can't 'propriate happiness by the skinful ef he is in contack wif sumbody's widder, an' is smart. Gin me a willin widder, the yeath over: what they don't know, haint worth larnin.
>
> (141)

Sensible in attitude and smooth in performance, widows are always willing in Sut's imagination to follow the lead of pleasure-seeking men. Sut's animal imagery emphasizes the earthiness of the women's desires and the type of skin-to-skin contact he anticipates. Yet the effect of Sut's language, which objectifies a class of women as spirited horses to be sexually ridden, is less descriptive than suggestive; the escalating accumulation of heated details—from their abject submission to their "naik-veins a-throbbin"—creates a critical, aesthetic distance between the narrator and the objects of his desire that suggests that these images are nothing more than the linguistic projections of Sut's pornographic fantasy. His stylistic stroking of these "smoof pacers" is surely the offspring of frustration rather than of consummation.

Sut's description of Sicily Burns may serve as an example of another version of his ideal female, at least in terms of external attributes and endowments. Her beauty marks her out as a possible "American Venus," almost a candidate for worship.

> She shows amung wimen like a sunflower amung dorg fennil, ur a hollyhawk in a patch ove smartweed. Sich a buzzim! Jis' think ove two snow balls wif a strawberry stuck but-ainded intu bof on em. . . . She kerried enuf devil about her tu run crazy a big settilment ove Job's children; her skin wer es white es the inside ove a frogstool, an' her cheeks an' lips es rosey es a pearch's gills in dorgwood blossom time—an' sich a smile!
>
> (75-76)[4]

Such sensuality seems to fit in well with Sut's philosophy, but distant worship cannot satisfy him for long: to be a candidate for his perfect woman, one must have the correct attitude and inclination; Sicily Burns is almost too classical (as Adams might say), existing "tu drive men folks plum crazy, an' then bring em too agin. Gin em a rale Orleans fever in five minits, an' then in five minits more, gin them a Floridy ager" (87). Unlike Sut's fantasized widows, who take direction at the touch of a bridle, Sicily manipulates Sut's fantasies and forcefully controls the reins of reality in **"Blown up with Soda."**

Sut's equivocating description of Sal Yardley reveals that he may have competing criteria for determining ideal womanhood. Beauty and sensuality are important, it is true, but neither is compelling unless the candidate possesses the right desires. As Sut struggles to judge Sal's qualities fairly, his clauses wind around like the tops of her stockings.

> Sal wer bilt at fust 'bout the laingth ove her mam, but wer never straiched eny by a par ove steers an' she wer fat enuf tu kill; she wer taller lyin down than she wer a-standin up. . . . She wer the fairest-lookin gal I ever seed. She allers wore thick woolin stockins 'bout six inches too long fur her laig; they rolled down over her garters, lookin like a par ove life-preservers up thar. I tell you she wer a tarin gal enyhow. Luved kissin, wrastlin, an' biled cabbige, an' hated tite clothes, hot weather, an' suckit-riders.
>
> (136-37)

In the end, Sal's enthusiasm outweighs her appearance. Twice Sut reminds us—as he reminds himself—of her value and utility. Her attitude, as he at last concludes, seems ideally suited to his needs and desires.

Yet throughout the *Yarns* women have quite different purposes from those imagined—needs and desires that often run contrary to Sut's simple equations. Sicily Burns, for example, after parading her pleasures before him, promising "a new sensashun," gives him soda powder as a love potion, curing rather than satisfying his immediate appetite. She is, like most spirited women in the *Yarns,* more serpent or siren than simply Eve. Even Sal, for all her willingness to be kissed, succeeds only in getting Sut kicked by her father.[5] In this rough-and-tumble, exaggerated, frontier world, wives do not long stay faithful to their loving husbands, the experienced widows do not experience Sut at all, the most respectable members of society are hypocrites, and even the proverbial nuptial bed is not what it once seemed.

Wat Mastin, because "at las' he jis cudn't stan the ticklin sensashuns anuther minnit" [230-31], marries widow McKildrin's daughter, Mary. Like many bridegrooms in the folklore tradition, Wat discovers that his bride is more than he bargained for; her sexual demands weaken him, make him physically thinner, and give him a backache. These unanticipated side effects encourage him to exchange her embrace for the grueling physical labor of a railroad factory.

> Oh yas, he married Mary tight an' fas', an' nex day he wer abil tu be about. His coat tho', an' his trousis look'd jis' a skrimshun too big, loose like, an' heavy tu tote. . . . Purty soon arter he hed made the garden, he tuck a noshun tu work a spell down tu Ataylanty, in the railroad shop, es he sed he hed a sorter ailin in his back, an' he tho't weldin rail car-tire an' ingine axil-trees, wer lighter work.
>
> (232)

Nothing is sacred or secure, and between appearance and reality, between imagined intention and actual intent, grows a widening gap. Sicily Burns, who had seemed to promise love (or at least a variety of physical equivalents), uses her sexuality as a weapon against Sut. Wat Mastin's "ticklin sensashuns" are irritated rather than relieved by marriage, and he eventually learns that his new bride, the previously and continuously unfaithful Mary, has lured him into matrimony so that her unborn child could have a legitimate father. Appropriately, they are married on April Fools' Day.

In Sut's world such attacks demand revenge. This forms a second theme in Harris's *Yarns,* one that seems to be a force of almost equal importance. Indeed, revenge is usually coupled with sensuality and functions as a form of confirmation: it can take a direct and immediate form, as in Sut's revenge on Parson Bullen, or it can be drawn out and intricate. In either case, however, return payment must be in kind.

The day Sicily marries the "suckit rider" Clapshaw, Sut manages to have the Burnses' bull, Sock, knock over their beehives and to lead "the bigges' an' the madest army ove bees in the world" [91] into the reception. The result is widespread damage, chaos, and sexual revenge.

> Sicily, she squatted in the cold spring, up tu her years, an' turn'd a milk crock over her head, while she wer a-drownin a mess ove bees onder her coats. I went tu her, an' sez I, "Yu hes got anuther new sensashun, haint yu?" Sez she—
>
> "Shet yer mouth, yu cussed fool!"
>
> Sez I, "Power'ful sarchin feelin bees gins a body, don't they?"
>
> "Oh, lordy, lordy, Sut, these yere 'bominabil insex is jis' burnin me up!"
>
> "Gin 'em a mess ove SODY," sez I, "that'll cool 'em off, an' skeer the las' durn'd one often the place. . . ."
>
> Ove all the durn'd misfortinit weddins ever since ole Adam married that heifer, what wer so fon' ove talkin tu snaix, an' eating appils, down ontil now . . . her an' him cudent sleep tugether fur ni ontu a week, on account ove the doins ove them ar hot-footed, 'vengeful, 'bominabil littil insex.
>
> (95, 96-97)

Not satisfied with this, however, Sut—or, noticing the less active role of simple George (he is only spoken to) and the verbal carnage created by such coinages as "suckit rider" and "insex,"[6] one is tempted to say Harris—completes his revenge in **"Sut Lovingood's Chest Story."** He discovers and drives off Sicily's lover, Gus, and leaves Sicily at the end "warin thin, her eyes am growin bigger, an she has no roses on her cheeks."[7] Sut destroys both her physical beauty and her sexual freedom—she will never tempt or taunt another man.

The revenge in the **"Rare Ripe Garden Seed"** trilogy takes a more complex form and brings to our attention almost by accident another "American Venus." At its conclusion the conniving and meddlesome widow McKildrin disappears, the adulterous Sheriff Doltin is humiliated and torn up by cats, Mary loses her lover and is frightened into fidelity and submission, and Sut, Wat, and Wirt are well avenged. Yet **"Rare Ripe"** is too densely packed with actions, emotion, and impostors to be summarized; it deserves to be read, as it is perhaps the finest story of revenge in the *Yarns.* I mention it first as a further instance in which revenge and sexuality are intertwined, and I will abstract from it a third variation of the Eve motif.

Wirt Staples's wife Susan appears briefly in **"Trapping a Sheriff,"** the conclusion of the **"Rare Ripe"** story. She is an interesting version of the "American Venus," who appeals, unlike Sicily or Sal, to Sut's stomach.

Wirt's wife got yearly supper, a rale suckit-rider's sup-per, whar the 'oman ove the hous' wer a rich b'lever. Thar wer chickens cut up, an' fried in butter, brown, white, flakey, light, hot biskit, made wif cream, scrambil'd aigs, yaller butter, fried ham, in slices es big es yure han, pickil'd beets, an' cowcumbers, roas'in ears, shaved down an' fried, sweet taters, baked, a stack ove buckwheat cakes, es full ove holes es a sifter, an' a bowl ove strained honey, tu fill the holes. . . . I kin tas'e em es low down es the bottim ove my trowsis po-kits. Fur drinks, she hed coffee, hot, clar an' brown, an' sweet milk es cold es a rich man's heart. Ontu the dresser sot a sorter lookin pot-bellied bottil, half full ove peach brandy, watchin a tumbler, a spoon, an' a sugar bowl. Oh! massy, massy, George! Fur the sake ove yure soul's 'tarnil wellfar, don't yu es long es yu live ever be temtid by money, ur buty, ur smartness, ur sweet huggin, ur shockin mersheen kisses, tu marry ur cum *ni* marryin eny gal a-top this livin green yeath, on-less yu hes seed her yursef cook jis' sich feedin es that wer. Durnashun, I kin tas'e hit now, jis' es plain es I tas'e that ar festergut, in that ar jug, an' I swar I tasis *hit* plain. I gets dorg hongry every time I sees Wirt's wife, ur even her side-saddil, ur her frocks a-hangin on the close-line.

Es we sot down, the las' glimmers ove the sun crep thru the histed winder, an' flutter'd on the white tabil cloth an' play'd a silver shine on her smoof black har, es she sot at the hed ove the tabil, a-pourin out the cof-fee, wif her sleeves push'd tight back on her white roun' arm, her full throbbin neck wer bar tu the swell ove her shoulders, an' the steam ove the coffee made a movin vail afore her face, es she slowly bursh'd hit away wif hur lef han', a-smilin an' a-flashin her talkin eyes lovinly at her hansum husbun. I thot ef I wer a picter-maker, I cud jis' take that ar supper an' that ar 'oman down on clean white paper, an' make more men hongry, an' hot tu marry, a-lookin at hit in one week, nor ever ole Whitfield convarted in his hole life.

(261-62)

I have quoted at length because Sut's description is lengthy, and the image of this "rale suckit-rider's sup-per" is pivotal: Sicily Burns may have a beautiful bo-som, and Sal Yardley may be willing, but Susan Staples actually satisfies. She understands that "'Less a feller hes his belly stretched wif vittils, he can't luv tu much pupus, that's so. Vittils, whisky, an' the spring ove the year, is what *makes* luv" (123). But perhaps this is too strong. Mrs. Staples, after all, only satisfies his hunger, not his sexual desire. Food may be a reasonable substi-tute for sex, may even take on the tactile, visual, and olfactory sensuality of the sexual act itself, but it is still only supper that Susan Staples serves Sut. Notwith-standing her desires, Sal Yardley is essentially a child, still dominated by the force of a paternal boot. And when Sicily marries Clapshaw, she loses her freedom, her ability to compete with Sut on his own cruel and chaotic terms. For to be bound to an institution of au-thority, be it family, church, or state, is to limit oneself and surrender the personal mobility necessary to ulti-mate victory.[8]

Susan Staples, however, is able to transcend these limi-tations and has not, although she is married, lost her ability to function actively as an effective—and force-ful—individual. Sut recognizes the wide range of her talents and pays her additional high tribute in the fol-lowing passage from **"Trapping A Sheriff."**

Wirt's wife did the planin, an' ef she aint smart fur an 'oman, I aint a nat'ral born durned fool. She aint one ove yure she-cat wimmin, allers spittin an' groanin, an' swellin thar tails 'bout thar vartu. She never talks a word about hit, no more nor if she didn't hev eny; an' she hes es true a heart es ever beat agin a shiff hem, ur a husban's shut. But she am full ove fun, an' I mout add es purty es a hen canary, an' I swar I don't b'l'eve the 'oman knows hit. She cum intu our boat jis' caze Wirt wer in hit, and she seed lots ove fun a-plantin, an' she wanted tu be at the reapin ove the crap.

(260)

Wirt's wife is a powerful combination of thinker, looker, and doer, a credible "American Venus." And, of perhaps most importance, she is aligned with Sut. This is not to imply that either Sut or Susan Staples is an agent of morality or universal justice, as Brom Weber suggests.[9] Indeed, they are decidedly amoral, and what justice they desire is personal revenge. What they do form is a rather loose community in search of momentary plea-sures, keen competition, and unlimited freedom: to com-pete is to assert one's individuality; to triumph is to se-cure it.

Susan Staples is undoubtedly the most successful woman in Sut's—and in Adams's—terms, and her ap-pearance at the conclusion of the **"Rare Ripe Garden Seed"** trilogy forms a locus of meaning. Harris allows Sut to dwell lovingly upon her portrait, insisting by ex-tended description on her integrity and importance. Her image—like her dinner—is obsessively detailed by Sut from her "full throbbin neck" to her "talkin eyes" (262), an image that insists self-reflexively upon its own icono-graphic power. A mere picture of Susan Staples and her supper would convert bachelors to the cause of mar-riage. Forceful and able, she is nevertheless "full ove fun," and while managing an ornery husband like Wirt, she still has the strength of will to maintain her identity as an individual. Like Sut, to whose character she is a key, Susan Staples celebrates the eternal joys of victory and survival and delights in the rejuvenating energy of vigorous action. If Sut can be seen as the prototypical Adam of the *Yarns,* she is certainly the most nearly Eve.

Yet Susan Staples is Wirt's wife, and her attractions, though great, must remain for Sut those of an unattain-able ideal; for in spite of the spirited women he en-counters, Sut is ultimately, like the conventional trick-ster or fool, bound by immutable laws to reveal what he cannot himself possess. As he so pointedly reminds us, he "gets dorg hongry" whenever he sees Susan Staples, or her sidesaddle (a reminder of her physical sexuality), or even most pathetically her dress on the clothesline (a symbol of her sexuality emptied of her physicality). But he has eaten at her table infrequently and, despite his elaborate description, recognizes that the fantasy of consumption must take the place of an impossible sexual consummation. Sut's fate consists of frustration, displacement, and denial. Full of "onregenerit pride," Sut shares with Natty Bumppo and Huckleberry Finn a clear if sobering perception of the price to be paid for independence: "Now ef a feller happens tu know what his pint am, he kin allers git along, sumhow, purvided he don't swar away his liberty tu a temprins s'ciety, live tu fur frum a still-'ous, an' too ni a chu'ch ur a jail" (88). The discovery of Adams's "American Venus" in a frontier landscape is all—and it is quite a lot—that he can accomplish.

Freedom can result in solitude, in escape, and the license it provides may go at first undetected. Wat Mastin must learn from Sut the benefits accompanying his newly earned liberty:

> "Sut, hell's tu pay at our hous'. Mary's been hid out sumwhar till this mornin. She cum up draggil'd an' hungry, an' won't say a durn'd word. An' ole Missis McKildrin's plum gone." Sez I—
>
> "Ain't yu glad?"
>
> He stretched his mouf intu the wides' smile yu ever seed, an' slappin me on the back, sez he—
>
> "I *is,* by golly!"
>
> (275)

It is this delight in and awareness of the moments of life, the reassertion that humor can provide a meaning, that vigorous living can restore one's purpose in defeat and confirm the integrity of the individual in triumph, that informs **Sut Lovingood. Yarns Spun by a "Nat'ral Born Durn'd Fool."** Sensuality and revenge are major forces in this world, stark frontier humor is the modus operandi, and the goal, or rather, the final achievement, is an undeniable affirmation of freedom.

Sal, Sicily, and Susan Staples reveal that on the imaginative frontier of Harris's **Yarns,** American women existed who would have been recognized by Adam and applauded by Adams. Their awareness that sex is a power before which men are helpless suggests a tradition of American women characters who flaunt their inheritance in a popular, male-dominated genre, one that Harris had the good fortune to discover and exploit.

Notes

1. Henry Adams, *The Education of Henry Adams* (1918; reprint, Boston: Houghton Mifflin, 1961), 384, 385.

2. Adams, we suppose, dismissed or carefully overlooked the heroines of Hawthorne, Howells, and Henry James as sensual but unsuccessful, ultimately impotent to change men's lives; and, if he knew them, the fates of Maggie Johnson, Edna Pontellier, and Sister Carrie must have seemed clear illustrations of the tragic extremes to which an emerging "American Venus" might easily be reduced.

3. George Washington Harris, *"Sut Lovingood. Yarns": A Facsimile of the 1867 Dick and Fitzgerald Edition,* ed. M. Thomas Inge (Memphis: Saint Lukes Press, 1987), 87. All future quotations will be from this edition with page numbers incorporated into the text.

4. Sicily's breasts are, to my knowledge, the first revealed in American literature. Although they suffer some obvious domestication through misspelling and metaphor, Sut's admiring description seems anything but "sexless"; Harris's humor is always subversive.

5. Although Sut is caught "convarsin wif a frien'" named "Sall" in "Parson John Bullen's Lizards," I do not believe this constitutes sufficient evidence against my point that Sut is frustrated. In both "Sicily Burns's Wedding" and "Dad's Dog School" Sut refers to his sister as "Sall." And in "Lizards," it must be admitted, Sut receives only pain from Bullen's boot.

6. These orthographic gymnastics, although occasionally careless, reveal an energy primarily sexual in nature and, as opposed to Sicily's "buzzim" discussed in note 4 above, attract attention to themselves as deliberate obscene neologisms. The enthusiasm Sut displays is here more obvious, perhaps—as I suggest—because the distance between Sut and Harris has greatly decreased. The effect and intention are quite different from those observed in "Trapping a Sheriff," where Mrs. Staples "seed lots ove fun a-plantin, an' she wanted tu be at the reapin of the crap" (260).

7. Inge's facsimile edition includes "Sut Lovingood's Chest Story," pages a-j.

8. In "Blown up with Soda," Sicily thought nothing of using a cruel deception to trick Sut. Milton Rickels, in his invaluable study, *George Washington Harris* (New York: Twayne Publishers, 1965), notes: "Sut has matched cruelty with Sicily. As long as she is free, she wins. When she binds herself with the institutions, she becomes respectable and has a social place to lose" (54).

9. See Brom Weber's introduction to *Sut Lovingood* (New York: Grove Press, 1954), ix-xxix, esp. xxv-xxvi. I also strongly disagree with what Weber

calls "the necessary task of simplifying the text" (xxvii), for in so doing much of the raw, untamed energy of the *Yarns* is reduced. As Sut warns in his preface to the 1867 edition, one should be very careful "afore yu takes eny ove my flesh ontu yer claws, ur my blood ontu yer bills" (x).

James E. Caron (essay date 1996)

SOURCE: Caron, James E. "Playin' Hell: Sut Lovingood as Durn'd Fool Preacher." In *Sut Lovingood's Nat'ral Born Yarnspinner: Essays on George Washington Harris,* edited by James E. Caron and M. Thomas Inge, pp. 272-98. Tuscaloosa: University of Alabama Press, 1996.

[*In the following essay, Caron examines the character of Sut Lovingood within the framework of traditional literary portrayals of the "fool." Caron argues that Sut represents the fringe of frontier Tennessee society while also embodying, and voicing, the values embraced by the mainstream. In this way, paradoxically, Sut defines the community from which he is ostensibly an outcast.*]

> "Suckit-riders am surjestif things tu me. They preaches agin me, an' I hes no chance tu preach back at them. Ef I cud I'd make the institushun behave hitsef better nur hit dus."

> **—"Sicily Burns's Wedding"**

Since Milton Rickels explored the idea at some length, a central point of commentary on the artistry of George Washington Harris is his use of long-standing conventions about the figure of the fool. Sut as fool allows Harris to depict behavior and express sentiments usually forbidden to writers in the antebellum United States. Rickels, however, draws a stark conclusion from his thesis. In his view Sut is hell-raising, whiskey-drinking, poor white trash—beyond the pale, detached both in life and spirit from his community and always threatening to overthrow authority. While his insight about Sut as fool remains valuable, Rickels, I will argue, veers from its truth when discussing the relationship between Sut and his community. Precisely because Sut enacts the role of fool and thus represents the fringe of society, he has the potential of representing the mainstream values of his east Tennessee, antebellum community.[1]

The paradox of the fool—on the margin yet potentially in the center—can be expressed as a structural relation with a community's ruler. Especially helpful for demonstrating that relationship is the trickster figure, a mythological form of the fool who is an enemy of order and boundaries: "since the disorder of which {the trickster} is the spirit is largely contained within his show {of foolishness}, he serves the boundary of which he is

the enemy; and in doing this, he sometimes even demonstrates an authority proper to the central figure of established order . . . such as the king."[2] Late medieval and Renaissance European courts illustrate this photographic-negative relationship: the licensed fool embodied disorder while the king or prince or duke embodied order. Yet, as King Lear's fool suggests, the fool's position endows him with the freedom to speak most forcefully for reason and order.

During ancient times, when kingship entailed a magical as well as political dimension, the king was not only the guarantor by force of arms of the kingdom's geographical boundaries but also the mediator between his people and the realm of the supernatural. He was the center of political and social life *and* the symbolic conduit through which divine life passed to ensure an abundant harvest. Within this aura of magic the doctrine of the divine right of kings assumed its full power. And with so much contingent upon the king, a hedge against failure became a necessary corollary: "the king came very early to have a double, who embodied the threat of natural catastrophe and was deliberately mocked by the people. . . . The mock king was not always a fool, but by the nature of his office the fool as court jester became a kind of mock king."[3] The roles of fool and king, then, ultimately functioned to preserve the community. Much the same way as ritual scapegoats provided a formal means whereby a community could rid itself of unwanted and unlucky elements, thus strengthening the group by reaffirming its proper members and by soliciting the goodwill of the gods, the fool, as mascot and scapegoat, either warded off antithetical powers or introduced them in order to ensure their defeat. While the fool generally evokes boundaries because of its marginal status yet has the potential to fulfill a central role, the king's central role is overlayed, at special times, by an evocation of the boundary between this world and the next. The king and fool thus were the symbolic center and margin of community, mapping by their dynamic the space wherein all other legitimate members resided.

If Milton Rickels's point about Sut as a fool makes sense, then the relation of fool and king as types that define a community argues for Sut's inclusion in his own historical community, Ducktown. Sut's wild behavior, however, runs counter to the order of a settled community, suggesting the ambiguity of a trickster fool. Indeed, Sut's liminality is also indicated by his status as a mountaineer who has moved into town.[4] Sut himself remains a candidate for purging yet explicitly performs the task of expelling the undesirable outsider—like a Yankee or an Irishman—and thus maintains the integrity of the town. Sut, then, is both potential scapegoat and the representative of the communal authority that performs the cleansing action of scapegoating. Sut is both Fool and Fool Killer.[5]

An objection to my point about the fool's relation to king and community might be that the European analogy applies only on the mythic or literary level and not on a social or political one. After all, where is the authority in frontier America's southern communities comparable to a king? In fact, one institution did exercise an influence pervasive enough and did create a cohesiveness strong enough to function as such a powerful center of community: evangelical Christianity.[6]

This essay will explore how Sut's foolishness playfully evokes and revokes this authoritative center of his specific community. Although Sut's role as fool inevitably contains elements of the scapegoat and the trickster, the essay's argument does not insist on a sense of magic in the yarns; there is, however, a permeating sense of the supernatural.[7] Indeed, Sut *must* commit his narratives to a running engagement with the other world. Just as the court jester clowned in front of his lord, taking license with the sacred and secular principles of order represented by the office of king, Sut's antics can be read as clownish presentations of evangelical Christianity, the center of his community. Sut is a mock preacher. As a fool who acts in the historical context of the antebellum United States, Sut cannot fulfill the role of mock king, but his particular manifestation as a fool nevertheless functions similarly within his community.[8]

Sut carries on his foolishness by appropriating religious discourse. Whether he mocks church or state, Sut as comic preacher delivers "sermons," the abiding text of which is human nature as he finds it both in himself and in his neighbors. Of course, Sut expounds anything but orthodox doctrine. His basic premise, however, echoes the Calvinistic view of human depravity: the hell-deserving nature of people. And he does acknowledge a basic division of sinners and saints, the unregenerate and the sanctified. Yet Sut himself is not a believer in the sense that he has experienced God's grace. His parodic fool's religion is as much folkish superstition as Christian tenet. Moreover, Sut's "preaching" does not represent a definable moral order inasmuch as a pursuit of play and freedom motivates everything Sut does. For Sut, license is always better than law. Yet, as we will see, woven into his pleasure principle is Sut's notion of proper behavior, a notion that, while falling short of a true ethic, establishes a right and a wrong way to act. I will not claim that all of Sut's behavior can be explained within a framework of religion. However, all the tales in *Sut Lovingood. Yarns Spun by a "Nat'ral Born Durn'd Fool"* are about the creation or maintenance of community according to his foolish notion of proper conduct, a notion that can be discussed by focusing on two other religious terms besides unregeneracy—tribulation and retribution. We will see that for all of the wildness of Sut's yarns, there is nevertheless a conservative element in the tales.

I

One example of how Sut mimics sermonizing comes in **"Eaves-dropping a Lodge of Free-masons,"** after Sut has interrupted George's nostalgic way of beginning the tale. Sut starts his version saying, "Ahem! I takes fur my tex, the fac' that eaves-drappin am a durn'd mean sorter way tu make a livin . . . an' hit hes hits retribushun, a orful wun" (116). An equally obvious example of Sut as comic preacher is in **"Sut Lovingood's Sermon—'Ye Cat Fishe Tavern,'"** a tale completed by **"Tripetown—Twenty Minutes for Breakfast."** The message of these stories has been repeated since antiquity: innkeepers are a herd of rascals. But Sut frames his diatribe with the conventions of a church sermon, again by announcing his text and by repeating part of that text at regular intervals as a refrain. Very much aware he is acting the role of preacher, Sut jokes about his credentials for preaching by noting five "facts": he has no soul, he is a lawless fool, he has the longest pair of legs of any creature, he can drink more whiskey without falling over than anyone else, and he can get into and out of more scary scrapes faster than anyone else. While this list bears a resemblance of form to the boast of the backwoods roarer, Sut is also making fun of the lack of formal training that usually characterized Methodist and Baptist preachers of the antebellum period: "ef these . . . pints ove karactar don't gin me the right tu preach ef I wants tu I wud like tu know whar sum preachers got *thar* papers frum" (172-73). Sut's negative credentials comically comment on an age when virtually any man with a religious turn of mind who felt the "call" could claim a right to preach.[9]

That Sut himself possesses the requisite religious mindset can be illustrated by a comment he makes that shows how he conceptualizes his own self in religious terms: "I hes a trustin reliance ontu the fidelity, injurance, an' speed ove these yere laigs ove mine tu tote me *an' my sins* away beyant all human retribushuns ur revenge" (xi, emphasis added). Moreover, there is Sut's readiness with biblical phrasing and his more direct references to the Holy Book, as he calls it (35). Appropriate to the tendency of evangelical Christianity, the allusions nearly all refer to the Old Testament.[10] Harris also has Sut close **"Dad's Dog School,"** the last of the *Yarns,* in a way that underscores Sut's mock religious orientation. Just before all who have been listening retire, Sut wishes them pleasant dreams. In particular he wishes George will "dream ove ownin three never-failin springs, so clost together yu kin lay on yure belly an' reach em all—the bigges wun runnin ole whiskey, the middil one strained honey, an' the leas' an' las'—cold warter" (298). This mountaineer's version of the biblical land of milk and honey is complemented by Sut's wish for himself: "Es tu me, ef I kin jis' miss dreamin ove hell ur {the circuit rider} ole Bullen's all I ax" (299). Sut's comic picture of paradise fits with his biblical allusions and phrasing, indicating the most basic credential for preaching: a mind shaped by the Good Book. Sut even mentions one of the most famous of the early evangelical preachers, Whitefield (262), showing a sense of history about the typical style of Christianity in antebellum east Tennessee.

For all of his apparent religious background, however, Sut has not "joined meeting." Sut is not part of the community of saints, nor is he even a believer in any usual sense of that word. His status in the community at large is summed up by the wanted poster Parson Bullen posts after Sut had interrupted his preaching by releasing lizards up his pant leg: "fur the raisin ove the devil pussonely, . . . an' a-makin the wickid larf" (48). Sut primarily acts as an agent of the pleasure principle, a trickster who disrupts community order. His willingness to mock, parody, and otherwise abuse religious discourse for unorthodox purposes illustrates the nature of his belief in Christian doctrine. Sut believes as the blasphemer believes, negatively.

The fundamental tenet of Sut's belief, however, is identical with his community's orthodox Christianity: "univarsal onregenerit human nater" (245). When, in **"Contempt of Court—Almost,"** Sut lists a number of concrete examples to show what he means by "onregenerit human nater," the thread running through them all is people's arbitrary and mean-spirited enmity for each other. The example par excellence of this enmity is Dad: "{the bulldog pup} wer the only critter I ever know'd dad tu be good tu, an' narra pusson yet" (278). This enmity is antithetical to community and thus represents the basic transgression against Sut's idea of proper behavior. Against this manifestation of unregeneracy Sut directs the force of his comic sermons, which usually consist of practical jokes.

Such scapegoating, however, does not constitute a morality, for Sut does not believe people will change. Rather, his motivation is an impulsive desire to expose someone's pretense of being outside the basic fact of unregeneracy, for the postulate about human nature most emphatically includes Sut and is part of the meaning of his constant reference to himself as a "nat'ral born durn'd fool."[11] When Parson Bullen says that Sut is "a livin proof ove the hell-desarvin natur ove man" (59), no one understands that better than Sut himself. What galls Sut is when people like Bullen act as though they are clearly exempt from the same statement. "Well, durn my rags ef gittin ove religun ain't the city ove rayfuge now-a-days; yu jis' let a raskil git hissef cotch, an' maul'd, *fur his dam meanness,* an' he jines chuch jis' es soon es he kin straitch his face long enuf tu fill the pius standurd" (274, emphasis added). Thus Bullen is guilty of the sin of pride, a fault that hollows out Bullen's claim of respectability and, like Dad's meanness, raises a threat to community. Yet Sut's "sermons"

against meanness do not erase his own obviously mean acts; together they illustrate the complexity of his role as fool, both threatening and maintaining the amity fundamental to any community.

A corollary of human nature's unregenerate quality is the propensity to indulge one's appetite. The figure for such "sins of the flesh" is, again, Hoss Lovingood. When Sut's father discards the sign of his humanity, clothes, and behaves like both a horse and a steer, he reveals everyone's link to the animal world of mere appetite, body. Denial of that link by sheriffs and parsons constitutes part of the claim to respectability by such folks, and exposure of that link—entailing a diminution of respectability—is a standard outcome of *Yarns.* Sheriff Doltin, for example, is exposed as an adulterer. Moreover, all the preachers in the stories are exposed as worldly because they succumb to the desires of the body. Thus, a black Baptist preacher and a white, Hardshell Baptist preacher both are fond of whiskey (161, 184), a Methodist preacher is fond of food (161), and Sut's archenemy, the Methodist Parson Bullen, is fond of both, for among the items that fly out of Bullen's clothes as he tries to shake the lizards Sut has released up his pant leg are "fifteen shorten'd biskits, a boiled chicken, . . . a hunk ove terbacker, {and} a sprinkil ove whisky" (55). Parson Clapshaw is the apex of this enslavement to creature comfort, for he retires from circuit riding to marry the well-endowed Sicily Burns, possessed not only of good looks but a dowry substantial enough to set him up as storekeeper.[12]

Sut is most acutely aware of the weakness of the flesh in his dealings with Sicily Burns, whose charms he describes vividly and to whom he reacts like a comic version of the traditional lovesick swain. An Aristophanic embodiment of comic principle, Sut is all for food and drink and sex. His animus against respectable folks, moreover, goes beyond a pretense to be above those desires: "George, this worl am all 'rong enyhow, more temtashun than perventitive; ef hit wer ekal, I'd stand hit. What kin the ole prechurs an' the ugly wimen 'spect ove us, 'sposed es we ar tu sich invenshuns es {Sicily} am? Oh, hits jis' no use in thar talkin, an' groanin, an' sweatin tharsefs about hit; they mus' jis' upset nater ontu her hed, an keep her thar, ur shet up" (77). Sut does not frame his problem in moral terms. More fundamental than hypocrisy or other social forms of controlling desire, the problem is human nature itself. Because desire is temptation *and* is built into human nature, prevention could exist only if human nature were changed. In reality, desires can neither be always satisfied nor always controlled. From the viewpoint of the durn'd fool preacher, "univarsal onregenerit human nater" is a problem without a solution—something to be ridiculed, not rectified.

II

Giving Sut the habit of expressing himself with biblical allusions and making the concept of universal unregeneracy a theme of several tales signal the commitment by Harris to representing Sut-as-fool through the role of comic preacher. Two other concepts depend upon the idea of unregeneracy and round out Sut's "religion": tribulation on earth and retribution in the hereafter.

In his enumeration of examples of universal unregeneracy Sut points out that pain and disappointment—tribulations—are what stand between an individual and the grave (246). In another instance, when Sut imitates the voice of Sicily Burns as part of a scheme to scare her lover, Gus Fabin, he refers to signs and wonders in the air that signify their sin and then exhorts Fabin to begin a "rale strong devil skurin prayr, . . . fur thars vexashun ove sperit an' bodily tribulashun ahead fur us bof."[13] Sut's speech wonderfully parodies the sinner who has seen the error of her ways. While Sut is aware that tribulations are spiritual as well as physical in nature (71) and that the ultimate tribulation is hell (176), the comic perspective of *Yarns* emphasizes bodily pain, even for animals. When his howling dog runs past him in the street, a victim of some town prankster, Sut thinks of "Dad's ho'net tribulashun, an' felt that thar wur such a thing as a tribulashun at las'" (151-52). Of course, someone always looks as though he or she has been soundly thrashed by the end of a tale. When Sut begins to peel away his starched shirt from his body (**"Sut's New-Fangled Shirt"**), he calls the awful pain a "quick-stingin trebulashun" (33).

Such representations of physical pain, usually the direct result of Sut's machinations, are the standard fare of *Yarns*. Equally ubiquitous is the fright that accompanies the pain. This combination of fright and pain is roughly equivalent to the religious notion that people must suffer. One of the foolish traits qualifying Sut as mock preacher is his ability to "git intu more durn'd misfortnit skeery scrapes, than enybody, an' then run outen them faster, by golly, nor enybody" (172). Scares or scrapes are the colloquial version of tribulations. It is not surprising to point out that the plots of all the tales in *Sut Lovingood. Yarns Spun by a "Nat'ral Born Durn'd Fool"* are structured by someone's involvement in a scary scrape. Less apparent is the way in which such scares and scrapes are sometimes directly presented as tribulations that function as a purification of the sufferer. Examples are the pain Sut endures from his shirt, the scare Gus Fabin receives, and, as we shall see, the series of scares Sut doles out in **"Frustrating a Funeral."** Even in the stories where religious discourse is not directly employed, the basically religious idea of purification remains a motive, for Sut either consciously wishes to purify his community of meanness of spirit or unconsciously wishes to purify himself of such a spirit.

Perhaps Sut's unconscious desire to purify himself can be more properly described as a thoughtless want, like scratching an itch. Such a trope is more consonant with the comic tone of *Yarns.*

However much tribulation is presented as purifying, at times Sut's tales question the religious idea that tribulations lead to purification. Such contradiction should be seen as commensurate with Sut's role as trickster, by definition the playful enemy of boundaries. Scares may therefore cause someone's faith to weaken. Such is the case with Clapshaw the circuit rider when he sees Sut riding toward him at the height of Sut's tribulation with the soda powder he has drunk, thinking it was a love potion: "As I cum tarin along, {Clapshaw} hilt up his hans like he wanted tu pray fur me; but es I wanted sumthin tu reach furder, an' take a ranker holt nur his prars cud, I jis' rambled ahead. I wer hot arter a ten-hoss dubbil-actin steam paunch-pump, wif wun aind sock'd deep intu my soda lake, an' a strong manbody doctur at tuther; hit wer my *big want* jis' then. *He* tuck a skeer, es I wer cumin strait fur him; his faith gin out" (82-83). The circuit rider's fear of physical harm is matched by Sut's desire for physical aid that reaches further and has an ability to "scratch" more vigorously than does prayer. Sut's practical response to his situation is, in fact, his fundamental reaction to tribulation. "When I'se in trubbil, skeer, ur tormint, I dus but wun thing, an' that's onresistabil, onekeled, an' durn'd fas' runnin, an' I jis' keeps at hit till I gits cumfort" (71). Such a response emphasizes the foolish presentation of religious discourse, not its morality. While Sut can unleash tribulation designed to purify the soul and can speak in biblical phrasing about manyfold tribulations this side of hell (176), he remains a *comic* preacher, one whose wish for fun is as least as strong as his wish for chastisement. While Sut can be earnest in his use of religious discourse to speak of the failings of people (himself included), he never loses his basic parodic function, to reduce spiritual values to material ones. Thus the comfort of spirituality will always lose out to the comfort gained from physically running from trouble because for Sut running is so immediate and instinctual.

I have been arguing that notions about what constitutes right and wrong behavior lie at the core of Sut's role as fool preacher. Such notions, of course, imply a system of justice. In Calvinistic terms, this system of justice becomes the idea of "divine retribution," God's punishment for transgressing sacred law. God's retribution is often represented by the threat of the devil and hell. That Sut maintains a belief in the idea of divine retribution is clear when we examine in some detail the stories **"Sut Lovingood's Daddy, Acting Horse"** and **"Sut's New-Fangled Shirt,"** which begin *Yarns,* as well as **"Dad's Dog School,"** which ends it. All are concerned with Sut's relationship to his family.

The opening stories should be read as complements of each other, Sut's mishap with a new, freshly starched shirt commenting upon Hoss Lovingood's encounter with a swarm of hornets while "acting horse." Though Sut does nothing to put his father into the role of victim, once Hoss Lovingood has jumped into the creek to avoid the hornets, Sut taunts his father, prompting vows of revenge and the necessity for Sut's departure. "Them words . . . mus' be my las, knowin dad's onmollified nater. I broke frum them parts, an' sorter cum over yere tu the copper mines" (27). Harris thus provides the rationale for Sut's career as fool, inasmuch as his departure is triggered by laughter, as well as the rationale for his presence in Ducktown. Harris's representation of Sut's break with his family follows the historical pattern for many actual antebellum men, the son breaking with the father by leaving home to seek a new fortune, in this case a piece of the economic boom associated with the copper mines near the Hiwasee River in Polk County.[14] In effect, the next story, **"Sut's New-Fangled Shirt,"** reveals the guilt Sut feels about that break. Summing up his misadventure for his favorite interlocutor, George, Sut says:

> Hits a retribushun sartin, the biggest kine ove a preacher's regular retribushun, what am to be foun' in the Holy Book.
>
> Dus yu mine my racin dad, wif sum ho'nets, an' so forth, intu the krick?
>
> Well, this am what cums ove hit. I'll drownd mysef, see ef I don't, that is ef I don't die frum that hellfired shut.
>
> (35-36)

Sut's familiarity with the fundamentalist emphasis on the ultimate retribution of hell-fire is apparently a long-standing one, as the last story in *Yarns,* **"Dad's Dog School,"** makes clear. Like the lead tale about dad "acting horse," this narrative recounts events from Sut's background, in this case when he was "'bout sixteen" (278). Also like the lead tale, this story partly functions as Sut's explanation for his own chronically foolish behavior: he is his father's child. But Sut sees the ridiculous attempt to train their dog, which takes place on a Sunday, as a parody of Sabbath solemnity too. He describes as a family devotion (286) his father's crawling inside the hide of a freshly skinned steer in order to teach their bulldog pup to grab its opponent and not let go. The joke has the fearful piquancy for Sut of any well-delivered blasphemy because he is quite aware that his family's behavior profanes the Lord's day: "I hearn a new soun in the thicket, an' hit bein Sunday, I wer sorter 'spectin a retribushun ove sum nater" (285).

But the sound of retribution Sut hears is only Squire Haney going to meeting on his horse.[15] Haney is one of the local gentry—money lender, landowner, and elder in the church. His piety is comically revealed through the actions of his livestock, for his horse is of a pious turn of mind (it does not kick, gallop, or chew its bridle) and his hens never lay on Sunday. The squire gives the whole of Sunday to the Lord, controls the purse strings of the church, and chastises backsliders. "He wer secon enjineer ove a mersheen, made outen . . . thin minded pussons, fur the pupus, es they sed, ove squelchin sin in the neighborhood, amung sich domestic heathins es us" (287). Squire Haney also represents the prototype for all the hypocrites that Sut will attack in his career at Ducktown. The Squire is known not only for his activities with the local church but also for "shaving notes of hand," that is, purchasing personal IOUs at a price reduced below the legal or customary rate in order to turn a quick profit. As if this kind of financial manipulation were not enough, Haney supplements the action by giving his victims religious tracts warning against the vanity of storing up earthly goods. Moreover, Sut's mother suggests Haney's sexual impropriety when she says that the squire should leave or he will be "late fur meetin, speshully ef he stops at *Missis Givinses*" (289).

That sarcastic remark from Mam is hardly an offhand one. When Squire Haney comes out from the woods on his horse and interrupts the Lovingoods' family devotion, he chastises them for tormenting animals and breaking the Sabbath, calling them "onregenerits" and demanding to know the whereabouts of the "patriark ove this depraved famerly" (288). The joke is that the patriarch is right in front of him, sewn into the hide of a steer and bellowing with pain because the bulldog pup now has a lockjaw hold on his nose. Yet Sut's reaction to the squire's sudden appearance is not a religious fear of Sabbath breaking but a social shame for the family's way of living, encompassed both by his dad's obvious folly and by Mam's "bar laigs an' open collar." Sut feels an overpowering urge to run from the scene but does not because he notices "the squar, blazin look mam met [the Squire] wif" (286). If she could stand the storm, Sut decides he can too. Mam's answer to the squire's question matches her look: "Look a-yere, Squire Haney . . . I'se {the} patriark jis' now; . . . yu'd bes' trot along tu yer meetin. This am a *privit soshul famerly 'musement* an' hit needs no wallin up ove eyes, nur groanin, nur second han low-quartered pray'rs tu make hit purfeck, 'sides, we's got no notes tu shave, nur gals ole enuf tu convart, so yu' better jis' go way wif yer four-laig'd, bal-faced pulpit, an' preach tu sich es yersef, sumwhat else; go 'long Squire, that's a good feller" (288-89).

Mam's answer reveals several things. First, she demonstrates the fierce southern pride that resents even the slightest aspersion against one's behavior and the equally fierce independence that resents any intrusion into one's privacy. But more to the point is Mam's translation of these qualities, which characterized all classes of the southern white population, into a blistering attack on the morality of one who sets himself up as a paragon of virtue in the community. Though my argument about Sut's foolish use of religious discourse downplays any consistent intent to use that discourse for moral purposes, clearly Mam's awareness of Squire Haney's worldliness (his financial dealings) and sensuality (Mrs. Givins and the reference to girls old enough to convert) provides Sut with a model for detecting hypocrisy. Moreover, Mam's response to Haney's righteousness illustrates the relationship Sut will maintain toward religion: a nonmeeting, quasibelief in evangelical Christianity laced, however, with comic, folkish attitudes. We have a sense of this mixture even before Squire Haney arrives when Mam reacts to her husband's plan for training the pup: "Lovingood, yu'll keep on wif yer devilmint an' nonsense, ontil yu fetch the day ove jedgement ontu our bar heds sum night, kerthrash, afore hits time, ur some uther ailment—collery—measils—pollygamy, ur sum sich like, jis' see ef yu don't" (279-80). The incident with Squire Haney, then, reveals Mam as the probable source of Sut's inchoate morality and considerable familiarity with the Bible and Christian tenets. Dad as the model for foolishness, Mam for perspicacity—both parents contribute to Sut as comic preacher.

If Mam should be thought of as Sut's role model for his preaching ways, her behavior in **"Dad's Dog School"** toward her husband provides a model for the comic manifestation of those preaching ways too: she beats Hoss Lovingood, still in the steer's hide on all fours and still trying to break the dog's hold, with a wooden bean-pole. This penultimate scene of the tale emblemizes the usual physical retribution of Sut's comic sermons. In addition, the scene creates an allegory basic to *Sut Lovingood. Yarns Spun by a "Nat'ral Born Durn'd Fool."* Mam represents conscience, not religiously orthodox but sincere. Dad is *the* symbol of original sin and the unregenerate, representing "the blind bull, Human nater" (123), that deserves to be punished, needs to be chastised, to achieve salvation. This allegory suggests the historical fact that most men in the antebellum South did not join churches while most women did and then tried to convert their stubborn husbands.[16] The allegory also represents what comes closest to morality in Sut's behavior: he is all too aware of his replication of Dad's unregenerate fool nature while, like Mam, he maintains his antipathy against those, like Dad or Haney, who refuse to acknowledge their foolish or hypocritical natures.

In *Yarns,* retribution from God often means evoking the devil. For Sut personally, Satan is never far away, and when he dreams of things that frighten him, the list includes the devil and hell (69, 299). This sense of the devil's presence is partly attributable to folk belief in supernatural powers, an attitude exemplified even by

Clapshaw, the circuit rider married to Sicily Burns who "believes in 'witches, an' warlocks, an' long nebbed things'" (j). Sut "b'leves strong in ghosts, an' in forewarnins too" (213). For most of the folk, the devil was a constant presence. Thus, when a man from North Carolina is caught up in a trick perpetrated by Sut, he says, "H——l's busted plumb open, an' this yere mountain's full ove the devils" (g), and one woman, fortunate to be only a spectator of another trick, says that what she saw must be "the Devil arter a tax collector" (47). Sut's profound belief in the nearby presence of the devil matches the evangelical emphasis on the necessary justice of God. His attitude toward the devil, however, is more complicated than most. When Sheriff Doltin says Sut has "'play'd hell,'" and Sut replies, "'Folks generlly sez that's my trade'" (259), clearly all concerned believe Sut to be a first-rate troublemaker of the sort usually referred to as a hell-raiser.

But, if Sut usually plays hell in the sense of behaving wildly and unsociably, at other times he can sound so much like a true preacher using hell-fire and brimstone that he seems to lose his parodic function and occupy the figurative center of his community. Sut "preaching" against a tavern, for example, says it is the worst place this side of hell, with a "brimstone retribushun . . . a-follerin clost arter hit" (179). Doggery owners are said to help the devil catch sinners (221), but being a tavern owner means losing one's soul: "When the devil takes a likin tu a feller, an' wants tu make a sure thing ove gittin him, he jis' puts hit intu his hed to open a catfish tavern" (177-78).

In **"Frustrating a Funeral"** Sut demonstrates more completely his ability to play hell and uphold traditional values, as a preacher would invoke demons in a sermon to bring sinners to an awareness of their ways. Sut finds himself an uninvited mourner at the wake of a slave because one of the town doctors wants the cadaver for dissection. Sut wants to avoid digging up the grave, so his plan is to substitute a drunk mourner for the corpse, but he is not satisfied with a simple swap. Major, the drunken slave, is made to look like "a purfeck dogratype ove the devil, tuck while he wer smokin mad 'bout sum raskil . . . jinin meetin on his deathbed, an' 'scapin" (212-13), while the mortal remains of Seize also resemble the Evil One, complete with snakes and a pitchfork. With Major installed in the coffin, Sut commences his exhortation of sinners, using Seize.

His first victim is Simon, known for preaching among his fellow slaves. At the moment Simon sees the "skeer makin mersheen" (213) Sut has made of Seize, Sut "imitates" the devil's voice, accusing Simon of stealing corn, which in fact Sut had seen him do. In a panic, Simon falls out the door, faints, and then runs off. More victims follow, including Mr. Hunnicut and Mrs. Loftin, symbolically accused of adultery by Sut when he tells

Mrs. Hunnicut he saw the two "way up in the air, ridin a-straddil ove a burnin ladder" (218). Both Mrs. Hunnicut and her black cook believe the sign, the cook saying that she "know dis tree munf Missis Loftin fotch de debil heah" (219). When Major wakes up in the coffin as it is on its way to the cemetery, he frightens not only all those in the procession but also (with the help of Sut's voice) the doggery keeper and the sheriff. The doctor Sut was supposed to help is especially included in Sut's list of sinners because, Sut says, a look at Seize "wud take away {the doctor's} appertite fur grave-yards . . . an' mout even make him jine meetins. I cudn't tell how much good hit mout du the onb'lever" (214). Perhaps more than any other tale except **"Sut's Sermon,"** **"Frustrating a Funeral"** reads like a deliberate effort on Sut's part to "preach a sermon," in this case using artful representations of hell-fire to chastise sinners. Nevertheless, Sut does not lose an essentially playful attitude about his own behavior. Finishing up the grotesquely comic tale, Sut says he performed two Christian duties: one, he buried Seize; two, he "minister'd ontu Wright's doggery, an' run hit till . . . hit went dry" (226). This presentation of religious discourse typifies Sut as mock preacher, for any sense of moral intent is undercut by the joke enwrapping the pious sentiment. Sut is not a parson *manque* but a parson *malgré lui.*

III

As comic fool, Sut has a license to flaunt order, and his antics target secular as well as sacred law. Throughout *Yarns* this flaunting produces ironic results because Sut's role as comic preacher functions to maintain community values. However, such improper maintenance would not be necessary if officials, such as preachers and sheriffs, behaved properly. In Sut's mind, phony sheriffs are indistinguishable from phony parsons, a basic attitude suggested in an insult directed against a judge by Wirt Staples, a good friend of Sut's: "yu ole false apostil ove lor" (251).

The intertwining of sacred and secular law is made clear in a number of places in *Yarns*. A particularly good example comes at the beginning of **"Rare Ripe Garden-Seed,"** which leads off a trio of stories (**"Contempt of Court—Almost"** and **"Trapping a Sheriff"** follow) that collectively tells of the downfall of the local sheriff, John Doltin, who is exposed as an adulterer by Sut, his friend Wirt Staples, and Wirt's wife Susan. At the outset, Sut speaks of his first scare. He is just a child, dressed in nothing but a shift that is split from neck to tail and held together with a drawstring and a hem. The scare will come from a sheriff's sudden appearance to confiscate the family's furniture, presumably for debts owed, but describing his attire causes Sut to digress, asking George what he would do if Sut came to George's city church dressed the same

and sat in George's pew. This image of license in sacred precincts is followed by a comic food chain, bishops at the top, that parodies the Great Chain of Being, implying that high church officials always get to the trough first. The flaunting of church-going decorum and the reducing of spiritual leadership to gluttony prefaces the tales about the sheriff because in them Sut and his accomplices will flaunt an official of secular law, revealing him to be like the bishops—nothing more than appetite. At bottom, the issue is hypocrisy or the *appearance* of respectability. The stories about preachers and sheriffs emphasize their hollow respectability and undeserved pride. Pride is dangerous to a democratic community because it stresses a better-than-thou attitude. This "sin" is doubly threatening when parsons and sheriffs act as though they are above the laws they preach or enforce.

I place "sin" in quotes because Sut's homespun backwoods dialect rewrites the religious discourse of *Yarns*. Thus tribulations become "skeers," while original sin and the consequent unregeneracy of human nature become "dam meanness." Because the enmity represented by meanness and pride is virtually a universal condition that threatens community by emphasizing separateness and strife, it would seem that *Yarns* argues against the existence of "grace," which might be defined as the neighborly amity that forms the bedrock of any community. This gloomy conclusion seems justified by the numerous examples of adulterous couples in the tales. How authentic can a community be when its backbone—the family—is represented by so many shams? Historically, Ducktown, like any antebellum southern community, no doubt had its share of worthy families, parsons, and sheriffs. And while *Yarns* may emphasize negative behavior for comic purposes, an example of an admirable family does exist in the persons of Susan and Wirt Staples. In effect, the Stapleses represent grace and salvation, the possibility of people who transcend mean-spirited behavior and unneighborly pride.

My use of theological vocabulary, especially transcendence, seems to make Susan and Wirt saints. They of course are as unorthodox an example of a worthy family as Sut is a preacher. Indeed, a whiskey-soaked boast by Wirt makes clear that he is a backwoods roarer (250-51).[17] And Susan is certainly as fun-loving and eager to unmask damn meanness as Sut, given her role as the architect of Sheriff Doltin's punishment. As comic versions of saints, Wirt and Susan do not stretch their faces to fit the dour mold of what passes for piety, nor do they pretend to abjure the body while in fact indulging it illicitly. Instead, descriptions of them suggest their physical beauty, Wirt with the strength typical of the roarer (253) and Susan "es purty es a hen canary" (260). Significantly, Susan's good looks are accompanied by a good nature that contrasts with the other beautiful woman of *Yarns,* Sicily Burns, a good nature manifested in Susan's demeanor, especially toward Wirt: "She aint one ove yure she-cat wimmin, allers spittin an' groanin, an' swellin thar tails 'bout thar vartu. She never talks a word about hit, no more nor if she didn't hev eny; an' she hes es true a heart es ever beat agin a shiff hem, . . . a-smilin an' a-flashin her talkin eyes lovinly at her hansum husbun" (260, 262).

Susan and Wirt's love represents the ties that bind not just family life but the neighborly life of a true community. Doltin's adulterous behavior cuts those ties, for he only pretends to live as a neighbor, a pretense dramatized by his answer when Wirt asks what Doltin is doing trying to kiss Susan: "'Yer—yer wife got her coatail tangled in the briars, an' I wer jis' in a neighborly way *ontanglin her*'" (264-65). Doltin's revises the rule "love thy neighbor" to "love thy neighbor till her husband comes home."

When parsons and sheriffs, pillars of communal law and order, actually enact disorder, the chaotic punishment that Sut constructs for them represents just deserts. The license of the fool is especially effective at revealing licentious behavior, and as self-proclaimed fool, Sut comically inverts what is already inverted when he appropriates the role of these so-called upholders of the law by righteously doling out justice for their transgressions. This inversion is obvious in Sut's use of comic deadpan to mimic piety, as when Sut fools Parson Bullen at the camp meeting by appearing with a face indicative of sorrow for sins (51) or when he mocks the rhetoric and manner of a "hard-shell" preacher (185). Another good example is Sut's retort to Mrs. Rogers, who implicitly accuses Sut and his friends of stealing her eggs and butter by sarcastically noting that their presence near her springhouse is not the holding of meeting. In a mock-pious fashion Sut claims that Hen Baily has been poisoned by Mrs. Rogers's dairy products (thus confirming her worst fears) when in fact he has swallowed turpentine and a live lizard: "Sez I, mouns'us solimn, straitenin mysef up wif foldid arms, 'Missis Rogers, . . . take a look at sum ove yu're work. That ar a-dyin feller bein; let jis' a few ove yer bowils melt, an' pour out rite yere in pity an' rey-morse'" (205). Sut not only uses deadpan to counter her reference to the crowd's unsanctified status but he also implies a rebuke for her notorious habit of feeding her workhands with buttermilk so sour "hit wud eat hits way outen a yeathen crock in wun nite" (206). Sut's consciousness of such mean-spirited acts and his readiness to chastise for them might have us agree with Sicily Burns's mother when she claims that Sut is not "one half es durn'd a fool es ole Burns, an' ten times more ove a Cristshun than Clapshaw" (105).

When Susan prepares a supper for Wirt and Sut after they have planned how to trap Doltin, the three at table constitute a community of comic saints. Sut refers to the meal as "a rale suckit-rider's supper, whar the 'oman ove the hous' wer a rich b'lever" (261), and in laughable fashion that is exactly what the scene represents. Sut *is* the preacher being served a lavish repast by a household that believes in his comic dogma, which extols generosity and states that the mean-spirited and hypocritical shall be punished or, as Sut puts it, initiated "intu the seekrit ove home-made durnashun" (263). The supper, lovingly recounted by Sut in copious detail, constitutes meeting for the "saints" Susan and Wirt and Sut. In keeping with the comic principle of reducing spiritual and moral values to a material plane, a principle about to be prosecuted upon the body of Sheriff Doltin, the supper is a parodic communion supper, celebrating not what bread and wine might symbolize but celebrating instead the material symbols themselves, food and drink. However, for all the amusement this inversion is designed to create, the supper also functions to bind people to a common purpose, just as Sut's role of fool places him at the margin yet allows him to mock the center in such a way as to usurp its power. The supper establishes a comic community marked by a spirit of generosity.

IV

Exemplified by an exalted notion of hospitality, a generous spirit was an important feature of southern culture before the Civil War. The supper taken by Sut with Susan and Wirt Staples presents a comic embodiment of that ideal. Such a presentation underscores the ambiguity of Sut playing the fool. On the one hand, he seems a champion of a core southern value; on the other, he remains a comic figure on the margin. As a self-proclaimed nat'ral born durn'd fool, Sut in effect represents an exaggeration of the fringe status of the mountaineer; that is, even in the mountains of east Tennessee, Sut the fool would be on the edge of his community, and that sense of being on the outside is doubled when he moves to Ducktown. I have argued, however, that by virtue of his homespun religious rhetoric Sut assumes a central role in the maintenance of an idea of community that could characterize a place like Ducktown. I now want to raise the stakes and claim that he is even more important. Sut is not only potentially the center of a particular southern community; he should also be seen as the comic bard of the Old South. Kenneth Lynn once said that "Sut" is an ugly contraction of "South." He was right. After all, the comic is a species of the ugly. Sut, as a yarnspinning, whiskey-drinking pleasure seeker, represents, in his own comic and not-so-pretty way, values besides generosity that were important to the antebellum South's sense of identity: leisure, liberty, and the communal function of talking.[18]

Leisure was probably as crucial as generosity to a sense of southern identity. I do not mean that no one in the antebellum South valued hard work or that hard work, and plenty of it, did not happen. However, hard work was not raised to an ideal in the South the way it was in New England. Undoubtedly this difference owed some of its existence to the slave system, which encouraged southerners to lead or aspire to an aristocratic life of ease. But it also stemmed from preexisting facts of climate and soil conditions as well as the Old World culture of many immigrants to the southern portions of North America. For very specific material reasons the southern white, whether high or low on the economic scale, attempted to create a life-style that did not emphasize personal hard labor.[19]

Though Sut seems to be that most notorious of stereotypes about the leisured life of a southerner, poor white trash, *Yarns* does sometimes show him capable of work. For example, he builds Betts Carr an ash hopper (30, 32). And Sut apparently earns money from a still, if his routine walk through town can be taken as a round of deliveries (158).[20] Nevertheless, work in the usual sense does not occupy much of Sut's life. His true avocations are *drinking* whiskey and telling stories. For Sut, these activities are virtually the same. When he narrates, Sut distills raw experience into something as pleasurable as whiskey—and as ubiquitous to the social scene. In a community where leisure time is highly valued, whiskey is very often the complement to yarns: one is poured into the mouth and the other pours from the mouth. Whiskey facilitates the yarn pouring forth, which in turn necessitates more whiskey pouring. In the comic, backwoods stories of the antebellum South, a tipping of a flask or bottle can precede a tale as surely as a throat-clearing call begins a bardic singer's epic song. As a yarnspinner who sounds like a comic preacher and makes whiskey, Sut unofficially challenges Parson Bullen, who is known for selling adulterated whiskey (86). Bullen as Sut's chief rival thus epitomizes those people against whom Sut always directs his comic sermons, the mean-spirited. In effect, Sut's impromptu campaigns are always against bad spirits.

If the South valued generosity and leisure, it also placed a premium on liberty, and boyhood in *Yarns* represents the comic version of liberty: freedom from responsibility. His intention for making the book, Sut tells us in his preface, is to raise "sich a laugh es is remembered [in] keerless boyhood" (xi). Sut, whose age one can never be sure of but who has white hair and is apparently old enough to remember what George and Lum did thirty-five years ago, never acts his age. His freedom from responsibility—manifested by his whiskey drinking, story telling, and wild pranks—makes him seem to deserve the epithet "yung man" a preacher gives him (184). Indeed, Sut's pranks are essentially boyish, designed to disrupt the serious business of society. When a number of Knoxvillians plot against a Yankee razor grinder who sets himself up to lecture to that southern community, Sut says that the Yankee's lecture

should not have included a comment about the depravity of man in boyhood, "fur hit wer boys what he wer dealin wif jis' then" (63). Sut's story about George and Lum Jones when they are thirteen, a story of eavesdropping on a meeting of Masons to learn their secrets, refers to the boys as "the durndest littil back-slidin devils outen jail" (116). At bottom, all the "devilment" that goes on in *Yarns* consists of boyish pranks.[21]

In this vein, *Sut Lovingood. Yarns Spun by a "Nat'ral Born Durn'd Fool"* resembles *The Adventures of Tom Sawyer*; both underline the liberty of youth. Despite Sut's interrupting George's eulogy to boyhood that is sentimental even by the standards of *Tom Sawyer*, Sut would agree when George speaks of a "happy, ragged, thoughtless" (115) quality of boyhood, for Sut embodies what George describes, a pleasurable freedom from rational thought. Yet, if *Tom Sawyer* is a hymn to boyhood, *Yarns* is a drinking song that comically emphasizes the continued presence of the boy in the man instead of a nostalgia for a boy forever gone. Moreover, Tom Sawyer's world does not contain the elemental level of fear and desire and gratification that Sut's world represents. Finally, Tom never remains for long outside his community; Sut never remains for long inside his. Like a natural fool, like a child, Sut seems to be excused from the censure of rational, responsible behavior.

The last aspect of Sut's character that suggests his role as comic bard involves the communal function of talking in the Old South. In a culture that valued oratory, both political and religious, as its highest form of literature, narrating, whether for information or for entertainment, assumed a vital role, binding together its participants with a sharing of events that established and reinforced the values of the social group. In this role, Sut as champion yarnspinner assumes a larger-than-life status. Yet Sut's talk, mirroring his role as fool, operates ambiguously in his community, whether at a particular or at a general level. His wild tales, reeking of whiskey and a careless freedom, partly function as the antics of sacred clowns do for Zuni Indians—as encouragement for a mass return of repressed impulses. For a brief interval, the audience is allowed to laugh at accounts or displays of how not to behave. It is this beyond-the-pale quality that is so celebrated or lamented in discussions of Sut's stories. My argument, however, suggests that a conservative thread also runs through *Yarns* and that Sut upholds values that were central to the Old South, even going so far as to mimic the religious rhetoric of evangelical Christianity. Perhaps narrating itself constitutes Sut's most conservative act. By plotting a story out of his wild, nonsensical actions, in effect Sut makes a bid to be taken as a rational, adult member of a community. There is truth in that last assertion if we also do not forget how the fool always undermines such effects as he apparently achieves them.

Sut's power comes not from being the bard of the Old South who speaks as a preacher but from playing hell with that role.

"He who would become wise must persist in his folly." William Blake's proverb of hell seems particularly apt for Sut Lovingood, who dispenses his own kind of perverse wisdom when he reminds us that he is a natural born durned fool. The notion that there is a wisdom in foolishness looks back to a favored figure of the Renaissance, the wise fool. My argument that Sut is a mock preacher insists on the similarity extending to the Christian background in which the tradition of the fool arose. As Blake in *The Marriage of Heaven and Hell* sought to overturn conventional wisdom about how to lead a religious life, Harris uses **Sut Lovingood. Yarns Spun by a "Nat'ral Born Durn'd Fool"** to challenge those who are complacent about their rectitude. That is the wisdom that may be extracted from the tales. But their comic power comes from the marvelous exploitation of the inherent ambiguity of the role of the fool. Licensed to do what ought not be done and thus to draw ridicule, the fool disrupts in order to remind a community of its self in two ways: that it too is ridiculous and that it should be better. Like the licensed fools in medieval and Renaissance European cultures or Amerindian cultures such as the Zuni, Sut is meant to entertain the audience with his presentations of chaos, but he is also meant to warn the audience against its own brands of foolishness. Like all fools, Sut helps willy-nilly to define community. Of course, Sut carries out this function in his own way. If *Yarns* argues for a proper way to behave in a community, that argument is not so much a moral imperative as an impulsive lashing out against those who threaten the community, a tongue-lashing that presents literal lashings of such undesirables. Those lashings are Sut's own style of comic wisdom.

Notes

1. Milton Rickels, *George Washington Harris* (New York: Twayne, 1965), 78, 83, 86, 96. Some of Rickels's comments appear in the selection reprinted for this collection. Kenneth S. Lynn, *Mark Twain and Southwestern Humor* (Boston: Little, Brown, 1959), 135-36, expresses a similar view on community and authority. For a view much closer to mine, see David C. Estes, "Sut Lovingood at the Camp Meeting: A Practical Joker Among the Backwoods Believers," *Southern Quarterly* 25 (1987): 53-65. Estes not only sees Sut as part of his community but also sees him as a "true pastor" (64). And for a discussion of Sut's public role that uses the notion of playing hell in a very different context, see John Wenke, "*Sut Lovingood's Yarns* {*sic*} and the Politics of Performance," *Studies in American Fiction* 15 (1987):

199-210. I have based my argument solely on Harris's book. The edition used is *"Sut Lovingood Yarns": A Facsimile of the 1867 Dick and Fitzgerald Edition,* ed. M. Thomas Inge (Memphis: Saint Lukes Press, 1987), and all parenthetical page insertions refer to this edition. Despite being published in 1867 and having one or two references to the Civil War, *Yarns* gives the feeling of taking place before the war and I will refer to the community represented in it as antebellum.

2. William Willeford, *The Fool and His Scepter: A Study in Clowns and Jesters and Their Audiences* (Chicago: Northwestern University Press, 1969), 133. See also Barbara Swain, *Fools and Folly During the Middle Ages and the Renaissance* (New York: Columbia University Press, 1932); Enid Welsford, *The Fool: His Social and Literary History* (London: Faber and Faber, 1935), esp. chap. 3; and Sandra Billington, *A Social History of the Fool* (New York: Saint Martin's Press, 1984).

3. Willeford, *Fool and His Scepter,* 158.

4. Although the town Sut lives in (or near) is never named and seems to be near Knoxville, we know that Harris met the historical Sut Miller in a place called Ducktown, in the southeastern corner of Tennessee. In order to emphasize the historical dimension of Sut's role as comic preacher, I will refer to his community as Ducktown. See Ben Harris McClary, "The Real Sut," in this volume [*Sut Lovingood's Nat'ral Born Yarnspinner: Essays on George Washington Harris* (Tuscaloosa: University of Alabama Press, 1996)], and Robert E. Barclay, *Ducktown Back in Raht's Time* (Chapel Hill: University of North Carolina Press, 1946). I follow Victor Turner's use of liminal: "Liminal to Liminoid in Play, Flow, Ritual: An Essay in Comparative Symbology," *Rice University Studies* 60 (1974): 53-92; and *The Ritual Process: Structure and Anti-Structure* (1969; reprint, Ithaca: Cornell University Press, 1977).

5. Ernest E. Leisy, "Jesse Holmes, The 'Fool Killer,'" *Publications of the Texas Folklore Society* 8 (1930): 152-54, and Ralph S. Boggs, "Running Down the Fool Killer," *Publications of the Texas Folklore Society* 14 (1938): 169-73, discuss a particular fool killer in nearby North Carolina, Jesse Holmes, who was popular particularly during the Civil War but also in the late 1850s. The fool killer is mentioned twice in *Yarns*: "Trapping a Sheriff" (264) and "Sut Lovingood's Chest Story" (h). In "Sut Lovingood Come to Life," Harris's first postwar Sut sketch, Sut is appointed "fool killer Gineril." The piece appeared originally in the *Nashville Union and American*, 3 May 1866. See M. Thomas Inge, ed., *High Times and Hard Times:*

Sketches and Tales by George Washington Harris (Nashville: Vanderbilt University Press, 1967), 276-81.

6. Donald G. Mathews, *Religion in the Old South* (Chicago: University of Chicago Press, 1977); John B. Boles, "Evangelical Protestantism in the Old South: From Religious Dissent to Cultural Dominance," in *Religion of the Old South,* ed. Charles R. Wilson (Jackson: University of Mississippi Press, 1985), 13-34; David Edwin Harrell, Jr., "The Evolution of Plain-Folk Religion in the South, 1835-1920," and Wade Clark Roof, "Religious Change in the American South: The Case of the Unchurched," in *Varieties of Southern Religious Experience,* ed. Samuel S. Hill (Baton Rouge: Louisiana State University Press, 1988), 24-51, 192-210. Compare to the way ritual clowns function in Pueblo Indian communities: Louis A. Hieb, "Meaning and Mismeaning: Toward an Understanding of the Ritual Clown," in *New Perspectives on the Pueblos,* ed. Alfonso Ortiz (Albuquerque: University of New Mexico Press, 1972), 163-95.

7. See Benjamin Franklin Fisher IV's article in this collection, "George Washington Harris and Supernaturalism."

8. Compare to Rickels's idea of Sut and religion: "Sut exists outside Christianity" (100); "Sut escapes the Christian conception of man. . . . He is the creator of his own being" (101)—both comments are in the selection for this collection; and Elmo Howell, "Timon in Tennessee: The Moral Fervor of George Washington Harris," also in this volume.

9. By 1850 only 20 percent of the clergy had any formal training. See Mathews, *Religion,* 23, 30, and esp. 85, 96. Also see *The Autobiography of Peter Cartwright, The Backwoods Preacher,* ed. W. P. Strickland (New York: Carlton and Porter, 1856), 4-7.

10. Biblical allusions include a light hidden under a basket (269), girding one's loins (191), and the call from labor to refreshment (119). Other references include Judas Iscariot (38), Job (76), Belteshazzar, comically spelled Beltashashur (79, 119), Joseph and Potiphar's wife (87-88), Beelzebub (83), Samson and the Philistines (191).

11. In medieval and Renaissance traditions, a "natural" fool is someone who is mentally defective, an idiot. Clearly, Sut is not an idiot in this sense, which makes him an "artificial" fool, acting foolishly for the entertainment and possible edification of others. See Welsford, *The Fool,* and Heather Arden, *Fool Plays: A Study of Satire in the "Sot-*

tie" (Cambridge: Cambridge University Press, 1980). Rickels, *George Washington Harris,* sees Sut as closest to this artificial or court fool (105), yet he also thinks Sut personifies "mindlessness" (98). Noel Polk criticizes Rickels, saying, "Sut is not mindless and he is no fool," in "The Blind Bull, Human Nature: Sut Lovingood and the Damned Human Race," which is reprinted in this collection. Polk sees the phrase "nat'ral born durn'd fool" as ironic self-deprecation and Sut as a backwoods Socrates, a moral gadfly. This claim, however, does not exclude Sut from the role of the artificial fool. Sut may be, as many have argued, a backwoods version of the "wise fool" so favored by Renaissance writers, but the degree of intention in any show of wisdom or satiric moral fervor is debatable. In my view, the fool figure always embodies the potential for exhibiting mindless clowning as well as wisdom. Compare to M. Thomas Inge, "Sut Lovingood: An Examination of the Nature of a 'Nat'ral Born Durn'd Fool,'" *Tennessee Historical Quarterly* 19 (1960): 231-51.

12. See Mathews, *Religion,* 86, for the Methodist habit of riding circuit for a while before marrying—often, a woman of means.

13. "Sut Lovingood's Chest Story," f. Inge's facsimile edition includes this tale left out of the original and paginates it with letters. See his "A Note on the Text."

14. Barclay characterizes the mining boom as follows: "the year 1850 . . . ushered in a decade that proved to be the most interesting and the most exciting that Ducktown had seen. . . . Every element which entered into similar stampedes throughout mining districts of the West in later years was present in the rush to Ducktown. Here was the scene of one of the most hectic scrambles of fortune seekers in the South" (*Ducktown,* 38). By 1854, the year Harris probably met Sut (Rickels, *George Washington Harris,* 28-29), the area was "thronged to overflowing with ardent speculators" (31-32).

15. The text also refers to this character as Squire Hanley.

16. See Mathews, *Religion,* for the role of women in the churches, 101-20.

17. Compare to Polk's description of Wirt and Susan. It is interesting that the snatch of a drinking song Wirt sings as part of his ring-tailed roarer's exhibition is called by Sut "one vearse ove the sixteen hundred an' ninety-ninth *hyme*" (251, emphasis added).

18. Lynn, *Mark Twain,* 137. The idea of the comic as a kind of ugliness is found in Aristotle's "Poetics"

(1449a, 32-37). The word he uses, "to geloion," is usually rendered as "the ridiculous," but it could be translated as "the laughable." See the Revised Oxford Translation of *The Complete Works of Aristotle,* ed. Jonathan Barnes, Bollingen Series 71, 2 vols. (Princeton: Princeton University Press, 1984), 2:2319. A discussion of the values of the Old South leads into a number of debates. The ground of these discussions is whether or not the antebellum South possessed a "character" distinctive from the North and thus generative of its own values. For a good overview of the historians' debate on this issue see Drew Gilpin Faust, "The Peculiar South Revisited: White Society, Culture, and Politics in the Antebellum Period, 1800-1860," in *Interpreting Southern History,* ed. John B. Boles and Evelyn Thomas Nolen (Baton Rouge: Louisiana State University Press, 1987), 78-119. Influential in making the argument for a distinct southern world view is the work of Eugene Genovese, starting with *The Political Economy of Slavery: Studies in the Economy and Society of the Slave South* (New York: Pantheon Books, 1965). Faust lists Genovese's later work. See also Edward Shapiro, "Frank L. Owsley and the Defense of Southern Identity," *Tennessee Historical Quarterly* 36 (1977): 75-94; Bertram Wyatt-Brown, *Southern Honor: Ethics and Behavior in the Old South* (New York: Oxford University Press, 1982); Randolph B. Campbell, "Planters and Plainfolks: The Social Structure of the Antebellum South," in Boles and Nolen, *Interpreting Southern History,* 49-77; and Grady McWhiney, *Cracker Culture: Celtic Ways in the Old South* (Tuscaloosa: University of Alabama Press, 1988). Eugene Current-Garcia argues that Sut symbolizes the Old South's "vigor and fertility." See "Sut Lovingood's Rare Ripe Southern Garden," *Studies in Short Fiction* 9 (1972): 129.

19. Leisure as a value has generated its own debate, one that is, again, intimately bound up with definitions of North and South. See David Bertelson, *The Lazy South* (New York: Oxford University Press, 1967); D. D. Bruce, Jr., "Play, Work and Ethics in the Old South," *Southern Folklore Quarterly* 41 (1977): 33-51; and C. Vann Woodward, "The Southern Ethic in a Puritan World," in his *American Counterpoint: Slavery and Racism in the North/South Dialogue* (New York: Oxford University Press, 1983). Bertelson and Woodward cast the debate about leisure versus laziness in the broad terms of Weber's analysis of capitalism and protestantism. For McWhiney, attitudes about work and leisure constitute the single most discernible cultural difference between North and South (*Cracker Culture,* 49).

20. Regardless of what might be said about the fictional character's work habits, Sut Miller, upon whom Sut Lovingood is based, was not a vagabond. McClary, in "The Real Sut," points out that Miller's farm was valued at $400 in the 1850 census. Blanche Henry Clark, *The Tennessee Yeoman, 1840-1860* (Nashville: Vanderbilt University Press, 1942), also uses 1850 census documents to establish the number of small or non-slaveholding farmers in the state. Miller's farm places him squarely in the yeoman class and probably makes him a member of the "Celtic" economy of farmers who were oriented as much toward grazing as farming and more toward self-subsistence than markets. McClary notes that Sut Miller's farm was planted mainly in corn, not unusual of course, but one might speculate how much of that corn became whiskey and how much that conversion (again, not unusual) influenced Harris's conversion of Sut Miller to Sut Lovingood. If Sut Miller had a still, then Sut Lovingood as still operator and distributor in the town seems likely. In any case, Ducktown in the 1850s saw "a great deal of drunkenness, fighting, debauchery, and other ill conduct" (Barclay, *Ducktown,* 39). An enterprising man with a good supply of corn and his own still could make hard cash selling whiskey to the miners.

21. Since Jeannette Tandy first spoke of Sut as a "debased country boy" in *Crackerbox Philosophers in American Humor and Satire* (New York: Columbia University Press, 1925), 93, many critics refer to Sut as a young man. Inge, in "Examination of the Nature of a 'Nat'ral Born Durn'd Fool,'" makes the best argument for Sut being an adult. The ambiguity of his age fits his role as fool.

Andrew Silver (essay date 2000)

SOURCE: Silver, Andrew. "Making Minstrelsy of Murder: George Washington Harris, the Ku Klux Klan, and the Reconstruction Aesthetic of Black Fright." *Prospects* 25 (2000): 339-62.

[*In the following essay, Silver examines elements of hatred and violence in Harris's later Sut Lovingood sketches. Silver argues that these later writings, while comical, suggest an elaborate fantasy of vengeance against the Northern states.*]

"Now, by golly, nobody can't tramp on *me,* wifout gettin thar foot bit"

GEORGE WASHINGTON HARRIS, *High Times and Hard Times* (164)

In George Washington Harris's Reconstruction sketch, **"Trapping a Sheriff, Almost,"** a rowdy Southern hero named Wirt Staples thunders outside of a courthouse waving a terrified African-American boy over his head in one hand and a dried venison steak in the other. With his muscles moving "like rabbits onder the skin," and his hips and thighs "[playing] like the swell on the river" (**Sut Lovingood,** 244), Wirt Staples represents Harris's fantasy of Southern superiority reemergent amidst Reconstruction chaos. The sketch ends with Wirt throwing the venison steak at a Reconstruction judge's head and kicking the boy through the shop window of a watch repairman, assaulting a figure of Northern authority and brutally exiling the black threat from Southern territory. As a final, triumphant gesture, Wirt saddles his horse and bellows, "The Lion's loose, shet your doors!" (**Sut Lovingood,** 254). The collection in which the sketch appeared, **Sut Lovingood: Yarns Spun by a "Nat'ral Born Durn'd Fool"** (1867), was published by a Northern press and advertised along with titles of parlor humor such as *Dick's Ethiopian Scenes, Tambo's End-Men's Gags,* and *Brudder Bons' Book of Stump Speeches.* "It would be difficult," the advertisement assures readers, "to cram a larger amount of pungent humor into 300 pages than will be found in this really funny book" (**Sut Lovingood,** 312).

Though Harris critics have largely continued the unproblematic reception of Harris's sketches as "rowdy slapstick fun" (Stewart, 304) written "just for the fun of it" (Inge, 236), his Reconstruction tales diverge from the good-natured chaos of Harris's earlier work and beg for an inquiry into both the lion that is his Reconstruction humor and, perhaps more importantly, those against whom Harris's comedy is loosed. While scholars have traditionally viewed humor as a positive release of antisocial aggression, the critical neglect of Harris's Reconstruction humor and the failure to acknowledge its relationship to postwar acts of terror originally conceived and popularly received as comic, have left unexplored humor's function in times of social upheaval as an organizing agent of cultural hostilities, occasionally blurring the distinction between comic fantasies of aggression and real enacted aggression.

Of course, George Washington Harris and his indefatigable comic alter ego, the Dionysian country bumpkin Sut Lovingood, represent a great deal more than the comic terror that defines much of his postwar career: Harris acknowledged and celebrated both male and female sexuality; he gave poor characters the liberty to critique and rebel against upper-class constraint; and it is he, not Mark Twain, who first developed a narrative technique in which dialect is rendered more descriptive and vivacious than official language itself. George Washington Harris is the Walt Whitman of Southern humor: as conservative as Whitman was progressive, Harris "indulged and expressed the chaos" (Buell, 330) that other humorists either overlooked, repressed, or feared.

Yet, though critics have been quick to point out the positive nature of Sut's rebellion, their investigations fail to situate much of his humor in the anxious and deeply divided culture of postwar Tennessee. Rather than explore the often suspect politics of Sut's comic victimizations, Harris critics celebrate them as either abstract, apolitical, and healthy rebellions against the conventions of civility or authentic expressions of rowdy frontier fun, at times going out of their way to excuse both Sut and Harris from the often violent Reconstruction politics of hatred against freed persons, Jews, and Northerners. "He does descend to intolerable depths, particularly in his treatment of the Negro," Lewis Leary writes as late as 1971, "but so each of us have our heights and depths, though often not so candidly revealed, or so successfully set forth" (114). M. Thomas Inge similarly inquires, "Is Sut any better or any worse than the rest of us? I somehow think he might come out, in comparison, a little better than most of us. At least he is candid and honest enough to evaluate society for what it is, and would rather withdraw from it, and oppose it, than yield to its influence to make him out to be what he is not. He understands himself well" (251). In a 1996 collection of essays on George Washington Harris, Sanford Pinsker praises those who assign Harris and "dare the campus 'thought police' to haul them in on charges of being racist, sexist, anti-Indian, anti-semitic, or just plain un-American" (299), and Hershel Parker boasts that "in all of nineteenth-century American literature, there is no politically correct meal that remotely compares to the riches of Harris's banquet" (299). The critic's role, then, is to defend humor from the corrosive energies of social criticism and instead view Sut Lovingood as either an eruption from the bestial floor of the psyche or an authentic Tennessee folk figure in the tradition of the ancient fool or *Eulenspiegel*: both incarnations safely situated outside of the complex culture of postwar Tennessee.

Although his career began in the early 1840s, roughly half of Harris's stories, including much of his best work in *Yarns Spun by a "Nat'ral Durn'd Born Fool,"* were written after the war and significantly diverge from his earlier sketches both in form and content. The Civil War and Reconstruction wrought a palpable change in Harris's humor, in which Sut gradually turns from grotesquely comic "other" to moral spokesman for the solidarity of the ideal Old South, from lone trickster to community scourge. Where the prewar sketches take the form of Sut acting the trickster and then running away, the Reconstruction sketches are characterized by the complicit and clandestine orchestration of terror and exile to regain control of a community. In the prewar **"Sicily Burns's Wedding"** (1858), for instance, Sut begins the sketch personally wronged (a woman has spurned his advances) and alienated from a communal ritual (a wedding ceremony), and then concludes the tale by disrupting the cultural rite, bringing disorder to a community, and himself fleeing into exile. Harris's postwar sketches **"Rare Ripe Garden Seed"** (1867), **"Bart Davis's Dance"** (1867), and **"Frustrating a Funeral"** (1867), on the other hand, begin with a threat to Sut's community and end with Sut and other accomplices humiliating and exiling that threat and preserving their community in the process. While in the earlier tales Sut's revenge is largely improvised or wholly accidental, in the later sketches terror becomes a highly orchestrated production undertaken, often with the help of others, to protect a community under siege.

Harris's later humor partakes of a distinctively Reconstruction fantasy of retribution: reversing the dislocating wartime forces that split his Tennessee community and drove Harris himself out of Tennessee and into Alabama and Georgia, Sut instead drives freedmen, freedwomen, Northerners, and loyalists into their lonely and separate exile. This displacement anxiety finds its ultimate fantasy in **"Sut Lovingood's Dream,"** in which Northern abolitionists lynched in a "constitutionalist" uprising (apparently with Harris's approval) are sent to Hell, only to be exiled and destroyed by Satan himself, who shoots them out of a mortar "[busting them] into a million pieces again the wall" (*High Times,* 290). At the heart of these Reconstruction sketches lies the desperate desire to imagine a newly ascendant middle-class patriarchy that could withstand Northern authority and threats from the rising power of African Americans and women. If, as David Estes argues, Sut wages a "guerrilla war against the conventional practices and values of his Tennessee community" (54), it is also a war fought against such unconventional authorities as the Freedmen's bureau and enfranchisement, and fought alongside fellow guerrilla warriors such as the Knights of White Camilla and the Ku Klux Klan, often borrowing the same images, language and tropes from these groups.

In February 1867, just as the state legislature began considering passage of the Reconstruction Acts that would make Tennessee the first Southern state to guarantee the mandatory suffrage of freedmen, the Ku Klux Klan nearly led the state into another civil war. In response to the rapid escalation of Klan activities, and fearing a showdown in the wake of the Reconstruction Acts, Gov. William G. "Parson" Brownlow called out the state militia and requested the presence of federal troops. When George Washington Harris prepared **Yarns Spun by a "Nat'ral Born Durn'd Fool"** for publication in the spring of 1867, his home state of Tennessee was in the process of federal occupation to quell what threatened to be a second Southern rebellion.

Though it would be pure speculation to identify Harris himself as a member of a specific Reconstruction terrorist group, Harris's brand of comic terror was an expression of a larger culture of terror in Tennessee that itself began as amusement, based on the laws of carnival. From every known account, the early Ku Klux Klan was formed in late 1865 or early 1866 in Pulaski, Tennessee, for the sole purpose of amusing the original members with practical jokes performed first on their own ranks and then on the larger community. Yet, though the original founders may have recalled the innocent nature of early Klan activities, the order almost immediately settled on the terrorization of African Americans and intractable Republicans as a proper extension of their original comic play, the carnival space of enacted fantasy quickly metamorphosing into an actual site of torture.

While it is clear that the Ku Klux Klan from the outset, and to the contrary of their leaders' claims, psychologically and physically tortured loyalists and African Americans, often murdering them in the process, Reconstruction-era Democratic newspapers and popular entertainment steadfastly and stubbornly translated such terror into comic discourse for public consumption. In the popular imagination, Klan terror, and the black fright that it created, remained a comic commodity far beyond the eventual public unveiling of the full extent of the Klan's brutality in 1869. Evidence from newspapers suggests that there was a good deal of overlap between minstrelsy, then popular in the South and the North, and the initial reception of the Klan. Amidst frequent bills advertising minstrel shows, the *Nashville Union and American* announced on January 1, 1868, the arrival of "Col. Minor's extravaganza of 'The Ku Klux Klan' . . . to be brought out for the first time at the St. Nicholas Varieties tonight" ("Ku Klux Klan Tonight," 5). "The rattling of dry bones and weird music of the unexplored spheres," the paper reads, "will make a ghostly carnival that the Grand Cyclops himself will wag his jaws with delight at witnessing" (5). In Reconstruction Tennessee, terror caught on the grooves of minstrel carnival, the bones of the end men here easily transformed into the "dry bones" of the Ku Klux ghosts. The show proved popular enough to later return to Nashville on March 31st. As in the case of minstrel shows, the sheet music from the "extravaganzas" was marketed to the public: in April, among the new music advertised in the paper, appears a "Ku Klux Klan Schottisch and Mazurka" by Steinhagen. On June 26, 1868, the newspaper explained that the Klan had grown into a kind of well-marketed fad:

> Since the "Ku-Klux fever" was at its highest pitch in our midst, we have had "Ku Klux Music" from the Music houses, "Ku-Klux Hats" from Furnishing emporiums, "Ku-Klux Cock-tails" from the different saloons, together with the many little "Ku-Klux etceteras" not in mind. And to cap the climax we now have the genuine "Ku-Klux Klan Knife," with the cabalistic letters and the terrible symbols of the order on its blade.

> ("K.K.K.," 3)

Here the "climax" of Klan terror produces a Reconstruction commodity culture that fetishizes both black terror and the vehicles of such terror.

Applying Mikhail Bakhtin's optimistic view of liberating carnival to American culture,[1] David Reynolds writes that, "As important as carnival was in the European culture Bakhtin studies, it was perhaps even more so in democratic America, which was a kind of carnival culture, one that abolished the social distance between people and yoked together high and low in an atmosphere of jolly relativity" (444). Rather than undermining hierarchy and replacing it with egalitarian festivity, the Klan's carnival space counters the specter of structural equality with carnival inequality, undermining the threat of egalitarian government with the reintroduction of hierarchy through carnival terror. Rather than abolishing social distance, the carnival atmosphere of the Reconstruction South aimed to solidify and widen it. Reynolds's assessment glosses over the actual cultural politics of the carnival space, which, in a 19th-century American culture split along lines of gender, race, and class, is hardly ever one of "jolly relativity." In Harris's Reconstruction Tennessee, carnival creates a revolutionary space, but it is only revolutionary for that portion of his Tennessee community that stands in opposition both to prevailing authorities as well as those marginalized people whom these authorities protected. Such humor is, as Reynolds argues, "subversive," but it does not promote "disorder" as a model; rather, it uses disorder to bring about a yet more conservative and deeply nostalgic order: it is a deposing terror that has an older King in mind for the throne.

For the carnival space to remain festive, anti-Republican newspapers consistently transformed black terror into slapstick comedy, often displacing any remaining anxieties about the enjoyment of actual black terror by portraying false alarms of Klan activity or relating practical jokes played on "loyal darkies" by white employers "disguised" as Klansmen. One such tale relates the fright of an African American janitor named "General," whose work superiors impersonate the Klan for a good laugh at his expense. The article describes General's "pop-eyed wonder" as his superiors, speaking through a speaking-tube, tell him that "the red-right hand of vengeance would steep its fingers in his heart's blood." The newspaper converts the dire and horrific nature of the threat into broad comedy: "'Prepare! prepare!' growled the hoarse voice from beneath. 'Oh, Lord! oh, Lord!' gasped poor Butler from above, and suddenly darted out of the room like a streak of oiled electricity, as the 'bottom-worker' gave a rap on the pipes that sounded like the discharge of a blunderbuss" ("A Voice," 3). The humor of fright and flight is central to these tales: here the conversion of a subjective being into "oiled electricity" makes comic the horrible promise to "steep fingers in heart's blood," the threat instead

becoming another element in the setup, delivery and punch-line of the joke. Another Klan "practical joke" relates that "with a loud yell of horror and dismay, a darkie sank upon the floor, where he doubled himself as if of India rubber" ("Ku-Klux in a Safe," 3). The black body in these sketches is relentlessly dehumanized in the face of terror, and it is precisely this dehumanization that amuses racist 19th-century audiences. Comic narratives such as these served both to condition the reception of terror as comic and to temper the tone of articles detailing real instances of Klan torture and murder, often appearing on the same pages as these practical jokes.

Articles concerning actual Klan terror were scarcely less comic. Humorous narratives of Klan activity focused especially upon black fright and flight as the primary means of evoking laughter. In the *Nashville Union and American*—a paper in which many of Harris's tales appeared—the following story was reported in March 1868 under the heading, "A Terrified Negro":

> A negro was met by one of the Ku-Klux near Franklin a few days ago, and the cowled knight of the black cross and scarlet robe cordially offered to shake hands. The negro grasped the extended palm, but no sooner had he touched it than it dropped off, leaving nothing but the bleeding stump of a gory wrist. Sambo, with a mingled shriek and yell of horror and fright, took to his heels and never once stopped until he had reached home, a distance of some five miles, where he curled up on his cabin floor, remaining in that position several hours before he could recover sufficiently to relate what happened.
>
> (3)

The "cordial" greeting here restages the Reconstruction attempt to bridge black and white cultures, and the freed slave is particularly eager to shake hands in a gesture of equality and friendship. His gesture, of course, is aborted by his discovery of the severed and gory wrist, whereupon he acts out the exile central to the scare: he is converted into a feminized "Sambo" who, with a "mingled shriek," takes to his heels and confines himself to the domestic sphere, the traditional domain of Southern women. Public spaces, then, are reclaimed in the scare by a ubiquitous white presence, and African Americans are chased once again to the margins of the community. The initial gesture of equality and reconciliation is merely a burlesque of peace, veiling instead another attempt to force African Americans into an antebellum submission.

If one's own trauma often leads to an encounter with another's trauma through "the very possibility and surprise of listening to another's wound" (Caruth, 8), the scare blocks such a startling recognition, in these newspaper accounts dissociating wartime Confederate trauma—in the foregoing story, the memory of dismembered and gory, war-torn, bodies—from its originary source, projecting it instead onto dehumanized black bodies. These popular Klan narratives convert trauma to pleasure, translating traumatic eruptions from the war into amusing minstrel routines. If blacking up is a method of cultural displacement and control, so too is enacting the blacked-up trauma of the scare: it controls and redirects traumatic repetition, projecting trauma onto black bodies and gaining control in the process both of the ex-Confederate's own trauma and the specter of African American power. The very first Klan scares, involving a Confederate soldier returning gory from the battlefields and demanding unquenchable amounts of water, were interchangeable at the time with an alternate version in which a murdered black man returns from the dead similarly demanding water. The scare amounts to a denial of history, a denial of trauma. The gesture is dismissive, decontextualizing, and dehistoricizing both of ex-Confederate trauma and (through its attempted reversal) African American trauma.

The scares themselves were often based upon folk humor: the prank just illustrated, in which a Klansman asked a victim for a handshake only to release a skeleton's gory wrist into his grip, was quite common, as was another borrowed from Washington Irving's "Legend of Sleepy Hollow," in which a Klansman presented a head-shaped gourd to the paralytic horror of the black victim. Of course, black fright was also one of the principal tropes of minstrelsy, and descriptions of such cowardice play an integral role in the comic reception of Klan activities in both Northern and Southern newspapers. When the Louisiana *Planters' Banner* narrates the story of a Klansman impersonating a soldier returned parched from hell, the writer takes particular pains to portray the imbecile slapstick comedy of black fright and flight: "The negro was astonished . . . [he] dropped the bucket, tumbled over two chairs and a table, escaped through a back window, and has not since been heard from" (Wade, 36). These postwar portrayals of black fright were part of a larger effort to counter the prevailing image of defeated and feminized Southern masculinity, dismissing the threat of black power by rendering black bodies clumsy and uncoordinated.

The newspaper accounts dehumanize terrorized men and women, present their explicit terror as desirable—both in terms of entertainment and justice—and end with the enforced exile and/or submission of the victims. As many contemporary witnesses noted, these newspaper accounts, popular in both the North and South, effectively aestheticized racial violence and transformed racial cruelty into comic discourse. The flavor of these stories, Louis Post writes, "was of *mardi gras* comedy rather than racial tragedy . . . with no purpose whatever except making sport of murder" (40). Nights when the Klan would ride, James Melville Beard maintains, were "holiday seasons" for the "festive

K.K.K." (32, 37) and, according to Verne S. Pease, Klan terror "was a huge joke—wild, fantastic, droll" (363). Newspapers North and South began "to herald [the Klan's] doings through the country as a huge joke," Albion Tourgee explains: "The nation held its sides with laughter, and the Ku-Klux took heart from those cheerful echoes and extended its borders without delay" (397).[2]

One of the first functions of the Ku Klux Klan was the disturbance and dissolution of public night meetings of freedmen that fostered widespread white paranoia about a sudden black rise to power in Tennessee.[3] James Melville Beard's *KKK Sketches: Humorous and Didactic* (1877) portrays the Klan terror that wracked Tennessee's Loyal League from 1866 onward as broadly comic, borrowing heavily from minstrel tropes to condition his Reconstruction audience's acceptance of black fright. In "KKK Dealings with the Loyal League," Beard first describes a league gathering of "ominous character" (53), yet the omniscient narrator, supposedly present and unseen at the time of the meeting, undercuts the dangers of radical Republican solidarity with scenes of comic incompetence and inwardly directed violence within: "Here, shouting and singing constituted the mercurial forces jurin de roasen 'ere and kant meetin' solstice, and here (*in hoc signo*) broken heads and scattered fragments of benches marked the political temperature" (53). Just when the speaker rises to his feet, bringing the chaos of the meeting to its height, the Klan arrives in their costumes and, as Beard's narrator explains, instead of "rebellion" (54), the meeting's congregants are frightened into "meek" submission (54). Beard farcically describes frightened congregants who "were engaged in a very animated game of leap-frog, directed toward . . . other angles of the building," and the doors are shortly blocked "with a mass of rolling, tumbling, somersaulting leaguers" (59). The leader himself had "executed three handslings and a somersault, and was at rest for the time being in a pile of superannuated furniture at the far end of the hall" (59). By the end of the Klan scare, the church in which the meeting was held has been left "completely deserted" and the Klansmen-tricksters give way "to an involuntary chuckle as they gazed . . . upon the wrecked surroundings" (59).

Importantly, the Klansmen's scare reveals the leaguers as harmless at precisely the moment in which their potential strength seems most threatening. Beard graphically illustrates this formula in a similar sketch later in the text, in which the loyal league chairman, engaged in a minstrel stump speech, inveighs against the Klan, climatically calling upon the body to "take immejit steps to surcumvalidate, deturrinerate, nomswogglemerate, and murder-r-r-r" (105). At the moment the minstrelized speaker calls upon the Union League to act in solidarity against the Klan, twenty "ghostly embodiments" enter the building and "great waves of panic . . . lashed the building side to side—at first converting all obstacles into a causeway for their terror" (105). The leader, whose speech had been interrupted at the height of its violent rhetorical power, proves the most cowardly among the congregation and, the narrator explains, "reaching a neighboring window at the end of two vigorous jumps, he passed into the night . . . as 'the startled ear of darkness' heard something like the report of 'murder' at brief intervals of time accommodated to long intervals of space, for about the period employed by an Erie express train in exhausting a winter horizon" (105-6). Though the leader's speech had called upon the League to kill members of the Klan, his panicked cry of "murder" as he flees the scene refers to the equal, opposite, and now comic fear that the Klan will murder him. The potential violence that the narrator had seen as inherent in the meeting is converted into minstrel fright at Klan violence and, once again, the meeting is "broken up" (121).

George Washington Harris's **"Sut at a Negro Night Meeting"** (1867), like Beard's sketches, provides a comic counterpart to such acts of terror, humorously describing how Sut and a doctor carefully rig a black meeting site to terrorize the congregants gathered there. Unlike Harris's antebellum tales, in this case there is no offense, no harm done to Sut, and no motive for his revenge; the enemy is the meeting itself. The sketch depends upon white anxieties about African Americans and black empowerment for its humor, and the extraordinarily sadistic and unparalleled violence that Sut unleashes on the crowd of worshipers, as well as the pleasure with which he narrates such terror, can only be comic if we share these Reconstruction sensibilities.

Though most of the Reconstruction sketches begin with the characterization of an offending interloper, raising audience anxiety about a character soon to be humiliated, Harris begins **"Sut at a Negro Night Meeting"** with a detailed description of the mass convergence of African Americans:

> Well, wun Sat'd'y nite, all the he, an' mos' ove the she niggers fur ten miles roun, started tu hold a big meetin. They cum a-foot, on hoss's, on muels, on oxes, on bulls, on sleds, in carts, waggins an' buggys. The meetin wer wuf ni ontu five hundred thousin dullars in flush times, an' yu cud a-smelt it a mile . . . nite cum, an' fotch wif hit the mos pufick 'sortmint of niggers yu ever seed outen Orleans ur Tophett, a big pine torch-lite at ni ontu every uther tree roun the shed, an' taller candils intu the chu'ch hous whar they cummenc'd thar work.

> (158, 160)

The description of hundreds of freedmen and women coming together at night functions in the same fashion as the listing of offenses that begins most of Sut's tales,

here exciting the audience's fear and its corresponding desire for revenge against a potential threat to white power.

Sut's characterization of the camp meeting focuses on appetite and the implicit connections between black physical, sexual, and political appetite that, the sketch implies, necessarily undo any intention of unified protest. He explains that the participants "hed hawl'd straw untill hit cum up ni ontu levil wif the tops ove the brainches, tu git happy in, an' du thar huggin an' wallerin on" (160), and he later recalls how "the sistren mos on em got ni ontu the pulpit, whar the straw wer deepist wif sich ove the he's es hed a appetite tu help du the huggin an' wallerin" (165). Sut describes the circuit rider and the Baptist preacher who lead the congregation in terms of appetite and hunger, both mistaking a bladder of carburated hydrogen that Sut hides under a pew for food or drink. "I seed him peep onder the seat es he sot down in the pulpit," Sut explains,

> whar he seed the bulge ove wun ove the bladders, stickin out frum onder the slab a littil. He licked his lips, then smak't em, an' wink'd a oily sort ove wink at a Baptis' nigger preacher, what sot by him, an' *he* show'd all ove his teef arter he'd tuck a peep, an' swaller'd like he wer gittin down a ho'n. They wer bof on em showin thar instincks.

> (161)

This conspiratorial communication between the leaders of the congregation, both of whom tacitly agree to keep their stash a secret for themselves alone, allows Harris to create a fictional world in which self-interest and the primacy of black physical desire work to deflate the possibility of real political solidarity in the meeting.

The text chosen for preaching similarly demonstrates both the insurrectionary nature of the meeting as well as the participants' natural "instincks" of appetite. *"Yu shall smell sweet-smellin yarbs, an' eat honey vittils dar,"* the Baptist "bull nigger" exhorts, *"fur thars no stink, nur bitter, whar you's gwine, in Caneyan"* (161). The utopian text is a familiar one, mirroring Reconstruction black theology and drawing an analogy between the bondage, liberation, and empowerment of the Israelites and the freed slave's own hopes for empowerment after liberation.[4] Yet, by placing the language of appetite immediately following the hungry exchange between the preachers, Harris hints that the threat is not so much a product of political desire as an expression of the Baptist preacher's physical hunger. Southern humor has typically proved adept at acknowledging threats to power while simultaneously dispelling them: Harris here recognizes and dismisses the more serious political issue of racial empowerment by recasting it in the more familiar terms of monstrously voracious black desire. After the farcical biblical citation, the preacher apparently loses control of his rhetoric altogether, and the incisive utopian message becomes lost in his hungry imagination. "He wer," Sut explains, "a-citin ove poseys, sinamint draps, fried bacon, an' the scent ove the cupboard, as good yeathly smells, a-gittin hot, an' a-breakin a holesum sweat" (161).

At the climax of the utopian sermon, Sut opens bladders filled with carbureted hydrogen into the crowd.[5] The strategic placement of the first attack, coming after the preacher summons the sweet smells of the promised land, reverses the utopian logic of the passage: the preacher's invocation to sweet liberation instead produces a noxious stench that the congregants take as a sign of the devil, finally driving the meeting out of its original location and into temporary exile. In Sut's world, the threat of a black promised land must be dispelled by white terror.

Sut's second prank on the congregation goes beyond the bounds of any of his antebellum sketches. Where in the antebellum **"Parson Bullens' Lizards,"** Sut releases lizards to crawl up the pants of a preacher who had exposed Sut's love affair to the girl's mother—a relatively innocuous prank against a personal enemy—here he unleashes thousands of bull hornets on an unsuspecting congregation innocent of any specific wrongdoing. After the preacher moves the location of the meeting, he presents another text, this one concerning the suffering of the wicked at the second coming: *"Thar shall be weepin an' railin an' chompin ove teef, bad,"* the preacher exhorts, *"an' then wif no teef, shall smash thar gums together like ontu wolf traps"* (165). Just as the preacher urges his congregation to a fevered crescendo that Sut characterizes as sexual, with "the niggers . . . a-mixin, he an' she, hollerin an' beginin to hug" (166), Sut releases hundreds of bull hornets into the crowd. Again, Harris recasts the political threat in terms of physical desire, envisioning an orgiastic chaos at precisely the moment where the preacher infers that divine retribution will be directed upon white society, the sinners who will soon be punished by God's wrath. The placement of Sut's revenge, however, reverses the damning logic of the passage and suggests that black revolt, rather than white oppression, is sinful, and that African Americans, not whites, will be made to suffer righteous vengeance for their sins. The orchestrated pain inflicted on black bodies dehumanizes the prayer congregants, provides a release of white anxiety, and supplies much of the Reconstruction comedy:

> Sich nises—screechin like painters, cryin, hollerin, a few a-cussin, an' more a-jinin em, beggin, prayin, groanin, gruntin, nickerin, an' wun or two fool wuns singin . . . [there were] millions of insix, jis' a-hoverin over the sufferers an' then divin down fur a sting . . . niggers wer a-shootin intu the woods in all direckshuns,

like ontu arrers shot frum orful bows, an' every durn'd nigger hed a brigade ove insex roun his hed . . . they went crashin outen site intu the brush like canyun shots.

(167)

The meeting, which began with threatening images of a mass gathering of black men and women, ends with their complete disempowerment, the community forced from their metaphorical homeland—their place of worship—and split into helpless individuals driven separately into the woods. Sut somehow escapes notice of the hornets, and he relates the scene as an omniscient, yet incorporeal, presence who regulates and disciplines his black victims from afar. "Thar warn't even a dorg lef on that campgroun'," Sut recalls, "an' yu cud hear nuffin but the humin ove the huntin ho'nets, an' the distunt nise ove scatterin niggers . . . frum that place ove torment, an' general discumfort" (170).

Sut's recollection of a black girl, stripped of all clothing except for her white stockings, running "tormented" through the woods, transforms the initial political threat of the meeting into a moment of sadistic sexual pleasure: "I seed sumthin dispersin hitssef intu the woods," Sut explains, "an' frum the glimpse I got hit look'd sorter like a black munkey shaved wif white hine laigs" (170). The sketch, then, manages to raise anxieties about collaborative black power, political and sexual, only to disperse them: the violated black woman's body serves as a larger metaphor for white ascendance and black vulnerability, reestablishing a pleasurable image of an individual black woman's sexual humiliation where there had been collective black strength. The end of the story has the meeting broken up, the congregants scattered, white power reasserted, and Sut assuring his readers that "thar haint been a nigger nite meetin hilt in the country since, an' they's mos' on em become pius, an' morril" (171). Though David Estes suggests that the congregants' religious sentiment at the sketch's conclusion has been reformed and "made purer than their hypocritical masters and mistresses" (58), clearly Sut's description of them bears no relation to their spiritual life. For African Americans to act pious and moral, in Sut's Reconstruction fantasy, simply means that they once again act like slaves. Sut has truly "'sisted" the meeting by cowing former slaves into orderly, peaceable submission through invisible and omnipresent physical torment.

The black body, in these sketches, becomes the canvas upon which Harris reverses anxieties about the sudden vulnerability of the white male body during the war and the loss of political control in its aftermath. The violability of both the Southern male body and the South itself during Reconstruction produces a commensurate pleasure in black physical terror and black submission in Harris's sketches, comically desensitizing the reader to pain inflicted on black bodies.[6] In **"Old Skissim's**

Middle Boy" Sut assists a white family in their quest to wake an extraordinarily indolent son by rigging an intricate device of torture to the chair in which he sleeps. Sut ties him to his chair, screws iron hand vices on his ears, ties a gridiron to one ankle and a pair of fire tongs to the other, pours red-pepper flakes down his back, turns loose a pint of June bugs in his shirt, ties a basket full of firecrackers to his chair back, his hair, and wrists, and buttons up an angry rat into his pants. Yet, before setting the firecrackers off, he paints the boy's "face the culler ove a nigger coal-burner, scept a white ring roun his eyes; an' frum the corners ove his mouf, sorter downards, slouch-wise . . . lef a white strip" (68). This seemingly random cosmetic change proves vital for the comedic effect: since the elaborate torture device seems an incommensurate punishment for a boy's sleepiness, such sadism can only be pleasurably unleashed on a "savidge" black body. The vices on his ears look like "over-grow'd yearrings," the irons on his ankles mimic a slave's chains, and the paint transforms the boy into a "devil" fit for "tresun, straterjim, an' tu spile things" (69), freeing his blacked-up body for the comic performance of minstrel terror which follows.[7]

If the comic performances of **"Sut at a Negro Night Meeting"** and **"Old Skissim's Middle Boy"** recall both ideology and strategies of the Ku Klux Klan, so too does Harris's chief Reconstruction trope: the reformative scare (or as Sut Livingood calls it, "skeer"). The Klan's belief in the reforming powers of the scare represents a complex Reconstruction desire to defend the principles of the Old South through the regulation, control, and comic emasculation of those who would threaten white authority. Rather than the brutally direct forms of punishment sanctioned in antebellum life, the scare aimed at a more subtle, devious, and discreet form of punishment that internalized discipline and constraint: "Be secret, be cautious, be terrible!" an 1868 Ku Klux Klan directive read (Lester and Wilson, 190). Instead of a discipline based on the visibility of power, no longer easily enforceable in Reconstruction Tennessee, the scare rendered authority invisible and its subjects highly visible.[8] "Dream as you sleep in the inmost recesses of your houses," a Ku Klux Klan warning read, "and hovering over your beds we gather your sleeping thoughts, while our daggers are at your throats" (Wade, 42). The Klan used the nocturnal scare to create a mechanism of continuous and anonymous night surveillance as a force of discipline especially against perceived threats of black thievery, sexual impropriety, sloth, and political empowerment. The Ku Klux Klan's terror, then, functioned as an extension of divine retribution and operated not on the basis of direct, empirical, individual evidence, but on the omniscient knowledge of a community's sins. "The far-piercing eye of the Grand Cyclops is upon you," another advertisement warns: "Fly the wrath to come!" (Wade, 64). The inten-

tion of the scare, as one white Alabaman woman put it, was not only to punish physically, but to strike "terror into the heart of the evil-doer" (Lester and Wilson, 96).

If the Klan waged psychological warfare on African Americans and offending whites in Reconstruction Tennessee, the early form of the scare itself effectively minstrelized terror, often using black bodies and black folk beliefs to enforce black submission. In his novel of a Reconstruction Tennessee saved by noble Klansmen, *In the Wake of War: A Tale of the South Under Carpet-Bagger Administration* (1900), Verne S. Pease has his aristocratic protagonist "black up" and "play de nigger" (320) in order to stop his black workers from striking. Early Ku Klux terror begins with this desire to black-up in an effort to render the black body docile even while vicariously participating in its supposed energies of disorder. Pease's genteel hero first fashions a folktale about a monster that eats black people at night, and then he himself dresses as one of the monster's black victims, returning from hell to terrorize any freedmen still determined to strike. "He was covered with an immense white mantle," Pease writes:

> An opening was made for his face, and slashes in the sides gave freedom to his arms. Two black horns stood up threateningly on the top of his head . . . If the frightened negroes in the cabin did not note all of these details, each marked the face of their former friend— for there was no doubt in their minds but it was Eli [the black victim]. The black features were drawn and twisted with agony; his great white teeth shone to the last molar. And the wheezy voice kept calling, "Water! water!"
>
> (369)

Pease's story of a man who has come back from Hell with an unquenchable thirst for water was also the most famous and widely circulated Ku Klux Klan scare in the Reconstruction South. "I's burnin'; burnin' insides; mo' water," the minstrel form cries: "Tell de boys to wuck, stiddy an' faitfu', or dey goes to Hell, shu'" (370).[9] As in **"Sut at a Negro Night Meeting,"** the freedmen are reformed through the "skeer," subsequently promise to "wucks good" (371), and Pease notes that "there was no general strike the next day" (372).

The passage demonstrates the perverse amalgamation of desires and anxieties present in the Ku Klux Klan's early scares: the plantation owner coauthors the narrative of the scare with his black servant—mimicking black folk belief and storytelling techniques—and subsequently acts out the cross-racial fantasy, participating, for a moment, in all of the assumed powers of the demonized black man. After the Klansmen create the rudimentary story of a man-eating monster, a loyal black servant "was then called in and the story was related to him. The alacrity with which he tacked on chapter after chapter of flesh-creeping details was astonishing. [One

Klansman] confessed the weakness of his own fancy" (351). For Pease, the scare participates in, borrows from, and is made effective by black discourse. Beard shares Pease's declared indebtedness to African American storytelling, calling African Americans superior "fiction venders" (68) who, though "grossly superstitious" (64), often use their powers of storytelling to gain power in a community: "An African," Beard explains, "is gratified beyond his expression by the knowledge that he possesses authority, no matter how brief or weak in extent, which may be exercised over his fellows" (68).[10] More importantly, Beard claims that enslaved people used the same methods to "gain ascendancy" over the minds of their "young masters and mistresses, whose influence was great at headquarters, and who would one day succeed to the estate" (69). The Klan, he argues, was "trained up in this school" (69) and so simply appropriated and reversed the disciplinary powers of the black "skeer": the color line may forbid African Americans from participating in "whiteness" but, in Beard's world, it does not forbid whites from successfully donning blackness.[11] In *In the Wake of War*, Pease's hero performs blackness so convincingly that he actually *becomes* threateningly black in the minds of his frightened black audience: his dialect is taken as authentic by the freedmen, and his blackened features prove convincing enough to leave "no doubt" in their minds that he is Eli.

Pease's text provides a fairly accurate portrayal of Klan activity in its first phase in which white men donned black potency to reestablish power over the black community. Klan dens commonly impersonated dead black men that their victims had known, now newly returned from hell, and used the props of minstrelsy in the pursuit of fright, often blacking up and lining their mouths with white rings as did minstrel performers.[12] Their costumes accentuated the phallic nature of black power; horns, sometimes as long as two feet, were affixed to the head, fifteen-foot tails were attached to costumes, and Klansmen often wore "huge teeth, either painted on the masks or made from quills or bone" (Fry, 126).[13] The Klan's terror torments and infantilizes black men even while validating white masculinity through the appropriation of the black body's symbolic strength and power.

The scare similarly allows Klansmen to assume the power of blackness even as it enables them to assign any autonomous black political desire to an irrational and infantile superstitiousness. "The superstition of the negro was a strong element of his character," Pease explains: "it outweighed gratitude, patriotism, hunger, and revenge" (373). Although there is considerable evidence that the black victims did not so much fear ghosts but the white men behind the supernatural disguise, this simply suggests the power of the fiction for these white men: not only did they think they knew "their" blacks

well enough to impersonate them, but they also knew their "primitive" beliefs well enough to expertly mimic and gain psychological control over their former slaves through them.[14] Since all of the Klansmen in *In the Wake of War* had blacked up at the same time and played the same dead black man in front of separate black audiences, word quickly circulated of an "omnipresent spirit" that "spread terror to hundreds of evildoers" (373). Pease relates that those who witness Eli's return from hell "were imbecile with fright; they could only groan and call, 'Gawd!'" (368) and explains that the circulation of "the foolish story . . . had frightened the negroes into a state of reasonable docility" (362).

Though George Washington Harris's **"Frustrating a Funeral"** was published just when Klan activities were reaching their height in the wake of the 1867 Reconstruction acts, and though it employs the same tropes commonly used in newspaper accounts of Ku Klux Klan raids in his home state, critics have overlooked both Harris's story and its participation in Tennessee's culture of terror. As in **"Sut at a Negro Night Meeting,"** the sketch concerns the desecration and "frustration" of an African American ritual, here a funeral procession, and once again involves the violation of African American physical integrity. **"Frustrating a Funeral"** begins with a young doctor who employs Sut Lovingood to steal a black man's corpse "tu chop up, an' bile" (**Yarns,** 212). Sut, however, never intends to steal the body, and instead uses its blackness and attendant prowess to scare and reform his community, purging it of undesirable white and black elements. First, Sut switches Seize's corpse with Maje, a black drunkard who was supposed to guard the body and has since passed out in a drunken stupor. Then he tends to Maje's face:

> Arter I got Maje intu the coffin, an' hed cut sum airholes, I sot in an' painted red an' white stripes, time about, runnin out frum his eyes like ontu the spokes ove a wheel, an' cross-bar'd his upper lip wif white, ontil hit looked like boars' tushes, an' I fastened a cuppil ove yearlin's ho'ns ontu his head, an' platted a ded black-snake roun the roots ove em, an durn my laigs ef I didn't cum ni ontu takin a runnin skeer mysef, fur he wer the purfeck dogratype ove the devil.
>
> (212)

The makeup recalls the common elements of Klan costuming: the red and white circles around the eyes, the animal horns attached to the head, and the exaggeration of the large, carnivorous teeth.[15] Sut's metaphor of the devil's "dogratype" reveals a fantasy of power in which the white gaze suspends and arrests demonic blackness through the controlling frame of the photographer's camera. The monstrous black devil, a "type" or likeness of a "dog" in Sut's tortured dialect, here becomes a docile tool of white control. Sut's artistic manipulation of the unconscious black man makes his living body indistinguishable, both literally and figuratively, from the black corpse upon which he next sets to work. "I'd got 'bout a tin cup full of litenin bugs," Sut explains:

> I smear'd em all over his face, har an' years, an' ontu the prongs ove a pitch-fork; I sot him up in the corner on aind, an' gin him the fork, prong aind up in his crossed arms. I then pried open his mouf, an' let his teef shet ontu the back ove a live bull-frog . . . an' pinned a littil live garter-snake by hits middil crosswise in his mouf . . . Now, rite thar boys, in that corner, stood the dolefulest skeer makin mersheen, mortal man ever seed outen a ghost camp.
>
> (213)

As in **"Sut at a Negro Night Meeting,"** the passage releases postwar white anxieties by violating black physical integrity. Sut's minstrelsy begins with the orchestration of dormant and docile blackness, inscribing the bodies of two comically innocuous black men—one a corpse and the other an unconscious drunkard—with opposite signs of phallically terrible blackness. As their names, Seize and Maje, indicate, the comedy of the scene depends on the profoundly ironic slippage between signifier and signified: the men must be rendered as powerless as their faces are made up to be powerful, as comic as their signs are terrible. The elements of the scene allow Harris to imagine the white nightmare of horrible blackness alongside the white fantasy of comically impotent blackness, at once recognizing and dismissing black power, using black bodies as minstrel puppets in the theatrical production of fright.

Sut's purgation of the community begins with Simon, "the ole preachin an' exhortin nigger ove the neighborhood" (218). As a preacher, Simon not only represents the threat of organized black religion and black empowerment, as in **"Sut at a Negro Meeting,"** but also of black threats against white property. Sut tells use that he has stolen corn from a white man's farm. The Ku Klux Klan often cited black theft, as well as potential black empowerment, as the foremost reason for their existence as purveyors of rough justice, responding to the difficulty of punishing those suspected of thievery by enacting their retribution in the guise of omniscient specters returned from the dead.[16] "The chief crime complained of [in the Reconstruction South]", Allen Trelease explains, "was petty thievery. Most thefts occurred after dark, with no witnesses, and it was almost impossible to discover the culprits. Cotton and corn were stolen from the fields, hams were abducted from smokehouses, tools and equipment disappeared from sheds and barns" (xix). In **"Frustrating a Funeral,"** the thieving Simon enters the cabin, catches sight of Seize's demonically painted corpse sitting in the corner, and becomes paralyzed with fright. Sut explains,

> Jis' then I moaned out in a orful doleful vise, '*Hiperkrit, cum tu hell, I hes a claim ontu yu fur holding the bag while Seize stole co'n.*' (I seed em a-doin that

job not long afore.) He jis' rar'd backwards, an' fell outen the door wif his hands locked, an' sed he in a weak, fever-ager sort ove vise, 'Please marster,' an' jis' fainted, he soon cum to a-runnin, fur I hearn the co'n crashin thru the big field like a in-gine wer runnin express thru hit. I haint seed 'Simon,' tu this day.

> (213-14)

All of the elements of this scare—the revenge taken under cover of darkness, the white man disguised as a familiar African American just returned from hell, the omniscient knowledge of an individual's sins, the use of the scare as a means of expulsion, and the detailed description of clumsy black fright—partake of the Reconstruction culture of terror waged especially against black men. Like the aristocratic protagonist in *In The Wake of War*, Sut effectively becomes Seize, marshaling the forces of demonic blackness in order to terrorize a black man into reform and, in this case, exile.

Later, Sut punishes Maje for helping Simon steal the corn. Maje has just burst from Seize's coffin in the midst of a funeral procession, frightening the black mourners who take him for the devil, and proceeds directly to the local tavern unaware of his costume and makeup. Sut is inexplicably present at the procession and somehow follows Maje to the bar, once again acting the part of omnipresent white authority and frightening his black subject into sudden reform. After Maje's grotesque costume frightens the owner from his tavern, Maje steals a bottle of "popskull" from behind the bar and, as he raises his head with the bottle in his hand, he "seed hissef fur the fust time in a big lookinglass." He takes the mirror to be a window, Sut explains,

> an' tho't what he seed wer in tuther room, a-watchin him. 'Yu—yu jis' lef me lon; I'se not yourn; *I b'longs tu meeting.*' sed Maje, as he back'd hissef to'ards the door. As he back'd, so did the taryfyin picter. Maje seed that. 'Gwine tu take a runnin butt, is yu,' sed Maje, as he fell a back summerset intu the street; as he lit, I groaned out at him: 'Major, my son, I'se cum fur the toll outen ole Hunicutt's co'n.' 'Simon dun got dat toll,' sed Maje, sorter sham'd like. He riz, showin a far sampil ove skared nigger runnin. 'Ho'ns an' butten go tugether, an' dat am de debil in dar,' sed Maje tu hissef. I holler'd . . . 'I'se farly arter yu now.' . . . He made down the street fur the river, an' clear'd the road ove every livin thing.

> (223)

Here Sut enacts the white fantasy of policing the black conscience: Maje looks in the mirror in the midst of a criminal act, and it is precisely at the moment when he acquires stolen property that he sees his demonic double and is transformed into a docile minstrel figure. Repulsed by his own image, he repents of his theft, gives back the bottle, and flees the community. As with Pease's Klan story, Sut uses the black body and black folk belief to regulate black behavior; Simon and Maje are ruled and reformed through their own black demons. Though Maje initially protests that he belongs to the meeting—an expression of spiritual independence and political autonomy—he is shortly controlled, regulated, and punished by a grotesque mirror image created by Sut Lovingood. This effort to split the black self into two stylized halves, the demonic and the cowardly, lies at the very heart of Harris's minstrelsy and the Klan's scares. In both, the white man appropriates the dark powers of the "demonic" black self in order to render infantile, terrorize, and discipline the "cowardly" black self. Sut's scares, like the newspaper reports of early Klan terror, end with the minstrel description of childish black fright: Simon tumbles through a doorway, pleads to his "marster," and faints, and Maje loses control of his body and backward "sommersets" out of the door and into the street.

"Frustrating a Funeral," however, expresses more than anxiety against African Americans: Sut purges his whole community of impurity, taking vengeance on the doctor who poisoned Caesar, an adulterous plantation owner, and, oddly enough, a sheriff who has recently lynched a black man named "Pomp." Again, this signals a new development in Harris's humor: where Sut's sadism in his antebellum sketches is founded purely on self-ish grounds—usually a character has done him some physical harm—here Sut's mischief is aimed at those who threaten his community.[17] For both the Klan and Harris, reforming black behavior was only part of a larger goal of returning the South to an ideal antebellum order. Both saw the Reconstruction South as an overturned hierarchy, with interlopers, corrupt politicians, and sinners occupying the top rungs of the social ladder, leaving defeated virtuous men at the bottom. "The shakin an' jumblin ove this yere war ove ourn," Sut explains: "hes fotch up tu the top ove the groun a new kine ove pisonus reptile" (**Yarns,** 173). J. C. Lester, one of the six founders of the Ku Klux Klan, uses the same metaphor of eruption, explaining that Klan scares were primarily aimed against "that class of men who, like scum, had been thrown to the surface in the great upheaval" (77). Rather than narrowly defining themselves as a group who disciplined freedmen, the Klan saw themselves in broader terms as an army of regulators who would defend chivalric ideals, aid the reestablishment of justice and, as Pease writes, "save the South from anarchy . . . in the name of Home" (365).

In one of his last stories, **"Sut Lovingood's Allegory,"** written late in 1868 at the height of the Reconstruction Ku Klux Klan's power, Harris laments Northern industrial progress and the passing of the ideal South, recalling the "good old days" of house raising, quiltings, and corn shuckings, "where the darkey's happy song was heard for the last time" (311). Though an antebellum Sut might have joyously undercut the narrator's senti-mental vein, here Sut joins in the elegy to the antebellum South, relating the tale of a once idyllic farm invaded by a promiscuous, "progressive billy-goat . . . as black as a coal cellar at midnight" (313). The black goat, a traditional symbol of the devil and the adulterer, here serves as a convenient proxy for Northern "progress" and black empowerment, both of which Harris links to rapacious sexual designs on Southern women and thus to his final nightmare of miscegenation. After stealing the farmer's corn and peaches, the black goat quickly crossbreeds with all of the other female farm animals, contaminating their pedigreed bloodlines and transforming them into grotesque, intractable hybrids of their original submissive breeds. The goat's rebellion plays on white accounts of black property theft and sexual potency, combining fears of economic as well as sexual emasculation under Northern occupation and African-American empowerment.

Of course, for Harris, sexual desires must precede and supply the motive for African-American political revolt and empowerment: following his sexual improprieties, the goat shortly becomes "impudent" and unruly, disrupting the natural hierarchy of the farm, attacking the farmer's wife and inquiring about purchasing the land itself. While the goat begins acting like a man, the feminized owner, Sut explains, "looked like a scared dorg, or a stepchild on the out aidge ove sufferance . . . He know'd that at the rate things were gwine on his stock, very soon, wouldent be worth a tinker's durn" (315). The landowner's solution to both his own disempowerment and the specter of the ruination of the farm's females is to castrate the black goat:

> Mister Benny, billy goat, instid ove chawin his cud, with a short, quick, sassey nip, nip, nip, arter that mornin', na' plum on, ontil he dried up, an' died in a sinkhole, he chaw'd it arter the fashion ove an old, lazy cow, when she is standin' onder the shade ove the willers, bellyfull an' bellydeep in the creek. His tail never agin flaunted the sky, surjestin 'youbedam.' He wer the very last one that you'd a thought ove axin about the price ove the farm. An *he dident raise any more family.*
>
> (316)

Through an act of terror that emasculates the threat to the farmer's own masculinity and authority, the farmer ensures the ownership of his farm, keeps pure both the lines of patriarchy and natural hierarchy among animals, and triumphantly returns to power. Of course, the act of castration, which destroys the threat to both the female community and "natural" forms of white male authority, evokes similar desires and reverses similar fears as had common Klan rituals of African American castration in the Reconstruction South.[18] Sut's comic metaphor provides a barely disguised approval of the use of terror against the enemies of antebellum ideals as a means to resuscitate antebellum Southern authority. The newspaper in which the sketch appeared, the *Knox-*

ville Press & Messenger, had only months before touted the Klan's powers of vengeance, calling upon its readers to "Organize your forces for the overthrow of Radicalism and Negro Domination, and the Establishment of a White Man's Government!" ("Prospectus," 3). The sketch presents the logical conclusion of the newspaper's own racist logic.

The fact that we can be highly amused by the terror and the pain of others has long been a truism of humor studies. Henri Bergson explains that laughter's function is "to intimidate by humiliating" (188), Freud connects jokes to "brutal hostility, forbidden by law" (122), and Ernst Kris theorizes that comic disparagement developed from doing harm to effigies, which developed in turn from doing harm to people themselves. However, the dehumanization that makes a harmless aggressive fantasy possible may, in a different context, lay the groundwork and provide the rationalization for actual aggression and acts of terror. Though recent critics like Gregg Camfield (who himself devotes half a chapter to Harris) have argued against a view of comedy as aggressive, claiming that such a perspective "reduces laughter to a simple weapon that articulates the joy of resistance, not the joy of being" (6), the joy of being can be realized only when the climate is right for joy, which it often is not in the humor of those who perceive themselves under cultural attack. While Camfield claims that, when we view humor as aggressive, "We miss [humor's] creative and playful as opposed to its destructive sides" (6), for Harris and the Klan, destruction itself is a form of creative play, yielding its own complex pleasures. The example of the Klan's racist carnival provides a close parallel to the tropes and themes at work in Harris's humor and reveals much about the possible collapse of the social space that separates "harmless" fantasies of comic terror from real enacted terror. The convergence of Harris's anxieties about sexuality, race, and power in his Reconstruction sketches found comic resolution in terror—what Sut calls "the *true* idear"—as a way to rethrone the Southern patriarch "for the sake ove this an' the nex generashun" (316).

The lines between humor and terror in Tennessee, then, had at times become fatally blurred during Reconstruction, the former often providing an aestheticization of the latter. Though the victims of Klan terror were nearly always freed people or Republicans, occasionally the terrible "joking" backfired on its perpetrators. In an article in March 1868, the *Nashville Union & American* reported that a white man "wearing a mask and enveloped in a sheet" had been killed by a freedman after he had demanded entry to the freedman's house, "saying he had business there and would kill the last one of them." The freedman reached for his rifle, opened the door, and fatally shot the man in the sheet. After the dead man's identity had been revealed as a good citizen

"with excellent character," the paper concluded that "the negro" was of "a vicious nature," the mask and cloak worn by the white man "were not the mask and robes worn by the Ku-Klux Klan . . . [but] one seen every day in our shop windows," and the intention of the "excellent" white man was to play a "practical joke" and "simply to frighten the negroes." The article's headline reads, "Killed in a Mask. Tragical Result of a Practical Joke—A Shrouded Masker Shot Dead by a Negro." Black terror, the newspaper implies, is in itself the logical conclusion of accepted Reconstruction humor. In the months before Harris wrote **"Sut Lovingood's Allegory,"** Klan activity reached its Reconstruction height, launching a bloody reign of terror throughout Tennessee that left the *Memphis Avalanche* predicting that the Klan would soon take over the state.[19] In Harris's hometown, the *Knoxville Whig* reported Klan notices hanging on street corners and speculated that the dire invocations might either represent a call to terror or the successful execution of "some huge joke" (Alexander, 205). In Reconstruction Tennessee, and in Harris's humor, such distinctions became increasingly difficult to make.

Notes

1. See Mikhail Bakhtin's *Rabelais and His World* (Bloomington: Indiana University Press, 1984).

2. It is important to note that the dissemination of humorous stories in the North equaled that of the South. Albion Tourgee reported that Northern "illustrated newspapers began to teem with caricatures of the disguised horsemen and frightened darkies . . . It was thought to be a very pleasant and innocent amusement for the chivalry of the South to play upon the superstitious fears of the recently emancipated colored people" (397). Louis F. Post similarly describes Northern caricatures and reports that relegated the Klan's activities "to the category of horseplay . . . fashioned to inspire doubts of their seriousness" (40). Northern reporters thus participated in the anxious humiliation of the superstitious and infantile African American, rewriting humorous accounts of practical jokes that reformed black behavior and conditioning the nation's initial reception of the Klan as comic.

3. "In Tennessee," Trelease explains, "the rallies held by the League were a source of fear and loathing to native whites. Like any political rally, League meetings included a good deal of bragging and ballyhoo; and to Southern whites, such license by crowds of 'free niggers' was a certain prelude to rape and rapine" (44). See Fry (150 ff.) for discussion of prayer meetings and Klan terror.

4. For more on Reconstruction black theology, see Theophus H. Smith's "Exodus" (*Conjuring Culture,* 66 ff.).

5. A doctor had lent him the gas specifically for the purposes of breaking up the meeting. Again, the note of complicity between Sut and other vengeful accomplices is new to the Reconstruction sketches.

6. These anxieties are also at work in the comic physical mutilation of Northerners, lawyers, and women in Harris's later sketches.

7. Of course, the boy's contrariness, indolence, and ensuing violent passion when waked make him a natural candidate for transformation into a stereotypical black man. The later rage against his family not only plays into white configurations of blackness, but also may symbolize black revolt and the ensuing chaos that results from that breach of patriarchy. In fact, the whole sketch may well be an allegorical satire of the Reconstruction: Old Skissim represents the schismatic North, since he is both Methodist and clock maker. (Harris associated Methodists with Brownlow, reform, and abolition; and clocks are invariably a symbol of the North in Harris's satires.) Skissim's middle son perhaps represents Harris's recurrent joke about abolitionists giving birth to black babies or, in fact, being black themselves.

8. I am indebted here to Michel Foucault's discussion of discipline, "The Means of Correct Training" (*Discipline and Punish,* 170-94).

9. In "Trapping a Sheriff," a Harris sketch written after the war, Sut drives a strong-minded widow from her house by disguising himself as her dead husband newly returned from hell: "Fetch me sum warter," he calls to her, "fur my tung's parch'd wif fervent heat" (271). Harris almost certainly borrows the elements of this scene from the Klan's favorite and popular "skeer," which he faithfully employs in the interest of preserving the sanctity of home. See McWhiney and Simkins (111) and Horn (19) for more on this notorious Ku Klux Klan scare.

10. Beard's analysis of a black imagination that thrives upon the domination of its fellows still circulates in chapter 2 of *Huckleberry Finn.* Here, Jim uses Tom Sawyer's "skeer" to gain control over his fellows, telling them that he had been "bewitched" by witches and "rode . . . all over the state" (36). In the wake of their newfound respect, Huck tells us, Jim becomes "most ruined, for a servant" (36). Though critics have read this scene as an indication of Twain's departure from popular conceptions of blackness, endowing Jim with unique shrewdness in his quest for power in the novel, this is not a particularly new or subversive portrait of a slave's unique powers of persuasion. Furthermore, since the audience here knows that Jim's empowerment originates in the white

imagination of Tom Sawyer, it is, if anything, less subversive a portrait even than Beard's: in *Adventures of Huckleberry Finn,* the superior "fiction venders" are not Jim or Nat, but Huck and Tom.

11. Indeed, the minstrel figure of the black dandy embodies the imagined incompetence of African Americans' attempts to cross the color line themselves. The dandy's humor originates in his profound failure to mimic and usurp white language and Western forms of knowledge (as we can see in Beard's stump speeches at the Union League gathering, for instance). "The black dandy," as Eric Lott explains, "literally embodied the amalgamationist threat of abolitionism, and allegorically represented the class threat of those who were advocating it" (134).

12. Although many Klansmen dressed as Confederate dead for their scares, there is significant evidence that blacking up was a common practice of the early Klan. Fry writes that "lampblack was sometimes used to completely blacken the face. It was presumed the onlooker would not be able to discern if the face underneath the coloring was Negro or white" (130). The Congressional investigation of the Klan in 1868 reveals similar costuming: "An oil-cloth patch [covered one of their faces], and his face [was] blacked up" (131), "The men were blacked or in disguise" (130), "Some had paper faces on, and some were just blacked and marked up" (130), "Those persons came in with their faces blacked, or were black men" (130).

13. See Wade (60, 111) and Fry (115, 125, 143, 145).

14. For a detailed discussion of black response to the Klan, see McWhiney and Simkins, "The Ghostly Legend of the Ku Klux Klan," *Negro History Bulletin* 14 (February 1951): 109-12; and Wade (36 ff.).

15. See Fry (124) and Wade (60) for the use of rings of red and white around eyes and mouth.

16. See Trelease (22).

17. It is also worth noting that Sut's revenge on both the doctor for poisoning Caesar and the sheriff for lynching a freedman shows that Harris clearly uses his lower-class character as a moral scourge, drawing a distinction between terror—the "skeer"—and murder. This was also a distinction that some leaders in the early Klan had attempted to articulate. Amidst the increasing citations of violence against freedmen and women, and as early as 1867, the leadership began to renounce instances of violence within the ranks of the Ku Klux Klan even while attempting to shift blame for these acts on Union League imposters bent on sullying the image of the Klan. The *Pulaski Citi-*

zen declared that the Klan had no intention of "harming the poor African" (Trelease, 33), and a general order from the Grand Dragon in the realm of Tennessee explained that the Klan

> is essentially, originally and inherently a protective organization. It proposes . . . to protect all good men, whether white or black, from the outrages and atrocities of bad men of both colors, who have been for the past three years a terror to society, and an injury to us all . . . imposters have, in some instances, whipped negroes. This is wrong! wrong! It is denounced by this Klan as it must be by all good and humane men.

> (Lester and Wilson, 110-11)

In fact, the Klan often ironically saw themselves as protectors of freedmen and women. In Pease's novel, for instance, the Klan drives carpetbaggers who had been stealing the "poor freedmen's" money from town. Pease concludes the chapter by declaring that "the negroes had defenders, or rather avengers; and vengeance is often the most available substitute for defense" (384). Though Pease's story and Harris's sketches indicate a more complex dynamic of mingled patriarchal protection and punishment as opposed to a narrower expression of murderous racial hatred, their advocacy of control through fright clearly encouraged the collapse of finer distinctions between psychological and physical terror that some of their rhetoric had attempted to draw.

18. For a detailed discussion of Klan lynchings and their representation in literature, see Trudier Harris.

19. See Trelease (44 ff.), Wade (46 ff.), and Alexander (205 ff.).

Works Cited

Alexander, Thomas B. "Ku Kluxism in Tennessee: 1865-69." *Tennessee Historical Quarterly* 8: 195-219.

Beard, James Melville. *KKK Sketches: Humorous and Didactic.* Philadelphia: Claxton, Remsen and Haffelfinger, 1877.

Bergson, Henri. "Laughter." *Comedy.* Ed. Wylie Sypher. New York: Doubleday Anchor, 1956.

Buell, Lawrence. *Literary Transcendentalism: Style and Vision in the American Renaissance.* Ithaca: Cornell University Press, 1973.

Camfield, Gregg. *Necessary Madness: The Humor of Domesticity in Nineteenth-Century American Literature.* New York: Oxford University Press, 1997.

Caruth, Cathy. *Unclaimed Experience: Trauma, Narrative, and History.* Baltimore: Johns Hopkins University Press, 1996.

"Doings of the Mysterious." *Nashville Union & American,* March 17, 1868: 3.

Estes, David. "Sut Lovingood at the Camp Meeting: A Practical Joker Among the Backwoods Believers." *Southern Quarterly* 25 (1987): 53-65.

Foucault, Michel. *Discipline and Punish: The Birth of the Prison.* New York: Vintage Books, 1991.

Freud, Sigmund. *Jokes and Their Relation to the Unconscious.* Trans. James Strachey. New York: W. W. Norton, 1989.

Fry, Gladys-Marie. *Night Riders in Black Folk History.* Knoxville: University of Tennessee Press, 1975.

Harris, George Washington. *High Times and Hard Times: Sketches and Tales by G. W. Harris.* Ed. M. Thomas Inge. Nashville: Vanderbilt University Press, 1967.

————. *Sut Lovingood: Yarns Spun by a "Nat'ral Born Durn'd Fool"—Warped and Wove for Public Wear.* New York: Dick and Fitzgerald, 1867.

————. *Sut Lovingood Yarns.* Ed. M. Thomas Inge. Memphis: St. Lukes, 1987.

Harris, Trudier. *Exorcising Blackness: History and Literary Lynching and Burning Rituals.* Bloomington: Indiana University Press, 1984.

Horn, Stanley F. *Invisible Empire.* Boston: Houghton Mifflin, 1939.

Inge, M. Thomas. "Sut Lovingood: An Examination of the Nature of a 'Nat'ral Born Durn'd Fool.'" *Tennessee Historical Quarterly* 19 (1960), 231-51.

"K.K.K." *Nashville Union & American,* June 26, 1868: 3.

"Killed in a Mask." *Nashville Union & American,* March 19, 1868: 3.

Kris, Ernst. *Psychoanalytic Explorations in Art.* London: G. Allen and Unwin, 1953.

"Ku-Klux in a Safe." *Nashville Union & American,* April 3, 1868: 3.

"The Ku Klux Klan To-night." *Nashville Union & American,* January 1, 1868: 5.

Leary, Lewis. "The Lovingoods: Notes Toward a Genealogy." *Southern Excursions: Essays on Mark Twain and Others.* Baton Rouge: Louisiana State University Press, 1971: 111-30.

Lester, J. C., and D. L. Wilson. *Ku Klux Klan: Its Origin, Growth and Disbandment.* New York: Neale, 1905.

Lott, Eric. *Love and Theft: Blackface Minstrelsy and the American Working Class.* New York: Oxford University Press, 1993.

McWhiney, H. Grady, and Francis B. Simkins. "The Ghostly Legend of the Ku Klux Klan." *Negro History Bulletin* 14 (1951): 109-12.

Parker, Hershel. "A Tribute to Harris's Sheriff Doltin Sequence." *Sut Lovingood's Nat'ral Born Yarnspinner: Essays on George Washington Harris.* Ed. James E. Caron and M. Thomas Inge. Tuscaloosa: University of Alabama Press, 1996: 217-27.

Pease, Verne S. *In the Wake of War: A Tale of the South Under Carpet-Bagger Administration.* New York: George M. Hill, 1900.

Pinsker, Sanford. "Uneasy Laughter: Sut Lovingood—Between Rip Van Winkle and Andrew Dice Clay." *Sut Lovingood's Nat'ral Born Yarnspinner: Essays on George Washington Harris.* Ed. James E. Caron and M. Thomas Inge. Tuscaloosa: University of Alabama Press, 1996: 299-314.

Post, Louis F. "A 'Carpetbagger' in South Carolina." *Journal of Negro History* 10 (1925): 10-79.

"Prospectus of the Press & Messenger for 1868." *Knoxville Press & Messenger,* May 14, 1868: 3.

Reynolds, David. *Beneath the American Renaissance: The Subversive Imagination in the Age of Emerson and Melville.* New York: Knopf, 1988.

Smith, Theophus H. *Conjuring Culture: Biblical Formations of Black America.* New York: Oxford University Press, 1994.

Stewart, Randall. "Tidewater and Frontier." *Georgia Review* 13 (1959): 296-307.

"A Terrified Negro." *Nashville Union and American,* March 1, 1868: 3.

Tourgee, Albion. *The Invisible Empire.* New York: Fords, Howard and Hulbert, 1880.

Trelease, Allen W. *White Terror: The Ku-Klux Klan Conspiracy and Southern Reconstruction.* New York: Harper and Row, 1971.

"A Voice from the Ku-Klux Tombs." *Nashville Union & American,* July 12, 1868: 3.

Wade, Wyn Craig. *The Fiery Cross: The Ku Klux Klan in America.* New York: Simon and Schuster, 1987.

FURTHER READING

Criticism

Brown, Carol S. "Sut Lovingood: A Nat'ral Born Durn'd Yarnspinner." *Southern Literary Journal* 18, no. 1 (fall 1985): 85-100.

Discusses Harris's Sut Lovingood sketches as they relate to the tall tale form.

De Voto, Bernard Augustine. *Mark Twain's America.* Cambridge: Houghton Mifflin, 1932, 351 p.

Includes a discussion of Harris's influence on the humor of Mark Twain, and argues that an inimitable exuberance and joy lie at the heart of the Sut Lovingood sketches.

Eddings, Dennis W. "The Emergence of Sut Lovingood." *Essays in Arts and Sciences* 26 (October 1997): 85-9.

Examines the role of Harris's Sut Lovingood stories in the emergence of Southern frontier humor.

Inge, M. Thomas. "William Faulkner and George Washington Harris: In the Tradition of Southwestern Humor." *Tennessee Studies in Literature* 7 (1962): 47-59.

Outlines certain key parallels between the two authors' work.

Keller, Mark. "That George W. Harris 'Christmas Story': A Reconsideration of Authorship." *American Literature* 54, no. 2 (May 1982): 284-87.

Takes issue with William J. Starr's assertion that the 1849 story "Home-Voices—A Tale for the Holy-Tide" was written by George Washington Harris.

Long, Hudson. "Sut Lovingood and Mark Twain's Joan of Arc." *Modern Language Notes* 64, no. 1 (January 1949): 37-9.

Examines the similarities between a joke in the popular Harris sketch "Sicily Burns's Wedding" and a scene from Mark Twain's *Joan of Arc.*

McClary, Ben Harris. "George Washington Harris's 'Special Vision': His *Yarns* as Historical Sourcebook." In *No Fairer Land: Studies in Southern Literature Before 1900,* edited by J. Lasley Dameron and James W. Mathews, pp. 226-41. Troy, N.Y.: Whitson Publishing Company, 1986.

Evaluates representations of Southern frontier culture in Harris's Sut Lovingood stories.

Penrod, James H. "Folk Humor in *Sut Lovingood's Yarns.*" *Tennessee Folklore Society Bulletin* 16, no. 4 (December 1950): 76-84.

Examines descriptions of Southern folk traditions in Harris's work.

Plater, Ormonde. "The Lovingood Patriarchy." *Appalachian Journal* 1 (1973): 82-93.

Offers a close reading of Harris's Lovingood sketches.

Ross, Stephen M. "Jason Compson and Sut Lovingood: Southwestern Humor as Stream of Consciousness." In *The Humor of the Old South,* edited by M. Thomas Inge and Edward J. Piacentino, pp. 236-46. Lexington: University Press of Kentucky, 2001.

Compares approaches to Southern humor in Harris's Sut Lovingood stories and William Faulkner's *The Sound and the Fury.*

Rourke, Constance. *American Humor, A Study of the National Character.* New York: Harcourt, Brace, 1931, 324 p.

Briefly discusses Harris's unique use of characterization and comedy in his Sut Lovingood sketches.

Stewart, Randall. "Tidewater and Frontier." *Georgia Review* 13, no. 3 (fall 1959): 296-307.

Examines echoes of Geoffrey Chaucer's *Canterbury Tales* in Harris's prose style and humor.

Tandy, Jennette Reid. *Crackerbox Philosophers in American Humor and Satire.* New York: Columbia University Press, 1925, 181 p.

Discusses the character of Sut Lovingood as an early example of the "rebel" in American literature.

Thorp, Willard. "Suggs and Sut in Modern Dress: The Latest Chapter in Southern Humor." *Mississippi Quarterly* 13, no. 4 (fall 1960): 169-75.

Examines the influence of Sut Lovingood on twentieth-century Southern writers such as Flannery O'Connor, Erskine Caldwell, and others.

Turner, Arlin. "Seeds of Literary Revolt in the Humor of the Old Southwest." *Louisiana Historical Quarterly* 39, no. 2 (April 1957): 143-51.

Evaluates the ways that Harris's Sut Lovingood sketches challenged literary and social conventions of the period.

Young, Thomas Daniel. "A Nat'ral Born Durn'd Fool." *Thalia* 6, no. 2 (fall-winter 1983): 51-6.

Analyzes aspects of hypocrisy and deception in Harris's Sut Lovingood stories.

Additional coverage of Harris's life and career is contained in the following sources published by Thomson Gale: *Dictionary of Literary Biography*, **Vols. 3, 11, 248;** *Literature Resource Center*; *Nineteenth-Century Literature Criticism*, **Vol. 23; and** *Reference Guide to American Literature*, **Ed. 4.**

Multatuli
1820-1887

(Born Eduard Douwes Dekker) Dutch novelist, essayist, poet, playwright, and short story writer.

INTRODUCTION

Many scholars and critics regard Multatuli as the most influential Dutch author of the late nineteenth century, a writer whose unorthodox approach to the novel form prefigured the emergence of modern Dutch literature. Multatuli, whose name means "I have suffered much," combined technical experimentation with a passionate commitment to social justice, creating a literature that was at once artistically daring and politically meaningful. A veteran of the civil service in the Dutch East Indies, Multatuli became one of the country's most outspoken critics of colonial government practices, and his fictional account of his experiences in Java, the 1860 novel *Max Havelaar,* remains a landmark of Dutch fiction. The novel was noteworthy not only for its powerful message, drawing attention to the political and human rights abuses perpetrated in the Dutch colonies during the period, but also for its unconventional structure and use of multiple narrative points of view. Although Multatuli's modern literary reputation rests almost solely on the impact of *Max Havelaar,* in recent years scholars have begun to consider the significance of his other writings, discovering in them an impressive range of sensibilities and styles. For more than one hundred years his works have inspired political activists in both Europe and Asia, in addition to exerting an influence on such diverse writers and thinkers as D. H. Lawrence, Sigmund Freud, and the twentieth-century Indonesian author Pramoedya Anata Toer.

BIOGRAPHICAL INFORMATION

Multatuli was born Eduard Douwes Dekker in Amsterdam on March 2, 1820, the son of Engel Douwes Dekker, a sea captain, and Sietske Eeltjes Klein. As a teenager, Multatuli attended the prestigious Barlaeus Grammar School in Amsterdam, but in 1835 he abandoned his education to take a job with a textile company. At the age of eighteen, Multatuli sailed to Java on his father's ship, the *Dorothea,* intent on securing a job in the General Audit Office in Batavia (modern-day Jakarta). By 1842 the young colonial official had risen to the rank of District Officer in Natal, a remote coastal

town in Western Sumatra. Multatuli's appointment in Natal proved tumultuous, however, and he soon found himself suspended from his post because of discrepancies in his bookkeeping, a circumstance that temporarily thrust him into dire poverty. Multatuli was eventually exonerated of any willful wrongdoing, and he received a new appointment to a post in Java. During this period Multatuli also began writing his first book, *Losse Bladen uit het Dagboek van een Oud Man,* an experimental novel which would remain unfinished. In 1846 Multatuli married Everdine (Tine) Huberte (the inspiration for the character of Tina in *Max Havelaar*). Over the next decade Multatuli and his family lived in various colonial outposts throughout the Dutch East Indies. He achieved his highest government rank in January 1856, when he was named Assistant Resident of Lebak, but the appointment was short-lived. Outraged by the abject poverty of the native population, Multatuli filed a damning report accusing the local Javanese prince, or Regent, on various charges of murder, brutality, and corruption. The Resident of Lebak refused to acknowledge the accusations, compelling Multatuli to take his report directly to the Governor-General of Java, a brazen circumvention of official protocol. Multatuli was promptly reprimanded for insubordination and was subsequently reassigned to the remote district of Ngawi. In April 1856, frustrated by the obstructive tactics of his superiors, as well as by his own failure to achieve justice on behalf of the Javanese, Multatuli resigned his commission.

Upon his return to Europe, the impoverished Multatuli moved with his family to Brussels, where they settled for a short time in a small hotel. While in Brussels Multatuli began writing *Max Havelaar,* a largely autobiographical novel based on his recent experiences in Java. After completing the manuscript, Multatuli put the material in the hands of an acquaintance, the lawyer and author Jacob van Lennep, with the hope of getting it published. Fearful that government censors would object to the work's explicit condemnation of colonial practices, van Lennep edited many of the novel's most inflammatory passages before submitting it to a publisher. Even so, the book's exposure of government malfeasance in Java caused a sensation in the Netherlands upon its publication in 1860, and it soon appeared in numerous translations throughout Europe. Although the work failed to effect immediate changes in Dutch colonial policy, its message was not lost on legislative officials, and Multatuli's novel eventually inspired lasting reform. Emboldened by the reception of his debut novel, Multatuli continued to write at a feverish pace over the succeeding two decades. His next work, *Minnebrieven,* a novel comprised of fictional letters depicting an epistolary relationship between Max Havelaar and two other characters, appeared in 1861. From 1862 to 1877 Multatuli composed and published his epic *Ideeën,* a radical seven-volume philosophical treatise comprised of several literary genres, which included the novel *De Geschiedenis van Woutertje Pieterse* (published separately in 1890; *Walter Pieterse*). Multatuli's later writings failed to stir the same passions in readers as *Max Havelaar,* however, and he struggled to earn a living during the remaining years of his life. Following the death of Tine in 1874, Multatuli married Maria Hamminck Schepel. A year later he published an unexpurgated edition of *Max Havelaar.* For the next decade Multatuli lived an itinerant existence in cities throughout Europe. He died of a severe asthma attack in Nieder-Ingelheim, Germany, on February 19, 1887.

MAJOR WORKS

Multatuli's literary reputation rests almost exclusively on his vanguard novel *Max Havelaar.* This idiosyncratic work of fiction revolves around an idealistic government official, Max Havelaar, whose efforts to fight corruption in colonial Java are met with stubborn resistance from his superiors. Taking the form of a frame narrative, the book's opening is told from the point of view of an affluent coffee merchant named Droogstoppel, who has an unexpected reunion with a former classmate who, the reader eventually learns, is Havelaar. Although Droogstoppel is reluctant to engage with his boyhood friend, whom he calls Sjaalman ("Scarfman") because of the man's threadbare attire, he soon finds himself moved by pity for his friend's impoverished condition, and agrees to review his friend's bundle of manuscripts with the aim of helping to get them published. Droogstoppel believes the book will offer him valuable information on the coffee trade in Java, but soon realizes that the work contains harsh accusations against the Dutch government's policies in the East Indies, leveled in a style and tone that offend his bourgeois sensibility. As Havelaar's story unfolds, it quickly begins to dominate the novel; Multatuli writes of his initial arrival in Java, his efforts to uncover the truth about political corruption, and his ultimate dismissal. The narrative weaves in and out of the two points of view, balancing Droogstoppel's obtuse sense of propriety with Havelaar's passionate, and ultimately futile, idealism. In the novel's final pages Multatuli makes his most radical narrative shift, introducing himself and exhorting the Dutch government, as well as his readers, to end political oppression by whatever means, even if that end requires force. Equal parts satire, polemic, and character study, *Max Havelaar* defies straightforward categorization and is as much a statement on the art of the novel as it is a portrayal of life in the Dutch East Indies.

In addition to *Max Havelaar,* Multatuli published several other works in a variety of genres, although none enjoyed the success of his debut novel. His next work, *Minnebrieven,* describes an intense epistolary relationship between Max Havelaar, his wife, and an ambiguous character named Fancy, who represents both a beautiful young woman and a poetic ideal. The novel uses a frame similar to the one in *Max Havelaar,* although in this case Multatuli allows his authorial persona to intrude into the narrative from the very beginning, and the work is a commentary on its own composition, as well as a story about its characters. In the epic *Ideeën,* Multatuli utilizes several literary forms, including aphorisms, fables, and poetry, to articulate the full breadth of his intellectual and spiritual beliefs. Buried within this massive text is Multatuli's second novel, *Walter Pieterse,* a semi-autobiographical account of a young boy coming of age in Amsterdam. *Millioenen-Studiën* (1870-73) follows a gambler-philosopher as he travels the European countryside, musing on love, literature, and the nature of human existence. Although substantially varied in style and focus, Multatuli's writings are interconnected, with certain key characters, scenarios, and themes recurring in each of his major works.

CRITICAL RECEPTION

Max Havelaar met with widespread critical and popular acclaim in Holland upon its original publication in 1860. Baron Alphonse Nahuÿs's 1868 translation of the novel introduced it to English-speaking readers, and early English reviewers lauded the work's integrity and political insight, although some believed its unorthodox construction was too radical for most readers. By the early twentieth century some readers came to regard the work as a bold and original work of fiction in its own right, and discussions of the novel's literary merits began to emerge. D. H. Lawrence's important introduction to the 1927 English translation examined the satirical aspects of the work, also extolling its defiantly "anti-novelistic" structure as a significant development in literary modernism. While most important criticism of Multatuli's overall body of work has been written in Dutch, some important studies have appeared in English in recent decades. Modern critical interpretations have focused not only on *Max Havelaar*, but also on Multatuli's lesser-known and equally noteworthy writings. Peter King's seminal 1972 study, *Multatuli*, provides an overview of Multatuli's major works and offers analysis of his stylistic innovations, as well as his profound humanism. Multatuli's attention to political abuses in the Dutch East Indies have also made his work a relevant subject for postcolonial criticism, and recent scholars, including Anne-Marie Feenberg, Gary Baker, and Carl H. Niekerk, have examined such topics as alienation, the politics of race, and the psychology of oppression in Multatuli's writings.

PRINCIPAL WORKS

Max Havelaar, of de Koffijveilingen der Nederlandsche Handelmaatschappij [*Max Havelaar; or, The Coffee Auctions of the Dutch Trading Company*] (novel) 1860; revised edition, 1875.

Het Gebed van den Onwetende (poetry) 1861

Minnebrieven (prose) 1861

Ideeën. 7 vols. (essays, poetry, short stories, plays, and novel) 1862-77

Millioenen-Studiën (prose) 1872-73

*Vorstenschool (play) 1875

†De Geschiedenis van Woutertje Pieterse [*Walter Pieterse: A Story of Holland*] (novel) 1890

Aleid (novel) 1891

Brieven van Multatuli. Bijdragen tot de kennis van zijn leven. 10 vols. (letters) 1891-96

Volledige Werken. 25 vols. (novels, essays, poetry, short stories, and plays) 1950-95

The Oyster and the Eagle: Selected Aphorisms and Parables of Multatuli (short stories) 1974

**1875 reflects the year of the first performance of this play. It had been published in *Ideeën*.

*†This novel first appeared in *Ideeën*.

CRITICISM

Westminster Review (review date January-April 1868)

SOURCE: Review of *Max Havelaar*, by Multatuli. *Westminster Review*, n.s., 33 (January-April 1868): 542-63.

[*In the following excerpt, the anonymous critic evaluates* Max Havelaar *as both a work of fiction and a political treatise, lauding the book for the authenticity of its characters and scenes, the inventiveness and humor of its style, and the unwavering force of its critique of Dutch imperialism.*]

It is difficult to say whether **Max Havelaar**[1] is more interesting as a novel or powerful as a political pamphlet. From either point of view it is of rare and first-rate excellence. In its life-like actuality it constantly recals Defoe, while in its tender and original humour it suggests Sterne in his best moods. The subject revolves round the Dutch government of Java and its other insular possessions in the East. The peculiarities of Dutch administration have been not long since held up to England as an object of admiration, and as a model we should do well to study and imitate. In **Max Havelaar** they are made the object of the most burning invective, and yet even from its pages it is easy to perceive how they could still in Europe maintain the high character which has been given them. The Dutch hold their Indian empire by a complete and undisputed conquest, but administer it through the native chiefs, interfering as little as possible with the social system they found prevailing in the islands. They know perfectly well how tyrannous in many of its features that system is, and they appoint residents and sub-residents to advise and control their "younger brother," the native Regent. These European officials, however, are but poorly paid, while the native chiefs have often truly princely incomes, which are increased by a percentage on all the exportable articles which are grown in their districts. Whole regions of the country are often reduced to starvation by these chiefs, who insist upon their subjects cultivating coffee, indigo, and spices, to the neglect of the rice fields, which yield their main crop and chief sustenance. The quasi-feudal rights which these regents have always possessed of demanding personal service, and levying contributions on the property of their subjects, enable them to subdue, or drive out of their districts, all who affect any independence. It is very true that the resident is appointed to restrain these excesses within endurable limits, but he is practically helpless and powerless in the matter. The oppressed native, who has appealed to him under cover of the night, will contradict his own indictment when he is, in rare cases, brought face to face with his "father" before the higher European officials, and the sub-resident who has endeavoured to do him justice acquires himself the character of a false accuser and disturber of the tranquillity of the colony. Private remonstrance is, indeed, deferentially listened to, but it is immediately disregarded by the regents. On the part of the higher officials, the settled principle is, that the exports to Europe must be kept up, and a fair face put upon matters to the home authorities. If a few natives, who have been driven by oppression to appeal to the nearest sub-resident, and in spite of the utmost precaution in approaching him for the purpose, have been discovered in doing so, are found the next morning to have been "drowned" on their return to their village; too much inquiry is thought by the colonial authorities to disturb the "tranquillity of the colony," to repeat a favourite phrase of theirs. The poor and peculative sub-residents are bribed by the chiefs, the weak are intimidated, and those who are neither dishonest nor timid run the greatest risk of finding something in some solemn feast to which they are invited that prevents their ever attending any other. And the superior officials will have it so. The evils are so great, and their cure so difficult, that each man puts off the day of reformation to the times of his successor. The Governor-General is usually a person who knows nothing of the colony before his arrival in it, and is immediately surrounded by men who have long since resolved to make the best of a bad matter. The most energetic soon succumb to the combined influences of the climate and such an entourage. To arouse the Dutch people to a full inquiry into the condition of their Indian empire is the object of the author. It is needless to compare this book in its aim and purpose with *Uncle Tom's Cabin*. It is far more convincing in its singularly life-like scenes and characters than that celebrated novel. Indeed, it is perfectly wonderful what an intimate feeling of insight into the whole social system of an oriental people the author succeeds in communicating to his readers. As digressive as Uncle Toby, the tale, during its progress, seems constantly to halt or wander from the point, and it is not until we arrive at the last chapters that the consummate art reveals itself by which an unwilling public is led to listen to a tale so repugnant to its prepossessions. The genuine and original humour with which the coffee broker of Amsterdam is drawn will leave Batavus Drystubble an immortal memory in the minds of all who here make his acquaintance. Many have descanted on the close alliance between humour and pathos. In the author of *Max Havelaar* they will find a fresh instance in support of their theory. The poetry of his oriental scenes, the sympathy he feels for the unredressed wrongs of the native Javanese, are as touching as his portraiture of Dutch self-complacency and narrow respectability is ironical and scorching. He is as true as Jan Steen in his pictures of his fellow-countrymen, while his oriental scenes affect you like some of the most beautiful of Cuyp's atmospheres. We regret greatly that our limits preclude us from extracting either Drystubble's self-portraiture or the affecting Indian idyl of Saidjah and Adinda. The publication of this book aroused a perfect storm in the author's native country. His bold and outspoken challenge to the government to contradict any of his assertions has never been replied to; but rather an effort has been made to restrict its sale. The author finding that he had unwittingly parted with the full copyright, no second edition has been allowed. He may well call himself "Multatuli." But his sub-residentship in Java has enabled him to add the name of Douwes Dekker to the very first rank of European novelists and philanthropists.

Note

1. *Max Havelaar; or the Coffee Plantations of the Dutch Trading Company.* By Multatuli. Translated from the original manuscript by Baron Alphonse Nahuys. Edinburgh: Edmonston and Douglas. 1868.

Contemporary Review (review date April 1868)

SOURCE: Review of *Max Havelaar*, by Multatuli. *Contemporary Review*, no. 4 (April 1868): 615-18.

[*In the following review, the anonymous critic finds* Max Havelaar *powerful and original, but takes Multatuli to task for attempting to integrate too many disparate styles and points of view into the novel.*]

This is a remarkable book. Yet it is one which it is very hard for a foreign critic to judge of fairly. The translator tells us in his preface that it was "published a few years ago, and caused such a sensation in Holland as was never before experienced in that country." He compares it to *Uncle Tom's Cabin*, but sets the author—Eduard Douwes Dekker, formerly Assistant-Resident of the Dutch Government in Java—far above Mrs. Stowe, as having "sacrificed future fortune, and all that makes life agreeable, for a principle—for right and equity." It is "immortal;" it will "do honour to the literature of any language;" it has been "written by a genius of that order which only appears at long intervals in the world's history." But distance is a dispassionate arbiter, and looked at from across the sea, the first impression which *Max Havelaar* produces is that of an attempt to blend in one a political pamphlet, a novel, and a collection of thoughts and opinions on things in general, which has spoilt all three. The pamphlet is high-toned and sincere, but is deprived of weight by the form adopted; the novel shows power, but loses interest through the intermixture of extraneous elements; the thoughts and opinions are often striking, but out of place. But after coming to such conclusions one feels that they are but platitudes, when the author, dismissing his personages with contempt, tells us that he will make no excuses for the form of his book; that he has simply written it to be read; that read he *will* be by statesmen, by men of letters, by merchants, by lady's-maids, by governors-general in retirement, by ministers, "by the lackeys of these excellencies, by mutes—who *more majorum* will say that I attack God Almighty where I attack only the god which they have made according to their own image—by the members of the representative chambers;" that "the greater the disapprobation of my book the better I shall be pleased, for the chance of being heard will be so much the greater;"—when he threatens to translate his book into all European languages, till in every capital the refrain shall be heard, "There is a band of robbers between Germany and the Scheldt;" if this fails, to translate it again into Malay, Javanese, & c., and sharpen scimitars and sabres by warlike songs, so as to give "delivery and help, lawfully if possible, *lawfully with violence* if need be—*and that would be very pernicious to the coffee auctions of the Dutch Trading Company!*" Clearly, a man like this must be followed upon his own ground, measured by his own standard. Though he may be only a Dutch-built leviathan, still he is of the breed; there is no putting "an hook into his nose," or boring "his jaw through with a thorn;" no playing with him "as with a bird," nor binding him for our maidens.

The only true way of judging the book, then, is not to view it as a book, but to look upon both book and man as facts—very surprising and portentous facts, it would seem, to the Dutch nation, and surprising, too, to some other nations also. For it had gone forth to the whole world that the Dutch Government of Java of late years was a great success—anomalous indeed, in some respects, according to political economy, since it rested upon monopoly and regulated cultivation, but undeniable, unmistakable. To the Dutchman himself this was a tenet of positive faith, which he drank down afresh with every cupful of his Java coffee, which he saw confirmed day after day at the auctions of his great *Handelsmaatschappy,* or Trading Company, in which his king was known to be a leading shareholder. Foreign visitors confirmed these conclusions, English above all—amongst whom it will be sufficient to name Mr. Money, whose "Java" is little more than a panegyric on Dutch, as compared with British, India.

In the midst of this state of things a book like **Max Havelaar** would explode like a shell. Here was a man, speaking from seventeen years' official experience, who declared that the profit of the Trading Company "was only obtained by paying the Javanese just enough to keep him from starving;" that he was "driven away from his rice-fields" in order to cultivate other products which the Government compelled him to grow, and compelled him to sell to itself, at the price it fixed for itself; that famine was often the consequence, by which sometimes "whole districts were depopulated, mothers offered to sell their children for food, mothers ate their own children"—as in our own Orissa, alas!—that labour was habitually exacted without payment both by native and European officials, cattle and produce taken away by robbery and extortion; that "endless expeditions" were sent, and "heroic deeds performed, against poor miserable creatures . . . reduced by starvation to skeletons . . . whose ill-treatment has driven them to revolt;" that European officials connived at wrong-doing, or were silent about it where they did not participate in it, knowing that an upright discharge of their duties would only bring on them reproof, disgrace, or ruin; that the official reports of the functionaries to the island Government, and those from the island to the mother country, were "for the greater and more important part untrue," the financial accounts ridiculously false; that a "mild and submissive" population "has complained year after year of tyranny," yet sees resident after resident depart without anything being ever done towards the redress of its grievances; that "the end of all this" would be a "Jacquerie."

The news in itself was startling, and the mode of delivering it was of a nature to make it more so. For a more stinging satire of the lower propensities of the Dutch character could hardly be conceived than that embodied in the Amsterdam coffee-broker, Batavus Drystubble, the supposed author of the work, the contrast between whom and the chivalrous, unworldly Havelaar is most powerfully brought out, though by very inartistic means. Overdone as the picture is, Batavus Drystubble certainly stands out as one of the most remarkable embodiments of money-grubbing Phariseeism which literature has yet produced; and this, although the first sketch of the personage is far from consistent with his fuller portrait,—giving a curious instance, in fact, of the way in which a character may grow into life and truth in the author's own mind, if only steadily looked at. Nothing can be better hit off than Drystubble's firm rich man's faith that a poor man must be a scoundrel:—

> Mark that Shawlman. He left the ways of the Lord; now he is poor, and lives in a little garret: that is the consequence of immorality and bad conduct. He does not now know what time it is, and his little boy wears knee breeches.

The *naïf* selfishness of this is equally masterly:—

> Why do they want buffaloes, those black fellows? *I* never had a buffalo, and yet I am contented; there are men who are always complaining. And as regards that

scoffing at forced labour, I perceive that he had not heard that sermon of Domine Wawelaar's, otherwise he would know how useful labour is in the extension of the kingdom of God. It is true he is a Lutheran.

Add this touch also to the last:—

> *I did not speak to him of the Lord, because he is a Lutheran*; but I worked on his mind and his honour.

This again is terrible:—

> Wawelaar himself has said that God so directs all things that orthodoxy leads to wealth. "Look only," he said, "is there not much wealth in Holland? That is because of the faith. Is there not in France every day murder and homicide? That is because there are Roman Catholics there. Are not the Javanese poor? They are Pagans. The more the Dutch have to do with the Javanese the more wealth will be here and the more poverty there." I am astonished at Wawelaar's penetration; for it is the truth that I, who am exact in religion, see that my business increases every year, and Busselinck and Waterman, who do not care about God or the Commandments, will remain bunglers as long as they live. The Rosemeyers, too, who trade in sugar, and have a Roman Catholic maid-servant, had a short time ago to accept 27 per cent. out of the estate of a Jew who became bankrupt. The more I reflect the further I advance in tracing the unspeakable ways of God. Lately it appeared that thirty millions had been gained on the sale of products furnished by Pagans, and in this is not included what I have gained thereby, and others who live by this business. Is not that as if the Lord said,—"Here you have thirty millions as a reward for your faith?" Is not that the finger of God who causes the wicked one to labour to preserve the righteous one? Is not that a hint for us to go on in the right way, and to cause those far away to produce much, and to stand fast here to the true religion? Is it not, therefore, "Pray and labour," that we should pray and have the work done by those who do not know the Lord's Prayer? Oh, how truly Wawelaar speaks when he calls the yoke of God light! How easy the burthen is to every one who believes! I am only a few years past forty, and can retire when I please to Driebergen, and *see how it ends with others who forsake the Lord.*

Thackeray himself could not have surpassed this scathing page. It is immortal, come what may to the book which contains it.

Max Havelaar himself, though the conception of his character is a subtle one, and is on the whole well brought out—at once dreamy and practical, lavish and self-stinting, indulgent and rigid, irregular in his impulses, and yet bent on enforcing order—is of far less worth artistically than the coffee-broker, and there is a constant tendency to rhetorical self-assertion about him which one fears is characteristic of the writer himself. The plot is really too slight to be worth analyzing in detail; suffice it to say that Havelaar is an Assistant-Resident in Java, intent on doing justice, and who

thereby only brings disgrace upon himself. More than one such tale might be told from the records of British India; and it is indeed remarkable that the worst excesses which the book complains of are laid to the charge of the native officials, although the burden of the vicious system of government, with which the tolerance of their malpractices seems almost irretrievably bound up, lies of course with the European rulers.

Havelaar's random opinions, *de omnibus rebus,* are often full of quaint power and humour; as when he complains of guide-book measurements which require you to have so many "feet of admiration at hand not to be taken for a Turk or a bagman," or inveighs against cataracts because they tell him nothing:—

> They make a noise, but don't speak. They cry, "rroo," "rroo," "rroo." Try crying, "rroo, rroo," for six thousand years or more, and you will see how few persons will think you an amusing man.

A full idea of the book cannot, however, be given without a sample of its pathos. Here is a perfectly exquisite piece of metreless poetry, which, if not translated from the Javanese, but the work of Mr. Douwes Dekker himself, is simply a nineteenth-century miracle:—

> I do not know when I shall die.
> I saw the great sea on the south coast
>   When I was there with my father making salt.[1]
> If I die at sea and my body is thrown into the
>   deep water, then sharks will come;
> They will swim round my corpse, and ask, "Which of
>   us shall devour the body that goes down into the
> water?"
>   —I shall not hear it.
>
>   I do not know where I shall die.
> I saw in a blaze the house of Pa-ansoe, which he
>   himself has set on fire, because he was *mata
> glap*;[2]
> If I die in a burning house, glowing embers
>   will fall on my corpse;
> And outside of the house there will be many cries of
>   men throwing water on the fire to kill it.
>   —I shall not hear it.
>
>   I do not know where I shall die.
> I saw the little Si-Oenah fall out of a klappa-tree,
>   When he plucked a *klappa* [cocoa-nut] for his
> mother;
> If I fall out of a klappa-tree I shall lie dead
>   below in the shrubs like Si-Oenah.
> Then my mother will not weep, for she is dead. But
>   others will say with a loud voice, "See, there lies
> Saidjah."
>   —I shall not hear it.
>
>   I do not know where I shall die.
> I have seen the corpse of Palisoe, who died of
>   old age, for his hairs were white:
> If I die of old age, with white hairs,
>   hired women will stand weeping near my corpse,

And they will make lamentation, as did the mourners
over
    Palisoe's corpse, and the grandchildren will
weep, very loud.
        —I shall not hear it.

  I do not know where I shall die.
I have seen at Badoer many that were dead. They
    were dressed in white shrouds, and were buried
in the earth.
If I die at Badoer, and am buried beyond the dessah
[village],
    eastward against the hill, where the grass is high,
Then will Adinda pass by there, and the border of
    her sarong will sweep softly along the grass.
        —I shall hear it.

Will not any gentlemen or ladies with volumes of poems ready, or preparing, or accumulating for publication, after reading the above, oblige their contemporaries and posterity by throwing their manuscripts into the fire?

There remains to be added that Mr. Douwes Dekker has, the preface tells us, in vain challenged a refutation of his charges—*e.g.*, at the International Congress for the Promotion of Social Science at Amsterdam in 1863—and that he has been declared to have understated rather than overstated the truth. One word must finally be said in favour of Baron Nahuijs's translation, the English of which might put to the blush many of our professed translators.

To conclude. Many English readers may, perhaps, hardly have patience to read through *Max Havelaar*; but few that do will deem their time misspent.

Notes

1. An offence in Java, as in British India, salt being a Government monopoly.

2. In a state of frenzy.

Athenaeum (review date 8 August 1868)

SOURCE: Review of *Max Havelaar*, by Multatuli. *Athenaeum*, no. 2128 (8 August 1868): 171-72.

[*In the following review, the anonymous critic praises Multatuli for writing truthfully about political oppression in the Dutch East Indies.*]

The Dutch have, no doubt, a number of valuable possessions in the East Indies, "that magnificent empire of Insulind, which winds about the equator like a garland of emeralds," as the favourite phrase runs; and the rest of the world hears so little and, what is more, cares so little about what is actually taking place, that it generally assumes tranquillity and prosperity there go hand in hand, and that the Dutch, a quiet, shrewd, peace-loving people, do know better than any other how to make colonies a source of direct profit rather than a dead loss to the mother-country. But on closer examination this pleasing assumption proves far from true. The Dutch, so far from avoiding the mistakes which the English, Spaniards, French and other nations have made in dealing with distant possessions, have reproduced them in even an exaggerated form, and do not seem to have learnt anything since those days when by their ultra-protectionist commercial policy and their wish to retain unjust monopolies they rendered themselves odious to the rest of the world. That the bulk of the Dutch nation does not know what is actually going on in their East-Indian possessions, we can well believe. The subject is far too complicated for any ordinary man to master, even if he has the wish and application to do so. But the difficulty is much increased by the fact that the Indian officials, desiring to make things look pleasant, do not, or rather are not allowed to furnish truthful *written* reports. They may make any number of *verbal* communications to proper quarters about the extortions, cruelties, and crimes of the native chiefs: but woe to the official who dares to put all this on paper. His doom is sealed: a mere dismissal from office, without pension, after spending the best part of his life in the sultry regions of the tropics, being the least punishment that awaits him. It is a fearful alternative that here presents itself.

Such, indeed, is the drift of *Max Havelaar,* the book placed at the head of our notice. It professes to be a novel, but a novel founded on facts, the author of which, we are told in the Preface, has boldly asked the Dutch Government to prove the substance of it to be false, and at the International Congress for the Promotion of Science at Amsterdam challenged his countrymen to refute him. But up to this moment no champion has come forward to disprove what is here asserted and hinted at; on the contrary, Mr. Veth, the well-known orientalist at Leyden, who made a special study of Indian matters, declared that the author understates rather than overstates the truth, and quoted Vitalis and others who had published accounts of scenes and facts much more shocking than those depicted in *Max Havelaar.*

The author wrote the book under the pseudonym of Multatuli; but his real name, Eduard D. Dekker, formerly Assistant-Resident of the Dutch Government of Java, at once became known; and the hero of the novel may be said to be an idealized portrait of the author himself. Max Havelaar then, a man of superior acquirements, finds himself appointed to a district in Java as Assistant-Resident, or Sub-Governor, and the first thing on his assumption of office is to convoke the native chiefs, by whose aid the machinery of government in the Dutch Indian dependencies is kept going, as well as the European official placed under his authority. He tells them that he is resolved to do his best to promote the prosperity of the impoverished district over which his jurisdiction extends, but that he expects the Regent, the highest native functionary, as well as the other native chiefs, will also do their duty, and not by cruel extortions drive the population away, and render the extension of cultivation a matter of impossibility. Fully aware of the existing abuses, and conscious that the system cannot be overthrown by the efforts of a single combatant, he endeavours to win over the Regent and others by telling them that he will let bygones be bygones, will not be too hard with them at first, but, at the same time, will not tolerate injustice in any shape. Havelaar soon perceives that his conciliatory policy is of no avail. The Regent's court has a large number of hangers-on, who commit all sorts of extortion and cruelties towards the natives. In the depth of night the boldest of the injured parties steal to Havelaar's house, and beseech him to protect them from the tyranny of their countrymen. But he finds it difficult to do anything for them. When he inquires officially into the matter the complainants, bearing in mind the punishments awaiting them from the hands of their native rulers for daring to prefer charges against them, revoke everything they have said, and offer the most humble and abject apologies. The Assistant-Resident goes home, disgusted with their cowardly behaviour, and the poor complainants are now subjected to all sorts of cruelties and tortures, if indeed they escape with their lives.

Havelaar soon discovers from papers left behind that his predecessor in office has also been a man resolved to do his duty, but that he died suddenly. How he died is known to his widow, who lives near Havelaar's premises, and fearing that the fate which befell her husband may also befall his successor, she closely watches and questions every native who comes to the Assistant-Resident's house. At first Havelaar attributes this to sheer inquisitiveness on her part, until she tells him plainly that it is done for his own and his family's protection; in fact, that she fears poison may be administered. Of course life under such circumstances is unbearable; and Havelaar, fully believing that the Head Government, when made aware of the real state of the district, will support him in remedying the evil, puts the whole case on record, and transmits it to the Resident, who for years has furnished the stereotyped statement that everything in the district is flourishing and progressing as rapidly as can be expected. The latter is much annoyed about this report, and desires Havelaar to withdraw it; but the Assistant-Resident is resolved to stand or fall by it. The consequence of this obstinacy is, that he is dismissed, and that all attempts to obtain an interview with the Governor-General for the purpose of justifying his conduct prove abortive. Havelaar goes to the wall, and the poor natives continue to be subjected to the same tyranny as they have always been liable to under Dutch rule.

In order to bring out the views entertained by a section of the commercial world in Holland itself about the subject, the author introduces a Mr. Drystubble, a rich coffee-broker and a great egotist, who is supposed to be editing the book and commenting upon the facts and opinions advanced. Drystubble is a mean, contemptible fellow, drawn by a masterly hand, who, we trust, may not be the type of a very large section of the Dutch nation. The book is written with considerable dash, and by a man who knows his subject thoroughly. It will naturally provoke a good deal of discussion, as containing charges of a most compromising nature against the administration of the Dutch Indian possessions,—not made, be it remembered, by a foreigner jealous of Holland's prosperity, but by a Dutchman to the backbone, anxious to remove what he considers foul blots from the national escutcheon.

Alphonse Johan Bernard Horstmar Nahuÿs (essay date 1868)

SOURCE: Nahuÿs, Alphonse Johan Bernard Horstmar. Preface to *Max Havelaar,* by Multatuli, translated by Alphonse Johan Bernard Horstmar Nahuÿs, pp. v-x. Edinburgh: Edmonston & Douglas, 1868.

[*In the following essay, Nahuÿs examines Multatuli's account of oppression and social injustice in the Dutch East Indies in* Max Havelaar, *while also evaluating the profound political repercussions of the work's original publication in the Netherlands.*]

Max Havelaar was published a few years ago, and caused such a sensation in Holland as was never before experienced in that country. The author wrote it under the pseudonym of Multatuli, but his real name, Eduard Douwes Dekker, formerly Assistant Resident of the Dutch Government in Java, at once became known. Full of fire, and overflowing with enthusiasm, the author presented it to his countrymen in the form of a novel,—a book wherein he made them acquainted with the incredible extortions and tyranny of which the natives of the Dutch Indies, "that magnificent empire of Insulind, which winds about the equator like a garland of emeralds," are the victims, and how he tried in vain, while still in the service of the Government, to put an end to the cruel oppressions that happen every day in those countries. Though some considered his book to be merely an interesting and captivating novel, the author maintained that it contained nothing but facts. He boldly asked the Dutch Government to prove the *substance* of his book to be false, but its truth has never been disputed. At the International Congress for the promotion of Social Sciences at Amsterdam, in 1863, he challenged his countrymen to refute him, but there was no champion to accept the challenge. In short, Mr. Douwes Dekker, who had been a functionary in the service of the Dutch Government for the space of seventeen years, rather understated than overstated the truth. Not a single fact was ever contested in Holland, and he is still ready to prove his statements.[1] In the Dutch Parliament nobody answered a single word, but Mr. Van Twist, ex-Governor-General of the Dutch Indies, who, on being appealed to by the Baron Van Hoevell, said that he could *perhaps* refute *Max Havelaar,* but that it was not his interest to do so.

The book proves that what was formerly written in *Uncle Tom's Cabin* of the cruelties perpetrated upon the slaves in America, is nothing in comparison to what happens every day in the Dutch Indies.

* * *

"Max Havelaar" is the name under which the author chooses to describe his experiences in the East; in the first chapters of the book he has just returned from India, and he meets an old school-companion, at that time a coffee-broker, a Mr. Drystubble. This Mr. Drystubble is very rich, and the author being just then very poor, the latter asks his old school-fellow to be security for the publishing of his book. At first Mr. Drystubble will not hear of this, but afterwards, when he perceives that it will be of some advantage to himself, he consents. Drystubble is a very characteristic person, knowing nothing beyond his trade, a great egotist, and is represented by the author with true wit and humour, in order to show the extreme contrast between him self and . . . some of his countrymen, whom he may perhaps have met with since his return from Java. At that time, the author wears a plaid or shawl, and Mr. Drystubble therefore speaks always of him as Mr. Shawlman. A few months after the publication of *Max Havelaar,* one of the most eminent members of the Dutch Parliament avowed that this book had struck the whole country with horror. In vain the Dutch tried to make a party question of it. The author openly declared that he belonged neither to the Liberal nor to the Conservative party; but that he placed himself under the banner of RIGHT, EQUITY, and HUMANITY. As soon, however, as he professed to be a mere friend of mankind, without bias to any political party, the official world avoided even to pronounce his name, and affected to have forgotten the man whose conduct had before been considered as a reproof, and whose influence menaced danger to people in place. Instead of accepting the challenge, it seemed more worthy to fight the battle out with the vile weapons of abuse and slander. Of course the reader will not regard Mr. Drystubble's nonsensical and hypocritical observations as the sentiments of our author. It is precisely Multatuli's intention to make Drystubble odious, and his philosophy absurd, though sometimes he speaks truth and common-sense—for he is a type of a part of the Dutch nation.

So much for the tendency of the book. Need I say that it will do honour to the literature of any language, and that it may be read as well for profit as for amusement?

But *Max Havelaar* is immortal, not because of literary art or talent, but because of the cause he advocates. I think that every one who admires Harriet Beecher Stowe's immortal pleading, ought likewise to read Multatuli's accusation. I compare *Max Havelaar* to *Uncle Tom's Cabin,* but I do not compare Multatuli, the champion and the martyr of humanity and justice, to Mrs. Stowe, for I am not aware that that lady, with all her merits, has sacrificed future fortune, and all that makes life agreeable, for a principle—for right and equity—as has been done by Eduard Douwes Dekker. *Max Havelaar* bears evidence of having been written by a genius of that order which only appears at long intervals in the world's history. His mind embraces in its intellectual compass all mankind, regardless of race or caste. By the diffusion of this book, a bond will be formed embracing all lovers of genius and justice throughout the world.

It was the intention of the author to have had his work translated into all the European languages. Unfortunately he *unwittingly* disposed of the property of his own book. And if it had not thus been "legally" withheld from the people of Holland, it is probably that I should not have been its translator, but I haven been constrained to make known as widely as possible the sad truth regarding the mal-administration of laws in themselves good, by the Dutch Government in her Indian dependencies. To the British nation the facts will be new, as the books published in England on Dutch India are few in number, superficial in character, and give no idea of the condition of the native population. I cannot judge of English politics or about British India, but however perfect British rule may be, it cannot be so perfect that it has nothing more to learn.

Note

1. Mr. Veth, the well-known learned Orientalist at Leyden, who made a special study of Indian matters, declared that Multatuli understated the truth, and quoted many authors, such as Mr. Vitalis and others, who had published accounts of scenes and facts much more shocking than he had depicted. Mr. Veth complimented Multatuli upon his moderation, saying that he displayed a mastership of art in not exhausting the subject.

Alfred Russel Wallace (essay date 1872)

SOURCE: Wallace, Alfred Russel. "Java." In *The Malay Archipelago, the Land of the Orang-utan and the Bird of Paradise; a Narrative of Travel, with Studies of Man and Nature,* rev. ed. 1872. Reprint, pp. 72-92. London: Macmillan and Co., 1898.

[*In the following excerpt, originally published in 1872, Wallace dismisses* Max Havelaar *as "tedious" and unfocused, while asserting that Multatuli's claims about Dutch colonial abuses are overstated.*]

A tale has lately been written in Holland, and translated into English, entitled *Max Havelaar; or, The Coffee Auctions of the Dutch Trading Company,* and with our usual one-sidedness in all relating to the Dutch Colonial System, this work has been excessively praised, both for its own merits, and for its supposed crushing exposure of the iniquities of the Dutch government of Java. Greatly to my surprise, I found it a very tedious and long-winded story, full of rambling digressions; and whose only point is to show that the Dutch Residents and Assistant Residents wink at the extortions of the native princes; and that in some districts the natives have to do work without payment, and have their goods taken away from them without compensation. Every statement of this kind is thickly interspersed with italics and capital letters; but as the names are all fictitious, and neither dates, figures, nor details are ever given, it is impossible to verify or answer them. Even if not exaggerated, the facts stated are not nearly so bad as those of the oppression by free-trade indigo-planters, and torturing by native tax-gatherers under British rule in India, with which the readers of English newspapers were familiar a few years ago. Such oppression, however, is not fairly to be imputed in either case to the particular form of government, but is rather due to the infirmity of human nature, and to the impossibility of at once destroying all trace of ages of despotism on the one side, and of slavish obedience to their chiefs on the other.

Austin Clarke (review date 2 April 1927)

SOURCE: Clarke, Austin. Review of *Max Havelaar,* by Multatuli. *Nation and Athenaeum* 40, no. 26 (2 April 1927): 930-32.

[*In the following excerpt, Clarke dismisses* Max Havelaar *as having little more than historical value for the modern reader.*]

The really interesting question about *Max Havelaar* is why Mr. D. H. Lawrence, who writes the introduction [in the 1927 edition], likes it at all. It has little colour or intensity. The neglected author of this Dutch novel of the fifties exposed the corruption of the coffee plantations in Java to annoy his countrymen; but satire on shopkeeping wears thin in this age of multiple shops and glorified merchant princes. "Multatuli" gives way to the discursive humour fashionable in the spaciousness of Victorian times, and the story never really moves by its own momentum, though it has fine moments and possibilities. Historical piety must be its due.

A. J. Barnouw (review date 2 April 1927)

SOURCE: Barnouw, A. J. "Romance and Reality." *Saturday Review of Literature* 3, no. 36 (2 April 1927): 693.

[*In the following review of* Max Havelaar, *Barnouw examines the historical and autobiographical aspects of*

the work. *Barnouw expresses high praise for the direct, plainspoken qualities of Multatuli's literary style.*]

Multatuli, "I have suffered much," was the pen-name of Eduard Douwes Dekker (1820-1887). The choice of that pseudonym was not a beggarly device for catching alms of literary notice from compassionate critics and a sentimental public. He did not shamelessly exploit his suffering; he proudly proclaimed it as the reason for his existence as an author, even as a martyr is made by his pain. Overcome in his single-handed fight for justice, Dekker drew in-inspiration from the bitterness of defeat and through the style of Multatuli vindicated Max Havelaar's cause. For the book is an autobiography, the story of Dekker's short career as a Government official in the Dutch East Indies.

As a *controleur* of Lebak, a district of the Bantam Residency, West Java, he found the native population over which he was made guardian impoverished by the extortions of their native prince and depleted by the emigration of those who preferred exile to misery at home. That native ruler was not a wicked despot, he only did what native ruders in Java had been accustomed to do from time immemorial. He was not worse than the majority of his type, the effect of his exactions was only more conspicuous in his regency because the soil there was less fertile than elsewhere and the people less able to bear up under the customary extortions. The Dutch authorities were loath to interfere, for the removal of a hereditary ruler was against their proved system of governing the natives through their own princes. They felt that Dekker, by insisting that the central government at Batavia should be notified of the Regent's malpractices, would detract from a great and time-honored tradition in order to redress a small abuse. Hence his zealous advocacy of the native fell on deaf ears. The Governor General, displeased with the manner in which he had proceeded, relieved him from his duties in Lebak and ordered his transfer to a different post. But Dekker, preferring martyrdom to discipline, asked and obtained his honorable discharge.

That is the reality which Dekker turned into the romantic story of Max Havelaar. It matters little whether the tale be untrue, as has been charged, to the facts of his experience. It suffices that Dekker honestly believed it to be true in every detail, and in the fire of his indignation he moulded his speech into a style that struck home by its directness and simple beauty. He was conscious of his art and of the power that it carried. "I do my best," he once wrote, "to write living Dutch, although I have gone to school." The sarcasm was prompted by a deeper feeling than mere pleasure in paradox. A rebel by temperament, he hated school for its choking grip on originality, and that same spirit of revolt made him resist the grip of officialdom on life in Java and, as a writer, shake off the grip of the literary standard upon the language, which squeezed all expression into stereotyped forms. The rebel in action becomes a reformer in retrospect, and Multatuli, whom his contemporaries denounced as a dangerous revolutionary, is now honored as a pioneer of liberating thought in education, in colonial government, and most of all in literary art.

Dekker was equally original and defiant of accepted standards in constructing his story. He set the picture of Havelaar among the Javanese in a framework of satirical allegory which was to reveal the ultimate cause of the evil that his hero opposed. The selfishness of Holland's *bourgeoisie satisfaite,* which fattened on the proceeds of Javanese labor and cared not for Javanese misery, was at the root of it all. In Batavus (i.e. Hollander) Drystubble, Amsterdam coffee broker, that bourgeoisie is personified and ridiculed. He is a complacent coxcomb and a hypocrite, he is prosaic and devoid of all sense of humor, prosperity is his gospel, and he considers his own success in business proof of divine satisfaction.

Drystubble, in the first person, opens the story, with his philistine ways. He has met an old schoolmate in the street, a destitute fellow without overcoat, of whose acquaintance he is rather ashamed. But the man may prove useful. For Shawlman, as he calls him—a shawl being his only protection against the cold—has sent him a pile of manuscripts in the hope that the rich broker, for old acquaintance' sake, would be willing to underwrite the publishing costs of a first issue, were it only of a small volume. Shawlman has been in the Dutch East Indies,—for he is identical with Multatuli and Max Havelaar—and among his miscellaneous writings are some articles on Java and native labor that contain matter of great value to coffee brokers. They have to be rewritten for Drystubble's purpose, and a young German in his office, Ernest Stern, undertakes the task on condition that Drystubble shall not change an iota of his story. This, it is true, does not please the broker, but the spring sale is at hand, and as no orders have come in yet from old Ludwig Stern, who is a great coffee merchant in Hamburg, Drystubble does not want to antagonize the son. Besides, he himself will write a chapter now and then to give the book an appearance of solidity. And so to their combined, or rather alternating, efforts the reading public in Holland owed the book that Stern calls *Max Havelaar,* but which Drystubble would entitle *The Coffee Sales of the Netherlands Trading Company.*

The fiction that the chapters containing Havelaar's story was the work of a German is part of the satire. A nation of Drystubbles does not produce the talent that can do justice to so moving a tale. It needed a son from the land of Goethe and Schiller to enter into the romantic spirit of Havelaar's tragedy. Among the pile of Shawlman's manuscripts, Drystubble found one on "The Homage paid to Schiller and Goethe in the German Middle-class." Drystubble, who is the middle-class of

Holland, calls all poetry a parcel of lies. And yet, that bourgeoisie of Drystubbles proved alive to the beauty of Stern's story of Max Havelaar. It had even sufficient sense of humor to enjoy its caricature in Batavus, the broker. His name became a byword, his type a laughing stock among the very nation which in him was satirized. Drystubble's success in literature became his defeat in life.

Multatuli (essay date 1967)

SOURCE: Multatuli. "Introductory Note (Abridged) by Multatuli to the Edition of 1875." In *Max Havelaar; or, The Coffee Auctions of the Dutch Trading Company,* edited and translated by Roy Edwards, pp. 321-27. Leyden, Netherlands: Sijthoff, 1967.

[*In the following essay, abridged from the 1875 edition of* Max Havelaar, *Multatuli describes his struggles to write the novel and also discusses at length the difficulties involved in getting it published. Although Multatuli acknowledges that* Max Havelaar *did little to effect substantive changes to colonial policies in Java, he also asserts that persistent administrative abuses in the East Indies are in fact a sign of waning Dutch influence in the region.*]

The delay in the appearance of this edition must be blamed on me, and certainly not on my very energetic publisher. Though it is doubtful whether the word *blame* is correct here. Blame presupposes *guilt;* and I wonder whether this can be applicable to my almost unconquerable aversion to experiencing once more page by page, word by word, letter by letter, the sad drama that gave birth to this book? This *book*! . . . the reader sees no more in it than that. But to *me* these pages are a chapter of my life . . . to me their correction was torment, one long torment! Over and over again the pen dropped from my hand, over and over again my eyes swam as I read the—incomplete and toned-down!—sketch of what happened twenty years ago in that formerly unknown spot on the map called Lᴇʙᴀᴋ. And I felt even more wretched when I looked back on what has taken place since the publication of *the book* **Havelaar,** fifteen years ago now. I repeatedly threw the printer's proofs aside and tried to fix my mental eyes on less tragic subjects than those which Havelaar's still fruitless struggle called to mind. Weeks, sometimes months—my publisher can vouch for it!—went by without my having the courage to look at the proofs. But somehow or other I have managed to stagger through the work of correction— correction which has taken more out of me than the writing of the book did. For in the winter of 1859, when I wrote my **Havelaar** in Brussels, partly in a little room without a fire, partly at a rickety, dirty table in a tavern amid good-natured but rather unaesthetically minded beer-drinkers, I thought I should *accomplish something,*

achieve something, bring something about. Hope gave
me courage, hope made me eloquent now and then. I
still remember the mood that inspired me when I wrote
and told *her*:[1] 'My book's finished, my book's finished!
Now everything will soon come right!' I had struggled
through—and wasted, alas!—four long, four difficult
years in trying, without publicity, without commotion,
above all without scandal, to do something that might
improve the situation in which the Javanese languishes.
The wretched Van Twist,[2] who would have been my
natural ally if any idea of honour and duty could have
been found in him, was not to be induced to lift a finger. The letter I addressed to him has been published
innumerable times, and contains virtually all the points
that form the gravamen of the Havelaar case. The man
has never replied, never shown a sign of wanting to do
what could be done to repair the damage he has caused.
I was *forced* at last, by his unprincipled indifference, to
publication—to the choice of a path other than that I
had been treading up to then. Indignation finally showed
me how to obtain what had seemed unobtainable: *a moment's hearing.* What lazy Van Twist would not grant
me, I managed to extort from the Nation: ***Max Havelaar*** was read. I was . . . heard. Alas, hearing is one
thing, reading another. The book was 'lovely', they assured me, and if I happened to have any more pretty
tales like that one . . .

Oh certainly, people found 'amusement' in reading it,
and never thought—or pretended not to think—that it
was not for 'amusement' that *I,* in middle age, threw up
my career, which had promised to be a brilliant one.
That *I* had not aimed at 'amusement' in defying death
by poison for myself, for my staunch and true wife, and
for our dear child! *Havelaar* was such an entertaining
book, people had the face to say to me; and these eulo-
gists included persons who would scream with terror if
confronted with the slightest, most ordinary danger—
not, I would add, to life and limb but to a small part of
their comfort. Most of my readers seem to think I exposed myself and mine to poverty, degradation and
death in order to provide them with some pleasant
reading-matter.

This error . . . but let us say no more about it. One
thing is certain: I had no idea that such a naïvely cruel
jocrissiade[3] lay before me when I cried with such exultation 'My book's finished, my book's finished!' My
conviction that I spoke truth, that I had brought to a
conclusion what I had been busy writing, and my oblivi-
ousness of the extent to which the reading and listening
public has grown accustomed to *cant* (sic—*Tr.*), to
empty talk, to almost perpetual contradiction between
words and deeds . . . all this filled me in 1859 with so
much hope as had indeed been *necessary* to make the
painful writing of ***Havelaar*** possible. But *now,* fifteen
years later, when I have seen only too well that the Nation takes the part of Van Twist and Co—i.e. the part of

rascality, robbery and murder—against me, i.e. against
Justice, Humanity and Enlightened Self-interest—now,
it has been infinitely harder for me to deal with these
pages than in 1859, albeit even then painful bitterness
repeatedly threatened to get the upper hand. And here
and there it breaks through in the book, however much
I should have liked to repress it. [. . .]

And . . . to all the grief over the continuing failure of
my endeavours has been added my grief over the loss
of *her* who stood shoulder to shoulder with me so heroically in the struggle against the world, and who will
not be there when the hour of triumph shall finally
come.

The hour of triumph, reader! For, whether you think it
strange or not, I *shall* triumph! Despite the tricks and
intrigues of the statesmanikins to whom the Netherlands entrusts its most vital concerns. Despite our stupid Constitution, which puts a premium on mediocrity
or, worse, on an attitude of mind that excludes everything which might arrest the universally recognized decay of our body politic. Despite the many who have a
vested interest in Injustice. Despite mean jealousy of
my 'writing talent' . . . isn't that what it's called? (I'm
not a writer—do believe me, gentlemen scribblers who
are determined to see a colleague and competitor in
me!) Despite coarse slander which considers nothing
too gross or too ridiculous if it will serve to smother
my voice and break my influence. And finally, despite
the pitiful laxity of the Nation, which goes on tolerating
all this . . . I shall triumph!

Of late, writers have risen to reproach me with not
achieving anything, or not enough, with changing nothing or not enough, with bringing about nothing or not
enough. I shall have something more to say presently
about the source of such reproaches. As regards the
point itself . . . I fully acknowledge that nothing has
improved in the Indies. But . . . *changed?* The individuals who took advantage of the furore made by
Havelaar to hoist themselves into the saddle, first immediately after the book's publication and then by
means of our wretched constitutional seesaw-system,
have done nothing else but change things. They had no
alternative, had they? Their profession of political acro-
bat required it. The partly incapable, partly not very
honest little bunch of politicians that 'fell upwards
through lack of weight' after '60 realized that something had to be *done,* though they preferred not to do
the right thing, which, if it comes to that—I can see
their point there!—would have been tantamount to suicide. Justice for the ill-used Javanese would have meant
elevating him; and that would have been a death sentence for most of our politicians. Nevertheless, a show
had to be put up of activity in a new direction, and the
People, 'shuddering' with indignation, had a succession
of bones thrown to them, not really to appease their

hunger for reform but to keep their jaws busy, even if it was only with blathering about what passed for economics and politics. The men in power threw titbits to their party caucuses, newspaper fabricators, and the rest of their coffeehouse public, one after the other—a policy to which I gave the definitive name of *duitenplaterij.*[4] For many years, even before **Havelaar,** freedom of labour had been the main dish, the *pièce de résistance* on the highly dangerous *menu.* By way of a change the gentlemen served to their unsuspecting guests trumped-up questions about the East Indian coinage. Then followed the land registration question, the Preanger question, the plantation-crop bonus question, the accountability question, the agricultural law question, the private ownership of land question, and a few more of the sort. One new law trod on the heels of another, and the men in office—whether conservative or liberal made not the slightest difference!—succeeded every time in hoodwinking the people into believing that the only possible solution *to the universally recognized difficulty* now lay really and truly and entirely in the very latest remedy to be proposed. Honestly, they cried, *this* one will work!

Thus every discredited experiment was followed by a new experiment. After each used-up quack medicine, a new quack medicine. With each new ministry, a new panacea. For each new panacea, new ministers, usually destined to burden the overburdened pension list for more years than they had burdened the throne of office for months. And the Second Chamber orating the while! And the party caucuses cracking-up or crying-down! And the People listening! All the novelties were examined, tested, adopted, applied. In the Indies the Chiefs, the European officials, and most of all the Population, were made dizzy by the ceaseless turning about . . . and nothing *changed* after **Havelaar**? Owing to **Havelaar**? Come off it! After and because of that book, the Indies suffered the same fate as Punch's watch. Someone told this philosopher that its works were dirty, and that was why it did not go right. He promptly threw it into the gutter and cleaned it with a stable broom. According to another tradition of the Hague puppet theatre our politician planted the heel of his wooden shoe on it. I can assure the reader that a great deal really has *changed* in that watch!

The Netherlands has not chosen to do justice in the Havelaar case. As sure as eggs are eggs, this omission—this *crime*!—will mark the starting-point of the loss of its East Indian possessions. Anyone who doubts this prophecy because today, i.e. only fifteen years after my *very reluctant* action, the Dutch flag still waves at Batavia, betrays the narrowness of his political vision. Do you think upheavals such as those in store for Insulinde, and which, in fact, have already begun—don't you see this, Dutchmen?—can take place in the same period of time as a commonplace incident in private life? In the life of States, fifteen years is less than a moment.

Nevertheless, the catastrophe will be consummated relatively quickly. The reckless war with ACHIN was one of the last *duitenplaterÿen* a certain minister needed in order to divert attention from his incompetence, and it will prove as disastrous in outcome and influence as it was rash and criminal in plan. The precarious authority of the Netherlands is not proof against such setbacks as we are suffering there. But, even before the manifestation of the more remote consequences which this piece of cruel stupidity is *bound* to entail . . . where, in this case, is the highly extolled *ministerial responsibility* to be found? Must the Nation simply resign itself to the fact that one Fransen van de Putte has thought fit to get it into a situation which is costing it so many millions of money, so many human lives—not to mention a shameful loss of prestige in the Malay Archipelago? Of course it must! *That* man's name is also on the pension list! Apparently the Dutch taxpayer has so much money he doesn't know what to do with it.

As regards the war with ACHIN, I shall presently be compelled to revert to it now and again in the notes to **Havelaar.** But before going any further I should like to say that in this context, too, I have noticed how carelessly people read the book. Hardly if ever have I had evidence that anyone had connected the present war, and my prediction of it elsewhere, with the contents of Chapter 13. In view of the wide circulation of **Havelaar** it is indeed strange that when, in September '72, my letter to the King appeared, and war was declared against ACHIN in the following spring, so few remembered that I had referred to our strained relations with that State as long before as '60, and given proof of knowing more about these matters than our hack journalists and Members of Parliament. If people *had* remembered, my well-meant warning of September '72 might have borne better fruit! Old Jupiter still makes the Kings and Nations he wishes to destroy blind, deaf, mad and conservative or . . . liberal, it's all the same. The main thing is and always will be: *to search for the truth, to recognize its importance, and, above all, to act on the information which, obtained thus, can be considered true.* All else is wrong, and Holland will lose the Indies because no justice was done to me in my endeavours to protect the Javanese against ill-treatment.

There are still people who cannot grasp the connexion between these two things. But is that my fault? The smothering of my complaints comes down to protection of untruth, encouragement of lying. Is it really so difficult to understand that in the long run such vast possessions cannot be administered when the powers that be are unwilling to receive any but untrue reports about the country and the population? Surely, in order to regulate, to administer, to govern something, the people responsible must first *know* in what condition the affairs concerned are? And so long as they disregard the information given in **Havelaar** they do *not* know!

And another thing. It appears from that book that the existing laws are not enforced. Then, pray, what is the good of behaving, in The Hague and during elections, as though there were any point in making *new* laws? I maintain that the old laws *in the main* were not so bad. But people chose not to observe them. *There* is the crux of the matter. There, and not in endless speechifying on subjects of supposed or simulated political importance, wranglings that undoubtedly serve to provide newspaper scribblers with texts for leading articles, keep ministers in power for one week longer, and occupy the entirely otiose imitation talents of Chamber debaters, but bring us not one step nearer to the only true goal: *protection of the Javanese against the rapacity of his Chiefs in complicity with a corrupt Dutch Administration.*

* * *

As regards this new edition [. . .] the pestilential dots with which Mr Van Lennep thought fit to spoil my work (e.g. P . . . K . . . ng for *Parang-Kujang*) have here, of course, been replaced by *readable words*. I have left unaltered the pseudonyms Slymering, Verbrugge, Duclari and Slotering because those names have become common property. My murdered predecessor was called Carolus. The real names of Controleur Verbrugge and Commandant Duclari were Van Hemert and Collard. The Resident of BANTAM was Brest van Kempen, and the petty Napoleon at PADANG was General Michiels. You may ask: what led me to change these names in the manuscript I entrusted to Mr Van Lennep? Let it suffice for me to refer to the end of Chapter 19 and say that I wanted to safeguard the honest but unheroic Controleur against victimization. He may not have supported me, but he had not opposed me either, and he had even supplied frank statements when I asked for them. That was already a great deal, and could have cost him dear. To continue . . . the name Slymering served to characterize my model. And finally, the change of the names of Carolus and Collard into Slotering and Duclari followed automatically from the other substitutions. I was certainly not out to observe secrecy—as, if it comes to that, is apparent from the whole purport of my book—but I found it distasteful to expose certain persons to criticism by the *lay* reading public. I considered that in the *official* world—and the matter was *their* concern—people would know whom they had to approach for further information on the facts I revealed. And they *did* know; for, after **Havelaar** had reached the Indies, Governor-General Pahud went post-haste to Lebak 'to investigate complaints about abuses there'. [. . .]

Notes

1. His wife, the 'Tina' of *Max Havelaar*. *Tr.*

2. Governor-General of the Dutch East Indies at the time of the events narrated in *Havelaar*. *Tr.*

3. From Jocrisse, a type in sixteenth-century French comedy. He is a stupid, clumsy servant, or a henpecked husband who does the housework. *Tr.*

4. In connexion with a new coinage for the Indies, the Government prepared and discussed pictures (*platen*) of the new coins (*duiten*). Such '*duitenplaterÿ*' was for Multatuli a ruse to distract attention from the fundamentals of the situation. *Tr.*

Peter King (essay date 1972)

SOURCE: King, Peter. "What's in a Pseudonym?" In *Multatuli*, pp. 11-26. New York: Twayne Publishers, 1972.

[*In the following essay, King examines how political and economic forces in nineteenth-century Holland helped shape Multatuli's attitudes toward social justice. King also analyzes the complex, often conflicting impulses behind the development of Multatuli's literary sensibility, particularly as they relate to his decision to adopt the pseudonym "Multatuli" ("I have suffered much"), arguing that his prose style was ultimately an extension of his alter ego.*]

I. MESSIANIC DREAMS

The scene on which Eduard Douwes Dekker first opened his eyes in 1820 was not a cheerful one. In the towns of Holland as many as one half of the population might be unemployed and a great economic depression was setting in throughout the countryside. It was a situation that promoted only retirement or enforced idleness. The country, on the brink of bankruptcy, dozed on, because it was morally and intellectually bankrupt too. Dekker was married in the year that the Dutch Parliament was forced by the events in France to reform the constitution—after debating the issue for a hundred years. As late as 1864 the Society for Public Welfare could still vote by a large majority against an inquiry into housing conditions,[1] and in this they were echoing the sentiments of the most popular literary annual which had just published this verse under an illustration of a poor family gazing at the purchases of a rich woman being helped into her carriage by her coachman:

Ye poor! Ye shall not covet.
Rich are ye if docility—
Averse to the feud of needy mortals
which leads them to rebellious hostility

'gainst those whom God grants a smoother way—
lays your table after the heat of the day
with sup of water and crusty morsels.
Your life task is: to suffer in silence
whatever torment privation may bring.[2]

Dekker shared the privations of the needy at this time, but he certainly did not suffer in silence. He made his presence known, and widely known, as Multatuli, the pseudonym he adopted from Horace's *Ars poetica* (1. 412):

Qui studet optatem cursu contingere metam,
Multa tulit fecitque puer, sudavit et alsit,
Abstinuit venere et vino.[3]

Yet the course run by Multatuli is marked not only by the austerity of Horace's athlete enduring sweating and cold in reaching for the highest goal, but also by a reckless self-indulgence totally incompatible with the athlete's self-discipline and abstinence from women and wine.

At an early age Eduard seems to have been very conscious of people's suffering and of his ambition to remedy it. "From my childhood days," he wrote to Mimi Hamminck Schepel in 1863, "I have always shown a lot of initiative, a desire for action. . . ." The wretched condition of people in general, he goes on, was as much on his conscience as the death of a fly. "As a child I translated that silly phrase: 'He bore the sins of the world' by: Tollit dolores mundi, the sorrows of the world. I am not complaining about this burden, only about my powerlessness to make that burden lighter for others. That powerlessness was my nightmare, my specter. Hence: craving for power, i.e. ambition, . . . to reach a situation where I could help people, save people. . . . So I struggled for power, . . . I really believe that my ambition is noble, and that I desire goodness. I do truly want to increase the sum total of universal happiness, and that in my view is virtue."[4]

In *Woutertje Pieterse,* a fictional tale reviving some of Multatuli's childhood memories, he said of the young hero, "Wouter's spirit was of an unusual character . . . a desire to achieve at once the *highest,* to reach the *farthest,* to be the *first,* in the arena into which his childish fantasy had led him."[5] Leentje, the sympathetic but simple maid servant in the Pieterse family, not unnaturally had some difficulty in understanding the lad. "Wouter sat with both elbows on the table with his head in his hands" and as he dreamed, the meaning of it all became clear to him. "He raised himself to his full height, fixed his proud gaze on the beams, placed his right hand on his heart and thrust his left arm out as if wrapping himself in a Spanish cloak and said, 'Leentje, I'm a prince!'"[6]

The Napoleonic gesture was natural enough in a boy born in a city which had nine years earlier welcomed the Emperor whom Multatuli called "The hero of my imagination. By this I do *not* mean that my imagination made such a hero of him. I mean the image of him that I created. . . . I have always disapproved of the abuse of the 'Corsican tyrant.' My own mother was very prone to that, and even as a lad I protested—*silently,* for I was not allowed to hold any opinion of my own."[7]

Dekker's first emotional crisis was his hazardous and ultimately unsuccessful courtship of Caroline Versteeg, two years after his arrival in the Dutch East Indies. In 1841, while he was at Djakarta and separated from Caroline, he wrote the first part of his earliest prose work, *Losse bladen uit het dagboek van een oud man.* In this fictional diary, August was a fourteen-year-old school friend of the old man's, who "spent his time, his skills, his clothes and savings, everything on others. He gave everything away." In order to save a bird's nest from a youthful collector, he gave him all his pocket money and a diamond pin (a present from his mother), then, while returning the nest to the tree, he fell and broke his arm. The following evening, a number of boys at the school were chatting together about happiness. August said that happiness was the enjoyment of what was most beautiful and most holy: "I'd die for what I loved. I can imagine no greater happiness!" Later, on his fifteenth birthday, August was drowned trying to rescue his brother in a skating accident. The old man concludes: "He had made the best wish;—he had received the finest reward."[8]

Seemingly Eduard's childhood altruism expressed itself in an act of complete self-giving in his first (and not only his first) erotic experience. This is even more explicit in his first play, *De Eerloze,* where self-sacrifice is confused with suffering, the suffering of his loss of Caroline at the time of his hardship and disgrace at Padang. Here the hero Holm, misjudged as dishonorable, defends his intention to commit suicide with the words "*Have you suffered as I have*? . . . I lived to sacrifice myself. . . . I *have* sacrificed myself."[9]

Two years later, in 1843, he continued these *Loose Pages from the Diary of an Old Man,* adding in 1845 after his reinstatement (and not in 1844 as stated by Mimi Hamminck Schepel[10]) a conclusion that need not concern us here. In the second part, with the subtitle *Jongelingsdromen,* a young man "pregnant with ideas" muses on his destiny in words reminiscent of Wouter's flights of fancy.

"Were the dreams of greatness in my youth untrue? Am I petty, wretched, despicable like the rest who call themselves people? . . . Am *I* not suited to an outlook unattainable to others? As a child I wanted to lord it over children, . . . is it required of me that I should . . . climb laboriously rung by rung? . . . What is to prevent my skipping the rungs and grasping the highest straight away? Bonaparte is great. And why?"[11] He was great because he had the will to greatness and achieved the mastery of his circumstances.

> Who or what prevents my striving after a crown? The desire alone merited a crown, . . .
>
> Embrace everything, sustain everything, read all things aright and always judge rightly. Let no one ever no ice that you can fail. Cover every fault with the scintillation of a brilliant wit. Do not say, this or that is impossible . . . it must take place! You must be able to resolve and destroy impossibility itself. . . .
>
> I must endure years of slavery; *I,* born to rule, must begin with obedience . . . so be it!
>
> . . . Is it not a fine goal to give happiness to a nation—nay rather—to create a happy people?[12]

Dekker's later references to this year of his life leave no doubt about the significance of the youthful Promethean dream in the old man's diary. In 1845 he wrote to his wife, Tine: "I honestly think that it is a pity I do not have a higher position in the world. I could climb—yes, but the times we live in are still close to 1790-1812. It will be years before the bottom comes up to the top again. . . . And yet two and a half years ago I had plans, mighty, perhaps impracticable plans which make my head spin!"[13] In 1863 he wrote to Mimi: "Long ago I realized that I need power, a lot of power, unlimited power. As always my whole policy was dictated by my heart. I never evolved it with insight or art. . . . In my 22nd year I promised myself . . . that I would be a genius who knew everything, understood everything, could do everything, and even now, when I find myself ignorant or incapable, I attribute it to a deliberate breach of promise rather than to an unintentional and regrettable weakness, which it often is, alas, especially in humdrum affairs."[14] Right up to the last year of his life, Napoleon was still as interesting to him as an object of study as he ever was. Looking back to the trivial stuff of his earliest days he still thinks that there was something there that was not unimportant, "something like a demarkation of my aim in life. There was some mention of Napoleon. I considered myself superior to him to this extent, that I had a *plan* (in my twenty-second year, what's more!) Whereas it seemed to me that he did not make his *own* way, but was *led.* Well, I still think I was right . . . it was *then* that I realized. I wanted then to change the world."[15]

II. HEROISM A REALITY

What, then, turned the young Multatuli's head from thoughts of self-effacement to plans of self-aggrandizement? From November, 1842, until August, 1843, he was at Natal where his first administrative appointment included responsibilities as head of the police, president of the native law court, civil registrar, postmaster, superintendent of buildings and works, and excise officer.[16] His own comment on this episode in his career is very revealing: "I was not even twenty-three, and 'commodore' of the province of Natal . . . the functions of such an administrator are extremely gratifying, and I have often in retrospect wished I were back in a position which because of my inexperience I did not sufficiently appreciate when I entered it. Until we have suffered, or suffered enough, we shall never learn. . . . In such a place one is not just at the top, one is *everything,* and many a Caesar might be well satisfied with that. It's true that the elevated position of such a district officer is actually created by a certain emptiness round him, since he is often the only European in the place, if not the whole province, apart from the military commander. But the man who arrives in the Indies young enough to have time to get well settled in, soon feels entirely at home in his dealings with the natives. The emptiness of the solitary life as a white man is made good by a kind of royal dignity in relation to the population, . . . the man who is lord has complete control and almost unlimited power."[17]

By a strange coincidence, one of the Chinese traders supplying Dekker at Natal had also supplied Napoleon on St. Helena. Less surprisingly, Dekker considered this significant, almost portentous.[18]

If his uncontested prefecture at the lonely trading station prompted unbridled dreams of a cosmic destiny, his later experience of high social life in the colony only heightened his awareness of a romantic and spectacular ideal. Describing his and Tine's life at Menado, where he had a post of considerable standing, accorded even more honor than was its due, he wrote to his brother Pieter, "Would you believe that parties are given here at least once and generally more than once a month for 100 to 150 people? There was a fancy-dress ball here in 1850, on the King's birthday, and it was a sight for sore eyes. I maintain that the highest circles in Europe would be unlikely to muster so many costly and beautiful costumes as there were here in remote Menado."[19] At Menado, too, he was saving up for his first leave in Holland, "for I fancy myself as a nabob." He will order food to be shared with all those brought in from the street by his servant or himself. He will give St. Nicholas presents to *all* the poor children in Europe. He will accept election to the Lower Chamber and "I will have the opera perform for me alone in The Hague. But it must say on the posters that it is for me."[20] And judging by his own actual estimates of his expenditure, he fully intended spending a very large part of his savings and income on parties, presents, clothes, and traveling.[21]

It is probably true, as Ett puts it, that he wanted wealth for others, not for himself, but it is not true that "money had no value for him personally."[22] Money was a very concrete form of power, the kind of power that could be purchased and advertised in a special performance of the opera or munificent public gestures—the kind of power that might be as effortlessly acquired at the gambling tables as the less tangible power of leadership could be acquired in dreams. But because it was so material, the lack of it was an obvious reminder of the lack of the power it symbolized. And this, as we shall see, was to be the nagging *evidence* of Multatuli's failure (according to his own terms of success) and the cause of the suffering which he now justified as a necessary *condition* of success. For whether through prodigal generosity or prodigal gambling, his life in Europe, on leave and after his final return in 1857, was for years a wretched saga of insecurity and separation for him and his family. During this period he learned the bitterness of being the victim of circumstance and the futility of self-sacrifice, so that his own August-like sentiments expressed by Holm in **De Eerloze** seemed absurd to him: "In '43 I did indeed believe that there was nothing more beautiful than throwing oneself away. Proof, surely, that I was not in my right mind."[23]

Yet long before humiliation had taught him to disavow August's humility he had been aware of his leanings towards Napoleonic grandeur, as his correspondence in 1845 shows. "I am strong enough for self-sacrifices," he wrote to Tine, "but not always, only rarely in fact, for simple devotion to duty . . . the doing of a simple duty does not exactly appeal to one's vanity!" "It was gratifying to my pride to be able to adopt the air of a protector."[24]

The events at Lebak, recounted in **Max Havelaar,** seem to have rudely awakened Multatuli from his Napoleonic dream of his younger days. The hand of destiny may have been laid upon him but his dreams, personified in his hero Max Havelaar, were not enough to save him from a fate little better than August's. At the end of the novel, "I, Multatuli, who have suffered much, take up the pen" for "I'm no fly-rescuing poet, no good-natured dreamer like that maltreated Havelaar."[25] Roused from his dream of greatness, he is only hardened by his frustrating experience in his resolve to confront the whole world with his mission. When Van Lennep, who had **Max Havelaar** published, failed to persuade Rochussen, the Minister of the Colonies, to reinstate him, Dekker wrote to Tine, "I'll take the whole East Indian Council on, and if that fails, then I am still Multatuli. I shall say like Luther: 'Here I stand (alone). God help me!' God means here my self, my being, my spirit, the ideals of my youth, my feeling, my heart, my genius! Despite everything I have hope and courage; I feel strong, yes, stronger than ever. I feel that one must suffer in order to succeed."[26]

To be true to his messianic calling he needed power.[27] His pen was now his only weapon and significantly **Max Havelaar** was, apart from a short fable, his first published work. His first aim in writing was to leave an honorable legacy to his children (and posterity). Secondly, "*I intend to be read!*"[28] But this is only a foretaste of the power that can be released if at first his words fall on deaf ears: "This book is an introduction . . . I shall wax in power and keenness of weapons, according as the needs dictate."[29] So his feeling, his heart, his genius will inspire his writing in which the world will recognize the reformer and on which the world will act to bring about the reforms. He will thus achieve the personal recognition sought by the despot as well as fulfilling his universal mission. In a more modest tone he states the same purpose in writing in his four-hundredth *Idee.* "For a long time I have toiled to remove a stone here and there from the path. And if I am unsuccessful, I shall still see to it that whoever comes after me will find traces of my attempts."[30]

The fact that circumstances forced him to publish when he did certainly does not mean, as is sometimes stated, that because of Dekker's resignation from the Colonial Service European literature gained an outstanding author. The emphasis on the greatness of Napoleon's thought in the young man's dreams, the significance of Fancy in Multatuli's writings and his title, **Ideas,** for over one third of his total work, all suggest a fertile imagination needing creative language to give it birth. In 1851, almost at the peak of his foreign service career, he wrote to an old friend, the publisher A. C. Kruseman, "I have never written like this before. It is a prelude to my firm intention of speaking to the people. I am pregnant with ideas; in a few days I shall be 31— now is the time, high time—now or never, that's to say, *soon* or never."[31] As well as containing examples of Multatuli's earlier writing, including **Losse bladen,** this letter (of some 20,000 words), like so much of his private correspondence, is in itself obviously an exercise in literary style.[32]

On the other hand, there is no evidence that at any time before 1859 he envisaged an author's career as an alternative to the Civil Service.[33] On the contrary, he implies a rejection of such a possibility by telling Kruseman in the same letter that though he can, like others, write for a living, this kind of writing is wearisome to him.[34] It frustrates him because it achieves neither of his stated purposes in writing, the creation of an honorable legacy and of something "to read," to read, that is, as a preparation for action. For the power he dreamed of *had* to be generated through other people in this way, since the seer's vision could not be kept clear unless there were disciples ready to act as intermediaries between the dream and the deed. Moreover, since experience soon taught him not to doubt the power of his own creative talent, he had no reason to abandon the most unrealistic visions of his adolescence.[35] Until he had tested his talent, however, it was the constant frustration caused by the impossible task of reconciling the power of the imagination to the impotence of reality that caused the creative suffering in Multatuli. "O, that accursed incompatibility between my powers and the scope of my will; why on earth must I feel and love what is great and perhaps noble without the power to achieve anything."[36] "There is no harmony between reason and desire; I want to enforce the impossible and tire myself out in the process."[37]

III. DREAM AND REALITY

After he had challenged the nation at large in *Max Havelaar,* discovering in the process the power of his own creative demon,[38] Multatuli's attitude changed and hardened. In the first place poverty, a humiliating reminder of the lack of personal recognition, dragged the creative suffering of his earlier tension "between reason and desire" down to the level of self-pity, as when he attributes his mean thoughts to his cramped environment.[39] In the second place, the disappointing response to the book was countered with a violent and lifelong contempt for "het Publiek," the reading public.[40] While he was writing *Max Havelaar* he described it as "a call to the reading public." When the royalties from the book, a public subscription, the mass sale of his portrait, and his candidature in two by-elections all failed miserably, he castigated the readers of *Minnebrieven* with "Public, I despise you with all my heart." Finally, and as a direct result of this contempt, anything that might appeal to the readers and everything they applauded in his work were also scorned by him as a betrayal of his mission and a travesty of his genius. Even the earliest signs of the disappointing sales of *Max Havelaar,* which Van Lennep had published in a limited edition and at an excessive price, produced a reaction from the author which foreshadows the years of bitterness to come. He wrote at that time from Brussels to Van Lennep: "No, I'm no novel writer. Fancy is a rag. What can I produce that is anything if people don't buy **M. H.** [*Max Havelaar*]? Indiscreet I may be, but I need money. . . . I intend to go to Holland. I shall give the King, the Ministry, the House, the Nation no peace. I *will* go to Holland. *I* shall announce my book!"[41]

In 1865 he wrote, "I have repeated with boring regularity that I am no writer,"[42] and so he had. But to understand what he meant by this, we have to read *Ideeën* 522-527. "I do not claim to be one of the best writers—or the best—but believe that there are few or none who write as well as I do just because I am no writer." To the person who says he has enjoyed reading *Max Havelaar* he says, "In that case you're a rotter!"[43] And when the whole reading public is guilty of deriving enjoyment from so much suffering he repeats his attack in *Minnebrieven,* "Publiek, ik veracht u met grote innigheid." Hence, "Anyone can see now that I am not a writer. A writer applies himself to giving pleasure. A writer is a flirt. A writer is a prostitute."[44]

The necessity to write for such a public in order to live was the most degrading reminder of his deep conflict between reality and dream. "It was in the evening. A female accosted me.—'Can't you do anything better than sell yourself?' I said, and thrust her away. The next evening she stood in my way again and threw my Ideas in my face. That hurt." And as a rider to this: "Jesus said many fine things. But all his fine statements would not fill half a sheet of copy (at 7½ cents)."[45]

This kind of solipsism and dramatized self-pity seems such a travesty of the Napoleonic concept that we might well agree with J. and A. Romein's verdict, that he is pleading too eloquently his defense for failing to achieve actual heroic mastery, and that he was "a writer from *inner* necessity because his unbreakable and inflexible 'proud spirit' could only achieve heroism in flights of the imagination."[46] This, however, is an unfair judgment. In comparison to his unrestrained will, his capacity was certainly inadequate. But equally, his actual power and indeed courage were far greater than his generation was willing or able to see.[47]

This forced him into a hostile isolation which often makes uninspiring as well as unentertaining reading. But as we have seen, Multatuli was himself aware of this. His bitterness is unedifying, but it is surely understandable. It may seem as if he is abusing "the keenness of his weapons" to flail the "public" that would not hear his message when, for instance, Kappelman (the individual "reader") says, "That's a good book but . . . the author is such a very nasty character . . ." and Multatuli retorts, "Kappelman, it would be such a bitter blow to me if you praised me!"[48] But the readers' acclamation of the wrong values in his work was in *fact,* and not just in his imagination, due to their congenital inability to understand the alien values he stood for.

Moreover, Multatuli's social position was insecure. His contempt for the middle-class respectability of the Droogstoppels, Hallemannetjes, and Kappelmans was probably aggravated by his resentment at being one of them himself, whereas his colonial career gave him a real taste of an aristocratic ideal dismally affronted by his penurious circumstances in Europe. The ambivalence of *Max Havelaar* between the crusade against corruption in the colonial administration and the lampooning of moral bankruptcy at home persists throughout his later writing, long after his championship of the natives' cause had lost its fervor. Later he rationalizes this by explaining to Mimi, "I want what is right. For that I need power. The Indies were my point of departure but remain only a part of it. (The whole world is full of senseless evil.) The name Insulinde represents from now on my general aspirations, like Nazareth in Christ's plan."[49] And in his notes to *Minnebrieven,* written two years after this, he explains that his duty there defined as the liberation of the Indies is to be understood in the wider sense of freeing the world from its ignorance.[50]

Yet the indisputable fact is that what was feasible with his position in the patrimonial bureaucracy of the Indies was pure illusion in his position in the domestic bureaucracy. He retained his aristocratic bearing—"There is a difference, a considerable difference, between one man and another—and there are other differences. The difference in mental development, tone, refinement, experience, taste. Certainly, all this distinguishes people in their kinds and classes. And I myself admit being very aristocratically set on maintaining that distinction."[51] But without the power of his office in the East Indies, how was he to assert that aristocratic superiority?

This is the core of his crisis in **Minnebrieven,** where Fancy, the personification of his fantasy,[52] finally tells him that he must adapt his will to his circumstances. The will to goodness is of itself not enough, he must find the ability to achieve what is right by desiring it in the right way. The author's final cry of triumph, "I have it . . . I know it . . . I feel it! . . . My heart is no longer empty . . . O God, I understand it all . . . Tine . . . I shall win through . . . ," suggests that there were prospects of some drastic change of circumstances in his own life or his wife's. But on the contrary, she was still the woman of aristocratic birth, now the mother of two children reduced to wretched circumstances by the transfer from high life in the Indies to begging hospitality in Holland. And his Fancy which had begun to take wing in the Colonies was now caged up and molested by uncouth hands as an object of beauty or curiosity.

There was, however, a third factor, expressed in the triangular relationship of these **Love Letters,** which at any rate momentarily resolved the dilemma; and being an emotional factor, it also brought the crisis itself to a head. This was the effect on Multatuli of the first personal and unconditional surrender to his demands, by an impressionable young girl. His relationship at this time with his niece Sietske Abrahamsz provided the momentary fulfillment of the dream in all its aspects. It provided an intimate friendship in his loneliness and removed his sense of insecurity by reaffirming his mastery, yet it also embodied the romantic ideal of an existence unencumbered by mundane realities, his wife and his family responsibilities. Multatuli, whose honesty about himself is itself characteristic of the idealist protesting against normal values, even those of tact and modesty, assumed, as only the fanatic could, that his wife would share his views. "Always remember when I have amorets or the like that this gives me verve . . . it is my kindling. Share this with me and write her an affectionate letter." "Romantic and adventurous enterprise inflames me, and middle-class probity stifles me. I do really love Siet intensely . . . after all, all my amorets come back to you in the end."[53] Such absurd unrealism is only possible in a man who so confused facts and fancy that he could regard his affection for Sietske as an expression of his love for Tine since both were mani-

festations of his dedication to his inspiration. "'All I know, understand, feel, dream, all that I give to *her!*' 'To your wife?' 'No, no. To Fancy . . . she is my wife!'"[54]

To Sietske, too, he could commit himself entirely, as August had in his act of self-giving, and also, since Sietske was also the embodiment of his Fancy, as Napoleon had to his dream. "Once, finding me alone," Sietske wrote later, "he declared in a kind of ecstasy that he was going to be Emperor, and this was the objective of his political planning . . . sons or daughters would not succeed to the throne but the sister's children, and Multatuli chose me as Crown Princess of Insulinde. My head would be portrayed on the coins of the new Empire. My provisional title would be Duchess of Sumatra."[55] This cannot entirely be attributed to flattery and bravado. The **"Tale of the Crucifixion"** in **Minnebrieven** reminds us that his identification with Christ was not confined to "tollit dolores mundi," for his Napoleonic dream was also a messianic mission. "Jesus began with fishermen, *I* start with *girls!*"[56]

The identification of the dreamer with his dream in the union with the (idealized) beloved is of course a common theme throughout romantic literature, and there is little doubt that the abnormally sensitive and quixotic boy, Eduard, would have sensed something of this erotic force. "Love is the tendency towards union . . . or would that tendency towards sharing, being together, being united, be in some people the desire for *goodness?* This was true of Wouter, though he did not know it."[57] Marie Anderson, one of his female admirers, remembers his telling her that he was sensual even as a child, and she adds her own comment that he did not outgrow this.[58]

IV. MULTATULI'S SELF-PORTRAIT

The foregoing portrait of Multatuli is clearly a self-portrait, whether it is signed Dekker, "an old man," Max Havelaar, or Multatuli. About this, too, he was completely honest, summing it up in *Idee* 34, "My Ideas are the 'Times' of my soul," and answering those who criticize him for this, in a series of *Ideeën* introduced by the refrain "You talk about yourself a lot . . . ." His answer in one of these is that the same could be said of other philosophers. "In *cogito ergo sum* the word 'I' occurs twice in three words."[59]

It is interesting that this should have occurred to Multatuli in this context because, though he gives no evidence of making a serious study of Descartes, or any other writer for that matter, the notion of thought proving being, of essence itself being dependent on thought, is entirely in keeping with Multatuli's "philosophy." The consequential reasoning, "I am what I think I am" and even "I am *only* what I think I am" would explain the predominance of "thinking," "understanding," "imagining," "fantasy," "dream," and "desire" in his concept of power and fulfillment. It would also explain his own central position in his thoughts, and the fact that these thoughts had to be recorded in order to affirm his own reality, including, of course, the thoughts that were less flattering to this "reality." But if he is *only* what he thinks he is, then we still really know very little about the man who left us those portraits. For when he talks of thought, understanding, or desire his manner suggests that his ultimate guide and sanction is *feeling,* a notoriously unreliable guarantee of objectivity. But even here, was this feeling "of the essence" or was it just part of the grand illusion? How seriously ought we to take his comment, "without my nervous agitation I am worth nothing"?[60] Mr. Lobo should know, for he was a kindly, simple man who saw a lot of Dekker in unguarded moments. When his money ran out in Amsterdam, Lobo took him into his Jewish home of nine children, and when Dekker remonstrated violently against the disturbance caused by the children's noise, Lobo calmed them, saying, "Mr. Dekker is a bit different from other people; but the man can't help it, he's got saltpeter in his blood."[61]

Multatuli has been credited[62] with unconditionally applying Spenser's dictum for the true artist, "Looke into thy heart and write." But when there is saltpeter in the blood, the result may be explosive. For the outcome may be far more than the expression of *Wahrheit* in *Dichtung*—of the kind justified by Multatuli in his postscript to **De Bruid daarboven**—it may take the form of a completely traumatic experience of reality itself; as when Multatuli gave pure fiction as *fact,* quoting, while he was the German correspondent of the *Oprechte Haarlemsche Courant,* the *Mainzer Beobachter,* a newspaper that simply did not exit.

This may have been intended as a joke,[63] but the obverse of this, his self-deception about his originality, was certainly not so intended. His reason for viciously and repeatedly attacking many of the greatest writers and thinkers was that by implication he, who repudiated any indebtedness to other people's ideas, was uniquely original. This, too, fits the picture of a man whose essential validity depended on the construct of his own mind. Similarly, anything which did not immediately contribute to this construct was branded as triviality, part of the inimical realm of "Necessity."[64] It was bad enough to toil at a manuscript that would only be misunderstood by the reader, but "my aversion to writing is even greater when it is a question of printing, correcting, and publishing."[65] "I'm sorry that *Hamlet* exists. I would write it if it weren't for that damned correction of the proofs."[66]

The frustration associated with this kind of obstacle to the instant realization of the dream was, of course, of the same order as the limitations imposed on him by his social and financial situation. Since this concrete Necessity was something he could *not* control, it represented his anathema, impotence, and was represented in emotional terms as suffering. The emotional rewards of successful personal relationships were, as we have seen, the reassurance he needed to cope with this Necessity which really did cause acute suffering because it prevented him from *being* the dream. When, however, such a relationship, idealized both for its own sake and as a flattering comment on his own imaginary self, came to grief, the suffering was doubly acute since the dream had engendered its own disillusionment. This is shown in the deep scar left on his life by Caroline's refusal to marry him, in the passing frenzy of the **"Tale of the Crucifixion,"** prompted by his humiliating separation from Tine, and in his later life, when he had for years been living openly with Miss Hamminck Schepel, by Tine's and the children's removal to Italy. Years later he could still write about this, blaming his son Edu for it and calling him "insanely wicked." "I have been burdened with this since he was fourteen, sixteen . . . especially since June 2, 1870, is this the case." Referring elsewhere to this date of Tine's departure, he writes, "After June of that year not a day dawned without my dreading it as a threatening, tormenting specter."[67]

It is inconceivable that a man who was so little prepared to stay with his family and suffer the consequences of trading his independence for humdrum realities could really have suffered so much from their alienation from him—unless it was his self-esteem or worse, his magic looking glass, that was shattered by this experience.

The conclusion to be drawn from this is, I believe, that Dekker's relationship with his imaginary self was as disharmonious as the coexistence of reality with his dream. We can only gauge the extent of this disharmony by the marks and effects of the suffering it caused, but the experience itself is described not by Dekker but by Multatuli, Dekker's idealized self, and the author of everything he wrote, whether "fictional" or "nonfictional." The result of this on the interrelationships between the authorial person and the fictional narrator will be seen when the construction of his works is examined.

The main purpose of this consideration of the authorial person was to show that Multatuli is more than a pseudonym. It represents a "bundle of contradictions"[68] between real and imaginary, contradictions which have produced as many conflicting views in his biographies. There is, however, considerable agreement that "it is with the best will in the world impossible to discover in Dekker such a youth" (as in Horace's lines quoted earlier) "and he himself forces us to give to his pseudonym roughly the same meaning as a contemporary of his afterwards expressed better with the name 'Multapatior' (I suffer much)."[69]

He was fifty-six when he wrote "If people want me as a dictator, all right! . . . Yes, I am and shall remain a despot just as long as the world gives me the impression that there is no other way to achieve something worthwhile! Yes, I am a deliberate, calculating, studied despot . . . but this above all, *unlimited* despotism, *unlimited!*"[70]

I think (I am a despot) therefore I am (a despot). The name Multatuli stands for the complete integrity and hence legitimacy of this conviction and all that it implies. Horace's athlete might proudly have looked back to the start of his training with the thought expressed by Multatuli in his sixty-fifth year: "*Then* I realized it. It was then that I wanted to change things. To that end I ordered my life. For that I denied myself the enjoyment of normal things."[71] Was the endeavor any less strenuous because it was made in the arena of the emotions and the imagination, as essential to this author as lungs and sinews to the athlete? The answer to this question lies surely in his achievements as an author, for that is the only man we know.

Notes

1. See J. and A. Romein, *De Lage Landen bij de zee* (Utrecht: De Haan, 1959), pp. 481, 487.

2. Quoted in J. J. Buskes, "Dominee Wawelaar," *De Nieuwe Stem,* XV (1960), 438 f.

3. Vosmaer's statement, "Multatuli took his name from Horace's well-known line . . ." was quoted by Multatuli himself (*Idee* 1035, *Volledige Werken* [Amsterdam: Van Oorschot, 1950-], VI, 349. Short title: *V. W.*). And although he was quoting Vosmaer in order to rebuff him, he did not challenge this statement. A. L. Sötemann does, however (*De structuur van "Max Havelaar." Bijdrage tot het onderzoek naar de interpretatie en evaluatie van de roman,* with a summary in English, Utrecht: Bijleveld, 1966, p. 199), on the grounds that Multatuli was not well-read in Latin. If he did not, he must have taken a lot of trouble scanning Horace's poem in order to complete Vosmaer's quotation (in *Idee* 1193d, *V. W.* VII, 303).

4. Multatuli, *Brieven. Bydragen tot de kennis van zyn leven.* Ed. M. Douwes Dekker-Hamminck Schepel (Amsterdam: Maatschappij voor goede en goedkoope Lectuur, 1912), VI, 113 f. (Short title: *Brieven*).

5. *V. W.* II, 610 f.

6. *V. W.* II, 612 f.

7. *Brieven van Multatuli aan Mr. Carel Vosmaer, R. J. A. Kallenberg van den Bosch en Dr. Vitus Bruinsma,* ed. Julius Pée (Brussels-Rotterdam: Manteau-Nijgh & Van Ditmar, 1942), p. 167 (Short title: *Vosmaer*).

8. *V. W.* VIII, 80-84.

9. *De Bruid daarboven* (the title of the published version of the play), Act IV, sc. i; *V. W.* III, 507. Italics are Multatuli's.

10. Cf. G. Stuiveling's note, *V. W.* VIII, 364, and *Brieven* I, 63. Stuiveling, however, appears to concur in Mimi's dating in stating that "Losse bladen II" was "voltooid te Padang," *V. W.* VIII, 105.

11. *V. W.* VIII, 364 f.

12. *V. W.* VIII, 370-73.

13. In a letter from Purwakarta dated October 24-27, 1845, *V. W.* VIII, 509; *Brieven* I, 127.

14. *Brieven* VI, 127.

15. Letter to Vosmaer, April 5, 1886, in *Vosmaer,* p. 251.

16. See G. Stuiveling in *V. W.* VIII, 102.

17. *Idee* 1048a, *V. W.* VI, 415 f.

18. See his note to *Idee* 1048a, *V. W.* VI, 422 f.

19. *V. W.* IX, 107; *Brieven* II, 87.

20. E. du Perron, *De Man van Lebak* (Amsterdam: Querido, 1937), p. 154 f. and *V. W.* IX, 156 ff.

21. *V. W.* IX, 276 f.

22. Henri A. Ett, "Multatuli bij Lobo," *De Nieuwe Stem* XV (1960), 597.

23. In a postscript of 1871 to *De Bruid daarboven, V. W.* III, 136.

24. *V. W.* VIII, 510, 532, 561; *Brieven* I, 128, 153, 187.

25. *Max Havelaar, of de Koffii-veilingen der Nederlandsche Handelmaatschappij* naar het authentieke handschrift uitgegeven door Dr. G. Stuiveling (Amsterdam: Van Oorschot, 1966), pp. 236, 238. (Short title: *M. H.* For a comparison of this with other editions see the bibliography.) Cf. the English translation by Roy Edwards *Max Havelaar or The Coffee Auctions of the Dutch Trading Company* (Leyden-London-New York: Sijthoff-Heinemann-London House & Maxwell, 1967), pp. 318, 320. (Short title: Translation).

26. November 29, 1859 in *V. W.* X, 138; *Brieven* IV, 12.

27. See his letter to Mimi, July 27, 1863, *Brieven* VI, 113 f. and the letters of July 29, 1863 and April 5, 1886 quoted on p. 14 f. above.

28. *M. H.,* p. 237; Translation, p. 318.

29. *M. H.,* p. 238; Translation, p. 320.

30. *V. W.* II, 607.

31. *V. W.* IX, 117; *Brieven* II, 102.

32. E.g. his letter to Tine of January 23, 1855. See Du Perron, *op. cit.,* p. 181 f. for a comparison of the narrative in this letter with the characterization in *Max Havelaar.*

33. There is no mention of an intention to resign in any of the correspondence referred to by D. de Vries in "Het ontstaan van de Max Havelaar," *Rekenschap* III, 1 (1956), 135-47, reprinted in "Geschriften van het Multatuli-genootschap" (1956). In a letter of October 29, 1845 (*V. W.* VIII, 519; *Brieven* I, 139), he refers to the possibility of writing as a profession, but only if he had a private income.

34. *V. W.* IX, 115.

35. See the letter of October 2-11, 1855, *V. W.* VIII, 466 f.; *Brieven* I, 77 f. and the conclusion of *Losse bladen, V. W.* VII, 380 f.

36. October 10, 1845, *V. W.* VIII, 481; *Brieven* I, 94.

37. November 27, 1845, *V. W.* VIII, 553; *Brieven* I, 178.

38. Cf. "I shall write as a god and as a devil. I shall bewitch them and start them trembling." Letter to Tine, June 12, 1861, *re Minnebrieven, V. W.* X, 474; *Brieven* V, 69.

39. E.g. in *Idee* 404, 405. Similarly, 249, 284; *V. W.* II, 609 f., 460, 479. Cf. *Idee* 649, *V. W.* IV, 391, written in the later period of eased financial circumstances.

40. *V. W.* X, 67; *Brieven* III, 49 and *V. W.* II, 22.

41. *V. W.* X, 236; *Brieven* IV, 148 f. "Fancy" was the original title of *Woutertje Pieterse,* which he had then begun writing.

42. In his first note to *Aan den Gouverneur-Generaal in ruste, V. W.* I, 240. Cf. "I am no writer. It makes me cross when they say I am. Just imagine, Christ after the Sermon on the Mount: a sermonizer!" *V. W.* X, 691; *Brieven* VI, 53.

43. *V. W.* III, 328. Cf. *Idee* 495, "It would seem that we *applaud* beauty . . . as our license for behaving in an ugly way," and 496, "The 'appreciation' of *Havelaar* is the justification of my contempt for the reader." *V. W.* III, 237, 239.

44. *V. W.* III, 329.

45. *Ideeën* 62, 63, *V. W.* II, 320.

46. J. and A. Romein, *op. cit.,* p. 714. My italics.

47. For Multatuli's bitterest feelings about this, see *Idee* 632, *V. W.* IV, 381 ff.

48. *Idee* 641, *V. W.* IV, 388.

49. September 10, 1862, *V. W.* X, 693; *Brieven* VI, 56.

50. *V. W.* II, 179.

51. *Idee* 451, *V. W.* III, 90.

52. *V. W.* X, 479; *Brieven* V, 71.

53. August 16 and September 4, 1860, *V. W.* X, 285, 306; *Brieven* IV, 92, 111.

54. *V. W.* II, 15.

55. E. Wienecke-Abrahamsz, "Multatuli-herinneringen," *Nederland,* I (1910), 78, quoted by G. Stuiveling in *V. W.* X, 378.

56. (A.) M. Anderson, *Uit Multatuli's leven. Bijdrage tot de kennis van zijn karakter* (Amsterdam: Daniels, s.d. [1901]), p. 50; and in a letter to Mimi: "Your letter gives me a feeling of holiness," *Brieven* VI, 87.

57. *Idee* 442, *V. W.* II, 647. Cf. Max Havelaar: "There is nothing, I would say, that so clearly reveals beauty in the abstract, the visible image of *truth,* of *spiritual purity,* as a beautiful woman . . ." Instinctively he wants "to gaze at her, to dream of her and . . . *to be good.*" *M. H.,* pp. 109, 113; Translation, pp. 151, 157.

58. (A.) M. Anderson, *op. cit.,* p. 73.

59. *Idee* 23, *V. W.* II, 314 f.

60. (A.) M. Anderson, *op. cit.,* p. 48.

61. H. A. Ett, *op. cit.,* p. 596.

62. By J. Prinsen J. Lzn. in *Uit de Ideeën van Multatuli* (Zwolle: Tjeenk Willink, 1910), p. XVIII.

63. See (A.) M. Anderson, *op. cit.,* p. 11.

64. The meaning of this word in Multatuli is discussed on pp. 75 f., 144 f. above.

65. "Fragmenten overgenomen uit het Multatuli-nummer van de Portefeuille" in *Ter gedachtenis aan Multatuli, 1887-19 de Februari-1892* (Amsterdam: Vereeniging "De Dageraad," 1892), p. 97.

66. *Brieven* VI, 87.

67. Letters dated July 22, 1880, to Van den Bosch and November 15, 1877, to Bruinsma in *Vosmaer,* pp. 92, 131.

68. ". . . vat vol tagenstrijdigheids," the description of Havelaar in *M. H.,* p. 61; Translation, p. 89.

69. J. te Winkel, *De Ontwikkelingsgang der Nederlandsche Letterkunde* (Haarlem: Bohn, 1927), VII, 291.

70. G. Brom, *Multatuli* (Utrecht-Antwerp: Spectrum, 1958), p. 229.

71. Letter to Vosmaer, April 5, 1886, in *Vosmaer,* p. 251.

Peter King (essay date 1972)

SOURCE: King, Peter. "*Ideeën.*" In *Multatuli,* pp. 68-89. New York: Twayne Publishers, 1972.

[*In the following essay, King offers an in-depth reading of Multatuli's seven-volume epic,* Ideeën, *the author's collection of reflections on philosophy, morality, and literature. King asserts that despite its fragmented, seemingly arbitrary structure, the work achieves cohesion through the forceful presence of the author's personality, as well as through the lively quality of the prose.*]

I. The Program for the *Ideas*

There is a tantalizing uncertainty about the ending of *Minnebrieven,* since new understanding and insights have clearly been gained by the author, and we are told that they will be expressed in the long overdue tenth Tale of Authority. Yet this tale is not provided. He starts it, as if it presents no problems: "There's a predatory state on the seaboard, between East Frisia and the Scheldt."[1] But he still needs Fancy's promised gift. And when he knows he has it—"My heart is no longer empty . . . She sent me . . . O God, I understand it all now!"—he does not continue the Tale.

That was in July, 1861. In December he started writing **"Over Vryen Arbeid in Nederlands Indië en de tegenwoordige Koloniale Agitatie,"** a pamphlet which might well be answering the call to the author to set Insulinde free.[2] With its motto "There is something rotten in the state of Denmark" it is also as concerned with the "predatory state between East Frisia and the Scheldt" as it is with the East Indies; so that it seems at least to have close connections with the final tale of authority. Yet it is overtly a pamphlet that is dated by the particular parliamentary crisis which necessitated its hasty publication. It seems inconceivable that this represents the new creative insights promised by the catharsis in *Minnebrieven.* But beneath the topical polemic on colonial policy lies an issue of really universal significance: the issue of truth and illusion implicit in *Max Havelaar* and explicit in *Minnebrieven.* For the burden of Multatuli's argument in his exposure of this particular question is that Free Labor, as the term is understood, is to be condemned, since Freedom in the false vocabulary of the Dutch Government means Servitude. The rottenness in the state is its corruption of the truth.

In the marginal notes added by Multatuli to a copy of the first edition of *Minnebrieven* in 1864, he wrote about Fancy's reference to the map: "Insulinde does *not*

mean: the East Indies. It is the point of departure for what I had envisaged as the road to *universal truth.*"[3] It is commonly held that this was Multatuli's rationalization of his enforced acceptance of the pen instead of the sword. This view is cogently put by J. and A. Romein: "Writing from sheer physical necessity—the emphatic reiteration of this theme by this born writer who constantly voiced his contempt of the talent so dear to him, which he rated among the greatest in world literature, all of this is his unremitting self-defense against his sense of failure in practical heroism. Writing from inner necessity because his indomitable and unyielding 'proud spirit' can only achieve heroism in an escape into fantasy."[4]

This view, I believe, does not do justice to the real issue in *Minnebrieven,* which was that neither "authority" (the sword, skepticism) nor "poetry" (the pen, romantic escape) could provide the tenth and authentic Tale of Authority. This, we are led to expect, will harmonize his "intense desire for the truth (exact, mathematical, logical) and his chronic hypersensitivity to imaginary impressions."[5] In future the poet's realistic campaign for the truth will be as practical as the hero's action. Indeed, Multatuli seems so preoccupied with his future program (the tenth Tale of Authority) that he breaks off his pamphlet on Free Labor in the East Indies to address his publisher:

> Dear d'Ablaing! No, it shall never be said that no one *attempted* to exorcise the curse on the nation. It shall not be said that no one attacked the disease, the gangrenous disease this nation is suffering from: the *lie.* I will do what I can. . . .
>
> In that writing I shall seek after *truth. That* is my program. That is my only program. I shall offer stories, anecdotes, accounts, parables, observations, recollections, novels, predictions, announcements, paradoxes. . . . I hope there will be an idea in every story, in every announcement, in every observation. So call my work: Ideeën. Just that. And give it the motto: "A sower went forth to sow." Announce it straight away. That work will be the banner I shall raise and hold aloft: parceque suivre bannière ne peux!6

These *Ideeën* would ultimately fill no less than seven volumes totaling nearly 2,500 pages. They were published like periodicals in separate parts as well as in complete volumes, appearing intermittently over a period of fifteen years. The first issue, of March, 1862, contained an important prologue beginning:

> Let Nature endow you with a desire for knowledge . . . make the pursuit of truth your chief aim in life, your only aim. . . . Sacrifice everything to that pursuit. . . . Go into the wilderness . . . gird a camel skin about your loins . . . feed on locusts and wild honey. . . .
>
> When you return from the desert with the truths you have learned there, some will call you evil, others will pay you lip service and others will disagree with you.

To all of these show the threadbare camel skin that was your garment in the desert. Then the people will cry out: Who is this who offers a worn-out garment as *proof*. . . . Answer then: My brothers, I pray you not to seek in my garment any proof of what I said, only an incentive to think upon what I have said.[7]

The images of the disciple denying father and mother for Christ's sake, and John the Baptist, proclaiming to those that have ears to hear, recall the shabby figure of Sjaalman, and the author of **Minnebrieven,** separated from his wife and child, sent back into the world after his lonely wrestling with the meaning of truth. These double associations in the prologue clearly convey the same message, that doubting Thomases can only be shown the *marks* of truth in the suffering that is needed to find it.

II. THE SEARCH FOR TRUTH

The first *Idee* pinpoints the author's problem: "Perhaps nothing is entirely true, including this." This does not of course absolve us from searching for the truth. ". . . If some one has not even looked he has no right to quote Socrates' description of agnosticism as the highest form of learning. I wish Socrates had never said that. He did not realize how it would be applied" (96).[8] This irony is typical of the man who also wrote, "The idea that is easily understood is rarely worth understanding" (68), and it partly explains the use of paradox and irony in his earlier work. It is also the result of his concept of suffering as a necessary condition of achievement, for it follows from this that an easy path is a valueless one. "It is better to look without finding than to find without looking" (97).

The most contemptible affront to the truth is an uncritical attitude to it. The arrogance of most people's ignorance is summed up in the cliché "'I know all about it', which really means: I am of the opinion that what *I* know about it is *everything*" (546). This is the defensive position of the majority who accept half-truths (2) and put up a common front against honesty (14), particularly in manifestly logical matters (141). The absurdity of the Christian religion is that it fails to make an absolute distinction between the potential *poetic* truth of the man Jesus and the logical absurdity of miracles (351). In upholding the truth of the Gospels, theology has made Jesus a charlatan (140), whereas in fact "Jesus met a gospel, and asked, who are you?" (93).

The distinction between factual and intuitive truths, expressed as a conflict between Droogstoppel and Stern (however much Stern pleaded the *factual* evidence) and between Max (to Tine) and Max (to Fancy), must be recognized by accepting poetic truths *only* when they do not flout reason. In fact, "There is nothing more poetic than the truth. Whoever cannot find poetry in *that* will always be just a poetaster on the outside" (263).

But how is the poet to get foolish people to recognize the truth, the unnatural child of his union with Parable? (Unnatural because she was married to him) (79). If Parable dresses the child in the pretty clothes she has made, the admirers look at these and not at the child (80). But if she presents them with the naked child, they exclaim "how indecent!" (81).

The truth will be shocking to those who are afraid of it, and our fear of the truth (143) and even of our inability to find it (144) inhibits our search for it. Yet error is as necessarily implied by truth as decomposition is implied by life, and mature men fear neither error nor decay (147). Indeed, "the man who has erred often should know the way better than anyone" (21), though to pride oneself on one's fallibility is a false form of humility (20). Nor does our acceptance of *dwaling,* the word Multatuli uses to express intellectual error, fallibility or doubt, mean that we must welcome it, for this leads to wilful dishonesty (145).

Multatuli's defense of agnosticism pivots on the distinction he makes between intellectual error and dishonesty, fallibility and falsehood, doubt and (wilful) ignorance. Triviality is one escape from doubt for those who are afraid of their ignorance. In their *horror vacui* they rush to all kinds of "unnecessary stuffing" to fill the blank spaces (464). Another escape is superstition, an opiate against the fear of uncertainty (144). In a dozen ways he ridicules the absurdity or dishonesty of the religious, and more specifically Christian hypothesis (e.g. 1233), deriving some consolation from the thought that since the greater the certainty the weaker is the spur to endeavor, there is some hope for those in doubt (440). But there is no cause for complacency. "To believe is to sleep. To doubt is to desire. To inquire is to labor. The laborers are few" (425). Belief here is tantamount to credulity, to an uncritical approach to the truth (353), either by confusing the precise meanings of ignorance, doubting, and negation (99), or by accepting package deals of the truth marketed by vested interests as principles, systems, or dogmas (100).

III. CUSTOM AND MORALITY

The adoption of collective attitudes not only dulls the critical faculties (493) but encourages mere lip service to a code of behavior. "Principles are things people use to avoid doing something unpleasant" (303). "Applause in the theater is a lie . . . it seems as if we *applaud* seemliness—and whatever looks like it—in payment for the right to do what is base" (495). "The approbation of Havelaar is the justification of my contempt for the Reading Public" (496).

If hypocrisy can "hide in the crowds," so can immorality. "Individual morality is for the most part cowardice" (328) since individuals would not dare to accept responsibility for much that they subscribe to collectively. "There is not a man who would not be considered a criminal if he permitted himself what the State permits itself. . . . I do not believe in the virtue of individuals who consider themselves innocent of the crimes of the nation 'because they weren't the only ones who did it'" (326). On the other hand moral principles vitiate enlightened government (191). What is the point of opening the cage when the bird is silly enough to pluck out its own wing feathers or has no desire to fly? (190). Worse still, "no law has ever been so bigoted and barbaric as moral principles."

The law punishes with limited sentences, moral convention adds rejection *for life*. The law says: the King . . . the moral code says His Majesty. The law upholds marriage in its social consequences, custom turns marriage into a religious, a moral—that is, very *im*moral—bond. The law protects the wife as a second-class citizen, the social norm makes her a bondswoman. The law recognizes a person's natural birthright, moral propriety spurns the child born without a passport. "The law is sometimes oppressive, custom always. For the most senseless law there are customs even more senseless. However cruel the law, custom can be more cruel" (192).

Convention, the norm for the lowest common denominator in society, is the ultimate anathema to Multatuli, since it lacks any kind of thrust, even the perverse thrust of moral principles. It is the prerogative of *les Sots*, rendered by Multatuli's *Kappellui* (the Killjoys) (73). "There are more gnats than wasps, more *Kappellui* than *droogstoppels*" (29). Their views are so valueless that even they do not act on them: "Whoever says twelve times: I would . . . is talking rubbish eleven times" (3). And they are of course, quite incapable of recognizing their own stupidity. "'You talk too much about yourself . . .' Yes, would you rather I talked about *you* . . . about your cat . . . about your dog . . . about your ass? Is *that* what you want? If so you should be pleased. I have often done so, but you weren't aware of it because you were getting yourself confused with your neighbor's ass. Your neighbor also complains, saying I always talked about *your* asses. Compensation. The asses themselves didn't complain, dear dumb animals" (25).

IV. RIGHTEOUS INDIGNATION

Moreover, the interaction of stupidity and confusion is a fit butt for irony since it is comic. And it is comic because it conforms to the muddled arbitrariness of Nature, which is the model for all humor (158). It is, however, only comic to the true artist whose sense of orderly perfection is affronted by the perversity of reality.[9] "I admit that the struggle with everyday matters, with pedestrian life, is in a sense necessary. The *true* artist derives from this the indispensable component of *humor* which is only ignored by the man who reduces art to a mere craft. In every notable creation of the human mind there is an undercurrent of Juvenalian *indignatio,* without which the artist's celestial vision would tax himself and us with a light all too brilliant, monotonous, and inartistic" (649). From this it follows that "the most vehement expression of affliction is sarcasm" (324).

There is an important distinction between the literary function of irony and ridicule which Multatuli failed to make, and was indeed incapable of making if the explicit confusion in **Minnebrieven** is any guide. *Indignatio* (hence humor and irony) becomes righteous indignation to the writer who makes a virtue of suffering (whence sarcasm and ridicule). "There is only *one* way to heaven: Golgotha. Anyone who tries to get there any other way is an infamous trickster" (57). Very occasionally he is able to stand back even from his own righteous indignation and look at it with ironic detachment, as in *Idee* 249 in which an impoverished hack asks the author's advice on what he should write about in order to make some money. He can write about anything, he is told, if he is fired by conviction. "'That's just what I haven't got. I'm as cold as your room. Ah, my mother!'—'No fire? I'll help you: yes, I'll have nothing to do with you. Freeze, you and your whole family. I can't be bothered with your kind. There's the door and the stairs are just beyond it . . .'—'All right, all right, I'm going! Disgraceful! That's no way to go on . . . it's enough to make you livid, just livid! I'll fix you. . . .' And the man *was* enflamed, and wrote an attack on me with great heat, and could pay for heating to provide his mother and his sisters with some warmth." More usually, however, the tone of his sarcasm reveals an ambivalent position between self-righteousness and self-pity, as in *Idee* 238, which is a blank, followed by *Idee* 284: "The preceding number contains several hundred Ideas that I didn't write because I had too many worries."

He is aware of projecting himself too large: "'You talk a lot about yourself.'—'Yes, so does a shopkeeper who delivered you the goods and presses for payment to no effect'" (298); "'—You talk a lot about yourself.'—'Yes, so would anyone if you showed him slander for justice'" (299). Yet, as in *Havelaar*—but now there is no possibility of anything but a self-portrait—he is unable to cut his hero down to life-size because he takes him too seriously, and there is no sign of the humor which Multatuli reckoned indispensable to true art. The heroic struggle against futilities is a recurrent theme,[10] but in *Idee* 67 it occurs with a difference. "A laborer sprained his ankle and the foreman cried, 'Carry on!' I have sprained my mind, and my master cries, 'Carry on!'—'Master, I *will*.'"

Who is Multatuli's master here? The association with the laborer's foreman suggests the tyranny of daily routine and economic necessity. But his obedience to his master is more reminiscent of his response to Fancy's charge "Do your duty!"[11] Yet Fancy expresses rather the freedom of the author's creative psyche[12] than the burden of drudgery. She might be the Knight's Lady but scarcely the workman's taskmaster. To understand the close affinity between the loftiest aspiration and humdrum survival in Multatuli's frequent concern with conflict and endeavor, we have to look at his philosophy—i. e. his attempt at an understanding (791)—of Necessity (*Noodzakelijkheid*).

V. Necessity and Reality

The very continuation of existence depends on the natural law of Necessity. The evidence for this is the mathematical fact—and the Law of Necessity is itself a mathematical law (1627)—that the *slightest* deviation in natural performance would, in an infinite progression, produce total disorder (198). The natural process of composition and decomposition (170) can be expressed as the law of *attraction*: "Whoever or whatever most strongly attracts gains substance. Whoever or whatever has the least attraction loses substance. Everything that happens has its origin in this eternal alternation of *more* with less" (172). The dynamic motivation which guarantees the continuity of this process is Necessity—the instinct to survive, closely associated in human life with the desire for knowledge and the sexual urge. This is the truth expressed by the legends of Paradise, Faust, and Woutertje Pieterse, discussed in the *Idee* **"Waarheid in Legende."** "We should not *exist* if we were not compelled to continue to exist by the properties of our *being*," the properties of attraction (the desire to know and to love) and conflict (rebellion against the frustration of these desires). "The truth demands *im*perfection" and "the bravest poet cannot conceive what would have become of Faust, of Adam, and hence of mankind, if Necessity—the god that closes paradises, because survival in paradises is impossible—had not driven us all out into the battlefield called *life*" (517). Human error is therefore necessary, as we have seen,[13] not as an end in itself, but to perpetuate the struggle for perfection.

"The totality of the properties of *Necessity* provides a unity which we try vaguely to express in all sorts of nouns with an emphatic prefix. Omnipresence, omnibenevolence, omnipotence, omniscience. Indeed, however, *un*knowing"—for the blindness of natural necessity is truly comic (158)—"this same necessity is in a sense *all*-knowing" (165). "Nature is *everything* and everything is *natural*. Where we are able to trace the progression of the logic of the facts we recognize this nature, this *necessity*. Where that logic eludes us—because we know so little—we think of a God" (166). Yet even the most devout Christian would not pray, "give me back yesterday, O Lord!" thereby acknowledging that even his Lord is subject to necessity. And it is *this* god

which existed before the anthropomorphic divinities, in the Roman *fatum* and the Indian *Trimourti* (170). Hence, "Necessity is God. There is no more to be said about God. And I'm sorry for that" (32).

Since "Nature is *everything*" (71) there can be no evidence for God in nature, since by definition God is supernatural (102). It is for this reason that the Christian belief in the Gospels with their miracles and deification of Jesus (265) is offensive to Multatuli, who still believes in the *man* Jesus "which means rather more than a god, or demigod, or God, according to choice" (264). So when Multatuli writes that he finds his God in goodness (277) we must read this in conjunction with *Idee* 16: ". . . When I say: God, I do so in a manner of speaking. For I don't know who God is." And he is presumably still talking of *his* God when he cries out "Some poetry, my God, you who exist only in poetry . . ." which clearly does not mean that God exists, though only in poetry, but that God is a poetic construct: "Some poetry, my God, if only because it created you. You do not, after all, exist?" (361).

The absolute rejection of God except in terms of poetry raises a serious question about Multatuli's use of the term "poetry." "Have faith and bow down, or reject it and stand upright. Naïve, childlike, sometimes sublime untruths are acceptable in *poetry*. But 2 x 2 = 5 will always be a monstrosity, so long as 2 x 2 is no more and no less than four" (141). "Untruths" must here be read as "illogicalities." The miraculous and supernatural are acceptable as myth, but when they are prescribed as articles of faith or facts of history they are falsehoods (*not* the same as untruths) which must be repudiated. This is the theme of truth in legend (517) which is further developed in *Idee* 513 where myth and history are contrasted as categories of truth and falsehood: "Once granted that nothing is entirely true (1), we have to admit that the study of a myth very often brings us nearer to the truth than the scrutiny of the deliberate lies of the historians." Since the poet is only the *maker,* giving *form* to what already *exists,* ". . . there is *always* truth in poetry (263), and where we fail to find it, the fault is ours." Mistrust of "poetic" wisdom is a Droogstoppel invention whereas the real deceit is in "prosaic" virtuosity, as much by its suppression as its distortion of the truth. This is the medium of historians, schoolmasters, clergymen, politicians, and literary men, all of whom have a vested interest in the manipulation of the truth. So "there isn't a man whose emotional case book would not be more important than the longest, most 'beautiful', *contrived* novel" (252). For "*Feeling, imagination and courage* are the essential motivations for the man who seeks to *know*. That is why philosophy and poetry are one" (513).

With this somewhat ingenuous semantic juggling, Multatuli can claim that his **Ideeën** are personal thoughts, therefore philosophy, therefore poetry (11-13, 34, 230), and that God can at most represent the abstract idea of something that does not exist, namely perfect truth and understanding (490). So whether Van Vloten was referring to systematic philosophy (which Multatuli classifies as "prose" in *Idee* 513) or the individual's *philosophia,* Multatuli is happy to quote him as an authority on style: "We cannot regard as productive any philosophy that cannot be expressed in everyday language" (125). He rates himself one of the best authors that have ever lived because he can express himself clearly (522), or rather, because of *what* he expresses so clearly, for *how* it is expressed is a matter of literary talent, and he is no writer (526). But since "the average standard of the reader is below the level of the most incompetent author" (524), the inimical *delectare* has to be introduced as a disguise for the *prodesse* (602-604). "I absolve *you* almost completely, you erring artists! It's Mr. 'Public' who loves cosmetics and shams. . . . The artist who does not crack under the 'Public's' demand for make-believe is a hero" (629). The author, too, can be guilty of *choosing* the easy option. "*The virginity of the impression* must be maintained despite *much suffering* . . . this makes heavy demands. Is it any wonder that poets are rare . . ." (1086). But if the suffering is a deterrent, it is also the mark of greatness. "The history of a great concept always reminds me of the text: In sorrow shalt thou bring forth children! If a grain of corn could speak, it would complain that germination is a painful process. Heroes, artists, and philosophers will understand me, as well as the complaint of that grain of corn" (30).

Undoubtedly his estimation of his own heroism is partly responsible for his high self-esteem, but his plain speaking is indeed so original that he was justifiably sensitive to those who would detract from his achievement either by underrating it (206) or imitating it. "Whoever tries to copy me is often my enemy, generally a bore, and always a fool" (51). "The adoption of an opinion 'because I said it myself' is a clear indication to me that I did not state it properly" (53). This is the ultimate claim to originality, for though it implies the modesty of a man whose opinions are always provisional, it equally implies a constant state of unindebtedness, even to himself. He may have said, as a protest against empty praise or to imply that he was not concerned with his own originality, "It is a sorry thing that the word 'original' is laudatory" (337), yet no judgment of his was as explicit and indeed as unbalanced as his condemnation of unoriginality (1265-69) and especially of the Renaissance ideal of *imitatio* (1268).

VI. FREEDOM OF THOUGHT

All this may lead us, as it has many of Multatuli's biographers, to remonstrate at the man's arrogance. He is as disarmingly frank about this, or at any rate seemingly so, as he is about himself in his private correspondence. How sincere, we are bound to ask, is the man who considered himself one of the world's greatest authors, when he writes, "The man who is satisfied with his work, has reason to be dissatisfied with his satisfaction" (61). We do not need to give the answer. He does himself. "All I know which I have not learned from others I would gladly exchange for everything I could have learned from others and haven't. I don't mean that. But I ought to" (106). At this, the hand poised to throw the stone has to drop it. Yet his apparent defenselessness is, we discover as we read on, an ambush. "I ought to mean it" is the world's judgment, not his. For humility is a virtue invented by little men afraid of being dwarfed. The upright man in Holland is labeled "pride" (107). "There is no pride. There is no humility. There is only truth and untruth" (108). Later, however, pride, *hoogmoed,* is honorably reinstated. "De hoogste graad van moed is hoogmoed" (220—Man's proudest endeavor is his pride) and, similarly, "Highmindedness is having a mind to stand high . . ." (246). *Hoogmoed* is clearly associated here with a high *ideal,* and this is confirmed by *Idee* 505: "No one rates highly enough what he could be. No one low enough what he *is*," which concurs with an earlier thought: "I should like to meet myself, to find out what I thought of myself. But I shall have to be in a good humor that day, since I don't like unpleasant experiences" (226).

The irony which is never far below the surface of Multatuli's thought, is again clearly audible here, for he takes humility from the semantic field of false modesty where he has found it in general use, and then shows its falsity by contrasting it with pride, an attribute condemned in the same field. Better, he says, to be proud if "Humility is a cowardly means of seeming to be worthwhile" (223), and better honest ambition than the modesty which cripples high endeavor. In the same way the meaning of the word "principles" acquires a negative charge from his opinion of the people most associated with them. "I have no principles" (933) since "principles are mean pretexts for dodging one's duty" (934). "Holland is full of principles" (936). "When Droogstoppel was accused of letting a child choke to death in a muddy ditch, his excuse was the Sunday coat he was wearing. I repeat, I have no principles. And my acceptance of this lack is made very simple for me by my observation of the actions of people who are subject to these things. The person who has to quote a principle in order to differentiate between good and evil is a knave" (935). This judgment summarizes Multatuli's frequently expressed hostility towards the immunity from independent inquiry obtained by the uncritical majority who seek protection in numbers.

Principles, dogmas, systems smother honest inquiry by prejudging the issue and treating the inquirer as a dangerous freethinker (128-29). They are promoted by interested parties who perpetuate them by claiming to serve social and moral order (111). They stultify independent thought and hence stimulate mediocrity, and "the sum of many mediocrities is always the same as one mediocrity" (5), or "The sum total of the judgments of many incompetents offers no greater guarantee of correctness than the judgment of one incompetent" (6). Democracy, therefore, is unlikely to work. The majority vote is a means not of arriving at the truth, but of expressing the law of the jungle without bloodshed—"If we fought, *we* should win . . . let's do without the fighting" (7). And it is even less likely to work when civil servants belong to a mutual admiration society (116) and when "representation" is impersonalized by collective responsibility. "The sharing of responsibility is the product of cowardice and mistrust. The mistrust of those who insist on it, cowardice in those who accept it" (334). "In an *emergency* the heart dictates *autocracy*. 'The doctor will know' the anxious voices round the sickbed will say. 'Captain, help us!' the terrified passengers call out. Consultations and ship's councils were devised, not to cure the sick or protect ships, but for convenience and the quasi-vindication of those who have lost ships and patients" (335). We should expect the admirer of Napoleon to advocate an enlightened despotism: "Parliamentary forms of government offer a system of insurance against abuses. I maintain that the sum of the premiums is higher than the likely cost of tyranny" (332). Yet he can offer no alternative to the constitutional monarchy with government by representation (121), perhaps because he is such an individualist that he could envisage no other despotism but his own. "I rarely write what I like, and never what any one else likes" (112).

To such an absolutist, mediocrity and moderation were almost synonymous. He ridicules compromise as a north-south solution to the dilemma of whether to look for the river bridge to the east or to the west (120) and is particularly virulent in his attacks on the liberal theologians—specifically the modernist J. C. Zaalberg (454)—because their moderation made territorial claims on *his* cynicism as well as on his enemies' theism: "They storm heaven and earth simultaneously" (940).

Since rigid systems and tolerant flexibility both compromised the integrity of the freethinker, Multatuli not unnaturally found himself accused of a destructive attitude to his environment. His answer is that testiness about trivial hindrances does not indicate a temperament incapable of higher purposes (260) and he refers to an earlier *Idee* about a sailor smoking his pipe through clenched teeth while his leg was being amputated without an anesthetic, but yelling when he was jabbed by the safety pin of the dressing. "'What . . . screaming like that, *you* who just now . . .'—'That's true . . . but you see Doctor, that pin prick shouldn't have been part of it'" (86). Moreover, the accusation itself is not true. "People think I 'protest against

everything.' That is the phrase. O, if only they knew how many things were sacred to me!" (253). Finally, to think freely, one must be *unencumbered,* and anyway: "Is the struggle *against* error not a struggle *for* truth?" (178).

Freedom of thought is never normally allowed to develop, since parents, who know far less about children than bird fanciers about birds (438), condition their children to a restricted development from the start. "The imposition of prejudices. We are subject to these right from birth" (555). "Even the body may not study freely"; rocking and overdressing the child and placing it in a playpen are the unnatural signs of parental love (557). "Silence is the first duty of the new world citizen. . . . It looks very much as if parents assess the true virtue of *existence* in terms of the child's behavior as if it did *not* exist" (558). "A few days ago a young girl suitably goody-goodied, catechized and domiciled, was taken by her family to a lunatic asylum in Utrecht. The lady in charge of the female patients in that asylum said to the family: 'Our regulations are simple. Gentleness is the main thing. Then, obviously, light, air, amusement, exercise, suitable relaxation. . . .'" Later, a younger daughter asked the father, "'. . . supposing we had begun with these things *before* our poor sister went mad?'" (209). Female emancipation is a particular concern of Multatuli's just because biblical morality and hence the law impose the most obviously unnatural conditions on women's freedom. "We have discovered morals, we apply them, we claim that we have to maintain them . . . morals that are perpetually at odds with the cardinal law of Nature. . . . We prescribe it as our duty to violate this Nature. This violation—or our constant futile attempt at it—we call virtue. Our whole upbringing of girls is a murderous revolt against goodness" (200).

This brings us back to our point of departure, ***Minnebrieven*** and the tenth Tale of Authority promised there. For the moral strictures on free love are just an acute form of the whole perversity of humanity's unnatural fears, superstitions, ignorances, and dishonesty about the simple truths in the laws of nature. Sexual love is goodness (508) because it is the fullest expression of man's understanding nature (489). It is goodness because it expresses man's acceptance of the Necessity of nature as something he is meant to understand because it is the motivation of life itself. "That dumb, unconscious, almighty, unknowing, Necessity is a *God of love*. . . . What *is, must* be. It is up to us—and it is this which is *God's will*—to be cautious, to take note, to beware of evil . . . It is up to us to *observe*, to reflect, to *put into practice* . . . to *desire* and to *work* . . . to *strive after growth* . . . to find *pleasure* in all this—in this sense—*is* virtue" (177). If "man's calling is to be man" (136), the prophetic artist's calling is to show him the way out of the caging structure of his society.[14] For true art stimulates the appreciation of beauty, hence pleasure and virtue. "Rulers who think that *art* is no matter for governments, are making government a commercial art" (459).

VII. IDEAS AS A LITERARY WORK

Whether or not we agree with P. Couperus[15] that in *Ideeën* Multatuli has discharged his promise to write the tenth Tale of Authority, there can be little doubt that in his *Ideeën* his primary concern is the program announced in the preface—to establish the authority of truth as it is found in the logical statements of the rationalist and in the mythical art of the poet. The very aim of this work gives it a hybrid quality which makes an objective appreciation of it unusually difficult. The aim is intellectual and abstract, but the means to that end are entirely literary and subjective. The cause may be rational but the effect is emotional. Our immediate response is to the literary effectiveness of metaphor, irony, hyperbole, satire, pathos, word play, rhythm, and so on, and Multatuli made no concealment of his deliberate use of this fact. What he had written in **"Over Vryen Arbeid"** applies to all his work. The newspaper reporters "say you *want* to read downright lies and futile bickering about lies. Is that so? I can't believe it. Honestly, now and then the truth is more pungent. Take my writings . . . everyone buys them. Now you know the secret of my so-called talent."[16]

In the usual types of "literature" the poet, dramatist, or author releases his individuality in his work with an ostensibly "take-it-or-leave-it" abandon; and the reader is free to adopt his own moral attitude to the literary work and to assess its credibility in terms of its literary effect. *Ideeën,* however, is in no sense handed over to the reader. It demands an all-or-nothing commitment, and, what is more, in the presence of the author.

Multatuli, of course, intended this and the necessary consequence, that the reader who disagrees with his views must reject his art. Brom, who is manifestly unable to suppress his ideological antipathy to Multatuli in his *literary* monograph on him, cannot do more than concede that "the vitality of *Ideeën* makes them readable (even when they dispense nonsense) whereas real thought often condemns itself to the graveyard."[17] More typical of Brom's general attitude is his comment: "The dilettante has the advantage of being able to speak remarkably fluently on any subject because he is never aware of the problems."[18] This, however, shows a remarkable unawareness of Multatuli's own serious study of his problems as an author and idealist, contained in *Ideeën* 591-783, under the title "On public lectures." This is a substantial essay of some 57,000 words discussing the very question of the author's ethical responsibilities to his readers, which so many of his critics either ignore or treat as their province and not his.

On the other hand, just because Multatuli's literary talent is particularly offensive to some readers, who feel that he is abusing it, they assume that others who recognize artistic integrity in his work, are intellectually and emotionally paralyzed by his persuasive manner. And a completely objective *literary* assessment is not made any easier by the blackmailing threat so often repeated by Multatuli, that if we should ascribe literary merit to his work we have not read it properly! But the proper reading of Multatuli obviously includes a proper understanding of this kind of statement, and our understanding is more likely to be objective if we consider Multatuli in his historical context.

We know that the "general reader" of Multatuli's day was very far removed from the most literate nation in the world today,[19] and, as we have seen,[20] Multatuli's was a very strange voice in a moral and social wilderness. But as an artist at least he shares many of the recognized characteristics of European romanticism, excess, hyperbole, extravagance together with naïveté, sentimentality, and idealism, and a tender social conscience harnessed to a ruthless disdain for social institutions.[21] The romantic, of course, can be highly contradictory without being inconsistent. "In his stand against religion he is a materialist, in his stand against social and economic oppression he is an idealist."[22] This is broadly true, but even this is, objectively speaking, consistently true of many acclaimed romantics. Even the most persistent and obvious contradiction, the idealist's contempt of the masses he is called to serve, is perfectly consistent with the romantic dilemma, in which the people (*het volk*) and the masses (*publiek*) are not synonymous. "The masses are . . . as Goethe says, 'was uns alle bändigt, das Gemeine.'" The masses, a mediocrity of individuals, can only be detested by the artist. The people, on the other hand, are an individual entity, a unity, a mystical community, from which the artist cannot isolate himself without producing his own sterilization; for the people have a soul expressing itself in myth, tradition, religion, art, and philosophy. "An artist must be in the community, but he can never be of the community."[23]

It is of course true that Multatuli was overtly conscious of this dilemma in a particularly acute form, since the pen was not the weapon of his choosing and it could not and did not produce the reforms he advocated. But again, his unequivocal recognition of this fact blunts the point of the attack that he had to write because of his "feelings of guilt about his failure to act, and the constant urge to compensate for that by fictional deeds and imaginary power to act."[24] As readers we are concerned with *what* he wrote, not with hypotheses about *why* he wrote. And he wrote of Napoleon: "He is great because of that *idea*; he would have been great even if the future had not brought this to fruition."[25] The question we have to answer is whether these *Ideeën* are of themselves "great" by evaluating the artistic form in relation to the total concept. Or, more basically, what, if anything, makes this verbal message a work of art?

The problem is obvious, and it has already been referred to. The verbal message is overtly addressed by the writer to the reader. The fragmentation of the whole into numbered units is a constant reminder that the author himself is the only cohesive factor, like the date on the columnist's newspaper or the artist's private diary. Lack of cohesion is not the only problem, however, for a personal diary (whether written for publication or not) like personal correspondence or even a series of lectures, could be classified as works of art if the diarist, letter writer, lecturer, columnist, essayist, historian, and so on wrote in a personal style that could be defined as literary. But the very diversity of style *and* structure in the **Ideeën** gives the work a polygenetic character which would obscure the common "factor" of the author if he did not take steps to remedy this.

A rereading of the **Ideeën** with this problem in mind leads to the general conclusion which we would have expected: the longer the *Idee*, the greater is the need for stylistic features that reveal the authorial person. The most obvious of these are the first and second person pronouns. But these are reinforced with a wide range of disruptive features such as sudden changes in the temporal or spatial points of view, rhetorical phrases and punctuation for emotive effect, and references to characters associated with the author (such as Droogstoppel, Kappelman, Fancy, Havelaar, Van Twist, Napoleon, de kleine Max) and to other *Ideeën* which may be more subjective than the text in front of us. This last comment requires elucidation. Cross-references, of course, always disrupt the stream of thought of the reader, but in their normal usage they do not disturb the objectivity of a sustained argument. In **Ideeën,** however, the use of a numeral in a relatively dispassionate passage reminds us, even if we do not look at the *Idee* referred to, that we are still in the presence of the emotional, impetuous, and ironic individual who communicates in this seemingly erratic way.

VIII. Structural and Stylistic Cohesion

A general statement about **Ideeën** as a literary work would therefore have to accept the paradox that the structural unity of the work resides *solely* in the fragmentation emphasized by the numbering of its parts. For these numbers do not operate as conventional markers of sequence but of division and reentry. A novel, a play, or a poem may of course have a numbered hiatus at the transition from one chapter, act, or stanza to the next. Here, where continuity is expected, the hiatus will express some spatial, temporal, modal, or situation transition and it prepares the reader for some kind of reorientation. But from the start of **Ideeën,** the reader cannot

begin to chart a course and take his bearings from it. Unlike the typographical markers in other literary works, the space announcing the end of each *Idee* and the numeral announcing the beginning of the next return us inevitably to the author, for we have nowhere else to go.

Since a structural assessment of this kind concerns the relationship of all the 1,282 parts to one whole, of 2,455 pages, it cannot easily be demonstrated. But the dual function of the numeration, to disrupt at one level (the textual) and reintegrate at another (the writer/reader point of view) can be illustrated for a set of *Ideeën* (**V. W.** [*Volledige Werken*] II, pp. 436-59) where there is also a *textual* sequence.

Idee 229 starts with the author's announcement of a tale he will tell. Sudden interventions from the author prevent the story from establishing its own fiction, until a substantial piece of third-person narrative draws us so far into its situation that the author's sudden return is an unwelcome intrusion (p. 437). The heading "Chapter Two" is followed only by an authorial explanation of the omission of "Chapter One" above the preceding section. *Idee* 230 relates only to the author's creative inspiration, concluding: "I no more think up my **Ideeën** than the attractive mother in 219 thought up her children." *Idee* 231 (p. 438) starts with the author's proposed contents of the second chapter, and the narrative is then resumed with only an occasional authorial "I," though since the narration is sustained, we are now, at most, aware only of a *narrator.*

The reader is, nevertheless, not so sure of his bearings in the tale that he is not slightly disorientated by the announcement "Tussen-hoofdstuk," seemingly an intermezzo, but also reminiscent of the complete destruction of the fictional illusion when Chapter Two was announced. Yet the narrative does in fact continue to the end of *Idee* 231 (p. 443), where the narrative subject of the comment: "Again I can't say . . . ," manifestly becomes an authorial person in "My publisher is asking for Ideeën. . . ."

The two *Ideeën* that follow (232-33) have no bearing on the tale they have interrupted. We are brought back to this in *Idee* 234 (p. 444) in which the first word, "I," is actually the narrator ("I don't know in which chapter of my story the group of passengers came on board . . .") but is, after the preceding *Ideeën*, inevitably read as the author. A short passage of third-person narrative is then interrupted by four lines of comment (235) which could have been the narrator's but for the cross-reference to *Idee* 21, which obviously belongs to the author's and not the narrator's realm.

Idee 236 (pp. 445-48), however, continues the narrative as if there had been no interruption. The narrator is only implicitly present in the pronoun "our" until the last page, and in particular the last paragraph, where the reader is conscious of the transition to the following *Idee* and hence aware of an ambiguity in the first-person pronoun. There is no longer any doubt at the start of *Idee* 237; only the author could write: "Now assuredly another chapter, . . . as it was told to me by Fancy." But for the rest of this, and indeed the following *Idee*, there is no evidence of the author and scarcely even of the narrator. The break between 237 and 238 has no function in the narrative, which calls for no more than a new paragraph at this point, and the *only* effect of the white space and marginal numeral is to disorientate the reader. The continuation of the tale reinforces the narrator-reader relationship, until the author suddenly steps out again from behind the narrator: "It reminds me of the child 'that loved his mother so much that he wanted to be able to give her a star'" (p. 452). This reference to Max Havelaar again takes us away from the narrator's realm to the author's. The disruptive effect of this paragraph within the tale can be compared with the effect of the paragraph numbered 239 which is less disruptive, because less unexpected, particularly since the punctuation at the end of *Idee* 238 (and the beginning of 240) clearly implies a digression.

Nowhere is the "suspension of belief" at the conclusion of each *Idee* more overtly exploited than in the transition to *Idee* 241, headed "Next chapter," and opening with the exclamation "They must be daft with their Sainte Vierge!" The reader is bound to be tricked here by the irony of an apparently obvious author-comment being in fact part of the narrative, which continues: "This, or something like it, was the only thought in the stranger's mind as he undressed. . . ."

In the "Penultimate chapter" (242) the tale continues with only one intrusion by the narrator (p. 458), but it is the author who has the last word: "The last chapter of this story is not for sale. I'll give it away to my special friends."

Just as the deliberate fragmentation of this story exposes the author at irregular intervals "through the cracks," so the whole seemingly haphazard mosaic of all the *Ideeën,* ranging in size from more than 25,000 words (451) to nil (283, 1197b), is really a tissue of pieces which, even when they are themselves not transparent, never obscure for long the author who is always in the background, the medium bonding them all.

Another cohesive factor throughout the *Ideeën* is, equally paradoxically, the diversity of style. Where this would normally disturb the unity of a sustained piece of writing, in such a piecemeal structure as this it helps to maintain the interest through the gaps. There is a fascinating and apparently arbitrary succession of different kinds of prose:[26] aphorism, essay, correspondence, fable, legend, satire, caricature (e.g. the Rammeslag mono-

logue in *Idee* 608), novel, drama, and even poetry (as in *Idee* 361, beginning "Some poetry, God, lest I succumb to nausea due to so much nausea *round* me!" and maintaining this iambic rhythm throughout two pages of a prose-like text.) The novel-length tale of Woutertje Pierse will, in the following chapter, be considered as part of **Ideeën,** and the five-act play **Vorstenschool** will be discussed with his other dramatic works. This, as an entirely autonomous work in its own right is, indeed, the only misfit in the structural scheme of **Ideeën.** So it is the more remarkable that he wrote of this same. "*Idee*": "How, why or whence the drama 'Vorstenschool' which follows came into being, I could not say. The main reason will probably be the urge to create, produce, fashion . . . O, everything boils down to arrangement! We can do no more than that" (929). And he refers to *Idee* 244, where poets are coupled with slanderers as people who cannot create but only arrange.

What he means by this is not that the poet expresses himself in formal orderliness but that he can only rearrange what already exists because no one can add to what is. In fact, one of his themes in **Ideeën,** which he returns to at great length in **Millioenen-Studiën,** is his conviction about the ultimate unity of creation, however diversified its parts. "Quite simply, in order to relate *everything* to *everything*—things are unitary by nature—I kept applying my previous experiences to other things" (539). "All is in all. Everything is held together in the relationship of cause to effect" (451). Multatuli has often been criticized for lacking the self-discipline essential to artistic expression. Certainly no one who has attempted the kind of summary of the thought in **Ideeën** which forms the main part of this chapter, could be in any doubt about the random disarray of this mosaic. But Multatuli himself refutes his critics by showing throughout **Ideeën** that he had a remarkable command of what he was doing by frequently cross-referencing the pieces, not only in the *Ideeën* themselves, but also in the copious notes which were added at various times in later years. In one such note, of 1872, when he had written five of the seven books of **Ideeën,** he wrote a comment on "My **Ideeën** are 'The Times' of my soul" (34), which gives an authorial view for comparison with a reader's view in the foregoing remarks in this chapter.

> It is said of "The Times" that it does not really follow any stated predetermined line, but reflects the opinions of the majority of the English people. To what extent this is true, or even possible, I do not know.
>
> The intention in my *Idee* is to give an assurance that I write according to my impression of the moment, without any concern for connections, homogeneity, or ultimate conclusions. Hence my constant change of subject.
>
> So in this lack of method, there is a sort of . . . method.[27]

Notes

1. *M. H.* [Multatuli, *Max Havelaar, of de Koffij-Veilingen der Nederlandsche Handelmaatschappij* (Amsterdam: van Oorschot, 1966)] p. 238; *V. W.* [Multatuli, *Volledige Werken* (Amsterdam: Van Oorschot, 1950-)] II, 157.

2. "Release *her* [Insulinde] . . . that is the calling I charge you with" (*V. W.* II, 155).

3. *V. W.* II, 179. These notes, 'which provide an extremely illuminating commentary on *Minnebrieven,* are available in *V. W.* II, 171-79.

4. [J. & A. Romein,] *Erflaters van onze beschaving* [(Rotterdam: 1990)], p. 714.

5. Cf. *V. W.* II, 178.

6. *V. W.* II, 261.

7. *V. W.* II, 309 f.

8. In this and the following chapter the number of the *Idee* referred to will be given in brackets with no further indication.

9. Bakhuizen van den Brink, in terms very similar to Multatuli's, describes humor as "the *comic* which has its natural roots in the incompatibilities of life: incompatibilities between reality and ideal, desire and fulfillment, rule and exception." *Studiën en Schetsen* III, 576, quoted in J. Prinsen J. Lz. *Multatuli en de Romantiek* (Rotterdam: Brusse, 1909), p. 15.

10. In *Ideeën* 55, 62, 70, 86, 90, 105, 216, 217, 260-62, 285, 942.

11. Cf. *Woutertje Pieterse*: "See to it that you are top of the school in three months," Femke said . . . "O, Femke, I'll do it!" (*Idee* 1063, *V. W.* VI, 660) and "Real high-mindedness," Holsma continued, "consists in doing what needs to be done, even in little things . . . and in thinking of nothing but your work. . . ."—"O, I *will,* I *will!*" (*Idee* 1186, *V. W.* VII, 276 f.).

12. See P. King, "Multatuli's psyche," *Modern Language Review* LIII, 1 (1958), 60-74.

13. See p. 71 above and *Ideeën* 144-49.

14. It is revealing that the letters to a widow condemned for her "free love" (448-50), lead into the longest *Idee* he wrote, a massive indictment of Dutch morality and the political administration that fostered it.

15. P. Th. Couperus, "Fantasie en Werkelijkheid. Eene beschouwing over Multatuli's Minnebrieven," *De Dageraad,* IV (1882), 109.

16. *V. W.* II, 218.

17. G. Brom, [*Multatuli* (Utrecht-Antwerp: Spectrum, 1958)] *op. cit.,* p. 93.

18. *Ibid.,* p. 70.

19. This cannot be substantiated. But current book sales, educational statistics, articles, and programs in the mass media and international opinion on the causes (high population density and exceptionally high general standard of education) of religious and political radicalism in Holland all point the same way.

20. See p. 11 above.

21. J. Prinsen J. Lzn., *op. cit.,* p. 43.

22. J. van der Bergh van Eysinga-Elias, *Multatuli als denker en dichter. Een keur uit zijn werken* (Amsterdam: Elsevier, 1919), p. 13.

23. J. A. Rispens, *Richtingen en figuren in de Nederlandse Letterkunde na 1880* (Kampen: Kok, 1938), p. 23 f.

24. J. & A. Romein, *Erflaters van onze beschaving,* p. 714.

25. *Losse bladen uit het dagboek van een oud man, V. W.* VIII, 370. My italics.

26. The words prose and poetry are used here only in the stylistic sense, and have none of the philosophical connotations given them by Multatuli.

27. *V. W.* II, 669 f.

A. van den Bergh (essay date fall 1984)

SOURCE: van den Bergh, A. "Multatuli and Romantic Indecision." *Canadian Journal of Netherlandic Studies/ Revue canadienne d'études néerlandaises* 5, no. 2 (fall 1984): 36-47a.

[*In the following essay, van den Bergh examines aspects of religiosity in Multatuli's work, arguing that Multatuli's profound ambivalence toward Christianity belongs to the larger tradition of European Romanticism.*]

At the Institute of Netherlandic Studies in Amsterdam, where I teach modern literature, the same problem presents itself every year: when romanticism comes up for discussion, the writers of this period seem to take an ambiguous attitude towards the Christian faith which is difficult to explain.

On the one hand the Dutch romanticists are children of "The Enlightenment" to such an extent that they are extremely critical of the dogmatic authority of the bible and of the church as a traditional institution. On the other hand the disappearance of the security of a joint religion leads to a desperate searching for new ties that are often found in a more emotional, more inward form of religiousness, which, in the thirties and forties of the last century led to a powerful movement of religious resurgence, the so-called 'Reveil' (=± Awakening). The students repeatedly have difficulties with that paradoxical, at the same time pro and anti-christian attitude. (At least we, the teachers, have difficulties explaining it).

Multatuli rises as a literary giant, head and shoulders above the mediocrity of his period, and thus he also represents the romantic ambivalence towards religion in a gigantic manner, in his works. Never have the christian doctrinal points been ridiculed with more sarcasm, and never professed with more avid conviction. He who looks into these points in his work and life, sets his eyes upon a highly enlightening illustration of the romantic paradox in question.

Douwes Dekker (the real name of Multatuli), born in 1820 in Amsterdam, grew up in a baptist milieu where Christianity was professed in an unorthodox, but fundamental way[1]: the baptists did not want to form an ordinary, neat congregation with all the institutions belonging to it, with elders and synods, but they took the true Christian message to the letter; they refused to carry weapons, to take an oath and did not take up any civic service. Often in those circles "home-practices" were held where laymen would explain the bible to each other.

Dekker's father was a captain in the foreign trade, who often was absent from home for months. The young Eduard, therefore, did not have much reason to stand up against religion, as could have been the case if it were imposed upon him with strict ecclesiastic and paternal authority. He went to the Latin School, because he was predestined to become a chaplain, just like his eldest brother Piet who was a chaplain for his whole life.

Did this milieu put its stamp on Douwes Dekker? Was he in his youth actually influenced by this gentle, but fundamental variety of the Protestant Christianity? Let us see what the writer tells us about this himself. In 1862, 42 years of age, he looks with a certain endearment back upon the image of God that he had in his youth. At least this was a God to whom people could relate and who would not hesitate to put his shoulder to the wheel: a strict but amiable father-figure.

In these memoirs[2] Multatuli asks for His help in his fight against the apathies of his fellow-countrymen and then writes—in the beautiful metrical prose that one can hardly render into equivalent English—"Up, up, thou God, help us! Hold out your hands, strike once to the left and once to the right and above all things do not be weaker in your acts than they described you in

the bible of my youth. There you sat on a high throne of clouds, looking grim (. . .) You were wrathful, jealous from time to time, sometimes capricious and disposed to bad moods, as can be expected from old gods, who, being alone for so long, and therefore in bad company, get bored. But still, although you did not look amiable, still I felt respect, fear or whatever it was . . . I felt *something,* when nanny reprimanded me because I asked if she had known you without a beard and if you had been young, as anyone else. Those were forbidden questions, the woman told me, and I would be damned if I asked them again. Fine. Henceforth I kept the questions to myself. And if I brewed some mischief . . . oh, do you recollect, how I once—it was awful—with charcoal drew glasses on your nose? Honestly, it was just a pastime, no malicious intent! (. . .) How scared I was! How my heart trembled at the thought that someone would discover the glasses and ask: who has put the glasses on God's nose? (. . .) But in those times I understood you. I lived *with* you, *in* you, and believed in good faith that *you,* too, lived in me".

Thus, apparently, for the forty-two year old Multatuli there was no doubt that in his youth God had been a reality, worthy of love. An even clearer sign of his early religious conviction can be found in a letter from his bosom schoolfriend, Bram des Amorie van der Hoeven, written when Dekker gets married on the Isle of Java in 1846. Van der Hoeven is then chaplain in Utrecht and knows Dekker's former spiritual world as no one else, due to their former close relationship. On the base of that knowledge he writes to the twenty-six year old government official in the colonies: "After a century people still must talk about the good and great works you did. You must also work for higher interests, for our Christianity. To keep the East Indies for the Netherlands and to win them for Christ, is nowadays our most urgent need (. . .)"[3] Undoubtedly the young chaplain sees in his friend Dekker nothing more or less than an ardent missionary amongst the heathens.

And it is certain that Dekker in those times expresses himself in his first literary experiments as an inspired Christian. Although in everyday life in the colonies he did not scorn earthly love, he knew very well that the theory of love should look like this, especially when one writes poetry:

> Wat zoekt ge, liefde en min? Mistrouw haar zoet genot:
> Geen liefde is als van God, bestendig, rein, verheven,
> Het stoffelijke is te zeer met ons bestaan doorweven,
> Gij vindt beneden niet, wat slechts bestaat bij God.[4]

I translate these traditional but smooth verses prosaically like this: "What are you looking for, for love? Mistrust her sweet delight: no love is as that of God, lasting, pure, sublime. Our earthly existence is too much determined by material things, you will not find down here, what exists only in God." This rendering is of course just amateurish, but there is an official translation of one of his early poems, because the writer included it in his autobiographical work, the famous ***Max Havelaar***; so, apparently, he himself thought it to be characteristic of the convictions of his youth, which he verbalised like this, standing on top of a volcano in Indonesia:

> 'T is sweeter here to praise aloud one's Mother . . .
> Prayer sounds more fair by mountainside and hill . . .
> The heart ascends higher than it does yonder—
> On mountains one is nearer to God's will!
> Here he created temple-choirs and altar,
> Where foot of man brings no impurity,
> Here he makes to Himself the tempest for his psalter
> . . .
> And rolling roars his thunder: Majesty![5]

But if he, twenty-five years old, so clearly hears God's thunder talking to him, what influences could then have led him to become a freemason just nine years later and soon after that a member of the society of free-thinkers, of which he even becomes one of the most prominent progagandists?

The years between 1845 and 1855 must have been years of feverish development for the colonial civic servant; what happened to him personally must have set him thinking about Holland's role as a Christian nation in a heathen colony. In order to get a clearer view on that question, it is good to outline concisely which biographical facts could have influenced his convictions. As a young man of twenty-one, Dekker meets in Batavia a beautiful Catholic girl, Caroline Versteegh, and falls in love with her. But she soon notifies him of the unshakeable standpoint of her father: should he want to have a slight chance of becoming engaged and of satisfying other obvious desires, he would have to convert to Catholicism. Dekker hesitates only briefly; the called in Pastor Scholten has a fatherly influence on him and he is baptised a catholic on August 28th, 1841. Alas . . . Caroline keeps on writing him cool notes and her father finally puts an end to the affair, stating in a letter that "their characters differ too much".[6]

It is generally accepted[7] that, for Dekker's romantic heart, the fact that he *in vain* had taken the step toward the Roman Catholic Church, must have given him a feeling of frustration. From that moment this feeling kept on influencing his convictions about belief as professed in the church, although he will never in his work show as much bitterness and sarcasm against Catholicism as against Protestantism, which was the official church of the country that would do him so much injustice.

In following years, he starts reading much, even very much for the conditions in the East, where the few books were hard to get and to preserve. According to

notes he made, he had read novels by Hugo and Balzac immediately after their appearance. His rational powers develop at the expense of his romantic feeling for nature, which before had led him to religion, especially on top of volcanoes. In 1845 he gets engaged to Tine van Wijnbergen, who is to be his first wife, and writes to her about his struggle between reason and sentiment; however, he does not yet admit that his recent critical analyses have had any influence upon his religious convictions. I quote from one of his renowned "engagement letters": "Oh, that wretched reason (. . .) With a tiny bit of reason one makes a farce out of the Revelations of John—with a tiny bit of feeling one grasps the whole idea of 'God', 'Christianity', 'Eternity'. So what is higher, fairer? Would an emotional human being with limited intellectual powers not come closer to the Creator than someone with the opposite qualities? (. . .) We feel the power of the Creator in Nature, but we do not understand, do not comprehend how a tree germinates from the seed. Which organ, therefore, is more exact, noble, perfect?"[8]

When Dekker is twenty-three, he already rules with almost absolute authority in a remote corner of the East Indies—the West coast of Sumatra—in a small out-of-the-way place, Natal. There he experiences how the "heathen" natives are often reliable and dedicated, and show highly developed ethical norms, while the Dutch authority, though based on Christian morals, can act mercilessly and cruelly, even towards himself. For instance, when out of carelessness a shortage in his government funds comes to light, it appears that Christianity and pettiness are only too compatible. Dekker was temporarily dismissed until the moment he was capable of refunding the deficit.

His first independent thoughts about church, Christianity and religion appear eloquently when in 1851 he writes a long letter from the Indies to his childhood friend Kruseman, who has in the meantime become a publisher in Haarlem. He considers it no longer possible to accept the christian creed, he says, because, if Christ had already existed and had reconciled humanity with God the Father, the Christian world would not be so terribly ill-organized. I quote from that letter: "I am not a christian, but I believe that I highly respect Christianity. So highly that I refuse to give that name to something that I have not yet seen on earth. And that is—among others—why I deny the truth of the New Testament. Christ would have been on Earth in vain—if he had ever been there. I honour Him more by denying his presence, than by believing that he has worked in vain and, therefore, wrongly."[9] Thus, Christ remains an inspiring example for the young romantic, a high standard by which he will permanently test his own and other people's behavior.

When in 1851 he prepares to go on a long European leave, he writes down a few thoughts that he wants to work out in peace. This document gives us, in its point by point enumeration of his society-assaulting ideas, a surprisingly clear view on his inner development[10]: "Every farmer a doctor in the arts" (a nice democratic idea that up till now nowhere has been successfully put into practice, as far as I know); "burning of the dead" (Multatuli was the first Dutchman who would let himself be cremated); "laziness is theft"—amplified by "poverty is a crime . . . either one committed by the poor man or by his neighbour"; "everybody educates his own children"; "taxes must be equal by unequality" (a formula that in its conciseness anticipates the principle of "equal ability to bear" to which all tax systems in the world have since been striving in vain); "women are human beings" (a highly revolutionary thought in those unemancipated days). Among these and similar social hand-grenades we also find a concise summary for himself of his religious conviction at that time; "New Religion. God is the Lord. People should serve him by loving nature which represents him. One's fellow-man is the principal part of that nature."

In fact, this dictum meant, in veiled terms, an abolition of religion embodied in the church and its replacement by the idea of loving one's neighbour based on a pantheistic view of the world: people should feel solidarity with their fellow-men because they share the same essence. Spontaneously Multatuli has arrived at the same conclusion as his compatriot Spinoza, two centuries earlier, when the latter wrote in his *Theological-political treaty*: "Piety and obedience to God exist only in love for one's fellow-man"[11]. Later Multatuli will remove from this conviction the metaphysical basis; his thinking then develops into an "existentialist" humanism, deduced from the naked fact of our common existence on earth.

But his wife Tine could hardly follow him in that train of thought. To her their attitude toward the traditional belief was unclear. What *were* they exactly: catholic? protestant? baptist? unchurchly? unchristian? unbelieving? When the family, after his resignation in the Indies, wanders through Europe—often not even together, she asks him in a letter to write her what his profession of faith is. His answer is a brilliant parable of one page, in which all his literary gifts suddenly manifest themselves very clearly; this is the first text of his hand that will be published, in—of course—*De dageraad* (*Daybreak*), the ephemeral paper of the Freethinkers movement.

Dekker's parable is about a father who leaves his children alone at home for some time and in order to keep them busy during that period, gives them the following riddle "What would he be doing during his absence?" The children, one by one, provide answers which are in accordance with their characters; for instance: "One of the children, who was wearing a blue jacket, said:—I

know. Father has gone to the tailor to get a blue jacket made."[12] But the youngest child is too busy caring for a thrush that had broken its leg, to be able to participate in the guessing game. When the father returns this child says that it has no idea where he could have been, because his thoughts have been too full of the thrush that is just now getting better. "Good", says the father, "that is also what the sick widow was doing whom I was visiting." End of the parable.

The meaning is clear: the child that did *not* form a notion about the absent father acted instinctively in accordance with his intentions. In other words, the different religions form their image of God after their own views and pull each other's hair—as the children in Multatuli's story do. But he who follows the impulse of his heart is "closest to the Father".

This turning away from the dogmatic religion and its ruling image of God is, of course, strongly fed by the writer's life experience. In 1856 he has come into conflict with the government machinery in the Dutch East Indies, and has handed in his resignation, because the Dutch administration did not enable him to protect the native population firmly enough against exploitation and oppression. When in 1860 he publishes his autobiographical report on these events, *Max Havelaar,* the book is praised everywhere as a work of art, but he gets neither real help, nor satisfaction or rehabilitation. Not even from the Church, that fulfils its missionary role in the colonies, so-called in the interest of the natives.

It is all the more striking for Douwes Dekker that he does receive moral and active support from the Freethinker movement. The atheistic chairman of "De Dageraad", d'Ablaing van Giessenburg, is his personal friend and also, for a few years, his publisher. When in 1865 Multatuli is completely broke, d'Ablaing even lets him use his attic, where a couple of free-thinking carpenters make a few inhabitable rooms. That same year he receives, after a speech to the organization, the famous golden pencil with the inscription: "To Multatuli—Society De Dageraad, March 29th 1865". A token of mutual appreciation in the wake of the fierce paper war Dekker has fought against the Church and for Free Thought. And indeed, Multatuli has in the meantime developed into what a contemporary critic, Busken Huet, called "the virtuoso of sarcasm"[13]. And that sarcasm (born of disappointed love[14]) is directed especially against the traditional Scripture and those who professionally preach it. Thus the writer introduces in *Max Havelaar* the boy Frits, son of Droogstoppel (Drystubble), who in his adolescent resistance against the doctrine imposed upon him by his father, asks the chaplain during confirmation class one painful question after the other: "Is my baby brother condemned to hell, because he died before he was baptized? What is the use of pigs in a country where pork is prohibited? What did they do with the inheritance of people who rose from the dead? Why does the devil still have so much power, if he has been beaten by Christ? What happens if, before a battle, the canons of both armies are blessed? Why is Jesus called a son of David, if Joseph, who really descended from David, is not his father? Where did Noah get a couple of polar bears for his ark? From where came those people who were not allowed to kill Cain?"[15]

To us this rationalistic bible criticism may seem innocent; nevertheless it is only too characteristic of Van Lennep, the first "editor" of **Max Havelaar,** that he considered these questions to be so improper that he struck out the passage; a censorship measure that apparently has worked through till the English edition of. . . . 1967![16]

On the other hand the "servants of the Word" who failed to take Havelaar's side in his conflict with the government are immortally ridiculed in the person of "parson Chatterbox"[17]. The best of it all is that this character is introduced in the book, described and quoted by an ardent admirer, who is supposed to have written the chapters set in Amsterdam. Thus in the text of the book Multatuli lets the ideas of the chaplain be enthusiastically admired, by which device the hidden criticism is left to the reader who sees through the irony. Yes, Chatterbox is in the text highly appreciated by Droogstoppel, because he knows how to explain why the Dutch—justly—become rich by the exploitation of the colonies, while the Javanese—also very justly—remain poor. This is the way Chatterbox puts it in a sermon: "Lo and behold, is there not much wealth in Holland? That is because we have the Faith. Are not battle, murder and sudden death the order of the day in France? That is because they are catholics. Are not the Javanese poor? They are heathens! The longer the Dutch have to do with the Javanese, the more wealth there will be here and the more poverty there will be there. It is God's will that it should be so! Isn't it clearly the finger of God, who makes the wicked labour to preserve the just? Isn't it a hint to get much produced over there and to stand firm in the true faith here? Isn't that why we're told to 'work and pray', meaning that *we* should pray and have the work done by the black scum which doesn't know its 'Our Father'?"[18]

Multatuli, by the way, is the first to admit that this portrait of Chatterbox is a caricature. When a missionary chaplain, parson Francken, a few months after the publication of **Max Havelaar** protests in the name of Christianity, the writer answers frankly that he has exaggerated and, therefore, lied in the description of Chatterbox. But then he justly asks this question: why doesn't the entire church protest, either against such abuse, as described by Multatuli, if it *exists,* or against the description of it, if it does *not* exist?"[19]

In the same reply by Multatuli, published in a journal, another passage catches the eye, where the writer magnanimously states that from an ethical point of view he and the christian doctrine are not so far apart: "No, you kind-hearted Christians, I am not far away from you. How could I be far away from you . . . I who have described Havelaar who sacrificed himself, from *you* who have based your faith on the altar of a sublime self-sacrifice?"[20] It is characteristic that here the following parallel is professed openly: Christ has sacrificed himself for the good of humanity, and . . . Havelaar has made a comparable elevated sacrifice.

It is this parallel that will obsess him for the rest of his life. Usually we know little about the daily reflections and statements of writers from a historic period. What they wrote in their diaries is mostly semi-unconsciously meant to be published and, therefore, filtered; and their conversations with friends are generally lost. But about Multatuli's informal association with his nearest friends a rare document is at our disposal: the booklet *From the life of Multatuli*[21], written shortly after his death by one of his (numerous) girlfriends, Marie Anderson. She looks at the writer with a mixture of critical distance and mollification that grants a high degree of reliability to many of her anecdotes. She tells us that Multatuli had gathered around him a group of young girls who were to help him in a revolutionary reformation of the world; he then says to Marie: "Jesus started with fishermen, I will start with girls."[22] With their help he hopes first to become emperor of the Netherlands East Indies, and afterwards something like "Lord of the World"—a significant term to someone who sees the parallel with Jesus in it. One day Marie is walking with Multatuli in a dark forest near Haarlem—as such, a daring act of shocking behaviour for an unmarried girl; she writes later: "In that dark forest his eyes, otherwise so faded, shone, when he imagined himself to be some sort of Jesus and when he praised Him because of His fulmination against the Pharisees."[23]

Yes, in that way Multatuli must have felt Jesus as his congenial spirit. He, too, had fiercely defended himself against the Chatterboxes of his time. At the end of the book the writer concludes that in her eyes Multatuli has gone through The Netherlands "in order to cast out devils". She must have been only half conscious of the fact that with the use of this terminology she joins her friend in his identification with Christ.

Often admirers of Multatuli's work observe that in tone and style too, he was inspired by the biblical example of Jesus. For one thing, he chooses parables to propagate his ideas, as for instance his famous **"Stories of Authority"**[24] show. Among those is the parable in which he ridicules the phenomenon of advertising which makes people believe in absurd qualities of the merchandise. This is the story: an Oriental, Hassan, only succeeds in selling his dates when he buys a parrot, which he teaches to repeat all day: "The dates of Hassan are thrice as big as they are." Immediately his sales boom.

In addition, he often takes his choice of words and sentence structures from the elevated style of the old-fashioned bible translation in Holland. He did not for nothing choose as the device for his collection of *Ideas*:

"A sower went out to sow."

Jesus[25]

But the whole, often flashingly concise formulation of many of these "ideas" has also the meaningful and aphoristic qualities of biblical sayings: "He who is satisfied with his work has a reason to be dissatisfied with his satisfaction"; "He who says 'I would' twelve times, says a stupidity eleven times"; "Where have all those nice kids gone?"; "He who talks humbly about himself, gets angry if you believe him".[26] Characteristic in this context is Idea 57: "There is only one way to Heaven: Golgotha". Here again we catch Douwes Dekker using his most typical form of "imitatio Christi". More and more Multatuli looks at his own hardships and his expulsion by the well-off society, as a parallel to Christ's martyrdom and crucifixion. Even in the choice of his pseudonym, his pen-name, this thought finds its expression. He is "multa-tuli", he who has suffered much and who, thereby, adds force to his task of rescuing mankind.

In a speech in Nijmegen in 1879, of which a lengthy newspaper report has been saved[27], he claims to respect the character of Jesus very much. Jesus suffered for his striving toward the good. But he had one privilege: he died young. If his disciples, who wanted to do anything to present him impressively, had had more knowledge of men, they would have let him live longer, in order to give him the opportunity to suffer more. Multatuli as Jesus' rival has then just become 59 . . . He considered his whole life of not being recognized as a reformer, of being ignored by the policy-makers, of enduring poverty and of having to write for a living, to be one of a real martyr.

When in 1861 Multatuli publishes the *Love Letters*[28], there appears in them a passage in verse, the well-known and most dramatic *Cross tale*[29]: a colourful and touching description of the delighted reactions of the public that marches after an unnamed convict, who drags his cross through the streets on the way to Golgotha. Enthusiastically they call to each other—and of course Multatuli despises them for that reason:

Something beautiful is to be seen on Golgotha (. . .)
That, by God, will be something nice this time!
He appears to be young and has something in his eyes
That indicates tenacity . . . look, there he sinks down
. . .

He yet seems to be weak . . . the cross is heavy . . .
I told you he was not strong, Nathan,
But still I think he is tenacious and will not
Cheat on us like the other thief last time,
Who had hung only half an hour, when his head
Fell aside and he was gone! He did not utter
One single word that rewarded us for our trouble.
Were you there? (Hold little Miriam a little higher,
Jochebed) Say, were you there, Nathan ben Daoud,
When that thief robbed us for so much vain trouble?

In the first edition the parallel is not brought to the fore until the end, but later Multatuli comes back to it in so many words. He then says in Idea 446 that he has heard from his publisher that "some readers have complained about the irregular way my *Ideas* appear." Promptly Multatuli reproaches these "some readers" because they, just like the obtrusive Jews around Golgotha, avidly want to enjoy his martyrdom. Just like these people, Multatuli's readers are afraid that he will not talk enough on his cross. It's all right, he assures the impatient readers, "the man on the cross is tenacious and will speak from the cross, but do not demand nor expect that he will keep on talking for ever. Jesus did say only seven short phrases and then died. I assure you, 'some readers', that from time to time I find it difficult to give you stories, that you for the greater part do not even understand, when my heart bleeds at the sight of my wife and children in need."[30]

In another Idea, Multatuli expressed his relationship to and admiration for Jesus in perhaps the purest and shortest way with all his undogmatic and subjective coloring: "Jesus is badly described in the Bible. He who does not feel that is not Jesus' friend. In order to appreciate Jesus, one must throw away the Bible."[31] "Jesus was not a Christian himself. And with that I do not mean that he was an Israelite[32]. But his whole phenomenon of psychological and actual identification with the Christ-figure would not be so important to the writer Multatuli, if his most fundamental message, his ultimate ethical opinions did not also coincide with the essence of the gospel. When Douwes Dekker calls Jesus "no Christian" in Idea 66, he means that he wants to clear the essence of Jesus' teaching of the religious connotation that does not belong to it. It is typical for Multatuli the romanticist that he craves for the fatherly God who would help mankind and would show it the right way; it is also characteristic that he refuses to believe in a God who would be responsible for all the injustice and suffering that he sees around himself.

Thus being torn apart and indecisive like a typical romantic, Multatuli writes in 1861 *Het gebed van den Onwetende* (*The Prayer of the Ignorant*), that will put such a strong stamp on the sceptical Christians of his generation. Already in its title the ambiguity in question reveals itself: after all the one who *really* is agnostic or an atheist will not pray. But the poem has shaken the belief in God of many a reader:

> I don't know if we are created with a goal : . .
> Or just exist by chance. Whether a God or . . . Gods
> Amuse themselves because of our pains and scoff
> At the imperfection of our existence. If that's the case
> It would be terrible! Who is to blame
> That the weak are weak, the sick sick and the fools
>   foolish?
> (. . .)
> What others claim to know about that God . . .
> Is of no use to *me* . . . I do *not* understand him! I
>   wonder
> Why He revealed Himself to others and not to me?
> Is one child closer to the Father than the other?
> If just one human being does not know that God,
> It will be slander to believe in such a God.
> The child who calls in vain his father does no harm,
> The father who permits his child to call in vain, acts
>   cruelly
> And fairer is the creed there is *no* father,
> Than that he would not listen to his child![33]

What Multatuli (again following Spinoza) completely rejects is ethical conduct to which a God as a kind of bogeyman would force us:

> I do not see what use a God can be, to separate
> The good from evil . . . Just the contrary! Those who
>   do good
> In order to receive rewards from heaven, turn the good
> Into something evil, into trade . . . And he who shuns
> All evil actions out of fear to burn one day in hell,
> Acts . . . cowardly!

Therefore Multatuli belongs to those who found a typically romantic solution for their indecision. He was convinced that in the end the rejection of all false images of God would mean a liberation, as a result of which mankind would reach its true destination. Only then the divine spark which is working inside us, would lead us unto a truth of our own making. The human being, left to its own responsibility, will want to do anything but good. Or in Multatuli's own words: "It is our task to observe, to think, to apply . . . It is our task to strive for development. It is our task to find pleasure in all this . . . that is, in one word: our task is to be virtuous, because pleasure, understood in this light, is virtue."[34]

That is why he ends ***The Prayer of the Ignorant*** with a flicker of this humanistically tinted hope:

> Or were you sure, oh Father, that I would do
> Your wish, even without knowing it? That I,
> Unconscious of Your being, would serve You,
> In accordance with your wish? Would that be true?

But the text ends with the famous ambivalent lament:

> The father does not answer . . . Oh God, there is no
>   God!

In this way Multatuli shows us the romantic indecision in optima forma. Reason had taught him there could not be a God; emotionally he longed for a God to be there; a God who would let him reach his essentially human destination on his own responsibility and out of his own free will. Or, as Dekker writes in a letter to Mimi, his second wife: "I do not believe that there is a God, but I dream of a good, wise, almighty being; and it always seemed to me as if he would ask me: how could you let it stay such a rotten mess? And I would say: how did you make it such a rotten mess? And he again: Indeed, I did it to find out if you could change it, it was a test."[35]

"Come, come, there is a man being crucified!"

And it is up to us, posterity, to decide if Multatuli has indeed passed this test.

Notes

1. Paul van 't Veer, *Het leven van Multatuli* (Amsterdam 1979), p. 34 etc.

2. Multatuli, *Volledige Werken* II, (Amsterdam 1951) p. 523. [Hereafter *VW.*]

3. idem, IX, p. 20.

4. Paul van 't Veer, o.c., p. 88.

5. Multatuli, *Max Havelaar or The coffee auctions of the Dutch Trading Company,* translated by Roy Edwards (Leyden, London, New York 1967), p. 120.

6. Paul van 't Veer, o.c., p. 95.

7. P. Spigt, *Keurig in de kontramine* (Amsterdam 1975), p. 32.

8. *VW.* VIII, p. 475.

9. *VW.* IX, p. 145.

10. *VW.* X, p. 172 and 282.

11. Spinoza, *Tractatus Theologico-Politicus,* [(1670; Gephardt Edition 1925),] caput 13.

12. *VW.* I, p. 9.

13. C. Busken Huet, "De virtuoos van het sarkasme" in: *Litt. Fantasien en Kritieken,* [(Amsterdam 1876)] deel II.

14. Garmt Stuiveling, "Multatuli's verhouding tot het Christendom" in: *Ontmoeting* 1954, p. 139 etc.

15. *VW.* I, p. 228.

16. see note 5.

17. Named 'Blatherer' in the English edition of 1967.

18. *Max Havelaar,* English edition, p. 251.

19. P. Spigt, o.c. p. 36.

20. *VW.* I, p. 385.

21. Marie Anderson, *Uit Multatuli's leven* (Utrecht 1981).

22. idem, p. 50.

23. idem, p. 72.

24. *VW.* II, p. 34 etc.

25. *VW.* II, p. 311.

26. *VW.* II, pp. 311-320.

27. P. Spigt, o.c., p. 176.

28. *Minnebrieven, VW.* II, 11-160.

29. *VW.* II, pp. 106-114.

30. Idee 446. *VW.* II, p. 654.

31. Idee 65. *VW.* II, p. 320.

32. Idee 66. *VW.* II, p. 321.

33. *VW.* I, pp. 475-477.

34. Idee 177. *VW.* II, p. 393.

35. *VW.* XI, p. 170.

Gary L. Baker (essay date 1990)

SOURCE: Baker, Gary L. "*Max Havelaar*: A Romantic Novel for Social Fluidity." In *The Low Countries: Multidisciplinary Studies,* edited by Margriet Bruijn Lacy, pp. 139-46. Lanham, Md.: University Press of America, 1990.

[*In the following essay, Baker examines Multatuli's radical approach to the novel form in* Max Havelaar, *tracing its influences to German Romanticism. Baker asserts that the work's unconventional structure and its liberal intermingling of literary genres effectively deepen the reader's engagement with the book's progressive political message.*]

Max Havelaar, written between the 10th of September and the 13th of October, 1859, is the first literary work ever published by Eduard Douwes Dekker (Multatuli). Jacob van Lennep, a poet and editor himself, called Dekker's manuscript a masterpiece and aided in the publication of the text, which appeared in May 1860 in the J. de Ruyter publishing house. There is a large amount of secondary literature dealing with the work of Multatuli, who is regarded as one of the most important Dutch writers of the 19th century. The novel *Max Havelaar: of de Koffij-veilingen der nederlandsche Handel-maatschappij* is considered to be his most accomplished work. The importance accorded this work is due to its combination of expository and fictional contents as well as its unique structure. Multatuli, like few authors before or after him, struck a rare harmony between form and intention in this particular work. However, the anti-linear approach to his subject matter has sparked much discussion, some of which expresses doubt that *Max Havelaar* is even a novel.

Is the structure of *Max Havelaar* novelistic or not? This is a question that has been posed repeatedly. D. H. Lawrence maintained: "As far as composition goes, it is the greatest mess possible."[1] Peter King discusses the literary situation in the Netherlands at that time and explains that Multatuli could not have used any Dutch novel from the 18th or 19th centuries as a model. He goes on to interpret the work as an "anti-novel."[2] Garmt Stuiveling, in an article entitled "De inzet van de moderne literatuur in Nederland," considered the text's structure to be unique and the most important aspect of its contribution to modernity in Dutch literature.[3] Even Multatuli himself felt it necessary to address the form of his work within the text itself: "Ik vraag geene verschooning voor den vorm van mijn boek, . . . die vorm kwam mij geschikt voor ter bereiking van mijn doel."[4] The author explicitly tells the reader that he chose a form to suit his intention and vice versa. An investigation of both form and content will demonstrate in what manner *Max Havelaar* is indeed novelistic and how its form is intended to reach a certain social, political, and historical goal.

Certainly, a novel with such a structure had never before appeared in Dutch literature. Analyzing the composition of this text, one believes to perceive an organizationally impaired product. The reader must practically become an archivist in order to read *Havelaar* without frustration. One must peruse its contents and follow the stories as must the family Droogstoppel, Rosemeijer, and the literary mediator Ernest Stern. The reader is invited into the book to have dessert at the Rosemeijers, "die in suiker doen," (p. 22) or the Havelaars, to hear the stories being read by Stern or told by Havelaar. S/he is often addressed and actually remains involved throughout the text. E. M. Beekman therefore evaluates the book as a type of letter—a "praatbrief"—which means the recipients of the story are addressed directly.[5] This collection of texts is a presentation to the reader from which the recipient may take as s/he wishes: ". . . het is eene staalkaart; bepaal uw keuze, . . ." (p. 172). Thus, the reader becomes a text-participant because subjective engagement of and intellectual reflection on the text is an essential task induced by form and style.

The novel's literary composition and its intrinsic desire to communicate with the reader invite its interpretation in light of German romanticism. One of the leading thinkers and writers of this literary epoch, Friedrich Schlegel, wrote: "Which travelogue, which collection of letters, which autobiography would not be a better novel for one who reads them in the romantic sense. . . ."[6] Reading in the romantic sense requires a type of subjective participation of the reader where s/he must ontologically transform the text into a personal story. Moreover, the text must be presented such that it may become part of the recipient's personal experience and thereby part of her/his consciousness. *Havelaar* lends itself well to this type of reading. The romantic aspect of *Havelaar* permeates the interaction of form, content, and reader.

German romanticism gave rise to the notion that the novel was the genre with the greatest possibilities for poetic and progressive materials, because it could include a constellation of several literary forms: "Indeed, I can scarcely visualize a novel but as a mixture of storytelling, song, and other forms."[7] Various forms within a form make it possible for a work to be read over and over again and always offer something new. Since *Max Havelaar* consists of letters, documents, poems, stories, anecdotes, fairy tales, essays, and notes, It presents an appearance of incompleteness. In Schlegel's famous fragment number 116 he states: "The romantic kind of poetry is still in the state of becoming; that in fact, is its real essence: that it should forever be becoming and never be perfected."[8] No form can offer more subjective freedom of interpretation and remain incompletely complete than a collection of fragments. Because the contents are preserved in their fragmentary form they can be subjectively completed with each new reading. Such a completion of the text requires the reader to become subjectively involved in its contents. In *Max Havelaar* the reader is called upon to employ her/his intellectual and emotional faculties so that the story becomes an intricate part of the reader's subjective makeup. Since romantic poetry, as Schlegel writes, "is a progressive, universal poetry,"[9] both the romantic notion of engaging the text and progressivity are valid for *Max Havelaar.* Progressive, in the romantic sense, means perpetually maturing, never taking solid form, and thus never congealing. This romantic progressivity pertains to the thematic level of the reader/text relationship as well as to the formal level of the text itself. For *Max Havelaar* it implies being historically based while remaining ahistorical, set in definitive time while being timeless. As D. H. Lawrence stated: "When there are no more Drystubbles, no more Governor-Generals or Slimerings, then *Max Havelaar* will be out of date."[10] Which novel then could be more romantic than one consisting of fragment upon fragment, including the diversity of many genres and human discourses? In this sense, *Max Havelaar* is a prime example of a romantic, i.e., novelistic piece of literature.

It is clear from the beginning of *Havelaar* that Dekker knew works by the German author Gotthold Ephraim Lessing. In the "Onuitgegeven Tooneelspel" (p. 2), one finds the situation in which a man named Lothario is unjustly accused of murder but proven beyond all doubt to be innocent. During the trial the judge repeats continuously: "Gij moet hangen" (p. 2). The alleged murder victim arrives in the courtroom to prove Lothario's innocence and give him an excellent character reference besides. Lothario says: "Gij hoort het, regter, ze zegt dat ik een braaf mensch ben, . . ." (p. 2). The judge then sentences him on other grounds: ". . . , hij moet hangen. Hij is schuldig aan eigenwaan" (p. 2). This ultra-rationalistic exercise of power represented in the command "You must hang" invariably echoes the dogmatic judgement of the patriarch against Nathan in Lessing's "dramatic poem," *Nathan the Wise:* "All one! The Jew must burn."[11] In *Nathan the Wise,* as in Multatuli's piece, Nathan and Lothario are not only innocent, but portrayed as intrinsically virtuous human beings as well. However, the petrified system—be it religious or judicial—is not flexible enough to recognize this fact. The "unpublished play" actually defines the underlying issue of the whole *Havelaar* novel—well-intentioned individual against rationalistic and dogmatic system. Thus, while the form remains timelessly fluid, we are confronted with contents that expose social stagnation as an inflexibility disproportionate to the flexibility of the form.

The system, as portrayed in *Havelaar,* perpetuates a condition where traditional Christian values of love and human ideals become interpreted in pure economic and instrumental terms. On the one side stands Lessing's patriarch, together with Multatuli's "regter," Droogstoppel, the Reverend Wawelaar, the Governor-General, and Slijmering. They represent the petrification and solidification of middle-class Dutch society by means of religion and economics. The symbol of its congealed state is Droogstoppel's incessant repetition of his address. He has an almost psychotic propensity to affirm his identity to the reader. It is as if he fears floating from the earth's surface at any moment: "—ik ben makelaar in koffij, en woon op de LAURIERGRACHT, No 37,—" and "Ik zeg: *waarheid en gezond verstand*; daar blijf ik bij" (p. 3). This "Ik ben" and "Ik blijf" is the petrification of which we are speaking and Droogstoppel's personal defense against dreaded *dweepzucht* or *Schwärmerei.* Droogstoppel's initial criticism of Sjaalman (i.e., Havelaar in Holland after his demise), and that which activates his suspicion the most, is: "Hij wist niet hoe laat het was" (p. 13). Droogstoppel needs place, time, and nomenclature in order to feel psychologically, socially, and politically secure. Since Sjaalman does not know how late it is, wears a scarf instead of a jacket, and obviously has no money, he deserves no identity, and therefore remains an object of Droogstoppel's derision throughout the novel. For Droogstoppel, Sjaalman obviously does not belong to the right class or have the proper faith. But Sjaalman is also not stagnant.

During the initial encounter between Sjaalman and Droogstoppel the reader experiences the latter's abuse of religion: ". . . hij scheen niet in goede omstandigheden te verkeeren, en ik houd niet van arme menschen, omdat er gewoonlijk eigen schuld onder loopt, daar de Heer niet iemand verlaten zou, die hem trouw gediend had" (p. 10). Wawelaar and Droogstoppel, like Lessing's patriarch, represent the perversion of religious values in their dogmatic perceptions of them. Droogstoppel uses religion as a weapon against threatening and suspicious outsiders or anybody who does not think as he. For example, his son Frits must pay money into the church coffers for criticism of Reverend Wawelaar. That was his punishment. Droogstoppel often interrupts Stern's readings in an attempt to set him and the reader ideologically straight. During one such intervention Droogstoppel contributes his debased views on religion and economics:

> Ik sta verbaasd over Wawelaar's doorzigt in zaken. Want het is de waarheid dat ik, die stipt op de godsdienst ben, mijne zaken zie vooruitgaan van jaar tot jaar, en Busselinck & Waterman die om God noch gebod geven, zullen knoeijers blijven hun leven lang. . . . Onlangs is gebleken dat er weer dertig millioenen zuiver gewonnen zijn op den verkoop van produkten die door de heidenen geleverd zijn, en daarbij is niet eens gerekend wat ik daarop verdiend heb, . . . Is dat nu niet alsof de Heer zeide: "Ziedaar dertig millioenen ter belooning van uw geloof?" Is dat niet de vinger Gods die den booze laat arbeiden om den regtvaardige te behouden? . . . Staat er niet dáárom in de Schrift: bidt en werkt, opdat *wij* zouden bidden, en het werk laten doen door het volk dat geen 'Onze Vader' kent?
>
> (p. 183)

The real antagonist in the book is then a mentality and not Droogstoppel himself. He is merely the embodiment of it. The utter perversion of religiously based values has produced a class of people with no heart. This is the class Multatuli desires to affect and consequently change.

Other congealing aspects of society are its narrowing field of interest and instrumental judgements on areas of study. The greatest contrast between Havelaar and Droogstoppel is obvious in the latter's lack of appreciation for the cases, testimonials, and essays in Sjaalman's "vervloekte pak" (p. 182). The list of contents covers four pages and includes many humanistic and scientific subjects. Droogstoppel finds little there that interests him and only lays articles concerning coffee to the side for future reference. In this example, Multatuli has demonstrated Havelaar's universality in order to present the one-dimensional thinking of middle-class Dutch society and of the Dutch government more crassly. Multatuli shows how much the middle-class sliced away from its image of the world as Droogstoppel cuts piece after piece from Sjaalman's package. Middle-class modes of thought are much too narrow;

that is one of Multatuli's most important projections. Multatuli demonstrates how the injustice in Java persists because of this home-grown mentality. He therefore begins the novel with Droogstoppel. He introduces the source of injustice and corruption in Holland while demonstrating its manifestation in the East Indies. The problems found on the islands could be at least partially solved with a loosening of the bourgeois perception of life at home. Thus, the same is valid for people like Slijmering and the Governor-General, who import such views into the Indies while exporting riches for Holland.

The configuration of the Havelaar-Sjaalman-Multatuli character is then similar to Nathan in methods of bringing about change. Like Nathan, Havelaar too is in favor of the fluidity or movement of stagnant society. The most important words of Havelaar's speech to Duclari and Verbrugge are: "Natuur is beweging . . . stilstand is de dood. Zonder beweging is geene smart, geen genot, geene aandoening" (p. 110). However, movement itself is not enough, the story and/or history must be the essential element of movement. Havelaar mentions waterfalls as being unimpressive phenomena, maintaining "Zij *zeggen* mij niets" (p. 109). Buildings speak somewhat more loudly to him because they are "bladzijden uit de geschiedenis" (p. 109). Duclari believes to detect a contradiction in Havelaar's philosophy and reminds him that waterfalls move. Havelaar retorts: "Ja, maar zonder *geschiedenis*. Zij bewegen, maar komen niet van de plaats" (p. 110). Although Havelaar is speaking about art and nature here, the social overtones cannot be denied. Both Nathan and Havelaar use stories—the opposite of a formalized education—to spur on social movement. Middle-class stagnation is indeed death—a figurative death-state in Holland, literal death in the colonies. Thus, storytelling becomes a type of education meant to keep the mind and heart open and not inculcate them to dormancy. Just as Nathan explodes religious dogmatism with his parable of the three rings, Multatuli hopes to discharge a heartless society out of its sleepy and self-contented state with his stories. This is the implicit link between form and intention (*doel*) in Multatuli's novel. In a truly romantic fashion, stories are utilized as fluidizing agents against the congealing aspects of society.

To be sure, **Max Havelaar** contains both doleful and delightful stories. One thinks here of the fairytale of the Japanese sculptor and the several ballads and poems contained in the text. The central story, of course, is the tale of Saïdjah and Adinda. But to what extent are the stories really accessible to the reader? The theme of **Havelaar** is much like the type described by Schlegel: ". . . that is romantic which presents a sentimental theme in a fantastic form."[12] "Romantic" refers to the genre itself, i.e., the novel; "fantastic" is the adjective of fantasy, meaning imaginative and original. "Sentimental," however, does not refer to the feelings aroused by human interest stories and trivial literature: "It is that which appeals to us where feeling prevails and . . . not a sensual but a spiritual feeling. The source and the soul of all these emotions is love, and the spirit of love must hover everywhere invisibly visible in romantic poetry."[13] The ultimate congealing of society is a critical lack of this type of sentimental feeling. Multatuli demonstrates this by juxtaposing the marriages of the Havelaars and the Droogstoppels. The former is clearly filled with love, and therefore an exception, while the latter is an economic convenience, and thus the rule. (As an essay in Sjaalman's package—"Over de prostitutie in het huwelijk" (p. 25)—insinuates, even marriage vows can be economically perverted.) An initial and natural feeling of love provides access to the progressivity inherent in the stories. Therefore, a willingness to progressivity is that which the reader must bring to the text. That which s/he fetches out of the novel are then progressive messages. The elder Droogstoppels are surrounded by this sentimental feeling but do not possess it themselves. Their son Frits, for example, digs about in the package for poetry. At one point he finds a sad poetic story and reads it for Luise Rosemeijer, causing her to cry (pp. 16-22). Their daughter Marie is also affected by the package; she refuses to read the Bible at breakfast one morning (pp. 180-181). And the fact that Stern is German, composes romantic poems—a textual connection to German romanticism—and is in charge of presenting pieces from the package is certainly no coincidence. It is also important to learn from Droogstoppel that Ernest Stern "schwärmt" (p. 22).

Droogstoppel's greatest and longest lament about the effect of Sjaalman's package on his family comes just before the reading of the tale of Saïdjah and Adinda. Droogstoppel is not interested in hearing it for the same reason Luise Rosemeijer wishes to, because "er van liefde zou inkomen" (p. 180). The author/mediator explains that this particular story is not for everybody and hopes: ". . . dat, wie gezegend is met blankheid en de daarmeê zamengaande beschaving, edelmoedigheid, handels—en Godskennis, deugd;—die blanke hoedanigheden zoude kunnen aanwenden op andere wijze dan tot nog toe ondervonden is door wie minder gezegend waren in huidskleur en zielevoortreffelijkheid" (pp. 178-179). All racist overtones aside, Multatuli is expressing hope that the sentimental feelings discussed above are somewhere at hand amongst his readers. With the introduction of this tale into the finer circles of Dutch society we experience the commencement of Multatuli's self-proposed errand, i.e., telling the story of oppression and exploitation of the Javanese people to those who could halt it but choose to perpetuate it. Thus, Multatuli demonstrated how, through a novelistic form of storytelling, sentimental feeling can be probed to fluidize petrified and stagnant aspects of society.

Notes

1. D. H. Lawrence, introd. *Max Havelaar: Or the Coffee Auctions of the Dutch Trading Company,* by Multatuli, trans. Roy Edwards, afterword E. M. Beekman (Amherst: University of Massachusetts Press, 1982), p. 12.

2. Peter King. *Multatuli.* Twayne's World Author Series 219 (New York: Twayne Publishers Inc., 1972), p. 42.

3. Garmt Stuiveling. "De inzet van de moderne literatuur in Nederland," *Levenslang* (Amsterdam: Huis aan de Drie Grachten, 1982), pp. 67-68.

4. Multatuli. *Max Havelaar: of de Koffij-veilingen der nederlandsche Handelmaatschappij,* ed. G. Stuiveling (Amsterdam: G. A. van Oorschot, n.d.), p. 236. All further references to this work occur in the text.

5. *Max Havelaar: Or the Coffee Auctions of the Dutch Trading Company,* p. 373.

6. Friedrich Schlegel. "Dialogue on Poetry," trans. Ernst Behler and Roman Struc, *German Romantic Criticism,* The German Library 21 (New York: Continuum Publishing Company, 1982), p. 110.

7. "Dialogue on Poetry," p. 108.

8. Friedrich Schlegel. "Athenaeum Fragments," in *Friedrich Schlegel's* Lucinde *and the Fragments,* trans. and introd. Peter Firchow (Minneapolis: University of Minnesota Press, 1971), p. 175.

9. "Athenaeum Fragments," p. 175.

10. Lawrence, p. 15.

11. Gotthold Ephraim Lessing, *Nathan the Wise,* trans. Bayard Quincy Morgan (New York: Frederick Ungar Publishing Co., 1955), p. 98.

12. "Dialogue on Poetry," p. 106.

13. "Dialogue on Poetry," p. 106.

Hans van den Bergh (essay date fall 1992)

SOURCE: van den Bergh, Hans. "Multatuli as a Writer of Letters." *Canadian Journal of Netherlandic Studies/ Revue canadienne d'études néerlandaises* 13, no. 2 (fall 1992): 17-22.

[*In the following essay, van den Bergh discusses the style and content of Multatuli's personal correspondence. Van den Bergh suggests that the author's letters provide valuable insight into his later literary output.*]

As the editor of Multatuli's **Complete Works,** I am currently working on volume XXIII (and the end of the road is in sight, for there are to be 25 volumes in all).[1]

In that capacity I quite often have to face irritated critics—especially from the ranks of the subsidizing institutions, since they are the ones who have had to cough up the necessary funds, each year since 1949. Again and again the question is raised whether the series still deserves to be continued, and more notably whether there is any point in publishing all those letters from the period after May 1877 until the author's death in February 1887. For in the last ten years of his life Multatuli no longer wrote for publication, and so the letters written during that period cannot be expected to tell us anything new about Multatuli as an author, which was after all the prime objective of the enterprise. Usually my answer to such questions is that precisely because Multatuli is no longer writing for the public at large—which, in a famous phrase of his, he professed to despise ("Publiek, ik veracht u met grote verachting!")—we need his letters to his friends in order to reveal the thoughts that preoccupied him in his final years.

Multatuli's literary talents continue to shine undiminished in the numerous letters he wrote after May 1877, as I hope to demonstrate. But that is not the only reason why these letters occupy such an important position in his oeuvre. What is more important, and even fundamental, is that in his correspondence he was able to meet one of the essential demands he made on literature, which he could not meet by writing proper literary works. At the root of Multatuli's idea of literature lay his aversion to everything to do with official literature, literariness or *letterkundery,* as he called it. Multatuli himself was, from the outset of his career as a writer, well aware of the paradoxical nature of his attitude. On the very first page of *Max Havelaar* (1859), the protagonist Droogstoppel expresses amazement at the "impudence with which poets and storytellers dare to palm off on you all sorts of things which never happened, and which usually never could happen." Soon after this initial show of indignation Droogstoppel launches into his glorious tirades against drama and poetry. The theatre is misleading because it accustoms us to lies, as he explains with persuasive arguments. He provides the following convincing example: "The hero of the play is pulled out of the water by someone who's on the point of going bankrupt. For this, he gives him half his fortune. That can't be true [. . .] because it's obvious that, in that way, you only have to fall into the water twice to be reduced to beggary." In his invective against poetry, Droogstoppel comes up with an even more incisive analysis of the problem. "Mind you," he says, "I've no objection to verses in themselves. If you want words to form fours, its all right with me! But don't say anything that isn't true." And again Droogstoppel proves his case with devastating logic. "It's all very well, he argues, for a poet to say 'The air is raw, the clock strikes four.' [. . .] But the versifier is bound to four o'clock by the *rawness* of the first line. For him it has to be ex-

actly four o'clock, or else the air cannot be raw. And so he starts tampering with the truth." In short, rhyme and meter, being typical of the literary form, get in the way of the poet seeking to give an accurate portrayal of reality.[2]

Of course it would not be fair to take Droogstoppel's down-to-earth outpourings as completely representing his creator's own views, but Multatuli returned to this very issue in one of the footnotes he added to *Max Havelaar* in the 1881 edition. He says, "I am far from disagreeing with *everything* I put into Droogstoppel's mouth. He normally never had anything to do with verses of the kind that follow here. Well, neither have I!" But in fact the dilemma was even more painful. For anyone seeking to create art will find himself obliged to deviate from completely truthful representation. In his Postscript to the play *De bruid daarboven* (*The Bride in Heaven*), Multatuli expresses his feelings about the necessity of exaggeration. "Het ideaal der kunst zou vorderen dat het vereist effekt werd te weeg gebracht zonder overdrijving". But art resists such absolute fidelity. For, he says,

> Lezer, hebt ge wel eens komedie gespeeld? Of zaagt ge wel eens de decoratieschermen van naby? De eis der "planken" [. . .] is: overdryving. Wat niet overdreven is in feite, vertoont zich by 't voetlicht laf, flauw, onbeduidend, kleurloos. Om effect te maken, moeten auteur, decoratieschilder en vertoners hun instrumenten enige tonen hoger stellen, dan binnenkamers voor correct zou gehouden worden.

And of course the conclusion Multatuli draws from his reflection on this inevitable distortion is that the author simply has no choice but to deviate from stark reality.

Remarkably, very similar arguments concerning the deficient veracity of art are to be found in Plato. The dialogue entitled *The Sophist,* in particular, offers comparable examples. A picture of a knife will always lack the prime "knifish" qualities: the picture itself cannot be sharp or hard or heavy. But worse than that, countless artists have discovered to their chagrin that they have to be *deliberately* untrue in their representations. Plato argues that if the columns of a temple were truly straight all the way to the top, they would not look straight. In order to appear straight to the viewer they have to be wider towards the capital. And Multatuli, for his part, sums it all up by saying: "Met burgerlyke droogstoppelige waarheid vervaardigt men geen drama."

The reason why this should be so is explained in more detail in a letter to Busken Huet.[3] A well-composed work of art must be to some extent untruthful, because, Multatuli says, "de betrekkelyke volkomenheid ligt niet in de natuur der dingen," and that therefore "een goed stuk onnatuurlyk moet zyn. De kunst eischt iets afgeronds, iets compleets, iets volkomens dat de natuur nooit levert [. . .] wie zich toelegt op waarheid moet wel hakkelige dingen voortbrengen."

There lies the dilemma. Unless one is resigned to creating fragmentary, "hakkelige" things, one is obliged to take liberties with reality, which is never comprehensive or perfectly formed. Multatuli himself had acquired this insight after considerable trials and tribulations of his own. He himself had had a bitter experience of the conflict between truth and beauty, in the years following the acclaimed publication of *Havelaar.* The showers of praise for the beauty of the book ultimately meant that it was regarded as just a romance, and therefore as fictitious. Havelaar had not been rehabilitated—truth had not triumphed!

Multatuli's most convincing exposé of his quandary is to be found in the first volume of *Ideeën.* It is convincing especially because he adopts an engaging literary form in the "parable" of the seamstress and her child. *Idee* 79 says that the prettier the clothes the woman dresses her baby in, the less people notice the child itself. The child's name is Truth, Multatuli explains. The child's father was the Poet. This story sums up Multatuli's own experience: the charming clothes, the beautiful literary form of *Max Havelaar,* prevented the public from seeing the real meaning of the novel, his child.

. . . . .

So the naked Truth, the complete absence of premeditated design, of literary form, seems to be the solution. And that is indeed the attitude Douwes Dekker, writing as Multatuli, often felt drawn to. Not surprisingly, Dekker relished the opportunity of letting himself go in his letters to friends—since those writings were not intended "for the press", as he put it, and his enjoyment of being released from the dictates of literary form is unmistakable. Thus on 24 January 1876 Multatuli started a long letter to his friend Loffelt.[4] He finished it two days later, adding a note about his untidiness at the top of the page: "Ik schryf altyd heel slordig als 't niet voor de pers is. Dat [. . .] vermaakt me [. . .] Corrigeer maar zelf, waar ik wat brabbel. Bedenk dat ik 'n hekel aan schryven heb."

The free form of the letter was a great advantage, since it dispensed with the need to manifest an acquired artistry. It is only in the letter, addressed to a single eager respondent, that the formal impositions of literature can be avoided, that there is no need to lie for the sake of beauty. In that sense, Multatuli meant what he said when he told van Hall, in a letter dated 27 December 1875, that he particularly enjoyed writing pieces that would not go to press: "Ik houd er zoo van als 't niet naar de pers moet. Van de 'pers' ben ik misselyk." He excuses himself to his friends for rambling on, but has no intention for the time being of changing his ways.

He likes to pretend that his letters are committed to paper spontaneously, without either premeditation or revision. In a letter to Tiele (9 December 1877) he offers an explanation, in a parenthetical aside, for the untidiness he permits himself: "ik ben zoo vry in brieven als dezen my slordigheden te veroorloven. Het tegendeel zou ik onvriendschappelyk vinden." In other words, you are a good reader, you do not need any embellishments. His allusions to the spontaneity of his writing in his correspondence with friends are remarkably frequent. In a postscript to a letter dated 15 September 1875 he mentions that he never rereads his letters: "ik lees m'n brieven niet na. Als er hier of daar 'n zin niet rondloopt, vul maar aan." In fact such allusions occur so frequently that one cannot avoid feeling that they represent a programmatic viewpoint rather than a mere statement of fact.

However, it is often possible to tell from minor corrections that the letters (or at least some of them) must have been read over before they were sent off, that they were scrutinized for stylistic impurities and obscure formulations. A typical example is to be found in one of his letters to Mimi, dated 26 February 1878. He tells her about his visit to her sister Frederique, after having sent a note to her husband Pool. His original words were: "Ik schreef reeds voor m'n bezoek aan Fredi aan Pool." But this casual turn of phrase evidently did not please him on second thoughts. So he changed the first *aan* into *by*—an obvious stylistic improvement, and sufficient reason for us editors of the recent volumes of the *Complete Works* to indicate this kind of correction from now on in the annotations to the letters. The emendations are almost without exception interesting, because they are implicit manifestations of Multatuli's epistolary aesthetic. When he changes "waaromtrent ik u eigenlyk schryven wou" into "waarover ik u eigenlyk schryven wou", it is of course because he wants to avoid officialese. Especially subtle is the painstaking removal of a typographical accent in a letter to Funke of 27 November 1876, in which his diagnosis of his new enemy, Buys,[5] reads: "hy stelt zich àls halfgek aan om de aandacht te trekken" (XVIII, 537). The stress had been on *àls* which, combined with "stelt zich aan", produces a form of pleonasm, so he crossed the accent out. Thus even a minimal stylistic imperfection could in his view do with improvement. The programmatic artlessness of the style of his letters evidently did not stop Multatuli from correcting shortcomings once he had noticed them. And there is a lot of circumstantial evidence that he re-read his longer epistles for this express purpose.

Multatuli's letters are, as we know, often composed of a succession of separate paragraphs, each dealing with a specific subject. As soon as such a subject had been exhausted (for the time being), Multatuli would mark it off with a horizontal dash several centimetres long, starting from the left margin. The vast majority of the letters, which are usually signed Dek, Douwes Dekker or with his initials DD, contain postscripts in which the letter is simply carried on, often until the sheet of paper is full. These second thoughts have partly to do with Multatuli's dislike of providing an orderly finish. It is no coincidence that **Havelaar** ends with a sort of explosion rather than with a conventionally elegant closure. **Woutertje Pieterse** and **Aleid** were not given a proper ending either. A well considered rounding-off of a narrative evidently represented for Dekker the ultimate untruth. For when do events in reality ever reach a formally pleasing conclusion?

But besides these what we might call poetical reasons for the continuation of a letter beyond the signature, there is another explanation. The postscript often contains afterthoughts about matters dealt with earlier in the body of the letter. The existence of such codas, in which he returns to the subjects discussed previously, proves in my view that Multatuli was in the habit of reading over what he had written and would then, inspired by his own exposé, put the finishing touches to his argument.

In spite of the apologies for his supposed carelessness, in the letters to his friends, he actually wants to make a candid and careless impression, and he achieves his aim thanks to his natural stylistic ability. Compared with the ornate and monumental style adopted by most other letter-writers of the period, Multatuli's letters are indeed masterpieces of artlessness.

. . . . .

Another curious paradox emerges on closer scrutiny of the letters. Multatuli, for all his self-centered outpourings about his own condition, ideas and circumstances, is always keenly aware of the character and intellectual level of the person he is writing to. As a letter-writer he adapts himself to the impression he expects his letter to make on the recipient. This is what I would call a rhetorically pragmatic approach: Multatuli the letter-writer is constantly taking into account the field of interest and the personal circumstances of the other person. A very straightforward illustration of this is to be found in a letter to Mimi dated 5 March 1878, in which he says: "Denk niet aan m'n haastig schryven dat ik zenuwachtig ben. Ik ben juist heel prettig en helder." He is obviously imagining how Mimi, at home in Wiesbaden, will pore over his letters in an effort to read between the lines. On other occasions, anticipating any misunderstandings that might arise with his correspondent, he makes a little drawing to show exactly what he means.

Multatuli's ability to identify with his correspondents is reflected in what I would like to call his chameleon-like skills. Here too his stylistic versatility produces a paradox: he who always prides himself on his entirely uninhibited attitude to his public, and who can afford to be even more candid in his correspondence with friends, in fact proves to be extremely sensitive to the conditions of the recipients of his letters. As a result, his letters to his various friends are remarkably different, not only in subject-matter but also in tone and style, and even in handwriting.

The literary scholar J. N. van Hall, editor of the journal *Het Nederlandsch Toneel,* received long letters on the subject of the dramatic arts. Multatuli's eloquent prose is interspersed with a great deal of exotic terminology. One of his letters to van Hall, dated 27 December 1875, contains 28 annotations referring to French expressions, five to German, and four to Latin! To the historian and linguist P. A. Tiele, Curator of the University Library in Leiden, Multatuli writes of his experiences with the historical works of Bor and Wagenaar, and at some length about his objections to Goethe's *Werther.* His style is drier here, more scholarly, and especially more tautly structured. This produces brilliant passages such as the following, which, it seems to me, embodies one of the fundamental principles underlying Multatuli's thinking in this period. It concerns the necessity of a basic unifying principle, an essential desire for oneness in both art and life:

> Geen poëzie zonder wellust. Poëzie, één met wysbegeerte, eischt het *volledig* gebruik van *alle* fakulteiten des gemoeds, dus ook van dien hoofdfactor in 't bewerktuigd *Zyn,* neen in alle stof, namelyk van de *zucht tot één zyn* die identisch is met *bestaan.* In physika noemen we 't aantrekkingskracht, in zielkunde heet het genegenheid, vriendschap, liefde. Alles wil (wahlverwantschaftlich) *naderen, in-zyn,* vereenigen. In chemie is *scheiden* niets dan voorkeur voor vereeniging met wat anders.

Multatuli's letters to Waltman[6] and Funke are warmer, more relaxed. At times he adopts a somewhat fatherly tone, offering advice on such things as what to do about Waltman's fits of coughing in the night, and about the size of Funke's family: after five children he thinks it is enough now. Fellow-writer Carel Vosmaer is one of his intimate friends during this period; he elicits a particular *parlando* tone, as if they were having a friendly conversation on the telephone.

> Je begrypt dat ik ook de andere stukken met de grootste belangstelling lezen zal (of herlezen). Maar houd me svp eens op de hoogte van de kritiek. Ik stel me daarvan ergernis voor, nu ja. Maar toch, ik wil nu eens goed opletten hoe dàt stuk, en Uw heelen III bundel ontvangen wordt! Met visschig zwygen? Ja, houd me op de hoogte! Hartelyk goeden nacht!

The letters to Mimi are in a class of their own. In them the psychological identification with the reader on the level of content, composition and style is the most marked. I would call it Mimi-cry. He sends her "heel erge kussen", and evokes the intimacy of the bedroom with little private jokes. Multatuli's chameleon-like qualities as a letter writer are even reflected in his handwriting. A. W. Sijthoff, publisher of the prestigious *Woordenboek der Nederlandsche Taal,* whom he did not know personally, received a letter written in a disciplined, extremely regular hand, while the notes he sent to Mimi in Germany when he was travelling in Holland are written in obvious haste, full of flourishes and long dashes.

Thus we see from Multatuli's own correspondence what sort of demands he made on the letter as a form of communication. Multatuli for his part also expected other letter-writers to aim at true contact, intense, free from conventions and polite inanities, full of understanding for the addressee. When he was away on tour in Holland, he begged Mimi to write to him daily, even if only briefly and about unimportant routine things, just so long as he received word from her every day. He could be upset for days on end when he believed a letter had been lost. The anxiety about things not reaching him could assume obsessive proportions. He sent instructions to the directors of all the main post offices about forwarding his mail, and he prepared detailed lists of dates and places where he could be reached, which he sent to all his correspondents.

Already when he was in Brussels in the 1860's, his fear that Tine's letters might get lost in the post is out of all proportion. Multatuli grumbled a lot about the postal services, which were quite a bit better then than what we have to put up with nowadays. He was still grumbling in 1878, when he calculated that a letter from Wiesbaden had taken 22 hours to reach him in Holland. He complained that since the journey itself took less than half that time, that was far too slow.

Not only did he insist on receiving mail from Mimi daily, he was also particular about what it contained. On 12 March 1878 he scolds Mimi for sending him a thick envelope, containing also a letter to someone else. "Ik ben nog steeds kwaad op je. Hoe kan je me 'n dik envelop zenden met 'n brief voor 'n ander?" And Multatuli himself has the delicacy to warn Mimi not to be disappointed when the special-delivery envelope he is sending her shortly turns out not to contain money: "Als de eerstvolgende brief aangetekend is, denk dan niet dat er geld in is; dat is zoo mal, want al heb je nu geen haast, het kon toch 'n teleurstelling wezen."

He demanded of others that they should show the same consideration for him. In February 1878 he received a letter in French from his daughter Nonni, after a long silence. He is offended because her hasty note contains so little apart from renewed requests for money. He replies with some severity: "Le chagrin me rend impuissant. J'avoue que cette fois-ci du moins je m'attendais à une lettre, une véritable lettre de ta part." A proper letter, in Multatuli's view, is one in which the writer's truthful expression of his feelings is coupled with sensitivity towards the correspondent.

. . . . .

But one of the strongest arguments in favour of publishing the correspondence from the last ten years of Multatuli's life is that, under more fortunate circumstances, those letters would have yielded the material for an eighth volume in the series of *Ideeën.* Take the following hilarious passage with "medical ideas" about the reasons why one catches cold. It comes from a letter to Waltman:

> De difteritische aandoeningen van de keel begonnen in de ziektegeschiedenis der menschen 'n hoofdrol te spelen in de periode der hooge stropdassen, bouffantes, cachenez & c. Dit nu is geen *bewys* dat keelziekten uit kunstmatig aangebrachten warmte voortspruit, maar 't geeft stof tot nadenken, vooral in verband met andere opmerkingen. De hals der vrouwen was ten-allen-tyde minder bedekt dan van de mannen. Als 't warmhouden nuttig was, moesten de vrouwen meer dan de mannen aan de keel souffreeren, *en dit is zoo niet.*

In a letter dated 5 April 1877 to the colonial administrator G. J. A. Boulet, he is more outspoken about his fears for the future of the colonies than he ever was in print:

> Indien men 't Hollandsch gezag verjaagt, vóór de stevige grondslagen van zelfregering gelegd zyn (waartoe grooter eensgezindheld in de oppositie vereischt wordt, dan er tot nog toe bestaat!) dan zie ik met schrik het moment te-gemoet dat men den 'hollandschen tyd' nog betreuren zal. Anarchie, heerschappy van Amerikaanse vrybuiters, van europeesch kanaille, zouden vreeselyke gevolgen hebben. Land en Volk zyn te goed voor zoo'n proef.

Convinced by the strength of his own arguments, it seems, Multatuli goes on to add, "ik geef u volkomen vryheid deze denkbeelden te verspreiden als ge weer op Java zult terug gekeerd zyn."

I myself am particularly fond of his scathing comments about professors of literature. In a letter to Loffelt, ridiculing van Vloten,[7] he says:

> V. Vl. was *hoogleeraar* in litteratuur (Zegge in 't *spreken* over litteratuur). Een medisch professor onderwyst: *hoe men zieken geneest,* d. w. z. hoe men *gezondheid produceert.* De professors in litteratuur bepalen zich voor 7/8 tot voorlezingen *over menschen die boeken gemaakt hebben,* en wachten zich gewoonlyk wel voor 't *leveren* van letterkundige pronkstukken. Hoeveel beroemde werken zyn er door *hoogleeraren* geleverd?

That the letters, in spite of their informal tone and composition, are often by no means inferior to the published works, is shown by the abundance of magnificently phrased passages. He sums up the idea that trying to convert heathens to Christianity without teaching them the basics of the creed is like trying to build a house without foundations, "men kan de rez de chaussée van 't gebouw niet missen." Whoever believes in heavenly salvation must also accept the alternative of damnation in hell, "anders is 't 'n schaar met één lemmet." And his assessment of the future of Insulinde becomes all the more ominous when he draws the almost Homeric comparison between the colony and a fine horse that must be bridled if it is to be saved from ruin:

> Insulinde is 'n prachtig paard waarop 'n dief zit. Dat men dien dief er afwerpt, is best. Maar men moet het niet doen voor men 't beest aan den teugel heeft, daar 't anders de wildernis inloopt en, onbestuurd, van de rotsen te-pletter valt.

Multatuli's correspondence can be divided into three main categories forming concentric circles around him. The first ring comprises the intimate letters with those closest to him, and it is largely made up of letters written to Mimi during his absences. The next ring comprises the letters to like-minded correspondents and friends, in which Multatuli indulges his fondness for plain speaking. The third, outer ring is made up of formal notes to business relations. It is especially the correspondence of the second category that can be seen, for reasons of both content and style, as the continuation of Multatuli's literary output after he stopped publishing. To someone like me, whose prime interest is in Dekker as a writer, there is no doubt whatsoever that the publication of all the letters, up to the bitter end in February 1887, must proceed.

Notes

1. Multatuli: *Volledige Werken* vols. 1-23, Amsterdam: van Oorschot, 1950-92. This year (1992) vol. 23 will appear, next year vol. 24, and in 1994 the last one, vol. 25, containing the indexes, repertoria etc. The more than two thousand letters of Multatuli that are preserved and edited in this edition are now kept in the Multatuli Museum, Korsjespoortsteeg 20, Amsterdam.

2. I quote from *Max Havelaar* in the English translation by Roy Edwards (London: Penguin Books, 1987). Droogstoppel's remarks are on p. 19 and 21, and the author's note about them on pp. 328-9. The translation is British, which is why the translator makes "four" and "raw" rhyme.

3. Conrad Busken Huet (1826-1886), Dutch writer and famous critic of his time.

4. Antonie C. Loffelt (1841-1906), a person of independent means who was a close friend of Multatuli. Van Hall and Tiele will be identified later in the paper.

5. George L. Funke (1836-1995), publisher of Multatuli's literary works since 1870, and his benefactor and friend. A[nton?] Buys (1842-1906), former disciple of Multatuli who later wrote a book against him entitled *Gedachten* (Amsterdam, 1878).

6. Jan Waltman jr. (1839-1891), publisher of some of Multatuli's earlier works.

7. Johannes van Vloten (1818-1883), Dutch author and philosopher, and early friend of Multatuli who later became his opponent.

Gary Lee Baker (essay date 1993)

SOURCE: Baker, Gary Lee. "Object of Desire and Undesired Knowledge in Multatuli's *Woutertje Pieterse*." In *The Low Countries and Beyond,* edited by Robert S. Kirsner, pp. 125-37. Lanham, Md.: University Press of America, 1993.

[*In the following essay, Baker discusses the central themes and narrative techniques of Multatuli's novel* Woutertje Pieterse. *Baker argues that the iconoclastic, unresolved qualities of the work embody the narrator's alienation from middle-class society.*]

Although Multatuli's **Woutertje Pieterse** is not a story in the traditional sense, i.e., one that incorporates a sense of closure or reconciliation, it is a narrative woven together by recurring themes and, of course, by its protagonist Wouter Pieterse. Peter King writes: "This is not a novel, he tells us, and if it were, it would not be written like this. It *is* a narration (*een geschiedenis*) but it is also poetry, the author's lyrical utterance."[1] The Woutertje-narrative lacks any kind of formal structure and defies traditional conceptions of genre. Nonetheless, as all narration, it contains, or is the result of, the desire to communicate something. As Peter Brooks states, "Desire is always there at the start of a narrative, often in a state of initial arousal, often having reached a state of intensity such that movement must be created, action undertaken, change begun."[2] Our narrator, who apparently works from archives, notes, and memory,[3] is courageous enough to commence with the story despite considering it a difficult task, "Er is moed nodig om 'n verhaal te doen aanvangen in een plaats die op 'dam' uitgaat."[4] (7) Of course the city is Amsterdam. A setting that ends in "dam" is already an indication that the story will not finish, because a "dam" is a blocking device, in this case blocking the flow of narrative. The fact that no reconciliation takes place in Woutertje's story indicates clearly that the narrator does not have control or mastery of his/her material.[5] This becomes most evident in Wouter as he shifts his focus from one object of desire to another.

One who intends to write something about *Woutertje Pieterse* is inclined to grasp for materials that deal with how books are structured, their openings, endings and middles. Edward Said states in his book *Beginnings,* ". . . for the writer, the historian, or the philosopher the beginning will emerge reflectively and, perhaps, unhappily, already engaging him in an awareness of its difficulty."[6] The story does not begin with Woutertje's birth but with the moment he is exposed to the influences of Fancy, meaning the initial point at which his desires in life scrape against the rough, solid, and petrified surface of Dutch middle-class values. The story-worthy conflict commences with the main character on his way to sell his New Testament for the works of a romance writer named Glorioso. The reader is offered a story with little sense of a beginning and even less of a feeling of conclusiveness. Frank Kermode explains in *The Sense of an Ending,* "We cannot, of course, be denied an end; it is one of the great charms of books that they have to end."[7] In *Woutertje* the reader is denied just that; there is a last word in the narrative, "introduceren" (501), which incidentally sounds more like the start of something than an ending. The ending we receive is obviously interrupted and not of the type intimated by Herrnstein Smith in *Poetic Closure,* "Perhaps all we can say . . . is that varying degrees or states of tension seem to be involved in all our experiences, and that the most gratifying ones are those in which whatever tensions are created are also released."[8] In *Woutertje* the reader is essentially left hanging in a state of tension. Will Wouter regain his proper clothing and become a solid middle-class citizen, or will Fancy become his ultimate object of desire, whereby he will grow to be a tragic and romantic outsider-figure like Max Havelaar? The courage spoken of above appears to run out by the end of the narrative; when Multatuli puts his pen down for the last time the reader (and narrator?) remains suspended in the story-line with the quest for Wouter's jacket and cap.

What was so compelling about Wouter's story that moved a narrator to fill over 500 pages of text without a reconciliation? Because Wouter represents hope or a utopian element in Dutch society. Without the story Wouter's romantic impulses would otherwise remain unnoticed within their framework of a congealed middle-class mentality, complete with moral codes, ideology, and sense of place. How does the narrator know that these impulses exist in Wouter? If s/he cannot know simple details, place names etc., how can s/he know and understand Wouter's mind and soul? Is Fancy the narrator? One is led to believe this from the fragment that precedes the Woutertje pieces; Fancy is asked to tell (actually whisper) a story, "LIEVE FANCY, wilt ge my een sprookje vóórzeggen?"[9] When one speaks of a good story, this is more a compliment to the narrator than the author. The author lends his/her name to the book, provides it with a title, and signs the copies you buy at his/her reading. The author provides a face to the work, often in the form of a picture on the dust cover. But, the narrator tells the story; s/he places one word after the other such that it grows into narrative. It is important, especially in *Woutertje Pieterse* not to confuse the two. The narrator is a poetic spirit that makes sense of the ideas and events that go together to make up the narrative. The narrator in *Woutertje Pieterse* understands the value of an imagination willing, courageous, and diverse enough to engage in the truth of poetic expression.

Woutertje's story depicts the life of a child who exists between being educated to become a competitive subject within society, and his attempts to transcend such boundaries and limitations by means of "Fancy" and/or imagination. Thus, his desire divides into ego-drives, which strive for death, and sexual drives, which are life affirmative, as Freud discusses them in "Beyond the Pleasure Principle," "The upshot of our enquiry so far has been the drawing of a sharp distinction between 'ego-instincts' and the sexual instincts, and the view that the former exercise pressure towards death and the latter towards a prolongation of life."[10] By the close (not closure) of the narrative we find Wouter's attention shifting from an object of desire that constitutes a life-affirmative attitude in "Fancy" to a death-affirmative drive depicted in his desire to re-acquire his middle-class attire. The Bible and clothing represent objects of desire that constitute an ideological, religious, and social consensus, which Wouter's mother and brother Stoffel insist he join. They signify a life of containment and formal training. According to Freud, "Death is rather a matter of expediency, a manifestation of adaptation to the external conditions of life . . ."[11] Wouter's desire for Fancy signifies his rejection of measures to form him into a competitive, and thereby, productive member of the Dutch middle-class. Thus, Wouter's bifurcated desire is caught between life and death affirmative impulses. Poetry is to be his savior from a life of dullness and triviality, hence Fancy's interest in him.

Wouter tells the wonder tale of Kusco, Telasco, and Aztalpha, which represents a poetic protest against competition for power, wealth, and influence. It is not by coincidence that the figures in the story are aristocratic and that it takes place, "Ver van hier en lang geleden . . ."[12] (90) Since the basis of middle-class existence is competition for possessions, Woutertje is risking his place in society by not joining in the struggle for material gain dictated by the middle-class mentality. Actually Wouter desires to abandon one form of competition for another. The struggle for power, money, and material is inherently life-negative. Life-positive is the competition for *knowledge* as we read in Multatuli's *Ideeën*:

> . . . overal is juist die brandende begeerte tot éénzyn met het onbekende, de oorzaak onzer beweging, dat is: van ons *bestaan*. Het spreekt dus vanzelf dat dit be-

staan vernietigd werd, wanneer het bereiken van 't doel mogelyk ware. En deze onmogelykheid stelt alzo de derde soort van kracht daar, die ons instand houdt: opstand tegen het verbod, behoefte aan *strijd*.[13]

Subjective, self-serving, ideological modes of thought have long since taken over where formerly there existed an objective, albeit aristocratic, world order, not based on money-acquiring structures, but on personages. For example, a king is a personage, not an office; aristocratic government cannot be effectively depicted as machine-like with interchangeable parts, like "enlightened," constitutional governments. As we find in **Max Havelaar** and in **Vorstenschool,** there exists a positive attitude toward monarchs, especially benevolent ones, which is also reflected in **Woutertje Pieterse,** "Er bestaat dan tevens kans, nader kennis te maken met prinses Erika, bij welke gelegenheid we misschien te weten komen, dat aristocratie van verstand en hart niet uitsluitend behoeft gezocht te worden in de . . . lagere standen . . ."[14] (335) The narrator insinuates that the middle-class has no capacity for emotional sensitivity when s/he explains that not everyone can understand Femke's emotions, "Femke zou begrepen zijn geworden door lager gemeen, of door adel. 't Is met gevoel, als met het goud der speelbanken. Dat komt niet in aller handen."[15] (101) One does not think of the aristocracy as having financial troubles, nonetheless, a prince or princess does not partake in petty competition to gain his/her wealth; at least they are not depicted this way in Multatuli's texts. There exists an express difference in the type or level of competition. Compared to the struggle for truth, which is intrinsically poetic for Multatuli,[16] and breaking out of the ego-boundaries that dictate competition on a trivial level, the struggle for money and other material goods is of a lower level. Nonetheless, Wouter must learn the lowest tasks in life, i.e., recognize his "naastbij-liggende werkelijkheid" (337) before he can rise up to the level of *Poëzie der Werkelijkheid*."[17] (335) Not surprisingly the lowest tasks in life are performed in the Owetijd & Kopperlith company. The type of competition Wouter enters into in the business world is in the words of one worker there, "Allemaal wind en 'n engelse *notting*."[18] (393)

It is interesting that the company in which Wouter learns the lowest tasks in society deals in textiles. The significance of laundry and linens in Multatuli's texts is undeniable. Femke and Vrouw Claus both work with laundry: Fancy, in the **Minnebrieven** works with clothing, washing them and mending them; in **Vorstenschool** the characters depicted with good hearts, Hanna and Landsheil, are a "naaister" (seamstress) and a "klerenmaker" (tailor) respectively. The two notions, textiles and poetics, come especially close as Albert, Hanna's fiancé, reads his latest creation as Hanna sews.[19] There is a definite relation between spiritual, emotional, and intellectual superiority, and persons who work with or make clothing. An explanation of this connection lies in the etymology of textile, which is derived from the Latin *texo,* meaning to weave, to entwine, or represent in tapestry. Interestingly, its third meaning in the *Oxford Latin Dictionary* is to construct a complex structure like a ship or "writings and other mental products."[20] Thus clothing or textiles represent an allegory of poetics and become a metaphor for Fancy's creation of narrative, "En spint de vlok tot draad / Tot doek, waarop zij, eindloos voortbordurend, / De loop van al wat is, te aanschouwen geeft. / En wie 't verband ontkent, is schuldig blind, / Ter nauwernood onschuldig wie 't niet kent!"[21] (247) The complex allegory of *poëzie* becomes clear. Princess Erika, for example, represents the sublime not only signified by her aristocratic heritage but also by her behavior. She is a cat-like figure difficult to pursue; as such she represents the sublime as aloof, unapproachable, undisciplined, yet noble. Opposite princess Erika stands Femke as a representation of daily existence and practical work. Furthermore, Erika has the desire to become a laundry girl like Femke (460), and Femke could have been aristocracy (309). Having felt Fancy's sting, the sublime and the practical blend in Wouter's perception (177). Together Femke, Fancy, and Erika represent a *teritum* (267 and 335), that influences Wouter in his desire for knowledge and Fancy, as well as his struggle against societal limitations. To be successful in his struggle to become *poëtisch,* Wouter must allow all three to influence him. He can receive love from all three while learning about the sublime, practicality (het gewone), and the power of imagination from the individual figures. All three are necessary for the ability to produce *poëzie*. Otherwise, as the narrator explains, the nature of Wouter's social class dictates that he remain "*onpoëtisch*" (122-123).

What prevents our narrator and author from finishing his/her "complex structure," about which we are reminded several times that it is not a novel but a story, a narration, "een geschiedenis." Are we as readers allowed to expect a reconciliation of the carefully wrought tensions in Wouter's life? It is obvious that Wouter is not pleased or satisfied with reality as he perceives it. He wishes to change what he sees, "'Later, later!' dacht hij. Later, als-i bevrijd zou zijn van schoolse en huiselijke banden. Dan zoud-i 'n werelddeel gelukkig maken. En nog een. En nóg een . . .'"[22] (177) Wouter's intentions are not only qualitatively noble but also in the simple fact that he wishes to make these continents happy as king—"koning van Afrika" (176) for example. However, our narrator conveys to us that pure dreaming has no place in the world and remains an illusion in the life-affirmative, reality-negative, posture of the dreamer. The person who rejects reality is certainly a utopian figure, but guiding such a figure requires that s/he remain within reality while maintaining utopian impulses of dreaming and a will toward change. We must bear in mind the motif of clothing and work with clothing; the metaphor of poetics is intertwined with the tasks of the day. After Pater Jansen praises how well Femke mends his underwear we read the lines, "De hoogheid van Fancy versmaadde 't rangverschil tussen paters onderbroeken en de melkweg."[23] (219) As the narrator explains, the poetics of reality stands much higher than "liefelijk bontgekleurde—maar kinderachtige, onvoedzame en verderfelijke—dromerij!"[24] (335) This explains why Femke tells him to be the best in school within three months (163) and Holsma's shift from an apparently free-thinking, liberal person to one who encourages Wouter to adjust his focus from the temporally and spatially far away, to the immediate here and now:

> ik was ook zo!—ze komt grotendeels voort uit luiheid. Het is gemakkelijker zich te verbeelden dat men zweeft boven 'n berg die heel in de verte ligt, dan in werkelijkheid z'n voet op te lichten om over 'n steentje te stappen. . . . Vraag altijd jezelf af: 'wat wordt er *op dit ogenblik* van me gevorderd?' en gebruik niet de ingenomenheid met het vermeend hogere, als voorwendsel tot verwaarlozing van wat je lager toeschijnt. Je bent ontevreden met je tegenwoordig standpunt? Wel, maak je 'n beter standpunt waard! . . . Vraag jezelf bij elke gelegenheid af: wat is m'n *naastbijliggende* plicht?[25]
>
> (331)

The narrator is making a case here for literature that not only rejects reality the way it is, but one that is suitable to bring about change in that reality. The task is not to switch worlds but to change the one in front of you. Poetics suited to aid in this cannot be "verdraaide poëzie en valse romantiek."[26] (163)

We should recall that Wouter first encountered Fancy at the windmills near Femke's house. She did not come to him in a dream or vision. Fancy spied a capable person as Wouter rid himself of his Bible, i.e., his ideological handbook for inclusion in the middle-class as a complete and solid citizen. She spies a soul that writes a poem about bandits instead of about virtue as he was supposed to. Fancy's voice comes to Wouter out of a machine. What could present a greater metaphor of the triumph of Dutch middle-class society than the windmill? When the winds (of change for example) blow against this machine they become even more resolute in their task of grinding or sawing for profit. The windmill becomes a metaphor for the way society works in all its intricacy and machine-like qualities; one is reminded here of Pennewip's hermetic categorizations of members of the Dutch middle-class (21). Fancy had to come to Wouter out of the run-of-the-mill, practical world in order to take advantage of his "romanziekte" (9), i.e., imagination and desire to change the world; she did not want to lose him to an escapist's mode of poetics. The dream world is not Fancy's home but rather the open niches of imagination and genuine love that she finds in reality. As he listens to the sawmills working they reveal their names "Morgenstond" and "Arend," signifying a new beginning (morning hour) above the earth (eagle). Together the mills sing the name Fancy (25).

Wouter's training is quite clear; he knows what he has to learn, but our narrator is not certain how to bring this about. A reader of the **Woutertje** narrative develops the impression that the ending is being avoided or even thwarted due to indecision about what to do with Wouter. He is caught between two objects of desire that comprise the oppositions that create tension throughout the text. When Holsma communicates to Wouter that he must first become acquainted "met het állerlaagste"[27] (335), in reality he meant trade and business, the arena of struggle for what the narrator termed "*machine infernale*" (9) or money. For Wouter, regaining his clothing means being accepted again in society, which is his main concern when the narrative ceases. He cannot simply break from society: "Hij was niet grof genoeg van inborst om de draden waarmed-i zich aan de maatschappij verbonden voelde, eenvoudig te verbreken en zich vrij te maken . . ."[28] (448) There is an obvious shift in the object of desire from a romantic quest for Fancy and poetics to the mundane matters of middle-class life, having the proper clothing in order to be seen on the street. The Bible, which Wouter gives up in the beginning and the jacket and hat he sells for the benefit of the Calbb family, to repay them for a parasol he broke, sandwich the multifaceted entity of Fancy, who gets repressed in Wouter's psyche. The initial line of the chapter, in which Wouter is depicted getting up for work, reads, "Fancy's luim had alzo voor ditmaal uitgestormd . . . en de lezer wordt nogmaals uitdrukkelijk uitgenodigd z'n verwachting op de leest van het dagelijkse te schoeien." (336) From here on Wouter is occupied with repressing his romantic impulses, "terzijdestelling van utopieën en fantastische begeerten . . ."[29] (336) Whenever he thinks of events or people in his life who might distract him from the hic et nunc he looks at the picture of Mercury, "die . . . ook geen kleren aan 't lijf had"[30] (346) hanging on the wall in the office. The desire for death manifests itself quite literally when Wouter decides he wants to commit suicide after breaking the parasol. But his spiritual death had already taken place in the office of Owetijd & Kopperlith:

> De romantiek was—niet voor altoos, waarschijnlijk—uitgeput, geknot, bedorven. Zijn worsteling tegen afdwalen begon vrucht te dragen, en de inspanning om zich met niets te bemoeien dan wat allernaast voor de hand lag, werd pijnlijker omdat hij met de hem ingegeven nietigheden z'n ziel niet voeden kon. Hij was iemand die men 't ongezond gebruik van snoeperij verbiedt, en inplaats daarvan op zaagsel en zand onthaalt, of . . . op niets.
>
> (389-390)[31]

In short, his whole time at work is characterized by control over his wishes for romantic endeavors and free thinking, because Wouter, "aan 't breidelen van z'n begeerten zo bijzonder behoefte had."[32] (416) The Fancy part of his psychological economy is not being developed and in fact being smothered and killed off. He has all but forfeited the desire devoted to Fancy and poetics, "De bloemen zijner fantasie waren verlept en geurloos geworden." and "Wouter had sedert einige tijd het poëtizeren verleerd. Hij durfde 't niet, omdat hij reden had zich te schamen voor 't liefelijke."[33] (435) Earlier Wouter had seen Femke on the street but was so ashamed of his life style that he did not call to her. The narrator explains that Wouter would have avoided his friends Dr. Holsma and Peter Jansen as well (426). Femke could save him from the stifling and damaging atmosphere of the Kopperlith household; he runs to her after the embarrassing incident with the parasol. However, the narrator does not allow him to see her and claims "—maar zo ver zijn we nog niet."[34] (436) The narrator does not wish to proceed further in any real sense and has injected here (another) delaying device so that the end is avoided. When Wouter breaks the parasol and the first serious thoughts of death enter his mind, the narrator refers to them as a "wenselijke uitweg" (444). Does s/he mean a way out of the narrative? Is this his/her opportunity for conclusiveness? The narrator cannot bring her/himself to terminate the narrative. To kill Wouter off would be to destroy a truly utopian element in the mundane world of middle-class existence.

But why should the narrator be reluctant to make just that statement: "Wouter cannot exist in our society, should we not change it to include people like him and be the better off for it?" There is a definite resistance to closure where the narrative ceases with a romantic on a rather unromantic quest, i.e., regaining his middle-class identity. D. A. Miller claims, "The text of obsession or idiosyncrasy is intrinsically interminable; as it can never be properly concluded, it can only be arbitrarily abandoned."[35] Peter King reminds us, "*Max Havelaar* was written in a few weeks, *Woutertje Pieterse* was unfinished after seventeen years."[36] Let us assume then that Woutertje did become an obsession of its author and narrator. Multatuli and his narrator were not wanting to work themselves out of the corner they had written themselves into. Either Wouter remains in his hideous looking jacket and the outsider he actually is, or he regains his clothes and returns to the Kopperliths with money for the parasol and reconciliation, in every sense of the word. Even this is made uncertain by the narrator as s/he depicts Wouter spending the money given to him by princess Erika for buying back his jacket. On the ferry to Haarlem many eyes have noticed that Wouter has money, will it get stolen? Will Wouter spend it all? Will he find the shop where he sold his jacket? At this point not even the narrator knows. If Multatuli had lived 30 years longer the Wouter-narrative would simply have been twice as long and little more than a collection of clever dilatory devices. The narrative's inconclusiveness is due to the undesired knowledge that Wouter cannot exist in middle-class society without either abandoning his desire for Fancy, or his desire to remain anchored in society. The former would doom him to an outsider's existence, in which he would physically perish, and the latter would mean a mundane existence, in which he would spiritually perish. There was no satisfying way to end the narrative. Suspended squarely between objects of desire, Wouter progresses nowhere due to the narrator's and Multatuli's undesired knowledge.

Notes

1. Peter King, *Multatuli,* Twayne World Authors Series 219 (New York: Twayne Publishers, Inc., 1972): 112.

2. Peter Brooks, *Reading for the Plot* (New York: Vintage Books, 1985): 38.

3. In talking about the type of collar Wouter wears to work, the narrator explains that s/he cannot say with certainty what the fashion was at the time, "Because of a regretful gap in my archive—unfortunately more traces of this will turn up" "Door 'n verdrietige gaping in m'n archief—daarvan zullen zich méér sporen vertonen, helaas!—. . ." Multatuli, *Woutertje Pieterse,* ed. Garmt Stuiveling (Amsterdam: G. A. van Oorschot, 1950): 338. The narrator's memory is part of that archive. S/he cannot remember specific places sometimes, "Also without referring to my complete lack of memory for locales—there is not a town, place, or village where I know the way—. . ." "Ook zonder me nu te beroepen op m'n volslagen gebrek aan lokaal-memorie—er is geen stad, vlek of dorp in de wereld, waar ik de weg weet—. . ." (304). When describing boys who sing a nasty song to a drunken preacher, the narrator admits; "I was not able to retain that poetic work. Which is a shame. And to *make up* something and pass it off as the exact text contradicts my principles." "Ik heb dat dichtstuk niet kunnen machtig worden. Wat jammer is. En iets te *maken* en dat uit te geven als de juiste tekst, strijdt tegen mijn principes" (57).

   It should be noted here that all further references to the text of *Woutertje Pieterse* in the present article are to the edition by Stuiveling cited above. All translations from Dutch into English are my own. To my knowledge, no decent translation of *Woutertje Pieterse* exists in English as yet.

4. "Courage is necessary in order to go ahead with a story in a place that ends in 'dam.'"

5. I will continue to refer to the narrator as his/her because I am not yet sure who it is. Though Multatuli, whoever that is, appears to be the author,

the narrator cannot be determined because s/he seems to have no body in the text. None of the persons in the novel reacts to the narrator although s/he is continuously present. And since the repetition of experience is often the motivation for narrative, the narrator could only be one of two figures. It is either "Fancy" retelling the unpleasant loss of Wouter as hope for imagination in society, or Wouter lamenting his loss of "Fancy" due to his quest for the middle-class lifestyle. Only these two could have been present in all instances in the text.

6. Edward Said, *Beginnings: Intention and Method* (New York: Basic Books, Inc., Publishers, 1975): 35.

7. Frank Kermode, *The Sense of an Ending: Studies in the Theory of Fiction* (New York: Oxford U P, 1967): 23.

8. Barbara Herrnstein Smith, *Poetic Closure: A Study of How Poems End* (Chicago: U of Chicago P, 1968): 3.

9. "DEAR FANCY, would you whisper a little tale to me?" Multatuli, *Ideeën,* 7 vols. (Amsterdam: Salamander Em. Querido's Uitgeverij, 1985) 1:240.

10. Sigmund Freud, *Beyond the Pleasure Principle,* trans. and ed. James Strachey, International Psycho-Analytical Library 4 (New York: Liveright Publishing, 1961): 38.

11. Freud, 40.

12. "Far from here and long ago . . ."

13. ". . . just that burning desire for unity with the unknown is everywhere, the cause of our movement, that is: of our *existence.* It goes without saying then that this existence would be destroyed if reaching that goal were possible. And this impossibility portrays thus the third type of force, which maintains us: rebellion against prohibition, need for *struggle.*" Multatuli, *Ideeën,* 7 vols. (Amsterdam: Salamander Em. Querido's Uitgeverij, 1985) 2:266.

14. "There exists also, then, a chance to make better acquaintance with princess Erika, by which opportunity we will perhaps come to know that aristocracy of the mind and heart does not exclusively have to be sought in the . . . lower classes . . ." As we can see "aristocratie" possesses its figurative and literal meaning. Aristocratic feelings and reason are the highest forms, which can, paradoxically, be found in the lowest classes of society. An aristocrat harbors here "aristocratic" emotions. The main point is that these emotions and this brand of reason are not found in the middle-class,

except in our protagonist. This is one reason Wouter is such a utopian element.

15. "Femke would be understood by the lower common folk, or by nobility. With feeling, it is the same as with the gold of the gambling houses. It does not come into just anybody's hands."

16. "There is nothing more poetic than the truth. He who finds no poetry in it, shall always remain out there a miserable little poet." "Er is niets poëtischer dan de waarheid. Wie dáárin geen poëzie vindt, zal steeds 'n pover poëetje blyven daarbuiten." Multatuli, *Ideeën* 1:168.

17. "most immediate reality" (337) and "*Poetics of Reality*" (335).

18. "Nothing but wind and an English *notting.*"

19. Multatuli, *Vorstenschool* (Amsterdam: Uitgevers-Maatschappij "Elsevier," 1919): 58-60.

20. "Texo," *Oxford Latin Dictionary,* 1982 ed.

21. "And spins the flock into thread / into cloth, upon which she, endlessly embroidering, / offers to behold, the course of everything that exists. / And he who denies the connection, is guilty of blindness, / barely innocent he who does not know it."

22. "'Later, later!' he thought. Later, if he were free from the bonds of school and home. Then he would make a continent happy. And another. And yet another . . ."

23. "The highness of Fancy spurned the difference in rank between father's underwear and the Milky Way."

24. "sweetly colored—but childlike, unsubstantial and pernicious—dreaminess."

25. "I was that way too!—it occurs for the most part due to laziness. It is easier to imagine that one is floating over a mountain that lies far off in the distance than to pick up one's foot to step over a little stone. . . . Always ask yourself: 'what is being demanded of me *at this moment?*' and do not use the satisfaction of the alleged sublime, as a pretext for neglecting what appears to you to be lower. You're dissatisfied with your present position? Well, make yourself worth a better position! . . . Ask yourself at every opportunity: what is my *most immediate* duty?"

26. "Disguised poetry and false romanticism." (163)

27. "With the absolute lowest."

28. "He did not have a rough enough disposition simply to break the strings, with which he felt bound to society, and make himself free."

29. "Fancy's mood is all stormed out for now . . . and the reader is again expressly invited to direct

his expectations along the lines of daily tasks" and "putting aside utopias and fantastic desires."

30. "who didn't have a stich of clothing on either."

31. "The romanticism was—not forever, probably—exhausted, knotted up, spoiled. His struggle against going astray began to carry fruit, and the effort to not trouble himself with anything but what immediately lay at hand, became more painful because he could not feed his soul with the trivialities dictated to him. He was someone for whom the unhealthy consumption of sweets is forbidden, and instead of that is given a diet of saw dust and sand, or . . . nothing."

32. "had such a great a need to bridle his desires."

33. "The flowers of his fantasy became wilted and without aroma" and "Wouter had since some time lost his talent for poetry. He didn't dare try it because he had reasons to be ashamed of that which is sweet."

34. "but we're not quite that far yet."

35. D. A. Miller, *Narrative and Its Discontents: Problems of Closure in the Traditional Novel* (Princeton: Princeton U P, 1981): 41.

36. King, 100.

Anne-Marie Feenberg (essay date December 1997)

SOURCE: Feenberg, Anne-Marie. "*Max Havelaar*: An Anti-imperialist Novel." *Modern Language Notes* 112, no. 5 (December 1997): 817-35.

[*In the following essay, Feenberg examines* Max Havelaar *as an indictment of the Dutch colonial government in Java. Feenberg argues that the radical narrative structure of the novel provides the perfect mode of expression for the author's anti-imperialist message, also suggesting that Multatuli's attitude toward European imperialism anticipates many of the postcolonial theories of politics and culture that emerged in the late twentieth century.*]

IMPERIALISM AND THE NOVEL

With the publication of Edward Said's *Orientalism*, colonialism and post-colonialism moved to the center of literary and cultural debates in the academic establishment. In his subsequent *Culture and Imperialism,* Said argues that nineteenth- and twentieth-century Western cultural formations have been structured by an imperialist vision that posits a fundamental ontological difference between Western and non-Western man, the difference residing in the superiority of the Westerner, justifying his domination over the rest of the world. Colonialism and imperialism were so profoundly influential that their existence as a formative mental structure determining the Western experience of the world was not recognized until very recently.

Said acknowledges that colonialism has had its detractors in the West, but distinguishes between anti-colonialism and anti-imperialism as follows:

> During the nineteenth century, if we exclude rare exceptions like the Dutch writer Multatuli, debate over colonies usually turned on their profitability, their management and mismanagement, and on theoretical questions such as whether and how colonialism might be squared with laissez-faire or tariff policies; an *imperialist* and Eurocentric framework is implicitly accepted. . . . Liberal anti-colonialists, in other words, take the humane position that colonies and slaves ought not too severely to be ruled or held, but—in the case of Enlightenment philosophers—do not dispute the fundamental superiority of Western man or, in some cases, of the white race.[1]

While this may be too sweeping a historical generalization—it is difficult to detect the superiority of the white European in Diderot's *Supplément au Voyage de Bougainville*—the distinction is useful for purposes of analysis. Whereas anti-colonialism advocates the humane treatment of colonies but remains Euro-centric, anti-imperialism repudiates colonialism altogether.

For Said, narratives, and especially novels, are privileged loci of the imperialist vision, which determines constitutive elements of plot and structure such as temporality and spatiality, as well as ideological biases. In the early nineteenth-century novel the empire is taken for granted and becomes visible only when it illuminates an element of the plot or the characters; in Jane Austen's *Mansfield Park,* for instance, Sir Thomas Bertram's wealth derives from his plantation in Antigua. When the reality of the empire assumes a more prominent place in public consciousness in the later half of the nineteenth-century, it also becomes more central in the novel, as in Conrad's *Heart of Darkness.* While *Heart of Darkness* has elements belying the imperialist vision, the dominant ideological bias reaffirms the "*mission civilisatrice*" of the West with respect to the non-Western world.

As Said notes, the nineteenth-century Dutch writer Multatuli does not share this prevailing imperialist vision. In fact, Multatuli's **Max Havelaar** denounces that vision as the justification for the oppression of the natives of Indonesia. The novel strikingly illustrates *avant la lettre* postcolonial theories about colonial psychology and imperialist ideologies. The complex narrative structure of this novel makes it an aesthetic and literary success in spite of the overt political rhetoric, as is evidenced by its enduring fame both in the Netherlands and in Indonesia.

When *Max Havelaar* appeared in 1860, it disturbed the torpor of Dutch literary life, which had been mainly concerned with religious questions. Its author, Edward Douwes-Dekker, was born in 1820 in Amsterdam, the son of a sea captain. At the age of 18, he went to Indonesia, one of the Dutch colonies, where he became a civil servant. In 1830, the Dutch government had instituted the *"cultuur-stelsel,"* a system of cultivation which forced native farmers to devote part of their land to crops for export; these they had to hand over to the government. This system led to the ruthless exploitation of the peasants. Often the Dutch colonial administration relied on native authorities to extract these taxes, which usually led to the intensification of exploitation. In spite of many troubles with the native as well as the Dutch hierarchy, Douwes-Dekker was eventually appointed the Assistant-Resident of Lebak in 1856.

Taking seriously his oath "to protect the native against exploitation and extortion," he officially accused the native Regent of corruption. The Dutch colonial government hastily transferred him to another region, deploring his "lack of prudence," whereupon Douwes-Dekker resigned indignantly. When it became clear to him that the Dutch Governor, whose help he had naively expected, was neither interested in the plight of the natives nor in Douwes-Dekker's own fate, he travelled back to Europe. There he wrote the story of the events on Lebak in *Max Havelaar* under the suggestive pseudonym *Multatuli,* "I have suffered much." With this novel, he hoped to alert public opinion to the appalling conditions in Indonesia as well as to vindicate himself. In *Max Havelaar,* the empire is thus very much at the heart of the novel, unlike most European fiction of the time.

One can hardly imagine a less auspicious starting point for a novel than Douwes-Dekker's didactic and propagandistic intent. *Max Havelaar* is loaded with digressions about Dutch colonial policy; its world is a manichean one in which the characters are good or evil, oppressor or oppressed, and where the hero is an all too noble Don Quixote whose identity with the author becomes obvious at the end of the story.

And yet the novel is aesthetically successful. In spite of its "defects," the novel "works" thanks to highly sophisticated narrative techniques.[2] Since the book is virtually unknown in this country, I will briefly describe the plot and bring out the complex narrative structure to which it owes much of its interest. The title *Max Havelaar,* and subtitle, *Or the Coffee Auctions of the Dutch Trading Company,* announce the double nature of the narrative: the story of Max Havelaar, the hero, and that of Droogstoppel, a coffee broker.[3] Coffee was one of the main crops which the natives were forced to cultivate and which accounted for the exorbitant profits of the Dutch Trading company. Droogstoppel's story is set in

Amsterdam. He receives a bundle of manuscripts from an impoverished acquaintance (Sjaalman, i.e. Shawl-man; see note 3) and believes he can make a book out of it useful to coffee brokers; he asks his young German apprentice, Stern, to put the different fragments from the bundle into a coherent whole. Stern's story is set in Indonesia and narrates the trials and tribulations of Max Havelaar, a Dutch colonial administrator whose life parallels Douwes-Dekker's. There are thus two narrators, Droogstoppel and Stern, and two locales, Holland and Indonesia.

In the conclusion, the author, "Multatuli," dismisses his hero as a romantic dreamer; he also dismisses Droogstoppel as a nauseating fiction representing real and despicable Dutch merchants. Multatuli writes that fiction though his novel may be, it should be read for the higher truth it contains, i.e., that the natives of Indonesia are exploited by their own nobility for the sake of their Dutch masters.

> Enough, my good Stern! I Multatuli take up the pen . . . I called you into being . . . It is enough, Stern, you may go! . . .
>
> Halt, wretched spawn of sordid money grubbing and blasphemous cant. I created you, you grew into a monster under my pen. I loathe my own creation: choke in coffee and disappear.
>
> (317)

Multatuli protests the expeditions against the poor, emaciated rebels, forced by mistreatment to revolt. His book proves that "there is a robber state between East Friesland and the Scheldt." He calls for:

> Deliverance and help, by legal means, if *possible* . . . by the *legitimate* means of force, if *necessary. And this would react most unfavorably on the* 'Coffee Auctions of the Dutch Trading Company!'
>
> (320)

Max Havelaar quickly became and remained the most widely read and famous of Dutch literary works. For a century, every educated Dutch person has read it, usually as an assignment in high school. But despite its great literary success, it did not have the political impact the author had hoped for; nor did it lead to his personal rehabilitation. Douwes-Dekker was forced to earn his living as a writer. He led a bohemian life, gambling, always broke, always travelling, until he died in 1877.

In Holland, *Max Havelaar* provoked an unending stream of astonishingly varied and often contradictory critical evaluations, mostly of a biographical nature: in some, the author is an idealistic dreamer, a romantic hero; in others he is a maniac, an arch egotist, a conservative, or an anarchist. The bulk of the critical literature concerns itself with the question of whether the events and characters recorded in the novel are realistically portrayed or whether the author distorted the truth in his own self interest. This emphasis is rather surprising since Douwes-Dekker himself points to the fictional character of the novel in the narrative and claims it represents a higher truth, a forthright admission that should have discouraged the matching of novelistic events with reality.[4]

Despite the controversy that surrounds it in Holland, Multatuli's enduring popularity in Indonesia justifies interpreting **Max Havelaar** as a repudiation of the imperialist vision. In Indonesia, where it was only available in Dutch until 1972, a small Indonesian elite read the novel in the Dutch-language schools. The novel had an important influence on Sukarno and other leaders of the nationalist liberation movement, which led the country to independence in 1945. In their book on Multatuli in Indonesia, Termorshuizen and Snoek cite Indonesian intellectuals and artists' testimony to Multatuli's influence on the liberation movement. They comment:

> Multatuli as symbol of humanity and as a natural supporter in the struggle for national independence: this is how he was seen by many young Indonesians and presented in nationalist speeches and writings.[5]

When the Indonesian translation appeared, the novel was also immediately successful among the population at large. Of course, the work had its share of detractors. Some deplored the unfavorable light in which the Indonesian aristocracy was portrayed, overlooking Multatuli's exposure of Dutch colonialism as the ultimate cause of the exploitation. Others, pleading for an Indonesia-centered viewpoint, commented that Multatuli had tried to impose Western notions of justice on an Asian feudal system. Some went so far as to say that the peasants were in fact happy to provide free labor to their Indonesian masters. Others again pointed to Douwes-Dekker's Eurocentric bias in naming the exploiting native princes by their real names while using fictive, if highly pejorative names for the Dutch colonial officials. A film based on the novel was made in 1976; interestingly, although this was a Dutch-Indonesian co-production, the Indonesian government deemed it so subversive that it forbade its release. The film was finally shown there in 1987.[6]

HISTORICAL CONTEXT

Nineteenth-century Holland is an unexpected place for the appearance of an anti-imperialist novel. The country was stagnating; industrialization had not yet taken place. There was practically no middle class nor industrial working class, not to mention, of course, a working class movement. According to contemporary social critics, Holland was characterized by narrow-mindedness, caution, lack of initiative and complete apathy. To quote but two of those: "In the northern Netherlands one can hear a leaf fall: everything there is as dead as possible." "There are many complaints about the sleepiness of the Dutch."[7] Intellectually, the situation was not much better. Literature from around 1850 to 1880 is dominated by ministers to such an extent that the period is characterized by the Dutch as the "domineescultuur" (minister-culture). It is not surprising that religious disputes should have had such importance in those days, given the lack of more modern issues and conflicts. Nevertheless, Romanticism did not fail to have its influence. Walter Scott, Byron, Victor Hugo and Lamartine had avid readers and imitators.

In Parliament, one of the dominant debates between the Liberal and Conservative parties concerned the *cultuurstelsel*. Conservatives wanted to keep this system of forced cultivation, administered by the Dutch state, while the Liberals wished to abolish it in favor of private enterprise. Both parties drew arguments from **Max Havelaar,** the Liberals to show the corruption of colonial management, the Conservatives to point out that given the rapacity of private entrepreneurs, Indonesian farmers would be exploited even more ruthlessly without the *cultuurstelsel*. The idea of abandoning colonies altogether was not widely articulated in nineteenth-century Europe.[8]

The most radical magazine seems to have been *De Dageraad,* the expression of the "freethinkers' union," founded in 1856, and intent on propagating Enlightenment ideas as well as the materialist and atheist concepts of the nineteenth century. In a certain sense religion was still a focal issue in as far as the free-thinkers militantly fought against it. Multatuli was one of the most important and progressive contributors to this magazine. Multatuli's political and social ideas do not form a consistent system. His critique of capitalism is romantic, primarily a ceaseless attack on the conventional and conservative aspects of Dutch life, on its bigotry and hypocrisy, its narrow-mindedness and self-righteousness.

In Holland, Enlightenment ideals had never had to stand the test of social and economic reality. True enough, the Dutch had known their revolution in 1795. This, as well as the annexation of the Netherlands by Napoleon, had brought about political changes—centralization, a new constitution, the abolition of guilds, to name but a few of them—but it did not pave the way for profound economic changes. On the contrary, economic decline set in as is evidenced by the flight of capital, loss of colonies, and most importantly by the collapse of Holland's maritime hegemony, with tremendous associated commercial losses.

Nevertheless, Holland had been a capitalist country in the strict sense of the term for centuries and it was pervaded by a "shopkeeper's mentality" intent on conservation rather than expansion in this period before industrialization. There was no question of the feverish excitement and dynamism of expanding capitalism that can be found in Balzac's novels.

This is why Max Havelaar could strive to be a Napoleon, but only a moral one. How was Douwes-Dekker able to rise above this general stagnation?

The belief in Enlightenment ideals and a Romantic sensibility must have contributed to a deeper insight into the fundamental issues raised in **Max Havelaar.** But it was Douwes-Dekker's personal experiences in Indonesia, which laid bare the real relation between colonizer and colonized, that enabled him to write a "realistic" novel in which a "type" does appear, where

> all the humanly and socially essential determinants are present on their highest level of development, in the ultimate unfolding of the possibilities latent in them, in extreme presentation of their extremes, rendering concrete the peaks and limits of men and epochs.[9]

NARRATIVE STRUCTURE IN *MAX HAVELAAR*

In the remainder of this essay I would like to present a detailed analysis of the form and content of **Max Havelaar.** I share with the early Lukács the view that one of the central themes of the nineteenth-century novel is the struggle between the individual and society. For Lukács, the novel is the portrayal of the degraded search for authentic values in a degraded world. The hero of the novel is always problematical: he is no longer part of a harmonious totality, as is clear from his search for authentic values in a world which has none. The hero's search is itself degraded and takes the form of a quest for worldly success: hence the predominance of the theme of ambition, the search for power and wealth in many nineteenth-century novels. The novel is characterized by irony, that of the creator; it is directed not only towards the hero, the vanity of whose search he or she knows, but also towards his or her own attempt to create a totality—the novel—which is doomed to remain the fruit of his or her subjective will. It is through irony that the implicit values are first posited, against which worldly values are judged and ultimately condemned.[10]

In the context of this central theme, I argue that values are affirmed or demystified in the interplay between formal elements and the contents that provide the raw materials of the novel. These values in turn can be traced back to historically conditioned ideologies.[11] In **Max Havelaar** both the hero's quest for justice as well as society's values, in this case the imperialist vision, are demystified. Unlike many nineteenth-century English novels, where the protagonist compromises and adapts to society, or French novels, where the quest often ends in death, **Max Havelaar** presents yet another type of dénouement, a political one.

At one level, **Max Havelaar** is a novel disillusionment; the hero is defeated, and exposed as a romantic. On the other hand, the novel affirms the hero's values, i.e., his quest for justice for the Indonesian natives, and condemns only his naivete in believing that he, as an individual, can eliminate exploitation within the bounds of the colonial system. His values, far from being discredited, are posited as ideals to be realized in the historical future. It is still a novel of disillusionment, but also a novel that refuses to give up hope. The use of several narrators hiding behind one another and providing different perspectives on characters and events, the to and fro in time and space between the present and the past, between Holland and Indonesia, the interplay between fact and fiction, all produce a complex narrative structure where irony weighs contrasting values.

The novel starts with a narrator in the first person: Batavus Droogstoppel. His point of view seems simple enough, that of a businessman full of common sense, suspicious of poetic fancy. However, his views are so extreme, so narrow-minded and bigoted that Droogstoppel becomes a caricature and is obviously not the locus of judgment of the characters and the action. He is himself being judged, and although the reader does not know yet by whom, it is clear that the unknown point of view is similar to that of the Sjaalman from whom Droogstoppel receives the bundle of manuscripts and whom he treats so contemptuously.

Although Droogstoppel is a caricature, he does represent the "world," Dutch society as a whole: he is successful, respectable and is received by "the best of society"; and it is in the interest of him and those like him—businessmen—that the Dutch state permits and encourages the exploitation of the Indonesian natives. The caricature of Droogstoppel, a satire of the Dutch bourgeoisie, is rendered even more powerful by the fact that his portrait is a self-portrait. Batavus does not seem conscious of the enormous contradictions in his views and his own hypocrisy, resulting from the need to justify morally uncharitable and cruel acts motivated by pure self-interest. Besides being a bigot and a hypocrite, Droogstoppel has all the other vices of the nineteenth-century bourgeois—as seen by the Romantic soul: he is a philistine, hates all literature and art in the name of literal truth; he is authoritarian and repressive and tries to kill spontaneity in his children. He thinks only in terms of stereotypes and clichés and is incapable of any imaginative thought, let alone action. Money comes first, respectability second. However, the reader has to take this ridiculous figure seriously because he, and what he stands for, is clearly the antagonist in the events that are yet to come.

According to Droogstoppel, the Dutch have a duty to rule the natives, since the latter are deprived of Christianity and hence of civilization; it is up to the white man to civilize these poor, lost souls and to help them overcome their lazy and indecent ways. But Droogstoppel cannot help constantly connecting the white man's "*mission civilisatrice*" to the necessity of making money with coffee production. The novel thus shows the hypocrisy of the "imperialist vision." Droogstoppel quotes with approval the Parson Waavelaar's ("Blatherer") sermon, which made a great impression on him:

> The ships of our Holland sail the great waters, to bring civilization, religion, Christianity, to the misguided Javanese! Nay, our happy Fatherland does not covet eternal bliss for itself alone: we wish to share it also with the wretched creatures on those distant shores who lie bound in the fetters of unbelief, superstition and immorality!
>
> (141)

With great satisfaction, Droogstoppel reflects on the perfect harmony between the Parson's ideas and his own belief that cultivating coffee is useful to the moral salvation of the Javanese.

The second narrator, Stern, seems rather too knowing for who he is supposed to be, namely a young, idealistic and romantic German who is just learning the Dutch language. This narrator is omniscient and sophisticated; he frequently comments in the first person and has an intimate knowledge of Max Havelaar and Indonesian affairs. Söteman argues that the "I" of the Stern narrative cannot be identified with a particular character in the novel but is the indefinite "I" of novelistic convention, through which the writer introduces an "auctorial medium" that stands outside of the story as such. The events and characters are judged from the point of view of this auctorial medium. He praises Havelaar's generosity and self-sacrifice, his noble, if impractical idealism, his poetic and fiery soul; he is utterly contemptuous of hypocrisy, greed, respectability, narrowmindedness and all other Droogstoppelian characteristics. Hence Droogstoppel stands doubly condemned: by his self-portrait in his own narration and by the parallel "Stern" narrative. The invisible hand behind Droogstoppel's self-caricature is the same as the "I" of the Stern narration.

However, the "I" of the Stern narration is not identical with Sjaalman, whose manuscript he uses. This can only be ascertained at the end of the novel, when it is clear that Sjaalman and Havelaar are one and the same. And the Stern narrator does take a certain distance from his hero and criticizes him at times.

A third narrator appears at the end of the novel, Multatuli himself, the "real" author (whose name is a pseudonym). He dismisses Droogstoppel and Stern, created by him to expose the situation in Indonesia. He relegates them to the world of fiction and does away with them now that they have served their purpose. He does not mind if his book is criticized on formal grounds; his aim was not so much to write well as to be heard. He concludes: "The substance of my work is irrefutable" (319). Although the novel as a whole is fiction, the reader has to accept the general lines of the story as reality. This ending is paradoxical: by emerging as the "real" author, the voice from the "real" world asks us to cease suspending disbelief and then reasserts the truth of his fiction.

This conclusion has been prepared throughout the book by the other two narrators. Droogstoppel constantly affirms that all literature is a lie and cannot be believed, and by arousing the strongest antipathy in the reader conditions the latter to believe the exact opposite, i.e. that literature is truth. Stern, the second narrator, discusses the relation of fiction to reality and comments again and again on his craft, on the nature of literature, as in his important passage on digressions. One is reminded of Laurence Sterne, an author whom Douwes-Dekker admired and after whom he may have named his own "Stern." The narrator also comments significantly on the tragic story of Saidjah and Adinda, a tale of peasant suffering and revolt within the novel, and presents a theory of literature at its conclusion. In Said's terms, the story of Saidjah and Adinda provides an element of "contrapuntal reading," i.e. a reading of the events from a native point of view, contrasting with the Droogstoppelian or imperialist vision. The parable does not idealize the native ("*le bon sauvage*") but shows the consequences of colonial exploitation for the ordinary peasant subjected to intensified exploitation by his feudal lords. When revolt breaks out, however, it becomes clear who the real culprits are: the Dutch army ruthlessly exterminates the rebels. The enduring popularity of the tale in Indonesia testifies to the legitimacy of such a contrapuntal reading. Saidjah and Adinda have played an enormous role in the Indonesian nationalist awakening.[12]

The tale is a kind of touchstone for **Max Havelaar** in as far as it presents the lived reality of the colonial system. The point of view initially is that of the all-knowing author but at the end the narrator confesses he does not know if the incidents he has recorded really happened. He has concrete data about the exploitation of the Indonesian peasant but he knows that just stating the facts does not move people while fiction does:

> Yes, a confession! Reader . . . I do not know whether Saidjah loved Adinda. Nor whether he went to Batavia. Nor whether he was murdered in the Lampong districts by Dutch Bayonets . . . I do not know all this! But I know *more*. I know, *and I can prove,* that there were *many* Adindas and Saidjahs, and that *what is fiction in particular is truth in general.*
>
> (278)

This "honesty" of the narrator of course creates the impression of an objective observer, which enables him to insert his comments on the economic, political and social situation in Indonesia with aesthetic impunity. The dialectic between fiction and reality is thus established and Multatuli's intervention at the end does not undermine the impact of the book; on the contrary, it strengthens it by further deconstructing the opposition between fictional narrative and truth.

The question remains of how, then, Multatuli can reaffirm the truth and reality of his hero's vision, claim it for his own and believe in its possible realization while showing the failure and inevitable defeat of the hero. Multatuli solves this problem by assuming the role of political analyst and stepping outside the narration to criticize the hero from a standpoint of superior knowledge. Havelaar thinks he can work through the system and Multatuli knows this is impossible. But there is an alternative. Havelaar's values are not irrevocably incompatible with the world; the narrator holds out the hope that they can be imposed by action of a type Havelaar cannot engage in. The narrator shares the same values as Havelaar but implies that *he* Multatuli will not fail, for "I am not a fly saving poet, no mild dreamer like Havelaar" (320). The novel is thus a political critique of romanticism.

ROMANTICISM TRANSCENDED

Multatuli promises that his future actions will be detrimental to the coffee auctions of the Dutch Trading Company. Why will he succeed? Because he is not a poet, a mild dreamer like Havelaar. In other words he reproaches his hero with being a romantic. And this is in fact how Havelaar is portrayed.

Droogstoppel introduces him to the reader: Havelaar is blond, blue-eyed and has an exotic air about him; he looks like a traveller or a foreigner. We learn that he is exceptionally intelligent and has a wide range of interests, as his bundle of manuscripts shows. He is unusual in every respect: his reputation among colonial circles in Indonesia is that of a "madman." He scorns bourgeois comforts, conventions and manners and moves with aristocratic charm and ease. The Stern narrator gives a detailed portrait of him:

> Havelaar was a man of thirty-five. He was slim, and quick in his movements. There was nothing remarkable in his appearance except . . . his large, pale-blue eyes, which had something dreamy about them when he was in a calm mood, but shot fire when a great idea took possession of him. His fair hair hung lank over his temples, and I can very well understand that people seeing him for the first time would get the impression that they were in the presence of one of the rare ones of the earth as regards both heart and head. He was a 'vessel of contradictions.' Sharp as a razor, yet tender-hearted as a young girl . . . Full of love for truth and justice . . . he was chivalrous and brave, but like that other Don Quixote, often wasted his valor on windmills. He burned with an insatiable ambition. No sci-

ence was wholly foreign to him. . . . His mind had a tendency to extravagance. . . .

(89-90)

Havelaar constitutes the romantic response to a society concerned only with profit. This becomes clear when one takes a closer look at the contrast between Havelaar and the base and prosaic Droogstoppel. Havelaar has all the human traits that are completely dysfunctional in a money-oriented society: he is generous to a fault, he considers people as ends and not as means and looks for authentic human relations as opposed to exploitative ones. His passionate search for truth and justice regardless of self sets him off sharply not only from the Droogstoppels but also from the well-meaning but timid bureaucrats and mummified government officials. His "loving heart" and concern for his fellow men brings out the cruel heartlessness and egoism of Droogstoppel's attitude toward his employees, Sjaalman in particular. The polar opposition between Havelaar and Droogstoppel makes the former a living critique of Dutch capitalism and the impoverishment of human life it engenders. This opposition is structurally necessary for the dramatic tension in the novel: Havelaar is all that Droogstoppel is not and vice-versa. And of course, tropical Indonesia, with its exoticism, where Havelaar feels at home, is a fitting counterpart to the horrible oppressiveness of Dutch daily life, with its respectability, its boredom and total lack of imagination.

The novel is a peculiar combination of a Flaubertian critique of daily bourgeois life and the most "romantic" expression of revolt. Havelaar could be characterized as a "romantic revolutionary" as defined by Barberis:

> Le romantisme révolutionnaire (Hugo, Michelet) refuse et condamne la réalité issue de la révolution bourgeoise, mais lui oppose des notions morales, des visions exaltantes de l'avenir, au lieu d'en faire l'analyse.[13]

Havelaar's vision and aspirations are unmistakably moral ones. The narrator underlines this fact by comparing him to Jesus and Socrates. Havelaar too suffered from being misunderstood by the world and failing in his moral mission. More important, however, are the comparisons with Don Quixote, both explicit and implicit. Of course this is another way in which the narrator acts as a literary critic, simultaneously approving and disapproving of his hero: Havelaar is the brave and courageous soul who fights valiantly but ineffectually for morally just causes.

Havelaar himself is aware of this; in his moments of self-mockery he also alludes to himself as a Don Quixote, but he feels he has to do his duty and takes a certain pride in being a martyr, and distinguishing himself in this manner from the morally weak and timid majority. The narrator in this way hints at a certain hubris in his hero, which is part of the latter's furious ambition, a moral ambition to be sure, but ambition nevertheless.

Havelaar dreams of being a sort of Napoleon of the moral realm. He does not search for his own happiness but for the happiness of humanity. Not only does he embody the revolt of the *poète maudit* or visionary against a stifling petty bourgeois society, but also older, prerevolutionary trends in European Romanticism. In the portrait of the hero elements can be found that are reminiscent of Schiller's vision of moral man: in Havelaar reason and the imagination as well as sensuousness are combined. The quest for beauty is the quest for the morally good, for perfection, for truth. But it should be added that as a man of action, however ineffectual, Havelaar sees the beautiful as a dynamic process, not as a static object of contemplation. This prerevolutionary aspect of Max Havelaar's romantic vision is indistinguishable from Enlightenment humanism with its quest for universal justice. Of course, to believe Enlightenment principles can be realized through sheer will circa 1860 is itself a romantic illusion. In that respect Havelaar is similar to characters such as Julien Sorel even if the former's illusions go back to an earlier stage in the history of bourgeois ideology. However, Havelaar can still believe in universal happiness, whereas Julien limits his search to the sphere of private happiness, which he knows does not coincide with the general welfare.

FROM AESTHETICS TO POLITICS

Havelaar believes to the bitter end that the obstacles he encounters are due to the weakness or cowardice of human individuals or the failings of bureaucracy, and his faith in the possibility of justice under Dutch rule remains virtually unshaken. As his personal history unfolds, the narrator prepares his downfall by his comments on the real nature of the bonds between Holland and Indonesia. Havelaar is the "colonizer who refuses" as he is portrayed by Memmi in *The Colonizer and Colonized*.[14] Memmi gives a psychological analysis of the dilemma of the colonizer who comes face to face with the injustices of colonialism. Either he learns to live with them and participates in the oppression of the natives, or he refuses to condone them and becomes a thorn in the side of his compatriots. It is impossible for him to remain a colonial administrator with a conscience: either he will have to resign in protest and leave the country, or be forced out.[15] Can he escape the dilemma by identifying with the natives and joining the struggle? That is not a realistic solution since he belongs and will always belong to the oppressors. For Memmi, the distinguishing trait of the moral colonizer is his political ineffectiveness.

At every stage of his journey towards defeat, Havelaar attributes the misery of the native population to breakdowns and abuses in the system rather than to the system itself. Until the very end of the novel he believes the intervention of the Governor General can change the situation and "prevent the sad and bloody events

which will soon result from the ignorance in which the Government chooses to be left concerning what is going on among the people" (317).

> Your Excellency has sanctioned: *the system of abuse of authority, of robbery and murder, under which the humble Javanese groans,* and it is that that I complain about.
>
> (316)

Repudiated by the Dutch colonial administration and having resigned in protest over his demotion to an even more obscure post, he resembles Memmi's colonial who refuses to condone the injustices of colonialism. Havelaar sympathizes with the revolts of the natives but cannot understand that they arise out of the very fact of colonialism rather than out of its excesses.

The narrator, however, does understand that the problem is systemic. Against Havelaar's romanticism, the narrator contrasts a stark analysis of reality. The exploitation of the peasant by the local aristocracy is not due to lack of energy on the part of Dutch civil servants but is a direct consequence of the Dutch colonial presence, which finds it convenient to have the natives taxed and controlled by their "natural" superiors. The burden of the Indonesian peasant, harsh enough under "normal" circumstances, is not lessened but multiplied by the introduction of Western civilization since he is now forced not only to provide for his own aristocracy but also to raise millions of florins of profit for Dutch coffers. The narrator writes:

> But strangers came from the West, who made themselves lords of his land. They wished to benefit from the fertility of the soil, and . . . if anyone should ask whether the man who grows the products receives an award proportionate to the yields the answer must be in the negative. The government compels him to grow on *his* land what pleases it; it punishes him when he sells the crop so produced to anyone else but it; and it fixes the price it pays him . . . The money given to the Chiefs to encourage them swells the purchase price further and . . . since, after all, the entire business must yield a profit, this profit can be made in no other way than by paying the Javanese just enough to keep him from starving, which would decrease the producing power of the nation. It is true then that the poor Javanese is lashed onward by the whip of dual authority; . . . it is true that famine is often the outcome of these measures. But . . . merrily flutter the flags at Batavia, Semarang, Surabaya, Pasaruan, Besuki, Probolingo, Patchitan, Chilachap, on board of ships which are being laden with the harvests that make Holland rich.
>
> (73)[16]

The colonial administration of which Havelaar is a part, far from enforcing justice, is set up to perpetuate injustice and make sure that the profits keep coming not just to Holland in general but to individuals in particular, such as Droogstoppel and his friend the tea merchant, whose interests the government diligently takes to heart. This ruthless exposition underlines the pathetic nature of Havelaar's quest and, as in Balzac and Stendhal, emphasizes the overwhelming obstacles to the hero realizing his ideals. It is hard to see how in 1860 anyone could have foreseen that decolonization could some day take place, let alone that the native population could ever defeat the military might of the mother country. Nevertheless, Multatuli sees revolt as inevitable, justifying his moral critique at the political level. The peculiar exhortation to the emperor at the end of the novel, to which the novel as a whole is an ironic refutation, should be interpreted as a desperate search for a historic solution in an impossible situation.

The salient feature of the **Max Havelaar** that distinguishes it from other novels of disillusionment is the attitude of the narrator toward the romantic illusion. "Stern" does indeed bring out the gap between reality and the hero's dreams, but his relation to his hero's values is more sympathetic than in most novels of this type. Usually the narrator either condemns the hero's aspirations, as in Dickens, or considers them anachronistic even if they are morally superior to the world, as in the case of Stendhal's Julien Sorel. There, the narrator represents the world's point of view, whatever his feelings about the hero's values. Multatuli, however, clearly approves of his hero's ideals but criticizes him for completely misunderstanding the conditions for their realization. This is probably why the fate of the hero is left indeterminate at the end of the novel. Multatuli leaves him wandering about, "poor and forsaken" after having been denied an audience with the Governor General. The last pages of the novel call on Havelaar to transcend his romanticism: not to abandon his ideals but to find other ways of realizing them. The validity of the romantic critique of capitalism and imperialism is affirmed in the context of a call for transcending the individual moral gestures of romantic practice.

In fact, the novel ends with what is essentially a political appeal. In literary terms this means that the author has moved from the aesthetic into the ethical realm; the implicit values of the novel become explicit. This of course explains why the author dismissed the characters in the book as merely fictional: literature ceases to exist as such when it becomes explicitly political.

Douwes-Dekker seems to have been fully conscious of this, as is apparent from some of the formal innovations of his novel. In characterizing his hero, he emphatically limits the similarities between Havelaar and "saints" such as Socrates and Jesus to their common suffering at the hands of the world, whereas Havelaar's resemblance to Don Quixote is fundamental. In other words, Havelaar is not the perfect bearer of ethical principles, but a "real" human being full of flaws and contradictions:

even if he tries to be a moral Napoleon, he still wants to be a Napoleon. It is significant that Havelaar, after the catastrophe of the "betrayal" by the Dutch colonial administration, disappears into the background of the novel as Sjaalman. A character who goes through life with a political message is no longer a novelistic hero.

Multatuli did not want this novel to end with the failure and disillusionment of his hero; this would have affirmed the unalterable nature of the world. However, the possibility of historical change could not be expressed aesthetically in a realistic novel; it could not yet be lived experience, especially not that of a Dutch colonial civil servant.

John Goode discusses a similar problem in the work of William Morris, who wanted to incorporate a socialist vision in his fiction in a historical situation in which such a vision had to remain at the level of a mere belief or dream. Under these circumstances, realism as a literary technique could only lead to despair:

> The danger of "realism" is that it can lose focus because it becomes overwhelmed by the phenomena it imitates and comes to see them as a permanent system of reality unconditioned by history. The voice of protest against the existing order of things may become the voice of despair through the intensity of its realization of that order; and despair is more comfortable than protest.[17]

Realism involves what Goode calls individualistic epistemology, the insistence on expressing reality through the lived experience of individuals. When historical conditions doom individual political resistance or rebellion, this individualistic epistemology will inevitably lead to a fiction of disillusionment and failure.

Multatuli's response to this limitation becomes clear in the authorial comments about the nature of literature, which affirm the difference between the aesthetic and the ethical in so many words. Responding to the possible accusation of untruthfulness because of the fictional character of his narration, Multatuli declares:

> What is fiction in particular is truth in general. It is not my purpose in this work to make statements as would be required by a tribunal sitting to pronounce judgment on the manner in which Dutch authority is exercised in the East Indies—statements which would only have power to convince those who had the patience to read through them with an attention and interest not to be expected from a public that reads for pleasure.

(278)

At the same time the author does worry about the reading public laying down his book without afterthoughts, having had its share of stirring emotions; he is concerned about what Marcuse calls the problem of "affirmative culture," the aesthetic realm becoming a world unto itself disconnected from reality. But Multatuli prefers to take this risk to that of not being read at all. Furthermore, he has what he thinks is a solution to the problem: he intervenes as a literary critic in his own novel, not only at the end but throughout the story. He interprets the hero's actions for us and provides us with the historical background that explains them. At the end he explains why the hero has to fail in terms of the real social and political conditions of historical change, in much the same way that Lukàcs, for example, talks about the failure of Julien Sorel in *Studies in European Realism.*

It is from the complex narrative structure of the novel as a whole that the anti-imperialist worldview emerges, regardless of the opinions and deeds of Douwes-Dekker, the man. Whether he was an anarchist or a reactionary, a romantic dreamer or ambitious egotist, is ultimately irrelevant. As Sitor Situmorang notes: "around the turn of the century, it was quite clear to the leaders of the emerging Indonesian nationalist movement that **Max Havelaar** contributed to their own awakening. Multatuli was in their eyes a fellow fighter against colonialism *avant la lettre.*"[18]

Notes

1. Edward Said, *Culture and Imperialism* (New York: Knopf, 1993), 240.

2. For an excellent analysis of the narrative structure see A. L. Sötemann, *De structuur van Max Havelaar* (Groningen: Wolters-Noordhoff NV, 1973).

3. As in eighteenth-century novels, many characters in Max Havelaar have names that say something about their personalities. Droogstoppel means Drystubble. Roy Edwards, the translator, comments on Droogstoppel's first name: "'Batavus,' referring as it does to the Batavi, the savage tribe which inhabited Holland at the beginning of the Christian era, suggests so many things: ancient virtues, sturdy John Bull-like common sense, parochialism, crass materialism, block-headed stupidity." *Max Havelaar* (Amherst: University of Massachusetts Press, 1982), 328. This English edition will be used throughout this article.

4. For a comprehensive overview of the *Max Havelaar* criticism, see Olf Praamstra, "Honderd jaar Max Havelaar-studie," in *Over Multatuli,* 29: 61-80.

5. Gerard Termorshuizen and Kees Snoek, *Adinda! Duizend vuurvliegjes tooien je loshangend haar. Multatuli in Indonesia* (Leiden: Dimensie, 1991), 14; my translation.

6. Termorshuizen and Snoek.

7. Termorshuizen and Snoek, 86.

8. For a short history of the *"cultuurstelsel"* and discussion of the local and colonial administrations in Java and Madoera during Douwes-Dekker's assistant-residency, see H. W. van den Doel, "Over 'brooddronkene vadzige regenten' en andere ambtenaren," in *Over Multatuli* 33 (1994).

9. Georg Lukács, *Studies in European Literature* (London, Hillway Publishing Co., 1950), 6.

10. Georg Lukács, *Die Theorie des Romans* [(1916; Darmstadt/Neuwied, 1982)].

11. See Anne-Marie Dibon, "From and Value in the French and English 19th-Century Novel," *MLN* 87.7 (1972).

12. See G. Termorshuizen and K. Snoek, *Adinda! Duizend vuurvliegjes tooien je loshangend haar. Multatuli in Indonesia* (Leiden: Dimensie, 1991).

13. Pierre Barberis, *Balzac et le mal du siècle,* 2 vols. (Paris: Editions Gallimard, 1970), I: 14.

14. Albert Memmi, *The Colonizer and the Colonized* (Boston: Beacon Press, 1967).

15. Shortly after the publication of *Max Havelaar,* three Dutch colonial administrators apparently committed suicide as they could no longer reconcile their offices with their consciences.

16. The Native Chiefs had become paid officials, who needed to extract from the peasants enough to pay taxes to the Dutch government and to keep up appearances. According to C. Fasseur, in *Onhoorbaar groeit de padi* (Amsterdam, 1987), profits from Indonesia made up 34% of the total income of the Dutch state in 1860.

17. John Goode, "William Morris and the Dream of Revolution" in *Literature and Politics in the Nineteenth Century* (ed. John Lucas, Methuen & Co. Ltd., 1971), 225.

18. Sitor Situmorang, "Multatuli en de Indonesische cultuur," in *Over Multatuli* 24 (1990), 5; my translation.

Carl H. Niekerk (essay date 2000)

SOURCE: Niekerk, Carl H. "Race and Gender in Multatuli's *Max Havelaar* and *Love Letters.*" In *One Hundred Years of Masochism: Literary Texts, Social and Cultural Contexts,* edited by Michael C. Finke and Carl Niekerk, pp. 171-90. Amsterdam: Rodopi, 2000.

[*In the following essay, Niekerk analyzes questions of race and identity in Multatuli's* Max Havelaar *and* Minniebrieven. *Niekerk also examines these works from a psychological perspective in relation to the later theories of Sigmund Freud.*]

Recent Freud scholarship focuses increasingly on issues of race and gender, and often closely connects the two. On the one hand, themes of race and gender seem, especially where they intersect, to be a repressed part of Freud's ongoing process of self-analysis and more broadly within the culture of psychoanalysis in general. On the other hand, these repressed themes also return. As Sander Gilman has shown, Freud's theory of psychoanalysis can be read as a product of and partial response to Freud's own insecurities concerning issues of race and gender.[1]

When Freud was asked in 1907 to name ten titles of books he considered good, he put Multatuli's *Letters and Works* at the top of his list.[2] Multatuli (meaning in Latin "I have suffered many things") is the pseudonym of Eduard Douwes Dekker (1820-1887), Dutch author and erstwhile colonial official, who is known outside of the Netherlands largely because of his novel *Max Havelaar or the Coffee Auctions of the Dutch Trading Company* (1860). I propose to read Freud's interest in Multatuli, and more specifically in Multatuli's colonial writings, as part of the culture of psychoanalysis and as an opportunity to contribute to the ongoing debate on issues of race and gender in Freud's life and thinking. Conventional wisdom holds that Freud favored Multatuli because of the enlightened views his works present—for instance, Freud quotes Multatuli favorably in an essay on the sexual education of children.[3] Indeed, Freud and Multatuli share a fundamental optimism regarding human nature, even when they are confronted with a reality that often seems to contradict that optimism. Both believe in the emancipatory potential of human beings, although neither author can be accused of naiveté. They are very aware of the obstacles in emancipation's path. But Freud and Multatuli also share a certain blindness regarding matters of race and discrimination. It is, for instance, as if their mutual opinion that race should not influence the process of emancipation results in an inability to perceive the concrete effects of racial discrimination in their immediate environment. To some extent this apparent blindness to contemporary problems may reflect a conscious attempt to not let those problems disrupt what they perceive to be their own objective and critically distant perspective and behavior. On the other hand—and much of what Gilman has recently discussed in relation to Freud seems to support this—such an attitude may have resulted in an unconscious strategy of avoiding specific, controversial topics.

Max Havelaar, the principal character of Multatuli's novel *Max Havelaar or the Coffee Auctions of the Dutch Trading Company,* is a young and idealistic colonial official in the Dutch East Indies in the mid-nineteenth century. As the main storyline begins, Havelaar moves with his wife and child to Lebak, a remote and poor district of the Dutch Indies, in order to assume a position as assistant resident of that district. Many of the problems Havelaar encounters have to do with the specifics of his official position (cf. e66ff./d1:58ff.).[4] As assistant resident, Havelaar is the highest local Dutch official in a subdistrict, and he works in conjunction with the local regent, a Native who is usually a member of local nobility. In contrast to the colonial strategies of other powers, the Dutch chose to use the existing precolonial hierarchies rather than to impose their own organization in the East Indies. This had little to do with respect for the relatively advanced organization of the indigenous society, and much to do with the fact that the Dutch lacked the manpower necessary to develop their own administrative structures. *Max Havelaar*'s main narrative is a report of the events leading to Havelaar's suspension and subsequent departure from the Dutch Indies. At least as interesting as *Max Havelaar* is the little-known sequel entitled *Love Letters,* published in 1861. In *Love Letters,* which Freud explicitly mentions in his letter of 1907 (Jones, 423), we find Havelaar back in the Netherlands alone and poor, reminiscing about his past experiences, the publication of his book, his social agenda after leaving the Indies, his relationships with women, and life in general.

Eduard Douwes Dekker, or Multatuli, is often categorized as a Romantic, as is repeatedly remarked in the secondary literature on him (cf. Nieuwenhuys, 92; Baker, 140; and Beekman, 211, 218, 221, 227). Indeed, Multatuli's protagonists are extremely idealistic, cultivate their emotions, and often act intuitively rather than deliberately. Max Havelaar almost always permits feelings rather than reason to guide his actions. However, in contrast to mainstream Dutch and German Romanticism, Multatuli's works exhibit a strong political and social agenda based on the ideals of the Enlightenment. Multatuli often refers to emotion in a calculated way. The title *Love Letters* for the sequel to *Max Havelaar* is motivated more by the belief that a book with such a title will sell well rather than by the work's content. The romantic love story "Saïdjah and Adinda" in *Max Havelaar* has a similarly pragmatic function, as it exposes the Romantic reader to the inhuman side of colonial reality.

Multatuli's characterization of Napoleon and the ideals of the French Revolution helps illuminate the alliance between Romantic and Enlightenment thought in his work. The slogan of the French revolution "liberty, equality, fraternity" as a radical version of Enlightenment values seems an apt summary of Dekker's political agenda. When Nieuwenhuys speaks of Dekker's "revolutionary impact" (Nieuwenhuys, 79), the kind of impact that Multatuli very much desired, he also inadvertently points out a connection between Multatuli and Napoleon. The Enlightenment agenda is pursued by Dekker/Multatuli with an uncanny fervor quite similar to Napoleon's. Multatuli's respect for Napoleon follows a more general trend of the restoration period (cf. Lützeler, 219ff.). Napoleon offers a good model for understanding how the Enlightenment's sociopolitical agenda and a certain Romantic spirit are combined in Multatuli's life and work.

For the moment, let us return to Freud. Within the European intellectual and also often rather conservative canon that Freud as a reader preferred (cf. Gilman 1994, 146), Multatuli is definitely one of the more experimental, more political, more progressive, and more outspoken authors. Freud's interest in Multatuli may on some level have had something to do with issues of race. It may seem daring to draw a parallel between the treatment of European Jews on the one hand and the object of the European colonial enterprise abroad on the other. However, Multatuli does just that in an anecdote that the narrator, Max Havelaar, tells toward the end of *Love Letters*. The anecdote alludes to the basic motivation underlying Multatuli's writings at that time; one could call it the "primal scene" of Multatuli's authorship. As a ten-year-old boy in Amsterdam, Havelaar watches as a Jewish child loses his yarmulke when it is blown into the water. The people around him do nothing to help the boy, and in fact are amused as soon as they notice how upset he is about his loss. Of course it is Max Havelaar who, motivated by what he calls his own inner "arrogance," decides to help the boy retrieve the "little beret" (d2:152).[5] The bystanders in the anecdote demonstrate the basic attitude of intolerance toward people of different ethnic and racial backgrounds that Multatuli ascribes to his Dutch readers—it relates an incident that could have happened in their own streets. Multatuli uses the anecdote to point out that intolerance also exists among those not directly involved in the colonial enterprise. Freud's interest in Multatuli may very well have been motivated by similar convictions on his own part, whether conscious or not. Perhaps Freud was intrigued by Multatuli's colonial writings because they treated issues related to race and ethnicity relevant to his own situation. They may have allowed him to work through some of those issues himself, but to do so indirectly rather than overtly. Such a use of literature would be entirely in line with Freud's own theories regarding the role that reading and interpretation play in the life of the psyche. Mention should also be made of an anti-Semitic incident involving Freud's father that bears remarkable similarities to Multatuli's story in *Love Letters*. Freud's father told his ten- or twelve-year-old son that he (Freud's father) once had had to retrieve his new fur cap from the gutter where it had been kicked by a Christian with clear anti-Semitic intentions. Gilman shows that this incident had a great, if not traumatic, impact on Freud (cf. Gilman 1993, 127, and Gilman 1994, 56,131,214).

Beyond the few remarks Freud made in his writings, we can only speculate about what exactly went through

his mind when he was reading Multatuli. What is possible, however, is a reading of Multatuli that focuses on topics relevant to the interaction of conceptions of race and gender in the middle-class European mind of the nineteenth and early twentieth centuries. I propose to use "masochism" as a key concept to capture the dynamics of power at work behind what appears initially to be Multatuli's very egalitarian political agenda, based on the Enlightenment's ideals and principles. Masochism helps to construct a promising theoretical framework especially because of the complex notions of power which are its correlate. Masochism always involves a double-bind with respect to power. On the one hand, it implies a sense of victimhood and therefore of lack of power. On the other hand, this lack of power is made into an instrument of power and a means to gain access to power. If such a mechanism were indeed at work in Multatuli's texts, it would certainly explain the very contradictory nature of his writings.

TRANSCULTURATION

Formally, *Max Havelaar* is a highly complex text, a quite uncommon feature given the direct, realistic literary style of the mid-nineteenth century. The text incorporates a number of different genres, material in very different forms, most of it listed at the beginning of the book (e45-50/d1:38-43) as the content of a package the coffee broker Batavus Droogstoppel—who frequently mentions that he lives at "No. 37 Lauriergracht, Amsterdam"—receives from a former high school acquaintance whom he calls Scarfman. Scarfman later turns out to be identical to Max Havelaar, the principal character of the novel. Droogstoppel is one of the narrators and the one who orders a book to be written based on the papers in the package he received from Scarfman, papers that he thinks have something to do with the coffee industry. There are a number of narrators in addition to Droogstoppel, each with his own specific agenda, and not all narrators are reliable sources of information. The reader does not always know who is speaking at a specific point in the text. This complex narrative structure,[6] I will argue, has much to do with what one could call Multatuli's notion of difference, the notion of cultural difference implicitly underlying his writing, and with his own interpretation of his role as a communicator and explicator of these differences.

E. M. Beekman has characterized Multatuli's novel with the help of the Bakhtinian notions of "dialogic" and "polyphonic" discourse (Beekman 229ff.).[7] To understand the formal complexities of the text, it is important to see that the person represented by Douwes Dekker (or Multatuli or Havelaar) does not consider himself a conqueror, but someone who will bring change and justice. Marie Louise Pratt describes this narrative position as one of "anti-conquest," a term that refers to "the strategies of representation whereby European bourgeois subjects seek to secure their innocence in the same moment as they assert European hegemony" (Pratt, 7)—strategies not uncommon among intellectuals facing colonial situations. Part of this position of "anti-conquest" is the vision Multatuli presents of himself as a mediator rather than a conqueror. Like Alexander von Humboldt not long before him (cf. Pratt, 135), Multatuli sees himself as a "transculturator." Marie Louise Pratt develops the concept of "transculturation" to describe the interaction, in the so-called "contact-zone," of dominant and subjugated culture, of the metropolis and the periphery, of empire and its subordinated subjects (Pratt, 6). Transculturation requires in the first instance an awareness of cultural difference, the ability to distinguish between one's own and the others' culture. Secondly, transculturation presupposes a willingness to mediate between two cultures. It is in this context, according to Marie Louise Pratt, not uncommon to find a "desire to achieve reciprocity" (Pratt, 80) as part of an ideology of transculturation—a desire that also can be found in *Max Havelaar,* as I will show momentarily.

Multatuli's position is in straightforward opposition to that of Batavus Droogstoppel, the first narrator of the novel, for whom "Holland has remained *Holland* because our old folk attended to their business, and because they had the true faith. That's all there is to it!" (e20/d1:16). Nevertheless, Multatuli needs Droogstoppel or a narrator like him. To be really convincing, he needs to be able to contrast the views of a stubborn and intolerant mid-nineteenth-century coffee merchant with those of more enlightened compatriots. Batavus Droogstoppel delegates the actual writing of the book to his son Frits and to "young Stern," the son of a German colleague who is in training in Droogstoppel's office. Young Stern and Frits, then, re-narrate Max Havelaar's tale, as found in Scarfman's package. At the novel's end, Multatuli himself breaks through its complex structure and confesses to be the author of the entire work:

> Enough, my good Stern! I, Multatuli, take up the pen. You are not required to write Havelaar's life story. I called you into being . . . I brought you from Hamburg . . . I taught you to write fairly good Dutch in a very short time . . . I let you kiss Louise Rosemeyer, who's in sugar . . . It is enough, Stern, you may go!
>
> [. . .]
>
> Yes, I Multatuli, 'who have borne much' take up the pen. I make no apology for the form of my book. That form seemed suitable to me for the attainment of my object.

>   (e317-18/d1:291-2)

To understand the function of the complex narrative structure of the novel, it is important to see nearly all narrators as mediators. Max Havelaar mediates between Natives of the Dutch Indies and the public at home in the Netherlands. Frits and young Stern mediate between Havelaar and Droogstoppel, who from the outset makes clear that he does not want anything to do with Scarfman. Droogstoppel mediates nothing, but simply represents Dutch nationalism and stubbornness. It is interesting that Multatuli opted for the somewhat unlikely route of having Stern—a German—write the actual text. Is young Stern, as a foreigner, more objective, more openminded, better suited to handle a message about abuse perpetrated by the author's and readers' fellow citizens? Or does the choice of a German narrator have something to do with the romantic spirit associated with Germans, as is suggested several times?

Transculturation as a strategy of anti-conquest, with interracial reciprocity as its goal, is maybe most visible in Havelaar's multilingualism. Havelaar is proud of his ability to communicate in foreign languages. Early on we hear that Scarfman's package contains documents "in several languages" (e50/d1:43). Droogstoppel finds this strange, as he does not see the point of learning other languages: "If each had stuck to his own language, it would have saved trouble" (e55/d1:48). Multatuli's self-positioning as a transcultural mediator is particularly clear at the end of *Max Havelaar,* after he reveals himself as the true author, when he envisions a future in which he will translate his book (if his voice is not heard in the Netherlands) "into the few languages I know, and into the many languages I can still learn" (e319/d1:293). And if all of Europe does not sing "*A pirate state lies on the sea, Between the Scheldt and Eastern Friesland!*" he will translate his book into "Malay, Javanese, Sundanese, Alfuro, Buginese, Battak . . ." (e319/d1:294). Literature functions in Multatuli's view as a forum of mediation; it continues the process of transculturation when communication in the real world is no longer possible. *Max Havelaar* not only contains a message for the colonial accomplices at home, at least according to Multatuli's intentions, but also for those who are the victims of colonialism.

Another aspect of Havelaar's multilingualism should be noted. It is no coincidence that Havelaar studies Sanskrit, as he indicates more than once (e:45/d1:38; d2:119). Multatuli may well have been aware of Friedrich Schlegel's claim "that Sanskrit and Persian on the one hand and Greek and German on the other had more affinities with each other than with the Semitic, Chinese, American, or African languages" (Said, 98). Today we still speak of "Indo-European" languages. Havelaar does not explicitly articulate what his interest in Sanskrit precisely is. It seems logical to assume, however, that he is interested in the Indo-European connection in the context of the construction of a "good" orient (cf. Said, 99)—"good" insofar as it relates to Europe. The issue of the existence of an Indo-European language helps to make this argument. For instance,

Havelaar praises Malay because of a supposedly natural simplicity long lost to European languages (e115/d1:104). Being exposed to Malay signifies to some extent a return to one's own origins.

RACE

Race is undoubtedly the domain in which the strategy of transculturation assumes the most urgent proportions. The issue of race is simultaneously omnipresent and barely visible in *Max Havelaar.* It is very directly connected to the injustices with which Havelaar has to deal continually. On a discursive level, however, race is rarely mentioned. The main cases of abuse described in *Max Havelaar* and later summarized in *Love Letters*—those involving murder, theft (especially of buffalo), unpaid labor, and unnecessary hunger, to name a few—have a clear racial dimension, but Multatuli prefers a non-racial explanation. In other words, the racial injustice is in Multatuli's eyes part of a broader phenomenon, of a more general form of injustice. Indeed, in relation to the abusive situations mentioned above, Multatuli is not only critical of the Europeans, but also of the highly hierarchical structure of Native society itself, a structure taken over and reinforced by the Dutch. The hierarchies existing among Europeans and Natives are mirrored by hierarchies among Natives themselves. The distinctions between European and Native culture are thus blurred.

Nevertheless, on the surface Havelaar's engagement with issues of racial injustice seems completely transparent. Perhaps one of the clearest examples illustrating both everyday colonialism and Havelaar's basic attitude toward it is represented by an anecdote related by one of the narrators:

> I am not quite certain, whether only a short time ago, when he [Havelaar] was on leave in Amsterdam, he did not pull down a signboard that displeased him because it showed a negro in chains, at the feet of a European with a long pipe in his mouth, and under it the inevitable words: 'The Smoking Young Trader'.
>
> (e94/d1:84)

Havelaar is strongly opposed to such a barbaric glorification of colonial abuse. On the surface his sympathies seem entirely on the side of the non-European. When Havelaar's wife Tine hears that the wife of Havelaar's predecessor—Mrs. Slotering, who will live with them for a while—is a Native woman, she responds with the remark that "that makes no difference" (e99/d1:89). As straightforward as this remark may sound, it is not entirely unproblematic. Does this mean that it is Mrs. Havelaar's opinion that racial difference even though recognized should not have any consequence for the way we treat the other person? Or does she mean that she ignores racial difference altogether? Or, and this would be the third possibility, does the first attitude, the

idea that race should make no difference in the way Europeans treat Natives, automatically create the second attitude, that of blindness toward race and the injustice that exists due to prejudice?

Multatuli's digressions in the novel illuminate such questions somewhat. He does occasionally make explicit comment on issues of race; he does not, however, make such comments in relation to Natives, but rather in relation to the problematic situation of "Mixed-Bloods" in the Dutch Indies. On the surface it seems Multatuli is concerned about practical matters, the inferior treatment of the Mixed-Blood, or "liplap" (a name Multatuli despises; cf. e100/d1:90), in colonial society and the subsequent creation of a class of inferior half-Europeans. Multatuli stresses the similarities between Europeans and Mixed-Bloods, stating that it is the inferior education of the Mixed-Blood alone which in general "hinders his being placed on an equality with the European, even when some individual liplap may perhaps deserve to be ranked above some individual European, as regards culture or scientific or artistic attainments" (e101/d1:91).

Multatuli's argument in favor of equal rights and equal treatment for Mixed-Bloods is nowhere to be found in his discussion of Natives. The "motto" that Multatuli chose at the end of his book—"*the Javanese is maltreated*" (e319/d1:293)—summarizes it quite well. He wants to abolish colonial abuse (maltreatment), but not necessarily colonialism itself. Multatuli does seem to be concerned about what one could call, using the vocabulary of the European Enlightenment, "the lack of a public sphere;" this is most visible in the passages in which Natives must sneak secretly to Havelaar's residence in the evening or at night, because if they were to visit him openly, the repercussions would be too huge (e238/d1:217). Multatuli laments the fact that Europeans can live in the Indies for more than thirty years without ever getting to know the indigenous population (e244/d1:223).

Why is Multatuli so concerned about the situation of Mixed-Bloods? One of the essays in Scarfman's package is entitled "On the influence of racial intermarriage on the mind" (e49/d1:43). A similar concern regarding interracial mixing is expressed in a footnote.[8] There is a long tradition in medical discourse and theories of race warning against such mixing (cf. Stafford 211ff.). The same concern, however—reflected, for instance, in Havelaar's fear of becoming a "hybrid"[9]—can be found on other levels as well. According to government instructions, the assistant resident is to treat the Native regent he has to work with as a "younger brother" (e71/d1:62). In practice, the regent enjoys great prestige in the local population and is often far more powerful than the assistant resident. In other words, "the inferior really commands the superior" (e70/d1:62). Why is Havelaar so concerned about this? Does it remind him too much of himself?

GENDER

Much of colonial literature presents a "vision of 'cultural harmony through romance'" (Pratt, 100). Racial inequality is flattened out by romantic, and therefore supposedly successful, relationships between representatives of different races or ethnic groups. This is not so in Multatuli's case. The one example of an interracial relationship in *Max Havelaar* has a tragic ending. Havelaar's predecessor, Mr. Slotering, who has married a Native woman, is killed by opponents among the Natives who are probably associated with the local regent. Multatuli clearly does not aim for what Todorov calls a "cross-breeding of cultures" (Todorov, 101). His reservations may be based in part on colonial reality. As I noted before, Multatuli was well aware of the problematic situation of Mixed-Bloods in the Indies. The reasons for his hesitation may also lie in what could be called the leftovers of his middle-class conscience: Dekker was proud of the noble background of his wife's family (cf. Beekman, 211, 213), and he hoped to get some money out of them.

In spite of all of this, Multatuli has a specific agenda in matters related to sex and gender. He compensates for the impossible ideal interracial or interethnic relationship by locating that ideal elsewhere—in Havelaar's happy family life. The idea is clearly not that private happiness compensates for professional hardship. Rather, a relationship based on equality rather than on hierarchy, a relationship that Havelaar cannot possibly achieve with the Natives, is nevertheless there, just in another form, as a relationship between the sexes. When Beekman calls Havelaar's wife "submissively devoted" (Beekman, 205) he is certainly right, but neither Multatuli nor Havelaar would agree. The text contains repeated references to the reciprocity and mutual dependence between husband and wife (cf. for instance e226/d1:206). Havelaar's relationship with Tine performs a utopian function within the framework of the novel. It shows that equality between partners is possible. A similar utopian model is visible in the story of the Natives "Saïdjah and Adinda." Again, a same-race relationship is presented as a model. The utopian moment in such relationships is part of a broader social agenda.

In *Max Havelaar* Multatuli presents arguments in favor of greater equality between the sexes, and in *Love Letters* he presents these arguments even more forcefully. After he has left the Indies, and it does not look like he will return there any time soon, he is clearly looking for a new social cause. Again, though, matters are less simple than they seem. An interesting document in this context is the first section of *Love Letters*. *Love Letters* is characterized by a rhapsodic style, which is certainly at times difficult to understand. It seems completely unrevised, which is plausible because we know that Multatuli wrote the book in just under two months (Oversteegen, 177). The introduction to *Love Letters* tells us a lot about the anxieties and fears that Havelaar/Multatuli is facing as the result of his political engagement.

According to Multatuli, a man who is interested in equal justice (whether concerning the rights of Natives or of women, a distinction that seems increasingly unimportant) is perceived as ill and emasculated; i.e., he is feminized.[10] "The woman is on the list of the exempting illnesses . . . in between cancer and impotence! The man is incapable of heroism and rifle brushing . . ." (d2:13). Multatuli here consciously invokes the topos of soldierhood as the quintessence of manhood (cf. Mosse, 50ff.). Shortly after this passage, it becomes clear that the feminization of the socially and politically engaged man is not just a metaphorical metamorphosis. The reader witnesses Multatuli's actual transformation into a woman. The passage is especially significant because in it Dekker plays with the pseudonym of Multatuli. Suddenly it is the readers who want to see him as Multatuli, he who has suffered so much:

> Buy and pay, all of you [i.e., you Dutchmen, Christians—old-fashioned and modern]! I have suffered enough to utter the tone that you like to hear so much! You have lied to me, you insulted and tortured me enough, to get something back for your torture, for your slander and lies!
>
> And if you are happy with the pitch of the scream which you kick out of my chest . . .
>
> (d2:22)

To understand this passage correctly, it may help to know that the Dutch word used for "scream" in this passage ("gil") implies that it is a very high scream. The quote demonstrates that Multatuli's transformation is not just discursive—the change does not merely involve an external symbolic stigma, but an internal process. Along with the public perception of identity, the perception of one's own sense of identity is involved. What began as a voluntary identification with a political cause turns out to be much more involving and involuntary. He (and the use of the masculine singular is intentional here) who defends a worthy cause is to some extent going to be identified with those he defends, those in the victim position, whether he wants to be or not. But the issue of identity and identification is even more complicated. In order to elucidate the complex and paradoxical processes of identification behind the political agenda in *Max Havelaar* and *Love Letters,* I propose turning to the concept of "masochism" as it is currently used and discussed in cultural theory.

MASOCHISM

Sander Gilman has recently proposed using the psychoanalytic concept of "masochism" to describe the cultural condition of intellectuals who place themselves, whether intentionally or no, on the faultlines between minority and majority culture.[11] In this respect, Gilman does not employ "masochism" as a psychoanalytic term in the narrow sense, as a clinical concept of analysis, but as a term for conceptualizing culture. At the core of his definition of "masochism" is the conviction of one's own powerlessness. This feeling of powerlessness is based upon the feeling, which may or may not be legitimate, of belonging to a group insufficiently represented in the majority culture. "Masochism" is then the mechanism through which a sense of powerlessness is used in order to gain access to power. The absence of power serves as partial legitimization for the attempt to acquire it. This requires the masochist to identify with those in power, and in fact to act as if he were indeed powerful himself. One could speak in this respect of a "double-bind." Masochism is a process of complex and paradoxical identification with feelings of power as well as of powerlessness. Such a mechanism is not necessarily conscious; the masochist may not be in the least aware of the fact that he or she has internalized attitudes of power or powerlessness. Gilman further assumes that, not surprisingly, the masochist's identification with the dominant group can never be completely successful. In other words, eventually the repressed feelings of powerlessness and inadequacy will return.

It is clear that Multatuli's own powerlessness helps justify his demand for power. It has often been remarked that there is a very selfish side to Multatuli's fight against injustice, against the maltreatment of the Natives. Indeed, he tends to make the impression of being more interested in his own case, in the injustices committed against himself, than in those committed against the Natives. This is especially clear in *Love Letters* and in the notes Multatuli later added to *Max Havelaar,* in which the main message seems to be about the wrongs perpetrated on the former colonial official Eduard Douwes Dekker rather than about the Natives' plight. Multatuli was at least to some extent aware of this; in *Love Letters,* one year after the publication of *Max Havelaar,* he responds to this potential critique by saying in effect that his arrogance is excusable because he is after all writing on behalf of a good cause (cf. d2:88).

What Multatuli overlooks here, however, is that the issue is clearly not just his "arrogance," but his dependence on a social structure he claims to reject. The inequality he so laments simultaneously provides the most fundamental legitimization of his existence. Without this inequality there would be no injustices to fight, no glorious cause to defend. In *Love Letters* Havelaar remarks that he "took such pleasure in relieving the burdens of those poor oppressed people" (d2:140). There are moments when the auctorial "we" in *Max Havelaar* comes close to analyzing the mechanism underlying this pleasure:

> We have said that difficulties attracted him, and that he had a craving for self-sacrifice. But he felt that the lure of such a sacrifice did not exist here, and feared that if, in the end, he had to engage in a serious battle against injustice, he would have to forego the chivalrous pleasure of beginning the battle as the weaker party.
>
> (e233/d1:212f.)

The words of the narrator(s) indicate an awareness of Havelaar's dependence on a self-perception of "weakness." The exact nature of this dependence is described as a "craving:" an irresistible urge, not something one can easily do without.

All of this still fits into the picture of the arrogant but noble Havelaar, the man who in his fight for a noble cause maybe gets a little bit too personally involved. In *Max Havelaar* Havelaar discusses an earlier incident regarding a satirical poem he wrote in which he criticized the man who was governor of the Dutch Indies at that time.

> And my epigram . . . that was even worse! He said *nothing,* and did *nothing*! Look . . . that was cruel! He grudged me the very least vestige of a martyr's crown, I was not allowed to become interesting through persecution, nor unhappy through excess of wit!
>
> (e178/d1:162)

At such moments, Multatuli's, as well as Havelaar's, own psychological structure clearly takes over to the point of jeopardizing his and the reader's consideration of the issues at stake. Although this passage is surely meant somewhat ironically, it is remarkably clear about the motives behind Multatuli's actions. Like Havelaar, Multatuli wants to be a martyr, and longs to be persecuted in order to "become interesting." The issue of racial injustice has moved completely to the background here. The fact that the incident concerns an "epigram" is even more interesting because it gives us another clue about the origins of Multatuli's authorship. Literature seems the ideal medium through which he can attract the attention he craves.

The pleasure of self-humiliation and of an identification with weakness is, as the passage cited above shows, closely tied to a feeling of power—and more specifically to the power of someone acknowledged by an audience as a public person. *Max Havelaar* ends with fantasies that confirm this need behind Havelaar's colonial engagement. Multatuli's desire for a "place in Parliament" to battle for the colonial cause is perhaps understandable (e319/d1:293), but not very realistic. Something similar applies in *Love Letters,* in which, notwithstanding the self-criticism regarding his arrogance, Multatuli does not hesitate to tell us again that he aims to become a parliamentarian (passim), that he hopes ("*because of the claims I think I have deserved by suffering so much*"; d2:66) to become an advisor to the governor of the Dutch Indies (d2:66,153), or to start a new political party (d2:75,154). He also compares his own sufferings to those of Christ (d2:84f.). Without the issue of racial injustice, Havelaar—and worse, Douwes Dekker—would be just another bad bookkeeper, someone who misappropriated funds (part of the reason for Havelaar's troubles in an earlier position was that he could not account for all the money he had spent for the Native population; cf. e18ff./d1:164f.). Behind Multatuli's engagement in matters related to colonial policy there exists ultimately the conviction that truth and Max Havelaar will triumph, or, more importantly, Multatuli will triumph. From this perspective it is not so striking that after *Max Havelaar* and *Love Letters,* after the creative phase of the late 1850s and early 1860s that enabled his definitive breakthrough as an author, Multatuli wrote no further substantial texts on colonialism. The great author had to move on, and dedicate himself to other subjects.

"Masochism," as redefined by Gilman, is not only Multatuli's way of dealing with his own conflicting identities. He also proposes it as a strategy to his readers, he invites them to share his masochistic fantasy. The claim is that only identification with, or at least some respect for, the position of the victim in these cases will pay off in the sense that it will guarantee the continuation of the Dutch colonial presence in the Indies. Multatuli says this very explicitly in a long introductory footnote to the 1875 edition of *Max Havelaar* (cf. e325/d1:301). One should indeed not forget that Multatuli is in essence a defender of colonialism. The question at stake for Multatuli is rather how colonialism could improve itself, and could, on the longer term, become more effective. "Masochism" forces us to rethink the strategy of "transculturation" present in Multatuli's text. The dialogic or polyphonic model structuring *Max Havelaar* clearly has its limits. Masochism, understood in the Gilmanian sense, interferes with the ongoing dialogue in Multatuli's novels. Whereas the use of concepts like dialogue and polyphony suggests communication as free exchange and desire for reciprocity, the fundamental masochistic scenario underlying the novel obstructs just such an exchange. The masochistic fantasy strategy not only constructs hierarchies, but in a complex and paradoxical way renders the author dependent on those hierarchies. To phrase it another way, Multatuli needs injustice to endure in order to legitimate his own position as the man who will fight it.

How is all of this relevant for Freud? If we agree with Freud that every text appeals to us for conscious and unconscious reasons, then we can rephrase that question: what conscious and unconscious reasons did Freud have for appreciating Multatuli? On a conscious level, Freud and Multatuli share a certain trust in the heritage of the Enlightenment, as I have already mentioned. Both are to some extent idealists, who believe that human behavior can be changed by rational means and who subscribe to a social agenda including a principle of equality. In matters of politics, Multatuli is no doubt the more daring of the two. Although I have pointed to inconsistencies in Multatuli's social and political engagement and reviewed some of its more questionable aspects, he undeniably was perceived as an activist and a real revolutionary. On an unconscious level, Multatuli's texts may have allowed Freud to work through certain fantasies he normally would not have allowed himself. Beyond that, reading Multatuli forced Freud to some extent to deal with the insecurities involved in his own racial and ethnic heritage and in the political agenda with which Freud sympathized. Freud must have been aware of Multatuli's masochism, and perhaps Freud's thought was influenced substantially by Multatuli. Both Freud and Multatuli live on the faultlines of different cultures, one of these cultures in a dominating position, the other one subjugated, suppressed and dominated. Both Freud and Multatuli are more or less hybrids and at the same time also fear their own hybridity.

William McGrath has pointed out that "Freud's favorite heroes—the Carthaginian general, Hannibal; Marcus Brutus, the defender of the Roman Republic; and Karl Moor, the Protagonist of Schiller's *The Robbers*—all shared a passionate dedication to freedom in the face of threatening tyranny" (McGrath, 59). The same can be said for Dekker/Multatuli/Havelaar. All of them have the stigma of the pariah. Of decisive importance, however, for all of these figures seems to be the fact that they acted upon their ideals, their belief in justice, and their desire for freedom. They did, in other words, what Freud was not allowed to do because of his ethnic background, his place in society, and his chosen career as a scientist. It is probably correct to say that "political radicalism" figured "prominently in Freud's adolescent fantasy life" (McGrath, 78), but this political interest was perhaps not entirely limited to his adolescence. Dekker/Multatuli/Havelaar may have acted out some of the things Freud wanted to do.

POSTSCRIPTUM

But what is or was the practical value of Dekker's/Multatuli's political activism? The insight in the masochistic nature of Multatuli's writing raises questions regarding the validity of his political agenda. Does not his masochism, the fact that his philosophy of more rights for the Natives and his identification with the poor ultimately serve only the purpose of acquiring justice for himself, disqualify him as a transculturator? To come to a fairer judgment regarding the political relevance and impact of Multatuli's writings, ideas, and the effectiveness of his masochistic strategies, I would like to follow one more trace. It is interesting to contrast Freud's mirroring of Multatuli with the work of a contemporary Indonesian author. Traces of Multatuli can also be found in Pramoedya Ananta Toer's *Buru Quartet,* a cycle of novels that Toer, who was born in 1925 on Java, initially relayed orally to fellow political prisoners on Buru Island, where he was confined by Indonesian authorities between 1965 and 1979. Toer had also been imprisoned by the Dutch authorities from 1947 to 1949 during the Indonesian war of independence, a time still commonly known in the Netherlands as the period of the "police actions" ("politionele acties"). Pramoedya's *Buru Quartet* is a cycle of historical novels covering the last two years of the nineteenth century and the first two decades of the twentieth, roughly half a century later than *Max Havelaar.* The principal character, narrator, and author of the first three volumes is Minke, a Native writer, furniture tradesman, sometime medical student, journalist, newspaper editor, organizer, political activist, and eventually exiled dissident. While *Max Havelaar* marked the beginning of a phase of intensified colonial self-criticism, *Buru Quartet* marks the next phase, which could be characterized as the beginning of Indonesian nationalism.

Minke's life is clearly influenced by Multatuli, who is initially an intellectual hero in Minke's eyes. He is mentioned as such many times. As his pen name, Minke chooses "Max Tollenaar"—an obvious reference to the main character and title of Multatuli's most famous novel; one of Minke's European friends and sympathizers calls him "the spiritual child of Multatuli" (2:259).[12] Multatuli gives Minke a frame of reference for his perceptions. When he leaves Java, his place of birth, for the first time, the scenery reminds him of Multatuli's "Emerald Horizon" (2:251). The controversial nature of Multatuli's writings is also clear occasionally. Sarah and Miriam, two of Minke's Dutch friends who attended the local Dutch high school a few years before he did, find it hard to believe his claim that Multatuli is starting to be discussed in the classroom (1:139). Indeed, the teacher who introduced him to her students is later forced to return to the Netherlands, although for different reasons.

Multatuli is not only portrayed as a friend to the Native oppressed, however. His work can be coopted by the other party. For instance, Minke discovers that Van Heutsz, who expanded the territory of the Dutch Indies and later became governor of that territory, is an admirer of Multatuli (cf. 3:139). A number of ideas that can either be traced back to Multatuli or whose general acceptance was aided by Multatuli's efforts reappear in *Buru Quartet.* The early twentieth century is the era of the so-called "ethical policy" (cf. volume 4 passim, and Max Lane's commentary, 4:361) in the colonies. In essence this "ethical policy" is a watered-down version of the idea of equality promulgated by the French Revolution, but adapted for colonial purposes. It promises Na-tives more responsibilities, more education, and more freedom—but all of this within a colonial superstructure. *Buru Quartet* complicates a number of the issues Multatuli raises in *Max Havelaar*; the issue of language is just one of these. Multilingualism as presented in *Buru Quartet* is not just a means to improve intercultural communication, but more often an instrument of power as well. Language itself is a battleground, as a number of scenes in *Buru Quartet* demonstrate. At court proceedings and other official meetings, but also at informal gatherings, the question of who is allowed to speak a specific language, and particularly of whether educated Natives are allowed to speak Dutch, has both practical and symbolic consequences. By regulating the use of language, those who are able to speak and understand those languages (the educationally privileged Europeans) have an advantage over Natives whose education was more limited; the Europeans have access to more knowledge. Symbolically, the right to decide who is allowed to speak which language is just another way to reinforce existing hierarchies and therefore existing power structures.

If *Buru Quartet* is written partially with Multatuli and his *Max Havelaar* in mind, to what extent does it provide its readers with an alternative model and indicate other solutions to the dilemmas sketched in *Max Havelaar*? First of all, there are few reasons to idealize the principal character of *Buru Quartet*. In contrast to Multatuli/Havelaar/Dekker, Minke does not survive his quest for greater justice. He is confronted with violence of a very immediate kind: frequent house arrests and intimidations by officials or semi-officials, the murder of his Mixed-Blood wife Annelies, kidnappings by officials, and finally exile and death due to lack of medical care. Significantly, however, Minke never desires to be nor enjoys being an underdog. Minke is no masochist.

What one could call the "masochistic type" is nevertheless a standard figure of the colonial world portrayed in *Buru Quartet*. In an early scene Mr. Mellema, the wealthy Dutch owner of a dairy product company, rudely disturbs the dinner of his Native Nyai (concubine), her children Robert and Annelies, Minke, and another guest. When he insults Minke because he is a Native, Nyai Ontosoroh tells him to shut his mouth and go to his room. Her explanation:

> "It is all for his own good. I treat him the way he wants. This is what he wants. It is the Europeans themselves who have taught me to act this way, Minke, the Europeans themselves." Her voice pleaded with me to believe. "Not at school, but in life."

> (1:49)

Europeans, in other words, want to be masochists, a perception supported in additional passages. Herbert de la Croix, an assistant resident like Max Havelaar and similar to Havelaar in several respects, must also leave his job for unclear reasons. After he has returned to the Netherlands, Minke receives a letter from de la Croix that is full of self-recrimination. Minke does not understand why de la Croix blames himself for what had happened, and finds this attitude unnecessary and not helpful (2:100). Minke has little respect for a masochistic way of dealing with this type of defeat.

To what extent does Minke himself then represent an alternative behavioral strategy for members of subjugated cultures? Jacques Pangamanann (the native but European-educated police commissioner and high government official who, after Minke has been arrested and banned to a remote island, also serves as the narrator of the final volume of *Buru Quartet*) calls Minke a "cultural hybrid" (4:117):

> [Minke's] values change as his situation changes. There is the influence of the environment on his personality, and the impact of his personality on the environment, changes in the means of communication and the people he communicates with, the role of racial discrimination and the law as its shadow, Europe as a teacher and a destroyer.
>
> (4:176)

Again, there are few reasons to idealize Minke, and the realities he faces are quite intimidating and horrendous. At moments, however, Minke is capable of a pluralism of behavioral patterns, of an independence of thinking unknown to Dekker/Multatuli/Havelaar. The principal character of the first three volumes of *Buru Quartet* is rather indifferent toward the question of the origin of his ideals, whether they are rooted in the European Enlightenment or in Native wisdom. Minke's hybridism and his ability to set aside such concerns result at moments in inner liberty—in the possibility to choose among different models of behavior rather than to be bound to just one. Maybe Pramoedya's lesson is that it is not so bad to be a hybrid after all.

Notes

1. Cf. Sander Gilman, *Freud, Race, and Gender* (1993), and *The Case of Sigmund Freud: Medicine and Identity at the Fin de Siècle* (1994).

2. Cf. Freud's letter to Hugo Heller (1907), quoted in: Ernest Jones, *The Life and Work of Sigmund Freud,* vol. 3: 422.

3. Freud "The Sexual Enlightenment of Children (an Open Letter to Dr. M. Fürst)," 133. Freud also quotes Multatuli in his paper "On the Economic Problem of Masochism," not in order to make a point about masochism, but about a more or less unrelated matter. Hillenaar and Schönau have collected a number of psychoanalytic readings of Multatuli in a Dutch volume with a special focus

on "Saïdjah and Adinda," part of *Max Havelaar.* Among these essays, Pietzcker's interpretation comes closest to reading Multatuli according to a concept of masochism, as he refers to Multatuli's "narcissistic-paranoid fantasies" (Hillenaar/ Schönau, 193ff.).

4. The first part of this page reference (e) refers to the English edition of *Max Havelaar,* and the second part (d) to the Dutch edition of Multatuli's collected works, followed by the volume number. The English translation of *Max Havelaar* does not contain all the footnotes which Multatuli added to later editions of his *Max Havelaar.* It does, however, contain many italics that cannot be found in the Dutch original, and those italics have been left out in the citations from this edition. There is no complete English translation of the *Minnebrieven.* Some fragments can be found in *The Oyster and the Eagle: Selected Aphorisms and Parables of Multatuli* (27-43).

5. The same anecdote can be found in a letter of Dekker to his fiancée, quoted by Beekman. The letter, however, is much more explicit about the meaning of the incident for Dekker's psyche: "I tore my clothes and scraped my hands, but not enough as far as I was concerned. There's hardly been any other pleasure in my life that would be capable of transcending the emotion I felt after I had climbed back up. I wouldn't mind having a portrait of me at that moment. Twenty or thirty people, all from the lesser classes and mostly Jews, hailed me . . . O, that damned vanity! I was glowing with pleasure. . . . Everyone looked up to me, everybody mentioned my name, everyone praised me! Those people would have obeyed me at that moment if I—a mere boy—if I had ordered them to . . . and I walked that day on stilts of pride" (Multatuli cited in Beekman, 214; the translation is Beekman's).

6. Gary L. Baker speaks in this context of the "antilinear approach" and "fluidity" in Multatuli's text (139). I would like to thank him for his very helpful criticism of an earlier version of this paper.

7. Beekman borrows these concepts from Bakhtin and seems to use them exclusively with a positive connotation; the "dialogic" and "polyphonic" nature of the text permits the author to let both sides speak. In the following pages I will show that the "dialogic" and "polyphonic" character of Multatuli's novel is interwoven with other, much less egalitarian mechanisms. On a theoretical level, one could also use Bakhtin to make that point. In his systematic overview of "double-voiced discourse" Bakhtin makes very clear that there is rarely a perfect balance of two voices, but that

usually one voice dominates or directs the other (Bakhtin, 199).

8. Cf. Multatuli's footnote regarding the beauty of the women living in the French city Arles: "The fact that the truly characteristic beauty of the women of Arles has been preserved better than at Marseilles may be due to the fact that there was less opportunity for intercourse with foreigners at Arles. In coastal towns such as Marseilles, races lose their purity very quickly." (e333/d1:337)

9. A theoretical overview of the history of the concept of "hybridity" in all its ambiguities is given by Robert J. C. Young in his first chapter "Hybridity and Diaspora" (1-28). In the following pages I will use the concept as a term of cultural criticism in order to indicate a mixing of different languages, cultures and conceptualizations of the world. Hybridity was originally, as Young shows, a category of racial theory. Herzog points out that the contemporary notions of "hybridity" often manifest traces of archaic, racially defined notions and more specifically the nineteenth-century model of the *Mischling*.

10. The fact that Max Havelaar's position is no exception can also be shown by comparing the book with Pramoedya Ananta Toer's *Buru Quartet,* a postcolonial cycle of novels that I discuss below in further detail. Minke, the male protagonist of the first three volumes, is repeatedly accused of being a "philogynist" on basis of his struggle in favor of equal rights for all.

11. I base my summary of Gilman's understanding of "masochism" on his analysis in *Franz Kafka, The Jewish Patient.* There he characterizes masochism ". . . not as self-abnegation or self-flagellation, but as a demand on the part of the author that the literary representation of the sense of powerlessness be understood as a tool to shape those who claim to have power over oneself. The projection of power may be onto the culture in its entirety or onto an individual in that culture. That sense of power and powerlessness is mirrored in the relationship that the individual has with the parent—the power of the parent having been internalized by the child, and the child needing that sense of power beyond him/herself, especially when the parent ages and weakens. Masochism comes to be an acting out of the conflict felt between the claims lodged against the individual and the inability of that individual to counter these claims completely because of the underlying incompleteness, the transitoriness of all constructions of the self. This is heightened when the model for this conflict is the model of child/parent interaction. In such a model the parent must remain powerful for the child to have any sense of his/her relationship to the source of power. The illusion of control that the child has becomes part of a real sense of loss as the child sees the parent's "power" waning. The inevitability of decay and death of the self becomes the repressed moment in this masochistic scene. Thus each person is incomplete within him/herself. *But in a culture in which the inevitability of decay is projected onto specific categories of difference, those who understand themselves as belonging to a stigmatized category can only partially repress this anxiety."* (Gilman 1995, 21-22).

12. All references to *Buru Quartet* list the volume number first, and then the page number. 1 = *This Earth of Mankind,* 2 = *Child of all Nations,* 3 = *Footsteps,* and 4 = *House of Glass.*

Works Cited

Baker, Gary L. 1990. "*Max Havelaar*: a Romantic Novel for Social Fluidity." In *The Low Countries: Multidisciplinary Studies. Publications of the American Association for Netherlandic Studies, vol. 3.* Ed. Margriet Bruijn Lacy. Lanham: UP of America.

Bakhtin, Mikhail. 1987. *Problems of Dostoevsky's Poetics.* Ed. and trans. Caryl Emerson, introd. Wayne C. Booth. Theory and History of Literature, vol. 8. Minneapolis: Minnesota UP.

Beekman, E. M. 1996. "Dekker/Multatuli (1820-1887): The Dialogic Truth from the Tropics." *Troubled Pleasures: Dutch Colonial Literature from the East Indies 1600-1950.* Oxford, New York a.o.: Oxford UP.

Freud, Sigmund. 1959. "The Sexual Enlightenment of Children (an Open Letter to Dr. M. Fürst)." *The Standard Edition of the Complete Psychological Works of Sigmund Freud. Vol. IX (1906-1908). Jensen's 'Gradiva' and Other Works.* Ed. James Strachey in coop. w. Anna Freud. London: The Hogarth Press/The Institute of Psycho-Analysis.

Gilman, Sander. 1993. *Freud, Race, and Gender.* Princeton: Princeton UP.

———. 1994. *The Case of Sigmund Freud: Medicine and Identity at the Fin de Siècle.* Baltimore, London: Johns Hopkins UP.

———. 1995. *Franz Kafka, the Jewish Patient.* New York, London: Routledge.

Herzog, Todd. 1997. "Hybrids and *Mischlinge*: Translating Anglo-American Cultural Theory into German." *German Quarterly* 70: 1-17.

Hillenaar, Henk, and Walter Schönau, eds. 1990. *Literatuur in psychoanalytisch perspectief. Een inleiding met interpretaties van Multatuli's 'Saidjah en Adinda.'* Amsterdam, Atlanta: Rodopi.

Jones, Ernest. 1957. *The Life and Work of Sigmund Freud, vol 3: 1919-1939 The Last Phase.* New York: Basic Books.

Lützeler, Paul Michael. 1990. "The Image of Napoleon in European Romanticism." In *European Romanticism: Literary Cross-Currents, Modes, and Models,* ed. Gerhart Hoffmeister. Detroit: Wayne State UP.

McGrath, William J. 1986. *Freud's Discovery of Psychoanalysis: the Politics of Hysteria.* Ithaca, London: Cornell UP.

Mosse, George L. 1996. *The Image of Man: The Creation of Modern Masculinity.* New York/Oxford: Oxford UP.

Multatuli. 1987. *Max Havelaar or the Coffee Auctions of the Dutch Trading Company.* Trans. Roy Edwards, introd. R. P. Meijer. London: Penguin.

———. 1974. *The Oyster and the Eagle: Selected Aphorisms and Parables of Multatuli.* Ed., trans. and introd. E. M. Beekman. Amherst: Massachusetts UP.

———. 1950. *Max Havelaar of de koffieveilingen der nederlandse handelsmaatschappij. Volledige werken, vol 1.* Amsterdam: G. A. van Oorschot.

———. 1951. *Minnebrieven. Volledige werken, vol 2.* Amsterdam: G. A. van Oorschot.

Nieuwenhuys, Rob. 1982. "Eduard Douwes Dekker." In *Mirror of the Indies: A History of Dutch Colonial Literature.* Trans. Frans van Rosevelt, introd. E. M. Beekman. Amherst: Massachusetts UP.

Oversteegen, J. J. 1984. "Nawoord." In: Multatuli, *Minnebrieven.* Amsterdam: Querido.

Pratt, Marie Louise. 1992. *Imperial Eyes: Travel Writing and Transculturation.* London, New York: Routledge.

Said, Edward W. 1994. *Orientalism.* New York: Vintage.

Stafford, Barbara Maria. 1993. *Body Criticism: Imaging the Unseen in Enlightenment Art and Medicine.* Cambridge MA: MIT UP.

Todorov, Tzvetan. 1992. *The Conquest of America: the Question of the Other.* Trans. Richard Howard. New York: HarperPerennial.

Toer, Pramoedya Ananta. 1996a. *This Earth of Mankind. The Buru Quartet, vol 1.* Trans. and afterward Max Lane. New York, London: Penguin.

———. 1996b. *Child of all Nations. The Buru Quartet, vol 2.* Trans. and introd. Max Lane. New York, London: Penguin.

———. 1996c. *Footsteps. The Buru Quartet, vol 3.* Trans. and introd. Max Lane. New York, London: Penguin.

———. 1996d. *House of Glass. The Buru Quartet, vol 4.* Trans. and introd. Max Lane. New York: Morrow.

Young, Robert J. C. 1995. *Colonial Desire: Hybridity in Theory, Culture and Race.* London, New York: Routledge.

FURTHER READING

Criticism

Baker, Gary L. "Multatuli's *Woutertje Pieterse* and *Vorstenschool*: The (Un)Poetic Truth of Upward Mobility." In *Contemporary Explorations in the Culture of the Low Countries,* edited by William Z. Shetter and Inge Van der Cruysse, pp. 1-11. Lanham, Md.: United Press of America, 1996.

> Examines Multatuli's hostile attitude toward the Dutch bourgeoisie and middle-class values in the works *Wouterje Pieterse* and *Vorstenschool.*

Dubois, Pierre Hubert. *Essays over Multatuli.* Rotterdam: Donker, 1962, 170 p.

> Offers a range of critical reactions to Multatuli's *Max Havelaar,* analyzing such aspects of the work as prose style and historical accuracy.

Hermans, Theo. "The Translator's Voice in Translated Narrative." *Target* 8, no. 1 (1996): 23-48.

> Examines various European translations of *Max Havelaar* in relation to the Dutch original.

King, Peter. "Multatuli's Psyche." *Modern Language Review* 53, no. 1 (January 1958): 60-74.

> Analyzes the character of Max Havelaar, while examining the ways in which Max serves as a representation of Multatuli's perception of himself.

———. *Multatuli.* New York: Twayne Publishers, 1972, 185 p.

> In-depth study of Multatuli's oeuvre.

———. *Gezelle and Multatuli: A Question of Literature and Social History.* Hull, England: University of Hull, 1978, 27 p.

> Compares Multatuli's life and literary career with that of Flemish poet Guido Gezelle, examining the authors' respective impacts on Dutch society and culture.

Lawrence, D. H. Introduction to *Max Havelaar; or, The Coffee Auctions of the Dutch Trading Company,* by Multatuli, edited and translated by Roy Edwards, pp. 11-15. Leyden, Netherlands: Sijthoff, 1967.

Introduction to the 1927 English translation of *Max Havelaar*. Analyzes the various shifts in literary attitudes that occurred in the decades after the novel's original publication.

Meijer, R. P. Introduction to *Max Havelaar; Or the Coffee Auctions of a Dutch Trading Company,* by Multatuli, translated by Roy Edwards, pp. 1-13. London: Penguin Books Ltd, 1987.

   Discusses the complicated circumstances that surrounded *Max Havelaar*'s original publication, while offering a brief analysis of the work's major themes.

Niekerk, Carl. "Rethinking a Problematic Constellation: Postcolonialism and Its Germanic Contexts." *Comparative Studies of South Asia, Africa and the Middle East* 23, nos. 1-2 (2003): 58-69.

   Compares representations of Dutch colonialism in Multatuli's *Max Havelaar* and Pramoedya Ananta Toer's *Buru Quartet.*

Nieuwenhuys, Rob. "Edward Douwes Dekker." In *Mirror of the Indies: A History of Dutch Colonial Literature,* translated by Frans van Rosevelt, pp. 77-93. Amherst: University of Massachusetts Press, 1982.

   Discusses the importance of *Max Havelaar* in Multatuli's development as a writer.

Schreurs, Peter. "Multatuli, a Soul-brother of Rizal." *Philippine Quarterly of Culture and Society* 14, no. 3 (September 1986): 189-95.

   Evaluates the influence of Multatuli's *Max Havelaar* on José Rizal's *Noli Me Tangere.*

Ter Braak, Menno, and Conrad Busken Huet. *Over Multatuli,* Amsterdam: Van Oorschot, 1950, 80 p.

   Includes critical interpretations of Multatuli's work from a number of leading Dutch scholars.

van den Bergh, Hans. "A Champion with a Cause? Conflicting Views of Multatuli." *Low Countries* (1996-97): 80-88.

   Investigates controversies surrounding Multatuli's critical reputation, his record as an administrator in the Dutch East Indies, and his anticolonial politics.

Van Niel, Robert. "A Perception of a Perception of a Perception: Multatuli's View of Java in the 1850's." *Canadian Journal of Netherlandic Studies/Revue canadienne d'études néerlandaises* 12, no. 1 (spring 1991): 21-9.

   Discusses Multatuli's portrayal of Dutch colonial culture in *Max Havelaar.*

van Oostrum, Duco. "Tina's Sneeze: Female Oppression in Multatuli's *Max Havelaar.*" *Dutch Crossing* 42 (autumn 1990): 85-95.

   Examines the issue of the exploitation of women in *Max Havelaar.*

Vanderauwera, Ria. "Texts and Contexts of Translation: A Dutch Classic in English." *Dispositio* 7, nos. 19-21 (1982): 111-21.

   Provides a detailed analysis of the three major English translations of *Max Havelaar.*

Additional coverage of Multatuli's life and career is contained in the following sources published by Thomson Gale: *Literature Resource Center*; **and** *Reference Guide to World Literature,* **Eds. 2, 3.**

How to Use This Index

> **Calvino, Italo**
> 1923-1985 .... CLC **5, 8, 11, 22, 33, 39,**
> **73; SSC 3, 48**

list all author entries in the following Gale Literary Criticism series:

AAL = Asian American Literature
BG = The Beat Generation: A Gale Critical Companion
BLC = Black Literature Criticism
BLCS = Black Literature Criticism Supplement
CLC = Contemporary Literary Criticism
CLR = Children's Literature Review
CMLC = Classical and Medieval Literature Criticism
DC = Drama Criticism
HLC = Hispanic Literature Criticism
HLCS = Hispanic Literature Criticism Supplement
HR = Harlem Renaissance: A Gale Critical Companion
LC = Literature Criticism from 1400 to 1800
NCLC = Nineteenth-Century Literature Criticism
NNAL = Native North American Literature
PC = Poetry Criticism
SSC = Short Story Criticism
TCLC = Twentieth-Century Literary Criticism
WLC = World Literature Criticism, 1500 to the Present
WLCS = World Literature Criticism Supplement

The cross-references

> See also CA 85-88, 116; CANR 23, 61;
> DAM NOV; DLB 196; EW 13; MTCW 1, 2;
> RGSF 2; RGWL 2; SFW 4; SSFS 12

list all author entries in the following Gale biographical and literary sources:

AAYA = Authors & Artists for Young Adults
AFAW = African American Writers
AFW = African Writers
AITN = Authors in the News
AMW = American Writers
AMWR = American Writers Retrospective Supplement
AMWS = American Writers Supplement
ANW = American Nature Writers
AW = Ancient Writers
BEST = Bestsellers
BPFB = Beacham's Encyclopedia of Popular Fiction: Biography and Resources
BRW = British Writers
BRWS = British Writers Supplement
BW = Black Writers
BYA = Beacham's Guide to Literature for Young Adults
CA = Contemporary Authors
CAAS = Contemporary Authors Autobiography Series
CABS = Contemporary Authors Bibliographical Series
CAD = Contemporary American Dramatists
CANR = Contemporary Authors New Revision Series
CAP = Contemporary Authors Permanent Series
CBD = Contemporary British Dramatists
CCA = Contemporary Canadian Authors
CD = Contemporary Dramatists
CDALB = Concise Dictionary of American Literary Biography
CDALBS = Concise Dictionary of American Literary Biography Supplement
CDBLB = Concise Dictionary of British Literary Biography

CMW = *St. James Guide to Crime & Mystery Writers*

CN = *Contemporary Novelists*

CP = *Contemporary Poets*

CPW = *Contemporary Popular Writers*

CSW = *Contemporary Southern Writers*

CWD = *Contemporary Women Dramatists*

CWP = *Contemporary Women Poets*

CWRI = *St. James Guide to Children's Writers*

CWW = *Contemporary World Writers*

DA = *DISCovering Authors*

DA3 = *DISCovering Authors 3.0*

DAB = *DISCovering Authors: British Edition*

DAC = *DISCovering Authors: Canadian Edition*

DAM = *DISCovering Authors: Modules*

   DRAM: *Dramatists Module;* **MST:** *Most-studied Authors Module;*

   MULT: *Multicultural Authors Module;* **NOV:** *Novelists Module;*

   POET: *Poets Module;* **POP:** *Popular Fiction and Genre Authors Module*

DFS = *Drama for Students*

DLB = *Dictionary of Literary Biography*

DLBD = *Dictionary of Literary Biography Documentary Series*

DLBY = *Dictionary of Literary Biography Yearbook*

DNFS = *Literature of Developing Nations for Students*

EFS = *Epics for Students*

EXPN = *Exploring Novels*

EXPP = *Exploring Poetry*

EXPS = *Exploring Short Stories*

EW = *European Writers*

FANT = *St. James Guide to Fantasy Writers*

FW = *Feminist Writers*

GFL = *Guide to French Literature,* Beginnings to 1789, 1798 to the Present

GLL = *Gay and Lesbian Literature*

HGG = *St. James Guide to Horror, Ghost & Gothic Writers*

HW = *Hispanic Writers*

IDFW = *International Dictionary of Films and Filmmakers: Writers and Production Artists*

IDTP = *International Dictionary of Theatre: Playwrights*

LAIT = *Literature and Its Times*

LAW = *Latin American Writers*

JRDA = *Junior DISCovering Authors*

MAICYA = *Major Authors and Illustrators for Children and Young Adults*

MAICYAS = *Major Authors and Illustrators for Children and Young Adults Supplement*

MAWW = *Modern American Women Writers*

MJW = *Modern Japanese Writers*

MTCW = *Major 20th-Century Writers*

NCFS = *Nonfiction Classics for Students*

NFS = *Novels for Students*

PAB = *Poets: American and British*

PFS = *Poetry for Students*

RGAL = *Reference Guide to American Literature*

RGEL = *Reference Guide to English Literature*

RGSF = *Reference Guide to Short Fiction*

RGWL = *Reference Guide to World Literature*

RHW = *Twentieth-Century Romance and Historical Writers*

SAAS = *Something about the Author Autobiography Series*

SATA = *Something about the Author*

SFW = *St. James Guide to Science Fiction Writers*

SSFS = *Short Stories for Students*

TCWW = *Twentieth-Century Western Writers*

WLIT = *World Literature and Its Times*

WP = *World Poets*

YABC = *Yesterday's Authors of Books for Children*

YAW = *St. James Guide to Young Adult Writers*

Literary Criticism Series
Cumulative Author Index

Alexie, Sherman (Joseph, Jr.)
1966- .... **CLC 96, 154; NNAL; PC 53**
See also AAYA 28; BYA 15; CA 138;
CANR 65, 95, 133; CN 7; DA3; DAM
MULT; DLB 175, 206, 278; LATS 1:2;
MTCW 2; MTFW 2005; NFS 17; SSFS
18

al-Farabi 870(?)-950 .... **CMLC 58**
See also DLB 115

Alfau, Felipe 1902-1999 .... **CLC 66**
See also CA 137

Alfieri, Vittorio 1749-1803 .... **NCLC 101**
See also EW 4; RGWL 2, 3; WLIT 7

Alfonso X 1221-1284 .... **CMLC 78**

Alfred, Jean Gaston
See Ponge, Francis

Alger, Horatio, Jr. 1832-1899 .... **NCLC 8, 83**
See also CLR 87; DLB 42; LAIT 2; RGAL
4; SATA 16; TUS

Al-Ghazali, Muhammad ibn Muhammad
1058-1111 .... **CMLC 50**
See also DLB 115

Algren, Nelson 1909-1981 ..... **CLC 4, 10, 33;**
SSC 33
See also AMWS 9; BPFB 1; CA 13-16R;
103; CANR 20, 61; CDALB 1941-1968;
CN 1, 2; DLB 9; DLBY 1981, 1982,
2000; EWL 3; MAL 5; MTCW 1, 2;
MTFW 2005; RGAL 4; RGSF 2

al-Hariri, al-Qasim ibn 'Ali Abu
Muhammad al-Basri
1054-1122 .... **CMLC 63**
See also RGWL 3

Ali, Ahmed 1908-1998 .... **CLC 69**
See also CA 25-28R; CANR 15, 34; CN 1,
2, 3, 4, 5; EWL 3

Ali, Tariq 1943- .... **CLC 173**
See also CA 25-28R; CANR 10, 99

Alighieri, Dante
See Dante
See also WLIT 7

al-Kindi, Abu Yusuf Ya'qub ibn Ishaq c.
801-c. 873 .... **CMLC 80**

Allan, John B.
See Westlake, Donald E(dwin)

Allan, Sidney
See Hartmann, Sadakichi

Allan, Sydney
See Hartmann, Sadakichi

Allard, Janet .... **CLC 59**

Allen, Edward 1948- .... **CLC 59**

Allen, Fred 1894-1956 .... **TCLC 87**

Allen, Paula Gunn 1939- .... **CLC 84, 202;**
NNAL
See also AMWS 4; CA 112; 143; CANR
63, 130; CWP; DA3; DAM MULT; DLB
175; FW; MTCW 2; MTFW 2005; RGAL
4; TCWW 2

Allen, Roland
See Ayckbourn, Alan

Allen, Sarah A.
See Hopkins, Pauline Elizabeth

Allen, Sidney H.
See Hartmann, Sadakichi

Allen, Woody 1935- .... **CLC 16, 52, 195**
See also AAYA 10, 51; AMWS 15; CA 33-
36R; CANR 27, 38, 63, 128; DAM POP;
DLB 44; MTCW 1; SSFS 21

Allende, Isabel 1942- ... **CLC 39, 57, 97, 170;**
HLC 1; SSC 65; WLCS
See also AAYA 18; CA 125; 130; CANR
51, 74, 129; CDWLB 3; CLR 99; CWW
2; DA3; DAM MULT, NOV; DLB 145;
DNFS 1; EWL 3; FL 1:5; FW; HW 1, 2;
INT CA-130; LAIT 5; LAWS 1; LMFS 2;
MTCW 1, 2; MTFW 2005; NCFS 1; NFS
6, 18; RGSF 2; RGWL 3; SATA 163;
SSFS 11, 16; WLIT 1

Alleyn, Ellen
See Rossetti, Christina

Alleyne, Carla D. .... **CLC 65**

Allingham, Margery (Louise)
1904-1966 .... **CLC 19**
See also CA 5-8R; 25-28R; CANR 4, 58;
CMW 4; DLB 77; MSW; MTCW 1, 2

Allingham, William 1824-1889 ...... **NCLC 25**
See also DLB 35; RGEL 2

Allison, Dorothy E. 1949- .... **CLC 78, 153**
See also AAYA 53; CA 140; CANR 66, 107;
CN 7; CSW; DA3; FW; MTCW 2; MTFW
2005; NFS 11; RGAL 4

Alloula, Malek .... **CLC 65**

Allston, Washington 1779-1843 .... **NCLC 2**
See also DLB 1, 235

Almedingen, E. M. .... **CLC 12**
See Almedingen, Martha Edith von
See also SATA 3

Almedingen, Martha Edith von 1898-1971
See Almedingen, E. M.
See also CA 1-4R; CANR 1

Almodovar, Pedro 1949(?)- .... **CLC 114;**
HLCS 1
See also CA 133; CANR 72; HW 2

Almqvist, Carl Jonas Love
1793-1866 .... **NCLC 42**

al-Mutanabbi, Ahmad ibn al-Husayn Abu
al-Tayyib al-Jufi al-Kindi
915-965 .... **CMLC 66**
See Mutanabbi, Al-
See also RGWL 3

Alonso, Damaso 1898-1990 .... **CLC 14**
See also CA 110; 131; 130; CANR 72; DLB
108; EWL 3; HW 1, 2

Alov
See Gogol, Nikolai (Vasilyevich)

al'Sadaawi, Nawal
See El Saadawi, Nawal
See also FW

Al-Shaykh 1945- .... **CLC 218**
See also CA 135; CANR 111; WLIT 6

Al Siddik
See Rolfe, Frederick (William Serafino Aus-
tin Lewis Mary)
See also GLL 1; RGEL 2

Alta 1942- .... **CLC 19**
See also CA 57-60

Alter, Robert B(ernard) 1935- .... **CLC 34**
See also CA 49-52; CANR 1, 47, 100

Alther, Lisa 1944- .... **CLC 7, 41**
See also BPFB 1; CA 65-68; CAAS 30;
CANR 12, 30, 51; CN 4, 5, 6, 7; CSW;
GLL 2; MTCW 1

Althusser, L.
See Althusser, Louis

Althusser, Louis 1918-1990 .... **CLC 106**
See also CA 131; 132; CANR 102; DLB
242

Altman, Robert 1925- .... **CLC 16, 116**
See also CA 73-76; CANR 43

Alurista .... **HLCS 1; PC 34**
See Urista (Heredia), Alberto (Baltazar)
See also CA 45-48R; DLB 82; LLW

Alvarez, A(lfred) 1929- .... **CLC 5, 13**
See also CA 1-4R; CANR 3, 33, 63, 101,
134; CN 3, 4, 5, 6; CP 1, 2, 3, 4, 5, 6, 7;
DLB 14, 40; MTFW 2005

Alvarez, Alejandro Rodriguez 1903-1965
See Casona, Alejandro
See also CA 131; 93-96; HW 1

Alvarez, Julia 1950- .... **CLC 93; HLCS 1**
See also AAYA 25; AMWS 7; CA 147;
CANR 69, 101, 133; DA3; DLB 282;
LATS 1:2; LLW; MTCW 2; MTFW 2005;
NFS 5, 9; SATA 129; WLIT 1

Alvaro, Corrado 1896-1956 .... **TCLC 60**
See also CA 163; DLB 264; EWL 3

Amado, Jorge 1912-2001 ... **CLC 13, 40, 106;**
HLC 1
See also CA 77-80; 201; CANR 35, 74, 135;
CWW 2; DAM MULT, NOV; DLB 113,
307; EWL 3; HW 2; LAW; LAWS 1;
MTCW 1, 2; MTFW 2005; RGWL 2, 3;
TWA; WLIT 1

Ambler, Eric 1909-1998 .... **CLC 4, 6, 9**
See also BRWS 4; CA 9-12R; 171; CANR
7, 38, 74; CMW 4; CN 1, 2, 3, 4, 5, 6;
DLB 77; MSW; MTCW 1, 2; TEA

Ambrose, Stephen E(dward)
1936-2002 .... **CLC 145**
See also AAYA 44; CA 1-4R; 209; CANR
3, 43, 57, 83, 105; MTFW 2005; NCFS 2;
SATA 40, 138

Amichai, Yehuda 1924-2000 .. **CLC 9, 22, 57,**
116; PC 38
See also CA 85-88; 189; CANR 46, 60, 99,
132; CWW 2; EWL 3; MTCW 1, 2;
MTFW 2005; WLIT 6

Amichai, Yehudah
See Amichai, Yehuda

Amiel, Henri Frederic 1821-1881 .... **NCLC 4**
See also DLB 217

Amis, Kingsley (William)
1922-1995 ...... **CLC 1, 2, 3, 5, 8, 13, 40,**
44, 129
See also AITN 2; BPFB 1; BRWS 2; CA
9-12R; 150; CANR 8, 28, 54; CDBLB
1945-1960; CN 1, 2, 3, 4, 5, 6; CP 1, 2,
3, 4; DA; DA3; DAB; DAC; DAM MST,
NOV; DLB 15, 27, 100, 139; DLBY 1996;
EWL 3; HGG; INT CANR-8; MTCW 1,
2; MTFW 2005; RGEL 2; RGSF 2; SFW
4

Amis, Martin (Louis) 1949- .... **CLC 4, 9, 38,**
62, 101, 213
See also BEST 90:3; BRWS 4; CA 65-68;
CANR 8, 27, 54, 73, 95, 132; CN 5, 6, 7;
DA3; DLB 14, 194; EWL 3; INT CANR-
27; MTCW 2; MTFW 2005

Ammianus Marcellinus c. 330-c.
395 .... **CMLC 60**
See also AW 2; DLB 211

Ammons, A(rchie) R(andolph)
1926-2001 ...... **CLC 2, 3, 5, 8, 9, 25, 57,**
108; PC 16
See also AITN 1; AMWS 7; CA 9-12R;
193; CANR 6, 36, 51, 73, 107; CP 1, 2,
3, 4, 5, 6, 7; CSW; DAM POET; DLB 5,
165; EWL 3; MAL 5; MTCW 1, 2; PFS
19; RGAL 4; TCLE 1:1

Amo, Tauraatua i
See Adams, Henry (Brooks)

Amory, Thomas 1691(?)-1788 .... **LC 48**
See also DLB 39

Anand, Mulk Raj 1905-2004 ...... **CLC 23, 93**
See also CA 65-68; 231; CANR 32, 64; CN
1, 2, 3, 4, 5, 6, 7; DAM NOV; EWL 3;
MTCW 1, 2; MTFW 2005; RGSF 2

Anatol
See Schnitzler, Arthur

Anaximander c. 611B.C.-c.
546B.C. .... **CMLC 22**

Anaya, Rudolfo A(lfonso) 1937- ...... **CLC 23,**
148; HLC 1
See also AAYA 20; BYA 13; CA 45-48;
CAAS 4; CANR 1, 32, 51, 124; CN 4, 5,
6, 7; DAM MULT, NOV; DLB 82, 206,
278; HW 1; LAIT 5; LLW; MAL 5;
MTCW 1, 2; MTFW 2005; NFS 12;
RGAL 4; RGSF 2; TCWW 2; WLIT 1

Andersen, Hans Christian
1805-1875 .... **NCLC 7, 79; SSC 6, 56;**
WLC
See also AAYA 57; CLR 6; DA; DA3;
DAB; DAC; DAM MST, POP; EW 6;
MAICYA 1, 2; RGSF 2; RGWL 2, 3;
SATA 100; TWA; WCH; YABC 1

Bishop, John Peale 1892-1944 ..... **TCLC 103**
See also CA 107; 155; DLB 4, 9, 45; MAL
5; RGAL 4

Bissett, Bill 1939- .... **CLC 18; PC 14**
See also CA 69-72; CAAS 19; CANR 15;
CCA 1; CP 1, 2, 3, 4, 5, 6, 7; DLB 53;
MTCW 1

Bissoondath, Neil (Devindra)
1955- .... **CLC 120**
See also CA 136; CANR 123; CN 6, 7;
DAC

Bitov, Andrei (Georgievich) 1937- ... **CLC 57**
See also CA 142; DLB 302

Biyidi, Alexandre 1932-
See Beti, Mongo
See also BW 1, 3; CA 114; 124; CANR 81;
DA3; MTCW 1, 2

Bjarme, Brynjolf
See Ibsen, Henrik (Johan)

Bjoernson, Bjoernstjerne (Martinius)
1832-1910 .... **TCLC 7, 37**
See also CA 104

Black, Robert
See Holdstock, Robert P.

Blackburn, Paul 1926-1971 .... **CLC 9, 43**
See also BG 1:2; CA 81-84; 33-36R; CANR
34; CP 1; DLB 16; DLBY 1981

Black Elk 1863-1950 .... **NNAL; TCLC 33**
See also CA 144; DAM MULT; MTCW 2;
MTFW 2005; WP

Black Hawk 1767-1838 .... **NNAL**

Black Hobart
See Sanders, (James) Ed(ward)

Blacklin, Malcolm
See Chambers, Aidan

Blackmore, R(ichard) D(oddridge)
1825-1900 .... **TCLC 27**
See also CA 120; DLB 18; RGEL 2

Blackmur, R(ichard) P(almer)
1904-1965 .... **CLC 2, 24**
See also AMWS 2; CA 11-12; 25-28R;
CANR 71; CAP 1; DLB 63; EWL 3;
MAL 5

Black Tarantula
See Acker, Kathy

Blackwood, Algernon (Henry)
1869-1951 .... **TCLC 5**
See also CA 105; 150; DLB 153, 156, 178;
HGG; SUFW 1

Blackwood, Caroline (Maureen)
1931-1996 .... **CLC 6, 9, 100**
See also BRWS 9; CA 85-88; 151; CANR
32, 61, 65; CN 3, 4, 5, 6; DLB 14, 207;
HGG; MTCW 1

Blade, Alexander
See Hamilton, Edmond; Silverberg, Robert

Blaga, Lucian 1895-1961 .... **CLC 75**
See also CA 157; DLB 220; EWL 3

Blair, Eric (Arthur) 1903-1950 .... **TCLC 123**
See Orwell, George
See also CA 104; 132; DA; DA3; DAB;
DAC; DAM MST, NOV; MTCW 1, 2;
MTFW 2005; SATA 29

Blair, Hugh 1718-1800 .... **NCLC 75**

Blais, Marie-Claire 1939- .... **CLC 2, 4, 6, 13,**
22
See also CA 21-24R; CAAS 4; CANR 38,
75, 93; CWW 2; DAC; DAM MST; DLB
53; EWL 3; FW; MTCW 1, 2; MTFW
2005; TWA

Blaise, Clark 1940- .... **CLC 29**
See also AITN 2; CA 53-56, 231; CAAE
231; CAAS 3; CANR 5, 66, 106; CN 4,
5, 6, 7; DLB 53; RGSF 2

Blake, Fairley
See De Voto, Bernard (Augustine)

Blake, Nicholas
See Day Lewis, C(ecil)
See also DLB 77; MSW

Blake, Sterling
See Benford, Gregory (Albert)

Blake, William 1757-1827 . **NCLC 13, 37, 57,**
127; PC 12, 63; WLC
See also AAYA 47; BRW 3; BRWR 1; CD-
BLB 1789-1832; CLR 52; DA; DA3;
DAB; DAC; DAM MST, POET; DLB 93,
163; EXPP; LATS 1:1; LMFS 1; MAI-
CYA 1, 2; PAB; PFS 2, 12; SATA 30;
TEA; WCH; WLIT 3; WP

Blanchot, Maurice 1907-2003 .... **CLC 135**
See also CA 117; 144; 213; CANR 138;
DLB 72, 296; EWL 3

Blasco Ibanez, Vicente 1867-1928 . **TCLC 12**
See Ibanez, Vicente Blasco
See also BPFB 1; CA 110; 131; CANR 81;
DA3; DAM NOV; EW 8; EWL 3; HW 1,
2; MTCW 1

Blatty, William Peter 1928- .... **CLC 2**
See also CA 5-8R; CANR 9, 124; DAM
POP; HGG

Bleeck, Oliver
See Thomas, Ross (Elmore)

Blessing, Lee (Knowlton) 1949- .... **CLC 54**
See also CA 236; CAD; CD 5, 6

Blight, Rose
See Greer, Germaine

Blish, James (Benjamin) 1921-1975 . **CLC 14**
See also BPFB 1; CA 1-4R; 57-60; CANR
3; CN 2; DLB 8; MTCW 1; SATA 66;
SCFW 1, 2; SFW 4

Bliss, Frederick
See Card, Orson Scott

Bliss, Reginald
See Wells, H(erbert) G(eorge)

Blixen, Karen (Christentze Dinesen)
1885-1962
See Dinesen, Isak
See also CA 25-28; CANR 22, 50; CAP 2;
DA3; DLB 214; LMFS 1; MTCW 1, 2;
SATA 44; SSFS 20

Bloch, Robert (Albert) 1917-1994 .... **CLC 33**
See also AAYA 29; CA 5-8R, 179; 146;
CAAE 179; CAAS 20; CANR 5, 78;
DA3; DLB 44; HGG; INT CANR-5;
MTCW 2; SATA 12; SATA-Obit 82; SFW
4; SUFW 1, 2

Blok, Alexander (Alexandrovich)
1880-1921 .... **PC 21; TCLC 5**
See also CA 104; 183; DLB 295; EW 9;
EWL 3; LMFS 2; RGWL 2, 3

Blom, Jan
See Breytenbach, Breyten

Bloom, Harold 1930- .... **CLC 24, 103**
See also CA 13-16R; CANR 39, 75, 92,
133; DLB 67; EWL 3; MTCW 2; MTFW
2005; RGAL 4

Bloomfield, Aurelius
See Bourne, Randolph S(illiman)

Bloomfield, Robert 1766-1823 ..... **NCLC 145**
See also DLB 93

Blount, Roy (Alton), Jr. 1941- .... **CLC 38**
See also CA 53-56; CANR 10, 28, 61, 125;
CSW; INT CANR-28; MTCW 1, 2;
MTFW 2005

Blowsnake, Sam 1875-(?) .... **NNAL**

Bloy, Leon 1846-1917 .... **TCLC 22**
See also CA 121; 183; DLB 123; GFL 1789
to the Present

Blue Cloud, Peter (Aroniawenrate)
1933- .... **NNAL**
See also CA 117; CANR 40; DAM MULT

Bluggage, Oranthy
See Alcott, Louisa May

Blume, Judy (Sussman) 1938- .... **CLC 12, 30**
See also AAYA 3, 26; BYA 1, 8, 12; CA 29-
32R; CANR 13, 37, 66, 124; CLR 2, 15,
69; CPW; DA3; DAM NOV, POP; DLB

52; JRDA; MAICYA 1, 2; MAICYAS 1;
MTCW 1, 2; MTFW 2005; SATA 2, 31,
79, 142; WYA; YAW

Blunden, Edmund (Charles)
1896-1974 .... **CLC 2, 56; PC 66**
See also BRW 6; BRWS 11; CA 17-18; 45-
48; CANR 54; CAP 2; CP 1, 2; DLB 20,
100, 155; MTCW 1; PAB

Bly, Robert (Elwood) 1926- .... **CLC 1, 2, 5,**
10, 15, 38, 128; PC 39
See also AMWS 4; CA 5-8R; CANR 41,
73, 125; CP 1, 2, 3, 4, 5, 6, 7; DA3; DAM
POET; DLB 5; EWL 3; MAL 5; MTCW
1, 2; MTFW 2005; PFS 6, 17; RGAL 4

Boas, Franz 1858-1942 .... **TCLC 56**
See also CA 115; 181

Bobette
See Simenon, Georges (Jacques Christian)

Boccaccio, Giovanni 1313-1375 ... **CMLC 13,**
57; SSC 10, 87
See also EW 2; RGSF 2; RGWL 2, 3; TWA;
WLIT 7

Bochco, Steven 1943- .... **CLC 35**
See also AAYA 11; CA 124; 138

Bode, Sigmund
See O'Doherty, Brian

Bodel, Jean 1167(?)-1210 .... **CMLC 28**

Bodenheim, Maxwell 1892-1954 .... **TCLC 44**
See also CA 110; 187; DLB 9, 45; MAL 5;
RGAL 4

Bodenheimer, Maxwell
See Bodenheim, Maxwell

Bodker, Cecil 1927-
See Bodker, Cecil

Bodker, Cecil 1927- .... **CLC 21**
See also CA 73-76; CANR 13, 44, 111;
CLR 23; MAICYA 1, 2; SATA 14, 133

Boell, Heinrich (Theodor)
1917-1985 ..... **CLC 2, 3, 6, 9, 11, 15, 27,**
32, 72; SSC 23; WLC
See Boll, Heinrich (Theodor)
See also CA 21-24R; 116; CANR 24; DA;
DA3; DAB; DAC; DAM MST, NOV;
DLB 69; DLBY 1985; MTCW 1, 2;
MTFW 2005; SSFS 20; TWA

Boerne, Alfred
See Doeblin, Alfred

Boethius c. 480-c. 524 .... **CMLC 15**
See also DLB 115; RGWL 2, 3

Boff, Leonardo (Genezio Darci)
1938- .... **CLC 70; HLC 1**
See also CA 150; DAM MULT; HW 2

Bogan, Louise 1897-1970 .... **CLC 4, 39, 46,**
93; PC 12
See also AMWS 3; CA 73-76; 25-28R;
CANR 33, 82; CP 1; DAM POET; DLB
45, 169; EWL 3; MAL 5; MAWW;
MTCW 1, 2; PFS 21; RGAL 4

Bogarde, Dirk
See Van Den Bogarde, Derek Jules Gaspard
Ulric Niven
See also DLB 14

Bogosian, Eric 1953- .... **CLC 45, 141**
See also CA 138; CAD; CANR 102; CD 5,
6

Bograd, Larry 1953- .... **CLC 35**
See also CA 93-96; CANR 57; SAAS 21;
SATA 33, 89; WYA

Boiardo, Matteo Maria 1441-1494 .... **LC 6**

Boileau-Despreaux, Nicolas 1636-1711 . **LC 3**
See also DLB 268; EW 3; GFL Beginnings
to 1789; RGWL 2, 3

Boissard, Maurice
See Leautaud, Paul

Bojer, Johan 1872-1959 .... **TCLC 64**
See also CA 189; EWL 3

Bok, Edward W(illiam)
1863-1930 .... **TCLC 101**
See also CA 217; DLB 91; DLBD 16

EXPN; EXPS; HGG; LAIT 3, 5; LATS
1:2; LMFS 2; MAL 5; MTCW 1, 2;
MTFW 2005; NFS 1, 22; RGAL 4; RGSF
2; SATA 11, 64, 123; SCFW 1, 2; SFW 4;
SSFS 1, 20; SUFW 1, 2; TUS; YAW

Braddon, Mary Elizabeth
1837-1915 .... **TCLC 111**
See also BRWS 8; CA 108; 179; CMW 4;
DLB 18, 70, 156; HGG

Bradfield, Scott (Michael) 1955- .... **SSC 65**
See also CA 147; CANR 90; HGG; SUFW
2

Bradford, Gamaliel 1863-1932 .... **TCLC 36**
See also CA 160; DLB 17

Bradford, William 1590-1657 .... **LC 64**
See also DLB 24, 30; RGAL 4

Bradley, David (Henry), Jr. 1950- .... **BLC 1;**
CLC 23, 118
See also BW 1, 3; CA 104; CANR 26, 81;
CN 4, 5, 6, 7; DAM MULT; DLB 33

Bradley, John Ed(mund, Jr.) 1958- . **CLC 55**
See also CA 139; CANR 99; CN 6, 7; CSW

Bradley, Marion Zimmer
1930-1999 .... **CLC 30**
See Chapman, Lee; Dexter, John; Gardner,
Miriam; Ives, Morgan; Rivers, Elfrida
See also AAYA 40; BPFB 1; CA 57-60; 185;
CAAS 10; CANR 7, 31, 51, 75, 107;
CPW; DA3; DAM POP; DLB 8; FANT;
FW; MTCW 1, 2; MTFW 2005; SATA 90,
139; SATA-Obit 116; SFW 4; SUFW 2;
YAW

Bradshaw, John 1933- .... **CLC 70**
See also CA 138; CANR 61

Bradstreet, Anne 1612(?)-1672 ...... **LC 4, 30;**
PC 10
See also AMWS 1; CDALB 1640-1865;
DA; DA3; DAC; DAM MST, POET; DLB
24; EXPP; FW; PFS 6; RGAL 4; TUS;
WP

Brady, Joan 1939- .... **CLC 86**
See also CA 141

Bragg, Melvyn 1939- .... **CLC 10**
See also BEST 89:3; CA 57-60; CANR 10,
48, 89; CN 1, 2, 3, 4, 5, 6, 7; DLB 14,
271; RHW

Brahe, Tycho 1546-1601 .... **LC 45**
See also DLB 300

Braine, John (Gerard) 1922-1986 . **CLC 1, 3,**
41
See also CA 1-4R; 120; CANR 1, 33; CD-
BLB 1945-1960; CN 1, 2, 3, 4; DLB 15;
DLBY 1986; EWL 3; MTCW 1

Braithwaite, William Stanley (Beaumont)
1878-1962 .... **BLC 1; HR 1:2; PC 52**
See also BW 1; CA 125; DAM MULT; DLB
50, 54; MAL 5

Bramah, Ernest 1868-1942 .... **TCLC 72**
See also CA 156; CMW 4; DLB 70; FANT

Brammer, Billy Lee
See Brammer, William

Brammer, William 1929-1978 .... **CLC 31**
See also CA 235; 77-80

Brancati, Vitaliano 1907-1954 .... **TCLC 12**
See also CA 109; DLB 264; EWL 3

Brancato, Robin F(idler) 1936- .... **CLC 35**
See also AAYA 9, 68; BYA 6; CA 69-72;
CANR 11, 45; CLR 32; JRDA; MAICYA
2; MAICYAS 1; SAAS 9; SATA 97;
WYA; YAW

Brand, Dionne 1953- .... **CLC 192**
See also BW 2; CA 143; CANR 143; CWP

Brand, Max
See Faust, Frederick (Schiller)
See also BPFB 1; TCWW 1, 2

Brand, Millen 1906-1980 .... **CLC 7**
See also CA 21-24R; 97-100; CANR 72

Branden, Barbara .... **CLC 44**
See also CA 148

Brandes, Georg (Morris Cohen)
1842-1927 .... **TCLC 10**
See also CA 105; 189; DLB 300

Brandys, Kazimierz 1916-2000 .... **CLC 62**
See also CA 239; EWL 3

Branley, Franklyn M(ansfield)
1915-2002 .... **CLC 21**
See also CA 33-36R; 207; CANR 14, 39;
CLR 13; MAICYA 1, 2; SAAS 16; SATA
4, 68, 136

Brant, Beth (E.) 1941- .... **NNAL**
See also CA 144; FW

Brant, Sebastian 1457-1521 .... **LC 112**
See also DLB 179; RGWL 2, 3

Brathwaite, Edward Kamau
1930- .... **BLCS; CLC 11; PC 56**
See also BW 2, 3; CA 25-28R; CANR 11,
26, 47, 107; CDWLB 3; CP 1, 2, 3, 4, 5,
6, 7; DAM POET; DLB 125; EWL 3

Brathwaite, Kamau
See Brathwaite, Edward Kamau

Brautigan, Richard (Gary)
1935-1984 .... **CLC 1, 3, 5, 9, 12, 34, 42;**
TCLC 133
See also BPFB 1; CA 53-56; 113; CANR
34; CN 1, 2, 3; CP 1, 2, 3, 4; DA3; DAM
NOV; DLB 2, 5, 206; DLBY 1980, 1984;
FANT; MAL 5; MTCW 1; RGAL 4;
SATA 56

Brave Bird, Mary .... **NNAL**
See Crow Dog, Mary (Ellen)

Braverman, Kate 1950- .... **CLC 67**
See also CA 89-92; CANR 141

Brecht, (Eugen) Bertolt (Friedrich)
1898-1956 ..... **DC 3; TCLC 1, 6, 13, 35,**
169; WLC
See also CA 104; 133; CANR 62; CDWLB
2; DA; DA3; DAB; DAC; DAM DRAM,
MST; DFS 4, 5, 9; DLB 56, 124; EW 11;
EWL 3; IDTP; MTCW 1, 2; MTFW 2005;
RGWL 2, 3; TWA

Brecht, Eugen Berthold Friedrich
See Brecht, (Eugen) Bertolt (Friedrich)

Bremer, Fredrika 1801-1865 .... **NCLC 11**
See also DLB 254

Brennan, Christopher John
1870-1932 .... **TCLC 17**
See also CA 117; 188; DLB 230; EWL 3

Brennan, Maeve 1917-1993 ... **CLC 5; TCLC**
124
See also CA 81-84; CANR 72, 100

Brenner, Jozef 1887-1919
See Csath, Geza
See also CA 240

Brent, Linda
See Jacobs, Harriet A(nn)

Brentano, Clemens (Maria)
1778-1842 .... **NCLC 1**
See also DLB 90; RGWL 2, 3

Brent of Bin Bin
See Franklin, (Stella Maria Sarah) Miles
(Lampe)

Brenton, Howard 1942- .... **CLC 31**
See also CA 69-72; CANR 33, 67; CBD;
CD 5, 6; DLB 13; MTCW 1

Breslin, James 1930-
See Breslin, Jimmy
See also CA 73-76; CANR 31, 75, 139;
DAM NOV; MTCW 1, 2; MTFW 2005

Breslin, Jimmy .... **CLC 4, 43**
See Breslin, James
See also AITN 1; DLB 185; MTCW 2

Bresson, Robert 1901(?)-1999 .... **CLC 16**
See also CA 110; 187; CANR 49

Breton, Andre 1896-1966 .. **CLC 2, 9, 15, 54;**
PC 15
See also CA 19-20; 25-28R; CANR 40, 60;
CAP 2; DLB 65, 258; EW 11; EWL 3;
GFL 1789 to the Present; LMFS 2;
MTCW 1, 2; MTFW 2005; RGWL 2, 3;
TWA; WP

Breytenbach, Breyten 1939(?)- .. **CLC 23, 37,**
126
See also CA 113; 129; CANR 61, 122;
CWW 2; DAM POET; DLB 225; EWL 3

Bridgers, Sue Ellen 1942- .... **CLC 26**
See also AAYA 8, 49; BYA 7, 8; CA 65-68;
CANR 11, 36; CLR 18; DLB 52; JRDA;
MAICYA 1, 2; SAAS 1; SATA 22, 90;
SATA-Essay 109; WYA; YAW

Bridges, Robert (Seymour)
1844-1930 .... **PC 28; TCLC 1**
See also BRW 6; CA 104; 152; CDBLB
1890-1914; DAM POET; DLB 19, 98

Bridie, James .... **TCLC 3**
See Mavor, Osborne Henry
See also DLB 10; EWL 3

Brin, David 1950- .... **CLC 34**
See also AAYA 21; CA 102; CANR 24, 70,
125, 127; INT CANR-24; SATA 65;
SCFW 2; SFW 4

Brink, Andre (Philippus) 1935- . **CLC 18, 36,**
106
See also AFW; BRWS 6; CA 104; CANR
39, 62, 109, 133; CN 4, 5, 6, 7; DLB 225;
EWL 3; INT CA-103; LATS 1:2; MTCW
1, 2; MTFW 2005; WLIT 2

Brinsmead, H. F(ay)
See Brinsmead, H(esba) F(ay)

Brinsmead, H. F.
See Brinsmead, H(esba) F(ay)

Brinsmead, H(esba) F(ay) 1922- ...... **CLC 21**
See also CA 21-24R; CANR 10; CLR 47;
CWRI 5; MAICYA 1, 2; SAAS 5; SATA
18, 78

Brittain, Vera (Mary) 1893(?)-1970 . **CLC 23**
See also BRWS 10; CA 13-16; 25-28R;
CANR 58; CAP 1; DLB 191; FW; MTCW
1, 2

Broch, Hermann 1886-1951 .... **TCLC 20**
See also CA 117; 211; CDWLB 2; DLB 85,
124; EW 10; EWL 3; RGWL 2, 3

Brock, Rose
See Hansen, Joseph
See also GLL 1

Brod, Max 1884-1968 .... **TCLC 115**
See also CA 5-8R; 25-28R; CANR 7; DLB
81; EWL 3

Brodkey, Harold (Roy) 1930-1996 .. **CLC 56;**
TCLC 123
See also CA 111; 151; CANR 71; CN 4, 5,
6; DLB 130

Brodsky, Iosif Alexandrovich 1940-1996
See Brodsky, Joseph
See also AITN 1; CA 41-44R; 151; CANR
37, 106; DA3; DAM POET; MTCW 1, 2;
MTFW 2005; RGWL 2, 3

Brodsky, Joseph . **CLC 4, 6, 13, 36, 100; PC**
9
See Brodsky, Iosif Alexandrovich
See also AMWS 8; CWW 2; DLB 285;
EWL 3; MTCW 1

Brodsky, Michael (Mark) 1948- .... **CLC 19**
See also CA 102; CANR 18, 41, 58; DLB
244

Brodzki, Bella ed. .... **CLC 65**

Brome, Richard 1590(?)-1652 .... **LC 61**
See also BRWS 10; DLB 58

Bromell, Henry 1947- .... **CLC 5**
See also CA 53-56; CANR 9, 115, 116

Bromfield, Louis (Brucker)
1896-1956 .... **TCLC 11**
See also CA 107; 155; DLB 4, 9, 86; RGAL 4; RHW

Broner, E(sther) M(asserman)
1930- .... **CLC 19**
See also CA 17-20R; CANR 8, 25, 72; CN 4, 5, 6; DLB 28

Bronk, William (M.) 1918-1999 .... **CLC 10**
See also CA 89-92; 177; CANR 23; CP 3, 4, 5, 6, 7; DLB 165

Bronstein, Lev Davidovich
See Trotsky, Leon

Bronte, Anne 1820-1849 ..... **NCLC 4, 71, 102**
See also BRW 5; BRWR 1; DA3; DLB 21, 199; TEA

Bronte, (Patrick) Branwell
1817-1848 .... **NCLC 109**

Bronte, Charlotte 1816-1855 ...... **NCLC 3, 8, 33, 58, 105, 155; WLC**
See also AAYA 17; BRW 5; BRWC 2; BRWR 1; BYA 2; CDBLB 1832-1890; DA; DA3; DAB; DAC; DAM MST, NOV; DLB 21, 159, 199; EXPN; FL 1:2; GL 2; LAIT 2; NFS 4; TEA; WLIT 4

Bronte, Emily (Jane) 1818-1848 ... **NCLC 16, 35, 165; PC 8; WLC**
See also AAYA 17; BPFB 1; BRW 5; BRWC 1; BRWR 1; BYA 2; CDBLB 1832-1890; DA; DA3; DAB; DAC; DAM MST, NOV, POET; DLB 21, 32, 199; EXPN; FL 1:2; GL 2; LAIT 1; TEA; WLIT 3

Brontes
See Bronte, Anne; Bronte, Charlotte; Bronte, Emily (Jane)

Brooke, Frances 1724-1789 .... **LC 6, 48**
See also DLB 39, 99

Brooke, Henry 1703(?)-1783 .... **LC 1**
See also DLB 39

Brooke, Rupert (Chawner)
1887-1915 ..... **PC 24; TCLC 2, 7; WLC**
See also BRWS 3; CA 104; 132; CANR 61; CDBLB 1914-1945; DA; DAB; DAC; DAM MST, POET; DLB 19, 216; EXPP; GLL 2; MTCW 1, 2; MTFW 2005; PFS 7; TEA

Brooke-Haven, P.
See Wodehouse, P(elham) G(renville)

Brooke-Rose, Christine 1926(?)- ..... **CLC 40, 184**
See also BRWS 4; CA 13-16R; CANR 58, 118; CN 1, 2, 3, 4, 5, 6, 7; DLB 14, 231; EWL 3; SFW 4

Brookner, Anita 1928- .. **CLC 32, 34, 51, 136**
See also BRWS 4; CA 114; 120; CANR 37, 56, 87, 130; CN 4, 5, 6, 7; CPW; DA3; DAB; DAM POP; DLB 194; DLBY 1987; EWL 3; MTCW 1, 2; MTFW 2005; TEA

Brooks, Cleanth 1906-1994 . **CLC 24, 86, 110**
See also AMWS 14; CA 17-20R; 145; CANR 33, 35; CSW; DLB 63; DLBY 1994; EWL 3; INT CANR-35; MAL 5; MTCW 1, 2; MTFW 2005

Brooks, George
See Baum, L(yman) Frank

Brooks, Gwendolyn (Elizabeth)
1917-2000 ... **BLC 1; CLC 1, 2, 4, 5, 15, 49, 125; PC 7; WLC**
See also AAYA 20; AFAW 1, 2; AITN 1; AMWS 3; BW 2, 3; CA 1-4R; 190; CANR 1, 27, 52, 75, 132; CDALB 1941-1968; CLR 27; CP 1, 2, 3, 4, 5, 6, 7; CWP; DA; DA3; DAC; DAM MST, MULT, POET; DLB 5, 76, 165; EWL 3; EXPP; FL 1:5; MAL 5; MAWW; MTCW 1, 2; MTFW 2005; PFS 1, 2, 4, 6; RGAL 4; SATA 6; SATA-Obit 123; TUS; WP

Brooks, Mel .... **CLC 12, 217**
See Kaminsky, Melvin
See also AAYA 13, 48; DLB 26

Brooks, Peter (Preston) 1938- .... **CLC 34**
See also CA 45-48; CANR 1, 107

Brooks, Van Wyck 1886-1963 .... **CLC 29**
See also AMW; CA 1-4R; CANR 6; DLB 45, 63, 103; MAL 5; TUS

Brophy, Brigid (Antonia)
1929-1995 .... **CLC 6, 11, 29, 105**
See also CA 5-8R; 149; CAAS 4; CANR 25, 53; CBD; CN 1, 2, 3, 4, 5, 6; CWD; DA3; DLB 14, 271; EWL 3; MTCW 1, 2

Brosman, Catharine Savage 1934- ..... **CLC 9**
See also CA 61-64; CANR 21, 46

Brossard, Nicole 1943- .... **CLC 115, 169**
See also CA 122; CAAS 16; CANR 140; CCA 1; CWP; CWW 2; DLB 53; EWL 3; FW; GLL 2; RGWL 3

Brother Antoninus
See Everson, William (Oliver)

The Brothers Quay
See Quay, Stephen; Quay, Timothy

Broughton, T(homas) Alan 1936- ..... **CLC 19**
See also CA 45-48; CANR 2, 23, 48, 111

Broumas, Olga 1949- .... **CLC 10, 73**
See also CA 85-88; CANR 20, 69, 110; CP 7; CWP; GLL 2

Broun, Heywood 1888-1939 .... **TCLC 104**
See also DLB 29, 171

Brown, Alan 1950- .... **CLC 99**
See also CA 156

Brown, Charles Brockden
1771-1810 .... **NCLC 22, 74, 122**
See also AMWS 1; CDALB 1640-1865; DLB 37, 59, 73; FW; GL 2; HGG; LMFS 1; RGAL 4; TUS

Brown, Christy 1932-1981 .... **CLC 63**
See also BYA 13; CA 105; 104; CANR 72; DLB 14

Brown, Claude 1937-2002 ... **BLC 1; CLC 30**
See also AAYA 7; BW 1, 3; CA 73-76; 205; CANR 81; DAM MULT

Brown, Dan 1964- .... **CLC 209**
See also AAYA 55; CA 217; MTFW 2005

Brown, Dee (Alexander)
1908-2002 .... **CLC 18, 47**
See also AAYA 30; CA 13-16R; 212; CAAS 6; CANR 11, 45, 60; CPW; CSW; DA3; DAM POP; DLBY 1980; LAIT 2; MTCW 1, 2; MTFW 2005; NCFS 5; SATA 5, 110; SATA-Obit 141; TCWW 1, 2

Brown, George
See Wertmueller, Lina

Brown, George Douglas
1869-1902 .... **TCLC 28**
See Douglas, George
See also CA 162

Brown, George Mackay 1921-1996 ... **CLC 5, 48, 100**
See also BRWS 6; CA 21-24R; 151; CAAS 6; CANR 12, 37, 67; CN 1, 2, 3, 4, 5, 6; CP 1, 2, 3, 4; DLB 14, 27, 139, 271; MTCW 1; RGSF 2; SATA 35

Brown, (William) Larry 1951-2004 . **CLC 73**
See also CA 130; 134; 233; CANR 117, 145; CSW; DLB 234; INT CA-134

Brown, Moses
See Barrett, William (Christopher)

Brown, Rita Mae 1944- .... **CLC 18, 43, 79**
See also BPFB 1; CA 45-48; CANR 2, 11, 35, 62, 95, 138; CN 5, 6, 7; CPW; CSW; DA3; DAM NOV, POP; FW; INT CANR-11; MAL 5; MTCW 1, 2; MTFW 2005; NFS 9; RGAL 4; TUS

Brown, Roderick (Langmere) Haig-
See Haig-Brown, Roderick (Langmere)

Brown, Rosellen 1939- .... **CLC 32, 170**
See also CA 77-80; CAAS 10; CANR 14, 44, 98; CN 6, 7

Brown, Sterling Allen 1901-1989 ...... **BLC 1; CLC 1, 23, 59; HR 1:2; PC 55**
See also AFAW 1, 2; BW 1, 3; CA 85-88; 127; CANR 26; CP 3, 4; DA3; DAM MULT, POET; DLB 48, 51, 63; MAL 5; MTCW 1, 2; MTFW 2005; RGAL 4; WP

Brown, Will
See Ainsworth, William Harrison

Brown, William Hill 1765-1793 .... **LC 93**
See also DLB 37

Brown, William Wells 1815-1884 ...... **BLC 1; DC 1; NCLC 2, 89**
See also DAM MULT; DLB 3, 50, 183, 248; RGAL 4

Browne, (Clyde) Jackson 1948(?)- ... **CLC 21**
See also CA 120

Browne, Sir Thomas 1605-1682 .... **LC 111**
See also BRW 2; DLB 151

Browning, Robert 1812-1889 . **NCLC 19, 79; PC 2, 61; WLCS**
See also BRW 4; BRWC 2; BRWR 2; CD-BLB 1832-1890; CLR 97; DA; DA3; DAB; DAC; DAM MST, POET; DLB 32, 163; EXPP; LATS 1:1; PAB; PFS 1, 15; RGEL 2; TEA; WLIT 4; WP; YABC 1

Browning, Tod 1882-1962 .... **CLC 16**
See also CA 141; 117

Brownmiller, Susan 1935- .... **CLC 159**
See also CA 103; CANR 35, 75, 137; DAM NOV; FW; MTCW 1, 2; MTFW 2005

Brownson, Orestes Augustus
1803-1876 .... **NCLC 50**
See also DLB 1, 59, 73, 243

Bruccoli, Matthew J(oseph) 1931- ... **CLC 34**
See also CA 9-12R; CANR 7, 87; DLB 103

Bruce, Lenny .... **CLC 21**
See Schneider, Leonard Alfred

Bruchac, Joseph III 1942- .... **NNAL**
See also AAYA 19; CA 33-36R; CANR 13, 47, 75, 94, 137; CLR 46; CWRI 5; DAM MULT; JRDA; MAICYA 2; MAICYAS 1; MTCW 2; MTFW 2005; SATA 42, 89, 131

Bruin, John
See Brutus, Dennis

Brulard, Henri
See Stendhal

Brulls, Christian
See Simenon, Georges (Jacques Christian)

Brunetto Latini c. 1220-1294 .... **CMLC 73**

Brunner, John (Kilian Houston)
1934-1995 .... **CLC 8, 10**
See also CA 1-4R; 149; CAAS 8; CANR 2, 37; CPW; DAM POP; DLB 261; MTCW 1, 2; SCFW 1, 2; SFW 4

Bruno, Giordano 1548-1600 .... **LC 27**
See also RGWL 2, 3

Brutus, Dennis 1924- ... **BLC 1; CLC 43; PC 24**
See also AFW; BW 2, 3; CA 49-52; CAAS 14; CANR 2, 27, 42, 81; CDWLB 3; CP 1, 2, 3, 4, 5, 6, 7; DAM MULT, POET; DLB 117, 225; EWL 3

Bryan, C(ourtlandt) D(ixon) B(arnes)
1936- .... **CLC 29**
See also CA 73-76; CANR 13, 68; DLB 185; INT CANR-13

Bryan, Michael
See Moore, Brian
See also CCA 1

Bryan, William Jennings
1860-1925 .... **TCLC 99**
See also DLB 303

Bryant, William Cullen 1794-1878 . **NCLC 6, 46; PC 20**
See also AMWS 1; CDALB 1640-1865; DA; DAB; DAC; DAM MST, POET; DLB 3, 43, 59, 189, 250; EXPP; PAB; RGAL 4; TUS

Bryusov, Valery Yakovlevich 1873-1924 .... **TCLC 10**
See also CA 107; 155; EWL 3; SFW 4

Buchan, John 1875-1940 .... **TCLC 41**
See also CA 108; 145; CMW 4; DAB; DAM POP; DLB 34, 70, 156; HGG; MSW; MTCW 2; RGEL 2; RHW; YABC 2

Buchanan, George 1506-1582 .... **LC 4**
See also DLB 132

Buchanan, Robert 1841-1901 .... **TCLC 107**
See also CA 179; DLB 18, 35

Buchheim, Lothar-Guenther 1918- .... **CLC 6**
See also CA 85-88

Buchner, (Karl) Georg 1813-1837 .... **NCLC 26, 146**
See also CDWLB 2; DLB 133; EW 6; RGSF 2; RGWL 2, 3; TWA

Buchwald, Art(hur) 1925- .... **CLC 33**
See also AITN 1; CA 5-8R; CANR 21, 67, 107; MTCW 1, 2; SATA 10

Buck, Pearl S(ydenstricker) 1892-1973 .... **CLC 7, 11, 18, 127**
See also AAYA 42; AITN 1; AMWS 2; BPFB 1; CA 1-4R; 41-44R; CANR 1, 34; CDALBS; CN 1; DA; DA3; DAB; DAC; DAM MST, NOV; DLB 9, 102; EWL 3; LAIT 3; MAL 5; MTCW 1, 2; MTFW 2005; RGAL 4; RHW; SATA 1, 25; TUS

Buckler, Ernest 1908-1984 .... **CLC 13**
See also CA 11-12; 114; CAP 1; CCA 1; CN 1, 2, 3; DAC; DAM MST; DLB 68; SATA 47

Buckley, Christopher (Taylor) 1952- .... **CLC 165**
See also CA 139; CANR 119

Buckley, Vincent (Thomas) 1925-1988 .... **CLC 57**
See also CA 101; CP 1, 2, 3, 4; DLB 289

Buckley, William F(rank), Jr. 1925- . **CLC 7, 18, 37**
See also AITN 1; BPFB 1; CA 1-4R; CANR 1, 24, 53, 93, 133; CMW 4; CPW; DA3; DAM POP; DLB 137; DLBY 1980; INT CANR-24; MTCW 1, 2; MTFW 2005; TUS

Buechner, (Carl) Frederick 1926- . **CLC 2, 4, 6, 9**
See also AMWS 12; BPFB 1; CA 13-16R; CANR 11, 39, 64, 114, 138; CN 1, 2, 3, 4, 5, 6, 7; DAM NOV; DLBY 1980; INT CANR-11; MAL 5; MTCW 1, 2; MTFW 2005; TCLE 1:1

Buell, John (Edward) 1927- .... **CLC 10**
See also CA 1-4R; CANR 71; DLB 53

Buero Vallejo, Antonio 1916-2000 ... **CLC 15, 46, 139; DC 18**
See also CA 106; 189; CANR 24, 49, 75; CWW 2; DFS 11; EWL 3; HW 1; MTCW 1, 2

Bufalino, Gesualdo 1920-1996 .... **CLC 74**
See also CA 209; CWW 2; DLB 196

Bugayev, Boris Nikolayevich 1880-1934 .... **PC 11; TCLC 7**
See Bely, Andrey; Belyi, Andrei
See also CA 104; 165; MTCW 2; MTFW 2005

Bukowski, Charles 1920-1994 ... **CLC 2, 5, 9, 41, 82, 108; PC 18; SSC 45**
See also CA 17-20R; 144; CANR 40, 62, 105; CN 4, 5; CP 1, 2, 3, 4; CPW; DA3; DAM NOV, POET; DLB 5, 130, 169; EWL 3; MAL 5; MTCW 1, 2; MTFW 2005

Bulgakov, Mikhail (Afanas'evich) 1891-1940 ..... **SSC 18; TCLC 2, 16, 159**
See also BPFB 1; CA 105; 152; DAM DRAM, NOV; DLB 272; EWL 3; MTCW 2; MTFW 2005; NFS 8; RGSF 2; RGWL 2, 3; SFW 4; TWA

Bulgya, Alexander Alexandrovich 1901-1956 .... **TCLC 53**
See Fadeev, Aleksandr Aleksandrovich; Fadeev, Alexandr Alexandrovich; Fadeyev, Alexander
See also CA 117; 181

Bullins, Ed 1935- ... **BLC 1; CLC 1, 5, 7; DC 6**
See also BW 2, 3; CA 49-52; CAAS 16; CAD; CANR 24, 46, 73, 134; CD 5, 6; DAM DRAM, MULT; DLB 7, 38, 249; EWL 3; MAL 5; MTCW 1, 2; MTFW 2005; RGAL 4

Bulosan, Carlos 1911-1956 .... **AAL**
See also CA 216; DLB 312; RGAL 4

Bulwer-Lytton, Edward (George Earle Lytton) 1803-1873 .... **NCLC 1, 45**
See also DLB 21; RGEL 2; SFW 4; SUFW 1; TEA

Bunin, Ivan Alexeyevich 1870-1953 ... **SSC 5; TCLC 6**
See also CA 104; DLB 317; EWL 3; RGSF 2; RGWL 2, 3; TWA

Bunting, Basil 1900-1985 ...... **CLC 10, 39, 47**
See also BRWS 7; CA 53-56; 115; CANR 7; CP 1, 2, 3, 4; DAM POET; DLB 20; EWL 3; RGEL 2

Bunuel, Luis 1900-1983 ... **CLC 16, 80; HLC 1**
See also CA 101; 110; CANR 32, 77; DAM MULT; HW 1

Bunyan, John 1628-1688 ..... **LC 4, 69; WLC**
See also BRW 2; BYA 5; CDBLB 1660-1789; DA; DAB; DAC; DAM MST; DLB 39; RGEL 2; TEA; WCH; WLIT 3

Buravsky, Alexandr .... **CLC 59**

Burckhardt, Jacob (Christoph) 1818-1897 .... **NCLC 49**
See also EW 6

Burford, Eleanor
See Hibbert, Eleanor Alice Burford

Burgess, Anthony . **CLC 1, 2, 4, 5, 8, 10, 13, 15, 22, 40, 62, 81, 94**
See Wilson, John (Anthony) Burgess
See also AAYA 25; AITN 1; BRWS 1; CD-BLB 1960 to Present; CN 1, 2, 3, 4, 5; DAB; DLB 14, 194, 261; DLBY 1998; EWL 3; RGEL 2; RHW; SFW 4; YAW

Burke, Edmund 1729(?)-1797 .... **LC 7, 36; WLC**
See also BRW 3; DA; DA3; DAB; DAC; DAM MST; DLB 104, 252; RGEL 2; TEA

Burke, Kenneth (Duva) 1897-1993 ... **CLC 2, 24**
See also AMW; CA 5-8R; 143; CANR 39, 74, 136; CN 1, 2; CP 1, 2, 3, 4; DLB 45, 63; EWL 3; MAL 5; MTCW 1, 2; MTFW 2005; RGAL 4

Burke, Leda
See Garnett, David

Burke, Ralph
See Silverberg, Robert

Burke, Thomas 1886-1945 .... **TCLC 63**
See also CA 113; 155; CMW 4; DLB 197

Burney, Fanny 1752-1840 .... **NCLC 12, 54, 107**
See also BRWS 3; DLB 39; FL 1:2; NFS 16; RGEL 2; TEA

Burney, Frances
See Burney, Fanny

Burns, Robert 1759-1796 ... **LC 3, 29, 40; PC 6; WLC**
See also AAYA 51; BRW 3; CDBLB 1789-1832; DA; DA3; DAB; DAC; DAM MST, POET; DLB 109; EXPP; PAB; RGEL 2; TEA; WP

Burns, Tex
See L'Amour, Louis (Dearborn)

Burnshaw, Stanley 1906- .... **CLC 3, 13, 44**
See also CA 9-12R; CP 1, 2, 3, 4, 5, 6, 7; DLB 48; DLBY 1997

Burr, Anne 1937- .... **CLC 6**
See also CA 25-28R

Burroughs, Edgar Rice 1875-1950 . **TCLC 2, 32**
See also AAYA 11; BPFB 1; BYA 4, 9; CA 104; 132; CANR 131; DA3; DAM NOV; DLB 8; FANT; MTCW 1, 2; MTFW 2005; RGAL 4; SATA 41; SCFW 1, 2; SFW 4; TCWW 1, 2; TUS; YAW

Burroughs, William S(eward) 1914-1997 .. **CLC 1, 2, 5, 15, 22, 42, 75, 109; TCLC 121; WLC**
See Lee, William; Lee, Willy
See also AAYA 60; AITN 2; AMWS 3; BG 1:2; BPFB 1; CA 9-12R; 160; CANR 20, 52, 104; CN 1, 2, 3, 4, 5, 6; CPW; DA; DA3; DAB; DAC; DAM MST, NOV, POP; DLB 2, 8, 16, 152, 237; DLBY 1981, 1997; EWL 3; HGG; LMFS 2; MAL 5; MTCW 1, 2; MTFW 2005; RGAL 4; SFW 4

Burton, Sir Richard F(rancis) 1821-1890 .... **NCLC 42**
See also DLB 55, 166, 184; SSFS 21

Burton, Robert 1577-1640 .... **LC 74**
See also DLB 151; RGEL 2

Buruma, Ian 1951- .... **CLC 163**
See also CA 128; CANR 65, 141

Busch, Frederick 1941- ... **CLC 7, 10, 18, 47, 166**
See also CA 33-36R; CAAS 1; CANR 45, 73, 92; CN 1, 2, 3, 4, 5, 6, 7; DLB 6, 218

Bush, Barney (Furman) 1946- .... **NNAL**
See also CA 145

Bush, Ronald 1946- .... **CLC 34**
See also CA 136

Bustos, F(rancisco)
See Borges, Jorge Luis

Bustos Domecq, H(onorio)
See Bioy Casares, Adolfo; Borges, Jorge Luis

Butler, Octavia E(stelle) 1947- .. **BLCS; CLC 38, 121**
See also AAYA 18, 48; AFAW 2; AMWS 13; BPFB 1; BW 2, 3; CA 73-76; CANR 12, 24, 38, 73, 145; CLR 65; CN 7; CPW; DA3; DAM MULT, POP; DLB 33; LATS 1:2; MTCW 1, 2; MTFW 2005; NFS 8, 21; SATA 84; SCFW 2; SFW 4; SSFS 6; TCLE 1:1; YAW

Butler, Robert Olen, (Jr.) 1945- ...... **CLC 81, 162**
See also AMWS 12; BPFB 1; CA 112; CANR 66, 138; CN 7; CSW; DAM POP; DLB 173; INT CA-112; MAL 5; MTCW 2; MTFW 2005; SSFS 11

Butler, Samuel 1612-1680 .... **LC 16, 43**
See also DLB 101, 126; RGEL 2

Butler, Samuel 1835-1902 .... **TCLC 1, 33; WLC**
See also BRWS 2; CA 143; CDBLB 1890-1914; DA; DA3; DAB; DAC; DAM MST, NOV; DLB 18, 57, 174; RGEL 2; SFW 4; TEA

Butler, Walter C.
See Faust, Frederick (Schiller)

Author Index

Canfield, Dorothea F.
See Fisher, Dorothy (Frances) Canfield

Canfield, Dorothea Frances
See Fisher, Dorothy (Frances) Canfield

Canfield, Dorothy
See Fisher, Dorothy (Frances) Canfield

Canin, Ethan 1960- .... **CLC 55; SSC 70**
See also CA 131; 135; MAL 5

Cankar, Ivan 1876-1918 .... **TCLC 105**
See also CDWLB 4; DLB 147; EWL 3

Cannon, Curt
See Hunter, Evan

Cao, Lan 1961- .... **CLC 109**
See also CA 165

Cape, Judith
See Page, P(atricia) K(athleen)
See also CCA 1

Capek, Karel 1890-1938 .... **DC 1; SSC 36; TCLC 6, 37; WLC**
See also CA 104; 140; CDWLB 4; DA; DA3; DAB; DAC; DAM DRAM, MST, NOV; DFS 7, 11; DLB 215; EW 10; EWL 3; MTCW 2; MTFW 2005; RGSF 2; RGWL 2, 3; SCFW 1, 2; SFW 4

Capote, Truman 1924-1984 . **CLC 1, 3, 8, 13, 19, 34, 38, 58; SSC 2, 47; TCLC 164; WLC**
See also AAYA 61; AMWS 3; BPFB 1; CA 5-8R; 113; CANR 18, 62; CDALB 1941-1968; CN 1, 2, 3; CPW; DA; DA3; DAB; DAC; DAM MST, NOV, POP; DLB 2, 185, 227; DLBY 1980, 1984; EWL 3; EXPS; GLL 1; LAIT 3; MAL 5; MTCW 1, 2; MTFW 2005; NCFS 2; RGAL 4; RGSF 2; SATA 91; SSFS 2; TUS

Capra, Frank 1897-1991 .... **CLC 16**
See also AAYA 52; CA 61-64; 135

Caputo, Philip 1941- .... **CLC 32**
See also AAYA 60; CA 73-76; CANR 40, 135; YAW

Caragiale, Ion Luca 1852-1912 ...... **TCLC 76**
See also CA 157

Card, Orson Scott 1951- .... **CLC 44, 47, 50**
See also AAYA 11, 42; BPFB 1; BYA 5, 8; CA 102; CANR 27, 47, 73, 102, 106, 133; CPW; DA3; DAM POP; FANT; INT CANR-27; MTCW 1, 2; MTFW 2005; NFS 5; SATA 83, 127; SCFW 2; SFW 4; SUFW 2; YAW

Cardenal, Ernesto 1925- .... **CLC 31, 161; HLC 1; PC 22**
See also CA 49-52; CANR 2, 32, 66, 138; CWW 2; DAM MULT, POET; DLB 290; EWL 3; HW 1, 2; LAWS 1; MTCW 1, 2; MTFW 2005; RGWL 2, 3

Cardinal, Marie 1929-2001 .... **CLC 189**
See also CA 177; CWW 2; DLB 83; FW

Cardozo, Benjamin N(athan)
1870-1938 .... **TCLC 65**
See also CA 117; 164

Carducci, Giosue (Alessandro Giuseppe)
1835-1907 .... **PC 46; TCLC 32**
See also CA 163; EW 7; RGWL 2, 3

Carew, Thomas 1595(?)-1640 . **LC 13; PC 29**
See also BRW 2; DLB 126; PAB; RGEL 2

Carey, Ernestine Gilbreth 1908- ...... **CLC 17**
See also CA 5-8R; CANR 71; SATA 2

Carey, Peter 1943- .... **CLC 40, 55, 96, 183**
See also CA 123; 127; CANR 53, 76, 117; CN 4, 5, 6, 7; DLB 289; EWL 3; INT CA-127; MTCW 1, 2; MTFW 2005; RGSF 2; SATA 94

Carleton, William 1794-1869 .... **NCLC 3**
See also DLB 159; RGEL 2; RGSF 2

Carlisle, Henry (Coffin) 1926- .... **CLC 33**
See also CA 13-16R; CANR 15, 85

Carlsen, Chris
See Holdstock, Robert P.

Carlson, Ron(ald F.) 1947- .... **CLC 54**
See also CA 105, 189; CAAE 189; CANR 27; DLB 244

Carlyle, Thomas 1795-1881 ..... **NCLC 22, 70**
See also BRW 4; CDBLB 1789-1832; DA; DAB; DAC; DAM MST; DLB 55, 144, 254; RGEL 2; TEA

Carman, (William) Bliss 1861-1929 ... **PC 34; TCLC 7**
See also CA 104; 152; DAC; DLB 92; RGEL 2

Carnegie, Dale 1888-1955 .... **TCLC 53**
See also CA 218

Carossa, Hans 1878-1956 .... **TCLC 48**
See also CA 170; DLB 66; EWL 3

Carpenter, Don(ald Richard)
1931-1995 .... **CLC 41**
See also CA 45-48; 149; CANR 1, 71

Carpenter, Edward 1844-1929 .... **TCLC 88**
See also CA 163; GLL 1

Carpenter, John (Howard) 1948- ... **CLC 161**
See also AAYA 2; CA 134; SATA 58

Carpenter, Johnny
See Carpenter, John (Howard)

Carpentier (y Valmont), Alejo
1904-1980 . **CLC 8, 11, 38, 110; HLC 1; SSC 35**
See also CA 65-68; 97-100; CANR 11, 70; CDWLB 3; DAM MULT; DLB 113; EWL 3; HW 1, 2; LAW; LMFS 2; RGSF 2; RGWL 2, 3; WLIT 1

Carr, Caleb 1955- .... **CLC 86**
See also CA 147; CANR 73, 134; DA3

Carr, Emily 1871-1945 .... **TCLC 32**
See also CA 159; DLB 68; FW; GLL 2

Carr, John Dickson 1906-1977 .... **CLC 3**
See Fairbairn, Roger
See also CA 49-52; 69-72; CANR 3, 33, 60; CMW 4; DLB 306; MSW; MTCW 1, 2

Carr, Philippa
See Hibbert, Eleanor Alice Burford

Carr, Virginia Spencer 1929- .... **CLC 34**
See also CA 61-64; DLB 111

Carrere, Emmanuel 1957- .... **CLC 89**
See also CA 200

Carrier, Roch 1937- .... **CLC 13, 78**
See also CA 130; CANR 61; CCA 1; DAC; DAM MST; DLB 53; SATA 105

Carroll, James Dennis
See Carroll, Jim

Carroll, James P. 1943(?)- .... **CLC 38**
See also CA 81-84; CANR 73, 139; MTCW 2; MTFW 2005

Carroll, Jim 1951- .... **CLC 35, 143**
See also AAYA 17; CA 45-48; CANR 42, 115; NCFS 5

Carroll, Lewis ..... **NCLC 2, 53, 139; PC 18; WLC**
See Dodgson, Charles L(utwidge)
See also AAYA 39; BRW 5; BYA 5, 13; CD-BLB 1832-1890; CLR 2, 18; DLB 18, 163, 178; DLBY 1998; EXPN; EXPP; FANT; JRDA; LAIT 1; NFS 7; PFS 11; RGEL 2; SUFW 1; TEA; WCH

Carroll, Paul Vincent 1900-1968 ...... **CLC 10**
See also CA 9-12R; 25-28R; DLB 10; EWL 3; RGEL 2

Carruth, Hayden 1921- ..... **CLC 4, 7, 10, 18, 84; PC 10**
See also CA 9-12R; CANR 4, 38, 59, 110; CP 1, 2, 3, 4, 5, 6, 7; DLB 5, 165; INT CANR-4; MTCW 1, 2; MTFW 2005; SATA 47

Carson, Anne 1950- .... **CLC 185; PC 64**
See also AMWS 12; CA 203; DLB 193; PFS 18; TCLE 1:1

Carson, Ciaran 1948- .... **CLC 201**
See also CA 112; 153; CANR 113; CP 7

Carson, Rachel
See Carson, Rachel Louise
See also AAYA 49; DLB 275

Carson, Rachel Louise 1907-1964 .... **CLC 71**
See Carson, Rachel
See also AMWS 9; ANW; CA 77-80; CANR 35; DA3; DAM POP; FW; LAIT 4; MAL 5; MTCW 1, 2; MTFW 2005; NCFS 1; SATA 23

Carter, Angela (Olive) 1940-1992 ...... **CLC 5, 41, 76; SSC 13, 85; TCLC 139**
See also BRWS 3; CA 53-56; 136; CANR 12, 36, 61, 106; CN 3, 4, 5; DA3; DLB 14, 207, 261, 319; EXPS; FANT; FW; GL 2; MTCW 1, 2; MTFW 2005; RGSF 2; SATA 66; SATA-Obit 70; SFW 4; SSFS 4, 12; SUFW 2; WLIT 4

Carter, Nick
See Smith, Martin Cruz

Carver, Raymond 1938-1988 ..... **CLC 22, 36, 53, 55, 126; PC 54; SSC 8, 51**
See also AAYA 44; AMWS 3; BPFB 1; CA 33-36R; 126; CANR 17, 34, 61, 103; CN 4; CPW; DA3; DAM NOV; DLB 130; DLBY 1984, 1988; EWL 3; MAL 5; MTCW 1, 2; MTFW 2005; PFS 17; RGAL 4; RGSF 2; SSFS 3, 6, 12, 13; TCLE 1:1; TCWW 2; TUS

Cary, Elizabeth, Lady Falkland
1585-1639 .... **LC 30**

Cary, (Arthur) Joyce (Lunel)
1888-1957 .... **TCLC 1, 29**
See also BRW 7; CA 104; 164; CDBLB 1914-1945; DLB 15, 100; EWL 3; MTCW 2; RGEL 2; TEA

Casal, Julian del 1863-1893 .... **NCLC 131**
See also DLB 283; LAW

Casanova, Giacomo
See Casanova de Seingalt, Giovanni Jacopo
See also WLIT 7

Casanova de Seingalt, Giovanni Jacopo
1725-1798 .... **LC 13**
See Casanova, Giacomo

Casares, Adolfo Bioy
See Bioy Casares, Adolfo
See also RGSF 2

Casas, Bartolome de las 1474-1566
See Las Casas, Bartolome de
See also WLIT 1

Casely-Hayford, J(oseph) E(phraim)
1866-1903 .... **BLC 1; TCLC 24**
See also BW 2; CA 123; 152; DAM MULT

Casey, John (Dudley) 1939- .... **CLC 59**
See also BEST 90:2; CA 69-72; CANR 23, 100

Casey, Michael 1947- .... **CLC 2**
See also CA 65-68; CANR 109; CP 2, 3; DLB 5

Casey, Patrick
See Thurman, Wallace (Henry)

Casey, Warren (Peter) 1935-1988 .... **CLC 12**
See also CA 101; 127; INT CA-101

Casona, Alejandro .... **CLC 49**
See Alvarez, Alejandro Rodriguez
See also EWL 3

Cassavetes, John 1929-1989 .... **CLC 20**
See also CA 85-88; 127; CANR 82

Cassian, Nina 1924- .... **PC 17**
See also CWP; CWW 2

Cassill, R(onald) V(erlin)
1919-2002 .... **CLC 4, 23**
See also CA 9-12R; 208; CAAS 1; CANR 7, 45; CN 1, 2, 3, 4, 5, 6, 7; DLB 6, 218; DLBY 2002

Cassiodorus, Flavius Magnus c. 490(?)-c.
583(?) .... **CMLC 43**

Cassirer, Ernst 1874-1945 .... **TCLC 61**
See also CA 157

Chapman, John Jay 1862-1933 .... **TCLC 7**
See also AMWS 14; CA 104; 191

Chapman, Lee
See Bradley, Marion Zimmer
See also GLL 1

Chapman, Walker
See Silverberg, Robert

Chappell, Fred (Davis) 1936- .... **CLC 40, 78, 162**
See also CA 5-8R, 198; CAAE 198; CAAS 4; CANR 8, 33, 67, 110; CN 6; CP 7; CSW; DLB 6, 105; HGG

Char, Rene(-Emile) 1907-1988 .... **CLC 9, 11, 14, 55; PC 56**
See also CA 13-16R; 124; CANR 32; DAM POET; DLB 258; EWL 3; GFL 1789 to the Present; MTCW 1, 2; RGWL 2, 3

Charby, Jay
See Ellison, Harlan (Jay)

Chardin, Pierre Teilhard de
See Teilhard de Chardin, (Marie Joseph) Pierre

Chariton fl. 1st cent. (?)- .... **CMLC 49**

Charlemagne 742-814 .... **CMLC 37**

Charles I 1600-1649 .... **LC 13**

Charriere, Isabelle de 1740-1805 .. **NCLC 66**
See also DLB 313

Chartier, Alain c. 1392-1430 .... **LC 94**
See also DLB 208

Chartier, Emile-Auguste
See Alain

Charyn, Jerome 1937- .... **CLC 5, 8, 18**
See also CA 5-8R; CAAS 1; CANR 7, 61, 101; CMW 4; CN 1, 2, 3, 4, 5, 6, 7; DLBY 1983; MTCW 1

Chase, Adam
See Marlowe, Stephen

Chase, Mary (Coyle) 1907-1981 .... **DC 1**
See also CA 77-80; 105; CAD; CWD; DFS 11; DLB 228; SATA 17; SATA-Obit 29

Chase, Mary Ellen 1887-1973 .... **CLC 2; TCLC 124**
See also CA 13-16; 41-44R; CAP 1; SATA 10

Chase, Nicholas
See Hyde, Anthony
See also CCA 1

Chateaubriand, Francois Rene de
1768-1848 .... **NCLC 3, 134**
See also DLB 119; EW 5; GFL 1789 to the Present; RGWL 2, 3; TWA

Chatelet, Gabrielle-Emilie Du
See du Chatelet, Emilie
See also DLB 313

Chatterje, Sarat Chandra 1876-1936(?)
See Chatterji, Saratchandra
See also CA 109

Chatterji, Bankim Chandra
1838-1894 .... **NCLC 19**

Chatterji, Saratchandra .... **TCLC 13**
See Chatterje, Sarat Chandra
See also CA 186; EWL 3

Chatterton, Thomas 1752-1770 .... **LC 3, 54**
See also DAM POET; DLB 109; RGEL 2

Chatwin, (Charles) Bruce
1940-1989 .... **CLC 28, 57, 59**
See also AAYA 4; BEST 90:1; BRWS 4; CA 85-88; 127; CPW; DAM POP; DLB 194, 204; EWL 3; MTFW 2005

Chaucer, Daniel
See Ford, Ford Madox
See also RHW

Chaucer, Geoffrey 1340(?)-1400 .. **LC 17, 56; PC 19, 58; WLCS**
See also BRW 1; BRWC 1; BRWR 2; CD-BLB Before 1660; DA; DA3; DAB; DAC; DAM MST, POET; DLB 146; LAIT 1; PAB; PFS 14; RGEL 2; TEA; WLIT 3; WP

Chavez, Denise (Elia) 1948- .... **HLC 1**
See also CA 131; CANR 56, 81, 137; DAM MULT; DLB 122; FW; HW 1, 2; LLW; MAL 5; MTCW 2; MTFW 2005

Chaviaras, Strates 1935-
See Haviaras, Stratis
See also CA 105

Chayefsky, Paddy .... **CLC 23**
See Chayefsky, Sidney
See also CAD; DLB 7, 44; DLBY 1981; RGAL 4

Chayefsky, Sidney 1923-1981
See Chayefsky, Paddy
See also CA 9-12R; 104; CANR 18; DAM DRAM

Chedid, Andree 1920- .... **CLC 47**
See also CA 145; CANR 95; EWL 3

Cheever, John 1912-1982 ..... **CLC 3, 7, 8, 11, 15, 25, 64; SSC 1, 38, 57; WLC**
See also AAYA 65; AMWS 1; BPFB 1; CA 5-8R; 106; CABS 1; CANR 5, 27, 76; CDALB 1941-1968; CN 1, 2, 3; CPW; DA; DA3; DAB; DAC; DAM MST, NOV, POP; DLB 2, 102, 227; DLBY 1980, 1982; EWL 3; EXPS; INT CANR-5; MAL 5; MTCW 1, 2; MTFW 2005; RGAL 4; RGSF 2; SSFS 2, 14; TUS

Cheever, Susan 1943- .... **CLC 18, 48**
See also CA 103; CANR 27, 51, 92; DLBY 1982; INT CANR-27

Chekhonte, Antosha
See Chekhov, Anton (Pavlovich)

Chekhov, Anton (Pavlovich)
1860-1904 .... **DC 9; SSC 2, 28, 41, 51, 85; TCLC 3, 10, 31, 55, 96, 163; WLC**
See also AAYA 68; BYA 14; CA 104; 124; DA; DA3; DAB; DAC; DAM DRAM, MST; DFS 1, 5, 10, 12; DLB 277; EW 7; EWL 3; EXPS; LAIT 3; LATS 1:1; RGSF 2; RGWL 2, 3; SATA 90; SSFS 5, 13, 14; TWA

Cheney, Lynne V. 1941- .... **CLC 70**
See also CA 89-92; CANR 58, 117; SATA 152

Chernyshevsky, Nikolai Gavrilovich
See Chernyshevsky, Nikolay Gavrilovich
See also DLB 238

Chernyshevsky, Nikolay Gavrilovich
1828-1889 .... **NCLC 1**
See Chernyshevsky, Nikolai Gavrilovich

Cherry, Carolyn Janice 1942-
See Cherryh, C. J.
See also CA 65-68; CANR 10

Cherryh, C. J. .... **CLC 35**
See Cherry, Carolyn Janice
See also AAYA 24; BPFB 1; DLBY 1980; FANT; SATA 93; SCFW 2; SFW 4; YAW

Chesnutt, Charles W(addell)
1858-1932 .... **BLC 1; SSC 7, 54; TCLC 5, 39**
See also AFAW 1, 2; AMWS 14; BW 1, 3; CA 106; 125; CANR 76; DAM MULT; DLB 12, 50, 78; EWL 3; MAL 5; MTCW 1, 2; MTFW 2005; RGAL 4; RGSF 2; SSFS 11

Chester, Alfred 1929(?)-1971 .... **CLC 49**
See also CA 196; 33-36R; DLB 130; MAL 5

Chesterton, G(ilbert) K(eith)
1874-1936 . **PC 28; SSC 1, 46; TCLC 1, 6, 64**
See also AAYA 57; BRW 6; CA 104; 132; CANR 73, 131; CDBLB 1914-1945; CMW 4; DAM NOV, POET; DLB 10, 19, 34, 70, 98, 149, 178; EWL 3; FANT; MSW; MTCW 1, 2; MTFW 2005; RGEL 2; RGSF 2; SATA 27; SUFW 1

Chettle, Henry 1560-1607(?) .... **LC 112**
See also DLB 136; RGEL 2

Chiang, Pin-chin 1904-1986
See Ding Ling
See also CA 118

Chief Joseph 1840-1904 .... **NNAL**
See also CA 152; DA3; DAM MULT

Chief Seattle 1786(?)-1866 .... **NNAL**
See also DA3; DAM MULT

Ch'ien, Chung-shu 1910-1998 .... **CLC 22**
See Qian Zhongshu
See also CA 130; CANR 73; MTCW 1, 2

Chikamatsu Monzaemon 1653-1724 ... **LC 66**
See also RGWL 2, 3

Child, L. Maria
See Child, Lydia Maria

Child, Lydia Maria 1802-1880 .. **NCLC 6, 73**
See also DLB 1, 74, 243; RGAL 4; SATA 67

Child, Mrs.
See Child, Lydia Maria

Child, Philip 1898-1978 .... **CLC 19, 68**
See also CA 13-14; CAP 1; CP 1; DLB 68; RHW; SATA 47

Childers, (Robert) Erskine
1870-1922 .... **TCLC 65**
See also CA 113; 153; DLB 70

Childress, Alice 1920-1994 . **BLC 1; CLC 12, 15, 86, 96; DC 4; TCLC 116**
See also AAYA 8; BW 2, 3; BYA 2; CA 45-48; 146; CAD; CANR 3, 27, 50, 74; CLR 14; CWD; DA3; DAM DRAM, MULT, NOV; DFS 2, 8, 14; DLB 7, 38, 249; JRDA; LAIT 5; MAICYA 1, 2; MAIC-YAS 1; MAL 5; MTCW 1, 2; MTFW 2005; RGAL 4; SATA 7, 48, 81; TUS; WYA; YAW

Chin, Frank (Chew, Jr.) 1940- .... **AAL; CLC 135; DC 7**
See also CA 33-36R; CAD; CANR 71; CD 5, 6; DAM MULT; DLB 206, 312; LAIT 5; RGAL 4

Chin, Marilyn (Mei Ling) 1955- .... **PC 40**
See also CA 129; CANR 70, 113; CWP; DLB 312

Chislett, (Margaret) Anne 1943- ...... **CLC 34**
See also CA 151

Chitty, Thomas Willes 1926- .... **CLC 11**
See Hinde, Thomas
See also CA 5-8R; CN 7

Chivers, Thomas Holley
1809-1858 .... **NCLC 49**
See also DLB 3, 248; RGAL 4

Choi, Susan 1969- .... **CLC 119**
See also CA 223

Chomette, Rene Lucien 1898-1981
See Clair, Rene
See also CA 103

Chomsky, (Avram) Noam 1928- ..... **CLC 132**
See also CA 17-20R; CANR 28, 62, 110, 132; DA3; DLB 246; MTCW 1, 2; MTFW 2005

Chona, Maria 1845(?)-1936 .... **NNAL**
See also CA 144

Chopin, Kate .... **SSC 8, 68; TCLC 127; WLCS**
See Chopin, Katherine
See also AAYA 33; AMWR 2; AMWS 1; BYA 11, 15; CDALB 1865-1917; DA; DAB; DLB 12, 78; EXPN; EXPS; FL 1:3; FW; LAIT 3; MAL 5; MAWW; NFS 3; RGAL 4; RGSF 2; SSFS 2, 13, 17; TUS

Chopin, Katherine 1851-1904
See Chopin, Kate
See also CA 104; 122; DA3; DAC; DAM MST, NOV

Chretien de Troyes c. 12th cent. - . **CMLC 10**
See also DLB 208; EW 1; RGWL 2, 3; TWA

Christie
See Ichikawa, Kon

Clutha, Janet Paterson Frame 1924-2004
See Frame, Janet
See also CA 1-4R; 224; CANR 2, 36, 76, 135; MTCW 1, 2; SATA 119

Clyne, Terence
See Blatty, William Peter

Cobalt, Martin
See Mayne, William (James Carter)

Cobb, Irvin S(hrewsbury)
1876-1944 .... **TCLC 77**
See also CA 175; DLB 11, 25, 86

Cobbett, William 1763-1835 .... **NCLC 49**
See also DLB 43, 107, 158; RGEL 2

Coburn, D(onald) L(ee) 1938- .... **CLC 10**
See also CA 89-92

Cocteau, Jean (Maurice Eugene Clement)
1889-1963 ...... **CLC 1, 8, 15, 16, 43; DC 17; TCLC 119; WLC**
See also CA 25-28; CANR 40; CAP 2; DA; DA3; DAB; DAC; DAM DRAM, MST, NOV; DLB 65, 258, 321; EW 10; EWL 3; GFL 1789 to the Present; MTCW 1, 2; RGWL 2, 3; TWA

Codrescu, Andrei 1946- .... **CLC 46, 121**
See also CA 33-36R; CAAS 19; CANR 13, 34, 53, 76, 125; CN 7; DA3; DAM POET; MAL 5; MTCW 2; MTFW 2005

Coe, Max
See Bourne, Randolph S(illiman)

Coe, Tucker
See Westlake, Donald E(dwin)

Coen, Ethan 1958- .... **CLC 108**
See also AAYA 54; CA 126; CANR 85

Coen, Joel 1955- .... **CLC 108**
See also AAYA 54; CA 126; CANR 119

The Coen Brothers
See Coen, Ethan; Coen, Joel

Coetzee, J(ohn) M(axwell) 1940- ..... **CLC 23, 33, 66, 117, 161, 162**
See also AAYA 37; AFW; BRWS 6; CA 77-80; CANR 41, 54, 74, 114, 133; CN 4, 5, 6, 7; DA3; DAM NOV; DLB 225; EWL 3; LMFS 2; MTCW 1, 2; MTFW 2005; NFS 21; WLIT 2; WWE 1

Coffey, Brian
See Koontz, Dean R.

Coffin, Robert P(eter) Tristram
1892-1955 .... **TCLC 95**
See also CA 123; 169; DLB 45

Cohan, George M(ichael)
1878-1942 .... **TCLC 60**
See also CA 157; DLB 249; RGAL 4

Cohen, Arthur A(llen) 1928-1986 ...... **CLC 7, 31**
See also CA 1-4R; 120; CANR 1, 17, 42; DLB 28

Cohen, Leonard (Norman) 1934- ...... **CLC 3, 38**
See also CA 21-24R; CANR 14, 69; CN 1, 2, 3, 4, 5, 6, 7; CP 1, 2, 3, 4, 5, 6, 7; DAC; DAM MST; DLB 53; EWL 3; MTCW 1

Cohen, Matt(hew) 1942-1999 .... **CLC 19**
See also CA 61-64; 187; CAAS 18; CANR 40; CN 1, 2, 3, 4, 5, 6; DAC; DLB 53

Cohen-Solal, Annie 1948- .... **CLC 50**
See also CA 239

Colegate, Isabel 1931- .... **CLC 36**
See also CA 17-20R; CANR 8, 22, 74; CN 4, 5, 6, 7; DLB 14, 231; INT CANR-22; MTCW 1

Coleman, Emmett
See Reed, Ishmael (Scott)

Coleridge, Hartley 1796-1849 .... **NCLC 90**
See also DLB 96

Coleridge, M. E.
See Coleridge, Mary E(lizabeth)

Coleridge, Mary E(lizabeth)
1861-1907 .... **TCLC 73**
See also CA 116; 166; DLB 19, 98

Coleridge, Samuel Taylor
1772-1834 ...... **NCLC 9, 54, 99, 111; PC 11, 39, 67; WLC**
See also AAYA 66; BRW 4; BRWR 2; BYA 4; CDBLB 1789-1832; DA; DA3; DAB; DAC; DAM MST, POET; DLB 93, 107; EXPP; LATS 1:1; LMFS 1; PAB; PFS 4, 5; RGEL 2; TEA; WLIT 3; WP

Coleridge, Sara 1802-1852 .... **NCLC 31**
See also DLB 199

Coles, Don 1928- .... **CLC 46**
See also CA 115; CANR 38; CP 7

Coles, Robert (Martin) 1929- .... **CLC 108**
See also CA 45-48; CANR 3, 32, 66, 70, 135; INT CANR-32; SATA 23

Colette, (Sidonie-Gabrielle)
1873-1954 .... **SSC 10; TCLC 1, 5, 16**
See Willy, Colette
See also CA 104; 131; DA3; DAM NOV; DLB 65; EW 9; EWL 3; GFL 1789 to the Present; MTCW 1, 2; MTFW 2005; RGWL 2, 3; TWA

Collett, (Jacobine) Camilla (Wergeland)
1813-1895 .... **NCLC 22**

Collier, Christopher 1930- .... **CLC 30**
See also AAYA 13; BYA 2; CA 33-36R; CANR 13, 33, 102; JRDA; MAICYA 1, 2; SATA 16, 70; WYA; YAW 1

Collier, James Lincoln 1928- .... **CLC 30**
See also AAYA 13; BYA 2; CA 9-12R; CANR 4, 33, 60, 102; CLR 3; DAM POP; JRDA; MAICYA 1, 2; SAAS 21; SATA 8, 70; WYA; YAW 1

Collier, Jeremy 1650-1726 .... **LC 6**

Collier, John 1901-1980 . **SSC 19; TCLC 127**
See also CA 65-68; 97-100; CANR 10; CN 1, 2; DLB 77, 255; FANT; SUFW 1

Collier, Mary 1690-1762 .... **LC 86**
See also DLB 95

Collingwood, R(obin) G(eorge)
1889(?)-1943 .... **TCLC 67**
See also CA 117; 155; DLB 262

Collins, Billy 1941- .... **PC 68**
See also AAYA 64; CA 151; CANR 92; MTFW 2005; PFS 18

Collins, Hunt
See Hunter, Evan

Collins, Linda 1931- .... **CLC 44**
See also CA 125

Collins, Tom
See Furphy, Joseph
See also RGEL 2

Collins, (William) Wilkie
1824-1889 .... **NCLC 1, 18, 93**
See also BRWS 6; CDBLB 1832-1890; CMW 4; DLB 18, 70, 159; GL 2; MSW; RGEL 2; RGSF 2; SUFW 1; WLIT 4

Collins, William 1721-1759 .... **LC 4, 40**
See also BRW 3; DAM POET; DLB 109; RGEL 2

Collodi, Carlo .... **NCLC 54**
See Lorenzini, Carlo
See also CLR 5; WCH; WLIT 7

Colman, George
See Glassco, John

Colman, George, the Elder
1732-1794 .... **LC 98**
See also RGEL 2

Colonna, Vittoria 1492-1547 .... **LC 71**
See also RGWL 2, 3

Colt, Winchester Remington
See Hubbard, L(afayette) Ron(ald)

Colter, Cyrus J. 1910-2002 .... **CLC 58**
See also BW 1; CA 65-68; 205; CANR 10, 66; CN 2, 3, 4, 5, 6; DLB 33

Colton, James
See Hansen, Joseph
See also GLL 1

Colum, Padraic 1881-1972 .... **CLC 28**
See also BYA 4; CA 73-76; 33-36R; CANR 35; CLR 36; CP 1; CWRI 5; DLB 19; MAICYA 1, 2; MTCW 1; RGEL 2; SATA 15; WCH

Colvin, James
See Moorcock, Michael (John)

Colwin, Laurie (E.) 1944-1992 .... **CLC 5, 13, 23, 84**
See also CA 89-92; 139; CANR 20, 46; DLB 218; DLBY 1980; MTCW 1

Comfort, Alex(ander) 1920-2000 .... **CLC 7**
See also CA 1-4R; 190; CANR 1, 45; CN 1, 2, 3, 4; CP 1, 2, 3, 4, 5, 6, 7; DAM POP; MTCW 2

Comfort, Montgomery
See Campbell, (John) Ramsey

Compton-Burnett, I(vy)
1892(?)-1969 .... **CLC 1, 3, 10, 15, 34**
See also BRW 7; CA 1-4R; 25-28R; CANR 4; DAM NOV; DLB 36; EWL 3; MTCW 1, 2; RGEL 2

Comstock, Anthony 1844-1915 ...... **TCLC 13**
See also CA 110; 169

Comte, Auguste 1798-1857 .... **NCLC 54**

Conan Doyle, Arthur
See Doyle, Sir Arthur Conan
See also BPFB 1; BYA 4, 5, 11

Conde (Abellan), Carmen
1901-1996 .... **HLCS 1**
See also CA 177; CWW 2; DLB 108; EWL 3; HW 2

Conde, Maryse 1937- ..... **BLCS; CLC 52, 92**
See also BW 2, 3; CA 110, 190; CAAE 190; CANR 30, 53, 76; CWW 2; DAM MULT; EWL 3; MTCW 2; MTFW 2005

Condillac, Etienne Bonnot de
1714-1780 .... **LC 26**
See also DLB 313

Condon, Richard (Thomas)
1915-1996 .... **CLC 4, 6, 8, 10, 45, 100**
See also BEST 90:3; BPFB 1; CA 1-4R; 151; CAAS 1; CANR 2, 23; CMW 4; CN 1, 2, 3, 4, 5, 6; DAM NOV; INT CANR-23; MAL 5; MTCW 1, 2

Condorcet .... **LC 104**
See Condorcet, marquis de Marie-Jean-Antoine-Nicolas Caritat
See also GFL Beginnings to 1789

Condorcet, marquis de
Marie-Jean-Antoine-Nicolas Caritat
1743-1794
See Condorcet
See also DLB 313

Confucius 551B.C.-479B.C. .... **CMLC 19, 65; WLCS**
See also DA; DA3; DAB; DAC; DAM MST

Congreve, William 1670-1729 ... **DC 2; LC 5, 21; WLC**
See also BRW 2; CDBLB 1660-1789; DA; DAB; DAC; DAM DRAM, MST, POET; DFS 15; DLB 39, 84; RGEL 2; WLIT 3

Conley, Robert J(ackson) 1940- .... **NNAL**
See also CA 41-44R; CANR 15, 34, 45, 96; DAM MULT; TCWW 2

Connell, Evan S(helby), Jr. 1924- . **CLC 4, 6, 45**
See also AAYA 7; AMWS 14; CA 1-4R; CAAS 2; CANR 2, 39, 76, 97, 140; CN 1, 2, 3, 4, 5, 6; DAM NOV; DLB 2; DLBY 1981; MAL 5; MTCW 1, 2; MTFW 2005

Connelly, Marc(us Cook) 1890-1980 . **CLC 7**
See also CA 85-88; 102; CAD; CANR 30; DFS 12; DLB 7; DLBY 1980; MAL 5; RGAL 4; SATA-Obit 25

Connor, Ralph .... **TCLC 31**
See Gordon, Charles William
See also DLB 92; TCWW 1, 2

Davis, Frank Marshall 1905-1987 ...... **BLC 1**
    See also BW 2, 3; CA 125; 123; CANR 42,
    80; DAM MULT; DLB 51

Davis, Gordon
    See Hunt, E(verette) Howard, (Jr.)

Davis, H(arold) L(enoir) 1896-1960 . **CLC 49**
    See also ANW; CA 178; 89-92; DLB 9,
    206; SATA 114; TCWW 1, 2

Davis, Natalie Zemon 1928- .... **CLC 204**
    See also CA 53-56; CANR 58, 100

Davis, Rebecca (Blaine) Harding
    1831-1910 .... **SSC 38; TCLC 6**
    See also CA 104; 179; DLB 74, 239; FW;
    NFS 14; RGAL 4; TUS

Davis, Richard Harding
    1864-1916 .... **TCLC 24**
    See also CA 114; 179; DLB 12, 23, 78, 79,
    189; DLBD 13; RGAL 4

Davison, Frank Dalby 1893-1970 ..... **CLC 15**
    See also CA 217; 116; DLB 260

Davison, Lawrence H.
    See Lawrence, D(avid) H(erbert Richards)

Davison, Peter (Hubert) 1928-2004 . **CLC 28**
    See also CA 9-12R; 234; CAAS 4; CANR
    3, 43, 84; CP 1, 2, 3, 4, 5, 6, 7; DLB 5

Davys, Mary 1674-1732 .... **LC 1, 46**
    See also DLB 39

Dawson, (Guy) Fielding (Lewis)
    1930-2002 .... **CLC 6**
    See also CA 85-88; 202; CANR 108; DLB
    130; DLBY 2002

Dawson, Peter
    See Faust, Frederick (Schiller)
    See also TCWW 1, 2

Day, Clarence (Shepard, Jr.)
    1874-1935 .... **TCLC 25**
    See also CA 108; 199; DLB 11

Day, John 1574(?)-1640(?) .... **LC 70**
    See also DLB 62, 170; RGEL 2

Day, Thomas 1748-1789 .... **LC 1**
    See also DLB 39; YABC 1

Day Lewis, C(ecil) 1904-1972 . **CLC 1, 6, 10;**
    PC 11
    See Blake, Nicholas; Lewis, C. Day
    See also BRWS 3; CA 13-16; 33-36R;
    CANR 34; CAP 1; CP 1; CWRI 5; DAM
    POET; DLB 15, 20; EWL 3; MTCW 1, 2;
    RGEL 2

Dazai Osamu .... **SSC 41; TCLC 11**
    See Tsushima, Shuji
    See also CA 164; DLB 182; EWL 3; MJW;
    RGSF 2; RGWL 2, 3; TWA

de Andrade, Carlos Drummond
    See Drummond de Andrade, Carlos

de Andrade, Mario 1892(?)-1945
    See Andrade, Mario de
    See also CA 178; HW 2

Deane, Norman
    See Creasey, John

Deane, Seamus (Francis) 1940- ...... **CLC 122**
    See also CA 118; CANR 42

de Beauvoir, Simone (Lucie Ernestine Marie
    Bertrand)
    See Beauvoir, Simone (Lucie Ernestine
    Marie Bertrand) de

de Beer, P.
    See Bosman, Herman Charles

De Botton, Alain 1969- .... **CLC 203**
    See also CA 159; CANR 96

de Brissac, Malcolm
    See Dickinson, Peter (Malcolm de Brissac)

de Campos, Alvaro
    See Pessoa, Fernando (Antonio Nogueira)

de Chardin, Pierre Teilhard
    See Teilhard de Chardin, (Marie Joseph)
    Pierre

de Crenne, Helisenne c. 1510-c.
    1560 .... **LC 113**

Dee, John 1527-1608 .... **LC 20**
    See also DLB 136, 213

Deer, Sandra 1940- .... **CLC 45**
    See also CA 186

De Ferrari, Gabriella 1941- .... **CLC 65**
    See also CA 146

de Filippo, Eduardo 1900-1984 ... **TCLC 127**
    See also CA 132; 114; EWL 3; MTCW 1;
    RGWL 2, 3

Defoe, Daniel 1660(?)-1731 .... **LC 1, 42, 108;**
    WLC
    See also AAYA 27; BRW 3; BRWR 1; BYA
    4; CDBLB 1660-1789; CLR 61; DA;
    DA3; DAB; DAC; DAM MST, NOV;
    DLB 39, 95, 101; JRDA; LAIT 1; LMFS
    1; MAICYA 1, 2; NFS 9, 13; RGEL 2;
    SATA 22; TEA; WCH; WLIT 3

de Gourmont, Remy(-Marie-Charles)
    See Gourmont, Remy(-Marie-Charles) de

de Gournay, Marie le Jars
    1566-1645 .... **LC 98**
    See also FW

de Hartog, Jan 1914-2002 .... **CLC 19**
    See also CA 1-4R; 210; CANR 1; DFS 12

de Hostos, E. M.
    See Hostos (y Bonilla), Eugenio Maria de

de Hostos, Eugenio M.
    See Hostos (y Bonilla), Eugenio Maria de

Deighton, Len .... **CLC 4, 7, 22, 46**
    See Deighton, Leonard Cyril
    See also AAYA 6; BEST 89:2; BPFB 1; CD-
    BLB 1960 to Present; CMW 4; CN 1, 2,
    3, 4, 5, 6, 7; CPW; DLB 87

Deighton, Leonard Cyril 1929-
    See Deighton, Len
    See also AAYA 57; CA 9-12R; CANR 19,
    33, 68; DA3; DAM NOV, POP; MTCW
    1, 2; MTFW 2005

Dekker, Thomas 1572(?)-1632 ..... **DC 12; LC**
    22
    See also CDBLB Before 1660; DAM
    DRAM; DLB 62, 172; LMFS 1; RGEL 2

de Laclos, Pierre Ambroise Franois
    See Laclos, Pierre-Ambroise Francois

Delacroix, (Ferdinand-Victor-)Eugene
    1798-1863 .... **NCLC 133**
    See also EW 5

Delafield, E. M. .... **TCLC 61**
    See Dashwood, Edmee Elizabeth Monica
    de la Pasture
    See also DLB 34; RHW

de la Mare, Walter (John)
    1873-1956 . **SSC 14; TCLC 4, 53; WLC**
    See also CA 163; CDBLB 1914-1945; CLR
    23; CWRI 5; DA3; DAB; DAC; DAM
    MST, POET; DLB 19, 153, 162, 255, 284;
    EWL 3; EXPP; HGG; MAICYA 1, 2;
    MTCW 2; MTFW 2005; RGEL 2; RGSF
    2; SATA 16; SUFW 1; TEA; WCH

de Lamartine, Alphonse (Marie Louis Prat)
    See Lamartine, Alphonse (Marie Louis Prat)
    de

Delaney, Franey
    See O'Hara, John (Henry)

Delaney, Shelagh 1939- .... **CLC 29**
    See also CA 17-20R; CANR 30, 67; CBD;
    CD 5, 6; CDBLB 1960 to Present; CWD;
    DAM DRAM; DFS 7; DLB 13; MTCW 1

Delany, Martin Robison
    1812-1885 .... **NCLC 93**
    See also DLB 50; RGAL 4

Delany, Mary (Granville Pendarves)
    1700-1788 .... **LC 12**

Delany, Samuel R(ay), Jr. 1942- .... **BLC 1;**
    CLC 8, 14, 38, 141
    See also AAYA 24; AFAW 2; BPFB 1; BW
    2, 3; CA 81-84; CANR 27, 43, 116; CN
    2, 3, 4, 5, 6, 7; DAM MULT; DLB 8, 33;
    FANT; MAL 5; MTCW 1, 2; RGAL 4;
    SATA 92; SCFW 1, 2; SFW 4; SUFW 2

De la Ramee, Marie Louise (Ouida)
    1839-1908
    See Ouida
    See also CA 204; SATA 20

de la Roche, Mazo 1879-1961 .... **CLC 14**
    See also CA 85-88; CANR 30; DLB 68;
    RGEL 2; RHW; SATA 64

De La Salle, Innocent
    See Hartmann, Sadakichi

de Laureamont, Comte
    See Lautreamont

Delbanco, Nicholas (Franklin)
    1942- .... **CLC 6, 13, 167**
    See also CA 17-20R, 189; CAAE 189;
    CAAS 2; CANR 29, 55, 116; CN 7; DLB
    6, 234

del Castillo, Michel 1933- .... **CLC 38**
    See also CA 109; CANR 77

Deledda, Grazia (Cosima)
    1875(?)-1936 .... **TCLC 23**
    See also CA 123; 205; DLB 264; EWL 3;
    RGWL 2, 3; WLIT 7

Deleuze, Gilles 1925-1995 .... **TCLC 116**
    See also DLB 296

Delgado, Abelardo (Lalo) B(arrientos)
    1930-2004 .... **HLC 1**
    See also CA 131; 230; CAAS 15; CANR
    90; DAM MST, MULT; DLB 82; HW 1,
    2

Delibes, Miguel .... **CLC 8, 18**
    See Delibes Setien, Miguel
    See also DLB 322; EWL 3

Delibes Setien, Miguel 1920-
    See Delibes, Miguel
    See also CA 45-48; CANR 1, 32; CWW 2;
    HW 1; MTCW 1

DeLillo, Don 1936- ..... **CLC 8, 10, 13, 27, 39,**
    54, 76, 143, 210, 213
    See also AMWC 2; AMWS 6; BEST 89:1;
    BPFB 1; CA 81-84; CANR 21, 76, 92,
    133; CN 3, 4, 5, 6, 7; CPW; DA3; DAM
    NOV, POP; DLB 6, 173; EWL 3; MAL 5;
    MTCW 1, 2; MTFW 2005; RGAL 4; TUS

de Lisser, H. G.
    See De Lisser, H(erbert) G(eorge)
    See also DLB 117

De Lisser, H(erbert) G(eorge)
    1878-1944 .... **TCLC 12**
    See de Lisser, H. G.
    See also BW 2; CA 109; 152

Deloire, Pierre
    See Peguy, Charles (Pierre)

Deloney, Thomas 1543(?)-1600 .... **LC 41**
    See also DLB 167; RGEL 2

Deloria, Ella (Cara) 1889-1971(?) ..... **NNAL**
    See also CA 152; DAM MULT; DLB 175

Deloria, Vine (Victor), Jr.
    1933-2005 .... **CLC 21, 122; NNAL**
    See also CA 53-56; CANR 5, 20, 48, 98;
    DAM MULT; DLB 175; MTCW 1; SATA
    21

del Valle-Inclan, Ramon (Maria)
    See Valle-Inclan, Ramon (Maria) del
    See also DLB 322

Del Vecchio, John M(ichael) 1947- .. **CLC 29**
    See also CA 110; DLBD 9

de Man, Paul (Adolph Michel)
    1919-1983 .... **CLC 55**
    See also CA 128; 111; CANR 61; DLB 67;
    MTCW 1, 2

DeMarinis, Rick 1934- .... **CLC 54**
    See also CA 57-60, 184; CAAE 184; CAAS
    24; CANR 9, 25, 50; DLB 218; TCWW 2

de Maupassant, (Henri Rene Albert) Guy
    See Maupassant, (Henri Rene Albert) Guy
    de

Dembry, R. Emmet
    See Murfree, Mary Noailles

Dimont, Penelope
See Mortimer, Penelope (Ruth)
Dinesen, Isak ..... **CLC 10, 29, 95; SSC 7, 75**
See Blixen, Karen (Christentze Dinesen)
See also EW 10; EWL 3; EXPS; FW; GL 2; HGG; LAIT 3; MTCW 1; NCFS 2; NFS 9; RGSF 2; RGWL 2, 3; SSFS 3, 6, 13; WLIT 2
Ding Ling .... **CLC 68**
See Chiang, Pin-chin
See also RGWL 3
Diphusa, Patty
See Almodovar, Pedro
Disch, Thomas M(ichael) 1940- ... **CLC 7, 36**
See Disch, Tom
See also AAYA 17; BPFB 1; CA 21-24R; CAAS 4; CANR 17, 36, 54, 89; CLR 18; CP 7; DA3; DLB 8; HGG; MAICYA 1, 2; MTCW 1, 2; MTFW 2005; SAAS 15; SATA 92; SCFW 1, 2; SFW 4; SUFW 2
Disch, Tom
See Disch, Thomas M(ichael)
See also DLB 282
d'Isly, Georges
See Simenon, Georges (Jacques Christian)
Disraeli, Benjamin 1804-1881 ... **NCLC 2, 39, 79**
See also BRW 4; DLB 21, 55; RGEL 2
Ditcum, Steve
See Crumb, R(obert)
Dixon, Paige
See Corcoran, Barbara (Asenath)
Dixon, Stephen 1936- .... **CLC 52; SSC 16**
See also AMWS 12; CA 89-92; CANR 17, 40, 54, 91; CN 4, 5, 6, 7; DLB 130; MAL 5
Dixon, Thomas, Jr. 1864-1946 ..... **TCLC 163**
See also RHW
Djebar, Assia 1936- .... **CLC 182**
See also CA 188; EWL 3; RGWL 3; WLIT 2
Doak, Annie
See Dillard, Annie
Dobell, Sydney Thompson
1824-1874 .... **NCLC 43**
See also DLB 32; RGEL 2
Doblin, Alfred .... **TCLC 13**
See Doeblin, Alfred
See also CDWLB 2; EWL 3; RGWL 2, 3
Dobroliubov, Nikolai Aleksandrovich
See Dobrolyubov, Nikolai Alexandrovich
See also DLB 277
Dobrolyubov, Nikolai Alexandrovich
1836-1861 .... **NCLC 5**
See Dobroliubov, Nikolai Aleksandrovich
Dobson, Austin 1840-1921 .... **TCLC 79**
See also DLB 35, 144
Dobyns, Stephen 1941- .... **CLC 37**
See also AMWS 13; CA 45-48; CANR 2, 18, 99; CMW 4; CP 4, 5, 6, 7; PFS 23
Doctorow, E(dgar) L(aurence)
1931- ...... **CLC 6, 11, 15, 18, 37, 44, 65, 113, 214**
See also AAYA 22; AITN 2; AMWS 4; BEST 89:3; BPFB 1; CA 45-48; CANR 2, 33, 51, 76, 97, 133; CDALB 1968-1988; CN 3, 4, 5, 6, 7; CPW; DA3; DAM NOV, POP; DLB 2, 28, 173; DLBY 1980; EWL 3; LAIT 3; MAL 5; MTCW 1, 2; MTFW 2005; NFS 6; RGAL 4; RHW; TCLE 1:1; TCWW 1, 2; TUS
Dodgson, Charles L(utwidge) 1832-1898
See Carroll, Lewis
See also CLR 2; DA; DA3; DAB; DAC; DAM MST, NOV, POET; MAICYA 1, 2; SATA 100; YABC 2
Dodsley, Robert 1703-1764 .... **LC 97**
See also DLB 95; RGEL 2

Dodson, Owen (Vincent) 1914-1983 .. **BLC 1; CLC 79**
See also BW 1; CA 65-68; 110; CANR 24; DAM MULT; DLB 76
Doeblin, Alfred 1878-1957 .... **TCLC 13**
See Doblin, Alfred
See also CA 110; 141; DLB 66
Doerr, Harriet 1910-2002 .... **CLC 34**
See also CA 117; 122; 213; CANR 47; INT CA-122; LATS 1:2
Domecq, H(onorio Bustos)
See Bioy Casares, Adolfo
Domecq, H(onorio) Bustos
See Bioy Casares, Adolfo; Borges, Jorge Luis
Domini, Rey
See Lorde, Audre (Geraldine)
See also GLL 1
Dominique
See Proust, (Valentin-Louis-George-Eugene) Marcel
Don, A
See Stephen, Sir Leslie
Donaldson, Stephen R(eeder)
1947- .... **CLC 46, 138**
See also AAYA 36; BPFB 1; CA 89-92; CANR 13, 55, 99; CPW; DAM POP; FANT; INT CANR-13; SATA 121; SFW 4; SUFW 1, 2
Donleavy, J(ames) P(atrick) 1926- .... **CLC 1, 4, 6, 10, 45**
See also AITN 2; BPFB 1; CA 9-12R; CANR 24, 49, 62, 80, 124; CBD; CD 5, 6; CN 1, 2, 3, 4, 5, 6, 7; DLB 6, 173; INT CANR-24; MAL 5; MTCW 1, 2; MTFW 2005; RGAL 4
Donnadieu, Marguerite
See Duras, Marguerite
Donne, John 1572-1631 ... **LC 10, 24, 91; PC 1, 43; WLC**
See also AAYA 67; BRW 1; BRWC 1; BRWR 2; CDBLB Before 1660; DA; DAB; DAC; DAM MST, POET; DLB 121, 151; EXPP; PAB; PFS 2, 11; RGEL 3; TEA; WLIT 3; WP
Donnell, David 1939(?)- .... **CLC 34**
See also CA 197
Donoghue, Denis 1928- .... **CLC 209**
See also CA 17-20R; CANR 16, 102
Donoghue, P. S.
See Hunt, E(verette) Howard, (Jr.)
Donoso (Yanez), Jose 1924-1996 ... **CLC 4, 8, 11, 32, 99; HLC 1; SSC 34; TCLC 133**
See also CA 81-84; 155; CANR 32, 73; CD-WLB 3; CWW 2; DAM MULT; DLB 113; EWL 3; HW 1, 2; LAW; LAWS 1; MTCW 1, 2; MTFW 2005; RGSF 2; WLIT 1
Donovan, John 1928-1992 .... **CLC 35**
See also AAYA 20; CA 97-100; 137; CLR 3; MAICYA 1, 2; SATA 72; SATA-Brief 29; YAW
Don Roberto
See Cunninghame Graham, Robert (Gallnigad) Bontine
Doolittle, Hilda 1886-1961 . **CLC 3, 8, 14, 31, 34, 73; PC 5; WLC**
See H. D.
See also AAYA 66; AMWS 1; CA 97-100; CANR 35, 131; DA; DAC; DAM MST, POET; DLB 4, 45; EWL 3; FW; GLL 1; LMFS 2; MAL 5; MAWW; MTCW 1, 2; MTFW 2005; PFS 6; RGAL 4
Doppo, Kunikida .... **TCLC 99**
See Kunikida Doppo
Dorfman, Ariel 1942- .... **CLC 48, 77, 189; HLC 1**
See also CA 124; 130; CANR 67, 70, 135; CWW 2; DAM MULT; DFS 4; EWL 3; HW 1, 2; INT CA-130; WLIT 1

Dorn, Edward (Merton)
1929-1999 .... **CLC 10, 18**
See also CA 93-96; 187; CANR 42, 79; CP 1, 2, 3, 4, 5, 6, 7; DLB 5; INT CA-93-96; WP
Dor-Ner, Zvi .... **CLC 70**
Dorris, Michael (Anthony)
1945-1997 .... **CLC 109; NNAL**
See also AAYA 20; BEST 90:1; BYA 12; CA 102; 157; CANR 19, 46, 75; CLR 58; DA3; DAM MULT, NOV; DLB 175; LAIT 5; MTCW 2; MTFW 2005; NFS 3; RGAL 4; SATA 75; SATA-Obit 94; TCWW 2; YAW
Dorris, Michael A.
See Dorris, Michael (Anthony)
Dorsan, Luc
See Simenon, Georges (Jacques Christian)
Dorsange, Jean
See Simenon, Georges (Jacques Christian)
Dorset
See Sackville, Thomas
Dos Passos, John (Roderigo)
1896-1970 ... **CLC 1, 4, 8, 11, 15, 25, 34, 82; WLC**
See also AMW; BPFB 1; CA 1-4R; 29-32R; CANR 3; CDALB 1929-1941; DA; DA3; DAB; DAC; DAM MST, NOV; DLB 4, 9, 274, 316; DLBD 1; DLBY 1996; EWL 3; MAL 5; MTCW 1, 2; MTFW 2005; NFS 14; RGAL 4; TUS
Dossage, Jean
See Simenon, Georges (Jacques Christian)
Dostoevsky, Fedor Mikhailovich
1821-1881 .. **NCLC 2, 7, 21, 33, 43, 119; SSC 2, 33, 44; WLC**
See Dostoevsky, Fyodor
See also AAYA 40; DA; DA3; DAB; DAC; DAM MST, NOV; EW 7; EXPN; NFS 3, 8; RGSF 2; RGWL 2, 3; SSFS 8; TWA
Dostoevsky, Fyodor
See Dostoevsky, Fedor Mikhailovich
See also DLB 238; LATS 1:1; LMFS 1, 2
Doty, M. R.
See Doty, Mark (Alan)
Doty, Mark
See Doty, Mark (Alan)
Doty, Mark (Alan) 1953(?)- .... **CLC 176; PC 53**
See also AMWS 11; CA 161, 183; CAAE 183; CANR 110
Doty, Mark A.
See Doty, Mark (Alan)
Doughty, Charles M(ontagu)
1843-1926 .... **TCLC 27**
See also CA 115; 178; DLB 19, 57, 174
Douglas, Ellen .... **CLC 73**
See Haxton, Josephine Ayres; Williamson, Ellen Douglas
See also CN 5, 6, 7; CSW; DLB 292
Douglas, Gavin 1475(?)-1522 .... **LC 20**
See also DLB 132; RGEL 2
Douglas, George
See Brown, George Douglas
See also RGEL 2
Douglas, Keith (Castellain)
1920-1944 .... **TCLC 40**
See also BRW 7; CA 160; DLB 27; EWL 3; PAB; RGEL 2
Douglas, Leonard
See Bradbury, Ray (Douglas)
Douglas, Michael
See Crichton, (John) Michael
Douglas, (George) Norman
1868-1952 .... **TCLC 68**
See also BRW 6; CA 119; 157; DLB 34, 195; RGEL 2
Douglas, William
See Brown, George Douglas

Duncan, Isadora 1877(?)-1927 .... **TCLC 68**
See also CA 118; 149

Duncan, Lois 1934- .... **CLC 26**
See also AAYA 4, 34; BYA 6, 8; CA 1-4R;
CANR 2, 23, 36, 111; CLR 29; JRDA;
MAICYA 1, 2; MAICYAS 1; MTFW
2005; SAAS 2; SATA 1, 36, 75, 133, 141;
SATA-Essay 141; WYA; YAW

Duncan, Robert (Edward)
1919-1988 .... **CLC 1, 2, 4, 7, 15, 41, 55;**
PC 2
See also BG 1:2; CA 9-12R; 124; CANR
28, 62; CP 1, 2, 3, 4; DAM POET; DLB
5, 16, 193; EWL 3; MAL 5; MTCW 1, 2;
MTFW 2005; PFS 13; RGAL 4; WP

Duncan, Sara Jeannette
1861-1922 .... **TCLC 60**
See also CA 157; DLB 92

Dunlap, William 1766-1839 .... **NCLC 2**
See also DLB 30, 37, 59; RGAL 4

Dunn, Douglas (Eaglesham) 1942- .... **CLC 6,**
40
See also BRWS 10; CA 45-48; CANR 2,
33, 126; CP 1, 2, 3, 4, 5, 6, 7; DLB 40;
MTCW 1

Dunn, Katherine (Karen) 1945- .... **CLC 71**
See also CA 33-36R; CANR 72; HGG;
MTCW 2; MTFW 2005

Dunn, Stephen (Elliott) 1939- .. **CLC 36, 206**
See also AMWS 11; CA 33-36R; CANR
12, 48, 53, 105; CP 3, 4, 5, 6, 7; DLB
105; PFS 21

Dunne, Finley Peter 1867-1936 ...... **TCLC 28**
See also CA 108; 178; DLB 11, 23; RGAL
4

Dunne, John Gregory 1932-2003 ..... **CLC 28**
See also CA 25-28R; 222; CANR 14, 50;
CN 5, 6, 7; DLBY 1980

Dunsany, Lord .... **TCLC 2, 59**
See Dunsany, Edward John Moreton Drax
Plunkett
See also DLB 77, 153, 156, 255; FANT;
IDTP; RGEL 2; SFW 4; SUFW 1

Dunsany, Edward John Moreton Drax
Plunkett 1878-1957
See Dunsany, Lord
See also CA 104; 148; DLB 10; MTCW 2

Duns Scotus, John 1266(?)-1308 ... **CMLC 59**
See also DLB 115

du Perry, Jean
See Simenon, Georges (Jacques Christian)

Durang, Christopher (Ferdinand)
1949- .... **CLC 27, 38**
See also CA 105; CAD; CANR 50, 76, 130;
CD 5, 6; MTCW 2; MTFW 2005

Duras, Claire de 1777-1832 .... **NCLC 154**

Duras, Marguerite 1914-1996 . **CLC 3, 6, 11,**
20, 34, 40, 68, 100; SSC 40
See also BPFB 1; CA 25-28R; 151; CANR
50; CWW 2; DFS 21; DLB 83, 321; EWL
3; FL 1:5; GFL 1789 to the Present; IDFW
4; MTCW 1, 2; RGWL 2, 3; TWA

Durban, (Rosa) Pam 1947- .... **CLC 39**
See also CA 123; CANR 98; CSW

Durcan, Paul 1944- .... **CLC 43, 70**
See also CA 134; CANR 123; CP 1, 7;
DAM POET; EWL 3

Durfey, Thomas 1653-1723 .... **LC 94**
See also DLB 80; RGEL 2

Durkheim, Emile 1858-1917 .... **TCLC 55**

Durrell, Lawrence (George)
1912-1990 ..... **CLC 1, 4, 6, 8, 13, 27, 41**
See also BPFB 1; BRWS 1; CA 9-12R; 132;
CANR 40, 77; CDBLB 1945-1960; CN 1,
2, 3, 4; CP 1, 2, 3, 4; DAM NOV; DLB
15, 27, 204; DLBY 1990; EWL 3; MTCW
1, 2; RGEL 2; SFW 4; TEA

Durrenmatt, Friedrich
See Duerrenmatt, Friedrich
See also CDWLB 2; EW 13; EWL 3;
RGWL 2, 3

Dutt, Michael Madhusudan
1824-1873 .... **NCLC 118**

Dutt, Toru 1856-1877 .... **NCLC 29**
See also DLB 240

Dwight, Timothy 1752-1817 .... **NCLC 13**
See also DLB 37; RGAL 4

Dworkin, Andrea 1946-2005 ..... **CLC 43, 123**
See also CA 77-80; 238; CAAS 21; CANR
16, 39, 76, 96; FL 1:5; FW; GLL 1; INT
CANR-16; MTCW 1, 2; MTFW 2005

Dwyer, Deanna
See Koontz, Dean R.

Dwyer, K. R.
See Koontz, Dean R.

Dybek, Stuart 1942- .... **CLC 114; SSC 55**
See also CA 97-100; CANR 39; DLB 130

Dye, Richard
See De Voto, Bernard (Augustine)

Dyer, Geoff 1958- .... **CLC 149**
See also CA 125; CANR 88

Dyer, George 1755-1841 .... **NCLC 129**
See also DLB 93

Dylan, Bob 1941- .... **CLC 3, 4, 6, 12, 77; PC**
37
See also CA 41-44R; CANR 108; CP 1, 2,
3, 4, 5, 6, 7; DLB 16

Dyson, John 1943- .... **CLC 70**
See also CA 144

Dzyubin, Eduard Georgievich 1895-1934
See Bagritsky, Eduard
See also CA 170

E. V. L.
See Lucas, E(dward) V(errall)

Eagleton, Terence (Francis) 1943- .. **CLC 63,**
132
See also CA 57-60; CANR 7, 23, 68, 115;
DLB 242; LMFS 2; MTCW 1, 2; MTFW
2005

Eagleton, Terry
See Eagleton, Terence (Francis)

Early, Jack
See Scoppettone, Sandra
See also GLL 1

East, Michael
See West, Morris L(anglo)

Eastaway, Edward
See Thomas, (Philip) Edward

Eastlake, William (Derry)
1917-1997 .... **CLC 8**
See also CA 5-8R; 158; CAAS 1; CANR 5,
63; CN 1, 2, 3, 4, 5, 6; DLB 6, 206; INT
CANR-5; MAL 5; TCWW 1, 2

Eastman, Charles A(lexander)
1858-1939 .... **NNAL; TCLC 55**
See also CA 179; CANR 91; DAM MULT;
DLB 175; YABC 1

Eaton, Edith Maude 1865-1914 .... **AAL**
See Far, Sui Sin
See also CA 154; DLB 221, 312; FW

Eaton, (Lillie) Winnifred 1875-1954 .... **AAL**
See also CA 217; DLB 221, 312; RGAL 4

Eberhart, Richard 1904-2005 ...... **CLC 3, 11,**
19, 56
See also AMW; CA 1-4R; 240; CANR 2,
125; CDALB 1941-1968; CP 1, 2, 3, 4, 5,
6, 7; DAM POET; DLB 48; MAL 5;
MTCW 1; RGAL 4

Eberhart, Richard Ghormley
See Eberhart, Richard

Eberstadt, Fernanda 1960- .... **CLC 39**
See also CA 136; CANR 69, 128

Echegaray (y Eizaguirre), Jose (Maria
Waldo) 1832-1916 .... **HLCS 1; TCLC 4**
See also CA 104; CANR 32; EWL 3; HW
1; MTCW 1

Echeverria, (Jose) Esteban (Antonino)
1805-1851 .... **NCLC 18**
See also LAW

Echo
See Proust, (Valentin-Louis-George-Eugene)
Marcel

Eckert, Allan W. 1931- .... **CLC 17**
See also AAYA 18; BYA 2; CA 13-16R;
CANR 14, 45; INT CANR-14; MAICYA
2; MAICYAS 1; SAAS 21; SATA 29, 91;
SATA-Brief 27

Eckhart, Meister 1260(?)-1327(?) .. **CMLC 9,**
80
See also DLB 115; LMFS 1

Eckmar, F. R.
See de Hartog, Jan

Eco, Umberto 1932- .... **CLC 28, 60, 142**
See also BEST 90:1; BPFB 1; CA 77-80;
CANR 12, 33, 55, 110, 131; CPW; CWW
2; DA3; DAM NOV, POP; DLB 196, 242;
EWL 3; MSW; MTCW 1, 2; MTFW
2005; NFS 22; RGWL 3; WLIT 7

Eddison, E(ric) R(ucker)
1882-1945 .... **TCLC 15**
See also CA 109; 156; DLB 255; FANT;
SFW 4; SUFW 1

Eddy, Mary (Ann Morse) Baker
1821-1910 .... **TCLC 71**
See also CA 113; 174

Edel, (Joseph) Leon 1907-1997 .. **CLC 29, 34**
See also CA 1-4R; 161; CANR 1, 22, 112;
DLB 103; INT CANR-22

Eden, Emily 1797-1869 .... **NCLC 10**

Edgar, David 1948- .... **CLC 42**
See also CA 57-60; CANR 12, 61, 112;
CBD; CD 5, 6; DAM DRAM; DFS 15;
DLB 13, 233; MTCW 1

Edgerton, Clyde (Carlyle) 1944- ..... **CLC 39**
See also AAYA 17; CA 118; 134; CANR
64, 125; CN 7; CSW; DLB 278; INT CA-
134; TCLE 1:1; YAW

Edgeworth, Maria 1768-1849 ... **NCLC 1, 51,**
158; SSC 86
See also BRWS 3; DLB 116, 159, 163; FL
1:3; FW; RGEL 2; SATA 21; TEA; WLIT
3

Edmonds, Paul
See Kuttner, Henry

Edmonds, Walter D(umaux)
1903-1998 .... **CLC 35**
See also BYA 2; CA 5-8R; CANR 2; CWRI
5; DLB 9; LAIT 1; MAICYA 1, 2; MAL
5; RHW; SAAS 4; SATA 1, 27; SATA-
Obit 99

Edmondson, Wallace
See Ellison, Harlan (Jay)

Edson, Margaret 1961- ...... **CLC 199; DC 24**
See also CA 190; DFS 13; DLB 266

Edson, Russell 1935- .... **CLC 13**
See also CA 33-36R; CANR 115; CP 2, 3,
4, 5, 6, 7; DLB 244; WP

Edwards, Bronwen Elizabeth
See Rose, Wendy

Edwards, G(erald) B(asil)
1899-1976 .... **CLC 25**
See also CA 201; 110

Edwards, Gus 1939- .... **CLC 43**
See also CA 108; INT CA-108

Edwards, Jonathan 1703-1758 .... **LC 7, 54**
See also AMW; DA; DAC; DAM MST;
DLB 24, 270; RGAL 4; TUS

Edwards, Sarah Pierpont 1710-1758 .. **LC 87**
See also DLB 200

Efron, Marina Ivanovna Tsvetaeva
See Tsvetaeva (Efron), Marina (Ivanovna)

Egeria fl. 4th cent. - .... **CMLC 70**

Egoyan, Atom 1960- .... **CLC 151**
See also AAYA 63; CA 157

Ehle, John (Marsden, Jr.) 1925- ...... CLC 27
See also CA 9-12R; CSW
Ehrenbourg, Ilya (Grigoryevich)
See Ehrenburg, Ilya (Grigoryevich)
Ehrenburg, Ilya (Grigoryevich)
1891-1967 .... CLC 18, 34, 62
See Erenburg, Il'ia Grigor'evich
See also CA 102; 25-28R; EWL 3
Ehrenburg, Ilyo (Grigoryevich)
See Ehrenburg, Ilya (Grigoryevich)
Ehrenreich, Barbara 1941- .... CLC 110
See also BEST 90:4; CA 73-76; CANR 16,
37, 62, 117; DLB 246; FW; MTCW 1, 2;
MTFW 2005
Eich, Gunter
See Eich, Gunter
See also RGWL 2, 3
Eich, Gunter 1907-1972 .... CLC 15
See Eich, Gunter
See also CA 111; 93-96; DLB 69, 124;
EWL 3
Eichendorff, Joseph 1788-1857 .... NCLC 8
See also DLB 90; RGWL 2, 3
Eigner, Larry .... CLC 9
See Eigner, Laurence (Joel)
See also CAAS 23; CP 1, 2, 3, 4; DLB 5;
WP
Eigner, Laurence (Joel) 1927-1996
See Eigner, Larry
See also CA 9-12R; 151; CANR 6, 84; CP
7; DLB 193
Eilhart von Oberge c. 1140-c.
1195 .... CMLC 67
See also DLB 148
Einhard c. 770-840 .... CMLC 50
See also DLB 148
Einstein, Albert 1879-1955 .... TCLC 65
See also CA 121; 133; MTCW 1, 2
Eiseley, Loren
See Eiseley, Loren Corey
See also DLB 275
Eiseley, Loren Corey 1907-1977 .... CLC 7
See Eiseley, Loren
See also AAYA 5; ANW; CA 1-4R; 73-76;
CANR 6; DLBD 17
Eisenstadt, Jill 1963- .... CLC 50
See also CA 140
Eisenstein, Sergei (Mikhailovich)
1898-1948 .... TCLC 57
See also CA 114; 149
Eisner, Simon
See Kornbluth, C(yril) M.
Ekeloef, (Bengt) Gunnar
1907-1968 .... CLC 27; PC 23
See Ekelof, (Bengt) Gunnar
See also CA 123; 25-28R; DAM POET
Ekelof, (Bengt) Gunnar 1907-1968
See Ekeloef, (Bengt) Gunnar
See also DLB 259; EW 12; EWL 3
Ekelund, Vilhelm 1880-1949 .... TCLC 75
See also CA 189; EWL 3
Ekwensi, C. O. D.
See Ekwensi, Cyprian (Odiatu Duaka)
Ekwensi, Cyprian (Odiatu Duaka)
1921- .... BLC 1; CLC 4
See also AFW; BW 2, 3; CA 29-32R;
CANR 18, 42, 74, 125; CDWLB 3; CN 1,
2, 3, 4, 5, 6; CWRI 5; DAM MULT; DLB
117; EWL 3; MTCW 1, 2; RGEL 2; SATA
66; WLIT 2
Elaine .... TCLC 18
See Leverson, Ada Esther
El Crummo
See Crumb, R(obert)
Elder, Lonne III 1931-1996 ..... BLC 1; DC 8
See also BW 1, 3; CA 81-84; 152; CAD;
CANR 25; DAM MULT; DLB 7, 38, 44;
MAL 5
Eleanor of Aquitaine 1122-1204 ... CMLC 39

Elia
See Lamb, Charles
Eliade, Mircea 1907-1986 .... CLC 19
See also CA 65-68; 119; CANR 30, 62; CD-
WLB 4; DLB 220; EWL 3; MTCW 1;
RGWL 3; SFW 4
Eliot, A. D.
See Jewett, (Theodora) Sarah Orne
Eliot, Alice
See Jewett, (Theodora) Sarah Orne
Eliot, Dan
See Silverberg, Robert
Eliot, George 1819-1880 ...... NCLC 4, 13, 23,
41, 49, 89, 118; PC 20; SSC 72; WLC
See Evans, Mary Ann
See also BRW 5; BRWC 1, 2; BRWR 2;
CDBLB 1832-1890; CN 7; CPW; DA;
DA3; DAB; DAC; DAM MST, NOV;
DLB 21, 35, 55; FL 1:3; LATS 1:1; LMFS
1; NFS 17, 20; RGEL 2; RGSF 2; SSFS
8; TEA; WLIT 3
Eliot, John 1604-1690 .... LC 5
See also DLB 24
Eliot, T(homas) S(tearns)
1888-1965 ...... CLC 1, 2, 3, 6, 9, 10, 13,
15, 24, 34, 41, 55, 57, 113; PC 5, 31;
WLC
See also AAYA 28; AMW; AMWC 1;
AMWR 1; BRW 7; BRWR 2; CA 5-8R;
25-28R; CANR 41; CBD; CDALB 1929-
1941; DA; DA3; DAB; DAC; DAM
DRAM, MST, POET; DFS 4, 13; DLB 7,
10, 45, 63, 245; DLBY 1988; EWL 3;
EXPP; LAIT 3; LATS 1:1; LMFS 2; MAL
5; MTCW 1, 2; MTFW 2005; NCFS 5;
PAB; PFS 1, 7, 20; RGAL 4; RGEL 2;
TUS; WLIT 4; WP
Elizabeth 1866-1941 .... TCLC 41
Elizabeth I 1533-1603 .... LC 118
See also DLB 136
Elkin, Stanley L(awrence)
1930-1995 .. CLC 4, 6, 9, 14, 27, 51, 91;
SSC 12
See also AMWS 6; BPFB 1; CA 9-12R;
148; CANR 8, 46; CN 1, 2, 3, 4, 5, 6;
CPW; DAM NOV, POP; DLB 2, 28, 218,
278; DLBY 1980; EWL 3; INT CANR-8;
MAL 5; MTCW 1, 2; MTFW 2005;
RGAL 4; TCLE 1:1
Elledge, Scott .... CLC 34
Eller, Scott
See Shepard, James R.
Elliott, Don
See Silverberg, Robert
Elliott, George P(aul) 1918-1980 .... CLC 2
See also CA 1-4R; 97-100; CANR 2; CN 1,
2; CP 3; DLB 244; MAL 5
Elliott, Janice 1931-1995 .... CLC 47
See also CA 13-16R; CANR 8, 29, 84; CN
5, 6, 7; DLB 14; SATA 119
Elliott, Sumner Locke 1917-1991 ..... CLC 38
See also CA 5-8R; 134; CANR 2, 21; DLB
289
Elliott, William
See Bradbury, Ray (Douglas)
Ellis, A. E. .... CLC 7
Ellis, Alice Thomas .... CLC 40
See Haycraft, Anna (Margaret)
See also CN 4, 5, 6; DLB 194
Ellis, Bret Easton 1964- ...... CLC 39, 71, 117
See also AAYA 2, 43; CA 118; 123; CANR
51, 74, 126; CN 6, 7; CPW; DA3; DAM
POP; DLB 292; HGG; INT CA-123;
MTCW 2; MTFW 2005; NFS 11
Ellis, (Henry) Havelock
1859-1939 .... TCLC 14
See also CA 109; 169; DLB 190
Ellis, Landon
See Ellison, Harlan (Jay)

Ellis, Trey 1962- .... CLC 55
See also CA 146; CANR 92; CN 7
Ellison, Harlan (Jay) 1934- ... CLC 1, 13, 42,
139; SSC 14
See also AAYA 29; BPFB 1; BYA 14; CA
5-8R; CANR 5, 46, 115; CPW; DAM
POP; DLB 8; HGG; INT CANR-5;
MTCW 1, 2; MTFW 2005; SCFW 2;
SFW 4; SSFS 13, 14, 15, 21; SUFW 1, 2
Ellison, Ralph (Waldo) 1914-1994 .... BLC 1;
CLC 1, 3, 11, 54, 86, 114; SSC 26, 79;
WLC
See also AAYA 19; AFAW 1, 2; AMWC 2;
AMWR 2; AMWS 2; BPFB 1; BW 1, 3;
BYA 2; CA 9-12R; 145; CANR 24, 53;
CDALB 1941-1968; CN 1, 2, 3, 4, 5;
CSW; DA; DA3; DAB; DAC; DAM MST,
MULT, NOV; DLB 2, 76, 227; DLBY
1994; EWL 3; EXPN; EXPS; LAIT 4;
MAL 5; MTCW 1, 2; MTFW 2005; NCFS
3; NFS 2, 21; RGAL 4; RGSF 2; SSFS 1,
11; YAW
Ellmann, Lucy (Elizabeth) 1956- ..... CLC 61
See also CA 128
Ellmann, Richard (David)
1918-1987 .... CLC 50
See also BEST 89:2; CA 1-4R; 122; CANR
2, 28, 61; DLB 103; DLBY 1987; MTCW
1, 2; MTFW 2005
Elman, Richard (Martin)
1934-1997 .... CLC 19
See also CA 17-20R; 163; CAAS 3; CANR
47; TCLE 1:1
Elron
See Hubbard, L(afayette) Ron(ald)
El Saadawi, Nawal 1931- .... CLC 196
See al'Sadaawi, Nawal; Sa'adawi, al-
Nawal; Saadawi, Nawal El; Sa'dawi,
Nawal al-
See also CA 118; CAAS 11; CANR 44, 92
Eluard, Paul .... PC 38; TCLC 7, 41
See Grindel, Eugene
See also EWL 3; GFL 1789 to the Present;
RGWL 2, 3
Elyot, Thomas 1490(?)-1546 .... LC 11
See also DLB 136; RGEL 2
Elytis, Odysseus 1911-1996 .... CLC 15, 49,
100; PC 21
See Alepoudelis, Odysseus
See also CA 102; 151; CANR 94; CWW 2;
DAM POET; EW 13; EWL 3; MTCW 1,
2; RGWL 2, 3
Emecheta, (Florence Onye) Buchi
1944- ...... BLC 2; CLC 14, 48, 128, 214
See also AAYA 67; AFW; BW 2, 3; CA 81-
84; CANR 27, 81, 126; CDWLB 3; CN
4, 5, 6, 7; CWRI 5; DA3; DAM MULT;
DLB 117; EWL 3; FL 1:5; FW; MTCW
1, 2; MTFW 2005; NFS 12, 14; SATA 66;
WLIT 2
Emerson, Mary Moody
1774-1863 .... NCLC 66
Emerson, Ralph Waldo 1803-1882 . NCLC 1,
38, 98; PC 18; WLC
See also AAYA 60; AMW; ANW; CDALB
1640-1865; DA; DA3; DAB; DAC; DAM
MST, POET; DLB 1, 59, 73, 183, 223,
270; EXPP; LAIT 2; LMFS 1; NCFS 3;
PFS 4, 17; RGAL 4; TUS; WP
Eminescu, Mihail 1850-1889 .. NCLC 33, 131
Empedocles 5th cent. B.C.- .... CMLC 50
See also DLB 176
Empson, William 1906-1984 ... CLC 3, 8, 19,
33, 34
See also BRWS 2; CA 17-20R; 112; CANR
31, 61; CP 1, 2, 3; DLB 20; EWL 3;
MTCW 1, 2; RGEL 2
Enchi, Fumiko (Ueda) 1905-1986 ..... CLC 31
See Enchi Fumiko
See also CA 129; 121; FW; MJW

Enchi Fumiko
See Enchi, Fumiko (Ueda)
See also DLB 182; EWL 3

Ende, Michael (Andreas Helmuth)
1929-1995 .... **CLC 31**
See also BYA 5; CA 118; 124; 149; CANR
36, 110; CLR 14; DLB 75; MAICYA 1,
2; MAICYAS 1; SATA 61, 130; SATA-
Brief 42; SATA-Obit 86

Endo, Shusaku 1923-1996 ..... **CLC 7, 14, 19,**
54, 99; SSC 48; TCLC 152
See Endo Shusaku
See also CA 29-32R; 153; CANR 21, 54,
131; DA3; DAM NOV; MTCW 1, 2;
MTFW 2005; RGSF 2; RGWL 2, 3

Endo Shusaku
See Endo, Shusaku
See also CWW 2; DLB 182; EWL 3

Engel, Marian 1933-1985 .... **CLC 36; TCLC**
137
See also CA 25-28R; CANR 12; CN 2, 3;
DLB 53; FW; INT CANR-12

Engelhardt, Frederick
See Hubbard, L(afayette) Ron(ald)

Engels, Friedrich 1820-1895 .. **NCLC 85, 114**
See also DLB 129; LATS 1:1

Enright, D(ennis) J(oseph)
1920-2002 .... **CLC 4, 8, 31**
See also CA 1-4R; 211; CANR 1, 42, 83;
CN 1, 2; CP 1, 2, 3, 4, 5, 6, 7; DLB 27;
EWL 3; SATA 25; SATA-Obit 140

Ensler, Eve 1953- .... **CLC 212**
See also CA 172; CANR 126

Enzensberger, Hans Magnus
1929- .... **CLC 43; PC 28**
See also CA 116; 119; CANR 103; CWW
2; EWL 3

Ephron, Nora 1941- .... **CLC 17, 31**
See also AAYA 35; AITN 2; CA 65-68;
CANR 12, 39, 83; DFS 22

Epicurus 341B.C.-270B.C. .... **CMLC 21**
See also DLB 176

Epsilon
See Betjeman, John

Epstein, Daniel Mark 1948- .... **CLC 7**
See also CA 49-52; CANR 2, 53, 90

Epstein, Jacob 1956- .... **CLC 19**
See also CA 114

Epstein, Jean 1897-1953 .... **TCLC 92**

Epstein, Joseph 1937- .... **CLC 39, 204**
See also AMWS 14; CA 112; 119; CANR
50, 65, 117

Epstein, Leslie 1938- .... **CLC 27**
See also AMWS 12; CA 73-76, 215; CAAE
215; CAAS 12; CANR 23, 69; DLB 299

Equiano, Olaudah 1745(?)-1797 . **BLC 2; LC**
16
See also AFAW 1, 2; CDWLB 3; DAM
MULT; DLB 37, 50; WLIT 2

Erasmus, Desiderius 1469(?)-1536 ..... **LC 16,**
93
See also DLB 136; EW 2; LMFS 1; RGWL
2, 3; TWA

Erdman, Paul E(mil) 1932- .... **CLC 25**
See also AITN 1; CA 61-64; CANR 13, 43,
84

Erdrich, (Karen) Louise 1954- .. **CLC 39, 54,**
120, 176; NNAL; PC 52
See also AAYA 10, 47; AMWS 4; BEST
89:1; BPFB 1; CA 114; CANR 41, 62,
118, 138; CDALBS; CN 5, 6, 7; CP 7;
CPW; CWP; DA3; DAM MULT, NOV,
POP; DLB 152, 175, 206; EWL 3; EXPP;
FL 1:5; LAIT 5; LATS 1:2; MAL 5;
MTCW 1, 2; MTFW 2005; NFS 5; PFS
14; RGAL 4; SATA 94, 141; SSFS 14;
TCWW 2

Erenburg, Ilya (Grigoryevich)
See Ehrenburg, Ilya (Grigoryevich)

Erickson, Stephen Michael 1950-
See Erickson, Steve
See also CA 129; SFW 4

Erickson, Steve .... **CLC 64**
See Erickson, Stephen Michael
See also CANR 60, 68, 136; MTFW 2005;
SUFW 2

Erickson, Walter
See Fast, Howard (Melvin)

Ericson, Walter
See Fast, Howard (Melvin)

Eriksson, Buntel
See Bergman, (Ernst) Ingmar

Eriugena, John Scottus c.
810-877 .... **CMLC 65**
See also DLB 115

Ernaux, Annie 1940- .... **CLC 88, 184**
See also CA 147; CANR 93; MTFW 2005;
NCFS 3, 5

Erskine, John 1879-1951 .... **TCLC 84**
See also CA 112; 159; DLB 9, 102; FANT

Eschenbach, Wolfram von
See Wolfram von Eschenbach
See also RGWL 3

Eseki, Bruno
See Mphahlele, Ezekiel

Esenin, Sergei (Alexandrovich)
1895-1925 .... **TCLC 4**
See Yesenin, Sergey
See also CA 104; RGWL 2, 3

Eshleman, Clayton 1935- .... **CLC 7**
See also CA 33-36R, 212; CAAE 212;
CAAS 6; CANR 93; CP 1, 2, 3, 4, 5, 6,
7; DLB 5

Espriella, Don Manuel Alvarez
See Southey, Robert

Espriu, Salvador 1913-1985 .... **CLC 9**
See also CA 154; 115; DLB 134; EWL 3

Espronceda, Jose de 1808-1842 ..... **NCLC 39**

Esquivel, Laura 1951(?)- ... **CLC 141; HLCS**
1
See also AAYA 29; CA 143; CANR 68, 113;
DA3; DNFS 2; LAIT 3; LMFS 2; MTCW
2; MTFW 2005; NFS 5; WLIT 1

Esse, James
See Stephens, James

Esterbrook, Tom
See Hubbard, L(afayette) Ron(ald)

Estleman, Loren D. 1952- .... **CLC 48**
See also AAYA 27; CA 85-88; CANR 27,
74, 139; CMW 4; CPW; DA3; DAM
NOV, POP; DLB 226; INT CANR-27;
MTCW 1, 2; MTFW 2005; TCWW 1, 2

Etherege, Sir George 1636-1692 . **DC 23; LC**
78
See also BRW 2; DAM DRAM; DLB 80;
PAB; RGEL 2

Euclid 306B.C.-283B.C. .... **CMLC 25**

Eugenides, Jeffrey 1960(?)- .... **CLC 81, 212**
See also AAYA 51; CA 144; CANR 120;
MTFW 2005

Euripides c. 484B.C.-406B.C. .... **CMLC 23,**
51; DC 4; WLCS
See also AW 1; CDWLB 1; DA; DA3;
DAB; DAC; DAM DRAM; MST; DFS 1,
4, 6; DLB 176; LAIT 1; LMFS 1; RGWL
2, 3

Evan, Evin
See Faust, Frederick (Schiller)

Evans, Caradoc 1878-1945 ... **SSC 43; TCLC**
85
See also DLB 162

Evans, Evan
See Faust, Frederick (Schiller)

Evans, Marian
See Eliot, George

Evans, Mary Ann
See Eliot, George
See also NFS 20

Evarts, Esther
See Benson, Sally

Everett, Percival
See Everett, Percival L.
See also CSW

Everett, Percival L. 1956- .... **CLC 57**
See Everett, Percival
See also BW 2; CA 129; CANR 94, 134;
CN 7; MTFW 2005

Everson, R(onald) G(ilmour)
1903-1992 .... **CLC 27**
See also CA 17-20R; CP 1, 2, 3, 4; DLB 88

Everson, William (Oliver)
1912-1994 .... **CLC 1, 5, 14**
See Antoninus, Brother
See also BG 1:2; CA 9-12R; 145; CANR
20; CP 2, 3, 4; DLB 5, 16, 212; MTCW 1

Evtushenko, Evgenii Aleksandrovich
See Yevtushenko, Yevgeny (Alexandrovich)
See also CWW 2; RGWL 2, 3

Ewart, Gavin (Buchanan)
1916-1995 .... **CLC 13, 46**
See also BRWS 7; CA 89-92; 150; CANR
17, 46; CP 1, 2, 3, 4; DLB 40; MTCW 1

Ewers, Hanns Heinz 1871-1943 ..... **TCLC 12**
See also CA 109; 149

Ewing, Frederick R.
See Sturgeon, Theodore (Hamilton)

Exley, Frederick (Earl) 1929-1992 .... **CLC 6,**
11
See also AITN 2; BPFB 1; CA 81-84; 138;
CANR 117; DLB 143; DLBY 1981

Eynhardt, Guillermo
See Quiroga, Horacio (Sylvestre)

Ezekiel, Nissim (Moses) 1924-2004 .. **CLC 61**
See also CA 61-64; 223; CP 1, 2, 3, 4, 5, 6,
7; EWL 3

Ezekiel, Tish O'Dowd 1943- .... **CLC 34**
See also CA 129

Fadeev, Aleksandr Aleksandrovich
See Bulgya, Alexander Alexandrovich
See also DLB 272

Fadeev, Alexandr Alexandrovich
See Bulgya, Alexander Alexandrovich
See also EWL 3

Fadeyev, A.
See Bulgya, Alexander Alexandrovich

Fadeyev, Alexander .... **TCLC 53**
See Bulgya, Alexander Alexandrovich

Fagen, Donald 1948- .... **CLC 26**

Fainzilberg, Ilya Arnoldovich 1897-1937
See Ilf, Ilya
See also CA 120; 165

Fair, Ronald L. 1932- .... **CLC 18**
See also BW 1; CA 69-72; CANR 25; DLB
33

Fairbairn, Roger
See Carr, John Dickson

Fairbairns, Zoe (Ann) 1948- .... **CLC 32**
See also CA 103; CANR 21, 85; CN 4, 5,
6, 7

Fairfield, Flora
See Alcott, Louisa May

Fairman, Paul W. 1916-1977
See Queen, Ellery
See also CA 114; SFW 4

Falco, Gian
See Papini, Giovanni

Falconer, James
See Kirkup, James

Falconer, Kenneth
See Kornbluth, C(yril) M.

Falkland, Samuel
See Heijermans, Herman

Fallaci, Oriana 1930- .... **CLC 11, 110**
See also CA 77-80; CANR 15, 58, 134; FW;
MTCW 1

Fielding, Helen 1958- .... **CLC 146, 217**
See also AAYA 65; CA 172; CANR 127; DLB 231; MTFW 2005

Fielding, Henry 1707-1754 .... **LC 1, 46, 85; WLC**
See also BRW 3; BRWR 1; CDBLB 1660-1789; DA; DA3; DAB; DAC; DAM DRAM, MST, NOV; DLB 39, 84, 101; NFS 18; RGEL 2; TEA; WLIT 3

Fielding, Sarah 1710-1768 .... **LC 1, 44**
See also DLB 39; RGEL 2; TEA

Fields, W. C. 1880-1946 .... **TCLC 80**
See also DLB 44

Fierstein, Harvey (Forbes) 1954- ..... **CLC 33**
See also CA 123; 129; CAD; CD 5, 6; CPW; DA3; DAM DRAM, POP; DFS 6; DLB 266; GLL; MAL 5

Figes, Eva 1932- .... **CLC 31**
See also CA 53-56; CANR 4, 44, 83; CN 2, 3, 4, 5, 6, 7; DLB 14, 271; FW

Filippo, Eduardo de
See de Filippo, Eduardo

Finch, Anne 1661-1720 .... **LC 3; PC 21**
See also BRWS 9; DLB 95

Finch, Robert (Duer Claydon)
1900-1995 .... **CLC 18**
See also CA 57-60; CANR 9, 24, 49; CP 1, 2, 3, 4; DLB 88

Findley, Timothy (Irving Frederick)
1930-2002 .... **CLC 27, 102**
See also CA 25-28R; 206; CANR 12, 42, 69, 109; CCA 1; CN 4, 5, 6, 7; DAC; DAM MST; DLB 53; FANT; RHW

Fink, William
See Mencken, H(enry) L(ouis)

Firbank, Louis 1942-
See Reed, Lou
See also CA 117

Firbank, (Arthur Annesley) Ronald
1886-1926 .... **TCLC 1**
See also BRWS 2; CA 104; 177; DLB 36; EWL 3; RGEL 2

Firdawsi, Abu al-Qasim
See Ferdowsi, Abu'l Qasem
See also WLIT 6

Fish, Stanley
See Fish, Stanley Eugene

Fish, Stanley E.
See Fish, Stanley Eugene

Fish, Stanley Eugene 1938- .... **CLC 142**
See also CA 112; 132; CANR 90; DLB 67

Fisher, Dorothy (Frances) Canfield
1879-1958 .... **TCLC 87**
See also CA 114; 136; CANR 80; CLR 71; CWRI 5; DLB 9, 102, 284; MAICYA 1, 2; MAL 5; YABC 1

Fisher, M(ary) F(rances) K(ennedy)
1908-1992 .... **CLC 76, 87**
See also CA 77-80; 138; CANR 44; MTCW 2

Fisher, Roy 1930- .... **CLC 25**
See also CA 81-84; CAAS 10; CANR 16; CP 1, 2, 3, 4, 5, 6, 7; DLB 40

Fisher, Rudolph 1897-1934 . **BLC 2; HR 1:2; SSC 25; TCLC 11**
See also BW 1, 3; CA 107; 124; CANR 80; DAM MULT; DLB 51, 102

Fisher, Vardis (Alvero) 1895-1968 .... **CLC 7; TCLC 140**
See also CA 5-8R; 25-28R; CANR 68; DLB 9, 206; MAL 5; RGAL 4; TCWW 1, 2

Fiske, Tarleton
See Bloch, Robert (Albert)

Fitch, Clarke
See Sinclair, Upton (Beall)

Fitch, John IV
See Cormier, Robert (Edmund)

Fitzgerald, Captain Hugh
See Baum, L(yman) Frank

FitzGerald, Edward 1809-1883 ...... **NCLC 9, 153**
See also BRW 4; DLB 32; RGEL 2

Fitzgerald, F(rancis) Scott (Key)
1896-1940 ... **SSC 6, 31, 75; TCLC 1, 6, 14, 28, 55, 157; WLC**
See also AAYA 24; AITN 1; AMW; AMWC 2; AMWR 1; BPFB 1; CA 110; 123; CDALB 1917-1929; DA; DA3; DAB; DAC; DAM MST, NOV; DLB 4, 9, 86, 219, 273; DLBD 1, 15, 16; DLBY 1981, 1996; EWL 3; EXPN; EXPS; LAIT 3; MAL 5; MTCW 1, 2; MTFW 2005; NFS 2, 19, 20; RGAL 4; RGSF 2; SSFS 4, 15, 21; TUS

Fitzgerald, Penelope 1916-2000 . **CLC 19, 51, 61, 143**
See also BRWS 5; CA 85-88; 190; CAAS 10; CANR 56, 86, 131; CN 3, 4, 5, 6, 7; DLB 14, 194; EWL 3; MTCW 2; MTFW 2005

Fitzgerald, Robert (Stuart)
1910-1985 .... **CLC 39**
See also CA 1-4R; 114; CANR 1; CP 1, 2, 3, 4; DLBY 1980; MAL 5

FitzGerald, Robert D(avid)
1902-1987 .... **CLC 19**
See also CA 17-20R; CP 1, 2, 3, 4; DLB 260; RGEL 2

Fitzgerald, Zelda (Sayre)
1900-1948 .... **TCLC 52**
See also AMWS 9; CA 117; 126; DLBY 1984

Flanagan, Thomas (James Bonner)
1923-2002 .... **CLC 25, 52**
See also CA 108; 206; CANR 55; CN 3, 4, 5, 6, 7; DLBY 1980; INT CA-108; MTCW 1; RHW; TCLE 1:1

Flaubert, Gustave 1821-1880 .... **NCLC 2, 10, 19, 62, 66, 135; SSC 11, 60; WLC**
See also DA; DA3; DAB; DAC; DAM MST, NOV; DLB 119, 301; EW 7; EXPS; GFL 1789 to the Present; LAIT 2; LMFS 1; NFS 14; RGSF 2; RGWL 2, 3; SSFS 6; TWA

Flavius Josephus
See Josephus, Flavius

Flecker, Herman Elroy
See Flecker, (Herman) James Elroy

Flecker, (Herman) James Elroy
1884-1915 .... **TCLC 43**
See also CA 109; 150; DLB 10, 19; RGEL 2

Fleming, Ian (Lancaster) 1908-1964 . **CLC 3, 30**
See also AAYA 26; BPFB 1; CA 5-8R; CANR 59; CDBLB 1945-1960; CMW 4; CPW; DA3; DAM POP; DLB 87, 201; MSW; MTCW 1, 2; MTFW 2005; RGEL 2; SATA 9; TEA; YAW

Fleming, Thomas (James) 1927- ...... **CLC 37**
See also CA 5-8R; CANR 10, 102; INT CANR-10; SATA 8

Fletcher, John 1579-1625 .... **DC 6; LC 33**
See also BRW 2; CDBLB Before 1660; DLB 58; RGEL 2; TEA

Fletcher, John Gould 1886-1950 .... **TCLC 35**
See also CA 107; 167; DLB 4, 45; LMFS 2; MAL 5; RGAL 4

Fleur, Paul
See Pohl, Frederik

Flieg, Helmut
See Heym, Stefan

Flooglebuckle, Al
See Spiegelman, Art

Flora, Fletcher 1914-1969
See Queen, Ellery
See also CA 1-4R; CANR 3, 85

Flying Officer X
See Bates, H(erbert) E(rnest)

Fo, Dario 1926- .... **CLC 32, 109; DC 10**
See also CA 116; 128; CANR 68, 114, 134; CWW 2; DA3; DAM DRAM; DLBY 1997; EWL 3; MTCW 1, 2; MTFW 2005; WLIT 7

Fogarty, Jonathan Titulescu Esq.
See Farrell, James T(homas)

Follett, Ken(neth Martin) 1949- .... **CLC 18**
See also AAYA 6, 50; BEST 89:4; BPFB 1; CA 81-84; CANR 13, 33, 54, 102; CMW 4; CPW; DA3; DAM NOV, POP; DLB 87; DLBY 1981; INT CANR-33; MTCW 1

Fondane, Benjamin 1898-1944 ..... **TCLC 159**

Fontane, Theodor 1819-1898 . **NCLC 26, 163**
See also CDWLB 2; DLB 129; EW 6; RGWL 2, 3; TWA

Fonte, Moderata 1555-1592 .... **LC 118**

Fontenot, Chester .... **CLC 65**

Fonvizin, Denis Ivanovich
1744(?)-1792 .... **LC 81**
See also DLB 150; RGWL 2, 3

Foote, Horton 1916- .... **CLC 51, 91**
See also CA 73-76; CAD; CANR 34, 51, 110; CD 5, 6; CSW; DA3; DAM DRAM; DFS 20; DLB 26, 266; EWL 3; INT CANR-34; MTFW 2005

Foote, Mary Hallock 1847-1938 .. **TCLC 108**
See also DLB 186, 188, 202, 221; TCWW 2

Foote, Samuel 1721-1777 .... **LC 106**
See also DLB 89; RGEL 2

Foote, Shelby 1916-2005 .... **CLC 75**
See also AAYA 40; CA 5-8R; 240; CANR 3, 45, 74, 131; CN 1, 2, 3, 4, 5, 6, 7; CPW; CSW; DA3; DAM NOV, POP; DLB 2, 17; MAL 5; MTCW 2; MTFW 2005; RHW

Forbes, Cosmo
See Lewton, Val

Forbes, Esther 1891-1967 .... **CLC 12**
See also AAYA 17; BYA 2; CA 13-14; 25-28R; CAP 1; CLR 27; DLB 22; JRDA; MAICYA 1, 2; RHW; SATA 2, 100; YAW

Forche, Carolyn (Louise) 1950- .... **CLC 25, 83, 86; PC 10**
See also CA 109; 117; CANR 50, 74, 138; CP 4, 5, 6, 7; CWP; DA3; DAM POET; DLB 5, 193; INT CA-117; MAL 5; MTCW 2; MTFW 2005; PFS 18; RGAL 4

Ford, Elbur
See Hibbert, Eleanor Alice Burford

Ford, Ford Madox 1873-1939 ... **TCLC 1, 15, 39, 57, 172**
See Chaucer, Daniel
See also BRW 6; CA 104; 132; CANR 74; CDBLB 1914-1945; DA3; DAM NOV; DLB 34, 98, 162; EWL 3; MTCW 1, 2; RGEL 2; TEA

Ford, Henry 1863-1947 .... **TCLC 73**
See also CA 115; 148

Ford, Jack
See Ford, John

Ford, John 1586-1639 .... **DC 8; LC 68**
See also BRW 2; CDBLB Before 1660; DA3; DAM DRAM; DFS 7; DLB 58; IDTP; RGEL 2

Ford, John 1895-1973 .... **CLC 16**
See also CA 187; 45-48

Ford, Richard 1944- .... **CLC 46, 99, 205**
See also AMWS 5; CA 69-72; CANR 11, 47, 86, 128; CN 5, 6, 7; CSW; DLB 227; EWL 3; MAL 5; MTCW 2; MTFW 2005; RGAL 4; RGSF 2

Ford, Webster
See Masters, Edgar Lee

Foreman, Richard 1937- .... **CLC 50**
See also CA 65-68; CAD; CANR 32, 63, 143; CD 5, 6
Forester, C(ecil) S(cott) 1899-1966 . **CLC 35; TCLC 152**
See also CA 73-76; 25-28R; CANR 83; DLB 191; RGEL 2; RHW; SATA 13
Forez
See Mauriac, Francois (Charles)
Forman, James
See Forman, James D(ouglas)
Forman, James D(ouglas) 1932- .... **CLC 21**
See also AAYA 17; CA 9-12R; CANR 4, 19, 42; JRDA; MAICYA 1, 2; SATA 8, 70; YAW
Forman, Milos 1932- .... **CLC 164**
See also AAYA 63; CA 109
Fornes, Maria Irene 1930- .... **CLC 39, 61, 187; DC 10; HLCS 1**
See also CA 25-28R; CAD; CANR 28, 81; CD 5, 6; CWD; DLB 7; HW 1, 2; INT CANR-28; LLW; MAL 5; MTCW 1; RGAL 4
Forrest, Leon (Richard)
1937-1997 .... **BLCS; CLC 4**
See also AFAW 2; BW 2; CA 89-92; 162; CAAS 7; CANR 25, 52, 87; CN 4, 5, 6; DLB 33
Forster, E(dward) M(organ)
1879-1970 ...... **CLC 1, 2, 3, 4, 9, 10, 13, 15, 22, 45, 77; SSC 27; TCLC 125; WLC**
See also AAYA 2, 37; BRW 6; BRWR 2; BYA 12; CA 13-14; 25-28R; CANR 45; CAP 1; CDBLB 1914-1945; DA; DA3; DAB; DAC; DAM MST, NOV; DLB 34, 98, 162, 178, 195; DLBD 10; EWL 3; EXPN; LAIT 3; LMFS 1; MTCW 1, 2; MTFW 2005; NCFS 1; NFS 3, 10, 11; RGEL 2; RGSF 2; SATA 57; SUFW 1; TEA; WLIT 4
Forster, John 1812-1876 .... **NCLC 11**
See also DLB 144, 184
Forster, Margaret 1938- .... **CLC 149**
See also CA 133; CANR 62, 115; CN 4, 5, 6, 7; DLB 155, 271
Forsyth, Frederick 1938- .... **CLC 2, 5, 36**
See also BEST 89:4; CA 85-88; CANR 38, 62, 115, 137; CMW 4; CN 3, 4, 5, 6, 7; CPW; DAM NOV, POP; DLB 87; MTCW 1, 2; MTFW 2005
Forten, Charlotte L. 1837-1914 .... **BLC 2; TCLC 16**
See Grimke, Charlotte L(ottie) Forten
See also DLB 50, 239
Fortinbras
See Grieg, (Johan) Nordahl (Brun)
Foscolo, Ugo 1778-1827 .... **NCLC 8, 97**
See also EW 5; WLIT 7
Fosse, Bob .... **CLC 20**
See Fosse, Robert Louis
Fosse, Robert Louis 1927-1987
See Fosse, Bob
See also CA 110; 123
Foster, Hannah Webster
1758-1840 .... **NCLC 99**
See also DLB 37, 200; RGAL 4
Foster, Stephen Collins
1826-1864 .... **NCLC 26**
See also RGAL 4
Foucault, Michel 1926-1984 . **CLC 31, 34, 69**
See also CA 105; 113; CANR 34; DLB 242; EW 13; EWL 3; GFL 1789 to the Present; GLL 1; LMFS 2; MTCW 1, 2; TWA
Fouque, Friedrich (Heinrich Karl) de·la Motte 1777-1843 .... **NCLC 2**
See also DLB 90; RGWL 2, 3; SUFW 1
Fourier, Charles 1772-1837 .... **NCLC 51**

Fournier, Henri-Alban 1886-1914
See Alain-Fournier
See also CA 104; 179
Fournier, Pierre 1916-1997 .... **CLC 11**
See Gascar, Pierre
See also CA 89-92; CANR 16, 40
Fowles, John (Robert) 1926- . **CLC 1, 2, 3, 4, 6, 9, 10, 15, 33, 87; SSC 33**
See also BPFB 1; BRWS 1; CA 5-8R; CANR 25, 71, 103; CDBLB 1960 to Present; CN 1, 2, 3, 4, 5, 6, 7; DA3; DAB; DAC; DAM MST; DLB 14, 139, 207; EWL 3; HGG; MTCW 1, 2; MTFW 2005; NFS 21; RGEL 2; RHW; SATA 22; TEA; WLIT 4
Fox, Paula 1923- .... **CLC 2, 8, 121**
See also AAYA 3, 37; BYA 3, 8; CA 73-76; CANR 20, 36, 62, 105; CLR 1, 44, 96; DLB 52; JRDA; MAICYA 1, 2; MTCW 1; NFS 12; SATA 17, 60, 120; WYA; YAW
Fox, William Price (Jr.) 1926- .... **CLC 22**
See also CA 17-20R; CAAS 19; CANR 11, 142; CSW; DLB 2; DLBY 1981
Foxe, John 1517(?)-1587 .... **LC 14**
See also DLB 132
Frame, Janet .. **CLC 2, 3, 6, 22, 66, 96; SSC 29**
See Clutha, Janet Paterson Frame
See also CN 1, 2, 3, 4, 5, 6, 7; CP 2, 3, 4; CWP; EWL 3; RGEL 2; RGSF 2; TWA
France, Anatole .... **TCLC 9**
See Thibault, Jacques Anatole Francois
See also DLB 123; EWL 3; GFL 1789 to the Present; RGWL 2, 3; SUFW 1
Francis, Claude .... **CLC 50**
See also CA 192
Francis, Dick
See Francis, Richard Stanley
See also CN 2, 3, 4, 5, 6
Francis, Richard Stanley 1920- ... **CLC 2, 22, 42, 102**
See Francis, Dick
See also AAYA 5, 21; BEST 89:3; BPFB 1; CA 5-8R; CANR 9, 42, 68, 100, 141; CD-BLB 1960 to Present; CMW 4; CN 7; DA3; DAM POP; DLB 87; INT CANR-9; MSW; MTCW 1, 2; MTFW 2005
Francis, Robert (Churchill)
1901-1987 .... **CLC 15; PC 34**
See also AMWS 9; CA 1-4R; 123; CANR 1; CP 1, 2, 3, 4; EXPP; PFS 12; TCLE 1:1
Francis, Lord Jeffrey
See Jeffrey, Francis
See also DLB 107
Frank, Anne(lies Marie)
1929-1945 .... **TCLC 17; WLC**
See also AAYA 12; BYA 1; CA 113; 133; CANR 68; CLR 101; DA; DA3; DAB; DAC; DAM MST; LAIT 4; MAICYA 2; MAICYAS 1; MTCW 1, 2; MTFW 2005; NCFS 2; SATA 87; SATA-Brief 42; WYA; YAW
Frank, Bruno 1887-1945 .... **TCLC 81**
See also CA 189; DLB 118; EWL 3
Frank, Elizabeth 1945- .... **CLC 39**
See also CA 121; 126; CANR 78; INT CA-126
Frankl, Viktor E(mil) 1905-1997 ...... **CLC 93**
See also CA 65-68; 161
Franklin, Benjamin
See Hasek, Jaroslav (Matej Frantisek)
Franklin, Benjamin 1706-1790 .... **LC 25; WLCS**
See also AMW; CDALB 1640-1865; DA; DA3; DAB; DAC; DAM MST; DLB 24, 43, 73, 183; LAIT 1; RGAL 4; TUS

Franklin, (Stella Maria Sarah) Miles (Lampe) 1879-1954 .... **TCLC 7**
See also CA 104; 164; DLB 230; FW; MTCW 2; RGEL 2; TWA
Franzen, Jonathan 1959- .... **CLC 202**
See also AAYA 65; CA 129; CANR 105
Fraser, Antonia (Pakenham) 1932- . **CLC 32, 107**
See also AAYA 57; CA 85-88; CANR 44, 65, 119; CMW; DLB 276; MTCW 1, 2; MTFW 2005; SATA-Brief 32
Fraser, George MacDonald 1925- ...... **CLC 7**
See also AAYA 48; CA 45-48, 180; CAAE 180; CANR 2, 48, 74; MTCW 2; RHW
Fraser, Sylvia 1935- .... **CLC 64**
See also CA 45-48; CANR 1, 16, 60; CCA 1
Frayn, Michael 1933- .... **CLC 3, 7, 31, 47, 176; DC 27**
See also BRWC 2; BRWS 7; CA 5-8R; CANR 30, 69, 114, 133; CBD; CD 5, 6; CN 1, 2, 3, 4, 5, 6, 7; DAM DRAM, NOV; DFS 22; DLB 13, 14, 194, 245; FANT; MTCW 1, 2; MTFW 2005; SFW 4
Fraze, Candida (Merrill) 1945- .... **CLC 50**
See also CA 126
Frazer, Andrew
See Marlowe, Stephen
Frazer, J(ames) G(eorge)
1854-1941 .... **TCLC 32**
See also BRWS 3; CA 118; NCFS 5
Frazer, Robert Caine
See Creasey, John
Frazer, Sir James George
See Frazer, J(ames) G(eorge)
Frazier, Charles 1950- .... **CLC 109**
See also AAYA 34; CA 161; CANR 126; CSW; DLB 292; MTFW 2005
Frazier, Ian 1951- .... **CLC 46**
See also CA 130; CANR 54, 93
Frederic, Harold 1856-1898 .... **NCLC 10**
See also AMW; DLB 12, 23; DLBD 13; MAL 5; NFS 22; RGAL 4
Frederick, John
See Faust, Frederick (Schiller)
See also TCWW 2
Frederick the Great 1712-1786 .... **LC 14**
Fredro, Aleksander 1793-1876 .... **NCLC 8**
Freeling, Nicolas 1927-2003 .... **CLC 38**
See also CA 49-52; 218; CAAS 12; CANR 1, 17, 50, 84; CMW 4; CN 1, 2, 3, 4, 5, 6; DLB 87
Freeman, Douglas Southall
1886-1953 .... **TCLC 11**
See also CA 109; 195; DLB 17; DLBD 17
Freeman, Judith 1946- .... **CLC 55**
See also CA 148; CANR 120; DLB 256
Freeman, Mary E(leanor) Wilkins
1852-1930 .... **SSC 1, 47; TCLC 9**
See also CA 106; 177; DLB 12, 78, 221; EXPS; FW; HGG; MAWW; RGAL 4; RGSF 2; SSFS 4, 8; SUFW 1; TUS
Freeman, R(ichard) Austin
1862-1943 .... **TCLC 21**
See also CA 113; CANR 84; CMW 4; DLB 70
French, Albert 1943- .... **CLC 86**
See also BW 3; CA 167
French, Antonia
See Kureishi, Hanif
French, Marilyn 1929- .. **CLC 10, 18, 60, 177**
See also BPFB 1; CA 69-72; CANR 3, 31, 134; CN 5, 6, 7; CPW; DAM DRAM, NOV, POP; FL 1:5; FW; INT CANR-31; MTCW 1, 2; MTFW 2005
French, Paul
See Asimov, Isaac

Freneau, Philip Morin 1752-1832 .. **NCLC 1, 111**
See also AMWS 2; DLB 37, 43; RGAL 4

Freud, Sigmund 1856-1939 .... **TCLC 52**
See also CA 115; 133; CANR 69; DLB 296; EW 8; EWL 3; LATS 1:1; MTCW 1, 2; MTFW 2005; NCFS 3; TWA

Freytag, Gustav 1816-1895 .... **NCLC 109**
See also DLB 129

Friedan, Betty (Naomi) 1921- .... **CLC 74**
See also CA 65-68; CANR 18, 45, 74; DLB 246; FW; MTCW 1, 2; MTFW 2005; NCFS 5

Friedlander, Saul 1932- .... **CLC 90**
See also CA 117; 130; CANR 72

Friedman, B(ernard) H(arper)
1926- .... **CLC 7**
See also CA 1-4R; CANR 3, 48

Friedman, Bruce Jay 1930- ...... **CLC 3, 5, 56**
See also CA 9-12R; CAD; CANR 25, 52, 101; CD 5, 6; CN 1, 2, 3, 4, 5, 6, 7; DLB 2, 28, 244; INT CANR-25; MAL 5; SSFS 18

Friel, Brian 1929- .... **CLC 5, 42, 59, 115; DC 8; SSC 76**
See also BRWS 5; CA 21-24R; CANR 33, 69, 131; CBD; CD 5, 6; DFS 11; DLB 13, 319; EWL 3; MTCW 1; RGEL 2; TEA

Friis-Baastad, Babbis Ellinor
1921-1970 .... **CLC 12**
See also CA 17-20R; 134; SATA 7

Frisch, Max (Rudolf) 1911-1991 ... **CLC 3, 9, 14, 18, 32, 44; TCLC 121**
See also CA 85-88; 134; CANR 32, 74; CD-WLB 2; DAM DRAM, NOV; DLB 69, 124; EW 13; EWL 3; MTCW 1, 2; MTFW 2005; RGWL 2, 3

Fromentin, Eugene (Samuel Auguste)
1820-1876 .... **NCLC 10, 125**
See also DLB 123; GFL 1789 to the Present

Frost, Frederick
See Faust, Frederick (Schiller)

Frost, Robert (Lee) 1874-1963 .. **CLC 1, 3, 4, 9, 10, 13, 15, 26, 34, 44; PC 1, 39; WLC**
See also AAYA 21; AMW; AMWR 1; CA 89-92; CANR 33; CDALB 1917-1929; CLR 67; DA; DA3; DAB; DAC; DAM MST, POET; DLB 54, 284; DLBD 7; EWL 3; EXPP; MAL 5; MTCW 1, 2; MTFW 2005; PAB; PFS 1, 2, 3, 4, 5, 6, 7, 10, 13; RGAL 4; SATA 14; TUS; WP; WYA

Froude, James Anthony
1818-1894 .... **NCLC 43**
See also DLB 18, 57, 144

Froy, Herald
See Waterhouse, Keith (Spencer)

Fry, Christopher 1907-2005 ... **CLC 2, 10, 14**
See also BRWS 3; CA 17-20R; 240; CAAS 23; CANR 9, 30, 74, 132; CBD; CD 5, 6; CP 1, 2, 3, 4, 5, 6, 7; DAM DRAM; DLB 13; EWL 3; MTCW 1, 2; MTFW 2005; RGEL 2; SATA 66; TEA

Frye, (Herman) Northrop
1912-1991 .... **CLC 24, 70; TCLC 165**
See also CA 5-8R; 133; CANR 8, 37; DLB 67, 68, 246; EWL 3; MTCW 1, 2; MTFW 2005; RGAL 4; TWA

Fuchs, Daniel 1909-1993 .... **CLC 8, 22**
See also CA 81-84; 142; CAAS 5; CANR 40; CN 1, 2, 3, 4, 5; DLB 9, 26, 28; DLBY 1993; MAL 5

Fuchs, Daniel 1934- .... **CLC 34**
See also CA 37-40R; CANR 14, 48

Fuentes, Carlos 1928- .. **CLC 3, 8, 10, 13, 22, 41, 60, 113; HLC 1; SSC 24; WLC**
See also AAYA 4, 45; AITN 2; BPFB 1; CA 69-72; CANR 10, 32, 68, 104, 138; CDWLB 3; CWW 2; DA; DA3; DAB;

DAC; DAM MST, MULT, NOV; DLB 113; DNFS 2; EWL 3; HW 1, 2; LAIT 3; LATS 1:2; LAW; LAWS 1; LMFS 2; MTCW 1, 2; MTFW 2005; NFS 8; RGSF 2; RGWL 2, 3; TWA; WLIT 1

Fuentes, Gregorio Lopez y
See Lopez y Fuentes, Gregorio

Fuertes, Gloria 1918-1998 .... **PC 27**
See also CA 178, 180; DLB 108; HW 2; SATA 115

Fugard, (Harold) Athol 1932- . **CLC 5, 9, 14, 25, 40, 80, 211; DC 3**
See also AAYA 17; AFW; CA 85-88; CANR 32, 54, 118; CD 5, 6; DAM DRAM; DFS 3, 6, 10; DLB 225; DNFS 1, 2; EWL 3; LATS 1:2; MTCW 1; MTFW 2005; RGEL 2; WLIT 2

Fugard, Sheila 1932- .... **CLC 48**
See also CA 125

Fujiwara no Teika 1162-1241 .... **CMLC 73**
See also DLB 203

Fukuyama, Francis 1952- .... **CLC 131**
See also CA 140; CANR 72, 125

Fuller, Charles (H.), (Jr.) 1939- .... **BLC 2; CLC 25; DC 1**
See also BW 2; CA 108; 112; CAD; CANR 87; CD 5, 6; DAM DRAM, MULT; DFS 8; DLB 38, 266; EWL 3; INT CA-112; MAL 5; MTCW 1

Fuller, Henry Blake 1857-1929 .... **TCLC 103**
See also CA 108; 177; DLB 12; RGAL 4

Fuller, John (Leopold) 1937- .... **CLC 62**
See also CA 21-24R; CANR 9, 44; CP 1, 2, 3, 4, 5, 6, 7; DLB 40

Fuller, Margaret
See Ossoli, Sarah Margaret (Fuller)
See also AMWS 2; DLB 183, 223, 239; FL 1:3

Fuller, Roy (Broadbent) 1912-1991 ... **CLC 4, 28**
See also BRWS 7; CA 5-8R; 135; CAAS 10; CANR 53, 83; CN 1, 2, 3, 4, 5; CP 1, 2, 3, 4; CWRI 5; DLB 15, 20; EWL 3; RGEL 2; SATA 87

Fuller, Sarah Margaret
See Ossoli, Sarah Margaret (Fuller)

Fuller, Sarah Margaret
See Ossoli, Sarah Margaret (Fuller)
See also DLB 1, 59, 73

Fuller, Thomas 1608-1661 .... **LC 111**
See also DLB 151

Fulton, Alice 1952- .... **CLC 52**
See also CA 116; CANR 57, 88; CP 7; CWP; DLB 193

Furphy, Joseph 1843-1912 .... **TCLC 25**
See Collins, Tom
See also CA 163; DLB 230; EWL 3; RGEL 2

Fuson, Robert H(enderson) 1927- .... **CLC 70**
See also CA 89-92; CANR 103

Fussell, Paul 1924- .... **CLC 74**
See also BEST 90:1; CA 17-20R; CANR 8, 21, 35, 69, 135; INT CANR-21; MTCW 1, 2; MTFW 2005

Futabatei, Shimei 1864-1909 .... **TCLC 44**
See Futabatei Shimei
See also CA 162; MJW

Futabatei Shimei
See Futabatei, Shimei
See also DLB 180; EWL 3

Futrelle, Jacques 1875-1912 .... **TCLC 19**
See also CA 113; 155; CMW 4

Gaboriau, Emile 1835-1873 .... **NCLC 14**
See also CMW 4; MSW

Gadda, Carlo Emilio 1893-1973 ...... **CLC 11; TCLC 144**
See also CA 89-92; DLB 177; EWL 3; WLIT 7

Gaddis, William 1922-1998 ... **CLC 1, 3, 6, 8, 10, 19, 43, 86**
See also AMWS 4; BPFB 1; CA 17-20R; 172; CANR 21, 48; CN 1, 2, 3, 4, 5, 6; DLB 2, 278; EWL 3; MAL 5; MTCW 1, 2; MTFW 2005; RGAL 4

Gaelique, Moruen le
See Jacob, (Cyprien-)Max

Gage, Walter
See Inge, William (Motter)

Gaiman, Neil (Richard) 1960- .... **CLC 195**
See also AAYA 19, 42; CA 133; CANR 81, 129; DLB 261; HGG; MTFW 2005; SATA 85, 146; SFW 4; SUFW 2

Gaines, Ernest J(ames) 1933- .. **BLC 2; CLC 3, 11, 18, 86, 181; SSC 68**
See also AAYA 18; AFAW 1, 2; AITN 1; BPFB 2; BW 2, 3; BYA 6; CA 9-12R; CANR 6, 24, 42, 75, 126; CDALB 1968-1988; CLR 62; CN 1, 2, 3, 4, 5, 6, 7; CSW; DA3; DAM MULT; DLB 2, 33, 152; DLBY 1980; EWL 3; EXPN; LAIT 5; LATS 1:2; MAL 5; MTCW 1, 2; MTFW 2005; NFS 5, 7, 16; RGAL 4; RGSF 2; RHW; SATA 86; SSFS 5; YAW

Gaitskill, Mary (Lawrence) 1954- .... **CLC 69**
See also CA 128; CANR 61; DLB 244; TCLE 1:1

Gaius Suetonius Tranquillus
See Suetonius

Galdos, Benito Perez
See Perez Galdos, Benito
See also EW 7

Gale, Zona 1874-1938 .... **TCLC 7**
See also CA 105; 153; CANR 84; DAM DRAM; DFS 17; DLB 9, 78, 228; RGAL 4

Galeano, Eduardo (Hughes) 1940- . **CLC 72; HLCS 1**
See also CA 29-32R; CANR 13, 32, 100; HW 1

Galiano, Juan Valera y Alcala
See Valera y Alcala-Galiano, Juan

Galilei, Galileo 1564-1642 .... **LC 45**

Gallagher, Tess 1943- ...... **CLC 18, 63; PC 9**
See also CA 106; CP 3, 4, 5, 6, 7; CWP; DAM POET; DLB 120, 212, 244; PFS 16

Gallant, Mavis 1922- ..... **CLC 7, 18, 38, 172; SSC 5, 78**
See also CA 69-72; CANR 29, 69, 117; CCA 1; CN 1, 2, 3, 4, 5, 6, 7; DAC; DAM MST; DLB 53; EWL 3; MTCW 1, 2; MTFW 2005; RGEL 2; RGSF 2

Gallant, Roy A(rthur) 1924- .... **CLC 17**
See also CA 5-8R; CANR 4, 29, 54, 117; CLR 30; MAICYA 1, 2; SATA 4, 68, 110

Gallico, Paul (William) 1897-1976 ...... **CLC 2**
See also AITN 1; CA 5-8R; 69-72; CANR 23; CN 1, 2; DLB 9, 171; FANT; MAICYA 1, 2; SATA 13

Gallo, Max Louis 1932- .... **CLC 95**
See also CA 85-88

Gallois, Lucien
See Desnos, Robert

Gallup, Ralph
See Whitemore, Hugh (John)

Galsworthy, John 1867-1933 .... **SSC 22; TCLC 1, 45; WLC**
See also BRW 6; CA 104; 141; CANR 75; CDBLB 1890-1914; DA; DA3; DAB; DAC; DAM DRAM, MST, NOV; DLB 10, 34, 98, 162; DLBD 16; EWL 3; MTCW 2; RGEL 2; SSFS 3; TEA

Galt, John 1779-1839 .... **NCLC 1, 110**
See also DLB 99, 116, 159; RGEL 2; RGSF 2

Galvin, James 1951- .... **CLC 38**
See also CA 108; CANR 26

George, Jean Craighead 1919- .... **CLC 35**
See also AAYA 8; BYA 2, 4; CA 5-8R;
CANR 25; CLR 1; 80; DLB 52; JRDA;
MAICYA 1, 2; SATA 2, 68, 124; WYA;
YAW

George, Stefan (Anton) 1868-1933 . **TCLC 2, 14**
See also CA 104; 193; EW 8; EWL 3

Georges, Georges Martin
See Simenon, Georges (Jacques Christian)

Gerald of Wales c. 1146-c. 1223 ... **CMLC 60**

Gerhardi, William Alexander
See Gerhardie, William Alexander

Gerhardie, William Alexander
1895-1977 .... **CLC 5**
See also CA 25-28R; 73-76; CANR 18; CN
1, 2; DLB 36; RGEL 2

Gerson, Jean 1363-1429 .... **LC 77**
See also DLB 208

Gersonides 1288-1344 .... **CMLC 49**
See also DLB 115

Gerstler, Amy 1956- .... **CLC 70**
See also CA 146; CANR 99

Gertler, T. .... **CLC 34**
See also CA 116; 121

Gertsen, Aleksandr Ivanovich
See Herzen, Aleksandr Ivanovich

Ghalib .... **NCLC 39, 78**
See Ghalib, Asadullah Khan

Ghalib, Asadullah Khan 1797-1869
See Ghalib
See also DAM POET; RGWL 2, 3

Ghelderode, Michel de 1898-1962 ..... **CLC 6, 11; DC 15**
See also CA 85-88; CANR 40, 77; DAM
DRAM; DLB 321; EW 11; EWL 3; TWA

Ghiselin, Brewster 1903-2001 .... **CLC 23**
See also CA 13-16R; CAAS 10; CANR 13;
CP 1, 2, 3, 4, 5, 6, 7

Ghose, Aurabinda 1872-1950 .... **TCLC 63**
See Ghose, Aurobindo
See also CA 163

Ghose, Aurobindo
See Ghose, Aurabinda
See also EWL 3

Ghose, Zulfikar 1935- .... **CLC 42, 200**
See also CA 65-68; CANR 67; CN 1, 2, 3,
4, 5, 6, 7; CP 1, 2, 3, 4, 5, 6, 7; EWL 3

Ghosh, Amitav 1956- .... **CLC 44, 153**
See also CA 147; CANR 80; CN 6, 7;
WWE 1

Giacosa, Giuseppe 1847-1906 .... **TCLC 7**
See also CA 104

Gibb, Lee
See Waterhouse, Keith (Spencer)

Gibbon, Edward 1737-1794 .... **LC 97**
See also BRW 3; DLB 104; RGEL 2

Gibbon, Lewis Grassic .... **TCLC 4**
See Mitchell, James Leslie
See also RGEL 2

Gibbons, Kaye 1960- .... **CLC 50, 88, 145**
See also AAYA 34; AMWS 10; CA 151;
CANR 75, 127; CN 7; CSW; DA3; DAM
POP; DLB 292; MTCW 2; MTFW 2005;
NFS 3; RGAL 4; SATA 117

Gibran, Kahlil 1883-1931 . **PC 9; TCLC 1, 9**
See also CA 104; 150; DA3; DAM POET,
POP; EWL 3; MTCW 2; WLIT 6

Gibran, Khalil
See Gibran, Kahlil

Gibson, Mel 1956- .... **CLC 215**

Gibson, William 1914- .... **CLC 23**
See also CA 9-12R; CAD; CANR 9, 42, 75,
125; CD 5, 6; DA; DAB; DAC; DAM
DRAM, MST; DFS 2; DLB 7; LAIT 2;
MAL 5; MTCW 2; MTFW 2005; SATA
66; YAW

Gibson, William (Ford) 1948- ... **CLC 39, 63, 186, 192; SSC 52**
See also AAYA 12, 59; BPFB 2; CA 126;
133; CANR 52, 90, 106; CN 6, 7; CPW;
DA3; DAM POP; DLB 251; MTCW 2;
MTFW 2005; SCFW 2; SFW 4

Gide, Andre (Paul Guillaume)
1869-1951 ..... **SSC 13; TCLC 5, 12, 36; WLC**
See also CA 104; 124; DA; DA3; DAB;
DAC; DAM MST, NOV; DLB 65, 321;
EW 8; EWL 3; GFL 1789 to the Present;
MTCW 1, 2; MTFW 2005; NFS 21;
RGSF 2; RGWL 2, 3; TWA

Gifford, Barry (Colby) 1946- .... **CLC 34**
See also CA 65-68; CANR 9, 30, 40, 90

Gilbert, Frank
See De Voto, Bernard (Augustine)

Gilbert, W(illiam) S(chwenck)
1836-1911 .... **TCLC 3**
See also CA 104; 173; DAM DRAM, POET;
RGEL 2; SATA 36

Gilbreth, Frank B(unker), Jr.
1911-2001 .... **CLC 17**
See also CA 9-12R; SATA 2

Gilchrist, Ellen (Louise) 1935- .. **CLC 34, 48, 143; SSC 14, 63**
See also BPFB 2; CA 113; 116; CANR 41,
61, 104; CN 4, 5, 6, 7; CPW; CSW; DAM
POP; DLB 130; EWL 3; EXPS; MTCW
1, 2; MTFW 2005; RGAL 4; RGSF 2;
SSFS 9

Giles, Molly 1942- .... **CLC 39**
See also CA 126; CANR 98

Gill, Eric .... **TCLC 85**
See Gill, (Arthur) Eric (Rowton Peter
Joseph)

Gill, (Arthur) Eric (Rowton Peter Joseph)
1882-1940
See Gill, Eric
See also CA 120; DLB 98

Gill, Patrick
See Creasey, John

Gillette, Douglas .... **CLC 70**

Gilliam, Terry (Vance) 1940- .... **CLC 21, 141**
See Monty Python
See also AAYA 19, 59; CA 108; 113; CANR
35; INT CA-113

Gillian, Jerry
See Gilliam, Terry (Vance)

Gilliatt, Penelope (Ann Douglass)
1932-1993 .... **CLC 2, 10, 13, 53**
See also AITN 2; CA 13-16R; 141; CANR
49; CN 1, 2, 3, 4, 5; DLB 14

Gilligan, Carol 1936- .... **CLC 208**
See also CA 142; CANR 121; FW

Gilman, Charlotte (Anna) Perkins (Stetson)
1860-1935 ...... **SSC 13, 62; TCLC 9, 37, 117**
See also AMWS 11; BYA 11; CA 106; 150;
DLB 221; EXPS; FL 1:5; FW; HGG;
LAIT 2; MAWW; MTCW 2; MTFW
2005; RGAL 4; RGSF 2; SFW 4; SSFS 1,
18

Gilmour, David 1946- .... **CLC 35**

Gilpin, William 1724-1804 .... **NCLC 30**

Gilray, J. D.
See Mencken, H(enry) L(ouis)

Gilroy, Frank D(aniel) 1925- .... **CLC 2**
See also CA 81-84; CAD; CANR 32, 64,
86; CD 5, 6; DFS 17; DLB 7

Gilstrap, John 1957(?)- .... **CLC 99**
See also AAYA 67; CA 160; CANR 101

Ginsberg, Allen 1926-1997 .... **CLC 1, 2, 3, 4, 6, 13, 36, 69, 109; PC 4, 47; TCLC 120; WLC**
See also AAYA 33; AITN 1; AMWC 1;
AMWS 2; BG 1:2; CA 1-4R; 157; CANR
2, 41, 63, 95; CDALB 1941-1968; CP 1,

2, 3, 4, 5, 6; DA; DA3; DAB; DAC; DAM
MST, POET; DLB 5, 16, 169, 237; EWL
3; GLL 1; LMFS 2; MAL 5; MTCW 1, 2;
MTFW 2005; PAB; PFS 5; RGAL 4;
TUS; WP

Ginzburg, Eugenia .... **CLC 59**
See Ginzburg, Evgeniia

Ginzburg, Evgeniia 1904-1977
See Ginzburg, Eugenia
See also DLB 302

Ginzburg, Natalia 1916-1991 .... **CLC 5, 11, 54, 70; SSC 65; TCLC 156**
See also CA 85-88; 135; CANR 33; DFS
14; DLB 177; EW 13; EWL 3; MTCW 1,
2; MTFW 2005; RGWL 2, 3

Giono, Jean 1895-1970 .... **CLC 4, 11; TCLC 124**
See also CA 45-48; 29-32R; CANR 2, 35;
DLB 72, 321; EWL 3; GFL 1789 to the
Present; MTCW 1; RGWL 2, 3

Giovanni, Nikki 1943- ...... **BLC 2; CLC 2, 4, 19, 64, 117; PC 19; WLCS**
See also AAYA 22; AITN 1; BW 2, 3; CA
29-32R; CAAS 6; CANR 18, 41, 60, 91,
130; CDALBS; CLR 6, 73; CP 2, 3, 4, 5,
6, 7; CSW; CWP; CWRI 5; DA; DA3;
DAB; DAC; DAM MST, MULT, POET;
DLB 5, 41; EWL 3; EXPP; INT CANR-
18; MAICYA 1, 2; MAL 5; MTCW 1, 2;
MTFW 2005; PFS 17; RGAL 4; SATA
24, 107; TUS; YAW

Giovene, Andrea 1904-1998 .... **CLC 7**
See also CA 85-88

Gippius, Zinaida (Nikolaevna) 1869-1945
See Hippius, Zinaida (Nikolaevna)
See also CA 106; 212

Giraudoux, Jean(-Hippolyte)
1882-1944 .... **TCLC 2, 7**
See also CA 104; 196; DAM DRAM; DLB
65, 321; EW 9; EWL 3; GFL 1789 to the
Present; RGWL 2, 3; TWA

Gironella, Jose Maria (Pous)
1917-2003 .... **CLC 11**
See also CA 101; 212; EWL 3; RGWL 2, 3

Gissing, George (Robert)
1857-1903 .... **SSC 37; TCLC 3, 24, 47**
See also BRW 5; CA 105; 167; DLB 18,
135, 184; RGEL 2; TEA

Gitlin, Todd 1943- .... **CLC 201**
See also CA 29-32R; CANR 25, 50, 88

Giurlani, Aldo
See Palazzeschi, Aldo

Gladkov, Fedor Vasil'evich
See Gladkov, Fyodor (Vasilyevich)
See also DLB 272

Gladkov, Fyodor (Vasilyevich)
1883-1958 .... **TCLC 27**
See Gladkov, Fedor Vasil'evich
See also CA 170; EWL 3

Glancy, Diane 1941- .... **CLC 210; NNAL**
See also CA 136; 225; CAAE 225; CAAS
24; CANR 87; DLB 175

Glanville, Brian (Lester) 1931- .... **CLC 6**
See also CA 5-8R; CAAS 9; CANR 3, 70;
CN 1, 2, 3, 4, 5, 6, 7; DLB 15, 139; SATA
42

Glasgow, Ellen (Anderson Gholson)
1873-1945 .... **SSC 34; TCLC 2, 7**
See also AMW; CA 104; 164; DLB 9, 12;
MAL 5; MAWW; MTCW 2; MTFW 2005;
RGAL 4; RHW; SSFS 9; TUS

Glaspell, Susan 1882(?)-1948 ..... **DC 10; SSC 41; TCLC 55**
See also AMWS 3; CA 110; 154; DFS 8,
18; DLB 7, 9, 78, 228; MAWW; RGAL
4; SSFS 3; TCWW 2; TUS; YABC 2

Glassco, John 1909-1981 .... **CLC 9**
See also CA 13-16R; 102; CANR 15; CN
1, 2; CP 1, 2, 3; DLB 68

Glasscock, Amnesia
See Steinbeck, John (Ernst)

Glasser, Ronald J. 1940(?)- .... **CLC 37**
See also CA 209

Glassman, Joyce
See Johnson, Joyce

Gleick, James (W.) 1954- .... **CLC 147**
See also CA 131; 137; CANR 97; INT CA-137

Glendinning, Victoria 1937- .... **CLC 50**
See also CA 120; 127; CANR 59, 89; DLB 155

Glissant, Edouard (Mathieu)
1928- .... **CLC 10, 68**
See also CA 153; CANR 111; CWW 2;
DAM MULT; EWL 3; RGWL 3

Gloag, Julian 1930- .... **CLC 40**
See also AITN 1; CA 65-68; CANR 10, 70;
CN 1, 2, 3, 4, 5, 6

Glowacki, Aleksander
See Prus, Boleslaw

Gluck, Louise (Elisabeth) 1943- .. **CLC 7, 22, 44, 81, 160; PC 16**
See also AMWS 5; CA 33-36R; CANR 40,
69, 108, 133; CP 1, 2, 3, 4, 5, 6, 7; CWP;
DA3; DAM POET; DLB 5; MAL 5;
MTCW 2; MTFW 2005; PFS 5, 15;
RGAL 4; TCLE 1:1

Glyn, Elinor 1864-1943 .... **TCLC 72**
See also DLB 153; RHW

Gobineau, Joseph-Arthur
1816-1882 .... **NCLC 17**
See also DLB 123; GFL 1789 to the Present

Godard, Jean-Luc 1930- .... **CLC 20**
See also CA 93-96

Godden, (Margaret) Rumer
1907-1998 .... **CLC 53**
See also AAYA 6; BPFB 2; BYA 2, 5; CA
5-8R; 172; CANR 4, 27, 36, 55, 80; CLR
20; CN 1, 2, 3, 4, 5, 6; CWRI 5; DLB
161; MAICYA 1, 2; RHW; SAAS 12;
SATA 3, 36; SATA-Obit 109; TEA

Godoy Alcayaga, Lucila 1899-1957 .. **HLC 2; PC 32; TCLC 2**
See Mistral, Gabriela
See also BW 2; CA 104; 131; CANR 81;
DAM MULT; DNFS; HW 1, 2; MTCW 1,
2; MTFW 2005

Godwin, Gail 1937- ...... **CLC 5, 8, 22, 31, 69, 125**
See also BPFB 2; CA 29-32R; CANR 15,
43, 69, 132; CN 3, 4, 5, 6, 7; CPW; CSW;
DA3; DAM POP; DLB 6, 234; INT
CANR-15; MAL 5; MTCW 1, 2; MTFW
2005

Godwin, Gail Kathleen
See Godwin, Gail

Godwin, William 1756-1836 .. **NCLC 14, 130**
See also CDBLB 1789-1832; CMW 4; DLB
39, 104, 142, 158, 163, 262; GL 2; HGG;
RGEL 2

Goebbels, Josef
See Goebbels, (Paul) Joseph

Goebbels, (Paul) Joseph
1897-1945 .... **TCLC 68**
See also CA 115; 148

Goebbels, Joseph Paul
See Goebbels, (Paul) Joseph

Goethe, Johann Wolfgang von
1749-1832 . **DC 20; NCLC 4, 22, 34, 90, 154; PC 5; SSC 38; WLC**
See also CDWLB 2; DA; DA3; DAB;
DAC; DAM DRAM, MST, POET; DLB
94; EW 5; GL 2; LATS 1; LMFS 1:1;
RGWL 2, 3; TWA

Gogarty, Oliver St. John
1878-1957 .... **TCLC 15**
See also CA 109; 150; DLB 15, 19; RGEL
2

Gogol, Nikolai (Vasilyevich)
1809-1852 .... **DC 1; NCLC 5, 15, 31, 162; SSC 4, 29, 52; WLC**
See also DA; DAB; DAC; DAM DRAM,
MST; DFS 12; DLB 198; EW 6; EXPS;
RGSF 2; RGWL 2, 3; SSFS 7; TWA

Goines, Donald 1937(?)-1974 ... **BLC 2; CLC 80**
See also AITN 1; BW 1, 3; CA 124; 114;
CANR 82; CMW 4; DA3; DAM MULT,
POP; DLB 33

Gold, Herbert 1924- ... **CLC 4, 7, 14, 42, 152**
See also CA 9-12R; CANR 17, 45, 125; CN
1, 2, 3, 4, 5, 6, 7; DLB 2; DLBY 1981;
MAL 5

Goldbarth, Albert 1948- .... **CLC 5, 38**
See also AMWS 12; CA 53-56; CANR 6,
40; CP 3, 4, 5, 6, 7; DLB 120

Goldberg, Anatol 1910-1982 .... **CLC 34**
See also CA 131; 117

Goldemberg, Isaac 1945- .... **CLC 52**
See also CA 69-72; CAAS 12; CANR 11,
32; EWL 3; HW 1; WLIT 1

Golding, Arthur 1536-1606 .... **LC 101**
See also DLB 136

Golding, William (Gerald)
1911-1993 ..... **CLC 1, 2, 3, 8, 10, 17, 27, 58, 81; WLC**
See also AAYA 5, 44; BPFB 2; BRWR 1;
BRWS 1; BYA 2, 5; CA 5-8R; 141; CANR
13, 33, 54; CD 5; CDBLB 1945-1960;
CLR 94; CN 1, 2, 3, 4; DA; DA3; DAB;
DAC; DAM MST, NOV; DLB 15, 100,
255; EWL 3; EXPN; HGG; LAIT 4;
MTCW 1, 2; MTFW 2005; NFS 2; RGEL
2; RHW; SFW 4; TEA; WLIT 4; YAW

Goldman, Emma 1869-1940 .... **TCLC 13**
See also CA 110; 150; DLB 221; FW;
RGAL 4; TUS

Goldman, Francisco 1954- .... **CLC 76**
See also CA 162

Goldman, William (W.) 1931- ...... **CLC 1, 48**
See also BPFB 2; CA 9-12R; CANR 29,
69, 106; CN 1, 2, 3, 4, 5, 6, 7; DLB 44;
FANT; IDFW 3, 4

Goldmann, Lucien 1913-1970 .... **CLC 24**
See also CA 25-28; CAP 2

Goldoni, Carlo 1707-1793 .... **LC 4**
See also DAM DRAM; EW 4; RGWL 2, 3;
WLIT 7

Goldsberry, Steven 1949- .... **CLC 34**
See also CA 131

Goldsmith, Oliver 1730-1774 .... **DC 8; LC 2, 48, 122; WLC**
See also BRW 3; CDBLB 1660-1789; DA;
DAB; DAC; DAM DRAM, MST, NOV,
POET; DFS 1; DLB 39, 89, 104, 109, 142;
IDTP; RGEL 2; SATA 26; TEA; WLIT 3

Goldsmith, Peter
See Priestley, J(ohn) B(oynton)

Gombrowicz, Witold 1904-1969 .... **CLC 4, 7, 11, 49**
See also CA 19-20; 25-28R; CANR 105;
CAP 2; CDWLB 4; DAM DRAM; DLB
215; EW 12; EWL 3; RGWL 2, 3; TWA

Gomez de Avellaneda, Gertrudis
1814-1873 .... **NCLC 111**
See also LAW

Gomez de la Serna, Ramon
1888-1963 .... **CLC 9**
See also CA 153; 116; CANR 79; EWL 3;
HW 1, 2

Goncharov, Ivan Alexandrovich
1812-1891 .... **NCLC 1, 63**
See also DLB 238; EW 6; RGWL 2, 3

Goncourt, Edmond (Louis Antoine Huot) de
1822-1896 .... **NCLC 7**
See also DLB 123; EW 7; GFL 1789 to the
Present; RGWL 2, 3

Goncourt, Jules (Alfred Huot) de
1830-1870 .... **NCLC 7**
See also DLB 123; EW 7; GFL 1789 to the
Present; RGWL 2, 3

Gongora (y Argote), Luis de
1561-1627 .... **LC 72**
See also RGWL 2, 3

Gontier, Fernande 19(?)- .... **CLC 50**

Gonzalez Martinez, Enrique
See Gonzalez Martinez, Enrique
See also DLB 290

Gonzalez Martinez, Enrique
1871-1952 .... **TCLC 72**
See Gonzalez Martinez, Enrique
See also CA 166; CANR 81; EWL 3; HW
1, 2

Goodison, Lorna 1947- .... **PC 36**
See also CA 142; CANR 88; CP 7; CWP;
DLB 157; EWL 3

Goodman, Paul 1911-1972 ..... **CLC 1, 2, 4, 7**
See also CA 19-20; 37-40R; CAD; CANR
34; CAP 2; CN 1; DLB 130, 246; MAL
5; MTCW 1; RGAL 4

GoodWeather, Harley
See King, Thomas

Googe, Barnabe 1540-1594 .... **LC 94**
See also DLB 132; RGEL 2

Gordimer, Nadine 1923- ...... **CLC 3, 5, 7, 10, 18, 33, 51, 70, 123, 160, 161; SSC 17, 80; WLCS**
See also AAYA 39; AFW; BRWS 2; CA
5-8R; CANR 3, 28, 56, 88, 131; CN 1, 2,
3, 4, 5, 6, 7; DA; DA3; DAB; DAC; DAM
MST, NOV; DLB 225; EWL 3; EXPS;
INT CANR-28; LATS 1:2; MTCW 1, 2;
MTFW 2005; NFS 4; RGEL 2; RGSF 2;
SSFS 2, 14, 19; TWA; WLIT 2; YAW

Gordon, Adam Lindsay
1833-1870 .... **NCLC 21**
See also DLB 230

Gordon, Caroline 1895-1981 . **CLC 6, 13, 29, 83; SSC 15**
See also AMW; CA 11-12; 103; CANR 36;
CAP 1; CN 1, 2; DLB 4, 9, 102; DLBD
17; DLBY 1981; EWL 3; MAL 5; MTCW
1, 2; MTFW 2005; RGAL 4; RGSF 2

Gordon, Charles William 1860-1937
See Connor, Ralph
See also CA 109

Gordon, Mary (Catherine) 1949- .... **CLC 13, 22, 128, 216; SSC 59**
See also AMWS 4; BPFB 2; CA 102;
CANR 44, 92; CN 4, 5, 6, 7; DLB 6;
DLBY 1981; FW; INT CA-102; MAL 5;
MTCW 1

Gordon, N. J.
See Bosman, Herman Charles

Gordon, Sol 1923- .... **CLC 26**
See also CA 53-56; CANR 4; SATA 11

Gordone, Charles 1925-1995 .. **CLC 1, 4; DC 8**
See also BW 1, 3; CA 93-96; 180; 150;
CAAE 180; CAD; CANR 55; DAM
DRAM; DLB 7; INT CA-93-96; MTCW
1

Gore, Catherine 1800-1861 .... **NCLC 65**
See also DLB 116; RGEL 2

Gorenko, Anna Andreevna
See Akhmatova, Anna

Gorky, Maxim .... **SSC 28; TCLC 8; WLC**
See Peshkov, Alexei Maximovich
See also DAB; DFS 9; DLB 295; EW 8;
EWL 3; TWA

Goryan, Sirak
See Saroyan, William

Gosse, Edmund (William)
1849-1928 .... **TCLC 28**
See also CA 117; DLB 57, 144, 184; RGEL
2

Gotlieb, Phyllis (Fay Bloom) 1926- .. **CLC 18**
See also CA 13-16R; CANR 7, 135; CN 7;
CP 1, 2, 3, 4; DLB 88, 251; SFW 4

Gottesman, S. D.
See Kornbluth, C(yril) M.; Pohl, Frederik

Gottfried von Strassburg fl. c.
1170-1215 .... **CMLC 10**
See also CDWLB 2; DLB 138; EW 1;
RGWL 2, 3

Gotthelf, Jeremias 1797-1854 .... **NCLC 117**
See also DLB 133; RGWL 2, 3

Gottschalk, Laura Riding
See Jackson, Laura (Riding)

Gould, Lois 1932(?)-2002 .... **CLC 4, 10**
See also CA 77-80; 208; CANR 29; MTCW
1

Gould, Stephen Jay 1941-2002 .... **CLC 163**
See also AAYA 26; BEST 90:2; CA 77-80;
205; CANR 10, 27, 56, 75, 125; CPW;
INT CANR-27; MTCW 1, 2; MTFW 2005

Gourmont, Remy(-Marie-Charles) de
1858-1915 .... **TCLC 17**
See also CA 109; 150; GFL 1789 to the
Present; MTCW 2

Gournay, Marie le Jars de
See de Gournay, Marie le Jars

Govier, Katherine 1948- .... **CLC 51**
See also CA 101; CANR 18, 40, 128; CCA
1

Gower, John c. 1330-1408 .... **LC 76; PC 59**
See also BRW 1; DLB 146; RGEL 2

Goyen, (Charles) William
1915-1983 .... **CLC 5, 8, 14, 40**
See also AITN 2; CA 5-8R; 110; CANR 6,
71; CN 1, 2, 3; DLB 2, 218; DLBY 1983;
EWL 3; INT CANR-6; MAL 5

Goytisolo, Juan 1931- .... **CLC 5, 10, 23, 133;
HLC 1**
See also CA 85-88; CANR 32, 61, 131;
CWW 2; DAM MULT; DLB 322; EWL
3; GLL 2; HW 1, 2; MTCW 1, 2; MTFW
2005

Gozzano, Guido 1883-1916 .... **PC 10**
See also CA 154; DLB 114; EWL 3

Gozzi, (Conte) Carlo 1720-1806 .... **NCLC 23**

Grabbe, Christian Dietrich
1801-1836 .... **NCLC 2**
See also DLB 133; RGWL 2, 3

Grace, Patricia Frances 1937- .... **CLC 56**
See also CA 176; CANR 118; CN 4, 5, 6,
7; EWL 3; RGSF 2

Gracian y Morales, Baltasar
1601-1658 .... **LC 15**

Gracq, Julien .... **CLC 11, 48**
See Poirier, Louis
See also CWW 2; DLB 83; GFL 1789 to
the Present

Grade, Chaim 1910-1982 .... **CLC 10**
See also CA 93-96; 107; EWL 3

Graduate of Oxford, A
See Ruskin, John

Grafton, Garth
See Duncan, Sara Jeannette

Grafton, Sue 1940- .... **CLC 163**
See also AAYA 11, 49; BEST 90:3; CA 108;
CANR 31, 55, 111, 134; CMW 4; CPW;
CSW; DA3; DAM POP; DLB 226; FW;
MSW; MTFW 2005

Graham, John
See Phillips, David Graham

Graham, Jorie 1950- .... **CLC 48, 118; PC 59**
See also AAYA 67; CA 111; CANR 63, 118;
CP 4, 5, 6, 7; CWP; DLB 120; EWL 3;
MTFW 2005; PFS 10, 17; TCLE 1:1

Graham, R(obert) B(ontine) Cunninghame
See Cunninghame Graham, Robert
(Gallnigad) Bontine
See also DLB 98, 135, 174; RGEL 2; RGSF
2

Graham, Robert
See Haldeman, Joe (William)

Graham, Tom
See Lewis, (Harry) Sinclair

Graham, W(illiam) S(idney)
1918-1986 .... **CLC 29**
See also BRWS 7; CA 73-76; 118; CP 1, 2,
3, 4; DLB 20; RGEL 2

Graham, Winston (Mawdsley)
1910-2003 .... **CLC 23**
See also CA 49-52; 218; CANR 2, 22, 45,
66; CMW 4; CN 1, 2, 3, 4, 5, 6, 7; DLB
77; RHW

Grahame, Kenneth 1859-1932 ...... **TCLC 64,
136**
See also BYA 5; CA 108; 136; CANR 80;
CLR 5; CWRI 5; DA3; DAB; DLB 34,
141, 178; FANT; MAICYA 1, 2; MTCW
2; NFS 20; RGEL 2; SATA 100; TEA;
WCH; YABC 1

Granger, Darius John
See Marlowe, Stephen

Granin, Daniil 1918- .... **CLC 59**
See also DLB 302

Granovsky, Timofei Nikolaevich
1813-1855 .... **NCLC 75**
See also DLB 198

Grant, Skeeter
See Spiegelman, Art

Granville-Barker, Harley
1877-1946 .... **TCLC 2**
See Barker, Harley Granville
See also CA 104; 204; DAM DRAM;
RGEL 2

Granzotto, Gianni
See Granzotto, Giovanni Battista

Granzotto, Giovanni Battista
1914-1985 .... **CLC 70**
See also CA 166

Grass, Guenter (Wilhelm) 1927- ... **CLC 1, 2,
4, 6, 11, 15, 22, 32, 49, 88, 207; WLC**
See Grass, Gunter (Wilhelm)
See also BPFB 2; CA 13-16R; CANR 20,
75, 93, 133; CDWLB 2; DA; DA3; DAB;
DAC; DAM MST, NOV; DLB 75, 124;
EW 13; EWL 3; MTCW 1, 2; MTFW
2005; RGWL 2, 3; TWA

Grass, Gunter (Wilhelm)
See Grass, Guenter (Wilhelm)
See also CWW 2

Gratton, Thomas
See Hulme, T(homas) E(rnest)

Grau, Shirley Ann 1929- .... **CLC 4, 9, 146;
SSC 15**
See also CA 89-92; CANR 22, 69; CN 1, 2,
3, 4, 5, 6, 7; CSW; DLB 2, 218; INT CA-
89-92; CANR-22; MTCW 1

Gravel, Fern
See Hall, James Norman

Graver, Elizabeth 1964- .... **CLC 70**
See also CA 135; CANR 71, 129

Graves, Richard Perceval
1895-1985 .... **CLC 44**
See also CA 65-68; CANR 9, 26, 51

Graves, Robert (von Ranke)
1895-1985 .. **CLC 1, 2, 6, 11, 39, 44, 45;
PC 6**
See also BPFB 2; BRW 7; BYA 4; CA 5-8R;
117; CANR 5, 36; CDBLB 1914-1945;
CN 1, 2, 3; CP 1, 2, 3, 4; DA3; DAB;
DAC; DAM MST, POET; DLB 20, 100,
191; DLBD 18; DLBY 1985; EWL 3;
LATS 1:1; MTCW 1, 2; MTFW 2005;
NCFS 2; NFS 21; RGEL 2; RHW; SATA
45; TEA

Graves, Valerie
See Bradley, Marion Zimmer

Gray, Alasdair (James) 1934- .... **CLC 41**
See also BRWS 9; CA 126; CANR 47, 69,
106, 140; CN 4, 5, 6, 7; DLB 194, 261,
319; HGG; INT CA-126; MTCW 1, 2;
MTFW 2005; RGSF 2; SUFW 2

Gray, Amlin 1946- .... **CLC 29**
See also CA 138

Gray, Francine du Plessix 1930- ..... **CLC 22,
153**
See also BEST 90:3; CA 61-64; CAAS 2;
CANR 11, 33, 75, 81; DAM NOV; INT
CANR-11; MTCW 1, 2; MTFW 2005

Gray, John (Henry) 1866-1934 ...... **TCLC 19**
See also CA 119; 162; RGEL 2

Gray, John Lee
See Jakes, John (William)

Gray, Simon (James Holliday)
1936- .... **CLC 9, 14, 36**
See also AITN 1; CA 21-24R; CAAS 3;
CANR 32, 69; CBD; CD 5, 6; CN 1, 2, 3;
DLB 13; EWL 3; MTCW 1; RGEL 2

Gray, Spalding 1941-2004 .... **CLC 49, 112;
DC 7**
See also AAYA 62; CA 128; 225; CAD;
CANR 74, 138; CD 5, 6; CPW; DAM
POP; MTCW 2; MTFW 2005

Gray, Thomas 1716-1771 .... **LC 4, 40; PC 2;
WLC**
See also BRW 3; CDBLB 1660-1789; DA;
DA3; DAB; DAC; DAM MST; DLB 109;
EXPP; PAB; PFS 9; RGEL 2; TEA; WP

Grayson, David
See Baker, Ray Stannard

Grayson, Richard (A.) 1951- .... **CLC 38**
See also CA 85-88, 210; CAAE 210; CANR
14, 31, 57; DLB 234

Greeley, Andrew M(oran) 1928- ...... **CLC 28**
See also BPFB 2; CA 5-8R; CAAS 7;
CANR 7, 43, 69, 104, 136; CMW 4;
CPW; DA3; DAM POP; MTCW 1, 2;
MTFW 2005

Green, Anna Katharine
1846-1935 .... **TCLC 63**
See also CA 112; 159; CMW 4; DLB 202,
221; MSW

Green, Brian
See Card, Orson Scott

Green, Hannah
See Greenberg, Joanne (Goldenberg)

Green, Hannah 1927(?)-1996 .... **CLC 3**
See also CA 73-76; CANR 59, 93; NFS 10

Green, Henry .... **CLC 2, 13, 97**
See Yorke, Henry Vincent
See also BRWS 2; CA 175; DLB 15; EWL
3; RGEL 2

Green, Julian .... **CLC 3, 11, 77**
See Green, Julien (Hartridge)
See also EWL 3; GFL 1789 to the Present;
MTCW 2

Green, Julien (Hartridge) 1900-1998
See Green, Julian
See also CA 21-24R; 169; CANR 33, 87;
CWW 2; DLB 4, 72; MTCW 1, 2; MTFW
2005

Green, Paul (Eliot) 1894-1981 .... **CLC 25**
See also AITN 1; CA 5-8R; 103; CAD;
CANR 3; DAM DRAM; DLB 7, 9, 249;
DLBY 1981; MAL 5; RGAL 4

Greenaway, Peter 1942- .... **CLC 159**
See also CA 127

Greenberg, Ivan 1908-1973
See Rahv, Philip
See also CA 85-88

Greenberg, Joanne (Goldenberg)
1932- .... **CLC 7, 30**
See also AAYA 12, 67; CA 5-8R; CANR
14, 32, 69; CN 6, 7; SATA 25; YAW

Greenberg, Richard 1959(?)- .... **CLC 57**
See also CA 138; CAD; CD 5, 6

Guinizelli, Guido c. 1230-1276 ...... **CMLC 49**
See Guinizzelli, Guido
Guinizzelli, Guido
See Guinizelli, Guido
See also WLIT 7
Guiraldes, Ricardo (Guillermo)
1886-1927 .... **TCLC 39**
See also CA 131; EWL 3; HW 1; LAW;
MTCW 1
Gumilev, Nikolai (Stepanovich)
1886-1921 .... **TCLC 60**
See Gumilyov, Nikolay Stepanovich
See also CA 165; DLB 295
Gumilyov, Nikolay Stepanovich
See Gumilev, Nikolai (Stepanovich)
See also EWL 3
Gump, P. Q.
See Card, Orson Scott
Gunesekera, Romesh 1954- .... **CLC 91**
See also BRWS 10; CA 159; CANR 140;
CN 6, 7; DLB 267
Gunn, Bill .... **CLC 5**
See Gunn, William Harrison
See also DLB 38
Gunn, Thom(son William)
1929-2004 . **CLC 3, 6, 18, 32, 81; PC 26**
See also BRWS 4; CA 17-20R; 227; CANR
9, 33, 116; CDBLB 1960 to Present; CP
1, 2, 3, 4, 5, 6, 7; DAM POET; DLB 27;
INT CANR-33; MTCW 1; PFS 9; RGEL
2
Gunn, William Harrison 1934(?)-1989
See Gunn, Bill
See also AITN 1; BW 1, 3; CA 13-16R;
128; CANR 12, 25, 76
Gunn Allen, Paula
See Allen, Paula Gunn
Gunnars, Kristjana 1948- .... **CLC 69**
See also CA 113; CCA 1; CP 7; CWP; DLB
60
Gunter, Erich
See Eich, Gunter
Gurdjieff, G(eorgei) I(vanovich)
1877(?)-1949 .... **TCLC 71**
See also CA 157
Gurganus, Allan 1947- .... **CLC 70**
See also BEST 90:1; CA 135; CANR 114;
CN 6, 7; CPW; CSW; DAM POP; GLL 1
Gurney, A. R.
See Gurney, A(lbert) R(amsdell), Jr.
See also DLB 266
Gurney, A(lbert) R(amsdell), Jr.
1930- .... **CLC 32, 50, 54**
See Gurney, A. R.
See also AMWS 5; CA 77-80; CAD; CANR
32, 64, 121; CD 5, 6; DAM DRAM; EWL
3
Gurney, Ivor (Bertie) 1890-1937 ... **TCLC 33**
See also BRW 6; CA 167; DLBY 2002;
PAB; RGEL 2
Gurney, Peter
See Gurney, A(lbert) R(amsdell), Jr.
Guro, Elena (Genrikhovna)
1877-1913 .... **TCLC 56**
See also DLB 295
Gustafson, James M(oody) 1925- ... **CLC 100**
See also CA 25-28R; CANR 37
Gustafson, Ralph (Barker)
1909-1995 .... **CLC 36**
See also CA 21-24R; CANR 8, 45, 84; CP
1, 2, 3, 4; DLB 88; RGEL 2
Gut, Gom
See Simenon, Georges (Jacques Christian)
Guterson, David 1956- .... **CLC 91**
See also CA 132; CANR 73, 126; CN 7;
DLB 292; MTCW 2; MTFW 2005; NFS
13

Guthrie, A(lfred) B(ertram), Jr.
1901-1991 .... **CLC 23**
See also CA 57-60; 134; CANR 24; CN 1,
2, 3; DLB 6, 212; MAL 5; SATA 62;
SATA-Obit 67; TCWW 1, 2
Guthrie, Isobel
See Grieve, C(hristopher) M(urray)
Guthrie, Woodrow Wilson 1912-1967
See Guthrie, Woody
See also CA 113; 93-96
Guthrie, Woody .... **CLC 35**
See Guthrie, Woodrow Wilson
See also DLB 303; LAIT 3
Gutierrez Najera, Manuel
1859-1895 .... **HLCS 2; NCLC 133**
See also DLB 290; LAW
Guy, Rosa (Cuthbert) 1925- .... **CLC 26**
See also AAYA 4, 37; BW 2; CA 17-20R;
CANR 14, 34, 83; CLR 13; DLB 33;
DNFS 1; JRDA; MAICYA 1, 2; SATA 14,
62, 122; YAW
Gwendolyn
See Bennett, (Enoch) Arnold
H. D. .... **CLC 3, 8, 14, 31, 34, 73; PC 5**
See Doolittle, Hilda
See also FL 1:5
H. de V.
See Buchan, John
Haavikko, Paavo Juhani 1931- .. **CLC 18, 34**
See also CA 106; CWW 2; EWL 3
Habbema, Koos
See Heijermans, Herman
Habermas, Juergen 1929- .... **CLC 104**
See also CA 109; CANR 85; DLB 242
Habermas, Jurgen
See Habermas, Juergen
Hacker, Marilyn 1942- ...... **CLC 5, 9, 23, 72,
91; PC 47**
See also CA 77-80; CANR 68, 129; CP 3,
4, 5, 6, 7; CWP; DAM POET; DLB 120,
282; FW; GLL 2; MAL 5; PFS 19
Hadewijch of Antwerp fl. 1250- ... **CMLC 61**
See also RGWL 3
Hadrian 76-138 .... **CMLC 52**
Haeckel, Ernst Heinrich (Philipp August)
1834-1919 .... **TCLC 83**
See also CA 157
Hafiz c. 1326-1389(?) .... **CMLC 34**
See also RGWL 2, 3; WLIT 6
Hagedorn, Jessica T(arahata)
1949- .... **CLC 185**
See also CA 139; CANR 69; CWP; DLB
312; RGAL 4
Haggard, H(enry) Rider
1856-1925 .... **TCLC 11**
See also BRWS 3; BYA 4, 5; CA 108; 148;
CANR 112; DLB 70, 156, 174, 178;
FANT; LMFS 1; MTCW 2; RGEL 2;
RHW; SATA 16; SCFW 1, 2; SFW 4;
SUFW 1; WLIT 4
Hagiosy, L.
See Larbaud, Valery (Nicolas)
Hagiwara, Sakutaro 1886-1942 .... **PC 18;
TCLC 60**
See Hagiwara Sakutaro
See also CA 154; RGWL 3
Hagiwara Sakutaro
See Hagiwara, Sakutaro
See also EWL 3
Haig, Fenil
See Ford, Ford Madox
Haig-Brown, Roderick (Langmere)
1908-1976 .... **CLC 21**
See also CA 5-8R; 69-72; CANR 4, 38, 83;
CLR 31; CWRI 5; DLB 88; MAICYA 1,
2; SATA 12; TCWW 2
Haight, Rip
See Carpenter, John (Howard)

Hailey, Arthur 1920-2004 .... **CLC 5**
See also AITN 2; BEST 90:3; BPFB 2; CA
1-4R; 233; CANR 2, 36, 75; CCA 1; CN
1, 2, 3, 4, 5, 6, 7; CPW; DAM NOV, POP;
DLB 88; DLBY 1982; MTCW 1, 2;
MTFW 2005
Hailey, Elizabeth Forsythe 1938- ..... **CLC 40**
See also CA 93-96, 188; CAAE 188; CAAS
1; CANR 15, 48; INT CANR-15
Haines, John (Meade) 1924- .... **CLC 58**
See also AMWS 12; CA 17-20R; CANR
13, 34; CP 1, 2, 3, 4; CSW; DLB 5, 212;
TCLE 1:1
Hakluyt, Richard 1552-1616 .... **LC 31**
See also DLB 136; RGEL 2
Haldeman, Joe (William) 1943- .... **CLC 61**
See Graham, Robert
See also AAYA 38; CA 53-56, 179; CAAE
179; CAAS 25; CANR 6, 70, 72, 130;
DLB 8; INT CANR-6; SCFW 2; SFW 4
Hale, Janet Campbell 1947- .... **NNAL**
See also CA 49-52; CANR 45, 75; DAM
MULT; DLB 175; MTCW 2; MTFW 2005
Hale, Sarah Josepha (Buell)
1788-1879 .... **NCLC 75**
See also DLB 1, 42, 73, 243
Halevy, Elie 1870-1937 .... **TCLC 104**
Haley, Alex(ander Murray Palmer)
1921-1992 .... **BLC 2; CLC 8, 12, 76;
TCLC 147**
See also AAYA 26; BPFB 2; BW 2, 3; CA
77-80; 136; CANR 61; CDALBS; CPW;
CSW; DA; DA3; DAB; DAC; DAM MST,
MULT, POP; DLB 38; LAIT 5; MTCW
1, 2; NFS 9
Haliburton, Thomas Chandler
1796-1865 .... **NCLC 15, 149**
See also DLB 11, 99; RGEL 2; RGSF 2
Hall, Donald (Andrew, Jr.) 1928- ...... **CLC 1,
13, 37, 59, 151**
See also AAYA 63; CA 5-8R; CAAS 7;
CANR 2, 44, 64, 106, 133; CP 1, 2, 3, 4,
5, 6, 7; DAM POET; DLB 5; MAL 5;
MTCW 2005; RGAL 4; SATA
23, 97
Hall, Frederic Sauser
See Sauser-Hall, Frederic
Hall, James
See Kuttner, Henry
Hall, James Norman 1887-1951 ..... **TCLC 23**
See also CA 123; 173; LAIT 1; RHW 1;
SATA 21
Hall, Joseph 1574-1656 .... **LC 91**
See also DLB 121, 151; RGEL 2
Hall, (Marguerite) Radclyffe
1880-1943 .... **TCLC 12**
See also BRWS 6; CA 110; 150; CANR 83;
DLB 191; MTCW 2; MTFW 2005; RGEL
2; RHW
Hall, Rodney 1935- .... **CLC 51**
See also CA 109; CANR 69; CN 6, 7; CP
1, 2, 3, 4, 5, 6, 7; DLB 289
Hallam, Arthur Henry
1811-1833 .... **NCLC 110**
See also DLB 32
Halldor Laxness .... **CLC 25**
See Gudjonsson, Halldor Kiljan
See also DLB 293; EW 12; EWL 3; RGWL
2, 3
Halleck, Fitz-Greene 1790-1867 .... **NCLC 47**
See also DLB 3, 250; RGAL 4
Halliday, Michael
See Creasey, John
Halpern, Daniel 1945- .... **CLC 14**
See also CA 33-36R; CANR 93; CP 3, 4, 5,
6, 7

Harriss, Will(ard Irvin) 1922- .... **CLC 34**
See also CA 111

Hart, Ellis
See Ellison, Harlan (Jay)

Hart, Josephine 1942(?)- .... **CLC 70**
See also CA 138; CANR 70; CPW; DAM
POP

Hart, Moss 1904-1961 .... **CLC 66**
See also CA 109; 89-92; CANR 84; DAM
DRAM; DFS 1; DLB 7, 266; RGAL 4

Harte, (Francis) Bret(t)
1836(?)-1902 ... **SSC 8, 59; TCLC 1, 25;**
WLC
See also AMWS 2; CA 104; 140; CANR
80; CDALB 1865-1917; DA; DA3; DAC;
DAM MST; DLB 12, 64, 74, 79, 186;
EXPS; LAIT 2; RGAL 4; RGSF 2; SATA
26; SSFS 3; TUS

Hartley, L(eslie) P(oles) 1895-1972 ... **CLC 2,**
22
See also BRWS 7; CA 45-48; 37-40R;
CANR 33; CN 1; DLB 15, 139; EWL 3;
HGG; MTCW 1, 2; MTFW 2005; RGEL
2; RGSF 2; SUFW 1

Hartman, Geoffrey H. 1929- .... **CLC 27**
See also CA 117; 125; CANR 79; DLB 67

Hartmann, Sadakichi 1869-1944 ... **TCLC 73**
See also CA 157; DLB 54

Hartmann von Aue c. 1170-c.
1210 .... **CMLC 15**
See also CDWLB 2; DLB 138; RGWL 2, 3

Hartog, Jan de
See de Hartog, Jan

Haruf, Kent 1943- .... **CLC 34**
See also AAYA 44; CA 149; CANR 91, 131

Harvey, Caroline
See Trollope, Joanna

Harvey, Gabriel 1550(?)-1631 .... **LC 88**
See also DLB 167, 213, 281

Harwood, Ronald 1934- .... **CLC 32**
See also CA 1-4R; CANR 4, 55; CBD; CD
5, 6; DAM DRAM, MST; DLB 13

Hasegawa Tatsunosuke
See Futabatei, Shimei

Hasek, Jaroslav (Matej Frantisek)
1883-1923 .... **SSC 69; TCLC 4**
See also CA 104; 129; CDWLB 4; DLB
215; EW 9; EWL 3; MTCW 1, 2; RGSF
2; RGWL 2, 3

Hass, Robert 1941- ... **CLC 18, 39, 99; PC 16**
See also AMWS 6; CA 111; CANR 30, 50,
71; CP 3, 4, 5, 6, 7; DLB 105, 206; EWL
3; MAL 5; MTFW 2005; RGAL 4; SATA
94; TCLE 1:1

Hastings, Hudson
See Kuttner, Henry

Hastings, Selina .... **CLC 44**

Hathorne, John 1641-1717 .... **LC 38**

Hatteras, Amelia
See Mencken, H(enry) L(ouis)

Hatteras, Owen .... **TCLC 18**
See Mencken, H(enry) L(ouis); Nathan,
George Jean

Hauptmann, Gerhart (Johann Robert)
1862-1946 .... **SSC 37; TCLC 4**
See also CA 104; 153; CDWLB 2; DAM
DRAM; DLB 66, 118; EW 8; EWL 3;
RGSF 2; RGWL 2, 3; TWA

Havel, Vaclav 1936- ..... **CLC 25, 58, 65, 123;**
DC 6
See also CA 104; CANR 36, 63, 124; CD-
WLB 4; CWW 2; DA3; DAM DRAM;
DFS 10; DLB 232; EWL 3; LMFS 2;
MTCW 1, 2; MTFW 2005; RGWL 3

Haviaras, Stratis .... **CLC 33**
See Chaviaras, Strates

Hawes, Stephen 1475(?)-1529(?) .... **LC 17**
See also DLB 132; RGEL 2

Hawkes, John (Clendennin Burne, Jr.)
1925-1998 .. **CLC 1, 2, 3, 4, 7, 9, 14, 15,**
27, 49
See also BPFB 2; CA 1-4R; 167; CANR 2,
47, 64; CN 1, 2, 3, 4, 5, 6; DLB 2, 7, 227;
DLBY 1980, 1998; EWL 3; MAL 5;
MTCW 1, 2; MTFW 2005; RGAL 4

Hawking, S. W.
See Hawking, Stephen W(illiam)

Hawking, Stephen W(illiam) 1942- . **CLC 63,**
105
See also AAYA 13; BEST 89:1; CA 126;
129; CANR 48, 115; CPW; DA3; MTCW
2; MTFW 2005

Hawkins, Anthony Hope
See Hope, Anthony

Hawthorne, Julian 1846-1934 .... **TCLC 25**
See also CA 165; HGG

Hawthorne, Nathaniel 1804-1864 ... **NCLC 2,**
10, 17, 23, 39, 79, 95, 158; SSC 3, 29,
39, 89; WLC
See also AAYA 18; AMW; AMWC 1;
AMWR 1; BPFB 2; BYA 3; CDALB
1640-1865; CLR 103; DA; DA3; DAB;
DAC; DAM MST, NOV; DLB 1, 74, 183,
223, 269; EXPN; EXPS; GL 2; HGG;
LAIT 1; NFS 1, 20; RGAL 4; RGSF 2;
SSFS 1, 7, 11, 15; SUFW 1; TUS; WCH;
YABC 2

Hawthorne, Sophia Peabody
1809-1871 .... **NCLC 150**
See also DLB 183, 239

Haxton, Josephine Ayres 1921-
See Douglas, Ellen
See also CA 115; CANR 41, 83

Hayaseca y Eizaguirre, Jorge
See Echegaray (y Eizaguirre), Jose (Maria
Waldo)

Hayashi, Fumiko 1904-1951 .... **TCLC 27**
See Hayashi Fumiko
See also CA 161

Hayashi Fumiko
See Hayashi, Fumiko
See also DLB 180; EWL 3

Haycraft, Anna (Margaret) 1932-2005
See Ellis, Alice Thomas
See also CA 122; 237; CANR 90, 141;
MTCW 2; MTFW 2005

Hayden, Robert E(arl) 1913-1980 ..... **BLC 2;**
CLC 5, 9, 14, 37; PC 6
See also AFAW 1, 2; AMWS 2; BW 1, 3;
CA 69-72; 97-100; CABS 2; CANR 24,
75, 82; CDALB 1941-1968; CP 1, 2, 3;
DA; DAC; DAM MST, MULT, POET;
DLB 5, 76; EWL 3; EXPP; MAL 5;
MTCW 1, 2; PFS 1; RGAL 4; SATA 19;
SATA-Obit 26; WP

Haydon, Benjamin Robert
1786-1846 .... **NCLC 146**
See also DLB 110

Hayek, F(riedrich) A(ugust von)
1899-1992 .... **TCLC 109**
See also CA 93-96; 137; CANR 20; MTCW
1, 2

Hayford, J(oseph) E(phraim) Casely
See Casely-Hayford, J(oseph) E(phraim)

Hayman, Ronald 1932- .... **CLC 44**
See also CA 25-28R; CANR 18, 50, 88; CD
5, 6; DLB 155

Hayne, Paul Hamilton 1830-1886 . **NCLC 94**
See also DLB 3, 64, 79, 248; RGAL 4

Hays, Mary 1760-1843 .... **NCLC 114**
See also DLB 142, 158; RGEL 2

Haywood, Eliza (Fowler)
1693(?)-1756 .... **LC 1, 44**
See also DLB 39; RGEL 2

Hazlitt, William 1778-1830 ...... **NCLC 29, 82**
See also BRW 4; DLB 110, 158; RGEL 2;
TEA

Hazzard, Shirley 1931- .... **CLC 18, 218**
See also CA 9-12R; CANR 4, 70, 127; CN
1, 2, 3, 4, 5, 6, 7; DLB 289; DLBY 1982;
MTCW 1

Head, Bessie 1937-1986 ...... **BLC 2; CLC 25,**
67; SSC 52
See also AFW; BW 2, 3; CA 29-32R; 119;
CANR 25, 82; CDWLB 3; CN 1, 2, 3, 4;
DA3; DAM MULT; DLB 117, 225; EWL
3; EXPS; FL 1:6; FW; MTCW 1, 2;
MTFW 2005; RGSF 2; SSFS 5, 13; WLIT
2; WWE 1

Headon, (Nicky) Topper 1956(?)- ..... **CLC 30**

Heaney, Seamus (Justin) 1939- .... **CLC 5, 7,**
14, 25, 37, 74, 91, 171; PC 18; WLCS
See also AAYA 61; BRWR 1; BRWS 2; CA
85-88; CANR 25, 48, 75, 91, 128; CD-
BLB 1960 to Present; CP 1, 2, 3, 4, 5, 6,
7; DA3; DAB; DAM POET; DLB 40;
DLBY 1995; EWL 3; EXPP; MTCW 1,
2; MTFW 2005; PAB; PFS 2, 5, 8, 17;
RGEL 2; TEA; WLIT 4

Hearn, (Patricio) Lafcadio (Tessima Carlos)
1850-1904 .... **TCLC 9**
See also CA 105; 166; DLB 12, 78, 189;
HGG; MAL 5; RGAL 4

Hearne, Samuel 1745-1792 .... **LC 95**
See also DLB 99

Hearne, Vicki 1946-2001 .... **CLC 56**
See also CA 139; 201

Hearon, Shelby 1931- .... **CLC 63**
See also AITN 2; AMWS 8; CA 25-28R;
CANR 18, 48, 103, 146; CSW

Heat-Moon, William Least .... **CLC 29**
See Trogdon, William (Lewis)
See also AAYA 9

Hebbel, Friedrich 1813-1863 . **DC 21; NCLC**
43
See also CDWLB 2; DAM DRAM; DLB
129; EW 6; RGWL 2, 3

Hebert, Anne 1916-2000 .... **CLC 4, 13, 29**
See also CA 85-88; 187; CANR 69, 126;
CCA 1; CWP; CWW 2; DA3; DAC;
DAM MST, POET; DLB 68; EWL 3; GFL
1789 to the Present; MTCW 1, 2; MTFW
2005; PFS 20

Hecht, Anthony (Evan) 1923-2004 .... **CLC 8,**
13, 19
See also AMWS 10; CA 9-12R; 232; CANR
6, 108; CP 1, 2, 3, 4, 5, 6, 7; DAM POET;
DLB 5, 169; EWL 3; PFS 6; WP

Hecht, Ben 1894-1964 ..... **CLC 8; TCLC 101**
See also CA 85-88; DFS 9; DLB 7, 9, 25,
26, 28, 86; FANT; IDFW 3, 4; RGAL 4

Hedayat, Sadeq 1903-1951 .... **TCLC 21**
See also CA 120; EWL 3; RGSF 2

Hegel, Georg Wilhelm Friedrich
1770-1831 .... **NCLC 46, 151**
See also DLB 90; TWA

Heidegger, Martin 1889-1976 .... **CLC 24**
See also CA 81-84; 65-68; CANR 34; DLB
296; MTCW 1, 2; MTFW 2005

Heidenstam, (Carl Gustaf) Verner von
1859-1940 .... **TCLC 5**
See also CA 104

Heidi Louise
See Erdrich, (Karen) Louise

Heifner, Jack 1946- .... **CLC 11**
See also CA 105; CANR 47

Heijermans, Herman 1864-1924 .... **TCLC 24**
See also CA 123; EWL 3

Heilbrun, Carolyn G(old)
1926-2003 .... **CLC 25, 173**
See Cross, Amanda
See also CA 45-48; 220; CANR 1, 28, 58,
94; FW

Hein, Christoph 1944- .... **CLC 154**
See also CA 158; CANR 108; CDWLB 2;
CWW 2; DLB 124

Heywood, Thomas 1573(?)-1641 .... **LC 111**
See also DAM DRAM; DLB 62; LMFS 1;
RGEL 2; TEA

Hibbert, Eleanor Alice Burford
1906-1993 .... **CLC 7**
See Holt, Victoria
See also BEST 90:4; CA 17-20R; 140;
CANR 9, 28, 59; CMW 4; CPW; DAM
POP; MTCW 2; MTFW 2005; RHW;
SATA 2; SATA-Obit 74

Hichens, Robert (Smythe)
1864-1950 .... **TCLC 64**
See also CA 162; DLB 153; HGG; RHW;
SUFW

Higgins, Aidan 1927- .... **SSC 68**
See also CA 9-12R; CANR 70, 115; CN 1,
2, 3, 4, 5, 6, 7; DLB 14

Higgins, George V(incent)
1939-1999 .... **CLC 4, 7, 10, 18**
See also BPFB 2; CA 77-80; 186; CAAS 5;
CANR 17, 51, 89, 96; CMW 4; CN 2, 3,
4, 5, 6; DLB 2; DLBY 1981, 1998; INT
CANR-17; MSW; MTCW 1

Higginson, Thomas Wentworth
1823-1911 .... **TCLC 36**
See also CA 162; DLB 1, 64, 243

Higgonet, Margaret ed. .... **CLC 65**

Highet, Helen
See MacInnes, Helen (Clark)

Highsmith, (Mary) Patricia
1921-1995 .... **CLC 2, 4, 14, 42, 102**
See Morgan, Claire
See also AAYA 48; BRWS 5; CA 1-4R; 147;
CANR 1, 20, 48, 62, 108; CMW 4; CN 1,
2, 3, 4, 5; CPW; DA3; DAM NOV, POP;
DLB 306; MSW; MTCW 1, 2; MTFW
2005

Highwater, Jamake (Mamake)
1942(?)-2001 .... **CLC 12**
See also AAYA 7; BPFB 2; BYA 4; CA 65-
68; 199; CAAS 7; CANR 10, 34, 84; CLR
17; CWRI 5; DLB 52; DLBY 1985;
JRDA; MAICYA 1, 2; SATA 32, 69;
SATA-Brief 30

Highway, Tomson 1951- ...... **CLC 92; NNAL**
See also CA 151; CANR 75; CCA 1; CD 5,
6; CN 7; DAC; DAM MULT; DFS 2;
MTCW 2

Hijuelos, Oscar 1951- .... **CLC 65; HLC 1**
See also AAYA 25; AMWS 8; BEST 90:1;
CA 123; CANR 50, 75, 125; CPW; DA3;
DAM MULT, POP; DLB 145; HW 1, 2;
LLW; MAL 5; MTCW 2; MTFW 2005;
NFS 17; RGAL 4; WLIT 1

Hikmet, Nazim 1902-1963 .... **CLC 40**
See Nizami of Ganja
See also CA 141; 93-96; EWL 3; WLIT 6

Hildegard von Bingen 1098-1179 . **CMLC 20**
See also DLB 148

Hildesheimer, Wolfgang 1916-1991 .. **CLC 49**
See also CA 101; 135; DLB 69, 124; EWL
3

Hill, Geoffrey (William) 1932- ...... **CLC 5, 8,
18, 45**
See also BRWS 5; CA 81-84; CANR 21,
89; CDBLB 1960 to Present; CP 1, 2, 3,
4, 5, 6, 7; DAM POET; DLB 40; EWL 3;
MTCW 1; RGEL 2

Hill, George Roy 1921-2002 .... **CLC 26**
See also CA 110; 122; 213

Hill, John
See Koontz, Dean R.

Hill, Susan (Elizabeth) 1942- ...... **CLC 4, 113**
See also CA 33-36R; CANR 29, 69, 129;
CN 2, 3, 4, 5, 6, 7; DAB; DAM MST,
NOV; DLB 14, 139; HGG; MTCW 1;
RHW

Hillard, Asa G. III .... **CLC 70**

Hillerman, Tony 1925- .... **CLC 62, 170**
See also AAYA 40; BEST 89:1; BPFB 2;
CA 29-32R; CANR 21, 42, 65, 97, 134;
CMW 4; CPW; DA3; DAM POP; DLB
206, 306; MAL 5; MSW; MTCW 2;
MTFW 2005; RGAL 4; SATA 6; TCWW
2; YAW

Hillesum, Etty 1914-1943 .... **TCLC 49**
See also CA 137

Hilliard, Noel (Harvey) 1929-1996 ... **CLC 15**
See also CA 9-12R; CANR 7, 69; CN 1, 2,
3, 4, 5, 6

Hillis, Rick 1956- .... **CLC 66**
See also CA 134

Hilton, James 1900-1954 .... **TCLC 21**
See also CA 108; 169; DLB 34, 77; FANT;
SATA 34

Hilton, Walter (?)-1396 .... **CMLC 58**
See also DLB 146; RGEL 2

Himes, Chester (Bomar) 1909-1984 .. **BLC 2;
CLC 2, 4, 7, 18, 58, 108; TCLC 139**
See also AFAW 2; BPFB 2; BW 2; CA 25-
28R; 114; CANR 22, 89; CMW 4; CN 1,
2, 3; DAM MULT; DLB 2, 76, 143, 226;
EWL 3; MAL 5; MSW; MTCW 1, 2;
MTFW 2005; RGAL 4

Himmelfarb, Gertrude 1922- .... **CLC 202**
See also CA 49-52; CANR 28, 66, 102

Hinde, Thomas .... **CLC 6, 11**
See Chitty, Thomas Willes
See also CN 1, 2, 3, 4, 5, 6; EWL 3

Hine, (William) Daryl 1936- .... **CLC 15**
See also CA 1-4R; CAAS 15; CANR 1, 20;
CP 1, 2, 3, 4, 5, 6, 7; DLB 60

Hinkson, Katharine Tynan
See Tynan, Katharine

Hinojosa(-Smith), Rolando (R.)
1929- .... **HLC 1**
See Hinojosa-Smith, Rolando
See also CA 131; CAAS 16; CANR 62;
DAM MULT; DLB 82; HW 1, 2; LLW;
MTCW 2; MTFW 2005; RGAL 4

Hinton, S(usan) E(loise) 1950- .. **CLC 30, 111**
See also AAYA 2, 33; BPFB 2; BYA 2, 3;
CA 81-84; CANR 32, 62, 92, 133;
CDALBS; CLR 3, 23; CPW; DA; DA3;
DAB; DAC; DAM MST, NOV; JRDA;
LAIT 5; MAICYA 1, 2; MTCW 1, 2;
MTFW 2005 !**; NFS 5, 9, 15, 16; SATA
19, 58, 115, 160; WYA; YAW

Hippius, Zinaida (Nikolaevna) .... **TCLC 9**
See Gippius, Zinaida (Nikolaevna)
See also DLB 295; EWL 3

Hiraoka, Kimitake 1925-1970
See Mishima, Yukio
See also CA 97-100; 29-32R; DA3; DAM
DRAM; GLL 1; MTCW 1, 2

Hirsch, E(ric) D(onald), Jr. 1928- .... **CLC 79**
See also CA 25-28R; CANR 27, 51; DLB
67; INT CANR-27; MTCW 1

Hirsch, Edward 1950- .... **CLC 31, 50**
See also CA 104; CANR 20, 42, 102; CP 7;
DLB 120; PFS 22

Hitchcock, Alfred (Joseph)
1899-1980 .... **CLC 16**
See also AAYA 22; CA 159; 97-100; SATA
27; SATA-Obit 24

Hitchens, Christopher (Eric)
1949- .... **CLC 157**
See also CA 152; CANR 89

Hitler, Adolf 1889-1945 .... **TCLC 53**
See also CA 117; 147

Hoagland, Edward (Morley) 1932- .. **CLC 28**
See also ANW; CA 1-4R; CANR 2, 31, 57,
107; CN 1, 2, 3, 4, 5, 6, 7; DLB 6; SATA
51; TCWW 2

Hoban, Russell (Conwell) 1925- ... **CLC 7, 25**
See also BPFB 2; CA 5-8R; CANR 23, 37,
66, 114, 138; CLR 3, 69; CN 4, 5, 6, 7;
CWRI 5; DAM NOV; DLB 52; FANT;
MAICYA 1, 2; MTCW 1, 2; MTFW 2005;
SATA 1, 40, 78, 136; SFW 4; SUFW 2;
TCLE 1:1

Hobbes, Thomas 1588-1679 .... **LC 36**
See also DLB 151, 252, 281; RGEL 2

Hobbs, Perry
See Blackmur, R(ichard) P(almer)

Hobson, Laura Z(ametkin)
1900-1986 .... **CLC 7, 25**
See also BPFB 2; CA 17-20R; 118; CANR
55; CN 1, 2, 3, 4; DLB 28; SATA 52

Hoccleve, Thomas c. 1368-c. 1437 ...... **LC 75**
See also DLB 146; RGEL 2

Hoch, Edward D(entinger) 1930-
See Queen, Ellery
See also CA 29-32R; CANR 11, 27, 51, 97;
CMW 4; DLB 306; SFW 4

Hochhuth, Rolf 1931- .... **CLC 4, 11, 18**
See also CA 5-8R; CANR 33, 75, 136;
CWW 2; DAM DRAM; DLB 124; EWL
3; MTCW 1, 2; MTFW 2005

Hochman, Sandra 1936- .... **CLC 3, 8**
See also CA 5-8R; CP 1, 2, 3, 4; DLB 5

Hochwaelder, Fritz 1911-1986 .... **CLC 36**
See Hochwalder, Fritz
See also CA 29-32R; 120; CANR 42; DAM
DRAM; MTCW 1; RGWL 3

Hochwalder, Fritz
See Hochwaelder, Fritz
See also EWL 3; RGWL 2

Hocking, Mary (Eunice) 1921- .... **CLC 13**
See also CA 101; CANR 18, 40

Hodgins, Jack 1938- .... **CLC 23**
See also CA 93-96; CN 4, 5, 6, 7; DLB 60

Hodgson, William Hope
1877(?)-1918 .... **TCLC 13**
See also CA 111; 164; CMW 4; DLB 70,
153, 156, 178; HGG; MTCW 2; SFW 4;
SUFW 1

Hoeg, Peter 1957- .... **CLC 95, 156**
See also CA 151; CANR 75; CMW 4; DA3;
DLB 214; EWL 3; MTCW 2; MTFW
2005; NFS 17; RGWL 3; SSFS 18

Hoffman, Alice 1952- .... **CLC 51**
See also AAYA 37; AMWS 10; CA 77-80;
CANR 34, 66, 100, 138; CN 4, 5, 6, 7;
CPW; DAM NOV; DLB 292; MAL 5;
MTCW 1, 2; MTFW 2005; TCLE 1:1

Hoffman, Daniel (Gerard) 1923- . **CLC 6, 13,
23**
See also CA 1-4R; CANR 4, 142; CP 1, 2,
3, 4, 5, 6, 7; DLB 5; TCLE 1:1

Hoffman, Eva 1945- .... **CLC 182**
See also CA 132; CANR 146

Hoffman, Stanley 1944- .... **CLC 5**
See also CA 77-80

Hoffman, William 1925- .... **CLC 141**
See also CA 21-24R; CANR 9, 103; CSW;
DLB 234; TCLE 1:1

Hoffman, William M.
See Hoffman, William M(oses)
See also CAD; CD 5, 6

Hoffman, William M(oses) 1939- ..... **CLC 40**
See Hoffman, William M.
See also CA 57-60; CANR 11, 71

Hoffmann, E(rnst) T(heodor) A(madeus)
1776-1822 .... **NCLC 2; SSC 13**
See also CDWLB 2; DLB 90; EW 5; GL 2;
RGSF 2; RGWL 2, 3; SATA 27; SUFW
1; WCH

Hofmann, Gert 1931-1993 .... **CLC 54**
See also CA 128; CANR 145; EWL 3

Hofmannsthal, Hugo von 1874-1929 ... **DC 4; TCLC 11**
See also CA 106; 153; CDWLB 2; DAM DRAM; DFS 17; DLB 81, 118; EW 9; EWL 3; RGWL 2, 3

Hogan, Linda 1947- ..... **CLC 73; NNAL; PC 35**
See also AMWS 4; ANW; BYA 12; CA 120, 226; CAAE 226; CANR 45, 73, 129; CWP; DAM MULT; DLB 175; SATA 132; TCWW 2

Hogarth, Charles
See Creasey, John

Hogarth, Emmett
See Polonsky, Abraham (Lincoln)

Hogarth, William 1697-1764 .... **LC 112**
See also AAYA 56

Hogg, James 1770-1835 .... **NCLC 4, 109**
See also BRWS 10; DLB 93, 116, 159; GL 2; HGG; RGEL 2; SUFW 1

Holbach, Paul-Henri Thiry
1723-1789 .... **LC 14**
See also DLB 313

Holberg, Ludvig 1684-1754 .... **LC 6**
See also DLB 300; RGWL 2, 3

Holcroft, Thomas 1745-1809 .... **NCLC 85**
See also DLB 39, 89, 158; RGEL 2

Holden, Ursula 1921- .... **CLC 18**
See also CA 101; CAAS 8; CANR 22

Holderlin, (Johann Christian) Friedrich
1770-1843 .... **NCLC 16; PC 4**
See also CDWLB 2; DLB 90; EW 5; RGWL 2, 3

Holdstock, Robert
See Holdstock, Robert P.

Holdstock, Robert P. 1948- .... **CLC 39**
See also CA 131; CANR 81; DLB 261; FANT; HGG; SFW 4; SUFW 2

Holinshed, Raphael fl. 1580- .... **LC 69**
See also DLB 167; RGEL 2

Holland, Isabelle (Christian)
1920-2002 .... **CLC 21**
See also AAYA 11, 64; CA 21-24R; 205; CAAE 181; CANR 10, 25, 47; CLR 57; CWRI 5; JRDA; LAIT 4; MAICYA 1, 2; SATA 8, 70; SATA-Essay 103; SATA-Obit 132; WYA

Holland, Marcus
See Caldwell, (Janet Miriam) Taylor (Holland)

Hollander, John 1929- .... **CLC 2, 5, 8, 14**
See also CA 1-4R; CANR 1, 52, 136; CP 1, 2, 3, 4, 5, 6, 7; DLB 5; MAL 5; SATA 13

Hollander, Paul
See Silverberg, Robert

Holleran, Andrew .... **CLC 38**
See Garber, Eric
See also CA 144; GLL 1

Holley, Marietta 1836(?)-1926 .... **TCLC 99**
See also CA 118; DLB 11; FL 1:3

Hollinghurst, Alan 1954- .... **CLC 55, 91**
See also BRWS 10; CA 114; CN 5, 6, 7; DLB 207; GLL 1

Hollis, Jim
See Summers, Hollis (Spurgeon, Jr.)

Holly, Buddy 1936-1959 .... **TCLC 65**
See also CA 213

Holmes, Gordon
See Shiel, M(atthew) P(hipps)

Holmes, John
See Souster, (Holmes) Raymond

Holmes, John Clellon 1926-1988 ...... **CLC 56**
See also BG 1:2; CA 9-12R; 125; CANR 4; CN 1, 2, 3, 4; DLB 16, 237

Holmes, Oliver Wendell, Jr.
1841-1935 .... **TCLC 77**
See also CA 114; 186

Holmes, Oliver Wendell
1809-1894 .... **NCLC 14, 81**
See also AMWS 1; CDALB 1640-1865; DLB 1, 189, 235; EXPP; RGAL 4; SATA 34

Holmes, Raymond
See Souster, (Holmes) Raymond

Holt, Victoria
See Hibbert, Eleanor Alice Burford
See also BPFB 2

Holub, Miroslav 1923-1998 .... **CLC 4**
See also CA 21-24R; 169; CANR 10; CD-WLB 4; CWW 2; DLB 232; EWL 3; RGWL 3

Holz, Detlev
See Benjamin, Walter

Homer c. 8th cent. B.C.- .... **CMLC 1, 16, 61; PC 23; WLCS**
See also AW 1; CDWLB 1; DA; DA3; DAB; DAC; DAM MST, POET; DLB 176; EFS 1; LAIT 1; LMFS 1; RGWL 2, 3; TWA; WP

Hongo, Garrett Kaoru 1951- .... **PC 23**
See also CA 133; CAAS 22; CP 7; DLB 120, 312; EWL 3; EXPP; RGAL 4

Honig, Edwin 1919- .... **CLC 33**
See also CA 5-8R; CAAS 8; CANR 4, 45, 144; CP 1, 2, 3, 4, 5, 6, 7; DLB 5

Hood, Hugh (John Blagdon) 1928- . **CLC 15, 28; SSC 42**
See also CA 49-52; CAAS 17; CANR 1, 33, 87; CN 1, 2, 3, 4, 5, 6, 7; DLB 53; RGSF 2

Hood, Thomas 1799-1845 .... **NCLC 16**
See also BRW 4; DLB 96; RGEL 2

Hooker, (Peter) Jeremy 1941- .... **CLC 43**
See also CA 77-80; CANR 22; CP 2, 3, 4, 5, 6, 7; DLB 40

Hooker, Richard 1554-1600 .... **LC 95**
See also BRW 1; DLB 132; RGEL 2

hooks, bell
See Watkins, Gloria Jean

Hope, A(lec) D(erwent) 1907-2000 .... **CLC 3, 51; PC 56**
See also BRWS 7; CA 21-24R; 188; CANR 33, 74; CP 1, 2, 3, 4; DLB 289; EWL 3; MTCW 1, 2; MTFW 2005; PFS 8; RGEL 2

Hope, Anthony 1863-1933 .... **TCLC 83**
See also CA 157; DLB 153, 156; RGEL 2; RHW

Hope, Brian
See Creasey, John

Hope, Christopher (David Tully)
1944- .... **CLC 52**
See also AFW; CA 106; CANR 47, 101; CN 4, 5, 6, 7; DLB 225; SATA 62

Hopkins, Gerard Manley
1844-1889 .... **NCLC 17; PC 15; WLC**
See also BRW 5; BRWR 2; CDBLB 1890-1914; DA; DA3; DAB; DAC; DAM MST, POET; DLB 35, 57; EXPP; PAB; RGEL 2; TEA; WP

Hopkins, John (Richard) 1931-1998 .. **CLC 4**
See also CA 85-88; 169; CBD; CD 5, 6

Hopkins, Pauline Elizabeth
1859-1930 .... **BLC 2; TCLC 28**
See also AFAW 2; BW 2, 3; CA 141; CANR 82; DAM MULT; DLB 50

Hopkinson, Francis 1737-1791 .... **LC 25**
See also DLB 31; RGAL 4

Hopley-Woolrich, Cornell George 1903-1968
See Woolrich, Cornell
See also CA 13-14; CANR 58; CAP 1; CMW 4; DLB 226; MTCW 2

Horace 65B.C.-8B.C. .... **CMLC 39; PC 46**
See also AW 2; CDWLB 1; DLB 211; RGWL 2, 3

Horatio
See Proust, (Valentin-Louis-George-Eugene) Marcel

Horgan, Paul (George Vincent
O'Shaughnessy) 1903-1995 .. **CLC 9, 53**
See also BPFB 2; CA 13-16R; 147; CANR 9, 35; CN 1, 2, 3, 4, 5; DAM NOV; DLB 102, 212; DLBY 1985; INT CANR-9; MTCW 1, 2; MTFW 2005; SATA 13; SATA-Obit 84; TCWW 1, 2

Horkheimer, Max 1895-1973 .... **TCLC 132**
See also CA 216; 41-44R; DLB 296

Horn, Peter
See Kuttner, Henry

Horne, Frank (Smith) 1899-1974 ...... **HR 1:2**
See also BW 1; CA 125; 53-56; DLB 51; WP

Horne, Richard Henry Hengist
1802(?)-1884 .... **NCLC 127**
See also DLB 32; SATA 29

Hornem, Horace Esq.
See Byron, George Gordon (Noel)

Horney, Karen (Clementine Theodore
Danielsen) 1885-1952 .... **TCLC 71**
See also CA 114; 165; DLB 246; FW

Hornung, E(rnest) W(illiam)
1866-1921 .... **TCLC 59**
See also CA 108; 160; CMW 4; DLB 70

Horovitz, Israel (Arthur) 1939- .... **CLC 56**
See also CA 33-36R; CAD; CANR 46, 59; CD 5, 6; DAM DRAM; DLB 7; MAL 5

Horton, George Moses
1797(?)-1883(?) .... **NCLC 87**
See also DLB 50

Horvath, odon von 1901-1938
See von Horvath, Odon
See also EWL 3

Horvath, Oedoen von -1938
See von Horvath, Odon

Horwitz, Julius 1920-1986 .... **CLC 14**
See also CA 9-12R; 119; CANR 12

Hospital, Janette Turner 1942- .... **CLC 42, 145**
See also CA 108; CANR 48; CN 5, 6, 7; DLBY 2002; RGSF 2

Hostos, E. M. de
See Hostos (y Bonilla), Eugenio Maria de

Hostos, Eugenio M. de
See Hostos (y Bonilla), Eugenio Maria de

Hostos, Eugenio Maria
See Hostos (y Bonilla), Eugenio Maria de

Hostos (y Bonilla), Eugenio Maria de
1839-1903 .... **TCLC 24**
See also CA 123; 131; HW 1

Houdini
See Lovecraft, H(oward) P(hillips)

Houellebecq, Michel 1958- .... **CLC 179**
See also CA 185; CANR 140; MTFW 2005

Hougan, Carolyn 1943- .... **CLC 34**
See also CA 139

Household, Geoffrey (Edward West)
1900-1988 .... **CLC 11**
See also CA 77-80; 126; CANR 58; CMW 4; CN 1, 2, 3, 4; DLB 87; SATA 14; SATA-Obit 59

Housman, A(lfred) E(dward)
1859-1936 .... **PC 2, 43; TCLC 1, 10; WLCS**
See also AAYA 66; BRW 6; CA 104; 125; DA; DA3; DAB; DAC; DAM MST, POET; DLB 19, 284; EWL 3; EXPP; MTCW 1, 2; MTFW 2005; PAB; PFS 4, 7; RGEL 2; TEA; WP

Housman, Laurence 1865-1959 .... **TCLC 7**
See also CA 106; 155; DLB 10; FANT; RGEL 2; SATA 25

Houston, Jeanne (Toyo) Wakatsuki
1934- .... **AAL**
See also AAYA 49; CA 103, 232; CAAE
232; CAAS 16; CANR 29, 123; LAIT 4;
SATA 78

Howard, Elizabeth Jane 1923- ..... **CLC 7, 29**
See also BRWS 11; CA 5-8R; CANR 8, 62,
146; CN 1, 2, 3, 4, 5, 6, 7

Howard, Maureen 1930- .... **CLC 5, 14, 46,
151**
See also CA 53-56; CANR 31, 75, 140; CN
4, 5, 6, 7; DLBY 1983; INT CANR-31;
MTCW 1, 2; MTFW 2005

Howard, Richard 1929- .... **CLC 7, 10, 47**
See also AITN 1; CA 85-88; CANR 25, 80;
CP 1, 2, 3, 4, 5, 6, 7; DLB 5; INT CANR-
25; MAL 5

Howard, Robert E(rvin)
1906-1936 .... **TCLC 8**
See also BPFB 2; BYA 5; CA 105; 157;
FANT; SUFW 1; TCWW 1, 2

Howard, Warren F.
See Pohl, Frederik

Howe, Fanny (Quincy) 1940- .... **CLC 47**
See also CA 117, 187; CAAE 187; CAAS
27; CANR 70, 116; CP 7; CWP; SATA-
Brief 52

Howe, Irving 1920-1993 .... **CLC 85**
See also AMWS 6; CA 9-12R; 141; CANR
21, 50; DLB 67; EWL 3; MAL 5; MTCW
1, 2; MTFW 2005

Howe, Julia Ward 1819-1910 .... **TCLC 21**
See also CA 117; 191; DLB 1, 189, 235;
FW

Howe, Susan 1937- .... **CLC 72, 152; PC 54**
See also AMWS 4; CA 160; CP 7; CWP;
DLB 120; FW; RGAL 4

Howe, Tina 1937- .... **CLC 48**
See also CA 109; CAD; CANR 125; CD 5,
6; CWD

Howell, James 1594(?)-1666 .... **LC 13**
See also DLB 151

Howells, W. D.
See Howells, William Dean

Howells, William D.
See Howells, William Dean

Howells, William Dean 1837-1920 ... **SSC 36;
TCLC 7, 17, 41**
See also AMW; CA 104; 134; CDALB
1865-1917; DLB 12, 64, 74, 79, 189;
LMFS 1; MAL 5; MTCW 2; RGAL 4;
TUS

Howes, Barbara 1914-1996 .... **CLC 15**
See also CA 9-12R; 151; CAAS 3; CANR
53; CP 1, 2, 3, 4; SATA 5; TCLE 1:1

Hrabal, Bohumil 1914-1997 ...... **CLC 13, 67;
TCLC 155**
See also CA 106; 156; CAAS 12; CANR
57; CWW 2; DLB 232; EWL 3; RGSF 2

Hrabanus Maurus 776(?)-856 .... **CMLC 78**
See also DLB 148

Hrotsvit of Gandersheim c. 935-c.
1000 .... **CMLC 29**
See also DLB 148

Hsi, Chu 1130-1200 .... **CMLC 42**

Hsun, Lu
See Lu Hsun

Hubbard, L(afayette) Ron(ald)
1911-1986 .... **CLC 43**
See also AAYA 64; CA 77-80; 118; CANR
52; CPW; DA3; DAM POP; FANT;
MTCW 2; MTFW 2005; SFW 4

Huch, Ricarda (Octavia)
1864-1947 .... **TCLC 13**
See Hugo, Richard
See also CA 111; 189; DLB 66; EWL 3

Huddle, David 1942- .... **CLC 49**
See also CA 57-60; CAAS 20; CANR 89;
DLB 130

Hudson, Jeffrey
See Crichton, (John) Michael

Hudson, W(illiam) H(enry)
1841-1922 .... **TCLC 29**
See also CA 115; 190; DLB 98, 153, 174;
RGEL 2; SATA 35

Hueffer, Ford Madox
See Ford, Ford Madox

Hughart, Barry 1934- .... **CLC 39**
See also CA 137; FANT; SFW 4; SUFW 2

Hughes, Colin
See Creasey, John

Hughes, David (John) 1930-2005 ..... **CLC 48**
See also CA 116; 129; 238; CN 4, 5, 6, 7;
DLB 14

Hughes, Edward James
See Hughes, Ted
See also DA3; DAM MST, POET

Hughes, (James Mercer) Langston
1902-1967 ..... **BLC 2; CLC 1, 5, 10, 15,
35, 44, 108; DC 3; HR 1:2; PC 1, 53;
SSC 6; WLC**
See also AAYA 12; AFAW 1, 2; AMWR 1;
AMWS 1; BW 1, 3; CA 1-4R; 25-28R;
CANR 1, 34, 82; CDALB 1929-1941;
CLR 17; DA; DA3; DAB; DAC; DAM
DRAM, MST, MULT, POET; DFS 6, 18;
DLB 4, 7, 48, 51, 86, 228, 315; EWL 3;
EXPP; EXPS; JRDA; LAIT 3; LMFS 2;
MAICYA 1, 2; MAL 5; MTCW 1, 2;
MTFW 2005; NFS 21; PAB; PFS 1, 3, 6,
10, 15; RGAL 4; RGSF 2; SATA 4, 33;
SSFS 4, 7; TUS; WCH; WP; YAW

Hughes, Richard (Arthur Warren)
1900-1976 .... **CLC 1, 11**
See also CA 5-8R; 65-68; CANR 4; CN 1,
2; DAM NOV; DLB 15, 161; EWL 3;
MTCW 1; RGEL 2; SATA 8; SATA-Obit
25

Hughes, Ted 1930-1998 . **CLC 2, 4, 9, 14, 37,
119; PC 7**
See Hughes, Edward James
See also BRWC 2; BRWR 2; BRWS 1; CA
1-4R; 171; CANR 1, 33, 66, 108; CLR 3;
CP 1, 2, 3, 4, 5, 6; DAB; DAC; DLB 40,
161; EWL 3; EXPP; MAICYA 1, 2;
MTCW 1, 2; MTFW 2005; PAB; PFS 4,
19; RGEL 2; SATA 49; SATA-Brief 27;
SATA-Obit 107; TEA; YAW

Hugo, Richard
See Huch, Ricarda (Octavia)
See also MAL 5

Hugo, Richard F(ranklin)
1923-1982 .... **CLC 6, 18, 32; PC 68**
See also AMWS 6; CA 49-52; 108; CANR
3; CP 1, 2, 3; DAM POET; DLB 5, 206;
EWL 3; PFS 17; RGAL 4

Hugo, Victor (Marie) 1802-1885 .... **NCLC 3,
10, 21, 161; PC 17; WLC**
See also AAYA 28; DA; DA3; DAB; DAC;
DAM DRAM, MST, NOV, POET; DLB
119, 192, 217; EFS 2; EW 6; EXPN; GFL
1789 to the Present; LAIT 1, 2; NFS 5,
20; RGWL 2, 3; SATA 47; TWA

Huidobro, Vicente
See Huidobro Fernandez, Vicente Garcia
See also DLB 283; EWL 3; LAW

Huidobro Fernandez, Vicente Garcia
1893-1948 .... **TCLC 31**
See Huidobro, Vicente
See also CA 131; HW 1

Hulme, Keri 1947- .... **CLC 39, 130**
See also CA 125; CANR 69; CN 4, 5, 6, 7;
CP 7; CWP; EWL 3; FW; INT CA-125

Hulme, T(homas) E(rnest)
1883-1917 .... **TCLC 21**
See also BRWS 6; CA 117; 203; DLB 19

Humboldt, Wilhelm von
1767-1835 .... **NCLC 134**
See also DLB 90

Hume, David 1711-1776 .... **LC 7, 56**
See also BRWS 3; DLB 104, 252; LMFS 1;
TEA

Humphrey, William 1924-1997 .... **CLC 45**
See also AMWS 9; CA 77-80; 160; CANR
68; CN 1, 2, 3, 4, 5, 6; CSW; DLB 6, 212,
234, 278; TCWW 1, 2

Humphreys, Emyr Owen 1919- .... **CLC 47**
See also CA 5-8R; CANR 3, 24; CN 1, 2,
3, 4, 5, 6, 7; DLB 15

Humphreys, Josephine 1945- ..... **CLC 34, 57**
See also CA 121; 127; CANR 97; CSW;
DLB 292; INT CA-127

Huneker, James Gibbons
1860-1921 .... **TCLC 65**
See also CA 193; DLB 71; RGAL 4

Hungerford, Hesba Fay
See Brinsmead, H(esba) F(ay)

Hungerford, Pixie
See Brinsmead, H(esba) F(ay)

Hunt, E(verette) Howard, (Jr.)
1918- .... **CLC 3**
See also AITN 1; CA 45-48; CANR 2, 47,
103; CMW 4

Hunt, Francesca
See Holland, Isabelle (Christian)

Hunt, Howard
See Hunt, E(verette) Howard, (Jr.)

Hunt, Kyle
See Creasey, John

Hunt, (James Henry) Leigh
1784-1859 .... **NCLC 1, 70**
See also DAM POET; DLB 96, 110, 144;
RGEL 2; TEA

Hunt, Marsha 1946- .... **CLC 70**
See also BW 2, 3; CA 143; CANR 79

Hunt, Violet 1866(?)-1942 .... **TCLC 53**
See also CA 184; DLB 162, 197

Hunter, E. Waldo
See Sturgeon, Theodore (Hamilton)

Hunter, Evan 1926-2005 .... **CLC 11, 31**
See McBain, Ed
See also AAYA 39; BPFB 2; CA 5-8R; 241;
CANR 5, 38, 62, 97; CMW 4; CN 1, 2, 3,
4, 5, 6, 7; CPW; DAM POP; DLB 306;
DLBY 1982; INT CANR-5; MSW;
MTCW 1; SATA 25; SFW 4

Hunter, Kristin
See Lattany, Kristin (Elaine Eggleston)
Hunter
See also CN 1, 2, 3, 4, 5, 6

Hunter, Mary
See Austin, Mary (Hunter)

Hunter, Mollie 1922- .... **CLC 21**
See McIlwraith, Maureen Mollie Hunter
See also AAYA 13; BYA 6; CANR 37, 78;
CLR 25; DLB 161; JRDA; MAICYA 1,
2; SAAS 7; SATA 54, 106, 139; SATA-
Essay 139; WYA; YAW

Hunter, Robert (?)-1734 .... **LC 7**

Hurston, Zora Neale 1891-1960 .... **BLC 2;
CLC 7, 30, 61; DC 12; HR 1:2; SSC 4,
80; TCLC 121, 131; WLCS**
See also AAYA 15; AFAW 1, 2; AMWS 6;
BW 1, 3; BYA 12; CA 85-88; CANR 61;
CDALBS; DA; DA3; DAC; DAM MST,
MULT, NOV; DFS 6; DLB 51, 86; EWL
3; EXPN; EXPS; FL 1:6; FW; LAIT 3;
LATS 1:1; LMFS 2; MAL 5; MAWW;
MTCW 1, 2; MTFW 2005; NFS 3; RGAL
4; RGSF 2; SSFS 1, 6, 11, 19, 21; TUS;
YAW

Husserl, E. G.
See Husserl, Edmund (Gustav Albrecht)

Husserl, Edmund (Gustav Albrecht)
1859-1938 .... **TCLC 100**
See also CA 116; 133; DLB 296

Jackson, Laura (Riding) 1901-1991 .... **PC 44**
See Riding, Laura
See also CA 65-68; 135; CANR 28, 89;
DLB 48

Jackson, Sam
See Trumbo, Dalton

Jackson, Sara
See Wingrove, David (John)

Jackson, Shirley 1919-1965 . **CLC 11, 60, 87;
SSC 9, 39; WLC**
See also AAYA 9; AMWS 9; BPFB 2; CA
1-4R; 25-28R; CANR 4, 52; CDALB
1941-1968; DA; DA3; DAC; DAM MST;
DLB 6, 234; EXPS; HGG; LAIT 4; MAL
5; MTCW 2; MTFW 2005; RGAL 4;
RGSF 2; SATA 2; SSFS 1; SUFW 1, 2

Jacob, (Cyprien-)Max 1876-1944 .... **TCLC 6**
See also CA 104; 193; DLB 258; EWL 3;
GFL 1789 to the Present; GLL 2; RGWL
2, 3

Jacobs, Harriet A(nn)
1813(?)-1897 .... **NCLC 67, 162**
See also AFAW 1, 2; DLB 239; FL 1:3; FW;
LAIT 2; RGAL 4

Jacobs, Jim 1942- .... **CLC 12**
See also CA 97-100; INT CA-97-100

Jacobs, W(illiam) W(ymark)
1863-1943 .... **SSC 73; TCLC 22**
See also CA 121; 167; DLB 135; EXPS;
HGG; RGEL 2; RGSF 2; SSFS 2; SUFW
1

Jacobsen, Jens Peter 1847-1885 .... **NCLC 34**

Jacobsen, Josephine (Winder)
1908-2003 .... **CLC 48, 102; PC 62**
See also CA 33-36R; 218; CAAS 18; CANR
23, 48; CCA 1; CP 2, 3, 4, 5, 6, 7; DLB
244; PFS 23; TCLE 1:1

Jacobson, Dan 1929- .... **CLC 4, 14**
See also AFW; CA 1-4R; CANR 2, 25, 66;
CN 1, 2, 3, 4, 5, 6, 7; DLB 14, 207, 225,
319; EWL 3; MTCW 1; RGSF 2

Jacqueline
See Carpentier (y Valmont), Alejo

Jacques de Vitry c. 1160-1240 ...... **CMLC 63**
See also DLB 208

Jagger, Michael Philip
See Jagger, Mick

Jagger, Mick 1943- .... **CLC 17**
See also CA 239

Jahiz, al- c. 780-c. 869 .... **CMLC 25**
See also DLB 311

Jakes, John (William) 1932- .... **CLC 29**
See also AAYA 32; BEST 89:4; BPFB 2;
CA 57-60, 214; CAAE 214; CANR 10,
43, 66, 111, 142; CPW; CSW; DA3; DAM
NOV, POP; DLB 278; DLBY 1983;
FANT; INT CANR-10; MTCW 1, 2;
MTFW 2005; RHW; SATA 62; SFW 4;
TCWW 1, 2

James I 1394-1437 .... **LC 20**
See also RGEL 2

James, Andrew
See Kirkup, James

James, C(yril) L(ionel) R(obert)
1901-1989 .... **BLCS; CLC 33**
See also BW 2; CA 117; 125; 128; CANR
62; CN 1, 2, 3, 4; DLB 125; MTCW 1

James, Daniel (Lewis) 1911-1988
See Santiago, Danny
See also CA 174; 125

James, Dynely
See Mayne, William (James Carter)

James, Henry Sr. 1811-1882 .... **NCLC 53**

James, Henry 1843-1916 .... **SSC 8, 32, 47;
TCLC 2, 11, 24, 40, 47, 64, 171; WLC**
See also AMW; AMWC 1; AMWR 1; BPFB
2; BRW 6; CA 104; 132; CDALB 1865-
1917; DA; DA3; DAB; DAC; DAM MST,
NOV; DLB 12, 71, 74, 189; DLBD 13;

EWL 3; EXPS; GL 2; HGG; LAIT 2;
MAL 5; MTCW 1, 2; MTFW 2005; NFS
12, 16, 19; RGAL 4; RGEL 2; RGSF 2;
SSFS 9; SUFW 1; TUS

James, M. R.
See James, Montague (Rhodes)
See also DLB 156, 201

James, Montague (Rhodes)
1862-1936 .... **SSC 16; TCLC 6**
See James, M. R.
See also CA 104; 203; HGG; RGEL 2;
RGSF 2; SUFW 1

James, P. D. .... **CLC 18, 46, 122**
See White, Phyllis Dorothy James
See also BEST 90:2; BPFB 2; BRWS 4;
CDBLB 1960 to Present; CN 4, 5, 6; DLB
87, 276; DLBD 17; MSW

James, Philip
See Moorcock, Michael (John)

James, Samuel
See Stephens, James

James, Seumas
See Stephens, James

James, Stephen
See Stephens, James

James, William 1842-1910 .... **TCLC 15, 32**
See also AMW; CA 109; 193; DLB 270,
284; MAL 5; NCFS 5; RGAL 4

Jameson, Anna 1794-1860 .... **NCLC 43**
See also DLB 99, 166

Jameson, Fredric (R.) 1934- .... **CLC 142**
See also CA 196; DLB 67; LMFS 2

James VI of Scotland 1566-1625 .... **LC 109**
See also DLB 151, 172

Jami, Nur al-Din 'Abd al-Rahman
1414-1492 .... **LC 9**

Jammes, Francis 1868-1938 .... **TCLC 75**
See also CA 198; EWL 3; GFL 1789 to the
Present

Jandl, Ernst 1925-2000 .... **CLC 34**
See also CA 200; EWL 3

Janowitz, Tama 1957- .... **CLC 43, 145**
See also CA 106; CANR 52, 89, 129; CN
5, 6, 7; CPW; DAM POP; DLB 292;
MTFW 2005

Japrisot, Sebastien 1931- .... **CLC 90**
See Rossi, Jean-Baptiste
See also CMW 4; NFS 18

Jarrell, Randall 1914-1965 .... **CLC 1, 2, 6, 9,
13, 49; PC 41**
See also AMW; BYA 5; CA 5-8R; 25-28R;
CABS 2; CANR 6, 34; CDALB 1941-
1968; CLR 6; CWRI 5; DAM POET;
DLB 48, 52; EWL 3; EXPP; MAICYA 1,
2; MAL 5; MTCW 1, 2; PAB; PFS 2;
RGAL 4; SATA 7

Jarry, Alfred 1873-1907 .... **SSC 20; TCLC 2,
14, 147**
See also CA 104; 153; DA3; DAM DRAM;
DFS 8; DLB 192, 258; EW 9; EWL 3;
GFL 1789 to the Present; RGWL 2, 3;
TWA

Jarvis, E. K.
See Ellison, Harlan (Jay)

Jawien, Andrzej
See John Paul II, Pope

Jaynes, Roderick
See Coen, Ethan

Jeake, Samuel, Jr.
See Aiken, Conrad (Potter)

Jean Paul 1763-1825 .... **NCLC 7**

Jefferies, (John) Richard
1848-1887 .... **NCLC 47**
See also DLB 98, 141; RGEL 2; SATA 16;
SFW 4

Jeffers, (John) Robinson 1887-1962 .. **CLC 2,
3, 11, 15, 54; PC 17; WLC**
See also AMWS 2; CA 85-88; CANR 35;
CDALB 1917-1929; DA; DAC; DAM
MST, POET; DLB 45, 212; EWL 3; MAL
5; MTCW 1, 2; MTFW 2005; PAB; PFS
3, 4; RGAL 4

Jefferson, Janet
See Mencken, H(enry) L(ouis)

Jefferson, Thomas 1743-1826 . **NCLC 11, 103**
See also AAYA 54; ANW; CDALB 1640-
1865; DA3; DLB 31, 183; LAIT 1; RGAL
4

Jeffrey, Francis 1773-1850 .... **NCLC 33**
See Francis, Lord Jeffrey

Jelakowitch, Ivan
See Heijermans, Herman

Jelinek, Elfriede 1946- .... **CLC 169**
See also AAYA 68; CA 154; DLB 85; FW

Jellicoe, (Patricia) Ann 1927- .... **CLC 27**
See also CA 85-88; CBD; CD 5, 6; CWD;
CWRI 5; DLB 13, 233; FW

Jelloun, Tahar ben 1944- .... **CLC 180**
See Ben Jelloun, Tahar
See also CA 162; CANR 100

Jemyma
See Holley, Marietta

Jen, Gish .... **AAL; CLC 70, 198**
See Jen, Lillian
See also AMWC 2; CN 7; DLB 312

Jen, Lillian 1955-
See Jen, Gish
See also CA 135; CANR 89, 130

Jenkins, (John) Robin 1912- .... **CLC 52**
See also CA 1-4R; CANR 1, 135; CN 1, 2,
3, 4, 5, 6, 7; DLB 14, 271

Jennings, Elizabeth (Joan)
1926-2001 .... **CLC 5, 14, 131**
See also BRWS 5; CA 61-64; 200; CAAS
5; CANR 8, 39, 66, 127; CP 1, 2, 3, 4, 5,
6, 7; CWP; DLB 27; EWL 3; MTCW 1;
SATA 66

Jennings, Waylon 1937-2002 .... **CLC 21**

Jensen, Johannes V(ilhelm)
1873-1950 .... **TCLC 41**
See also CA 170; DLB 214; EWL 3; RGWL
3

Jensen, Laura (Linnea) 1948- .... **CLC 37**
See also CA 103

Jerome, Saint 345-420 .... **CMLC 30**
See also RGWL 3

Jerome, Jerome K(lapka)
1859-1927 .... **TCLC 23**
See also CA 119; 177; DLB 10, 34, 135;
RGEL 2

Jerrold, Douglas William
1803-1857 .... **NCLC 2**
See also DLB 158, 159; RGEL 2

Jewett, (Theodora) Sarah Orne
1849-1909 .... **SSC 6, 44; TCLC 1, 22**
See also AMW; AMWC 2; AMWR 2; CA
108; 127; CANR 71; DLB 12, 74, 221;
EXPS; FL 1:3; FW; MAL 5; MAWW;
NFS 15; RGAL 4; RGSF 2; SATA 15;
SSFS 4

Jewsbury, Geraldine (Endsor)
1812-1880 .... **NCLC 22**
See also DLB 21

Jhabvala, Ruth Prawer 1927- . **CLC 4, 8, 29,
94, 138**
See also BRWS 5; CA 1-4R; CANR 2, 29,
51, 74, 91, 128; CN 1, 2, 3, 4, 5, 6, 7;
DAB; DAM NOV; DLB 139, 194; EWL
3; IDFW 3, 4; INT CANR-29; MTCW 1,
2; MTFW 2005; RGSF 2; RGWL 2;
RHW; TEA

Jibran, Kahlil
See Gibran, Kahlil

Jorgenson, Ivar
See Silverberg, Robert
Joseph, George Ghevarughese .... **CLC 70**
Josephson, Mary
See O'Doherty, Brian
Josephus, Flavius c. 37-100 .... **CMLC 13**
See also AW 2; DLB 176
Josiah Allen's Wife
See Holley, Marietta
Josipovici, Gabriel (David) 1940- ...... **CLC 6,**
43, 153
See also CA 37-40R, 224; CAAE 224;
CAAS 8; CANR 47, 84; CN 3, 4, 5, 6, 7;
DLB 14, 319
Joubert, Joseph 1754-1824 .... **NCLC 9**
Jouve, Pierre Jean 1887-1976 .... **CLC 47**
See also CA 65-68; DLB 258; EWL 3
Jovine, Francesco 1902-1950 .... **TCLC 79**
See also DLB 264; EWL 3
Joyce, James (Augustine Aloysius)
1882-1941 .... **DC 16; PC 22; SSC 3, 26,**
44, 64; TCLC 3, 8, 16, 35, 52, 159;
WLC
See also AAYA 42; BRW 7; BRWC 1;
BRWR 1; BYA 11, 13; CA 104; 126; CD-
BLB 1914-1945; DA; DA3; DAB; DAC;
DAM MST, NOV, POET; DLB 10, 19,
36, 162, 247; EWL 3; EXPN; EXPS;
LAIT 3; LMFS 1, 2; MTCW 1, 2; MTFW
2005; NFS 7; RGSF 2; SSFS 1, 19; TEA;
WLIT 4
Jozsef, Attila 1905-1937 .... **TCLC 22**
See also CA 116; 230; CDWLB 4; DLB
215; EWL 3
Juana Ines de la Cruz, Sor
1651(?)-1695 ...... **HLCS 1; LC 5; PC 24**
See also DLB 305; FW; LAW; RGWL 2, 3;
WLIT 1
Juana Inez de La Cruz, Sor
See Juana Ines de la Cruz, Sor
Judd, Cyril
See Kornbluth, C(yril) M.; Pohl, Frederik
Juenger, Ernst 1895-1998 .... **CLC 125**
See Junger, Ernst
See also CA 101; 167; CANR 21, 47, 106;
DLB 56
Julian of Norwich 1342(?)-1416(?) . **LC 6, 52**
See also DLB 146; LMFS 1
Julius Caesar 100B.C.-44B.C.
See Caesar, Julius
See also CDWLB 1; DLB 211
Junger, Ernst
See Juenger, Ernst
See also CDWLB 2; EWL 3; RGWL 2, 3
Junger, Sebastian 1962- .... **CLC 109**
See also AAYA 28; CA 165; CANR 130;
MTFW 2005
Juniper, Alex
See Hospital, Janette Turner
Junius
See Luxemburg, Rosa
Junzaburo, Nishiwaki
See Nishiwaki, Junzaburo
See also EWL 3
Just, Ward (Swift) 1935- .... **CLC 4, 27**
See also CA 25-28R; CANR 32, 87; CN 6,
7; INT CANR-32
Justice, Donald (Rodney)
1925-2004 .... **CLC 6, 19, 102; PC 64**
See also AMWS 7; CA 5-8R; 230; CANR
26, 54, 74, 121, 122; CP 1, 2, 3, 4, 5, 6,
7; CSW; DAM POET; DLBY 1983; EWL
3; INT CANR-26; MAL 5; MTCW 2; PFS
14; TCLE 1:1
Juvenal c. 60-c. 130 .... **CMLC 8**
See also AW 2; CDWLB 1; DLB 211;
RGWL 2, 3
Juvenis
See Bourne, Randolph S(illiman)

K., Alice
See Knapp, Caroline
Kabakov, Sasha .... **CLC 59**
Kabir 1398(?)-1448(?) .... **LC 109; PC 56**
See also RGWL 2, 3
Kacew, Romain 1914-1980
See Gary, Romain
See also CA 108; 102
Kadare, Ismail 1936- .... **CLC 52, 190**
See also CA 161; EWL 3; RGWL 3
Kadohata, Cynthia (Lynn)
1956(?)- .... **CLC 59, 122**
See also CA 140; CANR 124; SATA 155
Kafka, Franz 1883-1924 ... **SSC 5, 29, 35, 60;**
TCLC 2, 6, 13, 29, 47, 53, 112; WLC
See also AAYA 31; BPFB 2; CA 105; 126;
CDWLB 2; DA; DA3; DAB; DAC; DAM
MST, NOV; DLB 81; EW 9; EWL 3;
EXPS; LATS 1:1; LMFS 2; MTCW 1, 2;
MTFW 2005; NFS 7; RGSF 2; RGWL 2,
3; SFW 4; SSFS 3, 7, 12; TWA
Kahanovitsch, Pinkhes
See Der Nister
Kahn, Roger 1927- .... **CLC 30**
See also CA 25-28R; CANR 44, 69; DLB
171; SATA 37
Kain, Saul
See Sassoon, Siegfried (Lorraine)
Kaiser, Georg 1878-1945 .... **TCLC 9**
See also CA 106; 190; CDWLB 2; DLB
124; EWL 3; LMFS 2; RGWL 2, 3
Kaledin, Sergei .... **CLC 59**
Kaletski, Alexander 1946- .... **CLC 39**
See also CA 118; 143
Kalidasa fl. c. 400-455 .... **CMLC 9; PC 22**
See also RGWL 2, 3
Kallman, Chester (Simon)
1921-1975 .... **CLC 2**
See also CA 45-48; 53-56; CANR 3; CP 1,
2
Kaminsky, Melvin 1926-
See Brooks, Mel
See also CA 65-68; CANR 16; DFS 21
Kaminsky, Stuart M(elvin) 1934- ..... **CLC 59**
See also CA 73-76; CANR 29, 53, 89;
CMW 4
Kamo no Chomei 1153(?)-1216 .... **CMLC 66**
See also DLB 203
Kamo no Nagaakira
See Kamo no Chomei
Kandinsky, Wassily 1866-1944 .... **TCLC 92**
See also AAYA 64; CA 118; 155
Kane, Francis
See Robbins, Harold
Kane, Henry 1918-
See Queen, Ellery
See also CA 156; CMW 4
Kane, Paul
See Simon, Paul (Frederick)
Kanin, Garson 1912-1999 .... **CLC 22**
See also AITN 1; CA 5-8R; 177; CAD;
CANR 7, 78; DLB 7; IDFW 3, 4
Kaniuk, Yoram 1930- .... **CLC 19**
See also CA 134; DLB 299
Kant, Immanuel 1724-1804 ..... **NCLC 27, 67**
See also DLB 94
Kantor, MacKinlay 1904-1977 .... **CLC 7**
See also CA 61-64; 73-76; CANR 60, 63;
CN 1, 2; DLB 9, 102; MAL 5; MTCW 2;
RHW; TCWW 1, 2
Kanze Motokiyo
See Zeami
Kaplan, David Michael 1946- .... **CLC 50**
See also CA 187
Kaplan, James 1951- .... **CLC 59**
See also CA 135; CANR 121

Karadzic, Vuk Stefanovic
1787-1864 .... **NCLC 115**
See also CDWLB 4; DLB 147
Karageorge, Michael
See Anderson, Poul (William)
Karamzin, Nikolai Mikhailovich
1766-1826 .... **NCLC 3**
See also DLB 150; RGSF 2
Karapanou, Margarita 1946- .... **CLC 13**
See also CA 101
Karinthy, Frigyes 1887-1938 .... **TCLC 47**
See also CA 170; DLB 215; EWL 3
Karl, Frederick R(obert)
1927-2004 .... **CLC 34**
See also CA 5-8R; 226; CANR 3, 44, 143
Karr, Mary 1955- .... **CLC 188**
See also AMWS 11; CA 151; CANR 100;
MTFW 2005; NCFS 5
Kastel, Warren
See Silverberg, Robert
Kataev, Evgeny Petrovich 1903-1942
See Petrov, Evgeny
See also CA 120
Kataphusin
See Ruskin, John
Katz, Steve 1935- .... **CLC 47**
See also CA 25-28R; CAAS 14, 64; CANR
12; CN 4, 5, 6, 7; DLBY 1983
Kauffman, Janet 1945- .... **CLC 42**
See also CA 117; CANR 43, 84; DLB 218;
DLBY 1986
Kaufman, Bob (Garnell) 1925-1986 . **CLC 49**
See also BG 1:3; BW 1; CA 41-44R; 118;
CANR 22; CP 1; DLB 16, 41
Kaufman, George S. 1889-1961 ...... **CLC 38;**
DC 17
See also CA 108; 93-96; DAM DRAM;
DFS 1, 10; DLB 7; INT CA-108; MTCW
2; MTFW 2005; RGAL 4; TUS
Kaufman, Moises 1964- .... **DC 26**
See also CA 211; DFS 22; MTFW 2005
Kaufman, Sue .... **CLC 3, 8**
See Barondess, Sue K(aufman)
Kavafis, Konstantinos Petrou 1863-1933
See Cavafy, C(onstantine) P(eter)
See also CA 104
Kavan, Anna 1901-1968 .... **CLC 5, 13, 82**
See also BRWS 7; CA 5-8R; CANR 6, 57;
DLB 255; MTCW 1; RGEL 2; SFW 4
Kavanagh, Dan
See Barnes, Julian (Patrick)
Kavanagh, Julie 1952- .... **CLC 119**
See also CA 163
Kavanagh, Patrick (Joseph)
1904-1967 .... **CLC 22; PC 33**
See also BRWS 7; CA 123; 25-28R; DLB
15, 20; EWL 3; MTCW 1; RGEL 2
Kawabata, Yasunari 1899-1972 ..... **CLC 2, 5,**
9, 18, 107; SSC 17
See Kawabata Yasunari
See also CA 93-96; 33-36R; CANR 88;
DAM MULT; MJW; MTCW 2; MTFW
2005; RGSF 2; RGWL 2, 3
Kawabata Yasunari
See Kawabata, Yasunari
See also DLB 180; EWL 3
Kaye, M(ary) M(argaret)
1908-2004 .... **CLC 28**
See also CA 89-92; 223; CANR 24, 60, 102,
142; MTCW 1, 2; MTFW 2005; RHW;
SATA 62; SATA-Obit 152
Kaye, Mollie
See Kaye, M(ary) M(argaret)
Kaye-Smith, Sheila 1887-1956 .... **TCLC 20**
See also CA 118; 203; DLB 36
Kaymor, Patrice Maguilene
See Senghor, Leopold Sedar

Knight, Etheridge 1931-1991 ... **BLC 2; CLC 40; PC 14**
See also BW 1, 3; CA 21-24R; 133; CANR 23, 82; CP 1, 2, 3, 4; DAM POET; DLB 41; MTCW 2; MTFW 2005; RGAL 4; TCLE 1:1

Knight, Sarah Kemble 1666-1727 .... **LC 7**
See also DLB 24, 200

Knister, Raymond 1899-1932 .... **TCLC 56**
See also CA 186; DLB 68; RGEL 2

Knowles, John 1926-2001 ... **CLC 1, 4, 10, 26**
See also AAYA 10; AMWS 12; BPFB 2; BYA 3; CA 17-20R; 203; CANR 40, 74, 76, 132; CDALB 1968-1988; CLR 98; CN 1, 2, 3, 4, 5, 6, 7; DA; DAC; DAM MST, NOV; DLB 6; EXPN; MTCW 1, 2; MTFW 2005; NFS 2; RGAL 4; SATA 8, 89; SATA-Obit 134; YAW

Knox, Calvin M.
See Silverberg, Robert

Knox, John c. 1505-1572 .... **LC 37**
See also DLB 132

Knye, Cassandra
See Disch, Thomas M(ichael)

Koch, C(hristopher) J(ohn) 1932- .... **CLC 42**
See also CA 127; CANR 84; CN 3, 4, 5, 6, 7; DLB 289

Koch, Christopher
See Koch, C(hristopher) J(ohn)

Koch, Kenneth (Jay) 1925-2002 .... **CLC 5, 8, 44**
See also AMWS 15; CA 1-4R; 207; CAD; CANR 6, 36, 57, 97, 131; CD 5, 6; CP 1, 2, 3, 4, 5, 6, 7; DAM POET; DLB 5; INT CANR-36; MAL 5; MTCW 2; MTFW 2005; PFS 20; SATA 65; WP

Kochanowski, Jan 1530-1584 .... **LC 10**
See also RGWL 2, 3

Kock, Charles Paul de 1794-1871 . **NCLC 16**

Koda Rohan
See Koda Shigeyuki

Koda Rohan
See Koda Shigeyuki
See also DLB 180

Koda Shigeyuki 1867-1947 .... **TCLC 22**
See Koda Rohan
See also CA 121; 183

Koestler, Arthur 1905-1983 ... **CLC 1, 3, 6, 8, 15, 33**
See also BRWS 1; CA 1-4R; 109; CANR 1, 33; CDBLB 1945-1960; CN 1, 2, 3; DLBY 1983; EWL 3; MTCW 1, 2; MTFW 2005; NFS 19; RGEL 2

Kogawa, Joy Nozomi 1935- ...... **CLC 78, 129**
See also AAYA 47; CA 101; CANR 19, 62, 126; CN 6, 7; CP 1; CWP; DAC; DAM MST, MULT; FW; MTCW 2; MTFW 2005; NFS 3; SATA 99

Kohout, Pavel 1928- .... **CLC 13**
See also CA 45-48; CANR 3

Koizumi, Yakumo
See Hearn, (Patricio) Lafcadio (Tessima Carlos)

Kolmar, Gertrud 1894-1943 .... **TCLC 40**
See also CA 167; EWL 3

Komunyakaa, Yusef 1947- .. **BLCS; CLC 86, 94, 207; PC 51**
See also AFAW 2; AMWS 13; CA 147; CANR 83; CP 7; CSW; DLB 120; EWL 3; PFS 5, 20; RGAL 4

Konrad, George
See Konrad, Gyorgy

Konrad, Gyorgy 1933- .... **CLC 4, 10, 73**
See also CA 85-88; CANR 97; CDWLB 4; CWW 2; DLB 232; EWL 3

Konwicki, Tadeusz 1926- .... **CLC 8, 28, 54, 117**
See also CA 101; CAAS 9; CANR 39, 59; CWW 2; DLB 232; EWL 3; IDFW 3; MTCW 1

Koontz, Dean R. 1945- .... **CLC 78, 206**
See also AAYA 9, 31; BEST 89:3, 90:2; CA 108; CANR 19, 36, 52, 95, 138; CMW 4; CPW; DA3; DAM NOV, POP; DLB 292; HGG; MTCW 1; MTFW 2005; SATA 92, 165; SFW 4; SUFW 2; YAW

Koontz, Dean Ray
See Koontz, Dean R.

Koontz, Dean Ray
See Koontz, Dean R.

Kopernik, Mikolaj
See Copernicus, Nicolaus

Kopit, Arthur (Lee) 1937- ...... **CLC 1, 18, 33**
See also AITN 1; CA 81-84; CABS 3; CAD; CD 5, 6; DAM DRAM; DFS 7, 14; DLB 7; MAL 5; MTCW 1; RGAL 4

Kopitar, Jernej (Bartholomaus) 1780-1844 .... **NCLC 117**

Kops, Bernard 1926- .... **CLC 4**
See also CA 5-8R; CANR 84; CBD; CN 1, 2, 3, 4, 5, 6, 7; CP 1, 2, 3, 4, 5, 6, 7; DLB 13

Kornbluth, C(yril) M. 1923-1958 .... **TCLC 8**
See also CA 105; 160; DLB 8; SCFW 1, 2; SFW 4

Korolenko, V. G.
See Korolenko, Vladimir Galaktionovich

Korolenko, Vladimir
See Korolenko, Vladimir Galaktionovich

Korolenko, Vladimir G.
See Korolenko, Vladimir Galaktionovich

Korolenko, Vladimir Galaktionovich 1853-1921 .... **TCLC 22**
See also CA 121; DLB 277

Korzybski, Alfred (Habdank Skarbek) 1879-1950 .... **TCLC 61**
See also CA 123; 160

Kosinski, Jerzy (Nikodem) 1933-1991 .... **CLC 1, 2, 3, 6, 10, 15, 53, 70**
See also AMWS 7; BPFB 2; CA 17-20R; 134; CANR 9, 46; CN 1, 2, 3, 4; DA3; DAM NOV; DLB 2, 299; DLBY 1982; EWL 3; HGG; MAL 5; MTCW 1, 2; MTFW 2005; NFS 12; RGAL 4; TUS

Kostelanetz, Richard (Cory) 1940- .. **CLC 28**
See also CA 13-16R; CAAS 8; CANR 38, 77; CN 4, 5, 6; CP 2, 3, 4, 5, 6, 7

Kostrowitzki, Wilhelm Apollinaris de 1880-1918
See Apollinaire, Guillaume
See also CA 104

Kotlowitz, Robert 1924- .... **CLC 4**
See also CA 33-36R; CANR 36

Kotzebue, August (Friedrich Ferdinand) von 1761-1819 .... **NCLC 25**
See also DLB 94

Kotzwinkle, William 1938- ..... **CLC 5, 14, 35**
See also BPFB 2; CA 45-48; CANR 3, 44, 84, 129; CLR 6; CN 7; DLB 173; FANT; MAICYA 1, 2; SATA 24, 70, 146; SFW 4; SUFW 2; YAW

Kowna, Stancy
See Szymborska, Wislawa

Kozol, Jonathan 1936- .... **CLC 17**
See also AAYA 46; CA 61-64; CANR 16, 45, 96; MTFW 2005

Kozoll, Michael 1940(?)- .... **CLC 35**

Kramer, Kathryn 19(?)- .... **CLC 34**

Kramer, Larry 1935- .... **CLC 42; DC 8**
See also CA 124; 126; CANR 60, 132; DAM POP; DLB 249; GLL 1

Krasicki, Ignacy 1735-1801 .... **NCLC 8**

Krasinski, Zygmunt 1812-1859 .... **NCLC 4**
See also RGWL 2, 3

Kraus, Karl 1874-1936 .... **TCLC 5**
See also CA 104; 216; DLB 118; EWL 3

Kreve (Mickevicius), Vincas 1882-1954 .... **TCLC 27**
See also CA 170; DLB 220; EWL 3

Kristeva, Julia 1941- .... **CLC 77, 140**
See also CA 154; CANR 99; DLB 242; EWL 3; FW; LMFS 2

Kristofferson, Kris 1936- .... **CLC 26**
See also CA 104

Krizanc, John 1956- .... **CLC 57**
See also CA 187

Krleza, Miroslav 1893-1981 .... **CLC 8, 114**
See also CA 97-100; 105; CANR 50; CD-WLB 4; DLB 147; EW 11; RGWL 2, 3

Kroetsch, Robert (Paul) 1927- .... **CLC 5, 23, 57, 132**
See also CA 17-20R; CANR 8, 38; CCA 1; CN 2, 3, 4, 5, 6, 7; CP 7; DAC; DAM POET; DLB 53; MTCW 1

Kroetz, Franz
See Kroetz, Franz Xaver

Kroetz, Franz Xaver 1946- .... **CLC 41**
See also CA 130; CANR 142; CWW 2; EWL 3

Kroker, Arthur (W.) 1945- .... **CLC 77**
See also CA 161

Kroniuk, Lisa
See Berton, Pierre (Francis de Marigny)

Kropotkin, Peter (Aleksieevich) 1842-1921 .... **TCLC 36**
See Kropotkin, Petr Alekseevich
See also CA 119; 219

Kropotkin, Petr Alekseevich
See Kropotkin, Peter (Aleksieevich)
See also DLB 277

Krotkov, Yuri 1917-1981 .... **CLC 19**
See also CA 102

Krumb
See Crumb, R(obert)

Krumgold, Joseph (Quincy) 1908-1980 .... **CLC 12**
See also BYA 1, 2; CA 9-12R; 101; CANR 7; MAICYA 1, 2; SATA 1, 48; SATA-Obit 23; YAW

Krumwitz
See Crumb, R(obert)

Krutch, Joseph Wood 1893-1970 ..... **CLC 24**
See also ANW; CA 1-4R; 25-28R; CANR 4; DLB 63, 206, 275

Krutzch, Gus
See Eliot, T(homas) S(tearns)

Krylov, Ivan Andreevich 1768(?)-1844 .... **NCLC 1**
See also DLB 150

Kubin, Alfred (Leopold Isidor) 1877-1959 .... **TCLC 23**
See also CA 112; 149; CANR 104; DLB 81

Kubrick, Stanley 1928-1999 .... **CLC 16; TCLC 112**
See also AAYA 30; CA 81-84; 177; CANR 33; DLB 26

Kumin, Maxine (Winokur) 1925- ..... **CLC 5, 13, 28, 164; PC 15**
See also AITN 2; AMWS 4; ANW; CA 1-4R; CAAS 8; CANR 1, 21, 69, 115, 140; CP 2, 3, 4, 5, 6, 7; CWP; DA3; DAM POET; DLB 5; EWL 3; EXPP; MTCW 1, 2; MTFW 2005; PAB; PFS 18; SATA 12

Kundera, Milan 1929- . **CLC 4, 9, 19, 32, 68, 115, 135; SSC 24**
See also AAYA 2, 62; BPFB 2; CA 85-88; CANR 19, 52, 74, 144; CDWLB 4; CWW 2; DA3; DAM NOV; DLB 232; EW 13; EWL 3; MTCW 1, 2; MTFW 2005; NFS 18; RGSF 2; RGWL 3; SSFS 10

Kunene, Mazisi (Raymond) 1930- ... **CLC 85**
See also BW 1, 3; CA 125; CANR 81; CP
1, 7; DLB 117

Kung, Hans .... **CLC 130**
See Kung, Hans

Kung, Hans 1928-
See Kung, Hans
See also CA 53-56; CANR 66, 134; MTCW
1, 2; MTFW 2005

Kunikida Doppo 1869(?)-1908
See Doppo, Kunikida
See also DLB 180; EWL 3

Kunitz, Stanley (Jasspon) 1905- .. **CLC 6, 11,**
14, 148; PC 19
See also AMWS 3; CA 41-44R; CANR 26,
57, 98; CP 1, 2, 3, 4, 5, 6, 7; DA3; DLB
48; INT CANR-26; MAL 5; MTCW 1, 2;
MTFW 2005; PFS 11; RGAL 4

Kunze, Reiner 1933- .... **CLC 10**
See also CA 93-96; CWW 2; DLB 75; EWL
3

Kuprin, Aleksander Ivanovich
1870-1938 .... **TCLC 5**
See Kuprin, Aleksandr Ivanovich; Kuprin,
Alexandr Ivanovich
See also CA 104; 182

Kuprin, Aleksandr Ivanovich
See Kuprin, Aleksander Ivanovich
See also DLB 295

Kuprin, Alexandr Ivanovich
See Kuprin, Aleksander Ivanovich
See also EWL 3

Kureishi, Hanif 1954- .. **CLC 64, 135; DC 26**
See also BRWS 11; CA 139; CANR 113;
CBD; CD 5, 6; CN 6, 7; DLB 194, 245;
GLL 2; IDFW 4; WLIT 4; WWE 1

Kurosawa, Akira 1910-1998 .... **CLC 16, 119**
See also AAYA 11, 64; CA 101; 170; CANR
46; DAM MULT

Kushner, Tony 1956- .... **CLC 81, 203; DC 10**
See also AAYA 61; AMWS 9; CA 144;
CAD; CANR 74, 130; CD 5, 6; DA3;
DAM DRAM; DFS 5; DLB 228; EWL 3;
GLL 1; LAIT 5; MAL 5; MTCW 2;
MTFW 2005; RGAL 4; SATA 160

Kuttner, Henry 1915-1958 .... **TCLC 10**
See also CA 107; 157; DLB 8; FANT;
SCFW 1, 2; SFW 4

Kutty, Madhavi
See Das, Kamala

Kuzma, Greg 1944- .... **CLC 7**
See also CA 33-36R; CANR 70

Kuzmin, Mikhail (Alekseevich)
1872(?)-1936 .... **TCLC 40**
See also CA 170; DLB 295; EWL 3

Kyd, Thomas 1558-1594 .... **DC 3; LC 22**
See also BRW 1; DAM DRAM; DFS 21;
DLB 62; IDTP; LMFS 1; RGEL 2; TEA;
WLIT 3

Kyprianos, Iossif
See Samarakis, Antonis

L. S.
See Stephen, Sir Leslie

La3amon
See Layamon
See also DLB 146

Labe, Louise 1521-1566 .... **LC 120**

Labrunie, Gerard
See Nerval, Gerard de

La Bruyere, Jean de 1645-1696 .... **LC 17**
See also DLB 268; EW 3; GFL Beginnings
to 1789

Lacan, Jacques (Marie Emile)
1901-1981 .... **CLC 75**
See also CA 121; 104; DLB 296; EWL 3;
TWA

Laclos, Pierre-Ambroise Francois
1741-1803 .... **NCLC 4, 87**
See also DLB 313; EW 4; GFL Beginnings
to 1789; RGWL 2, 3

Lacolere, Francois
See Aragon, Louis

La Colere, Francois
See Aragon, Louis

La Deshabilleuse
See Simenon, Georges (Jacques Christian)

Lady Gregory
See Gregory, Lady Isabella Augusta (Persse)

Lady of Quality, A
See Bagnold, Enid

La Fayette, Marie-(Madelaine Pioche de la
Vergne) 1634-1693 .... **LC 2**
See Lafayette, Marie-Madeleine
See also GFL Beginnings to 1789; RGWL
2, 3

Lafayette, Marie-Madeleine
See La Fayette, Marie-(Madelaine Pioche
de la Vergne)
See also DLB 268

Lafayette, Rene
See Hubbard, L(afayette) Ron(ald)

La Flesche, Francis 1857(?)-1932 ...... **NNAL**
See also CA 144; CANR 83; DLB 175

La Fontaine, Jean de 1621-1695 .... **LC 50**
See also DLB 268; EW 3; GFL Beginnings
to 1789; MAICYA 1, 2; RGWL 2, 3;
SATA 18

Laforgue, Jules 1860-1887 . **NCLC 5, 53; PC**
14; SSC 20
See also DLB 217; EW 7; GFL 1789 to the
Present; RGWL 2, 3

Lagerkvist, Paer (Fabian)
1891-1974 ..... **CLC 7, 10, 13, 54; TCLC**
144
See Lagerkvist, Par
See also CA 85-88; 49-52; DA3; DAM
DRAM, NOV; MTCW 1, 2; MTFW 2005;
TWA

Lagerkvist, Par .... **SSC 12**
See Lagerkvist, Paer (Fabian)
See also DLB 259; EW 10; EWL 3; RGSF
2; RGWL 2, 3

Lagerloef, Selma (Ottiliana Lovisa)
.... **TCLC 4, 36**
See Lagerlof, Selma (Ottiliana Lovisa)
See also CA 108; MTCW 2

Lagerlof, Selma (Ottiliana Lovisa)
1858-1940
See Lagerloef, Selma (Ottiliana Lovisa)
See also CA 188; CLR 7; DLB 259; RGWL
2, 3; SATA 15; SSFS 18

La Guma, (Justin) Alex(ander)
1925-1985 . **BLCS; CLC 19; TCLC 140**
See also AFW; BW 1, 3; CA 49-52; 118;
CANR 25, 81; CDWLB 3; CN 1, 2, 3;
CP 1; DAM NOV; DLB 117, 225; EWL
3; MTCW 1, 2; MTFW 2005; WLIT 2;
WWE 1

Laidlaw, A. K.
See Grieve, C(hristopher) M(urray)

Lainez, Manuel Mujica
See Mujica Lainez, Manuel
See also HW 1

Laing, R(onald) D(avid) 1927-1989 . **CLC 95**
See also CA 107; 129; CANR 34; MTCW 1

Laishley, Alex
See Booth, Martin

Lamartine, Alphonse (Marie Louis Prat) de
1790-1869 .... **NCLC 11; PC 16**
See also DAM POET; DLB 217; GFL 1789
to the Present; RGWL 2, 3

Lamb, Charles 1775-1834 ..... **NCLC 10, 113;**
WLC
See also BRW 4; CDBLB 1789-1832; DA;
DAB; DAC; DAM MST; DLB 93, 107,
163; RGEL 2; SATA 17; TEA

Lamb, Lady Caroline 1785-1828 ... **NCLC 38**
See also DLB 116

Lamb, Mary Ann 1764-1847 .... **NCLC 125**
See also DLB 163; SATA 17

Lame Deer 1903(?)-1976 .... **NNAL**
See also CA 69-72

Lamming, George (William) 1927- .. **BLC 2;**
CLC 2, 4, 66, 144
See also BW 2, 3; CA 85-88; CANR 26,
76; CDWLB 3; CN 1, 2, 3, 4, 5, 6, 7; CP
1; DAM MULT; DLB 125; EWL 3;
MTCW 1, 2; MTFW 2005; NFS 15;
RGEL 2

L'Amour, Louis (Dearborn)
1908-1988 .... **CLC 25, 55**
See also AAYA 16; AITN 2; BEST 89:2;
BPFB 2; CA 1-4R; 125; CANR 3, 25, 40;
CPW; DA3; DAM NOV, POP; DLB 206;
DLBY 1980; MTCW 1, 2; MTFW 2005;
RGAL 4; TCWW 1, 2

Lampedusa, Giuseppe (Tomasi) di
.... **TCLC 13**
See Tomasi di Lampedusa, Giuseppe
See also CA 164; EW 11; MTCW 2; MTFW
2005; RGWL 2, 3

Lampman, Archibald 1861-1899 ... **NCLC 25**
See also DLB 92; RGEL 2; TWA

Lancaster, Bruce 1896-1963 .... **CLC 36**
See also CA 9-10; CANR 70; CAP 1; SATA
9

Lanchester, John 1962- .... **CLC 99**
See also CA 194; DLB 267

Landau, Mark Alexandrovich
See Aldanov, Mark (Alexandrovich)

Landau-Aldanov, Mark Alexandrovich
See Aldanov, Mark (Alexandrovich)

Landis, Jerry
See Simon, Paul (Frederick)

Landis, John 1950- .... **CLC 26**
See also CA 112; 122; CANR 128

Landolfi, Tommaso 1908-1979 .... **CLC 11, 49**
See also CA 127; 117; DLB 177; EWL 3

Landon, Letitia Elizabeth
1802-1838 .... **NCLC 15**
See also DLB 96

Landor, Walter Savage
1775-1864 .... **NCLC 14**
See also BRW 4; DLB 93, 107; RGEL 2

Landwirth, Heinz 1927-
See Lind, Jakov
See also CA 9-12R; CANR 7

Lane, Patrick 1939- .... **CLC 25**
See also CA 97-100; CANR 54; CP 3, 4, 5,
6, 7; DAM POET; DLB 53; INT CA-97-
100

Lang, Andrew 1844-1912 .... **TCLC 16**
See also CA 114; 137; CANR 85; CLR 101;
DLB 98, 141, 184; FANT; MAICYA 1, 2;
RGEL 2; SATA 16; WCH

Lang, Fritz 1890-1976 .... **CLC 20, 103**
See also AAYA 65; CA 77-80; 69-72;
CANR 30

Lange, John
See Crichton, (John) Michael

Langer, Elinor 1939- .... **CLC 34**
See also CA 121

Langland, William 1332(?)-1400(?) .... **LC 19,**
120
See also BRW 1; DA; DAB; DAC; DAM
MST, POET; DLB 146; RGEL 2; TEA;
WLIT 3

Langstaff, Launcelot
See Irving, Washington

le Carre, John .... **CLC 3, 5, 9, 15, 28**
　　See Cornwell, David (John Moore)
　　See also AAYA 42; BEST 89:4; BPFB 2;
　　　BRWS 2; CDBLB 1960 to Present; CMW
　　　4; CN 1, 2, 3, 4, 5, 6, 7; CPW; DLB 87;
　　　EWL 3; MSW; MTCW 2; RGEL 2; TEA

Le Clezio, J(ean) M(arie) G(ustave)
　　1940- .... **CLC 31, 155**
　　See also CA 116; 128; CWW 2; DLB 83;
　　　EWL 3; GFL 1789 to the Present; RGSF
　　　2

Leconte de Lisle, Charles-Marie-Rene
　　1818-1894 .... **NCLC 29**
　　See also DLB 217; EW 6; GFL 1789 to the
　　　Present

Le Coq, Monsieur
　　See Simenon, Georges (Jacques Christian)

Leduc, Violette 1907-1972 .... **CLC 22**
　　See also CA 13-14; 33-36R; CANR 69;
　　　CAP 1; EWL 3; GFL 1789 to the Present;
　　　GLL 1

Ledwidge, Francis 1887(?)-1917 .... **TCLC 23**
　　See also CA 123; 203; DLB 20

Lee, Andrea 1953- .... **BLC 2; CLC 36**
　　See also BW 1, 3; CA 125; CANR 82;
　　　DAM MULT

Lee, Andrew
　　See Auchincloss, Louis (Stanton)

Lee, Chang-rae 1965- .... **CLC 91**
　　See also CA 148; CANR 89; CN 7; DLB
　　　312; LATS 1:2

Lee, Don L. .... **CLC 2**
　　See Madhubuti, Haki R.
　　See also CP 2, 3, 4

Lee, George W(ashington)
　　1894-1976 .... **BLC 2; CLC 52**
　　See also BW 1; CA 125; CANR 83; DAM
　　　MULT; DLB 51

Lee, (Nelle) Harper 1926- . **CLC 12, 60, 194;**
　　WLC
　　See also AAYA 13; AMWS 8; BPFB 2;
　　　BYA 3; CA 13-16R; CANR 51, 128;
　　　CDALB 1941-1968; CSW; DA; DA3;
　　　DAB; DAC; DAM MST, NOV; DLB 6;
　　　EXPN; LAIT 3; MAL 5; MTCW 1, 2;
　　　MTFW 2005; NFS 2; SATA 11; WYA;
　　　YAW

Lee, Helen Elaine 1959(?)- .... **CLC 86**
　　See also CA 148

Lee, John .... **CLC 70**

Lee, Julian
　　See Latham, Jean Lee

Lee, Larry
　　See Lee, Lawrence

Lee, Laurie 1914-1997 .... **CLC 90**
　　See also CA 77-80; 158; CANR 33, 73; CP
　　　1, 2, 3, 4; CPW; DAB; DAM POP; DLB
　　　27; MTCW 1; RGEL 2

Lee, Lawrence 1941-1990 .... **CLC 34**
　　See also CA 131; CANR 43

Lee, Li-Young 1957- .... **CLC 164; PC 24**
　　See also AMWS 15; CA 153; CANR 118;
　　　CP 7; DLB 165, 312; LMFS 2; PFS 11,
　　　15, 17

Lee, Manfred B(ennington)
　　1905-1971 .... **CLC 11**
　　See Queen, Ellery
　　See also CA 1-4R; 29-32R; CANR 2; CMW
　　　4; DLB 137

Lee, Nathaniel 1645(?)-1692 .... **LC 103**
　　See also DLB 80; RGEL 2

Lee, Shelton Jackson 1957(?)- .. **BLCS; CLC
　　105**
　　See Lee, Spike
　　See also BW 2, 3; CA 125; CANR 42;
　　　DAM MULT

Lee, Spike
　　See Lee, Shelton Jackson
　　See also AAYA 4, 29

Lee, Stan 1922- .... **CLC 17**
　　See also AAYA 5, 49; CA 108; 111; CANR
　　　129; INT CA-111; MTFW 2005

Lee, Tanith 1947- .... **CLC 46**
　　See also AAYA 15; CA 37-40R; CANR 53,
　　　102, 145; DLB 261; FANT; SATA 8, 88,
　　　134; SFW 4; SUFW 1, 2; YAW

Lee, Vernon .... **SSC 33; TCLC 5**
　　See Paget, Violet
　　See also DLB 57, 153, 156, 174, 178; GLL
　　　1; SUFW 1

Lee, William
　　See Burroughs, William S(eward)
　　See also GLL 1

Lee, Willy
　　See Burroughs, William S(eward)
　　See also GLL 1

Lee-Hamilton, Eugene (Jacob)
　　1845-1907 .... **TCLC 22**
　　See also CA 117; 234

Leet, Judith 1935- .... **CLC 11**
　　See also CA 187

Le Fanu, Joseph Sheridan
　　1814-1873 .... **NCLC 9, 58; SSC 14, 84**
　　See also CMW 4; DA3; DAM POP; DLB
　　　21, 70, 159, 178; GL 3; HGG; RGEL 2;
　　　RGSF 2; SUFW 1

Leffland, Ella 1931- .... **CLC 19**
　　See also CA 29-32R; CANR 35, 78, 82;
　　　DLBY 1984; INT CANR-35; SATA 65

Leger, Alexis
　　See Leger, (Marie-Rene Auguste) Alexis
　　　Saint-Leger

Leger, (Marie-Rene Auguste) Alexis
　　Saint-Leger 1887-1975 .. **CLC 4, 11, 46;
　　PC 23**
　　See Perse, Saint-John; Saint-John Perse
　　See also CA 13-16R; 61-64; CANR 43;
　　　DAM POET; MTCW 1

Leger, Saintleger
　　See Leger, (Marie-Rene Auguste) Alexis
　　　Saint-Leger

Le Guin, Ursula K(roeber) 1929- ..... **CLC 8,
　　13, 22, 45, 71, 136; SSC 12, 69**
　　See also AAYA 9, 27; AITN 1; BPFB 2;
　　　BYA 5, 8, 11, 14; CA 21-24R; CANR 9,
　　　32, 52, 74, 132; CDALB 1968-1988; CLR
　　　3, 28, 91; CN 2, 3, 4, 5, 6, 7; CPW; DA3;
　　　DAB; DAC; DAM MST, POP; DLB 8,
　　　52, 256, 275; EXPS; FANT; FW; INT
　　　CANR-32; JRDA; LAIT 5; MAICYA 1,
　　　2; MAL 5; MTCW 1, 2; MTFW 2005;
　　　NFS 6, 9; SATA 4, 52, 99, 149; SCFW 1,
　　　2; SFW 4; SSFS 2; SUFW 1, 2; WYA;
　　　YAW

Lehmann, Rosamond (Nina)
　　1901-1990 .... **CLC 5**
　　See also CA 77-80; 131; CANR 8, 73; CN
　　　1, 2, 3, 4; DLB 15; MTCW 2; RGEL 2;
　　　RHW

Leiber, Fritz (Reuter, Jr.)
　　1910-1992 .... **CLC 25**
　　See also AAYA 65; BPFB 2; CA 45-48; 139;
　　　CANR 2, 40, 86; CN 2, 3, 4, 5; DLB 8;
　　　FANT; HGG; MTCW 1, 2; MTFW 2005;
　　　SATA 45; SATA-Obit 73; SCFW 1, 2;
　　　SFW 4; SUFW 1, 2

Leibniz, Gottfried Wilhelm von
　　1646-1716 .... **LC 35**
　　See also DLB 168

Leimbach, Martha 1963-
　　See Leimbach, Marti
　　See also CA 130

Leimbach, Marti .... **CLC 65**
　　See Leimbach, Martha

Leino, Eino .... **TCLC 24**
　　See Lonnbohm, Armas Eino Leopold
　　See also EWL 3

Leiris, Michel (Julien) 1901-1990 ..... **CLC 61**
　　See also CA 119; 128; 132; EWL 3; GFL
　　　1789 to the Present

Leithauser, Brad 1953- .... **CLC 27**
　　See also CA 107; CANR 27, 81; CP 7; DLB
　　　120, 282

le Jars de Gournay, Marie
　　See de Gournay, Marie le Jars

Lelchuk, Alan 1938- .... **CLC 5**
　　See also CA 45-48; CAAS 20; CANR 1,
　　　70; CN 3, 4, 5, 6, 7

Lem, Stanislaw 1921- ...... **CLC 8, 15, 40, 149**
　　See also CA 105; CAAS 1; CANR 32;
　　　CWW 2; MTCW 1; SCFW 1, 2; SFW 4

Lemann, Nancy (Elise) 1956- .... **CLC 39**
　　See also CA 118; 136; CANR 121

Lemonnier, (Antoine Louis) Camille
　　1844-1913 .... **TCLC 22**
　　See also CA 121

Lenau, Nikolaus 1802-1850 .... **NCLC 16**

L'Engle, Madeleine (Camp Franklin)
　　1918- .... **CLC 12**
　　See also AAYA 28; AITN 2; BPFB 2; BYA
　　　2, 4, 5, 7; CA 1-4R; CANR 3, 21, 39, 66,
　　　107; CLR 1, 14, 57; CPW; CWRI 5; DA3;
　　　DAM POP; DLB 52; JRDA; MAICYA 1,
　　　2; MTCW 1, 2; MTFW 2005; SAAS 15;
　　　SATA 1, 27, 75, 128; SFW 4; WYA; YAW

Lengyel, Jozsef 1896-1975 .... **CLC 7**
　　See also CA 85-88; 57-60; CANR 71;
　　　RGSF 2

Lenin 1870-1924
　　See Lenin, V. I.
　　See also CA 121; 168

Lenin, V. I. .... **TCLC 67**
　　See Lenin

Lennon, John (Ono) 1940-1980 .. **CLC 12, 35**
　　See also CA 102; SATA 114

Lennox, Charlotte Ramsay
　　1729(?)-1804 .... **NCLC 23, 134**
　　See also DLB 39; RGEL 2

Lentricchia, Frank, (Jr.) 1940- .... **CLC 34**
　　See also CA 25-28R; CANR 19, 106; DLB
　　　246

Lenz, Gunter .... **CLC 65**

Lenz, Jakob Michael Reinhold
　　1751-1792 .... **LC 100**
　　See also DLB 94; RGWL 2, 3

Lenz, Siegfried 1926- .... **CLC 27; SSC 33**
　　See also CA 89-92; CANR 80; CWW 2;
　　　DLB 75; EWL 3; RGSF 2; RGWL 2, 3

Leon, David
　　See Jacob, (Cyprien-)Max

Leonard, Elmore (John, Jr.) 1925- . **CLC 28,
　　34, 71, 120**
　　See also AAYA 22, 59; AITN 1; BEST 89:1,
　　　90:4; BPFB 2; CA 81-84; CANR 12, 28,
　　　53, 76, 96, 133; CMW 4; CN 5, 6, 7;
　　　CPW; DA3; DAM POP; DLB 173, 226;
　　　INT CANR-28; MSW; MTCW 1, 2;
　　　MTFW 2005; RGAL 4; SATA 163;
　　　TCWW 1, 2

Leonard, Hugh .... **CLC 19**
　　See Byrne, John Keyes
　　See also CBD; CD 5, 6; DFS 13; DLB 13

Leonov, Leonid (Maximovich)
　　1899-1994 .... **CLC 92**
　　See also CA 129; CANR 76; DAM NOV;
　　　EWL 3; MTCW 1, 2; MTFW 2005

Leonov, Leonid Maksimovich
　　See Leonov, Leonid (Maximovich)
　　See also DLB 272

Leopardi, (Conte) Giacomo
　　1798-1837 .... **NCLC 22, 129; PC 37**
　　See also EW 5; RGWL 2, 3; WLIT 7; WP

Le Reveler
　　See Artaud, Antonin (Marie Joseph)

Lin, Yutang 1895-1976 .... **TCLC 149**
See also CA 45-48; 65-68; CANR 2; RGAL 4

Lincoln, Abraham 1809-1865 .... **NCLC 18**
See also LAIT 2

Lind, Jakov .... **CLC 1, 2, 4, 27, 82**
See Landwirth, Heinz
See also CAAS 4; DLB 299; EWL 3

Lindbergh, Anne (Spencer) Morrow
1906-2001 .... **CLC 82**
See also BPFB 2; CA 17-20R; 193; CANR 16, 73; DAM NOV; MTCW 1, 2; MTFW 2005; SATA 33; SATA-Obit 125; TUS

Lindsay, David 1878(?)-1945 .... **TCLC 15**
See also CA 113; 187; DLB 255; FANT; SFW 4; SUFW 1

Lindsay, (Nicholas) Vachel
1879-1931 .... **PC 23; TCLC 17; WLC**
See also AMWS 1; CA 114; 135; CANR 79; CDALB 1865-1917; DA; DA3; DAC; DAM MST, POET; DLB 54; EWL 3; EXPP; MAL 5; RGAL 4; SATA 40; WP

Linke-Poot
See Doeblin, Alfred

Linney, Romulus 1930- .... **CLC 51**
See also CA 1-4R; CAD; CANR 40, 44, 79; CD 5, 6; CSW; RGAL 4

Linton, Eliza Lynn 1822-1898 .... **NCLC 41**
See also DLB 18

Li Po 701-763 .... **CMLC 2; PC 29**
See also PFS 20; WP

Lipsius, Justus 1547-1606 .... **LC 16**

Lipsyte, Robert (Michael) 1938- ..... **CLC 21**
See also AAYA 7, 45; CA 17-20R; CANR 8, 57; CLR 23, 76; DA; DAC; DAM MST, NOV; JRDA; LAIT 5; MAICYA 1, 2; SATA 5, 68, 113, 161; WYA; YAW

Lish, Gordon (Jay) 1934- ... **CLC 45; SSC 18**
See also CA 113; 117; CANR 79; DLB 130; INT CA-117

Lispector, Clarice 1925(?)-1977 .... **CLC 43; HLCS 2; SSC 34**
See also CA 139; 116; CANR 71; CDWLB 3; DLB 113, 307; DNFS 1; EWL 3; FW; HW 2; LAW; RGSF 2; RGWL 2, 3; WLIT 1

Littell, Robert 1935(?)- .... **CLC 42**
See also CA 109; 112; CANR 64, 115; CMW 4

Little, Malcolm 1925-1965
See Malcolm X
See also BW 1, 3; CA 125; 111; CANR 82; DA; DA3; DAB; DAC; DAM MST, MULT; MTCW 1, 2; MTFW 2005

Littlewit, Humphrey Gent.
See Lovecraft, H(oward) P(hillips)

Litwos
See Sienkiewicz, Henryk (Adam Alexander Pius)

Liu, E. 1857-1909 .... **TCLC 15**
See also CA 115; 190

Lively, Penelope 1933- .... **CLC 32, 50**
See also BPFB 2; CA 41-44R; CANR 29, 67, 79, 131; CLR 7; CN 5, 6, 7; CWRI 5; DAM NOV; DLB 14, 161, 207; FANT; JRDA; MAICYA 1, 2; MTCW 1, 2; MTFW 2005; SATA 7, 60, 101, 164; TEA

Lively, Penelope Margaret
See Lively, Penelope

Livesay, Dorothy (Kathleen)
1909-1996 .... **CLC 4, 15, 79**
See also AITN 2; CA 25-28R; CAAS 8; CANR 36, 67; CP 1, 2, 3, 4; DAC; DAM MST, POET; DLB 68; FW; MTCW 1; RGEL 2; TWA

Livy c. 59B.C.-c. 12 .... **CMLC 11**
See also AW 2; CDWLB 1; DLB 211; RGWL 2, 3

Lizardi, Jose Joaquin Fernandez de
1776-1827 .... **NCLC 30**
See also LAW

Llewellyn, Richard
See Llewellyn Lloyd, Richard Dafydd Vivian
See also DLB 15

Llewellyn Lloyd, Richard Dafydd Vivian
1906-1983 .... **CLC 7, 80**
See Llewellyn, Richard
See also CA 53-56; 111; CANR 7, 71; SATA 11; SATA-Obit 37

Llosa, (Jorge) Mario (Pedro) Vargas
See Vargas Llosa, (Jorge) Mario (Pedro)
See also RGWL 3

Llosa, Mario Vargas
See Vargas Llosa, (Jorge) Mario (Pedro)

Lloyd, Manda
See Mander, (Mary) Jane

Lloyd Webber, Andrew 1948-
See Webber, Andrew Lloyd
See also AAYA 1, 38; CA 116; 149; DAM DRAM; SATA 56

Llull, Ramon c. 1235-c. 1316 .... **CMLC 12**

Lobb, Ebenezer
See Upward, Allen

Locke, Alain (Le Roy)
1886-1954 .... **BLCS; HR 1:3; TCLC 43**
See also AMWS 14; BW 1, 3; CA 106; 124; CANR 79; DLB 51; LMFS 2; MAL 5; RGAL 4

Locke, John 1632-1704 .... **LC 7, 35**
See also DLB 31, 101, 213, 252; RGEL 2; WLIT 3

Locke-Elliott, Sumner
See Elliott, Sumner Locke

Lockhart, John Gibson 1794-1854 .. **NCLC 6**
See also DLB 110, 116, 144

Lockridge, Ross (Franklin), Jr.
1914-1948 .... **TCLC 111**
See also CA 108; 145; CANR 79; DLB 143; DLBY 1980; MAL 5; RGAL 4; RHW

Lockwood, Robert
See Johnson, Robert

Lodge, David (John) 1935- .... **CLC 36, 141**
See also BEST 90:1; BRWS 4; CA 17-20R; CANR 19, 53, 92, 139; CN 1, 2, 3, 4, 5, 6, 7; CPW; DAM POP; DLB 14, 194; EWL 3; INT CANR-19; MTCW 1, 2; MTFW 2005

Lodge, Thomas 1558-1625 .... **LC 41**
See also DLB 172; RGEL 2

Loewinsohn, Ron(ald William)
1937- .... **CLC 52**
See also CA 25-28R; CANR 71; CP 1, 2, 3, 4

Logan, Jake
See Smith, Martin Cruz

Logan, John (Burton) 1923-1987 .... **CLC 5**
See also CA 77-80; 124; CANR 45; CP 1, 2, 3, 4; DLB 5

Lo Kuan-chung 1330(?)-1400(?) .... **LC 12**

Lombard, Nap
See Johnson, Pamela Hansford

Lombard, Peter 1100(?)-1160(?) ... **CMLC 72**

London, Jack 1876-1916 .. **SSC 4, 49; TCLC 9, 15, 39; WLC**
See London, John Griffith
See also AAYA 13; AITN 2; AMW; BPFB 2; BYA 4, 13; CDALB 1865-1917; DLB 8, 12, 78, 212; EWL 3; EXPS; LAIT 3; MAL 5; NFS 8; RGAL 4; RGSF 2; SATA 18; SFW 4; SSFS 7; TCWW 1, 2; TUS; WYA; YAW

London, John Griffith 1876-1916
See London, Jack
See also CA 110; 119; CANR 73; DA; DA3; DAB; DAC; DAM MST, NOV; JRDA; MAICYA 1, 2; MTCW 1, 2; MTFW 2005; NFS 19

Long, Emmett
See Leonard, Elmore (John, Jr.)

Longbaugh, Harry
See Goldman, William (W.)

Longfellow, Henry Wadsworth
1807-1882 .... **NCLC 2, 45, 101, 103; PC 30; WLCS**
See also AMW; AMWR 2; CDALB 1640-1865; CLR 99; DA; DA3; DAC; DAM MST, POET; DLB 1, 59, 235; EXPP; PAB; PFS 2, 7, 17; RGAL 4; SATA 19; TUS; WP

Longinus c. 1st cent. - .... **CMLC 27**
See also AW 2; DLB 176

Longley, Michael 1939- .... **CLC 29**
See also BRWS 8; CA 102; CP 1, 2, 3, 4, 5, 6, 7; DLB 40

Longstreet, Augustus Baldwin
1790-1870 .... **NCLC 159**
See also DLB 3, 11, 74, 248; RGAL 4

Longus fl. c. 2nd cent. - .... **CMLC 7**

Longway, A. Hugh
See Lang, Andrew

Lonnbohm, Armas Eino Leopold 1878-1926
See Leino, Eino
See also CA 123

Lonnrot, Elias 1802-1884 .... **NCLC 53**
See also EFS 1

Lonsdale, Roger ed. .... **CLC 65**

Lopate, Phillip 1943- .... **CLC 29**
See also CA 97-100; CANR 88; DLBY 1980; INT CA-97-100

Lopez, Barry (Holstun) 1945- .... **CLC 70**
See also AAYA 9, 63; ANW; CA 65-68; CANR 7, 23, 47, 68, 92; DLB 256, 275; INT CANR-7, -23; MTCW 1; RGAL 4; SATA 67

Lopez de Mendoza, Inigo
See Santillana, Inigo Lopez de Mendoza, Marques de

Lopez Portillo (y Pacheco), Jose
1920-2004 .... **CLC 46**
See also CA 129; 224; HW 1

Lopez y Fuentes, Gregorio
1897(?)-1966 .... **CLC 32**
See also CA 131; EWL 3; HW 1

Lorca, Federico Garcia
See Garcia Lorca, Federico
See also DFS 4; EW 11; PFS 20; RGWL 2, 3; WP

Lord, Audre
See Lorde, Audre (Geraldine)
See also EWL 3

Lord, Bette Bao 1938- .... **AAL; CLC 23**
See also BEST 90:3; BPFB 2; CA 107; CANR 41, 79; INT CA-107; SATA 58

Lord Auch
See Bataille, Georges

Lord Brooke
See Greville, Fulke

Lord Byron
See Byron, George Gordon (Noel)

Lorde, Audre (Geraldine)
1934-1992 .... **BLC 2; CLC 18, 71; PC 12; TCLC 173**
See Domini, Rey; Lord, Audre
See also AFAW 1, 2; BW 1, 3; CA 25-28R; 142; CANR 16, 26, 46, 82; CP 2, 3, 4; DA3; DAM MULT, POET; DLB 41; FW; MAL 5; MTCW 1, 2; MTFW 2005; PFS 16; RGAL 4

Lord Houghton
See Milnes, Richard Monckton

MacDonald, John D(ann)
1916-1986 .... **CLC 3, 27, 44**
See also BPFB 2; CA 1-4R; 121; CANR 1, 19, 60; CMW 4; CPW; DAM NOV, POP; DLB 8, 306; DLBY 1986; MSW; MTCW 1, 2; MTFW 2005; SFW 4

Macdonald, John Ross
See Millar, Kenneth

Macdonald, Ross ..... **CLC 1, 2, 3, 14, 34, 41**
See Millar, Kenneth
See also AMWS 4; BPFB 2; CN 1, 2, 3; DLBD 6; MSW; RGAL 4

MacDougal, John
See Blish, James (Benjamin)

MacDougal, John
See Blish, James (Benjamin)

MacDowell, John
See Parks, Tim(othy Harold)

MacEwen, Gwendolyn (Margaret)
1941-1987 .... **CLC 13, 55**
See also CA 9-12R; 124; CANR 7, 22; CP 1, 2, 3, 4; DLB 53, 251; SATA 50; SATA-Obit 55

Macha, Karel Hynek 1810-1846 .... **NCLC 46**

Machado (y Ruiz), Antonio
1875-1939 .... **TCLC 3**
See also CA 104; 174; DLB 108; EW 9; EWL 3; HW 2; PFS 23; RGWL 2, 3

Machado de Assis, Joaquim Maria
1839-1908 .... **BLC 2; HLCS 2; SSC 24; TCLC 10**
See also CA 107; 153; CANR 91; DLB 307; LAW; RGSF 2; RGWL 2, 3; TWA; WLIT 1

Machaut, Guillaume de c.
1300-1377 .... **CMLC 64**
See also DLB 208

Machen, Arthur .... **SSC 20; TCLC 4**
See Jones, Arthur Llewellyn
See also CA 179; DLB 156, 178; RGEL 2; SUFW 1

Machiavelli, Niccolo 1469-1527 ... **DC 16; LC 8, 36; WLCS**
See also AAYA 58; DA; DAB; DAC; DAM MST; EW 2; LAIT 1; LMFS 1; NFS 9; RGWL 2, 3; TWA; WLIT 7

MacInnes, Colin 1914-1976 .... **CLC 4, 23**
See also CA 69-72; 65-68; CANR 21; CN 1, 2; DLB 14; MTCW 1, 2; RGEL 2; RHW

MacInnes, Helen (Clark)
1907-1985 .... **CLC 27, 39**
See also BPFB 2; CA 1-4R; 117; CANR 1, 28, 58; CMW 4; CN 1, 2; CPW; DAM POP; DLB 87; MSW; MTCW 1, 2; MTFW 2005; SATA 22; SATA-Obit 44

Mackay, Mary 1855-1924
See Corelli, Marie
See also CA 118; 177; FANT; RHW

Mackay, Shena 1944- .... **CLC 195**
See also CA 104; CANR 88, 139; DLB 231, 319; MTFW 2005

Mackenzie, Compton (Edward Montague)
1883-1972 .... **CLC 18; TCLC 116**
See also CA 21-22; 37-40R; CAP 2; CN 1; DLB 34, 100; RGEL 2

Mackenzie, Henry 1745-1831 .... **NCLC 41**
See also DLB 39; RGEL 2

Mackey, Nathaniel (Ernest) 1947- .... **PC 49**
See also CA 153; CANR 114; CP 7; DLB 169

MacKinnon, Catharine A. 1946- .... **CLC 181**
See also CA 128; 132; CANR 73, 140; FW; MTCW 2; MTFW 2005

Mackintosh, Elizabeth 1896(?)-1952
See Tey, Josephine
See also CA 110; CMW 4

MacLaren, James
See Grieve, C(hristopher) M(urray)

MacLaverty, Bernard 1942- .... **CLC 31**
See also CA 116; 118; CANR 43, 88; CN 5, 6, 7; DLB 267; INT CA-118; RGSF 2

MacLean, Alistair (Stuart)
1922(?)-1987 .... **CLC 3, 13, 50, 63**
See also CA 57-60; 121; CANR 28, 61; CMW 4; CP 2, 3, 4, 5, 6, 7; CPW; DAM POP; DLB 276; MTCW 1; SATA 23; SATA-Obit 50; TCWW 2

Maclean, Norman (Fitzroy)
1902-1990 .... **CLC 78; SSC 13**
See also AMWS 14; CA 102; 132; CANR 49; CPW; DAM POP; DLB 206; TCWW 2

MacLeish, Archibald 1892-1982 ... **CLC 3, 8, 14, 68; PC 47**
See also AMW; CA 9-12R; 106; CAD; CANR 33, 63; CDALBS; CP 1, 2; DAM POET; DFS 15; DLB 4, 7, 45; DLBY 1982; EWL 3; EXPP; MAL 5; MTCW 1, 2; MTFW 2005; PAB; PFS 5; RGAL 4; TUS

MacLennan, (John) Hugh
1907-1990 .... **CLC 2, 14, 92**
See also CA 5-8R; 142; CANR 33; CN 1, 2, 3, 4; DAC; DAM MST; DLB 68; EWL 3; MTCW 1, 2; MTFW 2005; RGEL 2; TWA

MacLeod, Alistair 1936- .... **CLC 56, 165**
See also CA 123; CCA 1; DAC; DAM MST; DLB 60; MTCW 2; MTFW 2005; RGSF 2; TCLE 1:2

Macleod, Fiona
See Sharp, William
See also RGEL 2; SUFW

MacNeice, (Frederick) Louis
1907-1963 .... **CLC 1, 4, 10, 53; PC 61**
See also BRW 7; CA 85-88; CANR 61; DAB; DAM POET; DLB 10, 20; EWL 3; MTCW 1, 2; MTFW 2005; RGEL 2

MacNeill, Dand
See Fraser, George MacDonald

Macpherson, James 1736-1796 .... **LC 29**
See Ossian
See also BRWS 8; DLB 109; RGEL 2

Macpherson, (Jean) Jay 1931- .... **CLC 14**
See also CA 5-8R; CANR 90; CP 1, 2, 3, 4, 5, 6, 7; CWP; DLB 53

Macrobius fl. 430- .... **CMLC 48**

MacShane, Frank 1927-1999 .... **CLC 39**
See also CA 9-12R; 186; CANR 3, 33; DLB 111

Macumber, Mari
See Sandoz, Mari(e Susette)

Madach, Imre 1823-1864 .... **NCLC 19**

Madden, (Jerry) David 1933- .... **CLC 5, 15**
See also CA 1-4R; CAAS 3; CANR 4, 45; CN 3, 4, 5, 6, 7; CSW; DLB 6; MTCW 1

Maddern, Al(an)
See Ellison, Harlan (Jay)

Madhubuti, Haki R. 1942- ... **BLC 2; CLC 6, 73; PC 5**
See Lee, Don L.
See also BW 2, 3; CA 73-76; CANR 24, 51, 73, 139; CP 5, 6, 7; CSW; DAM MULT, POET; DLB 5, 41; DLBD 8; EWL 3; MAL 5; MTCW 2; MTFW 2005; RGAL 4

Madison, James 1751-1836 .... **NCLC 126**
See also DLB 37

Maepenn, Hugh
See Kuttner, Henry

Maepenn, K. H.
See Kuttner, Henry

Maeterlinck, Maurice 1862-1949 ..... **TCLC 3**
See also CA 104; 136; CANR 80; DAM DRAM; DLB 192; EW 8; EWL 3; GFL 1789 to the Present; LMFS 2; RGWL 2, 3; SATA 66; TWA

Maginn, William 1794-1842 .... **NCLC 8**
See also DLB 110, 159

Mahapatra, Jayanta 1928- .... **CLC 33**
See also CA 73-76; CAAS 9; CANR 15, 33, 66, 87; CP 4, 5, 6, 7; DAM MULT

Mahfouz, Naguib (Abdel Aziz Al-Sabilgi)
1911(?)- .... **CLC 153; SSC 66**
See Mahfuz, Najib (Abdel Aziz al-Sabilgi)
See also AAYA 49; BEST 89:2; CA 128; CANR 55, 101; DA3; DAM NOV; MTCW 1, 2; MTFW 2005; RGWL 2, 3; SSFS 9

Mahfuz, Najib (Abdel Aziz al-Sabilgi)
.... **CLC 52, 55**
See Mahfouz, Naguib (Abdel Aziz Al-Sabilgi)
See also AFW; CWW 2; DLBY 1988; EWL 3; RGSF 2; WLIT 6

Mahon, Derek 1941- .... **CLC 27; PC 60**
See also BRWS 6; CA 113; 128; CANR 88; CP 1, 2, 3, 4, 5, 6, 7; DLB 40; EWL 3

Maiakovskii, Vladimir
See Mayakovski, Vladimir (Vladimirovich)
See also IDTP; RGWL 2, 3

Mailer, Norman (Kingsley) 1923- . **CLC 1, 2, 3, 4, 5, 8, 11, 14, 28, 39, 74, 111**
See also AAYA 31; AITN 2; AMW; AMWC 2; AMWR 2; BPFB 2; CA 9-12R; CABS 1; CANR 28, 74, 77, 130; CDALB 1968-1988; CN 1, 2, 3, 4, 5, 6, 7; CPW; DA; DA3; DAB; DAC; DAM MST, NOV, POP; DLB 2, 16, 28, 185, 278; DLBD 3; DLBY 1980, 1983; EWL 3; MAL 5; MTCW 1, 2; MTFW 2005; NFS 10; RGAL 4; TUS

Maillet, Antonine 1929- .... **CLC 54, 118**
See also CA 115; 120; CANR 46, 74, 77, 134; CCA 1; CWW 2; DAC; DLB 60; INT CA-120; MTCW 2; MTFW 2005

Maimonides, Moses 1135-1204 ..... **CMLC 76**
See also DLB 115

Mais, Roger 1905-1955 .... **TCLC 8**
See also BW 1, 3; CA 105; 124; CANR 82; CDWLB 3; DLB 125; EWL 3; MTCW 1; RGEL 2

Maistre, Joseph 1753-1821 .... **NCLC 37**
See also GFL 1789 to the Present

Maitland, Frederic William
1850-1906 .... **TCLC 65**

Maitland, Sara (Louise) 1950- .... **CLC 49**
See also BRWS 11; CA 69-72; CANR 13, 59; DLB 271; FW

Major, Clarence 1936- ... **BLC 2; CLC 3, 19, 48**
See also AFAW 2; BW 2, 3; CA 21-24R; CAAS 6; CANR 13, 25, 53, 82; CN 3, 4, 5, 6, 7; CP 2, 3, 4, 5, 6, 7; CSW; DAM MULT; DLB 33; EWL 3; MAL 5; MSW

Major, Kevin (Gerald) 1949- .... **CLC 26**
See also AAYA 16; CA 97-100; CANR 21, 38, 112; CLR 11; DAC; DLB 60; INT CANR-21; JRDA; MAICYA 1, 2; MAICYAS 1; SATA 32, 82, 134; WYA; YAW

Maki, James
See Ozu, Yasujiro

Makine, Andrei 1957- .... **CLC 198**
See also CA 176; CANR 103; MTFW 2005

Malabaila, Damiano
See Levi, Primo

Malamud, Bernard 1914-1986 .. **CLC 1, 2, 3, 5, 8, 9, 11, 18, 27, 44, 78, 85; SSC 15; TCLC 129; WLC**
See also AAYA 16; AMWS 1; BPFB 2; BYA 15; CA 5-8R; 118; CABS 1; CANR 28, 62, 114; CDALB 1941-1968; CN 1, 2, 3, 4; CPW; DA; DA3; DAB; DAC; DAM MST, NOV, POP; DLB 2, 28, 152; DLBY

McGinley, Patrick (Anthony) 1937- . **CLC 41**
See also CA 120; 127; CANR 56; INT CA-127

McGinley, Phyllis 1905-1978 .... **CLC 14**
See also CA 9-12R; 77-80; CANR 19; CP 1, 2; CWRI 5; DLB 11, 48; MAL 5; PFS 9, 13; SATA 2, 44; SATA-Obit 24

McGinniss, Joe 1942- .... **CLC 32**
See also AITN 2; BEST 89:2; CA 25-28R; CANR 26, 70; CPW; DLB 185; INT CANR-26

McGivern, Maureen Daly
See Daly, Maureen

McGrath, Patrick 1950- .... **CLC 55**
See also CA 136; CANR 65; CN 5, 6, 7; DLB 231; HGG; SUFW 2

McGrath, Thomas (Matthew)
1916-1990 .... **CLC 28, 59**
See also AMWS 10; CA 9-12R; 132; CANR 6, 33, 95; CP 1, 2, 3, 4; DAM POET; MAL 5; MTCW 1; SATA 41; SATA-Obit 66

McGuane, Thomas (Francis III)
1939- .... **CLC 3, 7, 18, 45, 127**
See also AITN 2; BPFB 2; CA 49-52; CANR 5, 24, 49, 94; CN 2, 3, 4, 5, 6, 7; DLB 2, 212; DLBY 1980; EWL 3; INT CANR-24; MAL 5; MTCW 1; MTFW 2005; TCWW 1, 2

McGuckian, Medbh 1950- .... **CLC 48, 174; PC 27**
See also BRWS 5; CA 143; CP 4, 5, 6, 7; CWP; DAM POET; DLB 40

McHale, Tom 1942(?)-1982 .... **CLC 3, 5**
See also AITN 1; CA 77-80; 106; CN 1, 2, 3

McHugh, Heather 1948- .... **PC 61**
See also CA 69-72; CANR 11, 28, 55, 92; CP 4, 5, 6, 7; CWP

McIlvanney, William 1936- .... **CLC 42**
See also CA 25-28R; CANR 61; CMW 4; DLB 14, 207

McIlwraith, Maureen Mollie Hunter
See Hunter, Mollie
See also SATA 2

McInerney, Jay 1955- .... **CLC 34, 112**
See also AAYA 18; BPFB 2; CA 116; 123; CANR 45, 68, 116; CN 5, 6, 7; CPW; DA3; DAM POP; DLB 292; INT CA-123; MAL 5; MTCW 2; MTFW 2005

McIntyre, Vonda N(eel) 1948- .... **CLC 18**
See also CA 81-84; CANR 17, 34, 69; MTCW 1; SFW 4; YAW

McKay, Claude .... **BLC 3; HR 1:3; PC 2; TCLC 7, 41; WLC**
See McKay, Festus Claudius
See also AFAW 1, 2; AMWS 10; DAB; DLB 4, 45, 51, 117; EWL 3; EXPP; GLL 2; LAIT 3; LMFS 2; MAL 5; PAB; PFS 4; RGAL 4; WP

McKay, Festus Claudius 1889-1948
See McKay, Claude
See also BW 1, 3; CA 104; 124; CANR 73; DA; DAC; DAM MST, MULT, NOV, POET; MTCW 1, 2; MTFW 2005; TUS

McKuen, Rod 1933- .... **CLC 1, 3**
See also AITN 1; CA 41-44R; CANR 40; CP 1

McLoughlin, R. B.
See Mencken, H(enry) L(ouis)

McLuhan, (Herbert) Marshall
1911-1980 .... **CLC 37, 83**
See also CA 9-12R; 102; CANR 12, 34, 61; DLB 88; INT CANR-12; MTCW 1, 2; MTFW 2005

McManus, Declan Patrick Aloysius
See Costello, Elvis

McMillan, Terry (L.) 1951- . **BLCS; CLC 50, 61, 112**
See also AAYA 21; AMWS 13; BPFB 2; BW 2, 3; CA 140; CANR 60, 104, 131; CN 7; CPW; DA3; DAM MULT, NOV, POP; MAL 5; MTCW 2; MTFW 2005; RGAL 4; YAW

McMurtry, Larry 1936- .... **CLC 2, 3, 7, 11, 27, 44, 127**
See also AAYA 15; AITN 2; AMWS 5; BEST 89:2; BPFB 2; CA 5-8R; CANR 19, 43, 64, 103; CDALB 1968-1988; CN 2, 3, 4, 5, 6, 7; CPW; CSW; DA3; DAM NOV, POP; DLB 2, 143, 256; DLBY 1980; EWL 3; MAL 5; MTCW 1, 2; MTFW 2005; RGAL 4; TCWW 1, 2

McNally, T. M. 1961- .... **CLC 82**

McNally, Terrence 1939- ... **CLC 4, 7, 41, 91; DC 27**
See also AAYA 62; AMWS 13; CA 45-48; CAD; CANR 2, 56, 116; CD 5, 6; DA3; DAM DRAM; DFS 16, 19; DLB 7, 249; EWL 3; GLL 1; MTCW 2; MTFW 2005

McNamer, Deirdre 1950- .... **CLC 70**

McNeal, Tom .... **CLC 119**

McNeile, Herman Cyril 1888-1937
See Sapper
See also CA 184; CMW 4; DLB 77

McNickle, (William) D'Arcy
1904-1977 .... **CLC 89; NNAL**
See also CA 9-12R; 85-88; CANR 5, 45; DAM MULT; DLB 175, 212; RGAL 4; SATA-Obit 22; TCWW 1, 2

McPhee, John (Angus) 1931- .... **CLC 36**
See also AAYA 61; AMWS 3; ANW; BEST 90:1; CA 65-68; CANR 20, 46, 64, 69, 121; CPW; DLB 185, 275; MTCW 1, 2; MTFW 2005; TUS

McPherson, James Alan 1943- . **BLCS; CLC 19, 77**
See also BW 1, 3; CA 25-28R; CAAS 17; CANR 24, 74, 140; CN 3, 4, 5, 6; CSW; DLB 38, 244; EWL 3; MTCW 1, 2; MTFW 2005; RGAL 4; RGSF 2

McPherson, William (Alexander)
1933- .... **CLC 34**
See also CA 69-72; CANR 28; INT CANR-28

McTaggart, J. McT. Ellis
See McTaggart, John McTaggart Ellis

McTaggart, John McTaggart Ellis
1866-1925 .... **TCLC 105**
See also CA 120; DLB 262

Mead, George Herbert 1863-1931 . **TCLC 89**
See also CA 212; DLB 270

Mead, Margaret 1901-1978 .... **CLC 37**
See also AITN 1; CA 1-4R; 81-84; CANR 4; DA3; FW; MTCW 1, 2; SATA-Obit 20

Meaker, Marijane (Agnes) 1927-
See Kerr, M. E.
See also CA 107; CANR 37, 63, 145; INT CA-107; JRDA; MAICYA 1, 2; MAIC-YAS 1; MTCW 1; SATA 20, 61, 99, 160; SATA-Essay 111; YAW

Medoff, Mark (Howard) 1940- .... **CLC 6, 23**
See also AITN 1; CA 53-56; CAD; CANR 5; CD 5, 6; DAM DRAM; DFS 4; DLB 7; INT CANR-5

Medvedev, P. N.
See Bakhtin, Mikhail Mikhailovich

Meged, Aharon
See Megged, Aharon

Meged, Aron
See Megged, Aharon

Megged, Aharon 1920- .... **CLC 9**
See also CA 49-52; CAAS 13; CANR 1, 140; EWL 3

Mehta, Deepa 1950- .... **CLC 208**

Mehta, Gita 1943- .... **CLC 179**
See also CA 225; CN 7; DNFS 2

Mehta, Ved (Parkash) 1934- .... **CLC 37**
See also CA 1-4R, 212; CAAE 212; CANR 2, 23, 69; MTCW 1; MTFW 2005

Melanchthon, Philipp 1497-1560 .... **LC 90**
See also DLB 179

Melanter
See Blackmore, R(ichard) D(oddridge)

Meleager c. 140B.C.-c. 70B.C. ...... **CMLC 53**

Melies, Georges 1861-1938 .... **TCLC 81**

Melikow, Loris
See Hofmannsthal, Hugo von

Melmoth, Sebastian
See Wilde, Oscar (Fingal O'Flahertie Wills)

Melo Neto, Joao Cabral de
See Cabral de Melo Neto, Joao
See also CWW 2; EWL 3

Meltzer, Milton 1915- .... **CLC 26**
See also AAYA 8, 45; BYA 2, 6; CA 13-16R; CANR 38, 92, 107; CLR 13; DLB 61; JRDA; MAICYA 1, 2; SAAS 1; SATA 1, 50, 80, 128; SATA-Essay 124; WYA; YAW

Melville, Herman 1819-1891 ..... **NCLC 3, 12, 29, 45, 49, 91, 93, 123, 157; SSC 1, 17, 46; WLC**
See also AAYA 25; AMW; AMWR 1; CDALB 1640-1865; DA; DA3; DAB; DAC; DAM MST, NOV; DLB 3, 74, 250, 254; EXPN; EXPS; GL 3; LAIT 1, 2; NFS 7, 9; RGAL 4; RGSF 2; SATA 59; SSFS 3; TUS

Members, Mark
See Powell, Anthony (Dymoke)

Membreno, Alejandro .... **CLC 59**

Menand, Louis 1952- .... **CLC 208**
See also CA 200

Menander c. 342B.C.-c. 293B.C. .... **CMLC 9, 51; DC 3**
See also AW 1; CDWLB 1; DAM DRAM; DLB 176; LMFS 1; RGWL 2, 3

Menchu, Rigoberta 1959- .. **CLC 160; HLCS 2**
See also CA 175; CANR 135; DNFS 1; WLIT 1

Mencken, H(enry) L(ouis)
1880-1956 .... **TCLC 13**
See also AMW; CA 105; 125; CDALB 1917-1929; DLB 11, 29, 63, 137, 222; EWL 3; MAL 5; MTCW 1, 2; MTFW 2005; NCFS 4; RGAL 4; TUS

Mendelsohn, Jane 1965- .... **CLC 99**
See also CA 154; CANR 94

Mendoza, Inigo Lopez de
See Santillana, Inigo Lopez de Mendoza, Marques de

Menton, Francisco de
See Chin, Frank (Chew, Jr.)

Mercer, David 1928-1980 .... **CLC 5**
See also CA 9-12R; 102; CANR 23; CBD; DAM DRAM; DLB 13, 310; MTCW 1; RGEL 2

Merchant, Paul
See Ellison, Harlan (Jay)

Meredith, George 1828-1909 .. **PC 60; TCLC 17, 43**
See also CA 117; 153; CANR 80; CDBLB 1832-1890; DAM POET; DLB 18, 35, 57, 159; RGEL 2; TEA

Meredith, William (Morris) 1919- .... **CLC 4, 13, 22, 55; PC 28**
See also CA 9-12R; CAAS 14; CANR 6, 40, 129; CP 1, 2, 3, 4, 5, 6, 7; DAM POET; DLB 5; MAL 5

Merezhkovsky, Dmitrii Sergeevich
See Merezhkovsky, Dmitry Sergeyevich
See also DLB 295

Merezhkovsky, Dmitry Sergeevich
See Merezhkovsky, Dmitry Sergeyevich
See also EWL 3

Merezhkovsky, Dmitry Sergeyevich
1865-1941 .... **TCLC 29**
See Merezhkovsky, Dmitrii Sergeevich;
Merezhkovsky, Dmitry Sergeevich
See also CA 169

Merimee, Prosper 1803-1870 ... **NCLC 6, 65;**
SSC 7, 77
See also DLB 119, 192; EW 6; EXPS; GFL
1789 to the Present; RGSF 2; RGWL 2,
3; SSFS 8; SUFW

Merkin, Daphne 1954- .... **CLC 44**
See also CA 123

Merleau-Ponty, Maurice
1908-1961 .... **TCLC 156**
See also CA 114; 89-92; DLB 296; GFL
1789 to the Present

Merlin, Arthur
See Blish, James (Benjamin)

Mernissi, Fatima 1940- .... **CLC 171**
See also CA 152; FW

Merrill, James (Ingram) 1926-1995 .. **CLC 2,**
3, 6, 8, 13, 18, 34, 91; PC 28; TCLC
173
See also AMWS 3; CA 13-16R; 147; CANR
10, 49, 63, 108; CP 1, 2, 3, 4; DA3; DAM
POET; DLB 5, 165; DLBY 1985; EWL 3;
INT CANR-10; MAL 5; MTCW 1, 2;
MTFW 2005; PAB; PFS 23; RGAL 4

Merriman, Alex
See Silverberg, Robert

Merriman, Brian 1747-1805 .... **NCLC 70**

Merritt, E. B.
See Waddington, Miriam

Merton, Thomas (James)
1915-1968 . **CLC 1, 3, 11, 34, 83; PC 10**
See also AAYA 61; AMWS 8; CA 5-8R;
25-28R; CANR 22, 53, 111, 131; DA3;
DLB 48; DLBY 1981; MAL 5; MTCW 1,
2; MTFW 2005

Merwin, W(illiam) S(tanley) 1927- ... **CLC 1,**
2, 3, 5, 8, 13, 18, 45, 88; PC 45
See also AMWS 3; CA 13-16R; CANR 15,
51, 112, 140; CP 1, 2, 3, 4, 5, 6, 7; DA3;
DAM POET; DLB 5, 169; EWL 3; INT
CANR-15; MAL 5; MTCW 1, 2; MTFW
2005; PAB; PFS 5, 15; RGAL 4

Metastasio, Pietro 1698-1782 .... **LC 115**
See also RGWL 2, 3

Metcalf, John 1938- .... **CLC 37; SSC 43**
See also CA 113; CN 4, 5, 6, 7; DLB 60;
RGSF 2; TWA

Metcalf, Suzanne
See Baum, L(yman) Frank

Mew, Charlotte (Mary) 1870-1928 .. **TCLC 8**
See also CA 105; 189; DLB 19, 135; RGEL
2

Mewshaw, Michael 1943- .... **CLC 9**
See also CA 53-56; CANR 7, 47; DLBY
1980

Meyer, Conrad Ferdinand
1825-1898 .... **NCLC 81; SSC 30**
See also DLB 129; EW; RGWL 2, 3

Meyer, Gustav 1868-1932
See Meyrink, Gustav
See also CA 117; 190

Meyer, June
See Jordan, June (Meyer)

Meyer, Lynn
See Slavitt, David R(ytman)

Meyers, Jeffrey 1939- .... **CLC 39**
See also CA 73-76, 186; CAAE 186; CANR
54, 102; DLB 111

Meynell, Alice (Christina Gertrude
Thompson) 1847-1922 .... **TCLC 6**
See also CA 104; 177; DLB 19, 98; RGEL
2

Meyrink, Gustav .... **TCLC 21**
See Meyer, Gustav
See also DLB 81; EWL 3

Michaels, Leonard 1933-2003 ..... **CLC 6, 25;**
SSC 16
See also CA 61-64; 216; CANR 21, 62, 119;
CN 3, 45, 6, 7; DLB 130; MTCW 1;
TCLE 1:2

Michaux, Henri 1899-1984 .... **CLC 8, 19**
See also CA 85-88; 114; DLB 258; EWL 3;
GFL 1789 to the Present; RGWL 2, 3

Micheaux, Oscar (Devereaux)
1884-1951 .... **TCLC 76**
See also BW 3; CA 174; DLB 50; TCWW
2

Michelangelo 1475-1564 .... **LC 12**
See also AAYA 43

Michelet, Jules 1798-1874 .... **NCLC 31**
See also EW 5; GFL 1789 to the Present

Michels, Robert 1876-1936 .... **TCLC 88**
See also CA 212

Michener, James A(lbert)
1907(?)-1997 .. **CLC 1, 5, 11, 29, 60, 109**
See also AAYA 27; AITN 1; BEST 90:1;
BPFB 2; CA 5-8R; 161; CANR 21, 45,
68; CN 1, 2, 3, 4, 5, 6; CPW; DA3; DAM
NOV, POP; DLB 6; MAL 5; MTCW 1, 2;
MTFW 2005; RHW; TCWW 1, 2

Mickiewicz, Adam 1798-1855 . **NCLC 3, 101;**
PC 38
See also EW 5; RGWL 2, 3

Middleton, (John) Christopher
1926- .... **CLC 13**
See also CA 13-16R; CANR 29, 54, 117;
CP 1, 2, 3, 4, 5, 6, 7; DLB 40

Middleton, Richard (Barham)
1882-1911 .... **TCLC 56**
See also CA 187; DLB 156; HGG

Middleton, Stanley 1919- .... **CLC 7, 38**
See also CA 25-28R; CAAS 23; CANR 21,
46, 81; CN 1, 2, 3, 4, 5, 6, 7; DLB 14

Middleton, Thomas 1580-1627 ...... **DC 5; LC**
33, 123
See also BRW 2; DAM DRAM, MST; DFS
18, 22; DLB 58; RGEL 2

Migueis, Jose Rodrigues 1901-1980 . **CLC 10**
See also DLB 287

Mikszath, Kalman 1847-1910 .... **TCLC 31**
See also CA 170

Miles, Jack .... **CLC 100**
See also CA 200

Miles, John Russiano
See Miles, Jack

Miles, Josephine (Louise)
1911-1985 .... **CLC 1, 2, 14, 34, 39**
See also CA 1-4R; 116; CANR 2, 55; CP 1,
2, 3, 4; DAM POET; DLB 48; MAL 5;
TCLE 1:2

Militant
See Sandburg, Carl (August)

Mill, Harriet (Hardy) Taylor
1807-1858 .... **NCLC 102**
See also FW

Mill, John Stuart 1806-1873 .... **NCLC 11, 58**
See also CDBLB 1832-1890; DLB 55, 190,
262; FW 1; RGEL 2; TEA

Millar, Kenneth 1915-1983 .... **CLC 14**
See Macdonald, Ross
See also CA 9-12R; 110; CANR 16, 63,
107; CMW 4; CPW; DA3; DAM POP;
DLB 2, 226; DLBD 6; DLBY 1983;
MTCW 1, 2; MTFW 2005

Millay, E. Vincent
See Millay, Edna St. Vincent

Millay, Edna St. Vincent 1892-1950 ..... **PC 6,**
61; TCLC 4, 49, 169; WLCS
See Boyd, Nancy
See also AMW; CA 104; 130; CDALB
1917-1929; DA; DA3; DAB; DAC; DAM
MST, POET; DLB 45, 249; EWL 3;
EXPP; FL 1:6; MAL 5; MAWW; MTCW
1, 2; MTFW 2005; PAB; PFS 3, 17;
RGAL 4; TUS; WP

Miller, Arthur 1915-2005 ..... **CLC 1, 2, 6, 10,**
15, 26, 47, 78, 179; DC 1; WLC
See also AAYA 15; AITN 1; AMW; AMWC
1; CA 1-4R; 236; CABS 3; CAD; CANR
2, 30, 54, 76, 132; CD 5, 6; CDALB
1941-1968; DA; DA3; DAB; DAC; DAM
DRAM, MST; DFS 1, 3, 8; DLB 7, 266;
EWL 3; LAIT 1, 4; LATS 1:2; MAL 5;
MTCW 1, 2; MTFW 2005; RGAL 4;
TUS; WYAS 1

Miller, Henry (Valentine)
1891-1980 .... **CLC 1, 2, 4, 9, 14, 43, 84;**
WLC
See also AMW; BPFB 2; CA 9-12R; 97-
100; CANR 33, 64; CDALB 1929-1941;
CN 1, 2; DA; DA3; DAB; DAC; DAM
MST, NOV; DLB 4, 9; DLBY 1980; EWL
3; MAL 5; MTCW 1, 2; MTFW 2005;
RGAL 4; TUS

Miller, Hugh 1802-1856 .... **NCLC 143**
See also DLB 190

Miller, Jason 1939(?)-2001 .... **CLC 2**
See also AITN 1; CA 73-76; 197; CAD;
CANR 130; DFS 12; DLB 7

Miller, Sue 1943- .... **CLC 44**
See also AMWS 12; BEST 90:3; CA 139;
CANR 59, 91, 128; DA3; DAM POP;
DLB 143

Miller, Walter M(ichael, Jr.)
1923-1996 .... **CLC 4, 30**
See also BPFB 2; CA 85-88; CANR 108;
DLB 8; SCFW 1, 2; SFW 4

Millett, Kate 1934- .... **CLC 67**
See also AITN 1; CA 73-76; CANR 32, 53,
76, 110; DA3; DLB 246; FW; GLL 1;
MTCW 1, 2; MTFW 2005

Millhauser, Steven (Lewis) 1943- .... **CLC 21,**
54, 109; SSC 57
See also CA 110; 111; CANR 63, 114, 133;
CN 6, 7; DA3; DLB 2; FANT; INT CA-
111; MAL 5; MTCW 2; MTFW 2005

Millin, Sarah Gertrude 1889-1968 ... **CLC 49**
See also CA 102; 93-96; DLB 225; EWL 3

Milne, A(lan) A(lexander)
1882-1956 .... **TCLC 6, 88**
See also BRWS 5; CA 104; 133; CLR 1,
26; CMW 4; CWRI 5; DA3; DAB; DAC;
DAM MST; DLB 10, 77, 100, 160; FANT;
MAICYA 1, 2; MTCW 1, 2; MTFW 2005;
RGEL 2; SATA 100; WCH; YABC 1

Milner, Ron(ald) 1938-2004 ..... **BLC 3; CLC**
56
See also AITN 1; BW 1; CA 73-76; 230;
CAD; CANR 24, 81; CD 5, 6; DAM
MULT; DLB 38; MAL 5; MTCW 1

Milnes, Richard Monckton
1809-1885 .... **NCLC 61**
See also DLB 32, 184

Milosz, Czeslaw 1911-2004 .... **CLC 5, 11, 22,**
31, 56, 82; PC 8; WLCS
See also AAYA 62; CA 81-84; 230; CANR
23, 51, 91, 126; CDWLB 4; CWW 2;
DA3; DAM MST, POET; DLB 215; EW
13; EWL 3; MTCW 1, 2; MTFW 2005;
PFS 16; RGWL 2, 3

Milton, John 1608-1674 ..... **LC 9, 43, 92; PC**
19, 72; WLC
See also AAYA 65; BRW 2; BRWR 2; CD-
BLB 1660-1789; DA; DA3; DAB; DAC;
DAM MST, POET; DLB 131, 151, 281;
EFS 1; EXPP; LAIT 1; PAB; PFS 3, 17;
RGEL 2; TEA; WLIT 3; WP

Min, Anchee 1957- .... **CLC 86**
See also CA 146; CANR 94, 137; MTFW 2005

Minehaha, Cornelius
See Wedekind, (Benjamin) Frank(lin)

Miner, Valerie 1947- .... **CLC 40**
See also CA 97-100; CANR 59; FW; GLL 2

Minimo, Duca
See D'Annunzio, Gabriele

Minot, Susan (Anderson) 1956- ...... **CLC 44, 159**
See also AMWS 6; CA 134; CANR 118; CN 6, 7

Minus, Ed 1938- .... **CLC 39**
See also CA 185

Mirabai 1498(?)-1550(?) .... **PC 48**

Miranda, Javier
See Bioy Casares, Adolfo
See also CWW 2

Mirbeau, Octave 1848-1917 .... **TCLC 55**
See also CA 216; DLB 123, 192; GFL 1789 to the Present

Mirikitani, Janice 1942- .... **AAL**
See also CA 211; DLB 312; RGAL 4

Mirk, John (?)-c. 1414 .... **LC 105**
See also DLB 146

Miro (Ferrer), Gabriel (Francisco Victor) 1879-1930 .... **TCLC 5**
See also CA 104; 185; DLB 322; EWL 3

Misharin, Alexandr .... **CLC 59**

Mishima, Yukio ..... **CLC 2, 4, 6, 9, 27; DC 1; SSC 4; TCLC 161**
See Hiraoka, Kimitake
See also AAYA 50; BPFB 2; GLL 1; MJW; RGSF 2; RGWL 2, 3; SSFS 5, 12

Mistral, Frederic 1830-1914 .... **TCLC 51**
See also CA 122; 213; GFL 1789 to the Present

Mistral, Gabriela
See Godoy Alcayaga, Lucila
See also DLB 283; DNFS 1; EWL 3; LAW; RGWL 2, 3; WP

Mistry, Rohinton 1952- ... **CLC 71, 196; SSC 73**
See also BRWS 10; CA 141; CANR 86, 114; CCA 1; CN 6, 7; DAC; SSFS 6

Mitchell, Clyde
See Ellison, Harlan (Jay)

Mitchell, Emerson Blackhorse Barney 1945- .... **NNAL**
See also CA 45-48

Mitchell, James Leslie 1901-1935
See Gibbon, Lewis Grassic
See also CA 104; 188; DLB 15

Mitchell, Joni 1943- .... **CLC 12**
See also CA 112; CCA 1

Mitchell, Joseph (Quincy) 1908-1996 .... **CLC 98**
See also CA 77-80; 152; CANR 69; CN 1, 2, 3, 4, 5, 6; CSW; DLB 185; DLBY 1996

Mitchell, Margaret (Munnerlyn) 1900-1949 .... **TCLC 11, 170**
See also AAYA 23; BPFB 2; BYA 1; CA 109; 125; CANR 55, 94; CDALBS; DA3; DAM NOV, POP; DLB 9; LAIT 2; MAL 5; MTCW 1, 2; MTFW 2005; NFS 9; RGAL 4; RHW; TUS; WYAS 1; YAW

Mitchell, Peggy
See Mitchell, Margaret (Munnerlyn)

Mitchell, S(ilas) Weir 1829-1914 .... **TCLC 36**
See also CA 165; DLB 202; RGAL 4

Mitchell, W(illiam) O(rmond) 1914-1998 .... **CLC 25**
See also CA 77-80; 165; CANR 15, 43; CN 1, 2, 3, 4, 5, 6; DAC; DAM MST; DLB 88; TCLE 1:2

Mitchell, William (Lendrum) 1879-1936 .... **TCLC 81**
See also CA 213

Mitford, Mary Russell 1787-1855 ... **NCLC 4**
See also DLB 110, 116; RGEL 2

Mitford, Nancy 1904-1973 .... **CLC 44**
See also BRWS 10; CA 9-12R; CN 1; DLB 191; RGEL 2

Miyamoto, (Chujo) Yuriko 1899-1951 .... **TCLC 37**
See Miyamoto Yuriko
See also CA 170, 174

Miyamoto Yuriko
See Miyamoto, (Chujo) Yuriko
See also DLB 180

Miyazawa, Kenji 1896-1933 .... **TCLC 76**
See Miyazawa Kenji
See also CA 157; RGWL 3

Miyazawa Kenji
See Miyazawa, Kenji
See also EWL 3

Mizoguchi, Kenji 1898-1956 .... **TCLC 72**
See also CA 167

Mo, Timothy (Peter) 1950- .... **CLC 46, 134**
See also CA 117; CANR 128; CN 5, 6, 7; DLB 194; MTCW 1; WLIT 4; WWE 1

Modarressi, Taghi (M.) 1931-1997 .... **CLC 44**
See also CA 121; 134; INT CA-134

Modiano, Patrick (Jean) 1945- .... **CLC 18, 218**
See also CA 85-88; CANR 17, 40, 115; CWW 2; DLB 83, 299; EWL 3

Mofolo, Thomas (Mokopu) 1875(?)-1948 .... **BLC 3; TCLC 22**
See also AFW; CA 121; 153; CANR 83; DAM MULT; DLB 225; EWL 3; MTCW 2; MTFW 2005; WLIT 2

Mohr, Nicholasa 1938- .... **CLC 12; HLC 2**
See also AAYA 8, 46; CA 49-52; CANR 1, 32, 64; CLR 22; DAM MULT; DLB 145; HW 1, 2; JRDA; LAIT 5; LLW; MAICYA 2; MAICYAS 1; RGAL 4; SAAS 8; SATA 8, 97; SATA-Essay 113; WYA; YAW

Moi, Toril 1953- .... **CLC 172**
See also CA 154; CANR 102; FW

Mojtabai, A(nn) G(race) 1938- ..... **CLC 5, 9, 15, 29**
See also CA 85-88; CANR 88

Moliere 1622-1673 ..... **DC 13; LC 10, 28, 64; WLC**
See also DA; DA3; DAB; DAC; DAM DRAM, MST; DFS 13, 18, 20; DLB 268; EW 3; GFL Beginnings to 1789; LATS 1:1; RGWL 2, 3; TWA

Molin, Charles
See Mayne, William (James Carter)

Molnar, Ferenc 1878-1952 .... **TCLC 20**
See also CA 109; 153; CANR 83; CDWLB 4; DAM DRAM; DLB 215; EWL 3; RGWL 2, 3

Momaday, N(avarre) Scott 1934- ...... **CLC 2, 19, 85, 95, 160; NNAL; PC 25; WLCS**
See also AAYA 11, 64; AMWS 4; ANW; BPFB 2; BYA 12; CA 25-28R; CANR 14, 34, 68, 134; CDALBS; CN 2, 3, 4, 5, 6, 7; CPW; DA; DA3; DAB; DAC; DAM MST, MULT, NOV, POP; DLB 143, 175, 256; EWL 3; EXPP; INT CANR-14; LAIT 4; LATS 1:2; MAL 5; MTCW 1, 2; MTFW 2005; NFS 10; PFS 2, 11; RGAL 4; SATA 48; SATA-Brief 30; TCWW 1, 2; WP; YAW

Monette, Paul 1945-1995 .... **CLC 82**
See also AMWS 10; CA 139; 147; CN 6; GLL 1

Monroe, Harriet 1860-1936 .... **TCLC 12**
See also CA 109; 204; DLB 54, 91

Monroe, Lyle
See Heinlein, Robert A(nson)

Montagu, Elizabeth 1720-1800 .... **NCLC 7, 117**
See also FW

Montagu, Mary (Pierrepont) Wortley 1689-1762 .... **LC 9, 57; PC 16**
See also DLB 95, 101; FL 1:1; RGEL 2

Montagu, W. H.
See Coleridge, Samuel Taylor

Montague, John (Patrick) 1929- ..... **CLC 13, 46**
See also CA 9-12R; CANR 9, 69, 121; CP 1, 2, 3, 4, 5, 6, 7; DLB 40; EWL 3; MTCW 1; PFS 12; RGEL 2; TCLE 1:2

Montaigne, Michel (Eyquem) de 1533-1592 .... **LC 8, 105; WLC**
See also DA; DAB; DAC; DAM MST; EW 2; GFL Beginnings to 1789; LMFS 1; RGWL 2, 3; TWA

Montale, Eugenio 1896-1981 ... **CLC 7, 9, 18; PC 13**
See also CA 17-20R; 104; CANR 30; DLB 114; EW 11; EWL 3; MTCW 1; PFS 22; RGWL 2, 3; TWA; WLIT 7

Montesquieu, Charles-Louis de Secondat 1689-1755 .... **LC 7, 69**
See also DLB 314; EW 3; GFL Beginnings to 1789; TWA

Montessori, Maria 1870-1952 ...... **TCLC 103**
See also CA 115; 147

Montgomery, (Robert) Bruce 1921(?)-1978
See Crispin, Edmund
See also CA 179; 104; CMW 4

Montgomery, L(ucy) M(aud) 1874-1942 .... **TCLC 51, 140**
See also AAYA 12; BYA 1; CA 108; 137; CLR 8, 91; DA3; DAC; DAM MST; DLB 92; DLBD 14; JRDA; MAICYA 1, 2; MTCW 2; MTFW 2005; RGEL 2; SATA 100; TWA; WCH; WYA; YABC 1

Montgomery, Marion H., Jr. 1925- .... **CLC 7**
See also AITN 1; CA 1-4R; CANR 3, 48; CSW; DLB 6

Montgomery, Max
See Davenport, Guy (Mattison, Jr.)

Montherlant, Henry (Milon) de 1896-1972 .... **CLC 8, 19**
See also CA 85-88; 37-40R; DAM DRAM; DLB 72, 321; EW 11; EWL 3; GFL 1789 to the Present; MTCW 1

Monty Python
See Chapman, Graham; Cleese, John (Marwood); Gilliam, Terry (Vance); Idle, Eric; Jones, Terence Graham Parry; Palin, Michael (Edward)
See also AAYA 7

Moodie, Susanna (Strickland) 1803-1885 .... **NCLC 14, 113**
See also DLB 99

Moody, Hiram (F. III) 1961-
See Moody, Rick
See also CA 138; CANR 64, 112; MTFW 2005

Moody, Minerva
See Alcott, Louisa May

Moody, Rick .... **CLC 147**
See Moody, Hiram (F. III)

Moody, William Vaughan 1869-1910 .... **TCLC 105**
See also CA 110; 178; DLB 7, 54; MAL 5; RGAL 4

Mooney, Edward 1951-
See Mooney, Ted
See also CA 130

Mooney, Ted .... **CLC 25**
See Mooney, Edward

Moorcock, Michael (John) 1939- ...... **CLC 5, 27, 58**
See Bradbury, Edward P.
See also AAYA 26; CA 45-48; CAAS 5; CANR 2, 17, 38, 64, 122; CN 5, 6, 7; DLB 14, 231, 261, 319; FANT; MTCW 1, 2; MTFW 2005; SATA 93; SCFW 1, 2; SFW 4; SUFW 1, 2

Moore, Brian 1921-1999 ... **CLC 1, 3, 5, 7, 8, 19, 32, 90**
See Bryan, Michael
See also BRWS 9; CA 1-4R; 174; CANR 1, 25, 42, 63; CCA 1; CN 1, 2, 3, 4, 5, 6; DAB; DAC; DAM MST; DLB 251; EWL 3; FANT; MTCW 1, 2; MTFW 2005; RGEL 2

Moore, Edward
See Muir, Edwin
See also RGEL 2

Moore, G. E. 1873-1958 .... **TCLC 89**
See also DLB 262

Moore, George Augustus 1852-1933 .... **SSC 19; TCLC 7**
See also BRW 6; CA 104; 177; DLB 10, 18, 57, 135; EWL 3; RGEL 2; RGSF 2

Moore, Lorrie .... **CLC 39, 45, 68**
See Moore, Marie Lorena
See also AMWS 10; CN 5, 6, 7; DLB 234; SSFS 19

Moore, Marianne (Craig) 1887-1972 .... **CLC 1, 2, 4, 8, 10, 13, 19, 47; PC 4, 49; WLCS**
See also AMW; CA 1-4R; 33-36R; CANR 3, 61; CDALB 1929-1941; CP 1; DA; DA3; DAB; DAC; DAM MST; POET; DLB 45; DLBD 7; EWL 3; EXPP; FL 1:6; MAL 5; MAWW; MTCW 1, 2; MTFW 2005; PAB; PFS 14, 17; RGAL 4; SATA 20; TUS; WP

Moore, Marie Lorena 1957- .... **CLC 165**
See Moore, Lorrie
See also CA 116; CANR 39, 83, 139; DLB 234; MTFW 2005

Moore, Michael 1954- .... **CLC 218**
See also AAYA 53; CA 166

Moore, Thomas 1779-1852 .... **NCLC 6, 110**
See also DLB 96, 144; RGEL 2

Moorhouse, Frank 1938- .... **SSC 40**
See also CA 118; CANR 92; CN 3, 4, 5, 6, 7; DLB 289; RGSF 2

Mora, Pat(ricia) 1942- .... **HLC 2**
See also AMWS 13; CA 129; CANR 57, 81, 112; CLR 58; DAM MULT; DLB 209; HW 1, 2; LLW; MAICYA 2; MTFW 2005; SATA 92, 134

Moraga, Cherrie 1952- ...... **CLC 126; DC 22**
See also CA 131; CANR 66; DAM MULT; DLB 82, 249; FW; GLL 1; HW 1, 2; LLW

Morand, Paul 1888-1976 .... **CLC 41; SSC 22**
See also CA 184; 69-72; DLB 65; EWL 3

Morante, Elsa 1918-1985 .... **CLC 8, 47**
See also CA 85-88; 117; CANR 35; DLB 177; EWL 3; MTCW 1, 2; MTFW 2005; RGWL 2, 3; WLIT 7

Moravia, Alberto .... **CLC 2, 7, 11, 27, 46; SSC 26**
See Pincherle, Alberto
See also DLB 177; EW 12; EWL 3; MTCW 2; RGSF 2; RGWL 2, 3; WLIT 7

More, Hannah 1745-1833 ...... **NCLC 27, 141**
See also DLB 107, 109, 116, 158; RGEL 2

More, Henry 1614-1687 .... **LC 9**
See also DLB 126, 252

More, Sir Thomas 1478(?)-1535 .... **LC 10, 32**
See also BRWC 1; BRWS 7; DLB 136, 281; LMFS 1; RGEL 2; TEA

Moreas, Jean .... **TCLC 18**
See Papadiamantopoulos, Johannes
See also GFL 1789 to the Present

Moreton, Andrew Esq.
See Defoe, Daniel

Morgan, Berry 1919-2002 .... **CLC 6**
See also CA 49-52; 208; DLB 6

Morgan, Claire
See Highsmith, (Mary) Patricia
See also GLL 1

Morgan, Edwin (George) 1920- .... **CLC 31**
See also BRWS 9; CA 5-8R; CANR 3, 43, 90; CP 1, 2, 3, 4, 5, 6, 7; DLB 27

Morgan, (George) Frederick 1922-2004 .... **CLC 23**
See also CA 17-20R; 224; CANR 21, 144; CP 2, 3, 4, 5, 6, 7

Morgan, Harriet
See Mencken, H(enry) L(ouis)

Morgan, Jane
See Cooper, James Fenimore

Morgan, Janet 1945- .... **CLC 39**
See also CA 65-68

Morgan, Lady 1776(?)-1859 .... **NCLC 29**
See also DLB 116, 158; RGEL 2

Morgan, Robin (Evonne) 1941- .... **CLC 2**
See also CA 69-72; CANR 29, 68; FW; GLL 2; MTCW 1; SATA 80

Morgan, Scott
See Kuttner, Henry

Morgan, Seth 1949(?)-1990 .... **CLC 65**
See also CA 185; 132

Morgenstern, Christian (Otto Josef Wolfgang) 1871-1914 .... **TCLC 8**
See also CA 105; 191; EWL 3

Morgenstern, S.
See Goldman, William (W.)

Mori, Rintaro
See Mori Ogai
See also CA 110

Mori, Toshio 1910-1980 .... **SSC 83**
See also CA 116; DLB 312; RGSF 2

Moricz, Zsigmond 1879-1942 .... **TCLC 33**
See also CA 165; DLB 215; EWL 3

Morike, Eduard (Friedrich) 1804-1875 .... **NCLC 10**
See also DLB 133; RGWL 2, 3

Mori Ogai 1862-1922 .... **TCLC 14**
See Ogai
See also CA 164; DLB 180; EWL 3; RGWL 3; TWA

Moritz, Karl Philipp 1756-1793 .... **LC 2**
See also DLB 94

Morland, Peter Henry
See Faust, Frederick (Schiller)

Morley, Christopher (Darlington) 1890-1957 .... **TCLC 87**
See also CA 112; 213; DLB 9; MAL 5; RGAL 4

Morren, Theophil
See Hofmannsthal, Hugo von

Morris, Bill 1952- .... **CLC 76**
See also CA 225

Morris, Julian
See West, Morris L(anglo)

Morris, Steveland Judkins 1950(?)-
See Wonder, Stevie
See also CA 111

Morris, William 1834-1896 . **NCLC 4; PC 55**
See also BRW 5; CDBLB 1832-1890; DLB 18, 35, 57, 156, 178, 184; FANT; RGEL 2; SFW 4; SUFW

Morris, Wright (Marion) 1910-1998 . **CLC 1, 3, 7, 18, 37; TCLC 107**
See also AMW; CA 9-12R; 167; CANR 21, 81; CN 1, 2, 3, 4, 5, 6; DLB 2, 206, 218; DLBY 1981; EWL 3; MAL 5; MTCW 1, 2; MTFW 2005; RGAL 4; TCWW 1, 2

Morrison, Arthur 1863-1945 .... **SSC 40; TCLC 72**
See also CA 120; 157; CMW 4; DLB 70, 135, 197; RGEL 2

Morrison, Chloe Anthony Wofford
See Morrison, Toni

Morrison, James Douglas 1943-1971
See Morrison, Jim
See also CA 73-76; CANR 40

Morrison, Jim .... **CLC 17**
See Morrison, James Douglas

Morrison, Toni 1931- ..... **BLC 3; CLC 4, 10, 22, 55, 81, 87, 173, 194**
See also AAYA 1, 22, 61; AFAW 1, 2; AMWC 1; AMWS 3; BPFB 2; BW 2, 3; CA 29-32R; CANR 27, 42, 67, 113, 124; CDALB 1968-1988; CLR 99; CN 3, 4, 5, 6, 7; CPW; DA; DA3; DAB; DAC; DAM MST, MULT, NOV, POP; DLB 6, 33, 143; DLBY 1981; EWL 3; EXPN; FL 1:6; FW; GL 3; LAIT 2, 4; LATS 1:2; LMFS 2; MAL 5; MAWW; MTCW 1, 2; MTFW 2005; NFS 1, 6, 8, 14; RGAL 4; RHW; SATA 57, 144; SSFS 5; TCLE 1:2; TUS; YAW

Morrison, Van 1945- .... **CLC 21**
See also CA 116; 168

Morrissy, Mary 1957- .... **CLC 99**
See also CA 205; DLB 267

Mortimer, John (Clifford) 1923- ..... **CLC 28, 43**
See also CA 13-16R; CANR 21, 69, 109; CBD; CD 5, 6; CDBLB 1960 to Present; CMW 4; CN 5, 6, 7; CPW; DA3; DAM DRAM, POP; DLB 13, 245, 271; INT CANR-21; MSW; MTCW 1, 2; MTFW 2005; RGEL 2

Mortimer, Penelope (Ruth) 1918-1999 .... **CLC 5**
See also CA 57-60; 187; CANR 45, 88; CN 1, 2, 3, 4, 5, 6

Mortimer, Sir John
See Mortimer, John (Clifford)

Morton, Anthony
See Creasey, John

Morton, Thomas 1579(?)-1647(?) .... **LC 72**
See also DLB 24; RGEL 2

Mosca, Gaetano 1858-1941 .... **TCLC 75**

Moses, Daniel David 1952- .... **NNAL**
See also CA 186

Mosher, Howard Frank 1943- .... **CLC 62**
See also CA 139; CANR 65, 115

Mosley, Nicholas 1923- .... **CLC 43, 70**
See also CA 69-72; CANR 41, 60, 108; CN 1, 2, 3, 4, 5, 6, 7; DLB 14, 207

Mosley, Walter 1952- .... **BLCS; CLC 97, 184**
See also AAYA 57; AMWS 13; BPFB 2; BW 2; CA 142; CANR 57, 92, 136; CMW 4; CN 7; CPW; DA3; DAM MULT, POP; DLB 306; MSW; MTCW 2; MTFW 2005

Moss, Howard 1922-1987 . **CLC 7, 14, 45, 50**
See also CA 1-4R; 123; CANR 1, 44; CP 1, 2, 3, 4; DAM POET; DLB 5

Mossgiel, Rab
See Burns, Robert

Motion, Andrew (Peter) 1952- .... **CLC 47**
See also BRWS 7; CA 146; CANR 90, 142; CP 4, 5, 6, 7; DLB 40; MTFW 2005

Motley, Willard (Francis) 1909-1965 .... **CLC 18**
See also BW 1; CA 117; 106; CANR 88; DLB 76, 143

Motoori, Norinaga 1730-1801 .... **NCLC 45**

Mott, Michael (Charles Alston) 1930- .... **CLC 15, 34**
See also CA 5-8R; CAAS 7; CANR 7, 29

Mountain Wolf Woman 1884-1960 . **CLC 92; NNAL**
See also CA 144; CANR 90

Moure, Erin 1955- .... **CLC 88**
See also CA 113; CP 7; CWP; DLB 60

Niven, Larry .... **CLC 8**
See Niven, Laurence Van Cott
See also AAYA 27; BPFB 2; BYA 10; DLB
8; SCFW 1, 2

Niven, Laurence Van Cott 1938-
See Niven, Larry
See also CA 21-24R, 207; CAAE 207;
CAAS 12; CANR 14, 44, 66, 113; CPW;
DAM POP; MTCW 1, 2; SATA 95; SFW
4

Nixon, Agnes Eckhardt 1927- .... **CLC 21**
See also CA 110

Nizan, Paul 1905-1940 .... **TCLC 40**
See also CA 161; DLB 72; EWL 3; GFL
1789 to the Present

Nkosi, Lewis 1936- .... **BLC 3; CLC 45**
See also BW 1, 3; CA 65-68; CANR 27,
81; CBD; CD 5, 6; DAM MULT; DLB
157, 225; WWE 1

Nodier, (Jean) Charles (Emmanuel)
1780-1844 .... **NCLC 19**
See also DLB 119; GFL 1789 to the Present

Noguchi, Yone 1875-1947 .... **TCLC 80**

Nolan, Christopher 1965- .... **CLC 58**
See also CA 111; CANR 88

Noon, Jeff 1957- .... **CLC 91**
See also CA 148; CANR 83; DLB 267;
SFW 4

Norden, Charles
See Durrell, Lawrence (George)

Nordhoff, Charles Bernard
1887-1947 .... **TCLC 23**
See also CA 108; 211; DLB 9; LAIT 1;
RHW 1; SATA 23

Norfolk, Lawrence 1963- .... **CLC 76**
See also CA 144; CANR 85; CN 6, 7; DLB
267

Norman, Marsha (Williams) 1947- . **CLC 28,
186; DC 8**
See also CA 105; CABS 3; CAD; CANR
41, 131; CD 5, 6; CSW; CWD; DAM
DRAM; DFS 2; DLB 266; DLBY 1984;
FW; MAL 5

Normyx
See Douglas, (George) Norman

Norris, (Benjamin) Frank(lin, Jr.)
1870-1902 .... **SSC 28; TCLC 24, 155**
See also AAYA 57; AMW; AMWC 2; BPFB
2; CA 110; 160; CDALB 1865-1917; DLB
12, 71, 186; LMFS 2; NFS 12; RGAL 4;
TCWW 1, 2; TUS

Norris, Leslie 1921- .... **CLC 14**
See also CA 11-12; CANR 14, 117; CAP 1;
CP 1, 2, 3, 4, 5, 6, 7; DLB 27, 256

North, Andrew
See Norton, Andre

North, Anthony
See Koontz, Dean R.

North, Captain George
See Stevenson, Robert Louis (Balfour)

North, Captain George
See Stevenson, Robert Louis (Balfour)

North, Milou
See Erdrich, (Karen) Louise

Northrup, B. A.
See Hubbard, L(afayette) Ron(ald)

North Staffs
See Hulme, T(homas) E(rnest)

Northup, Solomon 1808-1863 ...... **NCLC 105**

Norton, Alice Mary
See Norton, Andre
See also MAICYA 1; SATA 1, 43

Norton, Andre 1912-2005 .... **CLC 12**
See Norton, Alice Mary
See also AAYA 14; BPFB 2; BYA 4, 10,
12; CA 1-4R; 237; CANR 68; CLR 50;
DLB 8, 52; JRDA; MAICYA 2; MTCW
1; SATA 91; SUFW 1, 2; YAW

Norton, Caroline 1808-1877 .... **NCLC 47**
See also DLB 21, 159, 199

Norway, Nevil Shute 1899-1960
See Shute, Nevil
See also CA 102; 93-96; CANR 85; MTCW
2

Norwid, Cyprian Kamil
1821-1883 .... **NCLC 17**
See also RGWL 3

Nosille, Nabrah
See Ellison, Harlan (Jay)

Nossack, Hans Erich 1901-1978 .... **CLC 6**
See also CA 93-96; 85-88; DLB 69; EWL 3

Nostradamus 1503-1566 .... **LC 27**

Nosu, Chuji
See Ozu, Yasujiro

Notenburg, Eleanora (Genrikhovna) von
See Guro, Elena (Genrikhovna)

Nova, Craig 1945- .... **CLC 7, 31**
See also CA 45-48; CANR 2, 53, 127

Novak, Joseph
See Kosinski, Jerzy (Nikodem)

Novalis 1772-1801 .... **NCLC 13**
See also CDWLB 2; DLB 90; EW 5; RGWL
2, 3

Novick, Peter 1934- .... **CLC 164**
See also CA 188

Novis, Emile
See Weil, Simone (Adolphine)

Nowlan, Alden (Albert) 1933-1983 ... **CLC 15**
See also CA 9-12R; CANR 5; CP 1, 2, 3;
DAC; DAM MST; DLB 53; PFS 12

Noyes, Alfred 1880-1958 ...... **PC 27; TCLC 7**
See also CA 104; 188; DLB 20; EXPP;
FANT; PFS 4; RGEL 2

Nugent, Richard Bruce
1906(?)-1987 .... **HR 1:3**
See also BW 1; CA 125; DLB 51; GLL 2

Nunn, Kem .... **CLC 34**
See also CA 159

Nussbaum, Martha Craven 1947- .. **CLC 203**
See also CA 134; CANR 102

Nwapa, Flora (Nwanzuruaha)
1931-1993 .... **BLCS; CLC 133**
See also BW 2; CA 143; CANR 83; CD-
WLB 3; CWRI 5; DLB 125; EWL 3;
WLIT 2

Nye, Robert 1939- .... **CLC 13, 42**
See also BRWS 10; CA 33-36R; CANR 29,
67, 107; CN 1, 2, 3, 4, 5, 6, 7; CP 1, 2, 3,
4, 5, 6, 7; CWRI 5; DAM NOV; DLB 14,
271; FANT; HGG; MTCW 1; RHW;
SATA 6

Nyro, Laura 1947-1997 .... **CLC 17**
See also CA 194

Oates, Joyce Carol 1938- .. **CLC 1, 2, 3, 6, 9,
11, 15, 19, 33, 52, 108, 134; SSC 6, 70;
WLC**
See also AAYA 15, 52; AITN 1; AMWS 2;
BEST 89:2; BPFB 2; BYA 11; CA 5-8R;
CANR 25, 45, 74, 113, 129; CDALB
1968-1988; CN 1, 2, 3, 4, 5, 6, 7; CP 7;
CPW; CWP; DA; DA3; DAB; DAC;
DAM MST, NOV, POP; DLB 2, 5, 130;
DLBY 1981; EWL 3; EXPS; FL 1:6; FW;
GL 3; HGG; INT CANR-25; LAIT 4;
MAL 5; MAWW; MTCW 1, 2; MTFW
2005; NFS 8; RGAL 4; RGSF 2; SATA
159; SSFS 1, 8, 17; SUFW 2; TUS

O'Brian, E. G.
See Clarke, Arthur C(harles)

O'Brian, Patrick 1914-2000 .... **CLC 152**
See also AAYA 55; CA 144; 187; CANR
74; CPW; MTCW 2; MTFW 2005; RHW

O'Brien, Darcy 1939-1998 .... **CLC 11**
See also CA 21-24R; 167; CANR 8, 59

O'Brien, Edna 1932- ..... **CLC 3, 5, 8, 13, 36,
65, 116; SSC 10, 77**
See also BRWS 5; CA 1-4R; CANR 6, 41,
65, 102; CDBLB 1960 to Present; CN 1,
2, 3, 4, 5, 6, 7; DA3; DAM NOV; DLB
14, 231, 319; EWL 3; FW; MTCW 1, 2;
MTFW 2005; RGSF 2; WLIT 4

O'Brien, Fitz-James 1828-1862 ..... **NCLC 21**
See also DLB 74; RGAL 4; SUFW

O'Brien, Flann .... **CLC 1, 4, 5, 7, 10, 47**
See O Nuallain, Brian
See also BRWS 2; DLB 231; EWL 3;
RGEL 2

O'Brien, Richard 1942- .... **CLC 17**
See also CA 124

O'Brien, (William) Tim(othy) 1946- . **CLC 7,
19, 40, 103, 211; SSC 74**
See also AAYA 16; AMWS 5; CA 85-88;
CANR 40, 58, 133; CDALBS; CN 5, 6,
7; CPW; DA3; DAM POP; DLB 152;
DLBD 9; DLBY 1980; LATS 1:2; MAL
5; MTCW 2; MTFW 2005; RGAL 4;
SSFS 5, 15; TCLE 1:2

Obstfelder, Sigbjoern 1866-1900 .... **TCLC 23**
See also CA 123

O'Casey, Sean 1880-1964 .... **CLC 1, 5, 9, 11,
15, 88; DC 12; WLCS**
See also BRW 7; CA 89-92; CANR 62;
CBD; CDBLB 1914-1945; DA3; DAB;
DAC; DAM DRAM, MST; DFS 19; DLB
10; EWL 3; MTCW 1, 2; MTFW 2005;
RGEL 2; TEA; WLIT 4

O'Cathasaigh, Sean
See O'Casey, Sean

Occom, Samson 1723-1792 .... **LC 60; NNAL**
See also DLB 175

Ochs, Phil(ip David) 1940-1976 .... **CLC 17**
See also CA 185; 65-68

O'Connor, Edwin (Greene)
1918-1968 .... **CLC 14**
See also CA 93-96; 25-28R; MAL 5

O'Connor, (Mary) Flannery
1925-1964 .... **CLC 1, 2, 3, 6, 10, 13, 15,
21, 66, 104; SSC 1, 23, 61, 82; TCLC
132; WLC**
See also AAYA 7; AMW; AMWR 2; BPFB
3; BYA 16; CA 1-4R; CANR 3, 41;
CDALB 1941-1968; DA; DA3; DAB;
DAC; DAM MST, NOV; DLB 2, 152;
DLBD 12; DLBY 1980; EWL 3; EXPS;
LAIT 5; MAL 5; MAWW; MTCW 1, 2;
MTFW 2005; NFS 3, 21; RGAL 4; RGSF
2; SSFS 2, 7, 10, 19; TUS

O'Connor, Frank .... **CLC 23; SSC 5**
See O'Donovan, Michael Francis
See also DLB 162; EWL 3; RGSF 2; SSFS
5

O'Dell, Scott 1898-1989 .... **CLC 30**
See also AAYA 3, 44; BPFB 3; BYA 1, 2,
3, 5; CA 61-64; 129; CANR 12, 30, 112;
CLR 1, 16; DLB 52; JRDA; MAICYA 1,
2; SATA 12, 60, 134; WYA; YAW

Odets, Clifford 1906-1963 ..... **CLC 2, 28, 98;
DC 6**
See also AMWS 2; CA 85-88; CAD; CANR
62; DAM DRAM; DFS 3, 17, 20; DLB 7,
26; EWL 3; MAL 5; MTCW 1, 2; MTFW
2005; RGAL 4; TUS

O'Doherty, Brian 1928- .... **CLC 76**
See also CA 105; CANR 108

O'Donnell, K. M.
See Malzberg, Barry N(athaniel)

O'Donnell, Lawrence
See Kuttner, Henry

O'Donovan, Michael Francis
1903-1966 .... **CLC 14**
See O'Connor, Frank
See also CA 93-96; CANR 84

Oe, Kenzaburo 1935- .. **CLC 10, 36, 86, 187; SSC 20**
    See Oe Kenzaburo
    See also CA 97-100; CANR 36, 50, 74, 126; DA3; DAM NOV; DLB 182; DLBY 1994; LATS 1:2; MJW; MTCW 1, 2; MTFW 2005; RGSF 2; RGWL 2, 3

Oe Kenzaburo
    See Oe, Kenzaburo
    See also CWW 2; EWL 3

O'Faolain, Julia 1932- .... **CLC 6, 19, 47, 108**
    See also CA 81-84; CAAS 2; CANR 12, 61; CN 2, 3, 4, 5, 6, 7; DLB 14, 231, 319; FW; MTCW 1; RHW

O'Faolain, Sean 1900-1991 ...... **CLC 1, 7, 14, 32, 70; SSC 13; TCLC 143**
    See also CA 61-64; 134; CANR 12, 66; CN 1, 2, 3, 4; DLB 15, 162; MTCW 1, 2; MTFW 2005; RGEL 2; RGSF 2

O'Flaherty, Liam 1896-1984 .... **CLC 5, 34; SSC 6**
    See also CA 101; 113; CANR 35; CN 1, 2, 3; DLB 36, 162; DLBY 1984; MTCW 1, 2; MTFW 2005; RGEL 2; RGSF 2; SSFS 5, 20

Ogai
    See Mori Ogai
    See also MJW

Ogilvy, Gavin
    See Barrie, J(ames) M(atthew)

O'Grady, Standish (James) 1846-1928 .... **TCLC 5**
    See also CA 104; 157

O'Grady, Timothy 1951- .... **CLC 59**
    See also CA 138

O'Hara, Frank 1926-1966 .... **CLC 2, 5, 13, 78; PC 45**
    See also CA 9-12R; 25-28R; CANR 33; DA3; DAM POET; DLB 5, 16, 193; EWL 3; MAL 5; MTCW 1, 2; MTFW 2005; PFS 8, 12; RGAL 4; WP

O'Hara, John (Henry) 1905-1970 . **CLC 1, 2, 3, 6, 11, 42; SSC 15**
    See also AMW; BPFB 3; CA 5-8R; 25-28R; CANR 31, 60; CDALB 1929-1941; DAM NOV; DLB 9, 86; DLBD 2; EWL 3; MAL 5; MTCW 1, 2; MTFW 2005; NFS 11; RGAL 4; RGSF 2

O Hehir, Diana 1922- .... **CLC 41**
    See also CA 93-96

Ohiyesa
    See Eastman, Charles A(lexander)

Okada, John 1923-1971 .... **AAL**
    See also BYA 14; CA 212; DLB 312

Okigbo, Christopher (Ifenayichukwu) 1932-1967 .. **BLC 3; CLC 25, 84; PC 7; TCLC 171**
    See also AFW; BW 1, 3; CA 77-80; CANR 74; CDWLB 3; DAM MULT, POET; DLB 125; EWL 3; MTCW 1, 2; MTFW 2005; RGEL 2

Okri, Ben 1959- .... **CLC 87**
    See also AFW; BRWS 5; BW 2, 3; CA 130; 138; CANR 65, 128; CN 5, 6, 7; DLB 157, 231, 319; EWL 3; INT CA-138; MTCW 2; MTFW 2005; RGSF 2; SSFS 20; WLIT 2; WWE 1

Olds, Sharon 1942- .. **CLC 32, 39, 85; PC 22**
    See also AMWS 10; CA 101; CANR 18, 41, 66, 98, 135; CP 7; CPW; CWP; DAM POET; DLB 120; MAL 5; MTCW 2; MTFW 2005; PFS 17

Oldstyle, Jonathan
    See Irving, Washington

Olesha, Iurii
    See Olesha, Yuri (Karlovich)
    See also RGWL 2

Olesha, Iurii Karlovich
    See Olesha, Yuri (Karlovich)
    See also DLB 272

Olesha, Yuri (Karlovich) 1899-1960 . **CLC 8; SSC 69; TCLC 136**
    See Olesha, Iurii; Olesha, Iurii Karlovich; Olesha, Yury Karlovich
    See also CA 85-88; EW 11; RGWL 3

Olesha, Yury Karlovich
    See Olesha, Yuri (Karlovich)
    See also EWL 3

Oliphant, Mrs.
    See Oliphant, Margaret (Oliphant Wilson)
    See also SUFW

Oliphant, Laurence 1829(?)-1888 .. **NCLC 47**
    See also DLB 18, 166

Oliphant, Margaret (Oliphant Wilson) 1828-1897 .... **NCLC 11, 61; SSC 25**
    See Oliphant, Mrs.
    See also BRWS 10; DLB 18, 159, 190; HGG; RGEL 2; RGSF 2

Oliver, Mary 1935- .... **CLC 19, 34, 98**
    See also AMWS 7; CA 21-24R; CANR 9, 43, 84, 92, 138; CP 4, 5, 6, 7; CWP; DLB 5, 193; EWL 3; MTFW 2005; PFS 15

Olivier, Laurence (Kerr) 1907-1989 . **CLC 20**
    See also CA 111; 150; 129

Olsen, Tillie 1912- ... **CLC 4, 13, 114; SSC 11**
    See also AAYA 51; AMWS 13; BYA 11; CA 1-4R; CANR 1, 43, 74, 132; CDALBS; CN 2, 3, 4, 5, 6, 7; DA; DA3; DAB; DAC; DAM MST; DLB 28, 206; DLBY 1980; EWL 3; EXPS; FW; MAL 5; MTCW 1, 2; MTFW 2005; RGAL 4; RGSF 2; SSFS 1; TCLE 1:2; TCWW 2; TUS

Olson, Charles (John) 1910-1970 .. **CLC 1, 2, 5, 6, 9, 11, 29; PC 19**
    See also AMWS 2; CA 13-16; 25-28R; CABS 2; CANR 35, 61; CAP 1; CP 1; DAM POET; DLB 5, 16, 193; EWL 3; MAL 5; MTCW 1, 2; RGAL 4; WP

Olson, Toby 1937- .... **CLC 28**
    See also CA 65-68; CANR 9, 31, 84; CP 3, 4, 5, 6, 7

Olyesha, Yuri
    See Olesha, Yuri (Karlovich)

Olympiodorus of Thebes c. 375-c. 430 .... **CMLC 59**

Omar Khayyam
    See Khayyam, Omar
    See also RGWL 2, 3

Ondaatje, (Philip) Michael 1943- .... **CLC 14, 29, 51, 76, 180; PC 28**
    See also AAYA 66; CA 77-80; CANR 42, 74, 109, 133; CN 5, 6, 7; CP 1, 2, 3, 4, 5, 6, 7; DA3; DAB; DAC; DAM MST; DLB 60; EWL 3; LATS 1:2; LMFS 2; MTCW 2; MTFW 2005; PFS 8, 19; TCLE 1:2; TWA; WWE 1

Oneal, Elizabeth 1934-
    See Oneal, Zibby
    See also CA 106; CANR 28, 84; MAICYA 1, 2; SATA 30, 82; YAW

Oneal, Zibby .... **CLC 30**
    See Oneal, Elizabeth
    See also AAYA 5, 41; BYA 13; CLR 13; JRDA; WYA

O'Neill, Eugene (Gladstone) 1888-1953 ... **DC 20; TCLC 1, 6, 27, 49; WLC**
    See also AAYA 54; AITN 1; AMW; AMWC 1; CA 110; 132; CAD; CANR 131; CDALB 1929-1941; DA; DA3; DAB; DAC; DAM DRAM, MST; DFS 2, 4, 5, 6, 9, 11, 12, 16, 20; DLB 7; EWL 3; LAIT 3; LMFS 2; MAL 5; MTCW 1, 2; MTFW 2005; RGAL 4; TUS

Onetti, Juan Carlos 1909-1994 ... **CLC 7, 10; HLCS 2; SSC 23; TCLC 131**
    See also CA 85-88; 145; CANR 32, 63; CDWLB 3; CWW 2; DAM MULT, NOV; DLB 113; EWL 3; HW 1, 2; LAW; MTCW 1, 2; MTFW 2005; RGSF 2

O Nuallain, Brian 1911-1966
    See O'Brien, Flann
    See also CA 21-22; 25-28R; CAP 2; DLB 231; FANT; TEA

Ophuls, Max 1902-1957 .... **TCLC 79**
    See also CA 113

Opie, Amelia 1769-1853 .... **NCLC 65**
    See also DLB 116, 159; RGEL 2

Oppen, George 1908-1984 ..... **CLC 7, 13, 34; PC 35; TCLC 107**
    See also CA 13-16R; 113; CANR 8, 82; CP 1, 2, 3; DLB 5, 165

Oppenheim, E(dward) Phillips 1866-1946 .... **TCLC 45**
    See also CA 111; 202; CMW 4; DLB 70

Opuls, Max
    See Ophuls, Max

Orage, A(lfred) R(ichard) 1873-1934 .... **TCLC 157**
    See also CA 122

Origen c. 185-c. 254 .... **CMLC 19**

Orlovitz, Gil 1918-1973 .... **CLC 22**
    See also CA 77-80; 45-48; CN 1; CP 1, 2; DLB 2, 5

O'Rourke, P(atrick) J(ake) 1947- .. **CLC 209**
    See also CA 77-80; CANR 13, 41, 67, 111; CPW; DAM POP; DLB 185

Orris
    See Ingelow, Jean

Ortega y Gasset, Jose 1883-1955 ...... **HLC 2; TCLC 9**
    See also CA 106; 130; DAM MULT; EW 9; EWL 3; HW 1, 2; MTCW 1, 2; MTFW 2005

Ortese, Anna Maria 1914-1998 .... **CLC 89**
    See also DLB 177; EWL 3

Ortiz, Simon J(oseph) 1941- ... **CLC 45, 208; NNAL; PC 17**
    See also AMWS 4; CA 134; CANR 69, 118; CP 3, 4, 5, 6, 7; DAM MULT, POET; DLB 120, 175, 256; EXPP; MAL 5; PFS 4, 16; RGAL 4; TCWW 2

Orton, Joe ...... **CLC 4, 13, 43; DC 3; TCLC 157**
    See Orton, John Kingsley
    See also BRWS 5; CBD; CDBLB 1960 to Present; DFS 3, 6; DLB 13, 310; GLL 1; RGEL 2; TEA; WLIT 4

Orton, John Kingsley 1933-1967
    See Orton, Joe
    See also CA 85-88; CANR 35, 66; DAM DRAM; MTCW 1, 2; MTFW 2005

Orwell, George ...... **SSC 68; TCLC 2, 6, 15, 31, 51, 128, 129; WLC**
    See Blair, Eric (Arthur)
    See also BPFB 3; BRW 7; BYA 5; CDBLB 1945-1960; CLR 68; DAB; DLB 15, 98, 195, 255; EWL 3; EXPN; LAIT 4, 5; LATS 1:1; NFS 3, 7; RGEL 2; SCFW 1, 2; SFW 4; SSFS 4; TEA; WLIT 4; YAW

Osborne, David
    See Silverberg, Robert

Osborne, George
    See Silverberg, Robert

Osborne, John (James) 1929-1994 .... **CLC 1, 2, 5, 11, 45; TCLC 153; WLC**
    See also BRWS 1; CA 13-16R; 147; CANR 21, 56; CBD; CDBLB 1945-1960; DA; DAB; DAC; DAM DRAM, MST; DFS 4, 19; DLB 13; EWL 3; MTCW 1, 2; MTFW 2005; RGEL 2

Osborne, Lawrence 1958- .... **CLC 50**
    See also CA 189

Osbourne, Lloyd 1868-1947 .... **TCLC 93**

Osgood, Frances Sargent 1811-1850 .... **NCLC 141**
    See also DLB 250

Oshima, Nagisa 1932- .... **CLC 20**
    See also CA 116; 121; CANR 78

Oskison, John Milton
1874-1947 .... **NNAL; TCLC 35**
See also CA 144; CANR 84; DAM MULT;
DLB 175

Ossian c. 3rd cent. - .... **CMLC 28**
See Macpherson, James

Ossoli, Sarah Margaret (Fuller)
1810-1850 .... **NCLC 5, 50**
See Fuller, Margaret; Fuller, Sarah Margaret
See also CDALB 1640-1865; FW; LMFS 1;
SATA 25

Ostriker, Alicia (Suskin) 1937- .... **CLC 132**
See also CA 25-28R; CAAS 24; CANR 10,
30, 62, 99; CWP; DLB 120; EXPP; PFS
19

Ostrovsky, Aleksandr Nikolaevich
See Ostrovsky, Alexander
See also DLB 277

Ostrovsky, Alexander 1823-1886 .. **NCLC 30,
57**
See Ostrovsky, Aleksandr Nikolaevich

Otero, Blas de 1916-1979 .... **CLC 11**
See also CA 89-92; DLB 134; EWL 3

O'Trigger, Sir Lucius
See Horne, Richard Henry Hengist

Otto, Rudolf 1869-1937 .... **TCLC 85**

Otto, Whitney 1955- .... **CLC 70**
See also CA 140; CANR 120

Otway, Thomas 1652-1685 ... **DC 24; LC 106**
See also DAM DRAM; DLB 80; RGEL 2

Ouida .... **TCLC 43**
See De la Ramee, Marie Louise (Ouida)
See also DLB 18, 156; RGEL 2

Ouologuem, Yambo 1940- .... **CLC 146**
See also CA 111; 176

Ousmane, Sembene 1923- ... **BLC 3; CLC 66**
See Sembene, Ousmane
See also BW 1, 3; CA 117; 125; CANR 81;
CWW 2; MTCW 1

Ovid 43B.C.-17 .... **CMLC 7; PC 2**
See also AW 2; CDWLB 1; DA3; DAM
POET; DLB 211; PFS 22; RGWL 2, 3;
WP

Owen, Hugh
See Faust, Frederick (Schiller)

Owen, Wilfred (Edward Salter)
1893-1918 ... **PC 19; TCLC 5, 27; WLC**
See also BRW 6; CA 104; 141; CDBLB
1914-1945; DA; DAB; DAC; DAM MST,
POET; DLB 20; EWL 3; EXPP; MTCW
2; MTFW 2005; PFS 10; RGEL 2; WLIT
4

Owens, Louis (Dean) 1948-2002 .... **NNAL**
See also CA 137, 179; 207; CAAE 179;
CAAS 24; CANR 71

Owens, Rochelle 1936- .... **CLC 8**
See also CA 17-20R; CAAS 2; CAD;
CANR 39; CD 5, 6; CP 1, 2, 3, 4, 5, 6, 7;
CWD; CWP

Oz, Amos 1939- ...... **CLC 5, 8, 11, 27, 33, 54;
SSC 66**
See also CA 53-56; CANR 27, 47, 65, 113,
138; CWW 2; DAM NOV; EWL 3;
MTCW 1, 2; MTFW 2005; RGSF 2;
RGWL 3; WLIT 6

Ozick, Cynthia 1928- .... **CLC 3, 7, 28, 62,
155; SSC 15, 60**
See also AMWS 5; BEST 90:1; CA 17-20R;
CANR 23, 58, 116; CN 3, 4, 5, 6, 7;
CPW; DA3; DAM NOV, POP; DLB 28,
152, 299; DLBY 1982; EWL 3; EXPS;
INT CANR-23; MAL 5; MTCW 1, 2;
MTFW 2005; RGAL 4; RGSF 2; SSFS 3,
12

Ozu, Yasujiro 1903-1963 .... **CLC 16**
See also CA 112

Pabst, G. W. 1885-1967 .... **TCLC 127**

Pacheco, C.
See Pessoa, Fernando (Antonio Nogueira)

Pacheco, Jose Emilio 1939- .... **HLC 2**
See also CA 111; 131; CANR 65; CWW 2;
DAM MULT; DLB 290; EWL 3; HW 1,
2; RGSF 2

Pa Chin .... **CLC 18**
See Li Fei-kan
See also EWL 3

Pack, Robert 1929- .... **CLC 13**
See also CA 1-4R; CANR 3, 44, 82; CP 1,
2, 3, 4, 5, 6, 7; DLB 5; SATA 118

Padgett, Lewis
See Kuttner, Henry

Padilla (Lorenzo), Heberto
1932-2000 .... **CLC 38**
See also AITN 1; CA 123; 131; 189; CWW
2; EWL 3; HW 1

Page, James Patrick 1944-
See Page, Jimmy
See also CA 204

Page, Jimmy 1944- .... **CLC 12**
See Page, James Patrick

Page, Louise 1955- .... **CLC 40**
See also CA 140; CANR 76; CBD; CD 5,
6; CWD; DLB 233

Page, P(atricia) K(athleen) 1916- ...... **CLC 7,
18; PC 12**
See Cape, Judith
See also CA 53-56; CANR 4, 22, 65; CP 1,
2, 3, 4, 5, 6, 7; DAC; DAM MST; DLB
68; MTCW 1; RGEL 2

Page, Stanton
See Fuller, Henry Blake

Page, Stanton
See Fuller, Henry Blake

Page, Thomas Nelson 1853-1922 .... **SSC 23**
See also CA 118; 177; DLB 12, 78; DLBD
13; RGAL 2

Pagels, Elaine Hiesey 1943- .... **CLC 104**
See also CA 45-48; CANR 2, 24, 51; FW;
NCFS 4

Paget, Violet 1856-1935
See Lee, Vernon
See also CA 104; 166; GLL 1; HGG

Paget-Lowe, Henry
See Lovecraft, H(oward) P(hillips)

Paglia, Camille (Anna) 1947- .... **CLC 68**
See also CA 140; CANR 72, 139; CPW;
FW; GLL 2; MTCW 2; MTFW 2005

Paige, Richard
See Koontz, Dean R.

Paine, Thomas 1737-1809 .... **NCLC 62**
See also AMWS 1; CDALB 1640-1865;
DLB 31, 43, 73, 158; LAIT 1; RGAL 4;
RGEL 2; TUS

Pakenham, Antonia
See Fraser, Antonia (Pakenham)

Palamas, Costis
See Palamas, Kostes

Palamas, Kostes 1859-1943 .... **TCLC 5**
See Palamas, Kostis
See also CA 105; 190; RGWL 2, 3

Palamas, Kostis
See Palamas, Kostes
See also EWL 3

Palazzeschi, Aldo 1885-1974 .... **CLC 11**
See also CA 89-92; 53-56; DLB 114, 264;
EWL 3

Pales Matos, Luis 1898-1959 .... **HLCS 2**
See Pales Matos, Luis
See also DLB 290; HW 1; LAW

Paley, Grace 1922- .. **CLC 4, 6, 37, 140; SSC
8**
See also AMWS 6; CA 25-28R; CANR 13,
46, 74, 118; CN 2, 3, 4, 5, 6, 7; CPW;
DA3; DAM POP; DLB 28, 218; EWL 3;
EXPS; FW; INT CANR-13; MAL 5;
MAWW; MTCW 1, 2; MTFW 2005;
RGAL 4; RGSF 2; SSFS 3, 20

Palin, Michael (Edward) 1943- .... **CLC 21**
See Monty Python
See also CA 107; CANR 35, 109; SATA 67

Palliser, Charles 1947- .... **CLC 65**
See also CA 136; CANR 76; CN 5, 6, 7

Palma, Ricardo 1833-1919 .... **TCLC 29**
See also CA 168; LAW

Pamuk, Orhan 1952- .... **CLC 185**
See also CA 142; CANR 75, 127; CWW 2;
WLIT 6

Pancake, Breece Dexter 1952-1979
See Pancake, Breece D'J
See also CA 123; 109

Pancake, Breece D'J .... **CLC 29; SSC 61**
See Pancake, Breece Dexter
See also DLB 130

Panchenko, Nikolai .... **CLC 59**

Pankhurst, Emmeline (Goulden)
1858-1928 .... **TCLC 100**
See also CA 116; FW

Panko, Rudy
See Gogol, Nikolai (Vasilyevich)

Papadiamantis, Alexandros
1851-1911 .... **TCLC 29**
See also CA 168; EWL 3

Papadiamantopoulos, Johannes 1856-1910
See Moreas, Jean
See also CA 117

Papini, Giovanni 1881-1956 .... **TCLC 22**
See also CA 121; 180; DLB 264

Paracelsus 1493-1541 .... **LC 14**
See also DLB 179

Parasol, Peter
See Stevens, Wallace

Pardo Bazan, Emilia 1851-1921 .... **SSC 30**
See also EWL 3; FW; RGSF 2; RGWL 2, 3

Pareto, Vilfredo 1848-1923 .... **TCLC 69**
See also CA 175

Paretsky, Sara 1947- .... **CLC 135**
See also AAYA 30; BEST 90:3; CA 125;
129; CANR 59, 95; CMW 4; CPW; DA3;
DAM POP; DLB 306; INT CA-129;
MSW; RGAL 4

Parfenie, Maria
See Codrescu, Andrei

Parini, Jay (Lee) 1948- .... **CLC 54, 133**
See also CA 97-100, 229; CAAE 229;
CAAS 16; CANR 32, 87

Park, Jordan
See Kornbluth, C(yril) M.; Pohl, Frederik

Park, Robert E(zra) 1864-1944 ..... **TCLC 73**
See also CA 122; 165

Parker, Bert
See Ellison, Harlan (Jay)

Parker, Dorothy (Rothschild)
1893-1967 . **CLC 15, 68; PC 28; SSC 2;
TCLC 143**
See also AMWS 9; CA 19-20; 25-28R; CAP
2; DA3; DAM POET; DLB 11, 45, 86;
EXPP; FW; MAL 5; MAWW; MTCW 1,
2; MTFW 2005; PFS 18; RGAL 4; RGSF
2; TUS

Parker, Robert B(rown) 1932- .... **CLC 27**
See also AAYA 28; BEST 89:4; BPFB 3;
CA 49-52; CANR 1, 26, 52, 89, 128;
CMW 4; CPW; DAM NOV, POP; DLB
306; INT CANR-26; MSW; MTCW 1;
MTFW 2005

Parkin, Frank 1940- .... **CLC 43**
See also CA 147

Parkman, Francis, Jr. 1823-1893 .. **NCLC 12**
See also AMWS 2; DLB 1, 30, 183, 186,
235; RGAL 4

Parks, Gordon (Alexander Buchanan)
1912- .... **BLC 3; CLC 1, 16**
See also AAYA 36; AITN 2; BW 2, 3; CA
41-44R; CANR 26, 66, 145; DA3; DAM
MULT; DLB 33; MTCW 2; MTFW 2005;
SATA 8, 108

Pepys, Samuel 1633-1703 ... **LC 11, 58; WLC**
See also BRW 2; CDBLB 1660-1789; DA;
DA3; DAB; DAC; DAM MST; DLB 101,
213; NCFS 4; RGEL 2; TEA; WLIT 3

Percy, Thomas 1729-1811 .... **NCLC 95**
See also DLB 104

Percy, Walker 1916-1990 .... **CLC 2, 3, 6, 8,
14, 18, 47, 65**
See also AMWS 3; BPFB 3; CA 1-4R; 131;
CANR 1, 23, 64; CN 1, 2, 3, 4; CPW;
CSW; DA3; DAM NOV, POP; DLB 2;
DLBY 1980, 1990; EWL 3; MAL 5;
MTCW 1, 2; MTFW 2005; RGAL 4; TUS

Percy, William Alexander
1885-1942 .... **TCLC 84**
See also CA 163; MTCW 2

Perec, Georges 1936-1982 .... **CLC 56, 116**
See also CA 141; DLB 83, 299; EWL 3;
GFL 1789 to the Present; RGWL 3

**Pereda (y Sanchez de Porrua), Jose Maria
de** 1833-1906 .... **TCLC 16**
See also CA 117

Pereda y Porrua, Jose Maria de
See Pereda (y Sanchez de Porrua), Jose
Maria de

Peregoy, George Weems
See Mencken, H(enry) L(ouis)

Perelman, S(idney) J(oseph)
1904-1979 .. **CLC 3, 5, 9, 15, 23, 44, 49;
SSC 32**
See also AITN 1, 2; BPFB 3; CA 73-76;
89-92; CANR 18; DAM DRAM; DLB 11,
44; MTCW 1, 2; MTFW 2005; RGAL 4

Peret, Benjamin 1899-1959 .... **PC 33; TCLC
20**
See also CA 117; 186; GFL 1789 to the
Present

Peretz, Isaac Leib
See Peretz, Isaac Loeb
See also CA 201

Peretz, Isaac Loeb 1851(?)-1915 ...... **SSC 26;
TCLC 16**
See Peretz, Isaac Leib
See also CA 109

Peretz, Yitzkhok Leibush
See Peretz, Isaac Loeb

Perez Galdos, Benito 1843-1920 ..... **HLCS 2;
TCLC 27**
See Galdos, Benito Perez
See also CA 125; 153; EWL 3; HW 1;
RGWL 2, 3

Peri Rossi, Cristina 1941- .. **CLC 156; HLCS
2**
See also CA 131; CANR 59, 81; CWW 2;
DLB 145, 290; EWL 3; HW 1, 2

Perlata
See Peret, Benjamin

Perloff, Marjorie G(abrielle)
1931- .... **CLC 137**
See also CA 57-60; CANR 7, 22, 49, 104

Perrault, Charles 1628-1703 .... **LC 2, 56**
See also BYA 4; CLR 79; DLB 268; GFL
Beginnings to 1789; MAICYA 1, 2;
RGWL 2, 3; SATA 25; WCH

Perry, Anne 1938- .... **CLC 126**
See also CA 101; CANR 22, 50, 84; CMW
4; CN 6, 7; CPW; DLB 276

Perry, Brighton
See Sherwood, Robert E(mmet)

Perse, St.-John
See Leger, (Marie-Rene Auguste) Alexis
Saint-Leger

Perse, Saint-John
See Leger, (Marie-Rene Auguste) Alexis
Saint-Leger
See also DLB 258; RGWL 3

Persius 34-62 .... **CMLC 74**
See also AW 2; DLB 211; RGWL 2, 3

Perutz, Leo(pold) 1882-1957 .... **TCLC 60**
See also CA 147; DLB 81

Peseenz, Tulio F.
See Lopez y Fuentes, Gregorio

Pesetsky, Bette 1932- .... **CLC 28**
See also CA 133; DLB 130

Peshkov, Alexei Maximovich 1868-1936
See Gorky, Maxim
See also CA 105; 141; CANR 83; DA;
DAC; DAM DRAM, MST, NOV; MTCW
2; MTFW 2005

Pessoa, Fernando (Antonio Nogueira)
1888-1935 ..... **HLC 2; PC 20; TCLC 27**
See also CA 125; 183; DAM MULT; DLB
287; EW 10; EWL 3; RGWL 2, 3; WP

Peterkin, Julia Mood 1880-1961 ...... **CLC 31**
See also CA 102; DLB 9

Peters, Joan K(aren) 1945- .... **CLC 39**
See also CA 158; CANR 109

Peters, Robert L(ouis) 1924- .... **CLC 7**
See also CA 13-16R; CAAS 8; CP 1, 7;
DLB 105

Petofi, Sandor 1823-1849 .... **NCLC 21**
See also RGWL 2, 3

Petrakis, Harry Mark 1923- .... **CLC 3**
See also CA 9-12R; CANR 4, 30, 85; CN
1, 2, 3, 4, 5, 6, 7

Petrarch 1304-1374 .... **CMLC 20; PC 8**
See also DA3; DAM POET; EW 2; LMFS
1; RGWL 2, 3; WLIT 7

Petronius c. 20-66 .... **CMLC 34**
See also AW 2; CDWLB 1; DLB 211;
RGWL 2, 3

Petrov, Evgeny .... **TCLC 21**
See Kataev, Evgeny Petrovich

Petry, Ann (Lane) 1908-1997 .. **CLC 1, 7, 18;
TCLC 112**
See also AFAW 1, 2; BPFB 3; BW 1, 3;
BYA 2; CA 5-8R; 157; CAAS 6; CANR
4, 46; CLR 12; CN 1, 2, 3, 4, 5, 6; DLB
76; EWL 3; JRDA; LAIT 1; MAICYA 1,
2; MAICYAS 1; MTCW 1; RGAL 4;
SATA 5; SATA-Obit 94; TUS

Petursson, Halligrimur 1614-1674 .... **LC 8**

Peychinovich
See Vazov, Ivan (Minchov)

Phaedrus c. 15B.C.-c. 50 .... **CMLC 25**
See also DLB 211

Phelps (Ward), Elizabeth Stuart
See Phelps, Elizabeth Stuart
See also FW

Phelps, Elizabeth Stuart
1844-1911 .... **TCLC 113**
See Phelps (Ward), Elizabeth Stuart
See also DLB 74

Philips, Katherine 1632-1664 . **LC 30; PC 40**
See also DLB 131; RGEL 2

Philipson, Morris H. 1926- .... **CLC 53**
See also CA 1-4R; CANR 4

Phillips, Caryl 1958- .... **BLCS; CLC 96**
See also BRWS 5; BW 2; CA 141; CANR
63, 104, 140; CBD; CD 5, 6; CN 5, 6, 7;
DA3; DAM MULT; DLB 157; EWL 3;
MTCW 2; MTFW 2005; WLIT 4; WWE
1

Phillips, David Graham
1867-1911 .... **TCLC 44**
See also CA 108; 176; DLB 9, 12, 303;
RGAL 4

Phillips, Jack
See Sandburg, Carl (August)

Phillips, Jayne Anne 1952- .... **CLC 15, 33,
139; SSC 16**
See also AAYA 57; BPFB 3; CA 101;
CANR 24, 50, 96; CN 4, 5, 6, 7; CSW;
DLBY 1980; INT CANR-24; MTCW 1,
2; MTFW 2005; RGAL 4; RGSF 2; SSFS
4

Phillips, Richard
See Dick, Philip K(indred)

Phillips, Robert (Schaeffer) 1938- .... **CLC 28**
See also CA 17-20R; CAAS 13; CANR 8;
DLB 105

Phillips, Ward
See Lovecraft, H(oward) P(hillips)

Philostratus, Flavius c. 179-c.
244 .... **CMLC 62**

Piccolo, Lucio 1901-1969 .... **CLC 13**
See also CA 97-100; DLB 114; EWL 3

Pickthall, Marjorie L(owry) C(hristie)
1883-1922 .... **TCLC 21**
See also CA 107; DLB 92

Pico della Mirandola, Giovanni
1463-1494 .... **LC 15**
See also LMFS 1

Piercy, Marge 1936- .... **CLC 3, 6, 14, 18, 27,
62, 128; PC 29**
See also BPFB 3; CA 21-24R, 187; CAAE
187; CAAS 1; CANR 13, 43, 66, 111; CN
3, 4, 5, 6, 7; CP 1, 2, 3, 4, 5, 6, 7; CWP;
DLB 120, 227; EXPP; FW; MAL 5;
MTCW 1, 2; MTFW 2005; PFS 9, 22;
SFW 4

Piers, Robert
See Anthony, Piers

Pieyre de Mandiargues, Andre 1909-1991
See Mandiargues, Andre Pieyre de
See also CA 103; 136; CANR 22, 82; EWL
3; GFL 1789 to the Present

Pilnyak, Boris 1894-1938 . **SSC 48; TCLC 23**
See Vogau, Boris Andreyevich
See also EWL 3

Pinchback, Eugene
See Toomer, Jean

Pincherle, Alberto 1907-1990 ...... **CLC 11, 18**
See Moravia, Alberto
See also CA 25-28R; 132; CANR 33, 63,
142; DAM NOV; MTCW 1; MTFW 2005

Pinckney, Darryl 1953- .... **CLC 76**
See also BW 2, 3; CA 143; CANR 79

Pindar 518(?)B.C.-438(?)B.C. .... **CMLC 12;
PC 19**
See also AW 1; CDWLB 1; DLB 176;
RGWL 2

Pineda, Cecile 1942- .... **CLC 39**
See also CA 118; DLB 209

Pinero, Arthur Wing 1855-1934 .... **TCLC 32**
See also CA 110; 153; DAM DRAM; DLB
10; RGEL 2

Pinero, Miguel (Antonio Gomez)
1946-1988 .... **CLC 4, 55**
See also CA 61-64; 125; CAD; CANR 29,
90; DLB 266; HW 1; LLW

Pinget, Robert 1919-1997 .... **CLC 7, 13, 37**
See also CA 85-88; 160; CWW 2; DLB 83;
EWL 3; GFL 1789 to the Present

Pink Floyd
See Barrett, (Roger) Syd; Gilmour, David;
Mason, Nick; Waters, Roger; Wright, Rick

Pinkney, Edward 1802-1828 .... **NCLC 31**
See also DLB 248

Pinkwater, D. Manus
See Pinkwater, Daniel Manus

Pinkwater, Daniel
See Pinkwater, Daniel Manus

Pinkwater, Daniel M.
See Pinkwater, Daniel Manus

Pinkwater, Daniel Manus 1941- .... **CLC 35**
See also AAYA 1, 46; BYA 9; CA 29-32R;
CANR 12, 38, 89, 143; CLR 4; CSW;
FANT; JRDA; MAICYA 1, 2; SAAS 3;
SATA 8, 46, 76, 114, 158; SFW 4; YAW

Pinkwater, Manus
See Pinkwater, Daniel Manus

MAL 5; MAWW; MTCW 1, 2; MTFW 2005; NFS 14; RGAL 4; RGSF 2; SATA 39; SATA-Obit 23; SSFS 1, 8, 11, 16; TCWW 2; TUS

Porter, Peter (Neville Frederick)
1929- .... **CLC 5, 13, 33**
See also CA 85-88; CP 1, 2, 3, 4, 5, 6, 7; DLB 40, 289; WWE 1

Porter, William Sydney 1862-1910
See Henry, O.
See also CA 104; 131; CDALB 1865-1917; DA; DA3; DAB; DAC; DAM MST; DLB 12, 78, 79; MAL 5; MTCW 1, 2; MTFW 2005; TUS; YABC 2

Portillo (y Pacheco), Jose Lopez
See Lopez Portillo (y Pacheco), Jose

Portillo Trambley, Estela 1927-1998 .. **HLC 2**
See Trambley, Estela Portillo
See also CANR 32; DAM MULT; DLB 209; HW 1

Posey, Alexander (Lawrence)
1873-1908 .... **NNAL**
See also CA 144; CANR 80; DAM MULT; DLB 175

Posse, Abel .... **CLC 70**

Post, Melville Davisson
1869-1930 .... **TCLC 39**
See also CA 110; 202; CMW 4

Potok, Chaim 1929-2002 ... **CLC 2, 7, 14, 26, 112**
See also AAYA 15, 50; AITN 1, 2; BPFB 3; BYA 1; CA 17-20R; 208; CANR 19, 35, 64, 98; CLR 92; CN 4, 5, 6; DA3; DAM NOV; DLB 28, 152; EXPN; INT CANR-19; LAIT 4; MTCW 1, 2; MTFW 2005; NFS 4; SATA 33, 106; SATA-Obit 134; TUS; YAW

Potok, Herbert Harold -2002
See Potok, Chaim

Potok, Herman Harold
See Potok, Chaim

Potter, Dennis (Christopher George)
1935-1994 .... **CLC 58, 86, 123**
See also BRWS 10; CA 107; 145; CANR 33, 61; CBD; DLB 233; MTCW 1

Pound, Ezra (Weston Loomis)
1885-1972 .. **CLC 1, 2, 3, 4, 5, 7, 10, 13, 18, 34, 48, 50, 112; PC 4; WLC**
See also AAYA 47; AMW; AMWR 1; CA 5-8R; 37-40R; CANR 40; CDALB 1917-1929; CP 1; DA; DA3; DAB; DAC; DAM MST, POET; DLB 4, 45, 63; DLBD 15; EFS 2; EWL 3; EXPP; LMFS 2; MAL 5; MTCW 1, 2; MTFW 2005; PAB; PFS 2, 8, 16; RGAL 4; TUS; WP

Povod, Reinaldo 1959-1994 .... **CLC 44**
See also CA 136; 146; CANR 83

Powell, Adam Clayton, Jr.
1908-1972 .... **BLC 3; CLC 89**
See also BW 1, 3; CA 102; 33-36R; CANR 86; DAM MULT

Powell, Anthony (Dymoke)
1905-2000 .... **CLC 1, 3, 7, 9, 10, 31**
See also BRW 7; CA 1-4R; 189; CANR 1, 32, 62, 107; CDBLB 1945-1960; CN 1, 2, 3, 4, 5, 6; DLB 15; EWL 3; MTCW 1, 2; MTFW 2005; RGEL 2; TEA

Powell, Dawn 1896(?)-1965 .... **CLC 66**
See also CA 5-8R; CANR 121; DLBY 1997

Powell, Padgett 1952- .... **CLC 34**
See also CA 126; CANR 63, 101; CSW; DLB 234; DLBY 01

Powell, (Oval) Talmage 1920-2000
See Queen, Ellery
See also CA 5-8R; CANR 2, 80

Power, Susan 1961- .... **CLC 91**
See also BYA 14; CA 160; CANR 135; NFS 11

Powers, J(ames) F(arl) 1917-1999 ..... **CLC 1, 4, 8, 57; SSC 4**
See also CA 1-4R; 181; CANR 2, 61; CN 1, 2, 3, 4, 5, 6; DLB 130; MTCW 1; RGAL 4; RGSF 2

Powers, John J(ames) 1945-
See Powers, John R.
See also CA 69-72

Powers, John R. .... **CLC 66**
See Powers, John J(ames)

Powers, Richard (S.) 1957- .... **CLC 93**
See also AMWS 9; BPFB 3; CA 148; CANR 80; CN 6, 7; MTFW 2005; TCLE 1:2

Pownall, David 1938- .... **CLC 10**
See also CA 89-92, 180; CAAS 18; CANR 49, 101; CBD; CD 5, 6; CN 4, 5, 6, 7; DLB 14

Powys, John Cowper 1872-1963 ... **CLC 7, 9, 15, 46, 125**
See also CA 85-88; CANR 106; DLB 15, 255; EWL 3; FANT; MTCW 1, 2; MTFW 2005; RGEL 2; SUFW

Powys, T(heodore) F(rancis)
1875-1953 .... **TCLC 9**
See also BRWS 8; CA 106; 189; DLB 36, 162; EWL 3; FANT; RGEL 2; SUFW

Pozzo, Modesta
See Fonte, Moderata

Prado (Calvo), Pedro 1886-1952 ... **TCLC 75**
See also CA 131; DLB 283; HW 1; LAW

Prager, Emily 1952- .... **CLC 56**
See also CA 204

Pratchett, Terry 1948- .... **CLC 197**
See also AAYA 19, 54; BPFB 3; CA 143; CANR 87, 126; CLR 64; CN 6, 7; CPW; CWRI 5; FANT; MTFW 2005; SATA 82, 139; SFW 4; SUFW 2

Pratolini, Vasco 1913-1991 .... **TCLC 124**
See also CA 211; DLB 177; EWL 3; RGWL 2, 3

Pratt, E(dwin) J(ohn) 1883(?)-1964 . **CLC 19**
See also CA 141; 93-96; CANR 77; DAC; DAM POET; DLB 92; EWL 3; RGEL 2; TWA

Premchand .... **TCLC 21**
See Srivastava, Dhanpat Rai
See also EWL 3

Prescott, William Hickling
1796-1859 .... **NCLC 163**
See also DLB 1, 30, 59, 235

Preseren, France 1800-1849 .... **NCLC 127**
See also CDWLB 4; DLB 147

Preussler, Otfried 1923- .... **CLC 17**
See also CA 77-80; SATA 24

Prevert, Jacques (Henri Marie)
1900-1977 .... **CLC 15**
See also CA 77-80; 69-72; CANR 29, 61; DLB 258; EWL 3; GFL 1789 to the Present; IDFW 3, 4; MTCW 1; RGWL 2, 3; SATA-Obit 30

Prevost, (Antoine Francois)
1697-1763 .... **LC 1**
See also DLB 314; EW 4; GFL Beginnings to 1789; RGWL 2, 3

Price, (Edward) Reynolds 1933- ... **CLC 3, 6, 13, 43, 50, 63, 212; SSC 22**
See also AMWS 6; CA 1-4R; CANR 1, 37, 57, 87, 128; CN 1, 2, 3, 4, 5, 6, 7; CSW; DAM NOV; DLB 2, 218, 278; EWL 3; INT CANR-37; MAL 5; MTFW 2005; NFS 18

Price, Richard 1949- .... **CLC 6, 12**
See also CA 49-52; CANR 3; CN 7; DLBY 1981

Prichard, Katharine Susannah
1883-1969 .... **CLC 46**
See also CA 11-12; CANR 33; CAP 1; DLB 260; MTCW 1; RGEL 2; RGSF 2; SATA 66

Priestley, J(ohn) B(oynton)
1894-1984 .... **CLC 2, 5, 9, 34**
See also BRW 7; CA 9-12R; 113; CANR 33; CDBLB 1914-1945; CN 1, 2, 3; DA3; DAM DRAM, NOV; DLB 10, 34, 77, 100, 139; DLBY 1984; EWL 3; MTCW 1, 2; MTFW 2005; RGEL 2; SFW 4

Prince 1958- .... **CLC 35**
See also CA 213

Prince, F(rank) T(empleton)
1912-2003 .... **CLC 22**
See also CA 101; 219; CANR 43, 79; CP 1, 2, 3, 4, 5, 6, 7; DLB 20

Prince Kropotkin
See Kropotkin, Peter (Aleksieevich)

Prior, Matthew 1664-1721 .... **LC 4**
See also DLB 95; RGEL 2

Prishvin, Mikhail 1873-1954 .... **TCLC 75**
See Prishvin, Mikhail Mikhailovich

Prishvin, Mikhail Mikhailovich
See Prishvin, Mikhail
See also DLB 272; EWL 3

Pritchard, William H(arrison)
1932- .... **CLC 34**
See also CA 65-68; CANR 23, 95; DLB 111

Pritchett, V(ictor) S(awdon)
1900-1997 ... **CLC 5, 13, 15, 41; SSC 14**
See also BPFB 3; BRWS 3; CA 61-64; 157; CANR 31, 63; CN 1, 2, 3, 4, 5, 6; DAM NOV; DLB 15, 139; EWL 3; MTCW 1, 2; MTFW 2005; RGEL 2; RGSF 2; TEA

Private 19022
See Manning, Frederic

Probst, Mark 1925- .... **CLC 59**
See also CA 130

Procaccino, Michael
See Cristofer, Michael

Proclus c. 412-485 .... **CMLC 81**

Prokosch, Frederic 1908-1989 ...... **CLC 4, 48**
See also CA 73-76; 128; CANR 82; CN 1, 2, 3, 4; CP 1, 2, 3, 4; DLB 48; MTCW 2

Propertius, Sextus c. 50B.C.-c. 16B.C. .... **CMLC 32**
See also AW 2; CDWLB 1; DLB 211; RGWL 2, 3

Prophet, The
See Dreiser, Theodore (Herman Albert)

Prose, Francine 1947- .... **CLC 45**
See also CA 109; 112; CANR 46, 95, 132; DLB 234; MTFW 2005; SATA 101, 149

Proudhon
See Cunha, Euclides (Rodrigues Pimenta) da

Proulx, Annie
See Proulx, E. Annie

Proulx, E. Annie 1935- .... **CLC 81, 158**
See also AMWS 7; BPFB 3; CA 145; CANR 65, 110; CN 6, 7; CPW 1; DA3; DAM POP; MAL 5; MTCW 2; MTFW 2005; SSFS 18

Proulx, Edna Annie
See Proulx, E. Annie

Proust, (Valentin-Louis-George-Eugene) Marcel 1871-1922 ..... **SSC 75; TCLC 7, 13, 33; WLC**
See also AAYA 58; BPFB 3; CA 104; 120; CANR 110; DA; DA3; DAB; DAC; DAM MST, NOV; DLB 65; EW 8; EWL 3; GFL 1789 to the Present; MTCW 1, 2; MTFW 2005; RGWL 2, 3; TWA

Prowler, Harley
See Masters, Edgar Lee

Ralegh, Sir Walter
See Raleigh, Sir Walter
See also BRW 1; RGEL 2; WP

Raleigh, Richard
See Lovecraft, H(oward) P(hillips)

Raleigh, Sir Walter 1554(?)-1618 .... **LC 31, 39; PC 31**
See Ralegh, Sir Walter
See also CDBLB Before 1660; DLB 172; EXPP; PFS 14; TEA

Rallentando, H. P.
See Sayers, Dorothy L(eigh)

Ramal, Walter
See de la Mare, Walter (John)

Ramana Maharshi 1879-1950 .... **TCLC 84**

Ramoacn y Cajal, Santiago
1852-1934 .... **TCLC 93**

Ramon, Juan
See Jimenez (Mantecon), Juan Ramon

Ramos, Graciliano 1892-1953 .... **TCLC 32**
See also CA 167; DLB 307; EWL 3; HW 2; LAW; WLIT 1

Rampersad, Arnold 1941- .... **CLC 44**
See also BW 2, 3; CA 127; 133; CANR 81; DLB 111; INT CA-133

Rampling, Anne
See Rice, Anne
See also GLL 2

Ramsay, Allan 1686(?)-1758 .... **LC 29**
See also DLB 95; RGEL 2

Ramsay, Jay
See Campbell, (John) Ramsey

Ramuz, Charles-Ferdinand
1878-1947 .... **TCLC 33**
See also CA 165; EWL 3

Rand, Ayn 1905-1982 ...... **CLC 3, 30, 44, 79; WLC**
See also AAYA 10; AMWS 4; BPFB 3; BYA 12; CA 13-16R; 105; CANR 27, 73; CDALBS; CN 1, 2, 3; CPW; DA; DA3; DAC; DAM MST, NOV, POP; DLB 227, 279; MTCW 1, 2; MTFW 2005; NFS 10, 16; RGAL 4; SFW 4; TUS; YAW

Randall, Dudley (Felker) 1914-2000 . **BLC 3; CLC 1, 135**
See also BW 1, 3; CA 25-28R; 189; CANR 23, 82; CP 1, 2, 3, 4; DAM MULT; DLB 41; PFS 5

Randall, Robert
See Silverberg, Robert

Ranger, Ken
See Creasey, John

Rank, Otto 1884-1939 .... **TCLC 115**

Ransom, John Crowe 1888-1974 .. **CLC 2, 4, 5, 11, 24; PC 61**
See also AMW; CA 5-8R; 49-52; CANR 6, 34; CDALBS; CP 1, 2; DA3; DAM POET; DLB 45, 63; EWL 3; EXPP; MAL 5; MTCW 1, 2; MTFW 2005; RGAL 4; TUS

Rao, Raja 1909- .... **CLC 25, 56**
See also CA 73-76; CANR 51; CN 1, 2, 3, 4, 5, 6; DAM NOV; EWL 3; MTCW 1, 2; MTFW 2005; RGEL 2; RGSF 2

Raphael, Frederic (Michael) 1931- ... **CLC 2, 14**
See also CA 1-4R; CANR 1, 86; CN 1, 2, 3, 4, 5, 6, 7; DLB 14, 319; TCLE 1:2

Ratcliffe, James P.
See Mencken, H(enry) L(ouis)

Rathbone, Julian 1935- .... **CLC 41**
See also CA 101; CANR 34, 73

Rattigan, Terence (Mervyn)
1911-1977 .... **CLC 7; DC 18**
See also BRWS 7; CA 85-88; 73-76; CBD; CDBLB 1945-1960; DAM DRAM; DFS 8; DLB 13; IDFW 3, 4; MTCW 1, 2; MTFW 2005; RGEL 2

Ratushinskaya, Irina 1954- .... **CLC 54**
See also CA 129; CANR 68; CWW 2

Raven, Simon (Arthur Noel)
1927-2001 .... **CLC 14**
See also CA 81-84; 197; CANR 86; CN 1, 2, 3, 4, 5, 6; DLB 271

Ravenna, Michael
See Welty, Eudora (Alice)

Rawley, Callman 1903-2004
See Rakosi, Carl
See also CA 21-24R; 228; CANR 12, 32, 91

Rawlings, Marjorie Kinnan
1896-1953 .... **TCLC 4**
See also AAYA 20; AMWS 10; ANW; BPFB 3; BYA 3; CA 104; 137; CANR 74; CLR 63; DLB 9, 22, 102; DLBD 17; JRDA; MAICYA 1, 2; MAL 5; MTCW 2; MTFW 2005; RGAL 4; SATA 100; WCH; YABC 1; YAW

Ray, Satyajit 1921-1992 .... **CLC 16, 76**
See also CA 114; 137; DAM MULT

Read, Herbert Edward 1893-1968 ..... **CLC 4**
See also BRW 6; CA 85-88; 25-28R; DLB 20, 149; EWL 3; PAB; RGEL 2

Read, Piers Paul 1941- .... **CLC 4, 10, 25**
See also CA 21-24R; CANR 38, 86; CN 2, 3, 4, 5, 6, 7; DLB 14; SATA 21

Reade, Charles 1814-1884 .... **NCLC 2, 74**
See also DLB 21; RGEL 2

Reade, Hamish
See Gray, Simon (James Holliday)

Reading, Peter 1946- .... **CLC 47**
See also BRWS 8; CA 103; CANR 46, 96; CP 7; DLB 40

Reaney, James 1926- .... **CLC 13**
See also CA 41-44R; CAAS 15; CANR 42; CD 5, 6; CP 1, 2, 3, 4, 5, 6, 7; DAC; DAM MST; DLB 68; RGEL 2; SATA 43

Rebreanu, Liviu 1885-1944 .... **TCLC 28**
See also CA 165; DLB 220; EWL 3

Rechy, John (Francisco) 1934- ...... **CLC 1, 7, 14, 18, 107; HLC 2**
See also CA 5-8R; 195; CAAE 195; CAAS 4; CANR 6, 32, 64; CN 1, 2, 3, 4, 5, 6, 7; DAM MULT; DLB 122, 278; DLBY 1982; HW 1, 2; INT CANR-6; LLW; MAL 5; RGAL 4

Redcam, Tom 1870-1933 .... **TCLC 25**

Reddin, Keith 1956- .... **CLC 67**
See also CAD; CD 6

Redgrove, Peter (William)
1932-2003 .... **CLC 6, 41**
See also BRWS 6; CA 1-4R; 217; CANR 3, 39, 77; CP 1, 2, 3, 4, 5, 6, 7; DLB 40; TCLE 1:2

Redmon, Anne .... **CLC 22**
See Nightingale, Anne Redmon
See also DLBY 1986

Reed, Eliot
See Ambler, Eric

Reed, Ishmael (Scott) 1938- . **BLC 3; CLC 2, 3, 5, 6, 13, 32, 60, 174; PC 68**
See also AFAW 1, 2; AMWS 10; BPFB 3; BW 2, 3; CA 21-24R; CANR 25, 48, 74, 128; CN 1, 2, 3, 4, 5, 6, 7; CP 1, 2, 3, 4, 5, 6, 7; CSW; DA3; DAM MULT; DLB 2, 5, 33, 169, 227; DLBD 8; EWL 3; LMFS 2; MAL 5; MSW; MTCW 1, 2; MTFW 2005; PFS 6; RGAL 4; TCWW 2

Reed, John (Silas) 1887-1920 .... **TCLC 9**
See also CA 106; 195; MAL 5; TUS

Reed, Lou .... **CLC 21**
See Firbank, Louis

Reese, Lizette Woodworth 1856-1935 . **PC 29**
See also CA 180; DLB 54

Reeve, Clara 1729-1807 .... **NCLC 19**
See also DLB 39; RGEL 2

Reich, Wilhelm 1897-1957 .... **TCLC 57**
See also CA 199

Reid, Christopher (John) 1949- .... **CLC 33**
See also CA 140; CANR 89; CP 4, 5, 6, 7; DLB 40; EWL 3

Reid, Desmond
See Moorcock, Michael (John)

Reid Banks, Lynne 1929-
See Banks, Lynne Reid
See also AAYA 49; CA 1-4R; CANR 6, 22, 38, 87; CLR 24; CN 1, 2, 3, 7; JRDA; MAICYA 1, 2; SATA 22, 75, 111, 165; YAW

Reilly, William K.
See Creasey, John

Reiner, Max
See Caldwell, (Janet Miriam) Taylor (Holland)

Reis, Ricardo
See Pessoa, Fernando (Antonio Nogueira)

Reizenstein, Elmer Leopold
See Rice, Elmer (Leopold)
See also EWL 3

Remarque, Erich Maria 1898-1970 . **CLC 21**
See also AAYA 27; BPFB 3; CA 77-80; 29-32R; CDWLB 2; DA; DA3; DAB; DAC; DAM MST, NOV; DLB 56; EWL 3; EXPN; LAIT 3; MTCW 1, 2; MTFW 2005; NFS 4; RGWL 2, 3

Remington, Frederic S(ackrider)
1861-1909 .... **TCLC 89**
See also CA 108; 169; DLB 12, 186, 188; SATA 41; TCWW 2

Remizov, A.
See Remizov, Aleksei (Mikhailovich)

Remizov, A. M.
See Remizov, Aleksei (Mikhailovich)

Remizov, Aleksei (Mikhailovich)
1877-1957 .... **TCLC 27**
See Remizov, Alexey Mikhaylovich
See also CA 125; 133; DLB 295

Remizov, Alexey Mikhaylovich
See Remizov, Aleksei (Mikhailovich)
See also EWL 3

Renan, Joseph Ernest 1823-1892 . **NCLC 26, 145**
See also GFL 1789 to the Present

Renard, Jules(-Pierre) 1864-1910 .. **TCLC 17**
See also CA 117; 202; GFL 1789 to the Present

Renault, Mary .... **CLC 3, 11, 17**
See Challans, Mary
See also BPFB 3; BYA 2; CN 1, 2, 3; DLBY 1983; EWL 3; GLL 1; LAIT 1; RGEL 2; RHW

Rendell, Ruth (Barbara) 1930- .. **CLC 28, 48**
See Vine, Barbara
See also BPFB 3; BRWS 9; CA 109; CANR 32, 52, 74, 127; CN 5, 6, 7; CPW; DAM POP; DLB 87, 276; INT CANR-32; MSW; MTCW 1, 2; MTFW 2005

Renoir, Jean 1894-1979 .... **CLC 20**
See also CA 129; 85-88

Resnais, Alain 1922- .... **CLC 16**

Revard, Carter (Curtis) 1931- .... **NNAL**
See also CA 144; CANR 81; PFS 5

Reverdy, Pierre 1889-1960 .... **CLC 53**
See also CA 97-100; 89-92; DLB 258; EWL 3; GFL 1789 to the Present

Rexroth, Kenneth 1905-1982 .... **CLC 1, 2, 6, 11, 22, 49, 112; PC 20**
See also BG 1:3; CA 5-8R; 107; CANR 14, 34, 63; CDALB 1941-1968; CP 1, 2, 3; DAM POET; DLB 16, 48, 165, 212; DLBY 1982; EWL 3; INT CANR-14; MAL 5; MTCW 1, 2; MTFW 2005; RGAL 4

Reyes, Alfonso 1889-1959 .... **HLCS 2; TCLC 33**
See also CA 131; EWL 3; HW 1; LAW

Reyes y Basoalto, Ricardo Eliecer Neftali
See Neruda, Pablo
Reymont, Wladyslaw (Stanislaw)
1868(?)-1925 .... **TCLC 5**
See also CA 104; EWL 3
Reynolds, John Hamilton
1794-1852 .... **NCLC 146**
See also DLB 96
Reynolds, Jonathan 1942- .... **CLC 6, 38**
See also CA 65-68; CANR 28
Reynolds, Joshua 1723-1792 .... **LC 15**
See also DLB 104
Reynolds, Michael S(hane)
1937-2000 .... **CLC 44**
See also CA 65-68; 189; CANR 9, 89, 97
Reznikoff, Charles 1894-1976 .... **CLC 9**
See also AMWS 14; CA 33-36; 61-64; CAP
2; CP 1, 2; DLB 28, 45; WP
Rezzori (d'Arezzo), Gregor von
1914-1998 .... **CLC 25**
See also CA 122; 136; 167
Rhine, Richard
See Silverstein, Alvin; Silverstein, Virginia
B(arbara Opshelor)
Rhodes, Eugene Manlove
1869-1934 .... **TCLC 53**
See also CA 198; DLB 256; TCWW 1, 2
R'hoone, Lord
See Balzac, Honore de
Rhys, Jean 1890-1979 .... **CLC 2, 4, 6, 14, 19,**
51, 124; SSC 21, 76
See also BRWS 2; CA 25-28R; 85-88;
CANR 35, 62; CDBLB 1945-1960; CD-
WLB 3; CN 1, 2; DA3; DAM NOV; DLB
36, 117, 162; DNFS 2; EWL 3; LATS 1:1;
MTCW 1, 2; MTFW 2005; NFS 19;
RGEL 2; RGSF 2; RHW; TEA; WWE 1
Ribeiro, Darcy 1922-1997 .... **CLC 34**
See also CA 33-36R; 156; EWL 3
Ribeiro, Joao Ubaldo (Osorio Pimentel)
1941- .... **CLC 10, 67**
See also CA 81-84; CWW 2; EWL 3
Ribman, Ronald (Burt) 1932- .... **CLC 7**
See also CA 21-24R; CAD; CANR 46, 80;
CD 5, 6
Ricci, Nino (Pio) 1959- .... **CLC 70**
See also CA 137; CANR 130; CCA 1
Rice, Anne 1941- .... **CLC 41, 128**
See Rampling, Anne
See also AAYA 9, 53; AMWS 7; BEST
89:2; BPFB 3; CA 65-68; CANR 12, 36,
53, 74, 100, 133; CN 6, 7; CPW; CSW;
DA3; DAM POP; DLB 292; GL 3; GLL
2; HGG; MTCW 2; MTFW 2005; SUFW
2; YAW
Rice, Elmer (Leopold) 1892-1967 ...... **CLC 7,**
49
See Reizenstein, Elmer Leopold
See also CA 21-22; 25-28R; CAP 2; DAM
DRAM; DFS 12; DLB 4, 7; IDTP; MAL
5; MTCW 1, 2; RGAL 4
Rice, Tim(othy Miles Bindon)
1944- .... **CLC 21**
See also CA 103; CANR 46; DFS 7
Rich, Adrienne (Cecile) 1929- ... **CLC 3, 6, 7,**
11, 18, 36, 73, 76, 125; PC 5
See also AMWR 2; AMWS 1; CA 9-12R;
CANR 20, 53, 74, 128; CDALBS; CP 1,
2, 3, 4, 5, 6, 7; CSW; CWP; DA3; DAM
POET; DLB 5, 67; EWL 3; EXPP; FL 1:6;
FW; MAL 5; MAWW; MTCW 1, 2;
MTFW 2005; PAB; PFS 15; RGAL 4; WP
Rich, Barbara
See Graves, Robert (von Ranke)
Rich, Robert
See Trumbo, Dalton
Richard, Keith .... **CLC 17**
See Richards, Keith

Richards, David Adams 1950- .... **CLC 59**
See also CA 93-96; CANR 60, 110; CN 7;
DAC; DLB 53; TCLE 1:2
Richards, I(vor) A(rmstrong)
1893-1979 .... **CLC 14, 24**
See also BRWS 2; CA 41-44R; 89-92;
CANR 34, 74; CP 1, 2; DLB 27; EWL 3;
MTCW 2; RGEL 2
Richards, Keith 1943-
See Richard, Keith
See also CA 107; CANR 77
Richardson, Anne
See Roiphe, Anne (Richardson)
Richardson, Dorothy Miller
1873-1957 .... **TCLC 3**
See also CA 104; 192; DLB 36; EWL 3;
FW; RGEL 2
Richardson (Robertson), Ethel Florence
Lindesay 1870-1946
See Richardson, Henry Handel
See also CA 105; 190; DLB 230; RHW
Richardson, Henry Handel .... **TCLC 4**
See Richardson (Robertson), Ethel Florence
Lindesay
See also DLB 197; EWL 3; RGEL 2; RGSF
2
Richardson, John 1796-1852 .... **NCLC 55**
See also CCA 1; DAC; DLB 99
Richardson, Samuel 1689-1761 ...... **LC 1, 44;**
WLC
See also BRW 3; CDBLB 1660-1789; DA;
DAB; DAC; DAM MST, NOV; DLB 39;
RGEL 2; TEA; WLIT 3
Richardson, Willis 1889-1977 .... **HR 1:3**
See also BW 1; CA 124; DLB 51; SATA 60
Richler, Mordecai 1931-2001 .... **CLC 3, 5, 9,**
13, 18, 46, 70, 185
See also AITN 1; CA 65-68; 201; CANR
31, 62, 111; CCA 1; CLR 17; CN 1, 2, 3,
4, 5, 7; CWRI 5; DAC; DAM MST, NOV;
DLB 53; EWL 3; MAICYA 1, 2; MTCW
1, 2; MTFW 2005; RGEL 2; SATA 44,
98; SATA-Brief 27; TWA
Richter, Conrad (Michael)
1890-1968 .... **CLC 30**
See also AAYA 21; BYA 2; CA 5-8R; 25-
28R; CANR 23; DLB 9, 212; LAIT 1;
MAL 5; MTCW 1, 2; MTFW 2005;
RGAL 4; SATA 3; TCWW 1, 2; TUS;
YAW
Ricostranza, Tom
See Ellis, Trey
Riddell, Charlotte 1832-1906 .... **TCLC 40**
See Riddell, Mrs. J. H.
See also CA 165; DLB 156
Riddell, Mrs. J. H.
See Riddell, Charlotte
See also HGG; SUFW
Ridge, John Rollin 1827-1867 ...... **NCLC 82;**
NNAL
See also CA 144; DAM MULT; DLB 175
Ridgeway, Jason
See Marlowe, Stephen
Ridgway, Keith 1965- .... **CLC 119**
See also CA 172; CANR 144
Riding, Laura .... **CLC 3, 7**
See Jackson, Laura (Riding)
See also CP 1, 2, 3, 4; RGAL 4
Riefenstahl, Berta Helene Amalia 1902-2003
See Riefenstahl, Leni
See also CA 108; 220
Riefenstahl, Leni .... **CLC 16, 190**
See Riefenstahl, Berta Helene Amalia
Riffe, Ernest
See Bergman, (Ernst) Ingmar
Riggs, (Rolla) Lynn
1899-1954 .... **NNAL; TCLC 56**
See also CA 144; DAM MULT; DLB 175

Riis, Jacob A(ugust) 1849-1914 ..... **TCLC 80**
See also CA 113; 168; DLB 23
Riley, James Whitcomb 1849-1916 ... **PC 48;**
TCLC 51
See also CA 118; 137; DAM POET; MAI-
CYA 1, 2; RGAL 4; SATA 17
Riley, Tex
See Creasey, John
Rilke, Rainer Maria 1875-1926 .... **PC 2;**
TCLC 1, 6, 19
See also CA 104; 132; CANR 62, 99; CD-
WLB 2; DA3; DAM POET; DLB 81; EW
9; EWL 3; MTCW 1, 2; MTFW 2005;
PFS 19; RGWL 2, 3; TWA; WP
Rimbaud, (Jean Nicolas) Arthur
1854-1891 ... **NCLC 4, 35, 82; PC 3, 57;**
WLC
See also DA; DA3; DAB; DAC; DAM
MST, POET; DLB 217; EW 7; GFL 1789
to the Present; LMFS 2; RGWL 2, 3;
TWA; WP
Rinehart, Mary Roberts
1876-1958 .... **TCLC 52**
See also BPFB 3; CA 108; 166; RGAL 4;
RHW
Ringmaster, The
See Mencken, H(enry) L(ouis)
Ringwood, Gwen(dolyn Margaret) Pharis
1910-1984 .... **CLC 48**
See also CA 148; 112; DLB 88
Rio, Michel 1945(?)- .... **CLC 43**
See also CA 201
Rios, Alberto (Alvaro) 1952- .... **PC 57**
See also AAYA 66; AMWS 4; CA 113;
CANR 34, 79, 137; CP 7; DLB 122; HW
2; MTFW 2005; PFS 11
Ritsos, Giannes
See Ritsos, Yannis
Ritsos, Yannis 1909-1990 .... **CLC 6, 13, 31**
See also CA 77-80; 133; CANR 39, 61; EW
12; EWL 3; MTCW 1; RGWL 2, 3
Ritter, Erika 1948(?)- .... **CLC 52**
See also CD 5, 6; CWD
Rivera, Jose Eustasio 1889-1928 ... **TCLC 35**
See also CA 162; EWL 3; HW 1, 2; LAW
Rivera, Tomas 1935-1984 .... **HLCS 2**
See also CA 49-52; CANR 32; DLB 82;
HW 1; LLW; RGAL 4; SSFS 15; TCWW
2; WLIT 1
Rivers, Conrad Kent 1933-1968 .... **CLC 1**
See also BW 1; CA 85-88; DLB 41
Rivers, Elfrida
See Bradley, Marion Zimmer
See also GLL 1
Riverside, John
See Heinlein, Robert A(nson)
Rizal, Jose 1861-1896 .... **NCLC 27**
Roa Bastos, Augusto (Jose Antonio)
1917-2005 .... **CLC 45; HLC 2**
See also CA 131; 238; CWW 2; DAM
MULT; DLB 113; EWL 3; HW 1; LAW;
RGSF 2; WLIT 1
Robbe-Grillet, Alain 1922- .... **CLC 1, 2, 4, 6,**
8, 10, 14, 43, 128
See also BPFB 3; CA 9-12R; CANR 33,
65, 115; CWW 2; DLB 83; EW 13; EWL
3; GFL 1789 to the Present; IDFW 3, 4;
MTCW 1, 2; MTFW 2005; RGWL 2, 3;
SSFS 15
Robbins, Harold 1916-1997 .... **CLC 5**
See also BPFB 3; CA 73-76; 162; CANR
26, 54, 112; DA3; DAM NOV; MTCW 1,
2
Robbins, Thomas Eugene 1936-
See Robbins, Tom
See also CA 81-84; CANR 29, 59, 95, 139;
CN 7; CPW; CSW; DA3; DAM NOV,
POP; MTCW 1, 2; MTFW 2005

Robbins, Tom .... **CLC 9, 32, 64**
See Robbins, Thomas Eugene
See also AAYA 32; AMWS 10; BEST 90:3;
BPFB 3; CN 3, 4, 5, 6, 7; DLBY 1980

Robbins, Trina 1938- .... **CLC 21**
See also AAYA 61; CA 128

Roberts, Charles G(eorge) D(ouglas)
1860-1943 .... **TCLC 8**
See also CA 105; 188; CLR 33; CWRI 5;
DLB 92; RGEL 2; RGSF 2; SATA 88;
SATA-Brief 29

Roberts, Elizabeth Madox
1886-1941 .... **TCLC 68**
See also CA 111; 166; CLR 100; CWRI 5;
DLB 9, 54, 102; RGAL 4; RHW; SATA
33; SATA-Brief 27; TCWW 2; WCH

Roberts, Kate 1891-1985 .... **CLC 15**
See also CA 107; 116; DLB 319

Roberts, Keith (John Kingston)
1935-2000 .... **CLC 14**
See also BRWS 10; CA 25-28R; CANR 46;
DLB 261; SFW 4

Roberts, Kenneth (Lewis)
1885-1957 .... **TCLC 23**
See also CA 109; 199; DLB 9; MAL 5;
RGAL 4; RHW

Roberts, Michele (Brigitte) 1949- .... **CLC 48,
178**
See also CA 115; CANR 58, 120; CN 6, 7;
DLB 231; FW

Robertson, Ellis
See Ellison, Harlan (Jay); Silverberg, Robert

Robertson, Thomas William
1829-1871 .... **NCLC 35**
See Robertson, Tom
See also DAM DRAM

Robertson, Tom
See Robertson, Thomas William
See also RGEL 2

Robeson, Kenneth
See Dent, Lester

Robinson, Edwin Arlington
1869-1935 .... **PC 1, 35; TCLC 5, 101**
See also AMW; CA 104; 133; CDALB
1865-1917; DA; DAC; DAM MST;
POET; DLB 54; EWL 3; EXPP; MAL 5;
MTCW 1, 2; MTFW 2005; PAB; PFS 4;
RGAL 4; WP

Robinson, Henry Crabb
1775-1867 .... **NCLC 15**
See also DLB 107

Robinson, Jill 1936- .... **CLC 10**
See also CA 102; CANR 120; INT CA-102

Robinson, Kim Stanley 1952- .... **CLC 34**
See also AAYA 26; CA 126; CANR 113,
139; CN 6, 7; MTFW 2005; SATA 109;
SCFW 2; SFW 4

Robinson, Lloyd
See Silverberg, Robert

Robinson, Marilynne 1944- ...... **CLC 25, 180**
See also CA 116; CANR 80, 140; CN 4, 5,
6, 7; DLB 206; MTFW 2005

Robinson, Mary 1758-1800 .... **NCLC 142**
See also DLB 158; FW

Robinson, Smokey .... **CLC 21**
See Robinson, William, Jr.

Robinson, William, Jr. 1940-
See Robinson, Smokey
See also CA 116

Robison, Mary 1949- .... **CLC 42, 98**
See also CA 113; 116; CANR 87; CN 4, 5,
6, 7; DLB 130; INT CA-116; RGSF 2

Roches, Catherine des 1542-1587 ...... **LC 117**

Rochester
See Wilmot, John
See also RGEL 2

Rod, Edouard 1857-1910 .... **TCLC 52**

Roddenberry, Eugene Wesley 1921-1991
See Roddenberry, Gene
See also CA 110; 135; CANR 37; SATA 45;
SATA-Obit 69

Roddenberry, Gene .... **CLC 17**
See Roddenberry, Eugene Wesley
See also AAYA 5; SATA-Obit 69

Rodgers, Mary 1931- .... **CLC 12**
See also BYA 5; CA 49-52; CANR 8, 55,
90; CLR 20; CWRI 5; INT CANR-8;
JRDA; MAICYA 1, 2; SATA 8, 130

Rodgers, W(illiam) R(obert)
1909-1969 .... **CLC 7**
See also CA 85-88; DLB 20; RGEL 2

Rodman, Eric
See Silverberg, Robert

Rodman, Howard 1920(?)-1985 .... **CLC 65**
See also CA 118

Rodman, Maia
See Wojciechowska, Maia (Teresa)

Rodo, Jose Enrique 1871(?)-1917 .... **HLCS 2**
See also CA 178; EWL 3; HW 2; LAW

Rodolph, Utto
See Ouologuem, Yambo

Rodriguez, Claudio 1934-1999 .... **CLC 10**
See also CA 188; DLB 134

Rodriguez, Richard 1944- .... **CLC 155; HLC
2**
See also AMWS 14; CA 110; CANR 66,
116; DAM MULT; DLB 82, 256; HW 1,
2; LAIT 5; LLW; MTFW 2005; NCFS 3;
WLIT 1

Roelvaag, O(le) E(dvart) 1876-1931
See Rolvaag, O(le) E(dvart)
See also CA 117; 171

Roethke, Theodore (Huebner)
1908-1963 .... **CLC 1, 3, 8, 11, 19, 46,
101; PC 15**
See also AMW; CA 81-84; CABS 2;
CDALB 1941-1968; DA3; DAM POET;
DLB 5, 206; EWL 3; EXPP; MAL 5;
MTCW 1, 2; PAB; PFS 3; RGAL 4; WP

Rogers, Carl R(ansom)
1902-1987 .... **TCLC 125**
See also CA 1-4R; 121; CANR 1, 18;
MTCW 1

Rogers, Samuel 1763-1855 .... **NCLC 69**
See also DLB 93; RGEL 2

Rogers, Thomas Hunton 1927- .... **CLC 57**
See also CA 89-92; INT CA-89-92

Rogers, Will(iam Penn Adair)
1879-1935 .... **NNAL; TCLC 8, 71**
See also CA 105; 144; DA3; DAM MULT;
DLB 11; MTCW 2

Rogin, Gilbert 1929- .... **CLC 18**
See also CA 65-68; CANR 15

Rohan, Koda
See Koda Shigeyuki

Rohlfs, Anna Katharine Green
See Green, Anna Katharine

Rohmer, Eric .... **CLC 16**
See Scherer, Jean-Marie Maurice

Rohmer, Sax .... **TCLC 28**
See Ward, Arthur Henry Sarsfield
See also DLB 70; MSW; SUFW

Roiphe, Anne (Richardson) 1935- .. **CLC 3, 9**
See also CA 89-92; CANR 45, 73, 138;
DLBY 1980; INT CA-89-92

Rojas, Fernando de 1475-1541 ... **HLCS 1, 2;
LC 23**
See also DLB 286; RGWL 2, 3

Rojas, Gonzalo 1917- .... **HLCS 2**
See also CA 178; HW 2; LAWS 1

Roland (de la Platiere), Marie-Jeanne
1754-1793 .... **LC 98**
See also DLB 314

**Rolfe, Frederick (William Serafino Austin
Lewis Mary)** 1860-1913 .... **TCLC 12**
See Al Siddik
See also CA 107; 210; DLB 34, 156; RGEL
2

Rolland, Romain 1866-1944 .... **TCLC 23**
See also CA 118; 197; DLB 65, 284; EWL
3; GFL 1789 to the Present; RGWL 2, 3

Rolle, Richard c. 1300-c. 1349 ...... **CMLC 21**
See also DLB 146; LMFS 1; RGEL 2

Rolvaag, O(le) E(dvart) .... **TCLC 17**
See Roelvaag, O(le) E(dvart)
See also DLB 9, 212; MAL 5; NFS 5;
RGAL 4

Romain Arnaud, Saint
See Aragon, Louis

Romains, Jules 1885-1972 .... **CLC 7**
See also CA 85-88; CANR 34; DLB 65,
321; EWL 3; GFL 1789 to the Present;
MTCW 1

Romero, Jose Ruben 1890-1952 .... **TCLC 14**
See also CA 114; 131; EWL 3; HW 1; LAW

Ronsard, Pierre de 1524-1585 . **LC 6, 54; PC
11**
See also EW 2; GFL Beginnings to 1789;
RGWL 2, 3; TWA

Rooke, Leon 1934- .... **CLC 25, 34**
See also CA 25-28R; CANR 23, 53; CCA
1; CPW; DAM POP

Roosevelt, Franklin Delano
1882-1945 .... **TCLC 93**
See also CA 116; 173; LAIT 3

Roosevelt, Theodore 1858-1919 ..... **TCLC 69**
See also CA 115; 170; DLB 47, 186, 275

Roper, William 1498-1578 .... **LC 10**

Roquelaure, A. N.
See Rice, Anne

Rosa, Joao Guimaraes 1908-1967 ... **CLC 23;
HLCS 1**
See Guimaraes Rosa, Joao
See also CA 89-92; DLB 113, 307; EWL 3;
WLIT 1

Rose, Wendy 1948- . **CLC 85; NNAL; PC 13**
See also CA 53-56; CANR 5, 51; CWP;
DAM MULT; DLB 175; PFS 13; RGAL
4; SATA 12

Rosen, R. D.
See Rosen, Richard (Dean)

Rosen, Richard (Dean) 1949- .... **CLC 39**
See also CA 77-80; CANR 62, 120; CMW
4; INT CANR-30

Rosenberg, Isaac 1890-1918 .... **TCLC 12**
See also BRW 6; CA 107; 188; DLB 20,
216; EWL 3; PAB; RGEL 2

Rosenblatt, Joe .... **CLC 15**
See Rosenblatt, Joseph
See also CP 3, 4, 5, 6, 7

Rosenblatt, Joseph 1933-
See Rosenblatt, Joe
See also CA 89-92; CP 1, 2; INT CA-89-92

Rosenfeld, Samuel
See Tzara, Tristan

Rosenstock, Sami
See Tzara, Tristan

Rosenstock, Samuel
See Tzara, Tristan

Rosenthal, M(acha) L(ouis)
1917-1996 .... **CLC 28**
See also CA 1-4R; 152; CAAS 6; CANR 4,
51; CP 1, 2, 3, 4; DLB 5; SATA 59

Ross, Barnaby
See Dannay, Frederic

Ross, Bernard L.
See Follett, Ken(neth Martin)

Ross, J. H.
See Lawrence, T(homas) E(dward)

Ross, John Hume
See Lawrence, T(homas) E(dward)

Ryder, Jonathan
   See Ludlum, Robert
Ryga, George 1932-1987 .... **CLC 14**
   See also CA 101; 124; CANR 43, 90; CCA
   1; DAC; DAM MST; DLB 60
S. H.
   See Hartmann, Sadakichi
S. S.
   See Sassoon, Siegfried (Lorraine)
Sa'adawi, al- Nawal
   See El Saadawi, Nawal
   See also AFW; EWL 3
Saadawi, Nawal El
   See El Saadawi, Nawal
   See also WLIT 2
Saba, Umberto 1883-1957 .... **TCLC 33**
   See also CA 144; CANR 79; DLB 114;
   EWL 3; RGWL 2, 3
Sabatini, Rafael 1875-1950 .... **TCLC 47**
   See also BPFB 3; CA 162; RHW
Sabato, Ernesto (R.) 1911- .... **CLC 10, 23;**
   HLC 2
   See also CA 97-100; CANR 32, 65; CD-
   WLB 3; CWW 2; DAM MULT; DLB 145;
   EWL 3; HW 1, 2; LAW; MTCW 1, 2;
   MTFW 2005
Sa-Carneiro, Mario de 1890-1916 . **TCLC 83**
   See also DLB 287; EWL 3
Sacastru, Martin
   See Bioy Casares, Adolfo
   See also CWW 2
Sacher-Masoch, Leopold von
   1836(?)-1895 .... **NCLC 31**
Sachs, Hans 1494-1576 .... **LC 95**
   See also CDWLB 2; DLB 179; RGWL 2, 3
Sachs, Marilyn 1927- .... **CLC 35**
   See also AAYA 2; BYA 6; CA 17-20R;
   CANR 13, 47; CLR 2; JRDA; MAICYA
   1, 2; SAAS 2; SATA 3, 68, 164; SATA-
   Essay 110; WYA; YAW
Sachs, Marilyn Stickle
   See Sachs, Marilyn
Sachs, Nelly 1891-1970 .... **CLC 14, 98**
   See also CA 17-18; 25-28R; CANR 87;
   CAP 2; EWL 3; MTCW 2; MTFW 2005;
   PFS 20; RGWL 2, 3
Sackler, Howard (Oliver)
   1929-1982 .... **CLC 14**
   See also CA 61-64; 108; CAD; CANR 30;
   DFS 15; DLB 7
Sacks, Oliver (Wolf) 1933- .... **CLC 67, 202**
   See also CA 53-56; CANR 28, 50, 76;
   CPW; DA3; INT CANR-28; MTCW 1, 2;
   MTFW 2005
Sackville, Thomas 1536-1608 .... **LC 98**
   See also DAM DRAM; DLB 62, 132;
   RGEL 2
Sadakichi
   See Hartmann, Sadakichi
Sa'dawi, Nawal al-
   See El Saadawi, Nawal
   See also CWW 2
Sade, Donatien Alphonse Francois
   1740-1814 .... **NCLC 3, 47**
   See also DLB 314; EW 4; GFL Beginnings
   to 1789; RGWL 2, 3
Sade, Marquis de
   See Sade, Donatien Alphonse Francois
Sadoff, Ira 1945- .... **CLC 9**
   See also CA 53-56; CANR 5, 21, 109; DLB
   120
Saetone
   See Camus, Albert
Safire, William 1929- .... **CLC 10**
   See also CA 17-20R; CANR 31, 54, 91

Sagan, Carl (Edward) 1934-1996 .... **CLC 30,**
   112
   See also AAYA 2, 62; CA 25-28R; 155;
   CANR 11, 36, 74; CPW; DA3; MTCW 1,
   2; MTFW 2005; SATA 58; SATA-Obit 94
Sagan, Francoise .... **CLC 3, 6, 9, 17, 36**
   See Quoirez, Francoise
   See also CWW 2; DLB 83; EWL 3; GFL
   1789 to the Present; MTCW 2
Sahgal, Nayantara (Pandit) 1927- ... **CLC 41**
   See also CA 9-12R; CANR 11, 88; CN 1,
   2, 3, 4, 5, 6, 7
Said, Edward W. 1935-2003 .... **CLC 123**
   See also CA 21-24R; 220; CANR 45, 74,
   107, 131; DLB 67; MTCW 2; MTFW
   2005
Saint, H(arry) F. 1941- .... **CLC 50**
   See also CA 127
St. Aubin de Teran, Lisa 1953-
   See Teran, Lisa St. Aubin de
   See also CA 118; 126; CN 6, 7; INT CA-
   126
Saint Birgitta of Sweden c.
   1303-1373 .... **CMLC 24**
Sainte-Beuve, Charles Augustin
   1804-1869 .... **NCLC 5**
   See also DLB 217; EW 6; GFL 1789 to the
   Present
Saint-Exupery, Antoine (Jean Baptiste
   Marie Roger) de 1900-1944 .... **TCLC 2,**
   56, 169; WLC
   See also AAYA 63; BPFB 3; BYA 3; CA
   108; 132; CLR 10; DA3; DAM NOV;
   DLB 72; EW 12; EWL 3; GFL 1789 to
   the Present; LAIT 3; MAICYA 1, 2;
   MTCW 1, 2; MTFW 2005; RGWL 2, 3;
   SATA 20; TWA
St. John, David
   See Hunt, E(verette) Howard, (Jr.)
St. John, J. Hector
   See Crevecoeur, Michel Guillaume Jean de
Saint-John Perse
   See Leger, (Marie-Rene Auguste) Alexis
   Saint-Leger
   See also EW 10; EWL 3; GFL 1789 to the
   Present; RGWL 2
Saintsbury, George (Edward Bateman)
   1845-1933 .... **TCLC 31**
   See also CA 160; DLB 57, 149
Sait Faik .... **TCLC 23**
   See Abasiyanik, Sait Faik
Saki .... **SSC 12; TCLC 3**
   See Munro, H(ector) H(ugh)
   See also BRWS 6; BYA 11; LAIT 2; RGEL
   2; SSFS 1; SUFW
Sala, George Augustus 1828-1895 . **NCLC 46**
Saladin 1138-1193 .... **CMLC 38**
Salama, Hannu 1936- .... **CLC 18**
   See also EWL 3
Salamanca, J(ack) R(ichard) 1922- .. **CLC 4,**
   15
   See also CA 25-28R, 193; CAAE 193
Salas, Floyd Francis 1931- .... **HLC 2**
   See also CA 119; CAAS 27; CANR 44, 75,
   93; DAM MULT; DLB 82; HW 1, 2;
   MTCW 2; MTFW 2005
Sale, J. Kirkpatrick
   See Sale, Kirkpatrick
Sale, Kirkpatrick 1937- .... **CLC 68**
   See also CA 13-16R; CANR 10
Salinas, Luis Omar 1937- ... **CLC 90; HLC 2**
   See also AMWS 13; CA 131; CANR 81;
   DAM MULT; DLB 82; HW 1, 2
Salinas (y Serrano), Pedro
   1891(?)-1951 .... **TCLC 17**
   See also CA 117; DLB 134; EWL 3

Salinger, J(erome) D(avid) 1919- .. **CLC 1, 3,**
   8, 12, 55, 56, 138; SSC 2, 28, 65; WLC
   See also AAYA 2, 36; AMW; AMWC 1;
   BPFB 3; CA 5-8R; CANR 39, 129;
   CDALB 1941-1968; CLR 18; CN 1, 2, 3,
   4, 5, 6, 7; CPW 1; DA; DA3; DAB; DAC;
   DAM MST, NOV, POP; DLB 2, 102, 173;
   EWL 3; EXPN; LAIT 4; MAICYA 1, 2;
   MAL 5; MTCW 1, 2; MTFW 2005; NFS
   1; RGAL 4; RGSF 2; SATA 67; SSFS 17;
   TUS; WYA; YAW
Salisbury, John
   See Caute, (John) David
Sallust c. 86B.C.-35B.C. .... **CMLC 68**
   See also AW 2; CDWLB 1; DLB 211;
   RGWL 2, 3
Salter, James 1925- .. **CLC 7, 52, 59; SSC 58**
   See also AMWS 9; CA 73-76; CANR 107;
   DLB 130
Saltus, Edgar (Everton) 1855-1921 . **TCLC 8**
   See also CA 105; DLB 202; RGAL 4
Saltykov, Mikhail Evgrafovich
   1826-1889 .... **NCLC 16**
   See also DLB 238:
Saltykov-Shchedrin, N.
   See Saltykov, Mikhail Evgrafovich
Samarakis, Andonis
   See Samarakis, Antonis
   See also EWL 3
Samarakis, Antonis 1919-2003 .... **CLC 5**
   See Samarakis, Andonis
   See also CA 25-28R; 224; CAAS 16; CANR
   36
Sanchez, Florencio 1875-1910 .... **TCLC 37**
   See also CA 153; DLB 305; EWL 3; HW 1;
   LAW
Sanchez, Luis Rafael 1936- .... **CLC 23**
   See also CA 128; DLB 305; EWL 3; HW 1;
   WLIT 1
Sanchez, Sonia 1934- .... **BLC 3; CLC 5, 116,**
   215; PC 9
   See also BW 2, 3; CA 33-36R; CANR 24,
   49, 74, 115; CLR 18; CP 2, 3, 4, 5, 6, 7;
   CSW; CWP; DA3; DAM MULT; DLB 41;
   DLBD 8; EWL 3; MAICYA 1, 2; MAL 5;
   MTCW 1, 2; MTFW 2005; SATA 22, 136;
   WP
Sancho, Ignatius 1729-1780 .... **LC 84**
Sand, George 1804-1876 ..... **NCLC 2, 42, 57;**
   WLC
   See also DA; DA3; DAB; DAC; DAM
   MST, NOV; DLB 119, 192; EW 6; FL 1:3;
   FW; GFL 1789 to the Present; RGWL 2,
   3; TWA
Sandburg, Carl (August) 1878-1967 . **CLC 1,**
   4, 10, 15, 35; PC 2, 41; WLC
   See also AAYA 24; AMW; BYA 1, 3; CA
   5-8R; 25-28R; CANR 35; CDALB 1865-
   1917; CLR 67; DA; DA3; DAB; DAC;
   DAM MST, POET; DLB 17, 54, 284;
   EWL 3; EXPP; LAIT 2; MAICYA 1, 2;
   MAL 5; MTCW 1, 2; MTFW 2005; PAB;
   PFS 3, 6, 12; RGAL 4; SATA 8; TUS;
   WCH; WP; WYA
Sandburg, Charles
   See Sandburg, Carl (August)
Sandburg, Charles A.
   See Sandburg, Carl (August)
Sanders, (James) Ed(ward) 1939- .... **CLC 53**
   See Sanders, Edward
   See also BG 1:3; CA 13-16R; CAAS 21;
   CANR 13, 44, 78; CP 1, 2, 3, 4, 5, 6, 7;
   DAM POET; DLB 16, 244
Sanders, Edward
   See Sanders, (James) Ed(ward)
   See also DLB 244
Sanders, Lawrence 1920-1998 .... **CLC 41**
   See also BEST 89:4; BPFB 3; CA 81-84;
   165; CANR 33, 62; CMW 4; CPW; DA3;
   DAM POP; MTCW 1

Schnitzler, Arthur 1862-1931 ..... **DC 17; SSC 15, 61; TCLC 4**
  See also CA 104; CDWLB 2; DLB 81, 118; EW 8; EWL 3; RGSF 2; RGWL 2, 3

Schoenberg, Arnold Franz Walter 1874-1951 .... **TCLC 75**
  See also CA 109; 188

Schonberg, Arnold
  See Schoenberg, Arnold Franz Walter

Schopenhauer, Arthur 1788-1860 . **NCLC 51, 157**
  See also DLB 90; EW 5

Schor, Sandra (M.) 1932(?)-1990 ..... **CLC 65**
  See also CA 132

Schorer, Mark 1908-1977 .... **CLC 9**
  See also CA 5-8R; 73-76; CANR 7; CN 1, 2; DLB 103

Schrader, Paul (Joseph) 1946- . **CLC 26, 212**
  See also CA 37-40R; CANR 41; DLB 44

Schreber, Daniel 1842-1911 .... **TCLC 123**

Schreiner, Olive (Emilie Albertina) 1855-1920 .... **TCLC 9**
  See also AFW; BRWS 2; CA 105; 154; DLB 18, 156, 190, 225; FW; RGEL 2; TWA; WLIT 2; WWE 1

Schulberg, Budd (Wilson) 1914- .. **CLC 7, 48**
  See also BPFB 3; CA 25-28R; CANR 19, 87; CN 1, 2, 3, 4, 5, 6, 7; DLB 6, 26, 28; DLBY 1981, 2001; MAL 5

Schulman, Arnold
  See Trumbo, Dalton

Schulz, Bruno 1892-1942 .. **SSC 13; TCLC 5, 51**
  See also CA 115; 123; CANR 86; CDWLB 4; DLB 215; EWL 3; MTCW 2; MTFW 2005; RGSF 2; RGWL 2, 3

Schulz, Charles M. 1922-2000 .... **CLC 12**
  See also AAYA 39; CA 9-12R; 187; CANR 6, 132; INT CANR-6; MTFW 2005; SATA 10; SATA-Obit 118

Schulz, Charles Monroe
  See Schulz, Charles M.

Schumacher, E(rnst) F(riedrich) 1911-1977 .... **CLC 80**
  See also CA 81-84; 73-76; CANR 34, 85

Schumann, Robert 1810-1856 ...... **NCLC 143**

Schuyler, George Samuel 1895-1977 . **HR 1:3**
  See also BW 2; CA 81-84; 73-76; CANR 42; DLB 29, 51

Schuyler, James Marcus 1923-1991 .. **CLC 5, 23**
  See also CA 101; 134; CP 1, 2, 3, 4; DAM POET; DLB 5, 169; EWL 3; INT CA-101; MAL 5; WP

Schwartz, Delmore (David) 1913-1966 ... **CLC 2, 4, 10, 45, 87; PC 8**
  See also AMWS 2; CA 17-18; 25-28R; CANR 35; CAP 2; DLB 28, 48; EWL 3; MAL 5; MTCW 1, 2; MTFW 2005; PAB; RGAL 4; TUS

Schwartz, Ernst
  See Ozu, Yasujiro

Schwartz, John Burnham 1965- .... **CLC 59**
  See also CA 132; CANR 116

Schwartz, Lynne Sharon 1939- .... **CLC 31**
  See also CA 103; CANR 44, 89; DLB 218; MTCW 2; MTFW 2005

Schwartz, Muriel A.
  See Eliot, T(homas) S(tearns)

Schwarz-Bart, Andre 1928- .... **CLC 2, 4**
  See also CA 89-92; CANR 109; DLB 299

Schwarz-Bart, Simone 1938- . **BLCS; CLC 7**
  See also BW 2; CA 97-100; CANR 117; EWL 3

Schwerner, Armand 1927-1999 .... **PC 42**
  See also CA 9-12R; 179; CANR 50, 85; CP 2, 3, 4; DLB 165

Schwitters, Kurt (Hermann Edward Karl Julius) 1887-1948 .... **TCLC 95**
  See also CA 158

Schwob, Marcel (Mayer Andre) 1867-1905 .... **TCLC 20**
  See also CA 117; 168; DLB 123; GFL 1789 to the Present

Sciascia, Leonardo 1921-1989 .. **CLC 8, 9, 41**
  See also CA 85-88; 130; CANR 35; DLB 177; EWL 3; MTCW 1; RGWL 2, 3

Scoppettone, Sandra 1936- .... **CLC 26**
  See Early, Jack
  See also AAYA 11, 65; BYA 8; CA 5-8R; CANR 41, 73; GLL 1; MAICYA 2; MAICYAS 1; SATA 9, 92; WYA; YAW

Scorsese, Martin 1942- .... **CLC 20, 89, 207**
  See also AAYA 38; CA 110; 114; CANR 46, 85

Scotland, Jay
  See Jakes, John (William)

Scott, Duncan Campbell 1862-1947 .... **TCLC 6**
  See also CA 104; 153; DAC; DLB 92; RGEL 2

Scott, Evelyn 1893-1963 .... **CLC 43**
  See also CA 104; 112; CANR 64; DLB 9, 48; RHW

Scott, F(rancis) R(eginald) 1899-1985 .... **CLC 22**
  See also CA 101; 114; CANR 87; CP 1, 2, 3, 4; DLB 88; INT CA-101; RGEL 2

Scott, Frank
  See Scott, F(rancis) R(eginald)

Scott, Joan .... **CLC 65**

Scott, Joanna 1960- .... **CLC 50**
  See also CA 126; CANR 53, 92

Scott, Paul (Mark) 1920-1978 ...... **CLC 9, 60**
  See also BRWS 1; CA 81-84; 77-80; CANR 33; CN 1, 2; DLB 14, 207; EWL 3; MTCW 1; RGEL 2; RHW; WWE 1

Scott, Ridley 1937- .... **CLC 183**
  See also AAYA 13, 43

Scott, Sarah 1723-1795 .... **LC 44**
  See also DLB 39

Scott, Sir Walter 1771-1832 .... **NCLC 15, 69, 110; PC 13; SSC 32; WLC**
  See also AAYA 22; BRW 4; BYA 2; CDBLB 1789-1832; DA; DAB; DAC; DAM MST, NOV, POET; DLB 93, 107, 116, 144, 159; GL 3; HGG; LAIT 1; RGEL 2; RGSF 2; SSFS 10; SUFW 1; TEA; WLIT 3; YABC 2

Scribe, (Augustin) Eugene 1791-1861 . **DC 5; NCLC 16**
  See also DAM DRAM; DLB 192; GFL 1789 to the Present; RGWL 2, 3

Scrum, R.
  See Crumb, R(obert)

Scudery, Georges de 1601-1667 .... **LC 75**
  See also GFL Beginnings to 1789

Scudery, Madeleine de 1607-1701 .. **LC 2, 58**
  See also DLB 268; GFL Beginnings to 1789

Scum
  See Crumb, R(obert)

Scumbag, Little Bobby
  See Crumb, R(obert)

Seabrook, John
  See Hubbard, L(afayette) Ron(ald)

Seacole, Mary Jane Grant 1805-1881 .... **NCLC 147**
  See also DLB 166

Sealy, I(rwin) Allan 1951- .... **CLC 55**
  See also CA 136; CN 6, 7

Search, Alexander
  See Pessoa, Fernando (Antonio Nogueira)

Sebald, W(infried) G(eorg) 1944-2001 .... **CLC 194**
  See also BRWS 8; CA 159; 202; CANR 98; MTFW 2005

Sebastian, Lee
  See Silverberg, Robert

Sebastian Owl
  See Thompson, Hunter S(tockton)

Sebestyen, Igen
  See Sebestyen, Ouida

Sebestyen, Ouida 1924- .... **CLC 30**
  See also AAYA 8; BYA 7; CA 107; CANR 40, 114; CLR 17; JRDA; MAICYA 1, 2; SAAS 10; SATA 39, 140; WYA; YAW

Sebold, Alice 1963(?)- .... **CLC 193**
  See also AAYA 56; CA 203; MTFW 2005

Second Duke of Buckingham
  See Villiers, George

Secundus, H. Scriblerus
  See Fielding, Henry

Sedges, John
  See Buck, Pearl S(ydenstricker)

Sedgwick, Catharine Maria 1789-1867 .... **NCLC 19, 98**
  See also DLB 1, 74, 183, 239, 243, 254; FL 1:3; RGAL 4

Seelye, John (Douglas) 1931- .... **CLC 7**
  See also CA 97-100; CANR 70; INT CA-97-100; TCWW 1, 2

Seferiades, Giorgos Stylianou 1900-1971
  See Seferis, George
  See also CA 5-8R; 33-36R; CANR 5, 36; MTCW 1

Seferis, George .... **CLC 5, 11; PC 66**
  See Seferiades, Giorgos Stylianou
  See also EW 12; EWL 3; RGWL 2, 3

Segal, Erich (Wolf) 1937- .... **CLC 3, 10**
  See also BEST 89:1; BPFB 3; CA 25-28R; CANR 20, 36, 65, 113; CPW; DAM POP; DLBY 1986; INT CANR-20; MTCW 1

Seger, Bob 1945- .... **CLC 35**

Seghers, Anna .... **CLC 7**
  See Radvanyi, Netty
  See also CDWLB 2; DLB 69; EWL 3

Seidel, Frederick (Lewis) 1936- .... **CLC 18**
  See also CA 13-16R; CANR 8, 99; CP 1, 2, 3, 4, 5, 6, 7; DLBY 1984

Seifert, Jaroslav 1901-1986 . **CLC 34, 44, 93; PC 47**
  See also CA 127; CDWLB 4; DLB 215; EWL 3; MTCW 1, 2

Sei Shonagon c. 966-1017(?) .... **CMLC 6**

Sejour, Victor 1817-1874 .... **DC 10**
  See also DLB 50

Sejour Marcou et Ferrand, Juan Victor
  See Sejour, Victor

Selby, Hubert, Jr. 1928-2004 ..... **CLC 1, 2, 4, 8; SSC 20**
  See also CA 13-16R; 226; CANR 33, 85; CN 1, 2, 3, 4, 5, 6, 7; DLB 2, 227; MAL 5

Selzer, Richard 1928- .... **CLC 74**
  See also CA 65-68; CANR 14, 106

Sembene, Ousmane
  See Ousmane, Sembene
  See also AFW; EWL 3; WLIT 2

Senancour, Etienne Pivert de 1770-1846 .... **NCLC 16**
  See also DLB 119; GFL 1789 to the Present

Sender, Ramon (Jose) 1902-1982 ...... **CLC 8; HLC 2; TCLC 136**
  See also CA 5-8R; 105; CANR 8; DAM MULT; DLB 322; EWL 3; HW 1; MTCW 1; RGWL 2, 3

Seneca, Lucius Annaeus c. 4B.C.-c. 65 .... **CMLC 6; DC 5**
  See also AW 2; CDWLB 1; DAM DRAM; DLB 211; RGWL 2, 3; TWA

Shepherd, Michael
See Ludlum, Robert

Sherburne, Zoa (Lillian Morin)
1912-1995 .... CLC 30
See also AAYA 13; CA 1-4R; 176; CANR
3, 37; MAICYA 1, 2; SAAS 18; SATA 3;
YAW

Sheridan, Frances 1724-1766 .... LC 7
See also DLB 39, 84

Sheridan, Richard Brinsley
1751-1816 .... DC 1; NCLC 5, 91; WLC
See also BRW 3; CDBLB 1660-1789; DA;
DAB; DAC; DAM DRAM, MST; DFS
15; DLB 89; WLIT 3

Sherman, Jonathan Marc 1968- .... CLC 55
See also CA 230

Sherman, Martin 1941(?)- .... CLC 19
See also CA 116; 123; CAD; CANR 86;
CD 5, 6; DFS 20; DLB 228; GLL 1; IDTP

Sherwin, Judith Johnson
See Johnson, Judith (Emlyn)
See also CANR 85; CP 2, 3, 4; CWP

Sherwood, Frances 1940- .... CLC 81
See also CA 146, 220; CAAE 220

Sherwood, Robert E(mmet)
1896-1955 .... TCLC 3
See also CA 104; 153; CANR 86; DAM
DRAM; DFS 11, 15, 17; DLB 7, 26, 249;
IDFW 3, 4; MAL 5; RGAL 4

Shestov, Lev 1866-1938 .... TCLC 56

Shevchenko, Taras 1814-1861 .... NCLC 54

Shiel, M(atthew) P(hipps)
1865-1947 .... TCLC 8
See Holmes, Gordon
See also CA 106; 160; DLB 153; HGG;
MTCW 2; MTFW 2005; SCFW 1, 2;
SFW 4; SUFW

Shields, Carol (Ann) 1935-2003 ...... CLC 91,
113, 193
See also AMWS 7; CA 81-84; 218; CANR
51, 74, 98, 133; CCA 1; CN 6, 7; CPW;
DA3; DAC; MTCW 2; MTFW 2005

Shields, David (Jonathan) 1956- ...... CLC 97
See also CA 124; CANR 48, 99, 112

Shiga, Naoya 1883-1971 .... CLC 33; SSC 23;
TCLC 172
See Shiga Naoya
See also CA 101; 33-36R; MJW; RGWL 3

Shiga Naoya
See Shiga, Naoya
See also DLB 180; EWL 3; RGWL 3

Shilts, Randy 1951-1994 .... CLC 85
See also AAYA 19; CA 115; 127; 144;
CANR 45; DA3; GLL 1; INT CA-127;
MTCW 2; MTFW 2005

Shimazaki, Haruki 1872-1943
See Shimazaki Toson
See also CA 105; 134; CANR 84; RGWL 3

Shimazaki Toson .... TCLC 5
See Shimazaki, Haruki
See also DLB 180; EWL 3

Shirley, James 1596-1666 .... DC 25; LC 96
See also DLB 58; RGEL 2

Sholokhov, Mikhail (Aleksandrovich)
1905-1984 .... CLC 7, 15
See also CA 101; 112; DLB 272; EWL 3;
MTCW 1, 2; MTFW 2005; RGWL 2, 3;
SATA-Obit 36

Shone, Patric
See Hanley, James

Showalter, Elaine 1941- .... CLC 169
See also CA 57-60; CANR 58, 106; DLB
67; FW; GLL 2

Shreve, Susan
See Shreve, Susan Richards

Shreve, Susan Richards 1939- .... CLC 23
See also CA 49-52; CAAS 5; CANR 5, 38,
69, 100; MAICYA 1, 2; SATA 46, 95, 152;
SATA-Brief 41

Shue, Larry 1946-1985 .... CLC 52
See also CA 145; 117; DAM DRAM; DFS
7

Shu-Jen, Chou 1881-1936
See Lu Hsun
See also CA 104

Shulman, Alix Kates 1932- .... CLC 2, 10
See also CA 29-32R; CANR 43; FW; SATA
7

Shuster, Joe 1914-1992 .... CLC 21
See also AAYA 50

Shute, Nevil .... CLC 30
See Norway, Nevil Shute
See also BPFB 3; DLB 255; NFS 9; RHW;
SFW 4

Shuttle, Penelope (Diane) 1947- .... CLC 7
See also CA 93-96; CANR 39, 84, 92, 108;
CP 3, 4, 5, 6, 7; CWP; DLB 14, 40

Shvarts, Elena 1948- .... PC 50
See also CA 147

Sidhwa, Bapsi
See Sidhwa, Bapsy (N.)
See also CN 6, 7

Sidhwa, Bapsy (N.) 1938- .... CLC 168
See Sidhwa, Bapsi
See also CA 108; CANR 25, 57; FW

Sidney, Mary 1561-1621 .... LC 19, 39
See Sidney Herbert, Mary

Sidney, Sir Philip 1554-1586 . LC 19, 39; PC
32
See also BRW 1; BRWR 2; CDBLB Before
1660; DA; DA3; DAB; DAC; DAM MST,
POET; DLB 167; EXPP; PAB; RGEL 2;
TEA; WP

Sidney Herbert, Mary
See Sidney, Mary
See also DLB 167

Siegel, Jerome 1914-1996 .... CLC 21
See Siegel, Jerry
See also CA 116; 169; 151

Siegel, Jerry
See Siegel, Jerome
See also AAYA 50

Sienkiewicz, Henryk (Adam Alexander Pius)
1846-1916 .... TCLC 3
See also CA 104; 134; CANR 84; EWL 3;
RGSF 2; RGWL 2, 3

Sierra, Gregorio Martinez
See Martinez Sierra, Gregorio

Sierra, Maria (de la O'LeJarraga) Martinez
See Martinez Sierra, Maria (de la
O'LeJarraga)

Sigal, Clancy 1926- .... CLC 7
See also CA 1-4R; CANR 85; CN 1, 2, 3,
4, 5, 6, 7

Siger of Brabant 1240(?)-1284(?) . CMLC 69
See also DLB 115

Sigourney, Lydia H.
See Sigourney, Lydia Howard (Huntley)
See also DLB 73, 183

Sigourney, Lydia Howard (Huntley)
1791-1865 .... NCLC 21, 87
See Sigourney, Lydia H.; Sigourney, Lydia
Huntley
See also DLB 1

Sigourney, Lydia Huntley
See Sigourney, Lydia Howard (Huntley)
See also DLB 42, 239, 243

Siguenza y Gongora, Carlos de
1645-1700 .... HLCS 2; LC 8
See also LAW

Sigurjonsson, Johann
See Sigurjonsson, Johann

Sigurjonsson, Johann 1880-1919 ... TCLC 27
See also CA 170; DLB 293; EWL 3

Sikelianos, Angelos 1884-1951 .... PC 29;
TCLC 39
See also EWL 3; RGWL 2, 3

Silkin, Jon 1930-1997 .... CLC 2, 6, 43
See also CA 5-8R; CAAS 5; CANR 89; CP
1, 2, 3, 4, 5, 6; DLB 27

Silko, Leslie (Marmon) 1948- .... CLC 23, 74,
114, 211; NNAL; SSC 37, 66; WLCS
See also AAYA 14; AMWS 4; ANW; BYA
12; CA 115; 122; CANR 45, 65, 118; CN
4, 5, 6, 7; CP 4, 5, 6, 7; CPW 1; CWP;
DA; DA3; DAC; DAM MST, MULT,
POP; DLB 143, 175, 256, 275; EWL 3;
EXPP; EXPS; LAIT 4; MAL 5; MTCW
2; MTFW 2005; NFS 4; PFS 9, 16; RGAL
4; RGSF 2; SSFS 4, 8, 10, 11; TCWW 1,
2

Sillanpaa, Frans Eemil 1888-1964 ... CLC 19
See also CA 129; 93-96; EWL 3; MTCW 1

Sillitoe, Alan 1928- .. CLC 1, 3, 6, 10, 19, 57,
148
See also AITN 1; BRWS 5; CA 9-12R, 191;
CAAE 191; CAAS 2; CANR 8, 26, 55,
139; CDBLB 1960 to Present; CN 1, 2, 3,
4, 5, 6; CP 1, 2, 3, 4; DLB 14, 139; EWL
3; MTCW 1, 2; MTFW 2005; RGEL 2;
RGSF 2; SATA 61

Silone, Ignazio 1900-1978 .... CLC 4
See also CA 25-28; 81-84; CANR 34; CAP
2; DLB 264; EW 12; EWL 3; MTCW 1;
RGSF 2; RGWL 2, 3

Silone, Ignazione
See Silone, Ignazio

Silver, Joan Micklin 1935- .... CLC 20
See also CA 114; 121; INT CA-121

Silver, Nicholas
See Faust, Frederick (Schiller)

Silverberg, Robert 1935- .... CLC 7, 140
See also AAYA 24; BPFB 3; BYA 7, 9; CA
1-4R, 186; CAAE 186; CAAS 3; CANR
1, 20, 36, 85, 140; CLR 59; CN 6, 7;
CPW; DAM POP; DLB 8; INT CANR-
20; MAICYA 1, 2; MTCW 1, 2; MTFW
2005; SATA 13, 91; SATA-Essay 104;
SCFW 1, 2; SFW 4; SUFW 2

Silverstein, Alvin 1933- .... CLC 17
See also CA 49-52; CANR 2; CLR 25;
JRDA; MAICYA 1, 2; SATA 8, 69, 124

Silverstein, Shel(don Allan)
1932-1999 .... PC 49
See also AAYA 40; BW 3; CA 107; 179;
CANR 47, 74, 81; CLR 5, 96; CWRI 5;
JRDA; MAICYA 1, 2; MTCW 2; MTFW
2005; SATA 33, 92; SATA-Brief 27;
SATA-Obit 116

Silverstein, Virginia B(arbara Opshelor)
1937- .... CLC 17
See also CA 49-52; CANR 2; CLR 25;
JRDA; MAICYA 1, 2; SATA 8, 69, 124

Sim, Georges
See Simenon, Georges (Jacques Christian)

Simak, Clifford D(onald) 1904-1988 . CLC 1,
55
See also CA 1-4R; 125; CANR 1, 35; DLB
8; MTCW 1; SATA-Obit 56; SCFW 1, 2;
SFW 4

Simenon, Georges (Jacques Christian)
1903-1989 .... CLC 1, 2, 3, 8, 18, 47
See also BPFB 3; CA 85-88; 129; CANR
35; CMW 4; DA3; DAM POP; DLB 72;
DLBY 1989; EW 12; EWL 3; GFL 1789
to the Present; MSW; MTCW 1, 2; MTFW
2005; RGWL 2, 3

Simic, Charles 1938- .... CLC 6, 9, 22, 49, 68,
130; PC 69
See also AMWS 8; CA 29-32R; CAAS 4;
CANR 12, 33, 52, 61, 96, 140; CP 2, 3, 4,
5, 6, 7; DA3; DAM POET; DLB 105;
MAL 5; MTCW 2; MTFW 2005; PFS 7;
RGAL 4; WP

Simmel, Georg 1858-1918 .... TCLC 64
See also CA 157; DLB 296

Smith, Iain Crichton 1928-1998 .... **CLC 64**
 See also BRWS 9; CA 21-24R; 171; CN 1,
 2, 3, 4, 5, 6; CP 1, 2, 3, 4; DLB 40, 139,
 319; RGSF 2
Smith, John 1580(?)-1631 .... **LC 9**
 See also DLB 24, 30; TUS
Smith, Johnston
 See Crane, Stephen (Townley)
Smith, Joseph, Jr. 1805-1844 .... **NCLC 53**
Smith, Lee 1944- .... **CLC 25, 73**
 See also CA 114; 119; CANR 46, 118; CN
 7; CSW; DLB 143; DLBY 1983; EWL 3;
 INT CA-119; RGAL 4
Smith, Martin
 See Smith, Martin Cruz
Smith, Martin Cruz 1942- .. **CLC 25; NNAL**
 See also BEST 89:4; BPFB 3; CA 85-88;
 CANR 6, 23, 43, 65, 119; CMW 4; CPW;
 DAM MULT, POP; HGG; INT CANR-
 23; MTCW 2; MTFW 2005; RGAL 4
Smith, Patti 1946- .... **CLC 12**
 See also CA 93-96; CANR 63
Smith, Pauline (Urmson)
 1882-1959 .... **TCLC 25**
 See also DLB 225; EWL 3
Smith, Rosamond
 See Oates, Joyce Carol
Smith, Sheila Kaye
 See Kaye-Smith, Sheila
Smith, Stevie .... **CLC 3, 8, 25, 44; PC 12**
 See Smith, Florence Margaret
 See also BRWS 2; CP 1; DLB 20; EWL 3;
 PAB; PFS 3; RGEL 2
Smith, Wilbur (Addison) 1933- .... **CLC 33**
 See also CA 13-16R; CANR 7, 46, 66, 134;
 CPW; MTCW 1, 2; MTFW 2005
Smith, William Jay 1918- .... **CLC 6**
 See also AMWS 13; CA 5-8R; CANR 44,
 106; CP 1, 2, 3, 4, 5, 6, 7; CSW; CWRI
 5; DLB 5; MAICYA 1, 2; SAAS 22;
 SATA 2, 68, 154; SATA-Essay 154; TCLE
 1:2
Smith, Woodrow Wilson
 See Kuttner, Henry
Smith, Zadie 1976- .... **CLC 158**
 See also AAYA 50; CA 193; MTFW 2005
Smolenskin, Peretz 1842-1885 .... **NCLC 30**
Smollett, Tobias (George) 1721-1771 ... **LC 2,
 46**
 See also BRW 3; CDBLB 1660-1789; DLB
 39, 104; RGEL 2; TEA
Snodgrass, W(illiam) D(e Witt)
 1926- .... **CLC 2, 6, 10, 18, 68**
 See also AMWS 6; CA 1-4R; CANR 6, 36,
 65, 85; CP 1, 2, 3, 4, 5, 6, 7; DAM POET;
 DLB 5; MAL 5; MTCW 1, 2; MTFW
 2005; RGAL 4; TCLE 1:2
Snorri Sturluson 1179-1241 .... **CMLC 56**
 See also RGWL 2, 3
Snow, C(harles) P(ercy) 1905-1980 ... **CLC 1,
 4, 6, 9, 13, 19**
 See also BRW 7; CA 5-8R; 101; CANR 28;
 CDBLB 1945-1960; CN 1, 2; DAM NOV;
 DLB 15, 77; DLBD 17; EWL 3; MTCW
 1, 2; MTFW 2005; RGEL 2; TEA
Snow, Frances Compton
 See Adams, Henry (Brooks)
Snyder, Gary (Sherman) 1930- . **CLC 1, 2, 5,
 9, 32, 120; PC 21**
 See also AMWS 8; ANW; BG 1:3; CA 17-
 20R; CANR 30, 60, 125; CP 1, 2, 3, 4, 5,
 6, 7; DA3; DAM POET; DLB 5, 16, 165,
 212, 237, 275; EWL 3; MAL 5; MTCW
 2; MTFW 2005; PFS 9, 19; RGAL 4; WP
Snyder, Zilpha Keatley 1927- .... **CLC 17**
 See also AAYA 15; BYA 1; CA 9-12R;
 CANR 38; CLR 31; JRDA; MAICYA 1,
 2; SAAS 2; SATA 1, 28, 75, 110, 163;
 SATA-Essay 112, 163; YAW

Soares, Bernardo
 See Pessoa, Fernando (Antonio Nogueira)
Sobh, A.
 See Shamlu, Ahmad
Sobh, Alef
 See Shamlu, Ahmad
Sobol, Joshua 1939- .... **CLC 60**
 See Sobol, Yehoshua
 See also CA 200
Sobol, Yehoshua 1939-
 See Sobol, Joshua
 See also CWW 2
Socrates 470B.C.-399B.C. .... **CMLC 27**
Soderberg, Hjalmar 1869-1941 ...... **TCLC 39**
 See also DLB 259; EWL 3; RGSF 2
Soderbergh, Steven 1963- .... **CLC 154**
 See also AAYA 43
Sodergran, Edith (Irene) 1892-1923
 See Soedergran, Edith (Irene)
 See also CA 202; DLB 259; EW 11; EWL
 3; RGWL 2, 3
Soedergran, Edith (Irene)
 1892-1923 .... **TCLC 31**
 See Sodergran, Edith (Irene)
Softly, Edgar
 See Lovecraft, H(oward) P(hillips)
Softly, Edward
 See Lovecraft, H(oward) P(hillips)
Sokolov, Alexander V(sevolodovich) 1943-
 See Sokolov, Sasha
 See also CA 73-76
Sokolov, Raymond 1941- .... **CLC 7**
 See also CA 85-88
Sokolov, Sasha .... **CLC 59**
 See Sokolov, Alexander V(sevolodovich)
 See also CWW 2; DLB 285; EWL 3; RGWL
 2, 3
Solo, Jay
 See Ellison, Harlan (Jay)
Sologub, Fyodor .... **TCLC 9**
 See Teternikov, Fyodor Kuzmich
 See also EWL 3
Solomons, Ikey Esquir
 See Thackeray, William Makepeace
Solomos, Dionysios 1798-1857 .... **NCLC 15**
Solwoska, Mara
 See French, Marilyn
Solzhenitsyn, Aleksandr I(sayevich)
 1918- .. **CLC 1, 2, 4, 7, 9, 10, 18, 26, 34,
 78, 134; SSC 32; WLC**
 See Solzhenitsyn, Aleksandr Isaevich
 See also AAYA 49; AITN 1; BPFB 3; CA
 69-72; CANR 40, 65, 116; DA; DA3;
 DAB; DAC; DAM MST, NOV; DLB 302;
 EW 13; EXPS; LAIT 4; MTCW 1, 2;
 MTFW 2005; NFS 6; RGSF 2; RGWL 2,
 3; SSFS 9; TWA
Solzhenitsyn, Aleksandr Isaevich
 See Solzhenitsyn, Aleksandr I(sayevich)
 See also CWW 2; EWL 3
Somers, Jane
 See Lessing, Doris (May)
Somerville, Edith Oenone
 1858-1949 .... **SSC 56; TCLC 51**
 See also CA 196; DLB 135; RGEL 2; RGSF
 2
Somerville & Ross
 See Martin, Violet Florence; Somerville,
 Edith Oenone
Sommer, Scott 1951- .... **CLC 25**
 See also CA 106
Sommers, Christina Hoff 1950- ...... **CLC 197**
 See also CA 153; CANR 95
Sondheim, Stephen (Joshua) 1930- . **CLC 30,
 39, 147; DC 22**
 See also AAYA 11, 66; CA 103; CANR 47,
 67, 125; DAM DRAM; LAIT 4
Sone, Monica 1919- .... **AAL**
 See also DLB 312

Song, Cathy 1955- .... **AAL; PC 21**
 See also CA 154; CANR 118; CWP; DLB
 169, 312; EXPP; FW; PFS 5
Sontag, Susan 1933-2004 ... **CLC 1, 2, 10, 13,
 31, 105, 195**
 See also AMWS 3; CA 17-20R; 234; CANR
 25, 51, 74, 97; CN 1, 2, 3, 4, 5, 6, 7;
 CPW; DA3; DAM POP; DLB 2, 67; EWL
 3; MAL 5; MAWW; MTCW 1, 2; MTFW
 2005; RGAL 4; RHW; SSFS 10
Sophocles 496(?)B.C.-406(?)B.C. .... **CMLC 2,
 47, 51; DC 1; WLCS**
 See also AW 1; CDWLB 1; DA; DA3;
 DAB; DAC; DAM DRAM, MST; DFS 1,
 4, 8; DLB 176; LAIT 1; LATS 1:1; LMFS
 1; RGWL 2, 3; TWA
Sordello 1189-1269 .... **CMLC 15**
Sorel, Georges 1847-1922 .... **TCLC 91**
 See also CA 118; 188
Sorel, Julia
 See Drexler, Rosalyn
Sorokin, Vladimir .... **CLC 59**
 See Sorokin, Vladimir Georgievich
Sorokin, Vladimir Georgievich
 See Sorokin, Vladimir
 See also DLB 285
Sorrentino, Gilbert 1929- .. **CLC 3, 7, 14, 22,
 40**
 See also CA 77-80; CANR 14, 33, 115; CN
 3, 4, 5, 6, 7; CP 1, 2, 3, 4, 5, 6, 7; DLB 5,
 173; DLBY 1980; INT CANR-14
Soseki
 See Natsume, Soseki
 See also MJW
Soto, Gary 1952- ... **CLC 32, 80; HLC 2; PC
 28**
 See also AAYA 10, 37; BYA 11; CA 119;
 125; CANR 50, 74, 107; CLR 38; CP 4,
 5, 6, 7; DAM MULT; DLB 82; EWL 3;
 EXPP; HW 1, 2; INT CA-125; JRDA;
 LLW; MAICYA 2; MAICYAS 1; MAL 5;
 MTCW 2; MTFW 2005; PFS 7; RGAL 4;
 SATA 80, 120; WYA; YAW
Soupault, Philippe 1897-1990 .... **CLC 68**
 See also CA 116; 147; 131; EWL 3; GFL
 1789 to the Present; LMFS 2
Souster, (Holmes) Raymond 1921- .... **CLC 5,
 14**
 See also CA 13-16R; CAAS 14; CANR 13,
 29, 53; CP 1, 2, 3, 4, 5, 6, 7; DA3; DAC;
 DAM POET; DLB 88; RGEL 2; SATA 63
Southern, Terry 1924(?)-1995 .... **CLC 7**
 See also AMWS 11; BPFB 3; CA 1-4R;
 150; CANR 1, 55, 107; CN 1, 2, 3, 4, 5,
 6; DLB 2; IDFW 3, 4
Southerne, Thomas 1660-1746 .... **LC 99**
 See also DLB 80; RGEL 2
Southey, Robert 1774-1843 .... **NCLC 8, 97**
 See also BRW 4; DLB 93, 107, 142; RGEL
 2; SATA 54
Southwell, Robert 1561(?)-1595 .... **LC 108**
 See also DLB 167; RGEL 2; TEA
Southworth, Emma Dorothy Eliza Nevitte
 1819-1899 .... **NCLC 26**
 See also DLB 239
Souza, Ernest
 See Scott, Evelyn
Soyinka, Wole 1934- .. **BLC 3; CLC 3, 5, 14,
 36, 44, 179; DC 2; WLC**
 See also AFW; BW 2, 3; CA 13-16R;
 CANR 27, 39, 82, 136; CD 5, 6; CDWLB
 3; CN 6, 7; CP 1, 2, 3, 4, 5, 6 ,7; DA;
 DA3; DAB; DAC; DAM DRAM, MST,
 MULT; DFS 10; DLB 125; EWL 3;
 MTCW 1, 2; MTFW 2005; RGEL 2;
 TWA; WLIT 2; WWE 1
Spackman, W(illiam) M(ode)
 1905-1990 .... **CLC 46**
 See also CA 81-84; 132

Stephen, Adeline Virginia
See Woolf, (Adeline) Virginia
Stephen, Sir Leslie 1832-1904 .... **TCLC 23**
See also BRW 5; CA 123; DLB 57, 144, 190
Stephen, Sir Leslie
See Stephen, Sir Leslie
Stephen, Virginia
See Woolf, (Adeline) Virginia
Stephens, James 1882(?)-1950 .... **SSC 50; TCLC 4**
See also CA 104; 192; DLB 19, 153, 162; EWL 3; FANT; RGEL 2; SUFW
Stephens, Reed
See Donaldson, Stephen R(eeder)
Steptoe, Lydia
See Barnes, Djuna
See also GLL 1
Sterchi, Beat 1949- .... **CLC 65**
See also CA 203
Sterling, Brett
See Bradbury, Ray (Douglas); Hamilton, Edmond
Sterling, Bruce 1954- .... **CLC 72**
See also CA 119; CANR 44, 135; CN 7; MTFW 2005; SCFW 2; SFW 4
Sterling, George 1869-1926 .... **TCLC 20**
See also CA 117; 165; DLB 54
Stern, Gerald 1925- .... **CLC 40, 100**
See also AMWS 9; CA 81-84; CANR 28, 94; CP 3, 4, 5, 6, 7; DLB 105; RGAL 4
Stern, Richard (Gustave) 1928- .... **CLC 4, 39**
See also CA 1-4R; CANR 1, 25, 52, 120; CN 1, 2, 3, 4, 5, 6, 7; DLB 218; DLBY 1987; INT CANR-25
Sternberg, Josef von 1894-1969 .... **CLC 20**
See also CA 81-84
Sterne, Laurence 1713-1768 .... **LC 2, 48; WLC**
See also BRW 3; BRWC 1; CDBLB 1660-1789; DA; DAB; DAC; DAM MST, NOV; DLB 39; RGEL 2; TEA
Sternheim, (William Adolf) Carl 1878-1942 .... **TCLC 8**
See also CA 105; 193; DLB 56, 118; EWL 3; IDTP; RGWL 2, 3
Stevens, Margaret Dean
See Aldrich, Bess Streeter
Stevens, Mark 1951- .... **CLC 34**
See also CA 122
Stevens, Wallace 1879-1955 . **PC 6; TCLC 3, 12, 45; WLC**
See also AMW; AMWR 1; CA 104; 124; CDALB 1929-1941; DA; DA3; DAB; DAC; DAM MST, POET; DLB 54; EWL 3; EXPP; MAL 5; MTCW 1, 2; PAB; PFS 13, 16; RGAL 4; TUS; WP
Stevenson, Anne (Katharine) 1933- .. **CLC 7, 33**
See also BRWS 6; CA 17-20R; CAAS 9; CANR 9, 33, 123; CP 3, 4, 5, 6, 7; CWP; DLB 40; MTCW 1; RHW
Stevenson, Robert Louis (Balfour) 1850-1894 ...... **NCLC 5, 14, 63; SSC 11, 51; WLC**
See also AAYA 24; BPFB 3; BRW 5; BRWC 1; BRWR 1; BYA 1, 2, 4, 13; CD-BLB 1890-1914; CLR 10, 11; DA; DA3; DAB; DAC; DAM MST, NOV; DLB 18, 57, 141, 156, 174; DLBD 13; GL 3; HGG; JRDA; LAIT 1, 3; MAICYA 1, 2; NFS 11, 20; RGEL 2; RGSF 2; SATA 100; SUFW; TEA; WCH; WLIT 4; WYA; YABC 2; YAW
Stewart, J(ohn) I(nnes) M(ackintosh) 1906-1994 .... **CLC 7, 14, 32**
See Innes, Michael
See also CA 85-88; 147; CAAS 3; CANR 47; CMW 4; CN 1, 2, 3, 4, 5; MTCW 1, 2

Stewart, Mary (Florence Elinor) 1916- .... **CLC 7, 35, 117**
See also AAYA 29; BPFB 3; CA 1-4R; CANR 1, 59, 130; CMW 4; CPW; DAB; FANT; RHW; SATA 12; YAW
Stewart, Mary Rainbow
See Stewart, Mary (Florence Elinor)
Stifle, June
See Campbell, Maria
Stifter, Adalbert 1805-1868 .. **NCLC 41; SSC 28**
See also CDWLB 2; DLB 133; RGSF 2; RGWL 2, 3
Still, James 1906-2001 .... **CLC 49**
See also CA 65-68; 195; CAAS 17; CANR 10, 26; CSW; DLB 9; DLBY 01; SATA 29; SATA-Obit 127
Sting 1951-
See Sumner, Gordon Matthew
See also CA 167
Stirling, Arthur
See Sinclair, Upton (Beall)
Stitt, Milan 1941- .... **CLC 29**
See also CA 69-72
Stockton, Francis Richard 1834-1902
See Stockton, Frank R.
See also AAYA 68; CA 108; 137; MAICYA 1, 2; SATA 44; SFW 4
Stockton, Frank R. .... **TCLC 47**
See Stockton, Francis Richard
See also BYA 4, 13; DLB 42, 74; DLBD 13; EXPS; SATA-Brief 32; SSFS 3; SUFW; WCH
Stoddard, Charles
See Kuttner, Henry
Stoker, Abraham 1847-1912
See Stoker, Bram
See also CA 105; 150; DA; DA3; DAC; DAM MST, NOV; HGG; MTFW 2005; SATA 29
Stoker, Bram . **SSC 62; TCLC 8, 144; WLC**
See Stoker, Abraham
See also CA 23; BPFB 3; BRWS 3; BYA 5; CDBLB 1890-1914; DAB; DLB 304; GL 3; LATS 1:1; NFS 18; RGEL 2; SUFW; TEA; WLIT 4
Stolz, Mary (Slattery) 1920- .... **CLC 12**
See also AAYA 8; AITN 1; CA 5-8R; CANR 13, 41, 112; JRDA; MAICYA 1, 2; SAAS 3; SATA 10, 71, 133; YAW
Stone, Irving 1903-1989 .... **CLC 7**
See also AITN 1; BPFB 3; CA 1-4R; 129; CAAS 3; CANR 1, 23; CN 1, 2, 3, 4; CPW; DA3; DAM POP; INT CANR-23; MTCW 1, 2; MTFW 2005; RHW; SATA 3; SATA-Obit 64
Stone, Oliver (William) 1946- .... **CLC 73**
See also AAYA 15, 64; CA 110; CANR 55, 125
Stone, Robert (Anthony) 1937- ... **CLC 5, 23, 42, 175**
See also AMWS 5; BPFB 3; CA 85-88; CANR 23, 66, 95; CN 4, 5, 6, 7; DLB 152; EWL 3; INT CANR-23; MAL 5; MTCW 1; MTFW 2005
Stone, Ruth 1915- .... **PC 53**
See also CA 45-48; CANR 2, 91; CP 7; CSW; DLB 105; PFS 19
Stone, Zachary
See Follett, Ken(neth Martin)
Stoppard, Tom 1937- ... **CLC 1, 3, 4, 5, 8, 15, 29, 34, 63, 91; DC 6; WLC**
See also AAYA 63; BRWC 1; BRWR 2; BRWS 1; CA 81-84; CANR 39, 67, 125; CBD; CD 5, 6; CDBLB 1960 to Present; DA; DA3; DAB; DAC; DAM DRAM, MST; DFS 2, 5, 8, 11, 13, 16; DLB 13, 233; DLBY 1985; EWL 3; LATS 1:2; MTCW 1, 2; MTFW 2005; RGEL 2; TEA; WLIT 4

Storey, David (Malcolm) 1933- . **CLC 2, 4, 5, 8**
See also BRWS 1; CA 81-84; CANR 36; CBD; CD 5, 6; CN 1, 2, 3, 4, 5, 6; DAM DRAM; DLB 13, 14, 207, 245; EWL 3; MTCW 1; RGEL 2
Storm, Hyemeyohsts 1935- ... **CLC 3; NNAL**
See also CA 81-84; CANR 45; DAM MULT
Storm, (Hans) Theodor (Woldsen) 1817-1888 .... **NCLC 1; SSC 27**
See also CDWLB 2; DLB 129; EW; RGSF 2; RGWL 2, 3
Storni, Alfonsina 1892-1938 . **HLC 2; PC 33; TCLC 5**
See also CA 104; 131; DAM MULT; DLB 283; HW 1; LAW
Stoughton, William 1631-1701 .... **LC 38**
See also DLB 24
Stout, Rex (Todhunter) 1886-1975 ..... **CLC 3**
See also AITN 2; BPFB 3; CA 61-64; CANR 71; CMW 4; CN 2; DLB 306; MSW; RGAL 4
Stow, (Julian) Randolph 1935- ... **CLC 23, 48**
See also CA 13-16R; CANR 33; CN 1, 2, 3, 4, 5, 6, 7; CP 1, 2, 3, 4; DLB 260; MTCW 1; RGEL 2
Stowe, Harriet (Elizabeth) Beecher 1811-1896 .... **NCLC 3, 50, 133; WLC**
See also AAYA 53; AMWS 1; CDALB 1865-1917; DA; DA3; DAB; DAC; DAM MST, NOV; DLB 1, 12, 42, 74, 189, 239, 243; EXPN; FL 1:3; JRDA; LAIT 2; MAICYA 1, 2; NFS 6; RGAL 4; TUS; YABC 1
Strabo c. 64B.C.-c. 25 .... **CMLC 37**
See also DLB 176
Strachey, (Giles) Lytton 1880-1932 .... **TCLC 12**
See also BRWS 2; CA 110; 178; DLB 149; DLBD 10; EWL 3; MTCW 2; NCFS 4
Stramm, August 1874-1915 .... **PC 50**
See also CA 195; EWL 3
Strand, Mark 1934- .. **CLC 6, 18, 41, 71; PC 63**
See also AMWS 4; CA 21-24R; CANR 40, 65, 100; CP 1, 2, 3, 4, 5, 6, 7; DAM POET; DLB 5; EWL 3; MAL 5; PAB; PFS 9, 18; RGAL 4; SATA 41; TCLE 1:2
Stratton-Porter, Gene(va Grace) 1863-1924
See Porter, Gene(va Grace) Stratton
See also ANW; CA 137; CLR 87; DLB 221; DLBD 14; MAICYA 1, 2; SATA 15
Straub, Peter (Francis) 1943- ... **CLC 28, 107**
See also BEST 89:1; BPFB 3; CA 85-88; CANR 28, 65, 109; CPW; DAM POP; DLBY 1984; HGG; MTCW 1, 2; MTFW 2005; SUFW 2
Strauss, Botho 1944- .... **CLC 22**
See also CA 157; CWW 2; DLB 124
Strauss, Leo 1899-1973 .... **TCLC 141**
See also CA 101; 45-48; CANR 122
Streatfeild, (Mary) Noel 1897(?)-1986 .... **CLC 21**
See also CA 81-84; 120; CANR 31; CLR 17, 83; CWRI 5; DLB 160; MAICYA 1, 2; SATA 20; SATA-Obit 48
Stribling, T(homas) S(igismund) 1881-1965 .... **CLC 23**
See also CA 189; 107; CMW 4; DLB 9; RGAL 4
Strindberg, (Johan) August 1849-1912 ... **DC 18; TCLC 1, 8, 21, 47; WLC**
See also CA 104; 135; DA; DA3; DAB; DAC; DAM DRAM, MST; DFS 4, 9; DLB 259; EW 7; EWL 3; IDTP; LMFS 2; MTCW 2; MTFW 2005; RGWL 2, 3; TWA
Stringer, Arthur 1874-1950 .... **TCLC 37**
See also CA 161; DLB 92

Szirtes, George 1948- .... **CLC 46; PC 51**
See also CA 109; CANR 27, 61, 117; CP 4, 5, 6, 7

Szymborska, Wislawa 1923- ... **CLC 99, 190; PC 44**
See also CA 154; CANR 91, 133; CDWLB 4; CWP; CWW 2; DA3; DLB 232; DLBY 1996; EWL 3; MTCW 2; MTFW 2005; PFS 15; RGWL 3

T. O., Nik
See Annensky, Innokenty (Fyodorovich)

Tabori, George 1914- .... **CLC 19**
See also CA 49-52; CANR 4, 69; CBD; CD 5, 6; DLB 245

Tacitus c. 55-c. 117 .... **CMLC 56**
See also AW 2; CDWLB 1; DLB 211; RGWL 2, 3

Tagore, Rabindranath 1861-1941 .... **PC 8; SSC 48; TCLC 3, 53**
See also CA 104; 120; DA3; DAM DRAM, POET; EWL 3; MTCW 1, 2; MTFW 2005; PFS 18; RGEL 2; RGSF 2; RGWL 2, 3; TWA

Taine, Hippolyte Adolphe
1828-1893 .... **NCLC 15**
See also EW 7; GFL 1789 to the Present

Talayesva, Don C. 1890-(?) .... **NNAL**

Talese, Gay 1932- .... **CLC 37**
See also AITN 1; CA 1-4R; CANR 9, 58, 137; DLB 185; INT CANR-9; MTCW 1, 2; MTFW 2005

Tallent, Elizabeth (Ann) 1954- .... **CLC 45**
See also CA 117; CANR 72; DLB 130

Tallmountain, Mary 1918-1997 .... **NNAL**
See also CA 146; 161; DLB 193

Tally, Ted 1952- .... **CLC 42**
See also CA 120; 124; CAD; CANR 125; CD 5, 6; INT CA-124

Talvik, Heiti 1904-1947 .... **TCLC 87**
See also EWL 3

Tamayo y Baus, Manuel
1829-1898 .... **NCLC 1**

Tammsaare, A(nton) H(ansen)
1878-1940 .... **TCLC 27**
See also CA 164; CDWLB 4; DLB 220; EWL 3

Tam'si, Tchicaya U
See Tchicaya, Gerald Felix

Tan, Amy (Ruth) 1952- . **AAL; CLC 59, 120, 151**
See also AAYA 9, 48; AMWS 10; BEST 89:3; BPFB 3; CA 136; CANR 54, 105, 132; CDALBS; CN 6, 7; CPW 1; DA3; DAM MULT, NOV, POP; DLB 173, 312; EXPN; FL 1:6; FW; LAIT 3, 5; MAL 5; MTCW 2; MTFW 2005; NFS 1, 13, 16; RGAL 4; SATA 75; SSFS 9; YAW

Tandem, Felix
See Spitteler, Carl (Friedrich Georg)

Tanizaki, Jun'ichiro 1886-1965 ... **CLC 8, 14, 28; SSC 21**
See Tanizaki Jun'ichiro
See also CA 93-96; 25-28R; MJW; MTCW 2; MTFW 2005; RGSF 2; RGWL 2

Tanizaki Jun'ichiro
See Tanizaki, Jun'ichiro
See also DLB 180; EWL 3

Tannen, Deborah F(rances) 1945- .. **CLC 206**
See also CA 118; CANR 95

Tanner, William
See Amis, Kingsley (William)

Tao Lao
See Storni, Alfonsina

Tapahonso, Luci 1953- .... **NNAL; PC 65**
See also CA 145; CANR 72, 127; DLB 175

Tarantino, Quentin (Jerome)
1963- .... **CLC 125**
See also AAYA 58; CA 171; CANR 125

Tarassoff, Lev
See Troyat, Henri

Tarbell, Ida M(inerva) 1857-1944 . **TCLC 40**
See also CA 122; 181; DLB 47

Tarkington, (Newton) Booth
1869-1946 .... **TCLC 9**
See also BPFB 3; BYA 3; CA 110; 143; CWRI 5; DLB 9, 102; MAL 5; MTCW 2; RGAL 4; SATA 17

Tarkovskii, Andrei Arsen'evich
See Tarkovsky, Andrei (Arsenyevich)

Tarkovsky, Andrei (Arsenyevich)
1932-1986 .... **CLC 75**
See also CA 127

Tartt, Donna 1964(?)- .... **CLC 76**
See also AAYA 56; CA 142; CANR 135; MTFW 2005

Tasso, Torquato 1544-1595 .... **LC 5, 94**
See also EFS 2; EW 2; RGWL 2, 3; WLIT 7

Tate, (John Orley) Allen 1899-1979 .. **CLC 2, 4, 6, 9, 11, 14, 24; PC 50**
See also AMW; CA 5-8R; 85-88; CANR 32, 108; CN 1, 2; CP 1, 2; DLB 4, 45, 63; DLBD 17; EWL 3; MAL 5; MTCW 1, 2; MTFW 2005; RGAL 4; RHW

Tate, Ellalice
See Hibbert, Eleanor Alice Burford

Tate, James (Vincent) 1943- ..... **CLC 2, 6, 25**
See also CA 21-24R; CANR 29, 57, 114; CP 1, 2, 3, 4, 5, 6, 7; DLB 5, 169; EWL 3; PFS 10, 15; RGAL 4; WP

Tate, Nahum 1652(?)-1715 .... **LC 109**
See also DLB 80; RGEL 2

Tauler, Johannes c. 1300-1361 ...... **CMLC 37**
See also DLB 179; LMFS 1

Tavel, Ronald 1940- .... **CLC 6**
See also CA 21-24R; CAD; CANR 33; CD 5, 6

Taviani, Paolo 1931- .... **CLC 70**
See also CA 153

Taylor, Bayard 1825-1878 .... **NCLC 89**
See also DLB 3, 189, 250, 254; RGAL 4

Taylor, C(ecil) P(hilip) 1929-1981 .... **CLC 27**
See also CA 25-28R; 105; CANR 47; CBD

Taylor, Edward 1642(?)-1729 . **LC 11; PC 63**
See also AMW; DA; DAB; DAC; DAM MST, POET; DLB 24; EXPP; RGAL 4; TUS

Taylor, Eleanor Ross 1920- .... **CLC 5**
See also CA 81-84; CANR 70

Taylor, Elizabeth 1912-1975 ..... **CLC 2, 4, 29**
See also CA 13-16R; CANR 9, 70; CN 1, 2; DLB 139; MTCW 1; RGEL 2; SATA 13

Taylor, Frederick Winslow
1856-1915 .... **TCLC 76**
See also CA 188

Taylor, Henry (Splawn) 1942- .... **CLC 44**
See also CA 33-36R; CAAS 7; CANR 31; CP 7; DLB 5; PFS 10

Taylor, Kamala (Purnaiya) 1924-2004
See Markandaya, Kamala
See also CA 77-80; 227; MTFW 2005; NFS 13

Taylor, Mildred D(elois) 1943- .... **CLC 21**
See also AAYA 10, 47; BW 1; BYA 3, 8; CA 85-88; CANR 25, 115, 136; CLR 9, 59, 90; CSW; DLB 52; JRDA; LAIT 3; MAICYA 1, 2; MTFW 2005; SAAS 5; SATA 135; WYA; YAW

Taylor, Peter (Hillsman) 1917-1994 .. **CLC 1, 4, 18, 37, 44, 50, 71; SSC 10, 84**
See also AMWS 5; BPFB 3; CA 13-16R; 147; CANR 9, 50; CN 1, 2, 3, 4, 5; CSW; DLB 218, 278; DLBY 1981, 1994; EWL 3; EXPS; INT CANR-9; MAL 5; MTCW 1, 2; MTFW 2005; RGSF 2; SSFS 9; TUS

Taylor, Robert Lewis 1912-1998 .... **CLC 14**
See also CA 1-4R; 170; CANR 3, 64; CN 1, 2; SATA 10; TCWW 1, 2

Tchekhov, Anton
See Chekhov, Anton (Pavlovich)

Tchicaya, Gerald Felix 1931-1988 .. **CLC 101**
See Tchicaya U Tam'si
See also CA 129; 125; CANR 81

Tchicaya U Tam'si
See Tchicaya, Gerald Felix
See also EWL 3

Teasdale, Sara 1884-1933 .... **PC 31; TCLC 4**
See also CA 104; 163; DLB 45; GLL 1; PFS 14; RGAL 4; SATA 32; TUS

Tecumseh 1768-1813 .... **NNAL**
See also DAM MULT

Tegner, Esaias 1782-1846 .... **NCLC 2**

Teilhard de Chardin, (Marie Joseph) Pierre
1881-1955 .... **TCLC 9**
See also CA 105; 210; GFL 1789 to the Present

Temple, Ann
See Mortimer, Penelope (Ruth)

Tennant, Emma (Christina) 1937- .. **CLC 13, 52**
See also BRWS 9; CA 65-68; CAAS 9; CANR 10, 38, 59, 88; CN 3, 4, 5, 6, 7; DLB 14; EWL 3; SFW 4

Tenneshaw, S. M.
See Silverberg, Robert

Tenney, Tabitha Gilman
1762-1837 .... **NCLC 122**
See also DLB 37, 200

Tennyson, Alfred 1809-1892 ... **NCLC 30, 65, 115; PC 6; WLC**
See also AAYA 50; BRW 4; CDBLB 1832-1890; DA; DA3; DAB; DAC; DAM MST, POET; DLB 32; EXPP; PAB; PFS 1, 2, 4, 11, 15, 19; RGEL 2; TEA; WLIT 4; WP

Teran, Lisa St. Aubin de .... **CLC 36**
See St. Aubin de Teran, Lisa

Terence c. 184B.C.-c. 159B.C. ...... **CMLC 14; DC 7**
See also AW 1; CDWLB 1; DLB 211; RGWL 2, 3; TWA

Teresa de Jesus, St. 1515-1582 .... **LC 18**

Teresa of Avila, St.
See Teresa de Jesus, St.

Terkel, Louis 1912-
See Terkel, Studs
See also CA 57-60; CANR 18, 45, 67, 132; DA3; MTCW 1, 2; MTFW 2005

Terkel, Studs .... **CLC 38**
See Terkel, Louis
See also AAYA 32; AITN 1; MTCW 2; TUS

Terry, C. V.
See Slaughter, Frank G(ill)

Terry, Megan 1932- .... **CLC 19; DC 13**
See also CA 77-80; CABS 3; CAD; CANR 43; CD 5, 6; CWD; DFS 18; DLB 7, 249; GLL 2

Tertullian c. 155-c. 245 .... **CMLC 29**

Tertz, Abram
See Sinyavsky, Andrei (Donatevich)
See also RGSF 2

Tesich, Steve 1943(?)-1996 .... **CLC 40, 69**
See also CA 105; 152; CAD; DLBY 1983

Tesla, Nikola 1856-1943 .... **TCLC 88**

Teternikov, Fyodor Kuzmich 1863-1927
See Sologub, Fyodor
See also CA 104

Tevis, Walter 1928-1984 .... **CLC 42**
See also CA 113; SFW 4

Tey, Josephine .... **TCLC 14**
See Mackintosh, Elizabeth
See also DLB 77; MSW

1945; CLR 56; CN 1; CPW 1; CWRI 5;
DA; DA3; DAB; DAC; DAM MST, NOV,
POP; DLB 15, 160, 255; EFS 2; EWL 3;
FANT; JRDA; LAIT 1; LATS 1:2; LMFS
2; MAICYA 1, 2; MTCW 1, 2; MTFW
2005; NFS 8; RGEL 2; SATA 2, 32, 100;
SATA-Obit 24; SFW 4; SUFW; TEA;
WCH; WYA; YAW

Toller, Ernst 1893-1939 .... **TCLC 10**
See also CA 107; 186; DLB 124; EWL 3;
RGWL 2, 3

Tolson, M. B.
See Tolson, Melvin B(eaunorus)

Tolson, Melvin B(eaunorus)
1898(?)-1966 .... **BLC 3; CLC 36, 105**
See also AFAW 1, 2; BW 1, 3; CA 124; 89-
92; CANR 80; DAM MULT, POET; DLB
48, 76; MAL 5; RGAL 4

Tolstoi, Aleksei Nikolaevich
See Tolstoy, Alexey Nikolaevich

Tolstoi, Lev
See Tolstoy, Leo (Nikolaevich)
See also RGSF 2; RGWL 2, 3

Tolstoy, Aleksei Nikolaevich
See Tolstoy, Alexey Nikolaevich
See also DLB 272

Tolstoy, Alexey Nikolaevich
1882-1945 .... **TCLC 18**
See Tolstoy, Aleksei Nikolaevich
See also CA 107; 158; EWL 3; SFW 4

Tolstoy, Leo (Nikolaevich)
1828-1910 . **SSC 9, 30, 45, 54; TCLC 4,**
11, 17, 28, 44, 79, 173; WLC
See Tolstoi, Lev
See also AAYA 56; CA 104; 123; DA; DA3;
DAB; DAC; DAM MST, NOV; DLB 238;
EFS 2; EW 7; EXPS; IDTP; LAIT 2;
LATS 1:1; LMFS 1; NFS 10; SATA 26;
SSFS 5; TWA

Tolstoy, Count Leo
See Tolstoy, Leo (Nikolaevich)

Tomalin, Claire 1933- .... **CLC 166**
See also CA 89-92; CANR 52, 88; DLB
155

Tomasi di Lampedusa, Giuseppe 1896-1957
See Lampedusa, Giuseppe (Tomasi) di
See also CA 111; DLB 177; EWL 3; WLIT
7

Tomlin, Lily .... **CLC 17**
See Tomlin, Mary Jean

Tomlin, Mary Jean 1939(?)-
See Tomlin, Lily
See also CA 117

Tomline, F. Latour
See Gilbert, W(illiam) S(chwenck)

Tomlinson, (Alfred) Charles 1927- .... **CLC 2,**
4, 6, 13, 45; PC 17
See also CA 5-8R; CANR 33; CP 1, 2, 3, 4,
5, 6, 7; DAM POET; DLB 40; TCLE 1:2

Tomlinson, H(enry) M(ajor)
1873-1958 .... **TCLC 71**
See also CA 118; 161; DLB 36, 100, 195

Tonna, Charlotte Elizabeth
1790-1846 .... **NCLC 135**
See also DLB 163

Tonson, Jacob fl. 1655(?)-1736 .... **LC 86**
See also DLB 170

Toole, John Kennedy 1937-1969 ..... **CLC 19,**
64
See also BPFB 3; CA 104; DLBY 1981;
MTCW 2; MTFW 2005

Toomer, Eugene
See Toomer, Jean

Toomer, Eugene Pinchback
See Toomer, Jean

Toomer, Jean 1894-1967 .. **BLC 3; CLC 1, 4,**
13, 22; HR 1:3; PC 7; SSC 1, 45;
TCLC 172; WLCS
See also AFAW 1, 2; AMWS 3, 9; BW 1;
CA 85-88; CDALB 1917-1929; DA3;
DAM MULT; DLB 45, 51; EWL 3; EXPP;
EXPS; LMFS 2; MAL 5; MTCW 1, 2;
MTFW 2005; NFS 11; RGAL 4; RGSF 2;
SSFS 5

Toomer, Nathan Jean
See Toomer, Jean

Toomer, Nathan Pinchback
See Toomer, Jean

Torley, Luke
See Blish, James (Benjamin)

Tornimparte, Alessandra
See Ginzburg, Natalia

Torre, Raoul della
See Mencken, H(enry) L(ouis)

Torrence, Ridgely 1874-1950 .... **TCLC 97**
See also DLB 54, 249; MAL 5

Torrey, E(dwin) Fuller 1937- .... **CLC 34**
See also CA 119; CANR 71

Torsvan, Ben Traven
See Traven, B.

Torsvan, Benno Traven
See Traven, B.

Torsvan, Berick Traven
See Traven, B.

Torsvan, Berwick Traven
See Traven, B.

Torsvan, Bruno Traven
See Traven, B.

Torsvan, Traven
See Traven, B.

Tourneur, Cyril 1575(?)-1626 .... **LC 66**
See also BRW 2; DAM DRAM; DLB 58;
RGEL 2

Tournier, Michel (Edouard) 1924- .... **CLC 6,**
23, 36, 95; SSC 88
See also CA 49-52; CANR 3, 36, 74; CWW
2; DLB 83; EWL 3; GFL 1789 to the
Present; MTCW 1, 2; SATA 23

Tournimparte, Alessandra
See Ginzburg, Natalia

Towers, Ivar
See Kornbluth, C(yril) M.

Towne, Robert (Burton) 1936(?)- ..... **CLC 87**
See also CA 108; DLB 44; IDFW 3, 4

Townsend, Sue .... **CLC 61**
See Townsend, Susan Lilian
See also AAYA 28; CA 119; 127; CANR
65, 107; CBD; CD 5, 6; CPW; CWD;
DAB; DAC; DAM MST; DLB 271; INT
CA-127; SATA 55, 93; SATA-Brief 48;
YAW

Townsend, Susan Lilian 1946-
See Townsend, Sue

Townshend, Pete
See Townshend, Peter (Dennis Blandford)

Townshend, Peter (Dennis Blandford)
1945- .... **CLC 17, 42**
See also CA 107

Tozzi, Federigo 1883-1920 .... **TCLC 31**
See also CA 160; CANR 110; DLB 264;
EWL 3; WLIT 7

Tracy, Don(ald Fiske) 1905-1970(?)
See Queen, Ellery
See also CA 1-4R; 176; CANR 2

Trafford, F. G.
See Riddell, Charlotte

Traherne, Thomas 1637(?)-1674 .... **LC 99**
See also BRW 2; BRWS 11; DLB 131;
PAB; RGEL 2

Traill, Catharine Parr 1802-1899 .. **NCLC 31**
See also DLB 99

Trakl, Georg 1887-1914 .... **PC 20; TCLC 5**
See also CA 104; 165; EW 10; EWL 3;
LMFS 2; MTCW 2; RGWL 2, 3

Trambley, Estela Portillo .... **TCLC 163**
See Portillo Trambley, Estela
See also CA 77-80; RGAL 4

Tranquilli, Secondino
See Silone, Ignazio

Transtroemer, Tomas Gosta
See Transtromer, Tomas (Goesta)

Transtromer, Tomas (Gosta)
See Transtromer, Tomas (Goesta)
See also CWW 2

Transtromer, Tomas (Goesta)
1931- .... **CLC 52, 65**
See Transtromer, Tomas (Gosta)
See also CA 117; 129; CAAS 17; CANR
115; DAM POET; DLB 257; EWL 3; PFS
21

Transtromer, Tomas Gosta
See Transtromer, Tomas (Goesta)

Traven, B. 1882(?)-1969 .... **CLC 8, 11**
See also CA 19-20; 25-28R; CAP 2; DLB
9, 56; EWL 3; MTCW 1; RGAL 4

Trediakovsky, Vasilii Kirillovich
1703-1769 .... **LC 68**
See also DLB 150

Treitel, Jonathan 1959- .... **CLC 70**
See also CA 210; DLB 267

Trelawny, Edward John
1792-1881 .... **NCLC 85**
See also DLB 110, 116, 144

Tremain, Rose 1943- .... **CLC 42**
See also CA 97-100; CANR 44, 95; CN 4,
5, 6, 7; DLB 14, 271; RGSF 2; RHW

Tremblay, Michel 1942- .... **CLC 29, 102**
See also CA 116; 128; CCA 1; CWW 2;
DAC; DAM MST; DLB 60; EWL 3; GLL
1; MTCW 1, 2; MTFW 2005

Trevanian .... **CLC 29**
See Whitaker, Rod(ney)

Trevor, Glen
See Hilton, James

Trevor, William .. **CLC 7, 9, 14, 25, 71, 116;**
SSC 21, 58
See Cox, William Trevor
See also BRWS 4; CBD; CD 5, 6; CN 1, 2,
3, 4, 5, 6, 7; DLB 14, 139; EWL 3; LATS
1:2; RGEL 2; RGSF 2; SSFS 10; TCLE
1:2

Trifonov, Iurii (Valentinovich)
See Trifonov, Yuri (Valentinovich)
See also DLB 302; RGWL 2, 3

Trifonov, Yuri (Valentinovich)
1925-1981 .... **CLC 45**
See Trifonov, Iurii (Valentinovich); Trifonov, Yury Valentinovich
See also CA 126; 103; MTCW 1

Trifonov, Yury Valentinovich
See Trifonov, Yuri (Valentinovich)
See also EWL 3

Trilling, Diana (Rubin) 1905-1996 . **CLC 129**
See also CA 5-8R; 154; CANR 10, 46; INT
CANR-10; MTCW 1, 2

Trilling, Lionel 1905-1975 ..... **CLC 9, 11, 24;**
SSC 75
See also AMWS 3; CA 9-12R; 61-64;
CANR 10, 105; CN 1, 2; DLB 28, 63;
EWL 3; INT CANR-10; MAL 5; MTCW
1, 2; RGAL 4; TUS

Trimball, W. H.
See Mencken, H(enry) L(ouis)

Tristan
See Gomez de la Serna, Ramon

Tristram
See Housman, A(lfred) E(dward)

Trogdon, William (Lewis) 1939-
See Heat-Moon, William Least
See also AAYA 66; CA 115; 119; CANR
47, 89; CPW; INT CA-119

Ustinov, Peter (Alexander)
1921-2004 .... **CLC 1**
See also AITN 1; CA 13-16R; 225; CANR
25, 51; CBD; CD 5, 6; DLB 13; MTCW
2

U Tam'si, Gerald Felix Tchicaya
See Tchicaya, Gerald Felix

U Tam'si, Tchicaya
See Tchicaya, Gerald Felix

Vachss, Andrew (Henry) 1942- .... **CLC 106**
See also CA 118, 214; CAAE 214; CANR
44, 95; CMW 4

Vachss, Andrew H.
See Vachss, Andrew (Henry)

Vaculik, Ludvik 1926- .... **CLC 7**
See also CA 53-56; CANR 72; CWW 2;
DLB 232; EWL 3

Vaihinger, Hans 1852-1933 .... **TCLC 71**
See also CA 116; 166

Valdez, Luis (Miguel) 1940- ..... **CLC 84; DC
10; HLC 2**
See also CA 101; CAD; CANR 32, 81; CD
5, 6; DAM MULT; DFS 5; DLB 122;
EWL 3; HW 1; LAIT 4; LLW

Valenzuela, Luisa 1938- .... **CLC 31, 104;
HLCS 2; SSC 14, 82**
See also CA 101; CANR 32, 65, 123; CD-
WLB 3; CWW 2; DAM MULT; DLB 113;
EWL 3; FW; HW 1, 2; LAW; RGSF 2;
RGWL 3

Valera y Alcala-Galiano, Juan
1824-1905 .... **TCLC 10**
See also CA 106

Valerius Maximus fl. 20- .... **CMLC 64**
See also DLB 211

Valery, (Ambroise) Paul (Toussaint Jules)
1871-1945 .... **PC 9; TCLC 4, 15**
See also CA 104; 122; DA3; DAM POET;
DLB 258; EW 8; EWL 3; GFL 1789 to
the Present; MTCW 1, 2; MTFW 2005;
RGWL 2, 3; TWA

Valle-Inclan, Ramon (Maria) del
1866-1936 .... **HLC 2; TCLC 5**
See del Valle-Inclan, Ramon (Maria)
See also CA 106; 153; CANR 80; DAM
MULT; DLB 134; EW 8; EWL 3; HW 2;
RGSF 2; RGWL 2, 3

Vallejo, Antonio Buero
See Buero Vallejo, Antonio

Vallejo, Cesar (Abraham)
1892-1938 .... **HLC 2; TCLC 3, 56**
See also CA 105; 153; DAM MULT; DLB
290; EWL 3; HW 1; LAW; RGWL 2, 3

Valles, Jules 1832-1885 .... **NCLC 71**
See also DLB 123; GFL 1789 to the Present

Vallette, Marguerite Eymery
1860-1953 .... **TCLC 67**
See Rachilde
See also CA 182; DLB 123, 192

Valle Y Pena, Ramon del
See Valle-Inclan, Ramon (Maria) del

Van Ash, Cay 1918-1994 .... **CLC 34**
See also CA 220

Vanbrugh, Sir John 1664-1726 .... **LC 21**
See also BRW 2; DAM DRAM; DLB 80;
IDTP; RGEL 2

Van Campen, Karl
See Campbell, John W(ood, Jr.)

Vance, Gerald
See Silverberg, Robert

Vance, Jack .... **CLC 35**
See Vance, John Holbrook
See also DLB 8; FANT; SCFW 1, 2; SFW
4; SUFW 1, 2

Vance, John Holbrook 1916-
See Queen, Ellery; Vance, Jack
See also CA 29-32R; CANR 17, 65; CMW
4; MTCW 1

**Van Den Bogarde, Derek Jules Gaspard
Ulric Niven** 1921-1999 .... **CLC 14**
See Bogarde, Dirk
See also CA 77-80; 179

Vandenburgh, Jane .... **CLC 59**
See also CA 168

Vanderhaeghe, Guy 1951- .... **CLC 41**
See also BPFB 3; CA 113; CANR 72, 145;
CN 7

van der Post, Laurens (Jan)
1906-1996 .... **CLC 5**
See also AFW; CA 5-8R; 155; CANR 35;
CN 1, 2, 3, 4, 5, 6; DLB 204; RGEL 2

van de Wetering, Janwillem 1931- ... **CLC 47**
See also CA 49-52; CANR 4, 62, 90; CMW
4

Van Dine, S. S. .... **TCLC 23**
See Wright, Willard Huntington
See also DLB 306; MSW

Van Doren, Carl (Clinton)
1885-1950 .... **TCLC 18**
See also CA 111; 168

Van Doren, Mark 1894-1972 .... **CLC 6, 10**
See also CA 1-4R; 37-40R; CANR 3; CN
1; CP 1; DLB 45, 284; MAL 5; MTCW
1, 2; RGAL 4

Van Druten, John (William)
1901-1957 .... **TCLC 2**
See also CA 104; 161; DLB 10; MAL 5;
RGAL 4

Van Duyn, Mona (Jane) 1921-2004 .. **CLC 3,
7, 63, 116**
See also CA 9-12R; 234; CANR 7, 38, 60,
116; CP 1, 2, 3, 4, 5, 6, 7; CWP; DAM
POET; DLB 5; MAL 5; MTFW 2005;
PFS 20

Van Dyne, Edith
See Baum, L(yman) Frank

van Itallie, Jean-Claude 1936- .... **CLC 3**
See also CA 45-48; CAAS 2; CAD; CANR
1, 48; CD 5, 6; DLB 7

Van Loot, Cornelius Obenchain
See Roberts, Kenneth (Lewis)

van Ostaijen, Paul 1896-1928 .... **TCLC 33**
See also CA 163

Van Peebles, Melvin 1932- .... **CLC 2, 20**
See also BW 2, 3; CA 85-88; CANR 27,
67, 82; DAM MULT

van Schendel, Arthur(-Francois-Emile)
1874-1946 .... **TCLC 56**
See also EWL 3

Vansittart, Peter 1920- .... **CLC 42**
See also CA 1-4R; CANR 3, 49, 90; CN 4,
5, 6, 7; RHW

Van Vechten, Carl 1880-1964 ... **CLC 33; HR
1:3**
See also AMWS 2; CA 183; 89-92; DLB 4,
9, 51; RGAL 4

van Vogt, A(lfred) E(lton) 1912-2000 . **CLC 1**
See also BPFB 3; BYA 13, 14; CA 21-24R;
190; CANR 28; DLB 8, 251; SATA 14;
SATA-Obit 124; SCFW 1, 2; SFW 4

Vara, Madeleine
See Jackson, Laura (Riding)

Varda, Agnes 1928- .... **CLC 16**
See also CA 116; 122

Vargas Llosa, (Jorge) Mario (Pedro)
1936- .... **CLC 3, 6, 9, 10, 15, 31, 42, 85,
181; HLC 2**
See Llosa, (Jorge) Mario (Pedro) Vargas
See also BPFB 3; CA 73-76; CANR 18, 32,
42, 67, 116, 140; CDWLB 3; CWW 2;
DA; DA3; DAB; DAC; DAM MST,
MULT, NOV; DLB 145; DNFS 2; EWL
3; HW 1, 2; LAIT 5; LATS 1:2; LAW;
LAWS 1; MTCW 1, 2; MTFW 2005;
RGWL 2; SSFS 14; TWA; WLIT 1

Varnhagen von Ense, Rahel
1771-1833 .... **NCLC 130**
See also DLB 90

Vasari, Giorgio 1511-1574 .... **LC 114**

Vasiliu, George
See Bacovia, George

Vasiliu, Gheorghe
See Bacovia, George
See also CA 123; 189

Vassa, Gustavus
See Equiano, Olaudah

Vassilikos, Vassilis 1933- .... **CLC 4, 8**
See also CA 81-84; CANR 75; EWL 3

Vaughan, Henry 1621-1695 .... **LC 27**
See also BRW 2; DLB 131; PAB; RGEL 2

Vaughn, Stephanie .... **CLC 62**

Vazov, Ivan (Minchov) 1850-1921 . **TCLC 25**
See also CA 121; 167; CDWLB 4; DLB
147

Veblen, Thorstein B(unde)
1857-1929 .... **TCLC 31**
See also AMWS 1; CA 115; 165; DLB 246;
MAL 5

Vega, Lope de 1562-1635 ... **HLCS 2; LC 23,
119**
See also EW 2; RGWL 2, 3

Vendler, Helen (Hennessy) 1933- ... **CLC 138**
See also CA 41-44R; CANR 25, 72, 136;
MTCW 1, 2; MTFW 2005

Venison, Alfred
See Pound, Ezra (Weston Loomis)

Ventsel, Elena Sergeevna 1907-2002
See Grekova, I.
See also CA 154

Verdi, Marie de
See Mencken, H(enry) L(ouis)

Verdu, Matilde
See Cela, Camilo Jose

Verga, Giovanni (Carmelo)
1840-1922 .... **SSC 21, 87; TCLC 3**
See also CA 104; 123; CANR 101; EW 7;
EWL 3; RGSF 2; RGWL 2, 3; WLIT 7

Vergil 70B.C.-19B.C. ... **CMLC 9, 40; PC 12;
WLCS**
See Virgil
See also AW 2; DA; DA3; DAB; DAC;
DAM MST, POET; EFS 1; LMFS 1

Vergil, Polydore c. 1470-1555 .... **LC 108**
See also DLB 132

Verhaeren, Emile (Adolphe Gustave)
1855-1916 .... **TCLC 12**
See also CA 109; EWL 3; GFL 1789 to the
Present

Verlaine, Paul (Marie) 1844-1896 .. **NCLC 2,
51; PC 2, 32**
See also DAM POET; DLB 217; EW 7;
GFL 1789 to the Present; LMFS 2; RGWL
2, 3; TWA

Verne, Jules (Gabriel) 1828-1905 ... **TCLC 6,
52**
See also AAYA 16; BYA 4; CA 110; 131;
CLR 88; DA3; DLB 123; GFL 1789 to
the Present; JRDA; LAIT 2; LMFS 2;
MAICYA 1, 2; MTFW 2005; RGWL 2, 3;
SATA 21; SCFW 1, 2; SFW 4; TWA;
WCH

Verus, Marcus Annius
See Aurelius, Marcus

Very, Jones 1813-1880 .... **NCLC 9**
See also DLB 1, 243; RGAL 4

Vesaas, Tarjei 1897-1970 .... **CLC 48**
See also CA 190; 29-32R; DLB 297; EW
11; EWL 3; RGWL 3

Vialis, Gaston
See Simenon, Georges (Jacques Christian)

Vian, Boris 1920-1959(?) .... **TCLC 9**
See also CA 106; 164; CANR 111; DLB
72, 321; EWL 3; GFL 1789 to the Present;
MTCW 2; RGWL 2, 3

Wakefield, Herbert Russell
1888-1965 .... **TCLC 120**
See also CA 5-8R; CANR 77; HGG; SUFW

Wakoski, Diane 1937- ...... **CLC 2, 4, 7, 9, 11, 40; PC 15**
See also CA 13-16R, 216; CAAE 216; CAAS 1; CANR 9, 60, 106; CP 1, 2, 3, 4, 5, 6, 7; CWP; DAM POET; DLB 5; INT CANR-9; MAL 5; MTCW 2; MTFW 2005

Wakoski-Sherbell, Diane
See Wakoski, Diane

Walcott, Derek (Alton) 1930- ... **BLC 3; CLC 2, 4, 9, 14, 25, 42, 67, 76, 160; DC 7; PC 46**
See also BW 2; CA 89-92; CANR 26, 47, 75, 80, 130; CBD; CD 5, 6; CDWLB 3; CP 1, 2, 3, 4, 5, 6, 7; DA3; DAB; DAC; DAM MST, MULT, POET; DLB 117; DLBY 1981; DNFS 1; EFS 1; EWL 3; LMFS 2; MTCW 1, 2; MTFW 2005; PFS 6; RGEL 2; TWA; WWE 1

Waldman, Anne (Lesley) 1945- .... **CLC 7**
See also BG 1:3; CA 37-40R; CAAS 17; CANR 34, 69, 116; CP 1, 2, 3, 4, 5, 6, 7; CWP; DLB 16

Waldo, E. Hunter
See Sturgeon, Theodore (Hamilton)

Waldo, Edward Hamilton
See Sturgeon, Theodore (Hamilton)

Walker, Alice (Malsenior) 1944- .... **BLC 3; CLC 5, 6, 9, 19, 27, 46, 58, 103, 167; PC 30; SSC 5; WLCS**
See also AAYA 3, 33; AFAW 1, 2; AMWS 3; BEST 89:4; BPFB 3; BW 2, 3; CA 37-40R; CANR 9, 27, 49, 66, 82, 131; CDALB 1968-1988; CN 4, 5, 6, 7; CPW; CSW; DA; DA3; DAB; DAC; DAM MST, MULT, NOV, POET, POP; DLB 6, 33, 143; EWL 3; EXPN; EXPS; FL 1:6; FW; INT CANR-27; LAIT 3; MAL 5; MAWW; MTCW 1, 2; MTFW 2005; NFS 5; RGAL 4; RGSF 2; SATA 31; SSFS 2, 11; TUS; YAW

Walker, David Harry 1911-1992 ...... **CLC 14**
See also CA 1-4R; 137; CANR 1; CN 1, 2; CWRI 5; SATA 8; SATA-Obit 71

Walker, Edward Joseph 1934-2004
See Walker, Ted
See also CA 21-24R; 226; CANR 12, 28, 53

Walker, George F(rederick) 1947- .. **CLC 44, 61**
See also CA 103; CANR 21, 43, 59; CD 5, 6; DAB; DAC; DAM MST; DLB 60

Walker, Joseph A. 1935-2003 .... **CLC 19**
See also BW 1, 3; CA 89-92; CAD; CANR 26, 143; CD 5, 6; DAM DRAM, MST; DFS 12; DLB 38

Walker, Margaret (Abigail)
1915-1998 .... **BLC; CLC 1, 6; PC 20; TCLC 129**
See also AFAW 1, 2; BW 2, 3; CA 73-76; 172; CANR 26, 54, 76, 136; CN 1, 2, 3, 4, 5, 6; CP 1, 2, 3, 4; CSW; DAM MULT; DLB 76, 152; EXPP; FW; MAL 5; MTCW 1, 2; MTFW 2005; RGAL 4; RHW

Walker, Ted .... **CLC 13**
See Walker, Edward Joseph
See also CP 1, 2, 3, 4, 5, 6, 7; DLB 40

Wallace, David Foster 1962- ... **CLC 50, 114; SSC 68**
See also AAYA 50; AMWS 10; CA 132; CANR 59, 133; CN 7; DA3; MTCW 2; MTFW 2005

Wallace, Dexter
See Masters, Edgar Lee

Wallace, (Richard Horatio) Edgar
1875-1932 .... **TCLC 57**
See also CA 115; 218; CMW 4; DLB 70; MSW; RGEL 2

Wallace, Irving 1916-1990 .... **CLC 7, 13**
See also AITN 1; BPFB 3; CA 1-4R; 132; CAAS 1; CANR 1, 27; CPW; DAM NOV, POP; INT CANR-27; MTCW 1, 2

Wallant, Edward Lewis 1926-1962 ... **CLC 5, 10**
See also CA 1-4R; CANR 22; DLB 2, 28, 143, 299; EWL 3; MAL 5; MTCW 1, 2; RGAL 4

Wallas, Graham 1858-1932 .... **TCLC 91**

Waller, Edmund 1606-1687 .... **LC 86**
See also BRW 2; DAM POET; DLB 126; PAB; RGEL 2

Walley, Byron
See Card, Orson Scott

Walpole, Horace 1717-1797 .... **LC 2, 49**
See also BRW 3; DLB 39, 104, 213; GL 3; HGG; LMFS 1; RGEL 2; SUFW 1; TEA

Walpole, Hugh (Seymour)
1884-1941 .... **TCLC 5**
See also CA 104; 165; DLB 34; HGG; MTCW 2; RGEL 2; RHW

Walrond, Eric (Derwent) 1898-1966 . **HR 1:3**
See also BW 1; CA 125; DLB 51

Walser, Martin 1927- .... **CLC 27, 183**
See also CA 57-60; CANR 8, 46, 145; CWW 2; DLB 75, 124; EWL 3

Walser, Robert 1878-1956 ..... **SSC 20; TCLC 18**
See also CA 118; 165; CANR 100; DLB 66; EWL 3

Walsh, Gillian Paton
See Paton Walsh, Gillian

Walsh, Jill Paton .... **CLC 35**
See Paton Walsh, Gillian
See also CLR 2, 65; WYA

Walter, Villiam Christian
See Andersen, Hans Christian

Walters, Anna L(ee) 1946- .... **NNAL**
See also CA 73-76

Walther von der Vogelweide c.
1170-1228 .... **CMLC 56**

Walton, Izaak 1593-1683 .... **LC 72**
See also BRW 2; CDBLB Before 1660; DLB 151, 213; RGEL 2

Wambaugh, Joseph (Aloysius), Jr.
1937- .... **CLC 3, 18**
See also AITN 1; BEST 89:3; BPFB 3; CA 33-36R; CANR 42, 65, 115; CMW 4; CPW 1; DA3; DAM NOV, POP; DLB 6; DLBY 1983; MSW; MTCW 1, 2

Wang Wei 699(?)-761(?) .... **PC 18**
See also TWA

Warburton, William 1698-1779 .... **LC 97**
See also DLB 104

Ward, Arthur Henry Sarsfield 1883-1959
See Rohmer, Sax
See also CA 108; 173; CMW 4; HGG

Ward, Douglas Turner 1930- .... **CLC 19**
See also BW 1; CA 81-84; CAD; CANR 27; CD 5, 6; DLB 7, 38

Ward, E. D.
See Lucas, E(dward) V(errall)

Ward, Mrs. Humphry 1851-1920
See Ward, Mary Augusta
See also RGEL 2

Ward, Mary Augusta 1851-1920 ... **TCLC 55**
See Ward, Mrs. Humphry
See also DLB 18

Ward, Nathaniel 1578(?)-1652 .... **LC 114**
See also DLB 24

Ward, Peter
See Faust, Frederick (Schiller)

Warhol, Andy 1928(?)-1987 .... **CLC 20**
See also AAYA 12; BEST 89:4; CA 89-92; 121; CANR 34

Warner, Francis (Robert le Plastrier)
1937- .... **CLC 14**
See also CA 53-56; CANR 11; CP 1, 2, 3, 4

Warner, Marina 1946- .... **CLC 59**
See also CA 65-68; CANR 21, 55, 118; CN 5, 6, 7; DLB 194; MTFW 2005

Warner, Rex (Ernest) 1905-1986 ...... **CLC 45**
See also CA 89-92; 119; CN 1, 2, 3, 4; CP 1, 2, 3, 4; DLB 15; RGEL 2; RHW

Warner, Susan (Bogert)
1819-1885 .... **NCLC 31, 146**
See also DLB 3, 42, 239, 250, 254

Warner, Sylvia (Constance) Ashton
See Ashton-Warner, Sylvia (Constance)

Warner, Sylvia Townsend
1893-1978 .. **CLC 7, 19; SSC 23; TCLC 131**
See also BRWS 7; CA 61-64; 77-80; CANR 16, 60, 104; CN 1, 2; DLB 34, 139; EWL 3; FANT; FW; MTCW 1, 2; RGEL 2; RGSF 2; RHW

Warren, Mercy Otis 1728-1814 ..... **NCLC 13**
See also DLB 31, 200; RGAL 4; TUS

Warren, Robert Penn 1905-1989 .. **CLC 1, 4, 6, 8, 10, 13, 18, 39, 53, 59; PC 37; SSC 4, 58; WLC**
See also AITN 1; AMW; AMWC 2; BPFB 3; BYA 1; CA 13-16R; 129; CANR 10, 47; CDALB 1968-1988; CN 1, 2, 3, 4; CP 1, 2, 3, 4; DA; DA3; DAB; DAC; DAM MST, NOV, POET; DLB 2, 48, 152, 320; DLBY 1980, 1989; EWL 3; INT CANR-10; MAL 5; MTCW 1, 2; MTFW 2005; NFS 13; RGAL 4; RGSF 2; RHW; SATA 46; SATA-Obit 63; SSFS 8; TUS

Warrigal, Jack
See Furphy, Joseph

Warshofsky, Isaac
See Singer, Isaac Bashevis

Warton, Joseph 1722-1800 .... **NCLC 118**
See also DLB 104, 109; RGEL 2

Warton, Thomas 1728-1790 .... **LC 15, 82**
See also DAM POET; DLB 104, 109; RGEL 2

Waruk, Kona
See Harris, (Theodore) Wilson

Warung, Price .... **TCLC 45**
See Astley, William
See also DLB 230; RGEL 2

Warwick, Jarvis
See Garner, Hugh
See also CCA 1

Washington, Alex
See Harris, Mark

Washington, Booker T(aliaferro)
1856-1915 .... **BLC 3; TCLC 10**
See also BW 1; CA 114; 125; DA3; DAM MULT; LAIT 2; RGAL 4; SATA 28

Washington, George 1732-1799 .... **LC 25**
See also DLB 31

Wassermann, (Karl) Jakob
1873-1934 .... **TCLC 6**
See also CA 104; 163; DLB 66; EWL 3

Wasserstein, Wendy 1950-2006 . **CLC 32, 59, 90, 183; DC 4**
See also AMWS 15; CA 121; 129; CABS 3; CAD; CANR 53, 75, 128; CD 5, 6; CWD; DA3; DAM DRAM; DFS 5, 17; DLB 228; EWL 3; FW; INT CA-129; MAL 5; MTCW 2; MTFW 2005; SATA 94

Waterhouse, Keith (Spencer) 1929- . **CLC 47**
See also CA 5-8R; CANR 38, 67, 109; CBD; CD 6; CN 1, 2, 3, 4, 5, 6, 7; DLB 13, 15; MTCW 1, 2; MTFW 2005

Waters, Frank (Joseph) 1902-1995 .. **CLC 88**
See also CA 5-8R; 149; CAAS 13; CANR 3, 18, 63, 121; DLB 212; DLBY 1986; RGAL 4; TCWW 1, 2

Waters, Mary C. .... **CLC 70**

Waters, Roger 1944- .... **CLC 35**

Watkins, Frances Ellen
See Harper, Frances Ellen Watkins

Watkins, Gerrold
See Malzberg, Barry N(athaniel)

Watkins, Gloria Jean 1952(?)- .... **CLC 94**
See also BW 2; CA 143; CANR 87, 126; DLB 246; MTCW 2; MTFW 2005; SATA 115

Watkins, Paul 1964- .... **CLC 55**
See also CA 132; CANR 62, 98

Watkins, Vernon Phillips
1906-1967 .... **CLC 43**
See also CA 9-10; 25-28R; CAP 1; DLB 20; EWL 3; RGEL 2

Watson, Irving S.
See Mencken, H(enry) L(ouis)

Watson, John H.
See Farmer, Philip Jose

Watson, Richard F.
See Silverberg, Robert

Watts, Ephraim
See Horne, Richard Henry Hengist

Watts, Isaac 1674-1748 .... **LC 98**
See also DLB 95; RGEL 2; SATA 52

Waugh, Auberon (Alexander)
1939-2001 .... **CLC 7**
See also CA 45-48; 192; CANR 6, 22, 92; CN 1, 2, 3; DLB 14, 194

Waugh, Evelyn (Arthur St. John)
1903-1966 .. **CLC 1, 3, 8, 13, 19, 27, 44, 107; SSC 41; WLC**
See also BPFB 3; BRW 7; CA 85-88; 25-28R; CANR 22; CDBLB 1914-1945; DA; DA3; DAB; DAC; DAM MST, NOV, POP; DLB 15, 162, 195; EWL 3; MTCW 1, 2; MTFW 2005; NFS 13, 17; RGEL 2; RGSF 2; TEA; WLIT 4

Waugh, Harriet 1944- .... **CLC 6**
See also CA 85-88; CANR 22

Ways, C. R.
See Blount, Roy (Alton), Jr.

Waystaff, Simon
See Swift, Jonathan

Webb, Beatrice (Martha Potter)
1858-1943 .... **TCLC 22**
See also CA 117; 162; DLB 190; FW

Webb, Charles (Richard) 1939- .... **CLC 7**
See also CA 25-28R; CANR 114

Webb, Frank J. .... **NCLC 143**
See also DLB 50

Webb, James H(enry), Jr. 1946- ...... **CLC 22**
See also CA 81-84

Webb, Mary Gladys (Meredith)
1881-1927 .... **TCLC 24**
See also CA 182; 123; DLB 34; FW

Webb, Mrs. Sidney
See Webb, Beatrice (Martha Potter)

Webb, Phyllis 1927- .... **CLC 18**
See also CA 104; CANR 23; CCA 1; CP 1, 2, 3, 4, 5, 6, 7; CWP; DLB 53

Webb, Sidney (James) 1859-1947 .. **TCLC 22**
See also CA 117; 163; DLB 190

Webber, Andrew Lloyd .... **CLC 21**
See Lloyd Webber, Andrew
See also DFS 7

Weber, Lenora Mattingly
1895-1971 .... **CLC 12**
See also CA 19-20; 29-32R; CAP 1; SATA 2; SATA-Obit 26

Weber, Max 1864-1920 .... **TCLC 69**
See also CA 109; 189; DLB 296

Webster, John 1580(?)-1634(?) ...... **DC 2; LC 33, 84; WLC**
See also BRW 2; CDBLB Before 1660; DA; DAB; DAC; DAM DRAM, MST; DFS 17, 19; DLB 58; IDTP; RGEL 2; WLIT 3

Webster, Noah 1758-1843 .... **NCLC 30**
See also DLB 1, 37, 42, 43, 73, 243

Wedekind, (Benjamin) Frank(lin)
1864-1918 .... **TCLC 7**
See also CA 104; 153; CANR 121, 122; CDWLB 2; DAM DRAM; DLB 118; EW 8; EWL 3; LMFS 2; RGWL 2, 3

Wehr, Demaris .... **CLC 65**

Weidman, Jerome 1913-1998 .... **CLC 7**
See also AITN 2; CA 1-4R; 171; CAD; CANR 1; CD 1, 2, 3, 4, 5; DLB 28

Weil, Simone (Adolphine)
1909-1943 .... **TCLC 23**
See also CA 117; 159; EW 12; EWL 3; FW; GFL 1789 to the Present; MTCW 2

Weininger, Otto 1880-1903 .... **TCLC 84**

Weinstein, Nathan
See West, Nathanael

Weinstein, Nathan von Wallenstein
See West, Nathanael

Weir, Peter (Lindsay) 1944- .... **CLC 20**
See also CA 113; 123

Weiss, Peter (Ulrich) 1916-1982 .. **CLC 3, 15, 51; TCLC 152**
See also CA 45-48; 106; CANR 3; DAM DRAM; DFS 3; DLB 69, 124; EWL 3; RGWL 2, 3

Weiss, Theodore (Russell)
1916-2003 .... **CLC 3, 8, 14**
See also CA 9-12R; 189; 216; CAAE 189; CAAS 2; CANR 46, 94; CP 1, 2, 3, 4, 5, 6, 7; DLB 5; TCLE 1:2

Welch, (Maurice) Denton
1915-1948 .... **TCLC 22**
See also BRWS 8, 9; CA 121; 148; RGEL 2

Welch, James (Phillip) 1940-2003 ..... **CLC 6, 14, 52; NNAL; PC 62**
See also CA 85-88; 219; CANR 42, 66, 107; CN 5, 6, 7; CP 2, 3, 4, 5, 6, 7; CPW; DAM MULT, POP; DLB 175, 256; LATS 1:1; RGAL 4; TCWW 1, 2

Weldon, Fay 1931- . **CLC 6, 9, 11, 19, 36, 59, 122**
See also BRWS 4; CA 21-24R; CANR 16, 46, 63, 97, 137; CDBLB 1960 to Present; CN 3, 4, 5, 6, 7; CPW; DAM POP; DLB 14, 194, 319; EWL 3; FW; HGG; INT CANR-16; MTCW 1, 2; MTFW 2005; RGEL 2; RGSF 2

Wellek, Rene 1903-1995 .... **CLC 28**
See also CA 5-8R; 150; CAAS 7; CANR 8; DLB 63; EWL 3; INT CANR-8

Weller, Michael 1942- .... **CLC 10, 53**
See also CA 85-88; CAD; CD 5, 6

Weller, Paul 1958- .... **CLC 26**

Wellershoff, Dieter 1925- .... **CLC 46**
See also CA 89-92; CANR 16, 37

Welles, (George) Orson 1915-1985 .. **CLC 20, 80**
See also AAYA 40; CA 93-96; 117

Wellman, John McDowell 1945-
See Wellman, Mac
See also CA 166; CD 5

Wellman, Mac .... **CLC 65**
See Wellman, John McDowell; Wellman, John McDowell
See also CAD; CD 6; RGAL 4

Wellman, Manly Wade 1903-1986 ... **CLC 49**
See also CA 1-4R; 118; CANR 6, 16, 44; FANT; SATA 6; SATA-Obit 47; SFW 4; SUFW

Wells, Carolyn 1869(?)-1942 .... **TCLC 35**
See also CA 113; 185; CMW 4; DLB 11

Wells, H(erbert) G(eorge) 1866-1946 . **SSC 6, 70; TCLC 6, 12, 19, 133; WLC**
See also AAYA 18; BPFB 3; BRW 6; CA 110; 121; CDBLB 1914-1945; CLR 64; DA; DA3; DAB; DAC; DAM MST, NOV; DLB 34, 70, 156, 178; EWL 3; EXPS; HGG; LAIT 3; LMFS 2; MTCW 1, 2; MTFW 2005; NFS 17, 20; RGEL 2; RGSF 2; SATA 20; SCFW 1, 2; SFW 4; SSFS 3; SUFW; TEA; WCH; WLIT 4; YAW

Wells, Rosemary 1943- .... **CLC 12**
See also AAYA 13; BYA 7, 8; CA 85-88; CANR 48, 120; CLR 16, 69; CWRI 5; MAICYA 1, 2; SAAS 1; SATA 18, 69, 114, 156; YAW

Wells-Barnett, Ida B(ell)
1862-1931 .... **TCLC 125**
See also CA 182; DLB 23, 221

Welsh, Irvine 1958- .... **CLC 144**
See also CA 173; CANR 146; CN 7; DLB 271

Welty, Eudora (Alice) 1909-2001 .. **CLC 1, 2, 5, 14, 22, 33, 105; SSC 1, 27, 51; WLC**
See also AAYA 48; AMW; AMWR 1; BPFB 3; CA 9-12R; 199; CABS 1; CANR 32, 65, 128; CDALB 1941-1968; CN 1, 2, 3, 4, 5, 6, 7; CSW; DA; DA3; DAB; DAC; DAM MST, NOV; DLB 2, 102, 143; DLBD 12; DLBY 1987, 2001; EWL 3; EXPS; HGG; LAIT 3; MAL 5; MAWW; MTCW 1, 2; MTFW 2005; NFS 13, 15; RGAL 4; RGSF 2; RHW; SSFS 2, 10; TUS

Wen I-to 1899-1946 .... **TCLC 28**
See also EWL 3

Wentworth, Robert
See Hamilton, Edmond

Werfel, Franz (Viktor) 1890-1945 ... **TCLC 8**
See also CA 104; 161; DLB 81, 124; EWL 3; RGWL 2, 3

Wergeland, Henrik Arnold
1808-1845 .... **NCLC 5**

Wersba, Barbara 1932- .... **CLC 30**
See also AAYA 2, 30; BYA 6, 12, 13; CA 29-32R, 182; CAAE 182; CANR 16, 38; CLR 3, 78; DLB 52; JRDA; MAICYA 1, 2; SAAS 2; SATA 1, 58; SATA-Essay 103; WYA; YAW

Wertmueller, Lina 1928- .... **CLC 16**
See also CA 97-100; CANR 39, 78

Wescott, Glenway 1901-1987 .. **CLC 13; SSC 35**
See also CA 13-16R; 121; CANR 23, 70; CN 1, 2, 3, 4; DLB 4, 9, 102; MAL 5; RGAL 4

Wesker, Arnold 1932- .... **CLC 3, 5, 42**
See also CA 1-4R; CAAS 7; CANR 1, 33; CBD; CD 5, 6; CDBLB 1960 to Present; DAB; DAM DRAM; DLB 13, 310, 319; EWL 3; MTCW 1; RGEL 2; TEA

Wesley, John 1703-1791 .... **LC 88**
See also DLB 104

Wesley, Richard (Errol) 1945- .... **CLC 7**
See also BW 1; CA 57-60; CAD; CANR 27; CD 5, 6; DLB 38

Wessel, Johan Herman 1742-1785 .... **LC 7**
See also DLB 300

West, Anthony (Panther)
1914-1987 .... **CLC 50**
See also CA 45-48; 124; CANR 3, 19; CN 1, 2, 3, 4; DLB 15

West, C. P.
See Wodehouse, P(elham) G(renville)

West, Cornel (Ronald) 1953- .... **BLCS; CLC 134**
See also CA 144; CANR 91; DLB 246

West, Delno C(loyde), Jr. 1936- .... **CLC 70**
See also CA 57-60

West, Dorothy 1907-1998 ...... **HR 1:3; TCLC 108**
See also BW 2; CA 143; 169; DLB 76

West, (Mary) Jessamyn 1902-1984 ... **CLC 7, 17**
See also CA 9-12R; 112; CANR 27; CN 1, 2, 3; DLB 6; DLBY 1984; MTCW 1, 2; RGAL 4; RHW; SATA-Obit 37; TCWW 2; TUS; YAW

West, Morris L(anglo) 1916-1999 ..... **CLC 6, 33**
See also BPFB 3; CA 5-8R; 187; CANR 24, 49, 64; CN 1, 2, 3, 4, 5, 6; CPW; DLB 289; MTCW 1, 2; MTFW 2005

West, Nathanael 1903-1940 .. **SSC 16; TCLC 1, 14, 44**
See also AMW; AMWR 2; BPFB 3; CA 104; 125; CDALB 1929-1941; DA3; DLB 4, 9, 28; EWL 3; MAL 5; MTCW 1, 2; MTFW 2005; NFS 16; RGAL 4; TUS

West, Owen
See Koontz, Dean R.

West, Paul 1930- .... **CLC 7, 14, 96**
See also CA 13-16R; CAAS 7; CANR 22, 53, 76, 89, 136; CN 1, 2, 3, 4, 5, 6, 7; DLB 14; INT CANR-22; MTCW 2; MTFW 2005

West, Rebecca 1892-1983 ... **CLC 7, 9, 31, 50**
See also BPFB 3; BRWS 3; CA 5-8R; 109; CANR 19; CN 1, 2, 3; DLB 36; DLBY 1983; EWL 3; FW; MTCW 1, 2; MTFW 2005; NCFS 4; RGEL 2; TEA

Westall, Robert (Atkinson) 1929-1993 .... **CLC 17**
See also AAYA 12; BYA 2, 6, 7, 8, 9, 15; CA 69-72; 141; CANR 18, 68; CLR 13; FANT; JRDA; MAICYA 1, 2; MAICYAS 1; SAAS 2; SATA 23, 69; SATA-Obit 75; WYA; YAW

Westermarck, Edward 1862-1939 . **TCLC 87**

Westlake, Donald E(dwin) 1933- . **CLC 7, 33**
See also BPFB 3; CA 17-20R; CAAS 13; CANR 16, 44, 65, 94, 137; CMW 4; CPW; DAM POP; INT CANR-16; MSW; MTCW 2; MTFW 2005

Westmacott, Mary
See Christie, Agatha (Mary Clarissa)

Weston, Allen
See Norton, Andre

Wetcheek, J. L.
See Feuchtwanger, Lion

Wetering, Janwillem van de
See van de Wetering, Janwillem

Wetherald, Agnes Ethelwyn 1857-1940 .... **TCLC 81**
See also CA 202; DLB 99

Wetherell, Elizabeth
See Warner, Susan (Bogert)

Whale, James 1889-1957 .... **TCLC 63**

Whalen, Philip (Glenn) 1923-2002 .... **CLC 6, 29**
See also BG 1:3; CA 9-12R; 209; CANR 5, 39; CP 1, 2, 3, 4, 5, 6, 7; DLB 16; WP

Wharton, Edith (Newbold Jones) 1862-1937 ... **SSC 6, 84; TCLC 3, 9, 27, 53, 129, 149; WLC**
See also AAYA 25; AMW; AMWC 2; AMWR 1; BPFB 3; CA 104; 132; CDALB 1865-1917; DA; DA3; DAB; DAC; DAM MST, NOV; DLB 4, 9, 12, 78, 189; DLBD 13; EWL 3; EXPS; FL 1:6; GL 3; HGG; LAIT 2, 3; LATS 1:1; MAL 5; MAWW; MTCW 1, 2; MTFW 2005; NFS 5, 11, 15, 20; RGAL 4; RGSF 2; RHW; SSFS 6, 7; SUFW; TUS

Wharton, James
See Mencken, H(enry) L(ouis)

Wharton, William (a pseudonym) 1925- .... **CLC 18, 37**
See also CA 93-96; CN 4, 5, 6, 7; DLBY 1980; INT CA-93-96

Wheatley (Peters), Phillis 1753(?)-1784 ... **BLC 3; LC 3, 50; PC 3; WLC**
See also AFAW 1, 2; CDALB 1640-1865; DA; DA3; DAC; DAM MST, MULT, POET; DLB 31, 50; EXPP; FL 1:1; PFS 13; RGAL 4

Wheelock, John Hall 1886-1978 .... **CLC 14**
See also CA 13-16R; 77-80; CANR 14; CP 1, 2; DLB 45; MAL 5

Whim-Wham
See Curnow, (Thomas) Allen (Monro)

White, Babington
See Braddon, Mary Elizabeth

White, E(lwyn) B(rooks) 1899-1985 .... **CLC 10, 34, 39**
See also AAYA 62; AITN 2; AMWS 1; CA 13-16R; 116; CANR 16, 37; CDALBS; CLR 1, 21; CPW; DA3; DAM POP; DLB 11, 22; EWL 3; FANT; MAICYA 1, 2; MAL 5; MTCW 1, 2; MTFW 2005; NCFS 5; RGAL 4; SATA 2, 29, 100; SATA-Obit 44; TUS

White, Edmund (Valentine III) 1940- .... **CLC 27, 110**
See also AAYA 7; CA 45-48; CANR 3, 19, 36, 62, 107, 133; CN 5, 6, 7; DA3; DAM POP; DLB 227; MTCW 1, 2; MTFW 2005

White, Hayden V. 1928- .... **CLC 148**
See also CA 128; CANR 135; DLB 246

White, Patrick (Victor Martindale) 1912-1990 ...... **CLC 3, 4, 5, 7, 9, 18, 65, 69; SSC 39, TCLC 176**
See also BRWS 1; CA 81-84; 132; CANR 43; CN 1, 2, 3, 4; DLB 260; EWL 3; MTCW 1; RGEL 2; RGSF 2; RHW; TWA; WWE 1

White, Phyllis Dorothy James 1920-
See James, P. D.
See also CA 21-24R; CANR 17, 43, 65, 112; CMW 4; CN 7; CPW; DA3; DAM POP; MTCW 1, 2; MTFW 2005; TEA

White, T(erence) H(anbury) 1906-1964 .... **CLC 30**
See also AAYA 22; BPFB 3; BYA 4, 5; CA 73-76; CANR 37; DLB 160; FANT; JRDA; LAIT 1; MAICYA 1, 2; RGEL 2; SATA 12; SUFW 1; YAW

White, Terence de Vere 1912-1994 ... **CLC 49**
See also CA 49-52; 145; CANR 3

White, Walter
See White, Walter F(rancis)

White, Walter F(rancis) 1893-1955 ... **BLC 3; HR 1:3; TCLC 15**
See also BW 1; CA 115; 124; DAM MULT; DLB 51

White, William Hale 1831-1913
See Rutherford, Mark
See also CA 121; 189

Whitehead, Alfred North 1861-1947 .... **TCLC 97**
See also CA 117; 165; DLB 100, 262

Whitehead, E(dward) A(nthony) 1933- .... **CLC 5**
See Whitehead, Ted
See also CA 65-68; CANR 58, 118; CBD; CD 5; DLB 310

Whitehead, Ted
See Whitehead, E(dward) A(nthony)
See also CD 6

Whiteman, Roberta J. Hill 1947- ...... **NNAL**
See also CA 146

Whitemore, Hugh (John) 1936- .... **CLC 37**
See also CA 132; CANR 77; CBD; CD 5, 6; INT CA-132

Whitman, Sarah Helen (Power) 1803-1878 .... **NCLC 19**
See also DLB 1, 243

Whitman, Walt(er) 1819-1892 .. **NCLC 4, 31, 81; PC 3; WLC**
See also AAYA 42; AMW; AMWR 1; CDALB 1640-1865; DA; DA3; DAB; DAC; DAM MST, POET; DLB 3, 64, 224, 250; EXPP; LAIT 2; LMFS 1; PAB; PFS 2, 3, 13, 22; RGAL 4; SATA 20; TUS; WP; WYAS 1

Whitney, Phyllis A(yame) 1903- .... **CLC 42**
See also AAYA 36; AITN 2; BEST 90:3; CA 1-4R; CANR 3, 25, 38, 60; CLR 59; CMW 4; CPW; DA3; DAM POP; JRDA; MAICYA 1, 2; MTCW 2; RHW; SATA 1, 30; YAW

Whittemore, (Edward) Reed, Jr. 1919- .... **CLC 4**
See also CA 9-12R; 219; CAAE 219; CAAS 8; CANR 4, 119; CP 1, 2, 3, 4, 5, 6, 7; DLB 5; MAL 5

Whittier, John Greenleaf 1807-1892 .... **NCLC 8, 59**
See also AMWS 1; DLB 1, 243; RGAL 4

Whittlebot, Hernia
See Coward, Noel (Peirce)

Wicker, Thomas Grey 1926-
See Wicker, Tom
See also CA 65-68; CANR 21, 46, 141

Wicker, Tom .... **CLC 7**
See Wicker, Thomas Grey

Wideman, John Edgar 1941- ... **BLC 3; CLC 5, 34, 36, 67, 122; SSC 62**
See also AFAW 1, 2; AMWS 10; BPFB 4; BW 2, 3; CA 85-88; CANR 14, 42, 67, 109, 140; CN 4, 5, 6, 7; DAM MULT; DLB 33, 143; MAL 5; MTCW 2; MTFW 2005; RGAL 4; RGSF 2; SSFS 6, 12; TCLE 1:2

Wiebe, Rudy (Henry) 1934- .. **CLC 6, 11, 14, 138**
See also CA 37-40R; CANR 42, 67, 123; CN 1, 2, 3, 4, 5, 6, 7; DAC; DAM MST; DLB 60; RHW; SATA 156

Wieland, Christoph Martin 1733-1813 .... **NCLC 17**
See also DLB 97; EW 4; LMFS 1; RGWL 2, 3

Wiene, Robert 1881-1938 .... **TCLC 56**

Wieners, John 1934- .... **CLC 7**
See also BG 1:3; CA 13-16R; CP 1, 2, 3, 4, 5, 6, 7; DLB 16; WP

Wiesel, Elie(zer) 1928- .... **CLC 3, 5, 11, 37, 165; WLCS**
See also AAYA 7, 54; AITN 1; CA 5-8R; CAAS 4; CANR 8, 40, 65, 125; CDALBS; CWW 2; DA; DA3; DAB; DAC; DAM MST, NOV; DLB 83, 299; DLBY 1987; EWL 3; INT CANR-8; LAIT 4; MTCW 1, 2; MTFW 2005; NCFS 4; NFS 4; RGWL 3; SATA 56; YAW

Wiggins, Marianne 1947- .... **CLC 57**
See also BEST 89:3; CA 130; CANR 60, 139; CN 7

Wigglesworth, Michael 1631-1705 .... **LC 106**
See also DLB 24; RGAL 4

Wiggs, Susan .... **CLC 70**
See also CA 201

Wight, James Alfred 1916-1995
See Herriot, James
See also CA 77-80; SATA 55; SATA-Brief 44

Wilbur, Richard (Purdy) 1921- ..... **CLC 3, 6, 9, 14, 53, 110; PC 51**
See also AMWS 3; CA 1-4R; CABS 2; CANR 2, 29, 76, 93, 139; CDALBS; CP 1, 2, 3, 4, 5, 6, 7; DA; DAB; DAC; DAM MST, POET; DLB 5, 169; EWL 3; EXPP;

DAC; DAM MST, MULT, NOV; DLB 76, 102; DLBD 2; EWL 3; EXPN; LAIT 3, 4; MAL 5; MTCW 1, 2; MTFW 2005; NCFS 1; NFS 1, 7; RGAL 4; RGSF 2; SSFS 3, 9, 15, 20; TUS; YAW

Wright, Richard B(ruce) 1937- .... **CLC 6**
See also CA 85-88; CANR 120; DLB 53

Wright, Rick 1945- .... **CLC 35**

Wright, Rowland
See Wells, Carolyn

Wright, Stephen 1946- .... **CLC 33**
See also CA 237

Wright, Willard Huntington 1888-1939
See Van Dine, S. S.
See also CA 115; 189; CMW 4; DLBD 16

Wright, William 1930- .... **CLC 44**
See also CA 53-56; CANR 7, 23

Wroth, Lady Mary 1587-1653(?) .... **LC 30; PC 38**
See also DLB 121

Wu Ch'eng-en 1500(?)-1582(?) .... **LC 7**

Wu Ching-tzu 1701-1754 .... **LC 2**

Wulfstan c. 10th cent. -1023 .... **CMLC 59**

Wurlitzer, Rudolph 1938(?)- ... **CLC 2, 4, 15**
See also CA 85-88; CN 4, 5, 6, 7; DLB 173

Wyatt, Sir Thomas c. 1503-1542 . **LC 70; PC 27**
See also BRW 1; DLB 132; EXPP; RGEL 2; TEA

Wycherley, William 1640-1716 .... **LC 8, 21, 102**
See also BRW 2; CDBLB 1660-1789; DAM DRAM; DLB 80; RGEL 2

Wyclif, John c. 1330-1384 .... **CMLC 70**
See also DLB 146

Wylie, Elinor (Morton Hoyt) 1885-1928 .... **PC 23; TCLC 8**
See also AMWS 1; CA 105; 162; DLB 9, 45; EXPP; MAL 5; RGAL 4

Wylie, Philip (Gordon) 1902-1971 ... **CLC 43**
See also CA 21-22; 33-36R; CAP 2; CN 1; DLB 9; SFW 4

Wyndham, John .... **CLC 19**
See Harris, John (Wyndham Parkes Lucas) Beynon
See also DLB 255; SCFW 1, 2

Wyss, Johann David Von 1743-1818 .... **NCLC 10**
See also CLR 92; JRDA; MAICYA 1, 2; SATA 29; SATA-Brief 27

Xenophon c. 430B.C.-c. 354B.C. ... **CMLC 17**
See also AW 1; DLB 176; RGWL 2, 3

Xingjian, Gao 1940-
See Gao Xingjian
See also CA 193; DFS 21; RGWL 3

Yakamochi 718-785 .... **CMLC 45; PC 48**

Yakumo Koizumi
See Hearn, (Patricio) Lafcadio (Tessima Carlos)

Yamada, Mitsuye (May) 1923- .... **PC 44**
See also CA 77-80

Yamamoto, Hisaye 1921- .... **AAL; SSC 34**
See also CA 214; DAM MULT; DLB 312; LAIT 4; SSFS 14

Yamauchi, Wakako 1924- .... **AAL**
See also CA 214; DLB 312

Yanez, Jose Donoso
See Donoso (Yanez), Jose

Yanovsky, Basile S.
See Yanovsky, V(assily) S(emenovich)

Yanovsky, V(assily) S(emenovich) 1906-1989 .... **CLC 2, 18**
See also CA 97-100; 129

Yates, Richard 1926-1992 .... **CLC 7, 8, 23**
See also AMWS 11; CA 5-8R; 139; CANR 10, 43; CN 1, 2, 3, 4, 5; DLB 2, 234; DLBY 1981, 1992; INT CANR-10

Yau, John 1950- .... **PC 61**
See also CA 154; CANR 89; CP 4, 5, 6, 7; DLB 234, 312

Yeats, W. B.
See Yeats, William Butler

Yeats, William Butler 1865-1939 . **PC 20, 51; TCLC 1, 11, 18, 31, 93, 116; WLC**
See also AAYA 48; BRW 6; BRWR 1; CA 104; 127; CANR 45; CDBLB 1890-1914; DA; DA3; DAB; DAC; DAM DRAM, MST, POET; DLB 10, 19, 98, 156; EWL 3; EXPP; MTCW 1, 2; MTFW 2005; NCFS 3; PAB; PFS 1, 2, 5, 7, 13, 15; RGEL 2; TEA; WLIT 4; WP

Yehoshua, A(braham) B. 1936- .. **CLC 13, 31**
See also CA 33-36R; CANR 43, 90, 145; CWW 2; EWL 3; RGSF 2; RGWL 3; WLIT 6

Yellow Bird
See Ridge, John Rollin

Yep, Laurence Michael 1948- .... **CLC 35**
See also AAYA 5, 31; BYA 7; CA 49-52; CANR 1, 46, 92; CLR 3, 17, 54; DLB 52, 312; FANT; JRDA; MAICYA 1, 2; MAICYAS 1; SATA 7, 69, 123; WYA; YAW

Yerby, Frank G(arvin) 1916-1991 ..... **BLC 3; CLC 1, 7, 22**
See also BPFB 3; BW 1, 3; CA 9-12R; 136; CANR 16, 52; CN 1, 2, 3, 4, 5; DAM MULT; DLB 76; INT CANR-16; MTCW 1; RGAL 4; RHW

Yesenin, Sergei Alexandrovich
See Esenin, Sergei (Alexandrovich)

Yesenin, Sergey
See Esenin, Sergei (Alexandrovich)
See also EWL 3

Yevtushenko, Yevgeny (Alexandrovich) 1933- ...... **CLC 1, 3, 13, 26, 51, 126; PC 40**
See Evtushenko, Evgenii Aleksandrovich
See also CA 81-84; CANR 33, 54; DAM POET; EWL 3; MTCW 1

Yezierska, Anzia 1885(?)-1970 .... **CLC 46**
See also CA 126; 89-92; DLB 28, 221; FW; MTCW 1; RGAL 4; SSFS 15

Yglesias, Helen 1915- .... **CLC 7, 22**
See also CA 37-40R; CAAS 20; CANR 15, 65, 95; CN 4, 5, 6, 7; INT CANR-15; MTCW 1

Yokomitsu, Riichi 1898-1947 .... **TCLC 47**
See also CA 170; EWL 3

Yonge, Charlotte (Mary) 1823-1901 .... **TCLC 48**
See also CA 109; 163; DLB 18, 163; RGEL 2; SATA 17; WCH

York, Jeremy
See Creasey, John

York, Simon
See Heinlein, Robert A(nson)

Yorke, Henry Vincent 1905-1974 ..... **CLC 13**
See Green, Henry
See also CA 85-88; 49-52

Yosano Akiko 1878-1942 .... **PC 11; TCLC 59**
See also CA 161; EWL 3; RGWL 3

Yoshimoto, Banana .... **CLC 84**
See Yoshimoto, Mahoko
See also AAYA 50; NFS 7

Yoshimoto, Mahoko 1964-
See Yoshimoto, Banana
See also CA 144; CANR 98; SSFS 16

Young, Al(bert James) 1939- ... **BLC 3; CLC 19**
See also BW 2, 3; CA 29-32R; CANR 26, 65, 109; CN 2, 3, 4, 5, 6, 7; CP 1, 2, 3, 4, 5, 6, 7; DAM MULT; DLB 33

Young, Andrew (John) 1885-1971 ...... **CLC 5**
See also CA 5-8R; CANR 7, 29; CP 1; RGEL 2

Young, Collier
See Bloch, Robert (Albert)

Young, Edward 1683-1765 .... **LC 3, 40**
See also DLB 95; RGEL 2

Young, Marguerite (Vivian) 1909-1995 .... **CLC 82**
See also CA 13-16; 150; CAP 1; CN 1, 2, 3, 4, 5, 6

Young, Neil 1945- .... **CLC 17**
See also CA 110; CCA 1

Young Bear, Ray A. 1950- ... **CLC 94; NNAL**
See also CA 146; DAM MULT; DLB 175; MAL 5

Yourcenar, Marguerite 1903-1987 ... **CLC 19, 38, 50, 87**
See also BPFB 3; CA 69-72; CANR 23, 60, 93; DAM NOV; DLB 72; DLBY 1988; EW 12; EWL 3; GFL 1789 to the Present; GLL 1; MTCW 1, 2; MTFW 2005; RGWL 2, 3

Yuan, Chu 340(?)B.C.-278(?)B.C. . **CMLC 36**

Yurick, Sol 1925- .... **CLC 6**
See also CA 13-16R; CANR 25; CN 1, 2, 3, 4, 5, 6, 7; MAL 5

Zabolotsky, Nikolai Alekseevich 1903-1958 .... **TCLC 52**
See Zabolotsky, Nikolay Alekseevich
See also CA 116; 164

Zabolotsky, Nikolay Alekseevich
See Zabolotsky, Nikolai Alekseevich
See also EWL 3

Zagajewski, Adam 1945- .... **PC 27**
See also CA 186; DLB 232; EWL 3

Zalygin, Sergei -2000 .... **CLC 59**

Zalygin, Sergei (Pavlovich) 1913-2000 .... **CLC 59**
See also DLB 302

Zamiatin, Evgenii
See Zamyatin, Evgeny Ivanovich
See also RGSF 2; RGWL 2, 3

Zamiatin, Evgenii Ivanovich
See Zamyatin, Evgeny Ivanovich
See also DLB 272

Zamiatin, Yevgenii
See Zamyatin, Evgeny Ivanovich

Zamora, Bernice (B. Ortiz) 1938- .. **CLC 89; HLC 2**
See also CA 151; CANR 80; DAM MULT; DLB 82; HW 1, 2

Zamyatin, Evgeny Ivanovich 1884-1937 .... **SSC 89; TCLC 8, 37**
See Zamiatin, Evgenii; Zamiatin, Evgenii Ivanovich; Zamyatin, Yevgeny Ivanovich
See also CA 105; 166; SFW 4

Zamyatin, Yevgeny Ivanovich
See Zamyatin, Evgeny Ivanovich
See also EW 10; EWL 3

Zangwill, Israel 1864-1926 ... **SSC 44; TCLC 16**
See also CA 109; 167; CMW 4; DLB 10, 135, 197; RGEL 2

Zanzotto, Andrea 1921- .... **PC 65**
See also CA 208; CWW 2; DLB 128; EWL 3

Zappa, Francis Vincent, Jr. 1940-1993
See Zappa, Frank
See also CA 108; 143; CANR 57

Zappa, Frank .... **CLC 17**
See Zappa, Francis Vincent, Jr.

Zaturenska, Marya 1902-1982 ..... **CLC 6, 11**
See also CA 13-16R; 105; CANR 22; CP 1, 2, 3

Zayas y Sotomayor, Maria de 1590-c. 1661 .... **LC 102**
See also RGSF 2

Zeami 1363-1443 .... **DC 7; LC 86**
See also DLB 203; RGWL 2, 3

Author Index

Literary Criticism Series
Cumulative Topic Index

This index lists all topic entries in Gale's *Children's Literature Review* (CLR), *Classical and Medieval Literature Criticism* (CMLC), *Contemporary Literary Criticism* (CLC), *Drama Criticism* (DC), *Literature Criticism from 1400 to 1800* (LC), *Nineteenth-Century Literature Criticism* (NCLC), *Short Story Criticism* (SSC), and *Twentieth-Century Literary Criticism* (TCLC). The index also lists topic entries in the Gale Critical Companion Collection, which includes the following publications: *The Beat Generation* (BG), and *Harlem Renaissance* (HR).

NCLC Cumulative Nationality Index

AMERICAN

Adams, John **106**
Alcott, Amos Bronson **1**
Alcott, Louisa May **6, 58, 83**
Alger, Horatio Jr. **8, 83**
Allston, Washington **2**
Apess, William **73**
Audubon, John James **47**
Barlow, Joel **23**
Bartram, William **145**
Beecher, Catharine Esther **30**
Bellamy, Edward **4, 86, 147**
Bird, Robert Montgomery **1**
Boker, George Henry **125**
Boyesen, Hjalmar Hjorth **135**
Brackenridge, Hugh Henry **7**
Brentano, Clemens (Maria) **1**
Brown, Charles Brockden **22, 74, 122**
Brown, William Wells **2, 89**
Brownson, Orestes Augustus **50**
Bryant, William Cullen **6, 46**
Calhoun, John Caldwell **15**
Channing, William Ellery **17**
Child, Lydia Maria **6, 73**
Chivers, Thomas Holley **49**
Cooke, John Esten **5**
Cooke, Rose Terry **110**
Cooper, James Fenimore **1, 27, 54**
Cooper, Susan Fenimore **129**
Cranch, Christopher Pearse **115**
Crèvecoeur, Michel Guillaume Jean de **105**
Crockett, David **8**
Cummins, Maria Susanna **139**
Dana, Richard Henry Sr. **53**
Delany, Martin Robinson **93**
Dickinson, Emily (Elizabeth) **21, 77**
Douglass, Frederick **7, 55, 141**
Dunlap, William **2**
Dwight, Timothy **13**
Emerson, Mary Moody **66**
Emerson, Ralph Waldo **1, 38, 98**
Field, Eugene **3**
Foster, Hannah Webster **99**
Foster, Stephen Collins **26**
Frederic, Harold **10**
Freneau, Philip Morin **1, 111**
Garrison, William Lloyd **149**
Hale, Sarah Josepha (Buell) **75**
Halleck, Fitz-Greene **47**
Hamilton, Alexander **49**
Hammon, Jupiter **5**
Harris, George Washington **23**
Hawthorne, Nathaniel **2, 10, 17, 23, 39, 79, 95, 158**
Hawthorne, Sophia Peabody **150**
Hayne, Paul Hamilton **94**
Holmes, Oliver Wendell **14, 81**
Horton, George Moses **87**
Irving, Washington **2, 19, 95**
Jackson, Helen Hunt **90**
Jacobs, Harriet A(nn) **67, 162**
James, Henry Sr. **53**

Jefferson, Thomas **11, 103**
Kennedy, John Pendleton **2**
Kirkland, Caroline M. **85**
Lanier, Sidney **6, 118**
Lazarus, Emma **8, 109**
Lincoln, Abraham **18**
Longfellow, Henry Wadsworth **2, 45, 101, 103**
Longstreet, Augustus Baldwin **159**
Lowell, James Russell **2, 90**
Madison, James **126**
Melville, Herman **3, 12, 29, 45, 49, 91, 93, 123, 157**
Mowatt, Anna Cora **74**
Murray, Judith Sargent **63**
Neal, John **161**
Osgood, Frances Sargent **141**
Parkman, Francis Jr. **12**
Parton, Sara Payson Willis **86**
Paulding, James Kirke **2**
Pinkney, Edward **31**
Poe, Edgar Allan **1, 16, 55, 78, 94, 97, 117**
Prescott, William Hickling **163**
Rowson, Susanna Haswell **5, 69**
Sedgwick, Catharine Maria **19, 98**
Shaw, Henry Wheeler **15**
Sigourney, Lydia Howard (Huntley) **21, 87**
Simms, William Gilmore **3**
Smith, Joseph Jr. **53**
Solomon, Northup **105**
Southworth, Emma Dorothy Eliza Nevitte **26**
Stowe, Harriet (Elizabeth) Beecher **3, 50, 133**
Taylor, Bayard **89**
Tenney, Tabitha Gilman **122**
Thoreau, Henry David **7, 21, 61, 138**
Timrod, Henry **25**
Trumbull, John **30**
Truth, Sojourner **94**
Tyler, Royall **3**
Very, Jones **9**
Warner, Susan (Bogert) **31, 146**
Warren, Mercy Otis **13**
Webster, Noah **30**
Webb, Frank J. **143**
Whitman, Sarah Helen (Power) **19**
Whitman, Walt(er) **4, 31, 81**
Whittier, John Greenleaf **8, 59**
Wilson, Harriet E. Adams **78**
Winnemucca, Sarah **79**

ARGENTINIAN

Echeverria, (Jose) Esteban (Antonino) **18**
Hernández, José **17**
Sarmiento, Domingo Faustino **123**

AUSTRALIAN

Adams, Francis **33**
Clarke, Marcus (Andrew Hislop) **19**
Gordon, Adam Lindsay **21**
Harpur, Charles **114**
Kendall, Henry **12**

AUSTRIAN

Grillparzer, Franz **1, 102**
Lenau, Nikolaus **16**
Nestroy, Johann **42**
Raimund, Ferdinand Jakob **69**
Sacher-Masoch, Leopold von **31**
Stifter, Adalbert **41**

BRAZILIAN

Alencar, Jose de **157**

CANADIAN

Crawford, Isabella Valancy **12, 127**
De Mille, James **123**
Haliburton, Thomas Chandler **15, 149**
Lampman, Archibald **25**
Moodie, Susanna (Strickland) **14, 113**
Richardson, John **55**
Traill, Catharine Parr **31**

CHINESE

Li Ju-chen **137**

COLOMBIAN

Isaacs, Jorge Ricardo **70**
Silva, José Asunción **114**

CUBAN

Avellaneda, Gertrudis Gómez de **111**
Casal, Julián del **131**
Manzano, Juan Francisco **155**
Martí (y Pérez), José (Julian) **63**
Villaverde, Cirilo **121**

CZECH

Macha, Karel Hynek **46**

DANISH

Andersen, Hans Christian **7, 79**
Grundtvig, Nicolai Frederik Severin **1, 158**
Jacobsen, Jens Peter **34**
Kierkegaard, Søren **34, 78, 125**

ENGLISH

Ainsworth, William Harrison **13**
Arnold, Matthew **6, 29, 89, 126**
Arnold, Thomas **18**
Austen, Jane **1, 13, 19, 33, 51, 81, 95, 119, 150**
Bagehot, Walter **10**
Barbauld, Anna Laetitia **50**
Barham, Richard Harris **77**
Barnes, William **75**
Beardsley, Aubrey **6**
Beckford, William **16**
Beddoes, Thomas Lovell **3, 154**
Bentham, Jeremy **38**
Blake, William **13, 37, 57, 127**
Bloomfield, Robert **145**

Borrow, George (Henry) **9**
Bowles, William Lisle **103**
Brontë, Anne **4, 71, 102**
Brontë, Charlotte **3, 8, 33, 58, 105, 155**
Brontë, Emily (Jane) **16, 35**
Brontë, (Patrick) Branwell **109**
Browning, Elizabeth Barrett **1, 16, 61, 66**
Browning, Robert **19, 79**
Bulwer-Lytton, Edward (George Earle
   Lytton) **1, 45**
Burney, Fanny **12, 54, 107**
Burton, Richard F(rancis) **42**
Byron, George Gordon (Noel) **2, 12, 109,
   149**
Carlyle, Thomas **22, 70**
Carroll, Lewis **2, 53, 139**
Clare, John **9, 86**
Clough, Arthur Hugh **27, 163**
Cobbett, William **49**
Coleridge, Hartley **90**
Coleridge, Samuel Taylor **9, 54, 99, 111**
Coleridge, Sara **31**
Collins, (William) Wilkie **1, 18, 93**
Cowper, William **8, 94**
Crabbe, George **26, 121**
Craik, Dinah Maria (Mulock) **38**
Dacre, Charlotte **151**
Darwin, Charles **57**
Darwin, Erasmus **106**
De Quincey, Thomas **4, 87**
Dickens, Charles (John Huffam) **3, 8, 18, 26,
   37, 50, 86, 105, 113, 161**
Disraeli, Benjamin **2, 39, 79**
Dobell, Sydney Thompson **43**
Du Maurier, George **86**
Dyer, George **129**
Eden, Emily **10**
Eliot, George **4, 13, 23, 41, 49, 89, 118**
FitzGerald, Edward **9, 153**
Forster, John **11**
Froude, James Anthony **43**
Gaskell, Elizabeth Cleghorn **5, 70, 97, 137**
Gilpin, William **30**
Godwin, William **14, 130**
Gore, Catherine **65**
Hallam, Arthur Henry **110**
Hamilton, Elizabeth **153**
Haydon, Benjamin Robert **146**
Hays, Mary **114**
Hazlitt, William **29, 82**
Hemans, Felicia **29, 71**
Holcroft, Thomas **85**
Hood, Thomas **16**
Hopkins, Gerard Manley **17**
Horne, Richard Hengist **127**
Hunt, (James Henry) Leigh **1, 70**
Huxley, T(homas) H(enry) **67**
Inchbald, Elizabeth **62**
Ingelow, Jean **39, 107**
Jefferies, (John) Richard **47**
Jerrold, Douglas William **2**
Jewsbury, Geraldine (Endsor) **22**
Keats, John **8, 73, 121**
Keble, John **87**
Kemble, Fanny **18**
Kingsley, Charles **35**
Kingsley, Henry **107**
Lamb, Charles **10, 113**
Lamb, Lady Caroline **38**
Lamb, Mary **125**
Landon, Letitia Elizabeth **15**
Landor, Walter Savage **14**
Lear, Edward **3**
Lennox, Charlotte Ramsay **23, 134**
Lewes, George Henry **25**
Lewis, Matthew Gregory **11, 62**
Linton, Eliza Lynn **41**
Macaulay, Thomas Babington **42**
Malthus, Thomas Robert **145**
Marryat, Frederick **3**
Martineau, Harriet **26, 137**
Mayhew, Henry **31**

Mill, Harriet (Hardy) Taylor **102**
Mill, John Stuart **11, 58**
Mitford, Mary Russell **4**
Montagu, Elizabeth **117**
More, Hannah **27, 141**
Morris, William **4**
Newman, John Henry **38, 99**
Norton, Caroline **47**
Oliphant, Laurence **47**
Opie, Amelia **65**
Paine, Thomas **62**
Pater, Walter (Horatio) **7, 90, 159**
Patmore, Coventry Kersey Dighton **9**
Peacock, Thomas Love **22**
Percy, Thomas **95**
Piozzi, Hester Lynch (Thrale) **57**
Planché, James Robinson **42**
Polidori, John William **51**
Radcliffe, Ann (Ward) **6, 55, 106**
Reade, Charles **2, 74**
Reeve, Clara **19**
Reynolds, John Hamilton **146**
Robertson, Thomas William **35**
Robinson, Henry Crabb **15**
Robinson, Mary **142**
Rogers, Samuel **69**
Rossetti, Christina (Georgina) **2, 50, 66**
Rossetti, Dante Gabriel **4, 77**
Sala, George Augustus **46**
Shelley, Mary Wollstonecraft (Godwin) **14,
   59, 103**
Shelley, Percy Bysshe **18, 93, 143**
Smith, Charlotte (Turner) **23, 115**
Southey, Robert **8, 97**
Surtees, Robert Smith **14**
Symonds, John Addington **34**
Tennyson, Alfred **30, 65, 115**
Thackeray, William Makepeace **5, 14, 22, 43**
Thelwall, John **162**
Tonna, Charlotte Elizabeth **135**
Trelawny, Edward John **85**
Trollope, Anthony **6, 33, 101**
Trollope, Frances **30**
Warton, Joseph **118**
Williams, Helen Maria **135**
Wordsworth, Dorothy **25, 138**
Wordsworth, William **12, 38, 111**

FILIPINO

Rizal, José **27**

FINNISH

Kivi, Aleksis **30**
Lonnrot, Elias **53**
Runeberg, Johan **41**

FRENCH

Augier, Emile **31**
Balzac, Honoré de **5, 35, 53, 153**
Banville, Théodore (Faullain) de **9**
Barbey d'Aurevilly, Jules-Amédée **1**
Baudelaire, Charles **6, 29, 55, 155**
Becque, Henri **3**
Beranger, Pierre Jean de **34**
Bertrand, Aloysius **31**
Borel, Pétrus **41**
Chamisso, Adelbert von **82**
Chateaubriand, François René de **3, 134**
Comte, Auguste **54**
Constant (de Rebecque), (Henri) Benjamin **6**
Corbière, Tristan **43**
Crèvecoeur, Michel Guillaume Jean de **105**
Daudet, (Louis Marie) Alphonse **1**
Delacroix, Eugene **133**
Desbordes-Valmore, Marceline **97**
Dumas, Alexandre (fils) **9**
Dumas, Alexandre (pere) **11, 71**
Duras, Claire de **154**
Feuillet, Octave **45**
Flaubert, Gustave **2, 10, 19, 62, 66, 135**
Fourier, Charles **51**

Fromentin, Eugène (Samuel Auguste) **10,
   125**
Gaboriau, émile **14**
Gautier, Théophile **1, 59**
Gobineau, Joseph-Arthur **17**
Goncourt, Edmond (Louis Antoine Huot) de
   7
Goncourt, Jules (Alfred Huot) de **7**
Hugo, Victor (Marie) **3, 10, 21, 161**
Joubert, Joseph **9**
Kock, Charles Paul de **16**
Laclos, Pierre Ambroise François **4, 87**
Laforgue, Jules **5, 53**
Lamartine, Alphonse (Marie Louis Prat) de
   11
Lautréamont **12**
Leconte de Lisle, Charles-Marie-René **29**
Maistre, Joseph **37**
Mallarmé, Stéphane **4, 41**
Maupassant, (Henri René Albert) Guy de **1,
   42, 83**
Mérimée, Prosper **6, 65**
Michelet, Jules **31**
Musset, (Louis Charles) Alfred de **7, 150**
Nerval, Gérard de **1, 67**
Nodier, (Jean) Charles (Emmanuel) **19**
Pixérécourt, (René Charles) Guilbert de **39**
Renan, Joseph Ernest **26, 145**
Rimbaud, (Jean Nicolas) Arthur **4, 35, 82**
Sade, Donatien Alphonse François **3, 47**
Sainte-Beuve, Charles Augustin **5**
Sand, George **2, 42, 57**
Scribe, (Augustin) Eugène **16**
Senancour, Etienne Pivert de **16**
Staël-Holstein, Anne Louise Germaine
   Necker **3**
Stendhal **23, 46**
Sue, Eugene **1**
Taine, Hippolyte Adolphe **15**
Tocqueville, Alexis (Charles Henri Maurice
   Clérel Comte) de **7, 63**
Vallès, Jules **71**
Verlaine, Paul (Marie) **2, 51**
Vigny, Alfred (Victor) de **7, 102**
Villiers de l'Isle Adam, Jean Marie Mathias
   Philippe Auguste **3**

GERMAN

Arnim, Achim von (Ludwig Joachim von
   Arnim) **5, 159**
Arnim, Bettina von **38, 123**
Bonaventura **35**
Büchner, (Karl) Georg **26, 146**
Chamisso, Adelbert von **82**
Claudius, Matthias **75**
Droste-Hülshoff, Annette Freiin von **3, 133**
Eichendorff, Joseph **8**
Engels, Friedrich **85, 114**
Feuerbach, Ludwig **139**
Fichte, Johann Gottlieb **62**
Fontane, Theodor **26, 163**
Fouqué, Friedrich (Heinrich Karl) de la
   Motte **2**
Freytag, Gustav **109**
Goethe, Johann Wolfgang von **4, 22, 34, 90,
   154**
Grabbe, Christian Dietrich **2**
Grimm, Jacob Ludwig Karl **3, 77**
Grimm, Wilhelm Karl **3, 77**
Hebbel, Friedrich **43**
Hegel, Georg Wilhelm Friedrich **46, 151**
Heine, Heinrich **4, 54, 147**
Herder, Johann Gottfried von **8**
Hoffmann, E(rnst) T(heodor) A(madeus) **2**
Hölderlin, (Johann Christian) Friedrich **16**
Humboldt, Wilhelm von **134**
Immermann, Karl (Lebrecht) **4, 49**
Jean Paul **7**
Kant, Immanuel **27, 67**
Kleist, Heinrich von **2, 37**
Klinger, Friedrich Maximilian von **1**
Klopstock, Friedrich Gottlieb **11**

NCLC-165 Title Index

ISBN 0-7876-8649-2

90000